Jan 12: 1793	Paul Storr	Wa...
	Paul Storr	
Ap. 27 1793		John Marriott
August 8: 1794	Paul Storr	Walter Coles
Oct 8 1796	Paul Storr	Jn° Marriott
Jan 19 1793	Mary Jackson mark	Walter Coles

Aug 21 1807	Paul Storr	Rich Bratton
Feb 10 1808	Paul Storr	Rich Bratton
Dec 15 1808	Paul Storr	Rich Bratton
Oct 21 1813	Paul Storr	B Preston
Sep 12 1817	Paul Storr	B Patton
March 4 1819	Paul Storr	R Thompson

7 Sept 1833	Paul Storr	J Fuller
17 Dec 1834	Paul Storr	J Fuller

LONDON GOLDSMITHS
1697–1837

OTHER BOOKS BY THE AUTHOR

The Queen's Silver

Rococo Silver 1727–1765

Frontispiece The upper part of the first page for letter S in the first Largeworkers Book.

LONDON GOLDSMITHS
1697–1837

THEIR MARKS AND LIVES
from the Original Registers at Goldsmiths' Hall
and Other Sources

by

Arthur G. Grimwade, F.S.A.

ff
faber and faber

First published in 1976
by Faber and Faber
3 Queen Square London WC1N 3AU
Second, revised edition 1982
Third, revised and enlarged edition 1990

Printed in Great Britain
by TJI Digital, Padstow, Cornwall
All rights reserved

© Copyright Arthur G. Grimwade 1976, 1982, 1990

British Library Cataloguing in Publication Data is available
ISBN 10: 0-571-15238-4
ISBN 13: 978-0-571-15238-4

TO THE SHADES OF FOSTER LANE

Contents

List of Illustrations	ix
Note to Third Edition	x
Introduction	1

Part One

THE MARKS   9

    Note on Marks   11

    Abbreviations   12

I Registered Marks of Largeworkers and Smallworkers from the Goldsmiths' Hall Registers 1697–1837   13

II Registered Marks of Provincial Goldsmiths from the Goldsmiths' Hall Registers 1697–1837   239

III Unregistered Marks with tentative attributions   247

    Indexes of Marks of Categorized Makers not included in Sections I–III:

IV Smallworkers' Marks   281

V Incuse Marks of All Categories   287

VI Watchcasemakers' Cameo Marks   333

VII Goldworkers' Marks 1773–1837   355

VIII Bucklemakers' Marks 1773–1820   387

IX Hiltmakers' Marks 1773–1823   407

    Appendix to Section IX:

      Makers prior to 1773 and listed in Section I described as Haft- and Hiltmakers, Sword Cutlers, Free Cutlers and Cutlers   409

X Spectacle-makers' Marks 1794–1835   413

CONTENTS

Part Two

THE LIVES

I Biographical Dictionary of Makers listed in Part One, Sections I and III — 417

II Notices of Provincial Makers whose marks appear in the London Registers — 715

III Notes to Makers listed in Part One, Sections IV, V, VI and VII — 727

Appendix:

Index of Goldsmiths recorded in the Biographical Section who were Freemen of Livery Companies other than the Goldsmiths' — 729

Addenda to Biographical Dictionary — 733

Illustrations

1 *Frontispiece* The upper part of the first page for letter S in the first Largeworkers Book.

2 Apprenticeship entries of George Boothby and George Wicks 1712.
3 Apprenticeship entry of Thomas Chawner 1754.
4 Apprenticeship entry of Anthony Nelme 1672.
5 Entry of Hester Bateman's first mark 1761.
6 The entry of John Harvey's mark showing annotations for three changes of address.
7 Typical entries of Largeworkers' marks 1739.
8 *Endpapers* The entries of Paul Storr's marks from 1793 to 1834.

The arms of the Worshipful Company of Goldsmiths are reproduced on the cover and jacket by kind permission of the Wardens and Court of the Company.

Note to Third Edition

The call for a new edition of this work is gratifying evidence of the continued interest and research in the goldsmiths recorded, which the author may humbly feel has to some extent been stimulated by his own earlier efforts. The publication of John Culme's *The Directory of Gold and Silversmiths ... 1838–1914* is a logical and very welcome extension of my own chosen period and I am most grateful to the author for kind assistance and generosity in giving me free use of material which he has assembled outside the period of his own work, as also for enabling me to direct readers to his accounts of firms descended from makers recorded in these pages. I am much indebted as well to both Robert Barker and Sarah Tanner for their enthusiasm and hard work in uncovering many apprenticeship and other details of goldsmiths with masters outside the Goldsmiths' Company, as also to D. E. Wickham of the Clothworkers' Company and Helen Clifford for their generous contributions to the Addenda material. I am equally grateful to other friends for their additions which are acknowledged in the entries concerned.

As before, this edition contains further corrections and additions to both marks and biographical sections following the same plan, that is, with corrections to mark entries on the pages concerned and new biographical material added to and incorporating the previous Addenda.

A.G.G.

Introduction

The Task

The seeds of this book were sown, all unknown, in my mind soon after I began my working career at Christie's in 1932 under the enthusiastic tuition of Charles Brocklehurst, to whose kindness in guiding and stimulating my youthful interest I must here pay my long-remembered debt; as also to the memory of William Watts, then recently retired from the Victoria and Albert Museum, who made frequent visits to the Plate Room at 8 King Street to utter wise counsel and bestow his life-long knowledge with benevolent charm on the stripling who produced problems for his solution.

My first modest efforts in studying London goldsmiths' marks was then to keep for Charles Brocklehurst, in a small thumb-index book, a freehand drawn note of those we found not otherwise recorded, many of which, with his kind permission, are now embodied in Section III of the marks herein. The appearance in 1935 of Sir Ambrose Heal's *The London Goldsmiths 1200–1800* with its vast list of names, was of the greatest stimulus to our efforts and led to the tentative identification of some of the marks we had collected. As these increased, it became necessary to transfer them to a card index, which was completed at the beginning of the last war to act as a second record in case of war damage, and this has been continued down to today, although in the course of the preparation of this work many of the marks therein have been removed from the problematic to the certain.

The study of the makers' marks preserved in the registers at Goldsmiths' Hall has had a somewhat casual and erratic history. Although Octavius Morgan, the pioneer in the study of hallmarks in this country gave a lecture to the Society of Antiquaries in June 1852 'On the Assay Marks on Gold and Silver Plate' in which he naturally referred to makers' marks, it seems he knew only of the existence of the pre-1697 copper plate at Goldsmiths' Hall, for he makes no mention of the registers, nor does he seem to have pursued the matter further. The first deliberate attempt therefore to reveal the mystery of London goldsmiths' marks was left to the industrious William Chaffers who seems to have combined the business of art dealing with a typically Victorian energy in publishing much needed reference books for the growing band of collectors. Although today his name is mainly remembered by his works on pottery and porcelain, he also produced in 1863 his *Hallmarks on Gold and Silver Plate*, which immediately proved so successful that on 17 June 1864 he wrote a letter addressed to Walter Prideaux, Clerk of the Goldsmiths' Company:

'I must apologise for troubling you on a matter quite out of your usual routine; but being as you know interested in everything connected

INTRODUCTION

with the Goldsmiths' craft, I was talking a day or two ago with Mr Tite on the subject, especially as to the names of Goldsmiths whose initials appear stamped on plate; he said he was sure you would assist me in obtaining these names and if you will kindly allow me to inspect the books I will copy them out, together with the dates of their enrolment; whenever it may be convenient for me to attend. My little book on Hall Marks has had a good sale, the stock being in fact nearly exhausted and I am preparing a Second edition in which I hope to be able to throw some light on the Hall marks of other countries beside England.'

It will be noticed that Chaffers does not request permission to publish details of the marks and indeed attributes his desire to 'copy them out' to his personal interest in the matter, although one would think that his mention of a new edition of his *Hall Marks* should have indicated to the Clerk and Company what was in his mind. In fact, however, it seems that the appearance of his book *Gilda Aurifabrorum* in 1883 caused considerable surprise and offence to the Company, to judge by a letter from Wilfrid Cripps in 1892 to the collector H. D. Ellis, who, it seems, had asked the former for an introduction to the Company for research:

'You mention Chaffers' works; but I have some reason to believe that the reference to The Goldsmiths' Company in his book *Gilda Aurifabrorum* was unauthorised, and that the improper use of what permission he had to consult the Books, caused all permission in future to him to be forbidden; and has been the cause of much increased difficulty of access to those Books ever since. He in fact used the limited permission accorded him to make an entire transcript, as far as he possibly could in the time, of one or two of the Marks Books for the purpose of printing them in extenso. This he did, and added dedications etc. to the Company which he had over-reached. It is obvious that the Company would not care to have this sort of thing repeated.'

Cripps' 'dedications etc.' would appear to be the acknowledgement which Chaffers made in his preface to *Gilda Aurifabrorum* of its publication 'by the kind permission of the Warden and Court of Assistants of the Goldsmiths' Company, in which he has been materially assisted by the advice on all occasions of Mr Walter Prideaux and the obliging attention of the Deputy Warden Mr W. Robinson'. If this permission had been granted merely to inspect the registers as he asked in his first letter, Chaffers had certainly 'over-reached' himself in his publication, but one cannot avoid detecting a note of sour grapes in Cripps' letter. In his own *Old English Plate* he is loud in his praise of Octavius Morgan's pioneer work on the subject and studiously avoids mentioning Chaffers, while at the same time acknowledging the help of the Company and Clerk. Nevertheless, there is no evidence that he was allowed the use of the registers for the reproductions of the makers' marks in his work. That opposition to further use

INTRODUCTION

of the registers lingered on is reflected in the rumour that even Sir Charles Jackson found little co-operation in the production of *English Goldsmiths and their Marks* and certainly the fact that he reproduced the marks from actual impressions on plate under the chronological arrangement of the pieces themselves lends substance to this report. Happier has been my lot. From the first moment in 1953 when I outlined my project to Mr Walter Prideaux, the present Clerk of the Company I have met with enthusiastic and generous support from all concerned, among whom I would like to recall the late Charles Biggs, Prime Warden, who warmly encouraged me from the start. Mr Prideaux, Mr John Forbes and Miss Hare have all patiently suffered my inroads into their knowledge and time and I can only hope that the emergence of this volume at long last will prove that their kindness and help have not been wasted. As explained below the Company, through the Court, presented me with a full set of photostats of the registers for the construction of the mark lists, a very material contribution to the cost of the work for which I am deeply indebted. Many others have assisted me in researches, clerks and archivists of livery companies, librarians and archivists of municipalities and counties and silver collectors with a particular interest in some one goldsmith. To all these, some alas no longer alive, I pay my sincere thanks.

THE PLAN

To commend a new study of these marks to the student of English silver today appeared, on consideration, to demand a system of presentation in as easy and foolproof a dictionary form as could be devised. To achieve this in a reasonable format with the essential information at a glance, as well as detailed notes on the men themselves, it seemed desirable to divorce the marks from the biographical material, since otherwise, as in previous works in this or practically any other country, an index to the marks becomes necessary (instead of the marks forming their own index), thus adding both to the risk of error and waste of time in cross reference between index and marks. These considerations led, therefore, to the system adopted here of the marks arranged in three sections alphabetically and numbered consecutively throughout, followed by a biographical dictionary of the makers under surnames with reference by number to the individual marks of each man or woman. The three sections in which the marks are arranged are necessitated by two subsidiary factors, one the presence in the London registers of a number of provincial makers, who, for one reason or another, entered their marks at Goldsmiths' Hall, and secondly, the number of problematic marks without any certain identification, which, kept separate, can be referred to more easily and the section revised if more come to light. Marks which, although missing from the registers, as explained later (page 5), have been established by external evidence are included in Section I.

Having decided on the arrangement, the next problem was the mechanical one of reproduction. The only full and authoritative documentation of the

INTRODUCTION

marks is, of course, the registers at Goldsmiths' Hall, to which I return later, in which the makers' punches are reproduced by striking in lamp-black or later a suitable ink, so that the sunk or intaglio part of the punch itself, which produces the cameo portion of the impression when struck on the metal, is reproduced as white letters or devices against a black background of the surrounding portion of the punch out to its exterior edge, thus defining the shape. This has thus become the standard presentation of hall and makers' marks in nearly every country's literature on the subject, since at least the first edition of Rosenberg's *Der Goldschmiede Merkzeichen* of 1889. Why then do I now present a reverse representation in the marks reproduced here? The reason is a combination of accuracy, practicability and economy. On my first investigation of the problem I decided it was desirable to achieve maximum accuracy in facsimile reproduction of the impressions in the registers to assist identification between seemingly similar marks, allowed surprisingly frequently to different makers working at the same time. After a series of experiments with the kind assistance of Mr John Forbes, Deputy Warden at Goldsmiths' Hall, we jointly decided that a negative photostat of the pages of the register produced the least possible distortion of the original impressions that was practicable. The frequent demands made to the Company for information from the registers had decided the Court that a reproduction of them was needed for internal use at Goldsmiths' Hall, and Mr Forbes personally supervised the production of two photostat copies of the register, one of which the Court most generously presented to me for the construction of this book. To the Worshipful Company, through the Court, I am therefore deeply indebted, as also to Mr Forbes for his sympathetic interest and help in reaching what I am sure was the right solution to the problem of reproduction, before the advent of the electronic Xerox system.

The Registers

There is no trace of any books kept by the Company for the recording of makers' marks before 1697, when the Higher or Britannia Standard for silver was introduced. The only record of marks existing before that date is a copper plate at Goldsmiths' Hall struck with the marks of goldsmiths working from 1675 till the time of the change of standard, but this regrettably has no names accompanying the marks. A few of them can be identified by the similarity of punch and devices recurring in the Higher Standard marks using the first two letters of the surname in place of initials of Christian name and surname as before, but I have not included these since they lie outside the documented period commencing in April 1697.

At this date two books were begun for large and smallworkers respectively and these were used till the summer of 1739 when, following the Plate Act of 1738, all makers had to register fresh marks differing from their previous ones. Two new books were then commenced and used till 1758 of which unfortunately that for the smallworkers has been lost. The next book for smallworkers

INTRODUCTION

in use till 1773 has however survived, but that for largeworkers has been missing since at least 1863, when Chaffers first investigated the registers. As he then surmised, this seems almost certainly to have been removed by the parliamentary committee set up 'to enquire into the manner of conducting the several Assay Offices', which made its report in 1773. This seemed to me so likely a clue to its fate that I was emboldened to seek for it in the archives of the House of Commons, only to learn that nothing survived of the committee's papers except the printed report. We must imagine therefore that the vital clue to the identity of many of the makers of the earlier George III period perished in the fire that destroyed the old Houses of Parliament. After 1773 the distinction between large and smallworkers' books was ended and in one general volume commenced in that year, and in all others thereafter, specially ruled columns provide for the mark, name, date, address and category of the maker concerned. From this date plateworkers, smallworkers, spoonmakers, goldworkers, watchcasemakers, bucklemakers and occasionally even spectaclemakers are all specified. I have omitted from the reproduced marks and biographies all the last four categories of makers after 1773, since their inclusion would have increased the work by some 2000 marks and names, which I felt would have made reference more difficult by the interpolation of many which may rarely, if ever, be sought for. I have also omitted from the pre-1773 books a few smallworkers' marks, probably mostly for gold, which are so small that they could not possibly be reproduced facsimile, and of which magnification might have caused misidentification. The impressions of some of these in the registers are indeed almost illegible and only to be guessed at by the owners' initials. Also omitted are all incuse marks, i.e. initials and devices struck intaglio into the metal without surrounding punch, since these are largely the marks of watchcasemakers, albeit occasionally found on gold boxes, but only extremely rarely on silver. As a compromise I have listed the marks, names and addresses under these various categories in Sections IV to X. They have never been published before and many people, I believe, are unaware of the registration and therefore identification of watchcasemakers, bucklemakers and so on. To this extent, therefore, I hope the inclusion of the lists will prove of value.

The registers themselves present an interesting study in development from the carefree arrangement of the first few books to the orderly arrangement used from 1773 onwards. Although the largeworkers' register of 1697 starts with a finely engrossed title page under John Sutton's aegis as Touch Warden, it speedily deteriorates into a series of hastily written individual entries apparently in the hand of each individual maker, counter-signed by the Touch Warden, unless the maker was illiterate, when the entry seems to have been made by the Clerk and signed with a 'mark', either childish initials or a cross. While the majority of the entries are for a single mark, there are a certain number of early ones where the maker struck two or three slightly varying marks, as if, perhaps, he had been experimenting with several versions and wished to be able to use any at choice. All such variations are reproduced. There are often also two

INTRODUCTION

identical marks of different sizes and when this occurs I have reproduced the larger, stating that a smaller one also exists. Where, however, there is a difference discernible, however slight, I have reproduced both. After 1773 it seems that every new punch cut by a maker was conscientiously registered in his original entry space to the extent, in the early nineteenth century, of as many as ten or twelve versions over a few years. Here I have reproduced only the first of any similar series.

The divisions of the early books into large and smallworkers, while broadly observed, was at times overlooked and the wrong book used. Here and there we find notes by the Clerk or some assistant 'Looke for James Wilks marke in ye other booke ye Small Worker', 'Look for Avenell in the other book' and so on. Hurried entries under the wrong letter, usually that of the Christian name rather than surname, occur with corrections as 'Look for Anthony Calame in Letter A entered By a Mistake', 'Look for Anthony Du Chesne in the Letter R', this more difficult to account for. One is aware, through such glimpses, of a delightfully carefree attitude to the business of entering the marks, coupled with a desire at the same time to do the best to keep the books straight'.

At this point I should, perhaps, explain what to some may seem the somewhat arbitrary date of 1837 at which I decided to end this work. It must be remembered that this book was begun as long ago as 1953 at a time when nineteenth-century silver had few devotees. I felt therefore that the year of Victoria's accession—echoing the '7' of the starting year of the registers—provided a rational limit to my labours, since most makers entering their marks that year could be expected to have continued working until at least mid-century. Now, however, that Victorian silver has proved itself of increasing interest to collectors, I can only hope that some enthusiast in this field will be inspired, ere long, to produce some complementary volume to my own efforts for earlier years.

THE LIVES

The entry of a mark in the registers is throughout confined to the name, date, address and category of the maker concerned. It was necessary therefore to turn elsewhere for any attempt at biographical details of the craftsmen, who, with a handful of exceptions, have till now remained mere names attached to their marks since the registers were first read by Chaffers. It is true that in his pioneer work *Gilda Aurifabrorum* he produced short notes on a number of London goldsmiths from the earliest days, but a large proportion of these were of men either unidentifiable with known marks as working goldsmiths or categorically described by him as banker goldsmiths with little suggestion that they were ever, beyond probable apprentice instruction, practised in the craft to any serious degree. In this respect we should remember that the distinction between merchant or businessman and craftsman in the members of the Company goes back in fact to the mediaeval period.

Investigation showed that the beautifully kept and unbroken register of

INTRODUCTION

apprentices of the Company was an unworked mine of pure gold for information of the greatest interest and importance on the persons whose marks are recorded. Not only does it provide the paternity and place of origin of the new aspirant to the craft, but also his master to be, often with description and address, the term of his service, 'turn-overs' to another master if death or cessation of business of the first intervened, the premium paid and on occasions of need charitable gifts towards part or all of the premium. Examination of the material thus available demonstrated much valuable secondary information by cross reference, changes of address of masters, deaths established or dates fixed by reference to widows and executors, freedom of different companies disentangling identities of men of the same name and so on. This last problem has been present throughout the work. The possibility that a second entry of a mark under one name might be that of a son, hitherto unrecognized, even though the signature seemed similar, had constantly to be borne in mind, and although such problems have often been solved by the apprentice register or some other evidence, doubt inevitably remains in a certain number, in which case I have noted the uncertainty. Addresses, of course, have been of particular assistance in solving a number of puzzles of this kind.

Realizing early in my research into the material available that Sir Ambrose Heal had, in his *London Goldsmiths*, acquired many facts not apparent in the official records, I approached him for advice and possible assistance, hoping that his working material might still remain accessible and lighten my task. It was a sadness to realize that in his very great age—he died shortly afterwards—he had little recollection of the sources or of the survival of the working material for his publication. As I progressed, I realized, with something of a shock, from internal comparisons, that he had made no use either of the apprentice and freedom lists of the Company or of the marks registers in compiling his list, and that in consequence there were many omissions, particularly of small-workers, from what had previously been accepted as the fullest possible index of London goldsmiths from all known sources. His impressive work remains, however, one of my major inspirations and in learning its shortcomings I have not lost my admiration for its conception and presentation. I shall be lucky indeed if no worse is said of my own efforts to enlarge the available information on this absorbing subject.

One of the interesting and unexpected facts which emerge from the mark registers of the early years is the number of working goldsmiths who were, for one reason or another, free of another company other than that of their own craft. This discovery—as indeed it was, since no previous work seems to have noticed it—necessarily demanded research into the records of the companies in question, which has been fascinating and for the most part highly rewarding. The only gaps in this search are those caused by the destruction of a few companies' records in the last war. The appendix at the end of the biographical section reveals that there are forty-four other companies of which some goldsmiths, at least, were members. Of these only the Clockmakers and Cutlers

INTRODUCTION

had any craft connection with that of the Goldsmiths. Membership of these two companies seems almost certainly to indicate a specialist in either watchcases or knife and sword hafts and hilts respectively. For goldsmiths' membership of other companies we must look for varying reasons, either freedom by patrimony through a father not himself a goldsmith by trade, or by service to a working goldsmith who had acquired the freedom of a company unrelated to his craft from one of the same reasons. The mention of such freedoms in the register is also occasionally a determining factor in establishing the separate identities of two similarly named makers, hitherto confused as one, as John Edwards I and II.

While the apprenticeship registers provide such constant information as approximate birth-dates and the places from which the boys embarked on their career, the establishment of death or even retirement of any maker is much more elusive, made even more tantalizing by the practice of writing the single word 'Dead' across the entry of a man's mark with never a date added in a single case. If the indices to wills at Somerset House contained details of profession or trade we should have an invaluable list for any category of citizen, but this is, alas, not so, and apart from the rarer names, it seemed impossible to evolve any search system which would yield results without years of labour. I have had therefore to content myself obituarily with such scattered crumbs of information as have fallen to me from various hands. One of the most valuable of these was the index of obituary notices of goldsmiths from *The Gentleman's Magazine* kindly presented to me by Mrs G. E. P. How.

The enthusiasm of members of Huguenot families in England for their history, as revealed through the publications of the Huguenot Society, has provided by far the most fascinating information of personal details of the men who did so much to revivify the craft in London at the exact period when the registers begin. What has emerged from the records of the French churches and chapels in London at the time is the very close family relationship between so many of the best known goldsmiths as well as such unexpected pictures as the burglary at Pierre Harache's house when the Swallow Street communion cup was stolen, or the visit of David Willaume II to Metz as an apprentice of thirteen to claim his inheritance.

Interest in my researches, as they became known among many collectors and professionals in silver, has led to some unexpected and highly rewarding meetings with descendants of Hester Bateman, William Cafe, Paul Crespin, Pierre Platel and David Tanqueray, from all of whom I have acquired information on their ancestors and the warm feeling of a living contact with the past, which, however tenuous it may in fact be, is my own personal reward from my task. I have tried to clothe with some semblance of living flesh the dry bones of marks and names, which until now have been, with few exceptions, the sole link between the present and the men and women who conceived and executed the work which has come down to us from an age so close and yet seemingly so remote from ours. If my efforts have closed that gap even a little by revealing some small part of their lives and progress I shall feel content.

PART ONE

THE MARKS

Note on Marks

The marks in the three following sections are arranged alphabetically on the following plan:

1 Marks composed of mixed upper and lower case letters, e.g. Ab, in this order: Roman type, script letters and lastly Gothic or black-letter type.
2 Marks in capital letters, e.g. AB, in the same order, according to the three types.
3 Marks with more than one group of initials under the upper horizontal initials, or in marks of cross form under the horizontal initials, whether these relate to one man or as sometimes, through the diagonal arrangement of the two persons' initials, to part of each.

A complete order, therefore, inside one combination is as follows:

$$Ab, Ab, \mathfrak{Ab}, AB, AB, \mathfrak{AB},$$

$$\frac{Ab}{De}, \frac{Ab}{De}, \frac{\mathfrak{Ab}}{\mathfrak{De}}, \frac{D}{Ab}, \frac{AB}{DE}, \frac{AB}{DE}, \frac{\mathfrak{AB}}{\mathfrak{DE}}, \frac{D}{AB}$$

When virtually similar marks occur belonging to different makers (see, for instance, the plethora of 'IS'), the order is chronological according to entry date.

From the above strictly alphabetical arrangement it necessarily follows that Sterling and Britannia Standard marks of the same maker will be found in separate alphabetical positions, as also are marks of the same maker and standard but in varying types. All marks of any one maker can at once be found by reference to the numbers following each name in the Biographical Dictionary (Part Two, The Lives) and further reference is usually made in the last column of the name key to other mark numbers of the same maker.

The numbers I, II, III, etc., against names in the key, are used to indicate separately distinct makers of the same name in chronological order of registration, without necessarily indicating successive generations of the same family. Below each key column is printed a note of other marks or combinations within the limits of the particular page, which occur subsequently in Sections II and III. In such footnotes Italic initials, e.g. *AB*, refer to marks containing script letters. A mark not found in either of the first two sections may possibly, of course, be found in Section III.

The author will be grateful to hear—preferably with facsimile size photographs—of any marks apparently unestablished in any section.

Abbreviations

bm	bucklemaker
cm	casemaker
csm	candlestickmaker
gs	goldsmith
gw	goldworker
hfm	haftmaker
hlm	hiltmaker
khm	knifehaft-maker
lgw	largeworker
n.s.	not specified
pdm	pendantmaker
plw	plateworker
sbm	snuffboxmaker
stm	saltmaker
smw	smallworker
snm	snuffermaker
spm	spoonmaker
scm	spectaclemaker
ss	silversmith
sw	silverworker
wcm	watchcase-maker

Terms not found here are given in full

I
Registered Marks of Largeworkers and Smallworkers from the Goldsmiths' Hall Registers 1697–1837

Included in this section are a number of marks presumably to be found originally in the missing largeworkers' book of 1758–73, but sufficiently well established by external evidence as to have long-accepted attributions. Such marks are now reproduced from photographs of impressions on examples of silver by the particular maker and are so noted in the Notes column to their number.

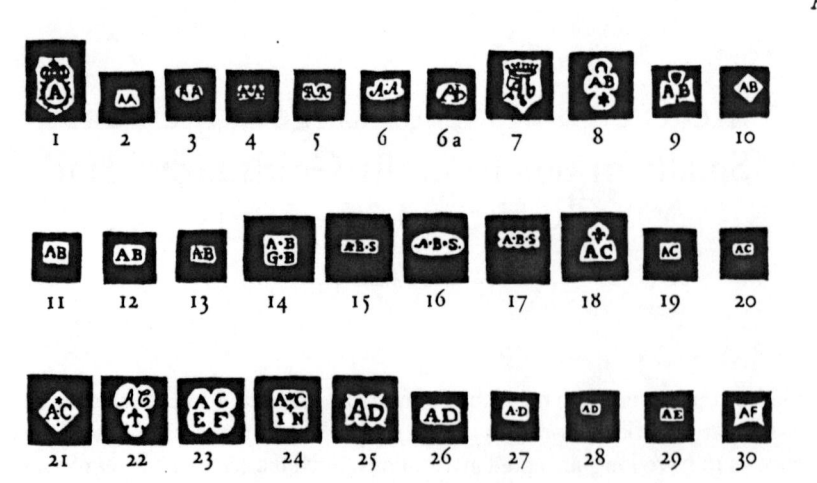

No.	Name	Category	Entered	Notes
1	Andrew Archer	lgw	11.8.1720	See also no. 84
2	Arthur Ashton	smw	13.3.1732	
3	Ann Andrews	smw	26.3.1759	
4	idem	smw	27.6.1760	
5	idem	smw	16.6.1761	
6	Arthur Annesley	lgw	23.3.1758	
6a	Robert Abercromby	lgw	29.4.1740	See also nos. 2254, 2258
7	John Abbott	lgw	5.7.1706	
8	Abraham Buteux	lgw	13.5.1721	See also no. 249
9	Abel Brokesby	lgw	24.8.1727	
10	Ann Barugh	smw	10.12.1731	For watchcases, see also Section V
11	Alexander Barnet	smw	8.8.1759	
12	Albrecht Borchers	lgw	14.6.1769	
13	Abraham Barrier	plw	18.5.1782	See also no. 3470. Also incuse mark 11.10.1775
14	Alice and George Burrows II	plw	10.7.1801	A smaller similar mark 7.11.1804. Others larger 21.2.1814 and 6.5.1818. See also nos. 762–3, 2419, 3581
15	Adey Bellamy Savory	plw	14.2.1826	See also no. 96
16	idem	plw	13.10.1826	
17	idem	plw	11.11.1826	Also five other marks in various punches of same date. Others 1829, 1830 and 1832
18	Augustin Courtauld	lgw	7.10.1729	See also nos. 22, 385
19	Abraham Cook	sbm	11.5.1759	A similar mark 2.11.1769
20	B. A. Chambrier	smw	14.10.1772	

LONDON GOLDSMITHS

No.	Name	Category	Entered	Notes
21	Ann Chesterman	smw	20.4.1775	
22	Augustin Courtauld	gs	6.7.1739	See also nos. 18, 385
23	Alexander Coats and Edward French	lgw	29.8.1734	A crudely cut punch. See also no. 578
24	Ann Craig and John Neville	gs	15.10.1740	A smaller similar mark without devices 27.5.1743 See also no. 1554
25	Charles Adam	lgw	1.2.1703	
26	Allen Dominy	smw	9.12.1789	
27	idem	smw	5.2.1790	
28	Archibald Douglas	plw	19.1.1826	A similar mark 26.3.1830. Another in oval punch 1.6.1836. See also no. 1256 and Section VII, A.D
29	Adrian Eastwick	smw	8.3.1768	A similar mark 23.11.1778
30	Anthony Francia	hfm	4.7.——	Approximate version of bad impression. Circa 1725

Also AB.LD. no. 3470; AC. no. 3471

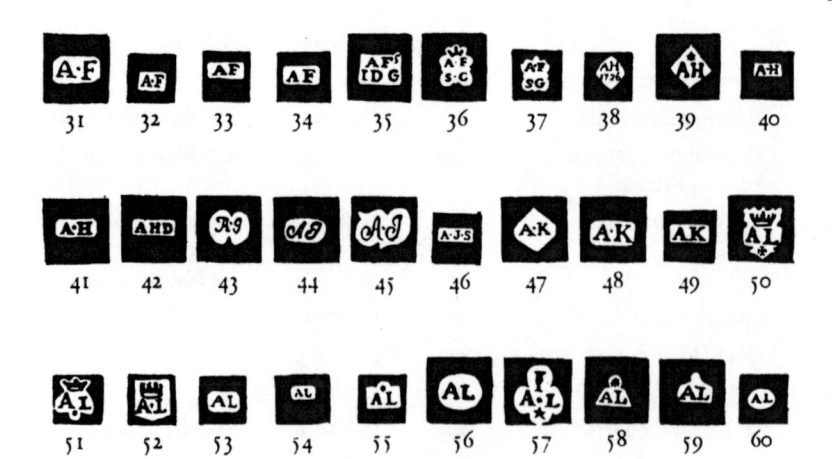

No.	Name	Category	Entered	Notes
31	Ann Farren	lgw	19.12.1743	Month written as 'Xber'
32	Andrew Fogelberg	plw	before March 1773	Not in register. Mark taken from cup of 1777. See also no. 36
33	Alexander Field	smw	14.7.1780	
34	idem	smw	19.6.1788	
35	Alexander Field and John De Gruchy	smw	20.4.1779	
36	Andrew Fogelberg and Stephen Gilbert	plw	17.7.1780	See also no. 32
37	idem	plw	idem	
38	Ann Hill	lgw	15.7.1726	
39	idem	lgw	undated	May 1734–Dec. 1735
40	Andrew Hogg	smw	8.12.1761	
41	Alexander Hewat	lgw	3.11.1810	
42	Abraham Harrison Day	plw	26.3.1836	
43	Anthony Jolland	lgw	27.6.1721	
44	Alexander Johnston	lgw	11.5.1733	
45	idem	lgw	22.1.1748	And two smaller similar marks same date
46	Alexander J. Strahan	smw	21.9.1799	And a smaller similar mark same date. Another 6.8.1823
47	Ann Kersill	lgw	16.6.1747	And a smaller similar mark same date
48	Andrew Killik	lgw	7.9.1749	
49	Abstainando King	snm	8.2.1791	And smaller similar marks, 6.7.1792, 12.12.1804 and 11.4.1806. See also no. 3473
50	Thomas Allen	lgw	April 1697	

LONDON GOLDSMITHS

No.	Name	Category	Entered	Notes
51	idem	lgw	idem	
52	idem	lgw	idem	
53	John Albright	smw	10.4.1718	See also no. 1094
54	Ambrose Lewis	smw	12.5.1725	
55	idem	smw	idem	
56	Abraham Le françois	lgw	1.12.1742(?3)	See also no. 62
57	Augustin Le Sage	lgw	before March 1773	Not in register. Mark taken from tureen 1774. See also no. 3474
58	Aaron Lestourgeon	smw	27.6.1771	A similar mark 11.11.1773. See also no. 63
59	idem	smw	4.1.1776	
60	Andrew Litzmann	gw	3.4.1784	See also no. 61

Also AJ. no. 3472; AK. no. 3473; AL. coronet above no. 3474

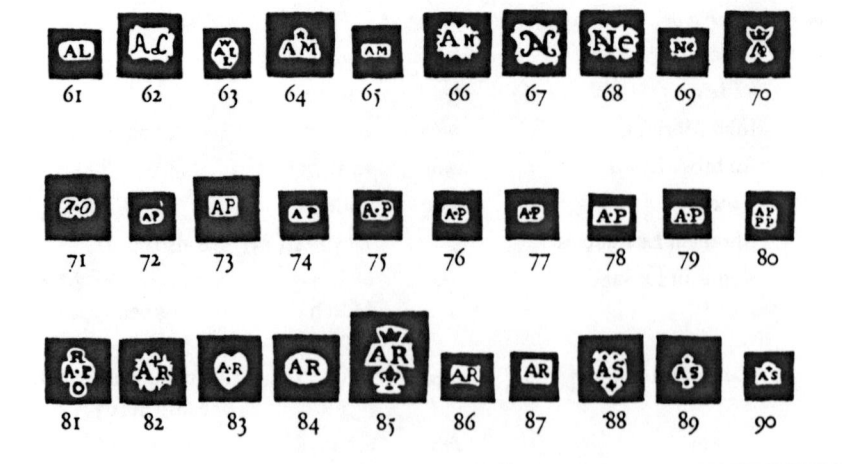

No.	Name	Category	Entered	Notes
61	Andrew Litzmann	gw	19.3.1803	
62	Abraham Le françois	lgw	22.10.1746	See also no. 56
63	William and Aaron Lestourgeon	smw	17.11.1767	Similar mark 8.12.1768. See also nos. 58, 59, 3227
64	A. Montgomery	lgw	27.6.1750	
65	Alexander Mullord	smw	6.2.1811	
66	William Andrews	lgw	April 1697	
67	Francis Nelme	lgw	20.3.1723	See also no. 702
68	Anthony Nelme	lgw	April 1697	See also no. 3741
69	idem	lgw	idem	
70	Abraham Lopes de Oliveyra	smw	undated c. 1725	
71	idem	lgw	3.7.1739	
72	Abraham Pope	smw	30.7.1720	See also no. 2208
73	Abraham Portal	lgw	26.10.1749	And a smaller similar mark same date
74	Andrew Price	smw	4.5.1763	
75	idem	smw	12.9.1766	
76	Alexperry Parkes	smw	20.6.1765	
77	Ann Pearee	smw	13.7.1765	
78	Abraham Peterson	plw	5.2.1790	A similar mark and a smaller 6.10.1792
79	Ann Payne	spm	25.10.1834	Similar mark 26.11.1834 and smaller similar mark in oval 5.12.1834
80	Abraham Peterson and Peter Podio	plw	1.5.1783	

LONDON GOLDSMITHS

No.	Name	Category	Entered	Notes
81	Hugh Arnett and Edward Pocock	lgw	15.2.1720	See also no. 993
82	Francis Archbold	lgw	April 1697	
83	Andrew Archbold	smw	31.3.1701	
84	Andrew Archer	lgw	27.10.1703	A smaller similar mark same date. See also no. 1
85	Peter Archambo I	lgw	9.3.1721	See also nos. 2127–8
86	Abraham Robert	smw	14.4.1727	See also no. 3475
87	Appolone Rudkins	smw	6.12.1766	
88	Thomas Ash	lgw	April 1697	See also nos. 95, 3476–7
89	Ambrose Stevenson	lgw	22.6.1720	See also no. 2638
90	William Ashbee	smw	11.1.1734	See also Section V, WA, star above

Also AM no. 3382; AR no. 3475; AS. nos. 3476–7

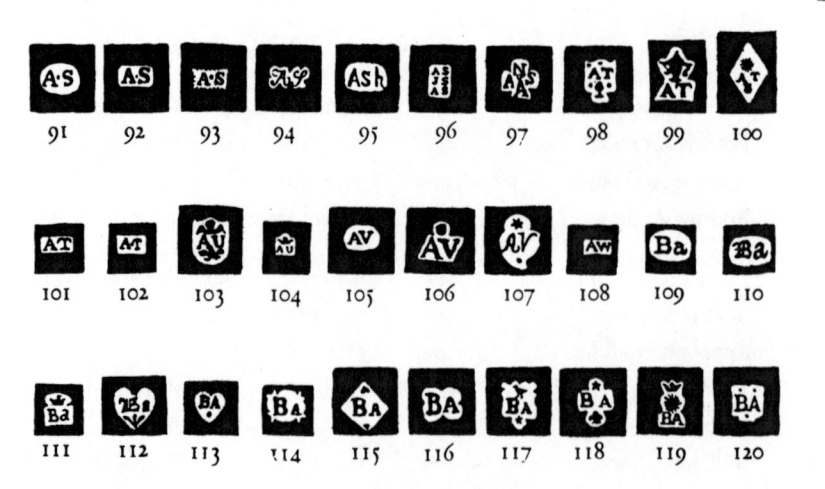

No.	Name	Category	Entered	Notes
91	Albartus Schurman	lgw	4.3.1756	See also no. 3478
92	Alexander Sa(u)nders	smw	17.7.1778	See also no. 94
93	Alexander Smith	smw	8.3.1819	
94	Alexander Saunders	lgw	3.9.1757	See also no. 92
95	Thomas Ash	lgw	April 1697	See also no. 88*
96	Adey Bellamy Savory, Joseph Savory II, Albert Savory	plw spm	7.9.1833	And another smaller same date and similar marks 5.7.1834
97†	Nathaniel Appleton and Anne Smith	smw	26.7.1771	Poor impression
98	Christopher Atkinson	lgw	23.10.1707	
99	William Atkinson	lgw	31.5.1725	See also no. 2999
100	Anne Tanqueray	lgw	undated c. 1725	Entered after her husband David's death
101	Abraham Taylor	smw	26.1.1796	And a smaller similar mark 6.2.1795 and similar marks in two sizes 2.11.1798 and 2.8.1803
102	Abraham Thurkle	smw	9.2.1827	See also Section IX, F.T
103	Henry Aubin	lgw	10.6.1700	
104	idem	lgw	13.3.1716	
105	Henry Avery	smw	23.8.1710	
106	Aymé Videau	lgw	By 1726	Missing from register (Cf. Jackson, p. 180). Mark taken from a creambucket 1735

* Cf. Jackson, page 154 for incuse monogram Ash struck over maker's mark MP on candlesticks of 1683. † Found on cream jugs of 1767 and 1780 (Goldsmiths' Company).

LONDON GOLDSMITHS

No.	Name	Category	Entered	Notes
107	idem	lgw	18.6.1739	
108	Arthur Worboys	smw	23.9.1758	
109	Thomas Bamford I	lgw	5.1.1720	See also nos. 2687, 2704
110	idem	lgw	idem	
111	Edmund Barton	smw	8.5.1734	
112	John Barnard I	lgw	April 1697	See also no. 3480
113	idem	lgw	12.10.1720*	Date uncertain but probably entered with Old Std. mark
114	William Bainbridge I	lgw	April 1697	
115	Mary Bainbridge	lgw	21.4.1707	
116	Richard Bayley	lgw	29.3.1708	And a smaller similar mark same date. See also nos. 2262, 2279, 3481, 3760-1
117	William Barnes	lgw	20.7.1702	
118	John Bache	lgw	1.11.1700	See also nos. 1115, 3482-3
119	Joseph Barbut	lgw	1.10.1703	Similar mark 27.7.1717. See also nos. 1114, 1176, 3481
120	Henry Bance	smw	4.9.1706	See also nos. 962, 964

Also AS nos. 3476-8; AU no. 3479; Ba no. 3480; BA nos. 3481-3

---

* But also found on pair of trencher salts of 1713 (Christie's).

21

BA BD

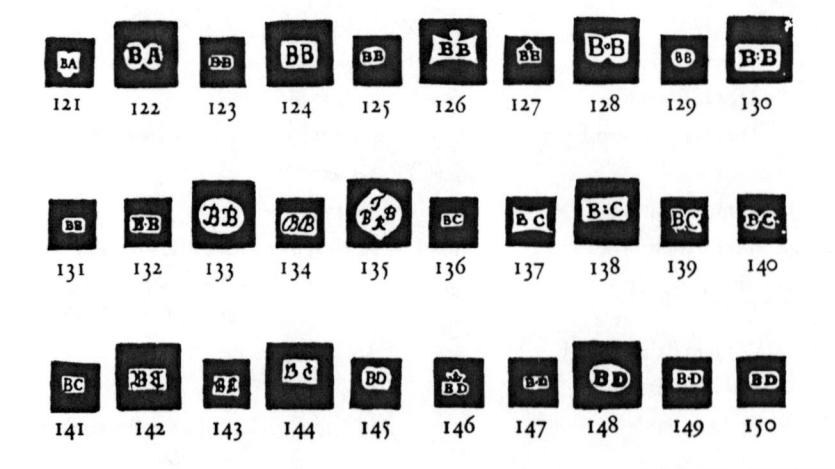

No.	Name	Category	Entered	Notes
121	Thomas Bass	smw	4.10.1708	See also no. 2685
122	Edward Barnett	lgw	18.11.1715	
123	Benjamin Bird	smw	16.2.1721	
124	Benjamin Blakely	lgw	29.6.1720	See also nos. 133, 185
125	idem	lgw	July 1738 –May 1739	
126	Benjamin Bentley	lgw	31.1.1728	See also no. 163
127	Benjamin Brewood I	smw	13.8.1729	
128	Benjamin Brewood II	lgw	9.8.1755	Apparently son of above
129	idem	lgw	idem	
130	idem	lgw	29.1.1757	
131	Benjamin Bickerton	smw	31.3.1762	Similar marks 10 and 26.6.1771. See also no. 134 and Section VIII, B.B. and BB.TB
132	Basil Bagshaw	plw, gw	27.3.1829	
133	Benjamin Blakeley	lgw	2.7.1739	See also no. 124
134	Benjamin Bickerton	smw	6.12.1762	See also no. 131
135	Bennett Bradshaw and Robert Tyrill	lgw	2.7.1739	See also nos. 2444, 2449
136	Benjamin Cooper I	smw	4.5.1724	
137	Benjamin Corbett	smw	8.8.1726	
138	Benjamin Cartwright II	lgw	22.4.1754	See also nos. 142–4
139	idem	lgw	7.9.1756	
140	idem	lgw	2.1.1770	
141	B(enjamin) Cooper II	smw	17.1.1764	Similar mark Sept. 1765
142	Benjamin Cartwright I	lgw	20.6.1739	See also nos. 138–40

LONDON GOLDSMITHS

No.	Name	Category	Entered	Notes
143	idem	*lgw*	19.5.1748	
144	idem	*lgw*	18.2.1757	
145	Basile Denn	*smw*	3.9.1729	
146	idem	*smw*	idem	And similar mark 31.3.1731
147	idem	*smw*	28.7.1758	A similar mark and another in lobed punch 22.7.1759
148	Burrage Davenport	*plw*	before March 1773	Not in register. Mark taken from mustard pot 1776
149	Benjamin Davis	*spm*	10.5.1823	And similar marks 24.1.1824 and 18.5.1826
150	Benjamin Reece Dexter	*plw*	30.9.1835	

Also BC no. 3484

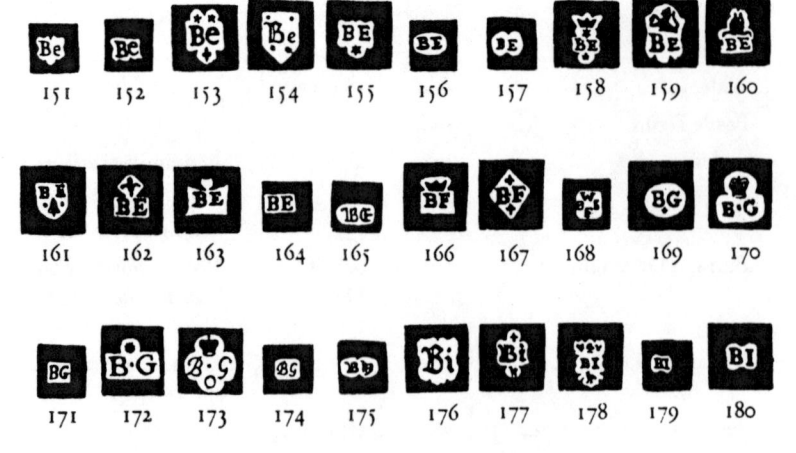

No.	Name	Category	Entered	Notes
151	John Berry	smw	20.12.1699	
152	Thomas Bevault	lgw	24.12.1712	
153	George Beale	lgw	1.6.1713	See also nos. 156, 3486
154	John Betts	lgw	25.4.1705	See also no. 1117
155	Benjamin Bentley	lgw	25.11.1698	See also no. 3485
156	George Beale	smw	27.10.1699	See also nos. 153, 3486
157	William Bedford	smw	10.5.1702	Month uncertain
158	James Beschefer	lgw	4.10.1704	
159	Henry Beesley	lgw	23.7.1714	And a smaller similar mark same date. See also no. 3600
160	William Bellassyse	lgw	16.3.1717	See also no. 3008
161	Joseph Bell I	lgw	1.10.1716	See also no. 2707
162	William Bellamy	lgw	1.10.1717	
163	Benjamin Bentley	lgw	31.1.1728	See also no. 126
164	Benjamin Elkin	plw	3.11.1817	
165	William Bertram	smw	April 1697	And a smaller similar mark in oval punch same date
166	Bernard Fletcher	lgw	17.9.1725	
167	Blanche Fralion	lgw	undated	Between Sept. 1727 and June 1728
168	Benjamin and William Flight	smw	20.12.1779	
169	Benjamin Godwin	lgw	15.1.1730	
170	Benjamin Godfrey	lgw	3.10.1732	See also nos. 173-4
171	Benjamin Griffin	lgw	27.1.1743	
172	Benjamin Gignac	lgw	28.2.1745	Another with square projecting upper portion found on pieces from 1750-63 (Christie's). See also no. 3489

LONDON GOLDSMITHS

No.	Name	Category	Entered	Notes
173	Benjamin Godfrey	*lgw*	18.6.1739	See also no. 170
174	idem	*lgw*	idem	
175	Bartholomew Harwood	*smw*	9.7.1733	
176	Francis Billingsley	*lgw*	April 1697	
177	Joseph Bird	*lgw*	April 1697	See also no. 1120
178	idem	*lgw*	idem	
179	idem	*lgw*	after 1702	
180	John Bignell	*lgw*	14.5.1718	See also no. 1116

Also BE nos. 3485-7; BC no. 3488; BG no. 3489

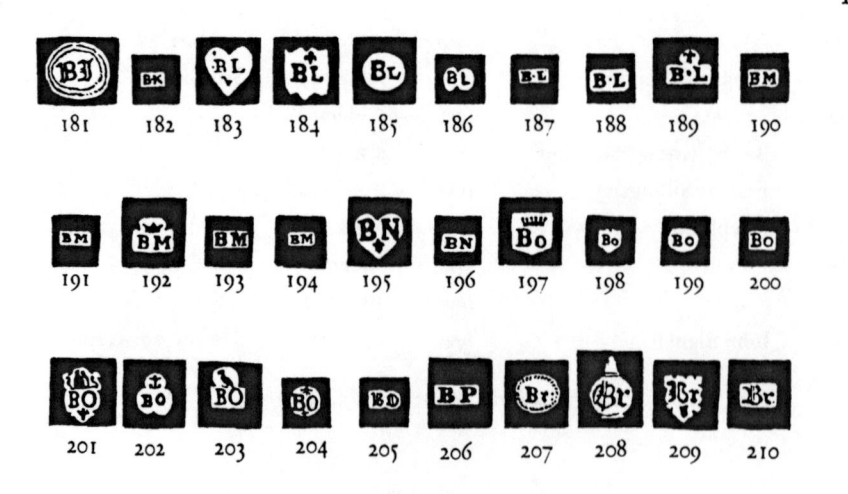

No.	Name	Category	Entered	Notes
181	Richard Bigge	lgw	23.11.1700	See also no. 3763
182	Louis Benoimont and Luke Kendall	smw	18.11.1761	See also nos. 1902, 1904
183	Anthony Blackford	lgw	12.6.1702	
184	Nathanvill Bland	lgw	10.7.1715	
185	Benjamin Blakely	lgw	10.10.1715	See also no. 124
186	Samuel Blackborow	lgw	4.9.1719	See also nos. 2474, 3789
187	Benjamin Lucas	smw	24.8.1758	
188	Benjamin Laver	plw	20.12.1781	And a smaller similar mark same date. Another 8.9.1782
189	idem	plw	1.7.1789	And two smaller similar marks same date
190	Benjamin Mordecai	smw	24.8.1770	And a smaller similar mark same date. See also no. 3490
191	Benjamin Mountigue	smw	26.4.1771	A similar mark 9.12.1771 and two others 4.9.1772 and 26.2.1773. See also nos. 1999, 3490 and Section VIII, B.M
192	Barak Mewburn	plw	31.8.1826	
193	idem	plw	1.5.1830	A similar mark 26.1.1831
194	Benjamin Massey	plw	19.8.1829	A similar mark slightly larger 23.9.1833
195	Bowles Nash	lgw	7.6.1721	
196	Benjamin North	hlm	15.2.1783	
197	Ishmael Bone	lgw	19.10.1699	
198	Samuel Bourne	smw	9.11.1700	
199	Robert Bodley	smw	4.4.1707	
200	Thomas Boulton	smw	19.12.1715	See also no. 2684
201	John Bodington	lgw	April 1697	

LONDON GOLDSMITHS

No.	Name	Category	Entered	Notes
202	Michael Boult	*lgw*	20.5.1713	See also no. 1993
203	George Boothby	*lgw*	1.3.1720	See also no. 746
204	Maurice Boheme	*smw*	29.6.1720	See also no. 1994
205	idem	*smw*	idem	
206	Benjamin Preston	*plw*	16.9.1825	And a smaller similar mark same date
207	Thomas Brydon	*lgw*	April 1697	See also no. 3493
208	William Brett	*lgw*	April 1697	
209	John Broake	*lgw*	8.7.1699	
210	Richard Bristow	*smw*	29.1.1707	

Also BM nos. 3490-2

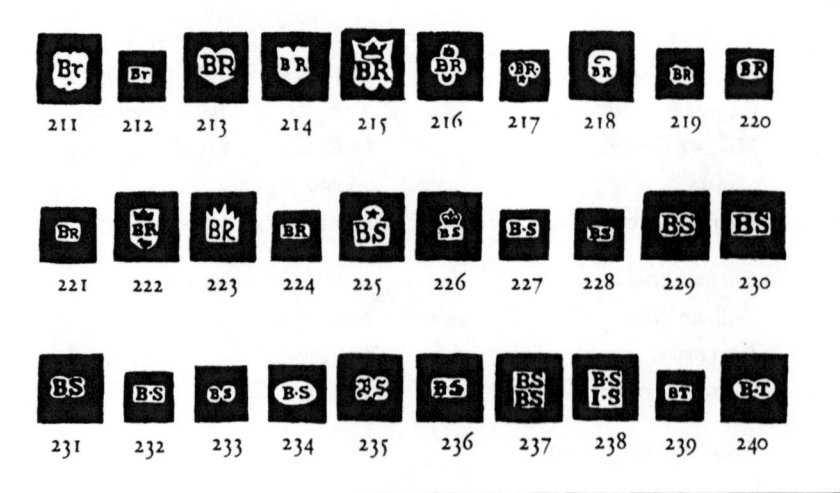

No.	Name	Category	Entered	Notes
211	Philip Brush	lgw	3.5.1707	
212	Erick Brandt	sbm	24.5.1726	See also no. 529
213	Moses Browne	lgw	April 1697	
214	John Brassey	lgw	April 1697	
215	Jonathan Bradley	lgw	April 1697	
216	Benjamin Braford	lgw	April 1697	
217	John Bromley	lgw	27.10 1703	
218	Stafford Briscoe	smw	23.7.1706	? A ring above. Poor impression
219	Hugh Brawne	smw	31.7.1710	
220	William Broadbent	smw	undated	Between 1702 and 1720
221	John Brind	smw	21.2.1716	
222	George Brydon	lgw	12.4.1720	See also no. 747
223	John Brumhall	lgw	undated	Between May 1721 and July 1723
224	Bartholomew Ross	smw	15.7.1822	
225	Benjamin Sanders	lgw	1.4.1737	See also nos. 235, 3494
226	Barnett Simons	smw	9.2.1767	Similar mark 11.6.1767
227	Benjamin Stephenson	plw	26.1.1775	And a smaller similar mark same date
228	Benjamin Simpson	smw	4.10.1800	
229	Benjamin Smith II	plw	25.6.1807	A smaller similar mark 11.5.1807
230	idem	plw	14.10.1812	And two smaller similar marks same date. Others similar 15.1.1814, 25.6.1818 and 24.5.1822
231	Benjamin Smith III	plw	1.12.1837	And a smaller similar mark same date

LONDON GOLDSMITHS

No.	Name	Category	Entered	Notes
232	Benoni Stephens	spm	14.8.1834	And a smaller same date. Another similar 9.10.1834
233	idem	spm	24.8.1836	
234	idem	plw	1.5.1835	And a smaller similar mark 18.6.1835
235	Benjamin Sanders	lgw	28.6.1739	See also nos. 225, 3494
236	Benjamin Smith III	plw	15.7.1818	And a smaller similar mark same date. See also nos. 231, 237
237	Benjamin Smith II and Benjamin Smith junr. (III)	plw	5.7.1816	And two smaller similar marks same date
238	Benjamin Smith II and James Smith III	plw	23.2.1809	And two smaller similar marks same date
239	Benjamin Tempest	spm	14.4.1826	
240	idem	spm	2.5.1826	Another in oval punch, undated, later

Also BR nos. 3383, 3493; BS no. 3384; *BS* no. 3494

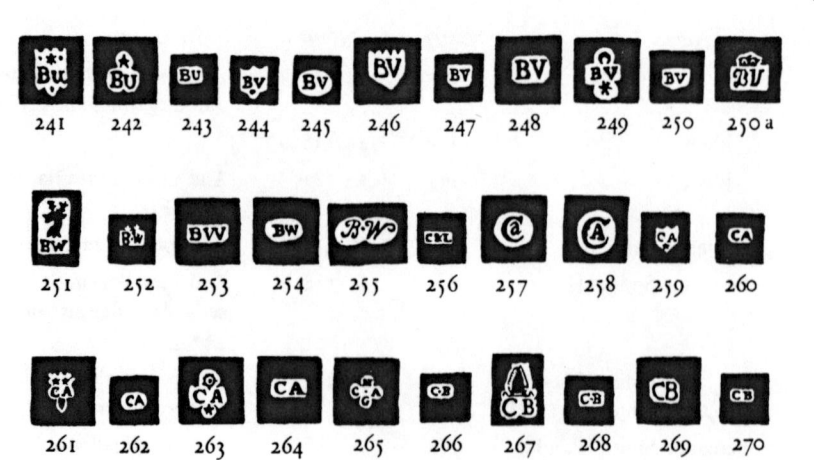

No.	Name	Category	Entered	Notes
241	Thomas Burridge	lgw	5.4.1706	See also no. 2686
242	idem	lgw	17.7.1717	
243	William Burkitt	smw	13.6.1716	
244	Thomas Bulley	smw	11.9.1707	See also nos. 250, 2688
245	John Burgh	smw	28.11.1716	See also no. 1119
246	William Bull	lgw	19.1.1699	See also no. 3495
247	Ed. Burkenhill	smw	12.8.1699	
248	Robert Butterfield	smw	undated	c. 1720
249	Abraham Buteux	lgw	13.5.1721	See also no. 8
250	Thomas Bulley	smw	undated	Jan./Feb. 1724. See also no. 244
250a	James Burne	lgw	4.3.1724	See also no. 1174
251	Benjamin Watts	lgw	7.9.1720	See also no. 2984
252	Benjamin Wood	smw	28.8.1729	
253	Bowyer Walker	lgw	10.4.1735	
254	Benjamin West	lgw	14.1.1738	
255	idem	lgw	8.6.1739	
256	William Lukin II	smw	7.11.1769	
257	Christopher Canner II	lgw	30.5.1716	See also no. 277
258	Christopher Canner I	lgw	April 1697	
259	John Carter I	smw	April 1697	
260	John Carman I	smw	4.5.1716	See also no. 1190
261	Isaac Callard	lgw	7.2.1726	See also nos. 1196, 1223-4
262	Charles Archer	smw	9.9.1726	
263	Charles Alchorne	lgw	9.10.1729	
264	Charles Aldridge	plw	20.9.1786	A smaller similar mark 25.9.1789

LONDON GOLDSMITHS

No.	Name	Category	Entered	Notes
265	Charles Aldridge and Henry Green	plw	19.8.1775	And a smaller similar mark same date. Also found earlier c. 1770.
266	Charles Bagshaw	smw	12.7.1731	
267	Charles Belasyse	lgw	21.7.1740	Bellasyse in Apprentice register
268	Christopher Binger I	smw	28.2.1771	See also no. 272 and Section VII, C.B
269	Cornelius Bland	smw	7.3.1772	
270	idem	plw	25.9.1788	See also no. 271

Also BV no. 3495; CB nos. 3496–7

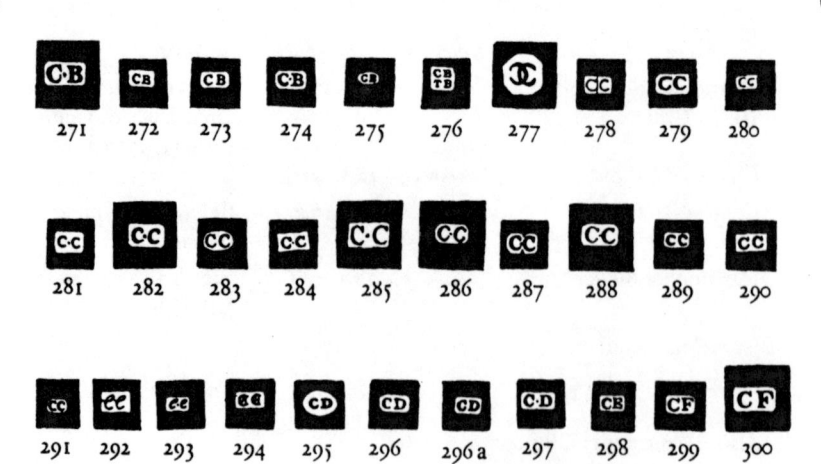

No.	Name	Category	Entered	Notes
271	Cornelius Bland	plw	9.12.1788	See also nos. 269, 270
272	Christopher Binger II	smw	24.2.1803	See also no. 268
273	Charles Boyton	spm	30.11.1825	
274	idem	spm	10.9.1830	And three similar marks 1830 to 1838
275	Charles Bull	smw	11.12.1832	
276	Christ. Barker and Thos. W. Barker	spm	11.10.1800	A similar mark 8.12.1804. See also nos. 2697, 3812
277	Christopher Canner II	lgw	8.7.1720	See also no. 257
278	Charles Cotterell I	smw	22.11.1723	See also no. 293
279	Christian Claris	lgw	16.6.1727	
280	Charles Chapman	smw	13.3.1734	
281	Charles Chesterman I	lgw	7.7.1741	See also no. 292
282	idem	lgw	20.11.1771	A similar mark to Charles Chesterman II as smallworker 14.2.1780
283	Charles Chesterman II	smw	6.3.1801	{ See above. And similar mark 10.1.1809
284	Charles Clark	lgw	12.9.1758	See also no. 294
285	idem	lgw	idem	
286	idem	lgw	14.3.1763	Another similar 20.4.1763
287	Catherine Clarke	smw	24.9.1761	
288	Charles Cathery	smw	3.7.1776	
289	Charles William Chilcott	smw	30.9.1822	
290	Clement Cheese	spm	30.6.1823	
291	Charles Conolly	plw	9.8.1824	
292	Charles Chesterman I	lgw	2.10.1752	See also nos. 281–2
293	Charles Cotterell II	smw	6.2.1760	See also no. 278

LONDON GOLDSMITHS

No.	Name	Category	Entered	Notes
294	Charles Clark	*lgw*	3.7.1739	See also nos. 284–6
295	Charles Dutton	*plw*	20.12.1790	
296	Charles Davy	*spm*	18.4.1817	
296a	Charles Day	*spm*	13.9.1822	See also no. 986
297	Charles Dimes	*plw*	28.2.1832	
298	Charles Eley	*spm*	19.1.1825	See also no. 3110
299	Crispin Fuller	*plw*	29.12.1792	And a smaller similar mark same date. Two similar marks 11.7.1796
300	idem	*plw*	5.8.1823	And a smaller similar mark same date

Also CC nos. 3498–9; CD no. 3500; *CE* no. 3501; CF. no. 3502

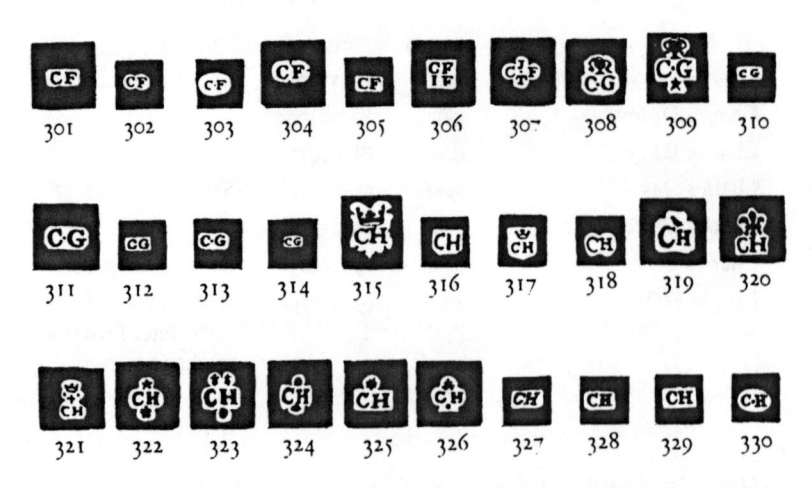

No.	Name	Category	Entered	Notes
301	Charles Fox I	plw	5.9.1804	See also no. 307
302	Charles Fox II	plw	19.2.1822	A similar mark 23.9.1823
303	idem	plw	27.1.1823	Similar marks of varying sizes 10.12.1823 and 9.5.1838
304	idem	plw	21.8.1823	And a similar mark same date
305	Charles Flint	plw	4.2.1826	
306	Charles and John Fry II	plw	29.8.1822	
307	James Turner and Charles Fox I	plw	20.10.1801	And a larger similar mark same date. See also nos. 301, 1716
308	Christopher Gerrard	lgw	2.7.1720	See also no. 790
309	Charles Gibbons	lgw	19.10.1732	
310	Charles Goodwin	smw	2.12.1799	
311	idem	smw	15.10.1803	
312	Charles Gibson	plw	21.2.1828	
313	Charles Gordon	smw	3.12.1828	
314	Christopher Gerock	smw	29.10.1831	
315	James Chadwick	lgw	April 1697	
316	William Chebsey	smw	undated	c. 1700
317	Richard Chapman	smw	undated	c. 1701. See also nos. 2282, 3765
318	Charles Chandler	smw	25.11.1701	
319	John Chamberlen	lgw	2.3.1704	
320	John Chartier	lgw	undated	April 1698–May 1699
321	idem	lgw	undated	April 1698–May 1699. See also no. 1194

LONDON GOLDSMITHS

No.	Name	Category	Entered	Notes
322	William Charnelhouse	lgw	19.6.1703	
323	Pierre Le Cheaube	lgw	21.11.1707	See also no. 2145
324	Charles Hatfield	lgw	21.6.1727	See also nos. 335, 944
325	Caleb Hill	lgw	17.9.1728	
326	Christian Hillan	lgw	20.4.1736	See also nos. 333–4
327	Charles Hougham	smw	11.1.1769	See also Section VIII, C.H
328	idem	smw	11.5.1769	
329	idem	plw	24.1.1785	And a smaller similar mark same date. Seven others 4.11.1786
330	Charles Hunter	smw	11.10.1771	
	Also CH no. 3503			

CH   CM

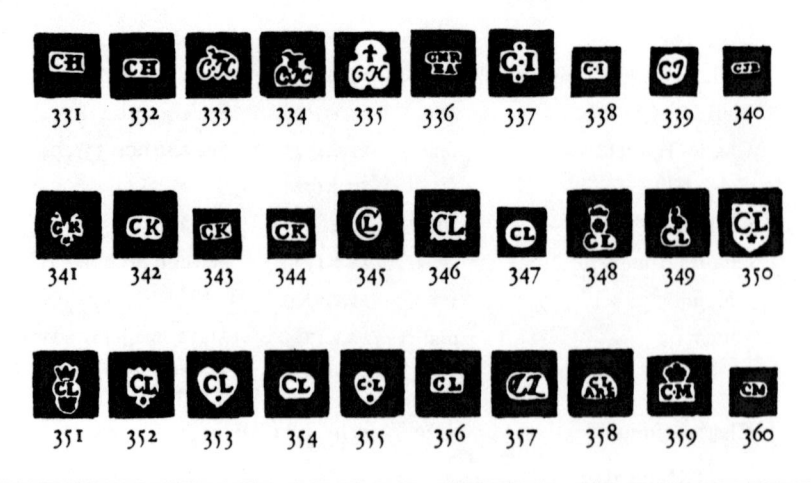

No.	Name	Category	Entered	Notes
331	Charles Hollinshed	plw	7.2.1807	And a smaller similar mark same date
332	idem	plw	23.4.1808	And a smaller similar mark same date. Another similar 16.3.1812
333	C(hristian) Hillan	lgw	4.6.1739	See also no. 326
334	idem	lgw	undated	On removal and a smaller similar mark in same entry
335	Charles Hatfield	lgw	10.8.1739	See also nos. 324, 944
336	Charles Hastings Rich and Elizabeth Adams	plw	13.6.1823	
337	Charles Jackson	lgw	6.7.1720	See also nos. 1095, 3611
338	Charles Johnson	lgw	4.8.1743	
339	Charles Jackson	lgw	18.6.1739	See also no. 337
340	Christopher John Buckler	smw	25.10.1804	
341	Charles Kandler I	lgw	29.8.1727	See also nos. 689, 691, 1540, 1862–3*
342	Charles Kandler II	plw	12.11.1778	And a smaller similar mark same date
343	Charles Kay	plw	15.3.1822	
344	Charles Kelk	n.s.	14.10.1828	
345	David Clayton	smw	9.7.1697	See also no. 452
346	Ruth Clayton	smw	31.12.1697	
347	John Clarke I	smw	12.9.1700	See also nos. 354, 1193
348	Jonah Clifton	lgw } smw	25.11.1703	And a smaller similar mark same date. See also no. 1191
349	Richard Clarke	lgw	21.10.1708	

* Another mark CK mitre above which must be his appears on the rococo kettle c. 1730 at the Victoria and Albert Museum.

LONDON GOLDSMITHS

No.	Name	Category	Entered	Notes
350	John Clifton	lgw	21.10.1708	
351	Niccolaus Clausen	lgw	10.6.1709	See also no. 2085
352	Henry Clarke I	lgw	28.6.1709	See also nos. 965–6, 968
353	Joseph Clare I	lgw	25.9.1713	See also no. 1189
354	John Clarke I	lgw	20.7.1722	See also nos. 347, 1193
355	Charles Laughton II	lgw	26.8.1741	*An earlier mark CL in circle, pellet above and below, 15.11.1738
356	Charles Lias	plw	13.5.1837	And a smaller similar mark same date and others 1842–6
357	Benjamin Clare	lgw	undated	? 1702
358	Joseph Clare II	smw	1.10.1767	A similar mark 16.9.1768. See also nos. 1208–9
359	Charles Martin	lgw	undated 1728?	Another similar with larger crown 23.1.1730. See also nos. 365, 3587
360	Charles Mackenzie	smw	3.5.1736	
	Also CM nos. 3385, 3504–5			

* Distorted and irreproducible.

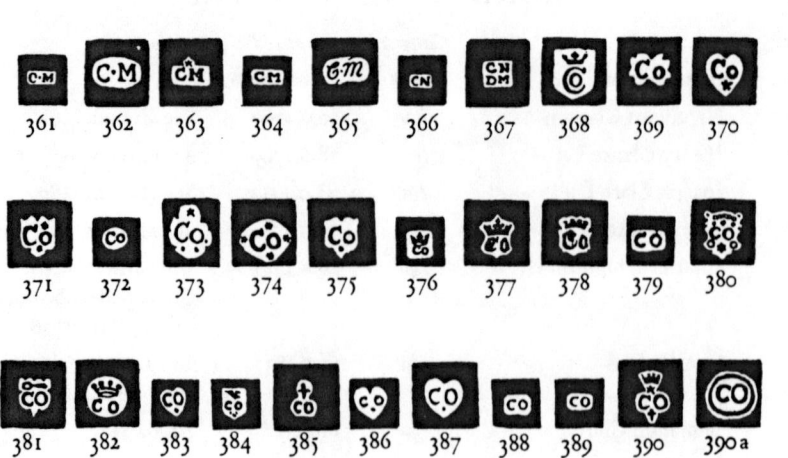

No.	Name	Category	Entered	Notes
361	Christopher Makemeid	smw	29.11.1758	
362	idem	plw	11.10.1771	A smaller similar mark 28.6.1773
363	Charles Mieg	smw	25.2.1767	
364	Charles Mansfield	spm	31.7.1828	
365	Charles Martin	lgw	20.2.1741	Entered by Sarah Martin in her husband's absence abroad. See also no. 359
366	Christopher Nicholle	smw	15.9.1720	See also no. 2096
367	Charles Neale and Daniel May I	smw	13.5.1783	See also no. 490
368	Henry Collins	lgw	undated	April 1698 – May 1699. See also no. 3507
369	Lawrence Coles	lgw	April 1697	
370	John Cole	lgw	April 1697	
371	George Cox	lgw	6.4.1698	
372	Edmund Cooper	smw	5.7.1699	And a similar mark with pellet over 'o'. Porringer and tumbler cup, 1705 (Christie's)
373	John Cope	lgw	25.6.1701	
374	John Cowsey	lgw	9.8.1701	See also no. 1192
375	idem	lgw	idem	
376	John Cooper I	smw	12.9.1721	'Gold mark'
377	John Cooke II	lgw	11.5.1699	
378	Matthew Cooper I	lgw	2.5.1702	See also no. 2003
379	Edward Courthope	lgw	April 1697	
380	Robert Cooper	lgw	April 1697	
381	Stephen Coleman	lgw	April 1697	

LONDON GOLDSMITHS

No.	Name	Category	Entered	Notes
382	John Cory	lgw	April 1697	
383	John Cooke I	smw	7.9.1699	
384	Thomas Corbet	lgw	12.12.1699	And a similar incuse mark same date
385	Augustine Courtauld	lgw	23.12.1708	See also nos. 18 and 22
386	Thomas Colvill	smw	14.7.1713	
387	Thomas Cooke I	smw	18.11.1713	
388	Samuel Colvill	smw	6.1.1716	See also no. 2488
389	Thomas Cooper	smw	18.4.1716	See also no. 2708
390	John Corporon	lgw	2.4.1717	?1716
390a	Edward Cornock	lgw	14.7.1707	See also no. 546

Also CN no. 3506; CO nos. 3386, 3507–9

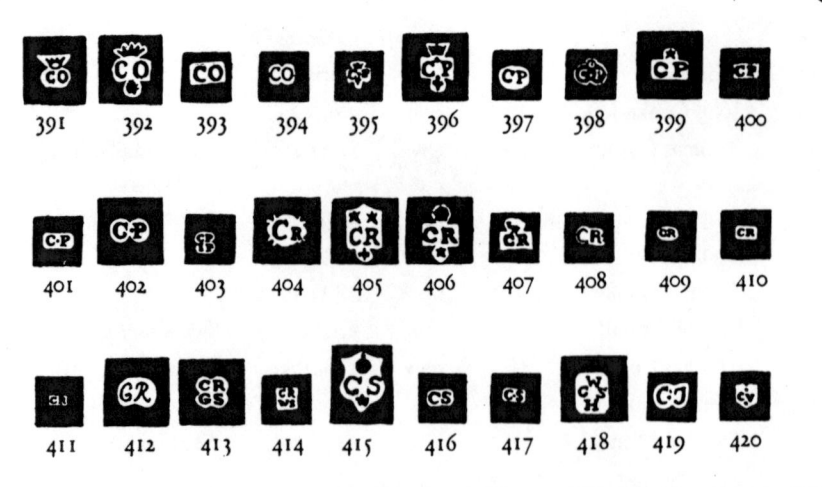

No.	Name	Category	Entered	Notes
391	Peter Courtauld	smw	15.6.1721	See also nos. 2144, 3509
392	Isaac Cornafleau	lgw	undated	July 1722–Dec. 1724. See also no. 1194a
393	Matthew Cooper II	lgw	9.9.1725	See also no. 2004
394	Peter Cornu	smw	8.10.1725	See also no. 2151
395	Charles Perier	lgw	6.1.1729	See also no. 2172
396	idem	lgw	21.6.1731	
397	Charles Pickering	smw	undated	May–August 1738
398	Catherine Pretty	smw	13.3.1759	
399	Christopher Potticary	smw	7.1.1767	See also Section V, N.P
400	Charles Plimpton	plw	27.5.1805	
401	Charles Price	plw	11.2.1812	
402	idem	plw	27.11.1823	A smaller similar mark 20.11.1826
403	Charles and John Plumley	plw	24.4.1822	
404	Jonathan Crutchfield	lgw	27.9.1697	
405	John Crutcher	lgw	29.6.1706	
406	Paul Crespin	lgw	undated	1720–1. See also nos. 412, 2143a, 2146, 2149
407	Jonathan (?) Croler	smw	7.12.1717	
408	Clifford Ray	smw	6.6.1737	
409	Charles Rawlings	plw	3.7.1817	
410	idem	smw	28.10.1819	And similar marks 1822 and 1826. Another in oval 1826
411	Charles Rich	plw	25.7.1817	
412	Paul Crespin	lgw	7.11.1740	See also nos. 406, 2143a, 2146, 2149
413	Charles Reily and George Storer	plw	1.1.1829	And a smaller similar mark same date

LONDON GOLDSMITHS

No.	Name	Category	Entered	Notes
414	Charles Rawlings and William Summers	smw	6.4.1829	And a smaller similar mark same date. See also Section VII, W.S
415	Charles Sprage	lgw	4.2.1734	
416	Charles Silk	smw	26.8.1817	
417	Charles Shipway	spm	25.1.1826	And a larger similar mark 8.5.1829. Another without pellet 17.6.1836
418	Charles Stewart and W.H	gs	4.7.1722	Second partner's name not given. See also no. 2647
419	Constantine Teulings	lgw	16.6.1755	
420	Christopher Cutting	smw	April 1697	

Also CR.DR no. 3387; CT.TTT no. 3388; CTW no. 3510

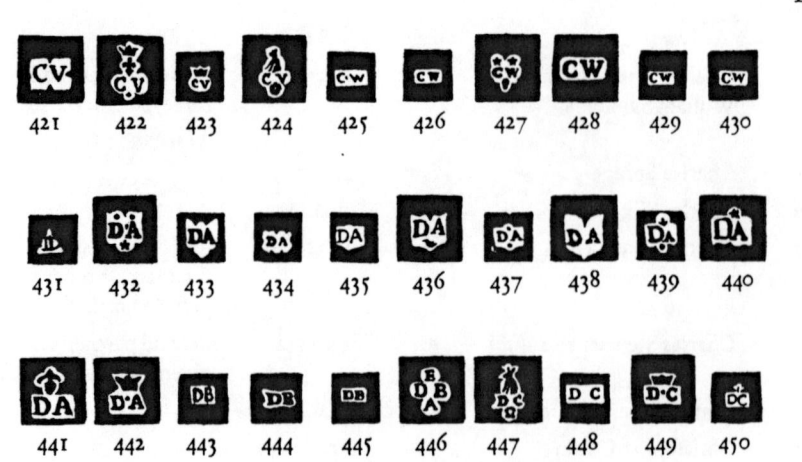

No.	Name	Category	Entered	Notes
421	Matthew Cuthbert	smw	April 1697	And a smaller similar mark same date
422	Louis Cuny	lgw	1.12.1703	See also no. 3715
423	idem	lgw	idem	Small mark
424	Daniel Cunningham	lgw	11.2.1717	See also no. 447
425	Charles Waldgrave	bm	21.1.1736	
426	Charles Woodward	lgw	10.4.1741	
427	Christopher Woods	plw	12.6.1775	And another slightly larger same date
428	Charles Wright	plw	22.7.1775	And two others similar with pellet between Feb. and Aug. 1780 and a smaller ditto. See also nos. 2976, 3510-11
429	Charles Watts	smw	5.1.1788	And others similar 1799, 1808 and 1813. Also incuse CW, Section V
430	Charles Weston	spm	13.10.1821	
431	John Delmestre	lgw	12.5.1755	See also no. 3630
432	Isaac Davenport	lgw	April 1697	
433	idem	lgw	idem	
434	idem	smw	2.2.1705	
435	John Daniels	smw	30.4.1703	See also no. 1238
436	Andrew Dalton	lgw	30.4.1708	
437	James Dalby	smw	2.8.1708	
438	Isaac Dalton	lgw	10.12.1711	See also no. 3512
439	idem	lgw	idem	
440	Josiah Daniel	lgw	21.2.1715	See also no. 3629
441	William Darker	lgw	10.1.1719	See also no. 3078

LONDON GOLDSMITHS

No.	Name	Category	Entered	Notes
442	Fleurant David	lgw	undated	After June 1724. See also no. 675
443	David Bell	lgw	30.11.1756	See also no. 3780
444	Daniel Boissonnade	smw	26.8.1775	
445	Daniel Bates	smw	23.6.1778	
446	William Denny and John Bache	lgw	April 1697	
447	Daniel Cunningham	lgw	4.7.1720	See also no. 424
448	Daniel Cowald	smw	29.6.1726	
449	Daniel Chapman	lgw	5.9.1729	
450	David Cartier	smw	25.9.1730	

Also CW no. 3511; DA no. 3512; DB.RM no. 3780

DC   DL

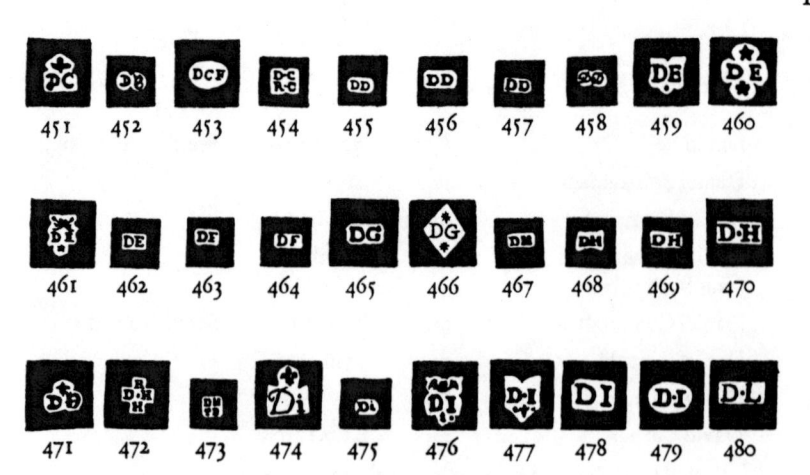

No.	Name	Category	Entered	Notes
451	Daniel Chartier	lgw	23.3.1740	
452	David Clayton	smw	6.7.1720	See also no. 345
453	Daniel Christian Fueter	lgw	8.12.1753	
454	Daniel Cole and Richard Calvert	smw	7.4.1762	
455	Dru Drury I	smw	8.8.1720	See also nos. 497–8
456	Daniel Denney	plw	24.7.1786	A similar mark 30.7.1799. See also no. 3513
457	Daniel Harmonas Dawes	smw	21.4.1827	
458	Dru Drury II	hfm, hlm	16.12.1767	
459	Samuel Dell	lgw	April 1697	
460	William Denny	lgw	April 1697	
461	James Desreumaux	smw	3.11.1716	See also no. 1237
462	James Delander	smw	undated	Before 24.10.1698
463	Daniel Fitch	smw	16.6.1773	
464	Donald Fraser	spm	5.7.1828	
465	David Green	lgw	22.6.1720	See also no. 875
466	Dinah Gamon	lgw	6.3.1740	
467	Daniel Heyford	smw	21.2.1730	And a similar mark 1.5.1739
468	Daniel Hall	smw	31.10.1734	
469	David Hennell I	lgw	23.6.1736	See also no. 471
470	Daniel Hockly	smw	16.1.1810	And a smaller similar mark same date
471	David Hennell I	lgw		Not in register. Probably June 1739. Mark taken from a saltcellar 1747
472	David and Robert Hennell I	lgw	9.6.1763	And a similar mark 9.7.1768

44

LONDON GOLDSMITHS

No.	Name	Category	Entered	Notes
473	Daniel Hockley and Thomas Bosworth	smw	6.4.1815	And a smaller similar mark same date
474	Arthur Dicken	lgw	18.6.1720	
475	William Dicker	smw	15.4.1720	See also no. 3077a
476	Isaac Dighton	lgw	April 1697	
477	John Diggle	lgw	April 1697	
478	Dike Impey	lgw	undated	Between Aug. 1727 and March 1729
479	idem	lgw	6.4.1736	
480	Dennis Langton	smw	26.6.1732	See also nos. 483, 1880, 3518

Also DD no. 3513; *DF* no. 3514; DH no. 3515; *DH* no. 3516; DK no. 3517; DL no. 3518

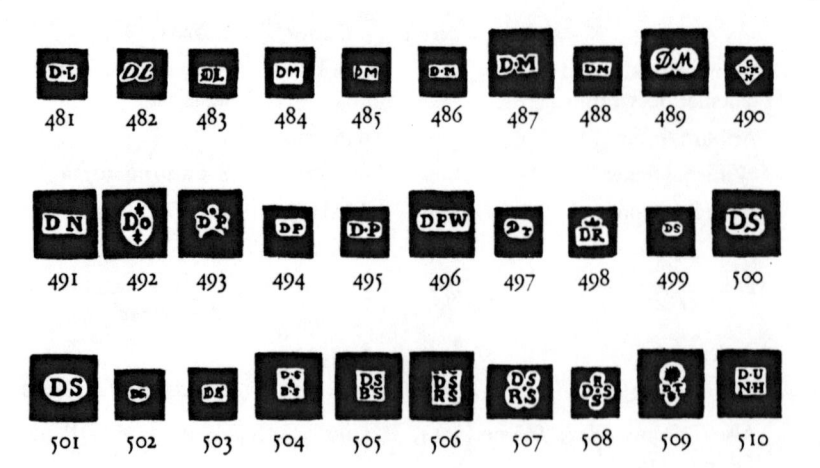

No.	Name	Category	Entered	Notes
481	Daniel Linthwait	smw	24.4.1761	
482	Daniel Lombard	wcm	4.3.1763	And a similar mark 26.11.1764
483	Dennis Langton	smw	28.10.1729	And a similar mark 17.3.1731. See also nos. 480, 1880, 3158
484	Donald Mackdonald	smw	21.7.1725	
485	Daniel Matthey	smw	25.1.1737	
486	David Mowden	slm	12.3.1739	
487	idem	smw	26.10.1774	
488	Daniel May I	smw	12.1.1784	
489	Dorothy Mills	lgw	6.4.1752	
490	Charles Neale and Daniel May I	smw	22.3.1783	See also no. 367
491	Desire Narcisse	plw	9.9.1824	And a smaller similar mark 26.4.1825
492	John Downes	lgw	April 1697	
493	Daniel Piers	lgw	3.11.1746	See also no. 3520
494	Daniel Pontifex	plw	10.9.1794	
495	David Phillips	spm	21.3.1834	And another similar 6.3.1835. A smaller mark without pellet 24.5.1839
496	Edward Dobson, William Pryor and James Williams	lgw	10.2.1755	
497	Dru Drury I	smw	7.7.1711	See also no. 455
498	idem	smw	14.10.1717	
499	Daniel Shelmerdine	sword cutler	22.6.1720	See also nos. 2523–4
500	Daniel Shaw	lgw	7.12.1748	
501	Dorothy Sarbitt	lgw	13.12.1753	See also no. 3519

LONDON GOLDSMITHS

No.	Name	Category	Entered	Notes
502	David Solomon	smw	19.9.1817	Also incuse mark DS 29.5.1813
503	Daniel Skinner	smw	20.6.1720	See also no. 2562
504	Digby Scott and Benjamin Smith II	plw	4.10.1802	See also no. 3522
505	idem	plw	21.3.1803	And smaller similar mark same date
506	Daniel Smith and Robert Sharp	plw	7.2.1780	And a smaller similar mark same date. See also nos. 2293, 2436
507	idem	plw	idem	
508	idem	plw	idem	Recorded by Jackson as early as 1768. See also nos. 3521, 3523
509	David Tanqueray	lgw	12.8.1720	See also no. 2675
510	Duncan Urquhart and Napthali Hart	bm	18.10.1791	And a smaller similar mark same date. Others similar 20.5.1795, 19.1.1802 and 22.8.1805. See also nos. 2094, 3743, 3849, and Section V, INH and NH.INH

Note: For an unidentified mark D & P see no. 1585 note. Also DM.TS no. 3519; DP no. 3520; *DS* no. 3521; DS.BS.IS no. 3522; *DS.RS.* no. 3523

DV   EB

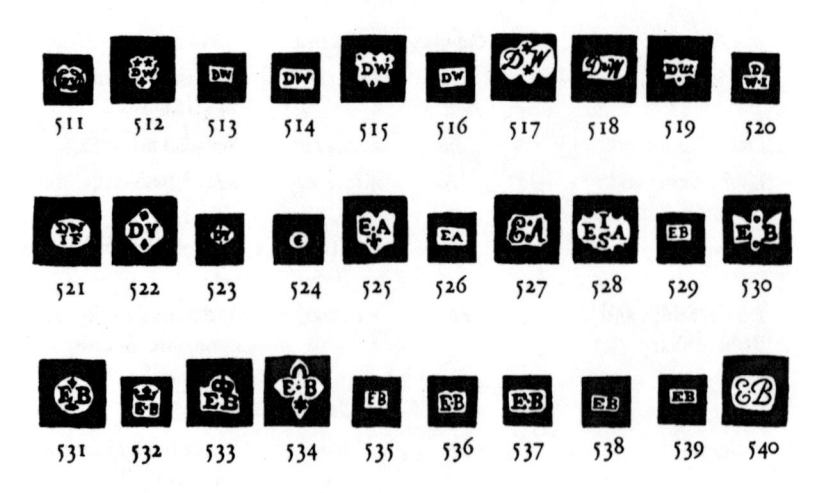

No.	Name	Category	Entered	Notes
511	Matthieu Durousseau	smw	27.8.1705	
512	David Willaume I	lgw	27.7.1720	See also nos. 3192-4
513	Daniel Wells	smw	23.9.1723	
514	David Willaume II	lgw	2.4.1728	See also nos. 517, 3195
515	Dennis Wilks	lgw	29.9.1737	See also no. 519
516	David Whitehouse	smw	25.11.1790	Also incuse DW, Section V
517	David Willaume II	lgw	19.6.1739	See also nos. 514, 3195
518	Thos. Devonshire and Wm. Watkins	lgw	9.2.1756	See also nos. 2739, 3374, 3857, 3910
519	Dennis Wilks	lgw	2.7.1739	And another similar 30.11.1747. See also no. 515
520	William and John Deane	smw	19.10.1762	And similar larger marks 3.11.1763, 10.8.1764, 12.10.1764 and 26.4.1768. See also nos. 1797 and 3090
521	Dennis Wilks and John Fray	lgw	19.7.1753	
522	Edward Dymond	lgw	1.12.1722	See also nos. 564-5
523	idem	lgw	idem	
524	James Edwards I	smw	30.7.1735	
525	John East	lgw	23.4.1697	See also no. 1266
526	Edward Aldridge	smw	5.2.1724	See also nos. 3528-35 and 3562
527	idem	lgw	29.6.1739	
528	Edward Aldridge and John Stamper	lgw	20.7.1753	And a smaller similar mark same date
529	Erick Brandt	sbm	24.5.1726	See also no. 212
530	Edward Bennett I	lgw	27.3.1727	See also nos. 533, 540, 544
531	Edmund Bodington	lgw	5.7.1727	See also no. 542

LONDON GOLDSMITHS

No.	Name	Category	Entered	Notes
532	Esaye Berthet	lgw	31.10.1728	
533	Edward Bennett I	lgw	25.6.1731	And a smaller similar mark 30.12.1737. See also nos. 530, 540, 544
534	Elizabeth Buteux	lgw	15.11.1731	
535	Ed. Broadhurst	smw	24.12.1731	
536	Edward Bradshaw	smw	14.6.1734	
537	Edward Bennett Jr. (II)	gs	26.6.1756	And a smaller similar mark same date. See also no. 541
538	Edward Betts	spm	23.12.1807	
539	Edward Barton	plw	14.1.1822	And a smaller similar mark same date. See also no. 3537
540	Edward Bennett I	gs	20.7.1747	See also 530, 533, 544

Also DW no. 3524; *DW* no. 3525; DW.WH no. 3526; DZ no. 3527; EA nos. 3528–30; *EA* no. 3531; 𝕰𝕬 nos. 3532–4; EA.EA nos. 3535; EB nos. 3536–7

EB   ED

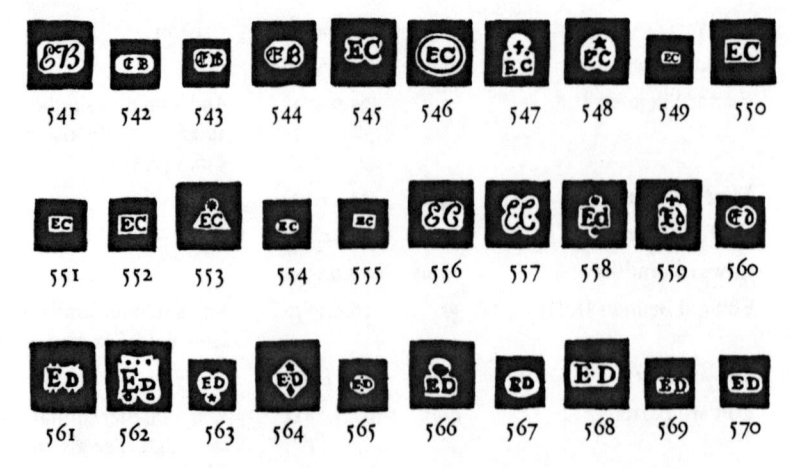

No.	Name	Category	Entered	Notes
541	Edward Bennett Jr. (II)	gs	26.6.1756	See also no. 537
542	Edmund Bodington	gs	8.10.1725	See also no. 531
543	Edward Bayley	smw	27.4.1738	
544	Edward Bennett I	gs	28.6.1739	See also nos. 530, 533, 540
545	John Eckfourd I	lgw	31.12.1698	See also no. 1264
546	Edward Cornock	lgw	25.11.1723	See also no. 390a
547	Edward Conen	lgw	8.12.1724	
548	John Eckford Jr. (II)	lgw	23.6.1725	See also no. 1269
549	Edward Cooke	smw	10.8.1735	
550	Ebenezer Coker	lgw	27.3.1738	See also nos. 556, 3538–9
551	Edmund Carrington	smw	16.5.1738	
552	Elizabeth Cooke	ss	24.1.1764	And a smaller similar mark with pellet between E.C. 9.3.1764. See also no. 3538
553	Edward Cooper	smw	27.7.1775	
554	E. Clark	smw	8.5.1790	
555	Edward Capper	smw	8.11.1792	And a larger similar mark 27.8.1813
556	Ebenezer Coker	lgw	25.6.1739	And a smaller similar mark 20.12.1751. Another in lobed punch 24.5.1745
557	Elias Cachart	lgw	17.6.1742	And another slightly smaller same date
558	Richard Edwards	lgw	13.8.1716	See also no. 2307
559	Samuel Edlin	smw	5.8.1704	See also no. 2508
560	idem	smw	idem	
561	James Edge (?Edgar)	lgw	April 1697	
562	Stephen Edmonds	lgw	13.6.1700	

50

LONDON GOLDSMITHS

No.	Name	Category	Entered	Notes
563	Moses Eden	smw	8.7.1719	See also no. 2022
564	Edward Dymond	lgw	1.12.1722	See also nos. 522–3
565	idem	lgw	idem	
566	John Edwards II	lgw	27.4.1724	See also nos. 573, 1267, 1277
567	Edward Dowdall	lgw	6.12.1748	
568	idem	lgw	9.11.1751	
569	Edward Dobson	lgw	9.9.1755	And a larger similar mark same date
570	Edward Darvill	lgw	23.3.1757	
	Also EC no. 3538; EC.TH no. 3539			

ED   EI

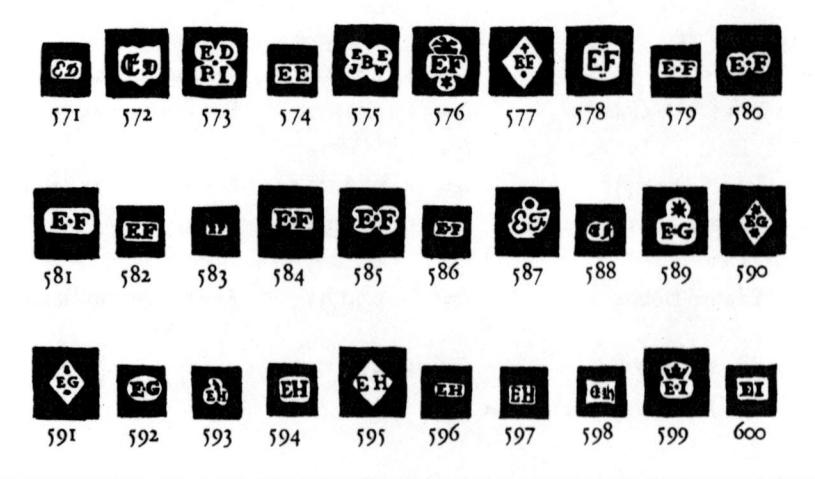

No.	Name	Category	Entered	Notes
571	Edward Dobson	spm	3.12.1778	
572	John Edwards I	lgw	April 1697	
573	John Edwards II and Georges Pitches	lgw	6.12.1723	See also no. 630
574	⎧ Edward Edwards I	plw	19.9.1816	And a smaller similar mark same date.
	⎩ Edward Edwards II	smw	11.4.1828	Others similar 1840 and 1841
575	Edward, Edward Jn., John and W. Barnard	plw	25.2.1829	And two others similar, larger and smaller, same date
576	Edward Feline	lgw	25.9.1720	See also nos. 587, 679
577	Edith Fle(t)cher	lgw	undated	Between Feb. 1729 and Jan. 1732
578	Edward French	lgw	undated	Between Aug. 1734 and May 1739. See also no. 23
579	Edward Fernell	plw	19.1.1780	And others similar 18.7.1787 and 3.8.1787. See also no. 3152
580	idem	plw	11.11.1780	
581	idem	plw	13.2.1781	And another similar 29.6.1787
582	idem	plw	8.8.1787	And another slightly larger 18.9.1787
583	Edward Fairbrother	smw	11.3.1793	And two others similar 18.9.1804 and see Section VIII, EF, pellet between
584	Edward Farrell	plw	27.4.1813	And a smaller similar mark 20.5.1813
585	idem	plw	17.3.1819	And a smaller similar mark same date
586	Edward Furnice	plw	2.8.1816	And another in rectangular punch, 5.1.1820. See also no. 2890

52

LONDON GOLDSMITHS

No.	Name	Category	Entered	Notes
587	Edward Feline	lgw	15.6.1739	See also no. 576
588	Epaphroditus Fowler	smw	27.7.1720	See also no. 704
589	Edward Gibbon	lgw	31.8.1723	And a larger similar mark same date. See also no. 826
590	Elizabeth Goodwin	lgw	2.12.1729	
591	Elizabeth Godfrey	lgw	29.6.1741	
592	Edmund Gouldsmith	smw	15.1.1796	
593	Edward Horne I	smw	27.7.1720	See also no. 1049
594	Edward Hall	lgw	14.1.1721	See also no. 943
595	Elizabeth Hartley	lgw	6.6.1748	
596	Edward Hunt II	smw	11.9.1762	
597	Edward Higgs	smw	30.3.1763	See also Section VIII, E.H and EH.JH
598	Edward Horne Junior (II)	smw	8.3.1739	
599	Edward Jennings	lgw	1.7.1720	See also nos. 1260, 1265
600	Elizabeth Jones	plw	15.1.1783	

Also €𝔅 no. 3540; EG nos. 3541-2; €𝕳𝔄 no. 3543; EI nos. 3544-5

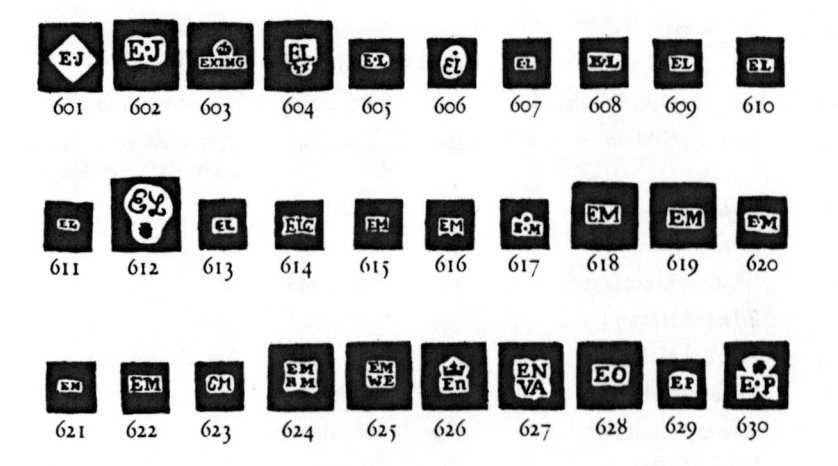

No.	Name	Category	Entered	Notes
601	Elizabeth Jackson	lgw	4.8.1748	See also no. 628 on re-marriage
602	Edward Jay	lgw	15.4.1757	And a smaller similar mark same date. See also no. 3545
603	Edmund King	smw	11.1.1717	Variant with ermine spot below K found on gilt box c. 1720
604	George Ellis	smw	15.11.1721	See also no. 791
605	Ed. Lee	smw	13.8.1729	
606	Edward Lambe I	lgw	31.7.1740	Impression distorted. See also nos. 612, 3546
607	Edward Lowe	smw	24.9.1760	And another similar 22.12.1769
608	idem	plw	15.8.1777	
609	Edward Leapidge	smw	22.8.1767	
610	Edward Lees	spm	22.2.1803	And another with canted top right corner to punch 30.6.1806
611	Edward Lambe II	plw	2.4.1824	
612	Edward Lambe I	lgw	3.9.1742	Impression distorted. See also no. 606
613	Robert Elliot	smw	15.2.1716	See also no. 2308
614	Elias Le Clerc	smw	11.1.1725	
615	Edward Mumford	smw	undated	Between Nov. 1721 and Feb. 1722
616	Elizabeth Marriott	smw	undated	May 1739
617	Edmund Medlycott	smw	30.6.1748	
618	Edward Moore	smw	20.7.1758	And another smaller 7.8.1758. Two others 14.12.1769. See also Section VII, E.M

LONDON GOLDSMITHS

No.	Name	Category	Entered	Notes
619	Elizabeth Muns	smw	3.5.1768	
620	Elizabeth Morley	smw	8.8.1794	And two others smaller 19.7.1796 and 1.10.1800
621	Edward Mayfield	smw	10.11.1706	
622	Edward Middlecott	plw	24.9.1817	See also no. 625
623	Edward Malluson	lgw	13.6.1743	
624	Elizabeth and Robert Mathews	plw	17.2.1825	And another similar 15.3.1825
625	Edward Middlecott and William Esterbrooke	plw	29.8.1816	See also no. 622
626	Thomas England	lgw	26.8.1725	See also nos. 2741, 2746
627	William England and John Vaen	lgw	22.7.1714	See also nos. 3850–1
628	Elizabeth Oldfield	lgw	19.12.1750	And a smaller similar mark 5.9.1754
629	Edmund Pearce	lgw	28.7.1720	See also nos. 2169, 3547
630	John Edwards II and George Pitches	lgw	6.12.1723	See also no. 573

Also EL no. 3389; *EL* no. 3546; EP nos. 3548–50

EP   Fa

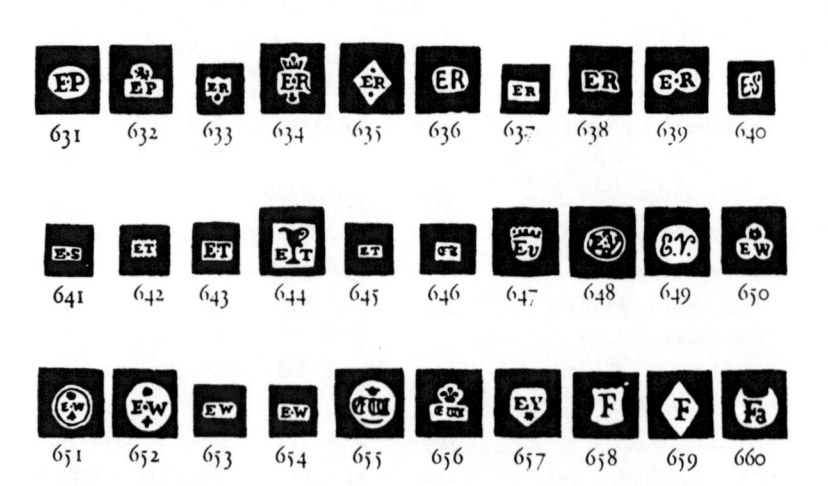

No.	Name	Category	Entered	Notes
631	Edward Peacock	lgw	5.9.1724	
632	Edward Pocock	lgw	11.12.1728	
633	Edward Raven(s)	smw	4.7.1720	See also no. 2250
634	Estienne Rongent	lgw	undated	c. 1731
635	Elizabeth Roode	smw	24.10.1738	
636	Edward Read	smw	3.3.1768	
637	idem	smw	16.3.1768	
638	Emick Romer	plw	before 1773	Not in register. Mark taken from mazareen
639	Elizabeth Roker	plw	11.10.1776	
640	Ernest Sieber	lgw	2.6.1746	Slightly distorted impression
641	Edward Stammers	smw	31.5.1816	And another larger 10.7.1828 as plateworker and a smaller ditto
642	Edward Thompson I	smw	undated	Between 1717 and 1720. See also no. 646
643	Evan Thomas	smw	25.4.1735	
644	Elizabeth Tuite	lgw	7.1.1741	
645	Elizabeth Taylor	smw	26.2.1767	And another similar, slightly larger 26.2.1771. See also no. 3559
646	Edward Thompson, Junr. (II)	smw	19.3.1728	See also no. 642
647	John Everit	smw	6.10.1701	
648	Edward Vincent	lgw	c. 1720	Missing from register. Mark taken from monteith 1724. See also nos. 2983, 3560, 3852
649	idem	lgw	25.6.1739	

56

LONDON GOLDSMITHS

No.	Name	Category	Entered	Notes
650	Thomas Ewesdin	lgw	6.5.1713	
651	Edward Wood	lgw	18.8.1722	See also nos. 655, 3246
652	idem	lgw	26.8.1735	
653	Edward Witham	smw	16.7.1813	And another slightly smaller 17.2.1814
654	Eden Wintle	spm	8.5.1828	
655	Edward Wood	lgw	30.9.1740	See also nos. 651–2, 3246
656	Edward Wakelin	lgw	17.11.1747	And a smaller similar mark same date
657	Edward Yorke	lgw	26.11.1730	See also no. 3381
658	William Fawdery	lgw	28.7.1720	See also nos. 664–5, 3563, 3873
659	Hester Fawdery	lgw	28.9.1727	
660	Thomas Fawler	lgw	3.9.1707	

Also ER no. 3551; ℭℜ no. 3552; *ER* nos. 3553–4; ER.S no. 3555; ES no. 3390; ℭ𝔖 no. 3556; ET nos. 3557–9; EV nos. 3560–1; EV.IA no. 3562

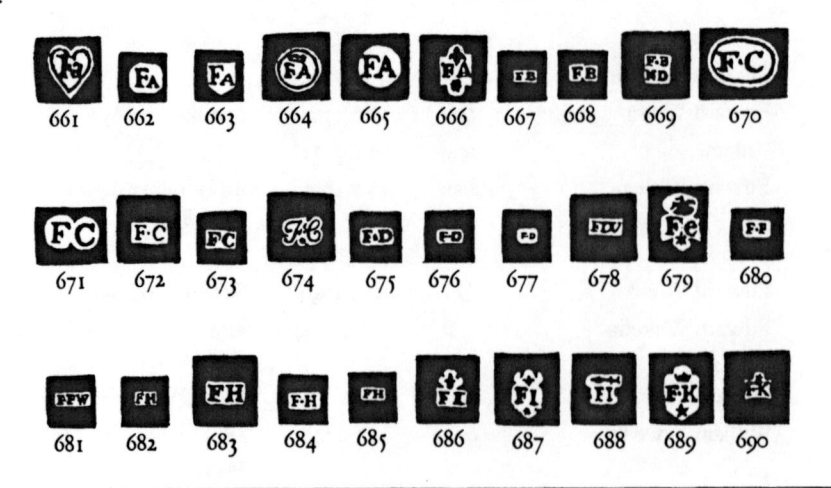

No.	Name	Category	Entered	Notes
661	John Farnell	lgw	26.6.1714	See also nos. 1283, 3565
662	John Fawdery I	lgw	April 1697	See also no. 1287
663	Peter Farettes	smw	15.6.1716	
664	William Fawdery	lgw	April 1697	See also nos. 658, 3563
665	idem	lgw	28.7.1720	
666	Thomas Farren	lgw	16.10.1707	See also nos. 2749, 2755, 3564
667	Francis Bazlinton	smw	27.6.1781	
668	Francis Blackbeard	plw	26.11.1824	
669	Francis Butty and Nicholas Dumee	lgw	by 1761	Not in register. Mark taken from a sauceboat 1765
670	Francis Crump	lgw	14.5.1745	See also no. 674
671	idem	lgw	30.3.1751	
672	idem	lgw	26.3.1756	And a larger similar mark 17.10.1761
673	Francis Clark*	plw	26.12.1826	And a smaller similar mark same date
674	Francis Crump	lgw	9.11.1741	See also nos. 670-2
675	Fleurant David	lgw	undated	After June 1724. See also no. 442
676	Francis Daniell	smw	26.5.1760	
677	Francis Douglas	smw	1.5.1837	And four others similar 1837-43
678	Frederick de Veer	smw	9.12.1731	
679	Edward Feline	lgw	25.9.1720	See also nos. 576, 3566
680	Flem(ing?) Forrester	smw	13.3.1772	
681	Frederick Foveaux Weiss	smw	30.6.1836	

* of Birmingham. Included here by error.

LONDON GOLDSMITHS

No.	Name	Category	Entered	Notes
682	Francis Harrache	smw	16.2.1738	
683	Francis Higgins	plw	31.10.1817	And a smaller similar mark same date and others 1821-9
684	idem	spm	3.12.1835	And others 1837-65
685	Frederick Hentsch	smw	4.11.1826	And also incuse FH 17.12.1818
686	Robert Finch	smw	April 1697	And a smaller similar mark same date
687	Joshua Field	lgw	3.12.1701	
688	William Fish	smw	10.6.1706	
689	Charles Frederick Kandler I	lgw	10.9.1735	See also nos. 341, 691, 1540, 1862
690	Frederick Knopfell	lgw	11.4.1752	

Also FA nos. 3563-5; Fe no. 3566; FE no. 3567; FF no. 3568; FG nos. 3569-70

FK   FS

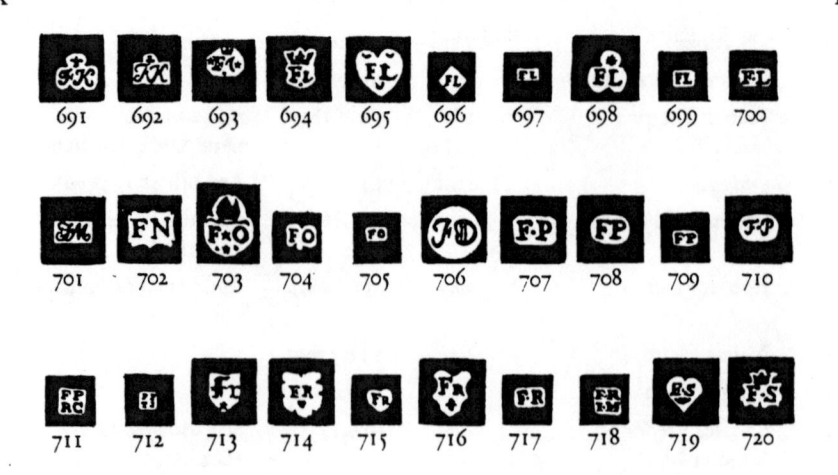

No.	Name	Category	Entered	Notes
691	Frederick Kandler	lgw	25.6.1739	See also nos. 689, 3571
692	idem	lgw	24.6.1758	
693	John Flavill	lgw	5.4.1726	See also no. 1285
694	William Fleming*	lgw	April 1697	
695	John Fletcher	lgw	undated	c. 1699–1700
696	Ann Fletcher	smw	April 1697	
697	Edward Fletcher	smw	4.4.1698	
698	John Flight	lgw	5.6.1710	
699	Francis Lawley	smw	31.12.1759	
700	idem	smw	16.5.1761	
701	Francis Magniac	plw	10.1.1798	
702	Francis Nelme	lgw	19.6.1739	See also no. 67
703	Thomas Folkingham	lgw	13.2.1707	See also no. 2750
704	Epaphroditus Fowler	smw	April 1697	See also no. 588
705	Frederick Obenaus	smw	17.7.1776	
706	William Fordham	lgw	31.1.1707	See also no. 3874
707	Francis Pages	lgw	—.—.1729	Day and month omitted in entry. See also no. 710
708	Frances Purton	smw	4.3.1783	And others smaller similar 16.6.1787 and 28.1.1795. See also no. 712
709	Francis Powell	smw	7.5.1818	See also no. 711
710	Francis Pages	lgw	18.6.1739	See also no. 707
711	Francis Powell and Robert Coates	smw	6.1.1818	
712	Frances Purton and Thomas Johnson	smw	28.2.1793	

* A similar mark with ermine spot at base found on teapot, 1718.

60

LONDON GOLDSMITHS

No.	Name	Category	Entered	Notes
713	James Fraillon	lgw	17.1.1711	See also no. 1284
714	William Francis	lgw	April 1697	
715	William Francys	smw	15.1.1704	
716	Joshua Frensham	lgw	12.9.1707	And another larger same date
717	Ralph Frith	lgw	24.6.1728	See also no. 2312
718	Francis Robine and John Macbride	smw	10.2.1810	
719	Francis Spilsbury I	lgw	24.7.1729	
720	idem	lgw	15.6.1739	See also no. 2621

Also *FK* 3571; 𝔍𝔐 no. 3572; FO no. 3573; FP.DG no. 3574; FP.SC no. 3575

FS   G B

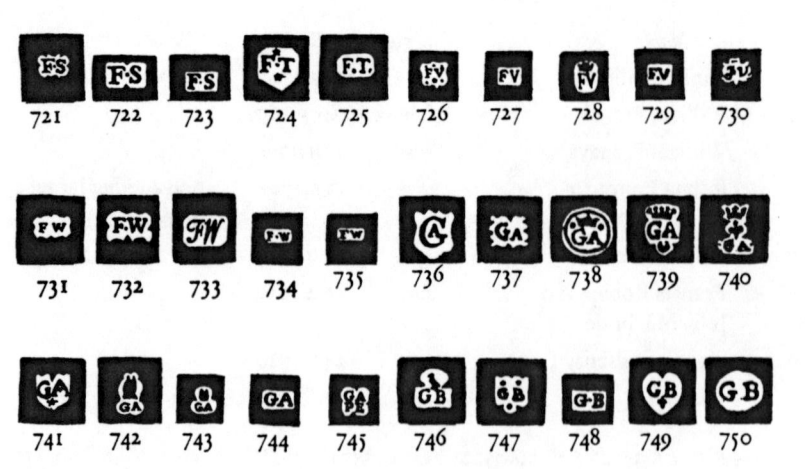

No.	Name	Category	Entered	Notes
721	Francis Spilsbury II	smw	24.11.1767	And a smaller similar mark same date
722	Frances Stamp	plw	12.5.1780	
723	idem	plw	idem	And a smaller similar mark same date
724	Francis Turner	lgw	5.8.1720	See also nos. 2950-1, 3576
725	Frances Theremin	smw	24.4.1772	
726	Richard Fuller	smw	April 1697	See also no. 2311
727	idem	smw	14.8.1717	
728	John Furnivall	smw	April 1697	A bad impression
729	Francis Verdier	smw	6.12.1730	
730	Frederick Vonham	lgw	22.12.1752	See also no. 3578
731	Fuller White	lgw	31.12.1744	See also no. 3579
732	idem	lgw	9.1.1751	
733	idem	lgw	5.7.1758	
734	Francis Waysmith	smw	20.8.1757	
735	Frederick Wade	smw	12.7.1820	
736	Francis Garthorne	lgw	April 1697	See also no. 3570
737	Richard Gardin	lgw	April 1697	
738	William Gamble	lgw	April 1697	
739	George Garthorne	lgw	April 1697	
740	Daniel Garnier	lgw	April 1697	
741	William Gardiner	smw	22.7.1700	
742	William Gattliffe	smw	22.9.1703	
743	James Gatliffe	smw	21.12.1713	
744	George Andrews	smw	13.4.1763	
745	John Garbett and James Pell	smw	30.6.1726	

62

LONDON GOLDSMITHS

No.	Name	Category	Entered	Notes
746	George Boothby	lgw	4.8.1720	See also nos. 203, 766
747	George Brydon	lgw	8.7.1720	See also no. 222
748	George Brome	lgw	31.10.1726	
749	George Baker I	smw	17.4.1733	See also no. 753
750	George Baskerville	lgw	9.2.1738	See also nos. 751, 754, 756, 768–9, 3580

Also FT nos. 3576–7; *FV* no. 3578; *FW* no. 3579; GA no. 3391

GB   GC

No.	Name	Category	Entered	Notes
751	George Baskerville	lgw	26.7.1745	And a larger similar mark 1.2.1751. See also no. 3580
752	George Bindon	lgw	13.12.1749	
753	George Baker II	lgw	31.7.1750	See also no. 749
754	George Baskerville	lgw	3.9.1755	See also nos. 750–1
755	George Burrows I	smw	14.12.1769	And a larger similar mark 10.12.1770
756	George Baskerville	smw	3.3.1780	See also nos. 750–1
757	George Brasier	smw	2.4.1785	And a smaller mark 4.3.1780. Another smaller similar mark 26.11.1789
758	idem	smw	19.10.1787	
759	idem	smw	31.1.1788	
760	George Beckwith	smw	7.3.1804	And a smaller similar mark same date
761	George Bower	smw	1.2.1813	
762	George Burrows II	plw	17.5.1819	See also nos. 14, 2419, 3581
763	idem	plw	27.8.1821	And a smaller similar mark same date
764	George Boggett	plw	10.2.1824	
765	George Bindoff	spm	5.11.1829	
766	George Boothby	lgw	22.6.1739	See also nos. 203, 746
767	George Blackway and John Hodsdon	smw	14.7.1790	
768	George Baskerville and Thomas Morley	plw	6.5.1775	And two smaller similar marks same date
769	George Baskerville and William Sampel	lgw	27.1.1755	
770	George Chebsey	smw	21.5.1722	
771	George Cowdery	smw	24.9.1771	And another similar 3.6.1784

LONDON GOLDSMITHS

No.	Name	Category	Entered	Notes
772	George Cowles	plw	30.10.1777	And a smaller similar same date. See also nos. 1907 and 3582
773	George Collins	smw	6.10.1800	
774	idem	smw	28.1.1804	
775	George Creak	plw	4.3.1802	
776	George Carsberg	smw	12.5.1803	And another larger 11.11.1810
777	Gabriel Couta	smw	29.10.1814	
778	George Clements	plw	29.6.1825	And a smaller similar mark same date
779	George Campar	lgw	7.11.1749	
780	George and John Cowie	plw	1.10.1822	Incuse mark 18.9.1822

Also GB no. 3580; GB.TB no. 3581; GC no. 3582

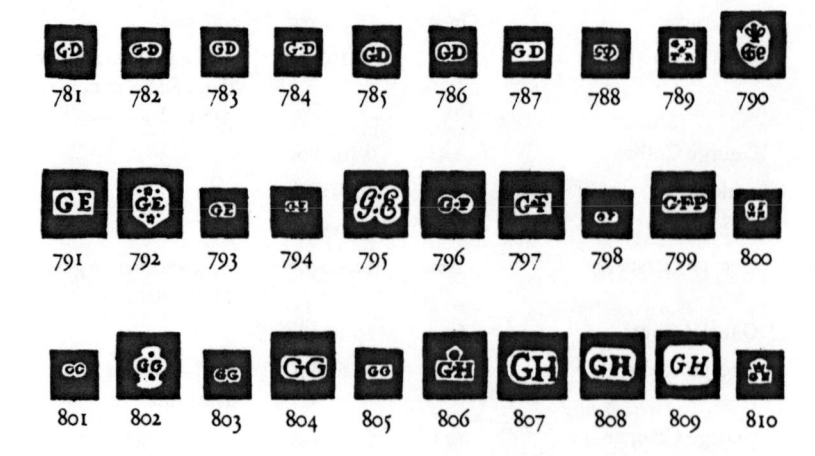

No.	Name	Category	Entered	Notes
781	George Dodds	smw	22.8.1738	
782	G. C. Dalmaine	smw	18.5.1797	
783	idem	smw	13.6.1801	
784	George Deighton	smw	24.9.1801	
785	George Day	spm	11.12.1809	
786	idem	spm	30.7.1812	
787	idem	spm	19.5.1814	
788	George Dowye	smw	18.9.1763	
789	George Dixon and Thomas Remmett	smw	6.2.1797	
790	Christopher Gerrard	lgw	27.11.1719	See also no. 308
791	George Ellis	smw	15.11.1721	See also no. 604
792	Griffith Edwards	lgw	8.1.1733	See also no. 795
793	George Evans	smw	4.4.1764	
794	George Davis Ewings	smw	29.3.1828	See also Section VIII, G.E
795	Griffith Edwards	lgw	4.7.1739	See also no. 792
796	George Foster	smw	27.10.1764	See also nos. 798, 800, 1311
797	George Fayle	smw	25.5.1767	And another similar mark 27.3.1771. See also Section IX, G.F
798	George Foster	smw	3.4.1772	
799	George Frederick Pinnell	smw	27.9.1830	And a larger similar mark same date. Others smaller 1840–2
800	George Foster and W. Hopper	smw	27.8.1771	
801	George Gines	smw	undated	c. 1720. See also no. 825
802	George Gillingham	lgw	11.9.1721	
803	George Giles	smw	8.7.1762	

LONDON GOLDSMITHS

No.	Name	Category	Entered	Notes
804	George Gray	smw	21.10.1782	And another slightly smaller mark same date. See also no. 3583
805	idem	smw	21.1.1789	
806	George Hodges	lgw	17.9.1728	See also no. 1055
807	George Hindmarsh	lgw	6.7.1731	
808	idem	lgw	undated	Between Dec. 1735 and 18.3.1736
809	idem	lgw	27.6.1739	And a smaller similar mark 15.9.1753
810	George Houston	smw	10.3.1737	

Also GD, note to no. 819; GG no. 3583; GG. HG no. 3584

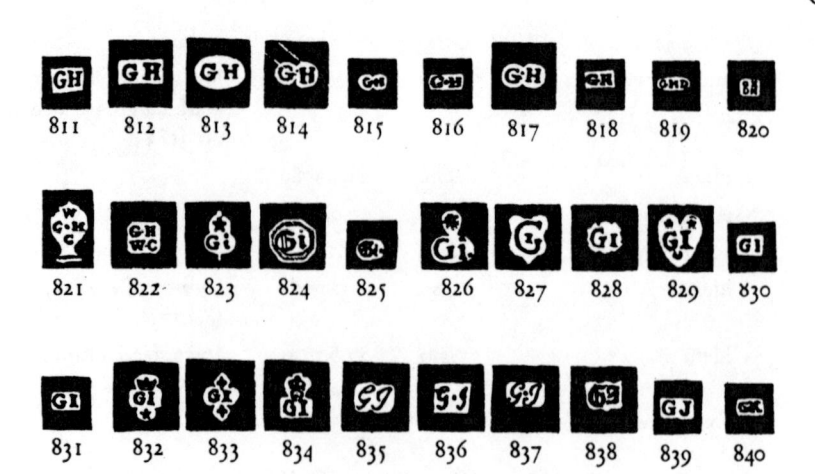

No.	Name	Category	Entered	Notes
811	George Hunter I	lgw	7.6.1748	
812	idem	lgw	31.10.1755	
813	idem	lgw	21.6.1765	
814	idem	lgw	14.11.1767	See also no. 817
815	George Harrison	smw	11.6.1760	Also incuse GH, Section V
816	George Hall	gw	16.3.1811	Incuse mark 10.4.1788. And a small mark 15.3.1793
817	George Hunter II	ns	20.3.1817	See also no. 814
818	George Harding	plw	30.8.1832	
819	George Henry Davis	smw	20.12.1827	And also GD in oval 7.10.1833
820	George Harris and Daniel May II	smw	30.7.1800	
821	George Heming and William Chawner I	plw	17.11.1774	
822	idem	plw	15.2.1781	And a similar smaller mark same date
823	John Gibbons	lgw	15.4.1700	See also nos. 1321, 3638
824	William Gibson	lgw	April 1697	
825	George Gines	smw	14.12.1715	See also no. 801
826	Edward Gibbon	lgw	6.8.1719	See also no. 589
827	George Gillingham	lgw	7.6.1703	See also no. 832
828	William Gimber	lgw	April 1697	See also no. 3586
829	Edward Gibson	lgw	April 1697	
830	Richard Gines	smw	18.4.1698	See also no. 838
831	John Gilbert	smw	27.3.1700	
832	George Gillingham	lgw	25.9.1718	See also no. 827
833	Glover Johnson	lgw	29.6.1720	See also no. 1560

LONDON GOLDSMITHS

No.	Name	Category	Entered	Notes
834	George Greenhill Jones	lgw	19.2.1726	
835	idem	lgw	27.6.1739	See also no. 1563
836	George Ibbot	lgw	6.8.1753	And a smaller similar mark same date
837	idem	lgw	28.11.1761	See also no. 1184
838	Richard Gines	lgw	7.10.1714	And another similar in varying shield 19.9.1717. See also nos. 830, 2314
839	George Jordon	smw	10.3.1835	
840	George Knight	smw	28.3.1818	And other similar marks 21.11.1820 and 4.7.1821

Also GH no. 3585; GI no. 3586

GK   GP

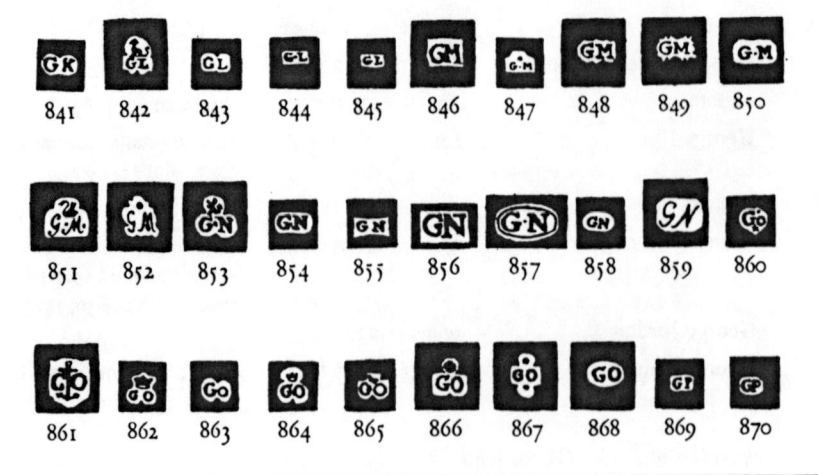

No.	Name	Category	Entered	Notes
841	George King	smw	11.11.1819	
842	Thomas Gladwin	lgw	4.12.1719	See also no. 2759
843	George Littleboy	smw	1.12.1731	Poor impression. Outline uncertain
844	George Love	smw	21.4.1763	See also no. 1312
845	George Longstaffe	smw	5.5.1799	And a smaller similar mark 15.4.1813
846	George Morland	sbm	6.9.1723	See also no. 3588
847	idem	sbm	30.6.1731	
848	George Meale	smw	15.4.1725	See also no. 2019
849	George Medley	smw	7.3.1737	
850	George Morris	lgw	18.5.1750	
851	idem	lgw	12.6.1751	
852	George Methuen	lgw	3.8.1743	Impression distorted by curvature of page
853	Gawen Nash	lgw	23.11.1726	See also nos. 859, 2084
854	idem	smw	1.7.1724	
855	George Natter	plw	23.10.1773	
856	idem	plw	idem	
857	idem	plw	idem	
858	George Nangle	smw	30.10.1797	And a similar mark in rectangle 21.3.1818
859	Gawen Nash	lgw	27.6.1739	See also nos. 853–4
860	James Gould	lgw	19.11.1722	See also nos. 1317, 1346, 3637
861	William Gossen	lgw	13.7.1700	
862	John Goode	lgw	25.7.1701	
863	James Goodwin	lgw	27.3.1710	See also no. 1342

LONDON GOLDSMITHS

No.	Name	Category	Entered	Notes
864	idem	lgw	idem	
865	Nathaniel Goldham	smw	28.9.1711	
866	Meschach Godwin	lgw	16.1.1723	See also no. 2029
867	Philip Goddard	lgw	23.1.1725	See also no. 2177
868	William Gould	lgw	24.7.1734	See also nos. 3134-5, 3149-50
869	George Padmore	smw	19.12.1764	And a smaller similar mark same date. See also Section VIII, E.P
870	George Powell	smw	9.8.1771	

Also GL no. 3392; GM no. 3587; GM no. 3588; GN no. 3589

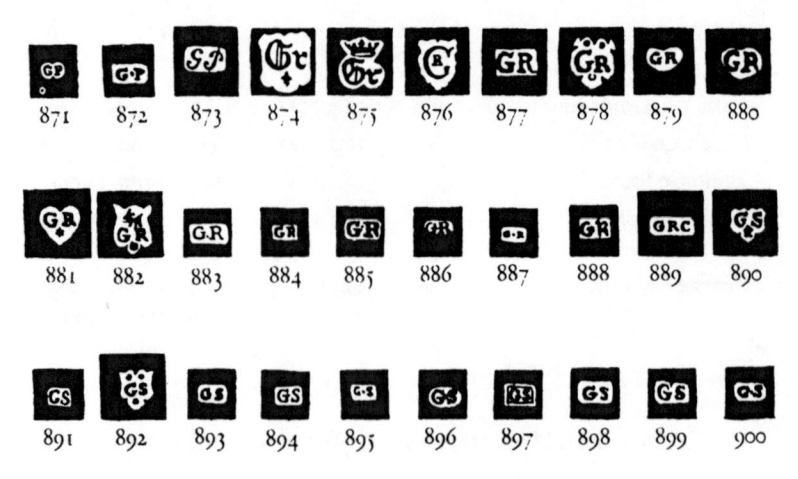

No.	Name	Category	Entered	Notes
871	George Pearson	smw	8.5.1817	
872	George Piercy	spm	16.12.1819	And a similar mark without pellet 7.12.1820
873	George Pizey	plw	23.12.1828	See also no. 2670, 3590
874	Nathaniel Greene	lgw	23.1.1699	
875	David Green	lgw	27.6.1701	See also no. 465
876	Richard Green	lgw	15.4.1703	And another with slight variations 4.10.1723. See also no. 2315
877	Dorothy Grant	lgw	April 1697	See also no. 3591
878	Henry Greene	lgw	31.8.1700	
879	John Gray	smw	4.1.1716	See also no. 1319
880	Gundry Roode	lgw	21.5.1721	See also nos. 2394, 3592
881	idem	lgw	9.9.1737	
882	Samuel Green	lgw	8.6.1721	See also nos. 2512-3
883	George Ridout	lgw	17.10.1743	
884	George Richardson	smw	12.7.1760	
885	George Rodenbostel	plw	5.12.1778	
886	George Reid	smw	6.3.1811	And smaller similar marks 1817, 1824, 1828 and 1829
887	George Richards	plw	20.7.1830	Other marks 1844-50
888	George Rous	smw	17.1.1765	Bad impression. G conjectural. See also no. 3593
889	George Richard Chatterton	spm	16.11.1836	And a smaller similar mark 2.12.1836
890	Gabriel Sleath	lgw	17.6.1720	See also nos. 904, 907, 2568
891	George Shaw	sword cutler	28.6.1720	
892	George Squire	lgw	25.11.1720	See also no. 2622

LONDON GOLDSMITHS

No.	Name	Category	Entered	Notes
893	Gorsper Soloro	smw	1.5.1724	
894	Giles Southam	smw	10.10.1734	
895	George Smith I	lgw	28.2.1732	See also nos. 905, 908
896	George Smith II	smw	undated	Before 7.8.1758. See also Section VIII, G.S, etc.
897	idem	smw	21.11.1767	See also nos. 906, 909–10
898	idem	smw	9.8.1771	
899	George Smith 'Junior' (IV)	spm	20.6.1799	And another smaller mark same date
900	idem	spm	8.11.1803	And a smaller mark same date. Similar marks without pellet 20.1.1812. See also no. 2294

Also *GP* no. 3590; GR nos. 3591–2; 𝕲𝕽 no. 3593; GRI no. 3594; GS nos. 3393, 3596

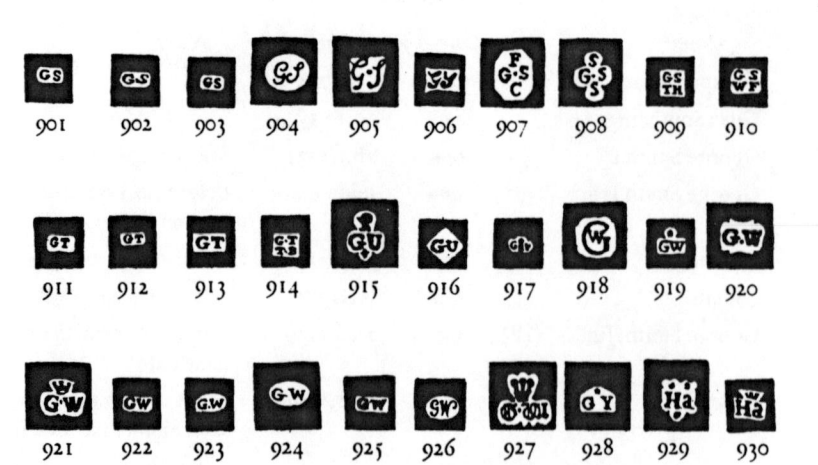

No.	Name	Category	Entered	Notes
901	George Sellers	smw	25.5.1802	And a similar mark 1.11.1820
902	George Stonhouse	plw	9.8.1824	And a smaller mark 19.11.1825. Other marks 14.12.1837
903	George Smith V	plw	5.1.1828	
904	Gabriel Sleath	lgw	18.6.1739	See also nos. 890, 907, 2568
905	George Smith I	lgw	4.9.1739	See also nos. 895–6
906	George Smith III	spm	1.2.1774	Various similar marks 1775–82 and see nos. 899–900
907	Gabriel Sleath and Francis Crump	lgw	22.11.1753	
908	Samuel Smith III and George Smith I	lgw	13.12.1750	
909	George Smith II and Thomas Hayter	plw	7.1.1792	And a smaller similar mark same date
910	George Smith III and William Fearn	plw	3.11.1786	
911	George Thurkle	smw	19.3.1800	And a similar mark with square corners 10.8.1821. See also Section IX, F.T
912	George Taylor	smw	26.3.1802	
913	George Turner	spm	22.11.1823	
914	George Turner and Thomas William Biddell	spm	29.3.1820	
915	John Guerrie	lgw	5.1.1717	
916	Nathaniel Gulliver	lgw	12.9.1722	See also no. 2090
917	George Vernon	smw	19.7.1728	
918	George Wickes	lgw	3.2.1722	See also nos. 921, 927, 3197
919	George Willcocks	smw	22.6.1720	See also no. 3189

LONDON GOLDSMITHS

No.	Name	Category	Entered	Notes
920	George Weir	lgw	27.7.1727	See also no. 3098
921	George Wickes	lgw	30.6.1735	See also nos. 918, 927, 3197
922	Gabriel Wirgman	smw	22.6.1772	See also Section VII, G.W
923	George Wintle	plw	28.2.1791	And a similar mark 6.12.1794
924	idem	spm	4.5.1801	And similar marks 1804 and 1818.
925	idem	spm	15.5.1813	And similar marks 1820 and 1823
926	idem	plw	2.1.1787	And a similar mark 25.6.1789. Also GW incuse, Section V
927	George Wickes	lgw	6.7.1739	And a smaller mark same date. See also nos. 918, 921
928	George Young	lgw	17.6.1746	Also GY incuse, Section V
929	John Harris I	lgw	21.3.1717	
930	John Harvey I	smw	9.1.1739	See also nos. 1367, 1372, 1401–3, 3644

Also GW no. 3394; *GW* no. 3597

HA   HB

No.	Name	Category	Entered	Notes
931	Benjamin Harris	lgw	April 1697	
932	George Havers	lgw	April 1697	
933	Jacob Harris	smw	27.4.1705	
934	William Harris	smw	25.2.1717	
935	Samuel Hawkes	lgw	April 1697	
936	Peter Harache I	lgw	April 1697	
937	Peeter Harrache Junior (II)	lgw	25.10.1698	
938	idem	lgw	idem	
939	idem	lgw	idem	
940	Joseph Haywood I	smw	15.2.1699	
941	Job Hanks	lgw	20.5.1699	
942	Paul Hanet	lgw	7.3.1716	Poor impression. See also no. 2189. Also HA incuse, Section V
943	Edward Hall	lgw	14.1.1721	See also no. 594
944	Charles Hatfield	lgw	21.6.1727	See also nos. 324, 335
945	Hugh Avenell	smw	29.3.1735	
946	Henry Alsept	smw	14.2.1820	
947	Henry Bruin	sword cutler	2.3.1726	A somewhat illiterate entry
948	Henry Burdett	gs	26.7.1732	
949	Henry Bates	lgw	12.7.1738	See also no. 963
950	Henry Brind	lgw	6.5.1742	
951	Henry Bailey	lgw	14.6.1750	See also no. 3601
952	Hugh Beard	smw	19.8.1758	
953	Henry Billinghurst	smw	11.10.1759	
954	Henry Bickerton	smw	26.8.1762	

LONDON GOLDSMITHS

No.	Name	Category	Entered	Notes
955	Hester Bateman	*plw*	28.6.1787	See also nos. 958–61
956	Henry Brockwell	*spm*	20.12.1821	
957	Harriet Bainbridge	*smw*	22.8.1831	
958	Hester Bateman	*smw*	16.4.1761	And another slightly larger mark with closed loop to B 3.12.1774
959	idem	*smw*	9.1.1771	And another similar mark but with closed loop to B 17.6.1774
960	idem	*spm*	5.6.1776	

Also HA nos. 3598–9; HB no. 3600; *HB* no. 3601

HB   HE

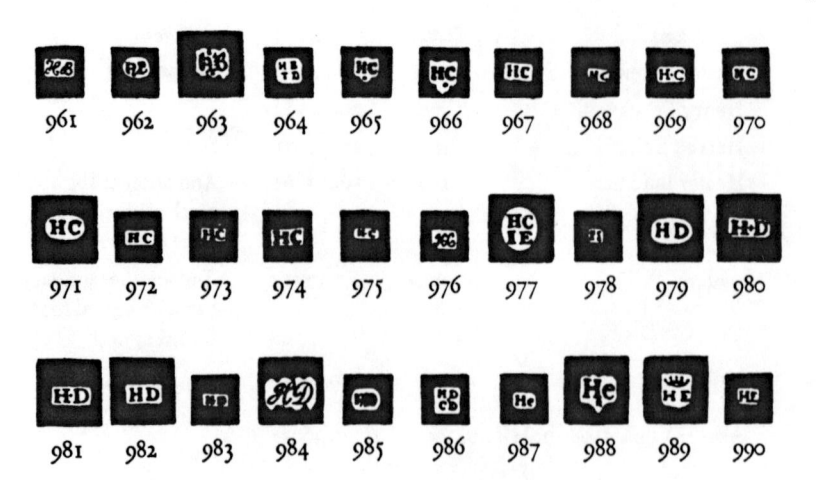

No.	Name	Category	Entered	Notes
961	Hester Bateman	plw	21.2.1778	And others similar 25.11.1781 and 3.8.1787
962	Henry Bance	smw	20.6.1720	See also nos. 120, 964
963	Henry Bates	lgw	19.7.1739	See also no. 949
964	Henry Bance and ?	smw	26.5.1721	See also nos. 120, 962
965	Henry Clarke I	lgw	undated	c. 1720–1. See also no. 352
966	idem	lgw	7.3.1723	
967	Henry Crook	smw	19.8.1734	Also HC incuse, Section V
968	Henry Clarke II	smw	21.7.1738	
969	Henry Corry	lgw	6.4.1754	And another similar mark 22.3.1764
970	Henry Cowper	plw	8.10.1782	See also no. 976
971	Henry Chawner	plw	11.11.1786	And a smaller similar mark same date
972	idem	plw	31.8.1787	And a larger similar mark same date
973	Henry Croswell I	smw	11.4.1804	And a similar mark for Henry Croswell II 21.12.1830. See also no. 978
974	Henry Cornman	plw	6.1.1813	And a smaller mark 31.8.1813
975	Henry Crowder	smw	23.1.1833	
976	Henry Cowper	plw	8.10.1782	See also no. 970
977	Henry Chawner and John Emes	plw	27.8.1796	And a smaller similar mark same date
978	Henry (I) and Richard Croswell	smw	5.8.1800	See also no. 973
979	Henry Dell	lgw	undated	Between Dec. 1722 and June 1724

LONDON GOLDSMITHS

No.	Name	Category	Entered	Notes
980	Henry Daniel	smw	30.12.1778	And a smaller similar mark same date
981	Henry Day	gw, spm	18.7.1817	And a smaller mark and a third in oval punch same date. A fourth 26.4.1821
982	James Henry Daniel	gw, sw	16.10.1820	And smaller similar marks 1821 and 1822. Also IHD. 1823 onwards, no. 1414
983	Henry Dolman	smw	6.1.1825	
984	Henry Dutton	lgw	16.12.1754	
985	Henry Duck	smw	20.10.1735	
986	Henry and Charles Day	plw	28.7.1821	See also no. 296a
987	Thomas Head I	smw	17.1.1716	
988	Joseph Healy	smw	19.8.1725	See also no. 1358
989	John Hely	lgw	11.3.1699	
990	James Hervot	smw	3.10.1712	See also no. 1356

HE   HJ

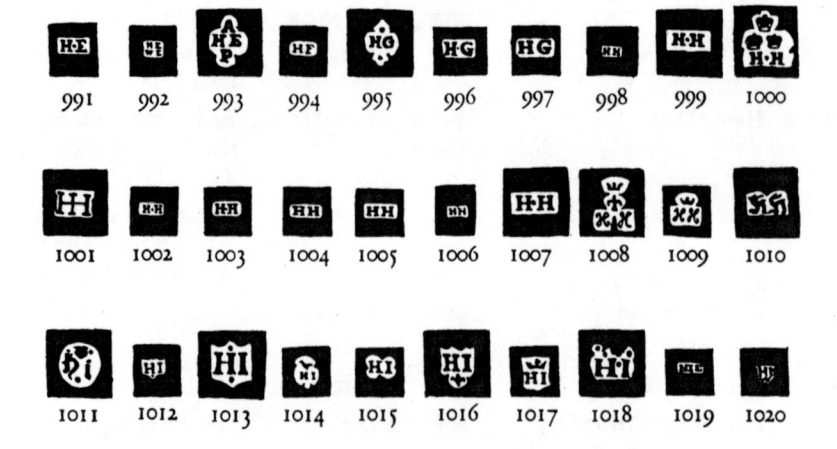

No.	Name	Category	Entered	Notes
991	Henrietta Eastwick	smw	26.6.1782	And another slightly larger mark without pellet 12.9.1789
992	Henrietta and William Eastwick	smw	11.9.1802	
993	Hugh Arnett and Edward Pocock	lgw	22.6.1720	See also no. 81
994	Henry Freeth	smw	14.6.1828	
995	Henry Greene	lgw	12.7.1720	See also no. 878
996	Henry Greenway	plw	24.11.1775	
997	Henry Green	plw	9.9.1786	And two smaller similar marks same date
998	Henry Hickman	smw	8.8.1722	
999	Henry Hebert	lgw	18.1.1734	See also nos. 1008–9
1000	idem	lgw	24.12.1735	
1001	Henry Hayens	lgw	13.10.1749	
1002	Henry Hobdell	smw	21.9.1767	And a similar mark without pellet 2.7.1770
1003	Henry Hall	plw	22.7.1788	
1004	Henry Househill	smw	18.5.1799	
1005	Hyam Hyams	plw	12.4.1821	And four similar marks of various sizes May–Oct. 1821
1006	Henry Hull	smw	3.4.1822	
1007	Henry Hyde	plw	23.5.1834	And two smaller similar marks same date. See also no. 2977
1008	Henry Hebert	lgw	28.6.1739	See also nos. 999–1000
1009	idem	lgw	idem	And a similar mark without coronet same date

80

LONDON GOLDSMITHS

No.	Name	Category	Entered	Notes
1010	Henry Hallsworth	lgw	before March 1773	Not in register. Mark taken from chamber-candlestick 1773*
1011	Robert Hill	lgw	13.1.1717	See also nos. 2335, 3775
1012	Thomas Hill	smw	27.6.1699	See also no. 1017
1013	William Hinton	lgw	7.10.1704	See also no. 1352
1014	John Hill	smw	27.11.1707	A bad impression. Somewhat conjectural. See also no. 1353
1015	Joseph Hitch	smw	1.2.1710	
1016	Samuel Hitchcock	lgw	24.11.1713	See also nos. 2526–7
1017	Thomas Hill	smw	9.5.1716	See also no. 1012
1018	Edmund Hickman	lgw	21.8.1719 or 1720	Year omitted in entry
1019	Henry John Edwards	smw	12.1.1832	
1020	Herman James Walther	smw	2.4.1770	

Also HG no. 3602; HH no. 3603; HJ no. 3604

---

* With this mark on candlesticks a small nozzle mark is also found of HH in Roman capitals and also used on body of sticks as well, 1774, 1778, 1780, and on branches, 1779.

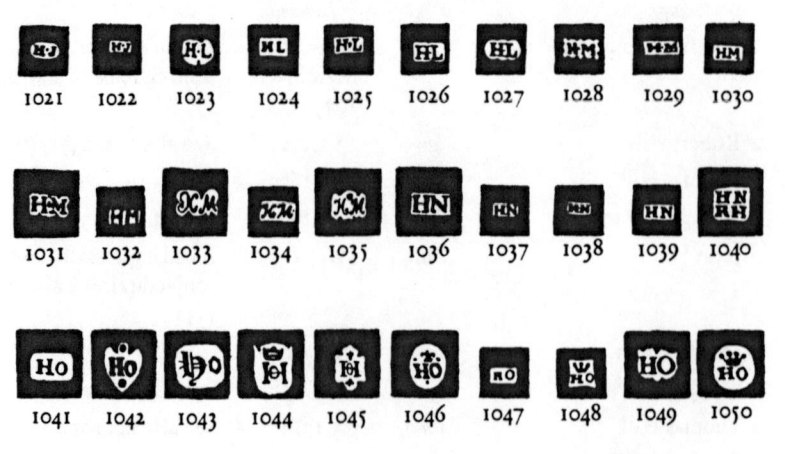

No.	Name	Category	Entered	Notes
1021	Henry Jefferys	plw	6.6.1793	And a smaller similar mark in rectangle same date
1022	Henry Johnson	smw	16.11.1829	
1023	Henry Long	smw	25.8.1721	Impression uncertain in upper section
1024	Henry Legg	smw	14.5.1728	
1025	Henry Land	smw	21.7.1767	
1026	Henry Ledger	plw	26.6.1827	And a smaller mark same date
1027	idem	plw	24.10.1828	
1028	Henry Miller I	lgw	9.7.1720	See also nos. 2036, 3738
1029	Henry Miller II	smw	8.5.1733	
1030	Henry Morris	smw	24.6.1720	See also nos. 1034-5, 2051, 3605
1031	idem	lgw	5.9.1749	
1032	Hugh Mills	lgw	23.5.1739	See also no. 3605
1033	idem	lgw	14.2.1746	
1034	Henry Morris	lgw	3.7.1739	See also nos. 1030-1
1035	idem	lgw	6.4.1744	
1036	Henry Nutting	plw	9.4.1796	
1037	idem	plw	idem	And a similar mark 3.10.1809
1038	Hannah Northcote	plw	6.6.1798	And a similar mark 3.12.1799
1039	Henry Nicholson	smw	29.3.1833	
1040	Henry Nutting and Robert Hennell II	plw	17.6.1808	And a smaller mark same date
1041	Edmund Holaday	lgw	1.11.1709	See also no. 1047
1042	William Hodgkins I	lgw	11.9.1719 or 1720	

LONDON GOLDSMITHS

No.	Name	Category	Entered	Notes
1043	Samuel Hood	lgw	April 1697	See also no. 1046
1044	John Hodson I	lgw	April 1697	
1045	Joshua Holland	lgw	22.8.1711	
1046	Samuel Hood	lgw	April 1697	See also no. 1043
1047	Edmund Holliday	smw	3.8.1703	See also no. 1041
1048	Elias Hosier	smw	26.4.1704	
1049	Edward Horne I	smw	25.10.1705	See also no. 593
1050	Thomas Holland I	lgw	23.9.1707	

Also HJ no. 3395; HM conjoined no. 3605; ℌ𝔐 no. 3606

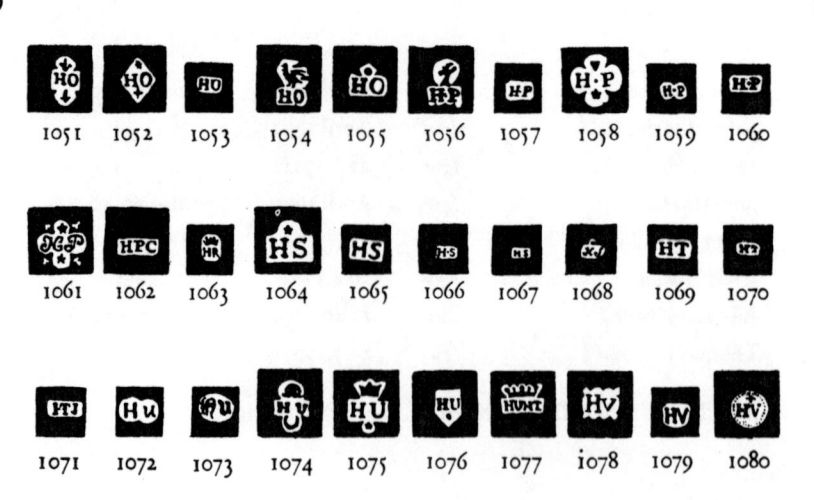

No.	Name	Category	Entered	Notes
1051	John Holland I	lgw	23.11.1711	See also no. 1354
1052	Sarah Holaday	lgw	22.7.1719	And a smaller similar mark same date. See also no. 2529
1053	William Hooker	smw	8.3.1720	
1054	John Hopkins	lgw	undated	1720–4. See also no. 1355
1055	George Hodges	lgw	17.9.1728	See also no. 806
1056	Harvey Price	lgw	10.2.1727	
1057	Humphrey Phillips	smw	undated	Between Feb. and May 1730
1058	Humphrey Payne	lgw	15.6.1739	See also nos. 1061, 2117–18
1059	Henry Plumpton	smw	14.11.1761	
1060	Henry Pennyfeather	smw	26.11.1783	Also HP incuse, Section V
1061	Humphrey Payne	lgw	undated	c. June 1720. See also nos. 1058, 2117–8
1062	Hannah and Peter Crammillion	smw	8.2.1762	See also Section V, PC
1063	Henry Renaud	smw	27.3.1727	
1064	Hugh Spring	lgw	27.10.1722	
1065	Humphrey Shinton	smw	21.1.1730	
1066	Henry Spree	smw	1.5.1738	
1067	Henry Skidman	sw	1.5.1821	
1068	Henry Sardet	smw	17.4.1765	
1069	Henry Thompson	smw	1.9.1730	
1070	Henry Tippen	smw	29.1.1805	And three similar marks 1805, 1808 and 1809
1071	Henry Thomas Jennings	plw	7.5.1801	
1072	Henry Hunt	smw	15.10.1712	
1073	William Hutchinson I	smw	23.3.1716	See also nos. 3156, 3884
1074	René Hudell	lgw	5.3.1718	

LONDON GOLDSMITHS

No.	Name	Category	Entered	Notes
1075	William Hudson	smw	19.11.1722	See also nos. 3154, 3883
1076	Samuel Hutton	lgw	7.1.1725	See also nos. 2528, 2544
1077	William Hunt	smw	21.6.1725	See also no. 3886–7
1078	Alexander Hudson	lgw	22.11.1704	See also no. 3609
1079	Edward Hunt I	smw	April 1697	
1080	James Hughes	smw	April 1697	Poor impression. Fleur-de-lys conjectural

Also Ho no. 3396; HP nos. 3607–8; HV nos. 3609–10

HV   IA

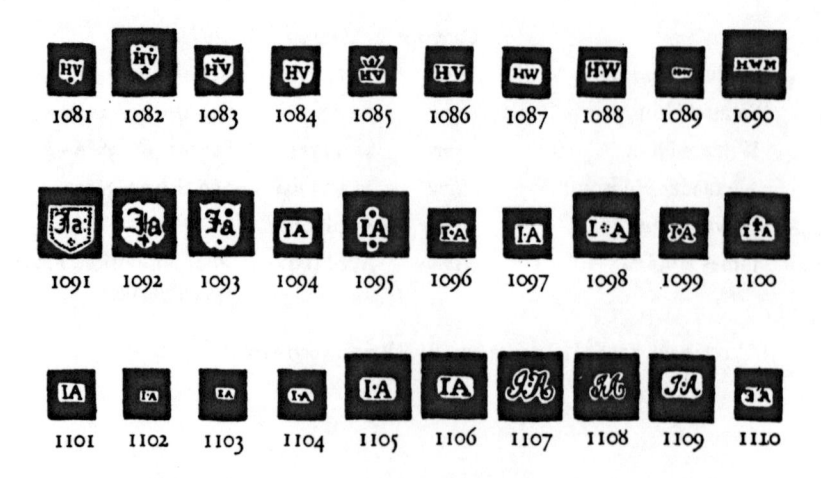

No.	Name	Category	Entered	Notes
1081	Edward Hunsdon	smw	April 1697	
1082	Philip Hulls	smw	April 1697	
1083	Ferdinando Hughes	smw	April 1697	
1084	John Humphrey	lgw	26.1.1711	
1085	Edward Hussey	smw	9.9.1735	
1086	Henry Vincent	smw	22.8.1783	
1087	Henry Wilcocke	smw	5.6.1721	
1088	Henry Walpole	smw	26.2.1765	
1089	Henry Webster	smw	29.12.1837	
1090	H. W. Mortimer	smw	7.5.1798	
1091	John Jackson I	lgw	April 1697	
1092	idem	lgw	idem	
1093	Henry Jay	lgw	undated	Between April 1714 and Dec. 1719*
1094	John Albright	smw	6.7.1720	See also no. 53
1095	Charles Jackson	lgw	2.4.1714	See also nos. 337, 3611
1096	John Allen I	smw	1.5.1733	
1097	John Allen II	smw	19.11.1736	
1098	John Alderhead	lgw	23.4.1750	
1099	John Andrews I	smw	9.8.1758	
1100	John Allen III	smw	10.6.1761	
1101	John Ashpinshaw	smw	26.5.1763	
1102	Isaac Aaron	smw	21.3.1791	
1103	Joseph Abraham	smw	19.4.1796	
1104	Joseph Ash I	smw	14.9.1801	

* Mark occurs with date-letter for 1716 on teapot, Assheton-Bennett Collection.

LONDON GOLDSMITHS

No.	Name	Category	Entered	Notes
1105	idem	smw	9.5.1810	And two smaller similar marks same date. Two other marks similar 3.1.1818
1106	Joseph Ash II	smw	23.9.1811	A separate identity?
1107	Jeconiah Ashley	lgw	12.11.1740	
1108	James Allen	smw	15.12.1766	
1109*	Jonathan Alleine	plw	by 1771	Not in register. Mark taken from taperstick 1781. See also no. 3703
1110	John Alcock	smw	22.7.1725	

Also *HV* conjoined no. 3397; IA nos. 3398, 3611; *IA* nos. 3399, 3612

---

* It now seems certain that this is the mark of John Arnell. See page 735.

IA IB

No.	Name	Category	Entered	Notes
1111	John Allen IV and Joshua Butler I	smw	16.3.1802	
1112	Joseph Allen and Mordecai Fox	lgw	9.3.1730	
1113	idem	lgw	21.8.1739	
1114	Joseph Barbut	lgw	c. 1720	Undated addition to 1703 entry. See also nos. 119, 1176
1115	John Bache	lgw	20.6.1720	See also no. 118
1116	John Bignell	lgw	6.7.1720	See also no. 180
1117	John Betts	lgw	9.8.1720	See also no. 154
1118	John Barnard I	lgw	12.10.1720	See also nos. 112–3
1119	John Burgh	smw	9.3.1721	See also no. 245
1120	Joseph Bird	lgw	19.6.1724	See also nos. 177–9, 3614–5
1121	John Barbot	smw	22.7.1726	
1122	John Bennett I	smw	30.4.1732	
1123	John Blunt I	smw	25.5.1732	
1124	John Blunt II	smw	12.11.1734	
1125	James Brooker	lgw	21.10.1734	
1126	John Barbe	lgw	16.1.1735	See also nos. 1177–8
1127	John Bryan	lgw	18.11.1735	See also no. 1183
1128	John Barrett	lgw	26.5.1737	
1129	John Berthellot	wcm	5.9.1738	See also nos. 1179, 3616
1130	James Betham	lgw	6.12.1743	
1131	Jas. Barker	lgw	17.4.1746	Also a small mark in oblong punch same date
1132	Joseph Bell II	lgw	25.10.1756	See also no. 3624
1133	St. John Barry	lgw	25.3.1758	
1134	James Barrett	smw	5.1.1759	

LONDON GOLDSMITHS

No.	Name	Category	Entered	Notes
1135	James Beatty	smw	13.3.1759	
1136	James Baker	smw	19.4.1759	See also no. 3617
1137	James Bellis	gw	16.5.1760	Also a small mark IB in oblong punch 22.12.1764
1138	John Brockus	smw	4.6.1760	
1139	John Bennett II	smw	9.12.1761	
1140	John Burrows	smw	13.2.1769	

Also IAC no. 3613; IB nos. 3400-1, 3614-3622

No.	Name	Category	Entered	Notes
1141	John Baker I	smw	28.9.1770	And a similar smaller mark same date. See also nos. 1147, 1773 and Section VIII, IB, pellet between etc.
1142	John Bassingwhite	smw	29.11.1770	And a slightly smaller mark 13.1.1771
1143	John Bayne	smw	20.6.1771	
1144	John Bourne	spm	2.2.1774	See also no. 1188 and Section VIII, IB.TM
1145	idem	spm	7.5.1774	And a similar mark without pellet for smallwork 22.7.1774
1146	idem	spm	24.1.1778	And a slightly smaller mark same date
1147	John Baker II	smw	17.5.1775	See also nos. 1141, 1773
1148	Joseph Bradley	smw	20.8.1776	
1149	John Broughton	plw	8.1.1779	See also no. 3617
1150	John Beldon	plw	13.3.1784	See also no. 3622
1151	John Blake	smw	5.9.1788	And other marks similar, slightly bolder 1792 and 1795
1152	James Beattie	smw	6.7.1790	See also no. 1774
1153	John Bull	smw	13.12.1790	
1154	John Brockwell	smw	13.3.1794	See also no. 1162
1155	John Boyer	smw	9.6.1794	See also no. 1182
1156	Joseph Barnard	smw	23.2.1798	And a smaller mark same date
1157	J. Berenger	smw	10.7.1798	
1158	James Barratt	smw	5.10.1801	And a slightly larger mark 20.6.1803

LONDON GOLDSMITHS

No.	Name	Category	Entered	Notes
1159	idem	smw	7.9.1803	And a much smaller mark same date. A similar smaller mark 29.6.1816
1160	John Blake	spm	16.5.1803	
1161	John Bunn	smw	10.5.1806	See also no. 2671
1162	John Brockwell	smw	6.4.1808	See also no. 1154
1163	John Blades	smw	9.6.1812	See also no. 1173
1164	John Brough	smw	7.8.1813	
1165	John Booth	plw	24.11.1813	
1166	Joseph Biggs	plw	26.1.1816	Two other marks with slight variations in punch 1819 and 1820
1167	John Baddeley	plw	8.10.1818	And a smaller similar mark same date
1168	James Bult	plw	13.7.1819	
1169	John Brent	smw	26.6.1820	
1170	John Brydie	spm	2.1.1823	And a smaller mark in rectangle punch 19.5.1824. Others 1825

Also IB nos. 3400–1, 3614–22

IB   IC

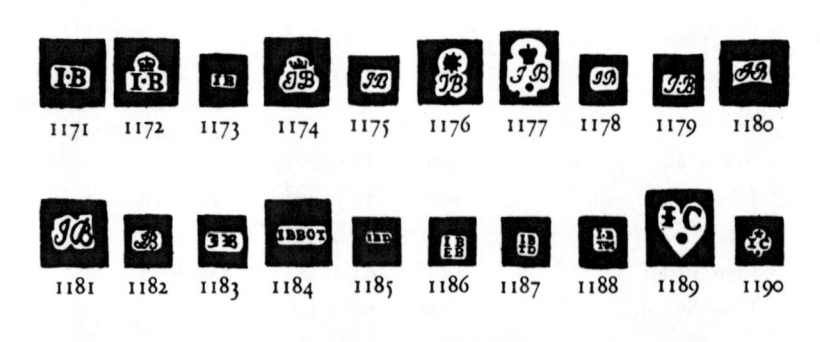

No.	Name	Category	Entered	Notes
1171	John Bridge	plw	13.11.1823	And three other marks graduating smaller same date. See also no. 3764
1172	idem	plw	25.11.1823	And three other marks graduating smaller same date
1173	John Blades	smw	8.12.1827	See also no. 1163
1174	James Burne	lgw	4.3.1724	See also no. 250a
1175	John Barrett	lgw	5.6.1739	
1176	Joseph Barbut	lgw	18.6.1739	See also nos. 119, 1114
1177	John Barbe	lgw	25.6.1739	See also no. 1126
1178	idem	lgw	idem	
1179	John Berthellot	lgw	26.7.1739	See also nos. 1129, 3616
1180	John Bayley	lgw	21.3.1751	
1181	John Buckett	sword cutler	28.1.1760	See also no. 3620
1182	John Boyer	smw	16.4.1772	See also no. 1155
1183	John Bryan	lgw	22.6.1739	See also no. 1127
1184	George Ibbot	smw	22.5.1759	See also nos. 836-7
1185	John Baptist Dubois	smw	8.12.1803	
1186	James and Elizabeth Bland	plw	16.9.1794	
1187	J. Brookes and Thomas Dare	smw	19.10.1764	
1188	John Bourne and Thomas Moore III	smw	26.6.1770	See also nos. 1144-5 and Section VIII, IB.TM and TM
1189	Joseph Clare I	lgw	23.6.1720	And a slightly smaller mark without crossbar to I, 15.12.1721. See also no. 353

92

LONDON GOLDSMITHS

No.	Name	Category	Entered	Notes
1190	John Carman I	smw	27.6.1720	See also no. 260
1191	Jonah Clifton	lgw	8.10.1720	See also nos. 348, 3627
1192	John Cowsey	lgw	11.11.1720	See also nos. 374–5
1193	John Clarke I	lgw	2.7.1722	See also nos. 347, 354
1194	John Chartier	lgw	10.7.1723	See also nos. 320–1
1194a	Isaac Cornafleau	lgw	undated	Between July 1722 and Dec. 1724. A poor impression somewhat conjectural. See also no. 392
1195	Jasper Cunst	smw	Sept. 1725	See also Section V, I.C and J.C
1196	Isaac Callard	lgw	7.2.1726	See also nos. 261, 1223–4
1197	John Carpender	smw	5.5.1727	
1198	Joseph Crane	smw	21.10.1728	
1199	John Chapman I	lgw	9.6.1730	
1200	John Cragg	smw	1.10.1730	

Also *IB* no. 3623; IBELL no. 3624; IB.IS no. 3625; IBO no. 3402; IB.WB. no. 3626; IC no. 3627

No.	Name	Category	Entered	Notes
1201	John Cann	lgw	8.3.1740	
1202	idem	lgw	30.6.1742	
1203	John Cafe	lgw	21.8.1740	See also no. 1228
1204	John Carman II	lgw	12.10.1756	See also nos. 1225, 3628
1205	J. Collins	lgw	17.5.1754	
1206	John Cormick	smw	15.3.1760	
1207	John Catt	smw	19.12.1762	See also Section V, BT.IC and I.C, star above
1208	Joseph Clare II	smw	2.3.1763	See also no. 358
1209	idem	smw	16.9.1768	
1210	John Clemenson	smw	4.5.1763	
1211	John Cox	smw	29.8.1763	
1212	Joseph Creswell	smw	16.5.1767	
1213	John Chapman II	smw	30.11.1774	
1214	John Carter II	plw	21.9.1776	A similar mark found earlier. Not in register
1215	idem	plw	30.10.1776	And a smaller mark same date
1216	Joshua Cooper	smw	14.9.1789	See also Section VIII, I.C
1217	John Cramer	plw	12.5.1797	See also no. 1235
1218	John Caney	smw	7.5.1800	Top curve of 'C' conjectural
1219	James Cull	smw	21.2.1804	
1220*	John Clarke II	plw	21.3.1807	
1221	Joseph Cradock	plw	13.10.1825	
1222	idem	plw	10.11.1827	
1223	Isaac Callard	lgw	20.6.1739	See also nos. 261, 1196

* This mark has a pellet between the initials and clear-cut rectangular outline.

LONDON GOLDSMITHS

No.	Name	Category	Entered	Notes
1224	idem	lgw	17.3.1747	And a slightly broader similar mark 3.12.1750
1225	John Carman II	lgw	4.7.1748	See also no. 1204
1226	Joseph Carpenter	smw	20.5.1768	And a similar mark 8.7.1771. See also Section V, I.C, axe above, and Section VI, I.C, coronet above
1227	John Clayton	smw	2.11.1736	
1228	John Cafe	lgw	13.12.1742	See also no. 1203
1229	James Clarke	smw	29.8.1769	Somewhat conjectural from poor impression. See also no. 1789 and Section VI, I.C, script
1230	John Cope Folkard	plw	12.3.1819	And a smaller similar mark same date

Also IC nos. 3403–4, 3628

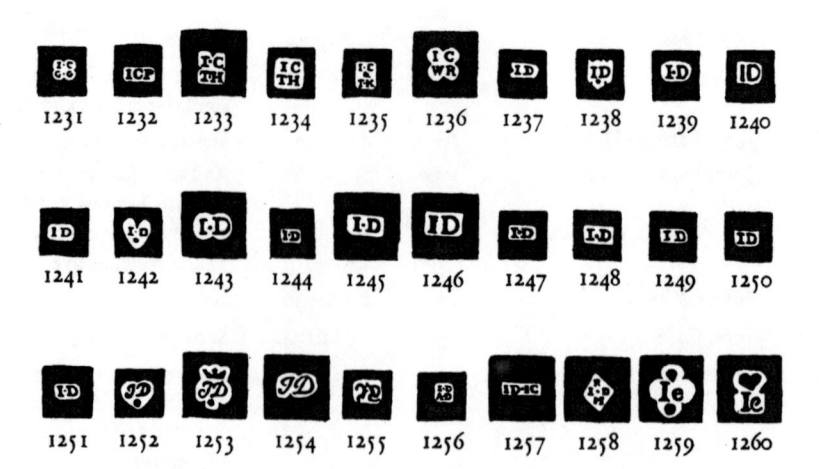

No.	Name	Category	Entered	Notes
1231	John Cooper and George Giles	smw	18.10.1765	See also Section V, I.C, pellet between
1232	John Cook Pettit	smw	30.6.1788	
1233	John Crouch I and Thomas Hannam	plw	by 1771	Not in register. Mark taken from salver 1784
1234	John Cotton and Thomas Head II	spm	8.12.1809	
1235	(Cramer ?) and Thomas Key	plw	21.9.1805	First name omitted in register and pencilled in as noted
1236	Joseph Cradock and William K. Reid	plw	8.6.1812	And smaller similar marks 19.8.1819 and 24.9.1824
1237	James Desreumaux	smw	23.6.1720	See also no. 461
1238	John Daniels	smw	19.8.1720	See also no. 435
1239	John Dearmor	smw	16.12.1724	See also Section V, I.D
1240	Joseph Drake	smw	25.8.1731	
1241	Jeremiah Davis	smw	12.5.1735	
1242	James Delas	smw	2.8.1737	See also no. 1252
1243	John Denwall	smw	20.10.1768	
1244	John Dare	smw	9.2.1773	
1245	John Dutton	smw	7.8.1776	
1246	John Deacon	plw	11.9.1776	Working by 1771
1247	James Darquits Junr.	smw	19.11.1787	
1248	Joseph Dodds	plw	13.6.1789	And two similar marks 22.7.1790
1249	John Death	smw	11.7.1803	And a larger similar mark 20.6.1808

LONDON GOLDSMITHS

No.	Name	Category	Entered	Notes
1250	John Douglas	smw	31.1.1804	And smaller marks, same date and 24.12.1813. See also nos. 1256, 2359. Also Section VIII, I.D
1251	John Danger	plw	6.1.1825	
1252	James Delas	smw	10.7.1723	See also no. 1242
1253	Isaac Duke	lgw	15.6.1743	
1254	Jabez Daniell	lgw	28.7.1749	See also nos. 3633-4
1255	John Denziloe	plw	27.10.1774	
1256	John and Archibald Douglas	smw	2.2.1821	And a slightly larger mark 22.11.1823. See also no. 28
1257	John James Detheridge and John Cottrill	plw	26.4.1826	See also Section VII, I.D
1258	Jane Dorrell and Richard May	smw	22.10.1766	And other marks similar 22.5.1769 and 3.5.1771. See also no. 2366
1259	Thomas Jenkins*	lgw	April 1697	
1260	Edward Jennings	lgw	26.1.1710	See also nos. 599, 1265

Also ID nos. 3405, 3529-31; *ID* no. 3632; ID.IM. no. 3633; ID.TD no. 3634

---

* Another mark IE in similar punch and scallop shell above and below appears on candlesticks of 1703 of the Fishmongers' Company.

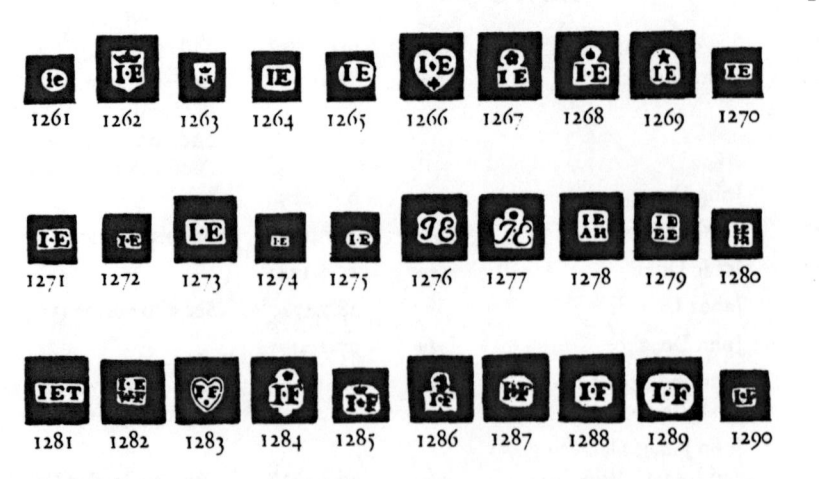

No.	Name	Category	Entered	Notes
1261	William Jelf	smw	undated	Between 1717 and 1720. See also no. 3196
1262	Samuel Jefferys	lgw	April 1697	
1263	James Englie	smw	29.6.1713	
1264	John Eckfourd I	lgw	undated	c. 1720. See also no. 545
1265	Edward Jennings	lgw	30.6.1720	See also nos. 599, 1260
1266	John East	lgw	24.5.1721	See also no. 525
1267	John Edwards II	lgw	27.4.1724	See also nos. 566, 1277
1268	idem	lgw	1.11.1753	Or perhaps son of above
1269	John Eckfourd Junior (II)	lgw	23.6.1725	See also nos. 548, 1276
1270	John Eaton	smw	15.7.1760	
1271	idem	smw	18.4.1761	And a smaller mark 2.12.1762
1272	James Evans	smw	7.2.1763	
1273	John Edwards III	plw	24.11.1788	And a smaller mark same date. Two others smaller 6.1.1792 and 2.8.1797
1274	John Edington	smw	16.5.1799	And a similar mark 18.8.1806
1275	idem	smw	5.12.1804	See also no. 1805 and Section VII, I.E
1276	John Eckford Jr. (II)	lgw	20.6.1739	See also nos. 548, 1269
1277	John Edwards II	lgw	9.8.1739	See also nos. 566, 1267-8
1278	James Ede and Alexander Hewat	lgw	6.12.1808	And a smaller mark same date
1279	John (III) and Edward (I) Edwards	plw	10.6.1811	And a smaller mark same date
1280	James Evans and John Russel	smw	31.8.1761	

LONDON GOLDSMITHS

No.	Name	Category	Entered	Notes
1281	John Edward Terrey	*plw*	26.1.1816	And a smaller mark same date. Others similar 1828 and 1835. See also nos. 1719, 2547
1282	John Edwards III and William Frisbee	*plw*	12.4.1791	And a smaller mark same date
1283	John Farnell	*lgw*	20.6.1720	See also no. 661
1284	James Fraillon	*lgw*	6.3.1723	See also no. 713
1285	John Flavill	*lgw*	5.4.1726	See also no. 693
1286	Jacob Foster	*lgw*	5.10.1726	
1287	John Fawdery II	*lgw*	27.2.1729	See also no. 662
1288	John Fossey	*lgw*	9.1.1733	See also no. 1310
1289	idem	*lgw*	undated	Between Jan. 1733 and Aug. 1734
1290	John Foote	*bm*	22.1.1735	See also no. 1309

IF   IG

No.	Name	Category	Entered	Notes
1291	John Fullford	smw	9.12.1735	
1292	John Fray	lgw	4.1.1748	And a smaller similar mark 28.8.1756. See also no. 1316
1293	James Freshfield	smw	undated	Sept. 1759–May 1761
1294	John Faux	smw	6.5.1763	And a larger mark 6.9.1763. See also no. 1312 and Section VIII, IF, script capitals
1295	John Foster I	smw	20.11.1764	
1296	John Fayle	smw	30.4.1772	
1297	John Fielding	smw	21.4.1775	
1298	John Foster II	smw	14.2.1778	See also Section IX, H.F
1299	idem	smw	8.10.1789	
1300	John Fountain	plw	1.5.1792	And a slightly smaller mark with pellet between 16.2.1797
1301	John Fisher	smw	22.2.1799	See also nos. 3129–30
1302	John Fuller	smw	26.1.1804	
1303	John Foskett	plw	27.10.1808	
1304	John Fry II	plw	18.4.1826	
1305	Joseph Flint	smw	17.9.1831	
1306	John Figg	plw	31.7.1834	And a smaller mark same date. Two others similar 10.5.1838
1307	John Frost I	lgw	30.8.1757	
1308	idem	lgw	idem	
1309	John Foote	smw	4.5.1761	See also no. 1290
1310	John Fossey	lgw	15.6.1739	See also nos. 1288–9
1311	John (I) and George Foster	smw	11.7.1764	

LONDON GOLDSMITHS

No.	Name	Category	Entered	Notes
1312	John Faux and George Love	smw	11.5.1764	And three other marks in quatrefoil punches Dec. 1764, Feb. 1767 and Feb. 1771. See no. 1294 and Section VIII, I.F
1313	John Fountain and John Beadnell	plw	10.5.1793	And a smaller mark same date
1314	John Foskett and John Stewart	plw	20.2.1810	
1315	John and William Frost	smw	18.11.1814	And a smaller similar mark 6.5.1816
1316	Fuller White and John Fray	lgw	4.3.1745	
1317	James Gould	lgw	19.11.1722	See also nos. 860, 1346–7
1318	idem	lgw	undated	Between Oct. 1732 and July 1734
1319	John Gray	smw	14.3.1722	And a smaller mark without pellet 20.4.1722. See also no. 879
1320	John Gale	smw	18.1.1723	

Also IF nos. 3406, 3635; *IF* no. 3636; IF.IW no. 3407

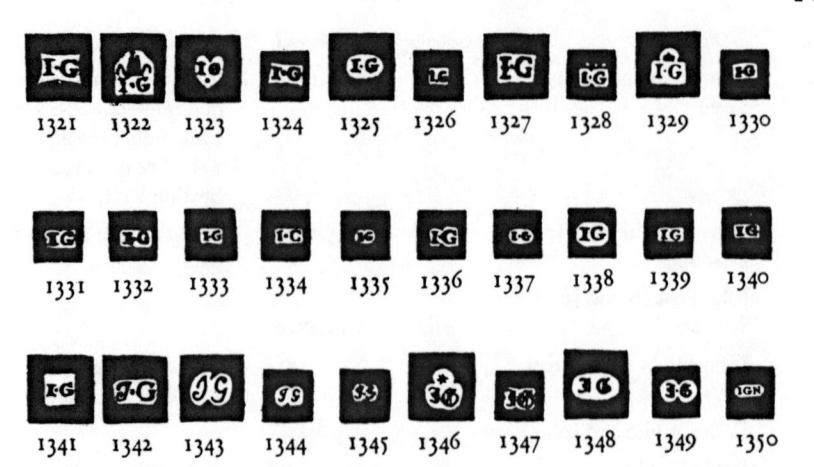

No.	Name	Category	Entered	Notes
1321	John Gibbons	lgw	2.3.1724	See also no. 823
1322	John Gorsuch	lgw	6.4.1726	See also no. 1348
1323	John Gamon	lgw	22.3.1727	
1324	John Gorham	lgw	11.12.1728	And a similar mark 8.9.1730. See also nos. 1343, 1349, 3640
1325	Jeffery Griffith	lgw	18.2.1732	See also no. 2558
1326	John Giles	smw	7.12.1733	
1327	John Gahegan	lgw	17.7.1734	
1328	John Goodrich	smw	14.10.1735	
1329	James Gould (entered by Mary Gould)	lgw	31.8.1747	
1330	James Graham	smw	26.7.1762	And a similar mark 15.4.1768
1331	idem	smw	3.8.1769	
1332	John Gurney	smw	23.12.1765	
1333	John Greenall	smw	2.4.1766	
1334	John Grace	smw	11.2.1772	
1335	Joseph Goulding	smw	29.8.1772	
1336	John Grant	gw	28.1.1774	And a smaller mark in rectangular punch 3.2.1780
1337	John Greer	smw	17.9.1791	
1338	John Gold	smw	27.3.1793	See also no. 3639
1339	John Girdler	spm	10.1.1803	
1340	John Gear	smw	27.8.1804	
1341	Joseph Guest	plw	16.5.1812	See also nos. 2771-2
1342	James Goodwin	lgw	4.9.1721	See also nos. 863-4

LONDON GOLDSMITHS

No.	Name	Category	Entered	Notes
1343	John Gorham	lgw	17.1.1757	Another mark with pellet between, found on spoons 1755 and 1759. See also nos. 1324, 1349, 3640
1344	Jane Gallant	smw	25.5.1760	
1345	James Gibbons	smw	7.8.1761	See also Section V, JG.SG
1346	James Gould	csm	30.5.1739	See also nos. 860 and 1317–8
1347	idem	csm	6.6.1743	
1348	John Gamon	lgw	15.6.1739	See also no. 1323
1349	John Gorham	lgw	27.6.1739	See also nos. 1324, 1343, 3640
1350	John George Nutting	plw	30.3.1831	Mark defaced 24.5.1833

Also IG nos. 3408, 3637–9; *IG* no. 3640

IGW   IH

No.	Name	Category	Entered	Notes
1351	John George Warner	smw	3.6.1819	See also Section VII, R.L & I.W
1352	William Hinton	lgw	7.10.1704	Possibly cut in error for H.I. See also no. 1013
1353	John Hill	smw	c. 1720	Very poor impression. Perhaps a bird above. See also no. 1014
1354	John Holland I	lgw	2.7.1720	See also no. 1051
1355	John Hopkins	lgw	undated	Between 1720 and 1724. See also no. 1054
1356	James Hervot	smw	20.1.1722	Entered as 'Gold marke'. See also no. 990
1357	James Heley	smw	undated	Between April 1724 and June 1726
1358	Joseph Healy	smw	19.8.1725	See also no. 988
1359	Isaac Harris	smw	23.9.1725	See also no. 1365
1360	Jean Harache	smw	22.6.1726	
1361	John Hiccox	smw	12.10.1730	
1362	John Henstridge	smw	24.5.1731	
1363	John Hilman	sword cutler	undated	Between June 1731 and March 1733
1364	Joseph Haywood II	smw	Nov. 1734	
1365	Isaac Harris	smw	22.9.1735	See also no. 1359
1366	John Hague I	smw	31.12.1735	See also no. 1371
1367	John Harvey I	smw	7.2.1738	See also nos. 930, 1372, 1401–3
1368	John Harwood	lgw	29.7.1739	See also no. 1411
1369	John Hyatt	lgw	26.1.1742	
1370	Joseph Heriot	lgw	30.6.1756	

LONDON GOLDSMITHS

No.	Name	Category	Entered	Notes
1371	John Hague I	smw	14.7.1758	And a smaller mark same date. See also no. 1366
1372	John (II) and Ann Harvey	smw	undated	Feb.–April 1759. And a similar mark 29.3.1768
1373	James Hunt	smw	30.7.1760	
1374	James Harmar	smw	9.4.1761	
1375	John Harris II	smw	15.5.1761	Also incuse mark 2.11.1765
1376	John Hardy	smw	6.10.1762	
1377	John Holloway	smw	undated	After 30.9.1772. And a similar mark 27.4.1773. See also no. 1385*
1378	John Hills	spm	19.11.1773	
1379	James Hine	smw	27.9.1774	
1380	James Hyde	smw	3.11.1777	See also no. 1407. And a similar and a smaller mark in oval 10.1.1786

Also IH nos. 3409, 3641–3.

---

* A very similar mark observed on pistol-mounts of 1766.

No.	Name	Category	Entered	Notes
1381	John Holman	smw	18.6.1778	
1382	John Hutson	plw	2.1.1784	
1383	Joseph Hastings	smw	11.3.1784	
1384	John Harris III	plw	2.3.1786	
1385	John Holloway	smw	16.1.1788	See also no. 1377
1386	John Hodgkinson	smw	2.10.1790	
1387	Joseph Hardy	plw	27.4.1799	And a smaller mark same date. See also no. 1416
1388	Joseph Hayward	smw	8.10.1800	
1389	John Hawkins	spm	2.11.1802	And a larger similar mark 12.11.1817. Others with pellet between 1821 and 1823 and without pellet 1825 to 1831
1390	John Gwyn Holmes	plw	10.7.1805	
1391	John Holdup	spm	11.11.1809	
1392	John Houle	plw	10.4.1811	And a smaller similar mark 23.2.1813
1393	John Hague II	spm	17.5.1819	
1394	Isaac Hebberd	smw	14.3.1822	And a slightly smaller mark 28.1.1825
1395	John Harris IV	spm	15.1.1818	
1396	idem	spm	9.2.1820	
1397	idem	spm	25.1.1822	
1398	idem	spm	12.7.1825	
1399	John Harris V	smw	22.11.1831	And a similar bolder mark 27.8.1834. Others in rectangles 1839 onwards
1400	Joseph Hodgson	plw	24.2.1827	

LONDON GOLDSMITHS

No.	Name	Category	Entered	Notes
1401	John Harvey I	*lgw*	18.6.1739	See also nos. 930, 1367, 1372, 3644
1402	idem	*lgw*	19.11.1745	
1403	idem	*lgw*	12.12.1746	Or perhaps 3.10.1748
1404	idem	*lgw*	16.8.1750	
1405	John Holland II	*lgw*	4.7.1739	
1406	John Huntly	*smw*	3.11.1759	See also nos. 3644–5
1407	James Hyde	*smw*	16.9.1778	See also no. 1380
1408	Jonathan Hayne	*lgw*	14.11.1808	And one larger and two smaller similar marks same date. Twelve others similar 1821–34. See also nos. 2978, 3646
1409	John Hayne	*plw*	31.5.1813	See also no. 1818
1410	John Holmes	*smw*	12.7.1733	

Also IH nos. 3409, 3641–3; *IH* nos. 3410, 3644–6

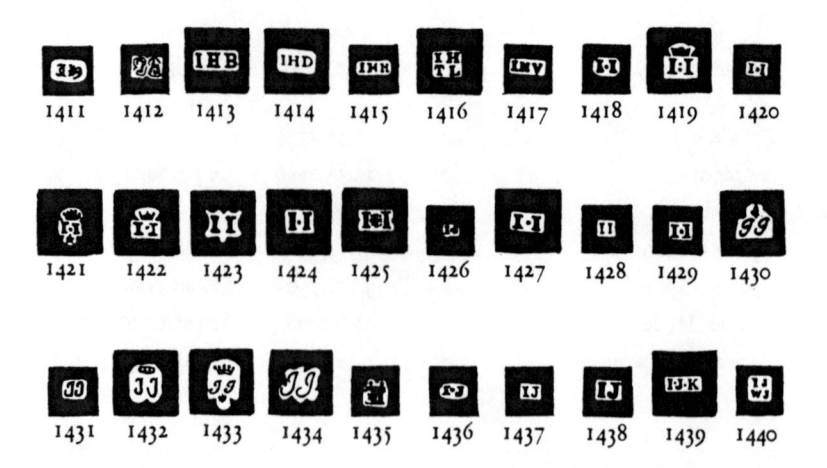

No.	Name	Category	Entered	Notes
1411	John Harwood	lgw	19.6.1739	See also no. 1368
1412	John Humphris	smw	10.6.1762	
1413	John Hawkins Barlow	plw	12.1.1815	
1414	James Henry Daniel	gw sw	20.1.1823	And a larger mark 8.11.1823 Another with pellets 20.7.1825. See also no. 982
1415	James and Henry Harding	smw	8.10.1768	
1416	Joseph Hardy and Thomas Lowndes	plw	26.5.1798	And a smaller similar mark same date. See also no. 1387
1417	John Henry Vere	smw	31.10.1769	
1418	John Jones I	lgw	27.3.1723	See also nos. 1431-2 and 1564
1419	idem	lgw	24.3.1729	
1420	John Jarvis	smw	30.6.1731	
1421	John Jacob	lgw	3.5.1734	See also no. 1433
1422	James Jenkins	lgw	15.1.1739	See also no. 1430
1423	John Jarratt	smw	22.7.1758	
1424	James Jennings	smw	27.2.1760	
1425	John Irvine	smw	11.8.1769	Repeated on moving 12.7.1771
1426	idem	smw	idem	idem
1427	Joshua Jackson	smw	6.5.1779	See also no. 1436 and Section V, J.J
1428	John Jackson III	smw	31.10.1792	See also no. 2819
1429	idem	smw	5.12.1795	
1430	James Jenkins	lgw	26.4.1731	See also no. 1422
1431	John Jones I	lgw	3.1.1733	See also nos. 1418-19, 1564
1432	idem	lgw	1.2.1739	Bad impression. First letter and crown conjectural

LONDON GOLDSMITHS

No.	Name	Category	Entered	Notes
1433	John Jacob	lgw	20.6.1739	And a smaller similar mark with three balls to coronet same date. See also no. 1421
1434	James Jones I	lgw	27.5.1755	
1435	John Johnson I	smw	28.6.1720	See also no. 1559
1436	Joshua Jackson	smw	1.7.1784	See also no. 1427. Two other marks similar 2.10.1787 and 14.1.1794
1437	Isaac Jones	smw	3.9.1800	See also Section VIII, II.WI, IJ and IJ.WJ
1438	John Jones III	plw	4.8.1824	And a smaller mark 7.2.1825
1439	John James Keith	plw	5.5.1824	
1440	Isaac and William (III) Jones	smw	5.5.1809	See also no. 1437 and Section VIII, II.WI, IJ and IJ.WJ

Also I.I no. 3647

IK   IL

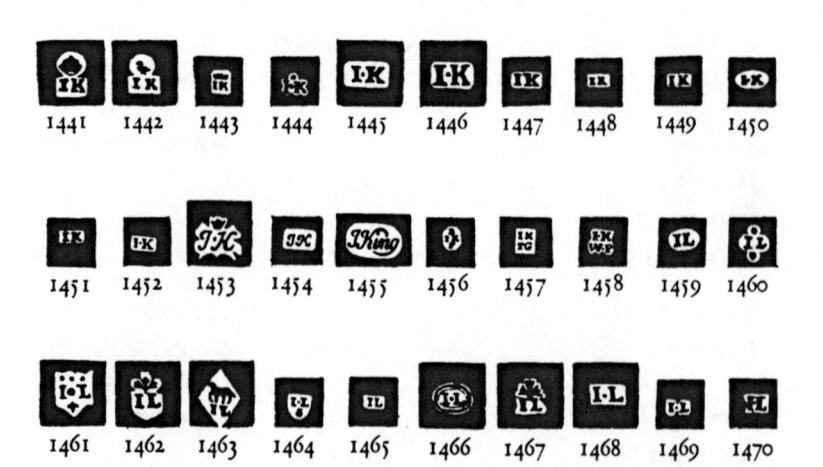

No.	Name	Category	Entered	Notes
1441	Jeremiah King	lgw	11.9.1723	See also nos. 1454–5, 1875
1442	idem	lgw	5.6.1736	Outline of punch conjectural, based on previous example
1443	John Kemp	smw	4.8.1724	
1444	James King I	smw	23.2.1764	And a similar mark 1.11.1769. See also nos. 1488, 3648
1445	John King	plw	22.4.1775	And other marks similar, varying sizes 1779 and 1785
1446	idem	plw	14.6.1775	And a similar mark 13.6.1777
1447	Jasper Kelly	gw	6.5.1779	
1448	John Kidder	plw	16.11.1780	
1449	John Köhler I	smw	1.3.1790	
1450	James Kidder	plw	2.3.1795	
1451	John Kerschner	spm	11.11.1808	And other marks similar, larger 1810, 1814, 1817
1452	John Köhler II	smw	3.3.1835	
1453	John Kincaid	lgw	17.10.1743	And a smaller nearly similar mark 23.8.1745
1454	Jeremiah King	lgw	18.6.1739	And other marks similar 26.1.1743 and 14.2.1744. See also nos. 1441–2
1455	idem	lgw	idem	
1456	Benjamin Flight and John Kelly	smw	19.1.1791	
1457	John Kentesber and Thomas Grove	lgw	14.6.1757	See also no. 3707
1458	William Portal and James King II	smw	10.11.1768	See also no. 3256
1459	John Lefebure	smw	21.6.1720	See also no. 1921

LONDON GOLDSMITHS

No.	Name	Category	Entered	Notes
1460	John Lingard	lgw	22.6.1720	See also nos. 1932–3, 3721
1461	John Ludlow	lgw	22.6.1720	Bad impression. Largely conjectural. See also nos. 1968, 3649
1462	Isaac Liger	lgw	5.9.1720	See also nos. 1467, 1931
1463	Jane Lambe	lgw	undated	Between January 1719 and July 1722. See also no. 1895
1464	John Luff	smw	2.10.1724	See also nos. 1487, 1498, 3651
1465	John Lee I	smw	12.11.1725	See also Section V, I.L and SI.IL
1466	Jeremiah Lee	smw	6.8.1728	See also nos. 1488, 3718
1467	John Liger	lgw	9.12.1730	See also no. 1462
1468	John Laver	lgw	19.5.1749	
1469	John Gibson Leadbetter	smw	28.7.1757	And two other larger similar marks 18.7.1758 and 3.2.1766
1470	idem	smw	22.8.1758	And a similar mark 11.5.1767. See also no. 3653

Also IK nos. 3648; IL 3649–55

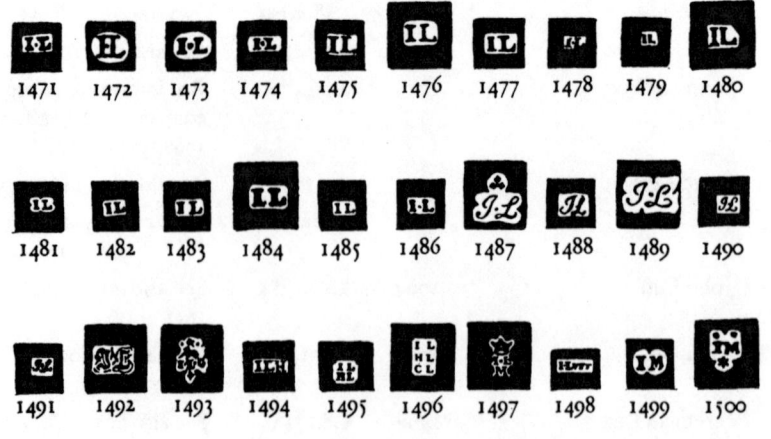

No.	Name	Category	Entered	Notes
1471	Joseph Lewis	smw	30.10.1767	And a similar mark 4.1.1768. See also nos. 1481, 1831 and Section VIII, I.L
1472	John Lambe	spm	8.2.1774	And a larger mark same date. Another similar mark in flatter oval 25.8.1780
1473	idem	spm	15.2.1782	And a smaller mark same date. Other marks similar same year and 1783
1474	idem	plw	4.7.1785	And other marks in oval 1785–91 and two small oblong punches 1791
1475	idem	plw	17.10.1791	
1476	John Lee II	plw	2.12.1782	
1477	John Lee III	gw	20.3.1793	See also no. 1832
1478	James Long	smw	17.11.1785	See also Section V, I.L
1479	John Ledie	smw	30.6.1789	
1480	idem	smw	1.4.1791	And two other marks smaller same date
1481	Joseph Lewis	plw	30.10.1792	See also nos. 1471, 1831 and Section VIII I.L
1482	John Lewis II	smw	3.6.1794	
1483	John Lias	plw	13.7.1799	And other marks with pellet 1802 and 1803; without pellet 1805–10. See also Section VIII, I.L and IL.DC
1484	idem	spm	31.10.1812	And a smaller mark same date. Others 16.6.1815. See also nos. 1495–6
1485	John Lawton	smw	30.9.1802	And a similar mark 24.10.1805

LONDON GOLDSMITHS

No.	Name	Category	Entered	Notes
1486	John London	smw	10.6.1808	And two other marks without pellet 9.1.1818
1487	John Luff	lgw	25.6.1739	*See also nos. 1464, 1498
1488	Jeremiah Lee	lgw	26.6.1739	See also nos. 1466, 3718
1489	John Lampfert	lgw	12.11.1748	And a slightly smaller mark same date
1490	idem	lgw	24.1.1749	
1491	John Linney	smw	20.10.1769	
1492	Joseph Lock	smw	18.6.1778	See also no. 1829
1493	James Bartholomew Langlois	lgw	6.4.1738	And a small mark very indistinct, probably IL, same date. See also no. 3651
1494	John Larans Hallardt	plw	10.9.1823	
1495	John and Henry Lias	spm	14.3.1818	And other marks similar 1819 and 1837 to 1845. See also nos. 1483-4 and Section VIII, I.L and IL.DC
1496	John, Henry and Charles Lias	plw	7.8.1823	And two other marks smaller same date. Others similar 1828-33
1497	John Lewis Marc	smw	27.6.1726	
1498	John Luff	smw	2.10.1724	See also nos. 1464, 1487
1499	John Munday	smw	2.8.1720	See also nos. 1508, 2078-9
1500	John Millington	lgw	23.6.1720	See also nos. 1511, 2037

Also IL nos. 3649-55; IL.IR no. 3411; IL.IS nos. 3656-7

---

* An unregistered small mark of script letters similar to no. 1487 but without device found together with large mark, both on the same piece, an incense boat of 1743.

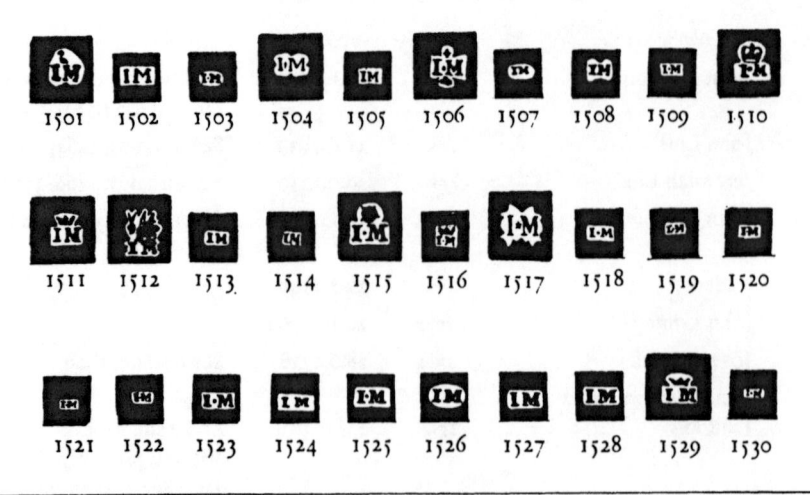

No.	Name	Category	Entered	Notes
1501	James Morson	lgw	20.6.1720	See also no. 2049
1502	Joseph Mumford	smw	27.7.1720	See also no. 2076
1503	idem	smw	idem	
1504	John Maggs	smw	1.9.1721	
1505	John Montgomery	smw	22.11.1721	
1506	idem	lgw	24.2.1729	
1507	idem	smw	18.10.1736	See also nos. 1535, 2050
1508	John Munday	smw	27.11.1721	See also nos. 1499, 2078-9
1509	John Mulford	smw	5.5.1725	See also no. 1970
1510	Jacob Margas	lgw	undated	Between 1720 and 1728
1511	John Millington	lgw	18.6.1728	See also nos. 1500, 2037
1512	James Maitland	lgw	undated	Between 18.6.1728 and 24.2.1729
1513	John Mansfield	smw	13.9.1731	
1514	John Mackfarlan	smw	23.2.1734	See also no. 1532
1515	James Manners	lgw	26.4.1734	See also no. 1538 and Section V, IM, six-petalled flower above
1516	James Montgomery	smw	29.9.1737	
1517	Jacob Marsh	lgw	24.4.1744	See also no. 3658
1518	John Muns	lgw	27.3.1753	And a larger mark 20.8.1757
1519	John Marder	smw	14.10.1760	
1520	John Mackhoule	smw	14.1.1765	
1521	James Morisset	smw	31.8.1770	See also Section VII, IM pellet between
1522	John Mince	smw	16.2.1773	
1523	John Moore	plw	18.7.1778	See also nos. 1536, 3658
1524	John Merry	smw	19.1.1782	

LONDON GOLDSMITHS

No.	Name	Category	Entered	Notes
1525	idem	smw	24.7.1789	And a smaller similar mark 13.11.1799
1526	James Mince	smw	5.2.1790	And two other smaller similar marks same date
1527	Josh. Marston	smw	30.1.1790	
1528	John Mewburn	plw	2.10.1793	See also no. 3659
1529	idem	plw	24.3.1823	
1530	John Myatt	smw	21.6.1799	See also Section VIII, IM, IM script capitals and IM.IM

Also IM nos. 3658–61

IM   Io

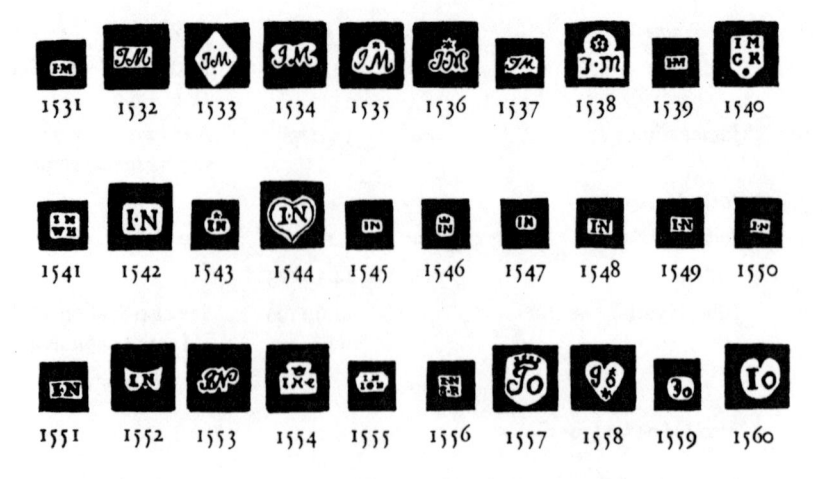

No.	Name	Category	Entered	Notes
1531	John Macbride	smw	13.9.1814	
1532	John Mackfarlen	lgw	25.6.1739	See also no. 1514
1533	Jse Mcfarlan	lgw	31.10.1739	
1534	James Morison	lgw	14.5.1740	And a smaller similar mark same date. Another intermediate size 28.11.1744
1535	John Montgomery	lgw	1.9.1742	See also nos. 1505–7
1536	John Moore	lgw	24.1.1758	See also nos. 1523, 3658
1537	James Marson	smw	21.3.1761	
1538	James Manners	lgw	21.6.1739	See also no. 1515
1539*	John Mcferlan	smw	13.3.1762	And a slightly larger mark as plateworker 9.5.1786
1540	James Murray and Charles Kandler I	lgw	29.8.1727	See also no. 1863
1541	James Mince and William Hodgkins II	plw	23.11.1780	
1542	Jonathan Newton	lgw	6.8.1720	See also nos. 2087–8
1543	John Nelson	smw	4.1.1721	
1544	John Newton	lgw	4.4.1726	See also no. 1553
1545	Joseph Norwood	smw	undated	Between July 1728 and Aug. 1731
1546	Jacob Neale	smw	25.8.1731	
1547	John Norris	smw	13.2.1735	
1548	James Nicolson	smw	23.7.1735	
1549	John Nicklin	smw	25.1.1760	
1550	Joseph Nutting	smw	12.2.1790	See also no. 1555
1551	John Nickolds	smw	21.9.1818	And a smaller mark. See also no. 1556
1552	John Nichols	plw	30.11.1825	

LONDON GOLDSMITHS

No.	Name	Category	Entered	Notes
1553	John Newton	lgw	21.6.1739	See also no. 1544
1554	John Neville	lgw	10.4.1745	
1555	Joseph and J. G. Nutting	smw	18.3.1803	
1556	John Nickolds and Samuel Roberts	smw	27.9.1808	And a larger similar mark as plateworkers 22.11.1813
1557	Lawrence Jones	lgw	April 1697	See also no. 3665
1558	Edward Jones	lgw	April 1697	And a smaller similar mark, lacking mullet above 'o' but with pellet between letters
1559	John Johnson I	smw	3.8.1708	See also no. 1435
1560	Glover Johnson	lgw	4.8.1712	See also no. 833

Also *IM* no. 3662; IM.DI no. 3663; *Io* nos. 3665–6

---

* No. 1539. The initials in this mark are in fact I·MF.

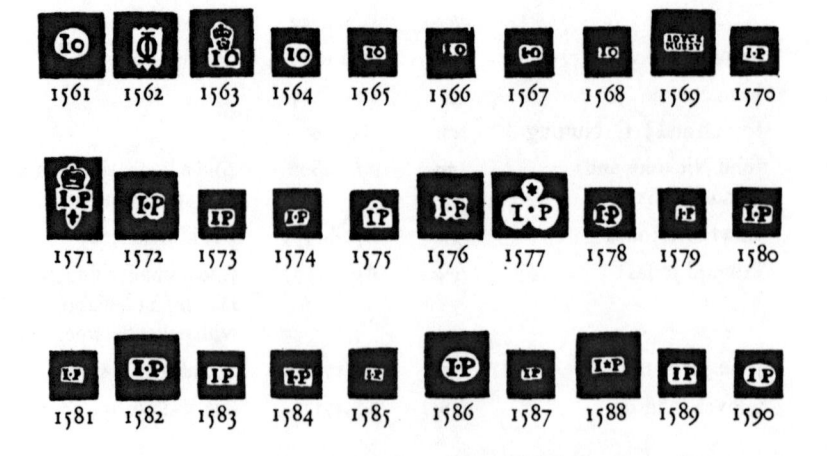

No.	Name	Category	Entered	Notes
1561	Simon Jouet	lgw	undated	Between 1724 and 1727
1562	John Overing	lgw	6.1.1725	See also nos. 2111, 3666
1563	George Greenhill Jones	lgw	5.12.1719	See also nos. 834–5
1564	John Jones I	lgw	27.3.1723	See also nos. 1418, 1431, 3664
1565	John Orme I	smw	20.9.1734	
1566	John Orme II	smw	2.4.1796	
1567	John Osborne	smw	3.5.1797	See also Section V, JO, pellet between
1568	Joseph Oliver	smw	23.3.1822	
1569	Hussey and Joyce	smw	12.5.1729	
1570	Jos(eph) Perkins I	smw	6.7.1720	And a similar mark without pellet 27.1.1735
1571	John Pero	lgw	23.11.1732	See also no. 1599
1572	John Pollock	lgw	16.10.1734	See also no. 1596
1573	John Penn	lgw	22.4.1736	
1574	John Pont	lgw	19.3.1739	See also no. 1578
1575	James Peltro	lgw	undated	Between 27 and 29 June 1739
1576	John Preist	lgw	24.6.1748	See also no. 3668
1577	John Perry	lgw	23.3.1757	See also nos. 3668–9
1578	John Pont	smw	5.2.1762	See also no. 1574
1579	Job Palmer	smw	3.8.1763	See also Section VI, I.P
1580	John Packwood	smw	26.10.1764	
1581	John Pickering	chaser	8.3.1765	
1582	James Perry	smw	28.6.1765	And other marks similar 1768 and 1773. See also nos. 1837–8 and Section IX, JP, pellet between

LONDON GOLDSMITHS

No.	Name	Category	Entered	Notes
1583	James Phipps I	smw	14.5.1767	And a smaller mark, pellet between 10.2.1772. See also no. 3049
1584	James Plumpton	smw	5.6.1767	
1585	James Peacock	smw	20.12.1769	Also D & P, perhaps at later date with unidentified partner
1586	John Plimmer	smw	18.12.1771	
1587	Joseph Preedy	plw	3.2.1777	
1588	idem	plw	20.1.1800	And a smaller similar mark same date
1589	John Priestman	spm	23.2.1786	
1590	John Prosser	smw	4.4.1796	

Also IO no. 3664; IP nos. 3412, 3667–70

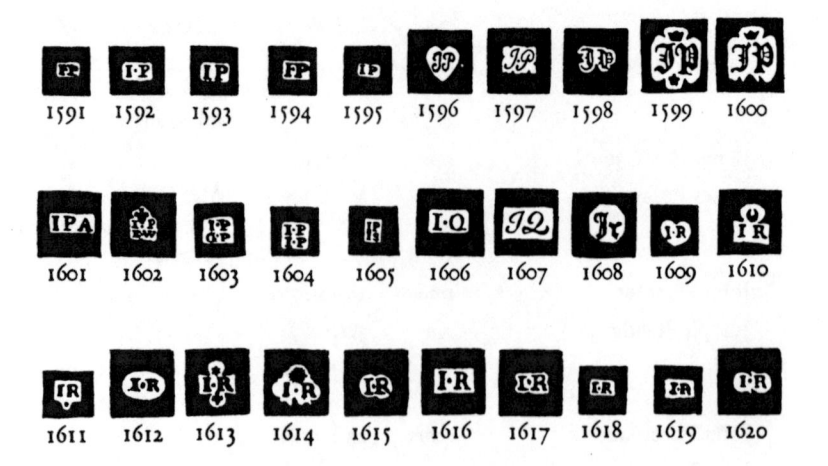

No.	Name	Category	Entered	Notes
1591	John Pritchard	smw	2.4.1799	See also Section VIII, I.P
1592	Jonathan Perkins I	plw	29.8.1800	And two similar marks 19.2.1803. See also nos. 1604, 1839 and Section VIII, IP and JP
1593	John Page	plw	8.1.1813	
1594	James Pratt	plw	11.8.1818	
1595	Joseph Pritchard	plw	10.2.1825	
1596	John Pollock	lgw	26.6.1739	See also no. 1572
1597	John Payne	lgw	13.4.1751	See also nos. 3671–2
1598	John Pitts	smw	26.10.1730	
1599	John Pero	lgw	22.6.1739	See also no. 1571
1600	Isabel Pero	lgw	1.5.1741	
1601	Jn. P. Acklam	plw	25.9.1832	And a smaller mark 22.6.1837
1602	John Parker I and Edward Wakelin	plw	after 1758	Not in register. Mark taken from a skewer. See also no. 3757
1603	Josiah and George Piercy	spm	4.1.1812	And a similar smaller mark same date
1604	Jonathan and Jonathan Perkins	plw	5.8.1795	And a similar smaller mark same date. See nos. 1592, 1839 and Section VIII, IP and JP
1605	John Peters and John Schaffer	smw	18.6.1810	See also Sections IV and VII, I.P
1606	John Quantock	lgw	undated	After 3.7.1739
1607	idem	lgw	30.5.1754	
1608	Edward Ironside	lgw	10.9.1702	See also no. 3675

LONDON GOLDSMITHS

No.	Name	Category	Entered	Notes
1609	Joseph Ridley	smw	30.8.1710	Old Std. style mark. ? For gold only
1610	Isaac Ribouleau	lgw	16.7.1724*	See also no. 2342
1611	Joseph Reason	smw	17.6.1720	See also no. 2304
1612	John Richardson I	lgw	8.7.1723	See also nos. 2344, 3778
1613	John Robinson I	lgw	4.11.1723	See also no. 2400
1614	John Robinson II	lgw	9.2.1738	See also nos. 1630, 3676
1615	James Ramsay	smw	18.2.1725	
1616	John Rowe	lgw	3.6.1749	
1617	John Radburn	smw	13.2.1762	And a smaller similar mark 18.4.1769. See also no. 3677
1618	John Raymond	smw	19.8.1762	See also no. 1633
1619	James Rudkins	smw	26.7.1763	
1620	John Reynolds	smw	10.10.1768	See also Section IX, IR, pellet between

Note: For a mark which might be read as IPG see no. 2182.
Also *IP* nos. 3671–3; *IP* monogram no. 3674; IP.TW no. 3413; IR nos. 3414, 3675–7

---

*Given as 1714 in register entry but lying between preceding and following entries of November 1723 and November 1724 respectively.

IR   IS

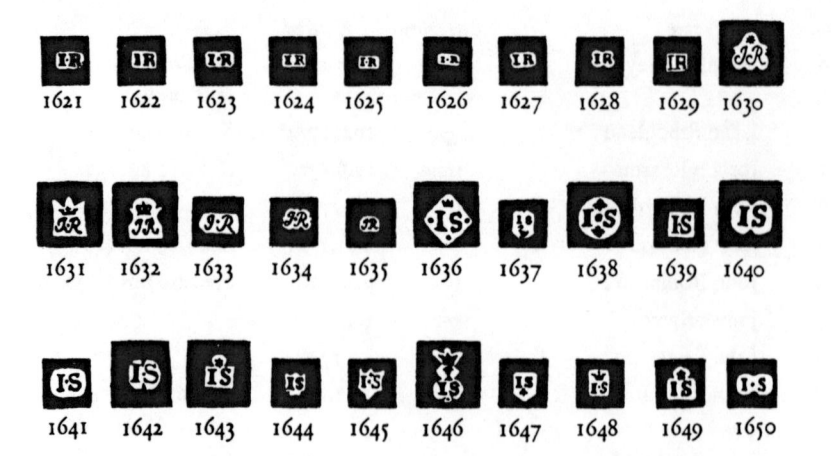

No.	Name	Category	Entered	Notes
1621	James Reasey	smw	23.10.1769	
1622	William Rogers	smw	11.4.1770	William presumably an error for John, James etc.
1623	John Robins	plw	20.10.1774	And two other similar marks, larger and smaller 7.8.1787. See also no. 3678
1624	James Ruell	smw	28.4.1795	
1625	John Robert	smw	14.10.1795	
1626	John Rotton	smw	16.3.1797	
1627	John Reily	smw	20.2.1801	And other marks smaller and larger similar 1802, 1805, 1823. See also no. 2033
1628	idem	smw	13.6.1823	
1629	John Robertson	smw	14.9.1802	And a smaller similar mark 8.10.1802. See also Section IV, JR and Section VII, IR and JR
1630	John Robinson II	lgw	3.7.1739	See also nos. 1614, 3676
1631	John Roker	lgw	13.9.1743	
1632	John Richardson II	lgw	13.8.1752	
1633	John Raymond	smw	19.8.1762	And a smaller similar mark without pellet 26.9.1768. See also no. 1618
1634	John Russel	smw	25.8.1764	And a similar mark 6.3.1767
1635	John Rich	smw	13.6.1765	See Section VIII, IR script capitals
1636	Joyce Issod	lgw	undated	Prior to 1702. Upper and lower portions of impression obscure

LONDON GOLDSMITHS

No.	Name	Category	Entered	Notes
1637	John Swann	smw	18.6.1714	Presumably mark for gold. See also no. 2651
1638	John Sanders I	lgw	27.6.1720	
1639	Joseph Simcoe	smw	29.6.1720	
1640	Joseph Smith I	lgw	6.7.1720	And a similar mark, pellet between letters 30.9.1723. See also nos. 2585, 3680
1641	idem	lgw	3.5.1728	
1642	James Seabrook	lgw	22.7.1720	See also no. 2507
1643	James Smith I	lgw	25.8.1720	See also no. 2586
1644	Joseph Steward I	lgw	7.9.1720	See also no. 2643
1645	Isaa(c) Stuart	smw	27.10.1721	Indifferent impression. Devices doubtful
1646	John Le Sage	lgw	26.7.1722	See also nos. 2469, 3678A (note) and 3683
1647	James Slater	lgw	undated	Between Oct. 1725 and Jan. 1728
1648	John Smallwood	smw	undated	Between Nov. 1725 and July 1726
1649	James Stone	smw	14.7.1726	
1650	James Savage	lgw	23.5.1728	

Note: For a mark apparently IR in script, a bunch of grapes between, see under TR no. 2913.
Also *IR* no. 3678; IS nos. 3679–81

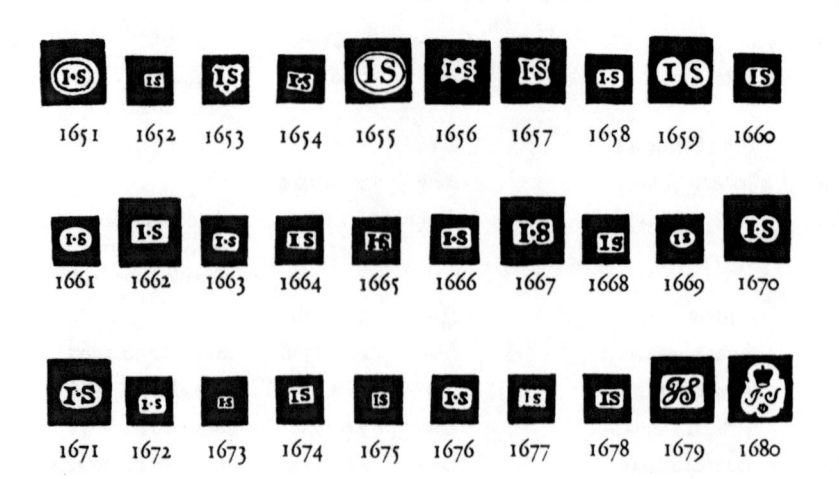

No.	Name	Category	Entered	Notes
1651	John Swift	smw	undated	Between May and Oct. 1728. See also no. 1689
1652	John Soux	smw	undated	Between May and Oct. 1728
1653	James Shruder	lgw	1.8.1737	See also nos. 1682–3
1654	John Spencer	smw	8.3.1739	
1655	Joseph Sanders	lgw	22.6.1739	See also no. 1679
1656	John Spackman II	lgw	11.9.1741	
1657	idem	lgw	24.11.1742	
1658	James Smith II	lgw	25.9.1746	See also no. 1685
1659	Joseph Steward II	lgw	29.1.1755	And other marks similar 8.4.1755 and 9.9.1762
1660	idem	smw	14.3.1768	
1661	idem	smw	7.3.1770	
1662	idem	smw	3.6.1773	And other smaller marks without pellet 18.6.1773, 4.4.1780 and 23.5.1783. See also no. 3681
1663	John Smith II	smw	19.2.1769	See also no. 1672
1664	Joseph Savory I	smw	31.1.1772	See also Section VII, JS, pellet between
1665	John Sadler	smw	15.4.1772	
1666	James Stamp	plw	6.7.1774	And other marks similar larger and smaller 1776, 1777, 1779
1667	idem	plw	14.10.1777	See also nos. 1691, 3708
1668	John Sanders II	smw	8.3.1775	See also no. 3687
1669	John Sidaway	smw	23.4.1777	

LONDON GOLDSMITHS

No.	Name	Category	Entered	Notes
1670	John Scofield	plw	13.1.1778	And a smaller mark 1.10.1787. See also nos. 2349, 3709, 3779
1671	James Sutton	plw	7.7.1780	And a smaller mark same date
1672	John Smith II	smw	28.2.1782	See also no. 1663
1673	John Steward	smw	19.5.1786	And other marks similar 1796–1800. See also no. 1687
1674	John Shekleton	smw	15.4.1799	And a slightly smaller mark with pellet same date and another similar 9.3.1809. See also no. 1677
1675	John Stapler	smw	9.2.1807	
1676	Joseph Smith II	smw	18.8.1808	
1677	John Shekleton	smw	8.3.1821	See also no. 1674
1678	John Sharp	plw	19.9.1821	
1679	Joseph Sanders	lgw	7.12.1730	See also no. 1655
1680	John Hugh Le Sage	lgw	25.6.1739	See also nos. 1646, 1681, 2469, 3683

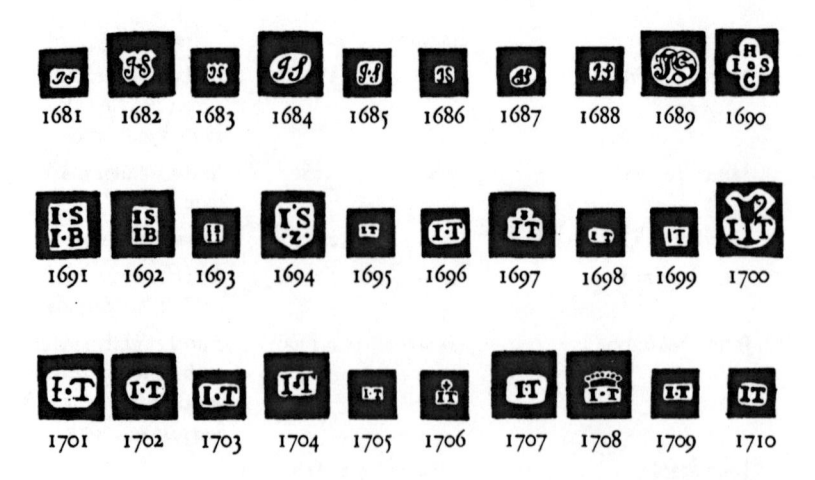

No.	Name	Category	Entered	Notes
1681	John Hugh Le Sage	lgw	25.6.1739	Mark found on candlestick nozzles with no. 1680 on bodies
1682	James Shruder	lgw	25.6.1739	See also no. 1653
1683	idem	lgw	idem	
1684	Joseph Steward I	lgw	28.6.1739	See also no. 2643
1685	James Smith II	lgw	14.9.1744	See also no. 1658
1686	John Schuppe	lgw	28.6.1753	
1687	John Steward	smw	26.6.1784	See also no. 1673. And other marks smaller similar in oblong punch 1784 and 1785
1688	Joseph Scammell	plw	11.8.1788	
1689	John Swift	lgw	29.6.1739	And a smaller similar mark 18.7.1757. A larger mark 22.8.1757. See also nos. 1651, 3686, 3708
1690	John Hyatt and Charles Semore	lgw	24.9.1757	
1691	James Stamp and John Baker I	smw	18.4.1764	And a smaller similar mark same date. Two similar marks 29.4.1768. See also nos. 1141, 1666-7, 1773
1692	James Sutton and James Bult	plw	4.10.1782	And a smaller mark same date. See also no. 3625
1693	John Sebille and James Jones II	plw	14.2.1798	See also no. 3656-7
1694	Thomas Issod	lgw	April 1697	
1695	John Thompson I	smw	15.8.1720	See also no. 2801
1696	John Tayler	lgw	6.6.1728	
1697	idem	lgw	14.1.1734	Device uncertain ? escallop

LONDON GOLDSMITHS

No.	Name	Category	Entered	Notes
1698	Jonathan Trenholme	smw	14.6.1734	Bad impression. Probably some device between but not recognizable
1699	John Tombs	smw	3.1.1738	A crude punch
1700	John Tuite	lgw	27.6.1739	See also no. 1722
1701	James Timberlake	lgw	19.4.1743	
1702	idem	lgw	5.4.1755	
1703	James Tookey	lgw	11.5.1750	
1704	idem	smw	25.1.1762	
1705	Job Tripp	lgw	27.7.1757	See also no. 1723
1706	John Turner	smw	26.2.1759	See also Section VI, IT, pellet between
1707	John Tayleur	plw	15.4.1775	And a smaller mark in oblong punch without pellet 4.12.1776. Styled buckle-maker 1779
1708	John Tringham	gw	9.3.1779	
1709	John Tweedie	plw	1.12.1783	
1710	John Touliet	smw	26.4.1784	And a smaller mark in oblong punch 9.2.1792

Also *IS* nos. 3683–7; IS.AN nos. 3688–9

IT   IW

No.	Name	Category	Entered	Notes
1711	John Troby	smw	29.3.1787	And other marks similar 1791 and 1800
1712	idem	plw	20.4.1803	And a smaller similar mark same date
1713	Isaac Trueman	smw	28.10.1788	And a smaller mark 26.11.1789
1714	Joseph Taconet	smw	20.2.1799	A poor impression
1715	Joseph Thredder	plw	19.8.1802	
1716	James Turner	plw	17.9.1804	See also no. 307
1717	James Trender	smw	27.8.1806	See also no. 1726 and Section VIII, I.T
1718	John Tripland	smw	8.4.1812	
1719	John Terry	smw	5.5.1818	See also nos. 1281, 2547
1720	John Tapley	sw	7.12.1833	
1721	idem	sw	8.7.1836	And a smaller mark same date. Also another in large 4-lobed punch 1840
1722	John Tuite	lgw	undated	Between Sept. 1721 and July 1725. A very poor impression
1723	Job Tripp	lgw	31.12.1754	See also no. 1705
1724	Joseph Tuckwell	smw	22.7.1720	See also no. 2954
1725	John Thomas Neate	smw	21.4.1837	
1726	James and Ann Trender	smw	29.11.1792	See also no. 1717
1727	John Tatum Sr and John Tatum Jr.	smw	21.7.1794	And a similar mark 28.2.1798
1728	William Juson	lgw	6.7.1704	See also no. 3690
1729	John Vincent	knife handle maker	undated	c. 1730

LONDON GOLDSMITHS

No.	Name	Category	Entered	Notes
1730	John Verlander	lgw	15.4.1747	See also no. 1732
1731	John Vickerman	smw	20.5.1768	
1732	John Verlander	lgw	9.8.1739	
1733	John Wisdome	lgw	26.8.1720	And a similar mark 14.10.1723
1734	James Wilks	lgw	31.12.1722	And a smaller mark 1728–9. See also no. 3198
1735	John White	lgw	4.1.1725	See also nos. 1751, 3153, 3881–2
1736	John Wrenn I	smw	14.11.1728	
1737	John Wichehalles	lgw	undated	Between April 1728 and April 1729
1738	John Woodward	smw	24.11.1730	
1739	James Willis	smw	undated	Between June 1732 and July 1735
1740	James Wright	smw	24.7.1735	

Also I.T. nos. 3415–7; IV nos. 3690–1; IW nos. 3418, 3692–9

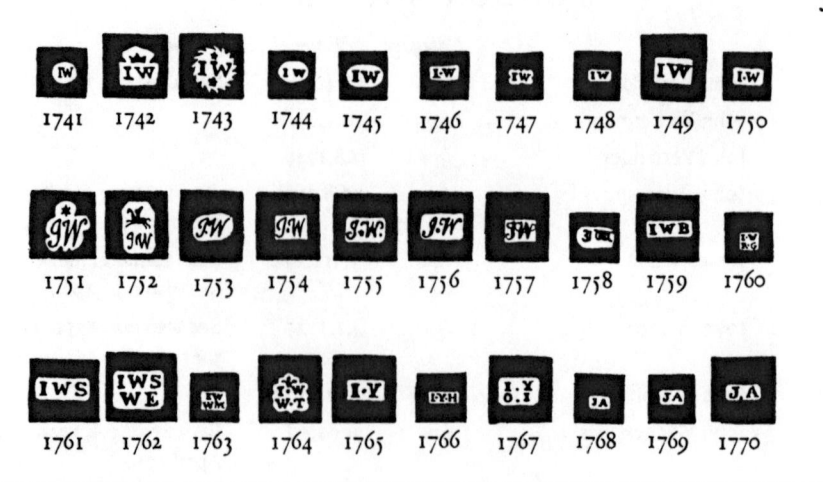

No.	Name	Category	Entered	Notes
1741	John Wingler	sbm	6.4.1738	
1742	James West	lgw	29.6.1739	
1743	James Waters	smw	24.5.1769	
1744	idem	smw	11.7.1775	
1745	John Wall	plw	7.1.1783	See also no. 2737
1746	John Whittingham	smw	1.2.1788	And a smaller mark in rounded oblong 13.8.1788
1747	John Warren	smw	19.12.1788	
1748	John Willis	smw	20.3.1789	And a slightly smaller mark 31.3.1796
1749	John Wakefield	smw	12.2.1806	And a smaller mark 22.8.1806. Two others with pellet between March and May 1818
1750	James Wintle	spm	15.2.1821	See also no. 1860
1751	John White	lgw	26.6.1739	See also nos. 1735, 3153, 3881-2
1752	James Willmot	lgw	3.8.1741	
1753	James Wilks	lgw	16.7.1742	See also no. 1758
1754	John Wirgman	lgw	13.5.1751	
1755	James Williams	lgw	30.7.1755	See also nos. 496, 2674
1756	John Wren II	spm	27.2.1777	
1757	John James Whiting	spm	7.10.1833	And other marks similar 1834, 1840, etc.
1758	James Wilks	lgw	20.6.1739	See also no. 1753
1759	John William Blake	spm	2.10.1823	And a smaller mark same date. Others similar Dec. 1823 and Sept. 1824
1760	John Wakelin and Robert Garrard I	plw	20.10.1792	See also no. 2320

LONDON GOLDSMITHS

No.	Name	Category	Entered	Notes
1761	Joseph William Story	smw	7.7.1803	
1762	J. W. Story and William Elliott	plw	6.10.1809	And a smaller mark same date
1763	John Wrangham and William Moulson	plw	28.3.1822	
1764	John Wakelin and William Taylor	plw	25.9.1776	And a smaller similar mark in straight-sided cut-corner punch 9.5.1777
1765	James Young	smw	21.7.1760	And similar marks as plate-worker April 1775 and April 1781
1766	Joseph York Hatton	smw	8.6.1810	And a smaller mark same date
1767	James Young and Orlando Jackson	plw	17.3.1774	And a smaller mark 13.5.1774
1768	James Aldridge	smw	22.2.1798	
1769	Joseph Angell	plw	7.10.1811	And a mark with bolder letters and pellet between 8.4.1824. See also no. 3703
1770	John Andrews II	smw	19.10.1818	And a smaller mark same date

Also IW nos. 3692–9; *IW* no. 3700; IW.TB no. 3701; IY no. 3702; JA no. 3703

JA   JD

No.	Name	Category	Entered	Notes
1771	James Arthur	plw	10.4.1823	
1772	Joseph and John Angell	plw	31.1.1831	And a smaller mark same date. See also nos. 1769, 3704
1773	John Baker I	smw	11.4.1770	And a smaller mark in oblong punch same date. See also nos. 1141, 1691
1774	James Beattie	smw	7.7.1790	See also no. 1152
1775	John Brough	smw	26.4.1803	And a smaller similar mark same date
1776	idem	smw	13.3.1807	
1777	Joseph Beckwith	smw	7.2.1807	
1778	James Beebe	spm	16.8.1811	And other marks similar 1829 and 1839
1779	idem	spm	11.9.1826	
1780	Joseph Bell III	spm	28.8.1818	
1781	James Britton	spm	25.8.1820	And a similar mark 10.10.1821
1782	Joshua Butler II	smw	24.10.1822	See also no. 1788
1783	James Buchanan	plw	1.4.1824	
1784	Joseph Josiah Burtt	spm	3.4.1828	
1785	John Beauchamp	plw	31.12.1828	And a smaller mark with pellet between same date
1786	Joseph Bidwell*	smw	16.1.1830	
1787	John Brough and John Mountford	smw	17.10.1806	

* 'of Norwhich'. Included here in error.

LONDON GOLDSMITHS

No.	Name	Category	Entered	Notes
1788	Joshua Butler II and Thomas Wise	smw	30.5.1835	Also in one line punch with pellet between B and T. See also no. 1782
1789	James Clarke	smw	31.10.1765	See also no. 1229 and Section VI, IC script
1790	Joseph Coles	smw	14.5.1800	
1791	John Crouch II	plw	11.2.1808	
1792	John Cowie	plw	23.1.1813	And a smaller mark same date. Another mark with thinner letters 4.3.1814
1793	John Clark	smw	30.7.1823	
1794	James Charles Edington	plw	6.2.1828	And other marks similar 1837–58
1795	Joseph Charles Reilly	plw	19.7.1819	
1796	John and Thomas Cutmore	plw	14.1.1829	And a smaller mark same date
1797	John Deane	smw	6.5.1768	See also no. 520
1798	John De Lafons	smw	2.3.1810	
1799	James Dicks	spm	2.11.1820	And a smaller mark same date
1800	Joseph Dunkin	plw	27.2.1824	And other marks smaller similar 3.10.1827 and 18.2.1835

Also JA no. 3703; JA.IA no. 3704; JB no. 3419; JC no. 3420; JD no. 3421

No.	Name	Category	Entered	Notes
1801	John Durandeau	spm	1.7.1824	
1802	John Driver	smw	24.12.1828	
1803	J. D. Goodlad	smw	16.9.1828	
1804	James Davis and William Powell	smw	2.10.1826	
1805	John Edington	smw	5.12.1804	See also nos. 1274–5
1806	John Emes	plw	10.1.1798	And a smaller mark same date
1807	idem	plw	idem	And a smaller mark same date. Another 21.7.1802
1808	Joseph Emanuel	plw	13.11.1820	And a smaller mark 27.3.1821. Other marks with pellet 1833 and 1834
1809	James Edwards II	plw	7.7.1824	
1810	John Evans II	smw	15.4.1834	
1811	John Eldershaw Brunt	smw	15.11.1836	
1812	Joseph Ford	smw	25.2.1764	
1813	idem	smw	17.9.1777	
1814	John Fry I	smw	13.9.1768	See also Section VII, J.F
1815	Joseph Foster	smw	31.8.1797	
1816	Joseph Fearn	plw	5.4.1810	And a smaller mark same date
1817	Jeremiah Garfield	plw	9.8.1813	And a similar mark without pellet same date. Another 25.9.1820
1818	John Hayne	plw	21.2.1816	And a larger mark with pellet between letters 8.7.1817. See also no. 1409
1819	John Harris VI	smw	26.5.1818	And another 5.5.1821

LONDON GOLDSMITHS

No.	Name	Category	Entered	Notes
1820	John Herbert*	smw	22.4.1828	And a smaller mark same date. Other marks similar 23.7.1836
1821	J. Horne and D. S. Ash	smw	20.10.1800	
1822	John Israel	smw	25.4.1786	
1823	John (II) and William (I) Jones	smw	23.8.1763	See also Section VIII, II, pellet between etc.
1824†	John Jago	smw	19.9.1783	And other marks similar of varying size, some with pellet, 1828
1825	Joshua Johnston	smw	23.1.1796	
1826	idem	smw	27.6.1799	
1827	James Jackson	smw	26.1.1805	See also Section V, J.J
1828	John Johnson II	spm	2.11.1835	
1829	Joseph Lock	smw	26.5.1775	See also no. 1492
1830	James Lea	smw	2.7.1790	

Also J E.EF no. 3705; JF no. 3422; JH no. 3706; JK no. 3707

---

* of Norwich. Included here in error.
† An almost identical mark for James Jago at same address 27.3.1828.

No.	Name	Category	Entered	Notes
1831	Joseph Lewis	smw	4.4.1795	See also nos. 1471, 1481 and Section VIII, I.L
1832	John Lee III	gw	20.7.1804	See also no. 1477
1833	John Linnit	smw	25.4.1815	And a mark with pellet between in cut-corner oblong punch 22.10.1821. See also Section VII, IL.WA
1834	idem	smw	31.1.1824	
1835	Jacob More	smw	16.1.1795	
1836	John Meek	spm	21.8.1821	And a larger similar mark in cut-corner punch 19.3.1828
1837	James Perry	smw	1.3.1763	See also no. 1582 and Section IX, JP, pellet between
1838	idem	smw	3.4.1767	And other marks similar 6.6.1768 and 7.1.1773
1839	Jonathan Perkins I	smw	23.4.1772	See also nos. 1592, 1604 and Section VIII, IP and JP
1840	Joseph Price	smw	10.8.1821	
1841	James Payne	spm	4.10.1824	And a similar mark 21.12.1833
1842	Josiah Piercy	spm	1.1.1828	
1843	Joseph Perkins II	smw	14.3.1834	
1844	John Parker III	smw	19.12.1836	See also no. 3670
1845	James Perchard and William Brooks II	smw	11.4.1808	
1846	Josephus Read	plw	10.8.1816	
1847	James Jordan Robertson	smw	15.7.1826	
1848	Josiah Snatt	smw	10.1.1798	
1849	John Shea	spm	6.11.1807	

LONDON GOLDSMITHS

No.	Name	Category	Entered	Notes
1850	James Shallis	plw	8.5.1811	And a smaller similar mark same date
1851	James Sambrook	smw	28.8.1819	
1852	Joseph Samways	plw	26.6.1832	
1853	Joseph (II) and Albert Savory	plw	2.1.1835	And a smaller mark same date. 'Trading as A B Savory & Sons'. Another similar mark 14.11.1835
1854	James Thomas	spm	10.8.1824	
1855	John Teare	smw	17.3.1828	And a larger mark 18.9.1833. Other marks in serrated and lobed punches 1840 and 1842
1856	John Turrill	smw	14.5.1836	
1857	James Vale	gw, sw	30.1.1836	
1858	Joseph Wyatt	smw	1.10.1789	And a smaller similar mark same date
1859	Joseph Willmore	smw	21.2.1805	And a smaller similar mark same date. Two other marks in serrated oval punches 1840
1860	James Wintle	spm	19.10.1812	And other marks in oval punches 1818–38. See also no. 1750

Also JS nos. 3423–4, 3708–9; JW nos. 3425–6

No.	Name	Category	Entered	Notes
1861	Joseph Widdowson	plw	2.1.1829	
1862	Charles Kandler I	lgw	undated	Probably Aug. 1727. See also nos. 341, 689, 691
1862a	idem	unregistered	1751	Mark taken from Britannia Std. inkstand in private ownership with much family plate by the same
1863	Charles Kandler I and James Murray	lgw	29.8.1727	See also no. 1540
1864	William Keatt	lgw	April 1697	See also nos. 1868-9
1865	John Kemble	smw	2.8.1706	
1866	Robert Keble	lgw	14.7.1710	See also no. 3711
1867	idem	lgw	13.1.1707	
1868	William Keatt	lgw	April 1697	See also no. 1864
1869	idem	lgw	idem	
1870	Thomas Kedden	smw	20.11.1700	
1871	John Kenton	smw	8.5.1701	
1872	Robert Kempton	lgw	12.6.1710	See also no. 3710
1873	John Keigwin	lgw	31.8.1710	
1874	Jona Kirke	lgw	April 1697	
1875	Jeremiah King	lgw	11.9.1723	See also nos. 1441-2, 1454-5
1876	David Kilmaine	lgw	14.9.1715	See also no. 3517
1877	William Knight I	hlm	undated	Before Nov. 1700
1878	Thomas Knagg	smw	26.10.1716	See also Section V, TK, coronet above
1879	Keirk Ryves	smw	20.1.1729	
1880	Dennis Langton	smw	28.3.1716	
1881	Charles Laughton I	smw	April 1697	
1882	idem	smw	idem	

LONDON GOLDSMITHS

No.	Name	Category	Entered	Notes
1883	Jeremiah Lammas	smw	18.10.1703	
1884	Edward Laughton	smw	April 1697	
1885	John Laughton I	smw	April 1697	
1886	Jane Laughton	smw	April 1697	
1887	William Laidman	smw	April 1697	
1888	William Lane	smw	10.12.1697	
1889	Jonathan Lambe	lgw	undated	Probably after freedom, July 1697
1890	Ann Laughton	smw	15.12.1701	

Also Ke nos. 3710-11; LA nos. 3712-14

LA   LE

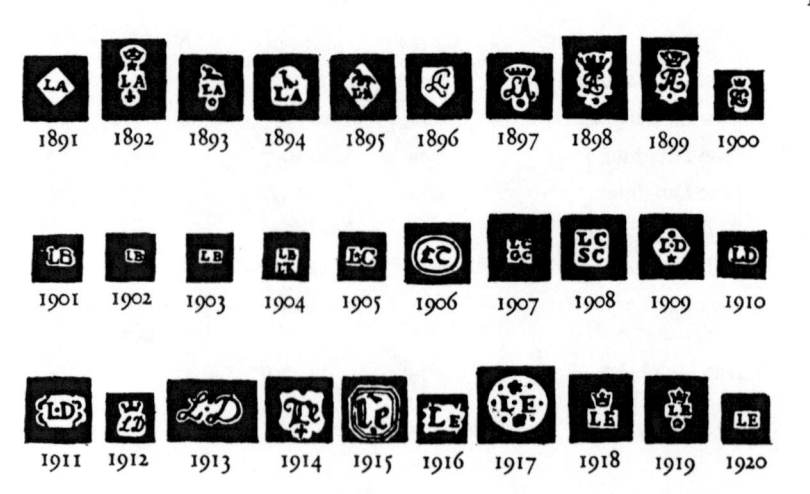

1891	1892	1893	1894	1895	1896	1897	1898	1899	1900
1901	1902	1903	1904	1905	1906	1907	1908	1909	1910
1911	1912	1913	1914	1915	1916	1917	1918	1919	1920

No.	Name	Category	Entered	Notes
1891	Mary Laughton	smw	31.10.1704	
1892*	Paul De Lamerie	lgw	5.2.1713	See also nos. 2203-4
1893	George Lambe	lgw	10.6.1713	
1894	Thomas Langford I	lgw	25.3.1715	
1895	Jane Lambe	lgw	undated	Between Jan. 1719 and July 1722. See also no. 1463
1896	John Langford I	smw	April 1697	
1897	John Ladyman	lgw	undated	Probably April 1697
1898	John Laughton Junior (II)	lgw	undated	idem
1899	idem	lgw	idem	idem
1900	idem	lgw	idem	idem
1901	Louis Black	lgw	30.7.1756	And another mark 11.12.1761
1902	Louis Benoimont	smw	21.8.1764	See also nos. 182, 1904
1903	Lewis Benjamin	plw	23.7.1834	
1904	Louis Benoimont and Luke Kendall	smw	18.11.1761	See also nos. 182, 1902
1905	Laurence Coughlan	smw	27.3.1762	And a similar mark without mullet 12.7.1763
1906†	Pierre Le Cheaube	lgw	21.11.1707	A poor impression. Subject to doubt. See also nos. 323, 2145

* For the recognition of two further unregistered New Standard marks by Lamerie, see page 744.
† Not the mark of Le Cheaube but a poor impression of Edward Cornock's mark no. 546, misstruck from the latter's entry immediately above that of Le Cheaube in the register.

LONDON GOLDSMITHS

No.	Name	Category	Entered	Notes
1907	Louisa Courtauld and George Cowles	plw	before 1773	Not in register. Mark taken from candelabrum 1772. And a smaller similar mark. See also no. 3716
1908	Louisa Perina and Samuel Courtauld II	plw	16.10.1777	See also nos. 2489–90
1909	Louis Dupont	lgw	20.9.1736	See also no. 1912
1910	Lewis Dumont	smw	4.12.1762	
1911	Louis Ducommieu	spm	12.10.1775	See also no. 3470
1912	Louis Dupont	lgw	2.7.1739	
1913	Louis Delisle	plw	27.7.1775	
1914	Ralph Leeke	lgw	undated	Between July 1697 and July 1699. See also no. 3717
1915	Petley Ley	lgw	30.6.1715	
1916	John Leach	lgw	undated	Probably April 1697
1917	Timothy Ley	lgw	April 1697	See also no. 3843
1918	George Lewis	lgw	22.12.1699	
1919	Samuel Lea	lgw	13.7.1711	See also no. 2571
1920	John Lewis I	smw	31.7.1714	

Also LA nos. 3712–14; LB no. 3427; LC nos. 3715–6; Le no. 3717

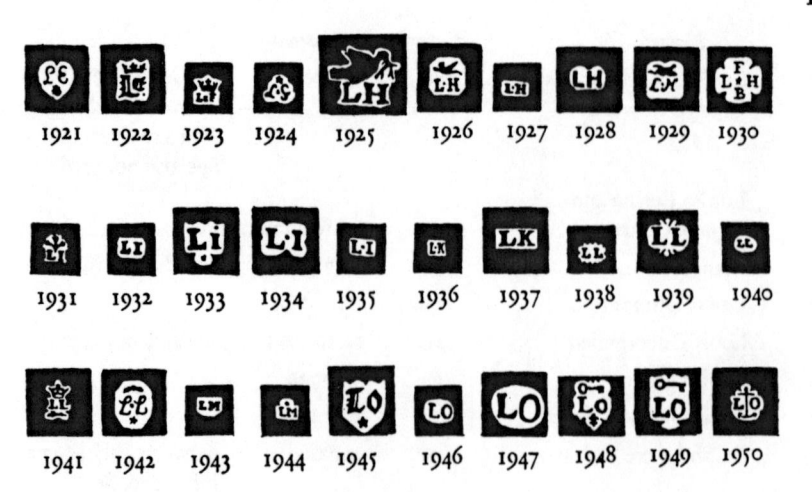

No.	Name	Category	Entered	Notes
1921	John Lefebure	smw	25.6.1714	See also no. 1459
1922	Samuel Lee	lgw	14.8.1701	See also no. 2570
1923	Daniel Lefebure	smw	20.11.1708	
1924	Louis Guichard	lgw	6.9.1748	
1925	Lewis Hamon	lgw	18.3.1736	See also nos. 1929, 3720
1926	idem	lgw	4.8.1738	
1927	Luke Hebden	smw	17.2.1759	
1928	L. Hauchar	smw	16.5.1772	
1929	Louis Hamon	lgw	20.6.1739	See also nos. 1925–6, 3720
1930	Lewis Herne and Francis Butty	lgw	13.7.1757	
1931	Isaac Liger	lgw	2.10.1704	See also no. 1462
1932	John Lingard	lgw	28.6.1718	See also nos. 1460, 3721
1933	idem	lgw	10.1.1719	
1934	Lawrence Johnson	lgw	3.4.1751	See also no. 3722
1935	idem	lgw	22.8.1752	
1936	Luke Kendall	smw	18.12.1766	See also nos. 182, 1904
1937	idem	smw	18.6.1772	
1938	Griffith Lloyd	smw	undated	c. 1700
1939	idem	smw	idem	
1940	Lewis Lefebure	smw	7.10.1725	
1941	Louis Laroche	lgw	19.11.1725	
1942	idem	lgw	31.7.1739	
1943	Lewis Mettayer	lgw	26.8.1720	See also nos. 2018, 3724
1944	Lewis Morel	smw	8.11.1737	

LONDON GOLDSMITHS

No.	Name	Category	Entered	Notes
1945	Seth Lofthouse	lgw	undated	Probably April 1697. A similar mark with smaller 'o' and another larger, same date
1946	Nathaniel Lock	smw	April 1697	
1947	idem	lgw	24.1.1699	
1948	idem	lgw	idem	
1949	idem	lgw	idem	
1950	Richard Lovell	smw	15.10.1701	See also no. 2354

Also Lee no. 3718; *LH* no. 3719; L𝖍 no. 3720; Li nos. 3721; LI no. 3722; *LL* no. 3723; LM nos. 3724-5; LO no. 3726

No.	Name	Category	Entered	Notes
1951	Robert Lovell	lgw	8.3.1703	
1952	William Looker	lgw	12.6.1713	See also nos. 3219, 3891
1953	Matthew E. Lofthouse	lgw	28.6.1705	See also nos. 2043, 3726
1954	Lewis Ourry	lgw	21.8.1740	See also no. 3726
1955	Lewis Plank	jeweller	26.8.1730	
1956	Lewis Pantin I	lgw	21.3.1734	See also no. 1962
1957	Louis Portal	smw	10.8.1758	
1958	Ellize Pyneton (?)	smw	9.9.1760	
1959	Lewis Pantin II	smw	28.7.1768	See Section VII, LP, pellet between
1960	Levy Phillips	smw	9.5.1770	
1961	Lewis Pantin Junr. (III)	smw	20.12.1798	And another similar smaller mark same date. See also Section VII, LP, pellet between
1962	Lewis Pantin I	lgw	29.6.1739	See also no. 1956
1963	Jason Ribouleau	smw	6.5.1761	
1964	Lancelot Simpson	smw	7.11.1769	
1965	Lewis Samuel*	spm	3.9.1830	And a similar mark with two pellets 11.6.1835
1966	William Lukin I	lgw	31.7.1699	And a smaller similar mark same date and re-entered 12.2.1702. See also no. 3220
1967	William Lutwich	smw	April 1697	
1968	John Ludlow	lgw	15.10.1713	See also nos. 1461, 3649
1969	Henry Lyon	smw	April 1697	
1970	John Mulford	smw	14.11.1716	'for gold'. See also no. 1509

* of Liverpool. Included here in error.

LONDON GOLDSMITHS

No.	Name	Category	Entered	Notes
1971	Thomas Mason	lgw	19.11.1716	See also nos. 2832–3, 2846–8
1972	Stephen Marram	smw	21.12.1715	
1973	George Manley	smw	April 1697	
1974	Matthew Madden	lgw	undated	c. 1699
1975	idem	lgw	undated	Between April and Dec. 1700
1976	William Mathew I	lgw	April 1697	See also no. 3730
1977	idem	lgw	20.4.1700	
1978	George Manjoy	smw	undated	c. 1700. See also nos. 3730–1
1979	idem	smw	idem	
1980	idem	smw	idem	

Also LP.FP no. 3727; LV no. 3728; M. no. 3729; MA nos. 3730–4
For an unusual mark MA with small W above see no. 3233.

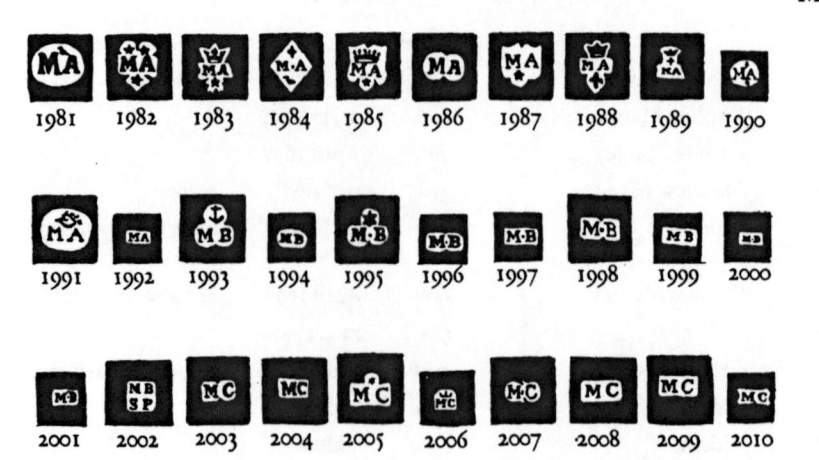

No.	Name	Category	Entered	Notes
1981	Willoughby Masham	lgw	24.5.1701	And a smaller mark with bird above A
1982	Jonathan Madden	lgw	2.12.1702	See also no. 3732
1983	Jacob Margas	lgw	19.8.1706	See also nos. 3733-4
1984	Mary Mathew	lgw	28.5.1707	
1985	John Mathew	lgw	13.9.1710	
1986	Isaac Malyn	lgw	24.11.1710	
1987	Thomas Mann	lgw	25.11.1713	See also nos. 2829-31, 2849
1988	Samuel Margas	lgw	14.2.1715	See also no. 2588
1989	James Mayo	smw	27.7.1716	
1990	Thomas Makepeace	smw	17.8.1716	See also no. 2835
1991	Elizabeth Marram	smw	6.4.1717	Crude punch and indistinct impression
1992	Miles Askew	smw	30.9.1784	
1993	Michael Boult	lgw	20.6.1720	See also no. 202
1994	Maurice Boheme	smw	29.6.1720	See also nos. 204-5
1995	Matthieu Brodier	lgw	11.4.1751	
1966	Mark Bock	smw	25.11.1761	See also no. 3735
1997	idem	smw	15.8.1764	
1998	Margaret Binley	smw	15.5.1764	And a smaller similar mark same date
1999	B. Mountigue	smw	20.6.1772	And a smaller mark BM 25.7.1772. See also nos. 191, 3490 and Section VIII, B.M
2000	Moses Brent	hfm	11.7.1775	And other marks similar 1782, 1788, 1791, 1795-6, 1799, 1800, 1804, 1806-7, 1809, 1811-13, 1815, 1817

LONDON GOLDSMITHS

No.	Name	Category	Entered	Notes
2001	Michael Barnett	smw	29.6.1781	And other marks similar as hiltmaker 1784 and 1791. Another mark 1820
2002	Moses William Brent and Sydenham William Peppin	plw	20.12.1815	And a smaller mark same date. A third smaller mark 2.6.1816
2003	Matthew Cooper I	lgw	13.7.1720	See also no. 378
2004	Matthew Cooper II	lgw	30.6.1725	See also no. 202
2005	Matthew Clayton	smw	23.1.1730	
2006	Michael Compigne	smw	27.2.1738	
2007	Mary Carman	hlm	20.1.1764	
2008	Mark Cripps	smw	25.4.1767	
2009	Mary Corry	smw	21.4.1768	
2010	Morris Cadman	smw	10.9.1800	

Also MA nos. 3730–4; MB no. 3735; *MC* no. 3736

No.	Name	Category	Enteted	Notes
2011	Mary Ann Croswell	smw	21.5.1805	And a similar mark 29.8.1816
2012	Mary Chawner	spm	14.4.1834	And a smaller mark same date. Other marks similar 25.3.1835
2013	Marmaduke Daintrey	smw	12.10.1737	
2014	idem	lgw	30.5.1747	
2015	idem	lgw	20.6.(1739?)	
2016	Martin Dell	smw	5.3.1763	
2017	Thomas Merry I	smw	19.6.1701	See also nos. 2837, 3737
2018	Lewis Mettayer	lgw	18.12.1700	See also nos. 1943, 3724
2019	George Meale	smw	22.6.1720	See also no. 848
2020	Matthew Ebborne	turner / sbm	20.12.1758	
2021	Moses Emanuel	spm	11.3.1800	
2022	Moses Eden	smw	22.6.1720	See also no. 563
2023	Morris and Michael Emanuel	plw	25.11.1825	And other marks smaller 29.7.1828 and 25.10.1830
2024	Matthew Ferris	smw	21.9.1759	
2025	Mordecai Fox	lgw	21.1.1747	
2026	idem	smw	18.6.1755	
2027	Magdalen Feline	lgw	15.5.1753	
2028	idem	lgw	18.1.1757	
2029	Meschach Godwin	lgw	15.3.1723	See also no. 866
2030	Mary Hussey	smw	undated	Between Oct. 1723 and April 1724
2031*	Margaret Harrison	smw	21.1.1764	

* Another mark MH is that of Margaret Hatton, 19.3.1764. See page 751.

148

LONDON GOLDSMITHS

No.	Name	Category	Entered	Notes
2032	Metcalf Hopgood	plw	14.8.1835	See also no. 2807
2033	Mary Hyde and John Reily	smw	28.11.1799	And a smaller mark same date. See also nos. 1627, 2066
2034	Matthew Coats Horsley and Robert Burton Cooper	smw	26.9.1821	
2035	William Middleton	lgw	undated	Between April and Dec. 1700
2036	Henry Miller I	lgw	14.7.1714	See also nos. 1028, 3738
2037	John Millington	lgw	22.9.1718	See also nos. 1500, 1511
2038	Mary Johnson	lgw	17.8.1727	
2039	Mathew Judkins	smw	8.5.1738	
2040	Michael Isaacs	smw	15.7.1782	And a similar mark 5.10.1784

Also *MC* no. 3736; Me no. 3737; MI no. 3738

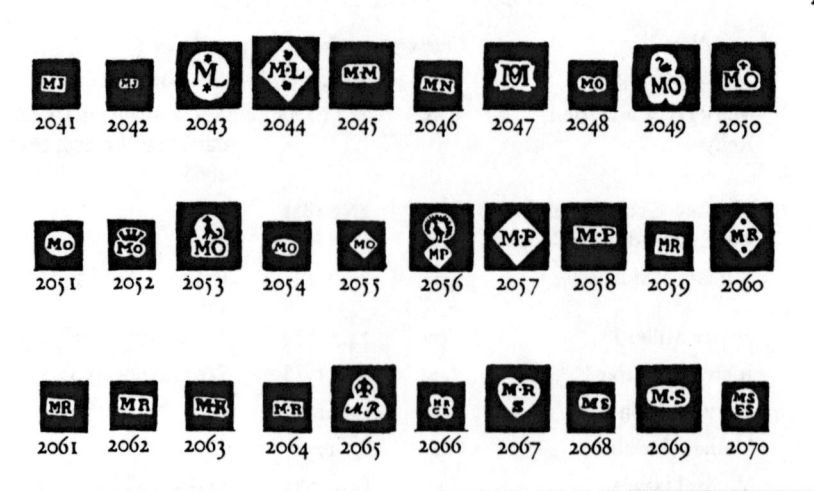

No.	Name	Category	Entered	Notes
2041	Moses Jacobs	smw	22.12.1760	
2042	Mahala Jago	smw	4.9.1830	
2043	Matthew E. Lofthouse	lgw	26.6.1721	See also nos. 1953, 3726
2044	Mary Lofthouse	lgw	30.3.1731	
2045	Mary Makemeid	plw	2.10.1773	
2046	Michael Nixon	spm	31.3.1832	
2047	Andrew Moore	lgw	undated	Between April and Dec. 1700
2048	George Moody	smw	17.2.1716	
2049	James Morson	lgw	17.10.1716	See also no. 1501
2050	John Montgomery	smw	11.3.1718	And two other smaller similar marks same date. See also nos. 1505–7, 1535
2051	Henry Morris	smw	1.12.1718	See also nos. 1030 etc., 3605
2052	John Motherby	lgw	22.2.1719	
2053	Thomas Morse	lgw	5.9.1718	See also no. 2834
2054	Thomas Moore I*	smw	27.6.1723	
2055	Mary Owen	smw	17.1.1739	
2056	Mary Pantin	lgw	14.8.1733	
2057	Mary Piers	lgw	2.6.1758	
2058	Michael Plummer	plw	5.10.1791	And a smaller similar mark same date
2059	Martha Ripshear	smw	1.12.1720	
2060	Mary Rood	lgw	2.12.1721	See also no. 2399
2061	Mary Richardson	smw	9.6.1763	And other marks similar 7.10.1763 and 12.7.1765

* *MO* (script) in indeterminate punch noted on sword hilt 1724 may be another mark of this maker.

LONDON GOLDSMITHS

No.	Name	Category	Entered	Notes
2062	Mary Ryder	smw	4.7.1769	
2063	Mary Reasey	smw	2.3.1773	
2064	Michael Rooke	smw	4.4.1796	
2065	Matthew Roker	lgw	29.4.1755	
2066	Mary Ann and Charles Reily	smw	31.5.1826	See also no. 2033
2067	Mary and Richard (II) Sibley	plw	23.2.1836	And a similar smaller mark same date
2068	Mary Sumner	spm	18.3.1807	See also no. 2070
2069	Michael Starkey	plw	19.1.1809	And a mark in oblong cut-corner punch 24.9.1822 and another 4.7.1834
2070	Mary and Eliza Sumner	spm	31.8.1809	And a smaller mark in square punch 21.8.1810

Also MO no. 3739

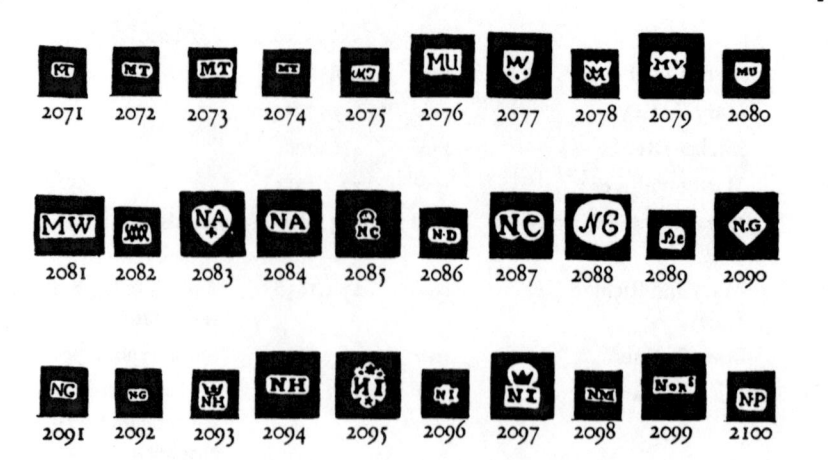

No.	Name	Category	Entered	Notes
2071	Marmaduke Tokett	smw	24.7.1762	
2072	Mehatabell Turton	smw	10.10.1798	And a smaller similar mark same date
2073	Mary Troby	smw	17.12.1804	
2074	Maria Tippen	smw	10.10.1821	
2075	Mark Thomegay	smw	10.9.1763	
2076	Joseph Mumford	smw	20.11.1711	See also nos. 1502–3
2077	Robert Munday	smw	April 1697	
2078	John Munday	smw	April 1697	See also nos. 1499, 1508
2079	idem	smw	undated	c. 1699
2080	Joseph Munday	smw	29.2.1716	A bad impression. ? U or u
2081	Michael Ward	lgw	undated	Between July 1750 and Feb. 1752
2082	Micah Wilkins	smw	11.6.1720	
2083	Bowles Nash	lgw	7.3.1721	
2084	Gawen Nash	smw	7.1.1726	See also nos. 853–4, 859
2085	Nicholas Clausen	lgw	29.7.1720	See also no. 351
2086	Nicholas Dumée	plw	13.4.1776	
2087	Jonathan Newton	lgw	17.10.1711	See also nos. 1542, 3741
2088	idem	lgw	1.5.1718	
2089	Robert Newman	smw	14.3.1720	See also no. 2377
2090	Nathaniel Gulliver	lgw	12.9.1722	See also no. 916
2091	Noah Goetze	smw	25.7.1804	
2092	idem	smw	3.10.1810	
2093	Nicolas Hodgson	smw	23.7.1719	Gold mark
2094	Naphthali Hart	plw	10.4.1812	See also nos. 510, 3743

LONDON GOLDSMITHS

No.	Name	Category	Entered	Notes
2095	Richard Nightingale	*lgw*	April 1697	Similar reversed N's sometimes observed in engraved letters. See also no. 3745
2096	Christopher Nicholle	*smw*	3.7.1719	See also no. 366
2097	Michael Nicholl	*lgw*	16.11.1723	
2098	Nicholas Middleton	*smw*	18.5.1795	
2099	Thomas Norris	*smw*	18.6.1725	
2100	Nathaniel Pack	*smw*	24.3.1732	

Also MW no. 3740; Ne no. 3741; NH nos. 3742–3; *NH* no. 3744; NI no. 3745

No.	Name	Category	Entered	Notes
2101	Niccolas Sprenkelsen	smw	8.7.1726	
2102	Nicholas Sprimont	lgw	25.1.1743	And a smaller similar mark same date
2103	Nicholas Thornburgh	smw	15.3.1738	
2104	Nathaniel Underwood	smw	19.12.1722	
2105	Nicholas Winkings	lgw	21.9.1751	
2106	Nathaniel Young	smw	undated	Between 1723 and 1736
2107	Orlando Jackson	smw	undated	Between Aug. 1759 and Feb. 1760. See also no. 3747
2108	Ozee Lhommedieu	smw	undated	During 1727
2109	Thomas Osborne	smw	18.3.1699	A crude punch
2110	Charles Overing	lgw	April 1697	
2111	John Overing	lgw	6.1.1725	See also no. 1562
2112	William Owen	smw	12.3.1716	See also no. 3247
2113	William Overton	smw	17.2.1716	See also no. 3245
2114	Phillip Oyles	lgw	9.10.1699	
2115	John Phillips	lgw	13.2.1717	
2116	Thomas Peirce	smw	24.2.1730	See also Section V, TP, pellet between
2117	Humphrey Payne	lgw	3.12.1701	See also nos. 1058, 1061
2118	idem	lgw	idem	
2119	William Paradise	lgw	7.7.1718	See also no. 3250
2120	Thomas Parr I	lgw	April 1697	
2121	idem	lgw	19.8.1717	
2122	Mark Paillet	lgw	undated	Between 22.4. and 21.10.1698
2123	Be...Page	smw	undated	c. 1700
2124	Simon Pantin I	lgw	23.6.1701	See also no. 2606

LONDON GOLDSMITHS

No.	Name	Category	Entered	Notes
2125	idem	lgw	16.9.1717	
2126	Thomas Page	smw	6.1.1719	See also no. 2869
2127	Peter Archambo I	lgw	2.11.1722	See also no. 85
2128	idem	lgw	27.6.1739	
2129	Peter Archambo II and Peter Meure	lgw	18.1.1750	
2130	Pierre Bouteiller	lgw	13.2.1727	

Also OF no. 3746; OJ no. 3747; P. no. 3748

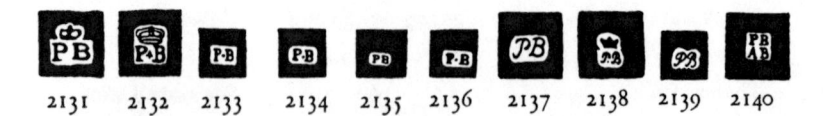

No.	Name	Category	Entered	Notes
2131	Peter Bennett	lgw	6.3.1732	See also no. 2137
2132	Philip Bruguier	lgw	19.3.1739	See also no. 2138
2133	Pointer Baker	smw	undated	Between 18.12.1759 and 28.1.1760
2134	Paul Barbot	gs	4.7.1771	
2135	Philip (?) Bocquet	smw	13.12.1771	See also no. 2139
2136	Philip Batchelor	smw	15.1.1770	
2137	Peter Bennett	lgw	22.6.1739	See also no. 2131
2138	Philip Bruguier	lgw	12.7.1739	And a similar mark 22.1.1753. See also no. 2132
2139	Paul Bocquet	smw	10.7.1762	See also no. 2135
2140	Peter and Ann Bateman	plw	2.5.1791	And two smaller similar marks same date
2141	Peter, Ann and William (I) Bateman	plw	Jan. 1800	And two smaller similar marks same date
2142	Peter and Jonathan Bateman	plw	7.12.1790	And two smaller similar marks same date. Another set of three similar marks re-entered two days later
2143	Peter and William (I) Bateman	plw	8.11.1805	And two smaller similar marks same date
2143a	Paul Crespin	lgw	undated	c. 1720. See also nos. 406, 412, 2146 and 2149
2144	Peter Courtauld	smw	21.7.1721	See also nos. 391, 3509
2145	Peter Le Chouabe	lgw	27.6.1726	See also no. 323
2146	Paul Crespin	lgw	22.1.1757	And a smaller mark same date. See also nos. 406, 412, 2143a, 2149
2147	Peter Carter	smw	24.3.1783	And a smaller similar mark 20.4.1791

LONDON GOLDSMITHS

No.	Name	Category	Entered	Notes
2148	Philip Cornman	smw	9.5.1793	And a mark in straight-sided oblong punch 18.10.1793
2149	Paul Crespin	lgw	4.7.1739	See also nos. 406, 412, 2143a, 2146
2150	Paul Callard	lgw	8.1.1752	And a very small oblong punch with Roman capitals 27.7.1759
2151	Peter Cornu	smw	8.10.1725	See also no. 394
2152	William Gwillim and Peter Castle	lgw	10.9.1744	See also no. 3140
2153	Peter Desvignes	smw	28.6.1771	
2154	Thomas Peele	lgw	2.3.1705	
2155	Edward Peacock	lgw	14.11.1710	
2156	John Penford	lgw	April 1697	See also no. 3674
2157	Robert Peake	lgw	April 1697	
2158	idem	lgw	idem	
2159	Henry Penstone	lgw	April 1697	
2160	William Penstone I	lgw	April 1697	See also no. 2161

Also PD no. 3428

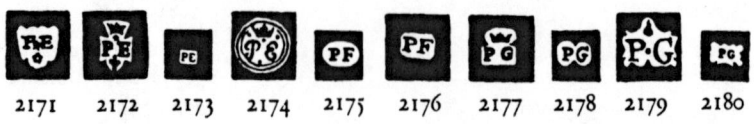

No.	Name	Category	Entered	Notes
2161	William Penstone II	lgw	4.10.1717	See also no. 2160
2162	James Pearce	lgw	22.4.1698	
2163	Vaughan Peake	smw	27.8.1701	
2164	John Penkethman	smw	6.5.1703	
2165	William Pearson	smw	22.5.1704	A poor impression. See also no. 3252
2166	idem	lgw	21.1.1710	
2167	idem	lgw	idem	
2168	idem	lgw	21.5.1717	
2169	Edmund Pearce	lgw	1.2.1705	See also nos. 629, 3547
2170	Jean Petrij	lgw	21.11.1707	
2170a	William Petley	lgw	22.7.1717	See also nos. 2174, 3251
2171	John Pero	lgw	24.8.1717	
2172	Charles Perier	lgw	6.1.1729	See nos. 395–6
2173	Paul Elin	smw	26.3.1736	
2174	William Petley	lgw	16.6.1699	See also no. 2170a
2175	Philip Freeman	smw	2.11.1772	And a similar mark 17.8.1773. Another similar as plate-worker 30.9.1773
2176	Philip Venner Firmin	smw	12.2.1822	And a smaller similar mark 17.3.1823
2177	Philip(s) Garden	lgw	3.1.1724	See also no. 867
2178	Philip Goddard	smw	12.6.1738	
2179	idem	lgw	12.3.1744	See also nos. 2184–5
2180	idem	lgw	idem	
2181	idem	lgw	18.4.1751	And a smaller similar mark 28.4.1756
2182	Peter Gillois	lgw	20.11.1754	

LONDON GOLDSMITHS

No.	Name	Category	Entered	Notes
2183	idem	*plw*	15.6.1782	
2184	Phillips Garden	*lgw*	23.6.1739	And a similar mark 29.10.1748
2185	idem	*lgw*	29.10.1748	
2186	P. G. Gresse	*smw*	16.8.1725	
2187	William Phillips	*smw*	11.10.1716	
2188	Phillip Phillis	*lgw*	20.2.1720	See also no. 2211
2189	Paul Hanet	*lgw*	24.5.1721	See also no. 942
2190	Israel Pinckn(e)y	*lgw*	April 1697	

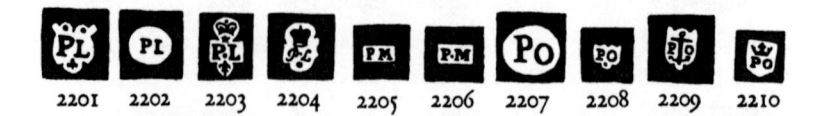

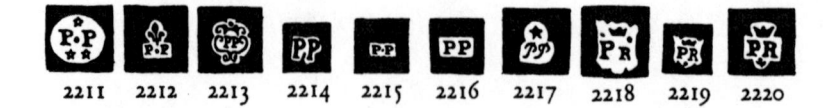

No.	Name	Category	Entered	Notes
2191	Clifford Pierce	smw	April 1697	
2192	idem	smw	11.5.1705	
2193	Matthew Pickering	lgw	23.9.1703	
2194	Thomas Pierce	smw	27.2.1717	
2195	Pezé Pilleau	lgw	undated	After 30.6.1720. See also nos. 2212, 2217
2196	Peter Jouet	smw	23.11.1723	
2197	Robert Pilkington	smw	undated	Between June 1724 and March 1725. See also nos. 2401, 2417
2198	Joseph Felix Podio	plw	2.8.1806	
2199	John Pix	smw	undated	c. 1725-6
2200	Pierre Platel	lgw	28.6.1699	
2201	Gabriel Player	lgw	3.8.1700	
2202	Francis Plymley	lgw	12.10.1715	
2203	Paul De Lamerie	lgw	17.3.1733	See also no. 1892
2204	idem	lgw	27.6.1739	
2205	Peter Moss	smw	12.8.1728	
2206	Peter Marsh	smw	26.10.1733	See also no. 3749A
2207	John Porter	lgw	21.10.1698	See also nos. 3571-2
2208	Abraham Pope	smw	30.8.1703	See also no. 72
2209	Thomas Port	lgw	3.6.1713	
2210	Benjamin Poole	smw	31.5.1717	
2211	Phillip Phillis	lgw	24.6.1720	See also no. 2188
2212	Pezé Pilleau	lgw	undated	After 30.6.1720. See also nos. 2195, 2217
2213	Philip Platel	lgw	25.11.1737	
2214	Paul Pinard	lgw	12.10.1751	

LONDON GOLDSMITHS

No.	Name	Category	Entered	Notes
2215	Peter Podio	plw	12.2.1790	
2216	Phillip Phillips	plw	28.8.1826	
2217	Pezé Pilleau	lgw	29.6.1739	See also nos. 2195, 2212
2218	Edmund Prockter	lgw	8.10.1700	A very poor impression. Reproduction largely conjectural
2219	Thomas Prichard	smw	April 1697	
2220	Thomas Prichard (?Junr.)	lgw	30.11.1709	

Also PI no. 3749; PM no. 3429; PN no. 3750; PO nos. 3751-2; P. ROKER no. 3753; PR nos. 3754-5

PR   RA

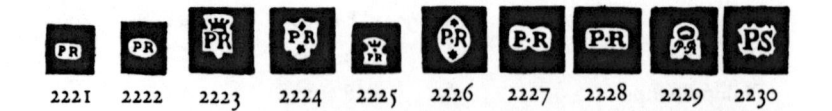

No.	Name	Category	Entered	Notes
2221	Walter Prosser	smw	23.3.1708	
2222	Thomas Prew	smw	16.7.1718	
2223	Philip Roker II	lgw	17.8.1720	See also nos. 2229, 2398, 3753–5
2224	Philip Rollos jnr. (II)	lgw	28.9.1720	See also no. 2392
2225	Philip Rainaud	lgw	26.10.1720	See also no. 2251
2226	Philip Robinson	lgw	29.4.1723	And a smaller similar mark same date
2227	Philip Roker III	spm	28.6.1776	
2228	Philip Rundell	plw	4.3.1819	And two other smaller similar marks same date. Three further marks without pellet 25.5.1819. Two other marks 31.10.1822. See also no. 3764
2229	Philip Roker II	lgw	20.6.1739	See also nos. 2223, 2398, 3753–5
2230	Peter Simon	lgw	14.5.1725	See also no. 2552
2231	Philip Shaw	smw	17.9.1730	Poor impression
2232	idem	smw	18.10.1733	
2233	Paul Storr	plw	12.1.1793	And a smaller similar mark same date
2234	idem	plw	27.4.1793	And smaller similar marks 1794 and 1799
2235	idem	plw	21.8.1807	And a smaller mark same date. Other marks in four sizes similar 1808, 1813, 1817, 1833, 1834
2236	Paul Siddall, John Wrangham and William Moulson	plw	15.11.1823	

LONDON GOLDSMITHS

No.	Name	Category	Entered	Notes
2237	Peter Tabart	lgw	7.7.1725	See also no. 2677
2238	idem	lgw	idem	
2239	Peter Taylor	lgw	11.11.1740	
2240	Philip Vincent	lgw	29.11.1757	
2241	Peter Wirgman I	smw	17.5.1738	
2242	Peter Werritzer	lgw	23.7.1750	See also no. 3756
2243	Paul Wright	smw	3.1.1771	And a smaller similar mark 15.5.1771. See also Section VII, P.W
2244	Benjamin Pyne	lgw	April 1697	See also no. 3748
2245	idem	lgw	idem	
2246	William Pyke	smw	April 1697	
2247	John Rand	lgw	13.1.1704	
2247a	John Rayne	smw	28.9.1736	See also no. 2259
2248	Andrew Raven	lgw	April 1697	Poor impression. See also no. 3475
2249	idem	lgw	idem	
2250	Edward Raven(s)	smw	April 1697	And a similar mark with pellet below same date. See also no. 633

Also PR nos. 3754–5; *PW* no. 3756; P & W no. 3757; RA no. 3758

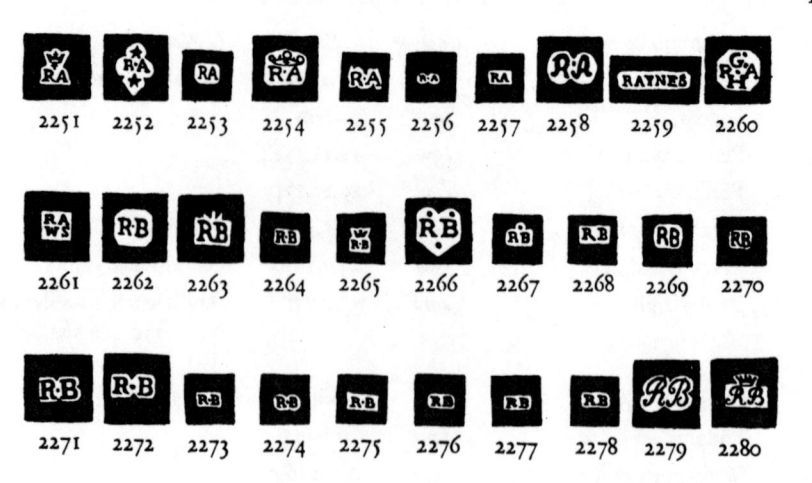

No.	Name	Category	Entered	Notes
2251	Philip Rainaud	lgw	14.2.1708	See also no. 2225
2252	Richard Raine	lgw	21.6.1712	
2253	Richard Adrian	bm spur maker	31.10.1723	
2254	Robert Abercromby	lgw	5.10.1731	See also nos. 6a, 2258
2255	Robert Andrews	spm	8.11.1745	
2256	Ralph Ayscough	smw	22.8.1769	
2257	Richard Andrews	smw	19.7.1773	
2258	Robert Abercromby	lgw	23.6.1739	See also nos. 6a, 2254
2259	John Raynes	smw	28.9.1736	See also no. 2247a
2260	Robert Abercromby and George Hindmarsh	lgw	11.5.1731	
2261	Richard William Atkins and William Nathaniel Somersall	plw	26.7.1824	And two smaller similar marks 31.3.1825 and 6.2.1830
2262	Richard Bayley	lgw	16.7.1720	See also nos. 116, 2279, 3481, 3760–1
2263	Rebekah Bird	smw	7.11.1721	
2264	Richard Burcombe	smw	10.2.1724	And a similar mark with initials of italic type 4.2.1735
2265	Rolland Bouchet	smw	27.7.1726	
2266	Richard Beale	lgw	1.10.1733	See also nos. 2280, 3762
2267	Richard Botfeild	smw	11.7.1734	
2268	Richard Bell	smw	22.8.1734	
2269	Richard Boucher	smw	7.5.1736	
2270	Robert Brown	lgw	8.10.1736	See also no. 2281
2271	Robert Burton	lgw	3.4.1758	

LONDON GOLDSMITHS

No.	Name	Category	Entered	Notes
2272	Richard Binley	smw	18.12.1760	A smaller mark similar 20.9.1760
2273	Roger Biggs	smw	14.5.1791	See also Section VII, RB, pellet between
2274	Robert Barker	smw	20.11.1793	
2275	Robert Bushby	smw	19.1.1803	
2276	Richard Buckton	smw	1.3.1806	
2277	Robert Beckwith	plw	27.5.1811	
2278	Richard Britton	spm	3.2.1812	Other marks with pellet between in oblong punch 1827 and 1842
2279	Richard Bayley	lgw	19.6.1739	See also nos. 116, 2262, 3481, 3760-1
2280	Richard Beale	lgw	22.6.1739	See also nos. 2266, 3762. Also a very small RB in oblong punch 25.2.1746

Also RA no. 3758; RB nos. 3759-62; RB no. 3763; RB & R no. 3764

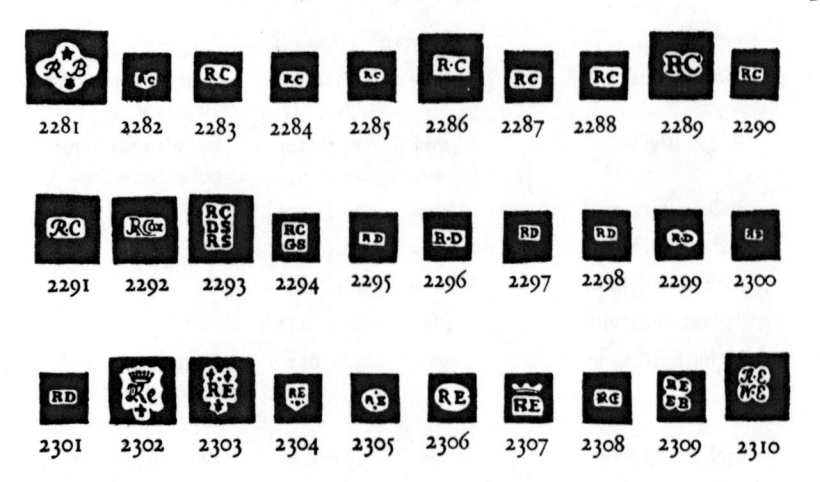

No.	Name	Category	Entered	Notes
2281	Robert Brown	lgw	26.6.1739	See also no. 2270
2282	Richard Chapman	smw	28.6.1720	And a similar mark, pellet below 2.3.1723. See also nos. 317, 3765
2283	Robert Cates	smw	22.6.1724	
2284	Robert Collier	smw	1.2.1727	And a mark with pellet between 6.10.1737. Also RC incuse
2285	Robert Cooke	smw	24.5.1731	
2286	Robert Albin Cox	lgw	10.7.1752	See also nos. 2291-2, 3767-9
2287	Robert Clark	smw	21.2.1765	
2288	Richard Crossley	plw	5.4.1782	And a smaller similar mark 9.12.1785. Other marks of two sizes 1795, 1804 and 1812. See also nos. 2294, 3334
2289	Richard Cooke	plw	28.6.1799	And a smaller similar mark same date
2290	Randall Chatterton	spm	17.10.1825	And a slightly larger mark 26.3.1829
2291	Robert Albin Cox	lgw	27.6.1759	See also nos. 2286, 3767-9
2292	idem	lgw	12.7.1758	
2293	Richard Carter, Daniel Smith and Robert Sharp	plw	9.12.1778	And a smaller similar mark same date. See also nos. 506-8, 2436
2294	Richard Crossley and George Smith IV	spm	9.4.1807	And a smaller similar mark same date
2295	Richard O'Niall Donel	smw	11.3.1731	
2296	Richard Dawley	smw	2.8.1734	
2297	Richard Davey	smw	26.9.1767	

LONDON GOLDSMITHS

No.	Name	Category	Entered	Notes
2298	Robert Dennison	smw	30.10.1767	And a similar mark with rounded ends to punch 25.1.1772
2299	idem	smw	24.11.1768	And other marks similar 2.11.1769 and 15.5.1771. See also Section VIII, A.R.D
2300	Richard Dovey	gs	9.6.1770	See also Section VIII, R.D
2301	Richard Devonshire	spm	14.10.1819	
2302	John Read	lgw	22.7.1704	Device at base uncertain from weak impression. See also no. 2442
2303	Joshua Readshaw	lgw	April 1697	
2304	Joseph Reason	smw	April 1697	See also no. 1611
2305	John Reason	smw	23.6.1698	
2306	Thomas Redhead	smw	4.5.1719	See also no. 2897
2307	Richard Edwards	lgw	25.11.1723	See also no. 558
2308	Robert Elliot	smw	17.6.1720	See also no. 613
2309	Rebecca Emes and Edward Barnard I	plw	14.10.1808	And a smaller similar mark same date. Other marks of various sizes 20.2.1821 and 29.10.1825
2310	Rebecca Emes and William Emes	plw	30.6.1808	And a smaller similar mark same date

Also RC nos. 3765–8; *RC* no. 3769; RE no. 3430

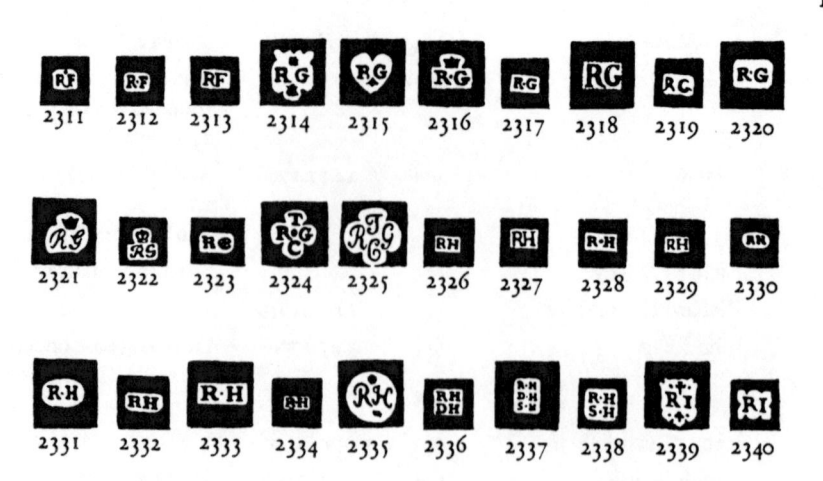

No.	Name	Category	Entered	Notes
2311	Richard Fuller	smw	24.6.1720	See also no. 726
2312	Ralph Frith	lgw	24.6.1728	See also no. 717
2313	Richard Foster	smw	22.6.1799	
2314	Richard Gines	lgw	21.6.1720	A poor impression the lower part uncertain. See also nos. 830, 838
2315	Richard Green	lgw	19.10.1726	See also no. 876
2316	Richard Gosling	smw	14.3.1733	And a smaller mark similar same date. See also nos. 2321, 3773
2317	Richard Glanville	gs	17.6.1768	See also Section V, R.G
2318	Robert Gaze	plw	5.1.1795	
2319	idem	plw	13.10.1797	A crudely cut punch
2320	Robert Garrard I	plw	11.8.1802	And a smaller similar mark same date. See also no. 1760
2321	Richard Gosling	lgw	28.6.1739	And a similar mark with lobed base 10.8.1748. See also nos. 2316, 3773
2322	Robert Garrard II	plw	17.1.1822	And smaller examples 1836, 1847
2323	idem	plw	18.4.1818	Mark actually RE. See 3769a
2324	Thomas Cooke II and Richard Gurney	lgw	19.10.1727	And a similar mark as 'Richard Gurney & Co' 23.12.1734 and another 30.7.1750
2325	Richard Gurney & Co.	lgw	28.6.1739	See also no. 2712
2326	Robert Higgs	smw	25.10.1721	
2327	Richard Holder	smw	28.1.1726	

LONDON GOLDSMITHS

No.	Name	Category	Entered	Notes
2328	Richard Hussey	smw	undated	During 1737
2329	Roger Hare	smw	6.3.1738	
2330	Robert Hennell I	smw	30.5.1772	
2331	idem	stm	9.10.1773	And a mark as no. 2330 same date
2332	Robert Hennell II	plw	3.11.1809	And a smaller similar mark same date. Other marks in rectangular punch, 11.8.1820 and 23.1.1826
2333	Robert Hennell III	plw	30.6.1834	With two smaller similar marks same date
2334	Richard Hillum	plw	10.9.1828	And a similar mark 6.12.1831
2335	Robert Hill	lgw	17.3.1740	Lower part of impression indistinct. See also nos. 1011, 3775
2336	Robert (I) and David (II) Hennell	plw	15.7.1795	
2337	Robert (I), David (II) and Samuel Hennell	plw	5.1.1802	And a smaller similar mark same date
2338	Robert (I) and Samuel Hennell	plw	28.10.1802	And a smaller similar mark same date
2339	Christopher Riley	lgw	April 1697	
2340	Thomas Ripshear	smw	April 1697	See also next no.

Also RG nos. 3431-2, 3770-2; R𝕲 nos. 3773-4; RH nos. 3433-4, 3775-6; RI 3777-8

No.	Name	Category	Entered	Notes
2341	Thomas Ripshear	smw	April 1697	See previous no.
2342	Isaac Ribouleau	lgw	16.7.1724	See also no. 1610, and note to same
2343	William Richards	smw	2.11.1719	
2344	John Richardson I	lgw	8.7.1723	See also nos. 1612, 3778
2345	Robert Innes	lgw	17.1.1743	And a similar smaller mark same date
2346	Robert Jones I	plw	1.2.1774	An unusually crudely cut punch for the period
2347	idem	plw	14.1.1778	Two other marks in oblong punch with rounded corners 29.1.1796 for son Robert Jones II
2348	Richard John Bilton	smw	20.9.1831	
2349	Robert Jones (I) and John Scofield	plw	10.2.1776	See also nos. 1670, 3709, 3779
2350	R. Johnston	smw	24.3.1800	Mark found on sword 1809 signed 'R. Johnston 68 St. James's Str London'
2351	Richard James Beckley	plw	18.2.1825	
2352	Richard Kersill	lgw	20.4.1744	
2353	Robert Kelley	smw	19.9.1807	
2354	Richard Lovell	smw	15.8.1720	See also no. 1950
2355	Robert Lucas	lgw	13.3.1727	See also no. 2358
2356	Richard Lee	plw	4.5.1782	
2357	Richard Lockwood	smw	20.5.1797	And a smaller mark in narrower punch 28.9.1797
2358	Robert Lucas	lgw	25.6.1739	See also no. 2355

LONDON GOLDSMITHS

No.	Name	Category	Entered	Notes
2359	Richard Lockwood and John Douglas	smw	12.8.1800	And a smaller similar mark 23.9.1800. See also nos. 1250, 1256
2360	Ralph Maidman	lgw	31.5.1731	
2361	Richard Mills	lgw	14.7.1755	Two other marks similar as smallworker 5.3.1760 and 15.12.1760. Another 29.6.1765
2362	idem	lgw	11.7.1758	See also nos. 2373, 3780, 3836
2363	Richard Meach	smw	29.3.1765	And a smaller similar mark same date
2364	idem	smw	2.3.1774	
2365	Richard Morrison	smw	18.10.1768	And a smaller similar mark same date
2366	Richard May	smw	14.5.1778	See also no. 2372
2367	Robert Makepeace II	plw	20.1.1795	And a smaller similar mark same date
2368	Robert Metham	plw	2.7.1808	
2369	Robert Mitchell	smw	4.9.1821	And a smaller mark 22.5.1823
2370	Rebecca Merfield	smw	27.1.1823	

Also $_{IS}^{R}$ no. 3779

RM   RO

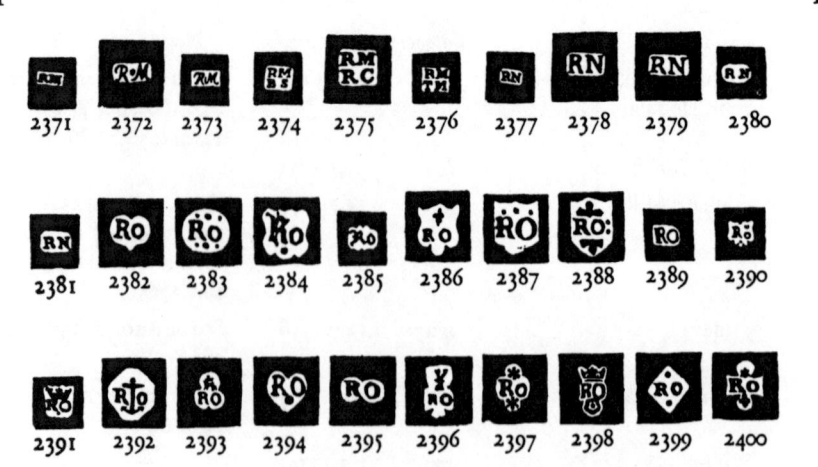

No.	Name	Category	Enteted	Notes
2371	Richard Mosley	smw	11.2.1835	See also Section VII, R.M
2372	Richard May	smw	12.5.1764	And a similar mark 3.10.1771 See also no. 2366
2373	Richard Mills	smw	2.11.1767	A weak impression. See also nos. 2361–2, 3780
2374	Richard Morson and Benjamin Stephenson	smw	27.10.1762	And a larger similar mark 9.7.1763
2375	Robert Makepeace I and Richard Carter	plw	20.1.1777	And a smaller similar mark
2376	Robert (II) and Thomas (II) Makepeace	plw	8.1.1794	And a smaller similar mark same date
2377	Robert Newman	smw	5.4.1721	See also no. 2089
2378	Richard Norman	smw	undated	After 21.7.1760. And a smaller mark in same entry
2379	idem	smw	31.8.1764	
2380	Robert Nicholls	smw	18.2.1772	
2381	Robert Nash	smw	24.12.1798	Smaller marks in rectangles 9.4.1782, 16.11.1789, 25.1.1799 and 5.9.1800
2382	Hugh Roberts	lgw	April 1697	
2383	Phillip Rollos I	lgw	April 1697	And a smaller similar mark same date
2384	Philip Roker I	lgw	April 1697	See also no. 3781
2385	John Roberts	smw	16.4.1716	
2386	Ann Roman	lgw	April 1697	
2387	idem	lgw	April 1697	
2388	Alexander Roode	lgw	idem	
2389	Nicholas Roe	smw	April 1697	

172

LONDON GOLDSMITHS

No	Name	Category	Entered	Notes
2390	Edward Robinson I	smw	10.12.1702	
2391	Thomas Roberts	smw	20.11.1703	
2392	Phillip Rollos Junr. (II)	lgw	20.8.1705	See also no. 2224*
2393	Ebenezer Roe	lgw	20.5.1709	Impression of animal indistinct
2394	Gundry Roode	lgw	1.3.1710	See also no. 880
2395	James Rood	lgw	27.10.1710	
2396	Nathaniel Roe	lgw	undated	Between Oct. 1710 and June 1712. Very poor impression. Largely conjectural
2397	Philip Robinson	lgw	10.3.1714	
2398	Philip Roker II	lgw	7.4.1720	See also nos. 2223, 2229
2399	Mary Rood	lgw	2.12.1721	See also no. 2060
2400	John Robinson I	lgw	4.11.1723	See also no. 1613

Also *RM* monogram no. 3435; RM.DB no. 3780; RO no. 3781

---

* Jackson shows octagonal punch in use 1708 and 1716.

RP RS

No.	Name	Category	Entered	Notes
2401	Robert Pilkington	smw	undated	Between June 1724 and March 1725. See also nos. 2197, 2417
2402	Richard Peters	smw	23.3.1725	
2403	Richard Pratt	smw	4.5.1730	
2404	Richard Pargeter	lgw	13.10.1730	See also no. 2418
2405	idem	smw	16.2.1737	A very indistinct impression
2406	R. Palmer	smw	25.6.1759	And a slightly larger similar mark 27.5.1763. See also Section V and VI, R.P
2407	Richard Payne I	smw	22.10.1762	
2408	Robert Platt	smw	21.9.1764	And a mark in incurved oblong punch 8.6.1768
2409	Richard Parr	smw	22.7.1772	See also Section VIII, R.P
2410	Robert Piercy	plw	21.7.1775	See also no. 3783
2411	Robert Purton	smw	23.1.1779	And other marks similar slightly smaller 13.4.1779 and 23.2.1780
2412	Richard Pearce	plw	10.10.1812	
2413	Robert Peppin	spm	15.12.1817	And a smaller mark same date. Other marks with pellet between in varying sizes 1818-24
2414	idem	spm	11.9.1829	
2415	Richard Poulden	smw	13.11.1818	And a smaller similar mark 13.10.1822
2416	Robert Pertt (?Perth)	lgw	21.7.1738	See also no. 3785
2417	Robert Pilkington	lgw	20.6.1739	See also nos. 2197, 2401
2418	Richard Pargeter	lgw	22.6.1739	See also nos. 2404-5

174

LONDON GOLDSMITHS

No.	Name	Category	Entered	Notes
2419	George Burrows II and Richard Pearce	plw	13.11.1826	And a smaller mark same date. Other marks similar 2.12.1835
2420	Richard Rugg	lgw	30.5.1754	
2421	idem	plw	18.3.1775	
2422	Robert Rew	lgw	10.8.1754	
2423	Richard Redrick	smw	7.4.1762	And other marks similar with pellet between 1763 and 1768. See also Section VI, C.R
2424	Richard Rowney	smw	1.4.1785	
2425	Robert Rutland	spm	21.8.1807	And other marks similar of various sizes 1808, 1811, 1812, 1815, 1819, 1821
2426	idem	spm	9.10.1822	And a similar mark 10.6.1826
2427	idem	spm	18.8.1824	
2428	Robert Ross	spm	13.10.1774	
2429	Richard Scarlett	lgw	24.6.1720	See also no. 2487
2430	idem	lgw	11.9.1723	

Also RP nos. 3782-4; *RP* no. 3785; RP.CP no. 3786

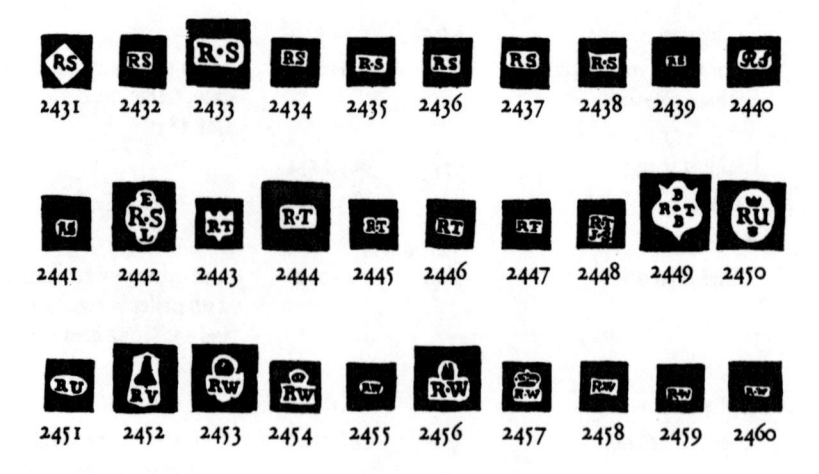

No.	Name	Category	Entered	Notes
2431	Rachel Simcoe	smw	20.2.1724	
2432	Robert Swanson	smw	18.3.(?1730)	Year omitted in date. See also no. 2441
2433	Robert Sallam	smw	6.11.1765	
2434	Richard Simpson	smw	31.7.1767	A blurred impression. See also Section VI RS, pellet between
2435	Richard Simkiss	smw	5.3.1770	And a similar mark and an incuse mark same date
2436	Robert Sharp*	plw	7.1.1788	And a smaller similar mark same date
2437	Robert Stevenson	smw	5.8.1802	
2438	Richard Sibley I	plw	11.3.1805	And a smaller similar mark same date. See also no. 2440
2439	Richard Sullivan	smw	11.7.1826	
2440	Richard Sibley I	plw	13.7.1812	And other marks of Richard Sibley II as spoonmaker smaller and larger similar 15.3.1837 and 21.6.1839. See also no. 2438
2441	Robert Swanson	lgw	18.10.1743	See also no. 2432
2442	John Read and Daniel Sleamaker	lgw	17.10.1701	
2443	Robert Turner	smw	17.3.1726	See also no. 2953
2444	Robert Tyrrill	lgw	10.5.1742	See also nos. 135, 2449
2445	Richard Thomas	lgw	20.3.1755	

* This mark is cut down from the combined mark of D. Smith and R. Sharp as can be clearly seen in the impression of the smaller punch. It has previously been ascribed to Robert Salmon for whom no mark whatever is registered.

LONDON GOLDSMITHS

No.	Name	Category	Entered	Notes
2446	Robert Twyford	smw	23.6.1784	
2447	Richard Turner	smw	28.10.1801	And a similar mark, pellet between, as spoonmaker 16.11.1809. See also Section VIII, R.T
2448	Richard Turner and John Shea	spm	23.4.1808	And a smaller similar mark same date
2449	Bennett Bradshaw and Robert Tyrrill	lgw	21.3.1737	See also nos. 135, 2444
2450	John Ruslen	lgw	April 1697	And a similar mark in more circular punch same date
2451	Robert Urquhart	smw	10.2.1801	
2452	Abraham Russell	lgw	24.7.1702	See also no. 3787
2453	Richard Watts	lgw	24.6.1720	See also nos. 2986–7, 3788
2454	idem	lgw	24.6.1720	Top of mark indistinct
2455	Robert White	smw	27.5.1723	
2456	Robert Williams	lgw	2.10.1726	See also no. 3199
2457	Robert Walker	smw	9.9.1731	
2458	Richard Weaver	snm	4.5.1738	
2459	Richard Lewis Wotton	smw	30.7.1760	
2460	Robert Waters	smw	29.7.1800	

Also RV no. 3787; RW nos. 3436, 3788

No.	Name	Category	Entered	Notes
2461	Robert Woolcomb	plw	12.11.1818	
2462	Robert Walliss	spm	28.11.1836	And a smaller similar mark 19.12.1836. Other marks various 1845–1849
2463	Ridg^y. Wm. Newland*	smw	15.3.1800	And a smaller similar mark same date
2464	Richard Zouch	lgw	31.3.1735	
2465	idem	lgw	27.6.1739	
2466	Thomas Sadler	lgw	25.8.1701	And a slightly smaller similar mark with scalloped edge to punch, same date. See also no. 2921
2467	John Sanders I	lgw	5.7.1717	
2468	Hugh Saunders	lgw	23.6.1718	
2469	John Hugh Le Sage	lgw	11.10.1718	See also nos. 1646, 1680–1
2470	Stephen Ardesoif	lgw	14.9.1756	
2471	idem	lgw	idem	
2472	Stephen Adams I	smw	8.10.1760	And other marks similar 1762, 1764, 1765, 1766, 1767 and 1769. See also no. 3203 and Section VIII, SA, pellet between, etc.
2473	Stephen Adams II	plw	14.11.1813	And a smaller mark 2.5.1815. See also Section VIII, S.A
2474	Samuel Blackborow	lgw	17.1.1721	See also nos. 186, 3789
2475	Samuel Bates	lgw	28.10.1728	
2476	idem	lgw	6.3.1744	

* of Farnham, Surrey. Included here in error.

178

LONDON GOLDSMITHS

No.	Name	Category	Entered	Notes
2477	Samuel Baker*	smw	20.12.1731	
2478	Sarah Buttall	lgw	10.5.1754	And a smaller similar mark same date. See also nos. 3790-1
2479	Susanna Barker	smw	25.6.1778	
2480	idem	smw	12.8.1789	And a smaller similar mark same date. Also another mark with pellet 26.8.1789
2481	Samuel Bellingham	smw	10.5.1806	See also Section VII, SB.SG
2482	Samuel Brough	smw	13.2.1808	See also Section VI, S.B
2483	Sarah and John William Blake	spm	15.6.1809	And other similar marks Jan. and Nov. 1821
2484	William Scarlett	lgw	April 1697	See also nos. 3292-3
2485	George Scrivener	smw	April 1697	Poor impression
2486	Dor (?ah) Scrivener	smw	April 1697	
2487	Richard Scarlett	lgw	24.9.1719	See also nos. 2429-30
2488	Samuel Colvill	smw	26.9.1722	See also no. 388
2489	Samuel Courtauld I	lgw	6.10.1746	
2490	idem	lgw	23.11.1751	

Also SB nos. 3789-91

---

* of Chatham. Included here in error.

No.	Name	Category	Entered	Notes
2491	Simeon Coley	smw	27.9.1761	See also Section VIII, S.C, various
2492	idem	smw	7.4.1763	
2493	Sarah Clarke	smw	22.5.1765	
2494	Samuel Chester	smw	23.6.1769	
2495	Sebastian Crespel II	lgw	3.8.1820	
2496	Samuel Lee Crees	spm	27.8.1833	
2497	Sebastian (I) and James Crespell	plw	not in register	Mark taken from meat-dish 1765. Another mark smaller also found
2498	Samuel Day	lgw	24.10.1698	Irregular mark for New Std. period
2499	Sandylands Drinkwater	smw	20.1.1735	See also no. 3792
2500	Samuel Dellaney	smw	19.3.1762	
2501	Samuel Davenport	plw	24.3.1786	See also no. 2504
2502	Samuel Davis	smw	2.7.1808	And a smaller similar mark same date
2503	Samuel Dutton	plw	8.5.1823	And a smaller similar mark same date. See also no. 2506
2504	Samuel and Edward Davenport	smw	8.4.1794	See also no. 2501
2505	Samuel Delaney and John Lee*	smw	5.1.1796	And a smaller similar mark same date
2506	Samuel Dutton ar. William Hattersley	plw	4.2.1822	See also no. 2503
2507	James Seabrook	lgw	11.10.1714	See also no. 1642
2508	Samuel Edlin	smw	19.9.1720	See also nos. 559–60

* of Bristol. Included here in error.

LONDON GOLDSMITHS

No.	Name	Category	Entered	Notes
2509	Samuel Eaton	smw	8.3.1736	
2510	idem	smw	5.2.1759	And other marks of various sizes some with pellet 1761, 1762, 1765, 1767 and 1768. See also no. 3793
2511	Samuel Fowler	smw	23.6.(?1730)	Year omitted in entry
2512	Samuel Green	lgw	8.6.1721	Poor impression
2513	idem	lgw	idem	See also no. 882
2514	Samuel Griffin	lgw	8.2.1731	
2515	Samuel Godbehere	plw	20.11.1784	And a smaller similar mark same date and also 27.11.1784
2516	Samuel Godbehere and Edward Wigan	plw	13.9.1786	And a smaller mark same date. Other marks 1789 and 1792
2517	S. Godbehere & Co.	plw	15.3.1800	As above with James Bult. And a smaller mark same date
2518	Samuel Goodbehere & James Bult	plw	16.9.1818	
2519	Samuel (II) and George Whitford	plw	23.7.1802	And a smaller similar mark same date
2520	John Shepherd	lgw	April 1697	This mark has two separate book entries

Also *SD* no. 3792; *SE* no. 3793

SH   SI

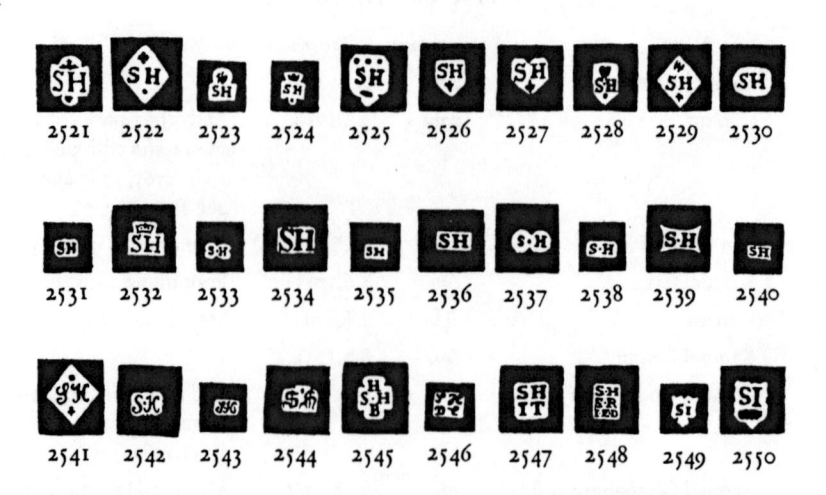

No.	Name	Category	Entered	Notes
2521	Joseph Sheene	lgw	April 1697	
2522	Alice Sheene	lgw	29.4.1700	
2523	Daniel Shelmerdine	smw	April 1697	Device uncertain. See also no. 499
2524	idem	smw	17.5.1717	
2525	Thomas Shermer	lgw	12.9.1717	Eleven impressions struck, all extremely poor, perhaps fleur-de-lys below
2526	Samuel Hitchcock	lgw	19.10.1720	See also no. 1016
2527	idem	lgw	5.10.1730	
2528	Samuel Hutton	lgw	7.10.1724	See also nos. 1076, 2544. Mark re-entered on moving 15.5.1734
2529	Sarah Holaday	lgw	15.6.1725	Upper device indistinct
2530	William Shaw I	lgw	16.1.1729	See also nos. 3299–300, 3329
2531	Samuel Holmes	smw	6.12.1734	
2532	Sarah Hutton	lgw	20.6.1740	
2533	Solomon Howland	smw	13.9.1760	
2534	idem	smw	11.11.1760	
2535	Samuel Harbert	smw	24.5.1771	See also nos. 2542, 2545
2536	Solomon Hougham	plw	1.2.1793	And two other marks smaller 6.2.1793. Other marks similar 13.11.1812. See also no. 2548
2537	Simon Harris	smw	30.10.1795	
2538	idem	smw	idem	
2539	Samuel Hennell	plw	22.6.1811	And a smaller similar mark same date. See also nos. 2337–8, 2547

LONDON GOLDSMITHS

No.	Name	Category	Entered	Notes
2540	Samuel Humphreys	plw	4.3.1822	
2541	Sussanah Hatfield	gs	14.4.1740	
2542	Samuel Herbert	lgw	9.10.1747	See nos 2535, 2545
2543	Samuel Hatton	smw	27.9.1758	See also Section VIII, S.H
2544	Samuel Hutton	gs	21.1.1740	See also nos. 1076, 2528
2545	Samuel Herbert & Co.	lgw	6.11.1750	See also nos. 2535, 2542
2546	Samuel Hayne and Dudley Cater	plw	5.7.1836	And a smaller mark same date. Other marks with Roman capitals 1837 and 1842
2547	Samuel Hennell and John Terrey	plw	6.4.1814	And a smaller mark same date. See also nos. 1281, 1719.
2548	Solomon Hougham, Solomon Royes and John East Dix	plw	13.9.1817	And a smaller mark same date. See also nos. 2536 and 2627
2549	Joseph Simson	smw	25.10.1703	
2550	Francis Singleton	lgw	April 1697	

Also SH no. 3437

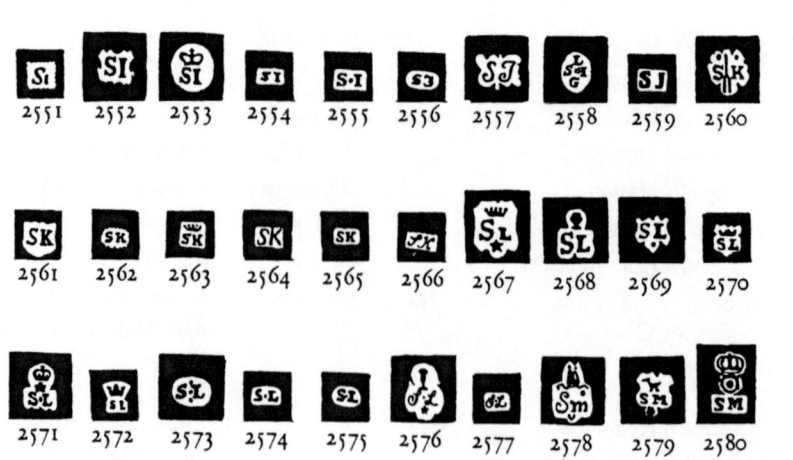

No.	Name	Category	Entered	Notes
2551	Joseph Simcoe	smw	1.12.1716	Largely conjectural. Impression nearly illegible
2552	Peter Simon	lgw	14.5.1725	See also no. 2230
2553	Simon Jouet	smw	21.7.1725	See also nos. 2556–7, 3794
2554	Samuel Johnson	smw	undated	Between 22.7. and 6.10.1725
2555	Stephen Joyce	smw	4.8.1759	And a smaller similar mark same date
2556	Simon Jouet	lgw	18.6.1739	See also nos. 2553, 3794
2557	idem	lgw	29.2.1748	
2558	Samuel Laundy and Jeffery Griffith	lgw	2.6.1731	See also nos. 1325, 2572–3
2559	Samuel Jackson	plw	22.4.1822	And a similar mark 3.6.1824
2560	George Skupholme	smw	April 1697	
2561	John Skupholme	smw	25.4.1705	
2562	Daniel Skinner	smw	3.7.1710	See also no. 503
2563	Abel Skinner	smw	19.8.1715	
2564	Samuel Knightly	smw	22.5.1761	And a similar mark with serif letters 30.8.1769. See also Section VIII, S.K
2565	Samuel Knight	plw	8.2.1816	See also no. 3218
2566	Samuel Key	lgw	15.10.1745	
2567	Daniel Sleamaker	lgw	15.8.1704	? mullet below
2568	Gabriel Sleath	lgw	14.3.1707	See also nos. 890, 904, 907
2569	idem	lgw	idem	
2570	Samuel Lee	lgw	1.7.1720	See also no. 1922
2571	Samuel Lea	lgw	12.12.1721	See also no. 1919
2572	Samuel Laundy	lgw	20.10.1727	See also no. 2558
2573	idem	lgw	idem	

LONDON GOLDSMITHS

No.	Name	Category	Entered	Notes
2574	Stephen Lane	bm	20.4.1738	
2575	Samuel Littlewood	smw	24.1.1772	
2576	Simon Le Sage	lgw	5.4.1754	
2577	idem	lgw	idem	
2578	Samuel Smith I	lgw	27.9.1700	
2579	John Smith I	lgw	April 1697	? bird above
2580	idem	lgw	idem	

Also *SI* no. 3794; SJ no. 3795; SM no. 3796

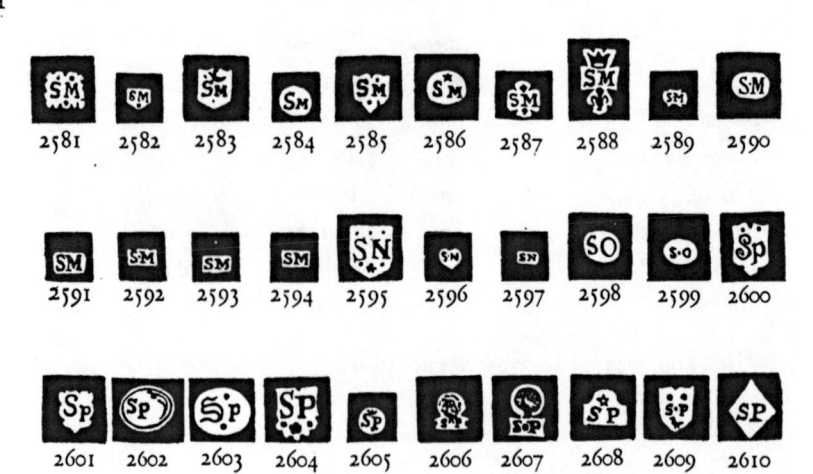

No.	Name	Category	Entered	Notes
2581	John Smithsend	lgw	April 1697	
2582	Ann Smith, Widow	smw	April 1697	
2583	Francis Smart	smw	22.1.1703	Upper part of mark very indistinct
2584	Benjamin Smith I	smw	26.7.1706	
2585	Joseph Smith I	lgw	11.4.1707	See also nos. 1640–1
2586	James Smith I	lgw	22.4.1718	See also no. 1643
2587	Samuel Smith II	lgw	26.9.1719	
2588	Samuel Margas	lgw	8.3.1721	See also no. 1988
2589	Samuel Meriton I	smw	10.5.1739	
2590	idem	lgw	7.7.1746	
2591	Samuel Meriton II	smw	8.5.1775	And a similar mark 16.10.1781
2592	Samuel Moulton	smw	30.3.1772	And a smaller mark 22.7.1774. Another larger 1.6.1781. Other marks smaller 1782 and 1788. See also Section VIII, S.M
2593	Samuel Mansell	khm	19.8.1773	
2594	Samuel Marshall	smw	18.7.1799	See also Section VII, SM, pellet between
2595	John Snelling	lgw	April 1697	
2596	Samuel Nichol	smw	23.3.1724	
2597	Stephen Noad	smw	30.6.1806	And a similar mark 6.2.1835
2598	William South	smw	April 1697	
2599	William Soame	lgw	19.1.1723	See also nos. 3295–7, 3328
2600	Thomas Spackman	lgw	25.5.1700	

LONDON GOLDSMITHS

No.	Name	Category	Entered	Notes
2601	idem	*lgw*	idem	And a smaller mark similar with two pellets above 15.1.1707
2602	William Spring	*lgw*	30.8.1701	Right hand side of punch very indistinct
2603	idem	*lgw*	idem	
2604	John Spackman I	*lgw*	April 1697	
2605	Francis Springgall	*smw*	15.12.1698	'Hiltmaker'
2606	Simon Pantin I	*lgw*	30.6.1720	See also nos. 2124–5
2607	Simon Pantin Junr. (II)	*lgw*	4.2.1729	And a similar mark 23.2.1731
2608	Hugh Spring	*lgw*	22.12.1721	
2609	William Spackman	*lgw*	1.11.1714	And a similar mark with pellets in place of annulets between Sept. 1723 and May 1725 with old Std. mark WS. See also no. 3294
2610	Sarah Parr	*lgw*	20.6.1728	

Also SM no. 3796; SP no. 3797

SP   ST

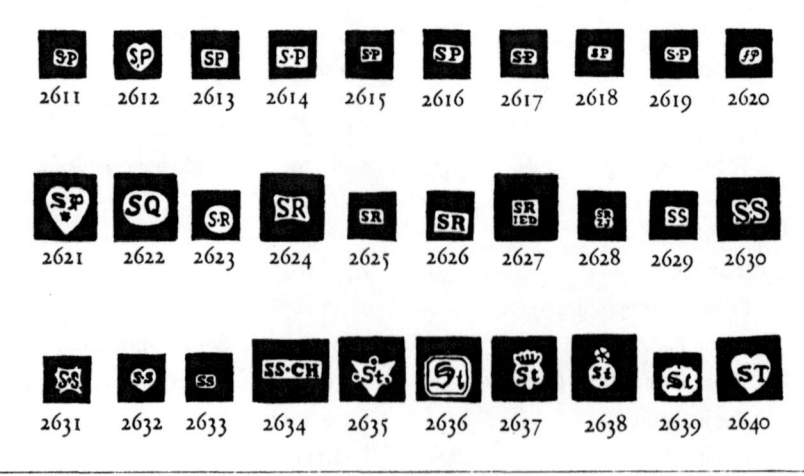

No.	Name	Category	Entered	Notes
2611	Samuel Parfit	smw	21.10.1734	
2612	John Spooner (?)	smw	25.1.1736	
2613	Samuel Priest	smw	24.3.1760	
2614	Sarey Price	smw	14.6.1763	See also no. 2620
2615	Stephen Picasse	smw	16.5.1770	
2616	Sydenham William Peppin	plw	25.7.1816	And a similar smaller mark 3.8.1816
2617	Sarah Purver	spm	23.9.1817	
2618	Sarah Pritchard	khm	19.2.1831	
2619	Susanna Peppin	smw	9.3.1835	
2620	Sarey Price	smw	27.6.1761	See also no. 2614
2621	Francis Spilsbury I	lgw	15.6.1739	See also no. 720
2622	George Squire	lgw	15.9.1720	See also no. 892
2623	Stephen Rainbow	smw	undated	c. 1721
2624	Samuel Roby	lgw	18.2.1740	
2625	Samuel Roberts	plw	22.7.1818	
2626	Solomon Royes	plw	22.2.1820	And a smaller similar mark same date. Other marks similar 26.11.1822
2627	Solomon Royes and John East Dix	plw	19.9.1818	And a smaller similar mark same date. See also nos. 3798 and 2536
2628	Samuel Rudduck and Zachariah Jennings	smw	27.3.1810	See also Section VII, S.R
2629	Samuel Shelley I	smw	24.10.1728	
2630	Samuel Smith III	lgw	4.2.1754	See also no. 908
2631	Samuel Siervent	lgw	20.6.1755	
2632	Samuel Shelley II	smw	6.12.1758	And a similar mark 3.7.1772. See also no. 3799

LONDON GOLDSMITHS

No.	Name	Category	Entered	Notes
2633	Sarah Snatt	smw	10.9.1817	
2634	Samuel Swain and Charles Hill	smw	25.7.1760	
2635	John Martin Stockar	lgw	April 1697	See also no. 2646
2636	idem	lgw	1.7.1710	Very poor impression. Largely conjectural
2637	Thomas Sturt	smw	April 1697	
2638	Ambrose Stevenson	lgw	1.2.1707	See also no. 89
2639	Thomas Stackhouse	smw	30.12.1715	See also no. 2920
2640	Joseph Stokes	lgw	April 1697	

Also SP no. 3797; SR.ID no. 3798; SS. no. 3799

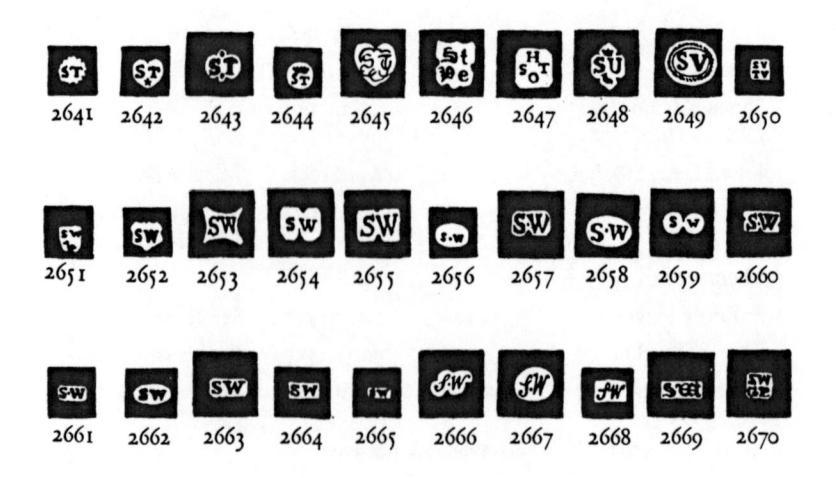

No.	Name	Category	Entered	Notes
2641	Thomas Steed	smw	April 1697	See also no. 2922
2642	William Street	lgw	26.2.1717	See also no. 3291
2643	Joseph Steward I	lgw	18.11.1719	See also no. 1684
2644	Daniel Stephens	smw	3.10.1720	
2645	Samuel Taylor	lgw	3.5.1744	And a similar mark 27.1.1757
2646	John Martin Stockar and Edward Peacock	lgw	20.10.1705	See also no. 2635
2647	Charles Stewart and W Ho?	lgw	4.7.1722	See also no. 418
2648	Thomas Sutton	lgw	7.1.1712	See also no. 3800
2649	John Sutton	lgw	15.4.1697	The first entry in the registers
2650	Samuel and Thomas Varden	smw	13.12.1775	
2651	John Swann	smw	19.12.1715	Almost illegible impression. Largely conjectural. See also no. 1637*
2652	Starling Wilford	lgw	30.6.1720	See also nos. 3191, 3802–3
2653	idem	lgw	22.4.1729	
2654	Samuel Welder	lgw	28.7.1720	See also nos. 3092–3, 3802–3, 3870
2655	idem	lgw	1.10.1729	
2656	Samuel Wood	lgw	3.7.1733	See also nos. 2666, 3808
2657	idem	lgw	undated	Between Sept. 1737 and Aug. 1738
2658	idem	lgw	15.7.1754	And a slightly smaller mark 2.10.1756

* Also confirmed by observation of actual punch on snuffbox c. 1720.

LONDON GOLDSMITHS

No.	Name	Category	Entered	Notes
2659	Samuel Wheat	*lgw*	11.5.1756	See also nos. 2668, 3807
2660	Sacheverel Wright	*smw*	23.8.1758	
2661	Samuel Whitford I	*smw*	27.3.1764	And a smaller similar mark same date. See also no. 3804
2662	Samuel Wintle	*smw*	27.5.1783	And a mark in oblong punch smaller 2.8.1792. See also Section VIII, S.W
2663	Samuel Whitford II	*plw*	10.6.1800	And a smaller similar mark same date. Other marks similar 5.10.1807 and 4.5.1812. See also no. 2669
2664	Samuel Wheatley	*plw*	23.8.1811	
2665	Samuel Webster II	*spm*	28.6.1826	
2666	Samuel Wood	*lgw*	15.6.1739	See also nos. 2656-8, 3808
2667	Samuel Welles	*lgw*	2.3.1741	
2668	Samuel Wheat	*lgw*	20.4.1757	See also nos. 2659, 3807
2669	Samuel Whitford II	*plw*	17.3.1817	And a larger similar mark 7.10.1817. See also no. 2663
2670	Samuel Whitford II and George Pizey	*plw*	27.8.1810	And a smaller similar mark same date

Also SU no. 3800; SW nos. 3801-4; *SW* no. 3805; 🙵 nos. 3806-8

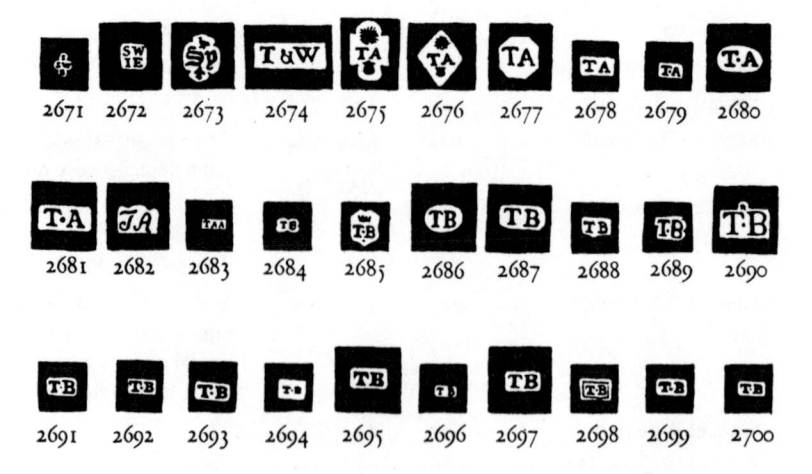

No.	Name	Category	Entered	Notes
2671	Samuel Webster I and John Bunn	smw	7.1.1806	
2672	Samuel Wheatley and John Evans I	plw	27.4.1810	
2673	Richard Syng	lgw	April 1697	And a similar mark in oval punch same date
2674	William Turner and James Williams	lgw	9.8.1753	And a smaller similar mark same date
2675	David Tanqueray	lgw	23.12.1713	And two smaller graduated similar marks same date. See also no. 509
2676	Anne Tanqueray	lgw	undated	Entered after former's death. See also no. 100
2677	Peter Tabart	lgw	7.7.1725	See also nos. 2237–8
2678	Thomas Arnold	smw	19.5.1770	And a similar mark 23.4.1776. See also no. 2682
2679	Thomas Adcock	smw	30.5.1772	
2680	Thomas Arden	plw	15.6.1805	And a smaller similar mark same date
2681	Thomas Austin	plw	8.4.1818	And a smaller similar mark same date. Another 22.11.1821
2682	Thomas Arnold	smw	6.4.1775	See also no. 2678
2683	Theodosia Ann Atkins	smw	27.9.1815	See also Section VIII, I.A and JA, pellet between
2684	Thomas Boulton	smw	20.6.1720	And a mark in oval punch 26.10.1727. See also no. 200
2685	Thomas Bass	smw	21.6.1720	Top outline of punch indistinct. See also no. 121
2686	Thomas Burridge	lgw	24.6.1720	See also nos. 241–2

LONDON GOLDSMITHS

No.	Name	Category	Entered	Notes
2687	Thomas Bamford I	*lgw*	27.6.1720	See also nos. 109–10, 2704
2688	Thomas Bulley	*smw*	undated	Jan.–Feb. 1724. See also nos. 244, 250
2689	Thomas Bowen I	*smw*	26.6.1732	
2690	Thomas Beare	*lgw*	18.12.1751	And a smaller similar mark same date
2691	Thomas Beezley	*lgw*	4.12.1755	See also no. 3811
2692	Thomas Bowen II	*smw*	7.6.1770	And two other marks similar, one slightly larger 29.6. and 5.8.1782
2693	Thomas Bamford II	*smw*	8.6.1770	
2694	Thomas Best	*smw*	28.4.1795	And two marks smaller 6.5.1795 and 23.5.1801
2695	Thomas Brough	*smw*	-.10.1795	And a smaller similar mark same date
2696	Thomas Bickerton	*smw*	10.7.1800	See also Section V, T.W.B
2697	Thomas Barker	*spm*	7.2.1805	And a smaller similar mark same date. Other marks with pellet 17.7.1811 and 1.12.1819. See also nos. 276, 3812
2698	Thomas Biddell	*smw*	6.11.1811	
2699	Thomas Balliston	*plw*	4.8.1812	And a similar mark 20.10.1815
2700	Thomas Ballam	*plw*	22.8.1820	And two marks similar, one larger 30.6.1821

Also TA no. 3809; *TA* no. 3810; TB nos. 3811–12

No.	Name	Category	Entered	Notes
2701	Thomas Burwash	plw	10.11.1821	
2702	Thomas Bannister	smw	19.1.1829	
2703	Thomas Burtt	smw	4.12.1834	
2704	Thomas Bamford I	lgw	18.7.1739	See also nos. 109-10, 2687
2705	Thomas B. Hopgood	plw	23.10.1828	See also no. 2807
2706	Thomas Bumfriss and Orlando Jackson	lgw	6.5.1766	
2707	Robert Timbrell and Joseph Bell I	lgw	undated	c. 1707. See also nos. 161, 2810
2708	Thomas Cooper	smw	24.6.1720	Another mark in oblong punch 11.5.1726. See also no. 389
2709	Thomas Cole	smw	13.8.1720	Annotated 'Goldwork'
2710	idem	smw	16.2.1732	
2711	Thomas Clark	lgw	2.3.1726	And a smaller mark with one pellet below same date. See also no. 3814
2712	Thomas Cooke	lgw	7.6.1727	See also nos. 2324-5
2713	Thomas Cock	smw	15.7.1736	
2714	Thomas Carlton	lgw	22.6.1744	
2715	Thomas Collier	lgw	5.6.1754	
2716	Thomas Congreve	lgw	18.9.1756	See also no. 3815
2717	Thomas Carter	smw	5.3.1762	
2718	Thomas Chawner	spm	15.10.1773	And a mark without pellet 1.11.1775
2719	idem	spm	31.5.1783	And a smaller similar mark same date. See also nos. 3510, 3816-17, 3869
2720	Thomas Crippin	smw	19.1.1779	

LONDON GOLDSMITHS

No.	Name	Category	Entered	Notes
2721	Thomas Combes	*smw*	30.9.1807	Poor impression. Somewhat conjectural. Others similar 21.6.1816 and 21.2.1817
2722	Thomas Clifford	*plw*	21.7.1820	
2723	Thomas Causton	*lgw*	7.12.1731	
2724	Thomas Cox Savory	*plw*	13.9.1827	And a larger mark 2.11.1827. Another mark 27.1.1832
2725	Tompson Davis	*lgw*	30.11.1757	See also no. 2734
2726	Thomas Dene	*smw*	22.7.1767	With another name? Vere Norman
2727	Thomas Daniell	*plw*	16.4.1774	See also nos. 2737, 3634
2728	idem	*plw*	10.5.1775	Other marks smaller similar same date and 8.3.1783
2729	idem	*plw*	8.10.1782	And a smaller similar mark same date
2730	Thomas Paine Dexter	*plw*	21.8.1805	And a smaller similar mark 10.10.1812

Also *TB* nos. 3438, 3813; *TC* nos. 3439, 3814–15; *TC* no. 3440; *TC.WC* nos. 3816–17; *TD* nos. 3441, 3818

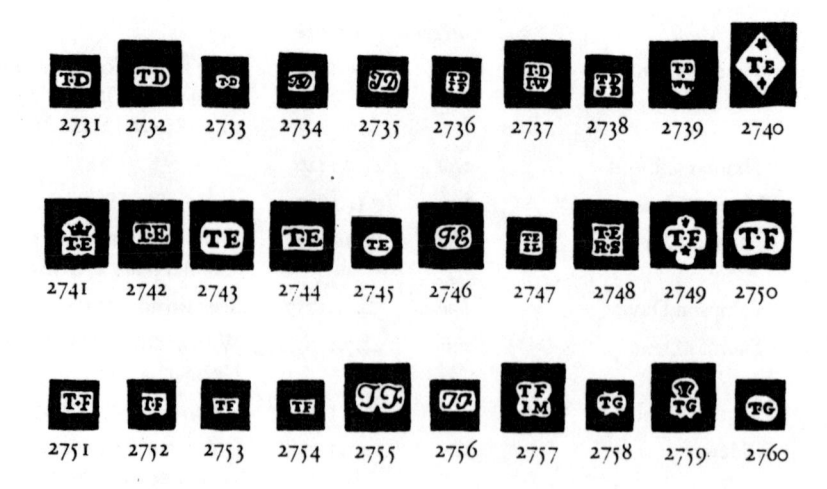

No.	Name	Category	Entered	Notes
2731	Thomas Dicks	spm	9.7.1811	And a smaller similar mark same date. See also no. 2738 and Section VIII, T.D, various
2732	Thomas Death	plw	17.2.1812	
2733	Thomas Diller	smw	5.12.1828	
2734	Tompson Davis	lgw	7.3.1758	See also no. 2725
2735	Thomas Dealtry	hfm, hlm	28.10.1765	
2736	Thomas Dee and John Fargus	smw	1.5.1830	
2737	Thomas Daniell and John Wall	plw	13.6.1781	See also nos. 1745, 2727–9
2738	Thomas and James Dicks	spm	20.9.1821	And other marks with larger cut corners 10.11.1821
2739	Thomas Devonshire and William Watkins	lgw	10.3.1756	And a similar mark in oval punch 24.6.1766. See also nos. 518, 3374, 3857, 3910
2740	Thomas Tearle	lgw	9.2.1719	Upper device indistinct ? a mullet. See also nos. 2938, 2947
2741	Thomas England	lgw	26.8.1725	See also nos. 626, 2746
2742	Thomas Evans	spm	11.3.1774	And a smaller similar mark same date. Other marks without pellet of various sizes 1779, 1782, 1784 and 1786
2743	Thomas Ellis	plw	20.4.1780	
2744	Thomas Ellerton	lgw	23.4.1805	

LONDON GOLDSMITHS

No.	Name	Category	Entered	Notes
2745	Thomas Edwards	plw	21.8.1816	And other marks in oblong cut-corner punches, pellet between, 1820 and 1823
2746	Thomas England	lgw	30.7.1739	See also nos. 626, 2741
2747	Thomas Evans and Jacob Levi	smw	20.2.1784	
2748	Thomas Ellerton and Richard Sibley I	plw	14.11.1803	And a smaller similar mark same date
2749	Thomas Farren	smw	11.11.1720	Upper device indistinct. See also nos. 666, 2755, 3564
2750	Thomas Folkingham	lgw	6.2.1721	See also no. 703
2751	Thomas Foster	smw	7.12.1769	And a slightly smaller mark with pellet between 29.7.1773. See also nos. 3822–3 and Sections V and VI, T.F
2752	Thomas Freeth I	smw	17.8.1773	Very poor impression. Conjectural reproduction. See also Section VIII, T.F
2753	Thomas Freeth II	spm	15.11.1820	
2754	Thomas Fairbairn	plw	15.12.1823	And similar marks as small-worker 1836
2755	Thomas Farren	lgw	15.6.1739	See also nos. 666, 2749
2756	Thomas Fair	smw	3.10.1768	
2757	Thomas Freeman and John Marshall	smw	13.9.1764	
2758	Thomas Gilpin	smw	24.9.1730	See also nos. 2768–9, 3825–6
2759	Thomas Gladwin	lgw	1.8.1737	See also no. 842
2760	Thomas Gopsill	smw	3.3.1786	

Also TE no. 3442; *TE* no. 3819; TE.GS no. 3820; TF nos. 3821–3; TG nos. 3443–4, 3824

TG   TH

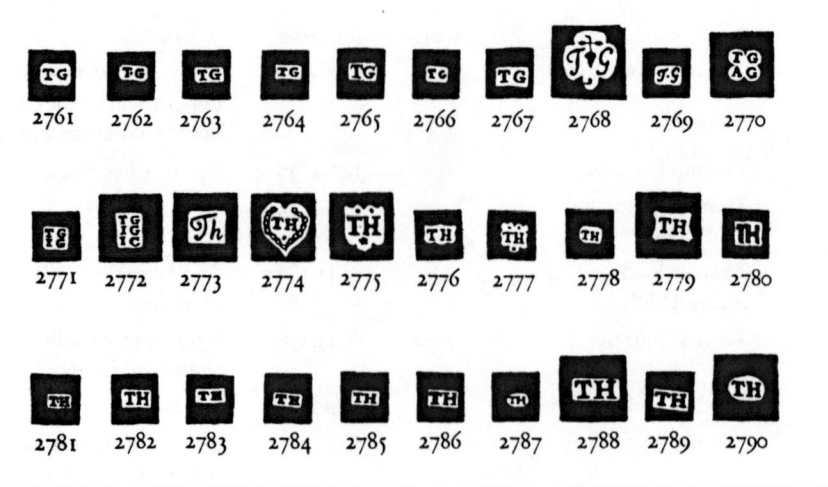

No.	Name	Category	Entered	Notes
2761	Thomas Gairdner	smw	30.11.1802	
2762	idem	plw	26.1.1818	
2763	Thomas Goddard	smw	25.6.1806	
2764	Thomas Goslee	smw	9.9.1819	
2765	Thomas Glover	plw	4.7.1821	And a smaller similar mark same date
2766	Thomas Gull	smw	17.12.1829	
2767	Thomas Galloway	plw	14.8.1837	
2768	Thomas Gilpin	lgw	2.7.1739	See also nos. 2758, 3826
2769	idem	lgw	idem	
2770	Thomas and Alfred Galloway	plw	12.8.1831	
2771	Thomas and Joseph Guest	plw	27.11.1805	
2772	T. & J. Guest and Joseph Cradock	plw	15.8.1806	And a similar mark 24.2.1808
2773	Benjamin Thomson	smw	6.1.1716	
2774	Samuel Thorne	lgw	April 1697	
2775	Simon Thriscross	lgw	April 1697	
2776	Francis Thompson	smw	21.10.1699	
2777	William Thompson I	smw	26.9.1701	
2778	John Thompson II	smw	10.5.1717	'maketh all sorts of knifes & forks'
2779	Thomas Hodgkinson	smw	17.7.1727	See also no. 3827
2780	Thomas Holyhead	smw	15.9.1731	
2781	Thomas Harrison	smw	18.8.1758	
2782	Thomas Hall	smw	7.5.1770	
2783	Thomas Hallows	smw	14.5.1771	And a similar mark 6.12.1790

LONDON GOLDSMITHS

No.	Name	Category	Entered	Notes
2784	Thomas Hyde	smw	3.2.1784	
2785	Thomas Hodge	smw	30.6.1787	See also no. 2802
2786	Thomas Harper I	smw	27.5.1790	And a smaller mark 5.5.1810. Another mark with pellet 11.7.1829
2787	Thomas Hoare	smw	28.4.1792	See also no. 2791
2788	Thomas Hobbs	smw	7.5.1796	And a smaller similar mark same date
2789	Thomas Holland II	plw	7.8.1798	
2790	Thomas Hayter	plw	21.5.1805	And a smaller similar mark same date

Also *TG* nos. 3825–6; TG.IW no. 3445; TH nos. 3446–7, 3827

TH   TJ

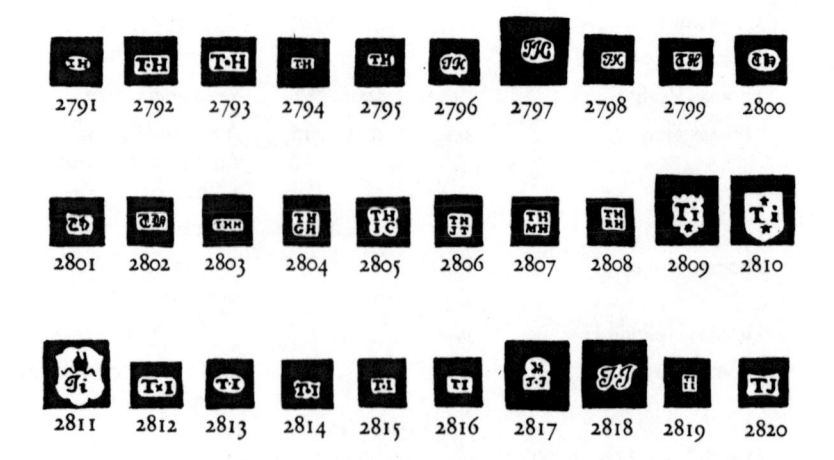

No.	Name	Category	Entered	Notes
2791	Thomas Hoare	smw	31.3.1806	See also no. 2787
2792	Thomas Harper II	spm	10.7.1806	
2793	Thomas Halford	plw	18.8.1807	And a smaller similar mark with pellet 23.9.1809. Another mark without pellet 14.11.1812. Two other marks with pellet 29.6.1820
2794	Thomas Hastings	smw	30.9.1811	And a mark in lobed punch 16.11.1836
2795	Thomas Hughes Headland	smw	30.5.1834	Also incuse mark THH 22.3.1834. See also no. 2803
2796	Thomas Heming	lgw	12.6.1745	See also no. 3828
2797	idem	lgw	after 1758	Not in register. Mark taken from dish 1763
2798	Thomas Hatton	smw	26.6.1762	See also no. 3829
2799	Thomas Harding	smw	12.9.1758	See also no. 3829
2800	James Thomasson	smw	17.3.1717	Poor impression. Somewhat conjectural
2801	John Thompson I	smw	9.4.1711	Indistinct impression. See also no. 1695
2802	Thomas Hodge	smw	10.3.1768	And a similar mark 5.9.1785. See also no. 2785
2803	Thomas Hughes Headland	smw	7.10.1834	And a larger mark 4.5.1837. See also no. 2795
2804	Thomas and George Hayter	plw	15.3.1816	And a smaller similar mark same date. Another in quatrefoil punch 7.12.1821
2805	Thomas Hannam and* John Crouch II	plw	13.4.1799	

* A nearly similar mark with pellets between letters is found from about 1765. This may be coincidentally similar and perhaps for Thomas Hannam and John Carter.

LONDON GOLDSMITHS

No.	Name	Category	Entered	Notes
2806	Thomas Hobbs and James Taylor	plw	27.10.1797	And a smaller similar mark same date
2807	Thomas Burn Hopgood and Metcalf Hopgood	plw	20.9.1833	See also nos. 2032, 2705
2808	Thomas and Rowland Hastings	smw	2.1.1808	
2809	George Titterton	lgw	April 1697	
2810	Robert Timbrell	lgw	April 1697	See also no. 2707
2811	John Tiffin	lgw	12.5.1701	
2812	Thomas Jackson I	lgw	7.12.1736	See also no. 2817
2813	Thomas Jackson II	lgw	30.9.1769	And a similar mark 10.5.1773. See also nos. 2819, 3840-1
2814	Thomas Justis	smw	24.11.1761	See also nos. 3840-1
2815	idem	smw	30.9.1762	And other marks similar 1763, 1765, and 1771. Others without pellet 1764 and 1765
2816	Thomas Joyce	smw	20.4.1791	
2817	Thomas Jackson I	lgw	26.6.1739	See also nos. 2812
2818	Thomas Jeanes	lgw	14.4.1750	
2819	Thomas (II) and John (III) Jackson	smw	16.4.1790	See also nos. 1428-9
2820	Thomas Johnson	smw	22.1.1800	

Also TH nos. 3446-7, 3827; *TH* nos. 3828-34; 𝔗𝔍 no. 3835; TH.RM. no. 3837; TH.RS. no. 3838; TH.SH no. 3839; TI no. 3840; *TI* no. 3841; TI.WI no. 3842

No.	Name	Category	Entered	Notes
2821	Thomas James	smw	30.10.1804	And a smaller similar mark same date
2822	Thomas Kendrick	smw	7.10.1731	
2823	Thomas Lawrence I	lgw	24.1.1743	See also Section V, TL, coronet above
2824	Thomas Lamborn	smw	2.9.1759	And a similar mark 27.4.1769
2825	Thomas Liddiard	smw	3.3.1770	
2826	Thomas Lister Junr.	smw	23.11.1803	And two marks smaller 17.6.1828, perhaps for son of the same
2827	Thomas Lloyd	plw	27.3.1821	
2828	Thomas Lawrence Junr. (II) and James Sage	smw	23.3.1771	
2829	Thomas Mann	lgw	1.7.1720	See also nos. 1987, 2849
2830	idem	smw	10.12.1729	
2831	idem	lgw	29.9.1736	
2832	Thomas Mason	lgw	1.7.1720	See also nos. 1971, 2846–8
2833	idem	lgw	28.9.1733	
2834	Thomas Morse	lgw	5.9.1718	See also no. 2053
2835	Thomas Makepeace I	smw	undated	c. 1720. See also no. 1990
2836	Thomas Moulden	smw	8.2.1722	
2837	Thomas Merry II	lgw	1.9.1731	
2838	Thomas Mercer	lgw	5.12.1740	
2839	Thomas Morley	smw	20.8.1778	And a slightly longer similar mark 17.1.1788
2840	Thomas Meriton	smw	1.3.1791	
2841	Theophilus Merry	smw	22.9.1824	
2842	Thomas McIntyre	plw	7.6.1832	
2843	Thomas Merrick	plw	19.4.1834	

LONDON GOLDSMITHS

No.	Name	Category	Entered	Notes
2844	T. Manning	*smw*	19.9.1738	
2845	Thomas Moore II	*lgw*	21.8.1750	First mark a very poor impression. Reproduction from similar mark 20.8.1757
2846	Thomas Mason	*lgw*	23.9.1745	See also nos. 1971, 2832-3
2847	idem	*lgw*	6.7.1739	
2848	idem	*lgw*	19.11.1740	
2849	Thomas Mann	*lgw*	13.7.1739	See also nos. 1987, 2829-31
2850	Thomas North	*smw*	4.5.1724	

Also TL nos. 3448, 3843-5; TM.IB.TM no. 3449; TN no. 3846

No.	Name	Category	Entered	Notes
2851	Thomas Newcomb	smw	21.7.1760	
2852	Thomas Nash I	smw	14.1.1767	See also nos. 2860, 3846, Section V, NASH and Section VIII, T.N various
2853	Thomas Northcote	spm	20.8.1776	And a smaller similar mark same date. Another mark 29.10.1777
2854	idem	spm	27.4.1779	And a smaller mark without pellet 16.5.1782
2855	idem	plw	19.11.1784	And other marks similar 27.11.1784, 4.12.1786 and 10.7.1792. Another with pellet 19.8.1789. Another 11.7.1797. See also no. 2861
2856	Thomas Nash II	smw	13.4.1786	
2857	Thomas Newby	plw	11.11.1816	
2858	Thomas Nortzell	smw	11.2.1817	See also no. 2862
2859	Thomas Nicholls	plw	10.8.1824	
2860	Thomas Nash I	smw	22.11.1759	And a smaller similar mark same date. See also nos. 2852, 3846
2861	Thomas Northcote and George Bourne	plw	5.6.1794	See also nos. 2853–5
2862	Thomas Nortzell and Henry Broughton	smw	29.12.1827	See also no. 2858
2863	William Toone	lgw	3.11.1725	See also no. 3336
2864	Edmund Townsend	lgw	April 1697	
2865	George Townsend	smw	10.3.1701	
2866	Richard Tomkins	smw	4.5.1709	See also Section V, R.T
2867	Thomas Moriah Otton	plw	4.6.1823	

LONDON GOLDSMITHS

No.	Name	Category	Entered	Notes
2868	Thomas Prew	smw	4.7.1720	Poor impression. Uncertain outline to punch
2869	Thomas Page	smw	12.8.1720	See also no. 2126
2870	Thomas Parr II	lgw	9.2.1733	See also nos. 2883-4
2871	Thomas Pettyfoot	smw	26.2.1733	
2872	Thomas Penn	smw	3.5.1738	Poor impression and crude punch
2873	Thomas Poynton	smw	22.8.1758	
2874	Thomas Pepper I	smw	23.2.1767	
2875	Thomas Pitts I	lgw	c. 1758	Not in register. Previously called Thos. Powell. Mark taken from epergne 1765
2876	Thomas Pitts II	plw	5.4.1804	
2877	Thomas Pattrick	smw	2.2.1797	A poorly cut mark
2878	Thomas Peacock	smw	23.10.1798	
2879	Thomas Price	smw	6.8.1802	
2880	Thomas P. Prothero	smw	29.10.1802	

Also TO nos. 3450-1; TP no. 3452

TP TR

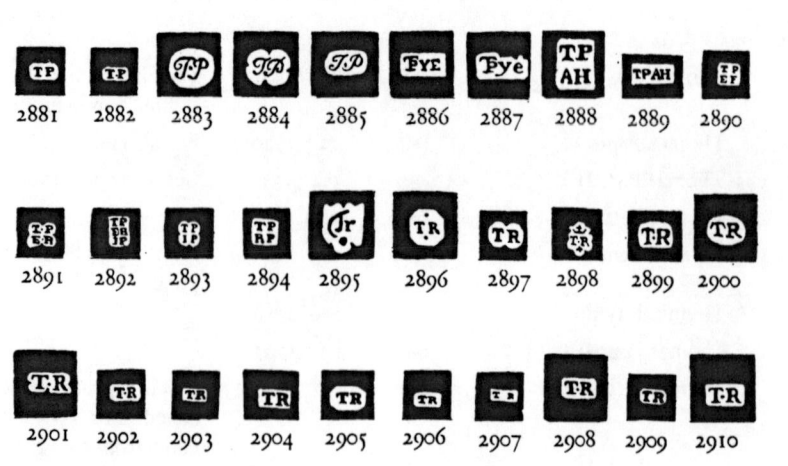

No.	Name	Category	Entered	Notes
2881	Thomas Pepper II	plw	30.12.1809	
2882	Thomas Purver	spm	6.10.1814	
2883	Thomas Parr II	lgw	19.6.1739	See also no. 2870
2884	idem	lgw	idem	
2885	Thomas Powell	lgw	8.5.1756	And a similar mark 10.2.1758
2886	Thomas Pye	lgw	17.7.1738	
2887	idem	lgw	14.6.1739	
2888	Thomas Pratt and Arthur Humphreys	plw	7.7.1780	And a smaller similar mark same date
2889	idem	plw	idem	
2890	Thomas Purver and Edward Furnice	spm	17.4.1815	See also no. 586
2891	Thomas Phipps and Edward Robinson II	smw	8.7.1783	And two other marks similar, one smaller 8.8.1789
2892	Thomas Phipps, James Phipps II and Edward Robinson II	smw	undated	No names to mark in register but countersigned by James Phipps. And a smaller similar mark same date
2893	Thomas and James Phipps II	smw	31.1.1816	And a smaller similar mark same date
2894	Thomas and Richard Payne	plw	30.10.1777	
2895	Benjamin Traherne	lgw	April 1697	
2896	William Truss	lgw	undated	Between July 1710 and Dec. 1713. See also nos. 3454, 3468
2897	Thomas Redhead	smw	29.6.1720	See also no. 2306
2898	Thomas Roberts	smw	6.7.1720	See also no. 2391
2899	Thomas Rush	lgw	25.11.1724	See also nos. 2913-4

LONDON GOLDSMITHS

No.	Name	Category	Entered	Notes
2900	idem	lgw	1.11.1731	
2901	Thomas Rowe	lgw	29.12.1753	And a slightly larger similar mark 23.2.1760
2902	Thomas Ray	smw	12.4.1759	See also Sections V and VI, T.R, etc.
2903	Thomas Read	smw	1.4.1772	See also no. 2919 and Section VIII, T.R
2904	Timothy Renou	plw	11.2.1792	
2905	idem	plw	2.8.1800	
2906	idem	plw	8.8.1800	
2907	Thomas Remmett	smw	17.10.1798	And a smaller mark with pellet 15.1.1799. Another without pellet 26.1.1804
2908	Thomas Robinson I	plw	5.3.1802	And a smaller similar mark same date
2909	idem	plw	2.12.1813	
2910	Thomas Radcliffe	smw	6.11.1802	And a similar mark as snuffermaker 28.11.1826. Another as smallworker 18.3.1828

Also TP no. 3452; TP.RM no. 3453; TR no. 3454

TR TT

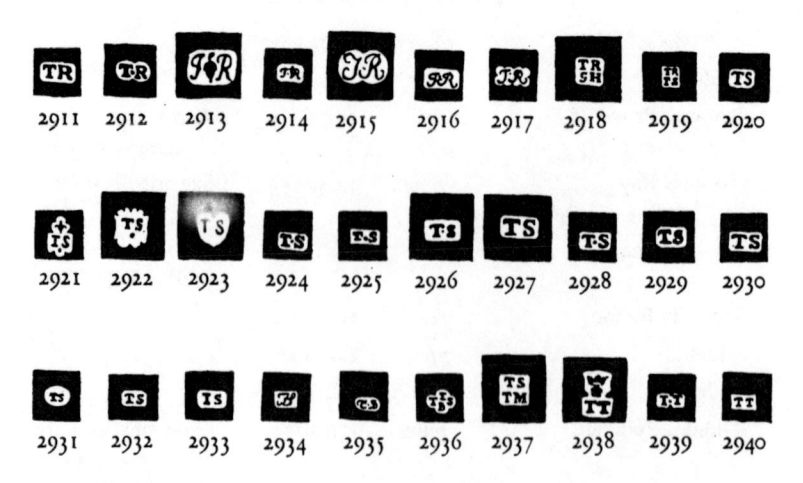

No.	Name	Category	Entered	Notes
2911	Thomas Richards	plw	23.5.1812	And a smaller similar mark same date
2912	Thomas Ross	plw	10.11.1819	See also nos. 2916–7
2913	Thomas Rush	lgw	18.6.1739	See also nos. 2899, 2900
2914	idem	lgw	idem	
2915	Thomas Robins	plw	10.1.1801	And a smaller similar mark same date
2916	Thomas Ross	plw	14.2.1821	See also no. 2912
2917	idem	plw	11.11.1825	
2918	Thomas Robinson II and S. Harding	smw	31.3.1810	
2919	Thomas Read and Thomas Smith II	smw	14.3.1771	See also no. 2903 and Section VIII, T.R
2920	Thomas Stackhouse	smw	21.6.1720	And a similar mark 6.5.1728. Other marks with pellet 9.8.1738 and 16.1.1739. See also no. 2639
2921	Thomas Sadler	lgw	undated	About June 1720. See also no. 2466
2922	Thomas Steed	smw	24.1.1723	Outline of shield indistinct. See also no. 2641
2923	Thomas Smith I	lgw	16.10.1750	Weak impression. Base of shield uncertain
2924	Thomas Swift	lgw	7.8.1758	
2925	idem	lgw	10.7.1762	
2926	Thomas Shepherd	smw	18.12.1769	And a similar mark without pellet 27.4.1773
2927	idem	smw	6.11.1782	And a smaller similar mark same date

LONDON GOLDSMITHS

No.	Name	Category	Entered	Notes
2928	idem	plw	20.10.1785	And a smaller mark without pellet in cut-corner oblong 5.4.1786
2929	Thomas Sharratt	smw	23.4.1772	And a similar mark 22.2.1776
2930	Thomas Streetin	plw	15.8.1794	And a similar mark 20.9.1802 and 16.7.1810. Another mark with pellet 13.4.1820
2931	idem	spm	10.8.1798	And a similar mark 25.10.1799. Another similar mark with pellet between initials entered 27.6.1806
2932	Thomas Shekleton	smw	10.2.1810	
2933	Timothy Smith	plw	21.7.1825	See also no. 2937
2934	Thomas Shaw	smw	22.6.1785	
2935	Thomas Sarson	smw	6.5.1737	
2936	Thomas Stilwell and Thomas Burbidge	smw	9.8.1763	See also Section V, T.S and T.S.B
2937	Timothy Smith and Thomas Merryweather	plw	10.1.1824	
2938	Thomas Tearle	lgw	30.6.1720	See also nos. 2740, 2947
2939	Thomas Thorne	gs	14.5.1736	
2940	Thomas Tombs	smw	14.6.1738	

Also TS no. 3455; TT no. 3456

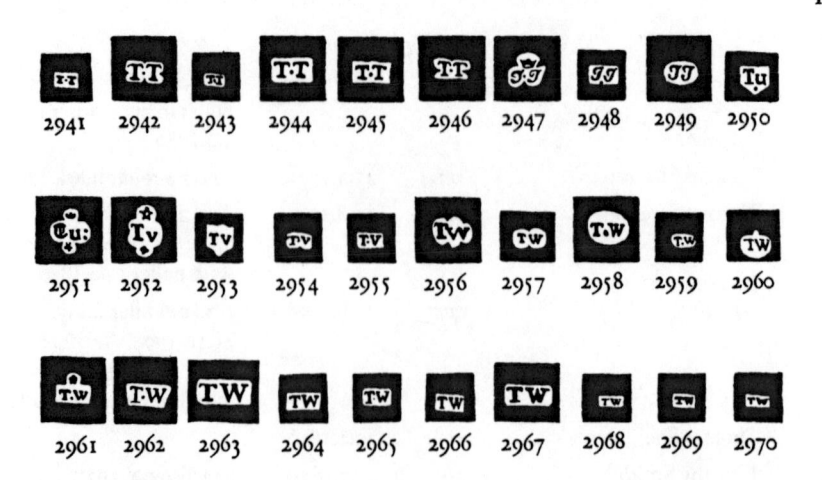

No.	Name	Category	Entered	Notes
2941	Thomas Townraw	smw	21.9.1738	And a similar mark 13.11.1753
2942	idem	smw	29.10.1754	
2943	Thomas Taylor I	smw	16.2.1767	And a longer similar mark 6.6.1772. Another similar without pellet 5.7.1771. See also Section VIII, TT, pellet between
2944	Thomas Tookey	spm	30.10.1773	And another smaller mark without pellet 2.11.1775. See also no. 2949
2945	Thomas Tayler	smw	21.5.1791	
2946	Thomas Taylor II	smw	19.10.1793	
2947	Thomas Tearle	lgw	22.6.1739	See also nos. 2740, 2938
2948	Trevillion Taylor	smw	10.2.1760	And a similar mark with three pellets below same date
2949	Thomas Tookey	spm	24.3.1779	And a similar mark 5.12.1780. See also no. 2944
2950	Francis Turner	lgw	25.2.1721	
2951	idem	lgw	5.4.1709	See also no. 724
2952	William Turbitt	lgw	7.7.1710	Weak impression. Devices doubtful
2953	Robert Turner	smw	29.6.1703	See also no. 2443
2954	Joseph Tuckwell	smw	15.4.1713	See also no. 1724
2955	Thomas Venn	smw	26.3.1764	See also Section V, TV, coronet above
2956	William Twell	lgw	28.3.1709	
2957	Thomas Wildman	smw	17.8.1720	
2958	Thomas Wright	lgw	6.9.1721	

LONDON GOLDSMITHS

No.	Name	Category	Entered	Notes
2959	idem	smw	9.11.1722	
2960	Thomas Wheeler	smw	10.2.1723	
2961	Thomas Whipham	lgw	20.6.1737	See also nos. 2974, 2976, 2979, 3510
2962	Thomas Wallis I	lgw	8.3.1758	And a smaller similar mark same date. Two others similar 22.1.1763
2963	Thomas Wallis I*	plw	7.11.1778	And two smaller graduated similar marks. See also nos. 2975, 2978 and Section VIII, T.W various
2964	Thomas Woodhouse	smw	4.10.1758	
2965	Thomas Wilson	smw	2.4.1761	And a mark in double lobed punch 25.8.1770. Another similar to first 3.11.1770. See also Sections V and VIII, T.W
2966	Thomas Wilkinson	smw	7.11.1763	And a slightly smaller mark 6.6.1767
2967	Thomas Watson	plw	1.1.1784	And a smaller similar mark same date
2968	Thomas Walker	smw	20.10.1800	See also Section V, IS.TW and T.W
2969	Thomas Wells	smw	29.8.1806	
2970	Thomas Wade	smw	21.5.1808	And other similar marks 15.3.1814 and 8.12.1821

Also TT no. 3456; TW nos. 3457-8, 3848

---

* Correctly Thomas Wallis I, the signature being clearly that of the father.

TW WA

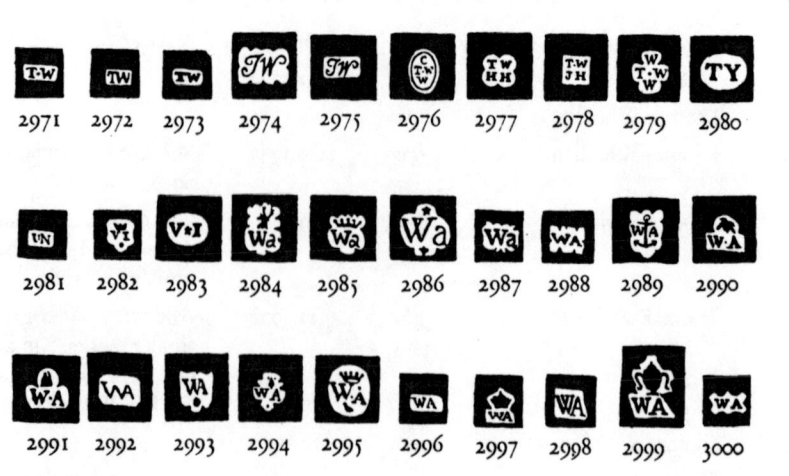

No.	Name	Category	Entered	Notes
2971	Thomas Willats	smw	15.7.1809	
2972	Thomas Whitehead	smw	2.1.1822	
2973	Thomas Wimbush	plw	27.11.1828	And a smaller similar mark same date
2974	Thomas Whipham I	lgw	18.6.1739	See also nos. 2961, 2976, 2979, 3847
2975	Thomas Wallis II	plw	15.9.1792	And a smaller similar mark same date. Others similar 16.8.1796 and 14.9.1801. See also nos. 2962–3
2976	Thomas Whipham II and Charles Wright	lgw	24.10.1757	Mark compressed from circle by curvature of book See also no. 3510, and page 771
2977	Thomas Wimbush and Henry Hyde	plw	27.1.1834	And two smaller similar marks same date
2978	Thomas Wallis II and Jonathan Hayne	plw	22.2.1810	And a smaller similar mark same date. Other marks larger and smaller 3.12.1817 and 17.2.1820
2979	Thomas Whipham and William Williams I	gs	1.5.1740	See also nos. 2961, 2974, 2976, 3362–3
2980	Thomas Yorke	smw	9.8.1721	
2981	Nathaniel Underwood	smw	12.1.1701	
2982	Thomas Vicaridge	hlm	April 1697	
2983	Edward Vincent	lgw	about 1712	Missing from register. Mark taken from a cup 1714. See also nos. 648–9, 3560, 3852
2984	Benjamin Watts	lgw	21.11.1698	And a smaller similar mark with straight sides to punch same date. See also no. 251
2985	White Walsh	lgw	25.11.1698	Weak impression

LONDON GOLDSMITHS

No.	Name	Category	Entered	Notes
2986	Richard Watts	lgw	10.2.1710	See also nos. 2453–4, 3788
2987	idem	lgw	idem	
2988	Richard Warter	smw	April 1697	
2989	Joseph Ward	lgw	April 1697	And a similar mark in slightly varying punch 19.9.1717. See also no. 3856
2990	Samuel Wastell	lgw	20.10.1701	See also no. 3801
2991	idem	lgw	idem	
2992	Thomas Waterhouse	lgw	22.7.1702	A crudely cut punch. Also similar mark in octagonal or hexagonal punch same date. Poor impression
2993	William Warham I	lgw	12.11.1703	Poor impression. Device below uncertain. See also nos. 3858–9
2994	William Warham Junior (II)	lgw	7.4.1705	
2995	Thomas Wall	lgw	25.9.1708	
2996	William Walters	smw	5.3.1716	Very vague impression. Largely conjectural
2997	William Allen I	smw	26.10.1724	
2998	idem	smw	22.8.1728	
2999	William Atkinson	lgw	31.5.1725	See also no. 99
3000	William Alexander	lgw	15.3.1743	See also no. 3860

Also TW nos. 3457–8, 3848; *TW* nos. 3459, 3847; U & H no. 3849; Va no. 3850; VA no. 3851; VI no. 3852; VN nos. 3853–5; VR no. 3460; Wa nos. 3856–7; WA nos. 3858–62

WA WB

No.	Name	Category	Entered	Notes
3001	William Abdy I	smw	24.6.1763	See also nos. 3860–1
3002	idem	smw	5.10.1767	And a smaller mark in rectangle punch, and two incuse marks same date. Other marks 15.10.1779
3003	idem	plw	1.9.1784	And two other marks smaller similar same date
3004	William Abdy II	plw	15.9.1790	And two other marks similar, larger and smaller 16.10.1790. See also no. 3862
3005	William Alldridge	smw	12.2.1768	
3006	William Allen II	smw	19.5.1769	See also Section VIII, W.A
3007	William Allen III	smw	10.8.1798	
3008	William Bellassyse	lgw	3.7.1723	See also no. 160
3009	William Bird I	smw	19.8.1731	See also no. 3021
3010	William Bagnall	lgw	6.6.1744	
3011	idem	lgw	idem	
3012	Walter Brind	lgw	7.2.1749	
3013	idem	lgw	31.8.17(51?)	And a smaller similar mark same date
3014	idem	lgw	11.10.1757	
3015	idem	plw	26.2.1781	See also no. 3864
3016	William Burton	smw	23.10.1758	See also Section V, W.B
3017	William Bayley I*	smw	19.2.1759	
3018	William Bell	smw	10.2.1759	And a smaller mark without bell in cut-corner punch 4.8.1772. Also Section V, WB, pellet between bell above and Section VII, W.B

* Another similar mark without pellet entered by William Bayley II, 2.11.1770.

214

LONDON GOLDSMITHS

No.	Name	Category	Entered	Notes
3019	William Brooks I	smw	23.9.1763	See also Section V, W.B and WB. TB, and Section VI
3020	William Bromfield	smw	31.5.1769	
3021	William Bird II	smw	13.7.1769	See also no. 3009 and Section VIII, W.B
3022	William Bissell	smw	24.10.1769	
3023	William Bromage	smw	24.9.1770	
3024	William Barrett I	smw	9.3.1771	
3025	idem	smw	14.9.1775	And other marks smaller similar 1777, 1780 and 1783. Another slightly larger 1790
3026	William Brockwell	smw	23.12.1776	And a smaller similar mark same date and also 20.10.1802
3027	Wilkes Booth	snm	11.10.1787	And a similar mark 8.7.1805
3028	William Burch	smw	7.3.1788	
3029	William Bennett	plw	1.6.1796	
3030	idem	plw	7.7.1808	And a smaller similar mark same date

Also *WA* no. 3863; WB nos. 3461-4, 3864-5

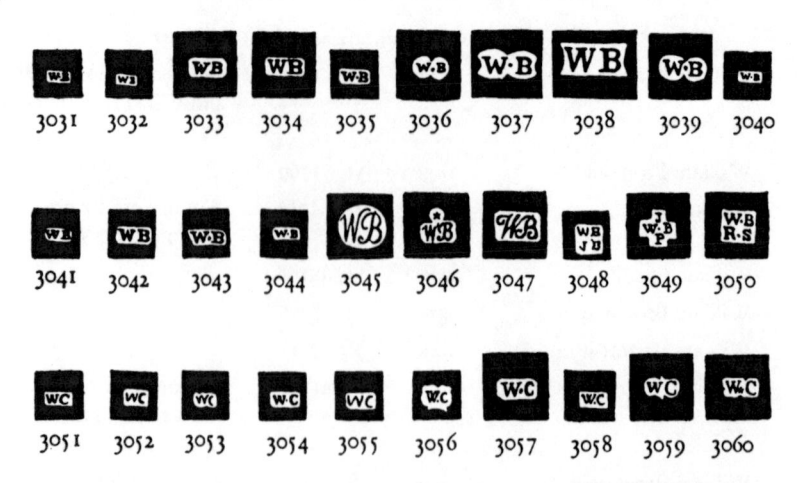

No.	Name	Category	Entered	Notes
3031	William Bryceson	smw	17.12.1796	Also incuse mark 30.12.1801
3032	William Barrott	smw	25.6.1807	
3033	William Barrett II	smw	17.2.1821	And another smaller similar same date. An earlier smaller similar mark 26.10.1812
3034	idem	plw	15.9.1828	And a smaller similar mark same date
3035	William Bruce	plw	18.6.1811	And a smaller similar mark same date
3036	William Burwash	plw	10.8.1812	And a slightly smaller similar mark same date. See also nos. 3047, 3050, 3866 and Section V, W.B, script
3037	William Bateman I	plw	15.2.1815	And three smaller similar marks same date
3038	William Bateman II	plw	9.2.1827	And three marks similar in smaller graduations same date. Another 22.5.1830
3039	William Brown	plw	24.1.1823	And a smaller similar mark same date
3040	William Bainbridge II	smw	8.12.1827	
3041	William Barber	spm	11.3.1828	
3042	William Boss	smw	20.6.1832	
3043	Walker Bluett	smw	6.9.1832	
3044	William Bain	smw	1.4.1837	
3045	William Bond	lgw	31.7.1753	See also no. 3049
3046	idem	lgw	idem	
3047	William Burwash	plw	23.4.1813	And a smaller similar mark same date. See also nos. 3036, 3866

LONDON GOLDSMITHS

No.	Name	Category	Entered	Notes
3048*	Wilkes and John Booth	smw	28.6.1810	Conjectural reading of almost illegible impression
3049	William Bond and James Phipps I	lgw	8.5.1754	See also nos. 1583, 3045-6
3050	William Burwash and Richard Sibley I	plw	7.10.1805	And a smaller similar mark same date
3051	Walter Crisp	smw	17.6.1730	
3052	William Cox I	smw	19.2.1739	
3053	William Cox II	smw	22.3.1763	See also Section VIII, W.C
3054	William Cox III	smw	20.3.1771	And a smaller mark without pellet 18.10.1784
3055	William Cowley	smw	18.12.1738	A poorly cut punch
3056	William Cripps	lgw	31.8.1743	
3057	idem	lgw	16.7.1746	
3058	idem	lgw	16.11.1751	
3059	William Caldecott	lgw	8.3.1756	
3060	William Chatterton	smw	7.4.1762	See also no. 3061

Also *WB* no. 3866; WB.IW no. 3465; WC nos. 3867-8

---

* No. 3048. Now established as WB over IB, as noted on a pair of snuffers.

WC   WD

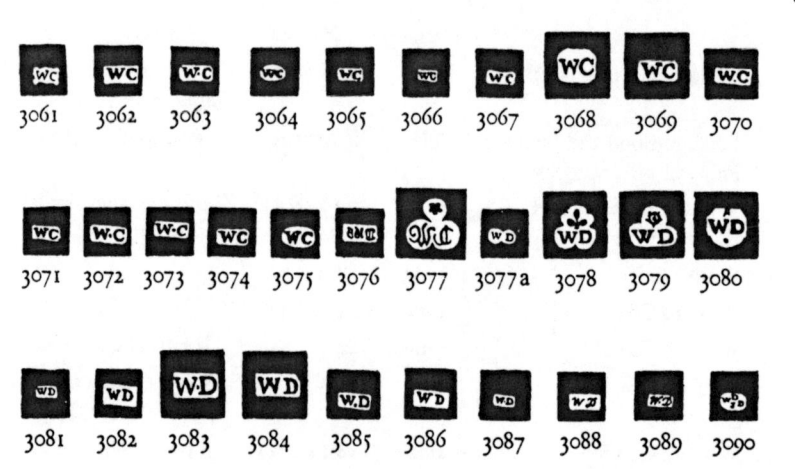

No.	Name	Category	Entered	Notes
3061	William Chatterton	smw	3.5.1763	Two other marks in oblong punches, one with pellet 14.12.1763, the other without 11.8.1766. See also no. 3060
3062	William Cattell	smw	2.2.1771	
3063	William Collings	smw	27.8.1771	
3064	William Champion	smw	22.4.1789	
3065	William Crowder	smw	11.3.1791	And a smaller similar mark same date. See also Section VIII, W.C
3066	Warner Cheesbrough	smw	14.8.1798	
3067	William Cartlidge	spm	9.10.1810	
3068	idem	spm	14.6.1827	And a mark in oblong cut-corner punch 29.6.1827
3069	William Chawner II	spm	9.2.1815	And a smaller similar mark same date and another 1819. See also no. 3868
3070	idem	spm	27.1.1820	And other marks similar 1821 and 1823. Another in cut-corner punch 1833
3071	William Capon	smw	9.6.1820	
3072	William Chinnery	plw	13.7.1825	
3073	William Collins	plw	4.3.1828	
3074	William Cooper	plw	11.11.1833	And a smaller similar mark same date. Other marks in circle 1844–5. Also large incuse initials 12.12.1823
3075	William Chandless	spm	8.9.1832	And a smaller similar mark same date. Other marks in lobed punches 1841 and 1851

LONDON GOLDSMITHS

No.	Name	Category	Entered	Notes
3076	William Coles	smw	5.8.1724	And incuse WC same date
3077	William Cafe	lgw	16.8.1757	And a smaller similar mark same date
3077a	William Dicker	smw	15.4.1720	See also no. 475
3078	William Darker	lgw	12.8.1720	And a similar mark 23.6.1724
3079	idem	lgw	1.4.1731	See also no. 441
3080	Wescombe Drake	lgw	undated	Between 1725 and April 1731
3081	William Deards	smw	23.11.1726	And a smaller similar mark same date
3082	William Dorrell	smw	11.2.1736	
3083	idem	smw	1.11.1764	Other marks similar 28.4.1762 and 3.5.1763
3084	William Day	smw	30.10.1759	Poor impression. See also Section VI, W.D
3085	William Downes	smw	16.1.1768	Poor impression. Pellet uncertain. Other marks 28.7.1768 and 8.11.1769. See also no. 3089
3086	William Dawson	smw	3.3.1768	See also Section V, E.D and W.D
3087	William Duncan	smw	20.1.1826	
3088	William Dean	smw	21.3.1765	
3089	William Downes	smw	12.3.1770	See also no. 3085
3090	John and William Deane	smw	6.8.1759	Poor impression. ?I or J at base. See also nos. 520 and 1797

Also WC.TC no. 3869

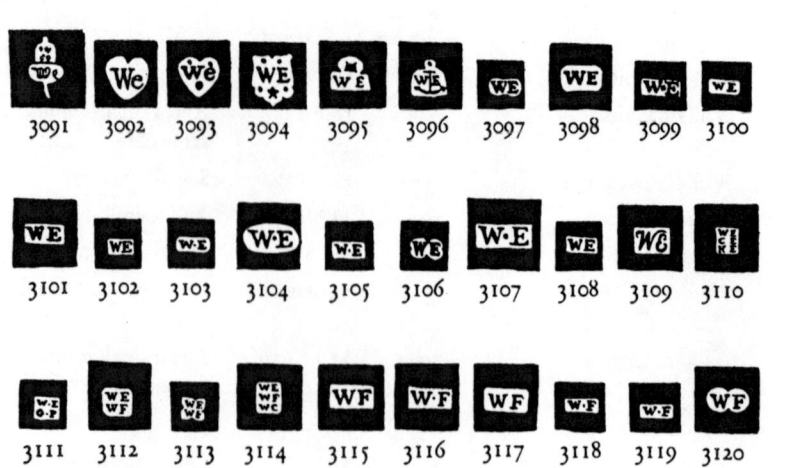

No.	Name	Category	Entered	Notes
3091	Henry Weever	smw	10.4.1701	
3092	Samuel Welder	lgw	11.8.1714	See also nos. 2654–5, 3802–3, 3870
3093	idem	lgw	30.9.1717	
3094	Mathew West	lgw	April 1697	
3095	Francis Wells	smw	19.8.1702	
3096	James Wethered	lgw	24.9.1709	Poor impression. Initials very weak
3097	John Wells	smw	29.11.1718	
3098	George Weir	lgw	27.7.1727	See also no. 920
3099	William J. Edwards	gw	13.1.1778	And a slightly smaller mark in oval and third very small in oblong, same date. Also very small mark 10.12.1774
3100	William Edwards	smw	11.12.1800	Another mark 22.9.1809. Another slightly larger with pellet 11.4.1823
3101	William Eley I	smw	3.11.1778	And a smaller similar mark 1.12.1778. See also nos. 3111–12, 3114, 3871 and Section VIII, W.E
3102	William Eley II	plw	20.6.1826	See also nos. 3109–10, 3113
3103	William Ellerby	smw	15.6.1802	And a smaller similar mark without pellet 9.4.1804
3104	idem	smw	13.8.1810	And a smaller similar mark same date

LONDON GOLDSMITHS

No.	Name	Category	Entered	Notes
3105	William Eaton	plw	18.5.1813	And a smaller similar mark without pellet same date. Another with pellet at base between initials 5.3.1824. Two others of varying size without pellet Oct. and Dec. 1825. See also Section VIII, W.E
3106	idem	plw	5.9.1828	And twelve other similar marks 1828, 1830, 1834, 1836, 1837 and 1840
3107	William Elliott	plw	7.9.1813	And a smaller similar mark same date
3108	William Esterbrook	spm	4.11.1817	And a similar mark 15.10.1824. Another with pellet 16.9.1834
3109	William Eley II	plw	19.1.1825	And two other smaller similar marks same date. See also nos. 3102, 3110, 3113
3110	William (II), Charles and Henry Eley	plw	14.7.1824	
3111	William Eley I and George Pierrepont	spm	11.11.1777	
3112	William Eley I and William Fearn	plw	4.1.1797	And a smaller similar mark same date and 29.1.1802. Two others as spoonmakers 6.10.1814
3113	William Eley II and William Fearn	plw	14.5.1824	
3114	William Eley I, William Fearn and William Chawner II	spm	10.4.1808	See also no. 3868
3115	William Flint	smw	21.6.1768	
3116	William Fearn	smw	-.4.1769	
3117	idem	spm	13.5.1774	
3118	William Lewis Foster	plw	31.1.1775	See also no. 3875
3119	William Frisbee	plw	11.1.1792	
3120	idem	plw	23.6.1798	And a smaller similar mark same date. See also no. 3121 and for comparison 3122

Also We no. 3870; WE no. 3871; WEH no. 3872; WF 3873-5

WF   WG

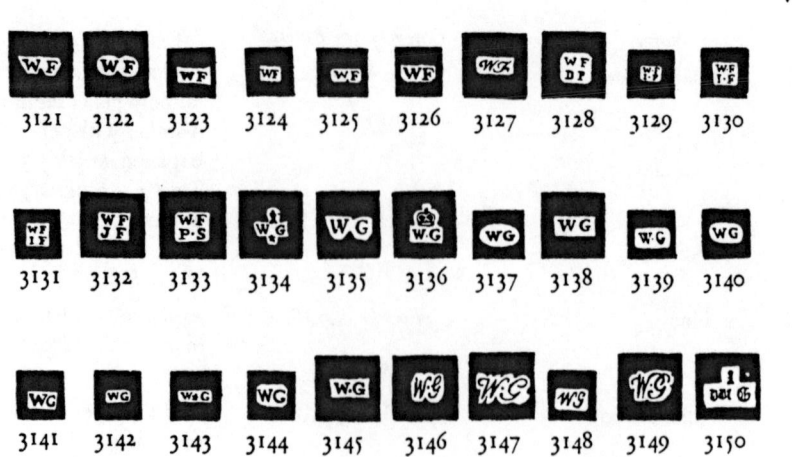

No.	Name	Category	Entered	Notes
3121	William Frisbee	plw	2.6.1801	And a smaller similar mark same date. See preceding no.
3122	William Fountain	plw	1.9.1794	And a smaller similar mark same date. See for comparison no. 3120. Also no. 3217
3123	idem	plw	5.2.1821	
3124	William Fisher	smw	10.11.1796	See also no. 3129–30
3125	William Furze	smw	23.11.1796	
3126	William Fell	smw	22.12.1818	And a smaller mark 27.11.1821
3127	William Fountain	plw	30.6.1798	And a slightly smaller mark same date. See also nos. 3122–3
3128	William Fountain and Daniel Pontifex	plw	29.7.1791	
3129	William and John Fisher	plw	16.8.1793	See also nos. 1301, 3124
3130	idem	spm	31.8.1797	
3131	William and John Frisbee	plw	11.5.1814	
3132	idem	plw	10.9.1811	
3133	William Frisbee and Paul Storr	plw	2.5.1792	And a smaller similar mark same date
3134	William Gould	lgw	20.10.1732	See also nos. 868, 3149–50
3135	idem	lgw	1.6.1748	Outline of punch uncertain
3136	William Gough	smw	14.11.1733	See also no. 3880
3137	William Garrard	lgw	1.4.1735	See also no. 3151
3138	idem	lgw	26.5.1749	
3139	idem	lgw	10.10.1755	
3140	William Gwillim	lgw	6.5.1740	See also no. 2152

LONDON GOLDSMITHS

No.	Name	Category	Entered	Notes
3141	William Goslee	smw	15.3.1771	
3142	William Godfrey	smw	8.1.1772	
3143	William Graham	smw	16.7.1795	
3144	W. Gardener	smw	11.3.1811	
3145	William Galloway	plw	28.7.1823	
3146	William Grundy	lgw	23.12.1743	And a similar mark 30.6.1748
3147	idem	lgw	24.6.1748	And a smaller similar mark same date
3148	idem	plw	20.9.1777	
3149	William Gould	lgw	24.9.1753	See also nos. 868, 3134–5
3150	idem	lgw	15.6.1739	

Also *WF* no. 3876; *WF* no. 3877; WF.IK no. 3878; WF.WO no. 3466; WG nos. 3879–80

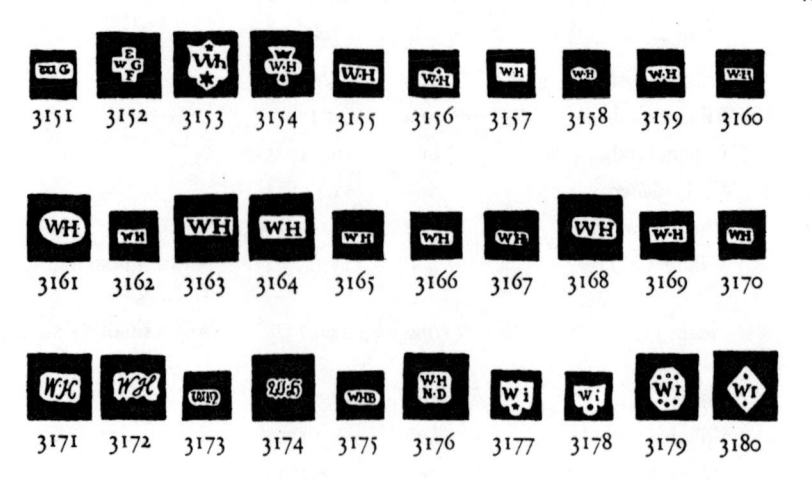

No.	Name	Category	Entered	Notes
3151	William Garrard	lgw	21.6.1739	See also nos. 3137–9
3152	William Grundy and Edward Fernell	plw	23.2.1779	See also nos. 579–82
3153	John White	lgw	10.12.1719	See also nos. 1735, 1751, 3881–2
3154	William Hudson	smw	22.4.1723	
3155	William Hopkins	smw	10.10.1723	And a very small similar mark 25.5.1739
3156	William Hutchinson II	smw	18.8.1736	See also nos. 1073, 3884
3157	William Hunter I	lgw	6.8.1756	See also nos. 3172, 3885
3158	William Harrison I	smw	18.7.1758	See also Section VIII, WH, pellet between
3159	idem	smw	20.5.1767	
3160	William How	smw	7.8.1771	
3161	William Holmes	plw	2.1.1776	A very similar mark probably entered about 1765 has been found on coffee-pots, tureens and dishes of 1767–71. See also nos. 3176, 3526
3162	idem	plw	21.3.1792	
3163	William Hall	plw	27.1.1795	And a smaller similar mark same date. See also no. 3872
3164	William Hunter (?II)	smw	15.3.1798	
3165	idem	smw	1.9.1824	Other marks with pellet between 1834 and 1839. Without pellet 1839–42
3166	William Hitchin	smw	20.8.1801	And a smaller similar mark 15.2.1825
3167	William Harrison II	smw	2.6.1810	Also incuse WH 1.2.1804

LONDON GOLDSMITHS

No.	Name	Category	Entered	Notes
3168	William Hattersley	plw	7.8.1828	
3169	William Hewitt	smw	24.2.1829	And a similar mark in oval punch 29.1.1834. Also Gothic initials 28.4.1843
3170	William Horton	smw	29.8.1837	
3171	William Homer	lgw	8.8.1750	And a smaller similar mark same date
3172	William Hunter I	lgw	28.7.1755	See also nos. 3157, 3885
3173	William Howes	smw	16.5.1732	
3174	William Howard	smw	19.8.1760	See also Section V, W.H
3175	W. H. Botwyle	smw	31.8.1772	
3176	William Holmes and Nicholas Dumée	plw	8.9.1773	See also nos. 3161-2, 3526
3177	Grace Winne	smw	13.2.1702	
3178	William Wildman	plw	15.4.1712	
3179	Edward Wimans	lgw	April 1697	
3180	Widow of above	lgw	undated	Subsequent to above

Also Wh no. 3881; WH nos. 3882-3, 3885, 3887; *WH* no. 3884; W. Hunt no. 3886

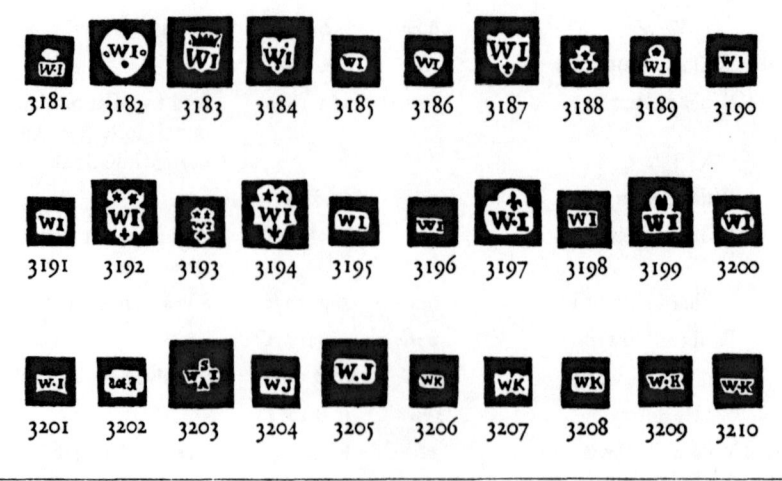

No.	Name	Category	Entered	Notes
3181	John Wilkins	smw	undated	c. 1699. Crudely cut punch. Upper part uncertain
3182	Charles Williams	lgw	April 1697	
3183	idem	lgw	idem	
3184	idem	lgw	idem	
3185	Joseph Wilcocke	smw	20.6.1701	
3186	Micah Wilkins	smw	16.3.1702	
3187	John Wisdome	lgw	17.6.1704	And a similar mark 7.8.1717
3188	Richard Williams	lgw	11.4.1712	
3189	George Willcocks	smw	2.5.1715	See also no. 919
3190	John Wildbore	diamond cutter	14.9.1715	
3191	Starling Wilford	lgw	17.1.1718	See also nos. 2652-3
3192	David Willaume I	lgw	April 1697	See also no. 512
3193	idem	lgw	idem	
3194	idem	lgw	29.1.1719	
3195	David Willaume II	lgw	2.4.1728	See also nos. 514, 517
3196	William Jelf	smw	27.7.1720	See also no. 1261
3197	George Wickes	lgw	3.2.1722	See also nos. 918, 921, 927
3198	James Wilks	lgw	31.12.1722	See also no. 1734
3199	Robert Williams	lgw	2.10.1726	See also no. 2456
3200	William Justis	lgw	undated	Between April 1731 and Jan. 1733. See also nos. 3202, 3888-9
3201	William Jury	smw	15.10.1760	
3202	William Justis	lgw	28.6.1739	See also nos. 3200, 3888-9

LONDON GOLDSMITHS

No.	Name	Category	Entered	Notes
3203	William Jury and Stephen Adams I	smw	29.10.1759	And another smaller similar mark same date. See also no. 2472
3204	William Johnson	spm	9.12.1822	And a similar mark 30.5.1835
3205	Walter Jorden	plw	29.3.1834	And a smaller similar mark same date
3206	William Kirk	smw	26.4.1733	
3207	William Kidney	lgw	7.6.1734	See also nos. 3216-7
3208	William Kersill	lgw	21.8.1749	
3209	idem	lgw	2.7.1757	
3210	William Kinman	smw	31.1.1759	

Also WI nos. 3888-9; *WI* no. 3890

No.	Name	Category	Entered	Notes
3211	W. King	smw	30.10.1761	Also incuse mark 21.10.1761
3212	William Key	smw	1.12.1783	
3213	William Kingdon	plw	9.7.1811	
3214	William Knight II	plw	8.2.1816	Other marks similar various sizes 1830 and 1839. See also no. 3218
3215	William King	plw	23.11.1826	
3216	William Kidney	lgw	15.6.1739	See also no. 3207
3217	idem	lgw	idem	
3217a	William Ker Reid	plw	3.5.1828	And two other smaller similar marks same date. See also no. 3286
3218	William (II) and Samuel Knight	smw	24.1.1810	See above no. 3214
3219	William Looker	lgw	6.7.1720	See also nos. 1952, 3891
3220	William Lukin I	lgw	10.6.1725	See also no. 1966
3221	Whitton Lawley	smw	1.7.1729	
3222	William Leaser	smw	26.5.1738	
3223	William London	smw	4.5.1761	And a similar mark 8.2.1762. See also no. 3230
3224	William Lilley	smw	30.9.1765	See also no. 3231
3225	William Lord	smw	6.2.1770	Also incuse mark 3.4.1770
3226	William Lancester	smw	18.8.1770	
3227	William Lestourgeon	smw	26.6.1771	See also no. 63
3228	William Lewis	smw	18.12.1783	See also Sections V and VI, W.L
3229	William Laver	plw	7.8.1789	

228

LONDON GOLDSMITHS

No.	Name	Category	Entered	Notes
3230	William London	smw	7.12.1762	See also no. 3223. Another mark perhaps without W 26.7.1765
3230a	William Le Bas	slm	2.11.1773	Also incuse mark Section V
3231	William Lilley	smw	13.8.1765	See also no. 3224
3232	William Mathew II	lgw	20.6.1720	
3233	idem	lgw	17.3.1712	A rare occurrence of Christian initial over New Std. maker's mark
3234	William Matthews	lgw	undated	Between 18.6.1728 and 24.2.1729
3235	William Moody	lgw	27.8.1756	
3236	William Maddocks	smw	16.2.1765	See also Section V, W.M
3237	William Mott	smw	6.8.1802	
3238	William Moore	spm	25.4.1827	
3239	Walter Morisse	smw	15.8.1831	And two other marks with pellet between 2.5.1843
3240	William Mackenzie	plw	29.2.1748	

Also WL nos. 3891–3; WM no. 3844

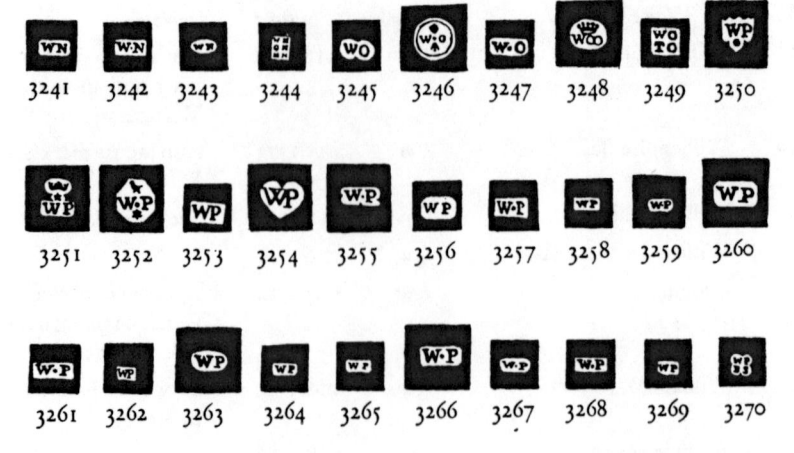

No.	Name	Category	Entered	Notes
3241	William Nixon	spm	11.6.1817	And a smaller mark 6.10.1817. Another 12.10.1821
3242	William Nickolds	plw	2.5.1827	And a smaller similar mark same date
3243	William Neal	plw	23.5.1829	And other marks similar 1845–60
3244	William, George and Martin Nangle	spm	14.9.1816	
3245	William Overton	smw	22.6.1720	See also no. 2113
3246	Edward Wood	lgw	18.8.1722	See also nos. 651–2, 655
3247	William Owen	lgw	14.3.1724	Same mark also struck in smallworkers' book. See also no. 2112
3248	Richard Woodhouse	smw	15.10.1725	
3249	William and Thomas Orme	smw	21.4.1784	
3250	William Paradise	lgw	24.6.1720	See also no. 2119
3251	William Petley	lgw	24.6.1720	See also nos. 2170a, 2174
3252	William Pearson	lgw	24.1.1721	See also nos. 2165–8
3253	William Phelps	smw	10.8.1738	
3254	William Peaston	lgw	8.1.1746	Also traces of two other marks, one in quatrefoil punch, the other oval, but both indecipherable. See also nos. 3275, 3897
3255	William Plummer	lgw	8.4.1755	And other similar marks 17.3.1774 and 7.5.1789
3256	William Portal	smw	7.9.1760	And a small mark 11.8.1760 (?). Another medium mark in oblong punch 21.4.1764. See also no. 1458

LONDON GOLDSMITHS

No.	Name	Category	Entered	Notes
3257	William Pickett	smw	16.1.1769	Slightly distorted impression
3258	William Pinder	smw	3.2.1770	And a slightly larger similar mark 30.5.1771. See also Section VIII, W.P
3259	William Peavey	smw	13.2.1773	
3260*	William Penstone III	spm	17.3.1774	
3261	William Potter	spm	26.2.1777	
3262	William Purrier	smw	27.10.1778	
3263	William Pitts	plw	18.12.1781	And other similar marks 4.5.1786, 21.12.1799 and 5.3.1806
3264	William Parkyns	smw	22.8.1792	See also no. 3269
3265	William Parker	smw	22.11.1798	
3266	idem	smw	25.6.1803	
3267	William Penn	smw	5.5.1801	
3268	William Price	smw	17.3.1812	
3269	William Parkin	plw	26.5.1824	See also no. 3264
3270	William Parker and Benjamin Simpson	smw	8.4.1799	And a smaller similar mark same date

Also WP no. 3895; WP no. 3896

---

* This mark has been found on a spoon of 1772 (Goldsmiths' Company).

WP   WS

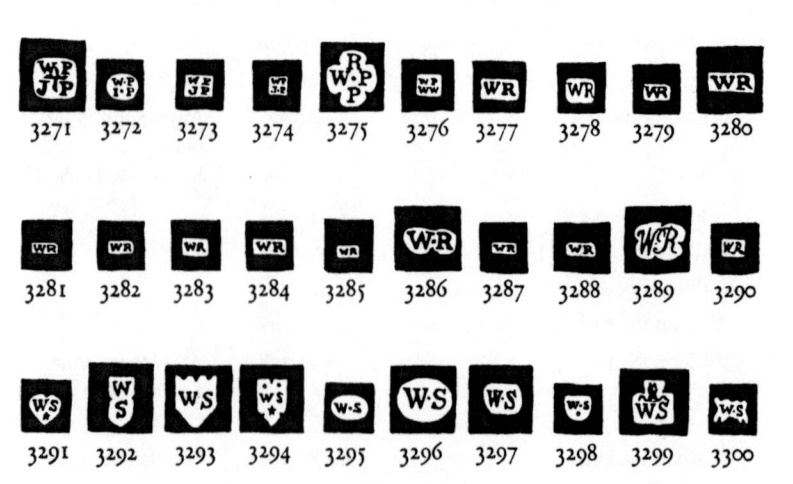

No.	Name	Category	Entered	Notes
3271	William and James Priest	lgw	by 1768	Not in register. Mark taken from tankard 1768
3272	William Pitts and Joseph Preedy	plw	11.1.1791	And a smaller similar mark same date
3273	William and Joseph Price	smw	28.1.1820	
3274	William and John Pike	plw	10.3.1824	
3275	William and Robert Peaston	lgw	12.7.1756	See also nos. 3254, 3782, 3784, 3897
3276	William Playfair and William Wilson	spm	16.5.1782	
3277	William Reeve(s?)	lgw	14.5.1731	
3278	William Reynolds(on?)	lgw	12.10.1757	See also no. 3899
3279	W(illiam) Rawle	smw	11.5.1769	See also Section IX, W.R
3280	William Roper	smw	13.10.1770	
3281	William Ralph	smw	26.8.1772	
3282	William Riccard	smw	18.11.1775	And a similar mark 8.3.1781
3283	William Rudkins	smw	12.3.1789	
3284	idem	smw	16.1.1796	And a similar mark 31.3.1797
3285	William Robson	smw	17.6.1822	Also incuse mark 23.7.1819
3286	William Ker Reid	plw	8.11.1825	And a smaller similar mark same date. See also no. 3217a
3287	W. Roberts	smw	20.3.1830	
3288	William Ripsher	smw	27.8.1834	And a larger mark, pellet between 27.4.1849
3289	William Robertson	lgw	3.10.1753	
3290	idem	lgw	23.9.1755	'Small mark'
3291	William Street	lgw	23.6.1720	See also no. 2642

LONDON GOLDSMITHS

No.	Name	Category	Entered	Notes
3292	William Scarlett	*lgw*	29.6.1720	And other marks similar 25.9.1722 and 18.10.1725. See also no. 2484
3293	idem	*lgw*	18.10.1725	
3294	William Spackman	*lgw*	14.7.1720	And a similar mark *c*. 1724. See also no. 2609
3295	William Soame	*lgw*	19.1.1723	See also nos. 2599, 3328
3296	idem	*lgw*	23.8.1732	
3297	idem	*lgw*	11.2.1739	
3298	William Strange	*smw*	9.6.1725	'Cutler'
3299	William Shaw I	*lgw*	16.1.1728	See also nos. 2530, 3329
3300	idem	*lgw*	24.4.1745	

Also WP.RP no. 3897; WR nos. 3898-9

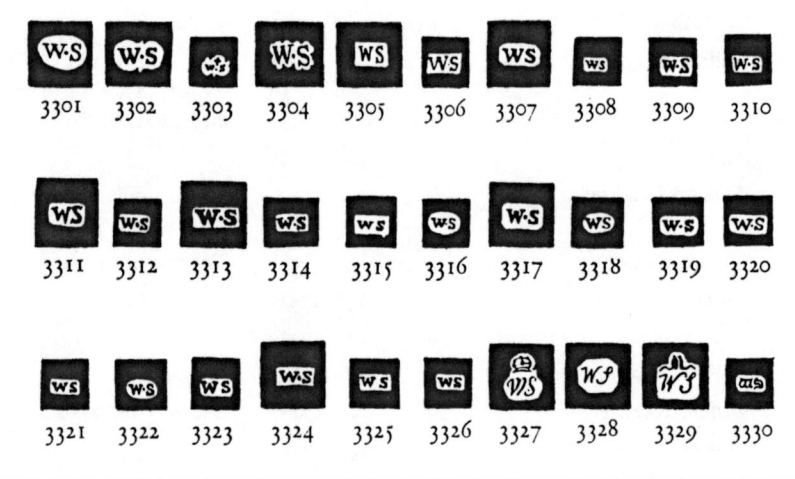

No.	Name	Category	Entered	Notes
3301	William Shaw II	lgw	3.1.1749	See also no. 3335
3302	William Solomon	lgw	19.10.1747	
3303	idem	lgw	idem	Small mark. And another similar 12.9.1751
3304	William Sanden	lgw	30.6.1755	
3305	William Sampel	lgw	29.8.1755	
3306	William Skeen	lgw	4.12.1755	Possibly distorted by position in book
3307	idem	plw	26.6.1775	And a similar mark 5.5.1783
3308	William Smith I	smw	28.10.1758	And a very small mark 25.9.1769
3309	idem	smw	12.6.1762	And a slightly smaller mark 30.10.1764. Another mark 13.7.1774
3310	William Sudell	smw	16.2.1767	And a smaller similar mark same date
3311	idem	smw	19.4.1774	Other marks smaller similar 16.11.1779 and 16.6.1788
3312	William Stephenson	smw	1.12.1775	Other marks similar 5.4.1780, 27.11.1781 and 23.6.1787
3313	idem	plw	17.6.1786	Other smaller similar marks 8.1.1790 and 17.12.1792
3314	William Simons	plw	18.1.1776	And a smaller mark without pellet 13.2.1776
3315	William Smith II	smw	10.6.1777	Apparently a separate maker from nos. 3308–9
3316	Wildman Smith	hfm	16.3.1781	
3317	William Sutton	plw	27.10.1784	And a smaller mark as smallworker 26.8.1784

LONDON GOLDSMITHS

No.	Name	Category	Entered	Notes
3318	William Sumner I	spm	14.12.1784	And other similar marks 9.5.1787, 7.6.1788, 15.10.1802 and 31.3.1803 (some with pellet). See also nos. 3331, 3334
3319	idem	spm	undated	After 7.6.1788
3320	William Sumner II	smw	12.5.1787	A separate maker from above
3321	William Stroud	plw	7.7.1788	See also no. 3332
3322	William Seaman	spm	29.2.1804	Other similar marks without pellet, larger and same size 15 and 18.10.1810, 1818, 1820
3323	William Southey	spm	3.2.1810	And a slightly smaller similar mark same date
3324	idem	spm	5.4.1821	And other similar marks without pellet, slightly smaller 2.1.1822 and 9.12.1825
3325	William Sharp	plw	31.3.1817	And a slightly larger mark with pellet 16.9.1824
3326	William Schofield	spm	10.11.1820	And a larger mark with pellet 17.5.1833
3327	William Swift	smw	21.4.1726	
3328	William Soame	lgw	20.6.1739	See also nos. 2599, 3295-7
3329	William Shaw I	lgw	24.6.1739	See also nos. 2530, 3299-300
3330	William Stocking	smw	21.2.1725	
·	Also WS no. 3467			

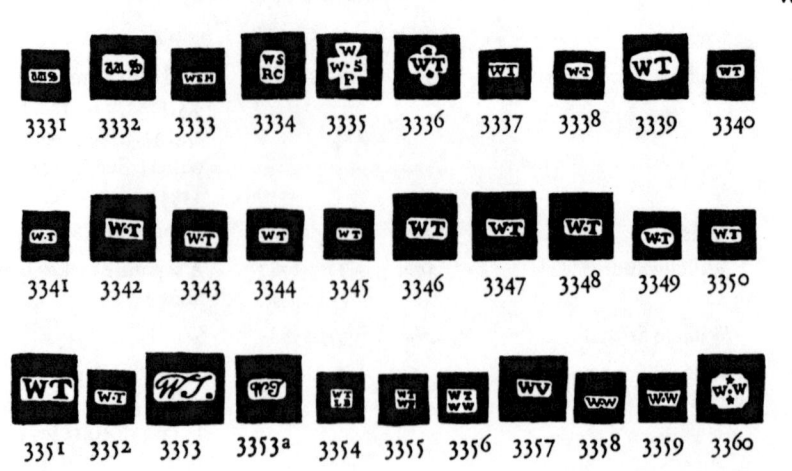

No.	Name	Category	Entered	Notes
3331	William Sumner I	plw	6.4.1782	See also nos. 3318-9
3332	William Stroud	plw	9.3.1821	Blurred impression somewhat conjectural. See also no. 3321
3333	William Snooke Hall	smw	21.3.1818	
3334	William Sumner I and Richard Crossley	plw	1.5.1775	And similar marks various sizes 27.1.1776, 10.5.1777, 27.1.1780
3335	William Shaw II and William Preist	lgw	12.10.1749	And a smaller similar mark same date. Another 27.6.1759
3336	William Toone	lgw	3.11.1725	See also no. 2863
3337	William Tey	smw	15.11.1725	
3338	William Trenholme	smw	23.10.(1730)	Year indistinct, perhaps 1731, 1732 or 1733. Very weak impression. Somewhat conjectural
3339	William Tuite	lgw	undated	Between Dec. 1755 and March 1758. See also nos. 3900-3
3340	William Taylor	smw	2.10.1764	See also Section VIII, W.T
3341	William Turton	smw	4.10.1773	And other similar marks without pellet 6.5.1782, 24.10.1783, 6.3.1791. See also no. 3356
3342	idem	smw	22.5.1780	
3343	Walter Tweedie	spm	7.12.1775	And other marks of two sizes similar without pellet as plateworker 25.9.1779. See also no. 3353a

LONDON GOLDSMITHS

No.	Name	Category	Entered	Notes
3344	William Thompson II*	smw	19.10.1802	And a similar mark 24.4.1804
3345	William Tanner	smw	26.9.1811	See also Section VII, W.T
3346	William Troby	plw	3.3.1812	And a smaller similar mark same date. Others similar in two sizes 18.7.1821
3347	William Traies	spm	4.6.1822	
3348	idem	spm	13.10.1823	And a smaller similar mark same date
3349	idem	spm	8.11.1824	And a small mark in oblong punch 25.8.1825
3350	William Theobalds	plw	14.1.1829	And a slightly smaller mark same date
3351	idem	plw	12.2.1835	And other marks of three sizes smaller, similar 27.2.1836
3352	William Treen	spm	11.1.1833	
3353	William Turner	lgw	21.6.1754	And two smaller similar marks same date. See also no. 3906
3353a	Walter Tweedie	spm	29.10.1781	And a smaller similar mark with mullet between same date. See also no. 3343
3354	William Theobalds and Lockington Bunn	plw } spm	30.6.1835	And a smaller similar mark same date
3355	William Thompson II and William Frost	plw	16.6.1818	
3356	William Turton and William Walbancke	smw	8.4.1784	And a smaller similar mark 26.6.1788. See also no. 3341
3357	William Vincent	lgw	not in register	Before 1773. Mark taken from tea-caddy 1783
3358	William Winne	smw	26.10.1720	See also Section V, WW, star above
3359	William Willson	smw	9.5.1726	
3360	William Woodward	lgw	20.8.1731	See also no. 3373

Also WT nos. 3469, 3900–4; *WY* nos. 3905–7; WV.IL no. 3908

---

* See Biographical section for probable William Thompson III.

WW   YO

No.	Name	Category	Entered	Notes
3361	William Woodcock	smw	7.1.1736	Month doubtful
3362	William Williams I	lgw	1.5.1740	Almost entirely conjectural. Mark much blurred. See also no. 2979
3363	idem	lgw	10.9.1742	
3364	William Wooller	lgw	14.5.1750	
3365	William Withers	smw	17.8.1762	
3366	William Worthington	smw	14.5.1771	And a similar mark without pellet 12.2.1772. See also Section VII, W.W
3367	William Williams II	smw	8.2.1797	See also nos. 3370, 3377
3368	William Weston	plw	18.9.1810	
3369	idem	spm	5.9.1822	
3370	Walter Williams II	plw	31.10.1815	And a smaller similar mark same date
3371	William Wheatcroft	smw	9.2.1831	
3372	William West	lgw	8.8.1738	
3373	William Woodward	lgw	19.10.1743	See also no. 3360
3374	William Watkins	lgw	9.2.1756	See also nos. 518, 2739, 3857, 3910
3375	William Winter	smw	25.1.1769	
3376	Walter Williams I	smw	7.10.1775	
3377	William (II) and John Williams	smw	14.4.1780	See no. 3367 and Section VIII, IW, pellet between
3378	William Young	lgw	31.3.1735	
3379	idem	lgw	29.6.1739	
3380	Daniel Yerbury	lgw	29.2.1716	
3381	Edward Yorke	lgw	3.7.1705	See also no. 657

Also *WW* no. 3909; *WWa* no. 3910

238

II
Registered Marks of Provincial Goldsmiths from the Goldsmiths' Hall Registers 1697-1837

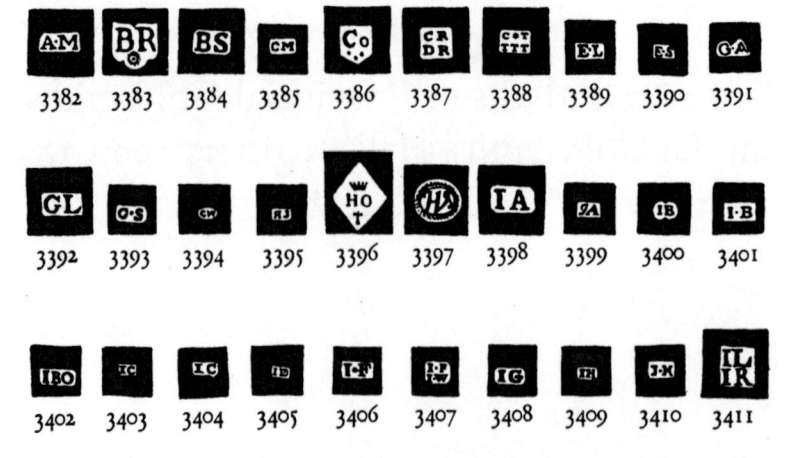

No.	Name	Category	Entered	Place and Notes
3382	Ann Miller	smw	16.1.1764	BRISTOL
3383	Edward Brockes	lgw	April 1697	DERBY
3384	Benjamin Swayne	smw	14.5.1781	DEVIZES. And a very small similar mark same date. See also Section VIII, F.S
3385	Charles Morgan	smw	9.2.1807	BRISTOL
3386	John Cove	lgw	4.1.1698	BRISTOL
3387	Christian Ker and David Reid	plw	10.10.1815	NEWCASTLE. And another smaller mark same date. Three others in quatrefoil shields 16.5.1828. Also CR only in small oblong punch 30.7.1817
3388	Charles and Thomas Terrett Taylor	plw	11.1.1837	BRISTOL
3389	Edward Lock	smw	30.7.1762	OXFORD. And a smaller similar mark same date
3390	Edward Stone	smw	1.7.1761	THAME
3391	George Andrews	smw	24.11.1737	LEICESTER. Poor impression. Somewhat conjectural
3392	George Lowe	smw	21.1.1791	CHESTER. And a smaller similar mark same date
3393	George Spender	smw	6.6.1763	BRADFORD, WILTS.
3394	George Washbourn	smw	7.4.1773	GLOUCESTER
3395	Hugh Jeboult	smw	25.5.1787	SALISBURY
3396	Frances Hoyte	lgw	April 1697	LITTLE RISENDON, GLOUCS. Somewhat light impression

PROVINCIAL GOLDSMITHS

No.	Name	Category	Entered	Place and Notes
3397	Richard Hutchinson I	lgw	13.12.1699	COLCHESTER. See also no. 3433
3398	Joseph Adams	smw	25.9.1772	WALSALL. See also Section VIII, I.A
3399	John Adams	smw	17.4.1787	EXETER
3400	John Brinds	smw	undated	NORFOLK. Nov./Dec. 1721
3401	John Brown	smw	23.7.1771	PLYMOUTH. See also Section VIII, IB, pellet between
3402	Joseph Boardman Orme	plw	14.2.1793	MANCHESTER
3403	John Chaldecott	smw	7.6.1769	CHICHESTER. And two smaller similar marks same date
3404	John Crowley Jr.	smw	24.8.1803	WOLVERHAMPTON
3405	Joseph Dickinson	smw	21.4.1780	GAINSBOROUGH
3406	John Farr	smw	3.1.1784	BRISTOL. Another very small mark 21.5.1791
3407	John Ford and John Williams	smw	6.5.1782	BATH. An earlier version in rectangular punch 10.3.1767
3408	John Grantham	smw	17.4.1771	NEWBURY. And a smaller similar mark same date
3409	John Harding	smw	5.4.1759	PORTSMOUTH
3410	John Hirst	smw	25.2.1765	FARFIELD, SHEFFIELD. And a similar mark 26.2.1770
3411	John Langlands and John Robertson	plw	3.3.1780	NEWCASTLE-ON-TYNE. And three smaller marks and one in single line same date

Note: Included in Section I are F. C. Francis Clark of Birmingham (no. 673); J. B. Joseph Bidwell of Norwich (no. 1786); J. H. John Herbert of Norwich (no. 1820). See also I. B. John Baxter of Banbury (no. 3619).

No.	Name	Category	Entered	Place and Notes
3412	John Powell	smw	12.11.1806	BRISTOL
3413	John Powell and Thomas Williamson	smw	8.10.1802	BRISTOL
3414	John Rowbotham	smw	14.12.1768	SHEFFIELD
3415	James Thorn	smw	20.9.1758	COLCHESTER. And a smaller similar mark same date
3416	John Townsend	plw	10.9.1783	BATH. And two other smaller similar marks same date
3417	John Thompson	plw	12.5.1785	SUNDERLAND. And a smaller similar mark same date
3418	James Welshman	plw	22.7.1813	BATH. Other marks similar 1819, 1822 and 1823
3419	James Bottle	plw	16.1.1819	BATH. And a smaller similar mark same date
3420	John Coakley	plw	3.9.1832	LIVERPOOL
3421*	Joseph Dallinger	plw	2.5.1828	IPSWICH. And a smaller mark in octagonal punch 15.5.1824
3422	Joshua French	smw	8.6.1763	BRISTOL. See also no. 3635
3423	John Smith	smw	25.2.1762	BIRMINGHAM
3424	James Sharp	plw	3.12.1817	NORTHAMPTON. And a smaller similar mark same date
3425	Jacob Willis	smw	7.4.1792	FROME

* The address for this mark entered as Norwich, the 1824 mark as Ipswich. See page 721.

PROVINCIAL GOLDSMITHS

No.	Name	Category	Entered	Place and Notes
3426	Joseph Walker	plw	24.12.1823	BIRMINGHAM. And a smaller similar mark 27.6.1823
3427	Lionel Bretton	plw	18.11.1784	BATH
3428	Phineas Daniell	smw	6.6.1790	BRISTOL
3429	Peter Merrett	smw	28.1.1793	BATH. And a smaller similar mark same date
3430	Richard Evans	smw	3.5.1779	SHREWSBURY. And a smaller mark at Birmingham 1.6.1787
3431	Richard Goldwire	smw	28.3.1753	OXFORD. Weak impression
3432	idem	smw	15.9.1763	OXFORD. See also no. 3770
3433	Richard Hutchinson II	lgw	28.6.1727	COLCHESTER. See also no. 3397
3434	Richard Hoskins	smw	6.5.1791	BRISTOL
3435	Richard Menefy	spm	28.11.1793	ANDOVER
3436	Richard Woods	smw	14.3.1822	NORWICH
3437	Samuel Harwood	spm	25.4.1836	SHEFFIELD
3438	Thomas Burrough	smw	26.5.1759	DEVIZES. And two other marks similar Oct. 1769. Other marks very small with Roman letters Nov. 1769 and Feb. 1778
3439	Thomas Cater	smw	13.6.1764	BIRMINGHAM. And a similar mark in serrated punch same date
3440	idem	smw	2.11.1765	idem
3441	Thomas Doncaster	smw	5.9.1758	WIGAN

Note: Included in Section I are L. S. Lewis Samuel of Liverpool (no. 1965); RWN. Ridgeway William Newland of Farnham, Surrey (no. 2463); SB. Samuel Baker of Chatham (no. 2477); $^{SD}_{JL}$ Samuel Delany and John Lee of Bristol (no. 2505).

No.	Name	Category	Entered	Place and Notes
3442	Thomas Eustace	plw	20.4.1779	EXETER. And a smaller similar mark same date
3443	Thomas Green	smw	17.3.1766	BIRMINGHAM
3444	Thomas Graham	plw	14.5.1792	BATH. And a slightly smaller similar mark same date
3445	Thomas Graham and Jacob Willis	plw	29.6.1789	BATH. And a similar smaller mark same date
3446	Thomas Howell	plw	27.5.1784	BATH
3447	idem	plw	11.6.1791	BATH. And a smaller similar mark same date. Two other marks 26.7.1792
3448	Thomas Lovidge	gw	12.:.1778	NEWBURY, BERKS. And a much smaller similar mark same date. See also no. 3844 and Section VII, T.L
3449	Thomas Mitchell, James Burden and Thomas Merrifield	plw	21.2.1831	BATH
3450	Thomas Ollivant	plw	12.5.1789	MANCHESTER
3451	Thomas Ollivant ?II	plw	3.11.1830	idem
3452	Thomas Peirce	smw	21.8.1765	BRISTOL. And a smaller similar mark 8.11.1763
3453	Thomas Pemberton and Robert Mitchell	smw	21.7.1813	BIRMINGHAM. See also Section VII, T.P
3454	William Truss	lgw	22.9.1721	READING. See also nos. 2896, 3468
3455	Thomas Spackman	smw	1.11.1725	MARLBOROUGH
3456	Thomas Tyas Jr.	smw	18.5.1769	SHEFFIELD

PROVINCIAL GOLDSMITHS

No.	Name	Category	Entered	Place sand Notes
3457	Thomas Wynne	lgw	18.10.1754	BATH. And a smaller similar mark same date
3458	Thomas Willmore	plw	23.3.1790	BIRMINGHAM
3459	Thomas Wigan	smw	11.7.1763	BRISTOL
3460	Samuel Urling	lgw	30.9.1701	CAMBRIDGE. And a smaller mark same date
3461	William Brimblecome	smw	11.6.1762	BRISTOL
3462	William Basnett	plw	3.9.1784	BATH
3463	idem	plw	idem	BATH
3464	William Bottle	plw	6.3.1800	BATH. And a smaller similar mark same date
3465	William Bottle and Jeremiah Willsher	plw	27.10.1796	BATH. And a smaller similar mark same date
3466	W. Folgate and William Osborne	plw	18.11.1825	NORWICH. And another mark with initials in one line same date
3467	William Sloden	smw	6.10.1764	BRISTOL
3468	William Truss	lgw	22.9.1721	READING. See also nos. 2896, 3454
3469	William Townsend	plw	7.9.1774	BATH

III
Unregistered Marks with Tentative Attributions

The marks in this Section are taken from two sources, distinguishable by their different presentation:

(i) Marks from Sir Charles Jackson's *English Goldsmiths and their Marks*, second edition, 1921, either with tentative attributions or as 'name not traced'. These marks, shown as in the above work with white letters in black punches, are reproduced by kind permission of the Trustees of the late Sir Charles Jackson through Mrs. G. E. P. How.

(ii) Marks, otherwise unmet with, collected since 1932 firstly by Mr. Charles Brockle-hurst and subsequently by the author, reproduced, as in the preceding sections, with black letters on white punches defined by black surrounds. These marks, having been noted freehand over a long period by two hands, are not to scale and should be regarded as diagrammatic rather than factual representations.

Note: The abbreviation 'PR. list' in the Notes column refers to the list of goldsmiths incorporated in the Parliamentary Report of 1773. In the Attribution column the phrase 'not traced' is quoted from Jackson's entries. 'Unidentified' is used for the marks new to this work.

AB   CC

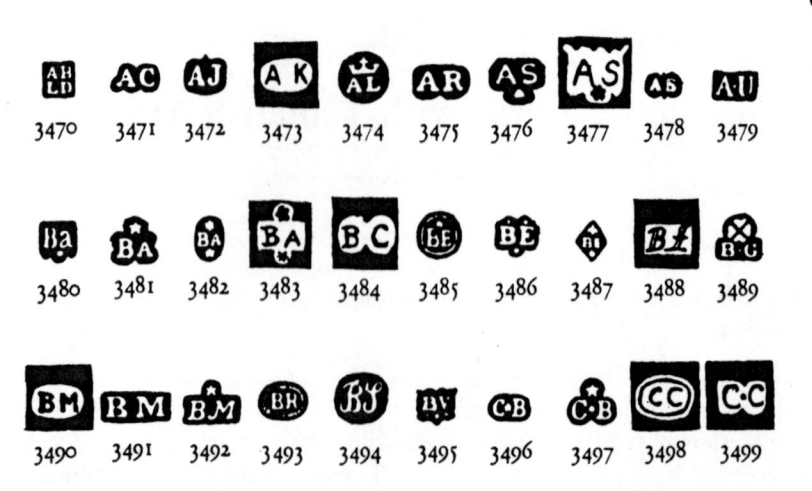

3470	3471	3472	3473	3474	3475	3476	3477	3478	3479
3480	3481	3482	3483	3484	3485	3486	3487	3488	3489
3490	3491	3492	3493	3494	3495	3496	3497	3498	3499

No.	Attribution, if any	Object bearing mark	Date	Notes
3470	Abraham Barrier and Lewis Ducommieu	spoon	1773	PR. list 'Ducommon'. See also no. 1911
3471	James Anthony Calame	candlesticks	1764	Two incuse marks only in register. See also no. 3613 and Section V
3472	not traced	milk-jug	1803	A mark of somewhat doubtful authenticity in appearance
3473	Abstainando King	mustard-pot 1798; salts 1802; sauce-tureens 1802; sugar-basin 1810	1798–1810	Cf. no. 49. Originally registered as snuffermaker
3474	Augustin Le Sage	tea-caddy	1769	Alternative attribution Aaron Le Stourgeon, see nos. 57–9
3475	Andrew Raven	teapot	1727	Cf. nos. 2248–9. Or possibly Abraham Robert, small-worker ent. 1727
3476	Thomas Ash	spoon	1697	Doubtful attribution. Evidence is that Ash was specialist candlestickmaker
3477	idem	candlestick	1706	
3478	Albert Schurman	sugar-tongs		Cf. no. 91. Doubtful attribution due to absence of date-letter on piece quoted
3479	A. Underwood	inkstand	1771	Only John U. in PR. list
3480	not traced (perhaps John Barnard I)	tobacco-box	1697	Cf. no. 112
3481	Joseph Barbitt (correctly Barbut)	spirit-lamp	1711	Attribution doubtful. Cf. no. 119. More likely Richard Bayley

UNREGISTERED MARKS

No.	Attribution, if any	Object bearing mark	Date	Notes
3482	John Bathe (correctly Bache)	communion paten, plate	1711 1713	Cf. no. 118
3483	John Bache	trencher-salts	no date	
3484	unidentified	brandy-saucepan	1734	Cf. nos. 139, 140 of later date
3485	Benjamin Bentley	spoon	1698	Cf. no. 155
3486	George Beale	strainer	1718	Cf. nos. 153, 156
3487	not traced	snuffbox	1727	Cf. no. 167 Blanche Fraillon
3488	unidentified	tablespoons	1750	?BF or BL
3489	Benjamin Gignac	communion cups	1770	Cf. no. 172
3490	? Benjamin Mordecai entered 1770, or Benjamin Mountigue entered 1771	salt-cellars	1767	Cf. nos. 190, 191
3491	not traced	tankard	1784	Possibly connected with no. 3490
3492	not traced	water-jug	1764	
3493	Thomas Brydon	tankard	1697	But cf. no. 207
3494	Benjamin Sanders	flagon	1743	Cf. nos. 225, 235
3495	William Bull	caster	1697	Cf. no. 246
3496	not traced	waiters, flagon	1758	No obvious attribution
3497	not traced	candlesticks	1767	No obvious attribution
3498	unidentified	sugar-bowl	1732	No obvious attribution
3499	unidentified	inkstand	1797	Cf. Catherine Clarke no. 287

CD   EA

No.	Attribution, if any	Object bearing mark	Date	Notes
3500	not traced	sugar-caster	1760	Description of piece as given by Jackson suggests a forgery and mark suspect
3501	unidentified	tea-service	1831 and 1834	
3502	unidentified	taperstick	1737	
3503	unidentified	inkstand, double sauce-boats	1764	Cf. Charles Hougham, nos. 327-8 ent. 1769
3504	not traced	sugar-basket	1764	Cf. Christopher Makemeid no. 361
3505	unidentified	snuffbox	1795	
3506	unidentified	mounts of shagreen caddy-case	(1756)	Tea-caddies of 1756 within
3507	Henry Collins	tankard	1698	But cf. no. 380, Robert Cooper
3508	not traced	sugar-caster	1714	
3509	? Peter Courtauld	pair of tapersticks	1718	Cf. no. 391 but not entered till 1721
3510	? Thomas Whipham and Charles Wright	soup-ladle	1764	Almost certainly correctly Thos. and William (I) Chawner. Cf. nos. 3816-7
3511	? Charles Wright	cup and tankard tea-urn	1768 1769	Cf. nos. 428, 2976
3512	Isaac Dalton	tablespoon	1711	Cf. nos. 438-9
3513	? Daniel Denney	dessertspoon	c. 1780	Cf. no. 456
3514*	David Field	nutmeg-grater caster muffineer	(1740) 1742 1743	

* See page 748.

250

UNREGISTERED MARKS

No.	Attribution, if any	Object bearing mark	Date	Notes
3515	unidentified	copy of Chinese libation cup	1797	
3516	unidentified	waiter	1739	
3516a	unidentified	jug	1765	Cf. Dike Impey, nos 478–9
3517	? David Kilmaine	alms-dish	1720	Untraced by Jackson. Cf. no. 1876
3518	? Dennis Langton	waiters	1732 and 1735	Untraced by Jackson. Cf. nos. 480, 483
3519	Dorothy Mills and Thomas Sarbitt	salt-cellars cream-jug	1748 1749	Identified from entry in A. Heal. See also no. 501
3520	Daniel Piers	tea-vase	1753	Cf. no. 493
3521	? Daniel Smith	pair of sauce-boats	1759	
3522	Digby Scott, Benjamin Smith II and James Smith III	plate	1811	Cf. nos. 229–230, 237–8, 504–5
3523*	Daniel Smith and Robert Sharp	salver	1763	Cf. nos. 506–8
3524	David Windsor (probably)	spoon	1809	
3525	? David Whyte	cup coffee-pots and jugs sauce-tureens	1762 1769 1771	Name in PR. list as plate-worker
3526	David Whyte and William Holmes	coffee-pot, sauce-boats, dishes, coffee-pot	1764 1767	Identified from entry in A. Heal
3527	unidentified	small mug	c. 1725	Maker's mark only. Possibly provincial
3528	Edward Aldridge	frame	1762	Cf. nos. 526–7
3529	idem	cake-basket	1763	

* No. 3523. This mark observed on coffee pot of 1761. (Information Mr K. Grant Peterkin.)

No.	Attribution, if any	Object bearing mark	Date	Notes
3530	? Widow of Edward Aldridge Senior	cruet and cake-basket	1766	
3531	Edward Aldridge	inkstand, salt-cellars	1763 1764	
3532	idem	caster	1740	
3533	idem	shells	1744	
3534	idem	cake-basket	1753	
3535	Edward Aldridge Junior and Senior	inkstand	1761	Mark actual size. Also jug 1762. Jackson, p. 208
3536	not traced	candlesticks	1791	
3537	? Edward Barton	silvergilt wine-cooler	1834	Cf. no. 539
3538	? Ebenezer Coker ? Elizabeth Cooke	candlestick	1764	Cf. nos. 550, 552, 556
3539	Ebenezer Coker and Thomas Hannam	salvers skewer	1759	Mark actual size
3540	not traced	plate	1721	If Britannia Standard, ? John Edwards I, cf. no. 572
3541	unidentified	dredger	1725	
3542	not traced	dessertspoon	1728	
3543	not traced	pap-boat	1749	
3544	not traced	paten	1735	Perhaps Edward Jennings. Cf. no. 599
3545	Edward Jay	salver paten	1771 1776	Cf. no. 602
3546	Edward Lambe I	tablespoon	1743	Cf. no. 612
3547	? Edmund Pearce	toilet-box cover	1720	Cf. no. 629
3548	unidentified	box and cover	1754	Some connection appears probable
3549	unidentified	circular box and cover	1775	

UNREGISTERED MARKS

No.	Attribution, if any	Object bearing mark	Date	Notes
3550	unidentified	tea-kettle, stand and lamp	1775	
3551	unidentified	snuffbox	c. 1730	? London or provincial. See no. 3555
3552	unidentified	cream-jug	1739	
3553	Elias Russell	gold snuffbox	1761	Mark actual size. Box signed, Parker and Wakelin
3554	idem	snuffbox	1777	Both this and preceding box in strong French taste
3555	unidentified	snuffbox	1751	Possibly connected with no. 3551
3556	not traced	communion cup	1740	? Possibly a misreading of nos. 3532 or 3533
3557	Elizabeth Tookey	tablespoon	1768	
3558	idem	tablespoons	1772	Name in PR. list 1773 only
3559	idem	marrowscoops tablespoons	1767 1774	See also Elizabeth Taylor no. 645

No. 3540A. Unidentified. EEE. Coffeepot 1768.

EV   GN

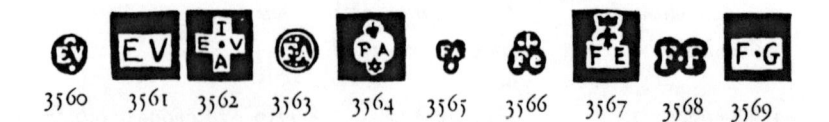

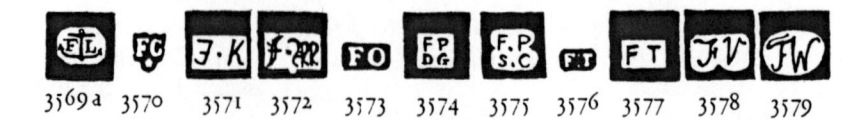

No.	Attribution, if any	Object bearing mark	Date	Notes
3560	Edward Vincent	communion cup tray	1721 1729	Perhaps a misreading of the usual mark. Cf. no. 648
3561*	Edmund Vincent	candlesticks dishes jug	1765 1768 1770	
3562†	Edmund Vincent and John Arnell	candlesticks	1763, 1764 and 1765	
3563	William Fawdery	ladle	1708	Cf. nos. 664–5
3564	Thomas Farren	pair salvers	1718	Cf. no. 666
3565	Joseph Fainell (?)	inkstand	1719	Name apparently misprint for John Farnell cf. no. 661
3566	Edward Feline	snuffbox	1720	Cf. no. 679
3567	unidentified	3 small silver-gilt spoons and forks, spirit flask	c. 1705 c. 1720	Maker's mark only. ? London or provincial
3568	not traced	clothes-brush	1824	? A misreading for no. 585
3569	unidentified	hotwater-jug sauce-tureen and stand	1763 1771	
3569a	unidentified	waiter	1726	
3570	Francis Garthorne	communion flagons	1725	As before 1697
3571	? Frederick Kandler	pair sauce-tureens	1776	? Too late for this ascription. Cf. nos. 691–2
3572	unidentified	two-handled cup	1766	Or possibly WF in reverse position
3573	not traced	coffee-pot	1703	? Epaphroditus Fowler cf. no. 704

* See page 689.   † See pages 769–70.

UNREGISTERED MARKS

No.	Attribution, if any	Object bearing mark	Date	Notes
3574	unidentified*	engraved sugar-tongs	c. 1800	? London or provincial
3575	unidentified*	cream-jug	c. 1790	? London or provincial
3576	Francis Turner	lady's tablet-case	1720	Questionable attribution. Cf. no. 724
3577	unidentified	epergne	1787	Also bearing mark of Thomas Pitts
3578	? Frederick Vonham	hotwater-jug	1762	Cf. no. 730
3579	? Fuller White	coffee-pot	1791	Cf. no. 733
3580	? George Baskerville	sweetmeat-basket	1765	Cf. nos. 751, 754
3581	G. and T. Burrows	teaspoons	1803	No other evidence for this ascription
3582	? George Cowles	cup and cover	1765	Cf. no. 772 not entered till 1777
3583	? George Gray	3 sugar-vases	1787	Cf. nos. 804-5
3584	unidentified	mustard-pot	1797	The piece probably an alteration of c. 1820 and maker's mark perhaps of that period
3585	unidentified	4 shellshaped salts	1802	
3586	William Gimber	rattail spoon	1697	Cf. no. 828
3587	not traced	noted by C.J.J.	1729	? a misreading of Charles Martin no. 359
3588	George Morland	2 snuffboxes	c. 1740	Probably an unrecorded new mark of 1739. Cf. nos. 846-7
3589	not traced	sugar-nippers	1777	

---

* Nos. 3574 and 3575. The second of these is definitely established as that of Francis Parsons and Stephen Crees of Exeter, working together from 1797 to 1800. The first (no. 3574) should probably read FP over BG, also found in Exeter silver for partnership of the same Francis Parsons and a member of the Goss family of silversmiths. (Information Mr T. Kent.) These two marks, originally noted without accompanying Exeter office hallmark, are now established therefore as having no London connotation.

No. 3586A. Unidentified. GI, mullet between, pellet above and below. Dessertspoons 1734 (Christie's).

GP   IB

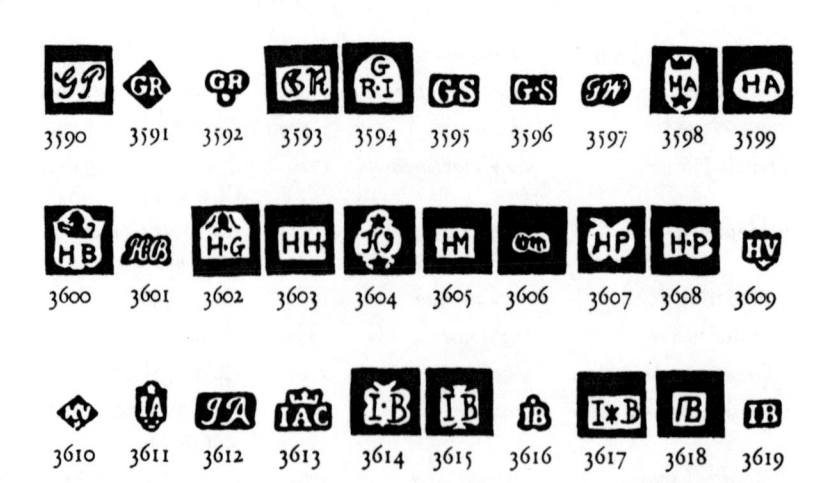

No.	Attribution, if any	Object bearing mark	Date	Notes
3590	unidentified	4 oval salts	1799	Cf. no. 873 but about twenty years later
3591	Dorothy Grant	communion paten	1711	Cf. no. 877
3592	Gundry Roode	tankard	1737	Cf. nos. 880-1
3593	? George Rous	cream-jug	1758	
		salt-cellars	1759 and 1762	Cf. no. 888
3594*	unidentified	tablespoons	1761	Also shoe-buckles undated
3595	not traced	candlesticks	1765	
3596	not traced	sauce-boat	1770	
3597	George Webb	butter-bowl	1837	
3598	unidentified	snuffbox	1717	
3599	unidentified	mustard-pot	1788	
		salt-cellars	1792 and 1801	
3600	Henry Beesley	2 snuffboxes	c. 1725–30	Cf. no. 159
3601	Henry Bayley	chamber-candlestick	1759	Cf. no. 951
3602	unidentified	tankard	1726	Communicated to author. Treat with caution
3603	unidentified	mustard-pot	1775	
3604	unidentified	sugar-bowl and cover	1737	
3605	Hugh Mills or Henry Morris?	salver	1739	Cf. nos. 1030-5
3606	idem	salver	1737	Actual size from photograph
3607	unidentified	porringer	1748	

* Probably the mark of Richard and Joseph Gosling, spoonmakers. See page 526. Mark also found on wine-labels.

UNREGISTERED MARKS

No.	Attribution, if any	Object bearing mark	Date	Notes
3608	unidentified	sugar-nippers	c. 1750	? London or provincial
3609	Alexander Hudson	tobacco-box	1701	Cf. no. 1078
3610	not traced	tablespoons	1736	
3611	Charles Jackson	paten	1714	
		spoon	1718	Cf. no. 1095
3612	John Austin	wine-labels	1803	Not otherwise known
3613	J. A. Calame	fish-trowel	1764	Only in register in incuse form. See also no. 3471 and Section V
3614	Joseph Bird	candlesticks	1726	Cf. no. 1120
3617	idem	tapersticks	1729 and 1734	
3616	John Berthelot	spoon-marrowscoop	1750	See also nos. 1129, 1179
3617	James Baker ?	mugs and jug	1765 and 1767	Or possibly for John Broughton (no. 1149)
3618	unidentified	2 pairs of ewers	1768 and 1769	Several possible attributions see nos. 1132–40
3619	John Baxter of Banbury	cruet-frame	1770	Name only known in PR. list 1773, as goldsmith

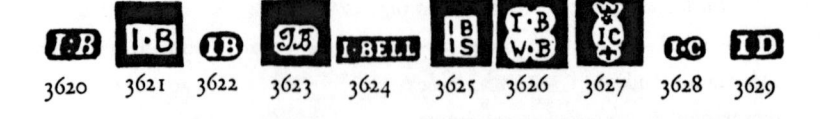

No.	Attribution, if any	Object bearing mark	Date	Notes
3620	? John Buckett	sugar-tongs	1770	Cf. no. 1181
3621	unidentified	dredger	1783	? John Broughton
		hotwater-jug	1789	? John Beldon
3622	John Beldon	tablespoons	1798	Cf. no. 1150
3623	unidentified	teapot	1813	
3624	Joseph Bell II	tablespoon, teaspoons	1758	Cf. no. 1132
3625	? James Bult and James Sutton	salver	1783	Cf. no. 1692
3626	unidentified	3 tea-caddies and cup	1764	
		sauce-boats	1765	
		saucepan	1766	
3627	? Jonah Clifton	candlesticks	1725	Cf. no. 1191
3628	John Carman II	punch-ladle	1752	Cf. no. 1204
3629	Josiah Daniel	teaspoons	1724	Cf. no. 440
3630*	John Delmester	mustard-pot	1759	
		flagon	1772	Cf. no. 431
3631	unidentified	muffineer	1764	
3632	unidentified	small circular box	c. 1735	? London or provincial
3633	Jabez Daniell and James Mince	casters and cruets	1766, 1767, 1769, 1770-5	
3634	Thomas and Jabez Daniell	not given	1771	Mark noted by Jackson
3635	? John French	mugs	1765 and 1766	Cf. no. 3422 as a possible alternative identification
3636	unidentified	fox mask stirrup-cup	1808	
3637	? James Gould	snuffers	1723	Top of punch uncertain

UNREGISTERED MARKS

No.	Attribution, if any	Object bearing mark	Date	Notes
3638	John Gibbons	large dish	1724	
3639	? John Gold	cruet-frame	1795	Cf. no. 1338
3640	? John Gorham	tumbler-cup	1753	Right hand of punch indistinct. Cf. no. 1343
3641	unidentified	candlesticks	1729	Or perhaps HI in reverse position
3642	John Horsley	candlesticks	1761	Name only known in PR. list 1773
3643	unidentified	sugar-basket	1792	
3644	? John Harvey or John Huntley	sauce-boat	1752	Cf. nos. 1403, 1406
3645	? John Huntley	mounts of coconut-cup	dated 1780	Or perhaps TH
3646	James Hobbs	communion cup and paten	1829	Doubtful attribution. Cf. also no. 1408 (Jonathan Hayne)
3647	John Innocent (probably)	tablespoons	1764	Or John Jackson II. Both in PR. list 1773 as spoon-makers
3648	? James King II or James Kingman	straining-funnel	1775	Other candidates John King and John Kidder. Cf. nos. 1444, 1445, 1448
3649	John Ludlow	taper-holder	1720	Cf. nos. 1461, 1968

---

* No. 3630. A similar mark, but with pellet between, presumably for the same maker. Cruet and caster 1769.

No. 3628A. Unidentified. IC over WC. Tablespoons 1769.

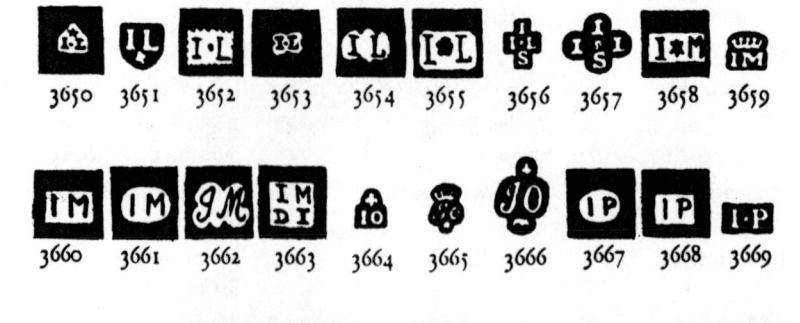

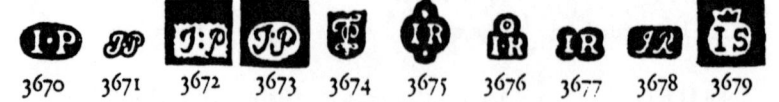

No.	Attribution, if any	Object bearing mark	Date	Notes
3650	unidentified	candlesticks	1735 and 1737	
		inkstand	1737	Mark actual size
3651	James Langlois	pair of candlesticks	1738	Cf. also no. 1464 (John Luff)
3652*	unidentified	tea-caddies	1772 and 1774	
		wine-coasters	1772	
		stirrup-cup	1773	
3653	? John Lawford	teapot and sauce-tureens	1768	Mark actual size. See page 756. Cf. no. 1469
3654	unidentified	feathered-edged spoons	1778 etc.	
3655	unidentified	2 hotwater-jugs	c. 1775	Pieces not fully marked. ? London or provincial
3656	John Langford II and John Sebille	cruet-frame	1766	Names only in PR. list 1773. Also inkstand 1763 (Chaffers). Cf. no. 1693
3657	idem	inkstand	1770	
3658	? Jacob Marsh or John Moore	mug	1763	
		coffee-pots	1767 and 1772	
		sauce-boats	1775	
3659	John Mewburn	tobacco-box	1796	Cf. no. 1529 of later date
3660	unidentified	candlesticks	1807	Cf. nos. 1527-8
		casters	1812	
		tray	1819	
3661	unidentified	soup-plates	1822	
3662	unidentified	pistol-mounts	c.1720-5	Pistols by Pickfatt
3663	John Moliere and Dyall Jones	tea-caddies	1767	Names only in PR. list 1773 and 1768 as plateworkers

260

UNREGISTERED MARKS

No.	Attribution, if any	Object bearing mark	Date	Notes
3664	John Jones I	rattail tablespoon	1719	Cf. no. 1564
3665	Lawrence Jones	paten	1697	Cf. nos. 1557, 1558
3666	? John Owing	three-pronged forks	1740	Cf. John Overing no. 1562
3667	unidentified	small tapersticks and snuffbox	c. 1720-35	? London or provincial
3668	? John Preist or John Perry	4 candlesticks	1755	Cf. nos. 1576-7
3669	John Perry	candlesticks	1759	Also observed on chamber candlesticks 1775. Cf. no. 1577
3670	John Parker II	tableforks, cream-jug	1801	Doubtful attribution. Cf. no. 1844
3671	John Payne	pair of candlesticks	1752	Doubtful attribution. Perhaps connected with nos. 3668-9
3672	? John Payne	tea-urn	1768	Cf. no. 1597
3673	Unidentified	teapot	1775	Or possibly TP
3674	John Penfold (probably)	alms-dish	1720	Cf. no. 2156
3675	Edward Ironside	paten-cover	1697	Cf. no. 1608
3676	John Robinson II	paten	1738	Cf. no. 1614
3677	John Romer	soup-tureen	1771	Name only in PR. list 1773. Also noted on tureens 1764, cake-basket 1765. Cf. also no. 1617
3678	? John Robins	wine-labels	1794	
3679	unidentified	salver	dated 1740/1	? London or provincial

---

* No. 3652A. Unidentified. IL in serrated oval, possibly another version of no. 3652. Stirrup-cup 1777. Possibly both for John Lambe, cf. nos. 1472-4.

No. 3678A. IS, cinquefoil and crown above, pellet below in shaped punch, exactly similar in style to no. 2469 for John Hugh Le Sage. Candlesticks 1721 (Mr H. Perovetz). Clearly the unregistered Old Standard mark of the above which should have been entered about June 1720.

IS   JS

No.	Attribution, if any	Object bearing mark	Date	Notes
3680	John Stewart (?)	paten	1741	No other record of name. Cf. also no. 1640 (Joseph Smith I)
3681	Joseph Steward II (?)	tea-caddy and tankard	1759	Cf. no. 1662
		pair caddies	1768	
3682	idem (?)	tankard and gold tumbler-cup	1765	
		hotwater-jug	1766	
3683	unidentified	pair of salts	1739	Possibly John Le Sage. Cf. no. 1680
3684	unidentified	wine-funnel	c. 1740	
3685	unidentified	tankard	1771	
3686	John Swift?	brandy-saucepan	1770	Cf. nos. 1689, 3708
3687	? John Sanders II	wine-labels	1812	Cf. no. 1668
3688	unidentified	sauce-boats	1760 and 1761	
3689	unidentified	cream-jugs	1768 and 1771	
3690	William Juson	marrow-scoop	1713	Cf. no. 1728
3691	unidentified	saucepan	1737	
3692	unidentified	salt-cellars	1736 and 1737	? A member of the Wood family
3693	unidentified	muffineer	1749	? idem
		salt-cellars	1751	
		cream-jugs	1757 and 1760	
3694	unidentified	silver-gilt beaker	1757	An imperfect mark probably the same also found on tea-vase 1763 and salts 1764

UNREGISTERED MARKS

No.	Attribution, if any	Object bearing mark	Date	Notes
3695	? John Wetherell	alms-plate	1751	Name not otherwise known
3696	? John Weldring or James Wiburd	sugar-vases	1763	
		candlesticks	1763, 1764, 1765	
		teacaddy-casket mounts	1765	
3697	? idem	octagonal dishes	1765	
3698	? idem	column candlesticks	1769	
3699	? idem	cake-basket	1772	
3700	unidentified	tea-kettle	1736	Or perhaps TW
3701	unidentified	epergne, candle-sticks	1763	
3702	unidentified	cream-jug	1737	
3703	Jonathan Alleine	communion patens	1777	Cf. no. 1769 (Joseph Angell, but 1811) ? date-letter b for 1817 misread for 1777
3704	J. and J. Aldous	beadle's staff	1821	Cf. no. 1772 (Joseph and John Angell)
3705	not traced	mounts of sugar-stand	1815	Cf. no. 1279 (John and Edward Edwards)
3706	unidentified	taperstick	1763	
3707	? John Kentenber (sic)	tablespoons	1759	Cf. no. 1457
3708	* John Swift	tankard	1772	
		candlesticks	1776	Cf. nos. 1689, 3686
3709	? John Scofield	waiter	1775	Accompanied by matching waiter by R. Jones and J. Scofield of the same year. Cf. nos. 1670, 2349, 3779

---

* Cf. also no. 1667 of James Stamp who seems a more likely attribution.

No. 3704A. Unidentified. JC, fleur-de-lis below, blurred device above, in lozenge punch. Tablespoon 1770. Possibly for the widow of Paul Callard (page 457), whose mark, like his father's, appears only on spoons.

No.	Attribution, if any	Object bearing mark	Date	Notes
3710	Launc. Keatt	caster	1709	Cf. no. 1872 (Robert Kempton)
3711	Robert Keble	casters	1711 and 1712	Cf. no. 1866
3712	unidentified	24 tablespoons	1704	And various teaspoons without date letters
3713	unidentified	teaspoons	c. 1705	Maker's mark only. Presumably related to no. 3712
3714	unidentified	candlesticks	1732	
3715	Louis Cuny	salvers	1732 and 1733	Actual size from photograph. Cf. no. 422
3716	Louisa Courtauld	tea-urn, table-bell	1766	Cf. nos. 1907–8
3717	Ralph Leeke	cup of porringer form	1701	Cf. no. 1914
3718	Jeremiah Lee	pair of sugar-nippers	c. 1760	Cf. nos. 1466, 1488
3719	not traced	loving-cup	1766	? Lewis Hamon, Louis Herne
3720	Lewis Hamon	tea-caddies	1752	Cf. nos. 1925–6, 1929
3721	John Lingard	three-pronged forks	1719	Cf. nos. 1460, 1932–3
3722	not traced	rosewater-salver	1784	? Laurence Johnson. Cf. nos. 1934–5
3723	unidentified	box	1811	
3724	Lewis Mettayer (?)	candlesticks	1734	Cf. nos. 1943, 2018
3725	Laurence M'Duff	3 tea-caddies	1764	
3726*	? Matt. Lofthouse	mark noted by C.J.J.	1732	Cf. nos. 1953, 2043
3727	unidentified	pair tea-vases	1762	Top letter noted as perhaps R in lieu of F
3728	not traced	communion paten	1773	
3729	not traced	child's mug	1729	

UNREGISTERED MARKS

No.	Attribution, if any	Object bearing mark	Date	Notes
3730	William Matthew I (?)	small bleeding-bowl	1698	More probably George Manjoy. Cf. no. 1978
3731	probably George Manjoy	toy candlesticks	1707	Cf. nos. 1978–80
3732	probably Jonathan Madden	porringer	1703	
		spirit-lamp	1705	
		tankard and cup	1709	Cf. no. 1982
3733	? Jacob Margas	cup	1702	Actual size from photograph
		candlesticks	1709	Cf. no. 1983
3734	Jacob Margas (?)	candlesticks	1710 and 1719	Cf. no. 1985, John Mathew
3735	? Mark Bock†	wine-funnel	1794	Cf. nos. 1996–7
3736	unidentified	chased sword-hilt	dated 1745	? London or possibly foreign
3737	Thomas Merry I (probably)	taper-holder	1711	Cf. no. 2017
3738	Henry Miller I	spoon	1720	Cf. no. 2036
3739	Hezekiah Mountfort	small engraved box	1710	Incuse mark only in register. See Section V, M.O

---

* No. 3726. This bears no comparison to the known marks of Matthew Lofthouse (nos. 1953 and 2043). It seems very probably a misreading by Jackson of no. 3715 above of Louis Cuny.
† This attribution by Jackson is negatived by the fact that Bock was dead by 1783. See page 443.

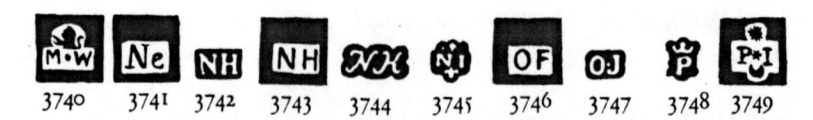

No.	Attribution, if any	Object bearing mark	Date	Notes
3740	unidentified	cream-jug	1721	Date-letter for that year. No other marks
3741	? Anthony Nelme or Jonathan Newton	mug	1714	Cf. nos. 69, 2087
3742*	Nicholas Hearnden	teapot	1778	Name only in PR. list 1773 as spoonmaker. Cf. no. 3744
3743*	? Napthali Hart	tea-service	1817–8	
3744†	not traced	teaspoons‡	c. 1763–4	? Nathaniel Horwood. PR. list 1773
3745	Richard Nightingale	rattail spoon	1697	Cf. no. 2095
3746	unidentified	snuffbox	1813	
3747	Orlando Jackson	argyle	1770	Cf. no. 2107
3748§	Benjamin Pyne	mace	1726	Cf. nos. 2244–5
3749	unidentified	pair candlesticks	1744	
3750	Philip Norman	snuffers and tray	1772	Name only in PR. list 1773
3751	John Porter	tankard	1698	Cf. no. 2207
3752	idem	communion cup	1711	
3753†	Philip Roker II	rattailed teaspoon	c. 1740	Cf. nos. 2223, 2229, 2398
3754	idem (?)	shell-bowled sauce-ladle	1753	
3755	idem (?)	spoon with *Wilkes* 'fancy-back'	c. 1765	

* These marks are almost certainly the same, the year indicated for no. 3742 being correctly 1818 and the maker Napthali Hart. See no. 2094 and page 752 under Hearnden.
† Almost certainly the mark of Nicholas Hearnden. See page 752.
‡ Also noted on a basting-spoon of 1759.
§ This mark also appears on six staves of 1723 of the University of Cambridge (H. C. Moffat, *Old Oxford Plate*).

UNREGISTERED MARKS

No.	Attribution, if any	Object bearing mark	Date	Notes
3756	? Peter Werritzer	gold and agate circular box	1744	Also snuff box c. 1740, makers' mark only. Cf. no. 2242
3757	? J. Parker I and E. Wakelin	tea-caddy	c. 1770	Accompanying another caddy of 1768. Cf. no. 1602
3758	not traced	spoon with marrow-scoop stem	1706	
3759	not traced	noted by C.J.J.	1722	
3760	Richard Bayley	teapot tankard cups	1724 1725 1726 and 1728	Cf. nos. 116, 2262, 2279, 3481
3761	Richard Bayley (?)	flagon	1730	Cf. no. 2267, Richard Botfield
3762	Richard Beale	bowl flagon	1732 1737	Cf. nos. 2266, 2280
3763	Richard Bigge (probably)	porringer	1724	Cf. no. 181 for only recorded mark
3764	Rundell, Bridge and Rundell	tea-service	1804	Cf. nos. 1171-2, 2228
3765	not traced	paten	1727	Possibly Richard Chapman. Cf. no. 2282
3765a	Robert Cruickshank	hotwater-jug	1781	
3766	not traced	tablespoons	1740	With a curious mark of a bird alongside
3767	Robert Cox	snuffbox	1752	Cf. nos. 2286, 2291-2, 3770
3768	idem (?)	epergne	1754	
3769	idem (?)	tea-caddies coffee-pot cup and cover	1766 1770 1772	

---

* No. 3746. Now recognized as the mark of Owen Fielding of Plymouth Dock (Exeter Assay Book), submitting boxes for assay from 1808 onwards. (Information Mr T. Kent).

† No. 3753. A very similar mark, possibly in undulating outline. Sauce-ladle 1767, Laing Art Gallery, Newcastle. Probably for Philip Roker III (page 645).

No. 3749A. PM in script in kidney-shaped punch. Sword-hilt 1739. Perhaps the new mark under the 1738 Act of Peter Marsh (no. 2206), whose address, New Street, Shoe Lane, was in the cutlers' area.

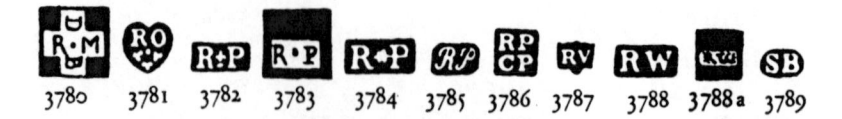

No.	Attribution, if any	Object bearing mark	Date	Notes
3769a	Robert Garrard II	inkstand	1817	First mark entered 16.4.1818, the 'G' wrongly cut as 'E'. See no. 2323
		plateau-mounts	1818	
3770	Richard Goldwire?	snuffboxes	1743 and 1744	The later date box engraved 'Richard Goldwyer Sarum'. Cf. nos. 3431–2, 3767
3771	Richard Gardner?	sauce-tureen	1770	
		teapot	1771	
		jug, salts	1773	
			1775	
3772	idem (?)	soup-plates, wine-coolers	1788	The time interval and type of pieces suggest another maker to no. 3771
3773	? Richard Gosling	cream-jug	c. 1745	Cf. nos. 2316, 2321
3774	unidentified	gold and agate box	1775	
3775	? Robert Hill	salver	1730	Cf. nos. 1011 and 2335
3776	unidentified	candlestick	1764	
3777	not traced	bleeding-bowl	1703	Cf. no. 2339, Christopher Riley
3778	? John Richardson I	paten	1728	Cf. also nos. 1612, 2344
3779	? Robert and Jno. Scofield	cup	1771	Cf. nos. 1670, 2349, 3709
3780	? Richard Mills and David Bell	salver	1752 or 1753	
3781	Philip Roker I	paten	1700	Cf. no. 2384
3782	R. Peaston	caster	1762	Cf. nos. 3275, 3784, 3897
3783	R. Piercy?	cup, waiter	1762	Cf. no. 2410
		casters	1765	
		cruet and casters	1767	

UNREGISTERED MARKS

No.	Attribution, if any	Object bearing mark	Date	Notes
3784*	Robert Piercy	Warwick cruet-frame	1765	Cf. no. 3275
3785	? Robert Perth	tablespoons	1754	Cf. no. 2416
3786	not traced	alms-dish	1834	Cf. no. 2419 (? Richard Pearce and possibly a son)
3787	Abm. Russell (?)	snuffer-stand	1710	Cf. no. 2452
3788	Richard Watts	teapot	1722	Cf. nos. 2453-4, 2986-7
3788a	unidentified	snuffbox	1740	
3789	Saml. Blackborow	communion cup	1737	Cf. nos. 186, 2474
3790	? Sarah Buttall	mustard-pot	1771	Cf. no. 2478
3791	idem (?)	inkstand	1771	Actual size from photo, probably the same as above
3792	Sandylands Drinkwater	wine-labels	c. 1745	Actual size from photo. Probably his new mark of 1739. Cf. no. 2499
3793	? Samuel Eaton	vase shaped jug	1774	Cf. nos. 2509-10
		4 sauce-tureens	1775	
3794	probably Simon Jouet	taperstick	1750	Cf. nos. 2556-7
3795	Samuel Jerman?	'fancy-back' teaspoons	c. 1775	
3796†	not traced	snuffer-tray	1698	Close affinities to the standard form of makers' marks in Rouen, France
3797	not traced	table and dessert-spoons, punch-ladle	1796	
3798	? Solomon Royes and John (East) Dix	meat-skewers	1819	Cf. no. 2627
3799	unidentified	sauce-boats	1771	? Samuel Shelley II. Cf. no. 2632

* See page 624.
† No. 3796. Closely similar to the mark of Samuel Margas senior of Rouen (1627–83) (C. G. Casson, *Les Orfèvres de Normandie*, Paris 1980). He was grandfather of Samuel and Jacob (see pages 590-1). This mark was probably used by their father, also Samuel, who was in London by 1688, aged thirty-two.

SU   TH

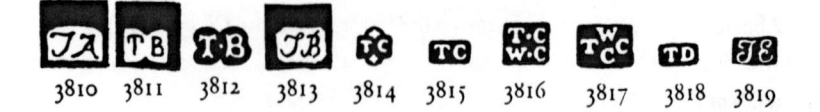

No.	Attribution, if any	Object bearing mark	Date	Notes
3800	? Thomas Sutton	punch-ladle	1721–3 or 1726–8	Top of punch indistinct. Cf. no. 2648
3801	Samuel Wastell	mug, teapot	1722 1725	Actual size from photo. Cf. no. 2991
3802	? Starling Wilford or Samuel Welder	muffineer	1724	Cf. nos. 2652–5
3803	idem	octagonal casters	1724 and 1726	
3804	? Samuel Whitford I or Samuel White	tankards	1764 and 1768	Cf. no. 2661
3805	unidentified	casters argyle salt-cellars	1796 1797 1804	
3806	unidentified	tablespoons	1747	
3807	? Samuel Wheat or White	altar candlesticks	1759	Cf. nos. 2659, 2668
3808	? Samuel Wood or Samuel White	tea and sugar-vases	1773	Cf. nos. 2656–9, 2666
3809	unidentified	rattailed spoons	c. 1720	? London or provincial. ? Peter Tabart, cf. no. 2677
3810	unidentified	gun-mounts	1742	
3811	? Thomas Beezley	coffee-pot beaker epergne	1767 1769 1770	Cf. no. 2691
3812	? T. Barker	mustard-spoons	1812	Cf. nos. 276, 2697
3813	unidentified	waiter	c. 1735	
3814	Thomas Clark	salver	1725	Cf. no. 2711
3815	Thomas Congreve	cream-jug	1759	Cf. no. 2716

270

UNREGISTERED MARKS

No.	Attribution, if any	Object bearing mark	Date	Notes
3816	T. & W. Chawner (probably)	tablespoons	1765	Cf. no. 2718–9, 3510
3817	idem	large skewer	1768	
3818*	Thomas Doxsey	tablespoons	1759	Incuse mark only in registers. See Section V, T.D
3819	not traced	lemon-strainer	1767	Cf. no. 2746 (Thomas England)
3820	not traced	teaspoons	c. 1763–4	
3821	unidentified	mug	1734	
3822	? Thomas Foster	sweetmeat-baskets	1767 and 1768	Cf. no. 2751
3823	Thomas Foster	sauce-boat	1771	Cf. no. 2751
3824	unidentified	pair candlesticks	1732	? Thomas Gilpin. Cf. no. 2758
3825	Thos. Gilpin	six three pronged forks	1741	Cf. nos. 2758, 2768–9
3826	? Thos. Gilpin	epergne	1756	Cf. nos. 2758, 2768–9
3827	unidentified	teapot	1729	? Thomas Hodgkinson. Cf. no. 2779
3828	Thomas Heming	maces sucrier	1767 1770	Cf. nos. 2796–7
3829	unidentified	coffee-pots	1771 and 1777	Cf. 2798–9

---

* More probably the mark of Thomas Devonshire. See page 746 under Doxsey.

TH   WA

No.	Attribution, if any	Object bearing mark	Date	Notes
3830	unidentified	saucepan sauce-boats	1780 1781	
3831	unidentified	salt-cellars	1790	
3832	unidentified	teapot and cradle-stand	1782	
3833	not traced	epergne	1783	
3834	unidentified	tea-caddy teapot	1786 1789	
3835	unidentified	cream-jug	1748	Identity of first letter uncertain
3836	? Thos. Hannam and Rich. Mills	waiters	1763 and 1764	
3837	unidentified	teapot	1803	No apparent connection with preceding mark
3838	unidentified	tea-caddy	1807	Also coffee-biggin of unrecorded date
3839	not traced	wine-labels	1810	Cf. no. 2808 for a possible connection
3840*	? Thomas Jackson II or Thomas Justis or Thomas Jones	candlestick A	1770	Also foxmask stirrup-cup 1779. Cf. nos. 2813–14
3841*	idem	candlestick B	1766	Also sweet and cake-baskets 1767. Kettle and stand 1768
3842	? T. Jefferys and W. Jones II	salt-cellars gilt cup and cover	1783 1784	Cf. Ambrose Heal
3843	Timothy Ley (as before 1697)	waterman's badge	1728	Cf. no. 1917. Presumably reverted to without re-registering in 1720

* These two marks actual size from photo on two matching candlesticks of dates given.

UNREGISTERED MARKS

No.	Attribution, if any	Object bearing mark	Date	Notes
3844	Thos. Langford II (probably)	plain goblet	1775	Name only in PR. list 1773. But cf. also no. 3448
3845	unidentified	tea-caddies	1770 and 1771	
3846	? Thomas Nash I	4 wine-coasters	1769	Cf. no. 2852
3847	? Thos. Whipham	flagon	1755	Cf. no. 2974
3848	unidentified	casters	1771 1782 1785	? Thos. Wallis cf. nos. 2962–3
3849	? D. Urquhart & N. Hart	child's rattle	c. 1815	Cf. nos. 510, 2094
3850	? John Vaen	tea-caddy caster, coffee-pot	1704 1709	Actual size from photo. Cf. no. 627
3851	idem	inkstand	1703	Actual size from photo
3852	? Edward Vincent	candlesticks	1705	Cf. no. 2983
3853	not traced	salver	1700	Cf. no. 2981 (Nathaniel Underwood)
3854	not traced	rattail spoon	1701	Cf. no. 2981
3855	unidentified	mug	1698	
3856	Joseph Ward	tea-caddy	1717	Cf. no. 2989
3857	? Wm. Watkins	candlesticks	1772	The mark suspect as of New Std. form at too late a date. Cf. no. 3910
3858	Wm. Warham II	dredger	1705	Cf. no. 2994.
3859	Wm. Warham I	scent-canister	1708	? A misreading of mark no. 3192 (David Willaume I)

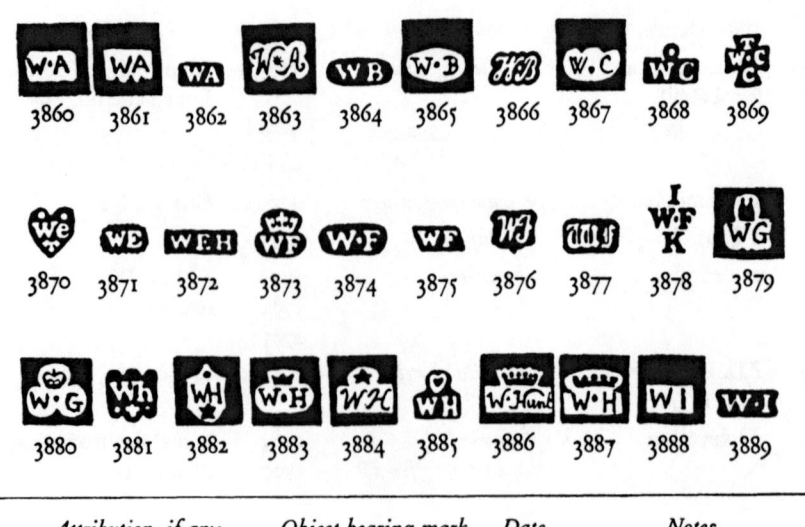

No.	Attribution, if any	Object bearing mark	Date	Notes
3860	? Wm. Alexander or Wm. Abdy I	Corinthian candlesticks	1759	Cf. nos. 3000-1 etc.
		3 tea-caddies	1762	
3861	? William Abdy I	dwarf candlesticks	1767	Cf. nos. 3001-4
3862	William Abdy II	cream-jug	1822	
3863	unidentified	tea-caddies	1756 and 1757	
3864	? Walter Brind	sugar-vase	1759	Cf. nos. 3012-5
3865*	Walter Brind	pair fluted sauce-boats	1782	
3866	William Burwash (?)	small tray	1802	Cf. no. 3047
3867	unidentified	candlesticks	1751	? William Cafe
3868	Wm. Chawner	spoon	1817	
3869	T. & W. Chawner (probably)	gravy-spoon	1763	Cf. nos. 2718-9, 3510, 3816-7
3870	Saml. Welder	octagonal muffineer	1714	Cf. nos. 2654-5, 3092-3, 3802-3
3871	Wm. Eley I	dessertspoons	1794	Cf. nos. 3101, 3111-2
3872	Wm. Hall	inkstand	1795	Cf. nos. 3163
3873	William Fawdery	small saucepan	1720	Cf. nos. 658, 664-5, 3563
3874	? Wm. Fordham†	cream-jug	1728	Cf. no. 706
3875	W. L. Foster	tablespoons etc.	1779	Cf. nos. 3115-8
3876	not traced	pair of soup-ladles	1768	? William Fisher (A. Heal, 1766-73)
3877	not traced	alms-dish	1765	Also tankards and mugs, 1766 Liverpool Corporation
3878	not traced	coffee pot	1767	

* See page 738.   † Or possibly William Fleming.

UNREGISTERED MARKS

No.	Attribution, if any	Object bearing mark	Date	Notes
3879	unidentified	tobacco-box dated	1702	? London or provincial
3880	? William Gough	taperstick	1750	Cf. no. 3136
3881	not traced	porringer and cover	1702	Cf. no. 3153 (John White)
3882	? John White	waiter	1723	Cf. no. 3153
3883	? William Hudson	mug	1727	Cf. nos. 1075, 3154
3884	? William Hutchinson II	snuffer-tray	1740	Cf. no. 3156
3885	? Wm. Hunter I	pair of tea-vases	1743	Of doubtful ascription. Cf. nos. 3157, 3172
3886	W. Hunt	finely chased gold chatelaine	1740	Cf. no. 1077
3887	idem (?)	gold chatelaine	1757	
3888	? Wiliam Justis	scallop dishes	1747	
		waiters and salvers	1749–1753	Cf. nos. 3200, 3202
3889	idem (?)	pair sauce-boats	1754	

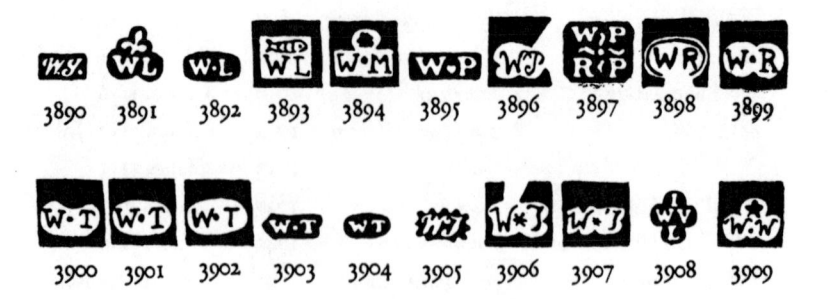

No.	Attribution, if any	Object bearing mark	Date	Notes
3890	not traced	taperstick	1799	
3891	William Looker	candlesticks	1720	Cf. nos. 1952, 3219
3892	not traced	sugar-nippers	c. 1760	
3893*	? William Lestourgeon	tobacco-box	1757	
		tray	1764	
		tea-caddy, mustard-pot	1765	
3894	unidentified	pair of tea-vases	1752	
		pair of tea-caddies	1753	
3895	William Purse	beaker	1804	Name not otherwise known
3896	unidentified	sauce-boat	1761	Top right corner of punch obscured
3897†	W. & R. Peaston	tankard	1764	Cf. nos. 3254, 3275, 3784
3898	unidentified	lid of tobacco-box	1710	Lower portion indistinct
3899	? William Reynolds	sauce-boats, dinner-plates	1759	Cf. no. 3278
3900	? William Tuite	Chinoiserie caddies	1758	Cf. nos. 3339 and 3903.
		candlestick	1759	Mark perhaps distorted in final working
3901	idem (?)	coffee and teapots	1760-1	
		sauce-tureens	1767	
		soup-tureen	1772	
3902	idem (?)	meat-dish	1763	
3903	idem (probably)	sauce-boat	1767	Cf. no. 3900
3904	William Tant	tumbler	1783	Name only in PR. list 1773 as spoonmaker

* See page 757.   † This may be the mark of William Preist and Richard Pargeter. See pages 761–2 under the latter.

UNREGISTERED MARKS

No.	Attribution, if any	Object bearing mark	Date	Notes
3905	William Tant (probably)	tablespoon	1762	
3906	unidentified	tankard	1764	? William Turner. Cf. no. 3353
3907	unidentified	taperstick	c. 1740	No other mark
		wirework sugar-basket	c. 1760	? version of no. 3906 or provincial
3908‡	? John Lawford and William Vincent	sauce-tureens	1764	Also coffee-pot 1762. ? John Vere and William Lutwyche. Cf. Heal, p. 260
3909	unidentified	watchcase	1739	Cf. no. 3372, William West
3910	William Watkins	marrow-scoop	1762	Cf. nos. 518, 2739, 3374, 3857

‡ See pages 756 and 770. See also no. 3357.

IV–X
Indexes of Marks of Categorized Makers not included in Sections I–III

The following Sections comprise indexes of all remaining marks in the registers from 1697 to 1837 not reproduced in the foregoing Sections I to III (see Introduction, pages 13–14). These indexes are arranged alphabetically by the initials composing the mark itself, and not by the makers' names, to enable the possible identification of a given mark to be attempted. Where initials are repeated in the first column for the same maker a further entry is indicated. Where only a further date is listed without initials a change of address only is indicated. It is obvious that without reproduction of the mark itself no final identification can be established except for rare combinations of initials or occasional examples with unusual devices included. There are unfortunately, only too often, duplications of similar initials in very similar punches registered at the same period, so that, even from the mark itself, final ownership may well remain in doubt. However, it would appear worthwhile to publish the categorized lists which follow herewith as a start, if no more, for further study of the various types of work produced by their makers.

IV
Smallworkers' Marks

All the marks in this section are in relief 'cameo' punches as in Sections I–III, but have been excluded from Section I, being too small for reproduction. Most are probably goldworkers'. The average punch width is less than an eighth of an inch.

Mark	Entered	Name	Address/Notes
AB, oblong	4.7.1770	*Aaron Bourne	Crown and Head, New Street, Covent Garden
AB, oblong	6.4.1810	Artaxerxes Brown	11 Bentick Street, Berwick Street, Soho
AL, shaped to letters	7.5.1716	†Robert Allison	'in the Minories'
AL, oblong	1.9.1792	Anthony Lobjort	Pimlico
AS, oblong	26.11.1828	*Abraham Scott	West Smithfield
AV, oblong	2.12.1726	Peter Aumonier	'Ryders Courte By Lester filds'
BA, oblong	19.3.1716	Joseph Barker	Bread Street. 'free Draper'
BB, oblong	17.2.1762	Benjamin Brooksby	'opposite Gerrards Hall Inn Basing Lane Jeweller'
BB, oblong	23.9.1815	Benjamin Barling	53 Princes Street, Soho
	28.8.1818	idem	Moved to 23 Broard Street, Golden Square
	22.11.1832	idem	Moved to Southampton Place, Camden Town
	14.1.1839	idem	Moved to 142 High Street, Camden Town
	30.6.1852	idem	New mark similar to first
BD, coronet of five balls above, oblong	31.5.1723	Benjamin Drayton	Little Britain. 'Goldworker'
BG, oblong	2.5.1740	Benjamin Gurdon	Noble Street
BH, oblong	15.9.1770	Benjamin Hawkins	Frying Pan Alley, Wood Street
BL, oblong	undated probably April 1697	Richard Blundell	Whites Alley, Coleman Street

Also A.R. 7.10.1831. Alfred Reeves, casemaker, 42 Spencer Street, Clerkenwell. See also Section V, page 288

* See Section VII, Goldworkers.   † Possibly a gun-mount maker from the address.

Mark	Entered	Name	Address/Notes
BW, oblong, cut corners	6.9.1830	Benjamin Wyon	2 Nassau Street, Soho
	18.5.1843	idem	Moved to 287 Regent Street
CB, oblong	10.6.1831	Charles Bradbrook	10 Serles Place, Carey Street
CI, oval	2.2.1722	*Sir Charles Jones	'Cripplegate, next door to ye Golden ball', 'free of ye Fonder'
CL, oblong	29.3.1770	Charles Leadbetter	9 Cary Lane
CL	20.9.1790	Caleb Lowe	'Thursbye near Godalman, Surrey'
CS, oblong, cut corners	11.7.1770	Charles Storey	Sidneys Alley, Leicesterfields
DC, oblong	24.12.1798	Dominick Collings	43 Bedfordbury
idem	23.10.1799	idem	Moved to 67 Chancery Lane
idem	23.2.1801	idem	Second mark
idem	no date	idem	Moved to 19 Water Street, Strand
idem	9.5.1804	idem	Moved to 2 Northumberland Court, Southampton Buildings, Holborn
DC	17.6.1830	David Cohen	5 Collingwood Street, NEWCASTLE
DF, incurved oblong	3.7.1792	Daniel Fellow	232 Piccadilly
DG, oblong	16.12.1771	Daniel Gottman	Milman Street, Bedford Row
EH, oblong	11.4.1770	†Edward Holmes	9 Foster Lane
EP, double lobe	27.10.1768	Edmund Price	17 Maiden Lane, Wood Street
EP, oblong, cut corners	15.9.1831	‡Edward Peacock	26 Grove Place, Goswell Street
ET, oblong	17.9.1770	Edmund Toulman	Mould Makers Row
EW, script capitals, shaped punch	23.9.1766	Edmund Wells	Bolt Court, Fleet Street
similar mark	8.5.1790	idem	36 Fetter Lane
EW, oblong	7.11.1767	Edward Wild	Water Lane, Fleet Street
FP, oblong, cut corners	27.3.1810	Francis Poiderin	15 Brewer Street, Golden Square
GB, oblong	2.12.1799	George Blakeway	37 Strand
GB, pellet between, oblong	27.8.1811	George Boggis	10 Adle Hill, Doctors Commons
GC, oblong	2.10.1770	†George Chalmers	Sidneys Alley, Leicester Fields

* See Section V. † See Section VII. ‡ See Section V.

SMALLWORKERS' MARKS

Mark	Entered	Name	Address/Notes
GR, rounded ends	2.2.1837	Gabriel Riddle	172 Blackfriars Road. See SM.GB below
GS, oblong	26.6.1770	George Seatoun	Gutter Lane
idem	30.9.1772	idem	idem
HC, oblong (two sizes)	3.5.1773	*Henry Cooper	Lancaster Court, Strand
IB, oblong	17.6.1772	*James Birkenhead	31 Gutter Lane
IB, oblong	20.8.1772	*James Birt	Silver Street, Wood Street
IC, oblong, cut corners	27.2.1759	John Cheney	St. Martins Lane. 'Bucklemaker'
IC, oblong	9.10.1770	John Clinton	Salisbury Street, Strand
IH, oblong	21.1.1773	James Hughes	Corner of Princes Square, Radcliff Highway
IH, oblong	16.10.1790	John Howlett	13 Little Compton Street, St. Anns, Soho
IH, oblong	10.12.1790	John Holden	Red Lion Court, Cock Lane, West Smithfield
II, oblong	13.1.1771	James Johnston	Cary Lane
idem	30.4.1771	idem	
II	27.3.1773	†James Jackson	BIRMINGHAM. By power attorney
IID, oval	1.2.1799	Joseph James Dallaway	4 George Lane, Botolph Lane
	19.10.1802	idem	Moved to 147 Tottenham Court Road
	29.3.1808	idem	Moved to Rowcrofts Building, STROUD, Glos
IL, oblong	26.1.1727	‡Job Lilley	At the Bull and Garter. 'Free Goldsmith'
IL, oblong	9.10.1772	John Lautier	20 Fleet Street
IM, oblong	17.10.1770	Joseph Malpas	Wood Street, Cheapside
IP, oblong	10.8.1812	§John Peters	20 Old Compton Street, Soho
IS, pellet between, oblong	3.3.1772	John Stirling	4 Queen Square, Bartholomew Close. 'Jeweller'
IS, oblong, cut corners	14.9.1791	Isaac Stokes	3 Salmon and Ball Court, Bunhill Row
IS, rough oblong	9.9.1809	John Sinclair	43 Union Street, Marylebone
IT, oblong	—.5.——	‖John Tatum I,	4 Poppins Court, Fleet Street
idem	22.10.1790	idem	idem
IT, oblong	28.3.1799	‖John Tatum, Junr.	53 Dorset Street, Salisbury Square

---

* See Section VII   † See also Section VII.
‡ See William Lilley (Section I, nos. 3224, 3231).
§ See Section I, no. 1605, and Section VII.   ‖ See Section I, no. 1727.

Mark	Entered	Name	Address/Notes
JF, oblong	15.1.1733	*John Ferris	Angel Street, St. Martin's Square. 'Goldsmith'
JJ, pellet between oblong	7.12.1771	John Johnson	7 Maiden Lane, Wood Street
JP, oblong	11.10.1769	John Phillips	Cold Bath Square, Clerkenwell
JR, oblong	28.6.1805	†John Robertson	Hen and Chickens Court, Fleet Street
LB, pellet between	20.4.1759	Loader Bourne	PORTSMOUTH
MG, oblong	9.10.1770	‡Michael Gamon	3 Paul's Court, Huggin Lane, Wood Street
MS	2.4.1759	Merducea Samuel	'of PORTSMOUTH Common'
MW, oblong	25.3.1762	Moses Willats	Poultry
NC, script	3.4.1776	Neil Campbell	AYLESBURY
NW, oblong	7.6.1810	Nathaniel Whitehouse	46 Red Lion Street, Clerkenwell
	21.7.1810	idem	Moved to 7 Bishops Court, Aylesbury Street
	22.4.1816	idem	Moved to 34 Leather Lane
	19.12.1817	idem	Moved to 5 Holborn
	4.12.1821	idem	Moved to 1 Cross Street, Hatton Garden
NW, oblong	7.4.1825	idem	29 Easton Street, Spa Fields
RH, oblong	7.2.1732	Robert Humphreys	'in Cheker Aly weight Cross Street Chripelgat'
RM, oblong	25.8.1761	Robert Maile	St. Ann's Lane
SH, oblong	1.9.1759	Stephen Hedges	Salisbury Court, Fleet Street
SM, oblong	12.2.1773	§Samuel Massey	'at Mr. Ford's, 8 Foster Lane'
SM, oblong idem	9.6.1823 4.1.1837	Sampson Mordan idem	22 Castle Street, City Road idem
SM.GB, oblong	30.4.1824	Sampson Mordan and Gabriel Riddle	idem
TB, pellet between, oblong, cut corners	3.2.1802	Thomas Bird	15 Beaufort Buildings, Strand
TC, oblong	10.6.1768	Thomas Collier	Giltspur Street, West Smithfield

* See Matthew Ferris (Section I, no. 2024).
† See Section I, no. 1629, and Section VII.
‡ Goldworker, Parl. Report list 1773. See also Section VII.
§ See Section VII.

SMALLWORKERS' MARKS

Mark	Entered	Name	Address/Notes
TC, oblong	12.8.1792	Thomas Chaldecot	East Street, CHICHESTER, Sussex
TE, pellet between, oblong	27.11.1732	Thomas Eeles	'att ye hand and spur in Wood Street'. 'Buckle and Spurmaker'
TH, oblong	4.3.1794	Thomas Hodges	127 St. John Street
	28.3.—	idem	Moved to 97 Old Street
	8.12.1798	idem	Moved to 39 Old Street
	27.5.1803	idem	Moved to 3 Chapel Row, Spa Fields
TM, oblong	27.2.1771	Thomas Millington	31 Gutter Lane, Cheapside
TP	5.4.1759	Thomas Pigott	PORTSMOUTH
TS, oblong	20.2.1770	*Thomas Satchwell	20 Paternoster Row. 'Jeweller'
idem	24.2.1770	idem	idem
TW, oblong	25.5.1837	†Thomas Wise	30 Coppice Row, Clerkenwell
TW, oblong, cut corners	10.8.1838	idem	idem
WE, oblong	19.10.1805	‡William Eastwick	102 Aldersgate Street
WF, oblong	18.11.1789	§William Forister	2 Charterhouse Lane
WH, oblong	7.3.1768	‖William Howes	Temple Bar
WM, oblong	28.3.1768	William Mears	New Rents, St. Martin's Le Grand
	19.12.1769	idem	Moved to 1 Oat Lane
WP, oblong	9.9.1790	William Peacock	18 Salisbury Court, Fleet Street
idem	30.11.1820	idem	18 Salisbury Square
WS, rough oblong	23.1.1795	William Smith	34 King Street, Cheapside
WS, oblong	23.4.1801	William Simcock	24 Red Lion Street, Clerkenwell
WS, oval	27.6.1828	William Stephenson	60 Queen Street, Lincoln's Inn
WW, oblong	28.11.1821	¶William Warren	9 Great Windmill Street, Haymarket

---

* See also Section VII.   † See also Section I, no. 1788.
‡ See also Section I, no. 992.   § See also Sections V and VII.
‖ See also Section I, no. 3173.   ¶ See also Section V.

V
Incuse Marks of All Categories

The marks listed below are struck directly into the metal in intaglio without a surrounding punch. Before 1773 they are probably mostly watchcasemakers' or goldworkers' marks. After 1773 they are categorized in the registers as abbreviated below.

Mark	Entered	Name	Category	Address/Notes
A	7.1.1734	Aaron Abrahams	smw	Layden Yard in ye Minories
AB	30.8.1721	*Ann Barugh	cm	Hind Court, Fleet Street 'Clockmaker'
AB	7.10.1730	Aaron Bates	smw	Field Lane. 'Silversmith', 'free Goldsmith'
AB	3.1.1820	Alfred Bendy	cm	52 Great Sutton Street, Clerkenwell
	12.9.1821	idem		Moved to 9 Vineyard Walk, Clerkenwell
AB	26.11.1823	Auguste Baillod	cm	7 Castle Street, Bloomsbury
idem	28.4.1824	idem		idem
	13.9.1826	idem		Moved to 14 Northampton Square, Clerkenwell
	20.6.1828	idem		Moved to 55 Myddleton Street
	25.1.1829	idem		Moved to 11 Exmouth Street
AC	10.10.1699	†William Achurch	cm	New Street, near Shoe Lane. 'free Clockmaker'
AC	22.2.1764	‡James Anthony Calame	smw	Strand, facing Exeter Change
AC, pellet between	8.10.1806	Abraham Conteste	gw	30 Ogle Street, St. Marylebone, later St. James' Street, Clerkenwell (no date)
ACF	11.5.1813	Alexander Chas. Faulder	gw	42 Seward Street
AD	5.10.1813	Ann Desvigny	cm	49 Rosoman Street, Clerkenwell
ADC	17.5.1731	Anthony Du Chesne	smw	Grafton Street, Seven Dials

* Widow of John Barugh. See Ba below, and Section I, no. 10.
† See also WA below.
‡ See also IAC below, and Section III, nos. 3471, 3613.

Mark	Entered	Name	Category	Address/Notes
AF	14.10.1734	Abraham Ferron	cm	Golden Fan, Great St. Andrew Street, St. Giles
AG	12.11.1790	Alexander Grant	smw	2 Winkworths Buildings, City Road
AG	12.9.1814	Ann Grove	cm	2 Vineyard Walk
AG JM }	20.12.1813	Ann Grove and James Melvill	cm	9 Vineyard Walk
AH, pellet between	25.1.1837	Alfred Hunt	cm	13 Shorts Building, Clerkenwell
AK, crown above	2.6.1788	Andrew King	cm	City Road, near Old Street
AM	5.7.1784	*Angela Marson	cm	Butchers Close, Upper Moorfields
AM	3.10.1810	Arthur Moring	cm	6 Pitman's Buildings, John's Row, St. Luke's
AM PD }	11.11.1793	Ann Macaire and Peter Desvignes	gw	13 Denmark Street, Soho
AN	4.11.1813	Augustus Newman	gw	7 Plumptree Street, Bloomsbury
idem	29.4.1817	idem		idem
AR	20.7.1827	Alfred Reeves	cm	42 Spencer Street, Clerkenwell
AS, coronet above	6.2.1735	Alexander Seret	cm	Malts Court, Fore Street, near Moorfields
AS	18.4.1822	Alexander Smith	smw	9 May's Buildings, St. Martin's Lane
AT	30.5.1789	†Alice Tringham	gw	3 Queen's Head Passage, Newgate Street
AT	23.12.1836	Alfred Thickbromm	cm	10 Galway Street, Bath Street
Ba, coronet above	11.9.1710	Thomas Baldwin	?cm	New Street. 'Free Clockmaker'
Ba	4.4.1718	‡John Barugh	?cm	Hind Court, Fleet Street. 'Free Clockmaker'
BA	undated prob. April 1697	Nathaniel Baseley	?cm	Gunpowder Alley, New Street. 'free Clockmaker'
BB	14.6.1799	Benjamin Bradberry	cm	Rose and Crown Court, Moorfields
BC	22.6.1732	§Benjamin Cartwright	?smw	3 Horse Shoes, Pedlars Lane, Cows Cross

* ? Widow of James Marson, Section I, no. 1537 and below.
† See John Tringham, Section I, no. 1708.
‡ See Ann Barugh above, and IB below.   § See Section I, nos. 142–4.

INCUSE MARKS OF ALL CATEGORIES

Mark	Entered	Name	Category	Address/Notes
BC, pellet between	27.2.1749	Benjamin Cooper	?cm	of Buringham (?BIRMINGHAM) by power of attorney by John Elton
BC, and BC ring above	9.7.1791	Benedict Couta	gw	3 Cross Lane, Long Acre
Be	14.3.1720	*John Beesly	?cm	The Sun, Holborn Bridge. 'Clockmaker'
BE	undated c. 1720-32	Ben Ellis	?smw	Golden Cup, Cary Lane. 'free Skinner'
BE, pellet in lozenge above	undated prob. April 1697	John Beckett	?cm	New Street
BE, coronet above	undated prob. April 1697	Urian Berrington	cm	Fetter Lane. 'free Clockmaker for watch cases'
BE	9.10.1795	Benjamin Eamonson	cm	9 Little Sutton Street Goswell Street
BI	22.3.1734	Richard Bignell	?cm	No address
BILLS	20.9.1736	Edward Bills	?cm	The Hand and Bucket, St. Martin's Court
BN, pellet between	6.8.1787	Bartholomew Need	cm	6 Cross Street, Clerkenwell
three similar marks	1788-96	idem		idem
BN	4.7.1804	†idem	cm	27 Rawstone Street, St. John's Road
BN, script	20.6.1809	idem		idem
BN, script conjoined	25.4.1820	Benjamin Norton	cm	59 Banner Street, St. Luke's
BN, pellets } IT, between	24.2.1783	Bartholomew Need and John Taylor	cm	13 Bridgewater Square
BO	undated prob. April 1697	Samuel Bowtell	?cm	Fetter Lane. 'free Clockmaker'
BP, crown above	10.2.1731	Benjamin Piron	?cm	Cabinet Court, Duke Street, Spitafields
BP	9.10.1802	‡Benjamin Pike	smw	48 Blue Anchor Alley, Bunhill Row
BS	26.7.1798	Benjamin Smart	gw	35 Frith Street, Soho
idem	8.5.1805	idem	gw	55 Princes Street, Leicester Square
BT, pellet between	18.10.1766	Benjamin Tristram	cm	Huggins Alley

* See IB below. † See Susanna Need below.
‡ See Samuel Pike below.

Mark	Entered	Name	Category	Address/Notes
I, B.T, C	24.8.1764	*Benjamin Tristram and John Catt	cm	Huggin Alley. 'Watchcase makers'
B, WL	30.7.1773	†William Le Bas		Red Lion Street, Theobalds Road (the entry struck through. See WLB, Section I)
? BW, ? RW (impression missing)	4.12.1805	Benjamin and Robert Webb	cm	21 St. John's Square, Clerkenwell
CB, pellet between	8.4.1836	Charles Brady	cm	34 Gloucester Street, Queen Square
CBH	22.5.1832	Cornelius Brook Holliday	cm	21 Queen Street, Percival Street, Clerkenwell
idem	28.8.1837	‡idem	cm	idem
CC, coronet above	16.4.1735	§Charles Clark	?cm	Gloucester Court, White Cross Street
CC, daisy above	31.10.1767	Charles Coleman	?cm	Tottenham Court Road
CC, script	23.1.1796	Charles Chassereau	cm	32 Ironmonger Row, Old Street
CC	4.7.1816	Charles Clarke	cm	70 Bunhill Row
CC, star above	11.7.1817	idem	cm	idem
CD	22.12.1828	Charles Dalton	cm	22 Mill Row, Kingsland Road
	22.12.1830	idem	cm	Moved to 4 Whitmore Road, Hoxton
	29.8.1833	idem	cm	Moved to 6 Mitchel Street, St. Luke's
	9.10.1834	idem	cm	Moved to 17 Ratcliff Gardens, St. Luke's
CD	27.9.1837	Charles Davenport	smw	33 Tabernacle Row, City Road
CE	7.10.1823	Charles Essex	smw	131 St. John Street, Clerkenwell
	22.5.1834	idem	smw	Moved to 2 Well Street, Grays Inn Road
	14.5.1838	idem	smw	Moved to 26 Southampton Row
CFN	12.10.1835	Charles Frederick Norvell	smw	8 Maidenhead Court Aldersgate Street
	26.9.1837	idem	smw	Moved to 4 Maidenhead Court, Aldersgate Street
	12.10.1857	idem	smw	Moved to 2 Haysward Place, Old Kent Road

* See Section I, no. 1207, and IC below.
‡ See also Section VI.
† See Section I, no. 3230a.
§ See Section I, nos. 284–6, 294.

INCUSE MARKS OF ALL CATEGORIES

Mark	Entered	Name	Category	Address/Notes
CG	22.3.1815	Charles Greenwood	cm	17 St. James's Street, Clerkenwell
CG	7.3.1823	Charles Green	pdm	24 Auther (?Arthur) Street, Goswell Street
CG JG }	23.12.1814	*Charles and Joseph Greenwood	cm	17 St. James's Street, Clerkenwell
CH, coronet above	11.12.1717	Charles Hyde	?smw	no address. 'of ye company of Broderers'
CH	10.4.1730	Charles Harrison	?smw	New Street Square, 'att Mr Goddards'
CH, script	10.11.1801	Charles Hubbard	cm	4 Johns Row, Brick Lane, St. Luke's
CH	13.7.1822	Charles Harle	cm	68 Wynyatt Street, Islington Road
CI	8.4.1720	†(Sir) Charles Jones	?smw	'at ye Dich side fonder'
CJ	10.1.1817	Charles Jaques	pdm	39 Red Lion Street, Clerkenwell
CL	13.12.1713	John Cleake (?)	?smw	Green Arbor Court, Little Old Bailey
CL, crown above	13.11.1732	Charles Lilliwhite	cm	New Street, near Fetter Lane
CL, pellet between	13.11.1815	Charles Lupton	cm	9 Red Lion Street, Clerkenwell
	15.3.1816	idem	cm	Moved to 6 St. James's Place, Clerkenwell
CL, scroll below	14.2.1817	idem	cm	idem
CL EL	6.1.1817	Charles and Edward Lupton	cm	6 St James's Place, Clerkenwell
CM, script	3.1.1800	Charles Mince	cm	6 St. James's Walk
idem, larger	21.2.1801	idem	cm	Moved to 1 Little Mitchel Street, St. Luke's
idem, interlaced	11.4.1808	idem	cm	59 Banner Square, St. Luke's
idem	4.1.1810	idem	cm	idem
CM	6.2.1816	‡Charles Muston	cm	13 St. James's Street, Clerkenwell
CM JM }	12.6.1809	Charles and Jeremiah Mince	cm	59 Banner Square, St. Luke's
C𝔭	27.10.1830	§Charles Plumley	plw	231 Strand
CR	11.2.1818	Charles Reid	cm	Mitchell Street, St. Luke's
CS	16.7.1789	Charles Simpson	smw	47 Old Bethlem

* See also Section VI. † See also Section IV.
‡ See also Section VI. § See Section I, no. 403.

291

Mark	Entered	Name	Category	Address/Notes
C.S	24.1.1797	Charles Saffell	cm	36 Clerkenwell Green
CT, pellet between	30.7.1778	Christian Thiems (?)	cm	20 Middle Street, Cloth Fair
	9.6.1780	idem	cm	Moved to 11 Bridgewater Gardens
	23.1.1782	idem	cm	Moved to 25 Whitecross Square
CT	3.9.1807	*Charles Tisdall	cm	13 Greenhill Rents
idem	12.12.1810	idem	cm	idem
idem	5.7.1822	idem	cm	idem
CW, pellet between	20.9.1783	†Charles Watts	smw	16 Wheeler Street, Spitalfields
DA	10.7.1717	Jenkin Davy	?smw	Old Bailey
DA, ? eagle above	16.2.1731	Daniel Aveline	?smw	Blue Ball, Tower Street, Seven Dials
DB, coronet above	15.6.1726	Denis Boursin	?cm	Golden Cup, Chandos Street
DD	22.3.1786	Daniel Dunnage	cm	5 Little Moorfields
DE	12.8.1707	Louis Derumaux	?cm	Blackfriars. 'free Clockmaker'
DL	undated May–Oct. 1725	Daniel Lemaire	?smw	Harvest Court by Half Moon Street, Strand
DP, pellet between	3.11.1758	David Pullin	cm	Coleman Street
idem	11.7.1776	idem	cm	9 Islington Road
DR, pellet between	25.6.1784	Daniel Rust	cm	1 Norman Buildings, Old Street
idem	20.6.1785	idem	cm	idem
	26.4.1790	idem	cm	Moved to 4 Old Street Square
DR, pellets II, between	1.2.1783	Daniel Rust and John Jones	cm	2 Norman's Buildings, Bunhill Row
idem	4.7.1783	idem	cm	idem
DW	24.1.1798	Daniel Walker	cm	9 Shorts Buildings, Clerkenwell Close
	30.9.1799	idem	cm	Moved to 49 Clerkenwell Close
idem	11.12.1802	idem	cm	idem
DW, script	11.12.1799	‡§David Whitehouse	smw	4 St. John's Street, Clerkenwell
	28.6.1810	idem	smw	Moved to 2 Sandyard, Turnmill Street

* See also IW CT below. † See Section I, no. 429.
‡ See Section I, no. 516. § Mark identified on silver spectacles 1823.

INCUSE MARKS OF ALL CATEGORIES

Mark	Entered	Name	Category	Address/Notes
DW	22.8.1805	Daniel Willmott	cm	7 Orchard Street, St. Luke's
EA	undated before Nov. 1721	Thomas East	?cm	Old Change. 'free Clockmaker'
EB	26.4.1725	Edward Butler	?smw	Ploughyard, Fetter Lane
EC	21.7.1725	Edward Chandler	?cm	Turnagain Lane, Snow Hill. 'free of ye Clockmaker Company'
EC, star above	13.12.1731	Edward Curill (?)	?smw	Giltspur Street without Newgate. 'free of the Goldsmith Company'
ED, star above	12.10.1719	Isaac Edwards	?cm	Arbor Court, Old Bailey. 'free Clockmaker'
ED	22.6.1778	*Elizabeth Dawson	cm	Oxford Arms Passage, Warwick Lane
ED	7.2.1827	Edward Abraham Delgrave	smw	St. Martin's Le Grand
EE, pellet between, star above	1.7.1775	Edward Ellicott	cm	17 Royal Exchange
EF	29.3.1814	Edward Feline	cm	7 Serle Row, Bath Street, St. Luke's
idem	3.1.1821	idem	cm	8 Pittman's Building, City Road
	4.9.1822	idem	cm	Removed to 2 Gloucester Street, Curtain Road
EG, daisy above	10.12.1736	Edward Gibbons	?cm	New Street Square, Shoe Lane. 'free Clockmaker'
EG	6.11.1817	Edmund Grove	cm	6 Albemarle Street
	22.4.1820	idem	cm	Moved to 5 Howards Place, Bowling Green Lane, Clerkenwell
EH, fleur-de-lys above	17.12.1772	Edlin Howard	cm	Little New Street, Shoe Lane
idem	3.6.1788	idem	cm	14 Ratcliff Row, City Road
E & JW	5.5.1826	Edward and Joseph Bonaparte Walker	cm	31 Rosoman Street, Clerkenwell
EK	27.11.1827	Edward Keat	cm	69 Banner Street
E. KING, large crown above	undated Jan. 1717–July 1720	Edward King	?smw	'Mint Street in the Mint'
EL	29.8.1781	Edward Leeming	cm	24 Giltspur Street
	4.1.1796	idem	cm	122 Bunhill Row
EL	9.8.1817	Edward Lupton	cm	110 Goswell Street

* See William Dawson, Section I, no. 3086, and WD below.

EL   GI

Mark	Entered	Name	Category	Address/Notes
EL	18.12.1830	Ebenezer Lowrie	cm	4 St. James's Place, Clerkenwell
EP	19.4.1833	*Edward Peacock	smw	18 Myrtle Street, Hoxton
EP	24.2.1809	Edward Potter	smw	15 Vere Street, Clare Market
ER, coronet above	19.5.1735	†E. Renou	?cm	'Lumber Street in ye mint Southwark'
ES, pellet between	3.6.1771	Edward Scales	?cm	99 Strand
ET	14.11.1806	Edward Terry	smw	2 Little Sutton Street, Clerkenwell
ET	21.2.1822	Edmund Taylor	smw	22 Fleet Lane, Old Bailey
	24.2.1825	idem	smw	Moved to 15 White Horse Yard, Stanhope Street
EW	6.9.1729	Elias Wilks	?smw	Union Court, Holborn
EW	25.8.1730	Edward Walker I	?cm	'Wits aley Cyanery Lane' (?) 'founder'
EW	29.7.1826	Edward Walker II	cm	31 Rosoman Street, Clerkenwell
idem	25.1.1830	idem	cm	46 Whiskin Street, Clerkenwell
	10.8.1835	idem		Moved to 48 Whiskin Street
	22.8.1836	idem		Moved to 2½ Foundling Terrace, Gray's Inn Road
EW	27.5.1834	Edwin Wilcox	pdm	13 Gibraltar Walk, Bethnal Green
FC } FH }	23.12.1808	Frederick Comtesse and Frederick Humbert	gw	34 King Street, Soho
	no date	idem		Moved to 21 Hyde Street, Bloomsbury
FH	14.12.1814	Frederick Humbert	cm	21 Hyde Street, Bloomsbury
FH } PM }	11.1.1826	Frederick Humbert and Philibert Mathey	cm	20 Hyde Street, Bloomsbury
FI	undated c. 1698	William Finch	?cm	Mulberry Court, Coleman Street. 'free Clockmaker'
FS	31.12.1813	Felix Shepard	scm	6 Bath Street, City Road
	23.11.1820	idem	idem	Moved to 1 Doby Court, Monkwell Street
	13.4.1822	idem		Moved to 1 George Yard, Old Street
	3.4.1828	idem	idem	Moved to 1 Great Sutton Street, Clerkenwell

* See also Section IV.   † See IR below.

INCUSE MARKS OF ALL CATEGORIES

Mark	Entered	Name	Category	Address/Notes
FS	13.9.1833	idem	idem	40 Wellington Street, St. Luke's
	1.2.1838	idem	idem	Moved to 5 Hoxton Market
FW	22.7.1807	Frances Wright	cm	7 King Street, Clerkenwell
GB	5.5.1821	George Brown I	cm	Bear Alley, Fleet Market
	11.3.1834	idem		Moved to 14 St. James's Buildings, Rosoman Street, Clerkenwell
GB	23.1.1835	idem	idem	idem
GB •	18.6.1822	George Brown II	gw	53 Green Street, Goswell Street
GC	21.6.1777	George Clerke I	cm	6 Round Court, St. Martin's Le Grand
GC	3.10.1806	George Clerke II	cm	18 Longs Buildings, White Cross Street
	19.1.1808 and 9.2.1810	idem		idem
GC	14.2.1821	George Conen	cm	6 Hull Street, St. Luke's
GC axe IC above	16.10.1804	*George and John Carpenter	cm	12 King Street, Clerkenwell
GD	28.9.1807	Griffith Downe	cm	4 Clerkenwell (?)
GD	11.3.1817	George Dane	gw	128 Great Porland Street
GE, pellet between	26.1.1807	George Eichorn	smw	44 Wardour Street, Soho
GG	18.4.1815	George Glenny	cm	21 Wynyatt Street, Goswell Street
GG RG	18.5.1814	George and Richard Garnett	smw	1 Perkins Rents, Peter Street, Westminster
GH, rayed sun above	11.9.1760	†George Harrison	?cm	Fenchurch Street
idem	18.12.1760	idem	cm	Goulston Square, Whitechapel
GH	27.10.1763	Giles Hooper	?cm	Gravil Street, Hatton Garden
GH	26.3.1776	George Hanet	gw	Porter Street, Newport Market
GH	6.3.1777	Gyles Hooper	cm	17 Union Court, Holborn
GH	11.2.1828	George Hammon	cm	2 Meredith Street
idem	19.3.1834	idem	cm	4 Skinner Street, Clekenwell
GI	3.8.1717	Solomon Gibbs	?cm	Plough Yard, Fetter Lane. 'free Clockmaker'

* See also IC Joseph Carpenter below.
† See Section I, no. 815.

GL   HH

Mark	Entered	Name	Category	Address/Notes
GL	23.3.1820	George Lassells	cm	16 Bateman's Buildings, Soho
GL	6.4.1820	idem	cm	idem
GM, star above	15.10.1789	*Gideon Macaire	gw	12 Denmark Street, St. Giles
GM	10.4.1816	George Meriton	cm	18 Clerkenwell Green
	9.7.1817	idem	cm	Moved to 6 St. John's Lane
	18.1.1821	idem	cm	Moved to 12 Europa Place, John Row, St. Luke's
GM	13.3.1822	idem	cm	5 Bathek (?) Street, St. Luke's
	21.10.1829	idem	cm	Moved to 17 Norman's Buildings, St. Luke's
GMB	20.6.1817	George Musgrave Batts	cm	8 Charterhouse Street
GN	9.1.1734	George Nixon	?cm	Little Green Arbour Court, Old Bailey
GN	30.3.1815	George Nichols	cm	27 Rawstone Street, Islington Road
GP	15.6.1822	George Parker	gw	11 Bulstrode Street, Manchester Square
GP	1.6.1831	George Poole	cm	6 Bartholomew Terrace, King Square, St. Luke's
GR	24.2.1794	Gaspard Richard	cm	3 Great St. Andrew Street, Seven Dials
idem	11.3.1794	idem	cm	idem
GR	4.9.1823	George Richards	cm	17 Bridgewater Square
GS	16.1.1736	George Smith	?cm	Poultry, against Grocers Alley. 'Clockmaker'
GS	23.1.1813	†George Smith	pdm	32 Red Lion Street
GS	12.3.1817	George Scott	cm	3 Phillips Court, Grub Street
idem	11.1.1822	idem	cm	19 Waterloo Street, St. Luke's
idem	23.9.1823	idem	cm	idem
	23.1.1826	idem	cm	Moved to 9 Norman Street, St. Luke's
	5.10.1827	idem	cm	Moved to 9 Regent Street, City Road
idem	15.2.1830	idem	cm	idem
idem	6.11.1830	idem	cm	35 Rahere Street, Goswell Road
	17.1.1837	idem	cm	Moved to 20 Moor Lane, Fore Street

* See Ann Macaire and Peter Desvignes above, also Section VII, GM, star above.
† See also Mary Smith below.

INCUSE MARKS OF ALL CATEGORIES

Mark	Entered	Name	Category	Address/Notes
GS	6.2.1835	George Sutton	gw	14 Bridge Road, Lambeth
	19.1.1847	idem	gw	Moved to 16 Bridge Road, Lambeth
GT	5.5.1738	Gray Townsend	cm	Wood's Coffee House, WoodStreet.'Clockmaker'
GW	30.5.1716	*George Watkins	?cm	Green Arbour Court, Old Bailey
GW	23.1.1776	George Walkers	cm	23 Salisbury Street, Strand
GW	7.10.1790	†George Wintle	plw	Aldersgate Street
GY	18.3.1723	‡George Young	smw	Glasshouse Yard, Blackfriars. 'free Cutler'
H	27.4.1733	Elisha Horne	?cm	New Street Square, near Shoe Lane
HA	9.5.1701	William Harrison	?cm	Great New Street. 'free Clockmaker'
HA	17.11.1717	§Paul Hanet	smw	Great St. Andrew Street, St. Giles. 'free Longbow Stringmaker'
HB	5.5.1769	Henry Blyth		'Gunmaker in the Minories'
HB	27.7.1826	Henry Berry	smw	14 Green Street, Theobalds Road
idem	15.9.1826	idem	smw	idem
HB } GB }	31.7.1826	Horatio and George Elliot Bartlett	cm	27 Greenhill Rents, Smithfields Bars
	29.12.1826	idem	cm	Moved to 3 King Square
HC	26.3.1740	‖Henry Crook	?cm	Brook's Market
HD	10.10.1797	John Henry De Larue	cm	24 Litchfield Street
HG	17.2.1816	Horace Gooch	cm	47 Clerkenwell Close
HG	3.8.1816	Henry Galloway	cm	49 Coppice Row, Clerkenwell
	no date	idem	cm	Moved to Woods Place, Bowling Green Lane
	25.2.1819	idem	cm	Moved to 8 Bartholomew Square, St. Luke's
	13.12.1821	idem	cm	Moved to 38 Reeves Place, Hoxton
	25.8.1826	idem		Moved to Upper Clifton Street, Finsbury
	22.4.1839	idem		Moved to Emmens Buildings, Chapple Street, Pentonville
HH	18.8.1721	Henry Hur(s)t?	cm	Princes Street. 'Clockmaker'

* See also WA below. † See Section I, nos. 923–6.
‡ See Section I, no. 928. § See Section I, nos. 942, 2189.
‖ See Section I, no. 967.

HH   IB

Mark	Entered	Name	Category	Address/Notes
HH	26.3.1778	*Henry Harding	cm	Princes Street, Barbican
HH	9.1.1830	Henry Hardy	cm	14 Rosomans Row, Clerkenwell
HHN	27.10.1834	†Henry Howard Nicholson	cm	5 Charles Street, Goswell Street, Road
Hi	undated c. 1697–8	John Higgs	?cm	Chequer Court, Old Bailey. 'free Clockmaker'
HJ	5.7.1816	Henry Jackson	cm	6 King Street, Clerkenwell
	19.10.1816	idem	cm	Moved to 5 Red Lion Square, Clerkenwell
HJ	28.3.1817	idem	cm	72 Compton Street, Clerkenwell
HP, pellet between	22.3.1763	‡Henry Pennyfeather	cm	'Prugians' Court, Old Bailey
HR	10.9.1723	Henry Rawlins	?cm	Cock Lane, Snow Hill. 'Clockmaker'
HR, coronet above	19.12.1733	idem	cm	'West Smithfield near yᵉ Red Cow'
HV	7.1.1715	§John Hughes	smw	Blackfriars. 'free Cutler'
HW	2.5.1823	Henry Whatmore	plw	35 Tothill Street, Westminster
Ia	undated c. 1700	William Jaques	?cm	Angel Court, Snow Hill. 'free Clockmaker'
IA, small crown between above	24.1.1734	Isaac Albert	cm	Still Court by the Bell and Magpy Without Bishops(gate)
IA, winged cherub's head (?) above	13.9.1733	James Allix	cm	'Dorset Street over against Doctor fletchers in Spittlefields'
IA, script monogram crescent above	1.12.1736	idem	cm	Half Moon, Porter Street, St. Anns
IA, pellet between	7.12.1760	Josiah Alderson	?cm	Pye Corner
IA, pellet between, star above	22.1.1776	John Allen	cm	16 Aldersgate Street Buildings
idem	23.11.1791	idem	cm	38 Gee Street, Goswell Street
IA	9.4.1795	idem	cm	12 King's Court, Bunhill Row
idem	18.4.1804	idem	cm	12 Pinks Road, City Road

* See Section I, no. 1415. † Also later cameo mark. See Section VI.
‡ See Section I, no. 1060. § See IH below for his gold mark.

INCUSE MARKS OF ALL CATEGORIES

Mark	Entered	Name	Category	Address/Notes
I.A, stop between	8.3.1793	John Atkinson	bm	10 Ball Alley, Lombard Street
IA, pellet between	13.1.1798	*Jacob Amedroz	gw	6 Meards Street, Soho
IAC, coronet above	15.5.1764	†James Anthony Calame	?smw	Strand, facing Exeter Change
IAT	28.2.1834	Joseph Abram Tyas	cm	36 Seward Street, Goswell Street
IB, pellet between	13.7.1716	‡John Barugh	?cm	'ye 2 White fryars in fleet Street'. 'free Clockmaker'. (Probably for gold)
IB	undated c. 1721	§John Benton	?cm	Half Moon Coffee House, Half Moon Passage, Gutter Lane. 'free Vinterner'
IB	14.3.1720	‖John Beesley	?cm	The Sun, Holborn Bridge. 'Clockmaker'
IB, small coronet above	4.1.1724	Joshua Barras	?smw	Elliott's Court, Little Old Bailey. 'gouldsmith'
JB	21.6.1731	idem	?smw	idem
IB, pellet between small star above	8.7.1746	¶John Berthellot	?smw	'Removed from Saffron Hill to the Bolling alley turnmill Street'
	30.11.1750	idem	?smw	Removed to White Horse Alley, Cow Cross
IB	4.5.1761	John Barrow	?cm	Golden Head, Tottenham Court Road
IB, ring above	11.8.1761	Joseph Buschman	?gw	Warwick Lane
IB, pellet between	8.7.1763	John Bingley	cm	Little Britain
IB	3.11.1774	idem	cm	13 Little Britain
IB	30.8.1782	John Bullocke	cm	40 Ironmonger Row, Old Street
IB, star above	29.1.1794	John Beadelcomb	cm	3 New Court, St. John Street, Clerkenwell
IB	23.1.1794	John Baxter	cm	113 Banner Street, Bunhill Row
IB, pellet between (two sizes)	8.8.1808	John Baxter	cm	28 North Street, City Road
	10.1.1809	idem	cm	Moved to 1 Church Row, St. Luke's
IB	1.12.1810	idem	cm	idem

* His mark identified on fine gold snuffboxes.
† See AC above and Section III, nos. 3471, 3613.
‡ See Anne Barugh, and Ba above.
§ Annotated 'my Husband being sick a bed witness my hand Mary benton'.
‖ See also Be above. ¶ See Section I, nos. 1129, 1179, 3616.

Mark	Entered	Name	Category	Address/Notes
IB	6.2.1812	idem	cm	idem
IB	16.3.1815	idem	cm	idem
IB	14.2.1817	idem	cm	3 Phillips Court, Grub Street
	23.12.1818	idem	cm	Moved to 12 Waterloo Street, St. Luke's
IB	5.4.1824	idem	cm	idem
IB	13.7.1829	idem	cm	idem
	18.6.1839	idem	cm	Moved to 54 Gee Street, Goswell Street
IB	3.10.1817	Joseph Burton	scm	15 Blackfriars Road
IC	19.9.1725	John Clarke	?cm	Cock Lane, Snow Hill. 'Free of ye Clockmakers Company'
IC	14.2.1727	John Cannans	?cm	Nagg's Head Court, Snow Hill. 'Clockmaker'
IC, star above	17.5.1726	James Crichet	?smw	Crown and Pearl, New Belton Street, St. Giles
IC	17.2.1727	John Cottenbelt	?book mounts	Duke Street, Lincoln's Inn Fields, 'at Mr Richmonds a Booksellers'
IC, star above	17.10.1766	*John Catt	cm	Noble Street
	no date	idem	cm	Rose Alley, Golden Lane
	30.10.1771	idem	cm	2 Bridgewater Gardens
IC	11.5.1776	†Jasper Const	gw	Salisbury Court, Fleet Street
IC, pellet between	13.12.1784	‡John Cooper	smw	5 Wardour Street, Soho
IC	no date	idem	smw	81 St. James's Street
IC, pellet between	13.3.1792	idem	smw	83 St. James's Street
IC, script, axe above	17.10.1774	§Joseph Carpenter	cm	Blue Anchor Alley, Bunhill Row
	28.3.1778	idem	cm	Moved to the Golden Horn, St. John Street Road
IC	19.8.1786	idem	cm	idem
IC, script	9.6.1779	John Clarke	cm	Ironmongers' Row, Old Street
IC, script	27.8.1790	idem	cm	idem
idem	1791 and 1802	idem	cm	Moved to Bunhill Row

* See BT.IC above, and Section I, no. 1207.
† See also JC below and Section I, no. 1195.
‡ See Section I, no. 1231. § See Section I, no. 1226 and Section VI.

INCUSE MARKS OF ALL CATEGORIES

Mark	Entered	Name	Category	Address/Notes
IC	13.12.1808	John Cuthbert	gw	11 Tottenham Court Road
IC	13.9.1828	John Crawley	smw	13 Great Newport Street, Leicester Square
IC	6.5.1836	John Canning	smw	50 Long Acre
IC, script	18.12.1801	Joseph Clarke	cm	71 Bunhill Row
IC, script	16.8.1817	John Crossland	cm	33 Ironmonger Street, St. Luke's
IC } FD	6.5.1812	James Cusins and Francis Dubois	cm	3 Richmond Building, Soho
IC } NC	18.7.1816	John and Nathaniel Crossland	cm	4 Pear Tree Street, Goswell Street
ID	28.7.1730	*John Dearmer I	?cm	Salisbury Court, Fleet Street. 'free Clockmaker'
ID	6.9.1736	John Dewilde	?cm	Ship Court, Old Bailey
ID, pellet between	17.1.1769	John Dimsdale	?cm	Goswell Street
ID	20.3.1782	John Dearmer II	cm	14 Featherstone Street, Bunhill Row
ID	19.12.1794	James Davenport	smw	1 Oat Lane, Noble Street
	4.7.1807	idem	smw	Moved to 1 George Street
ID	6.8.1807	idem	smw	idem
ID	20.2.1809	John Dyer	cm	85 Goswell Street
ID	18.12.1818	idem	cm	idem
	24.9.1819	idem	cm	Moved to 25 Plumber Street, City Road
	2.10.1826	idem	cm	Moved to 13 Dorset Crescent
ID	3.6.1814	James Dow	cm	15 St. James' Buildings, Clerkenwell
ID	30.6.1826	†James John Davenport	smw	14 London Wall
	21.9.1829	idem	smw	36 Wellington Street, Goswell Street
IE	10.7.1714	Benjamin Jeffes	?cm	New Street. 'Clockmaker'
IE, star above	12.10.1719	Isaac Edwards	?cm	Green Arbor Court, Old Bailey. 'free clockmaker'. 'Gold Mark'
IE	18.3.1799	Innocent Ekins	cm	2 Cumberland Curtain Road, Shoreditch
IE	12.3.1833	John Eagles	smw	5 Cock Lane, West Smithfield
	13.7.1844	idem	smw	Moved to 21 Cobourg Street, Clerkenwell

---

* See Section I, no. 1239.   † See James Davenport above, ? a son.

301

IF   IH

Mark	Entered	Name	Category	Address/Notes
IF, pellet between	9.10.1733	James Freman	?smw	Corner of Charterhouse Square
IF	3.10.1738(?)	James Fray	?cm	Little Old Bailey. 'Freeman of the Clockmaker's Company'
IF, script, star above	22.6.1765	John Foster	?cm	Goswell Street
IF	12.2.1799	John Field	ring maker	7 Bucklersbury
IF	7.2.1804	John Farren	gw	6 King Street, Goswell Street
IG	6.9.1736	James Gray	?cm	Hoxton Square Coffee House
IG	10.8.1787	*Joseph Griffin	bm	23 Red Cross Street
IG	10.5.1792	James Gouldsbrough	cm	5 Union Court, Holborn
IG	24.10.1792	Joseph Glenny	cm	13 Old Street Square
IG	19.8.1800	idem	cm	Moved to 22 Charles Square, Hoxton
IG (two sizes)	24.5.1804	idem	cm	Moved to 20 Red Lion Street, Clerkenwell
IG (two sizes)	14.12.1810	idem	cm	idem
IG	10.11.1812	idem	cm	idem
	16.7.1816	idem	cm	Moved to 6 Badger Yard, Red Lion Street
	16.5.1818	idem	cm	Moved to 23 St. John's Square, Clerkenwell
	16.1.1821	idem	cm	Moved to 21 Wynyatt Street, Clerkenwell
IG	1.12.1813	John Grisar	gw	23 Salisbury Street, Strand
IG	13.6.1814	John Green	pdm	20 Great Auther Street, Goswell Street
IG	15.7.1822	idem	pdm	24 Great Auther Street, Goswell Street
IG	24.7.1821	John Grove	cm	25 Ironmonger Row, St. Luke's
W } IG } V }	24.1.1770	John Gimblett and William Vale	?cm	BIRMINGHAM
IH, pellet between	8.2.1699	John Hickes (gold mark)	?cm	Plough Yard, Fetter Lane. 'free Clockmaker'
IH	7.4.1717	†John Hughes (gold mark)	smw	Blackfriars. 'free Cutler'
IH	22.7.1745	John Higginbotham	?cm	Whitehorse Court, Rosemary Lane

* See also Section VIII, IG.   † See HV above for Britannia Silver.

302

INCUSE MARKS OF ALL CATEGORIES

Mark	Entered	Name	Category	Address/Notes
IH, pellet between, coronet above	undated Mar.–Aug. 1729	Isaac Hochecorne	?cm	next door to Angel and Crown, Crispin Street, Spitalfields
IH, quatrefoil above	19.3.1733	John Hawkins	cm	Church year (sic) alley, Tuley Street, Southwarke. Watchcasemaker
IH	17.11.1767	John Hutchins	?cm	Bell Alley, Goswell Street
IH	22.10.1773	*John Harvey	gw	54 Snow Hill
IH	17.12.1789	John Hadley	cm	10 St. James Buildings, Rosomans Row
IH, pellet between	31.1.1801	idem	cm	idem
IH, pellet between	18.6.1801	idem	cm	Moved to 7 Rosomans Street
IH	9.8.1817	idem	cm	5 Austin Street, Shoreditch
	11.2.1818	idem	cm	Moved to 27 St. John Square
IH	7.6.1810	John Holmes	smw	Cherry Tree Alley, Whitecross Street
	11.2.1817	idem	smw	Moved to 2 Hospital Gate, West Smithfield
IH	26.10.1822	idem	smw	Moved to 14 Red Cross Square
IH, script	11.3.1817	John Harris	cm	41 Rawstone Street, Islington Road
idem, conjoined	17.9.1823	idem	cm	idem
IH	4.10.1819	James Haynes	gw	7 Plum Tree Street, Bloomsbury
IH	undated between July 1822 and Mar. 1825	John William Hammon	cm	91 Goswell Street
idem	4.3.1833	idem	cm	48 Whiskin Street
IH, pellet between	16.3.1837	idem	cm	11 Gloucester Street, St. John Street Road
IH, pellet between	9.9.1837	idem	cm	idem
IH, pellet between	3.1.1843	idem	cm	Moved to 26½ Sekford Street, Clerkenwell
	22.2.1844 30.4.1844 and 20.9.1854	idem	cm	Moved to 11 Sekford Street Two cameo marks at same address

* See Section I, no. 1372, perhaps his father.

IHG   IMH

Mark	Entered	Name	Category	Address/Notes
IHG	3.5.1819	John Henry Green	pdm	24 Great Arthur Street, Goswell Street
IHG	26.7.1820	idem	pdm	idem
	30.11.1820	idem	pdm	Moved to 17 Noble Street, Goswell Street
IHG	3.8.1836	idem	pdm	Moved to 36 Seward Street, Goswell Street
IHM	7.2.1829	John Hornby Maw	smw	55 Aldermanbury
II	9.7.1731	James Jones	?cm	'tithamham Corte Road near ye Rad Lion'
II	19.3.1807	John Jones	smw	9 Shoe Lane
IJ	6.12.1814	John Jaques	smw	1 George Street, Foster Lane
	no date	idem	smw	Moved to 14 London Wall
IJ, pellet between	2.8.1837	John Jackson	cm	33 Great Sutton Street, Clerkenwell
	14.3.1839	idem	cm	Moved to 10 Woodbridge Street, Clerkenwell
IJ	–.3.1844	idem	cm	idem
IK	undated Aug. 1724–Oct. 1731	John Kendrick	cm	White Hart Yard, Drury Lane. 'free Clockmaker'
IK, pellet between	4.5.1790	John Kenebel	gw	13 Thrift (Frith) Street, Soho
IL	15.2.1723	John Laing	?cm	Whites Alley, Coleman Street. 'Clockmaker'
IL	— 1725	*John Lee I	?cm	Angel Court, Snow Hill
IL, coronet above	13.11.1735	John La Salle	cm	Near Nassau Coffee House, King Street, St. Anns, Watchcasemaker
IL	23.5.1755	John Laithwait	?cm	LIVERPOOL. 'by power of attorney'
IL	16.11.1759	John Laithwait	?cm	Cold Bath Street
IL	9.6.1760	†Joseph Lejeune	?cm	Porter Street, Seven Dials
IL, pellet between fleur-de-lys above	15.1.1761	Jeremiah Lister	?cm	Old Fish Street
IL	4.7.1797	‡James Long	smw	Royal Exchange
IL, conjoined	21.7.1801	John Le Maitre	gw	23 Strand
	4.5.1804	idem	gw	Moved to 49 Stanhope Street, Clare Market
IL, conjoined	11.7.1804	idem	gw	Moved to 73 Long Acre
	28.6.1805	idem	gw	Moved to George Street, Adelphi

* See Section I, no. 1465 and SI.IL below.   † See ILI below.
‡ See Section I, no. 1478.

INCUSE MARKS OF ALL CATEGORIES

Mark	Entered	Name	Category	Address/Notes
IL, conjoined	6.10.1808	idem	smw	73 Great St. Martin's Lane
	4.11.1809	idem	smw	Moved to 2 Little Court, Castle Street
IL, conjoined	19.8.1811	idem	smw	10 Long Acre
	3.5.1813	idem	smw	Moved to Porter Street, Newport Market
	20.4.1815	idem	smw	Moved to 21 Cecil Court, St. Martin's Lane
	6.10.1817	idem	smw	Moved to 10 Crown Street, Leicester Square
IL	24.11.1808	John Noé Lamy	gw	2 Rathbone Place, Oxford Street
ILI	5.2.1778	Joseph Lejeune	?cm	Lichfield Street, Soho
IM, six petalled flower above	6.6.1726	*James Manners	?smw	Great St. Andrew Street, near Seven Dials
idem	26.9.1745	James Manners, 'Junior'	?smw	Villars Street, York Buildings
IM, pellet between	6.8.1762	John Mason	?cm	Silver Street, near Wood Street
IM, pellet between	27.7.1770	John Moore	spur-maker	Poland Street, Soho
IM	13.6.1775	James Marson	cm	Princes Street, Moorfields
IM	6.8.1777	James Macklin	cm	7 Plumtree Street, Bloomsbury
IM	29.10.1785	idem	gw	idem
IM	31.8.1805	James Merfield	smw	28 Allen Street, Clerkenwell
IM, pellet between	21.11.1793	†Jonah Mince	cm	8 Norman Street, Old Street
idem	9.6.1800	idem	cm	idem
IM	24.11.1814	John Marsh	cm	35 Clerkenwell Green
IM, pellet between	5.3.1819	Isaac Morgan	cm	33 St. John Street, Clerkenwell
IM, script conjoined	3.4.1805	‡Jeremiah Mince	cm	8 Norman Street, St. Luke's
idem	2.2.1809	idem	cm	idem
IMH	19.1.1824	John Martin Harding	cm	37 Great Sutton Street, Clerkenwell
	no date	idem	cm	Moved to 4 Old Street, St. Luke's
	16.3.1830	idem	cm	Moved to 4 Wellington Street, Goswell Street
	18.3.1836	idem	cm	Moved to 13 Powell Street, East Kings Square

* See Section I, nos. 1515, 1538.   † See Jeremiah Mince below.
‡ See JM JG below.

Mark	Entered	Name	Category	Address/Notes
IN	7.11.1786	John Nevill	cm	14 Cold Bath Square, Clerkenwell
IN	2.1.1789	idem	cm	idem
IN	8.1.1801	idem	cm	Moved to Vineyard Walk, Clerkenwell
IN	3.12.1801	idem	cm	idem
IN	5.7.1806	idem	cm	idem
IN, pellet between	24.5.1815	idem	cm	4 Vineyard Walk, Clerkenwell
IN, pellet between	28.4.1813	John Norvell	scm	Horseshoe Passage, Newgate
	19.7.1814	idem	scm	Moved to 2 Amen Corner, Paternoster Row
	14.9.1815	idem	scm	Moved to 66 Bartholomew Close
INH	3.1.1835	*John Napthali Hart	cm	5 King Street, Finsbury
IO, coronet above	undated c. 1697	Jonathan Jones	?cm	Bell Savage Court, Ludgate Hill. 'free Clockmaker'
IP, pellet between	20.2.1771	John Parker	?smw	'at Phillpotts Toy shop near the Bull and gate High Holborn'
IP	29.4.1777	John Penny	cm	14 Princes Street, Barbican
	6.1.1778	idem	cm	Moved to 2 Aldersgate Buildings
IPC, pellets between	7.1.1836	John Priston Cutts	scm	3 Crane Court, Fleet Street
IPF, coronet above	undated c. 1721	Jean Pierre Fontaine	cm	'Jacksons Court near breack neck stairs Black fryers'
IR	19.3.1722	John Roumieu	?cm	Drury Lane. 'free of ye Clockmakers Company'
IR, scroll cresting above	undated c. 1724	†James Renou	?cm	'In lonber Stris S gorge pariszouwar' (!)
idem	16.9.1735	idem	cm	'cat in and corte at sno hill nare holben bridge London'
IR, crown above	21.10.1765	John Reading	cm	Falcon Court, Coppice Row, Clerkenwell
	12.2.1771	idem	cm	Moved to 26 Sea Coal Lane
IR, crown above	24.10.1776	idem	cm	Hart Street, Covent Garden
	15.4.1780	idem	cm	King Street, Moorfields
	10.6.1782	idem	cm	3 Holywell Row, Moorfields
	2.8.1786	idem	cm	3 Garden Court, Red Cross Street

* See Section I, nos. 510 etc and NH.INH below.
† See ER above and RO below, the latter perhaps the same.

INCUSE MARKS OF ALL CATEGORIES

Mark	Entered	Name	Category	Address/Notes
IR, pellet between	18.1.1762	James Richards	cm	Red Lion Court, Silver Street
	16.1.1764	idem	cm	Moved to Bridgewater Square
IR, script	20.7.1771	idem	cm	Lamb Street, Spitalfields
IR, pellet between	16.9.1774	idem	cm	1 Bridgewater Square
IR, script, pellet between	19.10.1778	idem	cm	21 Shoemaker Row, Blackfriars Walk, Clerkenwell
	18.6.1779	idem	cm	Moved to St. James
IR, pellet between	10.4.1784	idem	cm	9 Bridgewater Square
IR	26.2.1790	idem	cm	idem
IR	13.4.1798	idem	cm	idem
IR, crown above	30.5.1799	idem	cm	15 Ratcliffe Row, City Road
IR	4.8.1802	idem	cm	?
IR	23.12.1813	idem	cm	Bridgewater Square
idem	9.3.1816	idem	cm	idem
IR	5.8.1797	John Richardson	smw	Little Queen Street, Holborn
IR	30.10.1822	John Robertson	gw	26 Villers Street (see Section VII)
IR	6.3.1833	John Read	smw	35 Regent Circus, Piccadilly
IR, script, pellet between	3.3.1796	Isaac Russell	cm	Little Mitchell Street, Old Street
IS	15.10.1718	James Shortall	?cm	West Smithfield. 'free of Clockmakers Company'
IS, scroll cresting above	21.8.1724	John Simmons	?smw	East Harding Street, New Street. 'Goldsmith'
IS, heart above	27.3.1729	Joseph Slight	?smw	Glasshouse Yard, Blackfriars. 'Goldsmith'
IS	5.2.1730	John Smither	cm	White Hart and Barley Mow, Old Street over against the New Church. 'free Cutler'
IS, coronet above	2.6.1735	idem	cm	Old Street, near St. Luke's Church
IS	7.7.1732	John Shaw*	?cm	*'Golden Sugar Loaf within four doors of ye Hay Markett'
IS	8.7.1775	Joseph Steward	sm	98 Wood Street

* See PS below for similar address.

Mark	Entered	Name	Category	Address/Notes
IS, script	25.6.1765	John Stubbs	?cm	Great Arthur Street, St. Luke's
IS } TW }	30.7.1800	*James Styring and Thomas Walker	cm	15 Dorrington Street, Cold Bath Fields
IT (drawn)	8.12.1755	John Townsend	?smw	Grays Inn Road
IT	29.3.1784	John Taylor	cm	67 Wood Street
	4.7.1785	idem	cm	Moved to 31 Ironmonger Row, Old Street
IT, pellet between	14.1.1788	idem	cm	idem
IT, pellet between	24.3.1790	†John Taylor	cm	13 Bridgewater Square
IT, pellet between	27.2.1800	idem	cm	Moved to 98 Leadenhall Street
	10.9.1802	idem	cm	Moved to 8 Wilderness Row
IT	15.10.1792	James Tetley	cm	10 Norman Street
IT, pellet between	28.3.1804	‡John Turner	cm	Greenhills Rents, Cow Cross
ITC	12.3.1810	§John Turner Carpenter	gw	Fleet Lane, Old Bailey
IT } IW }	25.6.1789	John Taylor and John Wackrill	cm	14 Bridgewater Square
ITP	16.11.1775	John Terrill Pain	cm	67 Shoe Lane
	16.10.1776	idem	cm	Moved to 7 Dean Street, Fetter Lane
IT } TJ }	16.6.1821	John Tipson and Thomas Juxon	cm	11 Doby Court, Monkwell Street
IU	18.3.1803	John Ustonson	smw	21 George Yard, Old Street
IV } TC }	31.1.1782	John Vincent and Thomas Cooke	cm	2 Wardour Street, Soho
IW, coronet above	11.3.1729	John Wynell	?cm	Brook Street, Holborn
IW, star above	26.6.1730	John Ward	?cm	Boars Head Court, Fleet Street. 'free Clockmaker'
IW	27.9.1758	John Watkins	?smw	'On London Bridge'
IW	2.2.1771	idem	?smw	Giltspur Street near Newgate
IW	22.10.1761	John Wright	gw	Duck Lane,
	14.4.1772	idem	gw	Red Lion Street
IW, pellet between	28.3.1799	John Wright (? son)	gw	43 Red Lion Street, Clerkenwell

* See Section I, no. 2968.
† Probably a separate identity to the previous John Taylor. See IT.IW below.
‡ See Section I, no. 1706. § See also Section VII.

INCUSE MARKS OF ALL CATEGORIES

Mark	Entered	Name	Category	Address/Notes
IW	13.1.1802	John Wood	cm	6 Banner Street, St. Luke's
	4.8.1804	idem	cm	Moved to 87 St. John's Street
IW, script	3.9.1807	John Williams	cm	11 White Cross Street
IW	24.7.1810	idem	cm	Moved to 56 Great Sutton Street
IW	1.2.1822	John Whitehouse	scm	27 Baldwin Gardens
	no date	idem	scm	Moved to 36 Leather Lane Holborn
	5.5.1823	idem	scm	Moved to 26 Grove Place, Goswell Street Road
	4.12.1823	idem	scm	Moved to 36 St. John's Lane
IW	15.3.1831	Joseph Wickes	cm	Wenlock Street, St. Luke's
IW, cameo mark	26.8.1831	idem	cm	Moved to 13 St. John's Lane
IW⎫ CT⎭	20.4.1807	*John Williams and Charles Tisdall	cm	12 Greenhill's Rents
IWP	17.6.1819	Joseph William Palmer	cm	49 Clerkenwell Close
JA, pellet between	20.5.1761	Joseph Allen	?cm	Featherstone Street, Bunhill Row; later (no date) Old Bailey
JA	26.9.1821	James Ariell Junr.	cm	23 St. John's Square, Clerkenwell
	6.7.1824	idem	cm	Moved to 12 Red Lion Street, Clerkenwell
	13.10.1826	idem	cm	Moved to 9 Ashby Street
JB	12.5.1719	John Birdwhissell	?cm	Green Arbour, Little Bailey. 'free of ye Clockmakers'
JB	17.4.1821	Josiah Barnett	cm	43 Galway Street, St. Luke's
idem	25.10.1838	idem	cm	15 Lower Charles Street, Southampton Square
JC	21.8.1776	†Jasper Cunst	gw	?69 Dorset Street
JC	2.7.1817	James Collings	scm	11 Johns Row, Brick Lane, St. Luke's
	1.4.1818	idem	scm	Moved to 3 Bishop Court, Alsberry (?Aylesbury) Street
	9.8.1819	idem	scm	Moved to 15 Vineyard Gardens, Bowling Green Lane
	2.10.1826	idem	scm	Moved to 9 Howards Place, Clerkenwell
	15.2.1830	idem	smw	Moved to 6 Skinner Street, Corporation Lane

* See CT above.   † See IC above and Section I, no. 1195.

Mark	Entered	Name	Category	Address/Notes
JC	9.9.1834	James Cox	scm	5 Barbican
JD	10.8.1815	James Dow	cm	15 St. James Buildings
idem	3.1.1824	idem	cm	idem
JD	1.12.1824	Joseph Dewin	cm	35 Charlotte Street, City Road
	6.9.1828	idem	cm	Moved to 91 Aldersgate Street
	3.5.1834	idem	cm	Moved to 17 Red Lion Street, Clerkenwell
JD	11.7.1837	idem	cm	idem
JF	12.6.1811	John Fogg	smw	Holloway
JF	12.6.1835	John Fraser	plw	36 York Street, St. Luke's
JG, SG	25.8.1763	*James Gibbons and Samuel Goostree	?cm	White Cross Alley, Moorfields
J & EG	9.4.1834	John and Edward Grafton	cm	42 Coleman Street, City Road
	21.8.1835	idem		Moved to 81 Fleet Street
JH	8.9.1806	John Howe	cm	220 Ironmonger Row, Old Street
JH	5.12.1806	John Hudson	smw	14 White Street, Little Moorfields
JH, pellet between	1.2.1814	idem	smw	1 Orange Court, Orange Street, Leicester Square
JJ, pellet between	12.7.1790	James Jackson I	cm	2 Bridgewater Street, Barbican
JJ, pellet between	27.10.1795	†Joshua Jackson	cm	10 Bridgewater Gardens
idem, smaller	3.6.1797	idem	cm	idem
	8.5.1798	idem	cm	Moved to Ferns (?) Alley, Aldersgate Street
JJ	13.2.1824	James Jackson II	cm	22 Richmond Street, Old Street
JJ	26.11.1835	John Jackson	pencil maker	52 Gee Street, Goswell Street
JM	10.9.1814	James Melvill	cm	4 King Street, Clerkenwell
JM, pellet between	3.4.1822	idem	cm	13 Spencer Street, Clerkenwell
JM	7.3.1822	Joseph Millard	scm	24 Coppice Row, Cold Bath Fields
JM, pellet between	22.11.1837	idem	scm	idem
JM	8.7.1822	James Martin	cm	42 Union Street, Hoxton New Town

* See Section I, no. 1345.   † See Section I, nos. 1427, 1436.

INCUSE MARKS OF ALL CATEGORIES

Mark	Entered	Name	Category	Address/Notes
JM	5.1.1827	idem	cm	15 Wingrove Place
JM	9.10.1832	James Martin	cm	48 Wynyatt Street, Clerkenwell
JM, cameo oblong	12.4.1833	idem	cm	idem
JM, pellet between	22.10.1834	idem	cm	idem
JM	2.1.1841	idem	cm	idem
JM, cameo oval	7.2.1849	idem	cm	idem
JM	10.7.1826	Justin Mathey	cm	20 Hyde Street, Bloomsbury
JM	7.3.1827	idem	cm	idem
JM	18.1.1827	James Mackie		16 Queen Street, Soho
JM	29.6.1833	John Symonds Marratt	scm	23 Meredith Street, Clerkenwell
	13.10.1837	idem	scm	Moved to 15 Great Winchester Street, London Wall
	14.9.1844	idem	scm	Moved to 63 King William Street, London Bridge
JM⎫ JG⎭	25.2.1811	Jeremiah Mince and James Gliddon	cm	20 Normans Buildings, St. Luke's
JO, pellet between	14.2.1801	*John Osborne	cm	31 Primrose Street, Bishopsgate Street
JO	31.7.1804	idem	cm	idem
JO	17.2.1823	John Butterworth Oswin	cm	COVENTRY. By power of Attorney entered by Joseph Taylor
JO	22.9.1837	James Overan	pdm	30 Smith Street, Northampton Square
JP, pellet between	21.12.1797	†Jane Peyton	cm	13 Old Street Square
JP, pellet between	13.7.1809	James Pellington	smw	3 Bedfordbury
JP	21.5.1821	James Pascall	pdm	18 Wilderness Row, Goswell Street
JP	13.1.1836	idem	pdm	idem
JP	9.5.1827	Joseph Potter	cm	47 Ironmonger Row
JR	22.5.1816	Joseph Rome	cm	Northampton Street, Clerkenwell
	12.9.1828	idem	cm	Moved to 6 Cross Street, Nicols Street, Shoreditch

* See Section I, no. 1567.   † See T.P, script initials for Thomas Peyton below.

311

Mark	Entered	Name	Category	Address/Notes
JS	21.7.1824	John Shaw	*plw*	18 Southampton Street, Pentonville
JS	7.8.1828	John Shales	*cm*	21 Bartholomew Terrace, St. Luke's
	31.7.1829	idem	*cm*	Moved to 73 Rahere Street St. Luke's
JS	8.2.1830	idem	*cm*	idem
JS	9.1.1832	idem	*cm*	Moved to 14 Rahere Street
	8.1.1836	idem	*cm*	Moved to 1 Rahere Street
	3.11.1842	idem	*cm*	Moved to 42 York Street, St. Luke's
JT	1.2.1832	James Thickbroom	*pdm*	10 Galway Street, St. Luke's
JW	2.4.1794	Joseph Wickes	*cm*	18 Islington Road
	31.7.1794	idem	*cm*	Moved to 22 Aylesbury Street, Clerkenwell
	no date	idem	*cm*	Moved to 29 Great Sutton Street
	20.4.1797	idem	*cm*	Moved to 114 Goswell Street
JW	20.10.1797	idem	*cm*	7 Hooper Street, Clerkenwell
JW	15.8.1799	idem	*cm*	5 St. James' Walk, Clerkenwell
JW	17.3.1826	John West	*cm*	99 White Cross Street
JW	4.7.1829	idem	*cm*	idem
JW, script	11.10.1833	idem	*cm*	24 Banner Square, St. Luke's
JW	28.1.1828	Joseph White	*cm*	4 Poole Street, City Road
	9.8.1828	idem	*cm*	Moved to 55 Bath Street, City Road
JW	13.3.1833	idem	*cm*	idem
JW	30.10.1830	Joseph Woodhead	*cm*	6 Hull Street, St. Luke's
JW	2.5.1831	Joseph Whitehouse	*scm*	3 Wimbleton Street, Wimbleton Square
JY	11.8.1804	John Yardley	*smw*	18 Plumtree Street, Bloomsbury
LA, pellet between	12.10.1772	*Laura Aveline	*?cm*	Denmark Street, St. Giles
LB	18.6.1816	Lewis Balding	*cm*	4 Red Lion Court, London Wall
LC, serpent (?) above	8.11.1804	Louis Comtesse	*gw*	13 Batemans Buildings, Soho

* See Daniel Aveline above (DA) and Mary Aveline and Gideon Macaire below (MA). (GM).

INCUSE MARKS OF ALL CATEGORIES

Mark	Entered	Name	Category	Address/Notes
LC	19.2.1824	idem	gw	idem
LL	30.5.1828	Lawrence Levy	smw	7 Windsor Street, Bishopsgate
LM, pellet between	10.1.1761	Lewis Masquerier	?cm	Brownlow Street, Long Acre
	19.4.1764	idem	?cm	Moved to Coventry Street
LR	30.12.1767	Mary Ribleou (?)	?cm	? by letter of attorney
LT	18.11.1784	Louis Thiebaw	bm	22 Warwick Street, Golden Square
MA	16.11.1811	Mary Atkins	cm	14 Bridgewater Square
MA ⎫ GM ⎭	19.7.1779	Mary Aveline and Gideon Macaire	cm	5 Denmark Street, St. Giles
MC, script	25.4.1805	Martha Clark	cm	70 Bunhill Row
MD, stag above	16.12.1800	Mary Dearmer	cm	14 Featherstone Street, Bunhill
MF	29.3.1769	Michael Ferron	cm	Church Street, St. Ann's
MG	26.3.1803	Matthew Govett	cm	46 Ironmonger Row, Old Street
MG	20.2.1813	idem	cm	47 Ironmonger Row, St. Luke's
MG	27.7.1814	idem	cm	idem
MG	14.3.1816	idem	cm	idem and four similar marks May and Dec. 1816, and July 1818
MH, pellet between	9.5.1826	Mary Ann Holmes	smw	14 Red Cross Square
MH, pellet between	17.4.1834	idem	smw	idem
MJ	19.1.1793	Mary Jackson	cm	2 Bridgewater Gardens
ML	12.5.1810	M. Linsey	cm	10 Norman Street, St. Luke's
ML	21.5.1816	idem	cm	idem
ML	24.10.1823	Montague Levyson	gw	125 Pall Mall
MN, script	28.4.1808	Matthew Need	cm	22 Featherstone Street, City Road
MO	15.1.1712	*Hezekiah Mountfort	?cm	Red Lion Court, Fleet Street
MO	14.2.1716	William Morley	?cm	Little Old Bailey. 'free Clockmaker'
MS	12.11.1812	Mary Smith	pdm	32 Red Lion Street ? widow George Smith (q.v.)

* See Section III, no. 3739.

Mark	Entered	Name	Category	Address/Notes
MT, crown above	8.3.1766	Mary Trowell	?cm	Featherstone Street
MW	5.3.1792	Mary Wall	bm	6 King's Head Court, St. Martin's Le Grand
MW (drawn)	22.2.1823	Mathew Coles Wyatt	plw	19 Henrietta Street, Cavendish Square
NA	31.7.1702	George Nan	?cm	New Street, near Shoe Lane. 'free Clockmaker'
NA in lozenge	no date	Margrett Nan 'Widd'	cm	idem
NASH	29.9.1759	*Thomas Nash	?smw	Bull and Mouth Street
	31.10.1761	idem	smw	Moved to Fletchers Court, Noble Street
NE	18.2.1800	Nicholas Edwards	smw	34 Butchers Row, Temple Bar
	29.3.1804	idem	smw	Moved to 98 Leadenhall Street
NF	18.2.1814	Nathaniel Fenner	pdm	17 Bridgewater Square
NH ⎱ INH ⎰	18.1.1833	†Napthali Hart and John Napthali Hart	cm	5 King Street, Finsbury Square
NM	15.8.1817	Nathan Magnus	cm	7 James Court, St. Mary Axe
NO	29.9.1718	William Noyes	?cm	New Street, near Shoe Lane
NP	1.11.1783	‡Nathaniel Potticary	cm	1 Bridgewater Square
NP	22.6.1784	idem	cm	Moved to 2 Princes Street, Bridgewater Square
	no date	idem	cm	Moved to 8 Finsbury Street, Moorfields
NTW, pellets between	3.9.1783	Nicholas Thomas Wood	cm	21 St. John's Square, Clerkenwell
OV	7.10.1717	James Overing	?cm	Cary Lane. 'Turner'
PA	8.6.1716	Isaac Pack	?cm	Carey Lane. 'free of the Turners'
PC	30.4.1736	§Peter Cromillou	?cm	Red Cross Court, Jewin Street
PD	11.10.1792	Peter Desvignes	gw	221 Piccadilly
PD	9.5.1796	idem	cm	13 Denmark Street, Soho
idem	19.1.1797	idem	gw	idem
PD	17.3.1808	idem	gw	Moved to 49 Rosamans Row, Clerkenwell

* See Section I, nos. 2852, 2860, 3846.
† See also INH above and Section I, nos. 510 etc.
‡ See Christopher Potticary, Section I, no. 399.
§ See Hannah and Peter Crammillion, Section I, no. 1062.

INCUSE MARKS OF ALL CATEGORIES

Mark	Entered	Name	Category	Address/Notes
PE	22.3.1716	John Peirce	?cm	New Street
PG	undated Mar.–Nov. 1733	Peter Guion	?cm	Princes Street, Leicester Fields
PG, a fish (?) above	15.12.1763	*Peter Goujon	?cm	The Star, Theobalds Row, near Bedford Row
PI	12.8.1717	James Piran	?cm	'att ye Dyall in the old jury free Clockmaker'
PL	30.7.1802	P. T. Lemaitre	cm	34 Castle Street, Holborn
PM	7.5.1761	Peter Mounier	cm	Frith Street, Soho
PS, crown above	undated c. 1726–7	Paul Seguier	?cm	'Goldsmith in Panton Street by Lester Fields att the Signe of the Golden Suger Leof a Grocers'
RA	2.3.1796	Robert Atkinson	cm	39 North Street, City Road
RB, a lozenge (?) above	12.3.1734	Richard Bignell	cm	'at Mr Servetings (?) White Cross Street near Cripplegate'
RB, pellet between	8.2.1813	Robert Butterfield	pdm	5 Chas Court, Hull Street, St. Luke's
	6.3.1818	idem	pdm	Moved to 3 Waterloo Street, St. Luke's
	4.2.1820	idem	pdm	Moved to 21 East Row, Mount Pleasant, City Row
	9.10.1822	idem	pdm	Moved to 2 Johns Row, St. Luke's
RB	3.2.1813	Richard Brown	pdm	96 St. John's Street
RB	4.7.1814	Richard Basell	pdm	26 Goswell Street
	3.5.1816	idem		Moved to 9 Cross Street, Curtain Road
RB	3.10.1828	Robert Bellows	pdm	11 Tonks Gardens, Bowling Green Lane, Clerkenwell
RB } GM	22.12.1840	Richard Ball and Gideon Macaire	cm	17 Middleton Street, Clerkenwell
RC, coronet above	–.9.1729	Richard Cahill	?cm	'in bonds Stables by fetter Lane'
RC	16.3.1765	Robert Clements	?cm	Aldermanbury
RC	13.3.1770	idem	cm	3 Little Britain
RC	undated	idem	cm	Moved to 18 Flett Lane (signed by Elizabeth Clements)
RC	26.9.1827	Robert Colley	cm	12 Grey Eagle Court, Spitalfields

* Cf. Stephen Goujon below.

RD SB

Mark	Entered	Name	Category	Address/Notes
RD	3.1.1772	Robert Devitt	?cm	7 Tottenham Court Road
RD	31.12.1788	*Richard Dawson	gw	3 Lillypot Lane
RD	26.7.1809	†Robert Death	plw	18 Lower Smith Street, King Street, Clerkenwell
RD	15.9.1814	Richard Dane	smw	11 Castle Street, Piccadilly
RD	24.2.1817	idem	smw	idem
RD	10.7.1820	Robert Dalton	cm	3 City Gardens, City Road
RG	23.1.1778	‡Richard Glanvill	smw	near St. Clements Church, Strand
RG, pellet between	1.12.1807	§Richard Grove	cm	Vineyard Walk, Clerkenwell
RG	26.7.1810	idem	cm	idem
RH	25.2.1825	Richard Harrison	smw	91 Paul Street, Finsbury
RH	22.6.1827	idem	smw	20 Sun Street
	31.12.1827	idem	smw	Moved to 11 Haberdashers Place, Hoxton
RH	4.6.1830	Robert Hall	smw	45 Kirby Street, City Road
RI	9.12.1726	Robert Jacques	?cm	Elliots Court, Little Old Bailey. 'free Clockmaker'
RIG, pellets between	3.2.1806	Richard and R. Joseph Grove	cm	Vineyard Walk, Clerkenwell
RJ	4.8.1835	Richard Jones	pdm	48 Wellington Street, St. Luke's
RM	16.6.1821	Robert Mansir	cm	5 St. James Place, Clerkenwell
RM, pellet between	10.11.1831	idem	cm	15 Lower Charles Street, Northampton Square
RN, pellet between	9.1.1759	Robert Nuttall	cm	Kirby Court
RN, pellet between	28.3.1760	idem	cm	idem
RN	28.8.1775	idem	cm	31 Clerkenwell Close
RO	undated c. 1697	‖James Rousnieu(?)	cm	'Black Fryers free Clockmaker'
RP	29.6.1724	Richard Payne	cm	'at Mr Carpenters in Bar^w Lane near ye Royal Exchange Citi-zn & Clockmaker'
RP	10.6.1769	¶Richard Palmer	cm	Red Lion Street, Clerkenwell

* See also Section VII. † See John Death (Section I, no. 1249).
‡ See Section I, no. 2317. § See RIG below.
‖ See IR above James Renou, possibly the same.
¶ See Section I, no. 2406 and Section VI.

INCUSE MARKS OF ALL CATEGORIES

Mark	Entered	Name	Category	Address/Notes
RP	22.10.1778	idem	cm	idem
RP	5.6.1798	Russell Pontifex	cm	24 Primrose Street, Bishopsgate Street
RR	24.3.1767	Richard Rawlings	?hlm	Cross Swords in Grafton Street, Soho
RR	16.3.1833	Robert Rowlands	cm	5 Meredith Street, Clerkenwell
RR	9.5.1834	idem	cm	idem (and later marks till 1864)
RT	undated 1730–4	*Richard Tomkins	?cm	'in Joneses lane ouver aganst the spred ghalesq' (?eagle)
RW, ? flower or star above	3.11.1735	Richard Wilson	?cm	'living in the Minories at ye Aintien Fowler'
RW, pellet between	16.1.1761	Robert Wherritt	?cm	Great Warner Street, Cold Bath Fields
RW	19.6.1800	Richard Walker	cm	57 New Compton Street
RW	26.3.1802	Robert Wolfe	cm	36 Clerkenwell Green
RY	30.3.1736	Ralph Yoemans	cm	'A Watch Case macker att Mr Lloyds A watchmaker in West Smith felde near Cow Laine'
SA, pellet between	15.9.1759	Samuel Armand	cm	Great White Lion Street, near Seven Dial
	no date	idem	cm	Moved to Bull Yard near Goswell Street Bars
SA, script, linked	3.6.1807	Samuel Atkins	cm	14 Bridgewater Square
SB, coronet above	undated July 1726–Oct. 1727	Salomon Delabare	?cm	St. Martin's Lane over aganst Slaters Coffee house in Castle Court
SB	11.6.1814	Samuel Brookes	cm	12 Rosoman Street, Clerkenwell
SB	26.10.1827	idem	cm	5 Ashby Street, Clerkenwell
SB	27.10.1815	Stephen Bryan	cm	5 Noble Street, Goswell Street
	no date	idem	cm	Moved to 42 Seward Street, Goswell Street
	31.3.1821	idem	cm	Moved to 14 Gastigney Place Radnor Street, Bath Street, St. Luke's
	no date	idem	cm	Moved to 42 Rahere Street, St. Luke's
SC (two sizes)	3.8.1791	†Sarah Carpenter	cm	9 Islington Road

* See Section I, no. 2866.   † See Thomas Carpenter below.

Mark	Entered	Name	Category	Address/Notes
SC	26.3.1793	idem	cm	idem
SC	11.1.1813	Sarah Clerke	cm	23 Banner Square. Also 28.4.1815
SC	24.4.1827	Samuel Cuendet	cm	20 Hyde Street, Bloomsbury
	25.4.1835	idem	cm	idem
SC, pellet between	13.10.1837	Samuel Clark	pcm	62 Wynyatt Street, Goswell Road
SD	9.12.1718	Samuel Dars (? smudged)	?cm	'old Bailey next door to the Coffee house'
SD	12.11.1813	Sarah Davenport	smw	George Street
SD	11.10.1816	Stephen Davies	gw	17 Great Sutton Street, Clerkenwell
SF, pellet between	21.4.1795	*Samuel Firmin	btm	153 Strand
SG, scroll cresting above	8.4.1720	†Stephen Goujon	?cm	Porter Street, corner of Newport Alley. 'free Clockmaker'
SG	12.2.1719	Solomon Gibbs	?cm	Plough Yard, Fetter Lane. 'free Clockmaker'
SG, coronet above	15.8.1732	idem	cm	'at ye Bakers in Phillip Lane near Addle Street'
SG, and SG heart above	13.5.1793	Stephen Gillet	cm	12 Compton Street, Soho
SH, pellet between	20.5.1786	Squire Hewkley	cm	199 St. John Street, Clerkenwell
SI	22.12.1813	Samuel Isaacs	pdm	9 New Court, Cread Lane, Aldgate
SI, IL, pellet between	21.3.1721	‡Sarah Jaques and John Lee I	?cm	Angel Court, Snow Hill. 'free Clockmaker'
SL	29.2.1728	Solomon Larrat	?cm	Water Lane, Blackfriars
SN	13.4.1804	§Susanna Need	cm	27 Rawstone Street, St. John's Street Road
SP	7.10.1807	Samuel Pike	cm	48 Blue Anchor Alley, Bunhill Row
SP, IR	28.3.1761	‖Samual Priest and John Rawley	?cm	Crown Court, Charterhouse Lane
SS, JH	21.2.1835	Samuel Saltmarsh and Joseph Hirst	cm	28 Coppice Row, Clerkenwell

* See Philip Venner Freeman (Section I, no. 2176).
† Cf. Peter Goujon above.
‡ See IL above, WI below, and Section I, no. 1465.
§ See BN above, Bartholomew Need at same address.
‖ See Samuel Priest Section I, no. 2613.

INCUSE MARKS OF ALL CATEGORIES

Mark	Entered	Name	Category	Address/Notes
SY, pellet between	4.5.1802	Samuel Yeoman	smw	8 Bishops Court, Clerkenwell
TA	24.7.1826	Thomas Law Andrews	gw	33 New Benet Street
	21.9.1827	idem	gw	Moved to 10 Hanover Place, Regents Park Road
	22.12.1842	idem	gw	Moved to 37 Coleshill Street, Pimlico
TB	20.4.1782	Thomas Barnard	gw	72 the corner of the Adelphi, Strand
TB	22.11.1797	Thomas Bligh	cm	16 Great Sutton Street, Clerkenwell
TB	4.1.1803	idem	cm	idem
TB, script, monogram and TB	30.12.1806	idem	cm	idem
TB	21.3.1809	idem	cm	40 Great Sutton Street, Clerkenwell
TB	28.8.1821	idem	cm	(below 16 Sutton Street entry)
TB, pellet between	5.2.1813	Thomas Burwash	pdm	120 St. John Street
TB	28.3.1820	Thomas Barrington	scm	2 Priest Court, Foster Lane
TB	19.7.1820	Thomas Burrows	pdm	19 Eagle Court, St. John's Lane, Clerkenwell
TB	13.5.1837	Thomas Blake	cm	11 Cross Street, Cambridge Road, Bethnal Green
	9.10.1837	idem	cm	Moved to 29 Southampton Street, John Street Road (and later addresses to 1843)
TB, script	9.7.1789	Thomas Brooke	cm	22 Golden Lane
TB, JP, pellet between	25.5.1830	Thomas Bull and James Plater	gw	107 Bunhill Row
TB ⎫ WH ⎭	12.6.1819	Thomas Burwash Jr. and William Hamilton Jr.	pdm	8 Princes Street, Percival Street, Clerkenwell
TC, pellet between	5.9.1782	Thomas Church	bm	6 Bull and Mouth Street
TC, figure 5 above	28.2.1788	*Thomas Carpenter	cm	5 Islington Road
TC	7.1.1790	idem	cm	idem
TC, axe above	20.7.1797	idem	cm	9 Islington Road

* See Sarah Carpenter above.
TB, unregistered. Gold watchcase 1747 (Mr K. Citroen).

Mark	Entered	Name	Category	Address/Notes
TC	5.2.1808	Thomas Cottril	smw	76 Leather Lane, Hoborn
TC	11.3.1808	*Thomas Crofts	gw	10 Winyat Street, Clerkenwell
TD	16.12.1756	†Thomas Doxsey	gw	near Great St. Helens, Bishopsgate Street
TD	17.4.1758	Theophilus Davys	?pm	King Street, Seven Dials 'at the sign of the hand penn'
TD	1.2.1793	Thomas Dennett	gw	35 Frith Street, Soho
TD	13.5.1824	‡Thomas Dane	gw	272 Regent Street
TE	14.12.1814	Thomas Emmett	pdm	16 Albemarle Street, Clerkenwell
TF, a device(?) above	13.3.1738	Thomas Farr	?smw	Shovel Alley, Wood Street
TF	11.8.1766	§Thomas Foster	cm	Pye Corner, West Smithfield
TF	6.11.1819	Thomas Ferris	cm	15 Upper Ashby Street, Northampton Square
TG	31.8.1716	Thomas Goore	?cm	Islington. 'free of Clockmakers'
TG	10.6.1723	Thomas Gorsuch	?cm	'in Shrewsbury Ent^d p Wm Carditch'
TG, pellet between	6.7.1768	Thomas Gibbard	cm	Quaker Building, Smithfield
TG	18.3.1784	idem	cm	28 Clerkenwell Close
TG	26.6.1777	Thomas Gosling	cm	2 Lilypot Lane
TG, goose above	3.12.1778	idem	cm	idem
TG	4.1.1794	Thomas Gooch	cm	23 Coppice Row, Clerkenwell
TG	26.3.1829 16.9.1835	Thomas Greves idem	cm cm	17 Camomile Street Moved to 4 Southampton Buildings, Rosomans Street, Clerkenwell
TH	undated 1727-38	Thomas Heavin	cm	Star Court, Butcher Row, Temple Bar
TH	12.3.1735	idem	cm	Blackfriars
TH	22.2.1771	Thomas Harper	?cm	Great St. Andrew Street, Seven Dials
TH	2.6.1781	Thomas Hardy	cm	14 Rosomans Row, Clerkenwell

* See also Section VII. † See Section I, no. 3818.
‡ See also Section VII. § See Section I, nos. 2751, 3822-3, and Section VI.

INCUSE MARKS OF ALL CATEGORIES

Mark	Entry	Name	Category	Address/Notes
TH	9.2.1793	idem	cm	12 Rosomans Row (also 22.3.1816)
TH, script, crescent above	16.7.1784	Thomas Hales	cm	8 Silver Street, Wood Street
TI	22.3.1721	Thomas Jollis	cm	Fetter Lane. 'free of the Clockmakers' Company'
TI	10.3.1775	Timothy Jordan	cm	156 Bishopsgate Street
TJ	28.6.1821	Timothy Jones	gw	20 Red Lion Street, Clerkenwell
TK, pellet between	26.10.1831	Thomas Key	smw	20 Charing Cross
TK	19.5.1835	idem	smw	idem
TK, coronet above	7.7.1720	*Thomas Knaggs	?cm	Lion Court, Fleet Street
TK	29.6.1832	Thomas Keeff	cm	Myddleton Street, Clerkenwell
TK, between dashes	24.12.1834	idem	cm	22 Rosomans Row, Clerkenwell
idem	18.11.1835	idem	cm	53 Myddleton Street (and other addresses in 1841–3)
T.L, coronet above	15.11.1748	†Thomas Lawrence I	?cm	George Court, St. John's Lane
idem	25.7.1754	idem	cm	idem
idem	13.4.1769	idem	cm	Clerkenwell
idem	15.4.1769	idem	cm	idem
idem	29.11.1770	idem	cm	St. John's Lane
T.L. cinquefoil above	21.7.1762	Thomas Layton	?cm	Dean Street, Fetter Lane
TL, star	26.3.1763	idem	cm	idem
TL	25.2.1809	Thomas Lock	cm	1 Rawstone Street, Islington
TM script	30.7.1808	Thomas Milliar	cm	1 Little Mitchell Street, St. Luke's
TM} HH}	20.7.1808	Tebaldo Monzani and Henry Hill	smw	3 Old Bond Street
	no date	idem	smw	Moved to 24 Dover Street, Piccadilly
	17.9.1819	idem	smw	Moved to Regent Street, Piccadilly
TN	30.7.1728	Thomas Nicholls	?cm	Green Dragon Court, Cow Lane. 'free Clockmaker'
TN	29.9.1759	Thomas Nash	?cm	Bull and Mouth Street

* See Section I, no. 1878. † See Section I, no. 2823.

Mark	Entered	Name	Category	Address/Notes
TN	1.2.1822	Thomas Norris	cm	8 Rawstone Street, St. John Street Road
TN, script	10.9.1823	idem	cm	idem
TN	11.5.1833	idem	cm	13 West Place, St. John's Row
TO	23.5.1765	Thomas Osborne	?cm	Shorts Gardens
TO	1.2.1813	Thomas Oades	pdm	41 Great Sutton Street, Clerkenwell
TP	26.2.1728	Thomas Potts	cm	Bolt Court, Fleet Street. 'free of the Clockmaker's Company'
	no date	idem	cm	Moved to Bull Head Court, Newgate Street
TP	17.5.1736	idem	cm	idem
TP, pellet between	23.11.1736	*Thomas Peirce	?cm	'over aganst ye hors sho ale hous in Westharding Street in fetter Lane'
TP, star above	14.11.1765	†Thomas Perry	?hlm	Shoe Lane
TP, script	12.2.1788	‡Thomas Peyton	cm	31 Old Street Square
TP	29.1.1791	idem	cm	idem
TP	6.12.1794	Thomas Phelps	smw	9 Cock Court, St. Martins Le Grand
TP	29.3.1797	idem	smw	idem
	15.3.1799	idem	smw	Moved to 36 Fetter Lane
	16.18.1800	idem	smw	Moved to 159 Fleet Street
	7.4.1802	idem	smw	Moved to 30 Red Lion Street, Holborn
	19.1.1814	idem	smw	Moved to 33 Monkwell Street
	31.10.1817	idem	smw	Moved to 18 Jewin Street
	14.8.1824	idem	smw	Moved to High Street, Peckham
TP, script	11.10.1826	idem	smw	idem
TP	3.4.1818	Thomas Phelps Jr.	scm	28 Holywell Lane, Curtain Road
TP	2.4.1832	idem	scm	Moved to 5 City Terrace, Old Street Road
TP	13.12.1823	Thomas Potter	plw	15 Vere Street, Clare Market
TR, crown above	4.12.1737	Timothy Renon	?cm	'at Linnin Draper (?Hall) Freeman of the Farer Company'

* See Section I, no. 2116. † See James Perry, Sections I, no. 1582, and IX.
‡ See Jane Peyton above.

INCUSE MARKS OF ALL CATEGORIES

Mark	Entered	Name	Category	Address/Notes
TR, pellet between. TR crown above	14.6.1777	*Thomas Ray	cm	9 Bridewell Precinct
TR	9.1.1813	Thomas Rowlands	pdm	Corporation Lane
	25.11.1815	idem	pdm	Moved to 10 Bartholomew Square, St. Luke's
	2.4.1822	idem	pdm	Moved to 10 Helmet Row, St. Luke's
TR	25.2.1829	idem	pdm	Nelson Street, St. Luke's
	28.2.1832	idem	pdm	Moved to 28 Wellington Street, Goswell Street
TR ⎫ WP ⎭	21.4.1819	†Thomas Rowlands and William Poulton	cm	53 Red Lion Street, Clerkenwell
TS, coronet above	10.10.1717	Tudor Smith	?cm	St. Martins Le Grand. 'free of Clockmakers' Company
TS, coronet above	16.6.1729	Thomas Smith	?cm	Noble Street. 'free Joyner'
TS	13.9.1764	‡Thomas Stilwell	?cm	St. Brides' Lane, Fleet Street
TS	8.12.1768	Thomas Sharratt	?cm	Ozier Lane, West Smithfield
TS, fleur-de-lys above	19.11.1770	Thomas Sones	?cm	Lilypot Lane
TS	29.3.1794	Thomas Stevens	cm	7 St. James' Walk, Clerkenwell
	29.1.1796	idem	cm	Moved to 33 Red Lion Street, Clerkenwell
TSB, fleur-de-lys above	14.12.1763	§Thomas Stilwell	?cm	Whitefriars Gateway, Fleet Street
TV, coronet above	26.10.1774	‖Thomas Venn	cm	Leopard Court, Baldwins Gardens
	10.2.1778	idem	cm	Moved to 18 Clerkenwell Green
TW, pellet between	12.7.1774	¶Thomas Whitford	smw	6 King's Head Court, St. Martins Le Grand
TW, pellet between	9.2.1790	idem	smw	idem
TW	26.6.1775	**Thomas Wilson	bm	Deptford, Kent

* See Section I, no. 2902, and Section VI.
† See William Poulton below.
‡ See TSB below and Section I, no. 2936.
§ See T.S above, and Section I, no. 2936.
‖ See Section I, no. 2955.   ¶ See Samuel Whitford I, Section I, no. 2661.
** See Section I, no. 2965, and Section VIII, T.W.

Mark	Entered	Name	Category	Address/Notes
TW	7.11.1787	*Thomas Worboys	gw	9 Bells Buildings, Salisbury Square, Fleet Street
TW	1.9.1800	†Thomas Walker I	cm	15 Dorrington Street, Cold Bath Fields
TW script	17.10.1810	idem	cm	6 Lamly Passage, Chiswell Street
	13.8.1817	idem	cm	Moved to 17 Gee Street, Goswell Street
TW	15.8.1814	Thomas Walker II	cm	16 Albemarle Street, Clerkenwell
TW, pellet between	17.3.1828	idem	cm	idem
TW	18.1.1831	idem	cm	idem
TWB	30.7.1819	‡Thomas Worsley Bickerton	smw	14 Jewin Street, Cripplegate
TWP	10.1.1832	Thomas William Parry	scm	8 Dean Street, New North Road
	5.4.1832	idem	scm	Moved to 14 Princes Street, Barbican
	15.5.1839	idem	scm	Moved to 24 Holywell Street, Strand
TY, coronet above	8.11.1722	§Thomas York I	?cm	Queens Head Court, Turnagain Lane, near Snow Hill. 'Free of ye Clockmakers'
TY, script, coronet above	30.9.1762	Thomas York II	?cm	Dyal & Golden Ball, Fleet Market
TY, pellet between	7.6.1765	idem	cm	idem
VW, pellet between	26.3.1782	Valentine Walker	cm	50 Liquer Pond Street, Grays Inn Lane
	8.10.1784	idem	cm	Moved to 8 St. John's Street Road
VW	23.7.1791	idem	cm	idem
VW (two sizes)	5.4.1796	idem	cm	12 Kirby Street, Hatton Garden
WA	30.5.1716	‖George Watkins	?cm	Green Arbor Court, Old Bailey
WA, star above	14.1.1730	¶William Ashbee	?cm	Black Boy and Crowne, Grape Street

* See Arthur Worboys, Section I, no. 108.
† See IS.TW above, and Section I, no. 2968.
‡ See Section I, no. 2696. § See also YO below.
‖ See also GW above. ¶ See Section I, no. 90.

INCUSE MARKS OF ALL CATEGORIES

Mark	Entered	Name	Category	Address/Notes
WA, coronet above	26.7.1733	*William Achurch	?cm	Bishop's Head, Little Old Bailey
WA, pellet between, fleur-de-lys above	19.2.1759	William Aveott	?cm	Pye Corner near West Smithfield
idem	3.11.1759	idem	cm	idem
WA	8.4.1797	William Atkins	gw	143 Leadenhall Street
WAB, pellets between	9.5.1810	W. A. Beckwith	gw	Skinner Street
WB, a device (?) above	14.6.1731	William Bankes	?cm	Elliots Court, Little Old Bailey. 'free Goldsmith'
WB	31.7.1734	Willson Buxton	?cm	Bridewell Walk, Clerkenwell. 'Clockmaker'
WB	13.12.1738	†William Burton	?cm	Mugwell Street. 'free gouldsmith'
WB, pellet between	20.1.1755	William Butcher I	?cm	Skinner Street, Bishopsgate Street
WB	18.12.1759	idem	?cm	Golden Lane
WB, pellet between, bell above	22.3.1763	‡William Bell	?cm	Featherstone Street
idem	8.3.1769	idem	cm	Bridgewater Square
WB	22.8.1777	§William Brooks	cm	1 Church Row, Old Street
WB, pellet between	20.11.1783	idem	cm	idem
idem	27.7.1786	idem	cm	idem
WB, script	30.7.1787	idem	cm	idem
WB	12.1.1792	idem	cm	idem
WB, pellet between crescent above	31.10.1782	William Blake	cm	White Cross Street
WB	23.9.1800	idem	cm	idem
WB	20.11.1802	idem	cm	28 White Cross Street
WB	26.8.1809	William Boulton	cm	49 Grays Inn Lane
	5.1.1820	idem	cm	Moved to 9 Kirby Street
WB, six-petal flower above	15.1.1819	William Bunting	cm	2 Jerusalem Passage, Clerkenwell

* See also AC above, perhaps father and son.
† See Section I, no. 3016.
‡ See Section I, no. 3018, and Section VII.
§ See also WB.TB below, Section VI and Section I, no. 3019.

Mark	Entered	Name	Category	Address/Notes
WB	13.5.1833	William Butcher II	scm	7 Queen's Square, Aldersgate Street
	6.6.1837	idem	scm	Moved to 2 St. John's Lane Clerkenwell
WB	25.2.1836	William Bennett	cm	10 Great Warner Street, Clerkenwell
WB, script, pellet between	16.8.1802	*William Burwash	cm	3 Red Lion Street, Clerkenwell
idem smaller	23.6.1803	idem	cm	idem
idem	6.7.1812	idem	plw	14 Bartholomew Close
WB⎫ CH⎭	23.4.1812	William Bush and Charles Hazle	cm	Bowling Green Lane, Clerkenwell
WB⎫ JH⎭	27.4.1819	William Brown and John Hands	cm	COVENTRY, by power of attorney
WB, pellets⎫ TB, between⎭	2.12.1786	William and Thomas Brooks	cm	1 Church Row, Old Street
WC	12.10.1731	William Coope	?cm	Lamb Court, Clerkenwell Green, 'near ye red Lyon tavern'
WC, pellet between	17.6.1774	William Carpenter	cm	45 Frith Street, St. Ann's
WC	10.12.1814	William Clarke	cm	40 Brunswick Street, Blackfriars Road
WC	12.6.1818	William Clark	gw	43 Kirby Street, Hatton Garden
WC	24.12.1827	William Collier	pdm	54 Bath Street
WC	12.1.1833	William Carter	cm	22 Gateway Street, St. Luke's
WC	28.7.1836	William Crawley	gw	21 Oxendon Street, Haymarket
WC⎫ SH⎭	14.9.1801	†William Cartwright and Samuel Horton	gw	BIRMINGHAM
WD	20.11.1781	‡William Dawson	cm	15 Gutter Lane
WD	31.8.1786	idem	cm	idem
WD			cm	and five similar marks 1795 to 1819
WD	17.1.1820	William Dane	gw	Regent Street, Oxford Street
WD	15.4.1831	William Dawkins	pdm	16 St. John's Lane, Clerkenwell
WF	27.4.1813	William Fielder	cm	51 St. John's Square, Clerkenwell

* See Section I, no. 3036 etc. † See also Section VII.
‡ See ED above and Section I, no. 3086.

INCUSE MARKS OF ALL CATEGORIES

Mark	Entered	Name	Category	Address/Notes
WF, script	27.2.1823	idem	cm	31 St. John's Square, Clerkenwell
WF	14.3.1825 and 12.5.1825	idem	cm	16 Clerkenwell Green
WF	21.7.1828	*William Forrester	gw	52 Red Lion Street, Clerkenwell
WF	24.1.1815	William Fisher	cm	5 Ironmonger Row, St. Luke's
WF	20.8.1833	William Francis	cm	15 King Street, Clerkenwell
WG	3.11.1785	William Garvie	gw	3 Thanet Place, Temple Bar
WG	15.12.1815	William Greely	cm	23 Banner Square, St. Luke's
WG	25.7.1826	William Griffiths	smw	136 Upper Street, Islington
Wh, star above	2.3.1716	James Whitlock	?cm	Old Bailey. 'free Clockmaker'
WH	undated c. 1700	Clay Whitton	?cm	Eagle Court, Strand. 'free Clockmaker'
WH	22.4.1720	William Hodges	?cm	Fenchurch Street. 'Free Clock-Maker'
WH	21.10.1777	William Huntley	smw	Brick Lane, Old Street
WH	26.3.1791	†William Howard	cm	48 Old Street
WH	13.12.1799	William Hodsoll	cm	31 Primrose Street, Bishopsgate
WH	30.9.1800	William Hammon I	cm	50 St. James's Buildings, Clerkenwell
WH	21.10.1819	‡William Hammon II	cm	28 Galway Street, St. Luke's
	12.4.1821	idem	cm	Moved to 14 Peartree Street, Goswell Street
	22.5.1822	idem	cm	Moved to 39 Monyers Street, Hoxton
WH	30.5.1828	idem	cm	idem
WH	31.1.1828	William Harris	cm	9 St James's Street, Clerkenwell
WI, coronet above	undated c. 1697	John Wightman	?cm	College Hill. 'free Clockmaker'
WI	undated c. 1698	John Willoughby	?cm	Old Bailey. 'free of the Clockmakers'

* See also Sections IV (Forister) and VII.
† See Section I, no. 3174, perhaps his father.
‡ See also WIH below.

Mark	Entered	Name	Category	Address/Notes
WI	6.10.1725	W. Jaques	?cm	Angel Court Snow Hill. 'Clockmaker'
WI, coronet above	8.7.1734	William Jackson	?cm	Great New Street, Fetter Lane
WIH, pellets between	23.11.1813	*William John Hammon	cm	20 Little Saffron Hill
	23.11.1814	idem	cm	Moved to 58 Wellington Street, Goswell Street
WIH, pellets between	19.2.1819	idem	cm	18 Percival Street, Clerkenwell
	6.4.1819	idem	cm	Moved to 28 Galloway Street, St. Luke's
	9.1.1821	idem	cm	Moved to 27 John Street, Spa Fields
	18.11.1823	idem	cm	Moved to 2 Whiskin Street
WIH	21.7.1832	idem	cm	3 Whiskin Street, Clerkenwell
	27.1.1834	idem	cm	Moved to 22 Gloucester Street
	10.11.1835	idem	cm	Moved to 9 John Street, Wilmington Square
WJ	6.4.1809	William Jackson I	cm	6 King Street, Clerkenwell
WJ	4.2.1813	idem	cm	idem
WJ	24.12.1819	William Jasper	cm	5 King's Head Court, Gutter Lane
WJ	1.1.1833	idem	cm	5 Red Lion Street, Clerkenwell
WJ	3.4.1834	William Jackson II	scm	3 Cross Street, Westmorland Place, City Road
WJ, pellet between	19.6.1832	William Johnson	smw	39 Kirby Street, Hatton Garden
WK, pellet between	26.6.1760	William Kendrick	gw	Queen Street, Seven Dials
WL	21.8.1766	William Lacy	cm	Saffron Hill. 'Watchcase Maker'
WL	8.4.1788	William Laithwait	cm	104 Gray's Inn Lane
WL	18.4.1793	†William Lewis	cm	11 Bridgewater Square
WL	10.2.1800	idem	cm	idem
WL	5.5.1801	idem	cm	Moved to 26 Red Lion Street, Clerkenwell
WL	6.9.1803	idem	cm	idem

* See also William Hammon II above.
† See Section VI, and Section I, no. 3228.

INCUSE MARKS OF ALL CATEGORIES

Mark	Entered	Name	Category	Address/Notes
WL, pellet between	28.7.1809	idem	cm	idem
WL, pellet between	3.5.1794	William Linsey	cm	2 Bridgewater Gardens
	26.9.1795	idem	cm	Moved to 10 Norman Street, St. Luke's
WL, C above	26.3.1800	William Linsley	cm	68 Banner Street, Bunhill Row
WL, stag above and WL	24.2.1802	idem	cm	idem
WL, stag above	1.2.1813 and 4.10.1814	idem	cm	idem
WL	24.10.1818	idem	cm	idem
	19.1.1827	idem	cm	Moved to 2 Cottage House
WL	26.1.1813	William Lupton	pdm	6 St. John's Walk, Clerkenwell
	3.8.1832	idem	pdm	4 Clerkenwell Close
WM, conjoined	16.9.1723	William Milward	cm	Hind Court, Fleet Street. 'Goldsmith'
WM	undated Oct. 1733– June 1735	*William Maddocks	?cm	Harding Street, near Fetter Lane
WM	4.6.1735	W. Michell	?cm	Twisters Alley, Bunhill Row
WM, coronet above	4.9.1735	William Marshall	cm	near the Three Tuns, New Street
WM, fleur-de-lys above	9.4.1783	William Mean	cm	8 St. John's Street Road
	15.8.1791	idem	cm	Moved to 7 Albemarle Street, St. John Square
	2.8.1799	idem	cm	Moved to 19 St. John Lane
WM, star above	5.10.1800	idem	cm	idem
	1.12.1818	idem	cm	Moved to 2 Jerusalem Passage
WM	17.6.1802	William Mansell	gw	32 Rosomond Street, Clerkenwell
WM	11.1.1809	idem	gw	29 Rosomond Street
WM	21.4.1818 and 8.6.1818	idem	gw	idem

* See Section I, no. 3236.

Mark	Entered	Name	Category	Address/Notes
WM	9.8.1816	William Murrell	gw	14 Little Saffron Hill
	8.7.1820	idem	gw	Moved to 16 Peartree Street
	13.8.1822	idem	gw	Moved to 26 Wellington Street, Goswell Street
	3.9.1833	idem	gw	Moved to 29 Wellington Street
	5.6.1841	idem	gw	Moved to 29 Upper Rosamond Street, Clerkenwell
WM	21.6.1821	William Mitchell	gw	18 Red Lion Street, Clerkenwell
	20.3.1823	idem	gw	Moved to 5 Newcastle Place, Clerkenwell
WM	15.1.1830	William Melville	cm	52 Red Lion Street, Clerkenwell
WM WM	5.2.1830	William Mansell and William Mansell	cm	32 Rosamund Street, Clerkenwell
	16.6.1830	idem	cm	Moved to 26 Spencer Street, Northampton Square
WN	12.4.1717	William Noyes	?cm	New Street, near Shoe Lane
WN PS	17.10.1718	William Noyes and Paul Sawyer	?cm	New Street, near Shoe Lane
WO	24.2.1826	William Osborne	cm	31 Rosoman Street, Clerkenwell
WP	23.10.1738	William Platt	?gw	'at Mr Longs Carpenter Guilt Spur Street Pye Corner West Smithfield Goldsmith'
WP, pellet between	29.11.1762	William Pretty	cm	West Smithfield
	21.11.1763	idem	cm	Moved to Clerkenwell Close
WP, pellet between	8.2.1773	idem	cm	6 Trinity Court, Aldersgate Street
	28.7.1780	idem	cm	38 Mugwell Street
WP	14.5.1785	idem	cm	16 Cross Key Street, Little Britain
WP	2.6.1792	William Phillips	cm	36 Hayden Yard, Minories
WP	10.12.1795	William Peachey	cm	186 High Holborn

INCUSE MARKS OF ALL CATEGORIES

Mark	Entered	Name	Category	Address/Notes
WP	17.1.1818	*William Poulton	pdm	34 Percival Street, St. John's Street, Clerkenwell
	26.9.1822	idem	pdm	Moved to 2 Union Building, Leather Lane
	16.8.1824	idem	pdm	Moved to 3 Exmouth Street, Spa Fields
	21.2.1828	idem	pdm	Moved to 15 Little Nelson Street, City Road
	19.6.1832	idem	pdm	Moved to 6 Hill Street, St. Luke's
WQ	12.6.1778	William Quinton	cm	31 New Street Square
WQ	31.7.1778	idem	cm	idem
WR	4.9.1788	William Robson	cm	11 Bridgewater Square, Barbican
WR	10.6.1817	William Rowlands	cm	13 Harper Street, Great Sutton Street
WR	2.8.1821	idem	cm	Moved to 32 Lower Smith Street, Northampton Square
WR	27.2.1830	idem	cm	idem
WR	25.10.1838	idem	cm	idem
WR	15.12.1831	William Ratcliff	scm	98 Britannia Street, City Road
WS	15.9.1734	William Shale	?cm	Benjamin Street, near Red Lion Street, Clerkenwell
WT	19.2.1759	William Thomas	cm	Garlick Hill
WT, coronet above	15.5.1771	idem	cm	Goldsmith Street, near Gough Square
idem	28.4.1778	idem	cm	85 Long Acre
WW, star above	19.6.1732	†William Wynn	cm	'att a Bakers in Bride Lane fleet Street free Goldsmith'
WW	12.10.1783	William West	cm	Jerusalem Court, St. John's Square
WW	24.11.1788	William Willson	gw	GLAMORGANSHIRE, South Wales
WW	15.11.1793	William Woodman	cm	18 Glasshouse Yard, Aldersgate
WW	4.4.1801	William Watson	gw	7 Red Lion Street, Clerkenwell
WW	31.5.1816	William Willis	gw	23 Goswell Terrace, Goswell Street Road

* See Thomas Rowlands and William Poulton above.
† See Section I, no. 3358.

Mark	Entered	Name	Category	Address/Notes
WW	27.10.1819	William Wickes	cm	34 Perceval Street, Clerkenwell
	26.10.1832	idem	cm	Moved to 8 Skinner Street, Clerkenwell
WW, pellet between	18.6.1821	William Wright	cm	15 Upper Ashby Street, Northampton Square
WW, zig-zag line above	13.10.1826	idem	cm	16 President Street, St. Luke's
WW	13.2.1819	idem	cm	idem
WW	19.11.1829	idem	cm	idem
WW, conjoined	4.7.1820	*William Warren	smw	9 Great Windmill Street, Haymarket
WW, script	12.10.1825	William Wilkin	cm	3 King Street, Clerkenwell
WWW, conjoined	29.12.1821	William Woolley Whall	gw	8 Gough Square, Fleet Street
YO, coronet above	8.11.1722	†Thomas York	?cm	Queens Head Court, Turnagain Lane, near Snow Hill. 'Free of ye Clockmakers Company'

* See also Section IV.   † See also TY above.

VI
Watchcasemakers' Cameo Marks

All the marks are in relief 'cameo' punches. Some pendantmakers' marks are included as well. The punches are categorized as follows: 1. rectangular; 2. rectangular with 'cut' corners; and 3. oval. The rare exceptions to the above have been described.
* against mark means see also Section V under the same initials.

Mark	Entered	Name	Address/Notes	Punch
AEP	15.10.1836	Abram Elisée Piguet	4 Richmond Buildings, Soho	1
AL	30.6.1790	[1]Ann Laithwait	104 Gray's Inn Lane	1
AM*	26.6.1822	Arthur Moring	6 Pitman's Buildings, John's Row, St. Luke's	1
AR*	7.10.1831	Alfred Reeves	42 Spencer Street, Clerkenwell	1
AS	30.9.1825	Andrew Scott	3 Eliza Place, Spa Fields	1
	13.10.1826	idem	Moved to 20 Northampton Square	
AT*	22.3.1829	Alford Thickbroom	10 Galway Street, Bath Street	2
AT*	30.11.1839	idem	idem	1
ℬℐ	24.1.1701	John Bayley	Butcher Hall Lane, Newgate Street. 'free clockmaker'	1
BE, pellet between	8.7.1777	Benjamin Eamonson	21 Bull and Mouth Street	2
BE	15.5.1798	idem	9 Little Sutton Street, Clerkenwell	2
BN, pellet between*	26.3.1784	Bartholomew Need	13 Bridgewater Square	2
BN*	20.7.1824	Benjamin Norton	59 Banner Square, St. Luke's	1
BN, pellet between	27.2.1830	idem	idem	2
BN	8.12.1834	idem	idem	2
BT	7.6.1777	Benjamin Tristram	5 Huggin Lane	1
BW, pellet between	20.3.1806	Benjamin Webb	3 Red Lion Street, Clerkenwell	2

[1] See IL below.

CAP FF

Mark	Entered	Name	Address/Notes	Punch
CAP	21.12.1828	[1]Charles Auguste Petterman	12 Upper King Street, Bloomsbury	2
CAP	2.12.1840	idem	idem	3
CBH*	1.7.1840	Charles Brook Holliday	21 Queen Street, Percival Street, Clerkenwell	2
CC*	6.12.1819	Charles Clarke	Charles Square, Hoxton	3
	2.7.1823	idem	Moved to 71 Bunhill Row	
CG ⎫ JG ⎭	1.5.1813	[2]Charles and Joseph Greenwood	17 St. James's Street, Clerkenwell	1
CH	20.11.1826	Charles Hubberd	6 Union Buildings, Kingsland Road	2
	6.10.1828	idem	Moved to 9 Pool Terrace, City Road	
CH	1834–1841	idem	idem (five marks)	1 and 2
CH	2.7.1834	Charles Howse	18 Richmond Street, Bartholomew Square (pendantmaker)	1, with round end to C
CJ, pellet between	9.7.1799	Charles Johnson	36 Clerkenwell Green	2
CJ	8.11.1804	Charles Jones	2 Arthur Street, Goswell Street	2
CJ, pellet between*	28.8.1817	Charles Jaques	39 Red Lion Street, Clerkenwell	3
CL*	10.3.1828	Charles Lupton	6 St. James's Place, Clerkenwell	2
CL*	22.1.1829	idem	idem	2
	7.8.1832	idem	Moved to 9 Wilmington Square	
	3.10.1833	idem	Moved to 2 York Place, Barnsbury Park	
CL	7.8.1834	idem	29 Brunswick Street, St. John Street	2
CL	17.8.1835	Charles Lorimier	4 Richmond Buildings, Soho (two marks)	1 and 3
CLC	1.1.1825	Charles Lorimier Calame	12 Bateman's Buildings, Soho	1
CM*	9.8.1824	Charles Muston	18 Red Lion Street, Clerkenwell	2
CM*	1825–1848	idem	idem (three marks)	2
CP	8.6.1833	Charles Pierrepont	9 Brick Lane, St. Luke's (pendantmaker)	1
	3.7.1833	idem	Moved to 7 Essex Street, Kingsland Road	

[1] See also CP below. [2] See WW.CG below.

WATCHCASEMAKERS' CAMEO MARKS

Mark	Entered	Name	Address/Notes	Punch
CP	21.11.1834	[1]Charles Auguste Petterman	12 Upper King Street, Bloomsbury	3
CR	17.6.1796	[2]Charles Redrick	37 Aldermanbury	1
CS*	6.7.1791	Charles Saffell	36 Clerkenwell Green	2
CS	18.3.1800	Charles Storer	25 Bowling Green Lane, Clerkenwell	1
CS	26.2.1801	idem	idem	2
CS, pellet between	17.1.1820	idem	8 Britannia Row, Islington	1
DF	23.10.1824	Drury Freeman	41 Gee Street, Goswell Street (pendantmaker)	1
DR	25.7.1782	Daniel Rust	2 Normans Buildings, Old Street	1
EF	25.7.1794	Edward Feline Jr.	3 Georges Row, City Road	1
	13.10.1795	idem	Moved to 8 Pittman's Buildings, City Road	
EK*	26.9.1827	Edward Keat	69 Banner Street	1
EL, pellet between	21.3.1777	Edward Leeming	24 Giltspur Street	1
	22.7.1785	idem	Moved to Cross Key Court, Little Britain	
EL	29.4.1796	idem	122 Bunhill Row	2
EL	30.6.1800	idem	Moved to 36 Monkwell Street	2
EL*	17.9.1823	Ebenezer Lowrie	8 Botolph Court, Botolph Lane	1
ES, pellet between	23.11.1798	Ezekiel Stevens	Falcon Place, Bay Street, Clerkenwell	2
ES	9.2.1819	idem (or son)	17 Percival Street, Clerkenwell	1
FC	19.5.1808	[3]Frederick Comtesse	34 King Street, Soho	1
FC, pellet between	11.12.1817	Frederick Clarke	23 Banner Square	2
FC	16.4.1819	idem	14 Mitchell Street, Brick Lane	1
	30.5.1820	idem	Moved to 13 Radnor Street, Bath Street, St. Luke's	
FD	3.7.1833	Frederick Dawkins	5 St. John's Street (pendantmaker)	1
FF, pellet between	10.3.1831	Frederick Feline	1 York Place, New Inn Street, Shoreditch	3

[1] See also CAP above.
[2] See also Section I, no. 2423.
[3] See also ID.FC below, and FC.FD Section VII.

FM   HD

Mark	Entered	Name	Address/Notes	Punch
FM	21.11.1823	Frederick Melvill	42 Spencer Street, Goswell Street	1
FP, pellet between	15.11.1794	Francis Purdom	22 Golden Lane	2
GA, mullet above	28.10.1763	George Ashton	Glasshouse Yard, Goswell Street	1, with curved top
GB	5.12.1804	George Byworth	13 Peartree Court, Clerkenwell Close	3
GC*	3.2.1786	George Clarke	3 Cherrytree Court, Aldersgate Street	2
GC*	13.12.1803	idem	18 Long's Buildings, Whitecross Street	2
GC*	19.1.1820 and 17.10.1821	[1]George Conen	6 Hull Street, St. Luke's	1
GC	20.7.1832	idem	idem	2
GD*	5.6.1804	George Donne	4 Clerkenwell (?)	2
GH	— 1737	[2]George Hanet	'Castle Street near St. Martins Court next door to the Angel, free of the Clockmakers'	1
GH*	6.8.1777	Gyles Hooper	17 Union Court, Holborn	1
GH*	12.7.1826	George Hammon	13 Tysoe Street, Clerkenwell	2
GH	17.7.1829	idem	2 Meredith Street	1
	2.2.1833	idem	Moved to 4 Skinner Street, Clerkenwell	
GL	9.3.1799	Gervas Lassells	Great Sutton Street, Clerkenwell	2
GM	14.2.1835	George Meriton	4 Little Mitchell Street, St. Luke's	1
GM	10.11.1835	idem	idem	3
GMB*	21.7.1823	George Musgrave Batts	9 Ashby Street, St John's Street	3
	1.11.1827	idem	Moved to 9 Clerkenwell Green	
GMB NVC	8.11.1826	[3]George Musgrave Batts and Nathaniel Valentine Crossland	5 Lizard Street, St. Luke's	2
GP*	30.7.1821	George Poole	23 Coppice Row, Clerkenwell	2

[1] See also GY.GC below.
[2] Probably son of Paul Hanet (Section I).
[3] See NC and NVC below.

WATCHCASEMAKERS' CAMEO MARKS

Mark	Entered	Name	Address/Notes	Punch
GP*	6.6.1831	idem	6 Bartholomew Terrace, King Square, St. Luke's	2
	10.10.1831	idem	Moved to 54 Rahere Street, Clerkenwell	
	18.7.1832	idem	Moved to 4 Wood Street, Rahere Street	
GP, pellet between	18.11.1837	idem	idem	2
GR*	28.7.1823	[1]George Richards	17 Bridgewater Square	1
GR	13.11.1834	idem	idem	2
	16.10.1837	idem	Moved to 19 Bridgwater Square	
GS	19.4.1800	George Swan	42 St. John's Square	1
GT	29.3.1819	[2]George Thickbroom	23 Richmond Street, St. Luke's	3
GT	18.8.1837	idem	10 Wellington Street, Clerkenwell	1
GV, script	8.11.1775	George Venables	162 Upper Thames Street	1, with curved top
	2.7.1776	idem	Moved to 38 Walbrook	
GY	24.12.1819	George Yeates	15 Mead Street, Bethnal Green	2
	2.2.1828	idem	Moved to 11 Doby Court	
GY GC }	3.3.1818	[3]George Yeates and George Conen	Jerusalem Court, St. John's Square	2
HB	4.4.1823	Horatio Bartlett	27 Greenhills' Rents, Smithfield Bars	2
HB }* GB	1.5.1826	Horatio and George Elliot Bartlett	idem	2
HD	31.3.1826	Henry Deacon	2 Upper Clifton Street, Finsbury	2
	30.1.1829	idem	Moved to 61 Goswell Street	
	21.10.1830	idem	Moved to 36 Reves Place, Hoxton	
	16.7.1836	idem	Moved to 13 White Street, Little Moorfields	
	5.7.1837	idem	Moved to 7 Orchard Street, St. Luke's	
HD	28.2.1843	idem	idem	2
	21.2.1845	idem	Moved to 36 Wellington Street, St. Luke's	

[1] See IR below.
[2] See also Alford Thickbroom above and Jane Thickbroom below.
[3] See GC above.

HG   IH

Mark	Entered	Name	Address/Notes	Punch
HG, pellet between*	14.5.1818	Horace Gooch	47 Clerkenwell Close	2
	19.3.1819	idem	Moved to 23 Coppice Row, Clerkenwell	
HG	15.5.1822	idem	idem	1
HH*	9.1.1830	Henry Hardy	14 Rosomans Row, Clerkenwell	2
HHN	18.10.1836	Henry Howard Nicholson	5 Charles Street, Goswell Street	1
HW	25.1.1806	Henry Williams	87 St. John's Street	1
HW, pellet between	11.11.1837	Henry Williamson	22 Percival Street, Clerkenwell	1
IA	30.5.1777	Joseph Allanson	15 Nixon Square, Jewin Street	1
IA*	23.4.1803	John Allen	26 Ratcliff Row	2
IA, pellet between	29.8.1805	idem	3 Gloucester Row, Curtain Road	2
IA	18.6.1806	idem	12 Parks Row, City Road	2
	22.12.1806	idem	Moved to 15 Craven Street, City Road	
	11.9.1807	idem	Moved to 9 Greenharbour Court, Goswell Street	
IB	31.8.1776	John Brotherton	Wells Row, Islington	2
IB	14.7.1780	James Boulton	11 King Court, Blue Anchor Alley, Bunhill Row	2
IB, pellet between mullet above*	7.2.1799	John Baxter	59 Banner Street, Bunhill Row	1, with curved top
IB, pellet between	2.3.1807	idem	idem	curved oblong
	no date	idem	Moved to 77 Sun Street, Bishopsgate	
	no date	idem	Moved to 28 North Street, City Road	
IB	20.11.1799	John Blast	43 Brick Lane, Old Street	2
IB	24.3.1812	James Bourne	26 Red Lion Street, Clerkenwell	1
IC, coronet above	1.4.1772	[1]Joseph Carpenter	Blue Anchor Alley, Bunhill Row	1, with sloping top sides
IC, script	27.2.1779	[2]James Clarke	58 Featherstone Street	3
IC, pellet between	29.12.1795	Joseph Collins	72 Wheeler Street, Spitalfields	2

[1] See Section I, no. 1226 and Section V.
[2] See Section I, nos. 1229, 1789, and IC, pellet between, below.

WATCHCASEMAKERS' CAMEO MARKS

Mark	Entered	Name	Address/Notes	Punch
IC, pellet between*	29.3.1775	John Clarke	Ironmongers Row, Old Street	1
IC, pellet between	27.8.1790	idem	idem	2
	21.1.1791	idem	Moved to 70 Bunhill Row	
IC, pellet between	26.1.1797	John Clerke	18 Long Buildings, Whitecross Street	1
IC, pellet between	10.10.1800	[1]James Clark	2 Type Street, Chiswell Street	double-lobed
IC	10.8.1800	James Callow	12 Bartholomew Close	2
IC, pellet between	14.6.1806	idem	idem	2
	9.4.1808	idem	Moved to 1 Elbow Place, City Road	
IC	14.10.1812	idem	idem	2
IC, pellet between	11.6.1814	John Church	11 Seward Street, Goswell Street	1
IC, pellet between	24.10.1818	James Critchfield	3 Rowston Street, Islington Road	1
IC, pellet between } IC, pellet between	12.11.1789	James Clark and James Callow	13 Bartholomew Close	2
ID	12.5.1772	John Day	Christopher Alley, Upper Moorfields	1
ID*	1.1.1836	John Dyer	55 Bath Street, City Road	2
ID	18.10.1837	idem	Moved to 21 Red Lion Street, Clerkenwell	2
	15.12.1841	idem	Moved to 11 Gloucester Street, Clerkenwell	
ID } FC	11.11.1807	[2]John De Saulles and Frederick Comtesse	34 King Street, Soho	2
IE*	4.7.1798	Innocent Ekins	2 Cumberland, Curtain Road, Shoreditch	2
IF, script	29.8.1811	John Fells	7 John's Row, Brick Lane	2
IG*	25.7.1812	Joseph Glenny	20 Red Lion (?St.), Clerkenwell	2
IG, script	14.5 1819	idem	21 Wynatt Street, Goswell Street	2
IH, pellet between	9.8.1787	John Hadley	3 Charterhouse Street	2
IH, pellet between	14.4.1792	John Hislop	16 Rawston Street, St. John Turnpike	1

[1] See IC script above, and IC.IC below   [2] See FC above.

I H   J B

Mark	Entered	Name	Address/Notes	Punch
IH*	11.7.1812	[1]John Harris	41 Rawstone Street, Islington Road	2
IH, pellet between	19.12.1835	idem	22 Gloucester Street, Clerkenwell	2
IH	21.8.1819	James Hood	8 Ivy Lane, Hoxton	1
	25.8.1821	idem	Moved to 4 Richard's Place, Old Street	
IH, pellet between*	26.7.1822	John William Hammon	91 Goswell Street	2
	11.3.1825	idem	Moved to 9 John Street	
	17.1.1826	idem	Moved to 48 Whiskin Street	
	12.3.1836	idem	Moved to 11 Gloucester Street, Clerkenwell	
IIG	16.8.1826	James John Gliddon	16 Red Lyon Passage, Red Lion Square	1
IL	3.3.1778	[2]John Laithwait	104 Gray's Inn Lane	oblong, shaped base
ILL, pellet after I	26.3.1796	John Lloyd	2 Crown Court, Charterhouse Lane	2
IM, pellet between	10.3.1767	[3]Jonah Mince	George Yard, Whitechapel	oblong, invected ends
IM	2.11.1778	idem	Old Street Road, No. 8 Norman Street	2
IN, pellet between	17.10.1805	John Nash	30 Brick Lane	2
IN	3.9.1813	idem	Moved to 17 King Street, Bethnal Green	2
IN, pellet between	29.7.1811	[4]James Norvill	14 James Buildings, Rosoman Street	3
IP	9.4.1805	[5]Job Palmer	2 Red Lion Street, Clerkenwell	3
IR, pellet between	19.1.1819	John Radcliffe	Prujean Square	2
IR, pellet between*	7.3.1822	James Richards	Bridgewater Square	2
IS, pellet between	16.8.1779	James Sage	24 Clerkenwell Green	2
idem	6.11.1779	idem	idem	1
IS, pellet between	5.7.1782	James Sharkey	19 Turnmill Street	2

[1] See also JH below. [2] See AL above.
[3] See also Section V. [4] See also JN below.
[5] See also IWP below and Section I, no. 1579.

WATCHCASEMAKERS' CAMEO MARKS

Mark	Entered	Name	Address/Notes	Punch
IS	27.3.1820	Joseph Saunders	13 Ironmonger Row, St. Luke's	incurved oblong
IS ⎫ IC ⎭	29.2.1820	Joseph Saunders and John Church	idem	1
IT, pellet between*	21.10.1777	[1]John Turner	13 Deans Rents	2
idem	21.11.1781	idem	idem	2
idem	12.10.1793	idem	Greenwells Rents	2
IW, pellet between	29.3.1779	[2]John Wills	2 Bull and Mouth Street	1
	24.12.1779	idem	Moved to 13 St. John's Lane, Smithfield	
IW	11.2.1800	idem	idem	3
IW (very small)	22.4.1813	John Weston	4 Pitman's Buildings, St. Luke's (pendantmaker)	2
IW*	1.3.1821	Joseph Wickes	Wenlock Street, St. Luke's	1
	11.5.1832	idem	Moved to 52 Sutton Street, Clerkenwell	
IWP*	21.7.1798	Job William Palmer	49 Clerkenwell Close	1
idem	16.10.1809	idem	2 Red Lion Street, Clerkenwell	2
IW ⎫ TI ⎭	14.4.1814	[3]John Weston and Thomas Iliff	47 Ironmonger's Row (pendantmakers)	2
JA	23.9.1814	Joseph Anderton	29 Brick Lane, Noble Street	3
JAT*	30.9.1829	John Abram Tyas	9 Clerkenwell Green	3
	25.6.1831	idem	Moved to 77 Rahere Street, Goswell Road	
	27.6.1833	idem	Moved to 36 Seward Street, Goswell Street	
	29.6.1836	idem	Moved to 11 Red Lion Street, Clerkenwell	
JB	5.1.1798	James Bridgman	8 Rose Street, St. Luke's	2
JB	7.10.1799	idem	idem	2
JB	27.6.1823	idem	14 Princes Street, Gravel Lane, Southwark	2
JB	12.1.1811	James Barwick	5 Norway Street, Old Street	2
JB	11.5.1819	James Bigg	4 Prujean Square, Old Bailey	2
JB*	8.11.1819	Josiah Barnett	52 Sutton Street, Clerkenwell	1
	22.3.1820	idem	Moved to 43 Galway Street, St. Luke's	

[1] See Section I, no. 1706. [2] See also IW.TI below. [3] See TI below.

JB   JP

Mark	Entered	Name	Address/Notes	Punch
JB	3.4.1823	idem	idem	1
JB	3.7.1833	idem	idem	1
	27.8.1835	idem	Moved to 15 Lower Charles Street, Northampton Square	
JC	8.11.1820	[1]John Church	16 Ironmonger's Row, St. Luke's	1
JC	28.9.1833	James Conen	6 Hull Street, St. Luke's	2
JC	8.6.1836	idem	idem	2
	13.6.1839	idem	Moved to 58 Wellington Street, Goswell Street	
JC	25.2.1840	idem	idem	3
JC	6.10.1842	idem	idem	1
JD*	7.9.1835	James Dow	54 Percival Street, Clerkenwell	2
JF, pellet between	29.6.1807	Joseph Field	9 St. James's Street, Clerkenwell	2
	27.1.1810	idem	Moved to 7 Red Lion Street, Clerkenwell	
JF, pellet between JP, pellet between	16.4.1800(?)	Joseph Field and John Palmer	9 St. James Street, Clerkenwell	2
JG	8.6.1815	Joseph Greenwood	3 Worship Street, Curtain Road	2
JG	6.8.1822	John Griffiths	22 West Place, John's Row, City Road	3
JG	2.2.1825	idem	idem	2
JG	14.2.1825	idem	idem	octagon
	12.11.1827	idem	Moved to 9 Regent Street, City Road	
	18.2.1828	idem	Moved to 23 Waterloo Street, St. Luke's	
	15.1.1831	idem	Moved to 2 Woods Buildings, New Inn Yard, Shoreditch	
JG, pellet between	12.11.1831	idem	idem	2
	5.5.1838	idem	Moved to 7 Clarence Place, Brick Square, St. Luke's	
	21.9.1840	idem	Moved to 5 Collingwood Street, Shoreditch	

[1] See IS.IC above.

WATCHCASEMAKERS' CAMEO MARKS

Mark	Entered	Name	Address/Notes	Punch
JG	13.12.1830	James Green	48 Ironmonger Row, St. Luke's	1
	1841–1856	idem	five other addresses	
JH*	17.9.1823	[1]John Harris	41 Rawstone Street, Islington Road	1
JH, pellet between	— 1829	[2]John Hartley	34 Wellington Street	1
JH	30.12.1833	John Hadwen	12 Willow Walk, Shoreditch	1
JH, pellet between	9.12.1836	[3]Joseph Hirst	153 St. John's Road	1
idem	11.2.1837	idem	idem	1
JH	18.9.1840	idem	idem	2
JH	21.6.1837	John Howell	4 Northampton Buildings, Rosoman Street (pendant-maker)	2
JJ, pellet between*	3.2.1785	[4]James Jackson I	2 Bridgwater Street, Barbican	2
JJ*	30.8.1832	[4]James Jackson II	10 Norman Street, St. Luke's	2
JJ	28.6.1839	idem	idem	1
JJ	5.10.1799	[5]John Johnson	38 Islington Road, St. John's Street	2
JM*	3.4.1822	James Melvill	13 Spencer Street, Clerkenwell	2
JM, pellet between*	27.6.1823	James Martin	9 Vineyard Walk, Clerkenwell	2
JM	12.4.1833	idem	48 Winyatt Street, Clerkenwell	2
JM	25.7.1826	James Moffat	2 James Street, Goswell Road	1
JN	30.1.1813	[6]James Norvill	Domingo Street, St. Luke's	3
JN, pellet between	8.3.1819	Jane Norvill	idem (presumably widow)	1
JP, pellet between	1.7.1807	[7]John Palmer	12 Berkley Court, Clerkenwell	2
JP, pellet between*	4.9.1820	James Pascall	18 Wilderness Row, Goswell Street (pendant-maker)	1

---

[1] See also IH above.
[2] Address entered in duplication in date column with pencil note '1829'.
[3] See also SS.JH below.   [4] See Section I, no. 1827.
[5] Conjectured from very blurred impression in register.
[6] See also IN above.   [7] See also JF.JP above.

Mark	Entered	Name	Address/Notes	Punch
JP, pellet between*	11.7.1832	Joseph Potter	47 Ironmonger Row	2
JR	17.2.1817	John Roberts	Ironmonger Row, St. Luke's (pendantmaker)	2
JS	21.12.1819	[1]James Storer	2 Rawstone Street, Islington Road	1
	11.8.1843	idem	Moved to 21 John Street Road	
JT	30.10.1837	[2]Jane Thickbroom	10 Wellington Street, Clerkenwell	1
JW*	28.2.1814	John Williams	56 Great Sutton Street	2
JW	29.7.1815	idem	idem	3
JW	28.7.1818	idem	idem	3
JW	26.2.1822	idem	idem	1
JW	26.3.1823	idem	idem	3
JW	7.4.1825	idem	idem	3
JW	18.11.1833	idem	idem	3
JW	15.8.1837	idem	idem	3
JW*	20.11.1817	John West	99 White Cross Street	1
JW, script	5.3.1822	idem	idem	2
JW	1.10.1836	idem	24 Banner Square, St. Luke's	2
JW	30.11.1838	idem	idem	1
JW, pellet between	27.5.1831	John Wells	31 Lower Northampton Street, Clerkenwell	2
	28.3.1833	idem	Moved to 20 Queen Street, Clerkenwell	
JW, pellet between	29.10.1834	idem	idem (and other marks to 1853)	2
LB	11.5.1813	Lewis Balding	4 Red Lion Court, London Wall (pendantmaker)	2
LC, three pellets below*	31.12.1827	Louis Comtesse	10 East Street, Red Lion Square	2
LC	19.1.1828	idem	idem	1
LC	1.6.1836	idem	idem	3
LC	5.3.1840	idem	idem	3
LN	14.7.1774	Lawrence Notley	8 Silver Street, Clerkenwell Green	2
MA, pellet between	1.2.1813	Michael Atkins	4 Red Lion Street, Clerkenwell (pendantmaker)	1

[1] See Section I, no. 413.
[2] See GT above.

WATCHCASEMAKERS' CAMEO MARKS

Mark	Entered	Name	Address/Notes	Punch
MD*	12.2.1798	Mary Dearmer	14 Featherstone Street, Bunhill Row	1, with incurved top
MG*	25.1.1809	[1]Matthew Govett	46 Ironmonger Row, Old Street	2
MG	7.2.1811	idem	idem	2
	31.8.1811	idem	Moved to 42 Ironmonger Row	
MN	12.1.1803	Matthew Need	2 Castle Street, City Road	2
MN	14.7.1806	idem	idem	2
	no date	idem	Moved to 22 Featherstone Street, City Road	
MT	23.1.1806	Matthew Travers	12 Great Sutton Street, Clerkenwell	1
MT	20.10.1809	idem	idem	2
MT, pellet between	18.2.1815	idem	7 Red Lion Street, Clerkenwell	1
NC, pellet between	2.8.1822	[2]Nathaniel Valentine Crossland	5 Lizard Street, St. Luke's	quatrefoil
NVC	1.1.1828	idem	idem	2
NC⎫ IP ⎭	20.11.1819	Nathaniel Crossland and John Phillips	idem	2
NTW*	13.4.1785	Nicholas Thomas Wood	21 St. John's Square, Clerkenwell	1
idem	1.8.1791	idem	idem	1
idem	16.1.1798	idem	idem	1
PM	5.11.1831	Philibert Matthey	5 Easton Street, Spafields	2
PM	7.12.1831	idem	idem	1
	7.4.1836	idem	Moved to 5 Baker Street, Clerkenwell	
PS, pellet between	7.7.1834	Peter Seddon	13 Lizard Street, Bartholomew Square (pendantmaker)	1
PS	8.3.1837	idem	idem	2
RB, pellet between*	10.8.1820	Robert Bellows	17 Looks (?) Gardens, Bowling Green Lane, Clerkenwell	1
	4.9.1833	idem	Moved to 14 Corporation Court, Corporation Row, Clerkenwell	
	8.10.1842	idem	Moved to 9 Whiskin Street, Clerkenwell	

[1] See also SG for his widow?
[2] See GMB.NVC above.

RB   SB

Mark	Entered	Name	Address/Notes	Punch
RB }* GM }	31.12.1806	Richard Ball and Gideon Macaire	6 St. James Street, Clerkenwell	1
	11.1.1809	idem	Moved to 33 Rosomon Street, Clerkenwell	
idem	21.11.1812	idem	idem	1
	6.6.1814	idem	Moved to 32 Northampton Square, Clerkenwell	
RB } GM }	24.7.1818	idem	idem	1
	4.6.1821	idem	Moved to 17 Middleton Street, Clerkenwell	
idem	25.2.1829	idem	idem	1
idem	31.10.1833	idem	26 Middleton Street, Clerkenwell	1
RC, pellet between	31.5.1787	Richard Clarke	58 Featherstone Street, Bunhill Row	2
	26.2.1789	idem	Moved to 126 Bunhill Row	
	12.4.1790	idem	Moved to 67 Wheeler Street, Smithfield	
RC, script	27.1.1792	idem	idem	2
RC	18.4.1796	idem	15 Ratcliff Row, City Road	2
	3.2.1800	idem	Moved to 4 Ship Court, Old Bailey	
RC	27.11.1805	idem	idem	2
RG	30.8.1792	Richard Grove	104 Gray's Inn Lane	2
RH, pellet between	12.8.1729	Richard Homesley	Golden Cup, St. Ann's Lane	2
RH	21.3.1836	Robert Hall	18 Norfolk Place, Curtain Road (pendantmaker)	2
	20.8.1836	idem	Moved to 5 Peerless Row, Bath Street, St. Luke's	
RM, pellet between*	25.10.1831	Robert Mansir	15 Lower Charles Street	2
RP*	15.7.1780	[1]Richard Palmer I	Red Lion Street, Clerkenwell	1, with shaped end to P
RP	22.12.1786	idem	2 Red Lion Street	2
RP	4.3.1791	idem	idem	1
RP	26.4.1793	idem	idem	2
RP, pellet between	17.3.1795	idem	idem	2
RP, mullet above	30.12.1793	Richard Palmer II	Bishops Court, Clerkenwell	1, top shaped
	9.7.1794	idem	Moved to 18 Sutton Street, Clerkenwell	

[1] See Section I, no. 2406 and Section V.

WATCHCASEMAKERS' CAMEO MARKS

Mark	Entered	Name	Address/Notes	Punch
RP, pellet between CS, pellet between	7.7.1785	Richard Palmer and Charles Saffell	2 Red Lion Street, Clerkenwell	2
RR GF	27.5.1818	Reuben Rice and George Fleming	4 Bishop's Court, Clerkenwell	2
	20.4.1819	idem	Moved to 49 Red Lion Street, Clerkenwell	
RS, pellet between	14.9.1720	Robet Sly	Adams Court, Broad Street, 'Clockmaker'	1
RS, pellet between	3.1.1776	[1]Richard Simpson	19 Albion Building, Aldersgate Street	2
RS	16.12.1784	idem	idem	2
RS	6.6.1800	idem	idem	1
RS	6.5.1795	Robert Skinner	3 White Street, Little Moorfields	3
RS	30.11.1796	idem	idem	3
RS	16.8.1805	Robert Styring	2 Brynes Row, Cold Bath Fields	2
SA, pellet between	28.6.1785	Samuel Armand	27 New Street, Cloth Fair	2
SA*	11.5.1801	Samuel Atkins	14 Bridgwater Square	2
SA, pellet between	13.3.1805	idem	idem	2
SB	13.8.1779	Samuel Bridge	29 St. John's Lane	2
SB	12.11.1792	[2]Samuel Brough	10 New Street, Cloth Fair	2
SB, pellet between	29.1.1794	idem	idem	2
SB	4.3.1794	idem	idem	hexagon
	30.6.1797	idem	Moved to 4 Berkley Street, Clerkenwell	
SB*	13.9.1796	Samuel Brookes	7 Aris's Buildings, Bowling Green Lane	1
	30.3.1799	idem	Moved to 20 Hosier Lane, West Smithfield	
SB	25.8.1801	idem	12 Rosomon Street, Clerkenwell	1
	30.9.1808	idem	Moved to 3 Ashby Street, Clerkenwell	
SB	10.3.1810	idem	idem	1
SB	18.5.1818	idem	idem	2
SB	7.3.1822	idem	idem	1

[1] See Section I, no. 2434.
[2] See Section I, no. 2482 for son (?).

Mark	Entered	Name	Address/Notes	Punch
SB, pellet between	7.10.1833	Stephen Bryan	48 Rahere Street, St. Luke's	2
SC*	29.7.1813	Sarah Clerke	23 Banner Square	3
S.C.*	25.4.1835	Samuel Cuendet	Wilmington Square (and 1848–9)	2
SG	2.12.1823	¹Sarah Govett	47 Ironmonger Row, St. Luke's	2
SK	29.6.1802	Samuel Keene	13 Bartholomew Close	2
	29.10.1804	idem	Moved to 7 Albion Buildings	
	12.10.1808	idem	Moved to 7 French Alley, Goswell Street	
SK	7.6.1810	idem	idem	2
SP, pellet between	8.5.1775	Southern Payne	17 Bridgwater Square	2
idem	31.3.1784	idem	idem	2
SP, pellet between*	16.12.1805	Samuel Pike	48 Blue Anchor Alley, Bunhill Row	2
SS, pellet between	22.2.1782	Samuel Stephens	5 Bull and Mouth Street	3
SS, pellet between	2.11.1805	Samuel Strahan	12 Great Prescot Street, Goodmans Fields	2
idem	18.2.1808	idem	1 Little Mitchell Street, St. Luke's	2
	13.10.1811	idem	Moved to 54 Lemon Street, Goodmans Fields	
	22.10.1811	idem	Moved to 36 Whites Row, Spitalfields	
SS, pellet between	1.9.1834	idem	idem (and again 29.11.1834)	2
SS	6.12.1836	Samuel Saltmarsh	74 Middleton Street, Clerkenwell (till 1845)	2
SS } * JH }	6.3.1835	Samuel Saltmarsh and Joseph Hirst	28 Coppice Row, Clerkenwell	1
TB*	16.2.1829	Thomas Burwash	7 St. James' Walk (pendantmaker)	2
	9.6.1841	idem	Moved to 11 Great Sutton Street	
TB, pellet between	17.7.1819	Thomas Balshaw	3 Bridgwater Gardens, Barbican	2
TB } IT }	11.4.1820	Thomas Britton and John Tipson	23 Goswell Terrace, Goswell Street	2
TB } * WL }	24.3.1798	²Thomas Bligh and William Linsley	16 Great Sutton Street, Clerkenwell	2

¹ See MG above.   ² See also WL below. TB

WATCHCASEMAKERS' CAMEO MARKS

Mark	Entered	Name	Address/Notes	Punch
TC*	27.9.1775	[1]Thomas Carpenter	5 Islington Road	2
TC, script	30.6.1792	idem	idem	2
TC	24.8.1796	idem	idem	2
TCC, pellets between	14.1.1804	Theodore C. Clark	19 St. John's Lane	2
T⎱ CC⎰	21.1.1804	idem	idem	1, with incurved top corners
TC⎱ RC⎰	7.12.1803	Thomas and Richard Carpenter	5 Islington Road	2
TC, pellet between RC, pellet between	12.6.1811	idem	5 St. John Street Road	2
TE*	27.1.1813	Thomas Emmett	16 Albemarle Street, Clerkenwell (pendant-maker)	3
TE	16.2.1813	idem	idem	2
TF, pellet between	30.12.1768	[2]Thomas Foster I	5 Pye Corner, West Smithfield	2
idem	26.9.1770	idem	idem	2
TF, pellet between	12.4.1790	Thomas Foster II	9 Oxford Arms Passage, Warwick Lane	2
	21.4.1790	idem	idem	2
TG*	14.2.1792	Thomas Gibbard	28 Clerkenwell Close	2
idem	23.7.1794	idem	idem	2
idem	25.9.1802	idem	idem	2
idem	7.11.1812	idem	idem	1
TG	1.5.1800	Thomas Gaunt	5 Bridgwater Gardens	1
TG, pellet between AB, pellet between	15.2.1799	Thomas Gaunt and Alexander Barker	idem	2
TG	20.10.1817	Thomas Grove	9 Vineyard Walk	2
*TH**	19.1.1776	Thomas Hardy I	30 Clerkenwell Close	1
TH	3.3.1788	idem	12 Rosomons Row, Clerkenwell	1
TH, pellet between	27.2.1813	Thomas Hardy II	1 Gwyn's Buildings, Goswell Street	2
TH, pellet between	24.1.1777	Thomas Hill	80 Aldersgate Street	2
TH	22.2.1779	idem	idem	2

[1] See TC.RC below.
[2] See Section I nos. 2751, 3822-3 and Section V

Mark	Entered	Name	Address/Notes	Punch
TH, pellet between	26.8.1781	idem	idem	2
TH	31.8.1783	idem	idem	1
TH, pellet between	13.12.1785	idem	idem	1
	7.2.1786	idem	Moved to 12 Little Moorfields	
TH	17.9.1777	Thomas Hailes	1 Huggin Lane, Trinity Lane	2
TH, mullet above	7.1.1779	idem	idem	1, with rounded top
	19.5.1779	idem	Moved to 5 Charterhouse Street	
	25.11.1779	idem	Moved to 13 Berkley Street, Clerkenwell	
TH, pellet between	28.1.1805	Thomas Harris	Horse Street, BATH	2
TI	20.10.1814	[1]Thomas Iliff	Ironmonger Row, St. Luke's (pendantmaker)	2, with shaped top
	22.5.1815	idem	Moved to Mount Pleasant, Gray's Inn Lane	
	12.1.1822	idem	Moved to 55 Rosomon Street, Clerkenwell	
	no date	idem	Moved to 22 Yardley Street, Clerkenwell	
	2.1.1824	idem	Moved to 2 Wiskin Street, Clerkenwell	
	9.2.1826	idem	Moved to 21 Rosomon Street	
TJ, pellet between	1.10.1805	Thomas Jemmett	22 Ironmonger Row, St. Luke's	2
TJ ⎫ GY ⎭	17.4.1822	Thomas Juxon and George Yeates	11 Doby Court, Monkwell Street	2
idem	17.2.1825	idem	idem	2
TJ, pellet between IH, pellet between	14.4.1804	Thomas Jemmett and John Howe	1 Wenlock Street, St. Luke's	2
TK*	21.7.1824	Thomas Keeff	41 Clerkenwell Close	2
TK, pellet between	undated before 19.6.1832	idem	Moved to Middleton Street	1

[1] See IW.TI above.

WATCHCASEMAKERS' CAMEO MARKS

Mark	Entered	Name	Address/Notes	Punch
TM*	7.2.1803	Thomas Milliar	37 Wynyatt Street, Goswell Street Road	2
	30.7.1808	idem	Moved to 1 Little Mitchell Street, St. Luke's	
	24.4.1818	idem	Moved to 130 Old Street	
	20.8.1819	idem	Moved to 24 Bartholomew Terrace, Brick Lane	
TN*	9.3.1822	Thomas Norris	8 Rawstone Street, St. John Street	2
TP, pellet between	24.1.1777	Thomas Primat	3 New Compton Street, Soho	2
TR, coronet above*	14.6.1777	[1]Thomas Ray	9 Bridewell Precinct	trefoil
TR	3.12.1824	Thomas Rogers	9 Vineyard Walk, Clerkenwell	2
	31.10.1828	idem	Moved to 63 Wheeler Street, Spitalfields	
	16.4.1832	idem	Moved to 19 Union Street, Bethnal Green Road	
	20.8.1836	idem	Moved to 9 James Street, St. Luke's	
TS	5.2.1774	Thomas Sones	5 Lilypot Lane, Noble Street	2
TS	1.5.1784	idem	idem	2
TW	7.1.1817	Thomas Warren	5 Susanna Row, Curtain Road	2
TW	20.9.1824	Thomas Wells	10 Short's Buildings, Clerkenwell (pendant-maker)	2
	9.8.1826	idem	Moved to 4 Fan Street, Goswell Street	
TW	25.10.1837	idem	4 Seward Street, St. Luke's	2
WB, pellet between	7.4.1777	William Boulton	55 Bread Street, Cheapside	1
	2.9.1781	idem	Moved to 12 Jerusalem Court, Clerkenwell	
WB, pellet between, crescent above*	18.2.1778	William Blake	5 Staining Lane	2, with curved top to crescent
	20.9.1781	idem	Moved to White Cross Street	

[1] See Section I, no. 2902.

Mark	Entered	Name	Address/Notes	Punch
WB, pellet between, crescent above	22.8.1788	idem	idem	1, with shaped top
WB	23.9.1800	idem	idem	2
WB	16.2.1801 and 3.6.1801	idem	28, White Cross Street	2
WB, pellet between*	31.8.1789	[1]William Brooks	1 Church Row, Old Street	2
WB, pellet between	10.9.1793	idem	idem	2
WB	29.6.1798	idem	idem	2
WB	26.1.1801	idem	idem	2
WB, pellet between	3.1.1805	idem	4 Susanna Row, Curtain Road	2
WB	5.7.1822	William Bush	20 Bowling Green Lane, Clerkenwell	1, with incurved top and base
WB	27.8.1822	William Brown	Well Street, COVENTRY	1
WC*	16.2.1813	William Collier	4 Rose Street, St. Luke's (pendantmaker)	3
WC, pellet between	11.3.1831	idem	54 Bath Street	2
WD	12.4.1777	[2]William Day	Broad Arrow Court, Grub Street	curved with invected top
WF, pellet between*	13.1.1809	William Fielder	2 George Yard, Snow Hill	1
WF	12.11.1811	idem	31 St. John's Square, Clerkenwell	2
WF*	5.10.1833	William Francis	15 King Street, Clerkenwell	2
WH*	24.1.1799	William Hodsoll	31 Primrose Street, Bishopsgate	2
WH, pellet between*	23.11.1813	[3]William John Hammon	20 Little Saffron Hill	2
	23.11.1814	idem	Moved to 58 Wellington Street, Goswell Street	
	9.4.1818	idem	Moved to 17 Percival Street	

[1] See Section I, no. 3019 and Section V.
[2] See Section I, no. 3084.
[3] See WIH below.

WATCHCASEMAKERS' CAMEO MARKS

Mark	Entered	Name	Address/Notes	Punch
WH, script*	24.6.1823	William Harris	6 Powell Street, Goswell Street	1
idem	27.11.1823	idem	idem	
	1.4.1824	idem	Moved to 9 St. James's Street, Clerkenwell	
WH, pellet between	19.1.1827	idem	idem	1
WH	9.5.1827	idem	idem	2
WH	7.10.1832	idem	21 Red Lion Street, Clerkenwell	3
WH ⎫ ES ⎭	20.11.1818 and 28.11.1818	William John Hammon and Ezekiel Stevens	17 Percival Street, Clerkenwell	2
WI, pellet between	8.2.1777	William Jones	18 Hosier Lane, Smithfield	2
WIH, pellets between	9.4.1818	William John Hammon	17 Percival Street, Clerkenwell	2
WJ*	31.3.1825	William Jasper	5 King's Head Court, Gutter Lane	2
WL, cross above	11.8.1766	William Lee	Opposite 19 Bunhill Row	1, with shaped top
WJ*	31.3.1825	William Jasper	5 King's Head Court, Gutter Lane	2
WL*	29.12.1798	[1]William Lewis	11 Bridgwater Square	2
WL, pellet between	25.4.1809	idem	26 Red Lion Street, Clerkenwell	2
WL*	14.11.1827	William Lupton	8 Lower Smith Street (pendantmaker)	1
WL ⎫ TB ⎭	1.3.1799	[2]William Linsley and Thomas Bligh	16 Great Sutton Street, Clerkenwell	2
WM	13.9.1820	William Mordan	5 Stangate Place, Stangate Street, Lambeth (pendantmaker)	2
	8.1.1820	idem	Moved to 49 Red Lion Street, Clerkenwell	
	10.7.1821	idem	Moved to 3 Berkley Street	
WP	15.6.1837	William Poulton	51 Ironmonger Row, St. Luke's (pendantmaker)	1
WR, pellet between	19.8.1784	William Russell	3 Crown Court, Foster Lane	1
WR, pellet between*	9.10.1813	William Rowlands	13 Harper Street, Great Sutton Street	2

---

[1] See Section I, no. 3228.   [2] See TB.WL above.

353

Mark	Entered	Name	Address/Notes	Punch
WR	17.8.1836	idem	32 Lower Smith Street, Northampton Square	1
WR ⎫ IB ⎬	16.1.1796	William Richards and John Blast	43 Brick Lane, Old Street,	2
WS, pellet between	25.5.1789	William Simpson	1 Bridgewater Gardens	2
WW, pellet between*	5.8.1800	William Woodman	18 Glasshouse Yard, Aldersgate	2
WW	4.3.1813	William Woolley	BIRMINGHAM (pendantmaker)	3
WW	1.5.1813	[1]William Webb	54 Great Sutton Street, Clerkenwell	2
	30.12.1833	idem	Moved to 6 Skinner Street, Clerkenwell	
WW	11.12.1834	idem	idem	2
WW	16.12.1818	William Wilcox	30 Great Sutton Street, Clerkenwell (pendant-maker)	1
WW*	30.4.1827	William Wright	15 Ashby Street, Northampton Square	1
idem	15.10.1827	idem	idem	1
WW ⎫ CG ⎬	19.6.1811	[2]William Webb and Charles Greenwood	54 Sutton Street, Clerkenwell	2
WY	6.2.1737	William Yearley	'at Mr. Rand's watch-maker at the sign of the Clock the Cornner of Noble Street Fishmonger'	1

---

[1] See WW.CG below.　　　[2] See CG.JG above.

VII

Goldworkers' Marks 1773–1837

All the marks are in relief 'cameo' punches and Roman capitals unless otherwise stated. The punches are generally rectangular or with 'cut' corners but their small size makes precise distinctions difficult. Only oval punches or other unusual examples have been noted. Some makers are categorized as 'jewellers' or 'ringmakers'.

Mark	Entered	Name	Address/Notes	Punch
AA, pellet between	6.7.1798	Andrew Avery	1 Alfred Court, Paul's Alley, Barbican	canted ends to punch
AB, pellet between	2.10.1773	*Aaron Bourne	New Street, Covent Garden (ringmaker)	
idem, larger	21.1.1774	idem	idem	
AB, pellet between	4.2.1775	Aaron Banting	12 St. Martin's Street, Leicester Fields	
AB	1.11.1831	Ann Burman	1 Exeter Place, Dover Road, Southwark	
AC	20.5.1783	Andrew Cooke	419 Oxford Street	
	14.1.1785	idem	92 Holborn Hill	
AC	31.7.1822 and 19.7.1823	Anthony Cox	38 Red Lion Street, Clerkenwell	
AD, pellet between	12.4.1796	Andrew Delauney	54 Jermyn Street, St. James's	
AD	1.5.1797	Adrian Decleve	50 Holywell Street, Strand	
AD	31.12.1818	Alexander Davidson	6 Blackheath Hill, Greenwich	
AD	23.9.1823	†Archibald Douglas	14 West Street	
AD	20.4.1826	idem	37 Penton Place, Pentonville	incurved side, cut corners
	14.12.1837	idem	Moved to 10 Wilderness Row, Chelsea	
AF	11.5.1782	Andrew Fowlds	8 St John Square.	
AF	6.2.1823	Andrew Findlater	44 Barbican	
AG	2.10.1809	Ann Glover	4 Noble Street	

* See Section IV.   † See Section I, nos. 28, 1256.

Mark	Entered	Name	Address/Notes	Punch
AH, pellet between	29.10.1784	Anthony Henderson	BRISTOL	
AH	8.6.1785	Abel Howell	SALISBURY	
AK	14.11.1777	Ann Knight	Noble Street	
AMR	2.2.1820	Alexander McRae	16 Devonshire Street, Bishopsgate	
AS	13.11.1830	*Abraham Scott	64 West Smithfield	
AS incuse	5.5.1835	idem	idem	
	30.9.1842	idem	Moved to 59–60 Red Lion Street	
AW, pellet between, and AW	28.1.1784	Alexander Walmsley	109 Wood Street	
BB ⎱ IY ⎰	11.8.1819	Benjamin Bull and James Young	24 Salisbury Street, Strand	
BC ⎱ WS ⎰	5.4.1826	Benjamin Colyer and William Spurr	13 Bateman's Row, Soho	
BG	31.8.1773	Benjamin Gurden	114 Wood Street (jeweller)	
BM	2.1.1824	†Benjamin Mayfield	18 Staining Lane	
	12.5.1828	idem	Moved to 63 St. John Street, Clerkenwell	
BP, pellet between	11.4.1821	Benjamin Pilkington	27 Coppice Row, Clerkenwell	
	9.4.1825	idem	Moved to 39 Percival Street	
BR	16.3.1822	Benjamin Rawlings	54 Leicester Square	
BS	30.8.1822	Benjamin Stephens	7 Searle Place, Carey Street	
BW	30.9.1809	‡Barnet Wisedill	6 North Place, West Square, Southwark	
	27.11.1823	idem	Moved to Prospect Place, West Square, Southwark	
CA	29.10.1808	Charles Ashling	3 Hind Court, Fleet Street	
	13.10.1824	idem	Moved to 3 Crown Court, Sherrard Street, Golden Square	
CB	21.7.1788	Cornelius Brown	56 Rupert Street 'near the Haymarket'	
CB	26.7.1788	idem	idem	oval
CB	27.4.1793	§Christopher Binger	3 Windmill Street	

* See Section IV   † See SUM and TM below.
‡ See RW below.   § See Section I, no. 268.
For AJS see Section I, no. 46.

GOLDWORKERS' MARKS 1773-1837

Mark	Entered	Name	Address/Notes	Punch
CB	21.12.1815	Charles Bell	5 Albion Buildings, Bartholomew Close, Clerkenwell	
	12.2.1829	idem	Moved to 19 King Street	
	3.11.1832	idem	Moved to 48 Compton Street, Clerkenwell	
CC	5.7.1813	Charles Cheese	19 Albany Street, Clerkenwell	
CCG	13.11.1833	Charles Cotton Godfrey	12 Princes Street, Clerkenwell	
	25.6.1834	idem	Moved to 15 St. James Street, Clerkenwell	
CG	27.11.1824	Charles Gay	15 Kirby Street, Hatton Garden	
CH, pellet between	4.12.1799	Charles Hancock	New Street, BIRMINGHAM	
idem	21.7.1814	idem	idem	also CH incuse
CH	7.6.1833	Charles Harris	25 Berwick Street, Soho	
	29.7.1837	idem	Moved to 3 Nassau Street, Soho	
CHW	18.7.1794	Charles Hitch Woolley	41 Hatton Garden	
CJ	13.10.1831	Charles Jones	9 Leather Lane, Holborn	oval
CM	18.5.1778	Charles Marsh	18 Giltspur Street	
CM, pellet between	23.11.1780	Charles Mackie	19 Princes Street, Leicester Fields	
	20.4.1785	idem	Moved to 6 Wine Office Court, Fleet Street	
	12.7.1785	idem	Moved to 7 York Buildings, George Street	
CM	29.8.1823	*Charles Mosley	113 Fetter Lane	
CO	16.10.1795	Charles Oswald	8 Little St. Martin's Lane	
	27.7.1804	idem	Moved to 15 Queen Street, Soho	
CS, pellet between	2.4.1828	Charles Sullivan	20 Goat Street, NORWICH	
idem	12.11.1831	idem	St. Andrew's Street, NORWICH	
CV	21.5.1825	Charles Varvell	3 Stewards Street, Soho	
CW	4.2.1788	†Charles Wheate	16 Bagnio Court, Newgate Street	
CW	19.2.1830	Charles Woods	17 Rahere Street, Goswell Road	

* See Richard and Robert Mosley below.
† See CW.IH below.

ES

Mark	Entered	Name	Address/Notes	Punch
CWIH	7.4.1780	Charles Wheate and Isaac Hartley	7 Priest Court, Foster Lane	
DA, pellet between	31.10.1775	Daniel Alt	9 Milk Alley, Dean Street, Soho	incurved oblong
DA	21.8.1823	*Denis Arnell	27 Percival Street, Clerkenwell	
	29.11.1836	idem	Moved to 11 Henry Street, Pentonville	
DC, pellet between	27.2.1836	Dennis Charie	3 Bridgwater Square, Barbican	
DF	2.6.1780	Daniel Field	LUTON, Bedfordshire	
	10.9.1789	idem	Moved to HITCHIN, Hertfordshire	
DJ	12.10.1773	Denis Jacob	Cockspur Street, Charing Cross	
DR	17.2.1824	Dennis Ransom	18 King Street, Soho	
DS	27.1.1789	Darby Sanders	3 Bridgwater Gardens	
DS	15.10.1823	Daniel Elgar Spink	2 Gracechurch Street	
DS, pellet between ES, pellet between	23.1.1836	David Simpson and Edward Starkey	29 Hatton Garden	
EC	24.9.1792	Elizabeth Cooke	BIRMINGHAM (by power of attorney)	
EC, pellet between SC, pellet between	28.8.1832	Edward and Sidney Cherrill	6 Newcastle Place, Clerkenwell	
EC.SC	18.6.1836	idem	idem	
ED	4.4.1835	Edmund Dear	33 Charles Street, City Road	
ED, pellet between TS, pellet between	15.10.1828	Edmond Duggan and Thomas Stroud	22 Denmark Street, Soho	
EE	13.8.1821	Edmund Ellison	Crown and Sceptre Court, St. James's Street	
EE, pellet between	24.4.1823	Evan Evans	102 Aldersgate Street	
	17.8.1835	idem	Moved to 101 Houndsditch	
EF	6.12.1775	Elizabeth Fry	6 Bull and Mouth Street	
EF	2.5.1801	Elizabeth Foster	1 Bartlett Passage, Holborn	

* See Richard Arnell below.

GOLDWORKERS' MARKS 1773-1837

Mark	Entered	Name	Address/Notes	Punch
EF, pellet between	6.4.1835	Edward Flower	5 Manchester Street, Gray's Inn Road	
EG	17.9.1813	Edward Griffiths	14 Cross Street, Hatton Garden	
EG	6.1.1815	idem	6 Blewitts Buildings, Fetter Lane	
EG	18.1.1826	Edward Gaubert	6 Searle Place, Lincoln's Inn	
EG, pellet between	22.2.1828	idem	idem	
EH	11.11.1784	*Edward Holmes	9 Foster Lane	
EH	11.10.1811	†Edmund Hopkins	3 Lilypot Lane	
EM	12.1.1774	‡Esther Moore	37 Gracechurch Street	oval
EM	22.6.1821	Edward Marr	24 Kirby Street, Hatton Garden	oval
	31.1.1823	idem	Moved to 13 Smith Street, Northampton Square	
EN	27.3.1824	Eliza Nash	2 Red Lion Street, Clerkenwell	
	29.4.1828	idem	Moved to 74 Myddleton Street	
EP, pellet between	25.1.1799	Edward Purdie	25 King Street, Soho	
EP, pellet between	10.10.1826	Edward Post	4 Brownlow Street, Holborn	
idem	7.9.1829	idem	idem	
EP ⎫ ES ⎭	11.12.1798	§Edward Purdie and Edmund Seymour	53 Greek Street, Soho	
ES	2.11.1775	Eusebius Sweet	30 Petticoat Lane, Whitechapel	oval
ES	16.4.1777	Edward Smity	4 Old Swan Lane, Upper Thames Street	
	22.4.1785	idem	Moved to 138 Martins Lane, Thames Street	
	12.6.1794	idem	Moved to 4 Britannia Row, Islington	
ES	19.5.1795	Edward Salter	20 Cary Street, London Stone	
ES	21.4.1804	Edmund Seymour	53 Greek Street, Soho	
ES, pellet between	16.6.1837	‖Edward Scargill	44 Coppice Row, Clerkenwell	

---

* See Section IV.   † See WH EH below.
‡ See Edward Moore, Section I, no. 618.
§ See ES below.   ‖ See IS.ES below.

Mark	Entered	Name	Address/Notes	Punch
ET	8.4.1837	Ebenezer Taylor	3 Crescent, Jewin Street	
ET⎫ IK⎭	17.8.1821	Ebenezer Taylor and John Kennard	Crescent, Jewin Street	
ET⎫ RK⎭	2.3.1824	Ebenezer Taylor and Robert Kennard	idem	
EW	5.5.1777	Eliezer Watson	24 Little Newport Street	
FB	25.2.1824	Francis Beland	1 Harford Place, Drury Lane	
	12.2.1831	idem	Moved to 5 Barron Street, Pentonville	
FB	29.4.1829	Frederick Barling	9 Upper Rosomand Street	
FB	11.12.1835	Francis Bower	8 Pollen Street, Hanover Square	
FC	16.5.1816	Francis Caton	107 Upper Thames Street	
FC	26.2.1833	idem	idem	
FC⎫ FD⎭	22.2.1808	*Fredrick Comtesse and Fredrick Droz	34 King Street, Soho	
FD, incuse	25.5.1826	François Dubois	12 Upper King Street, Bloomsbury	
FD	22.7.1828	idem	idem	
FD	20.7.1830	Frederick De Veaux	3 Leigh Street, Red Lion Square	
FF	20.10.1797	Frederick Fisher	41 Duke Street, West Smithfield	
FG, pellet between	1.9.1826	Frederick Ernst George Frederick Greenwood (sic)	23 Carburton Street, Fitzroy Square	
FH	28.6.1781	Francis Henault	43 Old Compton Street	
FH	16.12.1816	Frederick Hawsell	5 Church Court, Clements' Lane, Lombard Street	double-lobed
	10.11.1827	idem	Moved to 11 East Street, Kent Road	
FJ	17.6.1833	Frederick Jones	Adam and Eve Passage, BRISTOL	
FR	13.2.1816	Francis Robine	42 Gerrard Street, Soho	
FS	7.10.1812	Francis Stanley	14 St. James' Walk, Clerkenwell	
FS, pellet between	15.8.1821	Frederic Seagood	56 Red Lion Street, Clerkenwell	
idem	28.4.1823 and 11.5.1825	idem	idem	

* See FC, Section VI.

GOLDWORKERS' MARKS 1773-1837

Mark	Entered	Name	Address/Notes	Punch
FS, pellet between	6.5.1835	Frederick Sheppard	33 Ludgate Hill	
GA, pellet between	9.6.1791	George Auld	6 Monmouth Court, Witcomb Street	
GB	16.5.1825	G. Buckingham	10 Bridgwater Square, Barbican	
GB	30.5.1834	idem	31 Meridith Street, Clerkenwell	
GB } IB	23.2.1824	George and James Edward Blogg	129 Aldersgate Street	
GC	26.7.1775	*George Chalmers	Sidneys Alley, Leicester Fields	
GC	15.7.1777	George Cowdery	Near Mays Buildings, Bedfordbury	tapering sides
GC	17.2.1781	idem	idem	
GD	18.12.1837	George Dugard	34 Red Lion Street, Clerkenwell	
GE	6.8.1835	George Elliott	3 Charlton Place, Coldbrook Row, Islington	
	18.5.1836	idem	Moved to 2 Upper Ashby Street, Northampton Square	
GEC	22.7.1777	Gideon Ernest Charpentier	4 Great St. Andrew Street, Seven Dials	kidney shape
GF	23.8.1805	George Edward Fidler	47 Berwick Street, Soho	
GG	23.6.1818	George Griffiths	25 Cursiter Street, Chancery Lane	
GG	2.12.1837	George Gozzard	11 Baron Street, Pentonville	
GH	8.3.1824	George Horton	66 New Town Row, BIRMINGHAM	
GHA	24.4.1834	George Henry Allen	13 King Street, Soho	
GJC	15.6.1833 and 2.8.1834	George James Cox	30 Red Lion Street, Clerkenwell	
GL	28.10.1799	Giles Loyer	21 Denmark Street, St. Giles	
GM, star above	9.1.1783	†Gideon Macaire	17 Crown Street, St. Ann's, Soho	arched top over star
	17.10.1784	idem	Moved to 12 Denmark Street, St. Giles	

* See Section IV.
† Also incuse mark similar. See Section V.

361

GM   IB

Mark	Entered	Name	Address/Notes	Punch
GM	22.6.1821	George Mann	3 Upper Charles Street, Northampton Square	
GM	1.3.1834	Girardo Migotti	32 Southampton Street, Strand	
GMH	24.12.1824	George Melville Horton	52 High Holborn	
GMH	8.10.1828	idem	idem	
idem (incuse)	31.5.1834	idem	Moved to 17 Thavies Inn, Holborn	
	14.12.1836	idem	Moved to 32 Hatton Garden	
GP	22.8.1777	George Paris	4 Albion Buildings	rounded ends
GP	17.2.1819	George Phillips	4 Cobham Row, Clerkenwell	
GP	4.11.1824	George Pickering	10 Banner Street, Finsbury	
GP	13.5.1837	George Pickett	265 Oxford Street (jeweller)	
GP, pellet between	6.1.1836	George Philo	20 Hatton Wall, Hatton Garden	
GS	4.4.1823	George Stacy	2 Charlotte Street, Sadler's Wells, Clerkenwell	
	25.11.1826	idem	Moved to 65 Aldersgate Street	
GW (two sizes)	3.11.1785	*Gabriel Wirgman	11 Denmark Street, St. Giles	
GW	11.5.1819	Gervase Wheeler	28 Bartletts Building, Holborn	
HA	23.6.1828	Henry Collingwood Aumonier	58 King Street, Soho	
	no date	idem	Moved to 41 Frith Street, Soho	
HB	26.3.1793	Henry Brown	BRISTOL (entered by letter of attorney)	
HC	3.5.1773	†Henry Cooper	Lancaster Court, Strand. A re-entry of an earlier entry	
HC	23.7.1783	idem	33 Strand	
HC	4.10.1784	idem	33 Strand, near York Buildings	
HC	11.4.1786	idem	idem	
	17.2.1800	idem	Moved to 29 Charlton Street, Somers Town	

* See Section I, no. 922.   † See Section IV.

GOLDWORKERS' MARKS 1773-1837

Mark	Entered	Name	Address/Notes	Punch
HC	15.11.1799	Henry Chabaud	9 Plumtree Street, Bloomsbury	
HD (two sizes)	25.6.1816	Henry Edwyn Davies	14 Brewer Street, Golden Square	
HED	9.2.1820	idem	idem	
HED } JT	17.1.1818	Henry Edwyn Davies and James Thomson	idem	
HF	11.2.1829	Henry Frost	21 Denmark Street, Soho	
HF } WC	19.1.1835	*Henry Frost and William Charman	idem	
HK	14.4.1828	Henry Kitchin	10 Dufours Place, Golden Square	
HL	11.5.1829	Henry Ludlow	13 Winchester Street, Pentonville	
	3.8.1837	idem	Moved to 11 Castle Street, Falcon Square	
	27.9.1838	idem	Moved to 6 Goswell Road	
HM, pellet between	30.12.1780	Hector Maclean	17 Duke's Court, St. Martin's Lane	
HO	7.12.1821	William Henry Osborne	122 Great Russell Street, Bloomsbury	
HW	8.2.1834	Henry Williams	52 High Street, HASTINGS	
IA } IT	16.7.1823	John Aldred and John Tooke	30 Hatton Garden	
IB	6.8.1777	†James Berkenhead	31 Gutter Lane	
IB, pellet between	3.12.1789	Joseph Beauvais	15 Plumtree Street, Bloomsbury	
IB	9.12.1789	‡John Berkenhead	31 Gutter Lane	
IB	12.2.1789	§James Birt	5 Silver Street, Noble Street	
IB	5.1.1796	John Brogden	4 Ironmonger Row, Old Street	
	25.1.1805	idem	Moved to Bridgwater Square	
IB, pellet between	22.6.1816	idem	idem	
IB	15.3.1820 and 27.5.1824	idem	idem	
IB	12.12.1817	John Baldwin	Whitale Street, BIRMINGHAM	

* See William Charman alone, below.
† See Section IV, and John Berkenhead below.
‡ See IB SI below, and James Birkenhead above.
§ See Section IV.

Mark	Entered	Name	Address/Notes	Punch
IB, conjoined	3.8.1835	John Britain	54 Red Lion Street, Clerkenwell	
IB SI	10.1.1800	*John Berkenhead and Samuel Jobson	Gutter Lane	
IC	22.4.1777	John Coleman	16 Maiden Lane, Wood Street	
IC	27.8.1782	idem	Moved to 115 Newgate Street	
IC	21.11.1780	James Callard	10 Hungerford Street, Strand	
IC idem	13.3.1796 21.2.1799	Joseph Cooper idem	8 Furnival's Inn Court idem	
IC	23.11.1799	Joseph Cowing	36 Old Compton Street, Soho	
IC	21.11.1816	John Cooke	Crown and Sceptre Court, St. James's Street	
IC, pellet between	14.9.1821 27.10.1829	John Cross idem	35 Cursitor Street, Chancery Lane Moved to 3 Edward Street, Manchester Square	
IC idem	24.12.1821 7.3.1830	John Crofts idem	51 Wynyatt Street, Clerkenwell idem	
IC	10.4.1823	John Cole	25 Cursitor Street, Chancery Lane	
IC, pellet between	29.10.1825 23.2.1826 13.9.1828	Joshua Vernon Cooper idem idem	124 St. John Street, Smithfield Moved to 20 Queen Street, Clerkenwell Moved to 1 Brett's Buildings, Hoxton	
IC idem	1.2.1827 12.2.1833	John Garard Crisp idem	20 Goswell Terrace, Goswell Road idem	
ID	28.7.1810	John Da Saulles	13 Princes Street, Leicester Square	
ID	5.10.1811	†John Dethridge	9 Gee Street, Goswell Street	
ID	31.7.1826	James Davis	34 Southampton Street, Strand	
ID, pellet between TN, pellet between	10.9.1818	James Davies and Thomas Northwood	8 Plumtree Street, Bloomsbury	

* See IB above. † See Section I, no. 1257.

GOLDWORKERS' MARKS 1773-1837

Mark	Entered	Name	Address/Notes	Punch
IE	22.4.1789	John Elliott	15 Aldersgate Street Buildings	
IE	14.4.1837	*John James Edington	10 Portland Street, Soho Square	double-lobed
IF	24.2.1774	Isaac Foster	2 Hatton Street	
	10.8.1775	idem	Moved to 1 Bartlett Buildings, Holborn	
IF, pellet between	13.1.1778	idem	idem	
IF	19.9.1792	Joseph Froome	John Street, Blackfriars, Southwark	
IF	4.4.1795	idem	12 King Street, Bloomsbury	
IF	7.1.1805	John Freethy	106 Shoe Lane, Fleet Street	
	31.8.1816	idem	Moved to 9 Kirby Street, Hatton Garden	
	18.2.1820	idem	Moved to 17 Theobald's Road	
IF, pellet between	5.3.1813	John Frost	33 Arundel Street, Strand	
	25.9.1823	idem	Moved to 21 Denmark Street, Soho	
IF	26.2.1829	idem	idem	
IF	29.10.1835	idem	idem	
IG	15.8.1811	James Griffiths	45 Clerkenwell Close	
IG	11.2.1823	John Green	94 Hatton Gardens	
IG	12.4.1824	John Greswell	21 Portland Street, Soho	
IG	13.2.1835	John Gaubert	51 Berwick Street, St. James'	
IH	23.7.1777	John Hookham	7 Westmorland Buildings, Aldersgate	
IH	29.6.1778	idem	idem	
IH, pellet between	7.12.1792	idem	Moved to 53 Bartholomew Close	
IH, pellet between	19.9.1785	John Hedges	7 Laystall Street, Leather Lane	
	29.1.1788	idem	Moved to 32 Red Lion Street, Clerkenwell	
	20.4.1793	idem	Moved to 4 St. James' Place, Clerkenwell	
IH	28.3.1782	John Henderson	21 Cornhill	
IH	17.10.1821	John Hepburn	1 Cross Street, Great Sutton Street, Clerkenwell	
	21.3.1829	idem	Moved to 50 York Street, City Road	

* See JJE below, and John Edington, Section I, nos. 1274-5, 1805.

Mark	Entered	Name	Address/Notes	Punch
IH	29.2.1832	John Hopton	13 Pond Place, Chelsea Common	
IH, script	10.11.1778	Isaac Harley	14 Great Turnstile, Holborn	
IH, script and IH	26.8.1782	idem	7 Priest Court, Foster Lane	
	27.7.1787	idem	Moved to 6 Shack'lwell	
IHC	25.9.1822	J. H. Coles	92 Red Lion Street, Clerkenwell	
	7.8.1835	idem	Moved to 5 Skinner Street, Clerkenwell	
II, pellet between	19.10.1775	James Junod	47 Frith Street, Soho	
II, script pellet between	28.10.1779	*James Jackson	BIRMINGHAM (ring-maker)	
IJF, pellets between	5.2.1823	John James Franc	69 New Compton Street, Soho	
IIL, pellets between	14.1.1784	John Joseph Le Jeune	3 Stacey Street, Soho	
IK	7.6.1790	John Kirke	9 Foster Lane	
IK	5.12.1793	John Kenebel	13 Frith Street, Soho	
IK, pellet between (two sizes)	27.9.1808	idem	idem	
IK	26.2.1831	John King	3 Meredith Street, Clerkenwell	
IL	25.9.1775	John Lautier	23 Great Sheare Lane, Temple Bar	
IL	27.4.1776	John Loten	3 Carey Lane	
IL	25.2.1778	idem	idem	
IL	16.12.1777	John Lawson	4 Broad Street, St. Giles-in-the-Fields	
IL, pellet between	11.6.1784	James Law	18 Warwick Street, Charing Cross	
IL	19.11.1793	†Jonathan Lowe	126 St. Martin's Lane	
IL	16.12.1824	John Lacey	4 Bath Place, West Square, Lambeth	
IL, pellet between	8.4.1825	James Lewis	17 Corporation Court, Clerkenwell	
	30.7.1829	idem	Moved to 1 Berkley Street, Clerkenwell	

* Also an entry without mark, 27.3.1773, as 'Extract from the former Mark Book'.
‡ See also JL below.

GOLDWORKERS' MARKS 1773-1837

Mark	Entered	Name	Address/Notes	Punch
IL } RM }	30.12.1824	John Littleford and Robert Masters	6 Wilderness Row, Clerkenwell	
IL } WA }	24.7.1809	*John Linnit and William Atkinson	15 Fountain Court, Strand	
IM, pellet between	22.11.1787	†James Morisset	22 Denmark Street, Soho	
IM	6.11.1789	idem	idem	
IM	12.11.1789	idem	idem	
IM	19.8.1806	John Morgan	BRISTOL (by power of attorney)	
IM	27.8.1811	John Moore	Caroline Street, BIRMINGHAM	
IM	1.11.1821	‡James Montaguĕ	22 Denmark Street, Soho Square	
IM	15.2.1830	John Morris	26 Great Maze Pond (?), Borough	
	2.7.1841	idem	Moved to 119 Snows Fields	
IM	14.5.1830	John Mainwaring	8 Chichester Rents, Chancery Lane	
IMG, pellets between	22.1.1817	John MacGregor	14 Charterhouse Street	
idem	26.2.1817	idem	idem	
idem	3.1.1818	idem	idem	
IM SS, pellet between	8.1.1800	John Morgan and Samuel Sowerby	Wine Street, BRISTOL	
IN, pellet between	11.10.1775	§Joseph Newcomb	8 New Street, Shoe Lane	
IN, pellet between	13.7.1790	John Nash	23 Brewer Street	
IN	11.10.1793	¶John Northam	12 St. Martin's Street, Leicester Fields	
idem	9.5.1796	idem	12 Frith Street, Soho	
IN	29.3.1813	Jacob Nathan	Stonehouse, near PLYMOUTH (ringmaker)	
IO	16.2.1824	John Onions	31 Charles Street, Hatton Garden	
	12.9.1833	idem	Moved to 2 Benjamin Street, Cow Cross Street	
IP	4.5.1774	John Pukhaver	Grafton Street, Soho	

* Mark found on good quality gold snuffboxes. See Section I, nos. 1833-4.
† See Section I, no. 1521.
‡ See IR.IM below.
§ See JN.WN below.   ¶ Mark found on gold snuffboxes.

I P   I V

Mark	Entered	Name	Address/Notes	Punch
IP, pellet between	22.5.1779	John Pottinger	34 Ludgate Hill	
	12.6.1788	idem	Moved to Bells' Buildings, Salisbury Court, Fleet Street	
IP, pellet between	14.6.1788	John Phillips	1 Cold Bath Square	
idem	30.9.1802	idem	idem	
idem	11.1.1813	idem	2 Cold Bath Square	
idem	14.10.1815	idem	1 Cold Bath Square	
IP, pellet between	29.7.1829	John Phillips, Jr.	4 Cobham Row, Cold Bath Square	
IP	29.11.1837	idem	idem (till 1843)	
IP	21.7.1802	John Padbury	CIRENCESTER, Gloucestershire	
IP	2.10.1822	*John Peters	49 Rathbone Place	
IP	6.10.1823	John Perkins	13 Dean Street, Soho	oval
	no date	idem	Moved to 21 Frith Street	
	4.8.1828	idem	Moved to 31 Little Queen Street, Holborn	
	14.10.1830	idem	Moved to 7 North Place, Gray's Inn Lane	
IP & SR	20.11.1822	John Perkins and Samuel Robins	10 Great Newport Street	
IPW	14.9.1827	John Pitter Watts	25 Ive Lane	
IR, pellet between	13.5.1784	Jeremiah Ryon	53 New Cornton Street, St. Giles-in-the-Fields	
IR	30.10.1822	†John Robertson	26 Villers Street	
IR ⎫ IM ⎭	4.5.1800	‡John Ray and James Montague	Denmark Street	
IS	13.2.1777	John Simpson	DERBY	
IS, pellet between	28.10.1783	§James Stretch	4 Cock Court, St. Martin's Le Grand	
IS	5.3.1788	John Stirling	Shelburn Lane, Lombard Street	
IS	13.7.1799	‖John Stubbs I	241 Holborn	
IS, pellet between	12.9.1815	John Shearsmith	45 Moffatt Street, City Road	

* See Section I, no. 1605 and Section IV.
† See also JR below, Section I, no. 1629 and Section IV, J.R.
‡ See IM above. Mark found on gold sword hilt 1807 supplied by S. Goodbehere.
§ Also incuse mark, 8.5.1789.
‖ Exceptionally large mark for goldworker.

GOLDWORKERS' MARKS 1773–1837

Mark	Entered	Name	Address/Notes	Punch
IS	4.8.1818	John Stone	17 St. James' Street, Clerkenwell	
	1.1.1824	idem	Moved to 13 Red Lion Street, Clerkenwell	
	18.2.1827	idem	Moved to 7 Middleton Street (till 1849)	
IS	9.12.1819	John Shaw	17 Finsbury Street, Finsbury Square	
	8.3.1839	idem	Moved to 49 Clerkenwell Close	
IS	27.7.1821	John Stubbs II	6 Castle Street, Leicester Square	
	20.1.1838	idem	Moved to 28 Panton Street, Leicester Square (till 1844)	
IS	10.7.1821	*John Stephens	2 Castle Street, Holborn	
IS, pellet below	24.1.1820	†John Scargill	44 Coppice Row, Clerkenwell	
idem	18.9.1822	idem	idem	
IS	18.4.1823	John Sanden	10 Great Sutton Street, Clerkenwell	
IS, pellet between	12.7.1828	idem	idem	
IS	10.4.1828	John James Simons	47 Clerkenwell Green	
IS, pellet between / ES, pellet between	10.9.1818	John and Edward Scargill	44 Coppice Row, Clerkenwell	
IT	1.9.1788	John Tanner	St. Mary Port Street, BRISTOL	
IT	11.2.1795	idem	St. Augustins Back, BRISTOL	
IT, pellet between	13.4.1791	James Tringham	22 Noble Street, Falcon Square	oval
ITC, hatchet above	9. and 22.10.1807	‡John Turner Carpenter	58 Wynyatt Street, Goswell Road	
ITL, pellets between	18.9.1824	John Thomas Lindsey	4 Leathersellers Buildings, London Wall	
IT / AT	4.1.1803	John, Thomas and Ann Tringham	7 Priest Court, Foster Lane	
IT / SN	14.1.1780	John Thompson and Stephen Nost	1 George Street, St. Martin's Le Grand	
IV, pellet between	17.7.1815	John Vine	5 Staining Lane, Wood Street	
idem	27.8.1825	idem	idem	

* See also JS below.   † See IS.ES below and ES above.
‡ See also Section V for incuse mark.

Mark	Entered	Name	Address/Notes	Punch
IW	5.1.1819	James Warwick	3 Newcastle Place, Clerkenwell	
IW, pellet between	14.5.1821	James Willsher	6 Ryders Court, Leicester Square	
	4.1.1825	idem	Moved to 11 Lisle Street, St. Ann's	
	26.1.1827	idem	Moved to 12 Little Compton Street, Soho	
IW	18.6.1821	James Wilkinson	10 Castle Street, Holborn	curved top and base
IW	9.8.1823	James Woodhill	BIRMINGHAM	
IW	12.2.1825	John Woolley	11 Upper Clifton Street, Finsbury	
IW	14.11.1829	J. Whitehouse	7 Exmouth Street, Clerkenwell	
IW	25.6.1834	John Wellby	57 King Street, Soho	
	30.11.1837	idem	idem	
IWG (two marks)	8.8.1826	James Williams Garland	16 Bridgwater Square	
IWG (three marks)	25.9.1834	idem	idem	
IWP	13.7.1825	J. Wil on Pipe	Market Street, MANCHESTER	
JA	14.9.1797	James Alexandre	20 Greenhills Rents, Smithfield Bars	
JA	31.8.1836	John Abrahams	21 Bevis Marks	
JB	25.11.1834	John Bishop	3 Poland Street, Oxford Street	
JC	17.7.1785	Joseph Canter	6 Church Street, Soho	
JC	19.2.1823	Joseph Colinet	52 Princes Street, Leicester Square	
	30.7.1824	idem	Moved to 3 Pickering Place, St. James Street	
	3.3.1825	idem	Moved to 1 Brides' Lane, Fleet Street	
JC	11.10.1823	James Cooper	40 Gee Street	
JC, pellet between	6.9.1826	idem	18 Percival Street	
	22.8.1828	idem	Moved to 37 Percival Street	
idem	1.6.1836	idem	idem	
JC	3.8.1831	John Coulden	15 Rose Crescent, CAMBRIDGE	
JC	21.1.1837	idem	7 Gough Square, Fleet Street	

GOLDWORKERS' MARKS 1773-1837

Mark	Entered	Name	Address/Notes	Punch
JC and JH } JC.JH	14.11.1833	John Coulden and John Hodkinson	5 Wine Office Court, Fleet Street	
idem	21.5.1835	idem	idem	
JD, pellet between	30.5.1835	Joseph Downes	9 Owens Row, Islington	
JF	6.9.1775	*John Fry I	6 Bull and Mouth Street	
JF	10.7.1829	Jacob French	5 Newcastle Place, Clerkenwell	
JF, pellet between	27.1.1835	idem	idem, and till 1844	
JF.WM	20.9.1826	Jacob French and William Mitchell	idem	
JG	25.5.1776	John Green	NOTTINGHAM (by letter of attorney)	
JG, pellet between	5.10.1801	Joseph Gion	76 Berwick Street, Soho	
JG	25.5.1802	John Gibbs	6 St. Albans' Court, Wood Street, Cheapside	
idem	3.12.1812	idem	11 Castle Street, Cripplegate	
JG	25.1.1814 and 9.9.1818	idem	idem	
JG	5.2.1834	Jane Gill	10 Lower Smith Street, Northampton Square	
JG	9.12.1835	John Gramshaw	135 Goswell Street	
JH	27.7.1775	John Hedges	Neare (?) Street, Clare Market	
JH	16.9.1784	idem	8 Devereux Court, Strand	
JH	18.2.1802	idem	idem	
JH	1.6.1791	James Hill	9 Ball Alley, Lombard Street	
JH, pellet between	12.8.1828	James Horton	20 Norfolk Street, Stepney	
JH	10.1.1837	†John Hodkinson	5 Wine Office Court, Fleet Street	
JJ	19.12.1777	Jenkin Jones	61 St. James Street	
JJ, script	18.10.1779	John Israel	110 Whitechapel High Street	oval
idem	3.10.1780	idem	idem	
JJ	26.8.1789	Jean Alexandre Jonchon	32 Frith Street, Soho	
JJ	5.8.1819	Joseph Jones	44 Old Compton Street, Soho	
	28.4.1823	idem	Moved to 26 Charles Street, Parliament Street	

* See Section I, no. 1814. † See JC.JH above.

371

JJ   JW

Mark	Entered	Name	Address/Notes	Punch
JJ, pellet between	3.7.1821	John Jones	7 St. James Street, Clerkenwell	
idem	14.10.1830	idem	221 Hoxton Old Town	
JJE (two sizes)	16.6.1820	*John James Edington	10 Portland Street, Soho Square	
JJE, pellets between	6.1.1821	idem	idem	oval
JK	14.7.1774	Joseph Kent	7 Cross Key Court, Little Britain	
JK	8.11.1777	idem	idem	
JL	12.5.1780	Joseph Lea	2 Cock Court, St. Martins Le Grand	
JL	21.6.1788	idem	20 Silver Street, Wood Street	
JL	19.11.1793	†Jonathan Lowe	126 St. Martin's Lane	
JL	26.10.1827	John Davis Lea	20 Silver Street	
JL, pellet between	1.7.1833	John Littleford	8 St. James's Street, Clerkenwell	
JL / WR	7.11.1828	John Littleford and William Rapley	32 Rosomand Street, Clerkenwell	incurved ends
	28.6.1831	idem	Moved to 8 St. James' Street, Clerkenwell	
JM	28.2.1825	James Charles Money	13 Arlington Street, Clerkenwell	
JM	12.7.1826	idem	47 Red Lion Street	
	17.11.1826	idem	Moved to 47 Clerkenwell Close	
	24.9.1831	idem	Moved to 31 Percival Street, Clerkenwell	
JM	7.2.1834	idem	idem	
JM	18.9.1834	idem	idem	
JM / WM	28.10.1825	James Money and William Meyer	47 Red Lion Street, Clerkenwell	
JN, pellet between WN, pellet between	28.8.1824	‡Joseph and William Newcomb	8 Little New Street, Shoe Lane	
JO	13.9.1802	Jesse Oulet	23 Rathbone Place, Oxford Street	rounded ends
JO, pellet between	18.5.1825	James Osmond	11 Upper Rosomond Street, Clerkenwell	
JO	29.8.1831	James Ogden	17 Red Lion Street, Clerkenwell	

* See IE above and Section I, nos. 1274–5, 1805.
† See also IL above.   ‡ See IN above.

372

GOLDWORKERS' MARKS 1773-1837

Mark	Entered	Name	Address/Notes	Punch
JO	5.11.1831	idem	23 Red Lion Street, Clerkenwell	
	16.4.1834	idem	Moved to 11 St. James Street, Clerkenwell	
	9.5.1837	idem	idem, till 1856	
JP	3.4.1822	John Paradise	13 Newcastle Street, Strand	
JP	26.9.1826	James Price	8 Clifton Street, Finsbury	
JR, pellet between	21.8.1826	*John Robertson	62 Clarendon Street	
JR	25.7.1836	James Rapley	43 Northampton Street, Clerkenwell	
	5.3.1837	idem	Moved to 41 Skinner Street, Clerkenwell	
JR } WR }	17.7.1833	James and William Rapley	43 Northampton Square, Clerkenwell	
JS, pellet between	22.1.1782	†Joseph Savory	48 Cheapside	oval
JS	7.1.1822	‡John Stephens	2 Castle Street, Holborn	
	2.1.1824	idem	Moved to 47 Hatton Garden	
JS, pellet between	14.10.1825	John Smith	77 Berwick Street, Soho	
JS	4.2.1834	James Stevens	13 Princes Street, Leicester Square	
JT	28.4.1821	James Troup	233 Tooley Street	
	17.12.1831	idem	Moved to 120 Cheapside	
JT	30.9.1823	Joseph Tovey	3 Albion Buildings, Bartholomew Close	
JT	3.11.1826	John Tollit	13 Bartlett's Passage, Fetter Lane	
JV, pellet between	20.2.1833	John Vine	17 Clerkenwell Green	
JW	4.9.1775	Joseph Wade	4 Priest Court, Foster Lane	
JW	28.7.1777	idem	21 Noble Street	
	10.6.1788	idem	Moved to Bowman's Building, Aldersgate Street	
JW	2.5.1775	James Wheston	4 Foster Lane	
JW	10.10.1777	John Whichelow	3 Naked Boy Court, Ludgate Hill	oval
JW	18.6.1821	James Wilson	7 Denmark Street, St. Giles	
JW	17.9.1823	James Wood	6 Great Russell Street, Bedford Square	

* See also IR above, Section I, no. 1629 and Section IV, JR.
† See Section I, no. 1664.   ‡ See also IS above.

JW   RB

Mark	Entered	Name	Address/Notes	Punch
JW	7.4.1827	John Whitehorn	7 Leigh Street, Red Lion Square	
JW	19.7.1832	John Wilkinson	2 Skinner Street, Clerkenwell (till 1876)	
LL	21.12.1801	Lewis Landfriede	16 Craven Buildings, Drury Lane	
LL, script	26.2.1810	idem	idem	oval
LO	10.9.1811	*Leach Ozeley	2 Wood Street, Spitalfields	
LP, pellet between and LP	19.10.1782	†Lewis Pantin (II)	36 Southampton Street, Strand	
LP	12.4.1792	idem	8 Sloane Square, Chelsea	oval
	30.10.1795	idem	Moved to 6 Crown Street, Westminster	
	18.7.1800	idem	Moved to 17 Alfred Place, Newington Causeway	
LP, pellet between	22.6.1802	idem	30 Marsham Street, Westminster	
	17.7.1805	idem	Moved to 5 Canterbury Place, near Manor Place, Walworth	
LP, pellet between	22.3.1788	‡Lewis Pantin Junr. (III)	36 Southampton Street, Strand	
LT	15.9.1828	Lewis Tessier	13 Portland Street, St. James's	
LT ⎫ CH ⎭	2.1.1828	Lewis Tessier and Charles Harris	13 Portland Place, St. James's	
LT ⎫ IJE ⎭	10.7.1799	Lemuel Thomas and Joseph Jeffries Evans	Staining Lane	
LW	12.7.1826	Lambert Krannen Wirth	51 Penton Place, Pentonville	
MB	6.5.1788	Matthew Bance	HUNGERFORD, Berkshire	
MG	3.5.1786	§Michael Gamon	7 Well Yard, Little Britain	
MG	11.5.1786 5.7.1786	idem	38 Noble Street	
MH	3.5.1783	Matthew Hillback	6 Maiden Lane	
MK	27.8.1794	Michael Keys	23 Greek Street, Soho	
ML	15.1.1823	Myer Levi	10 Rampant Horse Street, NORWICH	
ML	22.10.1833	‖Montague Levyson	5 New Broad Street, Bishopsgate	

* Signs with +. See MO below.
† See Section no. I, 1959.   ‡ See Section I, no. 1961.
§ See Section IV.   ‖ See also Section V.

374

GOLDWORKERS' MARKS 1773-1837

Mark	Entered	Name	Address/Notes	Punch
ML, pellet between	1.8.1834	idem	idem	
ML	29.9.1825	Michael Lee	5 Hungerford Piazza, Strand	
MM	9.4.1836	*Mary Mainwaring	Chichester Rents, Chancery Lane	
MO	16.8.1809	†Marco Ozeley	2 Wood Street, Spitalfields	
MS	5.8.1824	Mark Small	4 St. Martin's Churchyard	
NP	21.4.1774	Nathaniel Pollard	Red Lion Street, Holborn	
PB	2.11.1780	Phineas Borrett	4 Staining Lane	
PB	3.12.1784	idem	21 Foster Lane	
PB	1.3.1787	idem	idem	
	8.9.1787	idem	Moved to 6 Queen Square, Aldersgate Street	
PB	4.11.1789	idem	93 Aldersgate Street	
PB	5.2.1805	idem	5 Staining Lane	
PC	11.11.1773	Peter Carpenter	York Buildings, Duke Street, Strand	
PC	28.9.1789	Peter Charman	3 York Buildings, Strand	
PD, pellet between GL, pellet between	1.8.1789	‡Peter Delauney and Giles Loyer	17 Crown Street, Soho	
PG	8.5.1780	Paul Gandon	6 Queen Street, Seven Dials	
PN, pellet between	21.7.1823	Phineas Nathan	9 Magdalen Row, Goodmanfields	
PP	1.3.1785	Philip Passavant	14 Red Lion Passage, Holborn	
PW	23.3.1782	§Paul Wright	10 George Yard, Aldersgate Street	
RA	7.11.1821	‖Richard Sayer Arnell	35 Percival Street, Clerkenwell	
RA	1.10.1830	Robert Aland	29 Gerrard Street, Soho	
RB, pellet between	19.6.1805	¶Richard Beland	3 Cross Court, Long Acre	
RB	15.2.1813	Richard Bright	9 Foster Lane	
RB, pellet between	30.12.1822	**Roger Biggs	2 Queen Square, Aldersgate Street	
RB	25.10.1826	idem	idem	

* See IM above. † See LO above.
‡ Mark found on fine gold snuffbox. § See Section I, no. 2243.
‖ See Dennis Arnell above. ¶ See Francis Beland above.
** See Section I, no. 2273.

RB	SB

Mark	Entered	Name	Address/Notes	Punch
RB	19.12.1826	Richard Brodnax	19 White Lion Street, Pentonville	
	25.9.1828	idem	Moved to 117 Upper Street, Islington	
	3.1.1830	idem	Moved to 24 Cross Street, Islington	
RC	26.2.1833	Robert James Chaplin	17 Red Cross Square (till 1851)	
RD	13.7.1778	Richard Dipple	17 Maiden Lane, Wood Street	
RD	6.7.1785	idem	4 Lillypot Lane	
RD	1.12.1781	Robert Davies	81 Bishopsgate Street	
RD	20.7.1789	*Richard Dawson	3 Lilypot Lane	
	4.11.1791	idem	Moved to 7 Basing Lane, Bread Street	
RD	14.3.1793	†Richard Dawsons	8 Bell Buildings, Salisbury Court	
RD	20.1.1825	Richard Daniel	22 Myddleton Street, Spa Fields	
RE, pellet between	7.1.1819	Robert Ellis	14 Garden Row, London Road, Southwark	
RE	6.7.1821	Robert Essex	224 Strand	
RF, pellet between	13.1.1823	Robert Fenn	1 Gray's Inn Lane	
RF	2.3.1827	idem	121 Gray's Inn Lane	
	31.8.1833	idem	Moved to 6 Cleveland Street, Mile End	
	16.9.1833	idem	Moved to 2 Vauxhall Street, Vauxhall	
RH	18.5.1790	‡Richard Hobdell	29 Addle Street, Aldermanbury	
RH, pellet between	25.4.1825	Robert Hughes	5 Medway Street, Westminster	
RH	16.8.1832	Richard Hebden	19 Clerkenwell Green	
	29.8.1832	idem	Moved to 15 Lower Smith Street, Clerkenwell	
	27.11.1832	idem	Moved to 12 Lower Smith Street, Clerkenwell	
RH, pellet between	23.9.1834	idem	idem	
	9.12.1837	idem	Moved to Dollis (Hill?), Hendon	

* See also Section V, incuse.
† Signature distinct from above.
‡ See Section I, no. 1002 for father (?).

GOLDWORKERS' MARKS 1773-1837

Mark	Entered	Name	Address/Notes	Punch
RI, pellet between	6.5.178–	Randall Jackson	46 Paternoster Row	
RI	27.5.1790	Robert Jones	1 Water Street, LIVERPOOL	
RI, pellet between	12.11.1822	Robert Jones	6 York Street, Covent Garden	
	2.12.1824	idem	Moved to 33 Henrietta Street, Covent Garden	
RK	4.12.1780	Robert Knight	Noble Street, Foster Lane	
	22.10.1785	idem	Moved to Love Lane, Wood Street	
R L & I W	23.3.1830	*Robert Latham and J. G. Warner	17 Denmark Street, Soho	
RM	5.6.1804	†Robert Mosley I	113 Fetter Lane, Holborn	
RM	21.2.1827	†Robert Mosley II	idem (until 1849)	
RM	30.12.1823	Richard Mosley	39 Castle Street, Holborn	
RM	14.7.1824	idem	idem	
RM	20.3.1825	idem	idem	
RS	11.11.1776	Richard Smith	Bridge Row	
RS	4.3.1825	Richard Hovil Seeley	7 Claremont Place, North Brixton	
	12.8.1825	idem	Moved to 13 Princes Street, Leicester Square	
	21.3.1831	idem	Moved to 35 Great Pulteney Street, Golden Square	
	16.2.1833	idem	Moved to 19 Broad Street, Golden Square	
𝕽𝕾	29.10.1830	Robert Spilsbury	8 Poland Street, Oxford Street	
RT	11.8.1801	Richard Teed	3 Lancaster Court, Strand	
RT	17.6.1833	Richard Townley	16 Cursitor Street, Chancery Lane	
RW	9.12.1831	Richard Wisedill	35 Union Row, New Kent Road	
RW pellet IC between	31.1.1794	Richard Wynne and John Chandler	57 Broad Street, Bloomsbury	
SA SEA CA	9.3.1814	Sarjeant, Sarjeant Edward and Claudius Ash	64 St. James' Street, St. James Square	
SB	7.11.1777	Samuel Burman I	51 Leming Street, Goodmans Fields	

* See Section I, no. 1351.   † See Section I, no. 2371.

Mark	Entered	Name	Address/Notes	Punch
SB	19.3.1819	Samuel Burman II	39 Hunter Street, St. George's Southwark	
SB	17.9.1821	Samuel Barnard	16 Duke Street, Adelphi, Strand	
SB } SG }	12.10.1793	*Samuel Bellingham and Samuel Gladman	8 Bell Square, St. Martin's Le Grand	
SC.MC	13.5.1837	Sidney and Montague Cherrill	6 Newcastle Place, Clerkenwell Close	
SG	21.11.1775	Samuel Glover	3 Mutton Court, Maiden Lane, Wood Street	
SG idem (five marks)	18.11.1791 1791–1807	idem idem	4 Noble Street idem	
	5.10.1809	idem	Moved to 4 Bull and Mouth Street	
idem	15.12.1812 and 1813	idem	idem	
SG	2.2.1816	idem	idem	oval
SG	27.9.1776	Sebastian Guerint	19 Beak Street, St. James's, Westminster	
	6.4.1785	idem	Moved to 6 Madox Street, Hanover Square	
SG, pellet between	24.4.1799	idem	37 Clerkenwell Close	
SG	1.7.1822	†Sarah Glover	4 Bull and Mouth Street	
SG	12.2.1831 8.11.1833	Stephen Gaubert idem	8 Carlisle Street, Soho Moved to 51 Berwick Street, Oxford Street	
SH	25.9.1789 18.6.1790	Samuel Hart idem	5 Staining Lane Moved to 15 Peartree Street, Goswell Street	
SH	30.1.1832	Samuel Hasluck	104 Hatton Garden (till 1841)	
SHG idem	30.3.1825 6.2.1829	‡Samuel Henry Glover idem	4 Bull and Mouth Street idem	
SHH	3.8.1836	Samuel Henry Hall	1 Brunswick Place, St. John Street Road	
SM	25.7.1780	§Samuel Massey	104 Leadenhall Street	
SM, pellet between	5.1.1821	‖Samuel Marshall	32 Great Bath Street, Clerkenwell	

---

* See Section I, no. 2481.
† See Samuel Glover above, presumably his widow.
‡ See Samuel Glover above. Probably a son of the former since Sarah Glover's mark intervenes in 1822.
§ See Section IV.   ‖ See Section I, no. 2594.

GOLDWORKERS' MARKS 1773-1837

Mark	Entered	Name	Address/Notes	Punch
SM	30.7.1823	Samuel Moss	140 Rosemary Lane	
SN	25.2.1782	Stephen Nost	1 George Street, St. Martin's Le Grand	
SN, pellet between	11.6.1782	idem	idem	
SP	9.8.1774	Samuel Peacock I	4 Cock Lane, Snow Hill (ringmaker)	
SP	28.7.1778	Samuel Pemberton	BIRMINGHAM	
SP	4.2.1784	Samuel Potticary	6 Well Street, Cripplegate	
SP, pellet between	10.8.1821	Samuel Peacock II	11 Charterhouse Street	
SR	2.6.1787	Samuel Ridgeway	137 St. Martin's Lane	
SR	29.6.1821	Samuel Reed	30 Fetter Lane	
idem (four marks	1822-1830	idem	idem	
SR	18.2.1831	*Samuel Ruddock	7 Denmark Street, Soho	double lobe
SS	17.8.1779	Samuel Spence	1 St. Peter's Alley, Cornhill	
SS	23.5.1806	Samuel Sowerby	High Street, BRISTOL	
SS	1.5.1823	Samuel Sadler	9 Wellington Street, Goswell Street	
SS	15.10.1828	Samuel Smith	14 Princes Street, Red Lion Street, Holborn	
SS	24.4.1829	Samuel Starkey	3 East Street, Hoxton	double lobe
	25.11.1829	idem	Moved to 9 Queen Square, Aldersgate Street	
SS	4.9.1833	idem	idem	
	19.5.1837	idem	Moved to 18 King Street, Clerkenwell	
SS & EF	14.3.1831	Samuel Sparrow and Edward Flower	18 Brook Street, Holborn	
ST	2.2.1792	Stephen Twycross	Newcastle Street, Strand	
ST	31.1.1822	Samuel James Townsend	2 Castle Street, Falcon Square	
ST, pellet between WB, pellet between	6.3.1793	Samson Tomlinson and William Bickley	Moor Street, BIRMINGHAM (by letter of attorney)	
SUM	24.1.1826	Samuel Udall Mayfield	18 Staining Lane	
	1.1.1828	idem	Moved to 12 Well Street	
	2.11.1830	idem	Moved to 12 Nicholls Square	

* See Section I, no. 2628, possibly father.

Mark	Entered	Name	Address/Notes	Punch
SW, pellet between	20.3.1779	Sarah Winter	21 Bunhill Row	
SW	20.6.1805 5.5.1809	Stephen Warwick idem	90 Shoe Lane Moved to Northampton Square, Clerkenwell	
SW	13.7.1825	idem	idem, till 1843	
TA	20.7.1825	Thomas Ausender	12 Short's Buildings, Clerkenwell	
TA, pellet between	29.2.1828	idem	idem, till 1838	
TA, pellet between	20.12.1834	*Thomas Benjamin Atkinson	32 Baker Street, Clerkenwell	
TB	10.7.1792	Thomas Blake	5 Elliotts Court, Old Bailey	
TB, pellet between	30.5.1826	Thomas Buss	20 Cirencester Street, Chancery Lane	
TBA	21.1.1829	Thomas Benjamin Atkinson	16 Kirby Street, Hatton Garden	
TC	15.3.1817	†Thomas Crofts	10 Winyat Street, Clerkenwell	
TC	19.11.1822	Thomas Clements	8 Green Street, Rathbone Lane	
TC	20.10.1823	Thomas Curby	22 Frith Street, Soho	
TD	4.6.1797	Thomas Dane	133 Oxford Street	
TD	6.1.1816	‡Thomas Davies	39 Brewer Street, Golden Square	
TD	10.2.1825	§Thomas Spicer Dismore	11 Clerkenwell Green	
TD	30.1.1834	idem	idem, till 1838	double lobe
TD	15.2.1825	§Thomas Downes	90 Hatton Gardens	
TD	28.7.1825	idem	idem	double lobe
	3.5.1827	idem	Moved to 8 High Street, Islington	
	12.7.1835	idem	Moved to 10 Great Portland Street, Oxford Street	
TD, pellet between DS, pellet between	19.11.1822	Thomas Dugard and David Simpson	34 Red Lion Street, Clerkenwell	
TD GD	5.2.1836	Thomas and George Dugard	idem	

* See TBA below.   † See also Section V.
‡ See TD.HD below.   § See TD.TD below.

GOLDWORKERS' MARKS 1773-1837

Mark	Entered	Name	Address/Notes	Punch
TD HD	27.2.1812	Thomas and Henry Davies	39 Brewer Street, Golden Square	
TD, pellet between TD, pellet between	10.8.1818	Thomas Downes and Thomas Dismore	11 Clerkenwell Green	
TD TD	8.9.1821	idem	idem, till 1824	
TEW	21.9.1829	Thomas Egerton White	4 Bull and Mouth Street	
	22.1.1835	idem	Moved to 12 Well Street, Cripplegate	
	11.3.1835	idem	Moved to 4 Bull and Mouth Street	
TF	21.7.1813	Thomas Flower	Chichester Rents, Chancery Lane	
TG	20.5.1783	Thomas Green	NOTTINGHAM	
TG	3.9.1823	Thomas Gleeson	19 Wynyatt Street, Goswell Street	
	20.8.1835	idem	Moved to 20 St. John's Square	
TG	13.10.1824	Thomas Gibbs	11 Castle Street, Falcon Square	
TG	26.11.1835	idem	idem	
TH	16.8.1775	Thomas Hawkins	139 Whitechapel (ringmaker)	
TH, pellet between	25.9.1783	Thomas Hitchman	Grafton Street, St. Anne's Square	
	26.2.1798	idem	Moved to 10 Portland Street, Soho	
TH	30.3.1803	Thomas Habgood	5 George Street, Foster Lane	
TH	30.12.1830	Thomas Haverson	19 Queen Street, Golden Square	
TI	20.11.1827	*Timothy Jones	5 Wine Office Court, Fleet Street	
idem	29.4.1835	idem	Moved to 18 Ludgate Street	
TJ	14.10.1779	†Thomas James	51 St. Martins Le Grand	
	19.9.1785	idem	Moved to 53 Tooley Street, Southwark	
TK	22.12.1802	Thomas Kearse	86 Queen Anne Street East, St. Marylebone	

* See also Section V.
† See Section I, no. 2821 for his probable son.

TL   WE

Mark	Entered	Name	Address/Notes	Punch
TL	23.10.1793	*Thomas Lovidge	NEWBURY, Berkshire (by letter of attorney)	
TL, pellet between	16.6.1825	Thomas Lovejoy	47 Red Lion Street, Clerkenwell	
TM	3.3.1790	†Thomas Mayfield	18 Staining Lane	
TN, pellet between	16.11.1779	Thomas Nowill	High Street, SHEFFIELD	
TP	29.11.1791	Thomas Palmer	13 St. John's Street, BRISTOL	
TP	27.3.1793	Thomas Parsons	BIRMINGHAM	
TP idem (three sizes)	18.8.1807 9.5.1826	‡Thomas Pemberton idem	Snow Hill, BIRMINGHAM idem	
TP	19.10.1826	Thomas Parkes	BIRMINGHAM (by power of attorney)	
TR	7.12.1778 21.2.1785	Thomas Ruggles idem	9 Westmorland Buildings, Aldersgate Street Moved to 89 London Wall	
TR	9.7.1785	Thomas Romilly	17 Frith Street, Soho	
TR	17.12.1785	idem	idem	
TR	26.1.1835	Thomas Read	75 George Street, Portman Square	
TS	30.6.1780 5.7.1785	§Thomas Satchwell idem	16 Noble Street Moved to 1 Purse Court, Old Change	
TS	7.10.1829	Thomas Stroud	13 Crown Street, Soho	
TS	3.5.1837	Thomas Stead	4 Owen's Row, St. John's Road	oval
TT, pellet between	25.7.1821	Thomas Tolfree	4 Bolt in Tun Passage, Fleet Street	
TT	3.12.1823	Thomas Thornton	35 Dean Street, Soho	oval
TT	2.10.1834	idem	idem	
TW	22.5.1826	Thomas Webster	33 Wellington Street, Kingsland Road	
TY	3.4.1824 no date	Thomas Young idem	50 Grub Street Moved to 11 Westmorland Buildings, Aldersgate Street	
WAP	20.11.1819	‖William Archer Price	Falcon Square	
WB, pellet between	21.12.1773	William Bulford	17 Bride Lane, Fleet Street	

* See Section II, no. 3448.
† See BM and SUM above and Section I, no. 621.   ‡ See Section II, no. 3453.
§ See also Section IV.   ‖ See WP below.

382

GOLDWORKERS' MARKS 1773-1837

Mark	Entered	Name	Address/Notes	Punch
WB	28.10.1774	*William Bell	10 Roles Building, Fetter Lane	
WB	6.8.1777	idem	idem	
WB	9.6.1779	William Baxter	33 Arundel Street, Strand	
WB	17.11.1824	William Beard	1 Craven Buildings, Drury Lane	
WC	11.8.1779	†William Charron	2 Little Marlborough Street, near Carnaby Market	
WC	4.11.1782	William Chapman	4 Leigh Street, Red Lion Square	
WC	8.3.1791	William Charpentier	3 Great Newport Street, Soho	
WC, pellet between	30.12.1823	William Clark	Camberwell	
WC	14.5.1821	William Carter	Mousham, CHELMSFORD, Essex	
WC	9.3.1830	William Cowbrick	40 Well Street, Oxford Street	
WC	23.10.1834 30.9.1837	‡William Clutton idem	48 Rupert Street Moved to 21 Denmark Street	
WC	11.2.1836	William Charman	63 Berwick Street, Oxford Street	
W.C. D.C }	30.10.1828	William Clutton and David Cox	48 Rupert Street	
WC SH }	25.1.1804	§William Cartwright and Samuel Horton	BIRMINGHAM	
WD	14.2.1825	William Davis	56 Leather Lane	
WD	13.9.1828	idem	9 Red Lion Street, Clerkenwell	
WD WL }	4.6.1823	William Davis and William Ludlow	6 St. James' Street, Clerkenwell	
WD.WL	15.12.1824	idem	idem	
WE	15.3.1791	William Edwards I	36 Coleman Street	
WE, pellet between	16.10.1794	idem	idem	
WE	22.5.1818 30.4.1830	William Edwards II idem	42 Little Britain Moved to 14 Smith Street, Northampton Square	
WE	13.10.1821	William Eady	26 Red Lion Street, Clerkenwell	

* See Section I, no. 3018 and Section V.
† Signed important Freedom Box of Admiral Keppel, 1779, 'Charron fecit' but which has maker's mark AF, pellet between (Guildhall Museum).
‡ See WC.DC below.   § See also Section V.

Mark	Entered	Name	Address/Notes	Punch
WE	27.1.1837	idem	idem	oval
WF	1.2.1803	W. Farthing	Cheapside	
WF	31.12.1825	*William Forrester	54 Red Lion Street, Clerkenwell	
	19.10.1830	idem	Moved to 16 Arlington Street, New River Head	
	14.10.1833	idem	Moved to 7 Amwell Street, New River Head	
	26.11.1834	idem	Moved to 23 Gerard Street, Soho	
WF, pellet between	7.6.1837	idem	idem	
	9.12.1837	idem	Moved to 32 Marylebone Street, St. James	
WG	6.1.1806	William Glover	1 Cross Key Square, Little Britain	
WG, pellet between	29.12.1827	William Gill	10 Smith Street, Clerkenwell	
WH	2.4.1774	William Holdsworth	42 Hoxton Square	
WH	25.6.1785	†William Hopkins	17 Maiden Lane, Wood Street	oval
WH	26.5.1791	idem	idem	
WH, pellet between	13.9.1826	William Henry Harrison	28 St. John's Square, Clerkenwell	
WH	11.2.1833	William Hinton	1 Paragon Place, Locks Fields, Walworth	
WH	8.7.1834	William Hitchcock	23 Red Lion Street, Clerkenwell	
WH⎫ EH⎭	4.1.1806	‡William and Edmund Hopkins	17 Maiden Street, Wood Street	quatre-foil
WH.EH	idem	idem	idem	
WJH	29.3.1825	William James Hemming	20 Cross Street, Hatton Garden	
WJL	25.5.1835	William James Leadbetter	4 Pollen Street, Hanover Square	
WK	6.4.1778	William Keates	117 Fleet Street	
WK	15.4.1820	William King	39 Red Cross Street, Cripplegate	
	7.9.1820	idem	Moved to 15 Bridgwater Square, Barbican	
	5.1.1824	idem	Moved to 18 Bridgwater Square, Barbican	
	12.2.1825	idem	Moved to 14 Red Lion Street, Holborn	

* See also Sections IV (Forister) and V.
† See WH.EH below.   ‡ See also EH and WH above.

GOLDWORKERS' MARKS 1773-1837

Mark	Entered	Name	Address/Notes	Punch
WK	6.1.1829	idem	idem	oval
	23.10.1834	idem	Moved to 11 Tavistock Row, Covent Garden (till 1843)	
WK, pellet between	16.7.1828	William Kilby	19 Silver Street, Wood Street	
WL	20.7.1815	William Leaver	33 Bartholomew Close	
WL	15.9.1833	William Ludlow	11 St. James Street, Clerkenwell	
WM	28.4.1774	William Murdoch	47 Chesil Street	
WM	19.12.1809	William Moore	13 Old Street, St. Luke's	
WM	10.1.1827	William Morgan	149 Holborn Bars	
WM	4.8.1832	William Daye Mills	4 Staple Inn Buildings, Middle Row, Holborn	
WN	22.11.1833 and 6.2.1835	William Nettleship	44 Kirby Street, Hatton Garden	
WN	3.2.1835	William Newbery	49 Greek Street, Soho	
WP	16.6.1781	William Pineau	31 Charles Street, Hatton Garden	
WP	1.11.1814	William Archer Price	17 Maiden Lane, Wood Street	
WP	20.4.1816	idem	idem	double lobe
WAP	20.11.1819	idem	Falcon Square	
WP	21.1.1822	idem	idem	oval
WP	5.3.1822	idem	17 Maiden Lane	oval
	7.9.1844	idem	Moved to 122 London Wall	
WP	1.5.1826	William Pawley	10 Short Buildings, Clerkenwell	
	12.1.1827	idem	Moved to 3 St. James Walk	
WP	16.10.1829	idem	11 St. James Walk	
	5.5.1834	idem	Moved to 22 Red Lion Street, Clerkenwell	
WP	29.5.1834	idem	idem	
WP, pellet between	3.8.1831	William Parker	10 New North Street, Red Lion Square	
WR	23.7.1821	William Reeves	10 Henrietta Street, Covent Garden	

Mark	Entered	Name	Address/Notes	Punch
WR conjoined	3.4.1824	William Rogers	16 Porter Street, Soho	
	13.10.1826	idem	Moved to 9 Great St. Andrew Street	
	21.4.1830	idem	Moved to 12 Clarkes Buildings, Bloomsbury	
	4.12.1832	idem	Moved to 54 High Street, St. Giles	
	17.10.1834	idem	Moved to 32 Greek Street, Soho	
	20.5.1840	idem	Moved to 10 St. Mary Street, Lambeth	
WR	12.3.1831	William Richards	35 Princes Street, Soho	
WR	16.7.1836	William Rapley	1 Brunswick Street, Southampton Street, Clerkenwell	
	3.4.1838	idem	Moved to 33 Northampton Street, Clerkenwell	
WS	6.11.1805	William Savory	2 Lillypot Lane	
WS	16.3.1826	*William Summers	19 Little Britain	
WSP	–.10.1837	William Swanwick Powell	3 Rahere Street, Goswell Street (ringmaker)	
WT	10.10.1803	†William Tanner	8 Georges Row, City Road	
WT	27.7.1810	William Tongue	22 High Street, BIRMINGHAM	
WV	17.8.1774	Walter Vavasour	SHEFFIELD, Yorkshire	
WW	19.5.1774	William Worsdell	7 Albion Buildings	
WW	13.3.1776	‡William Worthington	158 Fleet Street	
WW, pellet between	9.1.1778	William Watson	6 Ducks Court, St. Martin's Lane	
	6.2.1783	idem	Moved to 15 Church Street, Soho	
	24.7.1788	idem	Moved to 190 Strand	
WW	3.12.1781 and 24.10.1784	William Wright	211 Tooley Street	
WW	23.2.1801	William Warwick	9 Red Lion Street, Clerkenwell	
WW	9.5.1805	William Whitefield	9 Silver Street	
	10.11.1815	idem	Moved to 17 Crown Street, Soho	
WW	27.10.1831	Walter West	3 Eliza Place, Sadlers Wells	

* See Section I, no. 414. † See Section I, no. 3345.
‡ See Section I, no. 3366.

VIII

Bucklemakers' Marks 1773–1820

All the marks are in relief 'cameo' punches and Roman capitals unless otherwise stated. The punches have been categorized as follows: 1. rectangular; 2. rectangular with 'cut' corners; 3. oval. The rare exceptions to the above have been described. After 1810 the entries for bucklemakers vanish due presumably to diminishing production.

Mark	Entered	Name	Address/Notes	Punch
AB	10.8.1791	Alexander Bates	41 Clerkenwell Green	2
AG	23.6.1775	Alexander Glass	237 High Holborn	1
AH, pellet between	19.6.1789	Abraham Hazelhurst	Lumley Court, Bowling Green Alley, Chancery Lane	2
ARD	24.7.1776	*Anderson Robert Dennison	Cecil Court, St. Martin's Lane	2
BA	25.6.1776	Benjamin Ange	Gutter Lane	1
BA, pellet between	11.2.1777	Benjamin Aston	93 White Cross Street	2
BB, pellet between	29.3.1779	†Benjamin Bickerton	14 Jewin Street	2
BB	23.9.1789	idem	idem	1
BBTB	28.2.1791	Benjamin and Thomas Bickerton	idem	1
BM, pellet between	1.10.1773	‡Benjamin Mountigue	10 Clerkenwell Green	2
BM	17.11.1774	idem	idem	2
BM	18.7.1775	idem	idem	1
BM, pellet between	8.3.1776	idem	idem	2
BM	7.7.1779	idem	idem	2
BM, pellet between	24.11.1781 (two sizes)	idem	idem	2
BM, pellet between	16.6.1784 (two sizes)	idem	idem	2
BS	4.9.1783	Benjamin Swinfen	30 Greenhill's Rents, West Smithfield	1

* See Section I, nos. 2298–9.   † See Section I, nos. 131, 134.
‡ See Section I, nos. 191, 1999.

Mark	Entered	Name	Address/Notes	Punch
BS	11.9.1784	Benjamin Stubbs	5 Caroline Court, Saffron Hill	1
BW	29.10.1779	*Brook Walker	111 Salisbury Court, Fleet Street	2
	6.6.1788	idem	Moved to 6 Queen Court, Great Queen Street, Lincoln's Inn Fields	
BW	14.10.1785	Benjamin Wilson	5 Cherry Tree Court, Whitecross Street	1
	3.4.1787	idem	Moved to 11 Old Street Square	
CC (two marks, very poor rough letters)	19.1.1789	Charles Christian	27 Holborn	1 and 3
CE	7.12.1786	Charles Eaton	4 Princes Street, Barbican	1
	4.4.1789	idem	Moved to 4 Salisbury Court, Fleet Street	
CG / JG	19.1.1776	Charles and James Gilchrist	3 St. John's Square	2
CH	19.11.1773	†Charles Hougham	138 Aldersgate Street	1
CH (three sizes)	1775–1779	idem	idem	1
CL, pellet between	11.8.1777	Charles Lee	Turner Square, Hoxton	2
idem	4.7.1783	idem	11 Lamb's Conduit Passage	2
CR	8.11.1777	Charles Rapley	St. Martin's Court, Leicester Fields	1
CT	22.4.1784	Charles Thomson	89 Oxford Street	1
CW	7.4.1774	Cattern Whitford	Sugar Loaf Court, Salisbury Court, Fleet Street	2
CW	24.2.1795	Charles Wilson	4 Glasshouse Street, St. James'	1
DC	25.9.1787	David Chatterton	6 Brooks Gardens 'Totinham' Road	1
	27.5.1788	idem	Moved to 28 Greek Street, Soho	
	no date	idem	Moved to 1 Swallow Street, Piccadilly	
DK	3.2.1792	David Kennair	13 Bleeding Hart Yard, Charles Street, Hatton Garden	1

* See also TE.BW below. † See Section I, nos. 327–9.

BUCKLEMAKERS' MARKS 1773-1820

Mark	Entered	Name	Address/Notes	Punch
DP	27.6.1785	Dolphin Price	26 Charterhouse Lane	2
	10.5.1786	idem	Moved to 45 St. John Street	
EB ⎫ IW ⎭	6.3.1789	Elizabeth Barrows and Jane Williams	8 Bedford Street, Strand	1
idem	17.6.1789	idem	idem	2
EF, pellet between	24.5.1792	*Edward Farbrother	Clerkenwell Green	2
EH	28.8.1782	†Edward Higgs	Pitfield Street, Hoxton	1
EH, pellet between	4.2.1784	idem	Pitwell (sic) Street, Hoxton	3
EH	7.12.1786	idem	idem	1
EH, pellet between	14.6.1784	Edward Hatton	9 John's Court, Hanover Yard	2
	20.7.1804	idem	Moved to 21 Chapel Street, Soho	
EH ⎫ JH ⎭	29.12.1787	‡Edward and James Higgs	20 Pittfield Street	2
EI (crudely cut)	1.11.1782	Elias Jones	14 Goswell Street	1
EJ (two marks)	6.11.1782	idem	idem	2 and 3
EK, pellet between	14.10.1774	Edward King	Duck's Court, St. Martin's Lane	1
EL	20.7.1789	Edward Lycett	25 Noble Street	1
EL, pellet between	20.11.1790	idem	idem	2
EO	24.11.1787	Edward Owen	16 Ealey Place, Holborn	1
EO	31.7.1789	idem	idem	1
EP	29.8.1774	§Eliza Padmore	19 Frith Street, Soho	1
EP	21.4.1777	Edward Parsons	19 Long Lane, West Smithfield	1
FS (two sizes)	9.4.1783	¶Frances Swayne	DEVIZES, by letter of attorney	1
FS	idem	idem	idem	1, with indented top and base
GB	20.9.1780	George Burrows	10 Clerkenwell Close	2
GB (six sizes)	1781–1793	idem	idem	2
	12.6.1799	idem	Moved to 14 Red Lion Street, Clerkenwell	

---

* See Section I, no. 583.
† See EH.JH below and Section I, no. 597.   ‡ See EH above and Section I, no. 597.
§ See Section I, no. 869.   ¶ See Section II, no. 3384.

GB   IB

Mark	Entered	Name	Address/Notes	Punch
GB	18.10.1780	George Burnett	112 Fore Street	2
	18.12.1781	idem	Moved to 9 Pauls Alley, Red Cross Street	
GB	15.12.1784	George Butler	18 Holborn	3
GB, smaller	undated	idem	37 Chancery Lane	3
	28.6.1790	idem	Moved to 39 Norton Folgate	
	2.2.1792	idem	Moved to 7 Round Court, Strand	
	17.11.1792	idem	Moved to 78 Fetter Lane	
GB	4.10.1793	idem	idem	2
	4.11.1793	idem	Moved to 1 Dorminton Street, Leather Lane	
GE	23.1.1797	*George Ewings	10 Brook Street, Holborn	2
	4.4.1803	idem	Moved to 27 Rosamon Row, Clerkenwell	
	30.8.1804	idem	Moved to 9 Ratcliff Row, City Road	
GF	30.9.1784	George Frodsham	12 Kingsgate Street, Bloomsbury	2
GF	3.9.1785	idem	idem	1
GH	28.9.1786	George Hudson	41 Lower East Smithfield	1
GS	8.4.1775	†George Smith II	4 Huggin Lane	1
GS, script	21.9.1776	idem	idem	2
GS	14.5.1778	idem	idem	2
✸✸	25.1.1782	idem	idem	2
GS, star between	21.12.1782	idem	idem	2
GS (two sizes)	25.5.1784	idem	idem	2
GS, script	5.8.1786	idem	idem	2
GS	20.3.1787	idem	idem	2
GS, pellet between	24.9.1789	idem	idem	1
GS	21.7.1785	George Sanderson	28 Greenhills Rents, Smithfield	2
GS	28.10.1788	George Stewart	3 King's Head Court, Gutter Lane	2
GS	4.7.1789	George Stevens	Bottel Hay Yard, St. John's Street, Clerkenwell	2

* See Section I, no. 794.
† See Section I, nos. 896-8

BUCKLEMAKERS' MARKS 1773-1820

Mark	Entered	Name	Address/Notes	Punch
GT	22.4.1785	George Taylor	Blue Anchor Alley, Bunhill Row	2
GT	13.12.1792	George Thomas	10 Crown Court, Fleet Street	1
GW	26.7.1782	George Webster	8 Princes Street, Moorfields	1
GW	21.7.1794	idem	idem	1
GW	19.4.1787	George Wood	Long Acre	1
GW	31.12.1798	George Whitaker	12 Princes Street, Barbican	1
	18.4.1794	idem	Moved to 18 Noble Street, Goswell Street	
HB	5.5.1777	Henry Baker	King Street, Westminster	1
HM	19.2.1783	Henry McGrigor	7 Mercers Street, Long Acre	1
	16.4.1785	idem	Moved to 19 St. Martin's Street, Leicester Fields	
HP	28.3.1776	Henry Phillips	222 Radcliff Highway	1
HS, pellet between / IS, pellet between	1.11.1792	Henry and John Sweet	Christopher's Alley, Moorfields	1
IA (two sizes)	13.9.1776	*Joseph Adams	WALSALL, Staffordshire	1, incurved ends
IA, pellet between	27.3.1792	†James Atkins	12 Well Street	1
IB, pellet or star between / IB (large)	17.1.1774	‡John Baker	35 Snow Hill	1 / 1
	5.10.1775	idem	Moved to 4 Bull in Mouth Street	
IB	2.3.1786	idem	4 High Street, St. Giles	2
IB, pellet between	25.1.1774	§John Beedall	Newman's Row, Lincoln's Inn Fields	2
	9.4.1774	idem	Moved to 1 Orange Street, Red Lion Square	
IB	27.3.1777	John Beddoes	Red Lion Court, Charterhouse Lane	1
IB, pellet between	21.7.1778	‖John Brown	PLYMOUTH	2

* See Section II, no. 3398.
† See also IE.IA and JA below, and Section I, no. 2683.
‡ See also Section I, nos. 1141, 1691 and 1773.
§ See also IB.IB below. ‖ See Section II, no. 3401.

IB   II

Mark	Entered	Name	Address/Notes	Punch
IB, pellet between	25.2.1777	Joel Barns	Duke Street, West Smithfield	1, with incurved lobed ends
idem (smaller)	1.10.1778	idem	idem	idem
IB, script	18.8.1785	John Brown	149 Fleet Street	shaped oblong
IB AH}	17.2.1784	Abram Harcourt and John Backhous	4 Little Bartholomew Close	1
IB, pellet between IB, pellet between	29.7.1775	*John Beedall and John Bennett	1 Orange Street, Red Lion Square	2
IB } (two TM } sizes)	8.2.1775	†John Bourne and Thomas Moore	1 Queen's Square, Bartholomew Close	2
IC	30.5.1777 16.7.1779	John Chadwick idem	30 Minories Moved to 6 Raven Row, Spitalfields	1
IC, pellet between	20.8.1778	John Benjamin Cole	10 Bell Square, St. Martin's Le Grand	2
	3.7.1779	idem	54 Barbican	
IC	17.11.1785	idem	idem	1
IC, smaller	10.7.1789 and 8.3.1796	idem	idem	1
idem	23.8.1805 and 30.3.1809	idem	idem	1
IC	17.10.1786	‡Joshua Cooper	Brownlow Street, Holborn	2
IC	25.1.— (c. 1790)	John Cooper	8 Cock Court, St. Martin's Le Grand	2
IC	12.11.1794	Joshua Cook	Blue Anchor Alley, Bunhill Row	1
ID	25.11.1788	§John Douglas	4 Clerkenwell Close	1
ID, pellet between	17.4.1793	John Davis	153 Leadenhall Street	1
ID, pellet between	15.6.1796	John Davenport	3 King's Head Court, Gutter Lane	2
IE	23.1.1783	‖John Essex	11 Angle Court, Snow Hill	2

* See also I.B above.
† See also TM below and Section I, nos. 1144–6, 1188.
‡ See Section I, no. 1216.
§ See Section I, nos. 1250, 1256, 2359.   ‖ See also IE.IA below.

BUCKLEMAKERS' MARKS 1773-1820

Mark	Entered	Name	Address/Notes	Punch
IE, pellet between	23.10.1787	idem	idem	2
	5.6.1788	idem	Moved to 7 Clark's Buildings, Snow Hill	
IE	20.10.1789	idem	idem	1
IE, pellet between	2.10.1790	Joseph Egginton	2 Dean's Court, St. Martin's Le Grand	2
idem (two sizes)	1.12.1800	idem	idem	2
IE } IA }	19.7.1793	James Eaton	2 Salisbury Court, Fleet Street	2
IE	4.4.1791	*John Essex and James Atkins	12 Well Street	1
IF	27.6.1781	Joseph Fletcher	33 Greenhill's Rents, Smithfields Bars	1
	23.6.1783	idem	Moved to 45 St. John Street	
IF, script	6.12.1773	†John Faùx	Worship Street, Moorfields	2
idem (varying size)	3.9.1777, 4.11.1777 and 12.7.1784	idem	idem	2
IG	3.1.1788	Joseph Griffin	23 Red Cross Street	1
	no date	idem	Moved to 4 Princes Street, Barbican	
	2.10.1797	idem	Moved to 231 St. John's Street, Clerkenwell	
IG	14.11.1792	Joseph Girdler	13 Rose Street, Long Acre	2
IG, smaller	6.6.1793	idem	13 Covent Garden	
IH, pellet between	13.1.1789	Joseph Hedges	4 Change Court, Strand	1
idem	13.1.1789	idem	idem	double indented top and bottom
IH, pellet between	12.4.1791	John Husband	41 Noble Street	1
	16.4.1793	idem	Moved to 3 St. Martins Le Grand	
IH	28.7.1800	John Higgins	22 Arthur Street, Goswell Street	1
II, pellet between	26.7.1776	‡Joel Jacobson	10 St. James' Walk, Clerkenwell	1

* See also IA above and JA below. † See Section I, nos. 1294, 1312.
‡ See also II.IY and JJ below.

Mark	Entered	Name	Address/Notes	Punch
idem	16.7.1779	idem	88 High Holborn	1
II, pellet between	5.5.1777	*John Jones	46 Little Minories	1
II, star between	20.11.1777	idem	idem	1
	11.8.1783	idem	Moved to 6 Little Minories	
II } IC }	30.5.1775	John Jones and John Chadwick	46 Little Minories	1, with curved top
II, pellet between IY, pellet between	15.3.1780	Joel Jacobson and John Yardley	37 Charles Street, Hatton Garden	1
II } WI }	29.10.1787	†Isaac Jones and William Jones	26 Queen Street, Seven Dials	2
idem	15.1.1788	idem	idem	2
IJ	7.9.1780	†Isaac Jones	Great Wild Street, Lincoln's Inn Fields	double-lobed
IJ } WJ }	20.10.1787	†Isaac Jones and William Jones	26 Queen Street, Seven Dials	1
IK	26.4.1793	John Kirkham	13 Lombard Street, Fleet Street	1
	5.9.1793	idem	Moved to 4 King's Head, Court, St. Martin's le Grand	
IL	1.5.1775	‡Joseph Lewis	38 Foster Lane	2
IL	3.12.1779	idem	idem	2
IL	14.2.1783	idem	idem	2
IL, pellet between	29.3.1777	James Lockley	23 Peartree Court, Clerkenwell Close	2
IL	12.2.1783	John Lemay	10 New Inn, Oliver Mount Street	2
IL	18.2.1783	idem	idem	1
	3.9.1784	idem	Moved to 27 Ironmonger Row, Old Street	
IL	3.3.1788	idem	idem	1
	9.8.1791	idem	Moved to 4 King's Head Court, St. Martin's Le Grand	
IL, pellet between	10.11.1784	John Lisle	3 John's Court, Hanway Street, Oxford Street	2
IL	8.11.1791	§John Lias	15 Great Sutton Street	2

* See Section I, no. 1823.
† See Section I, nos. 1437, 1440 and IWI below.
‡ See Section I, nos. 1471, 1481, 1831.
§ See Section I, nos. 1483–4, 1495–6.

BUCKLEMAKERS' MARKS 1773-1820

Mark	Entered	Name	Address/Notes	Punch
IL, pellet between	3.7.1794	idem	13 Bethnal Green Road	2
	no date	idem	Moved to 3 Finsbury Street, Moorfields	
IL, script interlaced	19.10.1784	Jacob Levi	26 Mansell Street, Goodman's Fields	1
IL ⎫ DC ⎭	29.9.1792	*John Lias and Dennis Charie	16 Albemarle Street, St. John's Lane	1
IM	21.4.1775	†John Myatt	10 Little Wild Street, Clare Market	1
IM, pellet between	10.7.1783	John Mousell	26 Queen Street, Seven Dials	2
IM, pellet between	11.9.1787	John Moore	1 Great Bartholomew Close	3
IM, script	23.5.1783	John Myatt	13 Great Pultney Street	2
IMF, pellet between	24.2.1777	‡John Mcferlan	102 Thames Street	2
idem	24.10.-?	idem	idem	1
idem	22.5.1784	idem	idem	1
idem	22.9.1790	idem	Moved to 5 Bird Court, Phillip Lane	
IM, pellet between IM, pellet between	29.1.1780	John Myatt and John Mousell	26 Queen Street, Seven Dials	1
IN	26.2.1784	§John Nicson (sic)	56 Old Bailey	1
IN	29.4.1789	John Nixon	14 Union Court, Holborn	2
IN	12.11.1802	idem	23 Charles Street, Hatton Garden	1
IN	15.9.1807	idem	19 Atfield Street, Goswell Street	1
IN	6.10.1815	idem	31 Arthur Street, Goswell Street, later undated 5 Norway Street, Old Street	1
IN, pellet	11.8.1785	John Newey	20 Hyde Street, Bloomsbury	2
IN	5.12.1793	John Norman	15 Pear Street, Goswell Street	2
IN, pellet between WN, pellet between	12.2.1780	John and William Nicson	Bloomsbury Market	1

---

* See Section I, nos. 1483-4, 1495-6.
† See also IM script capitals and IM.IM below, and Section I, no. 1530.
‡ See Section I, no. 1539.   § See IN.WN below.

IO   JB

Mark	Entered	Name	Address/Notes	Punch
IO, pellet between	31.10.1789	John Oram	5 Grafton Street, Soho	1
IP	3.6.1776	*Jonathan Perkins	16 Hosier Lane, Smithfield	1
IP, pellet between	2.8.1777	idem	idem	1
IP, pellet between	26.2.1781	idem	idem	2
idem (three sizes)	1.7.1788	idem	idem	2
IP (two sizes)	6.11.1789	idem	idem	2
IP	19.10.1778	†John Pritchard	13 Sutton Street, Goswell Street	2
	1.8.1780	idem	Moved to 6 Goswell Street	
IP	9.5.1789	idem	idem	1
IP	12.2.1783	John Price	16 Fleet Lane	1
IR	23.2.1778	James Richardson	5 Racquet Court, Fleet Street	1
IR, pellet between	25.2.1778	John Radclyffe	1 King's Arms Yard, Holborn Bridge	1
IR	29.1.1780	Joseph Rogers	5 Bull and Mouth Street	1
	3.4.1781	idem	Moved to Greenhill's Rents, Smithfield	
IR, script	15.8.1780	‡John Rich	14 Tottenham Court Road	2
idem	idem	idem	idem	outline following letters
IS, pellet between	22.11.1773	Joseph Sutton	12 New Street, Covent Garden	1
IS	2.3.1774	Joseph Stainforth	Quee(?) Street, St. Ann's, Soho	1
	29.7.1777	idem	Moved to Middle Row, Holborn	
IS, pellet between	22.4.1776	John Stone	AYLESBURY, Buckinghamshire (by letter of attorney)	2
IS, pellet between	31.10.1781	John Stocker	16 Primrose Street, Bishopsgate	1
	23.8.1782	idem	Moved to 31 Houndsditch	
IS, pellet between	14.1.1783	idem	idem	1
	8.11.1787	idem	Moved to 15 Primrose Street, Bishopsgate	
	5.6.1788	idem	Moved to 5 Smith's Buildings, Leadenhall Street	

* See also JP below and Section I, nos. 1592, 1604, 1839.
† See Section I, no. 1591.   ‡ See Section I, no. 1635.

BUCKLEMAKERS' MARKS 1773-1820

Mark	Entered	Name	Address/Notes	Punch
IS, pellet between	25.5.1782	James Smith	8 Holywell Row, Moorfields	1
IS, pellet between	2.4.1784	John Sharp	2 Gravel Street, Hatton Garden	1
IS, pellet between	11.1.1789	John Simpson	5 Rose and Crown Court, Foster Lane	2
IT	28.8.1775	John Turner	Near the Nag's Head, Hackney Road	1
IT	18.10.1780	*John Turner	23 Charles Street, Hatton Garden	3
IT	19.4.1793	†James Trender	Princes Street, Barbican	2, with indented base
	9.8.1797	idem	Moved to 7 Long Lane, West Smithfield	
	no date	idem	Moved to Dove Court, 4 Leather Lane	
IT } EM }	22.3.1780	John Turner and Edward Morson	23 Lower Charles Street, Hatton Garden	2
IW, pellet between	11.3.1783	James Webb	7 New Street, Covent Garden	2
IW, pellet between	13.11.1790	‡John Williams	45 St. Martin's Lane	1
IW	19.11.1792	§John Wheeldon	10 Tower Street	1
	6.5.1796	idem	Moved to 3 Henrietta Street, Manchester Square	
IW	19.11.1792	§John Wickes	14 West Street, Seven Dials	2
IWI	14.10.1787	‖William and Isaac Jones	26 Queen Street, Seven Dials	1
IW } IW }	17.11.1790	John Wheeldon and John Wickes	14 West Street, Seven Dials	1
JA, pellet between	24.5.1793	¶James Atkins	12 Well Street	3
JA, pellet between	14.11.1797	idem	idem	incurved top and base
JA	31.3.1815	idem	idem	3
JB, pellet between	30.9.1782	John Barrow	52 New Compton Street, Soho	2
	18.9.1783	idem	Moved to 8 Bedford Street, Strand	

* Probably distinct from above as former signs with mark only. See IT.EM below.
† See Section I, nos. 1717, 1726. ‡ See Section I, no. 3377.
§ See IW.IW below and RP.IW.
‖ Noted below in Warden's hand 'A Rong Mark'. See II.WI above.
¶ See IA above.

JE   SB

Mark	Entered	Name	Address/Notes	Punch
JE } JS }	10.4.1790	James Eaton and John Sleap	3 Salisbury Court, Fleet Street	2
JJ, pellet between	16.6.1779	*Joel Jacobson	88 High Holborn	2
	31.12.1779	idem	Moved to 37 Charles Street, Hatton Garden	
JJ, pellet between	20.6.1786	idem	idem	2
JM	31.10.1782	John Maxwell	10 Brook Street, Holborn	2
JM	6.9.1785	idem	idem	1
JP, pellet between	30.3.1778	†Jonathan Perkins	16 Hosier Lane, Smithfield	2
JR	5.1.1784	John Reed	3 Dolphin Court, Holborn	1
JT, pellet between	9.7.1788	James Tidbury	8 Castle Street, Leicester Square	3
idem	4.12.1793	idem	idem	3, indented
	8.7.1796	idem	Moved to 95 Swallow Street, near Hanover Square	
MB } WY }	22.3.1780	‡Mary Beedall and William Yardley	23 Thorney Street, Bloomsbury	1
MW, pellet between	6.11.1778	Mary Whitford	6 St. Martin's Le Grand	2
MW	27.6.1798	Mary Willis	81 Bishopsgate Street	2
MW } WB } (two sizes)	12.1.1779	Mary Whitford and William Ballantine	6 St. Martin's Le Grand	2
NB, script conjoined	30.7.1774	Nathaniel Bentley	46 Leadenhall Street	1
PM	1.2.1789	Peter Mollett	20 Bowling Green Lane, Clerkenwell	1
	13.9.1790	idem	1 Clements Inn, Fleet Street	
PS	30.5.1788	Phillip Stallard	13 New Street Square, Shoe Lane	2
RD	17.3.1777	§Richard Dovey	'at Pimlico'	1
RE	19.11.1787	Robert Eaton	3 Salisbury Court, Fleet Street	2
RE	9.6.1789	idem	idem	1
RF } WF }	21.12.1787	Robert Fenton and William Flenley	7 Queen's Square, Aldersgate Street	1
RH	16.4.1777	Robert Hilton	93 White Cross Street	2

* See II, pellet between and II.IY above.
† See also IP above and Section I, no. 1592.
‡ See S.B. below. § See Section I, no. 2300.

BUCKLEMAKERS' MARKS 1773-1820

Mark	Entered	Name	Address/Notes	Punch
RP	4.9.1780	*Richard Parr (signs with mark)	11 Rolls Buildings, Fetter Lane	1
RP	28.7.1786	idem	idem	1
RP	21.11.1782	Richard Pugh	2 Coventry Court, Haymarket	1
RP } IW	22.10.1789	†Richard Pugh and John Wheeldon	Coventry Court, Haymarket	1
	5.8.1790	idem	'Out of the Trade'	
RS, pellet between	1.12.1783	Robert Smyth	Wood Close, 19 Compton Street	1
RS	16.6.1794	Robert Smith	11 Mount Row, City Road	1
	30.5.1801	idem	Moved to 24 Barons Buildings, Surrey Road	
RT	20.10.1783	‡Richard Turner	15 St. John Square	1
RT	7.1.1789	Richard Tyler	67 Bunhill Row	1
SA, pellet between	5.2.1774	§Stephen Adams I	3 St. Ann's Lane	1, with sloping right side
idem	26.3.1776	idem	idem	2
SA	30.3.1781	idem	idem	2
SA	6.3.1782	idem	idem	2
SA, pellet between	24.2.1787	idem	idem	2
SA	24.3.1792	‖Stephen Adams II	idem	2
SA	idem	idem	idem	3, scalloped
SA	21.5.1795	idem	idem	2
SA, pellet between	5.2.1802	idem	idem, till 1807	2
SA, pellet between	6.10.1792	Samuel Allen	15 Rosamund Street, Clerkenwell	1
idem	30.10.1792	idem	idem	2
SB	9.1.1776	¶Samuel Beedall	237 High Holborn	2
SB	4.7.1780	Simeon Bayley	21 Greenhills Rents, Smithfield	2
	12.3.1782	idem	Moved to 13 Charterhouse Lane	
	5.8.1782	idem	Moved to 26 Wardour Street, Soho	
SB	20.5.1790	Sarah Baxter	47 Monkwell Street	1

* See Section I, no. 2409.
‡ See Section I, nos. 2447-8.
‖ See Section I, no. 2473.
† See IW above and RP below.
§ See Section I, no. 2472.
¶ See MB.WY above.

399

Mark	Entered	Name	Address/Notes	Punch
SB⎫ BB⎭	10.2.1780	Simeon Alexander Bayley and Benjamin Benson	21 Quaker's Buildings, Smithfield	2
SC	16.12.1776	Samuel Cooke	Crown and Sceptre Court, St. James's Street	2
SC	27.8.1789	idem	idem	1
SC, script pellet between	30.11.1773	*Simeon Coley I	91 Fleet Street	1
SC, pellet between	15.10.1777	idem	35 Fetter Lane	1
SC	1.2.1779	idem	idem	2
SC	4.8.1780	idem	idem	3
SC, pellet between	2.10.1789	Simeon Coley II	idem	3
SCN	5.7.1782	Samuel Cardozo Nuñez	5 Little Minories	2
SH	23.3.1776	†Samuel Hatton	Rose Street, St. Ann's, Soho	1
SH, pellet between	18.2.1779	idem	idem	2
SI	29.6.1779	Samuel Jones	2 Halsey Court, Blackman Street, Borough	2
SK	3.7.1780	‡Samuel Knightly	24 East Smithfield	1
SL	9.1.1777	Simon Levine	11 Gun Yard, Houndsditch	1
SL, pellet between	25.6.1778	idem	idem	1
SM	28.9.1785	§Samuel Moulton	210 Borough (High Street?)	2
SN	4.7.1781	Samuel Nash	83 Fleet Street	1
	9.4.1782	idem	Moved to 10 Brook Street, Holborn	
	21.10.1782	idem	Moved to Kirby Street, Hatton Garden	
ST, pellet between	10.1.1782	Samuel Titmuss	33 Oxford Street	2
ST	9.3.1789	Samuel Touse	2 Lombard Street	1
ST	13.7.1793	Solomon Turvey	13 Coventry Court, Haymarket	1
ST	18.7.1794	Samuel Tibbs	1 Coles Row, Blackman Street	1
ST⎫ TH⎭	9.2.1788	Solomon Turvey and Thomas Hill	4 Coventry Court, Haymarket	2
idem	12.5.1792	idem	idem	1
	1.9.1792	idem	Moved to 13 Coventry Court, Haymarket	

* See Section I, nos. 2491–2. † See Section I, no. 2543.
‡ See Section I, no. 2564. § See Section I, no. 2592.

BUCKLEMAKERS' MARKS 1773-1820

Mark	Entered	Name	Address/Notes	Punch
SW	31.7.1779	*Samuel Wintle	'facing the Coach & Horses Long Lane, Southwark'	1
	no date	idem	Moved to Surrey Square, Kent Road	
TA	16.2.1786	Thomas Ayres	160 Fenchurch Street	2
TC	24.5.1776 and 13.7.1776	Thomas Church	12 Albion Buildings, Aldersgate Street	1
(TC incuse)	5.9.1782	idem	Moved to 6 Bull and Mouth Street	
	31.1.1795	idem	Moved to 12 East Harding Street	
TD	4.5.1792	†Thomas Dicks	39 Cow Lane, West Smithfield	1
TD, pellet between	11.1.1798	idem	36 Greenhills Rents, Smithfield	3
TD	idem	idem	idem	2
TD, pellet between	2.4.1801	idem	idem	2
TD	23.1.1818	idem	idem	1
TE	1.10.1779	Thomas Eaton	4 Salisbury Court, Fleet Street	2
TE, pellet between	7.5.1784	idem	idem	2
TE	6.2.1786	idem	idem	1
TE ⎫ BW ⎭	30.3.1778	‡Thomas Eaton and Brook Walker	4 Salisbury Court	1
TF	2.3.1787	§Thomas Freeth I	24 Clerkenwell Close	1
	16.6.1797	idem	Moved to 9 Queen Street, Islington	
TG, pellet between	24.3.1790	‖Thomas Goslee	5 Bath Row, Cold Bath Square	1
	20.7.1792	idem	Moved to 6 Hosier Lane, Smithfield	
TH	20.9.1788	Thomas Hill	9 Baldwin's Gardens	1
	no date	idem	Moved to 37 Aylesbury Street, Clerkenwell	
TH	31.7.1793	idem	1 Monmouth Court	3
	17.3.1796	idem	Moved to 28 Great Sutton Street, St. John's Street, Clerkenwell	
	27.8.1814	idem	Moved to 60 Old Bailey	
	2.9.1821	idem	Moved to 30 Stratton Place, Berkley Street, Clerkenwell	

* See Section I, no. 2662, and TW.SW below.
† See Section I, nos. 2731, 2738.   ‡ See BW above.
§ See Section I, no. 2752.   ‖ See WG below.

Mark	Entered	Name	Address/Notes	Punch
THH	20.2.1775	Thomas Hinde Hunsdon	'CHELSMORD', Essex	2
TI, pellet between	4.12.1782	Thomas Jones I	1 Great Rider Street, St. James'	2
TI	25.9.1788	idem	idem	2
TI (two sizes)	16.8.1792	idem	idem	3, indented
TI	23.12.1794	idem	idem	3, serrated
TI	17.7.1795	idem	idem	3, scalloped
TI	15.2.1792	Thomas Jones II	Buckley Court, Clerkenwell	1
TK	26.9.1786	Thomas Kirkham	2 Winsor Court, Monkwell Street	2
	no date	idem	Moved to 25 Chapel Street, Pentonville	
	20.1.1792	idem	Moved to Butcher Hall Lane	
	11.2.1793	idem	Moved to 7 Anderson's Buildings, City Road	
TK, pellet between (two)	6.6.1793	idem	idem	2 and 3
TL	27.9.1774	Thomas Latham	3 Blue Coat Buildings, Butcher Hall Lane	1
TL } EL }	1.10.1783	Thomas Lowndes and Edward Lycett	2 St. Ann's Lane, Aldersgate	1
	20.10.1788	idem	Moved to 25 Noble Street	
TL, pellet between TP, pellet between	9.2.1795	Thomas Larance and Thomas Price	15 Hog Lane, Norton Folgate	2
TM	2.5.1776	*Thomas Moore	93 Bartholomew Close	2
	10.1.1783	idem	Moved to 6 Butcher Hall Lane	
TM	24.2.1789	Thomas Meek	4 Fleet Row, Eyer Street Hill, Cold Bath Fields	1
TN, script pellet between (two sizes)	15.10.1773	†Thomas Nash	2 Water Lane, Fleet Street	1
TN, pellet between	idem	idem	idem	double lobe
TN, pellet between	3.6.1776	idem	idem	1

* See IB.TM above and Section I, no. 1188.
† See Section I, nos. 2852, etc. and Section V, NASH.

BUCKLEMAKERS' MARKS 1773-1820

Mark	Entered	Name	Address/Notes	Punch
TN	1.6.1790	Thomas Nicson	32 Cock Lane, Smithfield	1
TN	24.7.1792	idem	Moved to 2 Prujean Square, Old Bailey	1
TN	27.10.1792	idem, as Nixon	142 Tottenham Court Road	1
	18.10.1798	idem	Moved to 3 Paul's Place, Walworth	
	no date	idem	Moved to Charterhouse Lane	
TP, pellet between	13.4.1775	Thomas Parfit	Red Lion Street, Clerkenwell	'woolsack'
TR	11.6.1776	*Thomas Read	Caley Court, Holborn	1
TR, pellet between	30.7.1789	idem	idem	1
idem	5.12.1789	idem	idem	1
TR	3.9.1778	Thomas Richardson	447 Strand	1
TR	2.2.1782	Thomas Reeves	13 Albemarle Street, Clerkenwell	1
(TS)	19.4.1773	†Thomas Simons	near Holywell Mount, Shoreditch	
TT, pellet between	3.5.1774	‡Thomas Taylor I	White Cross Street	1
TT	11.8.1775	idem	idem	2
TW, pellet between	12.8.1774	Thomas Wright	Jewin Court, Jewin Street	1
TW	27.4.1778	idem	idem	1
	no date	idem	Moved to 10 Great Turnstile, Holborn	
	17.2.1802	idem	Moved to 30 Little Bell Alley, Coleman Street	
TW, star above, pellet between	24.4.1776	§Thomas Wilson	Near the Lower Watergate, Deptford	2, with 'gabled' top
TW, pellet between	24.4.1776	idem	idem	2
TW, script (two sizes)	6.1.1780	‖Thomas Wallis II	54 Red Lion Street, Clerkenwell	2
idem (various sizes)	⎧26.10.1786⎫ ⎨16.7.1787⎬ ⎩26.6.1789⎭	idem	idem	2

---

* See Section I, nos. 2903, 2919.
† No mark recorded. Entry reads 'Note this is only an Extract of the Entry of his Mark in the former Mark Book'.
‡ See Section I, no. 2943.
§ See Section I, no. 2965 and Section V
‖ See Section I, no. 2963.

Mark	Entered	Name	Address/Notes	Punch
TW } SW }	1.10.1778	*Thomas and Samuel Wintle	2 Blue Coat Buildings, Butcher Hall Lane	2
	16.7.1779	idem	Moved to 118 Fleet Street	
WA	14.4.1781	†William Allen II	92 Strand	1
WA	19.8.1786	idem	idem	1
WB	26.6.1782	William Burr	Paul's Alley, 9 Red Cross Street	2
	3.9.1783	idem	Moved to Leather Lane, Holborn	
WB	11.4.1786	William Blood	12 Benjamin Street, St. Sepulchre's	1
	31.5.1788	idem	Moved to 7 Salmon and Ball Court, Bunhill Row	
	23.11.1790	idem	Moved to 44 Featherstone Street	
WB (two sizes)	8.7.1788	William Ballantine	1 St. Martin's Le Grand	3
WB	9.9.1789	idem	idem	2
WB	24.7.1788	‡William Bird	219 Temple Bar	2
WB, pellet between	7.6.1792	William Bowsey	180 Bishopsgate Street	2
WC	1.2.1776	§William Cox II	18 Newgate Street	2
WC	2.8.1779	idem	6 Elliots Court, Old Bailey	1
	26.2.1791	idem	Moved to Green Arbor Court, Old Bailey	
	23.3.1792	idem	Moved to 2 Garden Court near Sutton Street, Goswell Street	
WC	22.6.1793	idem	idem	1
WC	11.3.1777	‖William Clarke	Lamb Street, Spittle Square	1
	1.3.1781	idem	Moved to Horma Street, Islington	
WC (two sizes)	14.1.1779	¶William Crowder	2 Cox Court, Aldersgate Street	2
	24.5.1781	idem	Moved to 126 Bunhill Row	
WC, pellet between	13.8.1785	Walker Chandler	BRISTOL	1, serrated
WC	17.8.1785	idem	idem	2
WE	19.3.1781	**William Eaton	6 Albion Buildings, Aldersgate Street	2
WE	22.4.(?)	idem	3 Adle Street, Wood Street	2, incurved top and base

* See SW above and Section I, no. 2662.
† See Section I, no. 3006.   ‡ See Section I, no. 3021.
§ See Section I, no. 3053.   ‖ See WH.WC below.
¶ See Section I, no. 3065.   ** See Section I, nos. 3105–6.

BUCKLEMAKERS' MARKS 1773-1820

Mark	Entered	Name	Address/Notes	Punch
WE (two sizes)	8.5.1786 and 20.8.1801	idem	idem	2
WE	29.4.1785	*William Eley I	14 Clerkenwell Green	1
WE	12.3.1790	idem	idem	3, serrated
WE (three sizes)	5.5.1795	idem	idem	3, serrated
WF, pellet between and WF	7.7.1796	William Farmer	20 Hanover Street, Hanover Square	2 1
WG, pellet between	21.9.1778	†William Goslee	4 Cold Bath Row, Cold Bath Square	1
WG	19.5.1784	idem	idem	1
WH, pellet between	17.11.1781	‡William Harrison	38 Monkwell Street	2
WH	12.7.1782	William Harris	28 Little Windmill Street	1
WH, pellet between	23.8.1782	idem	idem	2
WH, pellet between	8.1.1793	William Halliday	31 New Street, Cloth Fair	2
WHB	22.5.1776	William Henry Bouteville	17 Charterhouse Street	2
W H / W C	22.8.1777	William How and William Clarke	Lamb Street, Spittle Square	cross form
WH} WC	28.8.1777	idem	idem	2
WI, pellet between	20.11.1775	William Ivin	10 Norman Street, St. Luke's	1
WJ	4.5.1789	William Judd	Near the turnpike Islington Road	outline to letters
WJ} JA	7.5.1788	William Judd and Joseph Askew	19 Islington Road	2, incurved sides
WL	10.7.1789	William Lycett	6 St. John Square, Clerkenwell	3
	11.6.1791	idem	Moved to 10 Silver Street	
WM (two sizes)	24.3.1778	William Mason	146 High Street, Borough	1
WM	25.4.1778	idem	idem	2
WP	5.9.1775	§William Pinder	57 Bunhill Row	2

* See Section I, nos. 3101 etc. † See TG above.
‡ See Section I, nos. 3158-9. § See Section I, no. 3258.

405

Mark	Entered	Name	Address/Notes	Punch
WR	23.2.1792	William Rabon	23 Lower Charles Street, Hatton Garden	1
WS	6.3.1781	William Sharp	3 Princes Street, Barbican	2
WS, pellet between	27.2.1783	idem	idem	2
WS (two sizes)	30.5.1786	idem	idem	2
WS ⎫ MS ⎭	9.1.1786	William and Michael Spiggins	18 White Row, Spitalfields	1
WT	10.6.1774	*William Taylor	9 Huggin Lane	2
WT	25.11.1790 27.2.1792	William Tyler idem	67 Bunhill Row Moved to 45 Seaward Street, Brick Lane	1
WW, pellet between	14.6.1785	William Wilson	London Street, Tottenham Court Road	1
WY	7.11.1780	William Yardley	5 Thorney Street Bloomsbury	1
WY	5.12.1782	idem	idem	1

* See Section I, no. 3340.

IX
Hiltmakers' Marks 1773–1823

All the marks are in relief, 'cameo' punches and Roman capitals. The punches have been categorized as follows: 1. rectangular; 2. rectangular with 'cut' corners; 3. oval. The rare exceptions to the above have been described.

Mark	Entered	Name	Address/Notes	Punch
EB, pellet between	11.2.1823	*Elizabeth Barnett	Cock Lane, West Smithfield	2
FT, pellet between	8.10.1783	†Francis Thurkle	15 New Street Square	2
FT, pellet between	8.12.1792	idem	idem	1
FT	1.1.1794	idem	idem	1
GF	8.4.1782	‡George Fayle	36 Aldermanbury	2
HF	10.6.1795	§Hannah Foster	Fetter Lane	1
IF	2.1.1779	James Fisher	7 Gun Powder Alley, Shoe Lane	oblong with inverted ends
IR, pellet between	7.9.1775	‖John Reynolds	36 Little Old Bailey	1
IT, pellet between	11.8.1783	John Taylor	98 Strand	1
	4.7.1785	idem	Moved to 31 Ironmonger Row, Old Street	
IY	19.10.1813	John Yardley	5 Thorney Street, Bloomsbury	1
JP, pellet between	18.12.1777	¶James Perry	10 Crown Court, Fleet Street	2
NF, pellet between	5.1.1776	Nicholas Flint	1 Clements Lane, near Temple Bar	1
NF	23.9.1778	idem	29 Greenhills Rents, Smithfield	1
NW, pellet between	17.12.1778	Nathaniel Wilby	Churchyard, Bloomsbury	double-lobed

* Presumably widow of Michael Barnett (Section I, no. 2001).
† See Abraham and George Thurkle, Section I, nos. 102 and 911.
‡ See also Section I, no. 797. § See John Foster II, Section I, nos. 1298–9.
‖ See also Section I, no. 1620. ¶ See also Section I, nos. 1582, 1837–8.

Mark	Entered	Name	Address/Notes	Punch
RR	26.8.1777	Richard Rawlings	2 Sparrows Rents, near Pearpoole Lane	1
SB, pellet between	6.5.1796	Samuel Brunn	7 Charing Cross	1
SO, pellet between	8.10.1779	Sarah Owen	12 Magpie Alley, Fetter Lane	2
idem (larger)	15.4.1782	idem	Moved to 2 Dolphin Court, Ludgate Hill	
TF, pellet between	22.2.1774	Thomas Foster	16 King's Head Court, Fetter Lane	1
TJ	26.1.1776	Thomas Jones	*10 Crown Court, Fleet Street	1
VR, pellet between	21.2.1792	Valentine Rawle	23 Great Suffolk Street, Charing Cross	3
WC	20.3.1779	William Crow	16 Cursitor Street, Chancery Lane	2, with indents
WK, pellet	17.5.1782	William Kinman	9 New Street Square	outline to letters
WR	20.1.1776	†William Rawle	Corner of Cassell Court, Strand	1

* See James Perry above. † See also Section I, no. 3279.

APPENDIX TO SECTION IX

Makers prior to 1773 listed in Section I and described as haft and hiltmaker, sword cutler, Free Cutler or Cutler. (PR) = so described in Parliamentary Report list 1773.

Name	Date	Description	Address/Notes	Marks
Barnett, Michael	1781–1820	hlm	36 Cock Lane, Smithfield	2001
Bass, Thomas	1708	*'Free Cutler'*	Dean Street, Fetter Lane	121, 2685
Bennett, John II	1761–73	hlm (PR)	Threadneedle Street	1139
Bock, Mark	1761–83	sword cutler	King's Head Court, Shoe Lane	1996–7
Brawne, Hugh	1710	*'Free Cutler'*	Fleet Street	219
Brent, Moses	1775–1800	hfm	Hind Court, Noble Street, Foster Lane and five other addresses	2000
Brockus, John	1760–73	hlm	Shoe Lane, Fleet Street	1138
Bruin, Henry	1726	sword cutler	New Street, Fetter Lane	947
Bukett, John	1760	sword cutler	St. James's Street, Westminster	1181
Bulley, Thomas	1707–24	*'Free Cutler'*	Shoe Lane (1707), Hayden Yard, Minories (1724)	244, 250, 2688
Carman, John I	1716–20	*'Free Cutler'*	New Street	260, 1190
Carman, John II	1748–56	Sword cutler	New Street (1748), Hatton Garden (1752)	1204, 1225
Carman, Mary	1764	hlm	Holborn	2007
Chapman, Richard	c. 1701–23	*'Cutler'*	Lombard Street (c. 1701), Adams Court, Broad Street (1723)	317, 2282
Corbett, Benjamin	1726	*'Free Cutler'*	Gutter Lane	137
Dealtry, Thomas	1765–99	hlm (PR)	Sweething Alley (1765–73), 85 Cornhill (1783–99)	2735
Deards, William	1726–61	*'Free Cutler'*	Fleet Street ('Goldsmith & Toyman')	3081
Drury, Dru I	1711–47	hfm	Noble Street (1711), Lad Lane (1717–47)	455, 497–8
Drury, Dru II	1767–77	hfm	Wood Street (1767), Strand (1777)	458
Francia, Anthony	1729 (?)	hfm	Wood Street	30
Harris, William	1717	*'Free Cutler'*	White Friars, near Back Gate of Temple	934
Harrison, George	1760	? gun-mount maker	'at Mr. Jones Gunsmith in Fenchurch Street'	815

409

APPENDIX TO SECTION IX

Name	Date	Description	Address/Notes	Marks
Hilman, John	c. 1731-3	sword cutler	Russell Street, Covent Garden	1363
Hosier, Elias	1754	'Free Cutler'	New Street, near Shoe Lane	1048
Kenton, John	1701	'Free Cutler'	Lombard Street	1871
Knight, William I	c. 1700	hlm	New Street, Shoe Lane	1877
Littleboy, George	1731	'Free Cutler'	Noble Street, near Coachmaker's Arms	843
Mansell, Samuel	1773	knifehaft maker	48 Strand (1773), Orange Court, Leicester Fields (1774)	2593
North, Benjamin	1783	hlm	St. Thomas, Southwark	196
North, Thomas	1724	'Free Cutler'	Dean Street, Fetter Lane	2850
Perry, James	1763-1777	hlm (PR and 1777)	Shoe Lane (1763), Holborn (1765), Chancery Lane (1773)	1582, 1837-8
Pont, John	1739-62	hfm and hlm	Maiden Lane	1574, 1578
Portal, William	1760-73	hfm (PR)	Orange Street	1458, 3256
Pritchard, Joseph	1825-31	presumed hfm	4 Swinton Place, Bagnage Road (1825), 28 Steward Street (later)	1595
Pritchard, Sarah	1831	knifehaft maker	28 Steward Street	2618
Rawle, William	1769-73	hlm (PR)	Castle Court, Strand	3279
Reason, John	1698	'Free Cutler'	Heart Street, Covent Garden	2305
Reason, Joseph	1697-1720	'Free Cutler'	Burleigh Street, Strand	1611, 2304
Reynolds, John	1768-75	hlm (PR)	New Street, Fetter Lane (1768-73), 36 Little Old Bailey (1775)	1620
Roberts, John	1716	'Free Cutler'	Threadneedle Street	2385
Roberts, Thomas	1703	'Free Cutler'	Bread Street	2391, 2898
Scrivener, Dor(ah)	1697	'Free Cutler'	White Alley, Chancery Lane	2486
Shaw, George	1720	sword cutler	The Flaming Sword, Fullwoods Rents, Holborn	891
Shelmerdine, Daniel	1697-1729	sword cutler	Exchange Alley, Cornhill (1697), Golden Dagger, New Street (1720), Noble Street, Foster Lane (1729)	499, 2523-4
Smith, Wildman	1781	hfm	32 Cheapside	3316
Springgall, Francis	1698	hlm	New Street	2605
Strange, William	1725	'Cutler'	New Street Square	3298

APPENDIX TO SECTION IX

Name	Date	Description	Address/Notes	Marks
Stuart, Isaac	1721	*'Cutler'*	New Street, Shoe Lane	1645
Thompson, Francis	1699–25	hlm (Draper's Company records)	Abchurch Lane	2776
Vicaridge, Thomas	c. 1720	*'Free Cutler'* and hlm	New Street	2982
Vincent, John	c. 1730	knifehandle maker	Angel Court, Snow Hill	1729
Wilkins, John	c. 1699	*'Free Cutler'*	Exchange Alley	3181
Willcocks, George	1715–20	*'Free Cutler'*	Wine Office Court, Fleet Street	919, 3189
Wilson, William	1726	*'Free Cutler'*	New Street	3359

X
Spectaclemakers' Marks 1794–1835

All the marks are in 'cameo' rectangular punches except the two incuse examples as stated.

Marks	Entered	Name	Address/Notes
FE CN, pellet between	31.1.1834	Frederick Edwards and Charles Norvell	8 Maidenhead Court, Aldersgate Street
FE incuse	1.7.1835	Frederick Edwards	2 Hackney Road
FE	1.6.1840	idem	idem
	8.1.1845	idem	Moved to 39 Hoxton Square, Shoreditch
IR	21.3.1816	Joseph Reffell	9 Brownlow Street, Drury Lane
	26.9.1818	idem	Moved to 22 Fleet Lane, Fleet Market
	25.2.1822	idem	Moved to 44 Little Sutton Street
IR incuse	13.10.1822	idem	Moved to 19 Great Arthur Street, St. Luke's
	no date	idem	Moved to 24 Eagle Court, St. John's Lane
TP ID	6.11.1794	Thomas Phelps and James Davenport	9 Cock Court, St. Martin's Le Grand

413

PART TWO

The Lives

I
Biographical Dictionary of Makers listed in Part One, Sections I and III

The following dictionary contains an entry for every London maker with a mark reproduced in Section I or with an attributed mark in Section III of Part One. Provincial makers registered in London follow separately under their towns.

All apprenticeships and freedoms refer to the Goldsmiths' Company unless otherwise stated. Similarly the phrase 'No record of apprenticeship or freedom' applies only to the Goldsmiths' Company. It is always possible in these cases (unfortunately many) that the maker may have been free of another company not referred to in the entry of his mark, although it seems probable that in the latter part of the eighteenth century and thereafter many smallworkers particularly were allowed to work without having acquired freedom.

In giving the extracts from the Goldsmiths' Company apprentice register (nearly always at the beginning of the biographies), I have condensed the usual wordy form of the entry but in general retained the capital letters and lack of punctuation to convey the feeling of the old wording—except where doing so might have caused confusion.

The following abbreviations are used:

Arch. Journ.: Archaeological Journal
Chaffers: W. Chaffers, *Gilda Aurifabrorum*, new edition, 1899
Evans: Joan Evans, 'Huguenot Goldsmiths', *Huguenot Society Proceedings*, Vol. 14
Heal: Sir Ambrose Heal, *The London Goldsmiths 1200–1800*, 1935
Heal Add.: Unpublished addenda to the above made available to me by the author shortly before his death
Hug. Soc. Proc.: Huguenot Society Proceedings
Hug. Soc. Pub.: Huguenot Society Publication
Jackson: Sir C. J. Jackson, *English Goldsmiths and their Marks*, second edition, 1921
Parl. Report list 1773: The list of London working goldsmiths printed in the Report of the Parliamentary Committee

Note to third edition. As in the second edition, an asterisk before a name indicates that there is further information in the Addenda, pages 733ff.

HORS CONCOURS

ANDREWS, Phineas. Entered as a smallworker with mark, 26 September 1789, at 15 Brunswick Street, Blackfriars. The entry deleted and the following below: 'Memorandum the 3rd of March 1790. The name of Phineas Andrews was thus erased from this book by order of a Court of Wardens of the Goldsmiths Company, he being a Clerk to an informing Attorney (Sawbridge Alias Robinson) and not a Workman. No work brought by Phineas Andrews is to be taken in.'

A

AARON, Isaac (1102) No record of apprenticeship or freedom. Only mark as smallworker entered 21 March 1791. Address: Sparks Court, Dukes Place.

ABBOTT, John (7) Son of William Abbott Citizen and Wheelwright of London deceased, apprenticed to Robert Timbrell 15 March 1698. Free, 28 April 1705. Livery, April 1705. Only mark entered as largeworker, 5 July 1706. Address: Birchin Lane, where Heal records him till 1720.

*ABDY, William I (3001-3, 3860-1) Parentage undiscovered. Free by redemption, 2 May 1752. Livery, 1763. First mark entered as smallworker, 24 June 1763. Address: Noble Street, where Heal records him as haft and hiltmaker and goldsmith. Moved to (5) Oat Lane, 26 February 1765. Second and third marks, 5 October 1767. Fourth and fifth marks, 10 May 1769 (the latter incuse, sometimes found on small mounts such as wine-coaster parts). Appears as haftmaker, Oat Lane, Noble Street, in Parl. Report list 1773. Sixth mark (two sizes), 15 October 1779. Address: 5 Oat Lane. Seventh mark as plateworker (two sizes), 1 September 1784. His son Thomas apprenticed to him 6 August 1777. Died 6 September 1790, in Oat Lane. *European Magazine* and *The Gentleman's Magazine*.

ABDY, William II (3004, 3862) Son of William Abdy I. Free by patrimony, 4 April 1781, when described as goldsmith. Livery, February 1791. First mark entered 15 September 1790, shortly after his father's death. Second mark (two sizes), 16 October 1790. Moved to 11 Wilson Street, Finsbury, 3 February 1821. Resigned from Livery 1823, by which date retirement from trade may be assumed.

*ABERCROMBY, Robert (6a, 2254, 2258, 2260) No record of apprenticeship or freedom. First mark entered as largeworker, in partnership with George Hindmarsh, 11 May 1731. Address: Christopher's Court, St. Martin's Le Grand. Second mark alone, 5 October 1731. Address: New Rents, St. Martin's Le Grand. Third mark, 23 June 1739, same address. Fourth mark (New Standard), 29 April 1740. Appears to have specialized in salver making.

ABRAHAM, Joseph (1103) No record of apprenticeship or freedom. Mark entered as smallworker, 19 April 1796. Address: New Court, Leadenhall Street.

ACKLAM, Jn. P. (1601) No record of apprenticeship or freedom. Mark entered as plateworker, 25 September 1832. Address: 133·Strand. Second mark, 22 June 1837.

*ADAM, Charles (25) Son of Christopher Adam of Ranmash in the County of York clerk, apprenticed to Francis Archbold 12 September 1682. Free, 11 March 1689. Only mark entered as largeworker, 1 February 1703. Address: Foster Lane. The entry is annotated 'Left off' without a date, which suggests that he retired rather than died in business. Signatory as 'working goldsmith' to the petition complaining of the competition of 'necessitous strangers', December 1711. Appears from the occurrence of his mark to have specialized in caster making. Thomas Bamford (q.v.), also a castermaker, was apprenticed to him in 1703. See also Christopher Canner, another apprentice of Archbold and a specialist castermaker.

ADAMS, Elizabeth (336) No record of apprenticeship or freedom. Mark entered as plateworker in partnership with Charles Hastings Rich, 13 June 1823. Address: St. Ann's Lane.

*ADAMS, Stephen I (2472, 3203) Parentage undiscovered. Smallworker. First mark entered as partner with William Jury (q.v.), undated c. 1758, followed by another mark for both, 29 October 1759. Adams' first mark alone, 8 October 1760. Address: Lillypot Lane. Second mark (two sizes), 23 February 1762. Third mark, 11 January 1764. Address: St. Ann's Lane. Subsequent similar marks: 4 April 1765, 15 May 1766, 18 June 1767 and 15 August 1769. Appears as bucklemaker, St. Ann's Lane in Parl. Report list 1773, and his first mark as such entered 5 February 1774, with others, to 1787 (Section VIII). Adams is described as Citizen and Lorimer of London in the apprenticeship entry of his son (see below). (The records of the Lorimers' Company were destroyed in 1940-1.) From the occurrence of his mark and the turning over of Francis Higgins from John Manby, spoonmaker, to him in 1783, it

419

is clear that he was principally a spoon-maker. Heal records him at Lillypot Lane. 1760; and at St. Ann's Lane, 1784-99, with name of firm as Stephen Adams and Son from 1790-6. (Heal also records 'Stephen Abdy and William Jury' and 'Stephen Abdy and Son', both at the above addresses which must stem from old directory errors.) He seems to have retired about 1790, when his son entered his first mark as buckle-maker, and was probably dead by 5 February 1802, when the latter no longer styled himself 'Junior' in signing mark entries.

ADAMS, Stephen II (2473) Son of Stephen Adams (above) Citizen and Lorimer of London, apprenticed to Joseph Walton of Little Britain Citizen and Goldsmith, oilman 10 October 1777. Almost certainly an apprenticeship of convenience to acquire freedom of the Goldsmiths' Company which his father did not enjoy (See above.) Free, 6 October 1784. Livery, February 1791. Entered first mark as bucklemaker, 24 May 1792, and others to 1807 (Section VIII). First mark as plateworker, 14 November 1813. Address: 3 St. Ann's Lane. Second mark (small), 2 May 1815. Moved to 5 Wingrove Place, Clerkenwell, 13 March 1824. Moved to 70 Chapel Street, Islington, 21 January 1825. Died 15 July 1840.

ADCOCK, Thomas (2679) No record of apprenticeship or freedom. Only mark entered as smallworker, 30 May 1772. Address: Church Lane, near St. Martin's Church. Appears without category, Church Lane, St. Martin's, Strand, Parl. Report list 1773.

ADRIAN, Richard (2253) Son of Richard Adrian of Little Britain jeweller, apprenticed to Matthew Cuthbert 12 January 1716 on payment of £6. Turned over 6 April 1719 to William Overton in Ball Alley, Lombard Street, Goldsmith. Free, 7 March 1722. Mark entered as buckle and spurmaker, 31 October 1723. Address: Brick Lane, Old Street.

ALBRIGHT, John (53, 1094) Son of William Albright Citizen and Skinner of London deceased, apprenticed to William Twell 7 March 1711 on payment of £10 and later turned over to Thomas Killing Clothworker. Free, 3 April 1718. First mark entered, as smallworker 10 April 1718. Second (Sterling) mark, 6 July 1720. No address given. From surviving occurrence of marks appears to have specialized in the making of punch-ladles and strainers.

ALCHORNE, Charles (263) Son of Charles Alchorne of Little Laver in the County of Essex clerke, apprenticed to Samuel Welder 7 September 1721 on payment of £26.5s. Free, 3 September 1729. Livery, July 1731. Only mark entered as large-worker, 9 October 1729. 'Of ye Goldsmiths Company att the 3 Candlesticks in Forster Lane.' Heal shows him at this address until 1734. The baptism of five and the burial of four children of Charles Alchorne and his wife Martha are recorded in the registers of St. Michael le Quern between 1730 and 1744, the name variously spelt Alchorne, Alcorne and Alhorne.

ALCOCK, John (1110) Son of Thomas Alcock of St. Saviours' Southwark seedman, apprenticed to Daniel Skinner 12 September 1717 on payment of £20. Free, 1 October 1724. Mark entered as smallworker, 22 July 1725. Address: Wood Street. Livery, 1731. Presumably the Mr Alcock Goldsmith at ye Cup & Ring at Cripplegate' with whom Philip Shaw (q.v.) was living in 1730.

*ALDERHEAD, John (1098) Parentage undiscovered. Free by redemption, 7 October 1742. Only mark entered as largeworker, 23 April 1750. Address: Bishopsgate Street, where Heal records him as working goldsmith, at the Ring and Pearl near South Sea House, until 1766 and as goldsmith, jeweller and watchmaker at the same sign, 114 Bishopsgate Street, from 1768 to 1794. Appears as goldsmith, Bishopsgate Street, in Parl. Report list 1773. John Alderhead, goldsmith, also occurs at Bethnal Green, 1792. Livery, March 1758. Died between 1795 and 1801.

ALDOUS, J. and J. (3704) These names, which occur in Jackson against the particular mark, are not otherwise known and are unrecorded in apprenticeships or freedoms. There would appear possibly to be some confusion with the mark of Joseph and John Angell (q.v.).

ALDRIDGE, Charles (264-5) Son of Charles Aldridge of the parish of Slimbridge in the County of Gloucester staymaker, apprenticed to Edward Aldridge Citizen and Goldsmith (probably his uncle q.v.) 5 July 1758 and turned over the same day to Edward Aldridge Citizen and Clothworker. (Presumably a correction of the Clerk's mistake since Edward Aldridge appears as Clothworker in his entry of 1739.) In spite of

BIOGRAPHICAL DICTIONARY

which Charles is recorded Free of the Goldsmiths, 5 February 1766. First mark entered as plateworker in partnership with Henry Green, 19 August 1775. Address: 62 St. Martin's Le Grand. Second mark alone, 20 September 1786. Third small mark, 25 September 1789. There is no record of Charles Aldridge in the index of freemen of the Clothworkers' Company, but the Girdlers' Company list of freemen shows Charles Aldridge, free by redemption, 23 June 1772, followed immediately on the same day by Henry Green, which suggests that both partners acquired freedom of this company to enable them to set up business. Heal in fact records Aldridge as plateworker, Aldersgate Street, from 1772; and Green from 1773, before the entry of their mark; and the two together in the latter year (Parl. Report list 1773 without category) till 1777; and at 62 St. Martin's Le Grand, 1775-84. Aldridge alone appears at Aldersgate Street till 1786 and as goldsmith, Falcon Street, Aldersgate Street, 1790-3. Charles Aldridge and Elizabeth Andrews, goldsmiths, Cornhill, are also recorded as dissolving partnership in 1793.

*ALDRIDGE, Edward I (526-8, 3528-35, 3562) Parentage undiscovered. First mark as smallworker, 5 February 1724. Address: St. Lenrd (Leonards) Court, Foster Lane. Second mark as largeworker, then described as Clothworker, 29 June 1739. Address: In Lilley Pot Lane. Moved to Foster Lane, 20 April 1743. Third mark as partner with John Stamper, 20 July 1753, no address. Married, 19 October 1723 at Christchurch, Newgate, to Elizabeth Parker, both of St. Leonard, Foster Lane. Two daughters baptized at Christchurch, 1724 and 1725, a third at St. Vedast, 1733, and son John at same, 7 September 1737. In 1742 Aldridge was tried at the instigation of the Goldsmiths' Company for counterfeiting marks but acquitted by the jury 'Contrary to the opinion of the Court' (Minutes, 5 August 1742). Heal records him at the Golden Ewer, Lillypot Lane, 1739-43; and at the same sign Foster Lane, 1743 until after 1762; as London, 1763-5; also as in partnership with Stamper, 1753-7. It seems probable that he was dead by 1766-7 if, from the lozenge punch, we accept mark 3530 as that of his widow. Although described as Clothworker in his second entry of 1739 there is no record of his name in the index of freemen of that Company, but William Plummer (q.v.) was apprenticed to him as a Clothworker 4 February 1746/?7, when Aldridge is described as of Green Street, Leicester Fields, Goldsmith.

*ALDRIDGE, Edward II (3535, 3562) Son of Charles Aldridge of Slimbridge in the County of Gloucester staymaker (and brother of Charles, (q.v.), apprenticed to Starling Wilford 8 March 1751 and turned over to Edward Aldridge Clothworker (probably his uncle) the same day. Free, 5 April 1758. Livery, July 1763. Heal records Edward Aldridge Senior and Junior at the Golden Ewer, Foster Lane in 1762 as then dissolving partnership and the latter moving to George Street, St. Martin's Le Grand. He appears there, without category, in Parl. Report list 1773. Apparently shortly after this date Aldridge was in partnership with John Henry Vere (q.v.) although there is no entry in the register for either mark nor any in Heal for the latter partnership. In 1781 he is noted in Bishopsgate. Died between 1802 and 1811.

ALDRIDGE, James (1768) Son of James Aldridge of Plaistow in the County of Essex wheeler, apprenticed to Charles Aldridge of Aldersgate Street, Citizen and Goldsmith 8 April 1778. Free, 4 May 1785. Mark entered as smallworker, 22 February 1798. Address: 20 Strand. Moved to 10 Lancaster Court, Strand, 6 November 1800. Later (no date) to 11 Northumberland Street, Strand.

ALEXANDER, William (3000, 3860) Son of Richard Alexander of the parish of St. Peter (Marlborough?) Wilts maltster, apprenticed to Isabella Archer 1707 and free of the Tallow Chandlers' Company 1716 as a fine worker in brass of London Wall near Lorimers Hall. Master of the Tallow Chandlers 1747. Will proved 4 October 1762. Appears as William Alexander & Co Wood Street 1738-1758 and as Alexander & Shrimpton 1759 (Information of Robert Sherlock, author of 'London-made Chandeliers 1730-1830', *The Connoisseur*, June 1973). Mark entered as largeworker 15 March 1743. Address: Anchor and Key against St. Alban's Church in Wood Street. Probably the most important chandelier maker of the mid-eighteenth century. Apart from the remarkable Knesworth chandelier of 1752 of the Fishmongers' Company his work in silver is virtually unknown. However the interval between the entry of his mark and the date of the Knesworth chandelier suggests he may have received earlier commissions for silver examples which have not survived. In any case, he was acting as entrepreneur in the business since it is known from the Fishmongers' Company's account book of 1752-4 that the chandelier was made by William Gould (q.v.) and Alexander and one Joseph Dyer (not known as a goldsmith) returned the sum of £484.1s.3d. for frauds discovered to have been made by Gould.

ALLDRIDGE, William (3005) Son of Thomas Alldridge of Winslow in the County of Buckingham draper deceased, apprenticed to John Luff 3 September 1738 on payment of £31.10s. Free, 3 June 1748. Mark entered as smallworker, 12 February 1768. Address: Brook Street. Moved to Red Lion Passage, Holborn, 14 March 1776, where Heal records him as goldsmith at the Blackmoor's Head, from 1770-3 (with alternative spelling Allderidge), and at the same sign Fetter Lane in 1751. He appears as haftmaker, Red Lion Passage, Holborn, in the Parl. Report list 1773.

*ALLEINE, Jonathan (1109, 3703) Son of Jonathan Alleine of Andover in the County of Hants clerk, apprenticed to Richard Hussey 26 July 1739 on payment of £20. Free, 7 March 1749. Mark presumably entered in missing volume 1758-73, probably about 1771. Heal records him at Fenchurch Street, 1772-8, where he appears without category in Parl. Report list 1773. The mark 3703 seems of doubtful attribution. Mark found for the most part on candlesticks.

ALLEN, James (1108) No record of apprenticeship or freedom. Only mark entered as smallworker, 15 December 1766. Address: 'near the penny post office in Chichester rents, Chancery Lane', where Heal records him till 1771. He appears as bucklemaker at the same address in Parl. Report list 1773.

*ALLEN, John I (1096) No record of apprenticeship or freedom. Only mark entered as smallworker, 1 May 1733. Address: 'Wood Street over agane the Compter'. Heal records him as goldsmith, Bull Head Court, Wood Street, bankrupt, 1743.

ALLEN, John II (1097) Described in entry as Citizen and Founder. May therefore be either (1) son of Josiah Allen of Kingsbury in the County of Warwick farmer deceased, apprenticed to Robert Newman of the Founders' Company 2 January 1716. Free, 6 May 1723. Or (2) son of John Allen of the parish of St. Giles in the County of Middlesex Founder, apprenticed to Mary Allen of the Founders' Company 5 March 1716. Free, 5 August 1723. Only mark entered as smallworker, 19 November 1736. Address: Cock Lane, near Snowhill.

*ALLEN, John III (1100) Probably son of John Allen, apprenticed to John Bishop 1753 and turned over the same day to his father a Glover. Freedom date unknown. First mark entered as smallworker, 10 June 1761. Address: Carthusian Street, Charterhouse Square. Second mark, incuse, 17 November (?1761). Heal records him as watchcasemaker and plateworker, Carthusian Street, 1761-72 where he appears as watchcasemaker in the Parl. Report list 1773. He is presumably the father of John and William, described as watchcasemakers on receiving freedom by patrimony, 1781 and 1788. There is also a John Allen, son of John, apprenticed to his father as watchcasemaker in 1773 (See Section V, IA).

ALLEN, John IV (1111) Perhaps the John Allen, free by patrimony 1781, as watchcasemaker, son of John Allen (see above). Only mark entered as smallworker, in partnership with Joshua Butler, 16 March 1802. Address: 10 Bridgwater Gardens. Signs with X.

ALLEN, Joseph (1112-13) No record of apprenticeship or freedom. First mark entered as largeworker in partnership with Mordecai Fox, 9 March 1730. Address: St. Swithin's Lane, near Lombard Street. (The name of Mordecai Fox left blank in this entry.) Second mark, 21 August 1739, entered as 'Joseph Allen at the Sun in St. Swithin's Lane' and annotated at base 'Joseph Allen and Mordecai Fox in Comp'. Heal records them at this address till 1743.

*ALLEN, Thomas (50-2) Son of Thomas Allen of Kneighton (?) in the County of Leicester yeoman deceased, apprenticed to John King 30 September 1668. Free, 6 October 1675, and presumably working soon after. Described as Citizen and Goldsmith, bachelor about twenty-five, on his marriage to Mary Lincolne of Satterley, County of Suffolk, spinster about twenty-two, at St. Andrew, Holborn, with her father's consent, 3 March 1678/9 (Chester, *Registrar of Vicar General of Canterbury. London Marriage Licences*, 1887). Married secondly, 13 September 1688, at St. Dionis

Nov.d 29. Memorand that I George Boothby Son of Wm Boothby of Potter Marston in the County of Leicester Esq.r (He: being paid) to my Master Thirty & Five pounds doe put myself Apprentice to Matth:d Cooper Citizen & Goldsmith of London for his terms of Seven years from this day   George Boothby

Decemb.r 2. Memorand that I George Wicks Son of James Wicks late of St Edmonds bury in the County of Suffolk Upholsterer deced (there being paid to my Master Thirty pounds) doe put myself Apprentice to Samuell Wastell Citizen & Goldsmith of London for his terme of Seven years from this day   George Wicks

Above: Apprenticeship entries of George Boothby and George Wicks 1712.
Overleaf: *Top*, Apprenticeship entry of Thomas Chawner 1754. *Bottom*, Apprenticeship entry of Anthony Nelme 1672.

Memorandum that I Tho: Chaunor son of John Chaunor of the Parish of Church Broughton in the County of Derby yont do put myself Apprentice to Monsr Cohen Citizen & Goldsmith of London for the term of Seven Years from this Day. He being fit to my sd Master thirty pounds

Thomas Chaunor

The first of Novem[bre]
1658

Memorandum that Antony Nelms the son of John Nelms of the parish of Whitinaster in the County of Glouster Yeoman doe put my selfe Apprentice unto Richard Pitison and Goldsmith of London for the terme of Seaven years next from Christmas next comming.

Elizabeth Johnson

In the Præsence

Anthony Nelms

Top: Entry of Hester Bateman's first mark 1761.
Bottom: The entry of John Harvey's mark showing annotations for three changes of address.

Typical entries of Largeworkers marks 1739.

Backchurch, Mary Wilford of Enfield, County of Middlesex, when he is described as of St. Vedast, alias Foster, London. Isaac Davenport apprenticed to him 11 January 1689. Three daughters baptized at St. Vedast, 1689, 1693 and 1694, twin sons Richard and Edward 1697, and daughter 1700, when he is described as silversmith in Gutter Lane in this parish. Another son Thomas, who may have been of his first marriage was apprenticed to him, 24 June 1700. Three marks entered as largeworker, undated, probably in April 1697 on commencement of the register, with address Gutter Lane against the first, and Maidenhead Court in Aldersgate Street against the second. Heal records only the first address. His son Thomas, who has no registered mark, may perhaps be the —Allen, Subordinate Goldsmith to the King, 1723–45 (Major General H. W. D. Sitwell, 'The Jewel House and the Royal Goldsmiths', *Arch. Jour.*, CXVII, pages 154–5), but this remains uncertain. Thomas Allen, silversmith of Gutter Lane, is recorded as father of Charles aged eight admitted to St. Paul's School, 28 April 1757 (*Register of St. Paul's School*).

*ALLEN, William I (2997–8) Described in entry as Free Glover. Probably therefore the William Allen appearing in the list of orphan apprentices of the Glovers' Company dated June 1709 to June 1712. First mark entered as smallworker, 26 October 1724. Address: 'Aldersgate Street in ... Court', subsequently erased and 'Removed to Little Briton' added below. Second mark, 22 August 1728. Address: 'in Mold Maker Row in Saint Martins Lee Grand' erased and 'Removed to Little Briton' substituted.

ALLEN, William II (3006) Possibly son of William Allen, apprenticed to John Bingley 1761. Free, 3 August 1768. Only mark entered as smallworker, 19 May 1769. Address: Little Bartholomew's Close. Appears as bucklemaker at the same address in the Parl. Report list 1773, and entered two marks as such, 1781 and 1786, at 92 Strand (Section VIII).

ALLEN, William III (3007) Perhaps son of John Allen, free by patrimony 1 October 1788, described as watchcasemaker. Only mark entered as smallworker, 10 August 1798. Address: 35 Noble Street. Signs entry with X.

ALSEPT, Henry (946) No record of apprenticeship or freedom. Only mark entered 14 February 1820. Address: 13 Fullwoods Rents, Holborn. Moved, 2 July 1821, to 14 Kingsgate Street, Holborn, and 2 September 1829 to 69 Red Lion Street.

ANDREWS, Ann (3–5) Wife or widow of John Andrews I (q.v.). First mark entered as smallworker, 26 March 1759. Address: Brick Lane. Second mark, 27 June 1760. Third, 16 June 1761. The first two entries made below that of her husband.

ANDREWS, George (744) Perhaps son of John Andrews Citizen and Goldsmith, apprenticed to his father 2 August 1758. Freedom unrecorded. Only mark entered as smallworker, 13 April 1763. Address: Red Lion Street. Heal records him there as plateworker till 1773 (when he appears without category, at the same address, in Parl. Report list); also the same name as goldsmith, formerly of Moorfields, bankrupt, in Whitecross Street, 1769.

ANDREWS, John I (1099) Son of George Andrews of Colesbatch in the County of Leicestershire grazier deceased, apprenticed to George Andrews 5 June 1740 and turned over to Elizabeth his widow. Free, 6 September 1751. Mark entered as smallworker, 9 August 1758. Address: Brick Lane, Old Street. Probably dead by 26 March 1759, when his wife or widow Ann entered her first mark below his.

ANDREWS, John II (1770) Perhaps the son of John Andrews, free by patrimony 7 October 1800. Only mark entered as smallworker, 19 October 1818. Address: 18 Pall Mall.

*ANDREWS, Richard (2257) No record of apprenticeship or freedom. Only mark entered as smallworker, 19 July 1773. Address: 124 Edenhall Street (for Leadenhall Street), where Heal records him for this year only. He appears as goldworker, Leadenhall Street, in the Parl. Report list for the same year.

ANDREWS, Robert (2255) Son of William Andrews of St. Botolph without Bishopsgate Founder, apprenticed to John Holland 3 October 1738 on payment of £25. Free, 11 December 1745. Only mark entered as spoonmaker, 8 November 1745. Address: Gutter Lane.

ANDREWS, William (66) Either (1) the son of William Andrews Citizen and Vintner of London, apprenticed to Daniel Goddard 22 January 1664. Free, 2 August 1672.

423

Livery, April 1705. Or (2) the son of Toby Andrews late of Blackford in the County of Somerset gentleman, apprenticed to John East 27 May 1668. Mark entered as largeworker, undated, probably in April 1697 on commencement of the register. Address: Mugwell Street, where Heal records him till 1707. It may perhaps have been his son of the same name who was signatory as journeyman to the petition against assaying the work of foreigners not having served seven years apprenticeship, February 1716.

*ANGEL[L], John Charles (1772) Son of John Angel of Compton Street Clerkenwell silversmith, apprenticed to his father 5 October 1825. Free, 7 November 1832. Mark entered as plateworker in partnership with Joseph Angel his uncle, 31 January 1831. Address: 55 Compton Street, Clerkenwell. See below for the family interconnections.

*ANGEL[L], Joseph (1769, 1772) Son of Joseph Angel of Cow Cross London weaver, apprenticed to Henry Nutting of Noble Street Goldsmith 5 October 1796. Free, 3 October 1804. First mark entered as plateworker, 7 October 1811. Address: 55 Compton Street, Clerkenwell. Second mark, 8 April 1824. Third in partnership with nephew John Angel, 31 January 1831. Livery, February 1925. Died about 1851–3.

Joseph's brother John, described as son of Joseph of Battle Bridge in the County of Middlesex weaver, was apprenticed to William Elliott of Warwick Lane goldsmith in 1799 but does not appear to have entered a mark, although from his son's apprenticeship it is clear he was working with his brother in Compton Street in 1825. A third brother Abraham was apprenticed to Joseph in 1808. In 1825 Joseph's son Charles was apprenticed to his uncle John.

*ANNESLEY, Arthur (6) No record of apprenticeship or freedom. Only mark entered as largeworker, 23 March 1758. Address: Heathcock Court, Strand. Moved to Thatched House Alley, Strand, 19 April 1758. Recorded as goldsmith, Newcastle Court, bankrupt (*The Gentleman's Magazine*, April 1762). Heal records him as plateworker, Heathcock Street (? Court), for the same four years.

APPLETON, Nathaniel (97) Son of George Appleton of the parish of St. Giles without Cripplegate Cordwainer, apprenticed to James Waters 2 August 1751. Free, 7 March 1759. Mark entered as smallworker in partnership with Anne Smith, 26 July 1771. Address: Aldersgate Green. They appear as smallworkers, Cox's Court, Aldersgate Street, in the Parl. Report list 1773. Their mark is found chiefly on creamjugs and salt-cellars of a somewhat pedestrian nature.

ARCHAMBO, Peter I (85, 2127–8) Son of Peter Archambo of the parish of St. Martin's in the Field in the County of Middlesex staymaker, apprenticed to Jacob Margas Citizen and Butcher 6 April 1710. Free, 7 December 1720. First mark (New Standard) as largeworker, entered 9 March 1721, 'free of Butchers Company'. Address: the Golden Cup in Green Street. Second mark (Sterling), 2 November 1722, presumably at the same address, with note below: 'Removed to Hemings Row', but no date given. Third mark, 27 June 1739. Address: Golden Cup, Coventry Street, Piccadilly. According to Evans, ('Huguenot Goldsmiths', *Hug. Soc. Proc.*, 14) the family of Archambaud came from Oleron and Re and first appeared in England in the Bounty List of 1687, but there is also a Pierre Archambaut recorded in the Temoignages of the Threadneedle Street French Church, under the date 25 July 1680, as from Saumur, and this is perhaps the father of the goldsmith. He appears as 'tailleur d'habits' in the baptismal register of his daughter Anne, at Hungerford Market Church, 16 June 1695, where his wife is named Esther, and as 'tailleur', 10 December 1699, at the baptism of his son Jean. The goldsmith's baptism does not appear to have taken place in the same church. He was probably married in 1722–3 to Elizabeth Trube, to whom his son Peter II was born on 15 October 1724. In his will, dated 20 May 1759, he is described as of the parish of Twickenham, Middlesex, gentleman, implying retirement before this date, probably in 1750, when Peter II entered his mark at the Coventry Street address. The will was proved 7 August 1767 by Peter II, who is named with John Archambo, brother of Peter I, and Peter Meure his nephew as executors and trustees. He leaves £400 each to his three daughters, Ann, Elizabeth and Esther, the same sum to his sister Margaret Archambo and after her death back to the three daughters, and the same sum to his granddaughter Elizabeth Greenhow, daughter of another daughter Margaret, deceased. A codicil is added, 12 January 1776, and the will proved 7 August 1767 by Peter II, with power reserved for John Archambo and Peter Meure, and a second probate is granted 5 February 1768 to Peter Meure (P.C.C. Public Record Office, folio 294, Legard. Information Mervyn Medlycott Esq.). Although not in the same flight as Lamerie or Crespin, Archambo's work is of considerable importance in its period. He seems to have had a wide range of output of all the standard types of production. His most important patron was almost certainly George Booth, 2nd Earl of Warrington, for whom Archambo worked extensively, as witnessed by the contents of the Foley Grey sale of 1921 at Christie's which included the remarkable wine-urn with transposed marks of 1728 (Goldsmiths' Company), a wine-cistern of 1729 and six unusual sconces of 1730 as well as much dinner plate, salvers, sauce-boats and baskets.

ARCHAMBO, Peter II (2129) Son of the above, born 15 October and baptized 21 October 1724 at Hungerford Market Church, his godparents being his grandfather of the same name and Magdelane Trube his grandmother. Apprenticed to Paul De Lamerie 5 December 1738 without premium and turned over the same day to his father. Free, 3 February 1747. Mark entered as partner with his cousin Peter Meure (q.v.) as largeworkers, 18 January 1750, at same address as Peter I, Golden Cup, Coventry Street. Died 1768, probably before 5 February when second probate was granted to his father's will (see above). The mark of the two partners is found mainly on dinner plate of standard type.

ARCHBOLD, Andrew (83) Son of John Archbold Citizen and Goldsmith, apprenticed to his father 30 November 1693. Free, 10 March 1700. Only mark entered as smallworker, 31 March 1701. Address: Noble Street.

ARCHBOLD, Francis (82) Son of Edward Archbold of Kingsdowne Kent clerk, apprenticed to Jacob Harris for seven years 31 May 1671. Free, 18 July 1678. Probably working in his own right thereafter. Mark entered undated, probably April 1697 on commencement of register, as largeworker. Address: Foster Lane, where Heal records him till 1702 and as of London, 1724. Judeth, daughter by Judeth his wife, born 31 August, baptized 27 September and buried 7 October 1687 at St. Michael le Quern. Mrs Jone Archbold, widow 'out of Mr Frances Archbolds' (?mother or sister-in-law), buried 7 February 1692, and his wife Judeth 23 May 1700, when he is described as goldsmith at the signe of the Golden Cupp in Foster Lane. It is interesting to find one of the same name in the Parl. Report list 1773 working at Hanover Court, Grub Street, perhaps a great grandson.

ARCHER, Andrew (1, 84) Son of Andrew Archer of Arlington in the County of Gloucester tailor(?), apprenticed to Dorothy Grant (q.v.) widow of William Grant 6 July 1687 for eight years. Free, 9 February 1699. First mark entered as largeworker, 27 October 1703. Address: Fleet Street. Signatory as 'working goldsmith' to the petition complaining of the competition of 'necessitous strangers', December 1711. Livery, October 1712. Second mark, 11 August 1720. Address: Brides Lane, where Heal records him at the Rod and Crown from 1710 till death in 1725.

ARCHER, Charles (262) Son of Joseph Archer of Pla(i)stow in the County of Essex, apprenticed to John Johnson Citizen and Skinner 6 October 1713. Freedom unrecorded. Mark entered as smallworker, 9 September 1726. Address: Bromley by Bow. 'Free Skinner'.

ARDEN, Thomas (2680) No record of apprenticeship or freedom. Only mark entered as plateworker, 15 June 1805. Address: 1 Wenlock Street.

ARDESOIF, Stephen (2470-1) No record of apprenticeship or freedom. Two marks entered as largeworker, 14 September 1756. Address: Fountain Court, Strand, where Heal records him from 1755-1773, as goldsmith and jeweller, and where he is listed as goldworker in the Parl. Report list 1773. Of Huguenot origin, the family having arrived in London in 1687 when Charles Ardesoif and his children Peter and John are recorded as being denizened. Peter Ardesoif de Caen appears in the Bounty Lists for 1699-1709 and Renée A. d'Alençon in 1709. Phillipe François Ardesoif appears as Maitre Orfèvre in Paris in 1781. (Evans, 'Huguenot Goldsmiths', *Hug. Soc. Proc.*, 14).

ARNETT, Hugh (81, 993) Son of Hugh Arnett of Buckingham in the County of Buckingham grocer, apprenticed to Isaac Davenport 7 October 1701. Free, 8 February 1711. Signatory as journeyman to the petition against assaying the work of foreigners not having served seven years apprenticeship, February 1716. Marks entered as largeworker in partnership with Edward Pocock, New Standard 15 February 1720, Sterling 22 June 1720. No address in entry. Heal records him as plateworker, Foster Lane, 1719 and with his partner as goldsmiths, 1719-24. In 1723 their address appeared as Blackmoor's Head, Foster Lane (Heal Add.).

ARNOLD, Thomas (2678, 2682) Son of Edward Arnold late of the parish of St. Botolph without Aldgate London gentleman deceased, apprenticed to Thomas Thorne 6 October 1756. Free, 7 December 1763. First mark entered as smallworker, 19 May 1770. Address: London Wall. Second mark (small and probably for goldwork), 26 July 1771. Appears as smallworker, 89 London Wall, in Parl. Report list 1773. Third mark, 6 April 1775. Fourth mark, 23 April 1776. Address: 21 Aldersgate Street. Heal records him from 1770-2 only.

ARTHUR, James (1771) Son of Richard Arthur of Michelham in Surrey gardiner (sic), apprenticed to William Frisbee of Bridewell Hospital working goldsmith 1 March 1809 'by or at the sole charge of the Trustees or Governors of Bridewell Hospital out of the Charity monies thereof'. Free, 3 July 1816. Mark entered as plateworker, 10 April 1823. Address: 10 Craven Buildings, Drury Lane. Moved to 14 Clerkenwell Green, 13 October 1824. Moved to 7 St. John's Street Rents,, 21 April 1825.

ASH, D. S. (1821) No record of apprenticeship or freedom. Only mark entered as smallworker in partnership with J. Horne, 20 October 1800. Address: 64 St. James's Street.

*ASH, Joseph I (1104-5) No record of apprenticeship or freedom. First mark entered as smallworker, 14 September 1801. Address: 3 Angel Street, Butcher Hall Lane. Three new marks, 9 May 1810. Three further marks, 3 January 1818. Address: 146 Aldersgate. Moved to 12 Castle Street, Shoreditch, no date. His son James apprenticed to Joseph Bibbs (q.v.), 1818.

ASH, Joseph II (1106) No record of apprenticeship or freedom. Apparently distinct from above of the same name. Only mark entered as smallworker, 23 September 1811. Address: 28 Crown Street, Soho.

ASH, Thomas (88, 95, 3476-7) Son of Joseph Ash late of Aversbury (?) in the County of Dorset clerk, apprenticed to Joseph Ash 2 April 1675 for eight years. Freedom unrecorded. Two marks entered as largeworker, undated, probably April 1697 on commencement of register. Address: Staining Lane. Heal records him at Steyning Lane, 1697-1712; and another of the same name, probably related, as goldsmith, London, 1652-97.

ASHBEE, William (90) No record of apprenticeship or freedom. Incuse mark (Section V), probably as watchcasemaker, entered 14 January 1750. Address: Black Boy and Crowne, Grape Street. Second mark (New Standard) as smallworker, 11 January 1734. Address: Grape Street.

ASHLEY, Jeconiah (1107) Son of Bernard Ashley of Epsom in the County of Surrey joiner, apprenticed to Robert Cooper 25 February 1716 and turned over to Gislingham Cooper 11 November 1721. Free, 7 March 1737. Mark entered as largeworker, 12 November 1740. Address: Corner of Green Street, Leicester Fields. Heal records him as goldsmith 'at the Golden Acorn over again New Church in the Strand dead 1740'. The latter's mistake in his Christian name appears to stem from Chaffers' abbreviation 'Jereh'. Both apprenticeship and mark registers clearly show Jeconiah.

ASHPINSHAW, John (1101) No record of apprenticeship or freedom. Only mark entered as smallworker, 26 May 1763. Address: New Castle Street, Whitechapel. Heal records the name as Aspinshaw. Appears as Ashpinshaw, without category, at the same address in Parl. Report list 1773.

ASHTON, Arthur (2) No record of apprenticeship or freedom. Only mark entered as smallworker, 13 March 1732. Address: White's Alley, Chancery Lane.

ASKEW, Miles (1992) No record of apprenticeship or freedom. Only mark entered as smallworker, 30 September 1784. Address: 5 Aldersgate Street Buildings. Moved to 7 St. John's Court, St. Martin's Le Grand, 6 July 1785. Joseph Askew, in partnership with William Judd as bucklemakers, 1788 (Section VIII), may be related.

*ATKINS, Richard William (2261) No record of apprenticeship or freedom. First mark entered as plateworker in partnership with W. N. Somersall, 26 July 1824. Address: 11 Bridgwater Square. Second mark, 31

March 1825. Third mark, 6 February 1830. Their work is rarely met with. A large cup and cover bearing their mark belongs to the Painter-Stainers' Company.

ATKINS, Theodosia Ann (2683) No record of apprenticeship or freedom. Presumably widow of James Atkins, bucklemaker, 12 Well Street, mark entered 27 March 1792 and three further marks till 31 March 1815 (Section VIII). Her only mark entered as smallworker, 27 September 1815. Address: Well Street, Cripplegate.

ATKINSON, Christopher (98) Son of William Atkinson Citizen and Haberdasher of London, apprenticed to William Skinner 28 November 1694 and turned over 21 May 1698 to William Gibson. Free, 3 October 1707. Mark entered as largeworker, 23 October 1707. Address: Foster Lane. Heal records his death in 1753.

ATKINSON, William (99, 2999) Son of George Atkinson of York currier (?), apprenticed to William Bellasis of the Merchant Taylors' Company 5 February 1718. Free, 3 March 1725. Sterling and New Standard marks entered as largeworker, 31 May 1725. 'of Merchant Taylors' Company'. Address: 'at the Golden Cup, New Fish Street Hill'. Heal records him also as of London, 1736.

AUBIN, Henry (103-4) Son of Abraham Aubin of the Island of Jersey merchant, apprenticed to Edward Blagrave 26 August 1692. Free, 12 January 1699. Mark entered as largeworker, 10 June 1700. Address: Princes Court, Lothbury. Second mark, 13 March 1716, same address. Appears as witness to baptism (?godfather) of Henry La Loy, 29 September 1700, at the French Church, Threadneedle Street.

AUSTIN, John (3612) No record of apprenticeship or freedom. Nothing known other than the attribution by Jackson of this name to the mark in question.

AUSTIN, Thomas (2681) No record of apprenticeship or freedom. First mark entered as plateworker, 8 April 1818. Address: 3 Fanns Street, Aldersgate Street. Moved to 4 Goswell Street, 26 October 1819. Second mark, 22 November 1821.

AVENELL, Hugh (945) Son of John Avenell of the parish of St. James Westminster joyner, apprenticed to Job Lilley 2 August 1727 on payment of £15. Free, 7 January 1734. Mark entered as smallworker, 29 March 1735. Address: King Street, St. Ann's, near Soho Square.

*AVERY, Henry (105) Described as Free Cooper on entry of mark as smallworker, 23 August 1710. Address: Greater Carter Lane. Nothing else known of him.

AYSCOUGH, Ralph (2256) Son of Thomas Ayscough of Lombard Street gentleman, apprenticed to Edward Chowne 6 February 1739. Free, 3 December 1746. Livery, March 1758. Mark entered as smallworker, 22 August 1769. Address: Ludgate Street. Heal records him at the Ring and Pearl, Ludgate Street, having removed from Old Change, Cheapside, in 1753 until 1765; and at 18 Ludgate Street, being the same address until 1777. Appears here as goldworker in Parl. Report list 1773. He died before 1796.

B

BACHE, John (118, 446, 1115, 3482-3) Son of Thomas Bache of Avely(?) Salop yeoman, apprenticed to William Harrison 28 February 1673. Free, 5 March 1680. Court, 1703. Warden, 1718, 1722-3. Prime Warden, 1726. His first wife Margarett buried at St. Mary Woolnoth, 11 September 1682, when he is described as Silversmith; their son John baptized 5 June 1681. Married secondly 28 June 1683, at St. Mary Woolnoth, Suzanna Moore, when he is described as silversmith and both of that parish. Three sons and four daughters of this marriage baptized between 1684 and 1701, and an apprentice George Chapman buried 1687, when Bache is variously goldsmith or silversmith. First mark entered as largeworker in partnership with William Denny (also apprenticed to William Harrison, q.v.), undated, probably April 1697 on commencement of register. Address: Dove Court, Lombard Street. Signatory to the petition against the work of 'aliens and foreigners', 11 August 1697. Second mark alone as largeworker, 1 November 1700, and third (Sterling) mark, 20 June 1720, without address for either. Heal records him as working goldsmith, parish of St. Mary Woolnoth, 1688–1701; and plateworker, Dove Court, Lombard Street, 1700–29, with Denny and Backe at same address. In the church registers the spelling of the name varies between Bache, Backe and Batch.

BADDELEY, John (1167) No record of apprenticeship or freedom. Only mark entered as plateworker, 8 October 1818. Address: 27 Seward Street, Goswell Street.

BAGNALL, William (3010–11) Son of Thomas Bagnall of Uppingham in the County of Rutland shopkeeper, apprenticed to Gabriel Sleath 9 September 1736 on payment of £30. Free, March 1744. Mark in two sizes entered as largeworker, 6 June 1744. Address: 'North side of Smithfield'.

BAGSHAW, Basil (132) No record of apprenticeship or freedom. Only mark entered as plateworker, 27 March 1829. Address: 69 Red Lion Street, Holborn.

BAGSHAW, Charles (266) Son of Edward Bagshaw Citizen and Shipwright of London, apprenticed to Thomas Redhead of the Merchant Taylors' Company for seven years 3 June 1724 and free by servitude to Samuel Green (having been turned over) 7 July 1731. Mark entered as smallworker, 12 July 1731. Address: Ball Alley, Lombard Street. 'Free of Merchant Taylors' Company'.

*BAILEY, Henry (951, 3601) No record of apprenticeship or freedom. Only mark entered as largeworker, 14 June 1750. Address: Foster Lane. The ascription of mark 3601 to him by Jackson is very puzzling, as there is no record of a script mark in use by him. The date-letter of the piece quoted for this mark, the D of 1759, has often in the past been read in error for the O of 1769, and if this had been the case here, the mark shown may in fact be an incorrect version of that of Hester Bateman. On the other hand, Bailey may possibly have entered a second such mark in the missing largeworkers' book of 1758–73.

BAILEY See also BAYLEY

BAIN, William (3044) No record of apprenticeship or freedom. Only mark entered as smallworker, 1 April 1837. Address: 6 Museum Street.

BAINBRIDGE, Harriet (957) No record of apprenticeship or freedom. Only mark entered as smallworker, 22 August 1831. Address: 35 Holborn Hill. Presumably widow of William Bainbridge II (below).

BAINBRIDGE, Mary (115) No record of apprenticeship or freedom. Only mark entered as largeworker, 21 April 1707. Address: Oat Lane. Widow (presumably of William Bainbridge, below, although of different address).

BAINBRIDGE, William I (114) Son of Thomas Bainbridge of Bookford Derbyshire clerk, apprenticed to Robert Peake 19 October 1683. Free, 22 October 1690. Mark entered undated, probably on commencement of register April 1697. Address: Catherine Wheel Alley in Whitechapel.

BAINBRIDGE, William II (3040) No record of apprenticeship or freedom. Only mark entered as smallworker, 8 December 1827. Address: 35 Holborn Hill. Probably dead by 22 August 1831 when Harriet Bainbridge of same address (q.v.) entered her mark.

BAKER, George I (749) Probably son of Roger Baker of Gillingham in the County of Kent shipwright, apprenticed to Thomas Hill 18 May 1722 on payment of £20. Free, 2 July 1729. (Less probably perhaps, son of John Baker Citizen and Haberdasher of London, apprenticed to John Cooke 20 September 1698. Free, 14 November 1705. Livery, October 1708.) Only mark entered as smallworker, 17 April 1733, described as goldsmith. Address: 'At the Acorn in C(ros)s Lane', identifiable with —Baker, silversmith, Acorn near the Monument, 1732 (Heal), since Cross Lane is just to the east of the latter landmark.

BAKER, George II (753) No record of further apprenticeships or freedoms of this name beyond those above. Only mark entered as largeworker, 31 July 1750. Address: Five Bell Court, Foster Lane. Heal records him here as plateworker, 1724–50. He does not therefore appear to be identifiable with George Baker I.

BAKER, James (1136, 3617) No record of apprenticeship or freedom. Only mark entered as smallworker, 19 April 1759. Address: New Court, Bunhill Row, where he appears without category in Parl. Report list 1773. Heal records the name alone as goldsmith, London, 1758.

BIOGRAPHICAL DICTIONARY

*BAKER, John I (1691) Perhaps the son of Benjamin Baker Citizen and Gardener of London, apprenticed to Theophilus Spendelowe 3 July 1740 on payment of £30. Free, 3 February 1747. Livery, April 1765(?). Died before 1796(?). More probably the John Baker, free by redemption, 3 April 1765, as silversmith. First mark entered in partnership with James Stamp as smallworkers, 18 April 1764. Address: Cow Cross. Apparently moved to Ludgate Street, 18 February 1765, when second mark entered. Third mark, 29 April 1768. Died 1802-11.

*BAKER, John II (1141, 1773) Possibly but unlikely to be identified with the preceding, but no other record of apprenticeship or freedom suitable. First mark entered as smallworker, 11 April 1770. Address: 5 Old Bailey. Second mark, 28 September 1770. Heal records him as plateworker in this year only. He appears as goldsmith, at the same address, in the Parl. Report list 1773, and entered two further marks as bucklemaker, 17 January 1774. Address: 35 Snow Hill (Section VIII). Moved, 5 October 1775 to 4 Bull in Mouth Street, and entered another mark as bucklemaker, 2 March 1786. Address: 4 High Street, St. Giles.

*BAKER, John III (1147) No record of apprenticeship or freedom. Only mark entered as smallworker, 17 May 1775. Address: 89 Ray Street, Clerkenwell. Comparison of signatures in entries suggests separate identity to John Baker II.

BAKER, Pointer (2133) No record of apprenticeship or freedom. Only mark entered as smallworker, undated, between 18 December 1759 and 28 January 1760. Address: Compton Street, St. Anne's, Soho, where Heal records him as plateworker in 1773; as also the Parl. Report list of that year but without category.

BALLAM, Thomas (2700) No record of apprenticeship or freedom. First mark entered as plateworker, 22 August 1820. Address: 18 Gough Lane, Fleet Street. Second mark, 30 June 1821, on move to 25 Panton Street, Haymarket. He is presumably the Thomas Ballam of East Street, Walworth in Surrey, silversmith, whose son James Robert was apprenticed to Edward Barnard as silversmith and chaser 7 October 1818.

BALLISTON, Thomas (2699) No record of apprenticeship or freedom. Only mark entered as plateworker, 4 August 1812. Address: 1 Horse Shoe Court, Ludgate Hill. Moved to 13 Charles Street, City Road, 20 October 1815. Moved to 17 Rose Street, St. Luke's, 14 April 1817, and to 24 Banners Square, 18 April 1818.

BAMFORD, Thomas I (109-10, 2687, 2704) Son of Thomas Bamford of Uttoxeter in the County of Stafford maltster, apprenticed to Charles Adam 18 August 1703. Freedom unrecorded. Two marks as largeworker entered 5 January 1720. Third (Sterling) mark, 27 June 1720. Address: Gutter Lane. Fourth mark, 18 July 1739, Foster Lane. Three sons and two daughters of Thomas and Judith Bamford baptized between 1718 and 1726 at Christchurch, Newgate. The eldest son Thomas, born 1718, appears to be the Thomas Bamford buried 3 September 1732. Specialist castermaker, as was his master Adam and his apprentice Samuel Wood (q.v.).

BAMFORD, Thomas II (2693) No record of apprenticeship or freedom, and no apparent connection with above. Only mark entered as smallworker, 8 June 1770. Address: 'St. Clements' Lane near ye Strand', where the Parl. Report list records him without category in 1773.

BANCE, Henry (120, 962, 964) Son of Robert Bance late of Cue (Kew?) in the County of Surrey yeoman deceased, apprenticed to Anthony Nelme 9 January 1694. Freedom unrecorded. First mark entered as smallworker, 4 September 1706. Address: Gutter Lane. Second (Sterling) mark, 20 June 1720, in same entry. Third, separate entry with unnamed partner's initials TC included in punch, 26 May 1721.

BANNISTER, Thomas (2702) Perhaps son of Thomas Bannister who was free by patrimony as Goldsmith 4 December 1776. No record of apprenticeship or freedom suitable for date. Only mark entered as smallworker, 19 January 1829. Address: 68 John Street, Fitzroy Square.

*BARBE, John (1126, 1177-8) No record of apprenticeship or freedom. First mark entered as largeworker, 16 January 1735. Address: West Street, near Seven Dials. Second mark, 25 June 1739, same address. Third mark, 22 December 1742. Address: Little St. Andrew Street. Heal records him at the first address until 1773 when he appears as plateworker, at West Street, in Parl. Report list. Listed by Evans ('Huguenot Goldsmiths', *Hug. Soc. Proc.*, 14) as

Huguenot without further reference. The address supports the attribution.

BARBER, William (3041) No record of apprenticeship or freedom. Only mark entered as spoonmaker, 11 March 1828. Address: 15 Euston Street, Euston Square.

*BARBOT, John (1121) No record of apprenticeship or freedom. Only mark entered as smallworker, 22 July 1726. Address: 'Broad Street St. Giles att the Blackemors head a S$\underset{u}{u}$ff Chop' (?Snuff shop). Presumably a snuffbox maker. Heal records him as silversmith at the same address; and also as goldsmith, Golden Lion, Great St. Andrew's Street, Seven Dials, 1751. (There may perhaps be confusion here with John Barbe, above.)

BARBOT, Paul (2134) Presumably son of John Barbot (above). No record of apprenticeship or freedom. Only mark entered as 'Goldsmith', 4 July 1771. Address: Seven Dials, Golden Lion, and he appears as goldworker here in the Parl. Report list 1773. Heal records him as goldsmith, Great St. Andrew's Street, Seven Dials, 1768–79; and Tottenham Court Road, 1790–3.

BARBUT, Joseph (119, 1114, 1176, 3481) Parentage untraced but quoted as a Huguenot by W. H. Manchee, 'Huguenot London', Hug. Soc. Proc., 13, page 75. Previously wrongly titled Barbitt by Chaffers, through misreading of entry, and followed by Jackson and Heal. Heal records him as goldsmith, St. Martin's in the Fields, married 1690. Free by redemption, 1 October 1703. First mark entered as largeworker, 1 October 1703. Address: New Street, Covent Garden. Second mark, 27 July 1717, same address. Third mark (Sterling) entered without date under 1703 mark, probably June–July 1720. Fourth mark (Sterling), 18 June 1739, same address. Appears from the surviving occurrence of his mark to have been a specialist spoon and forkmaker.

*BARKER, Christopher (276) No record of apprenticeship or freedom. Appears as silversmith of Pemberton Row, Gough Square, London, in the apprenticeship of his son Thomas Wilkes (q.v.), 1787. First mark entered, in partnership with the latter as spoonmakers, 11 October 1800. Address: 9 Cross Street, Hatton Garden. Moved to 6 Kirby Street, Hatton Garden, and new marks entered, 8 December 1804.

*BARKER, James (1131) No record of apprenticeship or freedom. Only mark entered as smallworker, 17 April 1746. Address: Corner of Buckingham Street, Strand. Thomas Barker, aged ten, son of James Barker goldsmith of Searle Street admitted to St. Paul's School, 23 March 1758, presumably for the same at a subsequent address.

BARKER, Robert (2274) No record of apprenticeship or freedom. Presumably son of Susanna Barker (below). Only mark entered as smallworker, 20 November 1793. Address: 29 Gutter Lane, where Heal records him earlier, in 1789.

BARKER, Susanna (2479–80) No record of apprenticeship or freedom. First mark entered as smallworker, 25 June 1778. Address: 16 Gutter Lane. Second mark (two sizes), 12 August 1789. Third mark, 26 August 1789. Heal records her as working goldsmith, 29 Gutter Lane, 1790-3. Presumably dead by that year when Robert Barker entered his mark at the same address.

*BARKER, Thomas Wilkes (276, 2697, 3812) Son of Christopher Barker of Pemberton Row, Gough Square London silversmith (q.v.), apprenticed to William Fearn of Paternoster Row spoonmaker 5 December 1787 on payment of £5 of the Charity of Christ's Hospital London. First mark entered in partnership with his father as spoonmakers, 11 October 1800. Address: 9 Cross Street, Hatton Garden. Second mark, on moving to 6 Kirby Street, Hatton Garden, 8 December 1804. Third mark alone, 7 February 1805, same address. Fourth mark (two sizes), 17 July 1811. Fifth mark (two sizes), 1 December 1819.

BARLOW, John Hawkins (1413) Probably son of John Barlow late of Yarmouth in the County of Norfolk hairdresser deceased, apprenticed to Thomas Satchwell jeweller of Sutton Street Clerkenwell 1792. Free, 5 March 1800. Only mark entered as plateworker, 12 January 1815. Address: 1 Grange Court, Carey Street.

*BARNARD, Edward I (575, 2309) Son of Edward Barnard of Nichol Square London flatter, apprenticed to Charles Wright of Ave Maria Lane London Goldsmith 5 December 1781 on payment of £50. Turned over by consent 4 February 1784 to Thomas Chawner of Ave Maria Lane London goldsmith, Citizen and Goldsmith. Free, 4 February 1789. Livery, 1811. First mark entered as plateworker in partnership with Rebeccah Emes (q.v.), 14 October 1808. Address:

BIOGRAPHICAL DICTIONARY

Amen Corner. (The mark entered by power of attorney by William Emes.) Second mark, 29 April 1818. Third, 20 February 1821. Fourth, 29 October 1825. Fifth mark, in partnership with sons, Edward, John and William, 25 February 1829. Moved to Angel Street, St. Martin's Le Grand, 18 June 1838. Died c. 1853-5.

BARNARD, Edward II (575) Son of Edward Barnard of Paternoster Row silversmith (above), apprenticed to his father 7 February 1810. Free, March 1817. Livery January 1822. Mark entered with father and brothers John and William, 25 February 1829. Address: Amen Corner, Paternoster Row. Moved to Angel Street, St. Martin's Le Grand, 18 June 1838. Died, 26 December 1867.

BARNARD, John I (112-3, 1118, 3480) Son of Samuel Bernard (so entered by Clerk) of Crookerne in the County of Somerset maltster, apprenticed to Thomas Dymick Citizen and Goldsmith of London for eight years from 1 September 1677. Signs entry as 'barnard'. Free, 4 September 1685. The registers of St. Vedast, Foster Lane, contain entries for the baptism of children of John Barnard and Anne his wife from 1693 and in one of 1699 he is styled 'silversmith in Gutter Lane', thus identifying the earlier entries as of the same couple. (See also the entry for Job Hanks living with Barnard in 1699.) Two marks entered, undated, probably April 1697 on commencement of register. Address: Gutter Lane. Signatory as Jno. Bernard, working goldsmith, to the petition complaining of the competition of 'necessitous strangers', December 1711. Third mark (Sterling) added below the first entry, 12 October 1720 (the date thus wrongly given by Chaffers to the earlier New Standard marks).

BARNARD, John II (575) Son of Edward Barnard of Paternoster Row (q.v.), apprenticed to his father 1 January 1812. Free, 6 January 1819. Mark entered in partnership with his father and brothers Edward and William, 25 February 1829, as plateworkers. Address: Amen Corner, Paternoster Row. Livery, February 1831. Moved to Angel Street, St. Martin's Le Grand, 18 June 1838. Died c. 1877-81.

BARNARD, Joseph (1156) No record of apprenticeship or freedom. Only mark entered as smallworker, 23 February 1798. Address: 27 Brownlow Street, Drury Lane.

BARNARD, William (575) Son of Edward Barnard of Paternoster Row silversmith, apprenticed to his father 5 July 1815. Free, 5 February 1823. Mark entered in partnership with his father and brothers Edward and John, 25 February 1829, as plateworkers. Address: Amen Corner, Paternoster Row. Moved to Angel Street, St. Martin's Le Grand, 18 June 1838.

BARNES, William (117) Son of William Barnes Citizen and Leatherseller of London, apprenticed to Edmund Townsend 1 July 1695. Free, 17 July 1702. Mark entered as largeworker, 20 July 1702. Address: 'Without Ludgate'. Heal records him as goldsmith, by Ludgate on Ludgate Hill, 1702-31.

BARNET, Alexander (11) No record of apprenticeship or freedom. Only mark entered as smallworker, 8 August 1759. Address: 'in Woopen Naer Ormaditch Briedch'. This very phonetic entry is revealed as 'near the Hermitage Bridge, Wapping' in the Parl. Report list 1773, where he appears without category. Heal records him as ?St. Bride's Church, near Fleet Ditch', in 1759; and as London, 1777.

BARNETT, Edward (122) Son of Thomas Barnett late of Dimmocke in the County of Gloucester yeoman deceased, apprenticed to Anthony Nelme 3 December 1706. Free, 30 September 1715. Mark entered as largeworker, 18 November 1715. Address: Tooley Street, Southwark, where Heal records him till 1718.

*BARNETT, Michael (2001) No record of apprenticeship or freedom. First mark entered as smallworker, 29 June 1781. Address: 36 Cock Lane, Smithfield. Second mark, 6 January 1784, as hiltmaker. Third mark, 8 January 1785, as small plateworker. Fourth mark (two sizes), 26 October 1791, below the 1784 entry. Fifth and last mark as smallworker, 3 March 1820. Elizabeth Barnett, presumably his widow, entered her mark as hiltmaker (Section IX) at the same address, 11 February 1823.

BARRATT, James (1158-9) Son of James Barratt of Wakefield in the County of York gardener, apprenticed to William Abdy of Oat Lane Noble Street Goldsmith 6 May 1772. Freedom unrecorded. First mark entered as smallworker, 5 October 1801. Address: 7 Staining Lane. Moved to 24 Adelle (alias Addle) Street, 10 August 1802. Second mark, 20 June 1803. Third mark (two sizes), 7 September 1803. Fourth and last mark, 29 June 1816.

BARRETT, James (1134) No record of apprenticeship or freedom. Only mark entered as smallworker, 5 January 1759. Address: 'at Mr. Havercroft's Foster Lane', where he so appears without category in the Parl. Report list 1773.

BARRETT, John (1128, 1175) No record of apprenticeship or freedom. First mark entered as largeworker, 26 May 1737. Address: Castle Street Mews. 'a foriner'. Second mark, 5 June 1739. Address: Feathers Court, Holborn.

BARRETT, William I (3024-5) Son of John Barrett of Chesterfield in the County of Essex labourer, apprenticed to John Raymond 1762 and turned over to Joseph Steward of Gutter Lane 10 October 1768. Free, 1 November 1769. First mark entered as smallworker, 9 March 1771. Address: 1 Addle Street, Wood Street, where he appears as smallworker in Parl. Report list 1773. Second mark, 14 September 1775. Address: 50 Aldersgate Street. Third mark, 22 July 1777. Fourth, 13 April 1780; Fifth 30 May 1783; Sixth, 24 September 1784; Seventh (two sizes), 27 October 1790. Heal records him as working silversmith and clockmaker at 50 Aldersgate Street from 1777 to 1793; also a William Barrett, jeweller, 15 Charterhouse Street, 1790-6, but there would not seem any connection with the latter.

BARRETT, William II (3033-4) Son of Matthew Barrett of Shoreditch wharfinger, apprenticed to Thomas Rowe of Aldersgate Street as silver polisher 5 August 1800. Free, 6 April 1808. First mark entered as smallworker, 26 October 1812. Address: 3 Great Deane Court, St. Martin's Le Grand. Second mark, 17 February 1821, and moved to 18 Red Cross Square. Third mark as plateworker, 15 September 1828.

BARRIER, Abraham (14, 3470) No record of apprenticeship or freedom. First mark (incuse) entered as plateworker, 11 October 1775. Address: Stephen Street, Rathbone Place. Moved to St. Anne's Court, Soho, 15 December 1777. Moved to 19 Grafton Street, Soho, 16 November 1781. Second mark in standard type punch, 18 May 1782. Listed as spoonmaker in partnership with Louis Ducommon (Ducommieu), at Rathbone Place, in the Parl. Report list of 1773. The latter (q.v.) entered his mark separately, 12 October 1775, one day after Barrier's first mark. (A suggestion of sudden pressure from the Company to regularize their activities?) Listed with Ducommieu as Huguenots by Evans, 'Huguenot Goldsmiths', *Hug. Soc. Proc.*, 14.

BARROTT, William (3032) No record of apprenticeship or freedom. Only mark entered as smallworker, 25 June 1807. Address: Rose Street, Covent Garden.

BARRY, St. John (1133) Son of William Barry late of the parish of St. Dunstan in the West London woollen draper deceased, apprenticed to Robert Cooke 6 July 1748 on payment of £14 (£10 of which by the Churchwardens of the parish, the gift of Mrs. Laud). Turned over 18 October 1749 to William Shaw. Free, 6 October 1756. Livery, March 1781. Mark entered as largeworker, 25 March 1758. Address: Paternoster Row, where he appears as John Barry, goldsmith, in the Parl. Report list 1773. Heal records him as John B., Paternoster Row, 1758; and as St. John B., goldsmith and jeweller, 3 Minories, 1777-84; and 135 Leadenhall Street 1789-93. Died, August 1809.

BARTON, Edmund (111) No record of apprenticeship or freedom. Only mark entered as smallworker, 8 May 1734. Address: 'In Oxfordshire Passage, Warwick Lane'.

BARTON, Edward (539, 3537) No record of apprenticeship or freedom. Only mark entered as plateworker, 14 January 1822. Address: 104 Hatton Garden. Moved to 27 Hatton Garden, 5 June 1822.

BARUGH, Ann (10) No record of apprenticeship or freedom. Almost certainly widow of John Barugh, 'Free Clockmaker', who entered two marks in 1716 and 1718 (Section V). She entered a first mark (incuse), 30 August 1721, at his address. Second mark as smallworker, 10 December 1731. Address: Bolt Court, Fleet Street. Her illiterate writing which might read as Burugh is however proved to be Barugh by the 'Ba' New Standard mark of her husband.

BASKERVILLE, George (750-1, 754, 756, 768-9, 3580) Son of George Baskerville of Winterbourne upon Bassett in the County of Wiltshire yeoman, apprenticed to Joseph Sanders, undated but after 4 May 1732, on payment of £25. Freedom unrecorded. First mark entered as largeworker, 9 February 1738. Address: The Golden Acorn, Chandos Street. Second mark, 26 July 1745. Address: Cock Court, St. Martin's Le Grand.

Third mark, 1 February 1751. Address: Round Court, Strand. Fourth mark, in partnership with William Sampel, 27 January 1755. Address: New Inn Passage, Clare Market. Fifth mark alone, 3 September 1755, same address. Appears as goldsmith, Albion Buildings, in Parl. Report list 1773. Sixth mark in partnership with Thomas Morley as plateworkers, 6 May 1775. Address: 8 Albion Buildings. Last mark alone as smallworker, 3 March 1780. He appears to have had an exceptionally long working life but the signatures throughout the above entries appear to be from the same hand and there is no reference to a son of the same name. Heal records him as of London up to 1792.

*BASS, Thomas (121, 2685) Apprenticed to Joseph Reason of the Cutlers' Company. Free, 15 April 1708. Mark entered as smallworker, 4 October 1708. Address: Dean Street, Fetter Lane. 'Free Cutler'. Second mark (Sterling), 21 June 1720.

BASSINGWHITE, John (1142) No record of apprenticeship or freedom. First mark entered as smallworker, 29 November 1770. Address: 'at the French Baker's, Little Russell Street, Drury Lane'. Second mark, 13 January 1771. Address: 6 Dowlings Buildings, Purple Lane. Heal records him only as plateworker, Russell Street, 1770. He appears as John Basingwhite, bucklemaker, at the second address, in the Parl. Report list 1773.

BATCHELOR, Philip (2136) No record of apprenticeship or freedom. Only mark entered as smallworker, 15 January 1770. Address: Turnstile Row, Lincoln's Inn Fields. Appears as bucklemaker, Great Turnstile, Holborn, in the Parl. Report list 1773.

BATEMAN, Ann (2140-1) Born Dowling 1748. Married Jonathan Bateman (q.v.) 1769 at St. Luke's, Old Street. On her husband's death in 1791 joined her brother-in-law Peter (q.v.) in partnership, their mark entered 2 May 1791. Address: Bunhill Row. Her son William (q.v.) was added to the partnership in January 1800. She retired in 1805 and died before 1813. (For biographical information in this and following Bateman entries I am indebted to Miss Mary Fairbairns and her cousin Miss Annette Bull, both direct descendants in the female line from Hester Bateman.)

*BATEMAN, Hester (955, 958-61) Daughter of John Neden, baptized 7 October 1708 at St. Michael's, Paternoster Royal. Married 20 May 1732 John Bateman (c. 1704-60) of St. Bartholomew the Less at St. Botolph's Aldersgate, of which parish she then was. John Bateman, a chainmaker, died 1760 leaving all his property to his wife. First mark entered as smallworker, 16 April 1761, the entry signed by her with crude initials H B. Address: Bunhill Row. Second mark, 9 January 1771, no address. Appears as goldsmith, Bunhill Row, in Parl. Report list 1773. Third to sixth marks as spoonmaker, 17 June 1774, 5 June 1776, 21 February 1778, 25 November 1781, all at 107 Bunhill Row. Others as plateworker, 3 December 1774, 28 June 1787 (no. 955, her only mark using Roman in lieu of script letters, presumably by size intended for gold), and final mark 3 August 1787. Retired in 1790 on entry of Peter and Jonathan's mark, died 16 September 1794 and buried at St. Luke's, Old Street, 26 September, then living in parish of St. Andrew's, Holborn. Her five children were Letitia born 1733, Ann 1736, Peter 1740 (q.v.), John (? date) and Jonathan (q.v.) 1747.

*BATEMAN, Jonathan (2142) Third son of Hester Bateman (q.v.), born 18 November 1747. Apprenticed to Richard Clarke, husband of his sister Letitia, and entered the family business in 1769. Mark entered in partnership with his brother Peter, 7 December 1790, with six further marks on 9 December. Died 19 April 1791, leaving all his property to his wife Ann (q.v.) whom he had married in 1769, and by whom he had two sons Jonathan and William (q.v.), two daughters and five other children who died in infancy. Heal records him alone as goldsmith, Bunhill Row, 1784. On 7 July 1784 his son Jonathan was apprenticed to him, when the father is described as Citizen and Goldsmith of London. He was elected to the Livery, 5 October 1791.

*BATEMAN, Peter (2140-3) Second son of Hester Bateman (q.v.), born 1740. Apprenticed to Richard Clarke, husband of his sister Letitia. Married first, Elizabeth Beaver (widow) 1763, and second, Sarah — 1776. Lived at 86 Bunhill Row. First mark entered in partnership with Jonathan (q.v.), 7 December 1790, and six further marks on 9 December. On Jonathan's death entered mark with Ann Bateman, 2 May 1791. Third mark with Ann and William, January 1800.

Fourth mark with William, 8 November 1805. Probably retired in 1815 on entry of William Bateman's single mark (q.v.). He died 19 November 1825, leaving in his will £50 each to the Evangelical Institution at Newport Pagnall and the Baptist Academy, Stepney. In 1805 he gave a chandelier to the Meeting House at Newport Pagnall, whose minister William Bull, intimate of the poet Cowper, was a friend of the goldsmith and whose son, the Rev. T. B. Bull married Letitia, daughter of Jonathan and Ann Bateman.

BATEMAN, William I (2141, 2143, 3037) Second son of Jonathan and Ann Bateman (q.v.) and grandson of Hester. Born 17 December 1774. Apprenticed 7 January 1789 to his father and turned over on the latter's death to his mother 6 July 1791. Free by service, 6 February 1799. First mark entered in partnership with Peter and Ann, January 1800. Address: Bunhill Row. Second mark with Peter, 8 November 1805. Third mark alone (two sizes), 15 February 1815. Address: 108 Bunhill Row. Married Ann Wilson, 1800, at St. Mathew's, Friday Street, by whom he had three sons, William (q.v.), Henry and Josiah. William was apprenticed to him 1815, Henry 1816 (the latter turned over 1817 to Thomas Hacker timber merchant), and Josiah 1817. Livery, 1816. Court, 1828. Warden, 1833-5. Prime Warden, 1836. Warden, 1847-9. Sold the family business to Ben Car, c. 1840, having twenty years earlier entered the gas business. A Proprietor of the Chartered Gas, Light and Coke Company 1821, Director 1823, Deputy Governor 1840 and Governor 1846. Commissioner of Sewers for the Holborn and Finsbury Division. Died at Stoke Newington, January 1850. Subject of a lengthy and eulogistic obituary in *The Journal of Gas Lighting*, 11 February 1850.

BATEMAN, William II (3038) Son of William Bateman (above), apprenticed to his father 1 February 1815 and free by service 4 December 1822. First mark entered as plateworker, 9 February 1827 (three sizes). Second mark, 22 May 1830. Livery, 18 March 1829. Died between 1874 and 1877.

BATES, Daniel (445) No record of apprenticeship or freedom. Only mark entered as smallworker, 23 June 1778. Address: Featherstone Street, Bunhill Row. Alexander Bates, bucklemaker (Section VIII), is perhaps related.

BATES, Henry (949, 963) Son of Edward Bates of Ilson on the Hill in the County of Leicester yeoman, apprenticed to Jonathan Newton 14 May 1719 on payment of £30 and turned over to Francis Nelme at Amen Corner 6 May 1723. Free, 3 November 1726. Livery, 1737. First mark entered as largeworker, 12 July 1738. Address: Wide Gate Street, near Bishopsgate. Second mark, 19 July 1739, same address. Court, 1752. Warden, 1764-6. Resigned 1772. Died 1774.

BATES, Samuel (2475-6) Son of Richard Bates late of Sheffield in the County of York cutler deceased, apprenticed to John Boddington 17 December 1719 and turned over the same day to Captain Bird (presumably Joseph Bird, q.v.) in Foster Lane, Goldsmith. Free, 10 January 1728 (?9). First mark entered as largeworker, 28 October 1728. Address: Gutter Lane. Second mark, 6 March 1744. Address: Foster Lane, where Heal records him till 1755. Livery, February 1752. Warden, 1764-6. Resigned 19 November 1772. Died 1774. Samuel Bates, goldsmith, Islington, perhaps the same, appears in the Parl. Report list 1773.

BAYLEY, Edward (543) Parentage untraced. Only mark entered as smallworker, 27 April 1738. Address: Warwick Lane. 'Of ye Clockmakers' Company', but there is no trace of him in the existing registers of that company. Probably a watchcasemaker.

BAYLEY, John (1180) Probably son of John Bayley late of the parish of St. Botolph without Aldersgate London cabinetmaker deceased, apprenticed to William Richards 2 April 1729 on payment of £2 of the charity of the said parish. Turned over to John Betts 27 February 1735. Free, 6 September 1743. Livery, March 1750. Mark entered as largeworker, 21 March 1751. Address: Wood Street, where Heal records him as plateworker, at no. 106, from 1751 to 1781. Appears as goldsmith, Wood Street, in the Parl. Report list 1773. (An alternative identification is as son of Richard Bayley (q.v.), apprenticed to James Smith, 1732, and turned over to his father, whose freedom is however unrecorded, and who has no apparent further identity in company records.)

BAYLEY, Richard (116, 2262, 2279, 3481, 3760-1) Son of Anthony Bayly of Hampton near Highworth in the County of Wiltshire yeoman, apprenticed to Charles Overing 28 April 1699 and turned over to John Gibbons

26 April 1704. Signs Bayly. Free, 11 December 1706. First mark entered 29 March 1708. Address: Foster Lane. Livery, October 1712. Signatory as 'working goldsmith' to the petition complaining of the competition of 'necessitous strangers', December 1711, and to petition against assaying work of 'foreigners' not having served seven years apprenticeship, February 1716. Second mark (Sterling), 16 July 1720. Third, 19 June 1739. Court, 1732. Warden, 1746-8. Prime Warden, 1751. Heal records him in Foster Lane till 1748. His son Richard apprenticed to Samuel Spindler, 10 January 1753. Produced good plain hollow-ware such as tankards, jugs, tea and coffee-pots.

BAYLEY, William I (3017) No record of apprenticeship or freedom. Only mark entered as smallworker, 19 February 1759. Address: Blackhorse Court, Aldersgate Street, where he appears without category in the Parl. Report list 1773.

BAYLEY, William II (3017*) No record of apprenticeship or freedom. Mark entered as smallworker, 2 November 1770. Address: 78 Salisbury Court (Fleet Street), where he appears as bucklemaker in the Parl. Report list 1773. Heal records him as goldsmith, London, 1770-83.

BAYNE, John (1143) No record of apprenticeship or freedom. Only mark entered as smallworker, 20 June 1771. Address: Bartholomew Close. Appears without category, 16 Bartholomew Close, in Parl. Report list 1773.

BAZLINTON, Francis (667) No record of apprenticeship or freedom. Only mark entered as smallworker, 27 June 1781. Address: Red Lion Court, Charterhouse Lane No. 8.

BEADNELL, John (1313) Son of Robert Beadnell of Market Street, St. James's Market carpenter, apprenticed to Fendall Rushforth of Carey Lane Goldsmith 2 January 1782 and turned over 6 February 1782 to Daniel Smith Goldsmith and Merchant Taylor of Bartholomew Close. Free, 3 November 1790. Mark entered as plateworker in partnership with John Fountain, 10 May 1793. Address: 2 Carthusian Street, Charterhouse Square.

*BEALE, George (153, 156, 3486) Son of Rolfe Beale late of Winchcomb in the County of Gloucester yeoman deceased, apprenticed to Theophilus Albright Citizen and Skinner for seven years from 5 February 1688/9. Free, 7 April 1696. First mark entered as smallworker, 27 October 1699. Address: 'at Limehouse'. Second mark, 1 June 1713. Address: 'in Distaff Lane'. 'Free Skinner'. Heal records him as plateworker, Distaff Lane, 1713-19.

BEALE, Richard (2266, 2280, 3762) Son of — Beale of the town of Hull in the County of York draper, apprenticed to Jonathan Newton 13 June 1722 on payment of £25. Turned over to John Le Sage, Corner of Suffolk Street in the parish of St. Martin's in the Fields 23 July 1725. Freedom unrecorded. First mark entered as largeworker, 1 October 1733. Address: 'at ye Unicorn in Henaretter Street Covent Garden'. Second mark, 22 June 1739, same address. Third mark, probably for gold, 25 February 1746. Heal records him in Henrietta Street from 1731 to 1773. He appears as goldsmith, at the same address, in the Parl. Report list 1773.

BEARD, Hugh (952) No record of apprenticeship or freedom. Only mark entered as smallworker, 19 August 1758. Address: New Court, Brown Street, Bunhill Row. Appears without category in the Parl. Report list 1773.

BEARE, Thomas (2690) Son of Henry Beare of the parish of St. James Westminster gentleman, apprenticed to John Montgomery 3 December 1741 on premium of £30. Freedom unrecorded. Mark entered as largeworker, 18 December 1751. Address: D.ury Lane, St. Martin's, Westminster.

*BEATTIE, James (1152, 1774) No record of apprenticeship or freedom. First mark entered as smallworker, 6 July 1790. Address: 165 Strand. Second and third marks, 7 July and 27 August 1790.

*BEATTY, James (1135) No record of apprenticeship or freedom and no apparent connection with the above. Only mark entered as smallworker, 13 March 1759. Address: Greek Street, Soho. Heal records him as late of this address, deceased by 1762, but he appears as James Beaty, goldsmith, Greek Street, Soho, in the Parl. Report list 1773, perhaps an error for his widow carrying on business.

*BEAUCHAMP, John (1785) No record of apprenticeship or freedom. Only mark entered as plateworker, 31 December 1828. Address: 14 Holborn.

BECKLEY, Richard James (2351) Son of Edward Beckley deceased late of Hosier

Lane bookbinder, apprenticed to Joseph Angel of Red Lion Street as silversmith 7 November 1810 on payment of £26. 5s. Freedom unrecorded. Mark entered as plateworker, 18 February 1825. Address: 15 Southampton Street, Camberwell.

BECKWITH, George (760) Son of Jonah Beckwith of Church Row, St. Luke's (Old Street) goldsmith (brother of Joseph and Robert below), apprenticed to William Hunter of East Row Hoxton as goldsmith 3 March 1801 on payment of £5. 5s. of the charity of the Goldsmiths' Company. Freedom unrecorded. First mark entered as smallworker, 7 March 1804. Address: 6 Clerkenwell Green. Second larger mark entered without date.

BECKWITH, Joseph (1777) Son of Jonah Beckwith of St. Luke's in the County of Middlesex silver turner (and brother of George and Robert), apprenticed to Edward Edwards of Goswell Street as engraver and printer 1 December 1790 on payment of £7. 14s. of the charity of the Goldsmiths' Company. Freedom unrecorded. Only mark entered as smallworker, 7 February 1807. Address: 25 Wilderness Row, St. John Street (?Clerkenwell).

BECKWITH, Robert (2277) Robert William, son of Jonah Beckwith of the parish of St. Luke's silversmith, apprenticed to Samuel Hennell of Foster Lane as silversmith 3 March 1802 on payment of £7. 14s. of the charity of the Goldsmiths' Company. Free, 6 December 1809. Mark entered as plateworker, 27 May 1811. Address: 25 Wilderness Row, as his brother Joseph above.

*BEDFORD, William (157) Only mark entered as smallworker, 10 May (? a palimpsest) 1702. Address: New Street. 'Free of the Lorimers' (the records of this company unfortunately destroyed 1940).

BEEBE, James (1778–9) Son of John Beebe late of Compton Street Clerkenwell brewer's servant deceased, apprenticed to William Seaman of Pear Tree Street Goswell Street Middlesex silversmith, Citizen and Goldsmith 4 July 1804 on payment of £10. Free, 7 August 1811. First mark entered as spoonmaker, 16 August 1811. Address: 30 Red Lion Street, Clerkenwell. Moved to 26 Wilderness Row, 1 October 1817. Second mark, 11 September 1826. Moved to 65 Red Lion Street, 18 July 1827. Third and fourth marks, 21 October 1829 and 3 August 1839. Described as silver spoonmaker in the apprenticing to him of Henry Bickers 3 December 1817. Took another apprentice, Henry Hepburn, 2 July 1823.

BEESLEY, Henry (159, 3600) Perhaps the son of Richard Beesley of Twignorth in the County of Gloucester yeoman, apprenticed to Edward Gladwin 1682. Free, 1 April 1691. Signatory as 'working goldsmith' to the petition against competition from 'necessitous strangers', December 1711. Only mark entered as largeworker, 23 July 1714. Address: Nicholas Lane.

BEEZLEY, Thomas (2691, 3811) Son of John Beesley of Everton in the County of Northampton, apprenticed to Charles Hosier 26 February 1726. Freedom unrecorded. Mark entered as largeworker, 4 December 1755. Address: London Wall.

BELDON, John (1150, 3622) No record of apprenticeship or freedom. Only mark entered as plateworker, 13 March 1784. Address: Paternoster Row. Moved to 40 Hatton Garden, 12 March 1795. Heal records him at the first address only, from 1784 to 1789.

BELL, David (443, 3780) Son of James Bell of Ansford Inn in the County of Somerset gentleman, apprenticed to William Gould 3 October 1744. Turned over to Richard Rugg 13 January 1747. Freedom unrecorded. First mark (3780) entered as David Bell and Co., 11 January 1753, Greenhills Rents, Smithfield Bars and later the '& Co' and 'RM' portion of the mark struck through and a note added 'Look for ye mark in ye small book'. Second mark entered as largeworker, 30 November 1756. Address: Cary Street, Lincoln's Inn Fields. Heal records him as plateworker, Ironmonger Row, 1756 (cf. Joseph Bell II), and London, 1772.

BELL, Joseph I (161, 2707) Son of John Bell of Market Lavington in the County of Wiltshire, apprenticed to Robert Timbrell 7 May 1700. Free, 17 October 1707. Mark entered in partnership with Robert Timbrell as largeworkers, undated, below the original entry of the latter's mark alone, presumably after Bell's freedom about 1707. Address: Sherborne Lane. Signatory as 'working goldsmith' to the petition complaining of the competition of 'necessitous strangers', December 1711. Livery, October 1712. Second mark, alone as largeworker, 1 October 1716. Address: Cannon Street, where Heal records him till 1724. Court,

BIOGRAPHICAL DICTIONARY

1729. The second entry annotated 'Left off' in lieu of the usual 'dead'.

BELL, Joseph II (1132, 3624) Son of John Bell late of Bruton in the County of Lincoln butcher deceased, apprenticed to Richard Hawkins 5 October 1748. Free, 6 July 1757. Mark entered as largeworker, 25 October 1756. Address: 'near Ironmonger Row, Old Street. Later moved to Shoe Lane, where Heal records him in the same year.

*BELL, Joseph III (1780) No record of apprenticeship or freedom. Only mark entered as spoonmaker, 28 August 1818. Address: Little Dukes Street, Borough.

BELL, Richard (2268) Son of Richard Bell of St. Olaves Southwark gentleman, apprenticed to John Peirce 24 March 1724 on payment of £21. Free, 1 April 1735. Only mark entered as smallworker, 22 August 1734. Address: Mugwell Street, 'over against Surgeons Hall'.

BELL, William (3018) Son of John Bell late of Reading in the County of Berkshire linen draper deceased, apprenticed to William Burton 3 February 1748 on payment of £30. Free, 9 April 1755. Livery, March 1758. First mark entered as smallworker, 10 February 1759. Address: Monkwell Street. Moved to Featherstone Street, 31 October 1759, where he entered an incuse mark, 22 March 1763 (Section V). Moved to Silver Street, 3 April 1764. Third mark, incuse, 8 March 1769. Address: Bridgwater Square. Fourth mark, 4 August 1772. Address: (10) Rolls Buildings (Fetter Lane), where he appears as goldworker in the Parl. Report list 1773. Fifth and sixth marks as goldworker, 1774 and 1777, same address (Section VII). Heal records him as plateworker, Monkwell Street, 1759; watchcasemaker, Silver Street 1767; Pierpoint Row, Islington, 1771; and goldsmith, Rolls Buildings, 1773. He is presumably the William Bell appointed Junior Weigher in the Assay Office 9 December 1763 to succeed Gawen Nash (q.v.). If so he seems to have been able to carry on his own business as well, on the evidence of his mark entries after 1763. Resigned from Livery, August 1778, presumably on retirement from business.

BELLAMY, William (162) Son of Daniel Bellamy of Oxstidge (?Oxted) in the County of Surrey clerk, apprenticed to William Spring 3 March 1708 and turned over later to William Fawdery. Free, 21 September 1715. Signatory as journeyman to the petition against assaying the mark of foreigners not having served seven years apprenticeship, February 1716. Mark entered as largeworker, 1 October 1717. Address: Foster Lane.

BELLASYSE, Charles (267) Son of William Bellasyse (q.v.) Citizen and Merchant Taylor, apprenticed to James Wilkes 5 February 1734 on payment of £20. Turned over to Marmaduke Daintrey 27 July 1738. Signs apprentice register as Bellasyes. Free, 2 July 1741. Mark entered as largeworker, 21 July 1740. Address: Eagle Street, near Red Lion Square. Signs entry Belasyse. Heal records him at the Mitre at this address, for this year only.

BELLASSYSE, William (160, 3008) Son of Richard Bellasis late of Hangston in the Bishopric of Durham clerk, apprenticed to Seth Lofthouse (q.v.) of the Merchant Taylors' Company 5 October 1709. Free by servitude, 7 November 1716. First mark entered as largeworker, 16 March 1717. 'Free of Merchant Taylors'. Address: Monkwell Street. Second mark (Sterling), 3 July 1723. Address: Holborn. Signs this entry Bellassyes. Heal records him at the Mitre, Monkwell Street, 1716.

BELLINGHAM, Samuel (2481) No record of apprenticeship or freedom. First mark, in partnership with Samuel Gladman as goldworkers, 12 October 1793. Address: 8 Bell Square, St. Martin's Le Grand (Section VII). Second mark alone as smallworker, 10 May 1806, same address.

BELLIS, James (1137) No record of apprenticeship or freedom. First mark entered as goldworker, 16 May 1760. Address: King Street, Covent Garden. Second smaller mark, 22 December 1764, same address. Heal further records him at 9 Pall Mall from 1768 to 1788. Goldworker, Pall Mall, Parl. Report list 1773. Jeweller, Pall Mall, died 1 November 1788 (*The Gentleman's Magazine*).

BENJAMIN, Lewis (1903) No record of apprenticeship or freedom. Only mark entered as plateworker, 23 July 1834. Address: 12 John Street, Oxford Street. Moved to 37 Princes Street, Leicester Square, 23 February 1838.

BENNETT, Edward I (530, 533, 540, 544) Son of John Bennett late of Botolph without Aldersgate hair merchant deceased, apprenticed to Henry Miller 23 March 1720 on payment of £6 and turned over to Samuel

437

Hutton in Noble Street spoonmaker 6 April 1725. Free, 13 April 1727. First mark entered 27 March 1727. Address: Corsskee (?Crosskeys) Court, Little Britain. Second mark, 25 June 1731. Address: Noble Street. Livery March 1737. Third mark, 30 December 1737. Address: 'on London Bridg' Fourth mark, 28 June 1739. Same address. Fifth and sixth marks, 20 July 1747. Heal records him as plateworker, Little Britain, 1727; and as goldsmith, Blue Lion and Crown, Corner of Tooley Street, London Bridge, 1739–47.

BENNETT, Edward II (537, 541) Son of the above. Free by patrimony, 6 October 1756. First and second marks entered as 'Goldsmith' and signing 'Jr', 26 June 1756. Address: 'on London Bridge'. Third mark, 7 July 1758, still as 'Ju^r'. Address: Corner of Tueley Street, London Bridge, Southwark. Livery, July 1763. Died before 1796. The Parl. Report list 1773 contains the entry 'Edward Bennet, spoonmaker, Lombard Street', which seems difficult to reconcile with the foregoing addresses. The next entry is 'Edward Bennet Junior, spoonmaker Corner of Tooley Street, Southwark'. This suggests that the previous entry was a printer's error, which was corrected by the following line, but inadvertently left standing.

BENNETT, John I (1122) No record of apprenticeship or freedom. Only mark entered as smallworker, 20 April 1732. Address: New Street, near Shoe Lane, near the Three Tuns.

*BENNETT, John II (1139) Perhaps the son of John Bennett Citizen and Barber Surgeon of London, apprenticed to Aaron Bates 14 April 1747 on payment of £20. Freedom not recorded. Only mark entered as smallworker, 9 December 1761. Address: Threadneedle Street, where Heal records him as haftmaker in 1773. He appears as hiltmaker at the same address in the Parl. Report list 1773.

BENNETT, Peter (2131, 2137) Son of John Bennett of the parish of St. Botolph's Aldersgate hair merchant (and brother of Edward Bennett q.v.), apprenticed to Henry Miller 16 April 1724 on payment of £10. Apprenticed again (without explanation) 4 March 1725 to Hugh Arnett, no premium stated; turned over 3 November 1729 to his brother Edward Bennett Citizen and Goldsmith. Free, 23 May 1732. First mark entered as largeworker, 6 March 1732. Address: Little Britain. Second mark, 22 June 1739. Address: Goswell Street. Moved to 'Pages Walk the granged road Upper end of Barnaby Street Southwark', 13 March 1741. Moved to Brick Lane, Old Street, 17 January 1749. Heal records only the first two addresses.

BENNETT, William (3029–30) Son of John Bennett late of Rickmansworth in the County of Hertford blacksmith deceased, apprenticed to John Arnell of Little Britain London goldsmith, Citizen and Goldsmith 7 July 1784. Turned over by consent to John Perry of Bartholomew Close silversmith, Citizen and Goldsmith 2 August 1786. Turned over the second time to Solomon Hougham of Aldersgate Street goldsmith, Citizen and Goldsmith 3 October 1787. Free, 4 July 1792. First mark entered as plateworker, 1 June 1796. Address: 2 Half Moon Passage, Aldersgate Street. Moved to 19 Little Barthlomew Close, 25 September 1800. Second mark (three sizes), 7 July 1808. Heal records him at Bartholomew's Close in 1794, before the entry of his mark; and at Aldersgate Street, 1796–1800. Livery, April 1816. His mark appears chiefly on trays and salvers in which he seems to have specialized and has formerly been confused with that of William Bateman I, which was not entered till 1815. Died February 1825.

*BENOIMONT, Louis (182, 1902, 1904) Free by redemption as jeweller, 6 September 1749. Livery, April 1751. First mark entered as smallworker in partnership with Luke Kendall, 18 November 1761. Address: Carey Lane. Second mark alone, 21 August 1764, same address. Appears in Parl. Report list 1773 as goldsmith, Fenchurch Street. Listed as Huguenot by Evans ('Huguenot Goldsmiths', *Hug. Soc. Proc.*, 14).

BENTLEY, Benjamin (126, 155, 163, 3485) Son of William Bentley of Leicester mercer, apprenticed to Edmund Townsend 19 June 1691. Free, 11 November 1698. Livery, October 1708. First mark entered 25 November 1698, no address. Second and third marks (Sterling and New Standard), 31 January 1728. Address: Tooley Street. Jackson's association of his name in partnership with Robert Timbrell in place of Joseph Bell (q.v.) is an error followed by Heal and without any evidence. He was signatory as 'working goldsmith' to the petition complaining of the competition of 'necessitous strangers', December 1711.

BERENGER J(ohn) (1157) Son of Philip Berenger late of Salisbury Court Fleet Street watchmaker, apprenticed to Jn. Spindellow of Great New Street Fetter Lane 11 March 1772 as metal button maker on payment of £5.5s. Free, 7 April 1779. Livery, February 1791. Only mark entered as smallworker, 10 July 1798. Address: 24 Great New Street, Fetter Lane (as his master). Heal records him here as silver buckle maker in 1786. Died c. 1818-22.

BERNARD See BARNARD

BERRY, John (151) Either (1) the John Berry apprenticed to John Elsworth of the Clockmakers' Company 21 August 1684; free, 4 April 1692. Or (2) another of the same name apprenticed 22 December 1687 to John Benson; freedom unrecorded. Only mark entered as smallworker, 20 December 1699. Address: Shoe Lane. 'Free Clockmakers'. Presumably a watchcasemaker.

BERTHELLOT, John (1129, 1179, 3616) No record of apprenticeship or freedom. First mark entered as watchcasemaker, 5 September 1738. Address: Tower Street. Second mark in largeworkers' book, 26 July 1739. Address: Peter Street, corner of Holborn. Moved to Earl Street, corner of Tower Street, Seven Dials, no date. Moved to Long Lane, near Bermondsey Street, Southwark, 23 March 1742(?), and Saffron Hill, 28 July 1743. Incuse mark entered 8 July 1746, 'Removed from Saffron Hill to the Bolling alley turnmill Street', and another 30 November 1750, 'Removed to White Horse Alley, Cow Cross' (Section V). Heal records him at Peter Street, 1739; Long Lane, Holborn, 1741; and Cow Cross, Holborn, 1750-2. Listed as Huguenot by Evans ('Huguenot Goldsmiths', *Hug. Soc. Proc.*, 14).

BERTHET, Esaye (532) No record of apprenticeship or freedom. Only mark entered as largeworker, styling himself 'Silversmith', 31 October 1728. Address: 'at the Gold Ring Charing Cross'. Appears as godfather to Françoise Lavigne, 14 November 1720, in Hungerford Market Church register (*Hug. Soc. Pub.*, 31).

BERTRAM, William (165) Apprenticed to Samuel Horne of the Clockmakers' Company 7 May 1677. Free, 29 September 1684. Mark entered as smallworker, undated, probably April 1697 on commencement of register. Address: Old Bailey. 'Free Clockmaker'.

BESCHEFER, James (158) Son of James Beschefer of the Parish of St. Anne's Westm^r in the County of Middlesex, apprenticed to Daniel Garner (Garnier) 5 August 1697. He signs his name Bechefer. Free, 16 August 1704. Only mark entered as largeworker, 4 October 1704. Address: Porter Street, 'near Leisterfields'. He appears in the Naturalization Act list, 16 February 1705/6, as son of James Beschefer and Louise his wife, born at Vitry in Champaign in France. His sister Marie Anne was married, 3 January 1704, at the Tabernacle, Glasshouse Street, to Daniel Peltreau, merchant, when the parents were described as 'noble homme Jacques et dame Louise Villain'. The goldsmith appears as godfather to his niece Louise Peltreau, 15 August 1705, in the Leicester Fields Church register, and, as Capitaine Jacques Bechefer, godfather to Jacques Pelletreau, 15 May 1714, in West Street Church.

BEST, Thomas (2694) No record of apprenticeship or freedom. First mark entered as smallworker, 28 April 1795. Address: 3 Bayles Alley, Strand. Second mark, 6 May 1795. Moved to 1 Angel Court, Strand, 11 August 1797. Moved to 6 Red Lion Court, Fleet Street, 10 April 1799. Third mark, 23 May 1801. Address: 3 Richards Buildings, Shoe Lane. Moved to 17 Plough Court, Fetter Lane, 28 April 1806.

BETHAM, James (1130) Son of Robert Betham of Woodford in the County of Westmorland husbandman deceased, apprenticed to Thomas Farren 17 June 1735 on payment of £25. Free, 8 November 1743. Mark entered as largeworker, 6 December 1743. Address: Staining Lane, near Wood Street.

BETTS, Edward (538) No record of apprenticeship or freedom. Only mark entered as spoonmaker, 23 December 1807. Address: 11 Bedford Court, Covent Garden.

BETTS, John (154, 1117) Perhaps son of John Betts of London gentleman, apprenticed to John Hannam 2 June 1692. Free, 6 October 1699. He is however described as 'Free Lorimer' on the entry of his first mark as largeworker, 25 April 1705. Second (Sterling) mark, 9 August 1720. Address: 'in Holborn'. (The records of the Lorimers' Company were unfortunately destroyed in 1940.)

BEVAULT, Thomas (152) No record of apprenticeship or freedom. Only mark entered as largeworker, 24 December 1712. Address: Foster Lane. Listed by Evans as Huguenot, a Mary de Bevault appearing in the Bounty List of 1690. Evans also states he was free by apprenticeship in 1711 ('Huguenot Goldsmiths', *Hug. Soc. Proc.*, 14).

BICKERTON, Benjamin (131, 134) Son of John Bickerton Citizen and Baker of London, apprenticed to Henry Bickerton (probably his brother, q.v.) 7 June 1749 on payment of £20. Free, 6 October 1756. First mark entered as smallworker, 31 March 1762. Address: Jewin Street. Second mark, 6 December 1762. Third mark, 10 June 1771. Address: 41 Jewin Street. Fourth and fifth marks, 26 June 1771. Sixth and seventh marks as bucklemaker, 1779 and 1789, and eighth, with son Thomas, 1791 (Section VIII). Heal records him as silversmith, 14 (sic) Jewin Street, Aldersgate, from 1765–96. Livery, December 1771. Appears as smallworker, 41 Jewin Street, in Parl. Report list 1773. Died July 1808.

BICKERTON, Henry (954) Probably son of John Bickerton Citizen and Baker of London, apprenticed to John Alcock 2 May 1738 in consideration of £18. Turned over to William Wheate (Turner) 4 May 1738 and to his father 7 June 1741. Free, 3 July 1745. Livery, March 1758. Only mark entered 26 August 1762. Address: Monkwell Street. Died before 1796. It is interesting to note that he took his brother as apprentice in 1749 long before he is recorded entering his own mark, and it may be that an earlier mark is unrecorded.

BICKERTON, Thomas (2696) Thomas Worsley son of Benjamin Bickerton of Jewin Street London goldsmith, apprenticed to his father 1 July 1778. Free, 7 December 1785. Livery, February 1791. First mark, in partnership with his father as bucklemakers, 28 February 1791 (Section VIII). Second mark alone, entered as smallworker, 10 July 1800. Address: Jewin Street, where Heal records him in 1792. Entered incuse mark as smallworker, 30 July 1819. Address: 14 Jewin Street (Section V). Died before 1822.

BIDDELL, Thomas William (914, 2698) No record of apprenticeship or freedom. A Thomas Biddell, son of Richard, was free by patrimony 7 February 1759; and John son of Thomas Biddle of Windsor Court Monkwell Street goldsmith, Citizen and Goldsmith was apprenticed to Jonathan Perkins in 1780. There seems therefore to have been a family of this name practising as goldsmiths from about the mid-eighteenth century. The first mark (2698) may be that of the above, entered as smallworker, 6 November 1811. Address: 55 Drury Lane. Second mark (914) of Thomas William Biddell in partnership with George Turner as spoonmakers, 29 March 1820. Address: 55 Drury Lane. Partnership presumably dissolved by 22 November 1823, on entry of Turner's mark alone.

BIGGE, Richard (181, 3763) Son of John Bigg of Kimbell in the County of Buckingham yeoman, apprenticed to Thomas Bracey 21 July 1693, and turned over to Henry Collins. Free, 20 September 1700. Mark entered as largeworker, 23 November 1700. Address: 'Swethings Lane'. Heal records him at St. Swithin's Lane from 1700 to 1725(?).

BIGGS, Joseph (1166) Son of Thomas Biggs of Laystall Street Holborn gentleman, apprenticed to Robert Barker of Gutter Lane Goldsmith 6 May 1789 on payment of £20. Free, 3 May 1797. First mark entered as plateworker, 26 January 1816. Address: Winchester Street, Pentonville. Second mark, 28 June 1819. Third, 28 November 1820.

*BIGGS, Roger (2273) No record of apprenticeship or freedom. First mark entered as smallworker, 14 May 1791. Address: 64 Barbican. Moved to 5 Crescent, Jewin Street, 28 March 1797. Second and third marks as goldworker, 1822 and 1826. Address: 2 Queen Square, Aldersgate Street (Section VII).

BIGNELL, John (180, 1116) Son of George Bignell of Wilton in the County of Wiltshire farrier, apprenticed to Thomas Merry 22 December 1709. Signatory, as journeyman, to the petition against assaying the work of foreigners not having served seven years apprenticeship, February 1716. Free, 19 September 1717. First mark entered as largeworker, 14 May 1718. Probably the John Bignell of St. Benet Finck, bachelor, married to Mary Snow of St. Ann, Aldersgate, widow, 22 July 1718, at St. Bene't, Paul's Wharf. Second (Sterling) mark, 6 July 1720. Address: Staining Lane, where Heal records him as plateworker and silver caster from 1718 to 1729. Presumably identifiable with John Bignell, bachelor, goldsmith of St. Sepulchre's, married to Mary Weston, spinster of St. Michael Wood Street, in the Fleet Register of Marriages, Book 48. (The nature of these marriages of convenience at the Fleet does not necessarily imply that the contracting parties were imprisoned for debt. They were often legal fictions for financial transactions.) Buried at St. Alban Wood Street, 20 December 1739.

BILLINGHURST, Henry (953) No record of apprenticeship or freedom. Only mark entered as smallworker, 11 October 1759. Address: Aldersgate Street. Appears as watchcasemaker, Aldersgate Street, in the Parl. Report list 1773.

BILLINGSLEY, Francis (176) Son of Benjamin Billingsley of Greenstok in the County of Lincoln gentleman, apprenticed to William Eycott 18 April 1690 and turned over to Thomas Boulton. Free, 30 March 1698. Mark entered as largeworker, undated, probably on commencement of register in April 1697, but if so before grant of freedom. Address: Bedford Court, Covent Garden.

BILTON, Richard John (2348) No record of apprenticeship or freedom. Only mark entered as smallworker, 20 September 1831. Address: 9 Westminster Bridge Road.

BINDOFF, George (765) George Samuel son of Samuel Bindoff of Anchor Yard Old Street weaver, apprenticed to Thomas Wallis of Red Lion Street Clerkenwell 1 December 1813. Free, 3 November 1830. Mark entered as spoonmaker, 5 November 1829. Address: 2 Clarence Place, St. Luke's, Old Street.

BINDON, George (752) No record of apprenticeship or freedom. Only mark entered as largeworker, 13 December 1749. Address: 'at Mr Weavers in Theobalds Court in the Strand'.

*BINGER, Christopher I (268) No record of apprenticeship or freedom. Only mark entered as smallworker, 28 February 1771. Address: Windmill Street, Tottenham, where Heal records him as goldsmith, 1773. As goldworker at this address, Parl. Report list 1773, and entered a mark as such, 27 April 1793 (Section VII).

BINGER, Christopher II (272) Presumably son of above. Mark entered as smallworker, 24 February 1803. Address: 211 High Holborn.

*BINLEY, Margaret (1998) No record of apprenticeship or freedom. Presumably widow of Richard Binley below. Only mark entered as smallworker, 15 May 1764. Address: Gutter Lane, where Heal records her as goldsmith, 1771. Appears as Margaret Bingley, smallworker, at this address in Parl. Report list 1773. Like Richard Binley, her mark appears to be found only on winelabels.

BINLEY, Richard (2272) Son of William Binley of Little Wickstone in the County of Leicester farmer deceased, apprenticed to Sandylands Drinkwater 13 January 1732, on payment of £20. Free, 6 December 1739. First mark entered as smallworker, 20 September 1760. Address: Gutter Lane. The long interval since freedom may suggest that we have here the son of the above. Second mark, 18 December 1760. Presumably dead by 15 May 1764, on entry of Margaret Binley's mark (above). Like Drinkwater, his mark appears to be found only on wine-labels.

*BIRD, Benjamin (123) Son of William Bird free Waterman of the River Thames, apprenticed to Thomas Crooke of the Joyners' Company 9 September 1707. Free, 3 May 1715. Mark entered as smallworker, 16 February 1721. Address: Bell Savage Yard, Ludgate Hill. 'Free Joyner'. Called bucklemaker, in Bell Savage Yard, in the turn over to him of Richard Holder, apprentice, 14 November 1720.

*BIRD, Joseph (177-9, 1120, 3614-5) Largeworker. Two marks entered, undated, probably April 1697 on commencement of register. Address: Foster Lane. Described as Free Brewer. Third mark entered with no date or address. Fourth (Sterling) mark, 19 June 1724. His name does not appear in the registers of the Brewers' Company so far back as they have survived, 1685, so he was presumably a freeman before that date. Heal records him at Foster Lane from 1697 till his death in 1735 and he held the office of churchwarden of St. John Zachary in 1704. He was signatory as 'working goldsmith' to the petitition complaining of the competition of 'necessitous strangers', December 1711. His mark is usually found on candlesticks and it would seem probable that he may have been master of Henry Greene (q.v.), also a Brewer, and of David Green, whose

441

company is not recorded, but who was master in his turn of James Gould and the latter of John Cafe. He is presumably the 'Captain Bird', Foster Lane, Goldsmith, to whom Samuel Bates (q.v.) was apprenticed, 17 December 1719.

*BIRD, Rebekah (2263) No record of apprenticeship or freedom. Only mark entered as smallworker, 7 November 1721. Address: Star Court, Bread Street Hill.

BIRD, William I (3009) No record of apprenticeship or freedom. Only mark entered as smallworker, 19 August 1731. Address: Butchers Row, near Temple Bar.

BIRD, William II (3021) Probably son of above; but also possibly William son of John Bird recorded free by patrimony 5 May 1743. Mark entered as smallworker, 13 July 1769. Address: Strand, near Temple Bar. Appears as bucklemaker, near Temple Bar, Strand, in the Parl. Report list 1773, and entered mark as such in 1788 at 219 Temple Bar (Section VIII).

BISSELL, William (3022) Son of William Bissell of Rowley in the County of Stafford nailer, apprenticed to John Westray 7 February 1759. Free, 4 February 1767. Mark entered as smallworker, 24 October 1769. Address: 59 Hood Street.

BLACK, Louis (1901) No record of apprenticeship or freedom. First mark entered as largeworker, 30 July 1756. Address: James Street, near Haymarket. Second mark, 11 December 1761. From occurrence of mark apparently specializing in candlesticks.

BLACKBEARD, Francis (668) Son of Francis Blackbeard of Taylor Row, Islington silversmith, apprenticed to William Chawner of Lovells Court Paternoster Row 1 February 1809. Freedom unrecorded. Mark entered as plateworker, 26 November 1824. Address: 1 Lovell Court, Paternoster Row. Presumably remained as assistant to Eley and Fearn at this address, although he has no partnership mark with them.

BLACKBOROW, Samuel (186, 2474, 3789) Son of Henry Blackborow Citizen and Leatherseller of London, apprenticed to William Fawdery 13 October 1709. Signatory as journeyman to the petition against assaying the work of foreigners not having served seven years apprenticeship, February 1716. Free, 6 March 1717. First mark entered as largeworker, 4 September 1719. Address: Gutter Lane. Second (Sterling) mark, 17 January 1721. Address: Winchester Court, Mugwell Street.

BLACKFORD, Anthony (183) Son of Anthony Blackford late of the town and county of Warwick watchmaker, apprenticed to Samuel Hawkes 9 January 1694. Free, 18 July 1701. Livery, October 1708. Mark entered as largeworker, 12 June 1702. Address: Ball Alley, Lombard Street. Heal records him as goldsmith at the Golden Cup and Crown, Lombard Street, from 1702 till death in 1716. Hilton Price includes him in his *Handbook of London Bankers*.

BLACKWAY, George (767) No record of apprenticeship or freedom. Only mark entered as smallworker, in partnership with John Hodson, 14 July 1790. Address: 71 Strand.

BLADES, John (1163, 1173) No record of apprenticeship or freedom. First mark entered as smallworker, 9 June 1812. Address: 5 Ludgate Place. Second mark, 8 December 1827, same address.

*BLAKE, John (1151, 1160) No record of apprenticeship or freedom. First mark entered as smallworker, 5 September 1788. Address: 7 Cranborn Street, Leicester Fields. Moved to Long's Court, Leicester Fields, 26 October 1792. Second mark, 14 October 1795. Third mark as spoonmaker, 16 May 1803. Address: 16 Long Acre. Heal records him only at 5 Long's Court from 1790-1804. Probably died about June 1809, when Sarah and John William Blake entered a joint mark.

*BLAKE, John William (1759, 2483) No record of apprenticeship or freedom. Described as pewterer in apprenticeship to him of John Brydie, 1817, presumably free of that company. Presumably son of John Blake (above). Mark entered in partnership with Sarah Blake as spoonmakers, 15 June 1809. Address: 16 Long Acre. Second mark, 9 January 1821. Third, 7 November 1821. Four marks alone, 2 October 1823, same address. Fifth and sixth marks, 17 December 1823 and 30 September 1824.

BLAKE, Sarah (2483) Presumably widow of John Blake (q.v.). Mark entered in partnership with her son(?) John William, as spoonmakers, 15 June 1809. Address: 16 Long Acre. Second mark, 9 January 1821. Third, 7 November 1821. Dead or retired by 2 October 1823, when John William entered separate mark.

BLAKELY, Benjamin (124-5, 133, 185) Son

of Joseph Blakely Citizen and Joyner of London, free by patrimony of the Joyners' Company 6 September 1715. First mark entered as largeworker, 10 October 1715. Address: Strand. 'Free Joyner'. Second (Sterling) mark, 29 June 1720. Third mark, undated, after July 1738 and before May 1739. Address: Russell Street, Covent Garden. Fourth mark, 2 July 1739. Address: 'at Mr Carters Goldsmith Russell Street Covent Garden'. Heal records the above addresses and also London, 1768-9, the latter perhaps a son for whom there is no mark entered.

*BLAND, Cornelius (269-271) Son of Cornelius Bland of Henley upon Thames in the County of Oxford butcher, apprenticed to James Bishop 7 October 1761 on payment of £10. Free, 1 February 1769. First mark entered as smallworker, 7 March 1772. Address: 62 Aldersgate Street, where he appears as Cornelius Blane, without category, in the Parl. Report list 1773. Moved to 185 Fleet Street, 3 April 1773, at which address he was for a short time in partnership with George Natter as plateworkers. In the register against the date 2 August 1773 their joint names are entered without an impression of their mark with the note against Bland's name 'out of Trade' and 'Note this is only an Extract of the Entry of their Mark in the former Mark Book'. In 1779 Bland is described as 'Silver Chaser' when Thomas Young was apprenticed to him, which appears to confirm the note in the register above. Heal records him at Jewin Street in 1782, and he was there in 1786 when his son was apprenticed to him. He entered a second mark as plateworker, 25 September 1788. Address: 116 Aldersgate Street. Third mark, 9 December 1788. Moved to 126 Bunhill Row, 3 June 1790, where Heal records him till 1796. The Bland family were long established at Henley. John, son of Cornelius of Henley, was apprenticed to a member of the Haberdashers' Company in 1684.

BLAND, Elizabeth (1186) Presumably widow of Cornelius (above). Mark entered in partnership with James, the latter's son, 16 September 1794. Address: 126 Bunhill Row, where Heal records them from 1791, apparently overlapping the working period of Cornelius.

*BLAND, James (1186) James Huell Bland son of Cornelius (q.v.) of Jewin Street London silversmith, apprenticed to his father 1 November 1786 and turned over 7 February 1787 to Thomas Young of Aldersgate Street silversmith, Citizen and Goldsmith. Freedom unrecorded. Mark entered in partnership with Elizabeth, 16 September 1794, presumably on death or retirement of his father. Address: 126 Bunhill Row.

BLAND, Nathaniel (184) Son of Francis Bland Citizen and Vintner of London, apprenticed to John Cory 4 July 1700 and turned over to Anthony Blackford. Free, 1 December 1714. Mark entered as largeworker, 10 July 1715. Address: Noble Street.

BLUETT, Walker (3043) No record of apprenticeship or freedom. Only mark entered as smallworker, 6 September 1832. Address: 166 Fleet Street.

*BLUNT, John I (1123) No record of apprenticeship or freedom. Only mark entered as smallworker, 25 May 1732. Address: 'Noble Street over against ye Chapple in Old Street'.

BLUNT, John II (1124) Apparently a distinct entry from that above, the writing showing no similarity. No record of apprenticeship or freedom. Only entry as smallworker, 12 November 1734. Address: Huggin Alley, Wood Street. 'Gouldsmith'. Heal records one of this name as goldsmith, Cheapside, insolvent 1743.

BOCK, Mark (1996-7, 3735) No record of apprenticeship or freedom. First mark entered as smallworker, 25 November 1761. Address: King's Head Court, Shoe Lane. Second mark, 15 August 1764. Dead by 1 October 1783, when his son William was apprenticed to William Gyblett, Mark Bock being described as late of King's Head Court in Shoe Lane, sword cutler, deceased. The mark formerly much ascribed to him is that of Moses Brent (q.v.). Heal records Bock as goldsmith, Shoe Lane, 1773; and as London, 1799, the latter possibly derived from a misattribution to him of Brent's mark. He appears as hiltmaker at the above address in the Parl. Report list 1773.

BOCQUET, Paul (2139) No record of apprenticeship or freedom. Mark entered as smallworker, 10 July 1762. Address: 15 Great Kirby Street. Heal records Paul and Robert Bocquet, goldworkers, 12 Gloucester Street, Bloomsbury, 1772-4, which is presumably evidence of a later address and partnership of son or brother, for which there is no mark in the registers.

BOCQUET, Philip (2135) No record of apprenticeship or freedom. There may of course be some possibility of identity with the above, if for instance he had two names and interchanged them in use. Mark entered as smallworker, 13 December 1771. Address: 8 Bartholomew Close, where he appears as goldworker in the Parl. Report list 1773, which however conflicts with the address in Heal for Paul and Robert, as above.

BODINGTON, Edmund (531, 542) Son of Edmund Bodington late Citizen and Apothecary of London deceased, apprenticed to John Bodington 7 May 1706 and turned over 24 September 1706 to Giles Edmunds, Turner. Free, 5 May 1714. First mark entered in smallworkers' book as goldsmith, 8 October 1725. Address: Gutter Lane. Second mark as largeworker, 5 July 1727. Address: Foster Lane. 'Free Goldsmith'. Heal records him at the Mitre, Foster Lane, as successor to John Bodington (q.v.), from 1727 till insolvency in 1729. Livery, March 1736.

*****BODINGTON, John** (201) Son of John Boddington (sic) late of Marston in the County of Leicester clerk, apprenticed to Jacob Harris for eight years 2 November 1677. Free, 18 July 1688. Livery, April 1705. Mark entered as largeworker, undated, probably April 1697 on commencement of register. Address: Foster Lane, where Heal records him at the Mitre till 1727, and at Goldsmiths' Hall in 1727 (see below). Married Elizabeth Franklyn, 29 December 1692, at Christchurch, Newgate, he being of St. Leonard's, Foster Lane, and she of Christchurch. Two daughters, Elizabeth and Anne, baptized at the same church, 1693 and 1696. Signatory to the petition to the Company against the marking of foreigners' work, 1703, as 'working goldsmith' to that of 1711 against the competition of 'necessitous strangers'. His son John was apprenticed to him, 1 May 1718, but turned over the same December to Samuel Gatcliff of Abchurch Lane, jeweller, and again, in 1722, to W. Wright of Foster Lane. He does not appear to have entered any mark. Bodington must have come to financial grief by 1714 as in that year he was appointed Beadle to the Company, which post he held till his death in January 1727, to be followed by Benjamin Pyne equally impoverished in his turn. Heal records Edmund Bodington (q.v.), probably his nephew, as succeeding him in 1727, but if John had been Beadle since 1714 it is difficult to understand, and Edmund had himself entered a mark in 1725 separately. Bodington's surviving work shows a high standard and considerable Huguenot influence in spite of his antagonism to the immigrants. He may of course have employed some as journeymen.

BODLEY, Robert (199) Son of Thomas Bodle (sic) in Marfield in the County of Leicester, free of the Founders' Company by service seven years to Robert Newman 5 August 1706. Mark entered as smallworker, 4 April 1707. Address: Charles Court, Charing Cross. 'Free Founder'. Heal records him as Bodle—, silversmith at this address 1712.

BOGGETT, George (764) No record of apprenticeship or freedom. Only mark entered as plateworker, 10 February 1824. Address: 50 St. Martin's Lane.

BOHEME, Maurice (204-5, 1994) Son of George Boheme of Walcot in the County of Lincoln clerk, apprenticed to Joseph Willcox 9 November 1687. Free, 20 February 1694. Livery, October 1708. Signed petition against assaying work of foreigners not having served seven years apprenticeship, February 1716. Two marks (Sterling and New Standard) entered as smallworker, 29 June 1720. Address: Tokenhouse Yard, The Minories. Heal records him as goldsmith, Lad Lane, near Wood Street, 1709; and as in Goldsmith Street, 1724-7. It seems very probable that he was working independently from soon after his freedom but that his mark was omitted from the 1697 register.

BOISSONADE, Daniel (444) No record of apprenticeship or freedom. Described as goldworker of Gun Street Spitalfields in the apprenticeship of his son John to Nathaniel Appleton in 1773, and he appears as smallworker, 46 Gun Street, Spitalfields, in the Parl. Report list of the same year. Only mark entered as smallworker, 26 August 1775. Address: 11 Christopher Alley, Moorfields. Moved to 10 Lambeth Hill, Doctors' Commons, 16 August 1778.

BOND, William (3045-6, 3049) Son of Samuel Bond Citizen and Carpenter of London, apprenticed to David Hennell 5 May 1743 on payment of £15. Free, 10 April 1752. Two marks entered as largeworker, 31 July 1753. Address: Foster Lane. Third mark in partnership with James

Phipps, 8 May 1754, same address, where Heal records him till 1756.

BONE, Ishmael (197) Son of Edward Bone of Westmain (?West Meon) in the County of Hampshire carpenter, apprenticed to Stephen Coleman 15 June 1692 and turned over 6 May 1697 to John Ladyman. Free, 6 October 1699. Mark entered as largeworker, 19 October 1699. Address: Abchurch Lane, where Heal records him till 1704.

BOOTH, John (1165, 3048) No record of apprenticeship or freedom. First mark entered as smallworker in partnership with Wilks Booth (?father), 28 June 1810. Address: 8 Albemarle Street. Second mark alone, 24 November 1813, same address.

BOOTH, Wilkes (3027, 3048) No record of apprenticeship or freedom. First mark entered as snuffermaker, 11 October 1787. Address: 8 Albemarle Street. Second mark, 8 July 1805. Third mark, in partnership with John Booth (?son), 28 June 1810, same address.

BOOTHBY, George (203, 746, 766) Son of William Boothby of Potter Marston in the County of Leicester Esqre, apprenticed to Matthew Cooper 29 November 1712 on payment of £35. Signatory as journeyman to the petition against assaying the work of foreigners not having served seven years apprenticeship, February 1716. Free, 3 December 1719. First mark entered as largeworker, 1 March 1720. Address: 'at the Parrot in the Strand'. Second (Sterling) mark, 4 August 1720. Third (Sterling) mark, 22 June 1739, 'at ye Parrott Temple Bar'. Heal records him as goldsmith and banker, 1701 (but this must be an error); and at the Parrot without Temple Bar, from 1720 till 1741, when he appears in the *London Gazette* for 24 October 1741 as bankrupt described as 'Silversmith and Banker'. Listed as such by Hilton Price, *Handbook of London Bankers*.

*BORCHERS, Albrecht (12) No record of apprenticeship or freedom. Only mark entered as largeworker, 14 June 1769. Address: 3 Sparrow Fields, near Coldbath Fields, where he appears as goldworker in the Parl. Report list 1773.

BOSS, William (3042) No record of apprenticeship or freedom. Only mark entered as smallworker, 20 June 1832. Address: 7 Richmond Street, St. Bartholomew Square.

BOSWORTH, Thomas (473) No record of apprenticeship or freedom. Only mark entered as smallworker in partnership with Daniel Hockley, 6 April 1815. Address: 9 Brook Street, Holborn.

*BOTFEILD, Richard (2267) No record of apprenticeship or freedom. Only mark entered as smallworker, 11 July 1734. Address: Saffron Hill, near Potter Street.

BOTWYLE, William Henry (3175) No record of apprenticeship or freedom. Only mark entered as smallworker, 31 August 1772. Address: 'opposite the Rose and Crown in Clare Court, Blackmore Clare Market Street'. Appears as Botevyle, bucklemaker, Clare Court, Drury Lane, in the Parl. Report list 1773.

BOUCHER, Richard (2269) Son of William Boucher of Holston in the County of Wiltshire gentleman, apprenticed to John Fiddes 7 September 1726 on payment of £25. Freedom unrecorded. Only mark entered as smallworker, 7 May 1736. Address: Wheatsheaf, Tavistock Street, Covent Garden.

BOUCHET, Rolland (2265) No record of apprenticeship or freedom, although Peter Bouchet son of René is recorded apprenticed to Matthew Ducoussin in 1709. Only mark entered as smallworker, 27 July 1726. Address: Litchfield Street. Heal records René Bouchett as jeweller, St. Anne's, Westminster, 1709, and there may be some connection as in the apprenticeship quoted above. A Peter Bouket of Compton Street, Soho, appears without category in the Parl. Report list 1773, and seems possibly a grandson.

BOULT, Michael (202, 1993) Son of Richard Boult of St. Saviours Southwark in the County of Surrey lime merchant, apprenticed to Thomas Parr 3 April 1706. Free, 6 May 1713. Livery, December 1717. First mark entered 20 May 1713. Address: Cheapside, after which there is a further date in the entry, 11 April 1720, but no indication of another mark. Second (Sterling) mark, 20 June 1720, same address. Heal records him at the Blue Anchor and Star, Cheapside, over against Wood Street, from 1713 till retirement in 1745. A son was apprenticed to him in 1733, but has no mark recorded.

BOULTON, Thomas (200, 2684) Son of Thomas Boulton Citizen and Barber Surgeon of London, apprenticed to Henry Bance 6 May 1707. Free, 23 March 1714 (?5). First mark entered as smallworker,

19 December 1715. Address: Gold Street. Second (Sterling) mark, 20 June 1720. Third mark, 26 October 1727. Address: Goldsmiths' Street. Livery, March 1728. Court, February 1734.

BOURNE, George (2861) No record of apprenticeship or freedom. Perhaps connected with Aaron Bourne (Sections IV and VI). Only mark entered as plateworker in partnership with Thomas Northcote, 5 June 1794. Address: Berkley Street, Clerkenwell, where Heal records them in the same year noting 'partnership dissolved 1796', a fact substantiated by the entry of Northcote's separate mark, 11 July 1797.

BOURN(E), John (1144-6, 1188 No record of apprenticeship or freedom. First mark entered as smallworker in partnership with Thomas Moore, 26 June 1770, the entry made by power of attorney by Aaron Bourne, John Bourne being of Abbots Bromley in the County of Stafford and Thomas Moore of Bartholomew Close. Second mark of the partnership, 12 November 1770. They appear as John Browne and Thomas Moore, bucklemakers, Abbot Bromley, Staffordshire and Bartholomew Close, in the Parl. Report list 1773, and entered a mark as such at 1 Queen Square, 8 February 1775 (Section VIII). Separate mark of John Bourn as spoonmaker, 2 February 1774. Address: 93 Bartholomew Close. Second as such, 7 May 1774. Third as smallworker, 22 July 1774. Fourth as spoonmaker, 24 January 1778. Moved to 1 Queen Square, 11 March 1778. The original partnership between two men in London and Staffordshire is very extraordinary and it may perhaps be that Bourne was temporarily away from London or a sleeping partner.

BOURNE, Samuel (198) Son of Thomas Bourne of Wareham in the County of Leicester husbandman, apprenticed to Michael Borne 22 June 1683. Free, 27 November 1691. Mark entered as smallworker, 9 November 1700. Address: Gutter Lane, where Heal records him at the Queen's Head from 1696 to 1704. The registers of St. Vedast, Foster Lane, contain several relevant entries, including: 'A Female childe of Samuel Bourne, Goldsmith Liveing at ye Queens head in Gutter Lane in this parish was borne the 30th day of September 1699'. The first entry is the burial of a son, Samuel, on 24 September 1697, and the last the burial of daughter, Keziah (the second of the name), 5 October 1714. In all, three daughters and two sons, as well as Thomas Cooper, servant of Samuel Bourne, are recorded as buried.

BOUTEILLER, Pierre (2130) No record of apprenticeship or freedom. He appears however in the Bounty Lists as 'Pierre Bouteillé de Ré 55 ans, orfevre', 1722-7 (Evans, 'Huguenot Goldsmiths', *Hug. Soc. Proc.*, 14). Only mark entered as largeworker, 13 February 1727. Address: St. Martin's Court, where Heal records him, and as London, 1730-5. A John Bouteiller appears in the denization list, 19 August 1688 (Entry Book 67), but there is no apparent connection.

BOWEN, Thomas I (2689) Son of Thomas Bowen of the Stationers' Company, free by patrimony of that company 6 June 1732. Only mark entered as smallworker, 26 June 1732. Address: Green Arbour Court, Little Old Bailey. 'Free Stationer'.

BOWEN, Thomas II (2692) Son of Benjamin Bowen of Taunton in the County of Somerset gentleman, apprenticed to Thomas Thorne 9 June 1762. Freedom unrecorded. First mark entered as smallworker, 7 June 1770. Address: Albion Buildings. Appears as smallworker, 19 Albion's Buildings, in the Parl. Report list 1773. New address: 48 Lombard Street, 27 July (year omitted, presumably the same). Second mark, 29 June 1782. Address: 5 Naked Boy Court, Ludgate Hill. Third mark, 5 August 1782.

BOWER, George (761) No record of apprenticeship or freedom. Only mark entered as smallworker, 1 February 1813. Address: 17 Thavies Inn, Holborn.

BOYER, John (1155, 1182) No record of apprenticeship or freedom. First mark entered as smallworker, 16 April 1772. Address: Horseshoe Alley, Middle Moorfields. Appears as buttonmaker at this address, Parl. Report list 1773. Second mark, 9 June 1794, same address.

BOYTON, Charles (273-4) Son of George Boyton of Braintree in the County of Essex baize weaver, apprenticed to William Seaman of Hulls (?) Street, St. Luke's silversmith 4 November 1807 on payment of £15. Free, 4 April 1827. First mark entered as spoonmaker, 30 November 1825. Address: 12 Europia Place, St. Luke's. Second mark, 10 September 1830. Moved to 26 Wellington Street, St. Luke's, 29 October 1830. Three further marks, 30 December 1833, 4 February 1834 and 29 June 1838.

BIOGRAPHICAL DICTIONARY

BRADLEY, Jonathan (215) Son of Richard Bradley Citizen and Dyer of London, apprenticed to John Smith 6 June 1687 and later turned over to Lawrence Coles. Free, 8 June 1694. Mark entered, undated, probably April 1697 on commencement of register. Address: Carey Lane.

BRADLEY, Joseph (1148) Son of Joseph Bradley of the parish of St. Alban's Wood Street salesman, apprenticed to William Aldridge goldsmith 5 December 1764. Free, 1 July 1772. Mark entered as smallworker, 20 August 1776. Address: Red Lion Passage.

BRADSHAW, Bennett (135, 2449) Son of John Bradshaw of Tilton in the County of Leicester gentleman, apprenticed to Paul De Lamerie 21 April 1721 on payment of £20. Freedom unrecorded. First mark entered in partnership with Robert Tyrill as largeworkers, 21 March 1737. Address: The Golden Ball, Oxford Chapel, Cavendish Square. Second mark, 2 July 1739. Address: Oxford Chapel, both described as Free Goldsmiths. Heal gives address as Oxford Court, which he identifies as Chapel Court, Henrietta Street, St. Marylebone.

BRADSHAW, Edward (536) No record of apprenticeship or freedom. Only mark entered as smallworker, 14 June 1734. Address: Puddle Dock Hill. The name appears as watchcasemaker, Johnson's Court, Fleet Street, in the Parl. Report list 1773, which may perhaps be that of a son.

BRAFORD, Benjamin (216) Son of James Braford late of Tewkesbury in the County of Gloucester mercer deceased, apprenticed to John Cooke for eight years 1 December 1656. Free, 23 March 1665. Mark entered as largeworker, undated, probably on commencement of register April 1697. Address: St. Lawrence, Poultney Lane. Signatory to the petition against the work of 'aliens and foreigners', 11 August 1697.

BRANDT, Erick (212, 529) No record of apprenticeship or freedom. New Standard and Sterling marks entered in smallworkers' book as snuffboxmaker, 24 May 1726. Address: Mouldmakers Row, St. Martin's Le Grand.

BRASIER, George (757-9) Son of John Brasier late of Margate in the County of Kent yeoman deceased, apprenticed to John Westray of Little Britain goldsmith 3 October 1770. Free, 7 January 1778. First mark entered as smallworker, 4 March 1780. Address: 40 West Smithfield. Second mark, 2 April 1785. Address: 28 Giltspur Street. Third mark, 19 October 1787. Fourth, 31 January 1788. Fifth, 26 November 1789. Moved to 6 St. Ann's Lane, 27 April 1790, and to 114 Bishopsgate Street, 19 October 1790. Heal records him only as George Brassier, goldsmith, 28 Giltspur Street, 1790-3.

*BRASSEY, John (214) Son of John Brassey of Boston County of Lincoln goldsmith, apprenticed to John Tysoe for eight years 23 April 1675. Free, 26 April 1682. Livery, 1689. Court, 1705. Mark entered as largeworker, undated, probably April 1697 on commencement of register. Address: Lombard Street, where Heal records him at the Golden Acorn from 1691 till 1710, with a partner Caswall about 1700-7; and as without Aldgate from 1725 to 1731. His son Nathaniel was apprenticed to him, 30 January 1711, and the firm appears as John and Nathaniel Brassey from 1716 to 1720. In the London Gazette of 9 January 1720 they advertised the loss of £100 in banknotes for the recovery of which they would give £50 reward 'and ask no questions'. From 1730 to 1740 Nathaniel Brassey and Lee and with various partners till closure in 1835 (Hilton Price, Handbook of London Bankers, 1890).

*BRAWNE, Hugh (219) Apprentice of Henry Panton admitted to the freedom of the Cutlers' Company 16 November 1703. Mark entered as smallworker, 31 July 1710. Address: Fleet Street. 'Free Cutler'. Probably knife and/or sword-hilt maker.

BRENT, John (1169) Son of Moses Brent (q.v.), apprenticed to his father as silver haft maker 7 April 1790. Free, 8 March 1798, as silversmith. Mark entered as smallworker, 26 June 1820. Address: 3 Domingo Street, Old Street Road. Moved to 17 Menil Street, Old Street, 31 May 1822.

BRENT, Moses (2000) Son of William Brent of St. Mary Magdalen Bermondsey carpenter, apprenticed to Dru Drury knife handle maker (q.v.) 6 July 1763. Free, 7 November 1770. First mark entered as haftmaker, 11 July 1775. Address: Hind Court, Noble Street, Foster Lane. Second mark on removal to Well Yard, Little Britain, 28 June 1782. Third to seventh marks, 1788 to 1796. Eighth on removal to 42 Little Britain, 28 March 1799. Ninth as smallworker, 7 October 1800. Address: 12 Kirby Street, Hatton Garden. Tenth to twelfth marks as plateworker, 1804-7. Thirteenth to fifteenth marks as smallworker, 1809-12 Sixteenth mark as plateworker, 18 October 1813. Address: 22 Greville Street, Leather Lane. Seventeenth mark, 29 July 1815. Eighteenth, 18 February 1817. Address: 19 Leather Lane. From the very large number of his mark entries and the frequency they are met with on knifehafts and blades of his working period it is obvious that Brent had a virtual monopoly as specialist in this field to the retail trade of his day. His knives are constantly found accompanying 'flat ware' made by Eley, Fearn and Chawner as supplied to Rundell, Bridge and Rundell for all their best clients. Heal records him only at Bell Yard, 1783-9. His mark previously ascribed to Mark Bock (q.v.) who was dead by 1783.

BRENT, Moses William (2002) Son of Moses Brent of Little Britain knife haft maker, apprenticed to his father as such 6 May 1795. Free, 1 December 1802, as goldsmith. Mark entered as plateworker in partnership with S. W. Peppin, 20 December 1815. Address: 22 Greville Street. Second mark, 2 June 1816.

BRETT, William (208) No record of apprenticeship or freedom. Only mark entered as largeworker, undated, probably April 1697 on commencement of register. Address: Norris Street, near St. James's Market, where Heal records him from 1695-7, at which time he was one of the most westerly situated of the trade.

BREWOOD, Benjamin I (127) Son of Robert Brewood of Markfield in the County of Leicester yeoman, apprenticed to Samuel Bourne 24 February 1692. Free, 5 July 1699. Livery, October 1708. Mark entered as smallworker, 13 August 1729. Address: Bull in Mouth Street, 'Free Goldsmith'. There are three entries in the Fleet Register of Marriages which relate to him, but which appear to be confused:

(i) 4 September 1724: 'Benj. Breewood goldsmith widower and Mary Deacon, spr.'
(ii) 19 April 1729: 'Benj. Brewood goldsmith and Mary Deacon w. spr.'
(iii) 13 September 1729: 'Benjamin Brewood of St. Ann. Aldersgate widower goldsmith and Martha Deacon of St. Pancras Kentish Town spr.'

For comments on the Fleet Marriages see BIGNELL, John

It would appear to be a son of this marriage (whenever and to whomsoever it occurred!), Benjamin, who was apprenticed to William Grundy in 1745 (q.v.).

BREWOOD, Benjamin II (128-30) Son of the above, apprenticed to William Grundy 3 July 1745. Free, 7 May 1755. Two marks entered as largeworker, 9 August 1755. Address: Pemberton Square, near Gough Square. Third mark, 29 January 1757. His son Benjamin apprenticed to him 4 November 1767, and son Charles to him 6 May 1778. Heal records him in Pemberton Row, 1767. He appears as Benjamin Breewood, without category, at the same address, in the Parl. Report list 1773.

*BRIDGE, John (1171-2, 3764) Eldest son of Thomas Bridge of Piddle Trenthide Dorset, born 21 January 1755. Apprenticed 1769 to William Rogers of Bath on payment of £42. Arrived in London 1777, aged twenty-two, and became shopman at Pickett and Rundell (both q.v.). Said to have been recommended to George III by his cousin John, farmer of Wynford Eagle near Bridport, on the King's visit to Weymouth in 1789 (George Fox MS., Harvard University). Date of partnership with Philip Rundell was apparently 1788, and the two were appointed as Goldsmiths and Jewellers to the King by 1797 (Major General H. W. D. Sitwell, 'The Jewel House and the Royal Goldsmiths', *Arch. Journ.*, CXVII). First mark entered as plateworker (four sizes), 13 November 1823, presumably after the retirement of Philip Rundell whose mark had been entered after the secession of Paul Storr in 1819. Address: 76 Dean Street, Soho, presumably that of the workshop only. This mark, without crown, may never have been used since the second, with crown, was entered 25 November 1823 (three sizes). Bridge's nephew, John Gawler Bridge, had joined the firm in 1804 and became partner in 1817. The latter was free by redemption, 5 June 1816. Livery, 1818. Court, 1831. Prime Warden 1839 and died 1849. After the retirement of Edmond Rundell, John Bridge Senior formed a new firm in 1830 with his nephew and Thomas Bigge which lasted till 1834. In 1842 the stock was sold by auction at Christie's and the goodwill was said to have been purchased by Francis Lambert of Coventry Street (F. J. Britten, *Old Clocks and Watches and their Makers*). For the whole history of the firm of Rundell,

Bridge and Rundell see N. M. Penzer, *Paul Storr*, 1954, from whom the above is partly derived.

BRIND, Henry (950) Son of William Brind late of Highworth in the County of Wiltshire victualler deceased, apprenticed to Richard Bailey 5 March 1734 on payment of £31. 10s. Free, 6 May 1742. Livery, September 1746. Mark entered as largeworker, 6 May 1742. Address: Foster Lane, where Heal records him till 1749. Brother of Walter Brind (q.v.). Appears without category, Silver Street, in the Parl. Report list 1773.

BRIND, John (221) Mark entered as smallworker, 21 February 1716. Address: Love Lane, with the following note in the register: 'free of no Company but allowed to follow his trade by the Chamberlain's order as having been a soldier at the Battle of Allmanza'. Heal records him at Love Lane, West Smithfield, as insolvent 1724.

*BRIND, Walter (3012-15, 3864) Son of William Brind late of Highworth in the County of Wiltshire innholder deceased (and so brother to Henry, q.v.), apprenticed to John Raynes 7 October 1736 on payment of £25. Turned over to his brother Henry July 1742 (soon after the latter's entry of his mark). Free, 8 November 1743. Livery, March 1758. Mark entered as largeworker, 7 February 1749. Address: Foster Lane. Second mark (two sizes), 31 August 17(51?). Third mark, 11 October 1757. Same address, without category, in the Parl. Report list 1773. Fourth mark as plateworker, 26 February 1781. Address: 34 Foster Lane, where Heal records him till 1796. William, son of Walter and Ann Brind, was born 20 September, baptized 18 October 1749 at Christchurch, Newgate, and apprenticed to his father, 7 December 1763. Another son, Henry, aged nine, 'son of Walter Brind silversmith in Forster Lane' was admitted a scholar of St. Paul's School, 16 May 1764, and apprenticed to his father 5 April 1769. Third son, Thomas, was apprenticed to him 4 May 1774 and turned over 1777 to Thomas Clements of Gutter Lane ribbon weaver. (Presumably the Thomas Brind, Prime Warden 1813.) Fourth son, Walter, also apprenticed to him 4 February 1778 and turned over 1780 to George Jackson weaver. (He is presumably the Walter Brind, Prime Warden of 1820.) The baptism of three daughters is also recorded at Christchurch, Newgate, from 1750 to 1752. Mrs. Brind, wife of Walter Brind, goldsmith, Foster Lane, died 11 January 1791 (*The Gentleman's Magazine*). He died between 1795 and 1801.

BRISCOE, Stafford (218) Son of Richard Briscoe Citizen and Girdler of London, apprenticed to Daniel Antrobus 20 May 1699. Free, 25 May 1706. Mark entered as smallworker, 23 July 1706. Address: Wood Street. Livery, October 1708. Mary, daughter of Mr. Stafford Briscoe, goldsmith in Cheapside, and Abigail his wife, born and baptized 6 December 1711 at St. Vedast, Foster Lane. Heal records him as goldsmith, Bunch of Grapes, Cheapside, 1711-12; and as jeweller and goldsmith, at the Three Kings and Golden Ball or Golden Ball only, corner of Friday Street, Cheapside, variously from 1732-67; also in partnership with John Briscoe, 1742-60; and as Briscoe and Morrison, 1762-72. Described as silversmith, Cheapside, on death in November 1789. It would seem however, from the dates in question that this must be at least a son, if not grandson of the above.

BRISTOW, Richard (210) Son of John Bristoe of Ockin (?) in the County of Surrey yeoman deceased, apprenticed to Daniel Antrobus 28 July 1686. Free, 6 October 1693. Livery, 1698. Mark entered as smallworker, 29 January 1707. Address: Ludgate Street, where Heal records him as goldsmith, 1708; and at Three Balls or Bells, Fleet Street, corner of Bride Lane, 1716-36. Also listed by Hilton Price, *Handbook of London Bankers*, 1890. Court, 1716. Warden, 1726, 1732-3. Prime Warden, 1736.

*BRITTON, James (1781) No record of apprenticeship or freedom. First mark entered as spoonmaker, 25 August 1820. Address: 4 St. John Street Road, Clerkenwell. Moved to 8 Backhill, Hatton Garden, 17 July 1821. Second mark, 10 October 1821. Perhaps related to the following.

BRITTON, Richard (2278) Son of Henry Britton late of Kingston St. Michael in the County of Wiltshire baker deceased, apprenticed to John Hutson of St. John's Clerkenwell goldsmith 1 April 1798 and turned over to George Burrows of Red Lion Street Clerkenwell 1 January 1800. Free, 5 March 1806. First mark entered as spoonmaker, 3 February 1812. Address: 10 Hull(?) Street, St. Luke's. Moved to 48 Great Sutton Street, Clerkenwell, 17 May 1817. Second mark, 21 March 1827. Third mark, 15 December 1842.

BROADBENT, William (220) Apprenticeship untraced but free of the Vintners' Company 7 December 1687. Mark entered as smallworker, undated, between 1702 and 1720. Address: Bull and Mouth Street. 'Free Vintner'. Heal records only—Broadbent, jeweller, Warwick Lane, 1714–18, who may or may not be the same.

*BROADHURST, Ed. (535) No record of apprenticeship or freedom. Only mark entered as smallworker, 24 December 1731. Address: New Street, Cloth Fair near St. Luke's Head. Signs with 'B' as his mark.

BROAKE, John (209) No record of apprenticeship or freedom. Only mark entered as largeworker, 8 July 1699. Address: Gutter Lane, where Heal records him till 1704. The occurrence of his mark suggests he was a specialist spoonmaker.

*BROCKUS, John (1138) No record of apprenticeship or freedom. Only mark entered as smallworker, 4 June 1760. Address: Shoe Lane, Fleet Street. Heal records him as John Brockus, haftmaker, at this address 1773, and the Parl. Report list of same year as hiltmaker.

BROCKWELL, Henry (956) No record of apprenticeship or freedom. Possibly a son of John or William below. Only mark entered as spoonmaker, 20 December 1821. Address: 80 Leather Lane, Holborn.

*BROCKWELL, John (1154, 1162) Perhaps the son of William Brockwell of the parish of St. Giles without Cripplegate ivory pocket book maker, apprenticed to Henry Bickerton 2 May 1759. Freedom unrecorded. First mark entered as smallworker, 13 March 1794. Address: 31 George Street, Battle Bridge. Moved to Woolwich, Kent, 10 June 1799. Second mark, 6 April 1808. Address: 11 Peartree Street, Goswell Street.

BROCKWELL, William (3026) No record of apprenticeship or freedom. First mark entered as smallworker, 23 December 1776. Address: 4 Purse Court, Old Change. Moved to 11 Red Cross Square, 7 October 1786. Second mark, 20 October 1802. Moved to 12 Red Cross Square, 7 April 1804. Moved to 4 Pump Court, Snow Hill, 9 December 1825. Finally to 6 Royal Oak Walk, Hoxton, no date.

BRODIER, Matthieu (1955) No record of apprenticeship or freedom. Only mark entered as largeworker, 11 April 1751. Address: Newport Alley, St. Ann's Street, Westminster. Listed as Huguenot by Evans. ('Huguenot Goldsmiths', *Hug. Soc. Proc.*, 14.)

BROKESBY, Abel (9) Son of Abel Brocksby of Swithland in the County of Leicester clerk, apprenticed to Francis Turner of the Grocers' Company 'in St. Anns Lane silversmith' 18 June 1717. Free, 17 June 1726. Mark entered as largeworker, 24 August 1727. Address: St. Anne's Lane. 'Free Grocer'. Married Mackady King of St. John Zachary, London, spinster, at St. Bene't, Paul's Wharf, 23 November 1730; he is described as 'of St. Ann, Aldersgate, Lond. Bachelor'.

BROMAGE, William (3023) No record of apprenticeship or freedom. Only mark entered as smallworker, 24 September 1770. Address: 'In Litel Drurelain by the nuchurch in the srand'; a more than usually charming example of the orthography of the day. He appears without category in Little Drury Court, Strand, in the Parl. Report list 1773.

BROME, George (748) Son of George Brome late of Nottingham apothecary deceased, apprenticed to George Ellis of the Wax Chandlers' Company 10 June 1719 and turned over to James Wilkes Goldsmith in Fetter Lane near ye Whithouse Inn. Free, 6 October 1726. Mark entered as largeworker, 31 October 1726. Address: Fetter Lane. 'Free Waxchandler'.

BROMFIELD, William (3020) No record of apprenticeship or freedom. Only mark entered as smallworker, 31 May 1769. Address: Cow Lane, St. John's Court. Appears without category, John's Court, Cow Lane, in the Parl. Report list 1773.

BROMLEY, John (217) No record of apprenticeship or freedom. Only mark entered as largeworker, 27 October 1703. Address: Foster Lane, where Heal records him in 1720, and in St. Michael's Alley, 1732. Described as toyman, 1739. Also John Bromley, goldsmith, parish St. Dionis Backchurch, 1743. Died 1745. Perhaps the same as listed by Hilton Price (*Handbook of London Bankers*, 1890).

BROOKER, James (1125) Presumably the one of this name free by redemption 3 December 1745. Only mark entered as largeworker, 21 October 1734. Address: 'at the Golden Snail in Fleet Street'.

BIOGRAPHICAL DICTIONARY

BROOKES, J. (1187) Possibly James Brooke son of Richard Brooke, apprenticed to Charles Gardiner 1742. Free, 11 January 1750. Only mark entered as smallworker in partnership with Thomas Dare, 19 October 1764. Address: Southampton Buildings, Holborn.

BROOKS, William I (3019) Son of William Brooks Citizen and Clockmaker, apprenticed to Joseph Smithfield 3 June 1761 and turned over to his father May 1762. Freedom unrecorded. Mark entered as smallworker, 23 September 1763. Address: Snow Hill. Moved to Grub Street, 6 April 1764. Moved to Blue Anchor Alley, 31 July 1766. Presumably the William Brookes, watchcasemaker, Old Street, of the Parl. Report list 1773, and the William Brooks, 1 Church Row, Old Street, who entered incuse marks, 1777 to 1786 (Section V), and five marks as watchcasemaker, 1789-1805 (Section VI).

BROOKS, William II (1845) No identifiable apprenticeship or freedom recorded. Only mark entered as smallworker in partnership with James Perchard, 11 April 1808. Address: 14 Clerkenwell Green. Heal records them as goldsmiths and jewellers, 12 Charles Street, Hatton Garden, c. 1800, and at 14 Clerkenwell Green, 1808-17.

BROUGH, John (1164, 1775-6, 1787) No record of apprenticeship or freedom. First mark entered as smallworker, 26 April 1803. Address: 50 Aldersgate Street. (See Thomas Brough at this address, 1797.) Second mark, in partnership with John Mountford as smallworkers, 17 October 1806, same address. Third mark alone, 13 March 1807, same address. Fourth mark, 7 August 1813. Subsequently at the following addresses: 21 October 1813, 4 Queens Street, Hoxton; 6 August 1814, 3 King Street, Hoxton; 6 August 1818, 9 Gate Street, Lincoln's Inn Fields; 20 November 1821, 11 Little Wild Street, Lincoln's Inn Fields; 8 February 1823, 17 Paul's Alley.

BROUGH, Samuel (2482) No record of apprenticeship or freedom. Probably son of Samuel Brough, watchcasemaker (Section VI). Only mark entered as smallworker, 13 February 1808. Address: 3 King Street, Goswell Street.

BROUGH, Thomas (2695) Son of William Brough of Cloth Fair tailor, apprenticed to William Barrett of Aldersgate Street goldsmith 7 May 1788. Free, 5 August 1795. First mark entered as smallworker, October 1795. Address: 29 New Street, Cloth Fair. Moved to 50 Aldersgate, 24 July 1797. (See John Brough at this address, 1803.) Second mark noted in register but not struck, 16 January 1800. Heal records him as goldsmith at both addresses.

BROUGHTON, Henry (2862) No record of apprenticeship or freedom. Only mark entered as smallworker in partnership with Thomas Nortzele, 29 December 1827. Address: 21 Bouverie Street, Fleet Street.

BROUGHTON, John (1149, 3617) Son of Edward Broughton of the parish of St. Sepulchre in the County of Middlesex tallow chandler, apprenticed to Robert Albin Cox 8 June 1757 on payment of £15. Free, 4 July 1764. Mark entered as plateworker, 8 January 1779. Address: 11 Well Yard, Little Britain. Heal records him as silversmith, St. John's Square, Clerkenwell, from 1767-73 (where he appears as goldsmith in the Parl. Report list 1773); in Bartholomew Close, 1776; and in Little Britain, 1779. It is very probable, therefore, that he entered a mark c. 1765, in the missing largeworkers' book of 1758-73 (cf. for instance nos. 3618-19). This is supported by the fact of his taking Robert Gaze as apprentice, 6 February 1765 (q.v.).

BROWN, Robert (2270, 2281) Son of Richard Brown of Parish of St. Pulchers (?St. Sepulchre's) in the County of Middlesex butcher deceased, apprenticed to David Tanqueray 9 July 1723. Free, 10 January 1737. Mark entered as largeworker, 8 October 1736. Address: Piccadilly 'over against the Black Bear'. Second mark, 26 June 1739. Address: Piccadilly, 'Goldsmith', where Heal records him till 1743.

BROWN, William (3039) Perhaps William Thomas son of William Brown of Langbourn Chambers Fenchurch Street silversmith, apprenticed to George Munro of John Street St. George in the East working silversmith 2 February 1814. Freedom unrecorded. Only mark entered as plateworker, 24 January 1823. Address: 54 Little Bartholomew Close. Moved to 13 Silver Street, Wood Street, 31 August 1823.

BROWNE, Moses (213) Son of John Browne Citizen and Grocer of London, apprenticed to William Renalds 23 December 1687. Later turned over to John Diggle and John Corey. Free, 31 July 1695. Mark entered as largeworker, undated, probably April 1697

451

on commencement of register. Address: Russell Street, Covent Garden, where Heal records him till 1701.

BRUCE, William (3035) No record of apprenticeship or freedom. Only mark entered as plateworker, 18 June 1811. Address: 2 Ship Court, Old Bailey. Described as silversmith of this address in the apprenticeship of his son William to Thomas Robbins, 1 August 1810. It would seem therefore that he may have been established for some time before the entry of his mark.

BRUGUIER, Philip (2132, 2138) Son of James Bruguier merchant of London deceased, apprenticed to Philip Rainaud 13 March 1723. Free, 5 July 1749. First mark entered as largeworker, 19 March 1739. Address: Little St. Martin Street, near Leicester Fields. Second mark, 12 July 1739, same address. Moved to the Star, Bedford Street, Covent Garden, 22 January 1752 (or 3?). Heal, following Jackson, assumes that at this last date and address the entry is for a son of the same name, but there is no indication of this in the registers and the signature, allowing for age, looks the same as the earlier ones. Philip Bruguier, plateworker, does however appear in the Parl. Report list 1773 at the same address, and if it is assumed from the apprenticeship date that he was born about 1710, he would then be sixty-three, a not impossible age.

BRUIN, Henry (947) Apprentice of Thomas Bibb of the Cutlers' Company free of that company 29 October 1696. Mark entered in the smallworkers' book as sword cutler, 2 March 1726. Address: New Street, near Fetter Lane. He signs as 'Brun' with the second stroke of the 'u' dotted as if in his excitement or nervousness he miscounted his strokes!

BRUMHALL, John (223) No record of apprenticeship or freedom. Only mark entered as largeworker, undated, between others of May 1721 and July 1723. Address: Upper Moorfields. The mark is endorsed 'Nue Standard for my Bro' Brumhall Phi: Walker', the signatory presumably a brother-in-law. Heal records him as plateworker at this address, 1713-21.

BRUNT, John Eldershaw (1811) No record of apprenticeship or freedom. Only mark entered as smallworker, 15 November 1836. Address: 14 Greville Street, Hatton Garden. Described as jeweller of this address in the apprenticeship of his son Robert Peel Brunt to John Rumley as engraver, 2 December 1846.

BRUSH, Phillip (211) Son of Richard Brush of Tewkesbury in the County of Gloucester yeoman, apprenticed to Edward Maddox 28 July 1682. Free, 25 April 1707. Entered as largeworker, 3 May 1707. Address: George Alley, Lombard Street, where Heal records him as plateworker, and as London, 1714-23(?).

BRYAN, John (1127, 1183) Son of John Bryan of Somersetshire gentleman, apprenticed to William Paradise 8 September 1725 on payment of £20 and turned over 4 September 1732 to Edward Vincent Citizen and Goldsmith. Freedom unrecorded. First mark entered as largeworker, 18 November 1735. Address: Panner Alley, Newgate Street. Second mark, 22 June 1739. Address: Twisters Alley, Bunhill Row.

BRYCESON, William (3031) No record of apprenticeship or freedom. First mark entered as smallworker, 17 December 1796. Address: George Street, York Buildings. Second mark, 30 December 1801. Moved to 11 North Street, Pentonville, 2 February 1827.

BRYDIE, John (1170) Son of John Brydie of Alloa Clackmannanshire merchant deceased, apprenticed to John Cowie of Aldermanbury Postern silversmith 6 July 1814 and turned over to J. W. Blake of Long Acre spoonmaker and pewterer 1 January 1817. Free, 5 June 1822. First mark entered as spoonmaker, 2 January 1823. Address: 3 East Harding Street, Fetter Lane. Second mark, 19 May 1824. Third mark (two sizes), 28 January 1825. Moved to 40 Kirby Street, Hatton Garden, 23 August 1825.

BRYDON, George (222, 747) Son of Thomas and Ann Brydon, the former Citizen and Merchant Taylor of London, born 7 and baptized 23 April 1696, at Christchurch, Newgate. Apprenticed to Henry Green 4 June 1712 on payment of £5. Free, 5 February 1720. First mark (New Standard) entered as largeworker, 12 April 1720. Address: Maiden Lane. Second mark (Sterling), 8 July 1720.

BRYDON, Thomas (207, 3493) Son of Jasper Brydon of St. Edmunds Bury in the County of Suffolk gentleman, apprenticed to William Brett of the Merchant Taylors' Company of St. Martin's Le Grand goldsmith 6 July 1680. Free, 1 February 1688. Only mark entered as largeworker, undated, probably April 1697 on commencement of register. Address: New Rents, St. Martin's Le Grand, where Heal records him till 1702. The registers of Christchurch, Newgate, contain four entries for the children of Thomas and Ann (or Hannah) Brydon, commencing with Mary born 20 August 1694, George 1696 (see above), Thomas 1700, and Jasper born 1701, buried 1703.

BUCHANAN, James (1783) No record of apprenticeship or freedom. Only mark entered as plateworker, 1 April 1824. Address: 4 Raquet Court, Fleet Street.

BU(C)KETT, John (1181, 3620) No record of apprenticeship or freedom. Only mark entered as sword cutler, 28 January 1760. Address: St. James's Street, Westminster. Signs as 'Bukett' but appears as John Bockett, sword cutler, at the above address, in the Parl. Report list 1773.

BUCKLER, Christopher John (340) No record of apprenticeship or freedom. Only mark entered as smallworker, 25 October 1804. Address: 18 Great St. Martin's Lane. Later moved to 3 Garden Place, opposite Turnstile, Lincoln's Inn Fields.

BUCKTON, Richard (2276) No record of apprenticeship or freedom. First mark entered as smallworker, 1 March 1806. Address: 4 Brunswick Row, Queen Square, Bloomsbury. Second mark, incuse, 18 May 1814. Address: 8 Warwick Street, Charing Cross. Moved to 13 King Street, Westminster, 20 April 1825.

*BULL, Charles (275) No record of apprenticeship or freedom. Only mark entered as smallworker, 11 December 1832. Address: 10 New Court, Farrington Street.

BULL, John (1153) No record of apprenticeship or freedom. Only mark entered as smallworker, 13 December 1790. Address: 28 Anchor Street, Bethnal Green. Later (undated) moved to 5 Ironmonger Row.

*BULL, William (246, 3495) Free of the Haberdashers' Company by service to John Glover 18 March 1691 (apprenticeship record not found). Only mark entered as largeworker, 19 January 1699. Address: The Haymarket. 'Free Haberdasher'.

BULLEY, Thomas (244, 250, 2688) Described as Free Cutler in first entry of mark, but untraced in the apprenticeship or freedom lists of that company. First mark as smallworker, 11 September 1707. Address: Shoe Lane. Second entry, for Sterling and New standard marks, undated, between others of January and February 1724. Address: Hayden Yard, Minories. His first mark has been identified on the silver mounts of a pair of pistols in the Royal Collection, and on another pair of 1717 in the collection of Clay Bedford, U.S.A. His membership of the Cutlers' Company suggests his main activity was that of haft and hiltmaker to which pistol mounts appear naturally related.

BULT, James (1168, 1692, 2518, 3625) Son of Thomas Bult late of the parish of Kingston in the County of Somerset yeoman deceased, apprenticed to James Stamp of Cheapside London goldsmith 2 November 1774. Turned over to James Sutton of Cheapside Goldsmith 1 November 1780. Free, 7 November 1781. First mark entered in partnership with James Sutton (q.v.) as plateworkers, 4 October 1782. Address: 86 Cheapside. Second mark, as unnamed third partner with Samuel Godbehere and Edward Wigan, in register, 15 March 1800. Third mark, with S. Godbehere, 16 September 1818, same address. Fourth mark alone, 13 July 1819. The mark no. 3625, though possibly attributable to him and Sutton, occurs in 1783 before his first entry and places his initials above Sutton's, which seems unlikely as a junior partner, unless he had an unauthorized mark cut on his own initiative. After his survival as the last of the above three partners in the business, Bult turned to banking. James Bult Son and Co. first appear in the *London Directory* as bankers in 1841 at 85-6 Cheapside, the firm consisting of James, Philip and George Frederic Bult. They do not appear in the directory after 1852 (Hilton Price, *Handbook of London Bankers*, 1890). James Bult died 13 May 1846.

*BUMFRISS, Thomas (2706) No record of apprenticeship or freedom. Only mark entered as largeworker in partnership with Orlando Jackson, 6 May 1766. Address: Little Trinity Lane, Queenhithe, where Heal records them from 1768 to 1783. He appears as plateworker at this address in the Parl. Report list 1773. Thomas Bumfriss, chaser, of St. Martin's in the Fields appears as the father of Aaron Bumfriss, apprenticed to Henry Gubbin, 6 August 1760, and seems likely to be the same.

BUNN, John (1161, 2671) Son of Richard Bunn late of Red Cross Street baker deceased, apprenticed to Moses Brent of Little Britain 1 March 1797 on payment of £10 of the charity of the Drapers' Company from the gift of Richard Wynne deceased. Freedom unrecorded. First mark entered as smallworker in partnership with Samuel Webster, 7 January 1806. Address: 23 Charles Street, Hatton Garden. Second mark alone, 10 May 1806, same address. There seems no apparent connection with the John Bunn, goldsmith, Hoxton, 1782, recorded by Heal.

BUNN, Lockington (3354) No record of apprenticeship or freedom. Only mark entered as plate and spoon worker in partnership with William Theobalds, 30 June 1835. Address: 7 Salisbury Court, Fleet Street.

BURBIDGE, Thomas (2936) Son of Thomas Burbidge late of Wooburn in the County of Bedford husbandman deceased, apprenticed to Samuel Cawthorne 2 March 1757 and turned over the same day to Edward Bramstone Bayley Citizen and Clockmaker. Free, 6 June 1764. Mark entered as smallworker in partnership with Thomas Stilwell, 9 August 1763. Address: White Friars Gateway, Fleet Street. Incuse mark TSB (Section V) with Stilwell, 14 December 1763, at same address, where he appears alone as watchcasemaker in the Parl. Report list 1773.

BURCH, William (3028) Son of Joseph Burch of Maid Lane in the parish of St. Saviour Southwark India warehouseman, apprenticed to Thomas Shepherd of Bull and Mouth Street goldsmith 6 February 1771. Free, 5 August 1778. Only mark entered as smallworker, 7 March 1788. Address: 5 Bear Lane, Christchurch, Surrey. Moved to 8 Prices Street, Christchurch, 21 April 1795. Moved to 62 Gravel Lane, Surrey, 8 October 1798.

BURCOMBE, Richard (2264) Son of John Burcomb late of Colebrooke in the County of Buckingham mercer deceased, apprenticed to Abraham Pope of the Leathersellers' Company 1 June 1716. Free, 9 January 1724. First mark entered as smallworker, 10 February 1724. Address: Wine Office Court, Fleet Street. 'Free of Leathersellers Company'. Second mark, 4 February 1735. Address: 'at the Jack, Wood Street'.

*BURDETT, Henry (948) Free by redemption of the Goldsmiths' Company, 6 June 1732. Only mark entered as 'Goldsmith' 26, July 1732. Address: The Crown and Pearl, near the Monument. Heal records—Burdett, silversmith, Crown and Pearl, Little Old Bailey, 1732, but it is difficult to see the connection except for sign and date.

BURGH, John (245, 1119) Son of John Burgh of the parish of St. Mary Whitechapel gentleman, apprenticed to Abraham Pope of the Leathersellers' Company 4 August 1709. Free, 7 November 1716. First mark entered as smallworker, 28 November 1716. Address: Paternoster Row. 'Leatherseller'. Second (Sterling) mark, 9 March 1721. Address: Dowgate Hill. 'Goldsmith'.

BURKENHILL, Ed: (247) No record of apprenticeship or freedom. Only mark entered as smallworker, 12 August 1699. Address: Hanging Sword Alley, Fleet Street.

BURKITT, William (243) Free of the Carpenters' Company. Only mark entered, 13 June 1716. Address: Bear Alley, near Fleet Ditch, 'free Carpenter'.

BURNE, James (250a, 1174) No record of apprenticeship or freedom. Two marks, Sterling and New Standard, entered as largeworker, 4 March 1724. Address: Bedfordbury.

BURRIDGE, Thomas (241-2, 2686) Son of John Burridge late of the County and Town of Huntingdon butcher, apprenticed to Peter Downeham (?) 12 March 1675. Freedom unrecorded. First mark entered as largeworker, 5 April 1706. Address: Foster Lane. Second mark, 17 July 1717, same address. Third (Sterling) mark, 24 June 1720.

BURROWS, Alice (14) Presumably widow of George Burrows I (below). Mark entered as plateworker in partnership with George Burrows II, 10 July 1801 (two sizes). Address: 14 Red Lion Street, Clerkenwell. Second mark, 7 November 1804. Third mark (two sizes), 21 February 1810. Fourth mark, 6 May 1818. She presumably retired or died by 17 May 1819, when George Burrows entered a separate mark alone at the same address.

BURROWS, George I (755) No record of apprenticeship or freedom. First mark entered as smallworker, 14 December 1769. Address: Clerkenwell Close. Second mark, 10 December 1770. Subsequent marks as bucklemaker, 1780-99 (Section VIII). Described as goldsmith of Clerkenwell Close, 7 May 1783, on the apprenticeship of his son George (below), the latter being turned over to him, 6 July 1785. Presumably dead by 10 July 1801, when Alice and George II entered first mark.

BURROWS, George II (14, 762-3, 2419, 3581) Son of George Burrows of Clerkenwell Close goldsmith (above), apprenticed to George Smith of Huggin Lane London goldsmith 7 May 1783 and turned over to his father 6 July 1785. Free, 6 July 1791. First mark entered as plateworker in partnership with his mother (?) Alice, 10 July 1801 (two sizes). Address: 14 Red Lion Street, Clerkenwell. Second mark, 7 November 1804. Third mark (two sizes), 21 February 1814. Fourth, 6 May 1818. Fifth mark, alone, 17 May 1819. Moved to 41 Chapman Street, Islington, with sixth mark, 27 August 1821. New seventh mark, on commencing partnership with Richard Pearce, 13 November 1826. Address: 12 Banner Street, St. Luke's. Eighth mark (two sizes), 2 December 1835. The mark GB.TB (no. 3581) appears of somewhat doubtful connection with the above, since there is no record of another of the family with initial T.

*BURROWS, John (1140) No record of apprenticeship or freedom. Only mark entered as smallworker, 13 February 1769. Address: Bartlet Street. Appears as bucklemaker, Bartlett Street, Clerkenwell in the Parl. Report list 1773.

*BURTON, Robert (2271) No record of apprenticeship or freedom. Only mark entered as largeworker, 3 April 1758. Address: Noble Street.

BURTON, William (3016) Probably son of John Burton of Great Burstow in the County of Essex gentleman, apprenticed to William Richards 17 November 1728 on payment of £30. Free, 21 June 1739. Incuse mark, 13 December 1738. Address: Mugwell Street. 'Free gouldsmith' (Section V). Second mark entered as smallworker, 23 October 1758. Address: Bridgwater Square, where Heal records him as watchcasemaker 1767, as also in the Parl. Report list 1773.

*BURTT, Joseph Josiah (1784) No record of apprenticeship or freedom. Only mark entered as spoonmaker, 3 April 1828. Address: 45 Northampton Street, Clerkenwell.

BURTT, Thomas (2703) No record of apprenticeship or freedom. Presumably son or brother of the above. Only mark entered as smallworker, 4 December 1834. Address: 45 Northampton Street, Clerkenwell.

*BURWASH, Thomas (2701) Presumably a son of William Burwash (below). No record of apprenticeship or freedom. Only mark entered as plateworker, 10 November 1821. Address: 14 Bartholomew Close. The pendant maker of the same name at 120 St. John Street, 1813 (Section V), and other addresses later (Section VI), would seem to be unconnected.

*BURWASH, William (3036, 3047, 3050, 3866) No record of apprenticeship or freedom. Heal records William Burwash, watchcasemaker, at 45 Red Lion Street, Clerkenwell, from 1782-1804, for whom two incuse marks are entered in 1802 and 1803 at 3 Red Lion Street (Section V). It would seem very likely that he is the William Burwash of St. Stephen's, Wallbrook, married at that Church, 7 November 1781, to Elizabeth Salt of St. John's, Clerkenwell, and that they may be the parents of William Burwash of this entry. First mark entered in partnership with Richard Sibley, 7 October 1705. Address: 14 Bartholomew Close. Second mark alone, incuse, 6 July 1812. Third mark (two sizes), 10 August 1812. Fourth mark, 23 April 1813, all at the same address. His son George apprenticed to Richard Sibley 1 January 1806, and another son William to William Chawner 6 November 1816, who had married Mary Burwash earlier that year. See also Thomas (above).

BUSHBY, Robert (2275) No record of apprenticeship or freedom. Only mark entered as smallworker, 19 January 1803. Address: 34 St. Martin's Lane.

*BUTEUX, Abraham (8, 249) Son of Isaac Buteux and Elizabeth née Jonecourt, baptized 13 June 1698 at Threadneedle Street Church, godfather Simon Pantin, godmother Suzanne Lalau. (An earlier entry of the same name is Abraham Bulteaux, son of Jeremie and Marguerite, née Wilbe, baptized 18 September 1681 at the same church, but this is ruled out by the apprenticeship details.) Apprenticed as son of Isaac Butuex (sic) late of the parish of Stepney weaver deceased to William West of the Skinners' Company 4 December 1711. Free, 4 August 1719. Married Elizabeth Pentin (surely Pantin), both of the parish of St. Martin's in the Fields, with licence, at St. Paul's Cathedral, 11 February 1720 (St. Paul's Cathedral register). Two marks (Sterling and New Standard) entered as largeworker, 13 May 1721. Address: Green Street, Leicester Fields. 'Free of the Skinners'. Probably dead by 15 November 1731, when Elizabeth entered her mark, presumably as widow (q.v.). Buteux' master West, of the Skinners' Company, does not appear to have been a working goldsmith and the apprenticeship may have been a 'courtesy' one to acquire the necessary freedom of some company or other. It seems much more likely that the boy was working with one of the Huguenot makers, and who more likely than his godfather Simon Pantin, whose daughter was almost certainly Elizabeth Buteux. An indication of the probable connection of Buteux and Pantin is perhaps to be seen in a somewhat similar type of production, chiefly plain cups and other hollow-ware and salvers. Larger display pieces seem not to have come his way.

BUTEUX, Elizabeth (534) Presumably widow (née Pantin) of Abraham Buteux (above), since the form of mark is parallel to his. For their marriage see above. Mark entered as largeworker presumably on Abraham's death, 15 November 1731. Address: Norris Street, St. James. Married secondly Benjamin Godfrey (q.v.), February 1732, and later registered mark as Elizabeth Godfrey (q.v. also).

BUTLER, Joshua I (1111) No record of apprenticeship or freedom. Only mark entered as smallworker in partnership with John Allen, 16 March 1802. Address: 16 Bridgwater Gardens. Apparently distinct from the following.

BUTLER, Joshua II (1782, 1788) No apparent connection with the preceding unless perhaps a son. No record of apprenticeship or freedom. First mark entered as smallworker, 24 October 1822. Address: 15 Clough Court, Fetter Lane. Moved to 30 Coppice Row, Clerkenwell, 8 May 1833. Second mark in partnership with Thomas Wise, 30 May 1835, same address.

BUTTALL, Sarah (2478, 3790-1) No record of apprenticeship or freedom. Only mark entered as largeworker, 10 May 1754. Address: Minories. Heal also records her as of London, 1772.

BUTTERFIELD, Robert (248) Described as Free Merchant Taylor in entry of mark, but his name does not appear in the registers of that company. Only mark entered as smallworker, undated, c. 1720. Address: Crowderswell Alley.

*BUTTY, Francis (669, 1930) No record of apprenticeship or freedom. First mark entered as largeworker in partnership with Lewis Herne, 13 July 1757. Address: Clerkenwell Close. Herne absconded from that address, 1765. Second mark, in partnership with Nicholas Dumee, presumably entered sometime after 1758 in the missing register. They appear as goldsmiths in the Parl. Report list 1773, at the same address, where Heal records them till 1776. *The Gentleman's Magazine* records their bankruptcy, March 1773. Dumee (q.v.) entered a mark in partnership with William Holmes, September 1773, presumably as a result of the bankruptcy. Butty is listed as Huguenot by Evans ('Huguenot Goldsmiths', *Hug. Soc. Proc.*, 14).

C

CACHART, Elias (557) No record of apprenticeship or freedom. Only mark entered as largeworker, 17 June 1742. Address: 'Cundic' (?Conduit) Court, Long Acre, where Heal records him until 1752. His name occurs as overseer (? of parish) 1749, as quoted by W. R. Manchée ('Huguenot London, Covent Garden etc.', *Hug. Soc. Proc.*, 13, p. 70) and Evans ('Huguenot Goldsmiths', *op. cit.*, 14). From the surviving occurrence of his mark it is clear that he was probably the largest manufacturer of spoons and forks in the mid eighteenth century.

CADMAN, Morris (2010) No record of apprenticeship or freedom. Only mark entered as smallworker, 10 September 1800. Address: 5 St. Agnes Le Clear, Shoreditch.

*CAFE, John (1203, 1228) Son of Biles Cafe of the parish of Blackford in the County of Somerset yeoman, apprenticed to James Gould 15 December 1730. Free, 5 March 1740. Livery, September 1746. First mark entered as largeworker, 21 August 1740. Address: Foster Lane. Moved to Carey Lane, 13 April 1741. Second mark, 13 December 1742, 'the old one being broke'. Moved to Gutter Lane, 31 May 1743. Dead by 13 October 1757, when his apprentices

BIOGRAPHICAL DICTIONARY

Thomas Hannam and John Perry were turned over, by consent of his executor John Winning, to William Cafe. The Cafe family were long established at Blackford near Castle Cary. The last male descendant James Cafe died unmarried, aged eighty, at St. John's Wood in 1939 (information, Mrs. Lilian Cafe Thomson 1962).

*CAFE, William (3077) Son of Biles Cafe of the parish of Blackford in the County of Somerset yeoman, apprenticed to his brother John Cafe 11 March 1742. 'Turned himself over' to Simon Jouet Citizen and Goldsmith of London 'for the residue of ye turn' 19 March 1746. Free, 5 October 1757. Livery, March 1758. Mark entered as largeworker, 16 August 1757, probably on the death or illness of his brother John (q.v.), with whom he was presumably already working, to judge by their indistinguishable cast candlesticks of which, from surviving examples, they appear almost to have had a monopoly in the trade. Heal records him in Gutter Lane till bankruptcy in July 1772 (as appeared in *The Gentleman's Magazine*), but he appears without category, as working in 'Marybone', in the Parl. Report list 1773. On 2 July 1777 a Thomas Neale was apprenticed to him, when Cafe is described as 'of the same place' as the boy's father, 'High Street Marylebone'; on 1 December 1784 his own son Thomas was also apprenticed to him at the same address. Cafe died between 1802 and 1811.

CALAME, James Anthony (3471, 3613) No record of apprenticeship or freedom. Incuse marks only entered, 22 February and 15 May 1764, A C and I A C. Address: 'in the Strand facing Exeter change'. The attribution to him of the marks in question remains open to doubt. He appears as goldworker, opposite Exeter 'change, in the Parl. Report list 1773, which appears to confirm the entry of incuse marks as are met with in gold boxes and watchcases. Charles Lorimer Calame appears as watchcasemaker, 1825 (Section VI).

CALDECOTT, William (3059) Son of the Rev. Mr. George Caldecott of the parish of Great Bentley in the County of Essex clerk, apprenticed to Thomas Caldecott 6 March 1745 on payment of £20 of the charity money of the Stewards of the Corporation of the Sons of the Clergy. Turned over 4 May 1748 to John Montgomery and on 21 December 1750 by the administratrix of the latter to Thomas Hemming there being paid £4. 4s. Freedom unrecorded. Mark entered as largeworker, 8 March 1756. Address: 'At Mrs. Montgomerys in Silver Street near Golden Square', where Heal records him till 1766.

*CALLARD, Isaac (261, 1196, 1223-4) Possibly the son of Isaac Allar or Callard 'maitre tailleur d'habits âge de 55 ans ou environ' who married Elisabet Vivier 'âgée de 45 ans ou environ' at Hungerford Market Church 24 June 1688. Described as 'Free of no Company' when New and Sterling Standard marks entered as largeworker, 7 February 1726. Address: King Street, St. Giles in the Fields. Third mark, 20 June 1739. Address: The Crown, Tottenham Court Road. Fourth mark, 17 March 1747. Address: Earle Street, Seven Dials. Last mark, 3 December 1750. Address: 'Battersea Devision near to ye Black Raven'. A further date is added to this entry 27 July 1759, which is the same date as the entry of Paul Callard's second mark and may have been inserted in error for the latter and not deleted. Jackson, followed by Evans, suggests that the mark of 1739 is that of Isaac Callard Junior, but there is no evidence of this in the entries and the writing appears to be in the same hand throughout, with deterioration of age. From the occurrence of his mark it is clear that Callard was a spoonmaker and it is interesting to find him as a witness to the marriage on 4 June 1728, at the church of Le Carré, of Pierre des Champs and Elisabeth Hanet, almost certainly the daughter of Paul Hanet (q.v.), also a spoonmaker with whom Callard may well have learnt his trade. This supposition is virtually confirmed by the appearance of 'Hannett' as godfather to 'Paul Callar fils de Mr Isaac et de Marguerite', on 8 April 1724 at West Street Church.

*CALLARD, Paul (2150) Son of Isaac Callard (above) and Marguerite. Born 28 March, and baptized 8 April 1724 at West Street Church, godfather Paul Hanet (q.v.). Apprenticeship and freedom (if any) unrecorded. Mark entered as largeworker, 8 January 1752. Address: King Street, St. Ann, Soho. Second mark, a small one perhaps for gold, 27 July 1759. Heal records him only till 1755. James Callard, goldworker (Section VII), may perhaps be a son.

*CALVERT, Richard (454) No record of apprenticeship or freedom. Mark entered as

457

smallworker, in partnership with Daniel Cole, 7 April 1762. Address: 'at the Sun the corner of the Old Bailey'. Appears as watchcasemaker, Old Bailey, in the Parl. Report list 1773.

CAMPAR, George (779) John George son of Peter John Campar of the parish of St. Alphege London Wall weaver, apprenticed to Charles Pickering 3 April 1740 on payment of 10 guineas. Turned over to ? Roker November 1741. Free, 6 May 1747. Mark entered as largeworker, 7 November 1749. Address: Hart Street, Cripplegate. Moved to the Crown in Noble Street, 26 March 1752. Evans lists him as Huguenot (*Hug. Soc. Proc.*, 14).

CANEY, John (1218) No record of apprenticeship or freedom. Only mark entered as smallworker, 7 May 1800. Address: 10 Albemarle Street, Camberwell.

CANN, John (1201-2) No record of apprenticeship or freedom. He was probably free of the Coopers' Company, since a George Cann, after apprenticeship to Richard Gervas Williams in 1762, was turned over to John Cann Citizen and Cooper. First mark entered as largeworker, 8 March 1740. Address: Bridgwater Gardens, Charles Street, Barbican. Second mark, 30 June 1742, on removal to Boar's Head, Barbican.

CANNER, Christopher I (258) Son of Edward Canner late of Tewkesbury in the County of Gloucester hosier, apprenticed to Francis Archbold 18 June 1680 for eight years. Free, 20 June 1688. Livery, April 1705. Mark entered as largeworker, undated, probably April 1697 on commencement of register. Address: Gutter Lane, where Heal records him till his death in 1708, recorded in the register of St. Michael le Quern: 'Mr. Christopher Canner free of ye Goldsmiths was buried in ye New Vault from out of Gutter Lane Jany ye 12th 1707-8'. The register of St. Vedast, Foster Lane, contains baptismal entries for his son Christopher (q.v.) and two daughters, from 1691 to 1694, from which appears his wife's name Mary. His mark is found usually on casters, suggesting specialization, as also with Charles Adam (q.v.) another apprentice of Archbold's.

CANNER, Christopher II (257, 277) Son of Christopher Canner I, born and baptized 18 December 1692. Free by patrimony, 18 May 1716. First mark entered as largeworker, 30 May 1716. Address: Maiden Lane. Second (Sterling) mark, 8 July 1720. Address: Foster Lane. Probably the Christopher Canner of St. Michael le Quern, bachelor, who married Mary Page of St. Andrew, Holborn, spinster, at St. Bene't, Paul's Wharf, 16 February 1722-3; they were parents of two sons, both Christopher, buried at St. Michael le Quern 1723 and 1725.

CAPON, William (3071) No record of apprenticeship or freedom. Only mark entered as smallworker, 9 June 1820. Address: 2 New Bond Street.

CAPPER, Edward (555) No record of apprenticeship or freedom. First mark entered as smallworker, 8 November 1792. Address: 23 Stonecutter Street. Moved to 3 Georges Court, Clerkenwell, 14 September 1803, and to 12 Red Cross Square, Jewin Street, 1 February 1809. Second mark, 27 August 1813, at the last address above. Edward Capper, plateworker, Round Court, St. Martin's Le Grand, appears in the Parl. Report list 1773, and Heal records Edward Capper, silversmith at the same address, 1761-1777 (?), and at 23 Shoe Lane, 1795. It is difficult to determine whether the earlier address is that of the father of the above or the same man working for over fifty years. The former seems more likely. In any case the old confusion of the marks of this maker and Ebenezer Coker (q.v.) would seem to be eradicated by Coker's earlier and obviously more distinctive working life.

CARLTON, Thomas (2714) No record of apprenticeship or freedom. Only mark entered as largeworker, 22 June 1744. Address: 'next door to the Fan & Crowne in the Great Old Bailey'. Moved next door to the Sun Tavern, Ludgate Street, no date. Heal records him at the first address, 1744-8.

*CARMAN, John I (260, 1190) Apprentice of Thomas Vicaridge (q.v.) admitted to the freedom of the Cutlers' Company 19 April 1716. First mark entered as smallworker, 4 May 1716. Address: New Street. Described as 'Free Cutler'. Second (Sterling) mark, 27 June 1720. Heal records him as plateworker at New Street (Chancery Lane), till 1728. He was in fact probably a swordhilt and haftmaker. Dead by June 1743 (see below).

CARMAN, John II (1204, 1225, 3628) Son of the above. Admitted to freedom of the Cutlers' Company 30 June 1743 when his father is described as deceased. First mark entered as largeworker, 4 July 1748. Address: New Street. Moved to Holborn, near Hatton Garden, 30 September 1752. Second mark, 12 October 1756. Heal records him as working goldsmith and sword cutler, New Street, 1752; and Hatton Garden, 1755; and at the Ewer and Swords, near Bartletts Building, Holborn, c. 1760; also as plateworker, Holborn, 1748-52. He was dead by 10 January 1765 when Edward Carman, probably his son, described as late apprentice to John Carman Citizen and Cutler deceased, was admitted to the freedom of the same company.

CARMAN, Mary (2007) Almost certainly the widow of John Carman II. Mark entered as smallworker, 20 January 1764, described as silver hiltmaker, Holborn. Edward Carman, when made free of the Cutlers' Company, having been apprentice of John Carman II, was noted as 'at Mrs. Carman's Holborn'.

CARPENDER, John (1197) Son of George Carpender of the Town and County of Northampton yeoman, apprenticed to Thomas Sadler 7 April 1714 on payment of £30. Free, 27 July 1721. Mark entered as smallworker, 5 May 1727. Address: Snow Hill. Heal records him as goldsmith, next door to the Green Dragon Alehouse, Snow Hill, 1744-8.

CARPENTER, Joseph (1226) Probably son of Samuel Carpenter of Twyford near Reading in the County of Berkshire grocer, apprenticed to Joseph Allen 4 March 1761 and turned over to William Bell 1 December 1762. Free, 7 June 1769. First mark entered as smallworker, 20 May 1768. Address: Globe Court, Fish Street Hill. Moved to Drapers' Court, Princes Street, Lothbury, 9 March 1771. Second mark, 8 July 1771. Address: 81 West Smithfield. Livery March 1781. Died between 1781 and 1795. Heal records only Joseph Carpenter, watchcasemaker, Blue Anchor Alley, 1772, and the same appears in the Parl. Report list 1773, who seems of doubtful identity with the above (See Sections V and VI).

CARRINGTON, Edmund (551) No record of apprenticeship or freedom. Only mark entered as smallworker, 16 May 1738. Address: 15 Rutland Court, near Aldersgate Bars.

CARSBERG, George (776) No record of apprenticeship or freedom. First mark entered as smallworker, 12 May 1803. Address: 14 Old Street Square. Second mark on move to 8 Gloucester Row, Hoxton, 11 November 1810. Moved to 40 Britannia Street, City Road, no date.

CARTER, John I (259) Probably son of Thomas Carter of Denham in the County of Buckingham husbandman, apprenticed to William Salter of the Leathersellers' Company 4 March 1662. Free, 19 April 1670. Another John Carter was made free of the same company, 18 January 1694, but no details are given. Mark entered as smallworker, undated, probably April 1697 on commencement of register. Address: Burchin Lane. 'Free Leather Seller'.

*CARTER, John II (1214-5) No record of apprenticeship or freedom unless, as seems unlikely, son of John Carter late of Birmingham ironmonger, apprenticed to Robert Cooke 4 May 1732 and turned over to John Allen Glover 31 March 1735, of whom the freedom is unrecorded. Although his first mark in the register is 21 September 1776 (Address: Bartholomew Close), there is evidence that he was supplying candlesticks to the firm of Parker and Wakelin as early as 1769 (Wakelin, 'Workmen's Ledger', Garrard MSS, Victoria and Albert Museum). Second mark, 30 October 1776, this entry annotated 'Lef Trade Jan 20 1777'. The first mark of Richard Carter and Robert Makepiece was entered the same day at the same address. Heal records him as goldsmith, London, 1768-9, and at Westmorland Buildings, 1770, and he appears in the Parl. Report list at Bartholomew Close in 1773, when he gave evidence, being described as a manufacturer of large plate. There is almost certainly a relationship between him and Richard and Thomas Carter (q.v.) both of whom at some time were also in Westmoreland Buildings. From the survival of his mark Carter appears to have specialized almost exclusively on candlesticks and salvers. His mark is found overstruck on that of candlesticks bearing the early Sheffield hallmarks, presumably purchased by him to resell at a profit to meet the growing demand for stamped and filled examples in London.

CARTER, Peter (2147) No record of apprenticeship or freedom. First mark entered as smallworker, 24 March 1783. Address: 6 Fetter Lane. Second mark, 20 April 1791. Heal records him as goldsmith, Fleet Street, 1775; and in Foster Lane, 1787 (unless another of the same name).

*CARTER, Richard (2293, 2375) No record

of apprenticeship or freedom. Probably a younger brother or cousin of John Carter II (q.v.). First mark, in partnership with Robert Makepeace as plateworkers, entered 20 January 1777 (the same day as John Carter's entry is dated 'Left Trade'). Address: Bartholomew Close. Second mark, in partnership with Daniel Smith and Robert Sharp (q.v.), 9 December 1778. Address: 14 Westmoreland Buildings (Aldersgate Street). It is curious that Carter's mark should appear above those of his partners who had already been working together since 1763, and would have seemed senior to him. Heal records Carter and Makepeace as goldsmiths, 6 Serle Street, Lincoln's Inn, from 1772-7. It would seem probable that their 1777 mark was entered consequent on their moving to Bartholomew Close to take over the workshop of the retiring John Carter, and that an earlier mark had been entered in the missing register before 1773.

CARTER, Thomas (2717) Possibly son of John Carter of the parish of St. Brides brass turner, apprenticed to Henry Yates 6 September 1749. Free, 10 January 1759. Livery, July 1763. Resigned 1767. Only mark entered as smallworker, 5 March 1762. Address: Addle Street, Aldermanbury. Heal records Thomas Carter, goldsmith, Westmoreland Buildings, Aldersgate Street, 1778 (the same address as John and Richard Carter, Smith and Sharp), but there may be no connection with the present maker. There is also an undated entry without mark in the register 'Thos Carter Westmoreland' Buildings Aldersgate Street', which supports Heal.

*CARTIER, David (450) No record of apprenticeship or freedom. Only mark entered as smallworker, 25 September 1730. Address: 'Hanovay Street near St. Giles pound'. The mark curiously resembles that of Daniel Chartier (451) but the Christian names and addresses of the two entries are clearly distinct.

*CARTLIDGE, William (3067-8) No record of apprenticeship or freedom. First mark entered as spoonmaker, 9 October 1810. Address: 26 King Street, Lower Road, Islington. Moved to 10 Lower Road, 16 May 1821, and to 7 Red Lion Court, Charterhouse Lane, 11 January 1822. Second mark, 14 June 1827, on move to 3 Bridgwater Square. Third mark, 29 June 1827.

CARTWRIGHT, Benjamin I (142-4) No record of apprenticeship or freedom. Probably free of the Blacksmiths' Company, since William Tant was turned over to Benjamin Cartwright Citizen and Blacksmith 24 May 1758. (Lack of address prevents definite identification with Benjamin Cartwright I or II and records of the Blacksmiths' Company do not survive for this period.) First mark, incuse, entered as smallworker, 22 June 1732. Address: 3 Horse Shoes, Pedlars Lane, Cow Cross (Section V). Second mark as largeworker, 20 June 1739. Address: Crown and Pearl, Bartholomew Close. Third mark, 19 May 1748. Fourth mark, 18 February 1757. Heal records him as working goldsmith and toyman at this address, with variations of West Smithfield for Bartholomew Close, until 1774, and he appears without category, Paved Stones, Smithfield, in the Parl. Report list 1773.

CARTWRIGHT, Benjamin II (138-140) No record of apprenticeship or freedom, but see above. Described on entry of first mark as 'Junor' and presumably son of the above. First mark as largeworker, 22 April 1754. Address: Smithfield (presumably with his father). Second mark, 7 September 1756. Address: Kings Arms and Snuffers, in the Strand. Third mark, 2 January 1770. Address: Paved Alley, Pall Mall, where he appears without category in the Parl. Report list 1773. Heal records him as plateworker and toyman at the Strand address, from 1749-56, but the earlier date seems a confusion with Benjamin Cartwright I, who is not however recorded at this address.

CASTLE, Peter (2152) Son of Peter Castle Citizen and Dyer of London, apprenticed to Thomas Rush 12 November 1734 on payment of 25 guineas. Free, 4 February 1741/2 and 'de novo', 5 August 1742 (perhaps indicating an omission, later discovered, to make the affirmation required). Mark entered, in partnership with William Gwillim as largeworkers, 10 September 1774. Address: Cary Lane.

CATER, Dudley (Frank) (2546) Son of John Augustus Cater late of Guildford Street Russell Square gentleman deceased, apprenticed to Jonathan Hayne of Red Lion Street 5 March 1823. Free, 5 October 1836. First mark entered as plateworker, in partnership with Samuel Hayne, 5 July 1836. Address: 16 Red Lyon Street, Clerkenwell. Second mark (two sizes), 12 April 1837.

Third mark (six sizes), 26 May 1842. Fourth mark, 1 October 1842, and subsequent entries. Livery, 20 April 1842. Died c. 1881–85.

CATES, Robert (2283) Son of Ralph Cates Citizen and Clothworker, apprenticed to his father 14 April 1713. Free, 14 June 1720, and admitted to livery at unspecified date. Only mark entered as smallworker, 22 June 1724. Address: Tunbolt Street, 'at ye uper end of Clerkewel Green'. 'Clothworker'.

CATHERY, Charles (288) No record of apprenticeship or freedom. Only mark entered as smallworker, 3 July 1776. Address: Chapel Street, Soho. Moved to 21 Rupert Street, Soho, 25 April 1797. Described as chaser, of Rupert Street, 3 February 1796, on apprenticeship of his son William to John Thompson of Gutter Lane, engraver.

CATT, John (1207) Son of Thomas Catt late of Higham in the County of Kent husbandman deceased, apprenticed to Thomas Jones 1 March 1749. Free, 9 June 1762. First mark entered as smallworker, 19 December 1762. Address: Purse Court, Old Change. Second mark incuse, in partnership with Benjamin Tristram as watchcasemakers, 24 October 1764. Address: Huggin Alley. Other marks alone, at other addresses (Section V). Heal records him only as watchcasemaker, Bridgwater Gardens, 1772, his last address, as also in the Parl. Report list 1773.

CATTELL, William (3062) Son of John Cattell of Browton in the County of Northampton husbandman, apprenticed to John Easton 3 May 1753 and turned over the same day to Samuel Eaton leatherseller. Free, 7 May 1760. Only mark entered as smallworker, 2 February 1771. Address: Bull Head Court, Jewin Street, where he appears as smallworker in the Parl. Report list 1773. Moved to the Swan at Hoxton, 29 April 1773.

CAUSTON, Thomas (2723) Son of William Causton of the parish of St. Dunstan in the West gentleman, apprenticed to David Green 7 November 1723 on payment of £30. Turned over to Matthew Cooper Citizen and Goldsmith 7 May 1728. Freedom unrecorded. Mark entered as largeworker, 7 December 1731. Address: Foster Lane, where Heal records him in the same year as pawnbroker.

CHADWICK, James (315) Son of Edward Chadwick Citizen and Merchant Taylor of London, apprenticed to Joseph Shen (?Sheen) on 22 September 1686 'from Michaelmas next'. Later turned over to Francis Garthorne. Free, 9 March 1694. Mark entered as largeworker, undated, presumably April 1697 on commencement of register. Address: Maiden Lane, where Heal records him as plateworker from 1690 to 1703.

CHAMBERLEN, John (319) Son of Robert Chamberlen late of Hastings in the County of Sussex yeoman, apprenticed to Thomas Ash 18 September 1695. Later turned over to Jeremy Lammas. Free, 25 September 1702. Mark entered as largeworker, 2 March 1704. Address: Maiden Lane. Heal also records him as a goldsmith, St. Edmondsbury, 1704–1712. Evans lists him as a Huguenot (*Hug. Soc. Proc.*, 14) but his father's occupation makes this look unlikely. He is also recorded as such by W. H. Manchée, ('Huguenot London Covent Garden', *Hug. Soc. Proc.*, 13).

CHAMBRIER, B. A. (20) No record of apprenticeship or freedom. Only mark entered as smallworker, 14 October 1772. Address: Church Street, St. Ann's (Soho), where he appears as goldworker in the Parl. Report list 1773.

CHAMPION, William (3064) Son of James Champion late of Gravesend in County of Kent shopkeeper deceased. apprenticed to Thomas Evans of Wood Street Goldsmith 2 October 1771 on payment of £20. Free, 2 June 1779, as bucklemaker. Only mark entered as smallworker, 22 April 1789. Address: 100 Holywell Street, Shoreditch. Moved to 6 Pauls Court, Huggin Lane, 15 February 1791. Moved to 147 Aldersgate Street, 1 May 1792. Heal records him as goldsmith, 100 Shoreditch, 1790–3; and at Pauls Court, 1791.

CHANDLER, Charles (318) Son of Richard Chandler of Teddington in the County of Middlesex baker, apprenticed to Thomas Herbert 4 June 1675. Free, 27 October 1687. Mark entered as smallworker, 25 November 1701. Address: Fetter Lane.

*CHANDLESS, William (3075) No record of apprenticeship or freedom. First mark entered as spoonmaker, 8 September 1832. Address: 1 Crown Court, Aldersgate Street. Second mark (two sizes), on move to 3 Lant Street, Borough, 10 December 1840. Moved to 31 Banner Street, St. Luke's, 23 November 1841. Third mark (two sizes), on move to 2 Newcastle Place, Clerkenwell, 8 October 1851.

CHAPMAN, Charles (280) No record of apprenticeship or freedom. Only mark entered as smallworker, 13 March 1734. Address: Duck Lane, near Smithfield.

CHAPMAN, Daniel (449) Mark entered as largeworker, 5 September 1729. Address: Bunhill Row near Chiswell Street. 'Merchant Taylor'. Does not appear in that company's freedom lists but may probably have been son or grandson of Daniel Chapman, free of the Merchant Taylors 1681 after apprenticeship to a goldwire drawer. Heal records him at the above address till 1734.

CHAPMAN John I (1199) Son of Edward Chapman of Wormleighton in the County of Warwick grasier, apprenticed to Thomas Goodbarn 5 September 1720 on payment of £16. Only mark entered as largeworker, 9 June 1730. Address: Noble Street, near Foster Lane, where Heal records him from 1730-8.

CHAPMAN, John II (1213) No record of apprenticeship or freedom. Only mark entered as smallworker, 30 November 1774. Address: 53 Old Street. Moved to 133 Bunhill Row, 9 May 1777.

CHAPMAN, Richard (317, 2282, 3765) Free of the Cutlers' Company by redemption 10 January 1696. First mark entered as smallworker, undated, possibly 1701. Address: Lombard Street. 'Cutler'. Second (Sterling) mark, 28 June 1720. Third mark, 2 March 1723. Address: Adams Court, Broad Street.

CHARNELHOUSE, William (322) Son of Alexander Charnelhouse of Salford in the County of Oxford clerk, apprenticed to Robert Cooper 1 August 1688. Free, 27 May 1696. Livery, October 1708. Mark entered as largeworker, 19 June 1703. Address: Gutter Lane. Signatory as 'working goldsmith' to the petition complaining of the competition of 'necessitous strangers', December 1711. 'Mr Wm. Charnelhouse Goldsmith, was buried in ye New Vault March ye 16 1711-12' (register, St. Vedast).

CHARTIER, Daniel (451) Son of John Chartier (q.v.) Citizen and Goldsmith of London, apprenticed to his father 25 October 1720. Freedom unrecorded. Mark entered as largeworker, 23 March 1740. Address: Hemings Row, near St. Martin's Lane.

*CHARTIER, John (320-1, 1194) Presumably the son of Jean Chartier of Blois, who appears in the Reconnaissances of the French Church of the Savoy 17 May 1688. Endenizened 8 May 1697 with Peter and Claudius Platel and Lewis Cuny. Freeman of the Goldsmiths' Company by redemption, 13 April 1698. Married earlier, Suzanne Garnier. Their son Jean was baptized Leicester Fields Church, 23 December 1697. Two marks entered as largeworker, undated, but between April 1698 and May 1699, from register position. Third (Sterling) mark, 10 July 1723. His son Daniel (q.v.) was apprenticed to him 1720. His daughter Henriette was married, Christmas Day 1724, to Pezé Pilleau (q.v.), who had been apprenticed to Chartier in 1710. The goldsmith appears as godfather to Jean Pezé Pilleau in 1729, and Alexis Pilleau in 1731, in Hungerford Market Church registers. The Sterling mark of 1723 (no. 1194) was ascribed by Jackson to Jean II (i.e. the son baptized in 1697), but there is no internal evidence to support this. All three marks are contained in the single entry, which lies between others of 1698 and 1699 and the Sterling mark is added at the lower right hand corner with the date written in to follow the already existing address. This is in keeping with the majority of Sterling marks registered from 1720 onwards for workers already possessing New Standard marks. (See Sir Charles Clay, 'Notes on the Ancestors and Descendants of Pezé Pilleau'. *Hug. Soc. Proc.*, 16, No. 3.)

CHATTERTON, George Richard (889) No record of apprenticeship or freedom but from evidence of the address almost certainly son of Randall Chatterton (q.v.). First mark entered as spoonmaker, 16 November 1836. Address: 2 Peters Court, St. Martin's Lane. Second mark, 2 December 1836.

CHATTERTON, Randall (2290) Son of Joseph Chatterton of Monkwell Street, London Goldsmith, apprenticed to John Kerchner(?) of Giltspur Street, London goldsmith, Citizen and Goldsmith 6 January 1802. Free, 1 February 1809. Richard Chatterton son of Joseph Chatterton (presumably a younger brother), was apprenticed to him 3 April 1816 when Randall Chatterton is described as 'of City Garden Row, City Road, Silversmith and Spoonmaker, Citizen and Goldsmith'. His son Randall Robert Chatterton was apprenticed to him 7 August 1822 at Gwynne Buildings, Goswell Street and another son Joseph, 3 March 1824, at 5 Gwynne Buildings. First mark entered as spoonmaker, 17 October 1825. Address: 82 Gwynn's Buildings, Goswell Road. Moved to 6 Goldsmiths Row, St. Brides, 20 September 1827. Second mark, 26 March 1829. Third mark, 26 June 1829. Moved to 2 Peters Court, St. Martin's Lane, 22 February 1841.

CHATTERTON, William (3060-1) No record of apprenticeship or freedom. First mark entered as smallworker, 7 April 1762. Address: Beach Lane. Second mark, 3 May 1763. Third mark, 14 December 1763. Moved to Paternoster Row, Spitalfields, 8 November 1765. Fourth mark, 11 August 1766. Appears here without category in the Parl. Report list 1773, and is presumably the William Chatterton of the parish of Christchurch, in the county of Middlesex, working silversmith, prosecuted at Hick's Hall in 1767 for 'soldering bits of standard silver to Tea tongs and buckles and sending the same to the Company's Assay office, in order fraudulently to obtain their marks to the same' and named in the records of offenders against the hallmarking laws in the same Report.

*CHAWNER, Henry (971-2, 977) Only son of Thomas Chawner (q.v.). Born 14 November 1764. Free of Goldsmiths' Company by patrimony 7 December 1785. First mark entered as plateworker (two sizes), 11 November 1786. Address: Amen Corner. Second mark (two sizes), 31 August 1787. Married 2 March 1789, 'Mr Chawner working goldsmith of Ave Maria Lane to Miss Hore only daughter of Mr Hore wharfinger near the Hermitage' (*The Gentleman's Magazine*). According to Burke, *Landed Gentry*, where the marriage date is given as 3 March 1788, she was daughter and heiress of Edward Hore of Esher, Surrey. Livery, 19 April 1791. Third mark, as partner with John Emes, 27 August 1796, same address. Heal records him at Amen Corner till 1793; 34 Paternoster Row till 1796; and then with John Emes there, till 1808. Elected to Court of Assistants, 15 May 1801. Died March 1851. Henry Chawner purchased the Manor House of Newton Valence, Hampshire, and had two sons and three daughters. The family, represented by Captain Edward Hore Chawner, were still at Newton Valence in 1935. (Compiled from notes by Evelyn Howard Chaplin, granddaughter of the last named, with assistance from Rouge Dragon, 1935.)

CHAWNER, Mary (2012) Presumably widow of William Chawner II (q.v.). Mark entered as spoonmaker, 14 April 1834, he having died the previous month. Address: 16 Hosier Lane. Five new marks, 25 March 1835.

CHAWNER, Thomas (2718-9, 3510, 3816-7, 3869) Born 1734. Son of John Chawner and Ann, née Chaloner, of Muslane in the parishes of Church Broughton and Scropton in Derbyshire. John described as gentleman when Thomas apprenticed to Ebenezer Coker 4 December 1754 on payment of £30. Free, 13 January 1762. Livery, December 1771. Heal records him as plateworker, 60 Paternoster Row from 1759, both alone and in partnership with William Chawner; and at Red Lion Street, Clerkenwell, 1767; and he appears as spoonmaker, Pater Noster Row in the Parl. Report list 1773. He was obviously working at least from the date of his freedom but due to the hiatus in the registers his first mark entered is 15 October 1773. Address: 60 Paternoster Row. Second mark, 1 November 1775. Third mark, 31 May 1783. Address: 9 Ave Maria Lane, where Heal records him till 1785 (the address previously of Thomas Whipham and Charles Wright, q.v.). Married Sarah Emery and had one son Henry (q.v.). He is said to have held an appointment at the Mint(?). Arms: Sable a chevron between three cherubim or. Crest: A sea wolf's head erased. Died between 1802 and 1811. (Source as for Henry Chawner, above.)

*CHAWNER, William I (821-2, 3510, 3816-7) No record of apprenticeship or freedom. Appears likely to have been brother of Thomas Chawner (q.v.), since Heal records them in partnership from 1759 and the latter had been born in 1734. First mark in registers as plateworker, in partnership with George Heming, 17 November 1774. Address: Bond Street. Second mark, 15 February 1781. Address: Old Bond Street. Heal records him at 60 Paternoster Row, both alone and with Thomas, from 1759-68; and with Heming at King's Arms, New Bond Street, facing Clifford Street, 1773-81. He appears as goldsmith, New Bond Street, in the Parl. Report list 1773.

CHAWNER, William II (3069-70, 3114, 3868) Son of Jonathan Chawner of Horncastle in the County of Lincoln tanner, apprenticed to William Fearn of Clerkenwell Green Goldsmith 4 January 1797. Free, 4 April 1804. First mark entered 10 April 1808, in partnership with William Eley and

William Fearn, spoonmakers. Address: 1 Lovell's Court, Paternoster Row, partnership apparently terminated by 6 October 1814, when Eley and Fearn entered a new mark together. Chawner's first mark alone, as spoonmaker, 9 February 1815 (two sizes). Address: 16 Hosier Lane, West Smithfield. Described as silver spoonmaker in the apprenticeship to him of James Dovey, 1816. Second mark, 13 August 1819. Third mark, 27 January 1820. Fourth, 14 February 1820. Fifth, 11 August 1821. Sixth (two sizes), 11 June 1825. Seventh, 14 October 1833. Livery, 20 January 1824. He married, 16 June 1816 at St. Bartholomew the Great, Mary Burwash, presumably sister of William Burwash (q.v.). His son William, born 31 March 1817, was apprenticed to him 1831, free 1838. A daughter, Mary Ann was also born 26 April 1818. Chawner died 20 March 1834. (Information, Mr. M. T. Medlycott.)

*CHEBSEY, George (770) Mark entered as smallworker, 21 May 1722. Address: New Street, near Shoe Lane. 'Leather Seller'. Perhaps the George Chebsey recorded as free of the Leathersellers' Company, 26 April 1692, probably by patrimony as son of William Chebsey.

CHEBSEY, William (316) Mark entered as smallworker, undated, c. 1700. Address: Little Old Bailey. 'Free Leather Seller'. Probably the William Chebsey, Citizen and Leatherseller of London, to whom his son William was apprenticed 14 February 1708.

CHEESBROUGH, Warner (3066) No record of apprenticeship or freedom. Only mark entered as smallworker, 14 August 1798. Address: 4 Raquet Court, Fleet Street. Heal records him as gold and silvercaster and jeweller, 21 Beer Lane, Thomas Street, 1790-3; and at 4 Raquet Court, 1796.

*CHEESE, Clement (290) No record of apprenticeship or freedom. Mark entered as spoonmaker, 30 June 1823. Address: 29 Great Sutton Street, Clerkenwell. Moved to 14 Vineyard Walk, Clerkenwell, 22 April 1824. Moved to 40 Kirby Street, Hatton Garden, 16 July 1829. See Charles Cheese, goldworker (Section VII), perhaps related.

CHESTER, Samuel (2494) No record of apprenticeship or freedom. Only mark entered as smallworker, 23 June 1769. Address: Pear Tree Court, Clerkenwell, where he appears as bucklemaker in the Parl. Report list 1773.

CHESTERMAN, Ann (21) Widow of Charles Chesterman I (q.v.). Mark entered as smallworker, 20 April 1775. Address: Fleet Market. Dead by 5 April 1780, when her apprentice Samuel Wheatley (q.v.) was turned over by her executrix Sarah Chesterman to Charles Chesterman II (below) who had entered his mark on 14 February that year, which is presumably very near to Ann's death.

CHESTERMAN, Charles I (281-2, 292) Son of Thomas Chesterman Citizen and Joiner of London, apprenticed to George Greenhill Jones 21 May 1734 on payment of £25. Free, 2 November 1748. First mark entered as largeworker, 7 July 1741. Address: Horton Street, Clare Market. Second mark, 2 October 1752. Address: Carey Lane. Moved to Rose and Crown Court, Foster Lane, 1 August 1754. Third mark, 20 November 1771. Address: Fleet Market, where he had been since the apprenticeship to him of his son Charles in 1766. Apparently dead by 20 April 1775, on the registration of a mark by Ann Chesterman. Heal records him as goldsmith and pawnbroker, Clare Market, 1741; and at 62 Fleet Market till 1793, but this overlaps with Charles Chesterman II (q.v.). His son Charles was born 5, baptized 8 May 1752 at St. Vedast, Foster Lane, and daughter Anne, 25 March 1750 at St. Michael le Quern. There is a puzzling obituary notice of '—— Chesterman, goldsmith died 4 May 1770' in *The London Magazine*, which could suggest that the entry of the third mark in 1771 was by the son of the same name. On the other hand the signatures of the 1752 and 1771 entries appear identical (although a slight difference is observable between the first signature of 1741 and the second), and 1771 would seem rather early to expect a son to have taken over when still not free of his apprenticeship. Charles Chesterman, smallworker, Fleet Market, appears in the Parl. Report list 1773.

CHESTERMAN, Charles II (283) Born 5 May 1752, son of Charles Chesterman of the Fleet Market London Citizen and Goldsmith, apprenticed to his father 2 July 1766. Free, 4 May 1774. Mark entered as smallworker, 14 February 1780. Address: 62 Fleet Market. Second mark, 6 March 1801. Described as silversmith the same year in the apprenticeship to him of Richard Barker. Third mark, 10 January 1809.

CHILCOTT, Charles William (289) No

record of apprenticeship or freedom. Only mark entered as smallworker, 30 September 1822. Address: 16 Wheeler Street, Spitalfields. Moved to 18 Cow Lane, West Smithfield, 9 October 1823; to 2 Hunts Court, Castle Street, Leicester Square, 1 October 1828; and to 43 Essex Street, Strand, 23 May 1830.

CHINNERY, William (3072) No record of apprenticeship or freedom. Only mark entered as plateworker, 13 July 1825. Address: 141 Aldersgate Street.

CLARE, Benjamin (357) Son of Benjamin Clare Citizen and Glover of London, apprenticed to Thomas Impey of the Skinners' Company for seven years 6 November 1673. Free, 7 December 1680. Mark entered as largeworker, undated, perhaps 1702. Address: Bell Court, Gray's Inn Lane. 'free Skinner'. His son George was apprenticed to him, 5 March 1705/6. Benjamin Clare was dead by 4 November 1707, when John Johnson (q.v.), his apprentice, was made free.

CLARE, Joseph I (353, 1189) Son of Francis Clare Citizen and Baker of London, apprenticed to Nathaniel Locke 17 February 1702. Free, 4 November 1712. Livery, October 1721. First mark entered as largeworker, 25 September 1713. Address: Wood Street. Second (Sterling) mark, 23 June 1720. Address: Love Lane. Also written in a small hand, of later insertion, below his first mark: 'Lumbard Street', without a date. Third mark, 15 December 1721. Address: 'in Lumber Streete'. Heal records him as at Wood Street, by Love Lane, till 1720; and at the Blackamoor's Head, Lombard Street, from 1721 till death in 1728.

CLARE, Joseph II (358, 1208-9) Son of Joseph Clare late Citizen and Goldsmith of London deceased, apprenticed to Jeremiah Marlow Junr. 6 June 1732 on payment of £100 (an exceptional sum). Freedom unrecorded. First mark entered as smallworker, 2 March 1763. Address: Deanes Court, St. Martin's Le Grand. Second mark, 1 October 1767. Third mark, 16 September 1768. Heal records him merely as goldsmith, London, 1758.

CLARIS, Christian (279) No record of apprenticeship or freedom. Only mark entered as largeworker, 16 June 1727. Address: 'next to ye Ship in James Street, Covent Garden'. Listed as Huguenot, with first name as Christopher, by W. R. Manchée (*Hug. Soc. Proc.*, 13, p. 72).

CLARK(E), Charles (284-6, 294) Son of Charles Clark of St. Andrews Holborn in the County of Middlesex, apprenticed to William Collier 28 April 1726 on payment of £20. Freedom unrecorded. First mark, incuse, entered as smallworker (or watchcasemaker?), 16 April 1735. Address: Gloucester Court, Whitecross Street. Second mark as largeworker, 3 July 1739. Address: Chequers Alley, Bunhill Row, St. Luke's. Moved to Featherstone Street, 12 November 1750. Third mark (two sizes), 12 September 1758. Fourth mark, 14 March 1763. Fifth mark, 20 April 1763. Appears as watchcasemaker, Featherstone Street, in the Parl. Report list 1773. A possible descendant may be Charles Clarke, watchcasemaker (Section VI).

CLARK, E(benezer) (554) No record of apprenticeship or freedom. Only mark entered as smallworker, 8 May 1790. Address: Fleet Street. Initial of Christian name only in register, but Heal records him as Ebenezer Clark, silversmith 'removed from Fenchurch Street to near St. Dunstan's Church Fleet Street 1790-1817'.

CLARK, John (1793) No record of apprenticeship or freedom. Only mark entered as smallworker, 30 July 1823. Address: 38 Cow Cross.

CLARK, Robert (2287) No record of apprenticeship or freedom. Only mark entered as smallworker, 21 February 1765. Address: 'facing the Cock & Crown in Aldersgate Street'. Appears without category, Aldersgate Street, in the Parl. Report list 1773.

*CLARK, Thomas (2711, 3814) Son of James Clarke Citizen and Cordwainer of London, apprenticed to Richard Gines 7 January 1719 on payment of £52.10s. Free, 2 March 1726. Mark entered as largeworker, 2 March 1726. Address: Ball Alley, Lombard Street. Heal has nothing further. There is however another of the same name recorded by him as jeweller and toyman, Golden Head, Strand, near Arundell Street, c. 1750, without evidence of identity with the above. Thomas Clarke, without category, appears in the Parl. Report list 1773, at Great New Street, Fetter Lane.

CLARKE, Catherine (287) No record of apprenticeship or freedom. Only mark entered as smallworker, 24 September 1761. Address: Dorset Court, Salisbury Court, Fleet Street. Heal records her only as goldsmith, London, 1773-4. She appears without category, at this address, in the Parl. Report list 1773.

CLARKE, Henry I (352, 965-6) Son of Henry Clarke Citizen of the parish of St. James Westmin[r] in the County of Middlesex baker, apprenticed to William Scarlett Citizen and Brod(erer) of London 26 August 1700. Free, 2 October 1707, described as 'Henry Clarke Goldsmith at Mr Wm Scarletts in Gutter Lane'. First mark entered as largeworker, 28 June 1709. Address: Foster Lane. Signatory as 'working goldsmith' to the petition complaining of the competition of 'necessitous strangers', December 1711. Second mark (Sterling) undated, c. 1720. Address: St. Ann's Lane. 'Free Imbroiderer'. Third mark, 7 March 1723. Address: St. Ann's Lane. Livery, April 1731. Heal adds to the above addresses that he was in Gutter Lane in 1737, then insolvent. He also records Henry Clarke, goldsmith, Wood Street, from 1734 to death in 1777, but this would seem to be another man otherwise unrecorded.

CLARKE, Henry II (968) Son of John Clarke Citizen and Goldsmith of London (q.v.) apprenticed to his father 10 December 1716. Free, 22 September 1726. Mark entered as smallworker, 21 July 1738. Address: Dolphin Court, Ludgate Hill.

CLARKE, James (1229, 1789) No record of apprenticeship or freedom. First mark entered as smallworker, 31 October 1765. Address: Featherstone Street, Bunhill Row. Second mark, 29 August 1769, same address. Third mark, as watchcasemaker, 27 February 1779 (Section VI).

CLARKE, John I (347, 354, 1193) Either (1) son of John Clarke late Citizen and Grocer of London, apprenticed to Richard Alkin 14 August 1678. Freedom unrecorded. Or (2) son of Henry Clarke of Meare in the County of Wiltshire, dyer, apprenticed to Elizabeth Greene widow of Thomas 26 March 1680. Free, 29 June 1698. Livery, October 1708. First mark entered as smallworker, 12 September 1700. Address: Foster Lane. Signed petition against assaying work of foreigners not having served seven years apprenticeship, February 1716. Second mark as largeworker (Sterling), 2 July 1722. Third, New Standard mark, 20 July 1722, same address. The lapse of time between the first and second marks, and the fact that one would have expected an entry of the Sterling mark in 1720 on the return to the Standard, suggests a possibility that the 1722 marks might be that of a son. But there is no other evidence to this effect.

*CLARKE, John II (1220) Perhaps John Clark son of Robert of New Street, St. Luke's clockmaker, apprenticed to James Darquitt of St. Ann's Lane Goldsmith 1 January 1794. Freedom unrecorded. Mark entered as plateworker, 21 March 1807. Address: 12 Clerkenwell Green. Moved to 8 Aylesbury Street, Clerkenwell, 25 April 1814. Moved to 7 Broad Street, Golden Square, 18 March 1819. Moved to 15 Charterhouse Street, no date.

CLARKE, Richard (349) Son of William Clarke Citizen and Haberdasher of London, apprenticed to Benjamin Pyne 9 April 1701. Free, 15 July 1708. Mark entered as largeworker, 21 October 1708. Address: The Minories.

CLARKE, Sarah (2493) No record of apprenticeship or freedom. Only mark entered as smallworker, 22 May 1765. Address: 'in the Borough' (of Southwark). She appears as bucklemaker, Southwark, in the Parl. Report list 1773, and Heal records her as goldsmith, 1777.

*CLAUSEN, Nicholas (351, 2085) Appears as 'Nicholaus Clausen Parish St. Martin in the fields' in the Naturalization Act of 1709, with witnesses Godfried Wittich and Sven Holst, which suggests Swedish rather than German origin. Made free of the Haberdashers' Company by redemption 1 July 1709 as 'Niecolaus Clauson', without details of address or occupation, and there appears to be no other reference to him in that company's records. First mark entered as largeworker, 10 June 1709, a date earlier than that recorded for his freedom. Address: Orange Street, near Leicester Fields. 'Free of the Haberdashers'. Second (Sterling) mark, 29 July 1720. Heal records him at Orange Street till 1723. In spite of his Scandinavian origin his work, admittedly rare in survival, is typical of the Huguenot school, his latest and greatest achievement being the Imperial Throne of 1731 in the Hermitage, Leningrad.

*CLAYTON, David (345, 452) Free by patrimony of the Merchant Taylors' Company as son of David Clayton 10 September 1689. Livery, 28 February 1704. Mark entered as smallworker, 9 July 1697. Address: Cheapside. Second (Sterling) mark, 6 July 1720. 'Free Merchant Taylor'.

Heal records him as jeweller, Golden Unicorn, Cheapside, 1703-11; and at the same sign, Butcher Hall Lane, Newgate Street, in 1714. His mark is apparently found only on toys and was formerly attributed in error to Augustine Courtauld.

CLAYTON, John (1227) Probably son of David (above), since his mark is also found apparently exclusively on toys. No record of apprenticeship or freedom. Mark entered as smallworker, 2 November 1736. Address: 'Flower de Luce Court Blackfriars'. Heal records John Clayton, goldsmith, London, bankrupt 1737, who may be the same. There may also be a connection with John and Anthony Clayton, goldsmiths, Flower de Luce, Cheapside, 1704-6.

CLAYTON, Mat(hew) (2005) Son of Thomas Clayton of the town of Bedford maltster, apprenticed to Gundry Roode 8 December 1720 on payment of 10 guineas. Free, 3 April 1728. Mark entered as smallworker, 23 January 1730. Address: Noble Street. 'Free Goldsmith'.

CLAYTON, Ruth (346) No record of apprenticeship or freedom. Only mark entered as smallworker, 31 December 1697. Address: Ball Alley, Lombard Street.

CLEMENSON, John (1210) No record of apprenticeship or freedom. Only mark entered as smallworker, 4 May 1763. Address: Moorfields. Appears without category, at this address, in the Parl. Report list 1773.

CLEMENTS, George (778) Son of William Clements late of Bartholomew Close carver and gilder deceased, apprenticed to John Crouch of Marshall Street as silversmith and polisher 2 July 1806. Free, 1 June 1814. Mark entered as plateworker, 29 June 1825. Address: 400 Strand.

CLIFFORD, Thomas (2722) Son of Thomas Clifford late of Fan Street Aldersgate victualler deceased, apprenticed to Thomas F. Dexter of Goswell Street, St. Luke's as working goldsmith 4 October 1809. Free, 2 July 1817. Mark entered as plateworker, 21 July 1820. Address: 57 Charles Street, Goswell Street Road. Moved to 7 Bride Lane, Fleet Street, 19 October 1821, and to 7 Red Cross Square, Jewin Street, 5 February 1822.

CLIFTON, John (350) Possibly (1) son of Francis Clifton free by patrimony 5 July 1676. Or (2) son of John Clifton of Snitterton in the County of Derby gentleman, apprenticed to John King 6 November 1676 'as from Xmas next'. Both seem rather too early to be identified with this maker who entered his only mark as largeworker, 21 October 1708. Address: Foster Lane.

CLIFTON, Jonah (348, 1191, 3627) Son of William Clifton of Paulerspury in the County of Northampton gentleman, apprenticed to Benjamin Pyne 20 September 1693. Free, 7 November 1703. First mark entered as largeworker, 25 November 1703. Address: Tower Street, near St. Martin's Lane. Second (Sterling) mark, 8 October 1720. An identical entry with the two marks of the same size also appears in the smallworkers' book—a rare occurrence. Heal records him at Tower Street, till 1728. He also lists Jonas Clifton, goldsmith, Crown, Strand, 1718; and as at the Crown, Henrietta Street, Covent Garden, 'Removed a little beyond Hungerford in ye Strand', c. 1730. There seems however no apparent connection between the two names. He is probably identifiable with the James Clifton appearing as signatory as 'working goldsmith' to the petition complaining of the competition of 'necessitous strangers', December 1711, the list of signatories being a copy only in the Company records.

COATES, Robert (711) No record of apprenticeship or freedom. Only mark entered as smallworker, in partnership with Francis Powell, 6 January 1818. Address: 4 Fann Street, Aldersgate Street. Partnership apparently dissolved by 7 May 1818, when Powell entered a separate mark.

COATS, Alex(ander) (23) No record of apprenticeship or freedom. Mark entered as largeworker, in partnership with E. French, 29 August 1734. Address: Benet's Court, near Exeter Change, Strand.

COCK, Thomas (2713) Son of Richard Cock of Mutchmundin(?) in the County of Hertford yeoman, apprenticed to John Cooper 14 May 1718 on payment of £30. Free, 10 June 1725. Mark entered as smallworker, 15 July 1736. Address: Horseshoe Alley, Middle Moorfields.

COKER, Ebenezer (550, 556, 3538-9) Son of William Coker of Berkhampsted in the County of Hertford cheesemonger, apprenticed to Joseph Smith 21 October 1728. No premium stated. Free, 7 February 1740. First mark entered 27 March 1738. Address: Clerkenwell Green. Second mark, 25 June 1739. Third mark, 24 May 1745. Fourth mark, 20 December (?) 1751. A fifth mark probably entered after 1758 (3538), and another, in partnership with Thomas Hammond (?Hannam), 1759-60 (3539). Described as widower of St. James, Clerkenwell, Middlesex, on marriage to Elizabeth Ransey of the same parish, 1 December 1739, at St. Bene't, Pauls Wharf. Heal records him as plateworker at the Golden Cup and Rising Sun, Clerkenwell Close or Green, 1738; with Thomas Hammond (?Hannam) as goldsmiths, same address, dissolving partnership 1760; alone at Clerkenwell Close and 13 Wood Street, 1770. Appears as goldsmith, Clerkenwell Close, in the Parl. Report list 1773. His clerk and assistant gave evidence to the committee when Coker was described as large plate manufacturer. Bankrupt, 1781 (*The Gentleman's Magazine* for December that year). Died, 2 August 1783, 'Upon Clerkenwell Green Mr Coker, many years a goldsmith in Clerkenwell Close' (*The Gentleman's Magazine*). Like John Carter his chief productions were candlesticks and salvers.

*COLE, Daniel (454) No record of apprenticeship or freedom. Only mark entered as smallworker, in partnership with Richard Calvert, 7 April 1762. Address: 'at the Sun the Corner of the Old Bailey'. Appears without category, Old Bailey, in the Parl. Report list 1773.

COLE, John (370) Probably son of John Cole late of the town of Northampton fellmonger deceased, apprenticed to John Gray 20 September 1661. Free, 29 September 1669. Mark entered as largeworker, undated, probably April 1697 on commencement of register. Address: Silver Street.

*COLE, Thomas (2709-10) No record of apprenticeship or freedom. First mark entered as smallworker (annotated 'Goldwork'), 13 August 1720. Address: 'at the Lamb and Woolpack Cow Cross'. Second mark as smallworker, 16 February 1732, same address.

COLEMAN, Stephen (381) Son of Henry Coleman of Marlborough in the County of Wiltshire grocer, apprenticed to William Mathew 26 September 1683. Free, 8 October 1690. Mark entered as largeworker, undated, probably April 1697 on commencement of register. Address: Little Britain, where Heal records him till 1702.

COLES, Joseph (1790) No record of apprenticeship or freedom. Only mark entered as smallworker, 14 May 1800. Address: 173 Aldersgate Street.

COLES, Lawrence (369) Son of Hugh Coles of the Town and County of Northampton maltster, apprenticed to John Smith 22 August 1660 'from Michaelmas next coming'. Free, 23 October 1667. Mark entered as largeworker, undated, probably April 1697 on commencement of register. Address: Foster Lane. Heal records him as goldsmith, London, 1669-97, as goldsmith, parish of St. John Zachary, 1692-3; and as plateworker, Foster Lane, 1697-1714. Frances, daughter of Laurence Coles and Frances his wife, was born 5 and baptized 23 March 1685-6, at St. Michael le Quern, and the same buried there 13 April 1687. A son John was buried 8 April 1689 and his wife also on the same day 1692. Coles was elected to the Court in 1698 and Warden in 1712, 1715 and 1716, and was Deputy to the Common Council in 1701. Signatory to the petition against the work of 'aliens and foreigners', 11 August 1697. From the surviving appearances of his mark it is clear that Coles was a specialist spoonmaker.

COLES, William (3076) Son of Joseph Coles late of Ovinge in the County of Buckingham tobacconist deceased, apprenticed to Abraham Pope (q.v.) of the Leathersellers' Company 9 August 1715. Free, 7 December 1722. Mark entered as smallworker, 5 August 1724. Address: Shoe Lane. 'Leatherseller'. Heal records William Coles, silversmith, Silver Street, St. Olave's, 1744, but there seems no obvious connection. Coles was still working when his son William was apprenticed to him 19 January 1764, and free 1772.

COLEY, Simeon (2491-2) No record of apprenticeship or freedom. Born about 1725, and said at some time to have lived in North America and Jamaica. Freeman of the Glovers' Company 28 December 1773. First mark entered as smallworker, 27 September 1761. Address: Clerkenwell Green. Second mark, 7 April 1763, same address. Appears as bucklemaker, Aylesbury Street, Clerkenwell, in the Parl. Report list 1773, and entered four marks as such from 1773 to 1780, at 91 Fleet Street and 35 Fetter Lane, to be followed by his son of the same name in 1789 (Section VIII). His wife Elizabeth died 14 February 1778, and he 22 May 1798 leaving £3,000; both were buried at Bunhill Fields. He finally lived at Enfield. His son Simeon was born 5 August 1752, married 26 July 1788 at Bath Abbey, Frances, daughter of Rev. Peter Grigg, and died 13 January 1810 at Bedford leaving £25,000. Both father and son were members of the Moravian Church. Hannah, daughter of Simeon senior, married Thomas Northcote (see under both names). For all but the above mark details I am indebted to Mr. Brian G. C. Brooks, direct descendant of the Coleys.

COLLIER, Robert (2284) Son of Timothy Collier late of Bridge Norton in the County of Oxon. tallowchandler deceased, apprenticed to Robert Elliot of the Leathersellers' Company 7 May 1719. Free, 7 July 1726. First mark entered as smallworker, 1 February 1727, 'Living in Gutter Lane. Free of the Leathersellers'. Second mark, 6 October 1737. Address: 'At Mr Gorams in Gutter Lane' (presumably John Gorham, q.v.).

COLLIER, Thomas (2715) Son of Robert Collier of Whitney in the County of Oxford brasier, apprenticed to Jacob Marsh 12 October 1746 on payment of £20. Free, 10 January 1754. Mark entered as largeworker, 5 July 1754. Address: Foster Lane. One of the same name entered a smallworker's mark, 10 June 1768 (Section IV), and appears without category in the Parl. Report list 1773.

COLLINGS, William (3063) Son of John Collings late of Chichester in the County of Sussex taylor deceased, apprenticed to John Raymond 4 July 1754 on payment of £21. Free, 9 February 1763. Mark entered as smallworker, 27 August 1771. Address: 3 Fell Street, where he appears in same category in the Parl. Report list 1773.

COLLINS, George (773-4) No record of apprenticeship or freedom. First mark entered as smallworker, 6 October 1800. Address: 31 Clerkenwell Green. Moved to 50 Ray Street, Clerkenwell, 30 October 1802. Second mark, 28 January 1804.

COLLINS, Henry (368, 3507) Son of Henry Collins of Honeybourne Worcestershire yeoman, apprenticed to John Sutton 26 September 1673 for eight years. Free, 7 October 1681. Mark entered as largeworker, undated, but between April 1698 and May 1699 (surrounding dates). Address: Maiden Lane. Heal records him as plateworker, parish of All Hallows, Lombard Street, 1692-3; Maiden Lane, 1698; and London, 1714.

COLLINS, J. (1205) Perhaps Joseph son of William Collins Citizen and Cutler of London, apprenticed to Dru Drury 7 August 1728 on payment of £4 from the charity of the Drapers' Company. Free, 4 September 1735. Mark entered as largeworker, 17 May 1754. Address: Hind Court, Fleet Street. Moved to Paternoster Row, 18 April 1755. Heal records him at Hind Court, as plateworker, from 1754 to 1774.

COLLINS, William (3073) No record of apprenticeship or freedom. Only mark entered as plateworker, 4 March 1828. Address: 227 Strand.

COLVILL, Samuel (388, 2488) Son of Thomas Colvill late Citizen and Merchant Taylor of London, apprenticed to William Gatliffe 4 July 1704. Free, 12 February 1712. Mark entered as smallworker, 6 January 1716. Address: Talbot Court, Gracechurch Street. Second (Sterling) mark, 26 September 1722. Address: Lombard Street. 'of the Goldsmiths Company'.

COLVILL, Thomas (386) Son of the same Thomas Colvill (above) and brother of Samuel, apprenticed to William Francis 24 February 1701 and turned over to John Eckford. Free, 12 February 1712 (same day as his brother). Mark entered as smallworker, 14 July 1713. Address: St. Mary's Hill, near Billingsgate.

COMBES, Thomas (2721) No record of apprenticeship or freedom. First mark entered as smallworker, 30 September 1807. Address: 15 Little Wild Street, Lincoln's Inn Fields. Moved to Ship Yard, Wardens Street, Soho, 7 January 1812. Second mark, 21 June 1816. Third mark, 21 February 1817.

COMPIGNE, Michael (2006) No record of apprenticeship or freedom. Only mark entered as smallworker, 27 February 1738. Address: 'at the Six Bells, Long Acre. foriner'. Heal records him as Compiegne, without Christian name, as goldsmith at same date and address.

CONEN, Edward (547) Son of William Conen of London merchant, apprenticed to Philip Brush 12 November 1707 and turned over to Richard Watts. Free, 10 December 1714. Signatory as journeyman to the petition against assaying the work of foreigners not having served seven years apprenticeship, February 1716. Mark entered as largeworker, 8 December 1724. Address: Cary Lane. Free Goldsmith.

CONGREVE, Thomas (2716, 3815) No record of apprenticeship or freedom. Mark entered as largeworker, 18 September 1756. Address: St. Thomas' Church, Southwark, where Heal records him as plateworker from then till 1760. Dead by 1763, when his son William was apprenticed to Richard Clowdesly, the father described as Thomas Congreve, late of Borough of Southwark, jeweller, deceased.

CONOLLY, Charles (291) No record of apprenticeship or freedom. Only mark entered as plateworker, 9 August 1824. Address: 95 Piccadilly.

*COOK, Abraham (19) No record of apprenticeship or freedom. First mark entered as snuffboxmaker, 11 May 1759. Address: Little Cranborne Alley. Second mark, 2 November 1769. Address: Piccadilly, opposite the Haymarket.

COOKE, Edward (549) Son of James Cooke of St. Andrew's Holborn gentleman, apprenticed to Charles Jones 4 November 1713 on payment of £15.15s. Free, 1 December 1720. Livery, March 1737. Court of Assistants, 1755. Mark entered as smallworker, 10 August 1735. Address: Haymarket, Southwark. Free Goldsmith. Heal records him as goldsmith and jeweller, 210 Borough, in the Haymarket, Southwark, from 1760–77. He appears as goldsmith, Southwark, in the Parl. Report list 1773. Died 1774.

COOKE, Elizabeth (552, 3538) No record of apprenticeship or freedom. First mark entered as smallworker, 'Silversmith', 24 January 1764. Address: Foster Lane. Second mark, 9 March 1764. It seems possible from the address that she may have been the widow of Thomas Cooke II (below).

COOKE, John I (383) Son of Francis Cook Citizen and Goldsmith of London, apprenticed to John Cartlich 16 October 1690. Mark entered as smallworker, 7 September 1699. Address: Wood Street, where Heal records him as goldsmith, deceased 1706. Possibly identifiable with the Prime Warden of 1706 of the same name, but apparently unlikely.

COOKE, John II (377) Son of Joseph Cooke Citizen and Joyner of London, free by patrimony of the Joiners' Company 2 May 1699 on the attestation of William Lambe Citizen and Cutler and John Alexander Citizen and Cordwinder of London. Mark entered as largeworker, 11 May 1699, described as Free Joyner. Address: Strand. Heal records John Cooke, goldsmith, at the Porter, Gracechurch Street, 1690–1706, but there seems no apparent connection here.

COOKE, Richard (2289) No record of apprenticeship or freedom. Only mark entered as plateworker, 28 June 1799. Address: 29 Carey Street, Bell Yard. Moved to 3 Carey Street, 14 January 1805. His work, which has survived in reasonable quantity, shows a high standard and he probably supplied one of the leading retailers, Rundell and Co. or Jefferys, Jones and Gilbert. Most frequently met with are tea-sets and entrée-dishes, with some good covered cups of semi-classical inspiration.

COOKE, Robert (2285) Probably son of Joseph Cooke of the parish of All Saints Evesham in the County of Worcester barber, apprenticed to Henry Morris 4 July 1723 on payment of £17. Free, 9 September 1731. Mark entered as smallworker, 24 May 1731. Address: Chick Lane, near West Smithfields. Livery, May 1737.

COOKE, Thomas I (387) Probably son of Francis Cooke Citizen and Goldsmith of London, apprenticed to Henry Hoare 26 February 1702. Freedom unrecorded. Mark entered as smallworker, 18 November 1713. Address: 'at the Ditch-syde near holbourn Bridge'.

COOKE, Thomas II (2324–5, 2712) Son of John Cooke of the Town and County of Warwick weaver, apprenticed to Richard Bayley 11 June 1719 on payment of 25 guineas. Free, 22 September 1726. First mark entered as largeworker, 7 June 1727. Address: Foster Lane. 'Free Goldsmith'. Second mark, as partner with Richard Gurney, 19 October 1727. Address: Golden Cup, Foster Lane. Third mark, as Gurney and Co., 23 December 1734. Fourth mark, 28 June 1739. Fifth and sixth marks, 17 February 1749 and 30 July 1750. Livery, March 1739. Court, February 1752. Heal records Thomas Cooke, goldsmith, without address, 1721, died 1761, but this might be the preceding worker; Thomas Cooke and Richard Gurney as goldsmiths, Golden Cup, Foster Lane, 1721–73.

COOPER, Benjamin I (136) Son of George Cooper of Great Whitley in the County of Worcester yeoman, apprenticed to Richard Banks of the Haberdashers' Company St. Maryhill clockmaker 1 February 1717 and turned over in 1719 to Joseph Perkins Citizen and Merchant Taylor and in 1722 to Daniel Farmer Citizen and Glover. Free, 14 February 1723. Mark entered as smallworker, 4 May 1724. Address: Crooked Lane. 'Haberdasher'. Heal records him at the Wheelbarrow, Crooked Lane, 1725, and he seems to have been there till 1747. He may be the Benjamin Cooper of Buringham (?Birmingham), incuse mark entered 1749 (Section V). Since his first Haberdasher master is described as clockmaker, it would seem likely that the further two to whom he was turned over were the same, and that Cooper may have entered his mark for watchcases. See below.

COOPER, B(enjamin) II (141) No record of apprenticeship or freedom. Mark entered as smallworker, 17 January 1764. Address: Holborn. Second mark, September 1765. Heal records Benjamin Cooper, goldsmith, 7 Brownlow Street, Holborn, 1774-9. He appears as bucklemaker, High Holborn, in the Parl. Report list 1773. One of the same name is recorded as dead, 11 October 1786, aged eighty-eight (*The Gentleman's Magazine*, p. 910) and it is therefore possible that Benjamin Cooper I and II are identical although the two signatures differ.

*COOPER, Edmund (372) Parentage untraced. Described as 'Free Bowyer' on entry of mark as smallworker, 5 July 1699. Address: Old Change. 'Joyce daughter of Edmond Cooper a Goldsmith Liveing at ye signe of ye Crowne and Braslett in ye old Chaing in this parish and Joyce his wife was Born ye 20th of February and was Baptised the 6th day of March 1703' (Register, St. Vedast, Foster Lane). In entry for son John's baptism, 7 October 1707, Cooper is described as 'a Gold Chaine Maker', while in another entry for burial of John Goldwell, servant to Edmund Cooper, 27 October 1705, he is said to be 'at ye signe of ye Goldchaine'.

COOPER, Edward (553) No record of apprenticeship or freedom. Probably son of Benjamin Cooper II and brother of Joshua (q.v.). Mark entered as smallworker, 27 July 1775. Address: Brownlow Street, Holborn. Moved to 6 Turnpike Lane, Fleet Market, 6 May 1776.

COOPER, John I (376) Either (1) son of John Cooper Citizen and Bowyer of London, apprenticed to George Jackson 22 October 1690 and turned over to Edward Turner. Free, 15 March 1698 (?9). Or (2) son of Richard Cooper late of Epping in the County of Essex clerke deceased, apprenticed to Henry Jay 24 February 1708. Freedom unrecorded. Mark entered as smallworker, 12 September 1721, and noted alongside as 'Gold Mark', implying another entry for earlier Britannia Standard Silver mark, of which there is no evidence. Address: Gutter Lane. 'Goldsmith'. Heal records one of this name as goldsmith, Golden Ball over against the Maypole, Strand, 1712; and against the New Church, Strand, 1724-7, but this scarcely seems to be the same man.

COOPER, John II (1231) Perhaps (1) son of James Cooper of Dimock in the County of Gloucester yeoman, apprenticed to William Shaw 4 October 1749 on payment of £20. Free, 3 August 1757. Or (2) son of Robert Cooper of Stratford in the County of Essex apothecary, apprenticed to Vezy Haselfoot 11 October 1753. Free, 11 February 1761. Mark entered as smallworker, in partnership with George Giles, 18 October 1765. Address: 'in the Curtain near Holywell Mount, Shoreditch', where they appear without category in the Parl. Report list 1773. Perhaps identifiable with John Cooper, smallworker 1784-92 (Section V).

COOPER, Joshua (1216) No record of apprenticeship or freedom. Probably son of Benjamin Cooper II and brother of Edward (q.v.) of the same address. First mark entered as bucklemaker, 17 October 1786. Address: Brownlow Street, Holborn (Section VIII). Second mark as smallworker, 14 September 1789. Address: 7 Brownlow Street, Holborn. Moved to 1 Bartlett Passage, Fetter Lane, no date.

COOPER, Matthew I (378, 2003) Son of William Cooper late of Newport Pagnell in the County of Buckingham yeoman, apprenticed to Robert Cooper 20 January 1693 'as from Christmas last' for eight years. Turned over 19 May 1693 to Joseph Bird. Free, 21 April 1702. First mark entered as largeworker, 2 May 1702. Address: Foster Lane. Livery, October 1708. Signatory as 'working goldsmith' to the petition complaining of the competition of 'necessitous strangers', 1 December 1711, and to that against assaying work of foreigners not having served seven years apprenticeship, February 1716. Second (Sterling) mark, 13 July 1720. Son Robert apprenticed to him, 15 July 1725.

Bankrupt, December 1731, still in Foster Lane. His mark usually found on candlesticks, as is that of his master Joseph Bird. Heal records him in Foster Lane from 1699 and as insolvent in 1738, either a second occasion or misprint for above. He was churchwarden of St. John Zachary in 1713.

COOPER, Matthew II (393, 2004) No record of apprenticeship or freedom. First mark entered as largeworker, 30 June 1725. Address: Minories, followed by 'Spetel maker' (?Spectacle maker). Second mark (New Standard), 9 September 1725. An entry in the register without mark, 21 July 1726, gives his address as Pump Yard, Bishopsgate Street, near Norton Folgate.

COOPER, Robert (380) Son of William Cooper of Lasbury(?) in the County of Buckingham yeoman, apprenticed to Thomas George 8 January 1664 'from the Feast Day of the Purification of the Blessed Virgin next coming'. Free, 17 February 1670. Probably working independently by about 1675. Livery, 1682. Appears in the accounts of the banker Richard Hoare, 1685: 'June 18 Deld to Mr Cooper a Spitting Pot of Esqr. Peypes to alter wt. 14 oz. 12 dwt.', also: 'June 20 Deld to Mr Cooper a spit pot and hand candlestick of Esq. Peepys', and in a long account, 2 October 1685: '2 tankards to boil for Esqr. Peypes'. His Old Standard mark, pre-1697, is identifiable by comparison with his New Standard mark entered as largeworker, undated, probably April 1697 on commencement of register. Address: Strand. Court, 1693. Warden, 1707, 1711 and 1712 and Prime Warden, 1717, on the death of Benjamin Lane in office. Heal and Hilton Price record him as goldsmith, Golden Lion, corner of Arundel Street, Strand, 1694-1714; and as Robert Cooper and Co., same address, in 1717. He signed the report of the committee of the Goldsmiths' Company on the present state of the Company, 29 April 1708.

COOPER, Robert Burton (2034) No record of apprenticeship or freedom. Mark entered as smallworker, in partnership with Matthew Coats Horsley, 26 September 1821. Address: 461 Strand.

COOPER, Thomas (389, 2708) Son of John Cooper late of the parish of St. Saviour's Southwark gentleman deceased, apprenticed to Clifford Pearce 16 March 1709. Free, 10 April 1716. First mark entered as smallworker, 18 April 1716. Address: Aldersgate.

Second (Sterling) mark, 24 June 1720. Address: Noble Street. Third mark, 11 May 1726, same address.

COOPER, William (3074) Son of Michael Cooper of Holyday Yard Crud(?) Lane silversmith, apprenticed to Samuel Hennell of Foster Lane 2 March 1808. Freedom unrecorded. First mark (incuse) entered as plateworker, 12 December 1823. Address: 15 Bartholomew Square, Old Street. Second mark (normal type, two sizes), 11 November 1833, on move to 39 Kirby Street, Hatton Garden. Third mark (two sizes), 3rd December 1844. Fourth mark, 19 February 1845.

COPE, John (373) Son of Thomas Cope of Stamford in the County of Northampton taylor, apprenticed to Matthew West 23 March 1694. Free, 9 April 1701. Mark entered as largeworker, 25 June 1701. Address: Oat Lane, where Heal records him till 1703.

*CORBETT, Benjamin (137) Apprenticed to Charles Jackson of the Cutlers' Company and turned over to John Welles Goldsmith in Friday Street London 17 September 1718 and subsequently to Thomas Moulden. Free, 4 June 1726. Mark entered as smallworker, 8 August 1726. Address: Gutter Lane. 'Free of the Cutlers Comp'.

CORBETT, Thomas (384) Son of Symon Corbett of St. Martin's in the County of Middlesex gentleman, apprenticed (c. 1692) to Mathew Gyles of the Merchant Taylors' Company and subsequently turned over to Peter Platel. Free, 6 December 1699. Mark entered as largeworker, 12 December 1699. Address: St. Martins Lane. 'free Merchant Taylor'. Heal records him at this address till bankruptcy in 1706.

CORMICK, John (1206) No record of apprenticeship or freedom. Only mark entered as smallworker, 15 March 1760. Address: Horeshoe Alley, Middle Moorfields, where he appears in the same category in the Parl. Report list 1773.

CORNAFLEAU, Isaac (392, 1194a) Previously known as Cornasseau. His one signature in the register is misspelt and corrected 'Cornafleau'. This reading is supported by the following entries in the Huguenot Church registers of West Street and Crispin Street: 'Mr Isaac Cornafleau godfather to Isaac du Choux baptised 26 Jan. 1707' (West Street). 'Isaac Cornafleau Marie Pontin; mar. par Mr Laplace entre huict et neuf du matin. Annonces publiées en la par. St. Giles; certificat. Téms. Jean Harache. P. Harache. Mari Arache etc. etc. 13 June 1708' (West Street). 'Isaac Carnaflo godfather to Isaac Boinceau baptised 7 Mar. 1708. Tém. Isaac Cornafleaux' (Crispin Street. The first spelling presumably the clerk's and the second Cornafleaux' signature). Sterling and New Standard marks entered apparently at the same time but undated, between July 1722 and December 1724 from position in register. Address: The Acorn, Drury Lane. He does not appear to have been free of the Goldsmiths' or any other company. His work is rare, mostly of small domestic pieces, but of high quality.

CORNMAN, Henry (974) Presumably son of Philip Cornman, below. No record of apprenticeship or freedom. First mark entered as plateworker, 6 January 1813. Address: 5 Great Newport Street. Second and third marks (the latter incuse), 31 August 1813. Address: 29 Newman Street.

*CORNMAN, Philip (2148) No record of apprenticeship or freedom. First mark entered as smallworker, 9 May 1793. Address: 5 Great Newport Street, Long Acre. Second mark, 18 October 1793.

CORNOCK, Edward (390a, 546) Son of Thomas Cornock of St. Leonard Foster Lane London taylor, apprenticed to Henry Grant 9 February 1698 for eight years. Free, 27 March 1708. First mark entered as largeworker, 14 July 1707. Address: Carey Lane. Second (Sterling) mark, 25 November 1723. Heal records him with the alternative spelling of Cornac, at Carey Lane, 1707-23; and at Gutter Lane, 1723-31. From surviving examples apparently a specialist in tobaccoboxes.

CORNU, Peter (394, 2151) Peter Daniel son of Peter Cornu of St. Giles in the Fields chirurgion, apprenticed to John Lewis 20 August 1715 and turned over 28 January 1720 to John Bayley of Warwick Lane watchcasemaker. Free, 10 January 1723. Two marks (Sterling and New Standard) entered as smallworker, 8 October 1725. Address: Purse Court, Old Change. 'Goldsmith'. Probably from the evidence of his second master a watchcasemaker.

CORPORON, John (390) Son of John Corporon of St. Giles in the Fields in the County of Middlesex surgeon, apprenticed to Lewis Mettayer 24 May 1709. Free, 24 December 1716. He signs as 'Jean'. A note added to the entry reads: 'Certificate of the naturalization of the father dat. 13th instant signed by Richard Darby'. Mark entered as largeworker, 2 April 1717. Address: Prince Street. His work is rare. He or his father appears as a marriage witness in the Hungerford Market Church register, 25 April 1716.

CORRY, Henry (969) No record of apprenticeship or freedom. First mark entered as largeworker, 6 April 1754. Address: Aldersgate Street. Second small mark, 22 March 1764. Presumably dead by April 1768 when Mary Corry entered mark (see below).

CORRY, Mary (2009) No record of apprenticeship or freedom. Presumably widow of Henry (above). Mark entered as smallworker, 21 April 1768. Address: Aldersgate Street.

CORY, John (382) Son of Thomas Cory, free by patrimony 30 September 1687. (His father apprenticed to Edward Wade in 1646, free 1655, Livery, 1689.) Mark entered as largeworker, undated, probably April 1697 on commencement of register. Address: Fleet Street. Heal records him at the Golden Cup, Fleet Street, 1697-1722.

COTTERELL, Charles I (278) No record of apprenticeship or freedom. Only mark entered as smallworker, 22 November 1723. Address: Clerkenwell Close.

COTTERELL, Charles II (293) Perhaps son of the above. No record of apprenticeship or freedom. Only mark entered as smallworker, 6 February 1760. Address: Duck Lane. Moved to Salisbury Court, Fleet Street, 29 December 1764, where he appears without category in the Parl. Report list 1773.

COTTON, John (1234) John Hynde son of John Hynde Cotton of Shadwell in the County of Middlesex cooper, apprenticed to William Fearn of Pater Noster Row Goldsmith 1794 and turned over to George Smith 1 February 1797. (Both masters (q.v.) spoonmakers.) Free, 1 February 1801. Mark entered as spoonmaker, in partnership with Thomas Head, 8 December 1809. Address: 73 Wood Street, Cheapside.

COTTRILL, John (1257) No record of apprenticeship or freedom. Only mark entered as plateworker, in partnership with J. J. Detheridge, 26 April 1826. Address: 29 Great Sutton Street, Clerkenwell.

COUGHLAN, Laurence (1905) No record of apprenticeship or freedom. First mark entered as smallworker, 27 March 1762. Address: Brick Lane, Old Street. Second mark, 12 July 1763. At the same address without category in the Parl. Report list 1773. First mark found on buckles of rococo design (Lady Maufe Collection).

COURTAULD, Augustine (18, 22, 385) Son of Augustine Courtauld, 'marchand' of St. Pierre in the Ile d'Oleron and his first wife Julia Giron, born 1685-6 and brought to England as an infant, traditionally concealed in a basket of vegetables. His father was described as 'of the parish of St Anne's Westminster Wine Cooper' on the apprenticeship of Augustine to Simon Pantin (Pontaine), 9 August 1701. The entry also contains a 'Note. Made a denizen as appeared by a certificate from Mich. Hayward dat. 20th July 96', and he appears also in the Naturalization Act of 1709 as goldsmith, St. Martin in the Fields. Free of the Goldsmiths' Company by service, 20 October 1708. Married Anne Bardin, 1709. First mark entered as largeworker, 23 December 1708. Address: Church Court, St. Martin's Lane. Second (Sterling) mark, 7 October 1729. Address: Chandos Street. Third mark, 6 July 1739, same address with St. Martin's in the Fields added. Heal records him at Church Street, 1708-29; and Chandos Street from 1729. The mark described as his second mark for toys by E. Alfred Jones (*Some Silver wrought by the Courtauld Family*, privately printed, Oxford, 1940) is in fact that of David Clayton (q.v.), an error stemming from the ascription in Jackson, through a misreading of the Gothic letters. Courtauld died in Chandos Street and was buried at St. Luke's, Chelsea, leaving in his will all his utensils and patterns belonging to and used in his trade and business to his son Samuel (q.v.). His daughter Anne married, in 1738, John Jacob (q.v.). He appears to have had another son Augustine whose birth, 22 December 1710, and baptism 26 December, is recorded in the West Street Church register. He presumably died as an infant as another son was baptized Augustine, 24 July 1728, at Leicester Fields Church. The goldsmith's other children were Judy, born 1 July 1714, Catherine 13 June 1715, Pierre 2 August 1716, Augustine as above, and finally Samuel 13 September 1720, all baptized in Leicester Fields Church. The baptism of Anne, wife of John Jacob, seems to be unpublished. It is clear from Huguenot records that Courtauld played an active part in the community. He appears as godfather to Augustin Fouche, 1715 (Church of the Artillery), witness to the marriage of Jean Moulinais and Judith Pascal, 1718 (Tabernacle, Glasshouse Street), godfather to David Blanchard 1720, and Catherine Tanqueray 1726 (Hungerford Market Church), godfather to Augustin Goujon 1744 (Leicester Fields), and to a succession of grandchildren: Jean son of Jean Jacob 1743, Augustin another son of the same 1747, Anne, daughter of his son Augustine 1750, Samuel Jacob 1750, and Augustin son of Samuel Courtauld 1750. As a craftsman Courtauld was versatile and fairly prolific, although, like Simon Pantin his master, chiefly occupied with domestic pieces rather than the fine ornamental pieces to which Harache, Willaume and Lamerie aspired. His best known piece is probably the State Salt of the City of London of 1730. A representative collection of his work and that of his family following is illustrated in the work by E. Alfred Jones, quoted above, to which some of the above facts are acknowledged.

COURTAULD, Louisa Perina (1907-8, 3716) Daughter of Peter Ogier and his wife Catherine Rabaud, of Sigournay in Poitou. Married Samuel Courtauld (q.v.) at St. Luke's, Old Street 31 August 1749. Succeeded as head of her husband's business on his death in February 1765. First mark recorded on a cup of that year, but mark presumably entered in the missing largeworkers' volume. Second mark, as partner with George Cowles, also unregistered, about 1768. They appear together as goldsmiths in the Parl. Report list 1773. Third mark, with son Samuel, 16 October 1777. Address: Cornhill. Heal records her as goldsmith and jeweller, Crown, Cornhill 21 opposite to the Royal Exchange, from 1765-8; and with Cowles to 1778. Her charming portrait by Zoffany, still in family possession is reproduced by Jones, *op. cit.* (previous entry). She died at Clapton, 12 January 1807, and was buried in Spitalfields Church. Her work, chiefly surviving with the partnership marks of Cowles and her son shows, in the main, well executed classical motifs in the decoration of cups and coffee-pots.

COURTAULD, Peter (391, 2144, 3509) Son of Augustine Courtauld Senior and his second wife Esther Potier, born 10 January 1690, half brother to Augustine Courtauld (q.v.). Apprenticed to Simon Pantin 28 March 1705, when his father is described as Vintner as against Wine Cooper in Augustine's apprenticeship. Free, 3 December 1712. Married, 5 February 1709, Judith daughter of Esaie Pantin. First mark (New Standard) entered 15 June 1721. Address: Litchfield Street, St. John's, Westminster. Second mark (Sterling), 21 July 1721. Address: Lichfield Street St. Ann's, Soho. Took as apprentice Thomas Bonnet in 1723. Buried in St. Martin's in the Fields, 1729.

*COURTAULD, Samuel I (2489-90) Son of Augustine Courtauld (q.v.), born 10 September 1720, baptized 13 September, Leicester Fields Church. Apprenticed to his father 12 November 1734. Free, 3 February 1747. First mark entered as largeworker, 6 October 1746. Address: 'Shandois' Street, near St. Martin's Lane. Second mark, 23 November 1751. Married 31 August 1749, Louisa Perina Ogier (q.v.), at St. Luke's, Old Street. Their son Samuel was born 20 October 1752, followed by four daughters and two other sons. Livery, June 1763. Heal records him at the Rising Sun (see his mark), Chandos Street, 1746-51; and The Crown opposite Royal Exchange, 21 Cornhill, 1751-65. Died February 1765 and buried 24 February at Chelsea. He left all his property to his wife. Samuel's work does not appear to have survived in any great quantity. It is characterized by a mild rococo taste, attractively executed, though without evidence of great individuality.

COURTAULD, Samuel II (1908) Son of Samuel Courtauld I and Louisa Perina (both q.v.). Born 20 October 1752 and baptized 25 October, Threadneedle Street Church. Free by patrimony, 4 March 1778. Mark entered, as partner with his mother, 16 October 1777. Address: 21 Cornhill, where they remained to 1780, when they were succeeded by one John Henderson. Samuel later settled in America, apparently as a merchant, where he died in 1821 and was buried in the Old Swedes Churchyard, Wilmington, Delaware. Two portraits of him in family possession are illustrated by E. Alfred Jones, *op. cit.*, under Augustine Courtauld.

COURTHOPE, Edward (379) Son of George Courthope of Wadhurst in the County of Sussex gentleman, apprenticed to William Hall 7 November 1679. Free, 20 July 1687. Livery, October 1708. Mark entered as largeworker, undated, probably April 1697 on commencement of register. Address: Bishopsgate.

COUTA, Gabriel (777) No record of apprenticeship or freedom. Only mark entered as smallworker, 29 October 1814. Address: 12 Blenheim Street, Marlborough Street. Probably son of Benedict Couta who entered incuse marks as goldworker, 1791, at 3 Cross Lane, Long Acre (see Section V).

COWALD, Daniel (448) No record of apprenticeship or freedom. Only mark entered as smallworker, 29 June 1726. Address: 'Freuenpan Ally, Pettecot Laene' (A most curious piece of orthography suggesting a German origin for its author). He is presumably the Daniel Cowald of Christchurch, Spitalsfields, silversmith, whose son, also Daniel, was apprenticed to Charles Boyland, 27 July 1738.

COWDERY, George (771) No record of apprenticeship or freedom. First mark entered as smallworker, 24 September 1771. Address: Riders Court, Leicester Fields, and so appears in the Parl. Report list 1773. Second and third marks as goldworker, 1777 and 1781. Address: 'Near Mays Buildings, Bedfordbury' (Section VII). Fourth mark, 3 June 1784. Address: 1 Buckingham Street, York Building. Moved to 6 King Street, Holborn, 19 June 1800. Heal records him only as goldworker, 1 Buckingham Street, 1790-93.

COWIE, George (780) No record of apprenticeship or freedom. Presumably younger brother of John Cowie, following, with whom first mark (incuse) entered as plateworkers, 18 September 1822. Second mark (normal type), 1 October 1822. Address: 84 Long Acre.

COWIE, John (780, 1792) Son of John Jenn Cowie late of Falcon Square refiner deceased, apprenticed to William Sandland of Bunhill Row as engraver 4 March 1807 on payment of £20. Free, 6 April 1814. First mark entered as plateworker, 23 January 1813. Address: 4 Noble Street. Second mark, 4 March 1814, on move to Aldermanbury Postern. Moved to 3 Silver Street, 21 April 1818. Third mark (incuse), in partnership with George Cowie (above), 18 September 1822. Fourth mark, October 1822. Address: 84 Long Acre.

*COWLES, George (772, 1907, 3582) Son of George Cowles of the City of Gloucester carman, apprenticed to Samuel Courtauld

6 September 1751 on payment of £10 and turned over on former's death to Louisa Perina Courtauld. Free, 8 May 1765. Livery, 1781. First mark as plateworker, in partnership with Louisa Courtauld, probably included in missing register c. 1768. Heal has however self-contradictory records of Cowles as late partner with Mrs Courtauld, as goldsmith, in Swithin's Lane, 1766; followed by addresses for him alone at 26 Cornhill, 1770-93; 30 Cornhill, 1780-90; while at the same time having found the partnership at 21 Cornhill from 1768-77. They appear together as goldsmiths in the Parl. Report list 1773, when Cowles gave evidence to the committee. Even allowing for the fairly high probability of misprints in old directories it seems likely that there were two or three shops in operation at the same time. It is clear, however, that the partnership finished when Louisa entered another mark in partnership with Samuel II, 16 October 1777, and Cowles his second mark, alone as plateworker, 30 October 1777. Address: 5 George Yard, Lombard Street. He moved to No — Cornhill, 17 January 1778. (The first address may perhaps have been only his workshop.) Died 1811.

COWLEY, William (3055) No record of apprenticeship or freedom. Only mark entered as smallworker, 18 December 1738. Address: Snow Hill; possibly, from the locality, a hiltmaker.

COWPER, Henry (970, 976) No record of apprenticeship or freedom. Two marks entered as plateworker, 8 October 1782. Address: 1 Whitehall. Below his name the undated note 'Gone to Gib' (?Gibraltar). Heal records him at Whitehall till 1789.

COWSEY, John (374-5, 1192) Son of Henry Cowsey of St. Mary Whitechapel gentleman, apprenticed to Nathaniel Locke 6 March 1694. Free, 5 September 1701. Two marks entered as largeworker, 9 August 1701. Address: Foster Lane. Livery, October 1708. Signatory as Jno. Cowsy 'working goldsmith' to the petition complaining of the competition of 'necessitous strangers', December 1711. Third (Sterling) mark, 11 November 1720. Presumably dead by 1728 when John Cowsey, son of John deceased, was apprenticed to Edward Lammas. Chaffers, followed by Jackson and Heal misread this name as Corosey and on this spelling Evans included it as that of a Huguenot. The present reading is however confirmed by the apprenticeship and petition entries.

*COX, George (371) Apprenticed c. 1691 to William Scarlett Citizen and Broderer (q.v.). Free, 1 April 1698 as Broderer, when described as 'of Kery Lane London Silversmith'. (The apprentice register of this company survives only from 1694.) Mark entered as largeworker, 6 April 1698. Address: Carey Lane. 'free Imbroyderer'. Signatory as 'working goldsmith' to the petition complaining of the competition of 'necessitous strangers', December 1711.

COX, John (1211) No record of apprenticeship or freedom. Only mark entered as smallworker, 29 August 1763. Address: Hosier Lane, Smithfield, where he appears without category in the Parl. Report list 1773.

*COX, Robert Albin (2286, 2291-2, 3767-9) Son of Edward Cox of Bromham in the County of Somerset gentleman, apprenticed to Humphrey Payne 16 January 1745 on payment of 50 guineas. Turned over to John Payne 13 March 1750. Free, 2 July 1752. First mark entered as largeworker, 10 July 1752. Address: Fetter Lane. Second mark, 12 July 1758. Third mark, 27 June 1759. Heal records him at Fetter Lane till 1773 and at Little Britain 1769, where he appears as Robert Albion Cox, goldsmith, in the Parl. Report list 1773. The same name appears as elected to the livery, 20 May 1791. Court, 1813. Warden, 1815-17. Prime Warden, 1818 and died 1826, which if identifiable with the above would have made him about ninety-five at death and must surely indicate a son of the same name.

COX, William I (3052) No record of apprenticeship or freedom. Only mark entered as smallworker, 19 February 1739. Address: 'in ye neckinger(?) Road near ye coach and horses Southwark'.

COX, William II (3053) Perhaps son of William Cox late of the parish of St. Dunstan in the West Goldsmith deceased, apprenticed to John Bates 15 June 1750. Free, 1 October 1760. Mark entered as smallworker, 22 March 1763. Address: Magpie Alley, Fetter Lane, Holborn. Moved to Gray's Inn Lane, 10 April 1764, where he is recorded in 1773 in the Parl. Report list. Entered three marks as bucklemaker 1776-91. Addresses: 18 Newgate Street, 1776; 6 Eliots Court, Old Bailey, 1779; Green Arbor

BIOGRAPHICAL DICTIONARY

Court, Old Bailey, 1791. Final address: Garden Court, near Sutton Street, Goswell Street (Section VIII).

*COX, William III (3054) Apparently distinct from the above. No record of apprenticeship or freedom. First mark entered as smallworker, 20 March 1771. Address: Little Britain. Second mark, 18 October 1784. Address: 11 Aldersgate Street. Heal records him as goldsmith and jeweller at 7 Cox's Court, Little Britain, 1768-72; as goldsmith, St. Paul's Churchyard, 1773-4; as goldsmith and jeweller, in partnership with Thomas Watson, at 25 Aldersgate Street, 1774-84; and alone, 11 Aldersgate Street, 1784.

CRADOCK, Joseph (1221-2, 1236, 2772) No record of apprenticeship or freedom. First mark entered as partner with Thomas and Joseph Guest as plateworkers, 15 August 1806. Address: 67 Red Lion Street, Holborn. Second mark together, 24 February 1808. Moved to 67 Leather Lane, Holborn, 15 June 1808. Second partnership with William K. Reid. First mark, 8 June 1812, at the same address as the last above. New address: undated, 3 Carey Street, Lincoln's Inn Fields. Second mark (two sizes), 19 August 1819. Third mark, 24 September 1824. Alone as plateworker, first mark, 13 October 1825, same address. Second mark, 10 November 1827. (Seven entries in all). His son Charles Tyrwhitt Cradock was apprenticed to Alexander Thomas, silver planisher, in 1823.

CRAGG, John (1200) No record of apprenticeship or freedom. Mark entered as smallworker, 1 October 1730. Address: New Street, Cloth Fair. There seems to be no connection with John Craig following.

CRAIG, Ann (24) Presumably the widow of John Craig, for whom no mark is recorded, but who is recorded by Heal as partner with George Wickes from c. 1730-5 at the corner of Norris Street. A David Craig was apprenticed to George Wickes in 1731. Heal records John Craig at the same address from 1714 and as having died 1735. There is also an entry in *The Gentleman's Magazine*: 'Craig— silversmith, died 14 Dec. 1736', which appears to refer. Ann's first mark as largeworker, in partnership with John Neville, 15 October 1740. Address: Corner of Norris Street, St. James's, Haymarket. Second (small) mark, 27 May 1743. The partnership was presumably dissolved by her retirement or death by 10 April 1745, when Neville entered a separate mark. Heal however records the partnership from 1738-46. What little work has survived bearing this mark is of high quality and individual taste with a strong rococo tendency.

CRAMER, John (1217, 1235) No record of apprenticeship or freedom. Mark entered as plateworker, 12 May 1797. Address: 30 Charing Cross. Presumed partner with Thomas Key for the mark entered 21 September 1805. Address: 2 Pall Mall. While Key's name is written in ink, the second name is omitted and pencilled in is the note '?Cramer'.

CRAMMILLION, Hannah and Peter (1062) Hannah, widow of Peter Crammillion gold watchcase maker of the parish of St. James Clerkenwell who is presumably the Peter 'Cromillou' who entered an incuse mark 30 April 1736 at Red Cross Court, Jewin Street (Section V) already dead by 4 April 1754 when his son Peter was apprenticed to John Vowells and turned over the same day to his mother. Peter free of the Farriers' Company, 1761. Their mark entered as smallworkers, 'Han^h Crammillion & Son' and signed by both, 8 February 1762. Address: Clerkenwell Green, where Heal records Peter alone as watchcasemaker, 1767-9. They appear together, however, as such at the same address, in the Parl. Report list 1773.

CRANE, Joseph (1198) Son of Richard Crane Citizen and Merchant Taylor of London, apprenticed to Thomas Hill 6 June 1716. Free, 3 April 1729. Mark entered as smallworker, 21 October 1728. Address: Fryers Alley, Wood Street. His son Joseph was apprenticed to his father 1739, and free 3 July 1765.

CREAK, George (775) Son of James Creak of Monkwell Street Goldsmith, apprenticed to David Hennell of Foster Lane 8 December 1791. Free, 4 December 1799. (His father had been apprenticed to David Hennell I in 1761.) Mark entered as plateworker, 4 March 1802. Address: 40 Hare Street, Bethnal Green. Second mark (two sizes), 17 February 1812.

CREES, Samuel Lee (2496) No record of apprenticeship or freedom. Only mark entered as spoonmaker, 27 August 1833. Address: 145 White Cross Street, St. Luke's.

CRESPEL, James (2497) See below.

*CRESPEL, Sebastian I (2497) No record of apprenticeship or freedom of him or his presumed brother James, whom Heal records as working silversmiths, Whitcomb Street, Leicester Fields, from 1762 to 1773 (plateworkers, Parl. Report list 1773); and James Crespel alone in 1779. The mark which is clearly theirs must have been entered in the missing largeworkers' register somewhere about 1760. It seems highly probable that they may have learnt their trade in the establishment of Edward Wakelin, in view of the connection revealed by the ledgers of that firm (Garrard MSS, Victoria and Albert Museum). They first appear in the general workmen's ledger (which begins March 1766) in 1769 as supplying plates and dishes, which seem to constitute their greatest output throughout. From 1778 to 1806 a series of parallel ledgers survive kept by the Crespels and Wakelin and Taylor and their successors. These record the raw metal issued to the Crespels and the wrought plate supplied back by them, annotated with the client's name for whom ordered, or the word 'Shop', presumably for stock in Panton Street. In 1782 a definite financial connection between the Crespels and Wakelin and Taylor occurred, when the latter paid £380 for 'expenses, alterations and improvements done by them at the workshop no 25. Corner of Oxendon Street'; they further bought 'an annuity of £100 per Annum on both their lives and the survivor' for £1,000 and lent them £1,321.7s.3d. 'by their Joint Bond bearing 5% pr Annum with collateral security of all their Tools, Fixtures and Implements in Trade of all denominations'. It would seem, therefore, that from this date the Crespels were virtually owned by Wakelin and Taylor, and likely that all pieces bearing their mark went through the latters' hands. From 1788 the latters' ledger account is headed 'James Crespel', which may indicate Sebastian's death or retirement. The ledgers finish in October 1806 without any apparent successor to the business. James Crespel had at least four sons apprenticed in the trade: (1) Honoré, described as son of James Crespel of Panton Street silversmith, apprenticed to John Wakelin 3 February 1779 and free 1786. In 1801 his younger brother Sebastian was apprenticed to him, when Honoré is spelt Honorius and described as 'Flatter of the same parish' (i.e. as his father). (2) Andrew, apprenticed to the same 1785 and free 1792 (3) Sebastian (see below). (4) James, apprenticed to Thomas Gardner 1803 and free 1810. Sarah Crespel (1767–1824), presumably daughter of Sebastian married Robert Garrard I (q.v.) before 1793. The Crespels are listed as Huguenots by Evans, ('Huguenot Goldsmiths', *Hug. Soc. Proc.*, 14).

CRESPEL, Sebastian II (2495) Son of James Crespel of Panton Street St. Martin in the Fields silversmith (above), apprenticed to his brother Honorius Crespel flatter, Citizen and Goldsmith of the same parish 3 June 1801 and turned over to Robert Garrard 7 May 1806. Free, 3 May 1809. Mark entered as largeworker (an unusual description by this date), 3 August 1820. Address: 11 James Street, Haymarket. Moved to 11 White Hart Court, Castle Street, Leicester Square, 12 October 1836. His son Andrew free by patrimony, as silversmith, 6 May 1846.

*CRESPIN, Paul (406, 412, 2143a, 2146, 2149) Born 1694, son of Daniel Crespin of the parish of St. Giles Westminster, apprenticed to Jean Pons 24 June 1713 (*Index of Apprentice Books*, Society of Genealogists). The family appear to have been of long standing in the Huguenot colony in London. Paul Crespin, 'fils de Paul, natif de Londres et Rebecca Sprettle, fille de Thomas Sprettle, natif de Londres' were married, 4 December 1654, at the French Church, Threadneedle Street, and were possibly grandparents of the goldsmith. First two marks entered for Sterling and New Standard, undated, about July 1720 and before December 1721, when Crespin is described as 'free of the Longe bowe String'. (The records of the Longbowstring Makers, now merged with the Fletchers' Company, do not survive for this date. His freedom can have been by service to Pons, patrimony or redemption.) Address: Compton Street, 'overa' (probably unfinished for 'overagainst' followed by a location). He appears in the rate books from 1720 at the south-west junction of Compton Street and Greek Street. Third mark, 4 July 1739. Address: Compton Street, at the Golden Ball, St. Ann's, Soho. Fourth mark (New Standard), 7 November 1740. Fifth mark (two sizes), 22 January 1757, entered in chronological position in the register with reference to its date in the previous 1739–40 entry, an unusual occurrence. Same address. Heal adds nothing to this, but records Paul Crespin Junior, goldsmith, London, 1740, which however has no other supporting evidence and appears to stem from the ascription in Jackson, page 204.

Crespin's date and place of marriage do not seem to have been discovered, but it is known that his wife was Margaret Branboeuf, by whom he had five children between 1729 and 1743, all baptized at St. Anne's, Soho: Magdalen Bennin (sic) 1729, Lewis Vincent Paul 1732, Elias David 1734, Paul 1739 and Sarah 1743. Crespin is recorded bankrupt, February 1747 (*The Gentleman's Magazine*), but continued paying rates in Compton and Greek Street till 1759. He died aged seventy-six, 25 January 1770, at Southampton. By his will dated 17 December 1759, proved 26 March 1770, he left everything to his wife, appointing her sole executrix. She died the following year, describing herself in her will as of Southampton, where they must have retired about 1760. E. Alfred Jones discovered five letters from the goldsmith at Welbeck Abbey, where there is a considerable amount of plate by him. Four were written by Crespin to John Achard, tutor to the second Duke of Portland, anxious that his son Elias David should get to Cambridge. This was achieved through the help of the Bishop of St. Asaph, cousin of Margaret, Duchess of Portland, and Elias, after being at Merchant Taylors' School, was admitted a sizar at Gonville and Caius in 1752. He took orders and was subsequently Dean of Guernsey from 1765 till his death in 1795. The elder daughter Magdalene married Francis-Gabriel Barraud, the Huguenot clockmaker, from whom the family of artists of the nineteenth century are descended (E. M. Barraud, *Barraud. The Story of a Family*, The Research Publishing Company, 1967). A portrait, almost certainly of Crespin, showing him holding a silver vase of apparently late seventeenth century design is in Barraud family possession in New Zealand (illustrated, *op. cit.*).

Crespin's powers and reputation grew quickly after the first entry of his mark. *The Weekly Journal or British Gazetteer* contains the following, in the issue dated 23 July 1724: 'On Tuesday last there was made at Goldsmiths' Hall an Assay on a curious silver vessel for bathing, which weigh'd about 6030 ounces, said by some to be made for the King of Portugal', and on 15 August following: 'Some days ago Mr Crispin, a silversmith of this City carried the fine silver bathing vessel (made for the King of Portugal) to his Majesty at Kensington who was well pleased with so curious a piece of workmanship which can scarcely be match'd in all Europe' (R. W. Symonds, 'English Furniture in Portugal', *Connoisseur*, June 1940). Nothing more is now known of this seemingly extraordinary piece. The unusual large circular basin by Crespin of 1722 in the Wilding Collection, British Museum, may possibly be related to the former, having a Portuguese source when first on the London market about seventy years ago. Crespin's surviving work is of a consistently high standard, worthily rivalling Lamerie. He was perhaps at his highest powers around 1740 when his centrepiece in the Royal collection and the tureen of 1741, made for the Duke of Somerset, now at Toledo, Ohio, reveal qualities of execution matching the originality of design.

CRESWELL, Joseph (1212) No record of apprenticeship or freedom. Only mark entered as smallworker, 16 May 1767. Address: Golden Cross Court, Cateaton Street. Heal however records him as 'toyman (from Mr Chevenix)', Unicorn in Suffolk Street, *c.* 1760; and as goldsmith, corner of Adelphi, Strand, 1770–5. He appears as goldworker, Strand, in the Parl. Report list 1773.

CRIPPIN, Thomas (2720) No record of apprenticeship or freedom. Only mark entered as smallworker, 19 January 1779. Address: 16 Mitchell Street, Old Street Road.

CRIPPS, Mark (2008) No record of apprenticeship or freedom. Only mark entered as smallworker, 25 April 1767. Address: Golden Ball, St. James's Street, where he appears, as plateworker, in the Parl. Report list 1773. From evidence of the address presumably son of William Cripps (below).

*CRIPPS, William (3056-8) Son of Edward Cripps late of Newport in the County of Buckingham yeoman deceased, apprenticed to David Willaume (Junior) 8 January 1731. No premium stated. Free, 2 May 1738. First mark entered as largeworker, 31 August 1743. Address: Crown and Golden Ball, Compton Street. Second mark, 16 July 1746, on moving to Golden Ball, St. James's Street. Livery, January 1750. Third mark, 16 November 1751. Died about 1 September 1767, according to the apprenticeship to him of William Hall and the turning over of the latter 3 September of that year. As might be expected from his training under Willaume he became an accomplished craftsman and a versatile exponent of the rococo style; to judge from his surviving pieces he enjoyed a considerable clientele.

CRISP, Walter (3051) Son of Stephen Crisp of Pinner in the County of Middlesex clerk, apprenticed to Samuel Green of the Merchant Taylors' Company 12 June 1723 on payment of £21 and subsequently turned over to William Overton. Free, 2 December 1730. Mark entered as smallworker, 17 June 1730. Address: Nicholas Lane, Lombard Street. 'Merchant Taylor' (which at the date of entry was an anticipatory statement).

CROLER, Jn^t (?Jonathan) (407) No record of apprenticeship or freedom. Only mark entered as smallworker, 7 December 1717. Address: Chancery Lane.

CROOK, Henry (967) No record of apprenticeship or freedom. First mark entered as smallworker, 19 August 1734. Address: Brooks Market, near Hatton Garden. Incuse mark, 26 March 1740 (Section V), same address. Presumably watchcasemaker.

CROSSLEY, Richard (2288, 2294, 3334) Not apprenticed. Free by redemption, 1 May 1782. Livery, February 1791. First mark entered as spoonmaker, in partnership with William Sumner, 1 May 1775. Address: 1 Clerkenwell Close. Second mark (two sizes), 27 January 1776. Third mark, 10 May 1777. Fourth mark, 27 January 1780. Fifth mark alone, 5 April 1782. Address: 21 Foster Lane. Moved to Giltspur Street, 12 November 1783. Sixth mark, 9 December 1785. Seventh (two sizes), 6 January 1795. Eighth, 5 February 1802. Ninth, 14 May 1804. Tenth mark, in partnership with George Smith as spoonmakers, 9 April 1807. Eleventh mark alone as plateworker, 2 January 1812. Address: 14 Giltspur Street. Heal records him at Foster Lane till 1786 and at Giltspur Street, 1790 to 1798. He may of course have been running two workshops for part of the time. His output of flatware was obviously considerable and much remains in use. He died April 1815.

CROSWELL, Henry I (973, 978) Son of Henry Croswell of Cheriton in the County of Southampton yeoman, apprenticed to John Steward of Wood Street Goldsmith 7 October 1789, as was his brother Richard (q.v.). Free, 2 November 1796. Mark entered as smallworker, in partnership with Richard Croswell, 5 August 1800. Address: 8 Lambs Buildings, Bunhill Row. Moved to 31 Monkwell Street, 10 April 1801. Second mark alone, 11 April 1804, same address. Presumably dead by 21 May 1805, when Mary Ann Croswell of same address entered her mark; she is described as his widow in the apprenticeship of their son Henry in 1819.

CROSWELL, Henry II (973) Son of Henry Croswell (above) late of Monkwell Street silversmith deceased, apprenticed to his mother Mary Ann Croswell widow Citizen and Goldsmith 6 October 1819. Mark entered as smallworker 21 December 1830. Address 31 Monkwell Street.

CROSWELL, Mary Ann (2011) Widow of Henry Croswell I (above). Although styled 'Citizen and Goldsmith' in the apprenticeship record of her son Henry II, there is no record of her freedom. First mark entered as smallworker, 21 May 1805. Address: 31 Monkwell Street. Second mark, 29 August 1816.

CROSWELL, Richard (978) Son of Henry Croswell of Cheriton in the County of Hants farmer, apprenticed (as his elder brother, Henry) to John Steward of Wood Street as smallworker 7 November 1792. Free, 1 January 1800. Mark entered as smallworker, in partnership with his brother Henry, 5 August 1800. Address: 8 Lambs Buildings, Bunhill Row. Moved to 31 Monkwell Street, 10 April 1801. Partnership apparently dissolved by 11 April 1804, on entry of Henry's mark alone, or perhaps by Richard's death. (See under Henry Croswell I above.)

CROUCH, John I (1233) Son of Christopher Crouch late of the parish of St. Sepulchre in the County of Middlesex yeoman deceased, apprenticed to Richard Rugg 8 November 1758. Free, 4 December 1765. Mark, in partnership with Thomas Hannam (q.v.), occurs in the period of the missing register and dates from about 1770. They appear as plateworkers, 28 Giltspur Street, in the Parl. Report list 1773. Heal records them together at 23 Giltspur Street, 1766–93; and at 37 Monkwell Street, 1790; while Crouch appears alone as goldsmith, Giltspur Street, 1774–84. Specialist makers of salvers and trays with some candlesticks, but virtually no other type of piece.

CROUCH, John II (1791, 2805) Son of John Crouch of Giltspur Street London Citizen and Goldsmith, apprenticed to his father 6 January 1790. Free, 1 February 1797. Mark entered, as junior partner with Thomas Hannam, 13 April 1799. Address: 37 Monkwell Street. Second mark alone, presumably on death or retirement of Hannam, 11 February 1808, same address. Livery, March 1829. Died January 1837.

CROWDER, Henry (975) No record of apprenticeship or freedom. Only mark entered as smallworker, 23 January 1833. Address: 1 Artillery Row, West Bunhill Row. Probably son of William Crowder (below).

CROWDER, William (3065) No record of apprenticeship or freedom. Probably identifiable with the William Crowder who entered a mark as bucklemaker, 14 January 1779. Address: 2 Cox Court, Aldersgate Street, and moved, 24 May 1781, to 126 Bunhill Row (Section VIII); or possibly his son, as signatures show some difference. Only mark entered as smallworker, 11 March 1791. Address: 1 Bunhill Row, where Heal records him as goldsmith and jeweller from 1795-6. His son William was apprenticed to David Moore Water, gilder, 1792. Apparently succeeded by another son, Henry (above).

*CRUICKSHANK, Robert (3765a) Son of the late Rev. George Cruickshank of Aberbrothock in the Shire of Forfar in North Britain, apprenticed to Alexander Johnston Citizen and Goldsmith 4 April 1759. Free, 9 April 1766. Mark presumably entered in the missing register before 1773, when he appears as plateworker, Old Jewry, in the Parl. Report list. Heal records him as Cruickshanks, goldsmith, at this address from 1766-74; and of London, 1782.

*CRUMP, Francis (670-2, 674, 907) Son of John Crump of Bewdley in the County of Worcester cap maker, apprenticed to Gabriel Sleath 30 August 1726 on payment of 10 guineas, Free, 6 November 1741. First mark entered as largeworker, 9 November 1741. Address: Newcastle Street, near Fleet Market. Second mark, 14 May 1745. An entry without mark, 20 July 1750, records his move to 'the nine Elms, Battersea Parrish'. Moved to Fenchurch Street opposite Gracechurch and third mark, 30 March 1751. Fourth mark, in partnership with Gabriel Sleath, 27 November 1753. Fifth mark, alone. 26 March 1756. Address: Gutter Lane. Sixth mark, in smallworkers' book but of same size as preceding, 17 October 1761, same address. Heal records him as plateworker, Newcastle Street 1741-50, and Gutter Lane 1753-73 as he appears in the latter year in the Parl. Report list. Married 19 February 1760 as bachelor, Sarah Bulbeck of the parish of St. Mary, Woolwich in the County of Kent, spinster, at St. Vedast, Foster Lane. They had four children baptized at the same church: Mary 1761, John 1763, Francis 1765 and Sleath 1767. (Gabriel Sleath, his onetime master and partner, presumably acting as godfather.) *The Gentleman's Magazine* records the legacy to Francis Crump, Goldsmith, of £100 from John Cartlidge M.D. who died 29 August 1752. It is interesting to note that another Francis Crump, son of Daniel Crump of Bewdley, cordwainer, was also apprenticed to Gabriel Sleath, 5 October 1752. Free, 6 May 1761, but has no mark entered.

CRUTCHER, John (405) Son of John Crutcher Citizen and Carpenter of London, apprenticed to Francis Archbold 16 July 1698. Free, 14 February 1705. Mark entered as largeworker, 29 June 1706. Address: East Smithfield, where Heal records him 1706-7.

CRUTCHFIELD, Jonathan (404) Son of Edward Crutchfield Citizen and Merchant Taylor of London, apprenticed to Roger Grange 29 April 1690. Free, 3 May 1697. Mark entered as largeworker, 27 September 1697. Address: Garlick Hill, where Heal records him till 1703. Jonathan Crowchfeild a silversmith of the parish of St. James, Garlickhithe, and Sarah Branson of the parish of St. Mildred, Breadstreet, married on 2 February 1703 (Register, St. Martin Outwich).

CULL, James (1219) No record of apprenticeship or freedom. Only mark entered as smallworker, 21 February 1804. Address: 7 Brownlow Street, Holborn.

CUNNINGHAM, (Peter) Daniel (424, 447) Peter Daniel son of John Cunningham of Marybone in the County of Middlesex 'Sopeboyler', apprenticed to Peter Harache 11 November 1703 (the indenture then deleted with note 'not bound' in margin, but there is no record of a second binding). Free, 31 January 1716. Mark entered as largeworker, 11 February 1717, using only Daniel as Christian name. Address: Long Acre. Second (Sterling) mark, 4 July 1720. Heal records him as plateworker at above address, 1716-20; and as London, 1727-8. He appears as Peter Daniel Cunningham in the apprenticeship to him of Philip Renou in 1720. Daniel Cunningham, jeweller, Hatton Garden, is recorded as bankrupt (*The Gentleman's Magazine*, November 1755). His mark with the punning use of a rabbit (Coney) is perhaps the only example of this kind of heraldic humour to be noted.

*CUNST, Jasper (1195) No record of apprenticeship or freedom. Only mark entered as smallworker, September 1725. Address: Salisbury Court (Fleet Street). Cunst, presumably of German origin, if not himself an immigrant, was, in spite of the lack of official record one of the finest gold box-makers of the eighteenth century in London. His most accessible work is the gold freedom box presented by the City of London to Admiral Vernon in 1740 (National Maritime Museum, Greenwich) signed 'Iaspar Cunst London', and bearing an incuse mark. I C, apparently unentered at the Hall. Other examples are also known signed on the rim. It seems probable, since important gold boxes cannot have been ordered very frequently, that his main production may have been gold watchcases. Jasper Cunst, goldworker, Salisbury Court, appears in the Parl. Report list 1773, from which presumably Heal's sole date is taken. This is presumably the son of the same name who entered incuse mark JC, 21 August 1776. Address: 69 Dorset Street, as goldworker; and IC, 11 May 1776, at Salisbury Court, Fleet Street (Section V).

CUNY, Louis (422-3, 3715) Huguenot immigrant endenizened 8 May 1697, the same day as Peter and Claudius Platel and John Chartier. Free by redemption 1 December 1703, and first mark entered the same day. Address: Panton Street, where Heal records him as at the Three Crowns, corner of Panton Street and Hedge Lane, Leicester Fields, till 1727. His second (Sterling) mark (3715) is unrecorded in the register but must unquestionably be attributable to him from its parallel nature to the New Standard mark of 1703, and presumably dates from *c*. June 1720. Cuny was elected to the Livery in October 1708 (his name spelt Lewis Caney), and his son Samuel apprenticed to him 13 November 1710, and turned over to Daniel Shawe, Lorimer. Daniel became free 1724 but did not enter a mark. In 1705 Cuny appears as witness to the marriage of Louis Person (described as 'Meteur en oeuvre et jeolier' of St. Martin's in the Fields) and Elizabeth Millet at Hungerford Market Church. He also appears as witness to the marriage of Louise Millet in 1706 at West Street Church and to the naturalization of Ezekias Le Ber, 1709. His death is recorded in *The Gentleman's Magazine*, 14 December 1733: 'Mr de Cuney silversmith in Spur Street Leicester Fields'. Heal spells the name Cugny, but there is no such variation in any of the references above. Cuny's surviving work is for the most part of modest type and he does not appear to have been patronized by the great. His most unusual piece is probably the curious triangular salt of the Upholders' Company.

CUTHBERT, Matthew (421) Son of John Cuthbert late Citizen and Carpenter of London deceased, apprenticed to William Taylor 15 June 1683. Free, 10 September 1690. Livery, April 1705. Two marks entered as smallworker, undated, probably April 1697 on commencement of the register. Address: Little Britain. Heal records him as goldsmith, Aldersgate without, 1694, where Hilton Price also lists him till 1701 (*Handbook of London Bankers*, 1890). Heal also has Cross Keys, Little Britain, till 1724.

*CUTMORE, John and Thomas (1796) No record of apprenticeship of freedom of either. Mark entered as plateworkers, 14 January 1829. Address: 3 Lovels Court, Paternoster Row, the address from 1825 of the spoonmaking firm of the Eleys (q.v.), suggesting that the Cutmores were similarly occupied as part of the business or had succeeded to the premises in 1829.

CUTTING, Christopher (420) Apprenticed to Nat. Delaunder of the Clockmakers' Company for John Delaunder for seven years from 19 September 1687. No Freedom date given. Mark entered as smallworker, undated, probably April 1697 on commencement of register, Address: Old Bailey. 'free Clockmaker'. Probably a watchcase maker.

BIOGRAPHICAL DICTIONARY

D

DAINTREY, Marmaduke (2013-5) Son of Duke Daintrey of the parish of St. Giles without Cripplegate in the County of Middlesex cordwainer, apprenticed to Samuel Hutton 5 October 1730 on payment of £5. Free, 8 November 1737, First mark entered as smallworker, 12 October 1737. Address: Noble Street, Goswell Street. Second mark as largeworker, 20 June (?1739). Livery, September 1746. Third mark, on moving to The Crown, Old Street, 30 May 1747. Appears as spoonmaker, Hartley Row, Hampshire, in the Parl. Report list 1773, to which place he must have moved or retired sometime after the entry of his third mark.

DALBY, James (437) Son of James Dalby Citizen and Clothworker of London, apprenticed to Samuel Dell 10 February 1701 and turned over to Daniel Sleamaker. Free, 30 April 1708. Mark entered as smallworker, 2 August 1708. Address: 'at the Plough Cheapside'. Signatory as 'working goldsmith' to the petition complaining of the competition of 'necessitous strangers', December 1711.

DALMAINE, George (782-3) No record of apprenticeship or freedom. First mark entered as smallworker, 18 May 1797. Address: 7 Bow Street, Covent Garden. Second mark, 13 June 1801. Heal records Thomas Daleman, pawnbroker, Brown Bear, Bow Street, 1753, who seems likely to have been father of the above.

DALTON, Andrew (436) Free of the Broderers' Company by service with George Cox 21 April 1708. Mark entered as largeworker, 30 April 1708. Address: Ball Alley, Lombard Street. 'Free Imbroder'. Heal records him at the same address, 1705-15. Signatory as 'working goldsmith' to the petition complaining of the competition of 'necessitous strangers', December 1711.

DALTON, Isaac (438-9, 3512) Son of Samuel Dalton late of the parish of St Martin's in the Fields in the County of Middlesex baker, apprenticed to Isaac Davenport 1 September 1699. Free, 7 October 1709. Mark entered as largeworker, 10 December 1711. Address: George Street, St. Martin's Le Grand, where Heal records him to 1713. James, son of Isaac and Priscilla Dalton, born 9 January, baptized 27 January 1723, at Christchurch Newgate, may be his son.

DANGER, John (1251) No record of apprenticeship or freedom. Only mark entered as plateworker, 6 January 1825. Address: 2 Spanish Buildings, St. Pancras.

DANIEL, Henry (980) No record of apprenticeship or freedom. Only mark entered as smallworker, 30 December 1778. Address: 29 Goodmans Street, Summer Street.

DANIEL, James Henry (982, 1414) No record of apprenticeship or freedom. First mark entered as 'Gold & Silver Worker', 16 October 1820. Address: 6 Sloane Terrace, Sloane Street. Second mark, 1 September 1821. Third mark, 2 August 1822. Fourth, 9 December 1822. Fifth, 20 January 1823. Sixth, 8 November 1823. Seventh, 20 July 1825. With the exception of Daniel Fueter, for the brief time in the King's Road, Chelsea, James Daniel appears to be the most westerly address recorded in the registers.

DANIEL, Josiah (440, 3629) Son of Josiah Daniel late of Redriffe (?Rotherhithe) in the County of Surrey mariner deceased, apprenticed to Samuel Day 17 December 1703. Free, 4 June 1712. Mark entered as largeworker, 21 February 1715. Address: Wood Street. Heal records him as of London, 1725.

DANIELL, Francis (676) No record of apprenticeship or freedom. Only mark entered as smallworker, 26 May 1760. Address: Little Deans Court, St. Martin's Le Grand.

*DANIELL, Jabez (1254, 3633-4) Son of Jonathan Daniell of Aldgate London maltster, apprenticed to Samuel Wood 6 December 1739 (a premium erased in the entry). Free, 17 March 1747. First mark entered as largeworker, 28 July 1749. Address: Carey Lane, where Heal records him till 1768. Livery, May 1751. James Mince (q.v.), who was apprenticed to him in 1753 and free in 1761, appears to have worked in partnership with him from about 1766-75 on the evidence of mark no. 3633, found almost entirely on castors, and Mince was described as 'castormaker Carey Lane' in an apprenticeship entry of 1773. Daniell was then probably in partnership with his son Thomas (q.v.), from about 1771, as they appear together as goldsmiths, Carey Lane, in the Parl. Report list 1773 (although Mince is not found). This partnership was apparently shortlived as Thomas entered a mark alone in 1774, possibly indicating Jabez' death or retirement.

*DANIELL, Thomas (2727-9, 2737, 3634) Son of Jabez Daniell (q.v.). Free by patrimony, 8 May 1771, as goldsmith, Carey Lane. Livery, December 1771. First mark unrecorded, probably in missing register, with his father, c. 1771, with whom he appears together as goldsmiths, Carey Lane, in the Parl. Report list 1773. Second mark, alone, 16 April 1774. Address: 10 Carey Lane. Third mark, 10 May 1775. Fourth mark, in partnership with John Wall, 13 June 1781. Address: Foster Lane. Fifth mark alone, 8 October 1782. Sixth mark, 8 March 1783. Address: 10 Foster Lane. Died between 1795 and 1801. Heal records him alone at Carey Lane, from 1773 to 1774; with Randle Jackson, as goldsmiths, 10 Carey Lane, 1778 (partnership dissolved), with John Wall, as silversmiths and jewellers, 20 Foster Lane opposite Goldsmiths Hall, 1781-2; alone at the Silver Lion, 20 Foster Lane, 1782-93. I have seen a few pieces bearing his mark which are also engraved with his name and this last address, an unusual feature, e.g. a cup of 1786 at Lincoln College, Oxford, 'Made at the Silver Lyon Foster Lane London'.

DANIELS, John (435, 1238) Perhaps the son of John Daniel of the City of Oxford yeoman, apprenticed to Robert Finch 1681. Free, 19 August 1690. First mark entered as smallworker, 30 April 1703. Address: New Street. Second (Sterling) mark, 19 August 1720.

DARE, John (1244) Free by redemption 7 March 1770, when described as goldsmith in the Minories. Mark entered, 9 February 1773. Address: 103 Minories, and so appears in the Parl. Report list of the same year. Since he was free in 1770 he may have entered a largeworker's mark in the missing register.

DARE, Thomas (1187) No record of apprenticeship or freedom. Only mark entered as smallworker, in partnership with J. Brookes, 19 October 1764. Address: Southampton Buildings, Holborn.

DARKER, William (441, 3078-9) Son of John Darker of Sloughton in the County of Leicester gentleman, apprenticed to Richard Bailey 27 November 1711 on payment on 10 guineas. Free, 4 December 1718. First mark entered as largeworker, 10 January 1719. Address: 'Acron', Foster Lane. Second (Sterling) mark, 12 August 1720, same address. Third mark, 23 June 1724. Address: at the Rose 'over against St. Martin's Lane in ye Strand'. Livery, December 1725. Fourth mark, 1 April 1731, same address. Previously always published as Darkeratt, from an original error of transcription in Chaffers, so also Jackson and Heal. The latter records William Darkeratt Junior at the Rose, St. Martin's Lane, 1731-3, but there is no evidence for this otherwise than the ascriptions in Jackson.

DARQUITS, James, Junr. (1247) Son of James Darquits of Noble Street London silver turner, apprenticed to his father as silver turner 1772. Free, 1 February 1786. Mark entered as smallworker, 19 November 1787. Address: St. Ann's Passage, Noble Street. Moved to 22 Silver Street, 9 March 1797. Heal records the name without distinction of father in Gutter Lane, 1766-9; and Noble Street, 1772; also in Foster Lane, 1789; and Wood Street, 1800, again without distinction.

*DARVILL, Edward (570) No record of apprenticeship or freedom, although the occurrence of John Darvall apprenticed in 1707, and Thomas Darvill in 1780, suggests that he belonged to a family familiar with the trade. Only mark entered as largeworker, 23 March 1757. Address: Watling Street, near Bow Lane. Heal records him as at the Golden Ball, 64 Watling Street, from 1757 till bankruptcy in 1793. He appears as plateworker, Walting Street, in the Parl. Report list 1773.

*DAVENPORT, Burrage (148) No record of apprenticeship or freedom. His name appears only as plateworker in the Parl. Report list of 1773. Address: 6 Foster Lane. The mark long attributed to him must presumably have been registered during the period of the missing largeworkers' volume. There seems no other possible candidate for the mark in question. He may be the Burrage Davenport, bachelor, of St. Mary le Bow whose bans for marriage to Hannah

Kitchener of Russington, Sussex were published at St. Mary le Bow, January-February 1802, and whose son George was born 24 November and baptized 25 December at the same church.

DAVENPORT, Edward (2504) No record of apprenticeship or freedom. Only mark entered as smallworker, in partnership with Samuel Davenport, 8 April 1794. Address: 15 Lime Street, Leadenhall Street.

DAVENPORT, Isaac (432–4) Son of Richard Davenport of ? in the County of Leicester (?), apprenticed to Thomas Allen 11 January 1689. Free, 15 January 1696. Thomas, son of Isaac and Elizabeth Davenport, was born 17 January 1696 and baptized the same date at Christchurch, Newgate Street. Two marks entered as largeworker, undated, probably April 1697 on commencement of register. Address: Gutter Lane. In another hand on the entry: 'a proud Sur'. Third mark as smallworker, 2 February 1705, same address. After the record of his first child above, thirteen are recorded in the register of St. Vedast, Foster Lane, from 1697 to 1715. In the entry for his daughter Mary, 23 June 1700, he is described as 'silversmith at ye signe of the Blackmore head in gutter lane in this parish', and in the entry for Jane Sarah, 1710, as 'Spoone Maker'. Heal records Isaac Davenport, goldsmith, at the Queen's Head over against St. Clement's Church, Strand, 1731.

DAVENPORT, Samuel (2501, 2504) No record of apprenticeship or freedom. First mark entered as plateworker, 24 March 1786. Address: 15 Lime Street, Leadenhall Street. Second mark, in partnership with Edward Davenport as smallworkers, 8 April 1794, same address. His son Samuel was apprenticed to William Seaman of Hulls Street, St. Luke, silversmith, 3 May 1809. Cf. Sarah Davenport (Section V), incuse mark as smallworker, 1813, who may perhaps be his widow.

DAVEY, Richard (2297) No record of apprenticeship or freedom. Only mark entered as smallworker, 26 September 1767. Address: Corner Silver Street.

DAVID, Fleurant (442, 675) No record of apprenticeship or freedom. He is apparently the Florenc David who appears in the Denization Patent Roll, 12 September 1723, and also as godfather to Charlotte Hanet, daughter of Jean and Marie, at West Street Church, 31 January 1720. Two marks (Sterling and New Standard) entered, undated, after June 1724. Address: Green Street, Leicester Fields.

*DAVIS, Benjamin (149) No record of apprenticeship or freedom. First mark entered as spoonmaker, 10 May 1823. Address: 12 Well Street, Jewin Street. Second mark, 24 January 1824. Moved to 7 Carthusian Street, Charterhouse Square, 6 June 1825. Moved to 5 Wellington Street, Goswell Street, 27 September 1825. Third mark, 18 May 1826.

DAVIS, George Henry (819) Possibly identifiable with George Hugh Davis son of William of Red Lion Street Spitalfields grocer, apprenticed to John Harrison gold beater 5 May 1819. Free, 4 October 1826. First mark entered as smallworker, 20 December 1827. Address: 21 Cumberland Street, Curtain Road. Moved to 6 King's Head Square, Shoreditch, 25 April 1829. Second mark, 7 October 1833. Moved to 17 Anglesey Street, Bethnal Green, 5 August 1834. Moved to 12 Exmouth Street, Clerkenwell, 20 July 1835.

DAVIS, James (1804) No record of apprenticeship or freedom. Only mark entered as smallworker, in partnership with William Powell, 2 October 1826. Address: 7 Queen's Square, Aldersgate Street. James Davis, goldworker (Section VII), appears distinct from above.

DAVIS, Jeremiah (1241) No record of apprenticeship or freedom. Only mark entered as smallworker, 12 May 1735. Address: Aldersgate Street, 'near ye White Lyon Tavern'.

DAVIS, Samuel (2502) Possibly (1) son of William Davis of St. Catherine's near the Tower parish clerk, apprenticed to Edward Robinson of Gutter Lane 7 October 1794 on payment of £20. Free, 4 August 1802. Or (2) son of Samuel Davis late of Whitecorn Street, engraver deceased apprenticed to John Clarke of Bunhill Row 3 October 1796. Freedom unrecorded. Mark entered as smallworker, 2 July 1808. Address: 17 Bartholomew Close.

DAVIS, Tompson (2725, 2734). No record of apprenticeship or freedom. First mark entered as largeworker, 30 November 1757. Address: High Holborn, near Lincoln's Inn Fields. Second mark, 7 March 1758. Heal records him at the same address till 1764.

DAVY, Charles (296) No record of apprenticeship or freedom. Only mark entered as spoonmaker, 18 April 1817. Address: 10 Denmark Street, St. Giles.

DAWES, Daniel Harmonas (457) No record of apprenticeship or freedom. Only mark entered as smallworker, 21 April 1827. Address: 15 King Street, Covent Garden.

DAWLEY, Richard (2296) Son of Richard Dawley of Lewshem (sic) in the County of Kent yeoman, apprenticed to William Dicker 27 July 1721 on payment of £20. Freedom unrecorded. Mark entered as smallworker, 2 August 1734. Address: Crick Lane.

DAWSON, William (3086) No record of apprenticeship or freedom. Only mark entered as smallworker, 3 March 1768. Address: Oxford Arms Passage, Warwick Lane. He appears as watchcasemaker at this address, in the Parl. Report list 1773. His widow Elizabeth entered an incuse mark, at the same address, as casemaker, 22 June 1778 (Section V), and William Dawson, 1781-1819, may perhaps be their son (Section V).

DAY, Abraham Harrison (42) No record of apprenticeship or freedom. Only mark entered as plateworker, 26 March 1836. Address: 32 St. Martin's Lane, Charing Cross.

*DAY, Charles (296a, 986) Frederick Charles Day son of George Day of Eagle Court, St. John's Lane, spoonmaker, apprenticed to George Smith of Hosier Lane spoonmaker 3 June 1812 and turned over to Thomas Wilkes Barber of Kirby Street Hatton Garden spoonmaker and mercer 1 December 1813. Freedom unrecorded. Mark entered as plateworker, in partnership with his brother Henry, 28 July 1821. Address: 3 Wilderness Row. Second mark, 6 August 1821. Third mark alone, as spoonmaker, 13 September 1822. Address: 35 Clerkenwell Close.

DAY, George (785-7) Probably son of George Day, apprenticed to John Porter Goldsmith 1790. Freedom unrecorded. First mark entered as spoonmaker, 11 December 1809. Address: 17 Eagle Court, St. John's Lane. Second mark, 30 July 1812. Third mark, 19 May 1814. Moved to 13 Clerkenwell Green, 2 November 1814, where his son Henry (q.v.) joined or succeeded him in 1817.

DAY, Henry (981, 986) Son of George Day of Vinegar Yard, St. John's Lane Clerkenwell silversmith, apprenticed to John Kerchner silver spoonmaker of Silver Street 4 January 1809 on payment of £7.14s. of the charity of Goldsmiths' Company. Free, 5 November 1817. First mark entered as goldworker and spoonmaker, 18 July 1817. Address: 13 Clerkenwell Green (his father's address since 1814). Second mark, 11 March 1819. Third mark, 26 April 1821. Fourth, in partnership with his brother Charles as plateworkers, 28 July 1821. Fifth similar mark, 6 August 1821.

DAY, Samuel (2498) Son of John Day of Thurleigh in the County of Bedford gentleman, apprenticed to Edward Price 12 January 1670. Free, 31 March 1675 by redemption, having served two years before being bound. Livery, May 1694. Mark entered as largeworker, 24 October 1698. Address: Gutter Lane. Heal records him as buried 1705. His son Nathaniel free by patrimony, 8 February 1712.

DAY, William (3084) No record of apprenticeship or freedom. Only mark entered as smallworker, 30 October 1759. Address: Red Lion Court, Grub Street. He appears without category, at this address, in the Parl. Report list 1773, and entered mark as watchcasemaker, 12 April 1777. Address: Broad Arrow Court, Grub Street (Section VI).

DEACON, John (1246) Son of Cornelius Deacon of the parish of Tingrith in the County of Bedford husbandman, apprenticed to John Moore 19 January 1759 on payment of £40. Free, 2 July 1766. (Tingrith was the home of the Tanqueray-Willaume family, q.v.). Mark entered as plateworker, 11 September 1776. Address: 23 Greenhills Rents, St. John Street. An earlier mark was probably entered in the missing book before 1773. He appears as plateworker, 1 Love Lane, Wood Street, in the Parl. Report list 1773. Heal records him as goldsmith, Addle Street, 1771; Love Lane, Wood Street, 1773-5; and Greenhills Rents, 1773-9. He is recorded as bankrupt, April 1775, in Wood Street (*The Gentleman's Magazine*).

DEALTRY, Thomas (2735) Son of Wilsford Dealtry of the City of Nottingham farmer deceased, apprenticed to John Bennet Citizen and Cutler of London 12 June 1742. Free of the Cutlers' Company 29 June 1749. Mark entered as smallworker, 28 October 1765. Address: Sweething Alley, Royal Exchange. Heal records him as goldsmith and haftmaker, Royal Exchange, 1765; Sweating's Alley, 1773; and 85 Cornhill, 1783-99. He appears as hiltmaker, Sweeting's Alley, Royal Exchange, in the Parl. Report list 1773.

DEAN, William (3088) No record of apprenticeship or freedom. Only mark entered as smallworker, 21 March 1765. Address: Bridges Street, Covent Garden. He appears without category, at this address, in the Parl. Report list 1773.

DEANE, John (520, 1797, 3090) No record of apprenticeship or freedom. First mark entered as smallworker in partnership with William Deane (presumably brother), 6 August 1759. Address: Whitecross Street. Moved to Ironmonger Row, 7 April 1761. Second mark, 19 October 1762. Address: Ironmonger Row. Third mark, 3 November 1763. Fourth, 10 August 1764. Fifth, 12 October 1764. Address: Old Street. Sixth, 26 April 1768. Address: 60 Old Bailey. Seventh mark alone, 6 May 1768. Address: Old Bailey, where he appears without category in the Parl. Report list 1773.

DEANE, William (520, 3090) No record of apprenticeship or freedom. First mark entered as smallworker, in partnership with John Deane (above), 6 August 1759. Address: Whitecross Street. At the same date also a separate mark WD for himself alone. Subsequent marks as under John Deane. He appears without category, High Holborn, in the Parl. Report list 1773, and was apparently working alone from 7 May 1768 when John Deane entered a separate mark.

*DEARDS, William (3081) Son of John Deard, admitted a freeman of the Cutler's Company by patrimony 16 July 1724. Mark entered as smallworker, 23 November 1726. Address: Fleet Street. 'free of the Cutlers Company'. Heal records him as William Deard(s), goldsmith and toyman, opposite St. Dunstan's Church, Fleet Street, 1740; again in 1744; and as dying in 1761; another, presumably his son of the same name, Strand, 1765; and Dover Street, Piccadilly, 1777; also William and Mary Deards, goldsmiths and toymen, The Star, end of Pall Mall, near St. James's Haymarket, after 1765.

DEARMOR, John (1239) No record of apprenticeship or freedom. Only mark entered as smallworker, 16 December 1724. Address: Bell Court, Snow Hill. Perhaps identifiable with John Dearmer, 'free Clockmaker' incuse mark, 28 July 1730. Address: Salisbury Court, Fleet Street (Section V), but the writing and spelling of the two entries vary considerably.

DEATH, John (1249) Son of John Death of Grub Street St. Luke's hot presser, apprenticed to John Mewburn of Hare Court Aldersgate Street Goldsmith 7 January 1795 on payment of £5 of the charity of the Governors of the Protestant Dissenters School St. Bartholomew's Close West Smithfield. Free, 7 July 1802. First mark entered as smallworker, 11 July 1803. Address: 10 Grub Street. Second mark on move to 17 Lower Street, Clerkenwell, 29 June 1808. Robert Death, incuse mark as plateworker, 26 July 1809, 18 Lower Smith Street, King Street, Clerkenwell (Section V) is presumably connected.

DEATH, Thomas (2732) Son of John Death of Grub Street St. Luke's hot presser, apprenticed to his brother John (above) 4 May 1803 on payment of £4 of the charity of the Drapers' Company from the gift of Henry Dixon deceased. Free, 4 July 1810. Mark entered as plateworker, 17 February 1812. Address: 16 North Street, City Road. Moved to 39 St. John's Street, Clerkenwell, 2 February 1828.

DEE, Thomas (2736) No record of apprenticeship or freedom. Only mark entered as smallworker, in partnership with John Fargus, 1 May 1830. Address: 8 Sherard Street, Golden Square.

DE GRUCHY, John (35) Son the Rev. Philip de Gruchy late of the Island of Jersey deceased, apprenticed to John Swift 4 October 1758 on payment of £50. Freedom unrecorded. Appears in the Parl. Report list 1773 as goldsmith, Oxford. Heal records this as Oxford Street, but since the Parl. Report list records other provincial workers, e.g. at Portsmouth and Worcester, there is no necessity to assume a misprint in this case, since he may well have begun working in Oxford and came to London in 1779. First mark as smallworker, in partnership with Alexander Field, 20 April 1779. Address: City Road. The partnership apparently dissolved by 14 July 1780, when Field entered a separate mark.

DEIGHTON, George (784) No record of apprenticeship or freedom. Only mark entered as smallworker, 24 September 1801. Address: 21 Denmark Court, Strand.

DELAFONS, John (1798) Son of Philip

Delafons of Tottenham Court Road enameller, apprenticed to Isaac Chartier of Angel Court Throckmorton Street watchmaker 3 August 1768 on payment of £21. Free, 8 February 1788. Mark entered as smallworker, 2 March 1810. Address: 5 Rolls Buildings, Fetter Lane.

*DE LAMERIE, Paul (1892, 2203-4) Full name Paul Jacques, son of Paul Souchay de la Merie, officer in the army of William III, and Constance née Roux, Huguenots, baptized 14 April 1688, at the Walloon Church, Bois-le-Duc('s Hertogenbusch), Holland. Brought to England by his parents at the age of eleven and a half months, the family settling in Berwick Street, Soho, and subsequently living in considerable straits. Endenizened with his father 24 June 1703 and apprenticed without premium 6 August 1703 to Peter Plattel (Pierre Platel q.v.), when his father is described as 'Of the parish of St. Anne's Westminster Gent'. Free, 4 February 1713. First mark entered as largeworker, 5 February 1713. Address: Windmill Street, near the Haymarket. Goldsmith to the King 1716 (Major-General H. W. D. Sitwell. 'The Jewell House and the Royal Goldsmiths' *Arch. Journ.* CXVII, p. 152). Married, 11 February 1717, Louise Jolliott at Glasshouse Street Church with licence of Archbishop of Canterbury. To them six children were born: Margaret 1718, Mary 1720, Paul 1725, Daniel 1727, Susannah 1729 and Louisa Elizabeth 1730. Only Mary, Susannah and Louisa survived infancy. Livery, 18 July 1717. Defendant in 1722 in the case of *Armory* v. *Delamirie*, a text-book case well known to lawyers for the rights of a finder of property, in this case a chimney-sweeper's boy, to 'maintain trover', i.e. such a property as will enable him to keep it against all but the rightful owner. Court, 5 May 1731. Second (Sterling) mark as largeworker, 17 March 1733 Address: Golden Ball, Windmill Street, St. James's. Styled 'Captain' from 1736 and 'Major' from 1743, presumably as officer in one of the volunteer associations. Member of the committee of the Company in 1738 to prepare the petition and bill to Parliament for revision of hallmarking. Moved to Gerrard Street sometime in 1738. Heal records him here at No. 45 to 1739, 55 in 1742, and 42 from 1743-51, presumably due to directory or rate-book errors. Third mark, 27 June 1739. Address: 'Garard' Street. Fourth Warden 1743, third Warden 1746, second Warden 1747, but never Prime Warden, possibly from failing health. Second surviving daughter Susannah married, 29 March 1750, to Joseph Defaubre. Lamerie died 1 August 1751, and was buried at St. Anne's Soho. His will, dated 24 May 1750, ordered all plate in hand to be finished and stock to be auctioned by Langford of Covent Garden, his journeymen Frederick Knopfell and Samuel Collins to have £15 and £20 respectively, the latter 'to live with my executors until my Plate in hand shall be finished'. The short obituary from the *London General Evening Post*, Thursday August 1 -Saturday August 3, 1751 is worthy of recall: 'Last Thursday died Mr Paul de Lamerie of Gerrard Street much regretted by his Family and Acquaintance as a Tender Father, a kind Master and an upright Dealer'. Of the remaining daughters, Mary married John Malliett 11 November 1754, at St. Anne's Louisa died unmarried, 22 September 1761. Lamerie's widow Louisa died 8 June 1765. Full acknowledgement is made for the above biographical detail to the first and unsurpassable monograph on an English goldsmith, '*Paul De Lamerie*' by P. A. S. Phillips, 1935, whose enthusiasm and industry in research stands as a model for every disciple.

DELANDER, James (462) Described as Free Clockmaker in the entry of his mark, of which company he was probably free by patrimony since his name does not appear in the apprentice lists before 1700. Mark entered as smallworker, undated, but preceding another of 24 October 1698. Address: Bolt and Tun Court, Fleet Street. From the evidence of his company, presumably a watchcasemaker.

DELAS, James (1242, 1252) No record of apprenticeship or freedom. First mark entered as smallworker, 10 July 1723. Address: Angel Street, St. Martin's Le Grand. Second mark, 2 August 1737. Address: St. Martin's Le Grand, 'ye corner of Bagnio Alley'.

*DELISLE, Louis (1913) No record of apprenticeship or freedom. Only mark entered as plateworker, 27 July 1775. Address: 2 Angel Court, Strand. Heal records him as jeweller, Angel Court, 1773. Evans lists him as Huguenot (*Hug. Soc. Proc.* 14).

DELL, Henry (979) Free of the Glovers' Company, probably by patrimony since there is no entry for him in the apprentice register of the Company back to 1709. Mark entered as largeworker, undated, between December 1722 and June 1724. 'Free Glover'. Address: 'at ye Crowne and Dollphin in Moore Strett next Dore to ye Grayhound Tavern, Mullmouth (?Monmouth) Street End St. Gilles is Parrish'. Heal records him as goldsmith and jeweller, Crown and Pearl, Wood Street, 1706-14; and the above address and date of the entry as 1722. Hilton Price, *Handbook of London Bankers*, gives first address and date only.

DELL, Martin (2016) Son of Joseph Dell of Richmond in the County of Surrey calico printer, apprenticed to Thomas Chilcott 5 April 1753 on payment of £10.10s. Free, 6 August 1760. Mark entered as smallworker, 5 March 1763. Address: St. Ann's Lane. Moved to Warwick Lane, 15 July 1763. Appears as watchcasemaker, at this address, in the Parl. Report list 1773.

DELL, Samuel (459) Son of James Dell late of St. Michaels near the Towne of St. Albans Hertford yeoman deceased, apprenticed to Daniel Rutty 24 July 1671. Later turned over to William Wakefield. Free, 11 August 1679. Mark entered as largeworker, undated, probably on commencement of register April 1697. Address: Watling Street. Heal records him as plateworker, London (?) 1688; Watling Street, 1697-1703. His address is more closely indicated in the baptismal register of his daughter Sarah, 1699, at St. Mary Aldermary, as 'Watlin Street, nere the corner of Bowe laine'. She is the last of the family beginning with James, April 1683, followed by two other sons and six other daughters. His wife's name does not appear.

DELLANY, Samuel (2500) Son of Solomon Dellany Citizen and Weaver of London, apprenticed to Michael Boult 9 May 1754. Turned over the same day to John Allen(?) Citizen and Glover of London in consideration of £10.10s. Turned over (having served out his indentures) to William Harrison Citizen and Goldsmith 24 July 1758. Free, 3 June 1761. Mark entered as smallworker, 19 March 1762. Address: New Street Square, Shoe Lane, where he appears without category in the Parl. Report list 1773. Heal records him here as Dellamy. Evans considers him a Huguenot (*Hug. Soc. Proc.* 14).

*DELMESTRE, John (431, 3630) No record of apprenticeship or freedom. Only mark entered as largeworker, 12 May 1755. Address: Court Street, opposite Whitechapel Mount. Heal records him as plateworker, Whitechapel, till 1760. Evans lists him as Huguenot (*Hug. Soc. Proc.* 14).

DENE, Thomas (2726) No record of apprenticeship or freedom. Mark entered as smallworker, in partnership with another? Vere Norman (poor writing broken into two lines), 22 July 1767. Address: St. Luke's Buildings.

DENN, Basile (145-7) Son of Bazil Denn of St. George's Southwark tallowchandler, apprenticed to William Fawson 1 October 1715 and turned over to Captain Allison in the Minories 6 September 1720. Free, 21 October 1722. Livery, March 1739. First mark entered as smallworker, 3 September 1729. Address: Little Minories. 'free of the Goldsmiths Company'. Second mark, 31 March 1731. Third mark, 28 July 1758. Address: London Bridge. Fourth mark, 22 July 1759. Address: White Alley, Little Moorfields. Heal records him as goldsmith, Aldgate, insolvent 1729, which could perhaps be the father; also Basil Denn Junior, goldsmith and jeweller, at the Gold Ring, London Bridge, near Southwark, 1743-54; and Tooley Street, Southwark, 1771. There are two entries in the Parl. Report list 1773 which appear to indicate separate working identities still in that year: (1) Bassill Denn (misprinted Deun), ringmaker, White's Alley, Little Moorfields, as above for the 1759 mark entry; (2) Bassill Denn, bucklemaker, Tooley Street, Southwark, matching Heal's record for 1771 (above).

*DENNEY, Daniel (456, 3513) No record of apprenticeship or freedom. First mark entered as plateworker, 24 July 1786. Address: 11 St. Martin's Le Grand. Second mark, 30 July 1799. Address: 1 Cox's Court, Little Britain. Moved to 1 Ball Court, Giltspur Street, 18 July 1814. Heal records only the first date and address.

*DENNISON, Robert (2298-9) Free of the Joyners' Company. First mark entered as smallworker, 30 October 1767. Address: Cecil's Court, St. Martin's Lane. Second mark, 24 November 1768. Third mark, 2 November 1769. Fourth mark, 15 May 1771. Fifth, 25 January 1772. All at the same address. Appears as bucklemaker, at the same, in the Parl. Report list 1773. His son Anderson Robert was apprenticed to Edward Feline and turned over to his father,

1770, when the father is described as Citizen and Joyner of London, goldsmith. Anderson Robert entered a mark as bucklemaker, same address, 24 July 1776 (Section VIII).

*DENNY, William (446, 460) Son of Nathaniel Denny of Tutsbury Gloucester mercer, apprenticed to William Harrison 7 December 1670. Free, 3 October 1679. Appears as William Denne, silversmith, in the baptismal register of his daughter Elizabeth, at St. Mary Woolnoth, December 1681, and his son William, 1682. Mark entered as largeworker, in partnership with John Bache (also apprenticed to William Harrison q.v.), undated, probably April 1697 on commencement of register. Address: Dore Court, Lombard Street. Another entry of his mark alone, also undated (? at the same time). Address: Golden Ball, Swaythling Lane. Signatory to the petition against the work of 'aliens and forreigners', 11 August 1697. His wife Elizabeth was buried at St. Mary Woolnoth, 7 December 1705, and Denny himself 30 January 1707. Heal records him till 1733 but this may be a son, although the one born 1682 died the following year. The partnership with Bache is recorded by both Heal and Hilton Price to 1720, but this may be mere continuance of the name in directories.

DENWALL, John (1243) No record of apprenticeship or freedom. Only mark entered as smallworker, 20 October 1768. Address: Fisher Street, Red Lion Square, where he appears without category in the Parl. Report list 1773. The name was misread by Chaffers as Darwall, followed by Jackson and Heal. John Steventon Denwall son of John Steventon Denwall of Peartree Court Clerkenwell Goldsmith was apprenticed to James Mathews silver turner 3 February 1790.

DENZILOE, John (1255) Son of William Denziloe late of Bridport in the County of Dorset haberdasher, apprenticed to Charles Wright 9 January 1765 on payment of £20. Free, 6 May 1772. Livery, March 1781. Mark entered as plateworker, 27 October 1774. Address: 3 Westmoreland Buildings, Aldersgate Street, where Heal records him till 1793. His son Charles, aged eleven, was admitted to St. Paul's School, 13 August 1802, when it is clear Denziloe was still in business at Aldersgate Street. Died December 1820.

*DE OLIVEYRA, Abraham Lopez (70-1) A Sephardic Jew whose family had settled in Amsterdam after the dispersal from Spain. Son of Jacob, Warden of the Amsterdam Synagogue in 1654, born 1657. Reached London by 1697, when he was married there to Rebecca de Abraham Morais. Their daughter Sarah appears in the baptismal register of St. Helen's Bishopsgate, 1 November 1698, probably solely to establish her as English born, the only method then available. Oliveyra may very probably have been trained in Holland in both general goldsmithery and also engraving, since he appears as the engraver of the title page of a Spanish version of the Psalms of David by Daniel Lopez Laguna, published in London in 1720. The engraving signed 'Abm Lopes de Oliveira fecit' includes rebus pictures of a goldsmith's workshop and vessels suggesting a working acquaintance with the craft. There is, in any case, no record of apprenticeship or freedom in London. First mark entered as smallworker, undated, c. 1725. Address: St. Helen's Bishopsgate. The first recorded appearance of the mark is on two pairs of Rimonim (Bells for the Law) of 1724 at the Hambro and New Synagogues. Second mark as largeworker, 3 July 1739. Address: Houndsditch. Heal records him as plateworker, St. Helen's, Bishopsgate, 1725-7; and plateworker and engraver, Houndsditch, 1739. The records of Bevis Marks Synagogue, so close to which he worked and lived, show that de Oliveyra supplied the Synagogue with the Passover bread in 1736 and 1737, and that he made the silver salver for presentation to the Lord Mayor in the latter year at a cost of £40.10s.; this piece has not apparently survived. He died and was buried in Bevis Marks Cemetery in 1750, his tombstone stating his age as ninety-three (Lyson, *Environs of London*, Vol. III). His principal works are his Rimonim dating from 1724 to 1737 which display considerable invention with delicacy of execution (A. G. Grimwade, 'Anglo-Jewish Silver', *Transactions of the Jewish Historical Society*, Vol. XVIII, pp. 122-3).

*DESREUMAUX (DES RUMEAUX), James (461, 1237) Jacques des Rumaux son of John des Rumeaux of the parish of St. Ann's Westminster gentleman, apprenticed to Peter Harach Junior 16 March 1703. Free, 9 March 1715. First mark, as James Desreumaux, entered as smallworker, 3 November 1716. Address: Litchfield Street. Second (Sterling) mark, 23 June 1720.

BIOGRAPHICAL DICTIONARY

Address: West Street, St. Giles in the Fields. Heal records him only as goldsmith, London, 1714. Louis Derumaux who entered an incuse mark, 12 October 1707 (Address: Blackfriars. 'free Clockmaker') (Section V) is possibly related.

DESVIGNES, Peter (2153) No record of apprenticeship or freedom. Only mark entered as smallworker, 28 June 1771. Address: Old Benton Street, Long Acre (spelt 'Akee^r'). He appears as goldworker, Old Belton Street, Long Acre, in the Parl. Report list 1773. He or a son of the same name entered an incuse mark as goldworker, with Ann Macaire, 11 November 1793, at 13 Denmark Street, Soho, and he alone, 9 May 1796, at same address, probably after marrying her, since Ann Desvigny alone, presumably as widow, entered a further mark, 5 October 1813, at 44 Rosoman Street, Clerkenwell (Section V, $^{AM}_{PD}$, etc.). Desvignes should not be confused with Peter Devese, goldsmith, Queen Street, Golden Square, who also appears in the Parl. Report list. The name Peter Desergnes (Jackson, page 256) is apparently a misprint, the 'vi' of -vignes being read as 'er' at some point of transcription.

DETHERIDGE, John James (1257) No record of apprenticeship or freedom. Presumably identical with John Dethridge, entered as goldworker, 5 October 1811 (Section VII). Mark entered as plateworker, in partnership with John Cottrill, 26 April 1826. Address: 29 Great Sutton Street, Clerkenwell.

*DE VEER, Frederick (678) No record of apprenticeship or freedom. Only mark entered as smallworker, 9 December 1731. Address: With(White) Cross Alley, Middle Moorfields. Heal records Frederick Deveer, goldsmith, 7 Angel Court, Throgmorton Street, 1753–81, who must surely be the same, or perhaps a son. He appears as goldworker, at Angel Court, in the Parl. Report list 1773.

DEVONSHIRE, Richard (2301) Son of Israel Devonshire of St. Leonards Shoreditch Goldsmith (himself son of Thomas Devonshire (q.v.)), apprenticed to George Burrows of Clerkenwell Close Goldsmith 7 March 1792 on payment of £7. 14s. of the charity of the Goldsmiths' Company. Free, 2 December 1807. Mark entered as spoonmaker, 14 October 1819. Address: 24 Dove Row, Hackney Fields. Moved to 13 Bath Cort, Bath Street, Old Street Road, 9 March 1821.

DEVONSHIRE, Thomas (518, 2739) Son of Israel Devonshire of the parish of St. Mary Whitechapel labourer, apprenticed to Jeremiah Lee 6 May 1742. Freedom unrecorded. Mark entered as largeworker, in partnership with William Watkins, 9 February 1756. Address: Paternoster Row. Second mark, 10 March 1756. Third mark, 24 June 1766. Livery, December 1771. Heal records Watkins and Devonshire as spoonmakers, Paternoster Row, from 1756 to 1773, and Devonshire appears alone as spoonmaker here, in the Parl. Report list 1773. His son Israel was apprenticed to him, 4 August 1762, and his second son Joseph, 7 January 1778, when £7. 14s. of the charity of the Goldsmiths' Company was paid to the father, suggesting that Thomas must have been in a poor financial state to accept a premium for his own son; this is supported by the fact that he had resigned from the Livery, August 1775. The first son Israel appears in the Parl. Report list of 1773 as spoonmaker, 125 Aldersgate Street, but no mark is identifiable as his, which would presumably have been entered about 1769 in the missing register.

DEXTER, Benjamin Reece (150) No record of apprenticeship or freedom. Probably son of Thomas Paine Dexter (below). Only mark entered as plateworker, 30 September 1835. Address: 11 London Street, Upper North Street, Mile End.

DEXTER, Thomas Paine (2730) Son of Paine Dexter late of Whitechapel in the County of Middlesex shoemaker deceased, apprenticed to John Mewburn of Hare Court Aldersgate Street Goldsmith 1 June 1796. Free, 2 May 1804. Mark entered as plateworker, 21 August 1805. Address: 3 Blue Coat Building, Little Britain. Moved to 16 Goswell Place, 17 November :806. Second mark, 10 October 1812. Moved to 11 London Street, Upper North Street, Mile End Road, 6 September 1824. Described as working goldsmith of Goswell Street Road in the apprenticeship to him of James Ford, 5 August 1818.

DICKEN, Arthur (474) Son of John Dicken of ?Crewe in the County of Salop apothecary, apprenticed to William Fawdery 10 February 1702. Signatory to the petition against assaying the work of foreigners not having served seven years apprenticeship, February 1716. Free, 10 November 1719.

Mark entered as largeworker, 18 June 1720. Address: The Angel, Strand, where Heal records him till 1724.

*DICKER, William (475, 3077a) Son of Joseph Dicker late of Salehurst (?Selhurst) in the County of Sussex yeoman deceased, apprenticed to Nathaniel Gouldham 12 April 1711 on payment of £16 and turned over to George Caines. Free, 4 September 1718. Two marks (Sterling and New Standard) entered as smallworker, 15 April 1720. Address: Ball alley, Lombard Street. Heal records him in Lombard Street, from 1725 till bankruptcy in 1728.

DICKS, James (1799, 2738) No record of apprenticeship or freedom. First mark entered as spoonmaker, 2 November 1820. Address: 9 Bishop Court, Aylesbury Street, Clerkenwell. Second mark, in partnership with Thomas Dicks (q.v., ?father or elder brother), 20 September 1821. Address: 36 Greenhill Rents, West Smithfield. Third mark together, 6 November 1821. Fourth, 10 November 1821. Fifth mark alone, 23 January 1832.

DICKS, Thomas (2731, 2738) No record of apprenticeship or freedom. First mark entered as bucklemaker, 4 May 1792. Address: 39 Cow Lane, West Smithfield, and four further such, 1798-1818. Address: 39 Greenhills Rents, Smithfield (Section VIII). Sixth mark entered as spoonmaker, 9 July 1811. Address: 36 Greenhill Rents. Seventh mark, in partnership with James Dicks (q.v.), 20 September 1821, same address. Eighth mark, 6 November 1821. Ninth, 10 November 1821. The partnership was apparently dissolved by 23 January 1832 when James entered a separate mark, possibly on Thomas's death.

DIGGLE, John (477) Son of John Diggle of Herriard in the County of Southampton clerke, apprenticed to Thomas Littleton 20 December 1675. Free, 7 February 1683. Mark entered as largeworker, undated, probably on commencement of register April 1697. Address: Strand, near Charing Cross. Heal records him at the Cardinal's Cap or Red Hat in the Strand near Charing Cross, 1694-1701.

DIGHTON, Isaac (476) Son of Henry Dighton of the City of Bristol gentleman, apprenticed to William Browne Citizen and Haberdasher of London 26 May 1665. Free of the Haberdashers' Company, 7 June 1672. Mark entered as largeworker, undated, probably on commencement of register April 1697. Address: Gutter Lane. 'Free Haberdasher'. Signatory to the petition to the Goldsmiths' Company against the marking of foreigners work and extending the freedom to 'several Frenchmen', 1 October 1703. Described as 'Capt. Isaac Dighton goldsmith' in the register of his burial, 28 February 1707 in St. Vedast, Foster Lane. Mrs Catherine Dighton (presumably his widow) was buried in the same church, 3 July 1712.

DILLER, Thomas (2733) No record of apprenticeship or freedom. First mark enentered as smallworker, 5 December 1828. Address: 1 Richmond Building, Dean Street, Soho. Second mark, 12 January 1841.

DIMES, Charles (297) No record of apprenticeship or freedom, although others of the same surname occur from 1781. Only mark entered as plateworker, 28 February 1832. Address: 25 Robert Street, Hoxton.

DIX, John East (2548, 2627, 3798) Son of John Dix of Christchurch in the County of Surrey cooper, apprenticed to Solomon Hougham of Aldersgate Street Goldsmith 2 December 1795 on payment of £8 of the charity of the Governors of Christ's Hospital (presumably his school). Free, 5 January 1803. Livery, January 1824. First mark entered as plateworker, in partnership with Solomon Hougham and Solomon Royes, 13 September 1817. Address: 138 Aldersgate Street. Second mark, with Solomon Royes only, 19 September, 1818, same address. Livery, 20 January 1824. Died 12 October 1858.

DIXON, George (789) No record of apprenticeship or freedom. Only mark entered as smallworker, in partnership with Thomas Remmett, 6 February 1797. Address: Hemings Row, St. Martin's Lane.

DOBSON, Edward (496, 569, 571) Son of Edward Dobson late of Newmarket in the County of Cambridge barber deceased, apprenticed to Starling Wilford 2 August 1743. Free, 11 January 1751. Mark entered as largeworker, in partnership with James Williams and William Pryor, 10 February 1755. Address: Paternoster Row. Partnership dissolved 26 July 1755. Second mark alone, 9 September 1755. Address: Facing St. Bride's, Fleet Street. He appears as spoonmaker, Fleet Street, in the Parl. Report list 1773. Third mark as spoonmaker, 3 December 1778. Address: 12 Old Street Square. Heal records him as jeweller and working goldsmith at the Crown, Ring and Pearl, near Shoe Lane, 1755-73; and as goldsmith, Old Street, 1770-8. He was listed as bankrupt in 1758 (*The Gentleman's Magazine*).

DODDS, George (781) No record of apprenticeship or freedom. Only mark entered as smallworker, 22 August 1738. Address: Bartholomew Close.

*DODDS, Joseph (1248) No record of apprenticeship or freedom. First mark entered as plateworker, 13 June 1789. Address: 12 Aldersgate Street. Second mark (two sizes), 22 July 1790. Heal records him as goldsmith and jeweller at the above address, 1790-6; and also John Troutbeck and Joseph Dodds, goldsmiths, Aldersgate Street, dissolved partnership 1793, presumably begun after the entry of Dodds' second mark.

DOLMAN, Henry (983) No record of apprenticeship or freedom. First mark entered as smallworker, 6 January 1825. Address: 96 Curtain Road, Shoreditch. Second mark (incuse), on move to 2 Short Street, Tabernacle Square, 11 June 1850.

DOMINY, Allen (26-7) No record of apprenticeship or freedom. First mark entered as smallworker, 9 December 1789. Address: 55 Red Lion Street, Holborn. Second mark, 5 February 1790.

DONEL, Richard O'Niall (2295) No record of apprenticeship or freedom. Only mark entered as smallworker, 11 March 1731. Address: Turks Head, opposite St. Catherine Street, in the Strand.

DORRELL, Jane (1258) Probably the widow of William Dorrell (below). First mark entered as smallworker, in partnership with Richard May (formerly apprenticed to William Dorrell), 22 October 1766. Address: Quakers' Buildings. Second mark, 22 May 1769. Third mark, 3 May 1771. Address: 24 Quakers' Buildings. Appears alone as buttonmaker, Quaker's Building, Smithfield, in the Parl. Report list 1773. Heal records the partnership as plateworkers, only from 1771 to 1781, and suggests 'Quakers' Buildings' may indicate The Quakers' Meeting House, White Hart Yard, Lombard Street, but this is contradicted by the above.

DORRELL, William (3082-3) Son of Francis Dorrell Citizen and Clockmaker of London, apprenticed to John Clarke 3 April 1728 on payment of £5 of the Charity of Cripplegate School London. Free, 16 January 1745. First mark entered as smallworker, 11 February 1736. Address: Grub Street near the bell. His late freedom date may be due to his having worked outside the City limits. Second mark 28 April 1762. Address Smithfield Bars. Third mark 3 May 1763: same address. Fourth mark 1 November 1764. Probably dead by 22 October 1766 when Jane Dorrell (above) entered her mark. Another William Dorrell, described as son of William Dorrell Goldsmith was apprenticed to John Coster 1758 and turned over to his father in 1763 when the latter's first designation is altered to Wheelwright, possibly from initial confusion with subject of this entry.

DOUGLAS, Archibald (28, 1256) No record of apprenticeship or freedom. First mark entered as smallworker, in partnership with John Douglas (?father), 2 February 1821. Address: 52 Red Lion Street, Clerkenwell. Second mark as goldworker alone, 23 September 1823. Address: 14 West Street (Section VII). Third mark, with John Douglas, 22 November 1823. Address: 52 Red Lion Street. Fourth mark alone as plateworker, 19 January 1826. Fifth mark as goldworker, 20 April 1826. Address: 37 Penton Place, Pentonville. Moved to 57 Red Lion Street, 13 November 1827. Sixth mark, 26 March 1830. Seventh mark, 1 June 1836. Moved to 10 Wilderness Row, Chelsea, 14 December 1837, as goldworker.

DOUGLAS, Francis (677) No record of apprenticeship or freedom. Presumably son of Archibald (above). First mark entered as smallworker, 1 May 1837. Address: 57 Red Lion Street, Clerkenwell. Second mark, 20 October 1837. Third, 8 December 1837. Fourth, 17 February 1838. Moved to 13 St. James's Walk, Clerkenwell, 4 July 1838. Fifth mark, 11 July 1843.

DOUGLAS, John (1250, 1256, 2359) No record of apprenticeship or freedom. First mark entered as bucklemaker, 25 November 1788. Address: 4 Clerkenwell Close (Section VIII). Second mark entered as smallworker, in partnership with Richard Lockwood, 12 August 1800. Address: 8 Clerkenwell Green. Third mark, 23 September (without year, presumably the same). Fourth mark alone as smallworker, 31 January 1804. Address: 4 Clerkenwell Close. Fifth mark, 24 December 1813. Address: 52 Red Lion Street, Clerkenwell. Sixth mark, in partnership with Archibald Douglas (?son), 2 February 1821, same address. Seventh mark, with the same, 22 November 1823.

*DOVEY, Richard (2300) No record of apprenticeship or freedom. First mark entered as smallworker, 'Goldsmith', 9 June 1770. Address: 6 Craven Buildings, Drury Lane, where he appears as a goldworker in the Parl. Report list 1773. Heal records him as goldsmith and jeweller till 1774. Entered second mark as bucklemaker, 17 March 1777, 'at Pimlico' (Section VIII).

DOWDALL, Edward (567-8) No record of apprenticeship or freedom. First mark entered as largeworker, 6 December 1748. Address: Bishop's Court, Aylsbury Street, Clerkenwell. Moved to Bethnal Green, 7 August 1749. Second mark, on moving back to Aylesbury Street, Clerkenwell, 8 November 1751. Heal records him, with alternate spelling Doweall, as plateworker, Clerkenwell, till 1756.

DOWNES, John (492) Son of Robert Downes of Sheafold (?Sheffield) in the County of York cutler, apprenticed to George Garthorne 26 August 1681. Free, 4 September 1688. Mark entered as largeworker, undated, probably on commencement of register April 1697. Address: Wood Street, where Heal records him till 1703. Livery, October 1698. Another John Downes, jeweller is also listed by Heal, 'next door to the Cock in St. James's Street', 1731, perhaps a son.

DOWNES, William (3085, 3089) No record of apprenticeship or freedom. First mark entered as smallworker, 16 January 1768. Address: Little Love Lane, Wood Street. Second mark, 28 July 1768. Third, 8 November 1769. Fourth, 12 March 1770.

DOWYE, George (788) No record of apprenticeship or freedom. Only mark entered as smallworker, 18 September 1763. Address: Salisbury Court, 'near of Blue Post'(?)

*DOXSEY, Thomas (3818) No record of apprenticeship or freedom. Appears in the Parl. Report list 1773 as goldworker, and had entered an incuse mark, 16 December 1756 (Section V). Address: Near Great St. Helens, Bishopsgate Street. The mark ascribed to him above must remain doubtful.

DRAKE, Joseph (1240) No record of apprenticeship or freedom, although several of this surname, including Westcombe (below), appear in the freemen's register. Only mark entered as smallworker, 25 August 1731. Address: St. John Street, 'over against ye Cannon'. Heal records him, without Christian name, as silversmith at this address and date; also John Drake (?Joseph), goldsmith, Greenhills Rents, near West Smithfield, insolvent 1748.

DRAKE, Wescombe (3080) Son of John Drake of Kentish Town in the County of Middlesex (?gentleman), apprenticed to John Saunders 2 May 1721 on payment of £10 and turned over 20 December 1723 to George Wickes in Threadneedle Street plateworker. Free, 4 December 1728. Mark entered as largeworker, undated, after 1724 and before April 1731. Address: Golden Ball, Norton Folgate.

*DRINKWATER, Sandylands (2499, 3792) Son of William Drinkwater of St. Clement Danes in the County of Middlesex gentleman, apprenticed to Robert White 19 February 1719 on payment of £21 and turned over to Elizabeth White widow. Free, 22 December 1726. Livery, March 1737. Court, 1745. Warden, 1757-9. Prime Warden, 1761. Mark entered as smallworker, 20 January 1735. Address: Gutter Lane. The second mark (3792) is presumably his new style mark required under the 1738 Plate Act, but it not registered and remains conjectural. It would be a pity however to deprive one of this sober name of the connection with wine-labels, on which this mark appears, and which would appear to have been his principal if not entire output. Heal records him at the Hand and Coral, Gutter Lane, 1731-72. He appears as smallworker, Saint Alban's, in the Parl. Report list 1773, where he must presumably have retired at some point after his Prime Wardenship. Died 1776. Another of the name, presumably his son, was elected to the livery, November 1776.

DRIVER, John (1802) No record of apprenticeship or freedom. Only mark entered as smallworker, 24 December 1828. Address: 2 Holliwell Row, Worship Street.

DRURY, Dru I (455, 497-8) Fifth son of William Drury of Tannesford (Tempsford) in the County of Bedford gentleman previously at Godmanchester, born 1688, apprenticed to William Gardiner Goldsmith 8 July 1703. Free, 4 May 1711. Livery, June 1725. First mark entered as smallworker, 7 July 1711. Address: Noble Street. Second mark, 14 October 1717. Address: Lad Lane, Wood Street. Third mark (Sterling), 8 August 1720. Livery, June 1725. Heal records him at the last address as goldsmith

1724-7; and as Dan Drury, goldsmith and knife-haftmaker, 1742-66. It is obvious however from the occurrence of his mark that he was a specialist in knife-hafts and hilts, as was his son of the same name (below). He came to grief in 1741 as the following extract from the Court minutes of the Goldsmiths' Company reveals, 12 February 1741: 'Petition read of Dru Drury setting forth that he hath been inadvertently concerned in causing an impression of a stamp to be made resembling the Lion Passant and thereby incurring the displeasure of the Company and the penalty of £100; but that he hath never made any use of the stamp and hath now caused the same to be broken; and being sensible of his guilt, he is willing to submit himself to the Court, praying that the penalty may be moderated as the Court shall think fit and offering to pay the same with the charges incurred. In debate hereupon it is alleged that the petitioner, rather than be exposed at a public trial, is willing to pay the whole penalty with costs; but it is observed and taken notice of, that the Company, by the late Act of Parliament, seem to be entrusted with the care and direction of suits against persons committing frauds and abuses in gold and silver wares; and that should the Company upon application of any offenders (and more especially of members of the Company) accept the penalty with costs in a private way of consent, although the same may be as much or more than can be recovered by law, they may incur the displeasure of the Legislature, because it is probable a great part of the punishment of offenders, in such good circumstances as the petitioner is reputed to be, may be the exposing their characters at public trial, and be a greater concern to them than the charge of the penalty with costs. It is, besides, hoped that no prosecution of this kind will be set on foot for the sake of the penalty, or any other motive than to redress the fraud and abuse of counterfeit marks on wrought plate, especially as the standard of plate has always been deemed an honour to the nation and the great quantity of plate has now become a considerable part of the riches of the Kingdom; therefore it is moved and seconded that the said petition be rejected; and the question being put, it is carried in the affirmative; and the clerk is ordered to proceed against the petitioner in such manner as counsel shall advise.'

*DRURY, Dru II (458) Son of the above, born 4 February 1725, apprenticed to his father 1739. Free, 3 December 1746. Livery, March 1751. Married (date unknown) Easter, daughter of John Pedley of Wood Street in the City of London, soapmaker. Mark entered as smallworker, 16 December 1767. Address: Wood Street, possibly following his father's death. Described as haftmaker, Strand, in the Parl. Report list 1773. Heal records him as goldsmith, Wood Street, 1770, so he must have moved to the Strand soon after. Appears in the Strand, bankrupt, December 1777 (*The Gentleman's Magazine*). Heal further lists Drury Drury (successors to Nathaniel Jeffreys), goldsmith, (No. 32) Strand, corner of Villiers Street, 1770, bankrupt 1786; Drury Drury and Son at same address, 1781-93; and William Drury (his elder son, born 23 June 1752), goldsmith and jeweller, 32 Strand, 1796, by which time his father had apparently retired, since he was at Broxbourne by 1794. A second son Dru was born 22 March 1767. William married Margaret Charlotte Welch, April 1789 (*The Gentleman's Magazine*, and Drury Papers). Dru Drury's wife died at Enfield, 10 February 1787. A letter from Drury to the Goldsmiths' Company dated 4 February 1798 is however addressed Turnham Green. In this he calls himself 'the oldest Liveryman but one' and suggests that the money expended on Company dinners should instead be handed over to the Government to set against the financial stress caused by the current war. As a result, on February 8 the Committee recommended that the Company should forbear giving any public dinner during the continuance of the war, except on Lord Mayor's Day and should subscribe the sum of £1,000 per annum during the same time to aid the exigencies of the State. Drury's claim to fame lies, however, in an entirely different and surprising field, since he was one of the greatest entomological collectors of his day. His papers are preserved in the Entomological Library of the Natural History Section of the British Museum and reveal both his prowess in this field and others aspects of his character and life. In 1788 he published a description of his collection with a view to sale (probably with the idea of raising funds after his second bankruptcy). He wrote: 'There may be in Holland collections more numerous... yet no collection abounds with such a wonderful variety in all the different genera as this'. Bernard Smith, *European Vision and South Pacific 1768-1850*, 1960, has described his achievements. In order to augment his collection Drury printed *Directions for collecting Insects in Foreign Countries*, which he circulated widely among travellers embarking for distant regions. He also published *Thoughts on the Precious Metals, particularly Gold, with directions to Travellers etc. for obtaining them, and seeking other natural riches from the rough diamond down to the pebblestone*. Among others he commissioned the artist John William Lewin to collect insects in the South Seas, who reached Sydney in January 1800. Drury provided him with instructions for collecting insects and equipment for the task to the value of 51½ guineas which Lewin undertook to repay with a collection of insects from New South Wales as soon as possible, but the latter wrote that he found difficulty in collecting although he achieved twenty drawings 'with the larvae and chrysalise and moths compleat for engraving'. The papers contain a number of lists of boxes of equipment sent to travellers departing overseas to collect for him in the same way. The collection 'The most capital Assemblage probably ever offered to Public Sale consisting of upwards of Eleven Thousand different specimens' was eventually sold at auction after Drury's death by King and Lochee, 38 King Street, Covent Garden, on Thursday May 23 1805 and two following days. The priced catalogue is preserved in the Drury papers and contains 305 lots of insects, many in considerable groups, followed by 37 lots of cabinets and books and totalled £903.13s.6d., a very high sum for the time. The Drury papers also contain his letter book 1761-83, with a remarkable variety of correspondence (Prof. T. D. A. Cockerell, *The Scientific Monthly*, January 1922, indexed by C. D. Sherborn, *Journal for the Society for the Bibliography of Natural History*). The letters throw occasional light on Drury's business matters. In 1769 we find him dunning Lewis Pantin II (q.v.) for the settlement of an account for £44. 17s. 1d. outstanding for two and a half years: 'believe me I should not ask this favour of you if I was not so beset with difficulties as I am just now'. Drury buys knife-blades from James Woolhouse of Sheffield in 1769 and 'Mr. Trickett Snr', Gibraltar, Sheffield in 1768. In 1764 he writes to 'Mr. Kandler in Jermyn Street' (Charles Kandler, q.v.):

'Upon examining the Articles of yr Acco. in my Daybook I find an omission of an Article of 20 shillings being ye 24th May 1762 whereof I have neglected charging you with ye blades & 3 pronged forks to 24 hafts that weighed 31 oz. 9 d.' To John Langlands of Newcastle, 16 March 1769: 'I am favoured with yours have made an Assay of ye piece of Silver wch is 15 dwt & 06 (? grains) better (sc. 'than standard) for wch I am offered 5.11 p. oz. I have tried several persons & none have offered more. . . .' Another client was the goldsmith John Locker of Dublin whom he supplied with sets of knives described as 'shell haft'.

Drury's bankruptcy in 1777 was due to the machinations earlier that year of two confidence tricksters William Tate and John Thomas Wheate, with a shady knight Sir William Desse in the background. A long statement by Drury in his papers describes how they obtained £7,500 worth of stock from him in return for the supposed reversion on an estate in Yorkshire on the assurance of a lawyer put forward by them that the estate existed and that Tate's title to its inheritance was sound. On the eve of being declared bankrupt Drury drew up an account of his Estate commencing 'My own Fortune brought into Trade £6000' and claiming a 'total profit in Trade' (i.e. turnover) from the money received during six and a half years from 1771-77 as £70,558 with 'Proffit on do. at 17 pc. £11,986' and 'Extraordinary proffit this year' £1,500, showing a total revenue of £21,386. It would seem that Drury continued business in spite of the apparently disastrous confidence trick, since Heal records him at 32 Strand, bankrupt again in 1786. His attempted sale of his collection may have been due to this later trouble. By 1794, however, he seems to have retired to Broxbourne where he drew up a family tree found in his papers, from which various details above are derived. With the tree is a drawing of his coat of arms, argent on a chief vert a cross Tau between two mullets pierced or.

The most personal of all the papers are two paper-covered packet-books for memoranda ranging from 1794 to 1805, containing recipes, particularly for home-made wines, odd accounts and descriptions of his state of health, his self-dosings and other trivia. The second book is signed Dru Drury, No 32 Strand, to which he seems to have returned to live with his son William. Suddenly in 1803 there is a violent deterioration in the writing and he died on or before 16 January 1804, when his son signed a statement in the book that he had opened it 'in which was Mr. Dru Drury's will & also three Bank Notes of one Pound each'. This is followed by the melancholy account of a post mortem: 'Dr. Andrew, Mr. Demayes and 2 other Gentleman this day open'd Mr. D. Drury's Bladder & took therefrom 3 Large oval Stones . . . which together weigh 6 oz. 2 dw. 10 gr. of Troy weight . . . ye largest Stones ever seen in ye Body af any human Being as acknowledged by the Gentlemen who took them out'.

DUBOIS, John Baptist (1185) No record of apprenticeship or freedom. Only mark entered as smallworker, 8 December 1803. Address: 9 Aris Buildings, Vineyard Gardens, Clerkenwell.

DUCK, Henry (985) Probably the son or grandson of Henry Duck who was free of the Goldsmiths' Company in 1680 but there is no record of apprenticeship or freedom suitable in date for the entry in question. Only mark entered as smallworker, 20 October 1735. Address: St. Ann's Lane, Aldersgate. Another Henry Duck, son of John Duck Citizen and Goldsmith of London, was apprenticed to Henry Duck 3 December 1735, and free 4 May 1748, which suggests a working period for the present maker prior to the entry of his mark.

*DUCOMMIEU, Louis (1911, 3470) No record of apprenticeship or freedom. Listed as spoonmaker, in partnership with Abraham Barrier (q.v.), at Rathbone Place, in the Parl. Report list 1773. Only mark entered as spoonmaker, 12 October 1775, one day after his partner had entered his mark. Address: Stephen Street, Rathbone Place. Heal records him here till. 1778. Listed by Evans as Huguenot (*Hug. Soc. Proc.*, 14).

DUKE, Isaac (1253) Son of Francis Duke of Fulham smith, apprenticed to Edward Feline on payment of £10 27 May 1725. Free 4 July 1744. Mark entered as largeworker, 15 June 1743. Address: Witch (?Wych) Street, near Drury Lane. It is presumably his obituary in *The Gentleman's Magazine*, under the date 19 July 1789, as follows: 'Suddenly while at supper with his family, Mr. Duke, silversmith of Quakers Buildings near Smithfield. He had engaged but the preceding evening for the business of a tradesman in the city, who had been given over by his physician and supposed to be at the point of death; but who, from the hour of Mr. Duke's decease, has experienced a recovery not less rapid than astonishing'.

DUMEE, Nicholas (669, 2086, 3176) No record of apprenticeship or freedom. First mark, with Francis Butty, unrecorded, presumably shortly after the 1758 register was started. Listed in partnership thus, as goldsmiths, in Parl. Report list, which bears the date 8 March 1773, and as bankrupt in the same month (*The Gentleman's Magazine*). Second mark, in partnership with William Holmes as plateworkers, 8 September 1773. Address: 12 Clerkenwell Green. Third mark alone, 13 April 1776. Address: 9 Clerkenwell Close. Holmes had entered a separate mark in the previous January, remaining at the address of the partnership. Heal records the partnership as lasting till 1779, but this may be due to some unchanged directory entry. Listed as Huguenot by Evans (*Hug. Soc. Proc.*, 14).

DUMONT, Lewis (1910) No record of apprenticeship or freedom. Only mark entered as smallworker, 4 December 1762. Address: Seven Dials. Listed there, as goldworker, in Parl. Report list 1773.

DUNCAN, William (3087) No record of apprenticeship or freedom. Only mark entered as smallworker, 20 January 1826. Address: 62 St. James' Street (Clerkenwell?).

DUNKIN, Joseph (1800) No record of apprenticeship or freedom. First mark entered as plateworker, 27 February 1824. Address: 24 Dean Street, Fetter Lane. Moved to 3 Pemberton Row and Second mark, 3 October 1827. Third mark, 18 February 1835. Moved to 1 Goldsmith Street, Gough Square, 15 March 1844.

*DUPONT, Louis (1909, 1912) No record of apprenticeship or freedom. It would seem almost certain that he was the Louis Dupont, son of Pierre du Pont, goldsmith at Poitiers in Poitou, married to Marie Rachel Migault at Leicester Fields Church 12 February 1737, and whose daughter 'Susane' was baptized 1 January 1738, at the Savoy Church, and son Stephen at the same 4 February 1739. First mark entered as largeworker, 20 September 1736. Address: Wardour Street, Soho. Second mark, 2 July

1739. Address: Compton Street, near St. Anne's, Soho. Heal records him here till bankruptcy in 1747. Dupont was described as 'late of St. Anne's Westminster now of the Island of St. Domingo merchant' in the apprenticeship of his son Stephen to Samuel Courtauld in 1753. Another son, Oliver John, was apprenticed to Isaac Chartier, 1754. Listed as Huguenot by Evans (*Hug. Soc. Proc.*, 14).

*DURANDEAU, John (1801) No record of apprenticeship or freedom. Mark entered as spoonmaker, 1 July 1824. Address: 9 Baynes Row, Cold Bath Square. Moved to 32 Charles Street, St. Luke's, 21 January 1826.

DUROUSSEAU, Matthieu (511) Free by redemption, 17 May 1704. Mark entered as smallworker, 27 August 1705. Address: Rider's Court, near Leicester Fields. Heal however records him as goldsmith, King's Head, Gerrard Street, Soho, from 1704-10.

DUTTON, Charles (295) No record of apprenticeship or freedom. Only mark entered as plateworker, 20 December 1790. Address: 2 Rose Street, Covent Garden.

DUTTON, Henry (984) No record of apprenticeship or freedom. Only mark entered as largeworker, 16 December 1754. Address: Green Street, Leicester Fields, where Heal records him till 1773, when he appears, as plateworker, in the Parl. Report list.

*DUTTON, John (1245) Son of Betham Dutton late of Rotherhithe in the County of Surrey sawyer deceased, apprenticed to Thomas Burch of Moorfields cordwainer, Citizen and Goldsmith 5 February 1766. Freedom unrecorded. Mark entered as smallworker, 7 August 1776. Address: 6 Dartmouth Row, Westminster. The description of his master Burch as cordwainer suggests a possibility that he specialized in leather-covered goods with silver mounts, in which case Dutton might have continued in the same field, but this is conjecture.

DUTTON, Samuel (2503, 2506) No record of apprenticeship or freedom. First mark entered, in partnership with William Hattersley as plateworkers, 4 February 1822. Address: 7 Blewets Buildings. Second mark alone, 8 May 1823. Address: 99 Strand.

*DYMOND, Edward (522-3, 564-5) No record of apprenticeship or freedom. Four marks, two Sterling and two New Standard, entered at the same time, 1 December 1722 (a most unusual procedure suggesting high hopes of immediate business!). Address: St. Mary Hill, near Billingsgate. In spite of his enthusiasm for marks, little seems to have survived of his work.

E

*EAST, John (525, 1266) Son of John East Citizen and Turner of London, apprenticed to George Garthorne 7 August 1689. Free, 19 August 1696. First mark entered as largeworker, 23 April 1697 (the only one, apart from that of John Sutton (q.v.), with an actual date given in that year). Address: Foster Lane. Livery, October 1708. Probably identifiable with John East of St. John Zachary, married to Mary Wilkins of St. Ann, Aldersgate, at St. Lawrence Jewry, 18 August 1709, and churchwarden of St. John Zachary, 1709 and 1710. Signatory as 'working goldsmith' to the petition complaining of the competition of 'necessitous strangers', December 1711, and to that against assaying work of foreigners not having served seven years apprenticeship, February 1716. Second (Sterling) mark, 24 May 1721. Heal records him as plateworker, Foster Lane, 1697-1703: London, 1704-20; and St. Ann's Lane, Aldersgate, 1727-34. His father, since described as of the Turners' Company must be other than the John East, goldsmith and banker, at the Sun without Temple Bar, 1663-88, who is presumably identifiable with the Prime Warden of the Goldsmiths' Company in 1697, and probably the son of John East, goldsmith, Maiden Lane, 1641, both recorded by Heal.

EASTWICK, Adrian (29) Free of the Girdlers' Company by redemption 23 June 1772 (the same day as Charles Aldridge and Henry Green in the same company). First mark entered as smallworker 8 March 1768. Address: Cross Key Court, Little Britain, where he so appears in the Parl. Report list

BIOGRAPHICAL DICTIONARY

1773. Second mark, 23 November 1778. Address: 102 Aldersgate Street, where Heal records him till 1784. It seems probable however that he was dead by June 1782, when his widow Henrietta (below) entered her first mark.

EASTWICK, Henrietta (991-2) Presumed widow of Adrian (above). First mark entered as smallworker, 26 June 1782. Address: 102 Aldersgate Street. Second mark, 12 September 1789. Third, in partnership with William Eastwick (? son), 11 September 1802, same address.

EASTWICK, William (992) Son of Adrian and Henrietta (above), apprenticed to his mother 6 August 1794. Free, 4 November 1801. First mark entered as smallworker, in partnership with Henrietta, 11 September 1802. Second mark as smallworker, 19 October 1805 (Section IV).

EATON, John (1270-1) Son of John Eaton of Maidford in the County of Northampton husbandman, apprenticed to Edward Beddow Citizen and Goldsmith 3 October 1738 and turned over to Samuel Eaton 2 May 1745 (see below). Free, 11 December 1745. Livery, March 1758. First mark entered as smallworker, 15 July 1760. Address: Gutter Lane. Second mark, 18 April 1761. Third, 2 December 1762. Resigned from Livery 29 May 1767.

EATON, Samuel (2509-10, 3793) Son of George Eaton of Scaldwell in Northamptonshire husbandman, apprenticed to Robert Elliott of the Leathersellers' Company 13 December 1725. Free, 26 January 1733. Mark entered as smallworker, 8 March 1736. Address: Huggin Alley, Gutter Lane. 'Free Leatherseller.' Second mark, 8 June 1738. Third mark, 5 February 1759. Fourth, 13 October 1761. Fifth, 28 August 1762. Sixth, 3 August 1765. Seventh, 30 March 1767. Eighth, 17 September 1767. Ninth, 16 March 1768. Heal records him as plateworker, Huggin Court or Lane, 1759. It is possible to see a slight variation in the signature from the 1759 entry, which, after a lapse of twenty-one years from the previous one, may indicate a son of the same name, but there is no apprenticeship record to support this.

*EATON, William (3105-6) No record of apprenticeship or freedom. Perhaps identifiable with, or the son of the William Eaton who entered a mark as bucklemaker, 19 March 1781. Address: 6 Albion Buildings, Aldersgate Street. Second mark as such, 22 April 1784. Address: 3 Adle (sic) Street, Wood Street, with further marks 1786 and 1801 without change of address (Section VIII). First mark as plateworker entered 18 May 1813. Address: 30 Addler Street. Second mark, 5 March 1824. Third (two sizes), 18 October 1825. Moved to 16 Jewin Crescent, Jewin Street, 20 December 1825. Fourth mark, 5 September 1828. Moved to 2 Lovels Court, Paternoster Row, 10 December 1828. Fifth mark (two sizes), 31 December 1828. Sixth, 30 September 1830. Seventh, as spoonmaker (two sizes), 2 January 1834. Eighth (four punches), 27 January 1836. Ninth, on removal to 16 Jewin Crescent ('Manufactory and residence'), 2 June 1837. Tenth mark (two sizes), 22 February 1840. New Manufactory at 32 Banner Street, St. Luke's, 1 October 1844. Although only styled spoonmaker from 1834 onwards it seems probable that this was his special trade. The address in Lovels Court in 1828 suggests a connection, if only temporary, with the firm of Eley, Fearn and Chawner at the next number.

EBBORNE, Matthew (2020) No record of apprenticeship or freedom. Only mark entered as 'Turner and Snuff Box Maker', 20 December 1758. Address: Pittfield Street, Hoxton, where he appears as smallworker in the Parl. Report list 1773. A John Ebborne son of Golding Ebborne deceased, was apprenticed to John King as plateworker 1787.

ECKFO[U]RD, John I (545, 1264) Son of William Eckford of Berwick on Tweed smith deceased, apprenticed to John Whitfield tobacconist St. Martin's Lane of the Drapers' Company 12 April 1682. He was also entered in the Goldsmiths' Company apprentice register as bound to Anthony Nelme 11 September 1682, and the entry scored out. Free by Service, 29 June 1698 (a curiously long interval). Mark entered as largeworker, 31 December 1698. Address: Red Lyon Court, Drury Lane. 'Free Draper'. Second (Sterling) mark, undated, c. June 1720. Appears in the Draper's Company quarterage book as tobacconist, St. Martin's Lane, and silversmith, Covent Garden and it is significant that his mark is often found on tobacco-boxes of the period. Buried; 14 July 1730, St. Paul's, Covent Garden. Janett Eckford (presumably his widow) was buried there 12 December 1736.

ECKFOURD, John II (548, 1269, 1276) Son of John Eckfourd Citizen and Goldsmith of London (but see above, the latter presumably an assumption or error of laxity on the Clerk's part), apprenticed to John Fawdery 24 January 1712. Turned over 14 February same year to John Eckfourd and again 29 June 1714 to Philip Rollos. Free, 4 July 1723. Two marks entered as largeworker (Sterling and New Standard), 23 June 1725. Address: Three Tun Court, Red Cross Street. Third mark, 20 June 1739. His son Joseph apprenticed to Henry Brind, 3 September 1746, and another John to John Swift, 11 January 1753, when it is clear Eckfourd was still alive.

EDE, J(ame)s (1278) James son of Henry Ede late of the Strand in the County of Middlesex silversmith deceased, apprenticed to Solomon Hougham Goldsmith of Aldersgate Street, 5 March 1794. Free, 5 January 1803. Mark entered as largeworker, in partnership with Alexander Hewat, 6 December 1808. Address: 12 King Street, Goswell Street. Partnership apparently dissolved by 3 November 1810, when Hewat (q.v.) entered a separate mark at the same address.

EDEN, Moses (563, 2022) Son of Moses Eden of London cordwinder, apprenticed to Henry Bance 13 June 1712 on payment of £14. Free, 2 July 1719. First mark entered as smallworker, 8 July 1719. Second (Sterling) mark, 22 June 1720. Address: Foster Lane, where Heal records him as insolvent, 1725.

EDGE, James (561) Son of John Edge late Citizen and Innholder of London deceased, apprenticed to Thomas Demycke 25 August 1680. Free, 30 September 1687. Mark entered as largeworker, undated, probably on commencement of register April 1697. Address: Foster Lane. Chaffers wrongly read name as Edgar and address Gutter Lane, followed by Jackson and Heal.

EDINGTON, James Charles (1794) Son of James Edington of Berwick Street Soho plasterer, apprenticed to William Ker Reid of Carey Street Lincoln's Inn working goldsmith 5 November 1817. Free, 1 December 1824. Mark entered as plateworker, 6 February 1828. Address: 43 Berwick Street, Soho. Second mark, 10 November 1837. Moved to 23 Leicester Square, undated. Third mark, 22 January 1845. Fourth, 3 May 1854. Fifth, 10 December 1856. Sixth, 20 May 1858.

EDINGTON, John (1274-5, 1805) No record of apprenticeship or freedom. First mark entered as smallworker, 16 May 1799. Address: 10 Portland Street, Soho Square. Second mark (two punches), 5 December 1804. Third, 18 August 1806. Described as goldsmith, at same address, in the apprenticeship of his son John James to Stephen Gaubert, 1811. For the son see Section VII (IE and JJE).

EDLIN, Samuel (559-60, 2508) Son of Samuel Edlin of Watford in the County of Hertfordshire salesman, apprenticed to Matthew Cuthbert 20 April 1694. Free, 4 June 1701. Livery, October 1712. First and second marks entered 5 August 1704. Address: Foster Lane. Signed petition against assaying work of foreigners not having served seven years apprenticeship, February 1716. Third mark (Sterling), 19 September 1720. Heal records him as goldsmith, Corner of St. Mary Axe, 1712-14, as does Hilton Price in *London Bankers*. Heal adds Wood Street 1724-7, and Old Bailey 1734.

EDMONDS, Stephen (562) Son of Richard Edmonds of Oare in the County of Wiltshire, yeoman, apprenticed to John Spackman 29 October 1691. Free, 17 May 1700. Livery, October 1708. Mark entered as largeworker, 13 June 1700. Address: Pall Mall.

EDWARDS, Edward I (574, 1279) Son of John Edwards III of Bridgewater Square London silversmith (q.v.) apprenticed to John Mewburn of Hare Court Aldersgate Goldsmith 7 November 1797. Free, 6 March 1811. Mark entered as plateworker, in partnership with his father John, 10 June 1811. Address: 1 Bridgewater Square. Second and third marks alone, 19 September 1816, same address. Moved to 48 Banner Street, St. Luke's, 5 March 1823. Moved to 5 Radnor Street, St. Luke's, 18 March 1825.

EDWARDS, Edward II (574) No record of apprenticeship or freedom. Probably son of above. Mark entered as smallworker 11 April 1828. Address: 42 Fetter Lane. Moved to 60 Red Lion Street, 18 June 1829. Second mark, 12 May 1840. Third mark, 13 January 1841.

EDWARDS, Griffith (792, 795) Son of John Edwards I, free by patrimony, 21 April 1737. First mark entered as largeworker, 8 January 1733. Address: Hemlock Court, near Temple Bar (as his father in 1712). Second mark, 4 July 1739, same address. Heal records him at this address, being in Little Sheer Lane, Lincoln's Inn Fields from 1729-39.

EDWARDS, Henry John (1019) No record of apprenticeship or freedom. Only mark entered as smallworker, 12 January 1832. Address: 14 Little Britain.

*EDWARDS, James I (524) No record of apprenticeship or freedom. Only mark entered as smallworker, 30 July 1735. Address: Corner of St. Martin's Lane, Cannon Street. Heal records one of this name as goldsmith and jeweller, 149 Holborn Bars, 1767, but the connection appears doubtful.

EDWARDS, James II (1809) Probably son of William Edwards of Aldersgate Street silversmith, apprenticed to Thomas Rowe of Aldersgate Street silver polisher 5 May 1813 and turned over on the former's death 6 May 1818 to Thomas George Rowe. Mark entered as plateworker, 7 July 1824. Address: 92 Long Lane, Aldersgate Street.

EDWARDS, John I (572) Son of John Edwards late of Bangor in the County of Flint yeoman, apprenticed to Benjamin Pyne 2 April 1688. Free, 8 April 1695. Mark entered as largeworker, undated, probably April 1697 on commencement of register. Address: Gutter Lane. John Edwards of St. Leonard, Foster Lane, and Mary Terrill of the parish of St. Martin Outwich, married at the latter church, 13 May 1700. He is presumably the John Edwards, silversmith, recorded by Heal in Hemlock Court, Little Sheer Lane, Lincoln's Inn Fields, 1712 (see Griffith Edwards, above).

*EDWARDS, John II (566, 573, 630, 1267-8, 1277) Son of John Edwards of Oswestry Shropshire innholder, apprenticed to Thomas Prichard of the Grocers' Company (q.v.) 9 March 1708 for seven years, but did not take up his freedom till 7 November 1723, when the entry is witnessed by John Bache Citizen and Goldsmith (q.v.). Signatory as journeyman to the petition against assaying the work of foreigners not having served seven years apprenticeship, February 1716. Two marks (Sterling and New Standard) entered as largeworker, in partnership with George Pitches, 6 December 1723. Address: St. Swithin's Lane, near Lombard Street. Third and fourth marks alone, 27 April 1724, when described as 'Grocer'. Fifth mark, 9 August 1739, same address, where Heal records him till 1753.

A sixth mark, entered in new position, also reads John Edwards, St. Swithin's Lane, 1 November 1753, but for the first time the signature of the Christian name reads John as against Jn° for the previous entries. On the other hand the neat handwriting appears the same. We must, however, allow the possibility that this mark (1268) is that of a son. Edwards is probably the — Edwards, Subordinate Goldsmith to the King, who appears in the Jewel Office Records from 1723-1743 (Major General H. W. D. Sitwell, 'The Jewel Office and the Royal Goldsmiths' *Arch. Journ.* CXVII, p. 154-5). John, son of John and Catherine Healy, lodger at Mr. Edwards, silversmith in the parish of St. Mary Woolnoth, was baptized in the same church, 9 February 1745, and Sarah and Dinah, twin daughters of Stephen and Sarah Willson, lodgers at Mr. Edwards, the silversmith, baptized 27 May 1747, at the same. Is one wrong in suspecting that the Christian names in this last family sound very like those of Negro or mulatto servants? If so an establishment of some considerable status seems indicated. His work at best reaches remarkable quality of execution, as in the large rococo inkstand of 1744 (formerly in the Butlin Collection) and the outstanding tureen, with dolphin handles and crab finial, of 1737 (formerly in the Hurst Collection).

EDWARDS, John III (1273, 1279, 1282) Son of Edwards Edwards Citizen and Carpenter of London, free by patrimony of the Carpenters' Company 7 May 1782 and described as Citizen and Carpenter in the apprenticeship of his son John to William Frisbee 1789. First mark entered as plateworker, 24 November 1788. Address: 44 Jewin Street, Cripplegate. Second mark, in partnership with William Frisbee, 12 April 1791, at 48 Jewin Street. Third mark alone, 6 January 1792. Address: 4 Jewin Street. Moved to 1 Bridgwater Square, Barbican, 2 August 1797. Fourth mark, in partnership with his son Edward Edwards (q.v.), 10 June 1811, same address. The surviving work bearing any of his marks shows a high standard of design and execution. He seems to have produced a number of fine silver-gilt tea-services and other domestic plate. As partner with Frisbee for a short time he must have been in the circle which included the young Paul Storr.

EDWARDS, Richard (558, 2307) Son or Richard Edwards Citizen and Carpenter of

London, apprenticed to Benjamin Watts 1 July 1707. Free, 6 April 1715, Mark entered as largeworker, 13 August 1716. Address: Gutter Lane. Second (Sterling) mark, 25 November 1723. Address: Princes Street, near Leicester Fields, the latter address not recorded by Heal.

EDWARDS, Thomas (2745) Perhaps Thomas William son of John Edwards of Wimbledon taylor, apprenticed to John Robins of Aldersgate Street Goldsmith 3 June 1789. Freedom unrecorded. First mark entered as plateworker, 21 August 1816. Address: 7 Frog Lane, Islington. Moved to 19 Winsor Place, City Road, 19 October 1816, and to 4 Wellington Street, Goswell Street, 24 February 1820. Second mark, 25 October 1822. Address: 21 Wellington Street. Third, 1 November 1822. Fourth, 10 April 1823. Moved to 23 Ratcliff Row, 18 January 1836.

EDWARDS, William J. (3099) No record of apprenticeship or freedom. First mark entered as goldworker, 10 December 1774. Address: 21 Winchester Street. Second mark (two punches), 13 January 1778. He may be identifiable with William John Edwards recorded by Heal as goldsmith and jeweller, 36 Coleman Street, 1781-4; and 26 Coleman Street, 1790-6. There is also William Edwards, goldsmith, watchmaker and hardware-man (from Fetter Lane), Staples Inn Gate, Holborn Bars, 1775-83; and as goldsmith and jeweller, 121 Newgate Street, 1790-6. Evan Edwards, son of William Edwards, silversmith, of Coleman Street was admitted to St. Paul's School, 9 July 1793.

EDWARDS, William (3100) Son of Edward Edwards, apprenticed to his father as engraver 1 August 1792 on the same day as Joseph Guest to the same. First mark entered as smallworker, 11 December 1800. Address: 33 Goswell Street. Second mark, 22 September 1809. Moved to 4 George Row, St. Luke's, 4 April 1815. Moved to 5 Percival Street, Clerkenwell, 20 January 1819. Third mark, 11 April 1823. Moved to 42 Fetter Lane, 21 July 1826. Livery, July 1846. Died 28 February 1860. He may be the William Edwards of Little Britain, goldsmith, Citizen and Goldsmith, to whom John Jones was apprenticed, 1821.

ELEY, Charles (298, 3110) Son of William Eley I (q.v.), apprenticed to his father as silversmith 1 May 1811. Free, 4 November 1818. First mark entered as plateworker, in partnership with his brothers William and Henry, 14 July 1824. Address: 1 Lovell's Court, Paternoster Row. Second mark alone as spoonmaker, 19 January 1825. Address: 2 Lovell Court. Died 15 November 1785, aged seventy-eight and was buried at St. Lawrence, Isle of Wight, where his son was vicar (information, R. J. Malden Esq., great-grandson of the latter). See also Henry Eley, below.

ELEY, Henry (3110) Son of William Eley I (q.v.), apprenticed to his father 2 February 1814. Free, 6 February 1822. Mark entered as plateworker, in partnership with his brothers William II and Charles, 14 July 1824. Address: 1 Lovell's Court, Paternoster Row. Later took Holy Orders and became in 1841 vicar of Broomfield, Essex, eventually retiring to Brighton (information, R. J. Malden, as above).

*ELEY, William I (3101, 3111-2, 3114, 3871) Son of George Eley of Foston in the County of Derby yeoman, apprenticed to William Fearn 7 November 1770 on payment of £25. Free, 4 November 1778. Mark entered as spoonmaker, in partnership with George Pierrepont, 11 November 1777. Address: 46 Little Bartholomew Close. Second mark, alone as smallworker, 3 November 1778. Address: 4 New Street, Cloth Fair. Third mark, as such, 1 December 1778. Address: 2 George Street, St. Martin's Le Grand. Took out patent for 'Eley's New Constructed Buckles', 16 August 1784, then described as of Clerkenwell Green, bucklemaker. Fourth mark, as bucklemaker, 24 April 1785. Address: 14 Clerkenwell Green. Fifth and sixth marks as such, 12 March 1790 and 5 May 1795, same address. Seventh mark, in partnership with William Fearn as plateworker, 4 January 1797, same address. Eighth mark, with the same, 29 January 1802. Address: 1 Lovell's Court, Paternoster Row. Livery, October 1806. Ninth mark, in new partnership with William Fearn and William Chawner, 10 April 1808. Tenth mark, reverting to partnership with Fearn only, 6 October 1814. The signature to the next mark entry under the same heading is clearly that of William Eley II (q.v.). As well as the addresses above, Heal also records him as bucklemaker, Aylesbury Street (Clerkenwell), 1782. Died March 1824.

*ELEY, William II (3102, 3109, 3110, 3113)

Son of William Eley I, apprenticed to his father at Lovell's Court Paternoster Row 3 February 1808. Free, 1 March 1815. Livery, April 1816. First mark, in partnership with William Fearn, 14 May 1824. Address: 1 Lovell's Court. Second mark, in partnership with his brothers Charles and Henry, as plateworkers, 14 July 1824. Third mark alone as plateworker, 19 January 1825. Address: 3 Lovell's Court, Fourth-sixth marks, 22 June 1825, 20 June 1826 and 5 December 1826. Died June 1841. The business may have been taken over in 1829 by John and Thomas Cutmore (q.v.) at the same address.

ELIN, Paul (2173) No record of apprenticeship or freedom. Only mark entered as smallworker, 26 March 1736. Address: 'at the sign of the Parrot Compton Street, St. Ann's, Soho.' A Francis William Elin, son of Paul Elin of Kensington gentleman, was apprenticed to John Faulkner in 1764, which may indicate the same in a retired state.

ELKIN, Benjamin (164) No record of apprenticeship or freedom. Only mark entered as plateworker, 3 November 1817. Address: 8 Artillery Place, Finsbury Square.

ELLERBY, William (3103-4) No record of apprenticeship or freedom. First mark entered as smallworker, 15 June 1802. Address: 8 Ave Maria Lane, Ludgate Street. Second mark, 9 April 1804. Third mark (two sizes), 13 August 1810.

ELLERTON, Thomas (2744, 2748) No record of apprenticeship or freedom. First mark entered as plateworker, in partnership with Richard Sibley, 14 November 1803. Address: 14 Bartholomew Close. Second mark, alone as largeworker, 23 April 1805. Address: 1 Falcon Square.

ELLIOT, Robert (613, 2308) Son of Edward Elliott late of Witney in the County of Oxon. fellmonger deceased, apprenticed to Abraham Pope (q.v.) of the Leathersellers' Company 24 June 1708. Free, 27 January 1715. First mark entered as smallworker, 15 February 1716. Address: Carey Lane. 'Free Leatherseller'. Second (Sterling) mark, 17 June 1720. Heal records him as bucklemaker and small plateworker, Gutter Lane, 1723-4. There is clearly a connection between his membership of the Leathersellers and his speciality as bucklemaker.

ELLIOTT William (1762, 3107) Son of William Elliott of Warwick Lane, London plateworker, apprenticed to Richard Gardner of Silver Street Golden Square Middlesex goldsmith, Citizen and Goldsmith on payment of £7. 14s of the charity of the Worshipful Company of Goldsmiths, 7 May 1787. Free, 1 April 1795. Mark entered as plateworker, in partnership with J. W. Story, 6 October 1809. Address: 25 Compton Street, Clerkenwell. Second mark, alone, 7 September 1813, same address. Described as silversmith in the apprenticeship to him of James Parkin, 6 October 1819 at the same address, and still there 1823 (apprenticeship of John Evans) and 5 January 1825, when his son Richard William was also bound to him. Livery, January 1822. Died between 1853 and 1855.

ELLIS, George (604, 791) Son of Robert 'Elles' of the parish of St. Bride's London joyner, apprenticed to William Grosvenor, goldsmith and free of the Waxchandlers Company, 6 August 1686. Free, 30 June 1696. Two marks (New and Sterling Standard) entered 15 November 1721. Address: 'at the Ring in Wine Office Court Fleet Street'. 'Free Wax Chandler'.

ELLIS, Thomas (2743) No record of apprenticeship or freedom. Mark entered as plateworker (two sizes), 20 April 1780. Address: 9 Cow Cross. The Parl. Report list of 1773 shows him as plateworker, at Cow Cross, and he must probably therefore have entered an earlier mark in the missing register before 1773.

EMANUEL, Joseph (1808) No record of apprenticeship or freedom. First mark entered as plateworker, 13 November 1820. Address: 32 Muswell Street, Goodmans Fields. Moved to 3 Upper Street, Smithfield, 4 January 1821. Third mark, 11 January 1833. Address: 39 Nottingham Place, Charlotte Street, Whitechapel. Fourth mark, 29 April 1834. Address: 9 King Street, Aldgate.

EMANUEL, Michael (2023) No record of apprenticeship or freedom. First mark entered as plateworker, in partnership with Morris Emanuel, 25 November 1825. Address: 1 Bevis Marks, Camomile Street. Second mark, 29 July 1828. Third mark, 25 October 1830, same address.

EMANUEL, Morris (2023) See above.

EMANUEL, Moses (2021) No record of apprenticeship or freedom. Only mark entered as spoonmaker, 11 March 1800. Address: 23 Hanway Street, Oxford Street. Signs with cross.

*EMES, John (977, 1806-7) Presumably son of William Emes of Bowbridge Field near Derby surveyor, apprenticed to William Woollett of Green Street, Leicester Fields Citizen and Goldsmith, engraver on payment of £105 (one of the largest premiums recorded in the apprentice registers) 7 October 1778. Free, 5 July 1786. First mark (two sizes), entered as plateworker, in partnership with Henry Chawner (q.v.), 27 August 1796. Address: Amen Corner. Second and third marks alone, 10 January 1798. Fourth mark 21 July 1802. Presumably dead by 30 June 1808, when Rebeccah and William Emes entered their mark at the same address. His work, mostly tea and coffee-services with some tankards, shows a taste for elegant design and fine finish.

*EMES, Rebeccah (2309-10) Presumed widow of John Emes (above). First mark (two sizes) entered as plateworker, in partnership with William Emes, 30 June 1808. Address: Amen Corner. The mark was entered and signed by William Emes by virtue of a power of attorney, perhaps indicating that he was a brother of John and his executor. In any case this apparent partnership was short-lived and seems to have been a stop-gap measure, since on 14 October 1808 William entered, again by power of attorney, Rebeccah's second mark, this time in partnership with Edward Barnard (q.v.). Third mark, with the same, 29 April 1818. Fourth, 20 February 1821. Fifth, 29 October 1825. The firm was unquestionably one of the largest working in their period with wide connections in the trade. The surviving ledgers show that they supplied plate to Rundell, Bridge and Rundell and Cattle and Barber of York with racecups. For their continuation see under Barnard.

EMES, William (2310) See above.

ENGLAND, Thomas (626, 2741, 2746) Son of John England of Cranford in Middlesex gentleman, apprenticed to John Martin Stocker (or Stockar, q.v.) 4 August 1714 on payment of £30. Turned over 10 October 1716 to Samuel Margas (q.v.) butcher by Comp^d (?) 'lives in St. Martin's Lane'. Free, 2 October 1728. Two marks (Sterling and New Standard) entered as largeworker, 26 August 1725. Address: Long Acre, over against the Vine Tavern. Third mark, 30 July 1739. Address: Fleet Ditch. 'Free Goldsmith'. Moved to Newgate Street, 25 March 1740. Probably the Thomas England buried 31 May 1747 at Christchurch, Newgate.

ENGLAND, William (627) Son of William England late of Cirencester in the County of Gloucester woolcomber deceased, apprenticed to John Sutton 24 September 1703. Mark entered as largeworker, in partnership with John Vaen, 22 July 1714. Address: Bow Lane. Heal also records William England, goldsmith, parish of St. Anne's, Westminster, as insolvent 1748.

ENGLIE, James (1263) Free of the Haberdashers' Company by redemption, 1 May 1713. Mark entered as smallworker, 29 June 1713. Address: Fetter Lane. 'Free Haberdasher'.

*ESTERBROOK, William (625, 3108) No record of apprenticeship or freedom. First mark entered as plateworker, in partnership with Edward Middlecott, 29 August 1816. Address: 4 Long Acre. Second mark, alone as spoonmaker, 4 November 1817. Address: 4 Castle Street, Long Acre. Moved to 20 Hanover Street, Long Acre, 3 July 1822. Third mark, 15 October 1824. Fourth, 16 September 1834. Address: 13 Denzell Street, Clare Market. His son John apprenticed to Charles Mullins, engraver, in 1831.

*EVANS, George (793) No record of apprenticeship or freedom. Only mark entered as smallworker, 4 April 1764. Address: Fore Street, where he appears as bucklemaker in the Parl. Report list 1773. It was perhaps his father, or more likely grandfather, recorded without Christian name as silversmith and bucklemaker, Fore Street, Moorfields who died aged 101, 2 October 1794 (*The Gentleman's Magazine*, p. 965).

*EVANS, James (1272, 1280) No record of apprenticeship or freedom. First mark entered as smallworker, in partnership with John Russel (q.v.), 31 August 1761. Address: Golden Head, Greek Street, Soho. Second mark alone, 7 February 1763, same address. He appears here as James Morley Evans, goldworker, in the Parl. Report list 1773, where he is also mentioned as having been prosecuted in 1770 for making gold watchchains 'worse than standard'.

EVANS, John I (2672) Perhaps the son of George Evans of Swedeland Court, Tower Hill gentleman, apprenticed to Joseph Clarke of Bunhill Row Goldsmith 5 January 1803. Mark entered as plateworker, in partnership with Samuel Wheatley, 27

April 1810. Address: 3 Old Street, Goswell Street.

EVANS, John II (1810) Son of Benjamin Evans of Foster Buildings St. Luke's cordwainer, apprenticed to Thomas Johnson of Blue Anchor Alley Bunhill Row working silversmith 7 March 1821. Free, 7 December 1853, a long delay probably explained by the fact that he seems to have continued working for Johnson until the latter retired or died since his first mark entered 15 April 1834 at 26 Anchor Alley, Bunhill Row. No further mark entered, but the following moves: 14 January 1836, 7 Norman Street, St. Luke's; 15 October 1840, 111 Bunhill Row; 7 July 1842, 3 Wenlock Street, Old Street; 15 February 1854, 30 Russell Place, New North Road, Islington.

EVANS, Thomas (2742, 2747) Probably son of Thomas Evans of Aldersgate Street plateworker Citizen and Goldsmith, apprenticed to his father 8 January 1765 and turned over the same day to Thomas Wootton brazier in consideration of £8. 5s. of the charity of the Goldsmiths' Company. It is probably the elder Evans whom Heal records as spoonmaker, East Harding Street, 1766, and who appears in the Parl. Report list of 1773 as spoonmaker, Wood Street, but no mark is recorded for him before this date, probably because of the missing register. It may be possible that the following marks are those of the father rather than the son. First mark entered as spoonmaker, 11 March 1774. Address: 6 Barbican. Moved to 14 Giltspur Street, 23 September 1774; to 10 York Street, Covent Garden, 16 October 1775. Second mark (small), 30 December 1776. Appears as silversmith, Covent Garden, bankrupt 1779 (*The Gentleman's Magazine*). Third mark, 14 November 1779. Address: Rotherhithe Road, near Chiney Hall. Fourth mark, 22 November 1782. Address: 56 Houndsditch. Fifth mark as plateworker, 4 December 1782, same address. Moved to 32 Red Lion Square, Clerkenwell, 8 February 1783; to 20 Featherstone Street, near Bunhill Row, 7 January 1784. Sixth mark as smallworker, in partnership with Jacob Levi, 20 February 1784, same address. Seventh mark alone, 11 September 1784. Eighth, 11 May 1786. Ninth as smallworker, 11 November 1792. Address: 6 Royal Row, Lambeth. In all these entries the signature is unquestionably the same, with a distinctive Thos.

*EVERIT, John (647) Only mark entered as smallworker, 6 October 1701. Address: at Howells Coffee House in Gutter Lane. 'Free of the Sadlers Company'. His signature does not appear on the Company's freedom roll starting in 1684 and he was therefore probably already free by that date. Nothing more is known as most of the records of this company were destroyed in 1940.

EWESDIN, Thomas (650) Son of Thomas of Hitchin in the County of Hertford maltster, apprenticed to Henry Graunte 6 April 1703. Free, 7 May 1712. Mark entered as largeworker, 6 May 1713. Address: St. Martin's Le Grand. Probably the Thomas Everdon (so printed) married to Mary Barnard, 17 November 1715, at Christchurch, Newgate. Heal records him as plateworker, London, till 1721.

EWINGS, George Davis (794) No record of apprenticeship or freedom. Probably son of George Ewings, bucklemaker, 1797-1804 (Section VIII). Only mark entered as smallworker, 29 March 1828. Address: 14 Yardley Street, Clerkenwell.

F

FAIR, Thomas (2756) Son of Daniel Fair of the parish of St. Leonard's Shoreditch forkblade maker, apprenticed to William Phelps 6 July 1750 and turned over to Edward Hunt Goldsmith 6 June 1752 and to William Portal 23 January 1756. Free, 1 February 1764. Mark entered as smallworker, 3 October 1768. Address: 15 Castle Falcon Yard, Aldersgate Street. Moved to 'Angle of Porter Alley, Golding Lane', 23 April 1771. Appears as haftmaker, Golden Lane, in the Parl. Report list 1773.

FAIRBAIRN, Thomas (2754) No record of apprenticeship or freedom. First mark entered as plateworker, 15 December 1823. Address: 13 Little Wild Street. Second mark as smallworker, 14 April 1836, same address. Third mark, 29 April 1836.

FA[I]RBROTHER, Edward (583) Son of Robert Fairbrother of Abingdon in County of Berkshire locksmith, apprenticed to Joseph Lewis bucklemaker of Foster Lane 3 March 1779. First mark as bucklemaker (before freedom), 24 May 1792. Address: Clerkenwell Green (Section VIII). Free, 5 February 1794, as silversmith. Second mark as smallworker entered 11 March 1793. Address: 6 Paul's Alley, Huggin Lane. Third mark as plateworker, 18 September 1804. Address: 13 Bull and Mouth Street.

FARETTES, Peter (663) No record of apprenticeship or freedom. Only mark entered as smallworker, 15 June 1716. Address: St. Martin's Lane. 'Free Scrivener'. No applicable records of this company exist.

FARGUS, John (2736) No record of apprenticeship or freedom. Only mark entered as smallworker, in partnership with Thomas Dee, 1 May 1830. Address: 8 Sherard Street, Golden Square.

FARNELL, John (661, 1283, 3565) Son of William Farnell of Oakingham (?Wokingham) in the County of Berkshire blacksmith apprenticed to Thomas Ash 25 October 1706. Free, 3 February 1714. Mark entered as largeworker, 26 June 1714. Address: St. Ann's Lane. Second (Sterling) mark, 20 June 1720. Heal also records him at the Golden Ball, Corner of Plum-tree Court, Holbourn Bridge, 1729. Livery, March 1728. For a relation of a later generation see Edward Fernell. The ascription by Jackson of no. 3565 to John Fainell can only be a misprint since no maker of this name can be traced.

***FARRELL, Edward** (584–5) No record of apprenticeship or freedom. First mark entered as plateworker, 27 April 1813. Address: 18 King's Head Court, Holborn Hill. Second mark, 20 May 1813. Moved to 24 Bridge Street, Covent Garden, 26 September 1818. Third mark (two sizes), 17 March 1819. The mark of this maker, of whom as yet no more is known than stated above, is found on some of the most unusual productions of the Regency period, generally conceived in a kind of revival rococo style. He had a large output of heavy tea-services decorated with Dutch peasant scenes in the style of Teniers, and he also produced large ornamental plate of which perhaps the most remarkable is the Hercules candelabrum, made for the Duke of York in 1822 (Duke of York Sale, Christie's, 1827, Sir Clive Milnes Gaskell Collection, Christie's, 1967). It seems probable that he was the chief manufacturer for Thomas Hamlet, for whom no mark was entered, but whose stamped retailer's name is found on some pieces of this nature. For a sketch of Hamlet's career see W. Chaffers, *Gilda Aurifabrorum*.

FARREN, Ann (31) Presumably widow of Thomas Farren. Mark entered as largeworker, by virtue of a letter of attorney, by Thomas Whipham (q.v.) formerly apprenticed to Farren, 19 'Xber' (?December) 1743. Address: St. Swithin's Lane.

***FARREN, Thomas** (666, 2749, 2755, 3564) Son of John Farren of Tewkesbury in the County of Gloucester maltster, apprenticed to John Denny 8 April 1695. Free, 3 October 1707. First mark entered as largeworker, 16 October 1707. Address: 'Sweeting Lane'. Second (Sterling) mark, 11 November 1720. Address: 'St. Swethings Lane'. Third mark, 15 June 1739. Heal records him as plateworker, Unicorn, Swithin's Lane near the Post Office, from 1703 to 1741. His name appears variously as Farrar and Farrer, but apprentice and mark entries are spelt Farren. Livery, 1721. Court, 1731. Presumably dead by 19 October 1743, the date of the entry of Ann Farren's mark. Subordinate Goldsmith to the King, 1723–42 (Major General H. W. D. Sitwell, 'The Jewel House and the Royal Goldsmiths', *Arch. Journ.* CXVII, pp. 154–5). His work at best is of fine quality and shows some influence or perhaps the use of Huguenot work. His most important pieces may be the fountain and cistern of 1728 at Burghley. His best known apprentice was Thomas Whipham (q.v.).

FAUX, John (1294, 1312) No record of apprenticeship or freedom. First mark entered as smallworker, 6 May 1763. Address: 'In the Curtin near Moorfields'. Second mark, 6 September 1763. Third mark, in partnership with George Love, 11 May 1764. Address: 'in ye Curtain Holywell Mount, Shoreditch'. Fourth mark, 22 December 1764. Fifth, 10 February 1767. Moved to Worship Street near Moorfields, 14 August [1767 or later?]. Sixth mark, 6 February 1771. The two appear as bucklemakers, at this address, in the Parl. Report list 1773, and Faux alone entered four marks as such from 1773 to 1784 (Section VIII). Faux's son Thomas Thames was apprenticed to John Wren 1776, when John Faux was described as of Worship Street, Shoreditch, silversmith. Heal records him here till 1784, followed by Thomas, as bucklemaker, at the same address.

FAWDERY, Hester (659) Presumably widow of William Fawdery (q.v.). Mark entered as largeworker, 28 September 1727. Address: Goldsmith Street, near Cheapside.

FAWDERY, John I (662) Son of John Fawdery of Enstone in the County of Oxford yeoman (and younger brother of William, q.v.), apprenticed to Anthony Nelme 16 January 1688. Free, 11 September 1695. Mark entered as largeworker, undated, probably April 1697 on commencement of register. Address: Foster Lane. Livery, April 1705. Signatory as 'working goldsmith' to the petition complaining of the competition of 'necessitous strangers', December 1711, and to that against assaying work of foreigners not having served seven years apprenticeship, February 1716. Sarah, daughter of John and Elizabeth Fawdry, was born and baptized 24 November 1702 (Register, Christchurch, Newgate Street). Two other sons and daughters were baptized and buried there from 1705 to 1718, but the baptism of John II (q.v.) is not recorded. John Fawdry was buried 16 January 1724.

FAWDERY, John II (1287) Son of John Fawdery Citizen and Goldsmith of London, apprenticed to Edward Cornock 29 July 1719 on payment of 15 guineas. Freedom unrecorded. Mark entered 27 February 1729, 'Goldsmith'. Address: 'Hemenes Roe' (Hemings Row), St. Martin's Lane, where Heal records him till 1723. Possibly the Jno. Faudery of St. Fidei (presumably St. Faith with St. Augustine or a strange aberration for St. (Martin in the) Fields?), married at St. Lawrence Jewry to Hester Pain of Christchurch, Spitalfields, 1 April 1731.

FAWDERY, William (658, 664-5, 3563, 3873) Son of John Fawdery of Enstone in the County of Oxford gentleman (and elder brother of John, q.v.), apprenticed to Robert Cooper 15 December 1683. Free, 8 August 1694. First mark entered as largeworker, undated, probably April 1697 on commencement of register. Address: Goldsmith Street. Second Britannia Standard mark entered below the foregoing, 28 July 1720. Third mark, Sterling, entered separately on the same day. Address: 'Gold' Street. Livery, October 1708. Heal records him at Goldsmith Street from 1698; as at Gold Street, 1720; and of London, 1727. Signatory to the petition against the marking of foreigners' plate and extending the freedom to 'several Frenchmen', 1703, and to the similar petitions December 1711 and February 1716. Elected Renter Warden, 4 October 1721. Presumably dead by 28 September 1727 when Hester Fawdery his widow entered her mark at the same address.

FAWLER, Thomas (660) Thomas ffowler son of John Citizen and Distiller of London, apprenticed to Walter Perrey Haberdasher 4 September 1693 and turned over later to John Leach (q.v.) also Haberdasher. Free, 1700. Mark entered as largeworker, 3 September 1707. Address: Bull and Mouth Street. 'Free Haberdasher'.

FAYLE, George (797) No record of apprenticeship or freedom. First mark entered as smallworker, 25 May 1767. Address: Gillats(?) Coort, Little Old Bailey. Moved to Dogwell Court, Whitefriars, 13 July 1767. Second mark on move to King's Head Court, Helen Lane, 27 March 1771, signed by Sarah Fayle, which might suggest she was re-entering as widow, but George Fayle appears as hiltmaker, Dogwell Court, in the Parl. Report list 1773 and entered a mark as bucklemaker, 8 April 1782 (Section IX). Heal records him at Wilderness Lane, Salisbury Court, but this may be in error for John Fayle (below), presumably his son.

FAYLE, John (1296) Apparently son of the above. No record of apprenticeship or freedom. Mark entered as smallworker, 30 April 1772. Address: 31 Wilderness Court, Salisbury Lane. He appears as hiltmaker, at this address, Parl. Report list 1773.

FEARN, Joseph (1816) No record of apprenticeship or freedom, and no apparent connection with William Fearn (below). Only mark entered as plateworker, 5 April 1810. Address: 10 Cornhill.

FEARN, William (910, 3112-4, 3116-7) Son of William Fearn of the parish of Sedbury in the County of Derby farmer, apprenticed to Thomas Chawner 6 October 1762 on payment of £25. Free, 7 February 1770. Mark entered as smallworker April 1769. Address: 5 Brownlow Street, Holborn. Second mark as spoonmaker, 13 May 1774. Address: 75 Wood Street. Appears twice in the Parl. Report list 1773, as spoonmaker, No. 78 Wood Street, and without category, 5 Brownlow Street, Holborn, presumably at this time maintaining two workshops. Bankrupt, July 1777, as silversmith, Wood Street (*The Gentleman's Magazine*). Third mark, in partnership with George Smith as plateworkers, 3 November 1786. Address: 60 Paternoster Row. Moved to 1 Lovell's Court, Paternoster Row, 29 August 1790. Fourth mark, in partnership with William Eley, 4 January 1797. Address: 14 Clerkenwell Green (perhaps a branch workshop). Fifth mark with same, 27 January 1802. Address: 1 Lovell's Court. Sixth, with W. Eley and W. Chawner, 10 April 1808. Seventh, with W. Eley only, 6 October 1814. Eighth, with W. Eley II, 14 May 1824. On this last entry he omitted to sign the register. His signature is already shaky in 1814 when he must have been about sixty-six, so that by 1824 he was unusually old to be still in business, presumably as a sleeping partner. Heal also records him in Castle Street in 1783, of which there is no evidence in the registers.

FELINE, Edward (576, 587, 679, 3566) Son of Peter 'Fellen' of St. Martin's in the Fields tailor, apprenticed to Augustine Courtauld 31 March 1709. Free, 6 April 1721. An 'Edwards Pheline' married, 21 April 1720, Renee Barbut of the parish of St. Martin's, daughter of John Barbut (q.v.), at West Street Huguenot Church, to which 'Edward Feline' signs as witness. Two marks (Sterling and New Standard) entered as largeworker, 25 September 1720. Address: Rose Street, Covent Garden. Third mark, 15 June 1739. Address: King Street, Covent Garden. Livery, April 1731. His son Edward was apprenticed to him 3 April 1745. Feline was presumably dead by 15 May 1753, when his widow Magdalen entered her first mark, at the same address. One would have thought that the son might have taken over responsibility by this date, but a possible reason for this is the reference to him as 'of the Assay Office Goldsmiths Hall' in the apprenticeship to him of his son Edward III in 1786. There is no mark entered for Edward II, who was elected to the Livery, July 1763. On the other hand, Heal records the name (be it senior or junior) at King Street, Covent Garden till 1755, and again there, 1770–86. Yet the name does not appear in the Parl. Report list 1773. Edward Feline Junior, bachelor, was married to Mary Ann Gregg, spinster, at St. Mary Aldermary, 29 April 1796. He is presumably the watchcasemaker whose mark was entered in 1794 (Section VI) and who worked till 1822 (Section V). Frederick Feline, watchcasemaker, 1831, may be of a further generation (Section VI).

FELINE, Magdalen (2027–8) Presumably widow of Edward Feline (above). First mark entered as largeworker, 15 May 1753. Address: King Street, Covent Garden. Second mark, 18 January 1757. Heal records her as plateworker, Covent Garden, till 1762.

FELL, William (3126) No record of apprenticeship or freedom. First mark entered as smallworker, 22 December 1818. Address: 15 Provost Street, City Road. Second mark, 27 November 1821. Moved to Moneyer Street, Hoxton New Town, 9 July 1824.

FERNELL, Edward (579–82, 3152) Son of William Fernell of Oakingham (?Wokingham), in the County of Berkshire tallow chandler, apprenticed to William Grundy Goldsmith 4 August 1762. Free, 6 December 1769. (For a relative of an earlier generation see John Farnell.) First mark as plateworker, in partnership with William Grundy, 23 February 1779. Address: 119 Fetter Lane. Second mark alone, 19 January 1780, same address. Third mark, 11 November 1780. Fourth, 13 February 1781. Fifth, 29 June 1787. Sixth, 18 July 1787. Seventh, 3 August 1787. Eighth, 8 August 1787. Ninth, 18 September 1787. The reason for this spate of new marks in 1787 is mysterious. They should be distinguished carefully from those of Edward Farrell of later date (q.v.). Heal records him in Fetter Lane, as silversmith, in 1796.

FERRIS, Matthew (2024) Son of John Ferris Citizen and Goldsmith (see Section IV) of London, apprenticed to William Hunt 3 August 1748. Free, 5 October 1752. Mark entered as smallworker, 21 September 1759. Address: Lilley Pot Lane. Moved to 'Ozier' (Hosier) Lane, and second mark, 26 July 1771. Parl. Report list 1773, as smallworker, same address. Heal however records him at Lilly Pot Lane as early as 1754, when he was already free, although there is no evidence of an earlier mark.

FIELD, Alexander (33–5) Son of Alexander Field of Jewin Street clothworker, apprenticed to Thomas Pitts 5 October 1763. Free, 5 December 1770. First mark entered as smallworker, in partnership with John De Gruchy, 20 April 1779. Address: City Road. Second mark alone, 14 July 1780. Address:

BIOGRAPHICAL DICTIONARY

Facing Featherstone Street, City Road. Moved to 1 Bowling Green Walk, Hoxton, 3 September 1784. Third mark, 19 June 1788, same address, where Heal records him till 1790. His mark should be carefully distinguished from that of Andrew Fogelberg (32) to whom it is probable many pieces by Field have hitherto been attributed.

FIELD, Joshua (687) Son of John Field of Wellington in the County of Salop clerk, apprenticed to Philip Roker 13 December 1692 and turned over to Charles Overall. Free, 29 October 1701. Mark entered as largeworker, 3 December 1701. Address: Maiden Lane, where Heal records him only in the next year.

FIELDING, John (1297) Son of Thomas Fielding of Addle Street London hosier, Citizen and Paviour, apprenticed to John Westray of Little Britain, as goldsmith 2 March 1768 on payment of £20. Free, 8 March 1775. Mark entered as smallworker, 21 April 1775. Address: 6 Addle Street, Aldermanbury. Was he working in his father's house?

FIGG, John (1306) John Wilmin Figg son of William Figg of Kenton in the County of Middlesex farmer, apprenticed to William Elliott of Compton Street Clerkenwell 1 February 1826. Free, 5 June 1833. First mark entered as plateworker, 31 July 1834. Address: 25 St. John Street, Clerkenwell. Moved to 5 Wellington Street, St. Luke's, and second mark (two sizes), 10 May 1838. Moved to 6 Denmark Street St. Giles', 10 July 1848.

FINCH, Robert (686) Son of Thomas Finch of Walton in the County of Surrey yeoman, apprenticed to Francis Williams 14 March 1673. Free, 26 March 1680. Mark (two sizes) entered as smallworker, undated, probably April 1697 on commencement of register. Address: 'over against Bedford House in the Strand'.

FIRMIN, Philip Venner (2176) No record of apprenticeship or freedom. First mark entered as smallworker, 12 February 1822. Address: 153 Strand. Second mark, 17 March 1823. Probably son of Samuel Firmin who entered an incuse mark as buttonmaker, same address, 21 April 1795 (Section V).

*FISH, William (688) Free by patrimony, 9 May 1706, but his parentage unrecorded. Livery, 9 May 1706 also. Mark entered as smallworker, 10 June 1706. Address: Blue Anchor Alley, Bunhill Fields. He is perhaps the —Fish, goldsmith, recorded by Heal at the Lamb over against Half Moon Tavern, Cheapside, 1709-10. Signed petition against assaying work of foreigners not having served seven years apprenticeship, February 1716.

FISHER, John (1301, 3129-30) Son of William Fisher of Union Street Whitechapel silversmith, apprenticed to George Hazard of Whitehall Court Southwark goldsmith, Citizen and Goldsmith 1 February 1792. Freedom unrecorded. First mark entered as plateworker, in partnership with his father, 16 August 1793. Address: 1 Plumbers' Row, Whitechapel. Moved to 4 Osborn Place, Whitechapel, 5 May 1794. Second mark, together as spoonmakers, 31 August 1797. Moved to 33 Redman Row, Mile End, 3 July 1798. Third mark alone as smallworker, 22 February 1799, same address. Perhaps identifiable with John Spicer Fisher, elected to livery October 1801, and died 2 May 1846.

FISHER, William (3124, 3129-30, 3876) Possibly son of William Fisher of Millbrook in the County of Bedford warrener, apprenticed to Robert Albin Cox 2 June 1756. Free, 4 July 1764. Listed as plateworker, 73 Little Britain, in the Parl. Report list 1773, and by Heal from 1766. If this was so his mark would have appeared in the missing register. First recorded mark as plateworker, in partnership with his son (above), 16 August 1793. Address: 1 Plumbers' Row, Whitechapel. Moved to 4 Osborn Place, 5 May 1794. Second mark, alone as smallworker, 10 November 1796, same address. Third mark, in partnership as before as spoonmakers, 31 August 1797. Moved to 33 Redman's Row, Mile End, 3 July 1798.

*FITCH, Daniel (463) No record of apprenticeship or freedom. Only mark entered as smallworker, 16 June 1773. Address: Fulham, Middlesex. His name was re-entered as buttonmaker, apparently as a pattern entry, in the new register started the same year, with the same date and 'Note this is only an Extract of the Entry of his Mark in the former Mark Book'; the space provided for the mark was left blank.

FLAVILL, John (693, 1285) Son of John Flavill of Skowell(?) in the County of Leicester yeoman, apprenticed to James Rood 7 March 1717 on payment of £10. Free, 12 March 1724. Sterling and New

509

Standard marks entered as largeworker, 5 April 1726. Address: 'Maiden Lane at ye Maiden head'. Heal records a Thomas Flavill in Carey Lane, 1753, presumably a son.

FLEMING, William (694) Son of John Fleming Citizen and Haberdasher of London, apprenticed to Nathaniel Lock 22 February 1688. Free, 20 March 1695. Mark entered as largeworker, undated, presumably April 1697 on commencement of register. Address: Maiden Lane, without Cripplegate. Livery, October 1708. Signatory as 'working goldsmith' to the petition complaining of the competition of 'necessitous strangers', December 1711, and to that against assaying work of foreigners not having served seven years apprenticeship, February 1716. Churchwarden of St. John Zachary, 1716 and 1717. Heal records him as plateworker, Blackwell Lane Court, Cripplegate without, 1692-7 (the first date is curious as by then he could only have served four years of his apprenticeship); also in Gutter Lane, 1712; and Maiden Lane 1714 and 1727. His mark is frequently found on well executed small pieces of hollowware such as cream-jugs, saucepans, dredgers and miniature porringers.

FLETCHER, Ann (696) Only mark entered as smallworker undated, presumably April 1697 on commencement of register. Address: St. Martin's Le Grand. 'Free Clockmaker'. There is no apprenticeship record of her in that company's records. She was probably free by patrimony as several of the name were.

FLETCHER, Bernard (166) Son of Bernard Fletcher of St. Martin's in the Fields cook (?), apprenticed to Samuel Lea 5 July 1716. Free, 31 March 1726. Mark entered as largeworker, 17 September 1725. Address: Staining Lane. Dead by 1741/2, when his son Frederick was apprenticed. Heal records him in Staining Lane, 1723-7.

FLETCHER, Edith (577) Described as 'the widow Flecher' on the entry of her mark as largeworker undated, between February 1729 and January 1732. Address: 'Foster Lane'. Since neither of the preceding or following makers have this address, she cannot be definitely associated with a particular one. Heal records her at this address as plateworker, 1727-9.

FLETCHER, Edward (697) Apprenticed to Samuel Davis of the Clockmakers' Company 2 June 1679. Mark entered in smallworkers' book, probably for watchcases, 4 April 1698. Address: Fleet Lane. 'Free Clockmaker'.

FLETCHER, John (695) Probably son of Robert Fletcher of Creenel(?) Norton in the County of Northton miller, apprenticed to Thomas Porter 24 May 1661. Free, 23 March 1670. Mark entered as largeworker, undated, c. 1699-1700. Address: Silver Street, where Heal records him 1700-5.

FLIGHT, Benjamin (168, 1456) No record of apprenticeship or freedom. First mark entered as smallworker, in partnership with William Flight, 20 December 1779. Address: Exeter Change, Strand. Second mark, in partnership with John Kelly, 19 January 1791, same address.

FLIGHT, John (698) Son of John Flight of Great Canford in the County of Dorset clerk, apprenticed to Thomas Simons 21 June 1692. Free, 17 February 1710. Mark entered as largeworker, 5 June 1710. Address: Foster Lane. Signatory as journeyman to the petition against assaying the work of foreigners not having served seven years apprenticeship, February 1716.

FLIGHT, William (168) No record of apprenticeship or freedom. Mark entered as smallworker in partnership with Benjamin Flight, 20 December 1779. Address: Exeter Change, Strand. Dead or given up business by 1791, when the latter entered a new mark with John Kelly.

FLINT, Charles (305) Possibly son of Lewis Flint of Gutter Lane cordwainer, apprenticed to Moses Brent of Well Yard Little Britain knife-haft maker 4 March 1789. Free, 1 March 1797, as silversmith. Only mark entered as plateworker, 4 February 1826. Address: 3 Cross Street, Hatton Garden.

FLINT, Joseph (1305) No record of apprenticeship or freedom. Only mark entered as smallworker, 17 September 1831. Address: 36 Cock Lane.

FLINT, William (3115) No record of apprenticeship or freedom. Only mark entered as smallworker, 21 June 1768. Address: Dogwell Court, Whitefriars, where George Fayle (q.v.) also worked at the same time. He appears as hiltmaker at this address in the Parl. Report list 1773. Heal records him as Flints, William, haftmaker, Dogwell Street, in the same year. See also Nicholas Flint (Section IX).

BIOGRAPHICAL DICTIONARY

*FOGELBERG, Andrew (32, 36-7) No record of apprenticeship or freedom. His name suggests a Swedish origin and possibly arrival in this country already trained as a goldsmith. First appears in London as plateworker, Church Street, Soho, in the Parl. Report list 1773. His mark alone (32) was therefore presumably entered in the missing register a little before this. Second mark (two sizes) entered as plateworker, in partnership with Stephen Gilbert (q.v.), 17 July 1780. Address: 29 Church Street Ann^s (sc. St. Anne's, Soho). Heal records the partnership, at this address, till 1793; also Fogelberg alone till 1800. There is, however, I suspect, confusion at times with the mark of Alexander Field which may have led to a false assumption of the length of his working career. Either alone or with Gilbert his productions show an elegant restrained classicism, particularly in his speciality of the use of small cameo-like medallions based on the Tassie paste gems popular in England at that time. C. C. Oman has pointed out the parallel use of such decoration in Sweden, suggesting Fogelberg's influence returning to his country of origin (*Apollo*, August 1947).

FOLKARD, John Cope (1230) Son of Daniel Folkard of London Road Southwark pawnbroker, apprenticed to Edward Edwards silversmith of Bridgwater Square 1 May 1811 on payment of £50. Free, 6 May 1818. Mark entered as plateworker, 12 March 1819. Address: 35 King Street, Holborn.

FOLKINGHAM, Thomas (703, 2750) Son of Thomas Folkingham late of ? in the County of Derby clerk deceased, apprenticed to John Bache 9 March 1693. Free, 23 June 1703. Mark entered as largeworker, 13 February 1707. Address: Sweeting Lane. Livery, October 1708. Second (Sterling) mark, 6 February 1721, same address. He is however already recorded by Heal as Thomas Falkenham, goldsmith, London in 1700; and as Faulkeringham at the Golden Ball, corner of Bearbinder Lane, 1701; as Folkingham he appears at Golden Ball, Swithin's Lane near Stocks Market, from 1706-20; and at Golden Ball over against Sun Tavern, Royal Exchange, in 1724. He was married, 7 May 1700, to Elizabeth Denny, both of the parish of St. Mary Woolnoth, at the church of St. Martin Outwich. It seems almost certain that she must have been the daughter of William Denny (q.v.), born 1681, the latter being partner to John Bache, Folkingham's master. Their three daughters and a son, Denny, were baptized at St. Mary Woolnoth from 1701 to 1715. In January 1710, Folkingham advertised in *The Daily Courant* for a runaway apprentice Jabez Tench, 'a young man near 21 years of age, of low stature, wears a brown coat and a brown natural wig' (Hilton Price, *Handbook of London Bankers*). Signatory as 'working goldsmith' to the petition complaining of the competition of 'necessitous strangers', December 1711, and to that against assaying work of foreigners not having served seven years apprenticeship, February 1716. He died 23 October 1729. 'Two days before died Mr Falkenham, a very noted goldsmith, said to have left upwards of 30,000 l' (*Political State of Great Britain*, 25 October 1729, Vol. XXXVIII). It is fairly clear that in Folkingham we have a banker-goldsmith of considerable status. His best work shows strong Huguenot influence and it is highly likely he employed émigrés as journeymen, in spite of his support of the petitions of 1711 and 1716.

FOOTE, John (1290, 1309) No record of apprenticeship or freedom. First mark entered as bucklemaker, 22 January 1735. Original address: 'Queen Street near Tower Hill at a shoemaker' has been deleted and Red Cross Square added later, undated. Second mark as smallworker without description as above, 4 May 1761. Address: Aldersgate Street, where he appears without category in the Parl. Report list 1773. Livery, November 1776. Court, February 1777. Warden, 1790-1. Prime Warden, 1792. Died 1795-1801. But this career may refer to a son.

FORD, Joseph (1812-3) No record of apprenticeship or freedom. First mark entered as smallworker, 25 February 1764. Address: New Street, Shoe Lane. Signs with mark. Second mark, 17 September 1777. Address: Brownlow Street, Long Acre. He appears without category, at Robinhood Court, Shoe Lane, in the Parl. Report list 1773.

FORDHAM, William (706, 3874) Son of Richard ffordham of Tharfield in the County of Hertford gentleman, apprenticed to Melior Benskin widow of Richard Benskin late Citizen and Waxchandler of London 1 December 1686. Free of the Waxchandlers' Company, ?1693. Mark entered as largeworker, 31 January 1707. Address:

Lombard Street. 'Free of the Wax Chandlers'. His entry has the Sterling mark of Thomas Folkingham stamped in error at the bottom corner.

FORRESTER, Lancelot Fleming (680) Son of Richard Forrester of the parish of St. Andrew Holborn gentleman, apprenticed to William Barnesley 3 October 1764. Freedom unrecorded. Mark entered as smallworker, 13 March 1772. Address: 2 Orange Street, Red Lion Square. Signs 'Flem^g' for second name. Appears as Fleming Forrester, without category, 2 Orange Court, Red Lion Square, in the Parl. Report list 1773.

FOSKETT, John (1303, 1314) Son of Samuel Foskett of Saffron Hill in the County of Middlesex silversmith, apprenticed to William Frisbee as goldsmith 7 October 1795 on payment of £7. 14s. of the charity of the Worshipful Company of Goldsmiths. Free, 3 November 1802. First mark entered as plateworker, 27 October 1808. Address: 45 Leather Lane, Holborn. Moved to 27 St. John's Square, 18 December 1809. Second mark, in partnership with John Stewart, 20 February 1810, same address.

FOSSEY, John (1288-9, 1310) Son of Daniel Fossey of the parish of Hempstead in the County of Hertford draper deceased, apprenticed to Thomas Tearle 7 May 1724 on payment of £20. Free, 9 September 1731. Mark entered as largeworker, 9 January 1733. Address: 'at ye Hand & Seale in Gutter Lane'. Second mark, undated but before August 1734, on moving to 'Next Door ye 3 Tunn tavern Wood Street'. Third mark, 15 June 1739. Address: Wood Street. Heal records him at the Hand and Seal, Gutter Lane from 1724 to 1733; as goldsmith, Lombard Street, died 1746; also presumably a son, John Fossey, goldsmith, Golden Ring, corner of Ball Alley, Lombard Street, 1746-8; and goldsmith and jeweller, Blackammor's Head, Corner of Ball Alley in Lombard Street, 1748.

FOSTER, George (796, 798, 800, 1311) No record of apprenticeship or freedom. First mark entered as smallworker, in partnership with brother(?) John (q.v.), 11 July 1764. Address: Carter Lane. Second mark alone, 27 October 1764. Address: Mile End Green. Third mark, in partnership with W. Hopper, 27 August 1771. Address: White Swan, Friars Street, Blackfriars. Fourth alone, 3 April 1772, same address. None of these dates or addresses is noted by Heal, who gives only George Foster, goldsmith, Purple(?) Lane, Holborn, bankrupt 1769. The name appears as bucklemaker, Red Lion Street, Clerkenwell, in the Parl. Report list 1773.

FOSTER, Jacob (1286) Son of Joseph ffoster late of Peckham watchmaker deceased, apprenticed to Glover Johnson of the Haberdashers' Company Noble Street goldsmith 10 July 1719. Free, 1726. Mark entered as largeworker, 5 October 1726. Address: 'at the Pearl & Crown in the Borough of Southwark', where Heal records him till 1728.

FOSTER, John I (1295, 1311) Probably son of Robert Foster of the parish of St. Sepulchre's London gentleman, apprenticed to John Bishop 3 May 1753 on payment of £30. Freedom unrecorded. First mark entered as smallworker, in partnership with brother(?) George, 11 July 1764. Address: Carter Lane. Second mark, alone, 20 November 1764. Address: Little Carter Lane. Heal records only John Foster, silversmith, Mint Street, Southwark, bankrupt 1769, who seems unlikely to be the same. Another of the same name entered an incuse mark, 1765, in Goswell Street (Section V), and appears without category, at this address, in the Parl. Report list 1773.

FOSTER, John II (1298-9) No record of apprenticeship or freedom. Presumably son or brother of Thomas Foster of the same address (q.v.). First mark entered as smallworker, 14 February 1778. Address: King's Head Court, Fetter Lane. Second mark, on moving to 65 Fetter Lane, 8 October 1789. Presumably dead by 10 June 1795, when Hannah Foster entered a mark as hiltmaker at the same address (Section IX); she was succeeded by Richard Foster (q.v.), 1799. A similar mark to his first, without pellet, is found on sword-hilts of 1788-91, signed 'Bland and Foster' (information, Mr Vesey Norman).

FOSTER, Joseph (1815) No record of apprenticeship or freedom. Only mark entered as smallworker, 31 August 1797. Address: 5 Carpenter Street, Westminster.

FOSTER, Richard (2313) No record of apprenticeship or freedom. Probably son of John Foster II, at same address. Only mark entered as smallworker, 22 June 1799. Address: 65 Fetter Lane.

FOSTER, Thomas (2751, 3822-3) Possibly son of Thomas Foster late Citizen and Barber Surgeon of London deceased, apprenticed to Josiah Daniel 3 December 1734 and turned over same day to his mother Mary Foster. There seems, however, too long an interval before the entry of his first mark as smallworker, 7 December 1769. Address: 16 King's Head Court, Fetter Lane. Second mark, 29 July 1773. Heal records him as haftmaker at this address for the years above. Listed in Parl. Report list 1773 at hiltmaker. Succeeded by son or brother John Foster II (q.v.). The incuse mark of 1766 entered by the same name (Section V) and those as watchcasemaker (Section VI) show slight difference in the signature but may refer also to him. If he was principally a hilt and haftmaker it seems a little difficult to reconcile the marks of nos. 3822–3, found on pierced baskets, to him.

FOSTER, William Lewis (3118, 3875) Presumably William Foster son of Paul Foster of Tottenham High Cross in the County of Middlesex husbandman, apprenticed to William Watkins 7 May 1760 on payment of £15 and turned over later to Thomas Chawner. Free, 4 April 1770. Mark entered as plateworker, 31 January 1775. Address: 10 Blue Anchor Alley, Bunhill Row, where Heal records him as W. L. Foster till 1780. There is however a curious note against the entry of his mark: 'Later Charcoal Man: Bishopsgate', and William Foster, spoonmaker, without Bishopsgate, appears in the Parl. Report list 1773, which suggests the same individual working at the specialist craft he would have learnt from Chawner, while the address agrees with the 'Charcoal Man'. Did he perhaps run a sideline as purveyor of furnace charcoal to the trade?

FOUNTAIN, John (1300, 1313) Son of John Fountain late of Poplar shipwright (and elder brother of William, q.v.), apprenticed to Robert Grace Cleets of Bell Yard, Doctors' Commons silver chaser 12 January 1774 and turned over to Daniel Smith of Aldersgate goldsmith, Citizen and Merchant Taylor, as was his brother. Free, 2 November 1791. First mark entered as plateworker, 1 May 1792. Address: 2 Carthusian Street, Aldersgate Street. Second mark, in partnership with John Beadnell, 10 May 1793, same address. Third mark alone, 16 February 1797. Address: Vere Street, Clare Market. Heal prints the date at Aldersgate Street as '1762 (? 1792)', the latter being correct as above.

FOUNTAIN, William (3122–3, 3127–8) Son of John Fountain late of Poplar in the County of Middlesex shipwright deceased (and younger brother of John, above) apprenticed to Fendall Rushworth of Goldsmiths' Hall Citizen and Goldsmith 1 October 1777. Turned over the same day by consent to Daniel Smith of Aldermanbury London Citizen and Merchant Taylor. Free, 2 February 1785. Mark entered as plateworker, in partnership with Daniel Pontifex, 29 July 1791. Address: 13 Hosher (Hosier) Lane, West Smithfield. Second mark alone, 1 September 1794. Address: 47 Red Lion Street, Clerkenwell. Third mark 30 June 1798. Moved to King Street, Clerkenwell, 1 April 1811. Fourth mark, 5 February 1821. Address: Harford Place, Haggerston Bridge. Heal records him as plateworker, Charterhouse Lane, 1787, before the entry of his first mark; otherwise up to 1800 as above.

FOWLER, Epaphroditus (588, 704) Free of the Merchant Taylors' Company by service to Robert Monday 6 October 1687. Elected to the Livery, 23 October 1696. Mark entered as smallworker, undated, probably April 1697 on commencement of register. Address: 'at the Hermitage Bridge in Wapping'. 'Free Merchant Taylor'. Second (Sterling) mark, 27 July 1720.

FOWLER, Samuel (2511) Son of Richard Fowler Citizen and Grocer of London, apprenticed to Matthew Cuthbert 3 August 1721 on payment of £25 and turned over to Richard Gosling in Barbican Goldsmith 27 October 1724. Free, 3 April 1729. Mark entered as smallworker, 23 June (?1730). Address: Fox and Crown in Aldersgate Street.

*FOX, Charles I (301, 307) No record of apprenticeship or freedom. First mark entered as plateworker, in partnership with James Turner, 20 October 1801. Address: 3 Old Street, Goswell Street. Second mark alone, 5 September 1804. Address: 139 Old Street. Apparently succeeded by his son Charles (q.v.) in 1822.

*FOX, Charles II (302–4) Presumably son of Charles Fox I. No record of apprenticeship or freedom. First mark entered as plateworker, signed Charles Fox Junr, 19 February 1822. Address: 139 Old Street. Second mark, 27 January 1823. Third, 21 August 1823. Fourth, 23 September 1823. Fifth, 10 December 1823. Sixth, 9 May 1838. His work shows consistently high quality. The rapid entry of marks suggests a fairly large establishment with varying marks used for different categories of work. Fox was perhaps the last individualist plateworker before the debacle of Victorian mass production.

FOX, Mordecai (1112-3, 2025-6) No record of apprenticeship or freedom. First mark entered as largeworker, in partnership with Joseph Allen, 9 March 1730. Address: St. Swithin's Lane, near Lombard Street (Fox's name is left blank in the entry but established by the second entry, 21 August 1739: 'Joseph Allen and Mordecai Fox in Comp' at the Sun in St Swithin's Lane.) Third mark alone, 21 January 1747. Address: St. Swithin's Lane. Fourth mark as smallworker, 18 June 1755. Heal records the partnership till 1743, and Fox alone till 1755. He is probably the —Fox, Subordinate Goldsmith to the King 1746-59 (Major General H. W. D. Sitwell, 'The Jewel House and the Royal Goldsmiths', *Arch. Journ.*, CXVII, p. 155).

FRAILLON, Blanche (167) Signs 'Blance Ffailion'. Presumably widow of James Fraillon (below). Mark entered as largeworker, undated, between September 1727 and June 1728. Address: 'Lanchester Court in ye Strand'. She appears as witness to the baptism of Salomon Claude Fraillon, son of Pierre Fraillon, 3 June 1716, and again to his daughter Elizabeth, 4 October 1719, both at Threadneedle Street Church.

FRAILLON, James (713, 1284) Son of Claude Fraillon of St. Martin's Lane in the County of Middlesex, apprenticed to Philip Roker 25 February 1699. Free, 1 May 1706. Appears in Denizations List, 29 September 1698, as Jacobus Fraillon. Mark entered as largeworker, 17 January 1711. Address: Maiden Lane, Covent Garden. Moved to Lanchester Court in the Strand, undated. Second (Sterling) mark, 6 March 1723, same address. Probably dead by a date between September 1727 and June 1728, when Blanche Fraillon enters her mark at the same address. He appears as a witness to the baptism of Elizabeth Anne Fraillon, daughter of Pierre Fraillon, calico printer, and Anne Suzanne his wife, in Gray Eagle Street, Stepney, at Threadneedle Street Church, 12 April 1702. Although he does not seem to have been commissioned by the great for any large decorative pieces, the quality of his work as seen in such items as his double-lipped sauce-boats shows his standard to have been high.

FRANCIA, Anthony (30) Son of Joseph Francia of Islington gentleman, apprenticed to John Thompson (q.v.) of the Skinners' Company 28 June 1721. Free, 5 July 1725? Mark entered as haftmaker, 4 July (no year) circa 1725. Address: Wood Street. 'Skinners Company'.

FRANCIS, William (714) Probably son of Roger Francis of Shrewsbury yeoman, apprenticed to Thomas Littleton 26 September 1673. Freedom unrecorded. Mark entered as largeworker, undated, probably 1697 on commencement of register. Address: St. Martin's Lane near Charing Cross, where Heal records him at the Black Lion, as goldsmith, 1692-1712; and the same or another of the name, Shoreditch, 1724-7. Livery, August 1705. See below.

FRANCYS, William (715) Son of Christopher ffrancyes of Woodham Water in the County of Essex gentleman, apprenticed to Charles Tendring 21 March 1683 (signs 'ffrancyes'). Free, 19 November 1690. Mark entered as largeworker, 15 January 1704. Address: Sherborn Lane. Signs register 'ffrancys'. Livery, October 1708. Court, 1705.

FRASER, Donald (464) No record of apprenticeship or freedom. Only mark entered as spoonmaker, 5 July 1828. Address: 10 Collingwood Street, Shoreditch.

FRAY, John (521, 1292, 1316) Son of David Fray of the parish of St. Giles Cripplegate in the County of Middlesex innholder, apprenticed to William Fawdery 19 October 1726 on payment of £5. Turned over to Charles Martin 3 September 1729. Free, 16 December 1736. Mark entered as largeworker, in partnership with Fuller White, 4 March 1745. Address: 'at ye Golden Ball & Pearl in Noble Street'. Second mark alone, 4 January 1748. Address: Three Crown Court, Foster Lane. Third mark, in partnership with Dennis Wilks, 19 July 1753. Address: Fore Street. Fourth mark alone, 28 August 1756. Address: Field(?) Lane. Heal records him at 3 Crown Court from 1744 to 1748, otherwise as above. He was alive 4 May 1768, when his son Dennis (presumably a godson of his partner Dennis Wilks fifteen years before) was apprenticed to William Barnesley.

FREEMAN, Philip (2175) Son of Philip Freeman late Citizen and Glover of London deceased, apprenticed to Edward Aldridge Citizen and Goldsmith 2 August 1758 and turned over the same day to Edward Aldridge Citizen and Clothworker in consideration of £31 10s. (This is apparently a clerical device to avoid erasing the entry, as Aldridge was in fact not free of the Goldsmiths but of the Clothworkers. See the same device in the apprenticeship of Charles Aldridge.) Freedom unrecorded. Mark entered as smallworker, 2 November 1772. Address: Baker's Place, Whitechapel. Appears as smallworker, Baker's Row, Whitechapel, in the Parl. Report list 1773. Second mark, 17 August 1773. Third as plateworker, 30 September 1773. Address: 66 Bartholomew Close.

FREEMAN, Thomas (2757) No record of apprenticeship or freedom. Mark entered as smallworker in partnership with John Marshall, 13 September 1764. Address: Little Bartholomew Close, while Marshall's address is given separately as Princes Street, Bridgwater Square, an unusual occurrence. Appears alone as plateworker, Westmoreland Buildings, Aldersgate Street, in Parl. Report list 1773.

FREETH, Henry (994) No record of apprenticeship or freedom. Only mark entered as smallworker, 14 June 1828. Address: Little Sutton Street.

FREETH, Thomas I (2752) No record of apprenticeship or freedom. Only mark entered as smallworker, 17 August 1773. Address: St. Martin's Church Lane, Strand. Heal records Thomas Freeth, silversmith, Clerkenwell Close, 1790-3, who may be the same, and who entered two marks as bucklemaker, 1790-2, first at 24 Clerkenwell Close and secondly at 9 Queen Street, Islington (Section VIII).

FREETH, Thomas II (2753) No record of apprenticeship or freedom. Presumably son of the foregoing. Only mark entered as spoonmaker, 15 November 1820. Address: 9 Queen Street, Islington.

FRENCH, Edward (23, 578) No record of apprenticeship or freedom. First mark entered as largeworker, in partnership with Alexander Coats, 29 August 1734. Address: Benet's Court, near Exeter Change, Strand. Second mark alone, undated, between August 1734 and May 1739. Address: Great Benet's Court in the Strand.

*FRENCH, John (3635) Free by redemption, 5 June 1755. Appears as plateworker, Paul's Alley, Redcross Street, as having a mark entered, in the Parl. Report list 1773. Heal records him as goldsmith and jeweller at the same address and date; at 2 Tavistock Street, Covent Garden, 1779-84; and 21 Tavistock Street, 1790-3; also John French and Brian Markland as goldsmiths, 2 Tavistock Street, partnership dissolved 1781.

FRENSHAM, Joshua (716) Son of Joshua Frensham late of Clothfair London tailor deceased, apprenticed to Samuel Dell 12 January 1699 as from the first day of March next, and turned over later to Seth Lofthouse. Free, 27 March 1707. Mark entered as largeworker, 12 September 1707. Address: Shoe Lane. Heal records him at this address as plateworker from 1697 to 1707, a period which is proved incorrect by his apprenticeship date. Signatory as 'working goldsmith' to the petition complaining of the competition of 'necessitous strangers', December. 1711.

FRESHFIELD, James (1293) No record of apprenticeship or freedom. Only mark entered as smallworker, undated, between September 1759 and May 1761. Address: Great St. Andrew's Street, where he appears as watchcasemaker in the Parl. Report list 1773.

FRISBEE, John (3131-2) Son of William Frisbee of Cow Lane Goldsmith, apprenticed to his father as goldsmith 6 March 1799. Free, 2 April 1806. Mark entered as plateworker, with his father, 10 September 1811. Address: Bridewell Hospital. Second mark, 11 May 1814, same address.

FRISBEE, William (1282, 3119-21, 3131-3) Son of John Frisbee of the Old Bailey Citizen and Tallow Chandler of London, apprenticed to John Crouch of Giltspur Street London Goldsmith on payment of £10 5 October 1774. Free, 6 February 1782. Mark entered as plateworker, in partnership with John Edwards, 12 April 1791. Address: 48 Jewin Street. Second mark alone, 11 January 1792. Address: 51 Cock Lane, Snowhill. Third mark, in partnership with Paul Storr, 2 May 1792. Address: 5 (?51) Cock Lane. Fourth mark alone, 23 June 1798. (Storr had entered his own separate mark, January 1793, so that Frisbee's activities between that date and his 1798 mark remain conjectural. Was he perhaps still working with Storr?) Fifth mark, 2 June 1801. Address: Inner Court, Bridewell Hospital. Livery, October 1806. Sixth mark, in partnership with his son John, 10 September 1811. Address: Bridewell Hospital. Seventh similar mark, 11 May 1814. Three of his sons were apprenticed to their father: the first John, 6 March 1799, when William Frisbee is 'Of Cow Lane London', the second William, 1 October 1806, and the third Daniel Luffman, 4 January 1809. He died 9 December 1820.

FRITH, Ralph (717, 2312) Son of Robert Frith late of March of the County of Cambridge yeoman deceased, apprenticed to James Smith 10 October 1721 on payment of £22 and turned over 28 October 1723 to Meschach Godwin. Freedom unrecorded. Sterling and New Standard marks entered as largeworker, 24 June 1728. Address: 'in Shoreditch att ye sine of ye Golden Cup. Goldsmith'.

FROST, John I (1307-8) Son of George Frost of Wirestone (?) in the County of Derby yeoman, apprenticed to Gawen Nash 7 March 1750 and turned over same day to Thomas Gladwin Citizen and Merchant Taylor in consideration of £15. Free, 4 May 1757. Two marks, large and small, entered as largeworker, 30 August 1757. Address: Cornhill. Heal records him as goldsmith and jeweller, Golden Cup, opposite St. Peter's Church, Cornhill, 1757. He is listed bankrupt as silversmith, Cornhill, February 1758 (*The Gentleman's Magazine*).

FROST, John II (1315) No record of apprenticeshop or freedom. First mark entered as smallworker, in partnership with William Frost, 18 November 1814. Address: 11 Air Street, Piccadilly. Second mark, smaller, 6 May 1816. John Frost, goldworker, 1813-29 (Section VII) appears a separate identity.

FROST, William (1315, 3355) No record of apprenticeship or freedom. First mark entered as smallworker, in partnership with John Frost (above), 18 November 1814. Second (smaller) mark, 6 May 1816. Third mark, in partnership with William Thompson, 16 June 1818, same address.

FRY, Charles (306) Son of John Fry late of Clapham in the County of Surrey fishmonger, apprenticed to William Elliott of Compton Street Clerkenwell as silver plateworker 6 December 1809. Free, 2 July 1817. Mark entered as plateworker, in partnership with John Fry II, 29 August 1822. Address: 17 Perceevl Street, Clerkenwell. Moved to 60 Red Lion Street, Clerkenwell, 9 July 1823.

FRY, John I (1814) Son of Samuel Fry of St. Luke's in the County of Middlesex sergemaker, apprenticed to Henry Hobdell 2 August 1758. Free, 7 August 1765. Mark entered as smallworker, 13 September 1768. Address: Bull and Mouth Street, where Heal records him from 1770-3. He appears here as goldworker in the Parl. Report list 1773, and entered a mark as such at 6 Bull and Mouth Street, 6 September 1775 (Section VII).

FRY, John II (306, 1304) Son of John Fry late of Clapham in the County of Surrey fishmonger, apprenticed (like his brother Charles, above) to William Elliott as silversmith 6 March 1811, 'at the sole charge of the Governors of the Orphan Charity School in the City Road'. Free, 7 October 1818. First mark entered as plateworker, in partnership with his brother Charles, 29 August 1822. Address: 17 Perceval Street, Clerkenwell. Moved to 60 Red Lion Street, Clerkenwell, 9 July 1823. Second mark alone, 18 April 1826, same address. Moved to 13 Center Street, Minerva Street, Hackney Road, 30 July 1827.

FUETER, Daniel Christian (453) Born at Berne, Switzerland, 14 April 1720. Worked as goldsmith there till 1749, when he took part in the conspiracy of Samuel Henzi to overthrow the aristocratic regime, was condemned to death, but escaped to London. Mark entered as largeworker, 8 December 1753. Address: King's Road, Chelsea, 'next door to the Man in the Moon'. His stay here was very brief since he was advertising in New York in the spring of 1754 and worked there till 1779, when his death sentence in Switzerland was annulled and he returned home to Berne, dying there 31 December 1785. (Martha Gandy Fales, *American Silver in the Henry Francis Dupont Winterthur Museum*, 1958.)

*FULLER, Crispin (299, 300) No record of apprenticeship or freedom. First mark entered as plateworker, 29 December 1792. Address: 42 Monkwell Street. Second and third marks (two sizes), 11 July 1796. Moved to 3 Windsor Court, Monkwell Street, 14 August 1791. Fourth mark, 5 August 1823. His son Jeremiah was apprenticed to James Shallis as oil and colourman, 2 June 1813, when Fuller was still at Windsor Court.

FULLER, John (1302) No record of apprenticeship or freedom. Only mark entered as smallworker, 26 January 1804. Address: 65 Chapel Street, Pentonville.

FULLER, Richard (726-7, 2311) Son of Richard Fuller of Stocke in the County of Essex carpenter, apprenticed to William Chebsey of the Leathersellers Company 14 June 1670. Free, 23 January 1678. Mark entered as smallworker, undated, probably April 1697 on commencement of register. Address: New Street, Fetter Lane. 'Free Leatherseller'. Second mark, 14 August 1717, same address. Third (Sterling) mark, 24 June 1720.

FULLFORD, John (1291) No record of apprenticeship or freedom. Only mark entered as smallworker, 9 December 1735. Address: 'at the Crown and Tobacco Riole (? Roll) in Newte Street near ye Watch House in High Holborn'. The sign suggests a snuff and tobacco-box maker.

FURNICE, Edward (586, 2890) Son of Richard Furnice of Pemberton Row London baker, apprenticed to George Smith of Paternoster Row 6 November 1799 and turned over to William Fearn of Lovell's Court Paternoster Row 7 December 1803. Free, 1 April 1807. First mark entered as spoonmaker, in partnership with Thomas Purver, 17 April 1815. Address: 2 Clerkenwell Close. Second mark alone as plateworker, 2 August 1816. Address: 72 Red Lion Street, Clerkenwell. Third mark, 5 January 1820.

FURNIVALL, John (728) Son of John Furnivall deceased free by patrimony of the Merchant Taylors' Company 7 June 1664. Mark entered as smallworker, undated, probably April 1697 on commencement of the register. Address: 'In Shoe Lane near Fleet Street'. 'Free Merchant Taylor'.

FURZE, William (3125) William Henry Furze son of John Furze of Islington shopkeeper, apprenticed to Edward Robinson of Gutter Lane as goldsmith on payment of £20 7 June 1786. Free, 4 June 1794. Mark entered as smallworker, 23 November 1796. Address: High Street, Croydon, Surrey.

G

GAHEGAN, John (1327) No record of apprenticeship or freedom. Only mark entered as largeworker, 17 July 1734. Address: Three Dove Court, St. Martin's Le Grand.

GAIRDNER, Thomas (2761-2) Son of George Gairdner of St. Martin's Lane Westminster gentleman, apprenticed to John Wakelin as goldsmith 3 October 1792 on payment of £20 of the charity of Watson Hospital of the City of Edinburgh. Free, 7 October 1800. First mark entered as smallworker, 30 November 1802. Address: 5 George Court, Strand. Second mark as plateworker, 26 January 1818. Address: 23 Maiden Lane, Covent Garden. Apparently succeeded by William Galloway (q.v.), at the same address, 1823.

GALE, John (1320) Son of John Gale late of London gentleman deceased, apprenticed to William Pearson 11 March 1713. Free, 19 December 1721. Mark entered as smallworker, 18 January 1723. Address: Newgate Street. 'Free Goldsmith'. Heal has only —Gale, goldsmith and jeweller, Strand near Essex Street, 1756 (perhaps a son, who may be the John Gale elected to the livery, 8 March 1781, died c. 1820, but more likely a grandson).

*GALLANT, Jane (1344) No record of apprenticeship or freedom. Only mark entered as smallworker, 25 May 1760. Address: Smarts Building, Holborn. Signs with X. Appears as watchcasemaker, at this address, in the Parl. Report list 1773.

GALLOWAY, Alfred (2770) Probably with Thomas (below) sons of William Galloway (q.v.). No record of apprenticeship or freedom. Mark entered with Thomas as plateworkers, 12 August 1831. Address: 23 Maiden Lane, Covent Garden.

GALLOWAY, Thomas (2767, 2770) See Alfred (above) with whom first mark entered as plateworkers, 12 August 1831. Address: 23 Maiden Lane, Covent Garden. Second mark alone, 14 August 1837. Address: 8 Great Mays Buildings, St. Martin's Lane. Moved to 4 Horseferry Road, Westminster, 24 March 1840.

GALLOWAY, William (3145) No record of

GAMBLE

apprenticeship or freedom. Only mark entered as plateworker, 28 July 1823. Address: 23 Maiden Lane, where Thomas Gairdner had been since 1818. Succeeded in his turn at this address by Alfred and Thomas Galloway (above) in 1831.

GAMBLE, William (738) Son of Thomas Gamble late Citizen and Carpenter of London, apprenticed to John Sutton 18 June 1680 'from the XVIth day of November next'. Free, 2 March 1688. Mark entered as largeworker, undated, probably April 1697 on commencement of register. Address: Foster Lane. William Gamble of St. Leonard, Foster Lane, married Mary Saunders of Christchurch, London, at Christchurch, Newgate, by licence, 26 February 1690. Three short-lived children are recorded from 1700 to 1708 and a son William born 16 and baptised 27 May 1709, to be followed by his mother's burial 4 June 1709. Gamble was elected to the Livery, April 1705. Signatory as 'working goldsmith' to the petition complaining of the competition of 'necessitous strangers', December 1711, and to that against assaying work of foreigners not having served seven years apprenticeship, February 1716. Court, 1724. Warden, 1730. In 1732, after Benjamin Pyne's death, he applied for the post of Beadle but being over sixty was not eligible. Heal records him at Foster Lane from 1692(?)-1703, and states that he was succeeded by his son Ellis (to whom Hogarth was apprenticed). It is obvious, however, that William was active till 1730 and there is no evidence from the baptismal entries for the family of a son of this name. Furthermore, Ellis Gamble's only recorded address is Cranbourn Street, Leicester Fields, he has no recorded mark and Hogarth was apprenticed to him in 1712, when, as clear above, William was in the middle of his working life. Heal also records William Gambel, goldsmith, Red Lion Street, Clerkenwell, 1727, which may possibly be a later address for Gamble.

GAMON, Dinah (466) Widow of John Gamon (q.v.). Mark entered as largeworker, 6 March 1740. Address: Staining Lane, near Goldsmiths' Hall.

GAMON, John (1323, 1348) Son of Michael Gamon late Citizen and Haberdasher of London deceased, apprenticed to William Fawdery 22 January 1717 on payment of £20. Free, 16 April 1724. Mark entered as

GARRARD

largeworker, 22 March 1727. Address: Gutter Lane. Second mark, 15 June 1739. Address: Staining Lane. Two sons of William and Dinah Gamon appear in the register of St. Vedast: William, born 26 May 1728 and John, born 17 February 1730. The latter was apprenticed to John Ruffin of the Goldsmiths' Company, 4 June 1746, when his father is described as 'late', and had presumably died before the entry of Dinah Gamon's mark in March 1740. Evans lists John Gamon, Senior and Junior, and Michael as Huguenots (*Hug. Soc. Proc.*, 14). The latter two, if indeed goldsmiths, have no registered marks and the evidence of their French ancestry seems based on the name. Michael Gamon, goldworker, 3 Paul's Court, Hogan Lane, appears in the Parl. Report list 1773, and he may well have been another son of John, named after his grandfather (Section IV and Section VII).

GARBETT, John (745) Son of Thomas Garbett of Buttaigton(?) in the County of Montgomery gentleman deceased, apprenticed to John Pearson 20 September 1718 on payment of £31. 10s. Free, 7 October 1725. Mark entered as smallworker, in partnership with James Pell, 30 June 1726. Address: 'at the Half Moon and Star against ye Church in Foster Lane'. 'Free Goldsmith'. Heal records them here at the same date, and also John Garbett, goldsmith, Anchor and Crown, Lombard Street, deceased 1747, presumably the same.

*GARDEN, Phil(l)ip(s) (2178-81, 2184-5) Philip Garden son of John Garden late Citizen and Draper of London deceased, apprenticed to Gawen Nash 4 February 1730 on payment of £5 of the charity of Christ's Hospital London. Free, 3 October 1738. Mark entered as smallworker, 12 June 1738. Address: Gutter Lane. 'Free of Goldsmiths'. Second mark as largeworker, 23 June 1739. Third, 12 March 1744. Address: St. Paul's Churchyard. Livery, September 1746. Fourth mark, 29 October 1748. Fifth, 18 April 1751. Heal records him as Phillips Garden, working goldsmith and jeweller, Gutter Lane, 1739; and at the Golden Lion, North side of St. Paul's Churchyard, 1739 to 1762 when bankrupt, and states he was succeeded by John Townsend in the latter year. Resigned from Livery, 9 December 1763. Phillips Garden, goldsmith, Mary(le)bone, appears in the Parl. Report list 1773. Henry Garden, son of Philip Garden, goldsmith, of St. Paul's Churchyard was admitted

518

BIOGRAPHICAL DICTIONARY

to St. Paul's School (almost alongside his father's shop), 7 April 1749, aged nine. At his best Garden is an admirable exponent of the rococo style.

*GARDENER, W. (3144) Perhaps William Gardner son of William Gardner deceased, apprenticed to James Swindells as watchcasemaker 1795. Only mark entered as smallworker, 11 March 1811. Address: 37 King Street, Soho.

GARDIN, Richard (737) Free of the Haberdashers' Company by servitude to Thomas Chaplin 24 February 1693. Mark entered as largeworker, undated, probably April 1697 on commencement of register. Address: Turnagain Lane. 'Free Haberdasher'.

GARDINER, William (741) Perhaps William Gardner son of Robert Gardner of the parish of St. Edmundsbury of London gentleman, apprenticed to Richard Jordan 11 May 1681. Free, 18 December 1689. Livery, October 1708, as Gardner. First mark entered as smallworker, 22 July 1700. Address: Ely Court in Holborn, near Hatton Garden. Second (Sterling) mark, 22 June 1720. No further address.

GARDNER, Richard (3771-2) Son of John Gardner of the parish of Hamstead Middlesex gardener, apprenticed to William Cripps 3 July 1745 on payment of £12 of the charity of Lady Langhorne to the parish of Hamstead. Free, 5 March 1766. Appears in Parl. Report list 1773 as plateworker, Archer Street, Haymarket, and recorded by Heal as such and Silver Street, 1782-7. The variety of pieces on which the mark now attributed to him is found suggests a fairly large output. The second mark of 1788 might perhaps not be his, but no other candidate seems available.

*GARFIELD, Jeremiah (1817) Jeremy son of Thomas Garfield late of Clerkenwell in the County of Middlesex butter factor, apprenticed to John Hudson of St. John's Square Clerkenwell as goldsmith 7 August 1793 on payment of £20. Free, 7 October 1800. First mark entered as plateworker, 9 August 1813. Address: 25 Bridgewater Gardens, Cripplegate. Moved to 4 Badger Road, Red Lion Street, and second mark undated. Third mark on move to 1 Vineyard Gardens, Clerkenwell, 25 September 1820. Moved to 17 Little Knightrider Street, Doctors' Commons, no date.

GARNIER, Daniel (740) Either (1) the son of Isaac Garnier, who is named with other children of the latter in the Denization List of 24 August 1684; or (2) as Evans considers, son of Michael Garnier and Mary his wife in the Denization List of 9 April 1687, and in the Naturalization Act of 1702 as born at Caen in Normandy. Another Daniel Garnier appears as witness in the register of the French Church, Threadneedle Street, in 1671, but this may be unrelated coincidence. Made free of the Goldsmiths' Company, 29 May 1696, 'by Redemption according to an order of the Lord Mayor and Court of Aldermen'. Mark entered as largeworker, undated, probably April 1697 on commencement of register. Address: Pall Mall. It is clear that he had been working earlier, since a Sterling mark, D.G., of the same general design occurs on pieces before 1697, and he must have arrived in the country fully qualified as a craftsman of high standards. Livery, October 1698. His surviving masterpiece is the outstanding toilet service at Melbury, Dorset. The chandelier of about 1710 from the Sneyd heirlooms now at Colonial Williamsburg is also important.

GARRARD, Robert I (1760, 2320) Son of Robert Haslefoot Garrard of Cheapside London linen draper, born 1758, apprenticed to Stephen Unwin of the Grocers' Company hardwareman in Cheapside 7 October 1773 'on consideration of love and affection' (presumably a relation). Free, 2 November 1780, as 'at Messrs Wakelin & Co Goldsmiths Panton Street Haymarket'. Mark entered as plateworker, in partnership with John Wakelin, 20 October 1792. Address: Panton Street. Married before 1793 Sarah Crespel (1767-1824) presumably daughter of Sebastian Crespel (q.v.) since the Garrard's third son was christened Sebastian (born and died 1797) to be followed by a surviving son Sebastian born 1798. Second mark alone, 11 August 1802, same address. Heal records him as plateworker, Panton Street, 1792-1802. Died 1818. Three sons, Robert, James and Sebastian succeeded their father. (Family details from information of Mrs. Meade-Fetherstonaugh per Mr. Christopher Lever.)

*GARRARD, Robert II (2322-3, 3769a) Son of Robert Garrard (above) born 1793. Free by patrimony of the Grocers' Company 1816. First mark entered as plateworker, 16 April 1818. Address: Panton Street. (This mark, by an oversight or misunderstanding of the cutter is actually ℜℭ. Although this is

519

apparent in the impression in the register, I very naturally assumed it was a poor impression and corrected it for reproduction as no. 2323 until I found a clear impression on an inkstand of 1817-18, reproduced as no. 3769a under the original belief that it was an unrecorded mark of a goldsmith with surname initial E.) Second mark, 17 January 1822. Married 11 June 1825, at St. George's Hanover Square, Esther Whippy, by whom he had three sons and three daughters. Moved to 29 Panton Street, 27 February 1836. Third and fourth marks (both small, probably for gold), 29 June 1847. Heal records Robert Garrard Junior as plateworker, 31 Panton Street, 1802-21, but the signature to the mark of 1802 is clearly that of the father. Heal next lists Robert Garrard and Bros. (Robert, James and Sebastian), late Wakelin and Garrard, Panton Street, 1818. Robert Garrard II was Master of the Grocers' Company, 1853. Died 1881. The firm was appointed Goldsmiths and Jewellers to the King in 1830 and has held the Royal appointment continuously to the present day (Major General H. W. D. Sitwell, 'The Jewel House and the Royal Goldsmiths', *Arch. Journ.*, CXVII, p. 153).

GARRARD, William (3137-9, 3151) Son of James Garrard Citizen and Carpenter of London, apprenticed to Samuel Laundry 4 June 1729 on payment of 16 guineas. Turned over 30 March 1732 to Jeffery Griffith and again 26 September 1732 to Ralph Maidman. Freedom unrecorded. Mark entered as largeworker, 1 April 1735. Address: Staining Lane. Second mark, 21 June 1739. Address: Noble Street. Third mark, 26 May 1749. Address: Short's Buildings, Clerkenwell. Moved to Noble Street, 10 October 1755, where he appears as haftmaker in the Parl. Report list 1773. He is described as Citizen and Carpenter (presumably free by patrimony, see above), in the turning over to him of George Hunter (q.v.) in 1741.

GARTHORNE, Francis (736, 3570) Described as Free Girdler in the entry of his mark. This company's freemen's list survives only from 20 July 1694 and he is therefore not identifiable therein. Mark entered as largeworker, undated, probably April 1697 on commencement of register. Address: Sweeting Lane. 'Free Girdler'. One of the petitioners against the work of 'aliens or foreigners', 11 August 1697, and as 'working goldsmith' to that complaining of the competition of 'necessitous strangers',

December 1711. After the return of Sterling Standard he is presumed to have reverted to his pre-1697 mark on the evidence of its similarity of form to that ascribed to George Garthorne for the same period. Heal records him as plateworker at the Sun, St. Swithin's Lane, 1677(?)-1726, and he appears in the list of Subordinate Goldsmiths to the Queen and King, 1702-1723 (Major General H. W. D. Sitwell, 'The Jewel House and the Royal Goldsmiths', *Arch. Journ.*, CXVII, p. 154).

*GARTHORNE, George (739) Son of John Garthorne of Cleasby(?) in the County of York farmer, apprenticed to Thomas Payne 18 August 1669 and turned over later to Francis Garthorne (q.v.). Free, 11 August 1680. Heal records him as plateworker, Carey Lane, from 1674 to 1697. Judeth, daughter of Mr. George Garthorne and Judeth his wife, was baptized at St. Vedast, Foster Lane, 2 August 1687. Only documented mark entered as largeworker, undated, probably April 1697 on commencement of register. Address: Keyre (Carey) Lane. Signatory to the petition against the work of 'aliens and foreigners', 11 August 1697. Heal also records the same name as plateworker, Monkwell Street, 1724-7. Died between August and November 1730, when he was 'weigher' in the Assay Office.

GATLIFFE, James (743) Son of Samuel Gatliffe of Great Markham in the County of Nottingham clerke deceased, apprenticed to his brother William (below) 9 June 1702, before the entry of the latter's mark. Free, 30 June 1709. Mark entered as smallworker, 21 December 1713. Address: Noble Street.

GAT(T)LIFFE, William (742) Son of the same Samuel Gatliffe deceased, apprenticed to William Francis 8 July 1692. Free, 7 October 1700. Mark entered as smallworker, 22 September 1703. Address: Abchurch Lane. His brother James already apprenticed to him in 1702. Heal records him as goldsmith, parish of St. Olave's, Silver Street, insolvent 1725.

GAZE, Robert (2318-9) No record of apprenticeship or freedom but Robert son of John Gaze late of Wherstead in the County of Norfolk husbandman deceased was apprenticed to John Broughton 6 February 1765 (perhaps the father of the above). First mark entered as plateworker, 5 January 1795. Address: Shoe Lane. Second mark, 13 October 1797.

BIOGRAPHICAL DICTIONARY

GEAR, John (1340) No record of apprenticeship or freedom. Only mark entered as smallworker, 27 August 1804. Address: 9 Brains Row, Spawfields. He signs with difficulty.

GEROCK, Christopher (314) No record of apprenticeship or freedom. Only mark entered as smallworker, 29 October 1831. Address: 79 Cornhill.

GERRARD, Christopher (308, 790) Son of John Gerrard of Wimborne Minster in the County of Dorset butcher, apprenticed to Matthew West 28 June 1709 and turned over later to William Gamble. Free, 25 October 1716. Signatory as journeyman to the petition against assaying the work of foreigners not having served seven years apprenticeship, February 1716. Mark entered as largeworker, 27 November 1719. Address: Portugal Street. Second mark (Sterling) 2 July 1720.

GIBBON, Edward (589, 826) Son of Robert Gibbon Citizen and Weaver of London, apprenticed to Thomas Ash 7 May 1712 on payment of £12. Turned over 14 March 1715 to John Farnell Goldsmith in St. Anne's Lane for the residue of his term. Free, 31 July 1719. Mark entered as largeworker, 6 August 1719. Address: Aldersgate Street. Second (Sterling) mark, 31 August 1723. Address: Lad Lane, where Heal records him till 1727.

GIBBONS, Charles (309) Son of John Gibbons Citizen and Goldsmith of London (q.v.), apprenticed to Gabriel Sleath 16 July 1724. Free, 2 October 1735. Mark entered as largeworker, 19 October 1732. Address: Round Court, St. Martin's Le Grand, where Heal records him till 1734.

GIBBONS, James (1345) No record of apprenticeship or freedom. First mark entered as smallworker, 7 August 1761. Address: 'in the Curtain near Moorfields.' Incuse mark, in partnership with Samuel Goostree, 25 August 1763. Address: White Cross Alley, Moorfields. Gibbons alone appears at same address, without category, in the Parl. Report list 1773.

GIBBONS, John (823, 1321, 3638) Son of John Gibbons of Chipping Wykham (High Wycombe?) in the County of Buckingham yeoman, apprenticed to Francis Singleton 12 November 1691. Married, 12 November 1699, Jane Singleton of St. John Zachary, without doubt his master's daughter. Free, 16 January 1700. First mark entered as largeworker, 15 April 1700. Address: Foster Lane. Livery, October 1708. Signatory as 'working goldsmith' to the petition complaining of the competition of 'necessitous strangers', December 1711. Second (Sterling) mark, 2 March 1724. Address: Eagle Street, near Red Lion Square. Heal records him as goldsmith, Orange Street, near Red Lion Square, 1712-7; and Red Lion Street, 1723-6. Court, 1729. Resigned 1744. Four children of John and Jane Gibbons were baptized at Christchurch, Newgate, from 1700 to 1708, and others of John and Elizabeth Gibbons in 1728. Whether this latter entry refers to a second marriage remains doubtful. His son Charles (q.v.) is not among the baptisms recorded. Two sons and daughters of Mr. Jn° Gibbons were buried at St. Vedast, Foster Lane, 1710-12.

GIBSON, Charles (312) No record of apprenticeship or freedom. Only mark entered as plateworker, 21 February 1828. Address: 171 Bishopsgate Street. Possibly a descendant of Edward Gibson, below (cf. the addresses)

GIBSON, Edward (829) Son of John Gibson late Citizen and Carpenter of London, apprenticed to Thomas Tyso Citizen and Haberdasher of that company 2 November 1683. Free of the Haberdashers, 14 November 1690. Mark entered as largeworker, undated, probably April 1697 on commencement of register. Address: Bishopsgate Street. 'Free Haberdasher'. Heal records him as plateworker, near Half Moon Alley, Bishopsgate Without, 1691-1713; and Bishopsgate Street, 1697-1721; also Mrs. Gibson, silversmith, Bishopsgate Street, 1755, perhaps a widowed daughter-in-law. See also Charles Gibson (above).

GIBSON, William (824) Son of William Gibson of High Cunsclife in ye Bishopric of Durham gentleman, apprenticed to George Garthorne 14 June 1682. Free, 11 March 1690. Mark entered as largeworker, undated, probably April 1697 on commencement of register. Address: Carey Lane. Livery, April 1705. Heal records this date and address, and also William Gibson, goldsmith, St. Anne's, Westminster, 1705. This is confirmed by the following entries in the Register, St. Vedast, Foster Lane: Jane, daughter of William Gibson, 'a Goldsmith liveing in Gutter Lane', born 27 October, baptized 11 November 1703; Martha, daughter of William Gibson, 'liveing at St. Anne, Westminster', buried 'in ye New Vault', 18 July 1705. There follows later the

521

interesting entry: 'A maile child of Mr. Wm Gibson, her Majties Lyon Keeper in the Tower was buried in the New Vault Jany ye 10th 1709-10'. Another daughter, Mary, was buried 14 January 1711-12. Finally, Elizabeth, wife of Willm Gibson of Her Majesty's Tower of London, was buried 22 February 1712-13. If we have here, as seems highly probable, entries relating to the same man, they provide evidence of the most unlikely change of occupation for a goldsmith one could imagine.

*GIGNAC, Benjamin (172, 3489) No record of apprenticeship or freedom. Mark entered as largeworker, 28 February 1745. Address: 'de karner Gre den kort', annotated by Charles Fletcher countersigning the entry as 'Deans Court St. Martins Lee Grand'. Heal records him here as plateworker, 1741-8 and he still appears as such in the Parl. Report list 1773. His son William was apprenticed to Thomas Symonds, 4 May 1774, when Benjamin was still 'of Deane St. in St. Martins Le Grand in the county of Middlesex Goldsmith'. Listed by Evans as Huguenot (*Hug. Soc. Proc.*, 14, p. 538). His very odd attempt at spelling with the k's for c's leaves a feeling of Flemish or German origin, but 'Gre' remains a mystery, possibly an abbreviation of 'Great'.

GILBERT, John (831) Probably son of Thomas Gilbert late of the parish of St. Mary Overies labourer deceased, apprenticed to Francis Millington 21 May 1692. Free, 18 October 1699. Mark entered as smallworker, 27 March 1700. Address: Foster Lane.

GILBERT, Stephen (36-7) Son of John Gilbert late of Hixton in the County of Stafford yeoman deceased, apprenticed to Edward Wakelin 8 May 1752, but before this appears in the ledgers of the latter (*Garrard MSS*, Victoria and Albert Museum) as being paid £5 in 1750 and £6 in 1751 for wages, the payments finishing on the day of his apprenticeship. Presumably he occupied some menial post in these early years. Free, 1 February 1764. He appears in the same ledgers, from before 1766, with James Ansill as working for the Wakelin establishment in the same manner as the Crespels (q.v.). Their output varies between 17,837 ounces in 1767-8 (Michaelmas) up to 29,780 ounces in 1772. The arrangement may have lasted further. No mark has however been identified with this partnership and presumably

their work went out bearing their sponsors' mark (Parker and Wakelin). Gilbert eventually entered two marks as largeworker, in partnership with Andrew Fogelberg (q.v.), 17 July 1780. Address: 29 Church Street, St. Anne's, Soho. Heal records him alone as goldsmith, Panton Street (in the vicinity or even on the premises of Parker and Wakelin), 1776-81; at Church Street from 1784 to 1794; and with Fogelberg at the same address, 1780-93.

*GILES, George (803, 1231) No record of apprenticeship or freedom. First mark entered as smallworker, 8 July 1762. Address: London Wall, near Wood Street. Moved to the Curtain, Holywell Mount, undated. Second mark as smallworker, in partnership with John Cooper, 18 October 1765. Address: 'in the Curtain near Holywell Mount Shoreditch'. Heal records them here as silversmiths, 1773, when they appear without category, at the same address, in the Parl. Report list of that year. For the mark formerly attributed to Giles and found overstruck on pieces by Hester Bateman, see George Gray (below).

GILES, John (1326) No record of apprenticeship or freedom. Only mark entered as smallworker, 7 December 1733. Address: 'at the Cannon, Lingan Street'.

GILLINGHAM, George (802, 827, 832) Son of Richard Gillingham of Oakley(?) in the County of Dorset gentleman, apprenticed to Anthony Nelme 2 July 1692. Free, 5 July 1699. Mark entered as largeworker, 7 June 1703. Address: Black Lion in the Strand, near Temple Bar. Signatory as journeyman to petition against assaying the work of foreigners not having served seven years apprenticeship, February 1716. Second mark, 25 September 1718. Address: Guildford Street, near Pye Corner. Third (Sterling) mark, 11 September 1721. Address: Giltspur Street, near Pye Corner, where Heal records him till 1728.

GILLOIS, P(eter) (2182-3) The name appears in the records of Dublin goldsmiths in 1753-4, but no details of a working career there can be traced. First mark entered (in London) as largeworker, 20 November 1754. Address: Wardour Street, St. Ann, Soho, where he appears as plateworker in the Parl. Report list 1773. Second mark, 15 June 1782. Address: 25 Queen Street, Seven Dials. Jackson, followed by Heal and Evans ascribes this mark to Peter Gillois Junior,

BIOGRAPHICAL DICTIONARY

but there is no documentary evidence for this and an inspection of the two signatures shows the repetition of the same unusual 'P' with flat-based loop and lengthy script 'G' with tightly curled upper end. Gillois' work appears from surviving examples to have been confined almost entirely to tea-caddy and sugar-box sets of a delicate rococo flavour.

*GILPIN, Thomas (2758, 2768-9, 3825-6) Son of Robert Gilpin late of Hockliff in the County of Bedford innholder deceased, apprenticed to John Wells 7 January 1720 on payment of £40. Freedom unrecorded. Mark entered as smallworker, 24 September 1730. 'Goldsmith at ye Acorn in ye Strand'. Second mark as largeworker, with third small mark accompanying it, 2 July 1739. Address: 'Lincoln's Inn Back Gate'. This Heal expands to Serle Street, next door to Will's Coffee-house, where he succeeded Gilbert Langley, 1731-73. He appears as goldsmith, Serle Street, Lincoln's Inn, in the Parl. Report list 1773. His son Richard was apprenticed as an engraver to John Fielding, Citizen and Goldsmith, 1 July 1767. At his best Gilpin is an extremely accomplished exponent of the rococo style. He is well represented by candlesticks and tureens in the collection at Althorp.

GIMBER, William (828, 3586) Possibly (1) son of William Gimber late of Milton in the County of Kent carpenter deceased, apprenticed to Mathew Mills 4 June 1647. Free, 30 June 1654. Or (2) he might be a son of the former. Mark entered as largeworker, undated, probably April 1697 on commencement of register. Address: Ratcliff Highway.

GINES, George (801, 825) Son of Richard Gines of Compton in the County of Wiltshire yeoman, apprenticed to his brother Richard Gines (q.v.) of the Merchant Taylors' Company 5 July 1697. Free, 6 August 1712. Mark entered as smallworker, 14 December 1715. Address: Lombard Street. 'Free of the Merchant Taylors'. Second (Sterling) mark, undated, c. 1720. Elected to Livery of Merchant Taylors, 1736. Heal records him as goldsmith, Ship and Crown, Gracechurch Street, 1721-44; Gines and Pewtress, goldsmiths, Gracechurch Street, 1748; and William Gines, bankers and (?) goldsmiths, Rose and Crown, 50 Lombard Street, 1751-68, succeeded by Gines and Atkinson, 1770-81. The former also listed by Hilton Price, Handbook of London Bankers.

GINES, Richard (830, 838, 2314) Son of Richard Gines of Compton in the County of Wiltshire farmer (and therefore elder brother of George Gines above), apprenticed to Robert Monday of the Merchant Taylors' Company for nine years (unusually long term) 12 January 1688. Free, 6 April 1698. Mark entered as smallworker, 18 April 1698. Address: Fenchurch Street. 'free Merchant Taylor'. Second mark as largeworker, 7 October 1714. Address: Lombard Street. Third mark, slightly varying from second, 19 September 1717, same address. Fourth (Sterling) mark, 21 June 1720. Elected to Livery of Merchant Taylors' Company, 15 October 1706, and Court 17 October 1728. Heal records him (with a variant spelling Gaynes) as goldsmith, Rose and Crown, corner of Nag's Head Court (or corner of Ball Alley), Lombard Street, 1698 till death in 1742; also in Hilton Price, Handbook of London Bankers.

GIRDLER, John (1339) No record of apprenticeship or freedom. Only mark entered as spoonmaker, 10 January 1803. Address: 33 Bridge Road, Lambeth. Perhaps related to Joseph Girdler, bucklemaker, 1792-3 (Section VIII).

GLADWIN, Thomas (842, 2759) Son of Joseph Gladwin of Bythorpe in the County of Derby, apprenticed to John Rand of the Merchant Taylors' Company 25 November 1712 and later turned over to Thomas Langford. Free of the Merchant Taylors, 3 December 1719. Mark entered as largeworker, 4 December 1719. Address: 'at the Spotted Dog Lombard Street' (probably still with Langford). There is no record of his entering a Sterling mark until second mark, 1 August 1737. Address: Marylebone Street, St. James. 'Merchant Taylor'. Heal records both addresses at entry dates of marks, and he also appears in Hilton Price's Handbook of London Bankers. He took Daniel Smith (q.v.) as apprentice, 6 November 1740. Thomas Gladwin, plateworker, Houndsditch, who may be a son, appears in the Parl. Report list 1773.

*GLANVILLE, Richard (2317) No record of apprenticeship or freedom. Only mark entered as smallworker, 17 June 1768. 'Goldsmith'. Address: opposite St. Clement's Church in the Strand. Appears as smallworker, Great Bell Alley, Coleman Street, in the Parl. Report list 1773, and immediately below repeated with the former address, 'opposite St. Clement's Church Yard' (?a printer's error in the first entry for another name). Incuse mark as smallworker, 23 January 1778, same address (Section V).

GLOVER, Thomas (2765) Probably son of Samuel Glover, free by patrimony 6 December 1820. Described as chaser. Mark entered as plateworker, 4 July 1821. Address: 6 King's Head Court, St. Martin's Le Grand.

*GODBEHERE, Samuel (2515-8) No record of apprenticeship or freedom. First mark (two sizes) entered as plateworker, 20 November 1784. Address: Cheapside. Second mark, 27 November 1784. Third (two sizes), in partnership with Edward Wigan, 13 September 1786. Address: 86 Cheapside. Fourth mark (three sizes), with the same, 14 August 1789. Fifth (three sizes), 26 July 1792. Sixth, in partnership with Edward Wigan and James Bult, entered as S. Goodbehere and Co., 15 March 1800, when he signs as Goodbehere as opposed to Godbehere in the first entries. Seventh mark, in partnership with James Bult only, 16 September 1818. Address: 86 Cheapside. This partnership was apparently dissolved by 13 July 1819, when Bult's mark alone was entered. Samuel Godbehere 'Of Cheapside Goldsmith' married, 13 November 1790, Miss Wood of Great George Street, Westminster (*The Gentleman's Magazine*, p. 1052). Heal records him as succeeding James Stamp (q.v.), goldsmith and jeweller, 86 Cheapside, next Mercers' Chapel, 1784; with Wigan as plateworkers, Cheapside, 1786; and as Godbehere, Wigan and Co. (late Mr. Stamp's), working goldsmiths, at the same address, 1787-96. Godbehere had power of attorney to sign the entry of William Bottle's mark, a Bath goldsmith (q.v. below), 6 March 1800, when he signs as 'Ald.' (?Alderman). A George Fred. Bult also had power of attorney in 1831 for James Burden of Bath (q.v.) which suggests a fairly long connection of the Cheapside establishment with Bath goldsmiths, perhaps as supplying the latter with London goods.

GODDARD, Philip (867, 2177) Son of Philip Goddard of Bookham in the County of Berkshire (no occupation given), apprenticed to Peter White 27 September 1711 on payment of 30 guineas. Free, 3 March 1720. Mark entered as largeworker, 3 January 1724. Goldsmith. Address: Fountain Court, Cheapside. Second (New Standard) mark, 23 January 1725.

GODDARD, Thomas (2763) Son of Robert Goddard of Lambeth in the County of Surrey blacksmith, apprenticed to John Langton of White Cross Street as goldsmith 6 October 1790. Free, 6 December 1797. Mark entered as smallworker, 25 June 1806. Address: 40 Brick Lane, Old Street.

*GODFREY, Benjamin (170, 173-4) No record of apprenticeship or freedom. Was probably working as journeyman for Elizabeth Buteux (q.v.) after she set up in Norris Street, 15 November 1731. He married her at St. Bene't, Paul's Wharf, 6 February 1732, when he is described as of St. James', Westminster, bachelor and she as Elisabeth Bettew of St. James', Westminster, widow. Benjamin then entered his first mark as largeworker, 3 October 1732. Address: 'at the Hand Ring & Crown Norris Street Haymarket'. Second and third marks, 18 June 1739, same address. The last entry annotated 'Dead', presumably by 29 June 1741 when Elizabeth, widow of a goldsmith for the second time, entered a separate mark (see below).

*GODFREY, Eliza(beth) (591) Née Pantin. Married first to Abraham Buteux (q.v.) whom she survived to carry on business as his widow until marriage the following year to Benjamin Godfrey (above). Mark entered, 29 June 1741, presumably on Benjamin's death. Address: Norris Street, Haymarket, where Heal records her till 1758. Described in her trade card as 'Goldsmith, Silversmith and Jeweller to His Royal Highness the Duke of Cumberland (Heal, *London Goldsmiths*, Plate XXXIII.) Her work, which has survived in considerable quantity, shows, as might be expected, strong Huguenot characteristics of design and fine execution.

GODFREY, William (3142) No record of apprenticeship or freedom. Only mark entered as smallworker, 8 January 1772. Address: Castle Street, behind Shoreditch Church. Appears without category, at this address, in Parl. Report list 1773.

GODWIN, Benjamin (169) Son of Edward Godwin of Newbury in the County of Berkshire, gentleman deceased, apprenticed to Joseph Clare 25 August 1722 on payment of £30. Turned over 13 July 1727 to Wm. Darker at Charing Cross. Free, 14 January 1730. Mark entered as largeworker, 15 January 1730. Address: Gutter Lane, where Heal records him to 1732.

BIOGRAPHICAL DICTIONARY

GODWIN, Meschach (866, 2029) Son of Shadreck Godwin of Hemstead in the County of Hertford farrier, apprenticed to Humphrey Paine (sic) 18 August 1709. Signatory as journeyman to the petition against assaying the work of foreigners not having served seven years apprenticeship, February 1716. Free, 17 July 1718. New Standard mark entered as largeworker, 16 January 1723. Address: 'Fauster Lane'. 'Free Goldsmith.' Second (Sterling) mark, 15 March 1723. Heal records him at Foster Lane from 1722 to 1726. Presumably the Meshack Godwin of St. John Zachary, London, bachelor, married to Elisabeth Lester of St. Mildred, Bread Street, widow, at St. Ben't, Paul's Wharf, 4 November 1726.

GOETZE, Noah (2091-2) No record of apprenticeship or freedom. First mark entered as smallworker, 25 July 1804. Address: 18 Bedford Court, Covent Garden. Second mark, 3 October 1810. Moved to 8 Wardour Street, Soho, no date.

GOLD, John (1338, 3639) Son of George Gold of West Ham Essex Independent minister, apprenticed to Robert Purton of Carey Lane as goldsmith 7 August 1782 (the same day as Thomas Johnson to the same master). Free, 2 December 1789. Mark entered as smallworker, 27 March 1793. Address: 156 Aldersgate. Moved to 40 Foster Lane, 24 July 1794. Moved to 118 Fleet Street, 14 November 1808. Heal records him as goldsmith, Priest Court, Foster Lane, 1796.

GOLDHAM, Nathaniel (865) Son of Nathaniel Goldham Citizen and Turner of London, apprenticed to William Lutwych 6 August 1700. Free, 18 October 1708. Mark entered as smallworker, 28 September 1711. Address: Robinson Court, Milk Street.

GOODBEHERE see GODBEHERE

*GOODE, John (862) Free of the Longbowstring Makers' Company (now incorporated with the Fletchers' Company but records for this period are no longer extant). Mark entered as largeworker, 25 July 1701. Address: Hemings Row, followed by record of his freedom as above. The company in question seems to have been used as a convenient one of which to obtain the freedom by other Huguenots, and it seems possible that in Goode we have an anglicized name, since the year after the entry of his mark it appears on the highly accomplished strapwork pilgrim-bottles of the strongest Huguenot character in the ambassadorial plate of the Duke of Marlborough at Althorp, supplied at the same time as the wine-cisterns and ewers and dishes by Pierre Harache. These are certainly his masterpieces and he never seems to have accomplished anything comparable afterwards, and indeed his mark is rarely met with. It is possible as an alternative that he was a banker-goldsmith commissioning the pieces, but Hemings Row is not an address associated with such. More likely would seem the possibility that he had been a journeyman to one of the important Huguenots, Harache or Willaume, and had set up alone, perhaps even been handed over the Marlborough bottles by them, and then faded into obscurity or met an early death.

GOODLAD, J. D. (1803) No record of apprenticeship, freedom or Christian names. Only mark entered as smallworker, 16 September 1828. Address: 25 Villers Street, Strand.

GOODRICH, John (1328) No record of apprenticeship or freedom. Only mark entered as smallworker, 14 October 1735. Address: 'in Swithins Alley att ye Royal Exchange next door to a hatter'.

GOODWIN, Charles (310-11) No record of apprenticeship or freedom. First mark entered as smallworker, 2 December 1799. Address: 39 Red Lion Street, Clerkenwell. Second mark, 15 October 1803.

GOODWIN, Elizabeth (590) Widow of James Goodwin (q.v.) and so described in the apprenticeship to her of John Spackman II (q.v.) 21 October 1730. Mark entered as largeworker, 2 December 1729. Address: Noble Street.

GOODWIN, James (863-4, 1342) Son of James Goodwyn of Watford in the County of Hertford innholder, apprenticed to John Cowsey (q.v.) 21 January 1703. Free, 23 March 1710. Two marks entered as largeworker, 27 March 1710. Address: Foster Lane. Signatory as 'working goldsmith' to the petition complaining of the competition of 'necessitous strangers', December 1711. Third (Sterling) mark, 4 September 1721. Address: Noble Street. Presumably dead by 2 December 1729 when Elizabeth Goodwin, at same address, entered mark.

GOPSILL, Thomas (2760) No record of apprenticeship or freedom. Only mark entered as smallworker, 3 March 1786. Address: 9 Bridgewater Square.

525

GORDON, Charles (313) No record of apprenticeship or freedom. Only mark entered as smallworker, 3 December 1828. Address: 36 Southampton Street, Pentonville.

GORHAM, John (1324, 1343, 1349, 3640) Son of Henry Goreham of St. Neots in the County of Huntingdon grocer, apprenticed to Gundry Rood 30 September 1715. Re-apprenticed to Lawrence Coles 2 October 1718 on payment of £10. 10s. Turned over to 'Mr. Arnet at ye Blackamoors head in Foster Lane Goldsmith'. Free, 14 December 1725. First mark entered as largeworker, 11 December 1728. Address: Gutter Lane. Goldsmith. Second mark, 8 September 1730. Address: 'at the Blackamoors Head in Gutter Lane'. Third mark, 27 June 1739. Address: Gutter Lane. Fourth, 7 January 1757. Livery, March 1737. In 1737 Robert Collier (q.v.) entered his second mark, 'at Mr. Gorams in Gutter Lane'. Heal records Gorham's death in 1761.

GORSUCH, John (1322) Son of Daniel Gorsuch of Weston in the County of Hertford yeoman, apprenticed to James Smith 31 July 1718 on payment of £18. Free, 6 August 1725. Mark entered as largeworker, 6 April 1726. Address: Little Eastcheap. 'Free of Gouldsmiths Company'. There seems no connection with Thomas Gorsuch of Shrewsbury (Section V).

GOSLEE, Thomas (2764) No record of apprenticeship or freedom. Presumably the son of William Goslee (below). First and second marks entered as bucklemaker, 24 March 1790. Address: 5 Bath Row, Cold Bath Square; and 20 July 1792. Address: 6 Hosier Lane, Smithfield (Section VIII). Third mark as smallworker, 9 September 1819. Address: 51 Fore Street. His son Thomas apprenticed to Thomas Willmott in 1820, when his father is described as silversmith.

GOSLEE, William (3141) No record of apprenticeship or freedom. First mark entered as smallworker, 15 March 1771. Address: Ellis Row, Cold Bath Square, where he appears as bucklemaker in the Parl. Report list 1773, and entered two marks as such, 1778 and 1784, with address 4 Cold Bath Row (Section VIII).

GOSLING, Richard (2316, 2321, 3773) Son of Richard Gosling late Citizen and Haberdasher of London deceased, apprenticed to Matthew Cuthbert 28 May 1712 on payment of £25. Free, 3 September 1719 Mark entered as smallworker, 14 March 1733. Address: 'at ye Fox and Crown Barbican'. Second mark as largeworker, 28 June 1739. Address: Barbican. Moved to Cornhill, 7 July 1743. Third mark, 10 August 1748. Heal records him at Cornhill till 1754. Tried and convicted at the instigation of the Company for counterfeiting marks, and fined £100 (Court Minutes, 5 August 1742). This fall from grace did not, however, put him out of business since Richard and Joseph Gosling, spoonmakers, Cornhill, who appear in the Parl. Report list 1773, are presumably his sons.

GOSSEN, William (861) Son of William Gossen of Burford in the County of Oxford innholder, apprenticed to John Yate, 2 December 1691. Turned over to John Ward. Free, 31 March 1699. Mark entered as largeworker, 13 July 1700. Address: Foster Lane. Heal records him as Gosson.

GOUGH, William (3136, 3880) No record of apprenticeship or freedom. Only mark entered as largeworker, 14 November 1733. Address: Kerby Street, Hatton Garden.

*****GOULD, James** (860, 1317-8, 1346-7, 3637) Son of James Gould of Kingsbury in the County of Somerset grasier, apprenticed to David Green 26 October 1714 on payment of £25. Free, 8 November 1722. Two marks (Sterling and New Standard), entered 19 November 1722. Address: 'at the three Golden Lions in Gutter Lane.' 'Free of the Goldsmiths Company'. Third mark undated, between October 1732 and July 1734, same address. Livery, 1739. Fourth mark, 30 May 1739. 'Candlestick Maker'. An entry of 25 March 1743, with large blot where mark may have been struck, reads 'removed out of Gutter Lane to the Golden Bottle in Avy Mary Lane'. Fifth mark, 6 June 1743. Court, 1745. Presumably dead by 31 August 1747, when 'Mrs. James Gould' entered mark. Heal records him as plateworker, Golden Lion or Three Golden Lions, Gutter Lane, 1722–37; Candlestick, Gutter Lane, 1739–43; and Golden Bottle, Ave Mary Lane, 1741–4. James, son of James Gould and Mary his wife, was born 22 February 1730, and baptized 24 February at St. Vedast, Foster Lane. Apprenticed to his father, 3 October 1744. He is presumably the James Gould, candlestick-maker, Ave Maria Lane, in the Parl. Report list 1773, but no mark seems attributable to him. The baptisms of three other sons, William 1731, Henry 1732 and John 1735 are recorded in the St. Vedast registers and also, pathetically, three daughters Mary, 1734, 1736 and 1737, the same name repeated in hope each time.

*GOULD, Mary (1329) Widow of James Gould (above). Mark entered as largeworker, 'Mrs James Gould', 31 August 1747.

*GOULD, William (868, 3134-5, 3149-50) Son of James Gould of Kingsbury in the County of Somerset gentleman (cf. grasier in the apprenticeship of James Gould, above), apprenticed to his brother James Gould on payment of £10 9 January 1724. Free, 5 April 1733. First mark entered as largeworker, 20 October 1732. Address: 'Wheat Sheff in Gutter Lane'. Second (New Standard) mark, 24 July 1734. Address: 'at ye Candelstick in Foster Lane'. Third mark (Sterling), 15 June 1739. Livery, September 1746. Fourth mark, 1 June 1748. Fifth, 24 September 1753. Address: Old Street. Moved (back) to Foster Lane, 14 May 1756. Heal however records him at Old Street to 1757. Like his brother's, his mark is found virtually on candlesticks alone, but his greatest work bears the mark of William Alexander (q.v.). This is the great Knesworth chandelier of the Fishmongers' Company, of 1752, for which the Renter Warden's account book for 1752-54 shows a repayment of £484. 1s. 3d. from Joseph Dyer and William Alexander for frauds discovered to have been made by 'William Gould the workman'. Since Alexander's work is otherwise virtually unknown, it seems certain that he acted as sponsor for the piece and that on the evidence of the above statement Gould was the actual craftsman responsible for one of the greatest pieces of rococo silver surviving. Gould's misdemeanour was not forgotten by his own Company when he applied in December 1763 for the post of Junior Weigher in the Assay Office. The minutes record 'it was observed that the said Willm Gould had some years ago been guilty of a fraud in concealing a great quantity of copper in a silver chandelier made for the Fishmongers Company & that the same was a fact well known to many of the gentlemen of the Court and therefore it was moved & seconded that the sd Wm Gould's petition be rejected . . .'. A few days later Gould petitioned for the return of his Livery fine of £20 on the grounds 'that thro' divers lossess and misfortunes he is now straitened in his circumstances and in great want of some charitable assistance'. His petition was granted on his executing a release of all his privileges as a Liveryman and he fades from sight.

GOULDING, Joseph (1335) Son of William Goulding Citizen and Cook of London, apprenticed to William Bell 6 October 1756. Turned over to John Morecock, 19 July 1763. Free, 1 August 1764. Mark entered as smallworker, 29 August 1772. Address: Great Arthur Street, near Golden Lane, where he appears without category in the Parl. Report list 1773.

GOULDSMITH, Edmund (592) Son of Thomas Gouldsmith. Free by redemption, 7 April 1802, as jeweller. Mark entered as smallworker, 15 January 1796. Address: 9 Castle Street, Aldersgate Street.

GRACE, John (1334) No record of apprenticeship or freedom. Only mark entered as smallworker, 11 February 1772. Address: 12 Newgate Street, where he appears as bucklemaker in the Parl. Report list 1773.

GRAHAM, James (1330-1) No record of apprenticeship or freedom. First mark entered as smallworker, 26 July 1762. Address: Queen Square, Bartholomew Close. Moved to Christopher's Court, St. Martin's Le Grand, 14 November 1764. Second mark, undated. Address: 'in Whitechapel Road opposite the Mount'. Moved to White Cross Alley, Moorfields, 15 April 1768. Third mark, 3 August 1769. Appears as bucklemaker, at this last address, in the Parl. Report list 1773.

GRAHAM, William (3143) No record of apprenticeship or freedom. Only mark entered as smallworker, 16 July 1795. Address: 104 Old Street Road.

GRANT, Dorothy (877, 3591) Widow of William Gra(u)nt Citizen and Goldsmith of London, described as such in the apprenticeship to her, 10 September 1679, of Thomas Grant son of Augustine Grant late of Allington in the County of Lincoln yeoman. Her husband, also son of Augustine, probably of the previous generation, had been apprenticed to Peter Downham 1658, free 1666, and elected to Livery 1671. Dorothy's son Benjamin was apprenticed to his mother 1686, followed by William 1691. Her mark entered as largeworker, undated, probably April 1697 on commencement of register. Address: 'in the Borough Southwark', where Heal records her till 1712.

GRANT, John (1336) No record of apprenticeship or freedom. First mark entered as goldworker, 28 January 1774. Address: 49 Clare Market. Second mark, 3 February 1780. Address: 6 Wine Office Court, Fleet Street. Heal records the same name as jeweller and goldsmith, 3 Cockspur Street, Haymarket, 1784-93.

GRAY, George (804-5, 3583) Free by redemption, 1 May 1782 as jeweller. First mark entered as smallworker, 21 October 1782. Address: India House, 4 Billeter Square. Second mark, 21 January 1789, same address. Heal records the same name as jeweller, 24 Dean Street, Fetter Lane, 1777; then at 4 Billeter Square, 1779-99; as also J. and G. Gray, jewellers, at the same address, 1796. His first mark appears frequently overstruck on those of Hester Bateman and her successors Peter and Anne, and it would seem likely that he bought extensively from them such small items as creamjugs.

GRAY, John (879, 1319) An orphan, apprenticed to Francis Townsen of the Poulterers' Company 16 June 1704. Free, 20 May 1715. First mark entered as smallworker, 4 January 1716. Address: Field Lane. Second (Sterling) mark, 14 March 1722. Third mark, 20 April 1722. 'Free Poulterer'.

GREEN, David (465, 875) Son of George Green late of Monmouth in the County of Monmouth yeoman deceased, apprenticed to Thomas Gardner 8 May 1691 and turned over to Joseph Bird. Free, 16 January 1699 or 1700. First mark entered as largeworker, 27 June 1701. Address: Foster Lane. Second (Sterling) mark, 22 June 1720. His mark usually found on candlesticks and tapersticks, in which he seems to have specialized, following his second master Joseph Bird.

*GREEN, Henry (265, 997) Free by redemption of the Girdlers' Company 23 June 1772, immediately following the name of Charles Aldridge (q.v.). Mark entered as plateworker, in partnership with Charles Aldridge, 19 August 1775. Address: 62 St. Martin's Le Grand. Second mark (three sizes) alone, 9 September 1786. Address: 62 Aldersgate. Heal records him alone, either Aldersgate Street or 62 St. Martin's Le Grand, 1773-96; and with Aldridge at both varieties of address, 1773-84.

GREEN(E) Nath(aniel) (874) Son of Daniel Green of Hulmodish(?) in the County of Norfolk clerke, apprenticed to Jacob Bodendike 3 July 1678. Free, 24 September 1690. Mark entered as largeworker, 23 January 1699. Address: St. Martin's Lane. Heal records him as goldsmith, Black Lion, Leicester Fields, 1694-7; and St. Martin's Lane, 1698-1704. In 1696 he offered a reward of £10 for plate stolen from the home of the Duke of Ormond (Hilton Price, *Handbook of London Bankers*). Heal further records Nathaniel Green, jeweller to His Majesty, Dover Street, died 1728, who is presumably the same.

GREEN, Richard (876, 2315) Son of Francis Green late of Enfield in the County of Middlesex mealman deceased, apprenticed to George Moore 20 April 1691. Free, 9 April 1703. Mark entered as largeworker, 15 April 1703. Address: Foster Lane. Livery, October 1708. Signatory as 'working goldsmith' to the petition complaining of the competition of 'necessitous strangers', December 1711, and to that against assaying the work of foreigners not having served seven years apprenticeship, February 1716. Churchwarden of St. John Zachary in 1713 and 1714. Second mark, 4 October 1723, presumably intended as Sterling mark, although of same form as first New Standard mark, made possible by the rare identity of letters in initials and first two letters of surname used as monogram. Third mark, 19 October 1726. Heal records him as plateworker (Green or Greene) at Foster Lane till 1734. He also has Richard Green, goldsmith and jeweller, Strand opposite Royal Exchange, c. 1750, who appears in the apprenticeship register as the former's son.

*GREEN, Samuel (882, 2512-3) Son of Benoni Green Citizen and Blacksmith of London, apprenticed to Richard Gines (q.v.) of the Merchant Taylors' Company 5 May 1714. Free, 7 June 1721. Three marks entered 8 June 1721: one New Standard as largeworker. Address: Ball Alley, Lombard Street. 'Free of Merchant Taylors', with the note 'Look ye old Std marke in ye other book'; and two Sterling marks in the smallworkers' book, with same address and freedom note. Heal records him as bankrupt at the Three Half Moons, Lombard Street, 1726.

GREENALL, John (1333) No record of apprenticeship or freedom. Only mark entered as smallworker, 2 April 1766. Address: 'at ye corner of Great Queen Street Lincoln inn Fields', where he appears, without category, in the Parl. Report list 1773.

GREENE, Henry (878, 995) Son of Henry Green of Stepney in the County of Middlesex gentleman, apprenticed to Thomas Allen, 11 August 1693. Probably turned over at some time to Joseph Bird (q.v.). Free, 23 August 1700. Mark entered as largeworker, 31 August 1700. Address: Gold Street. Described in the entry as 'Brewer', which suggests the turn-over presumed above, although there is no record of him in the apprentice list of that company back to 1685. Bird was himself a Brewer and had David Green (q.v.), a possible relative of Henry, also as apprentice. Livery, October 1708. Signatory as 'working goldsmith' to the petition complaining of the competition of 'necessitous strangers', December 1711, and to that against assaying work of foreigners not having served seven years apprenticeship, February 1716. Second (Sterling) mark, 12 July 1720. Address: 'in Cary Lane'. Heal records him as plateworker, Gold Street, 1700–20; and Noble Street, 1724–34; also as silversmith, Carey Lane, near Foster Lane, Cheapside, 1710–18. The name also appears, as goldsmith, in the parish of St. John Zachary, 1727.

GREENWAY, Henry (996) Son of Francis Greenway Citizen and Bowyer of London, apprenticed to Charles Wright 9 January 1765. Free, 6 May 1772. Mark entered as largeworker, 24 November 1775. Address: 14 Gilt Spur Street, where Heal records him till 1778, and as plateworker, London 1790. Livery, March 1781. Died between 1818 and 1822.

GREER, John (1337) No record of apprenticeship or freedom. Only mark entered as smallworker, 17 September 1791 Address: 13 Ludgate Street.

GRESSE, P. G. (2186) No record of apprenticeship or freedom. Only mark entered as smallworker, 16 August 1725. Address: Dean Street, Soho, near Tyburn Road.

GRIFFIN, Benjamin (171) No record of apprenticeship or freedom. Only mark entered as largeworker, 27 January 1743. Address: Bond Street, where Heal records him as plateworker from 1742 to 1748. He appears without category here in the Parl. Report list 1773.

GRIFFIN, Samuel (2514) No record of apprenticeship or freedom. Only mark entered as largeworker, 8 February 1731. Address: 'at ye Carpenters Arms in Woods Close Clerkenwell'. He signs only with a crude 'G'. Heal records him without Christian name at the same address, 1730.

GRIFFITH, Jeff[e]ry (1325, 2558) Son of Robert Griffith Citizen and Clockmaker of London deceased, apprenticed to James Goodwin 12 May 1724 on payment of 20 guineas. Free, 9 September 1731. Mark entered as largeworker, in partnership with Samuel Laundy, 2 June 1731. Address: Staining Lane. Second mark alone, 18 February 1732, same address, where Heal records him till 1740. He also has an earlier entry, Jeffrey Griffith, plateworker, Over against the New Bagnio St. James's Street, 1700, which obviously cannot refer to the present worker, but might perhaps be that of his grandfather, so often of the same Christian name. The fact that the former's father above was free of the Clockmakers lends some support to this possibility.

GROVE, Thomas (1457) No record of apprenticeship or freedom. Mark entered as largeworker, in partnership with John Kentesber (q.v.) 14 June 1757. Address: Red Lyon Street, St. John's Clerkenwell, where Heal records them as plateworkers till 1773, when they appear in the Parl. Report list.

GRUNDY, William (3146–8, 3152) Son of Charles Grundy late of the parish of St. Giles without Cripplegate dyer deceased, apprenticed to Edward Vincent 2 April 1731. Free, 6 February 1739. First mark entered as largeworker, 23 December 1743. Address: Fetter Lane. Second mark (two sizes), 24 June 1748. Address: Pemberton Row, Goff (sic) Square. Third mark, 30 June 1748. Livery, January 1750. Moved to 'Fatter Lane', 26 May 1754 (entry in register without mark). Appears as plateworker in the Parl. Report list 1773. Fourth mark, 20 September 1777. Address: Fetter Lane. Fifth mark, in partnership with Edward Fernell, 23 February 1779. Address: 119 Fetter Lane. Heal records him as above, with additional 'Golden Cup' to the Pemberton Row address in 1751. Fernell entered a separate mark, 19 January 1780, so it is possible that Grundy had died by this date. His entry is annotated in the usual undated way, 'Dead'.

GUERRIER, John Peter (915) Son of John Guerrier of St. Anne's Westminster in the County of Middlesex tailor, apprenticed to Peter Harache 26 September 1700, his name or his father's 'John Guerrier' having appeared in the Denization List, 29 September 1698. Free, 24 December 1716. Mark entered as largeworker, 5 January 1717. Address: 'at the Mitre in the Strand.' Work by him appears almost unknown and he may have been forced by circumstances to work for one of the larger establishments, either Huguenot or English, and to see his productions marked as another's.

GUEST, Joseph (1341, 2771-2) Joseph Thomas son of Thomas Guest of Little Britain silversmith, apprenticed to Edward Edwards of Goswell Street as engraver 1 August 1792 on the same day as William Edwards to his father. Free, 3 November 1802, as silversmith. First mark entered as plateworker, in partnership with his father (below), 27 November 1805. Address: 57 Red Lion Street, Holborn. Second mark, in partnership with addition of Joseph Craddock, 15 August 1806, same address. Third mark, 24 February 1808. Moved to 67 Leather Lane, Holborn, 15 June 1808. Fifth mark, alone as plateworker, 16 May 1812. Address: Red Lion Street, Clerkenwell. Moved to 12 Rose Street, Long Acre, 25 March 1824.

GUEST, Thomas (2771-2) No record of apprenticeship or freedom. Described as silversmith Little Britain 1792 in the apprenticeship of his son Joseph (above). First mark entered as plateworker, in partnership with the latter, 27 November 1805. Address: 67 Red Lion Street, Holborn. Second mark, in partnership with addition of Joseph Craddock, 15 August 1806, same address. Third mark together, 24 February 1808. Moved to 67 Leather Lane, Holborn, 15 June 1808.

GUICHARD, Louis (1924) No record of apprenticeship or freedom. Only mark entered as largeworker, 6 September 1748. Address: King Street, St. Ann's, Soho. Moved to Hemings Row, 13 December 1754. Listed by Evans as Huguenot (*Hug. Soc. Proc.*, 14).

GULL, Thomas (2766) No record of apprenticeship or freedom. Only mark entered as smallworker, 17 December 1827. Address: 19 Princes Street, Leicester Square.

GULLIVER, Nathaniel (916, 2090) Son of Samuel Gulliver late of Banbury in the County of Oxford wheelwright deceased, apprenticed to Jonathan Newton 23 August 1715 on payment of £14. Turned over 27 January 1716 to Ambrose Stevenson in Foster Lane, again 14 April 1719 to Wm. Gulliver in Gutter Lane gilder, again 8 December 1719 to Thomas Gladwin in Lombard Street, again 11 March 1720 to John Pero, Charing Cross Goldsmith. Does this unusually high number of transfers infer a stormy and uncontrollable nature or was he seeking wide experience at his own request? There is no mention of the death of any of the masters concerned. Free, 6 September 1722. Two marks (Sterling and New Standard) entered as largeworker, 12 September 1722. Address: Gutter Lane. 'Murall (Muriel?) ye daugh' of Nath[ll] Gulliver by Mary his Wife was Baptized March ye 19th 1724-5 by Mr. Berriman' (Register, St. Vedast, Foster Lane).

GURNEY, John (1332) Perhaps son of George Gurney late of Tuddington in the County of Bedford butcher deceased, apprenticed to his brother Richard (q.v.) 9 October 1730. Freedom unrecorded. Only mark entered as smallworker, 23 December 1765. Address: Lower Street, Islington, where he appears without category in the Parl. Report list 1773. The connection with the above apprenticeship appears tenuous due to the time interval.

GURNEY, Richard (2324-5) Son of George Gurney of Turrington in the County of Bedford butcher, apprenticed to Richard Bayley 2 May 1717 on payment of £10. Free, 3 September 1724. Mark entered as largeworker, in partnership with Thomas Cooke II, 19 October 1727. Address: Golden Cup, Foster Lane. Second mark, as 'Richard Gurney and Co.', 23 December 1734, same address. Livery, 1737. Third mark, as above, 28 June 1739. Fourth, 17 February 1749. Fifth, 30 July 1750. Court, 1752. Warden, 1763, 1764 and 1765. Heal lists Richard Gurney goldsmith, Foster Lane, 1721-7; Richard Gurney and Co., plateworkers, Foster Lane, 1734-50; T. and R. Gurney (which must be a directory error), silversmiths, Foster Lane, 1744; R. Gurney and T. Cook, goldsmiths, same address, 1721-73. His younger brother John was apprenticed to him 9 October 1730, when the father was dead. The freedom of the latter is unrecorded. He may possibly be the John Gurney above.

GWILLIM, William (2152, 3140) Son of Richard Gwillim late of Golden Lane London gentleman, apprenticed to John Gamon 28 July 1731 on payment of £15. Free, 9 January 1739. Mark entered as largeworker, 6 May 1740. Address: Cary Lane. 'Goldsmith'. Second mark, in partnership with Peter Castle, 10 September 1744. Address: Cary Lane.

BIOGRAPHICAL DICTIONARY
H

*HAGUE, John I (1366, 1371) Free of the Lorimers' Company (records destroyed). First, mark entered as smallworker 31 December 1735. Address: Noble Street. 'Lorrymer'. Second mark (two sizes), 14 July 1758, same address. Listed as Huguenot by Evans (*Hug. Soc. Proc.*, 14) with alternative Hagne. The writing in both entries is however perfectly clear and the 'u' distinct.

*HAGUE, John II (1393) No record of apprenticeship or freedom. Possibly a grandson of the above. Only mark entered as spoonmaker, 17 May 1819. Address: 37 John Street, Holland Street, Blackfriars Road.

HALFORD, Thomas (2793) Son of Thomas Halford of the City Road in the County of Middlesex haberdasher, apprenticed to Alexander Field of Hoxton in the same county goldsmith, Citizen and Goldsmith 2 October 1799 on payment of £30. Free, 5 November 1786. Mark entered as plateworker, 18 August 1807. Address: 34 City Road. Second mark, 23 September 1809. Third, 14 November 1812. Fourth mark (two sizes), 29 June 1820. Moved to Earl Street, Stratford, Essex, 24 March 1829.

*HALL, Daniel (468) No record of apprenticeship or freedom. Only mark entered as smallworker, 31 October 1734. Address: 'at the Sun Fleet Street'. 'Casemaker'.

HALL, Edward (594, 943) Son of John Hall of Dartford in the County of Kent clerk, apprenticed to Isaac Davenport 11 November 1712 on payment of £25. Free, 1 December 1720. New Standard mark entered as largeworker, 14 January 1721, with 'Old Standard' (Sterling) immediately below but undated, presumably at the same time. Address: Maiden Lane.

HALL, George (816) No record of apprenticeship or freedom. First mark, incuse, entered as goldworker, 10 April 1788. Address: 482 Strand. Second mark (small punch), 15 March 1793. Third mark, again incuse, 16 March 1811. Heal records him only as working goldsmith at the same address, 1790.

HALL, Henry (1003) No apparent record of apprenticeship or freedom, although there is a Henry Hall, son of Henry deceased late of Duke Street, Grosvenor Square yeoman, apprenticed to John Lambe of Fetter Lane as goldsmith 1 July 1788. Freedom unrecorded. The above mark however was entered only three weeks later as plateworker, 22 July 1788. Address: 11 Sutton Street, Clerkenwell and can scarcely refer to the same, unless the apprenticeship was a mere formality, for which there does seem to be some evidence in other cases.

HALL, Thomas (2782) Either (1) son of Nathaniel Hall Citizen and Butcher of London, apprenticed to Sandylands Drinkwater 3 May 1749 on payment of £21. Free, 7 November 1759. Or (2) son of George Hall Citizen and Goldsmith of London, apprenticed to James Ryder 2 July 1752 on payment of £8 of the charity of Christ's Hospital and £8. 5s. of the Goldsmiths' Company and turned over April 1753 to Richard Reily Citizen and Stationer. Free, 2 August 1759. Mark entered as smallworker, 7 May 1770. Address: Denmark Court, Strand. Appears as goldworker Denmark Street, Strand, in the Parl. Report list 1773, and so Heal.

HALL, William (3163, 3872) Son of Charles Hall deceased of Bunhill Row saddletree maker, apprenticed to Jonathan Bateman 3 October 1787 on payment of £25 and turned over to Ann Bateman widow 6 July 1791. Free, 5 November 1794, as saddletree maker. Mark (two sizes) entered as plateworker, 27 January 1795. Address: 7 Finsbury Street. Since Jonathan Bateman is described as Citizen and Goldsmith in the apprenticeship to him on his own son, it is difficult to understand the emergence of William Hall as 'saddletree maker'. If this was indeed his trade why was he apprenticed to a working silversmith and is the mark above that of the same man?

HALL, William Snooke (3333) Possibly son of Richard Hall of St. John, Westminster brewer, apprenticed to William Stroud in Denbigh Street Strand as silver polisher 7 October 1789 on payment of £5. Free, 4 May 1803. Mark entered as smallworker, 21 March 1818. Address: 7 Asby Street, Northampton Square.

HALLARDT, John Larans (1494) No record

of apprenticeship or freedom. Only mark entered as plateworker, 10 September 1823. Address: 28 Elliotts Row, Prospect Place, Southwark.

HALLOWS, Thomas (2783) No record of apprenticeship or freedom. First mark entered as smallworker, 14 May 1771. Address: Near South^n Street, Strand, where he appears as goldworker in the Parl. Report list 1773. Second mark, 6 December 1790. Address: 4 Hunts Court, St. Martin's Lane. Moved to 77 St. Martin's Lane, 24 November 1806. Heal records Thomas Hallows or Hallowes, goldsmith, Southampton Street, Strand, 1773; and Strand alone, as insolvent, 1774. It is possible that the second mark is that of a son of the same name, although the signatures are not noticeably different.

HALLSWORTH, Henry (1010) Son of Henry Hallsworth late of the parish of St. Martin's Le Grand victualler deceased, apprenticed to William Cafe 3 March 1762. Free, 2 August 1769. Mark not in register, presumably entered in missing book c. 1769. Appears in Parl. Report list of 1773 as plateworker, 24 Bull and Mouth Street, and Heal records him also at Angel Street, 1774–81. The marks attributed to him appear on candlesticks noted from 1773 to 1780, which, it is reasonable, from his apprenticeship, to consider was his main output.

*HAMON, Louis (1925–6, 1929, 3719–20) No record of apprenticeship or freedom. First mark entered 18 March 1736. Address: Great Newport Street, Long Acre. Second mark, 4 August 1738. Address: Church Street, St. Ann's. Third mark, 20 June 1739, same address. 'Goldsmith'. Heal records him as Lewis Hamon, plateworker, Great Newport Street, from 1716–35; and Church Street, Soho, 1738–39. Listed by Evans as Huguenot (*Hug. Soc. Proc.*, 14). He appears as godfather to Jeanne Madelaine Harrache, at the Savoy Church, 1735, and to Louis Tavernier at Threadneedle Street, 1738. His work, though rarely met with, displays considerable power of rococo invention.

*HANET, Paul (942, 2189) The first appearance of the name in London records of the Huguenots appears to be that of Catherine Hanet, widow, forty-eight years, Paul (nine) and Magdelaine Catherine (fourteen), her children, from Paris, in the Reconnaissances of the French Church of the Savoy, 29 August 1686; the former is presumably the same as Catherine Hanet, widow of a clockmaker, in the Bounty List of 1687/8 and 1705. Paul Hanet 'de Paris' married Francoise Hyard, 'de lad(ite) ville', 19 March 1699, at Leicester Fields Church, when, if identifiable with the previous Paul, he would be twenty-two. There follows the baptism of a daughter Magdeleine, 'ff. de Paul (Hanet) orphèvre in Tower Street à côté de la Tête du Roy, par. de St. Gilles' (Savoy Church register), followed by that of Marie in 1705 and four other sons and daughters, at West Street Church, from 1707 to 1721. Among the godparents recorded are Louis Mettayer and René Hudell (q.v.). In spite of all this evidence of a large family and existence as goldsmith, Paul Hanet's first mark as largeworker was not entered till 7 March 1716. Address: Great St. Andrews Street, St. Giles. One must assume he had been working as journeyman till then. On entry of mark he is described as 'Free of the Longbow String Makers', probably by redemption to establish freedom to work as others. Second mark, incuse, 17 November 1717 (Section V). Third (Sterling) mark, 24 May 1721. Heal records him as plateworker, Savoy, 1705–8 (the address probably transposed from the Church register, see above); 'Next to the Golden Boy', Castle Street, St. Martin's Court, 1710–28 (also recorded by Hilton Price, *Handbook of London Bankers*); Great St. Andrew's Street, 1715–28; and Rider's Court, Soho, 1733 (the latter appears another transposition from the fact that Hanet appears as godfather in the register of Rider Court Church in that year). From the evidence of the survival of pieces bearing his mark, Hanet was clearly one of the principal Huguenot spoonmakers of his day. For his connection with Isaac and Paul Callard, also such specialists, see their entries (above). George Hanet, presumably a son, entered a mark as watchcasemaker in 1737 (Section VI) with the address Castle Street, near St. Martin's Court, next door to the Angel (cf. 'Golden Boy' above), free of the Clockmakers.

HANKS, Job (941) Son of Robert Hanks of Abbington (?Abingdon) in the County of Berkshire labourer, apprenticed to William Eyrott(?) 13 June 1684 for eight years from the preceding 1 May. He signs his name Hainks. Free, 26 May 1693. Mark entered as largeworker, 20 May 1699. Address: Gutter Lane. 'Anne the daughter of Job Hankes, silversmith, Lodge in John

Bernard's house in Gutter Lane in this parish was Buried in ye Churchyard the 17th day of December 1699' (Register, St. Vedast, Foster Lane). (See also John Barnard.)

HANNAM, Thomas (1233, 2805, 3539, 3836-7) Son of William Hannam late of Blackford in the County of Somerset tallowchandler deceased, apprenticed to John Cafe 6 November 1754 on payment of 30 guineas. Turned over by consent of John Winning executor to Mr. Cafe to William Cafe. Free, 2 December 1761. Heal records Ebenezer Coker and Thomas Hammond, goldsmiths, Clerkenwell Close, as dissolving partnership in 1760, and this appears to agree with the occasional occurrence of the mark 3539 in 1759. Hammond & Co. also appear in the Wakelin ledgers as supplying waiters. Next occurs Thomas Hannam and Richard Mills, Goldsmiths, 1765 (3836). Heal finds Thomas Hannam and John Crouch, goldsmiths, 23 Giltspur Street, 1766-93, and at 37 Monkwell Street, 1790. They appear in the reverse order as plateworkers, 28 Giltspur Street, in the Parl. Report list 1773. In view of the priority given in the above mentions of the partnership it is curious to find the IC over TH mark (1233). The first documented mark is that with John Crouch junior (who had been apprenticed to his father in 1790), 13 April 1799. Address: 37 Monkwell Street. Crouch entered a separate mark, 11 February 1808, by which time it would seem probable that Hannam had either retired or died. The two partnerships of this firm appear to have had a virtual monopoly in the trade as makers of fine quality salvers and waiters. The earlier marks also appear on cast candlesticks, which in view of Hannam's apprenticeship to the Cafes is not surprising, but this side of their business seems to have died out later.

*HARACHE, Francis (682) No record of apprenticeship or freedom. Only mark entered as smallworker, 16 February 1738. Address: 'Silversmith att ye Seven Dyals in great St. Andrew Street att ye blackmoors head St. Gilses'. Heal records him at this address as silversmith and toyman, 1732-58. Evans lists him as Huguenot (*Hug. Soc. Proc.*, 14). His relationship to others (below) of the same name remains undetermined. He signs the register as Harrache but the single 'r' appears more commonly with the others' records.

*HARACHE, Jean (1360) He appears as 'de Rouen orfevre, Riders Court' 1722 in the Bounty List for that year, and as godfather in Le Tabernacle and Rider Court Church registers from 1698 to 1709, and may be the John Harache endenizened in 1687 (Evans, *Hug. Soc. Proc.*, 14). Only mark entered as smallworker, 22 June 1726. Address: Riders Court, St. Ann's parish, near Leicester Fields. 'forriner'. Surviving examples of his work appear almost confined to small finely engraved teaspoons, which have previously been dated *c*. 1690. It is of course possible that Harache had been working before 1697, using the same mark and that he re-entered it in 1722, but there is no intervening New Standard mark entered by him.

*HARACHE, Peter I (936) His place of origin and birth in France are as yet untraced. He appears in the Denization List (Entry Book 67, S.P. Dom., Chas. II) 26 June 1682, together with his wife Anna. Free of the Goldsmiths' Company by redemption on payment of £10, 21 July 1682, by order of the Court of Aldermen, 'lately come from France to avoid persecution'. Livery, 1687. By comparison with his New Standard mark his Sterling mark can be identified in 1683 as on candlesticks at Althorp. New Standard mark as largeworker, undated, probably April 1697 on commencement of register. Address: Suffolk Street, near Charing Cross. This is annotated 'Dead' as so many entries of marks are, without any date. Heal records his death in 1700, and the marriage of 'Abraham Arache fils de defunt Pierre Arache', dated 27 June 1703, appears in the register of Le Petit Charenton Church. There is however a reference to 'la vefue Harache' as witness to the baptism of Pierre Gaillard to whom Pierre Harache (?II) was godfather, 17 June 1694, at the Leicester Fields Church, and Heal has Mrs. Harrache, silversmith, corner of Great Suffolk Street, 1699, which lends supposition to the possibility that Peter Harache I of the 1682 freedom may have already died and that the entry of 1697 (above) is that of Peter Harache II, who would not in that case have used the suffix 'Junior' as Peter Harache II (?III) did in 1698. There is however also a reference to 'Pierre Harache 60 ans Orfevre Grafton Street' in the Bounty Lists of 1713-4, who must therefore have been born in 1653 and would appear to be identifiable with Peter Harache II, who might possibly have continued to work at the Suffolk Street address after his father's death and only enter a new mark on moving to Compton Street in 1698 (see below). For further development of this problem see Peter Harache II, below. The name of Pierre Harache, to whichever generation it may belong, makes frequent appearances in the Huguenot Church registers of London at the time, as a witness to marriages or as godfather. These are tabulated below in an endeavour to clarify the picture. There is a particularly interesting entry in the records of the Church of St. James' Square or Swallow Street (*Hug. Soc. Pub.*, 35, p. xxxiii) under December 1691:

'La coupe d'argent qui servit à la Communion a esté desrobée chez Mr Harache par les voleurs entrés par les fenestres de sa chambre, et il a esté résolu qu'on consultera les principaux chefs de famille pour savoir d'eux s'ils trouveront convenable qu'on remplace ladite coupe par une coupe de bois de Calambourg (a scented Indian wood) doublée par dedans de vermeil doré, dont le prix ne montera pas à plus de trente shillings que Monsieur Harache a tesmoigné vouloir payer de sa propre bourse, a quoi la Compaignie a unaniment refusé d'aquiescer, attendir que la coupe volée estoit un dépost dont luy dépositaire est tant moins responsable qu'il a eu le malheur d'estre volé aussi luy mesme.'

Harache's offer to pay for a new cup does him credit, as also his fellow churchmen's refusal to let him do so. One wonders whether the cup was in his hands for repair or merely safe-keeping. The earliest pieces certainly attributable to Harache are the four candlesticks of 1683 at Althorp and another pair of the same date formerly in the Noble collection. The cut-card porringer of 1685 in the Farrer Collection (Ashmolean Museum) is another fine early example. The chocolate-pot of 1695 (formerly Noble Collection), so clearly derived from French design, shows his allegiance to his native country. His rarest piece is undoubtedly the gold porringer and stand of 1691 belonging to the Duke of Brunswick (Jones, *Old English Gold Plate*, Introduction). From 1697 come the important ewer and dish from Chatsworth, now in the Wilding Collection (British Museum), and the wine-cistern of the Barber Surgeons' Company, from 1699 comes the pair of pilgrim-bottles from the Farrer Collection now belonging to Eton College. After 1698 most recorded pieces are probably the work of Pierre II, although unfortunately few catalogues or authors distinguish between the marks, and re-examination is needed to clarify the situation.

*HARACHE, Peter II (937-9) Presumably son of the above, born 1653. Denization, 29 September 1698. Free by redemption, 24 October 1698, by order of the Court of Aldermen. Three marks entered as large-worker on same day, 25 October 1698. Address: Compton Street, St. Ann's Church. Heal records him here till 1705; and at Grafton Street, 1714-17. He is presumably the Peter Harach Junior to whom Jacques Des Rumeaux was apprenticed, 16 March 1703, although Peter Harache I was dead in 1700, according to Heal. Married to Jeanne le Magnan (alias Mannaye) before 1690; a son Pierre, born 27 March, baptised 6 April 1690, must have died young as another of the same name was born 30 December 1696, baptised 10 January 1696/7. A daughter Marianne, born 5 November, baptized 19 November 1693, is also recorded. (See also below.)

The surviving output of Pierre II is considerably larger than that of his father: e.g.

1700 Ewer with arms of William III (Earl of Ancaster)
1701 The Marlborough ewers and dishes and wine-cistern and fountain (Earl Spencer)
1702 Ewer and dish (Duke of Portland)
1703 Dish (Ex Methuen Collection; Farrer Collection)
1704 Punch-bowl (Barber Surgeons' Company)
1705 Gold Race cup (formerly Noble Collection)

His work is of the highest standard of design and execution and perhaps more restrained than that of his great rival David Willaume. His patronage of Simon Gribelin for the engraving of important pieces such as the Burghley toilet-service well demonstrates the impeccability of his taste.

Chronological appearances of the name Peter Harache in Huguenot Church registers:
A. Presumed Peter Harache I or II:
  1688, November 22: Godfather to Pierre Paul Chagneaux. Hungerford Market Church.
  1689, November 25: Surname only. Witness to marriage of Bernard du Faux and

Marie Montballier. Hungerford Market Church.

1693, January 8: Gives away his daughter Gabrielle to Antoine Morgan. Swallow Street Church.

B. Presumed Peter Harache II:

1690, April 6: Pierre, son of Pierre Harache and Jeanne Magnan, born 27 March, baptized 6 April at Swallow Street Church. Godfather, Pierre Harache (presumably grandfather, Pierre Harache I).

1691, January 25: Witness with Magdelaine Harache (?a sister) to baptism of Susanne Bourgain. Threadneedle Street Church.

1691, February 25: Godfather to Pierre Anthoine Boulee. Le Carré Church.

1692, May 29: Godfather to Jeanne Perigal. Swallow Street Church.

1693, November 19: Marianne daughter of Pierre Harache and Jeanne 'Ramagna' (sic), born 5 November, baptized 19 November. Leicester Fields Church.

1694, June 17: Godfather to Pierre Gaillard. Leicester Fields Church. Witness, 'la vefue Harache'.

1697, January 10: Pierre, son of Pierre Harache, born 30 December 1696, baptized 10 January 1696/7. Godmother, Susanne Finet, wife of Jan Harache. Leicester Fields Church.

1699, April 30: Godfather to Catherine Poret. Hungerford Market Church.

1699, November 4: Witness to marriage of Izac Papavoine and Jeudy Mameau. Swallow Street Church.

1700: Ancient of French Church, Swallow Street.

1700, April 1: Witness to marriage of Estienne Hobbema and Anne Harache (Arrache). Swallow Street Church.

1700, August 26: Godfather to Isaac Papavoine. Hungerford Market Church.

1703, June 27: Witness to marriage of Abraham Arache ('fils de defunt Pierre Arache et d'Elisabeth Guerin') and Marie Louise Bonnivers. Le Petit Charenton Church.

1708, June 13: Witness to marriage of Isaac Cornafleau and Marie Pontin. West Street Church.

HARBERT, Samuel (2535) No record of apprenticeship or freedom. Only mark entered as smallworker, 24 May 1771. Address: Ironmonger Row, Old Street, where he appears without category in the Parl. Report list 1773. There is no apparent connection with Samuel Herbert (below). The addresses are different and the present signature of an illiterate nature.

HARDING, George (818) George Christmas son of George Harding of 9 Pear Tree Court Clerkenwell silversmith, apprenticed to William Ker Reid of Carey Street Chancery Lane as silversmith 7 January 1824. Freedom unrecorded. Mark entered as plateworker, 30 August 1832. Address: 9 Pear Tree Court, Coppice Row, Clerkenwell, presumably taking over from his father, for whom no mark is recorded.

HARDING, James and Henry (1415) Henry perhaps son of Robert Harding of Palmers Green County of Middlesex peruke maker, apprenticed to John Morecock 6 August 1760. Free, 11 March 1772, as watchcasemaker. No record of apprenticeship or freedom for James. Mark entered as smallworkers, 8 October 1768. Address: Salisbury Court, where they appear, without category in the Parl. Report list 1773. Henry Harding removed to Fleet Lane, 27 July 1773, 'By power of aturney of Rushforth', the latter assayer at Goldsmiths' Hall at the time. Henry entered an incuse mark, 26 March 1778, at Princes Street, Barbican (Section V). John Martin Harding (Section V) may be related.

HARDING, S. (2918) Perhaps Samuel son of Thomas Harding deceased late of Old Street, St. Luke's watchglass-maker, apprenticed to John Clarke of Bunhill Row as watchcasemaker 5 August 1800. Free, 6 July 1808. Mark entered as smallworker, in partnership with Thomas Robinson, 31 March 1810. Address: 4 Dean's Court, St. Martin's Le Grand.

HARDING, Thomas (2799, 3829) Perhaps son of Thomas Harding of the parish of St. Bennett's Paul's Wharf milkman, apprenticed to Richard Holder 4 March 1735 on payment of £21. Free, 1 April 1742. Livery, July 1768. Mark entered as smallworker, 12 September 1758. Address: Minories, where he appears, as goldsmith, in the Parl. Report list 1773. Heal records him as working goldsmith and jeweller, Crown and Spur, 43 Minories, 1751-81; also Thomas Harding & Co., goldsmiths, 43 Minories, 1760-1802. His son Thomas was free by patrimony, 5 August 1772, as goldsmith, Minories, followed by two further sons, John in 1774 and Benjamin 1775, but no evidence of their trade. Heal also records the name as goldsmith, Paul's Court, 1782; and Harp Lane, 1795. Thomas Harding, silversmith, from the parish of St. Botolph Without, Aldgate, was buried 'in the Middle Aile of the Church', 7 March 1787, at St. Bene't, Paul's Wharf, which connects with the apprenticeship given above.

HARDY, John (1376) Probably son of James Hardy late of Runwell in the County of Essex husbandman deceased, apprenticed to James Henley 5 July 1751 on payment of £15.15s. Free, 2 August 1758. Mark entered as smallworker, 6 October 1762. Address: Ball Court, Pye Corner. Moved to 8 Bridgewater Square, 23 July 1771, where he appears as watchcasemaker in the Parl. Report list 1773.

HARDY, Joseph (1387, 1416) Possibly son of John Hardy of the parish of St. Sepulchre watchcasemaker, apprenticed to John Davis 1762. Free 1 February 1786. Livery, February 1791. First mark (two sizes) entered as plateworker, in partnership with Thomas Lowndes, 26 May 1798. Address: 26 Clements Lane, Lombard Street. Second mark (two sizes) alone, 27 April 1799, same address. He is presumably the Joseph Hardy in partnership with T. B. Pratt and W. E. Smith as goldsmiths and jewellers, 82 Cheapside, 1790-6, recorded by Heal. Died 1827-9.

HARE, Roger (2329) No record of apprenticeship or freedom. Only mark entered as smallworker, 6 March 1738. Address: 'at the Hand and Spur', Clerkenwell Close, near Clerkenwell Green. Was he a silver spurmaker from his sign? Heal records him at the above address and date without Christian name.

HARMAR, James (1374) No record of apprenticeship or freedom. Only mark entered as smallworker, 9 April 1761. Address: Wharton Court, Holborn Bars, where he appears as bucklemaker in the Parl. Report list 1773. Heal, however, records the same name as silversmith, Ship Yard, Temple Bar, 1747.

HARPER, Thomas I (2786) Probably born at Bristol c. 1735-40. No record of apprenticeship or freedom, nor evidence of working life in London until later. Made a Mason of Lodge no. 24 at Bristol, 1761, and paid dues till 1763, sometime after which he emigrated to America. Became Royal Arch-Mason at Charlestown, South Carolina, 1770, and Junior Warden of Lodge 190 meeting there in 1774. Advertised in the *South Carolina Gazette*, 14 January 1773, as 'Working Jeweller and Goldsmith, Has opened a shop in Broad-Street, where all kinds of work in the above branches will be completely executed upon the cheapest Terms, and with all possible dispatch. N.B. The utmost value given for old Gold, Silver or Jewels', and on 31 January 1774: 'At his Shop in Broad-Street near the Exchange, Has just imported in the Heart of Oak, Capt. Gunn from London, A neat assortment of Jewellery, &c. &c. Also a Quantity of Jeweller's and Silversmith's tools, which he will dispose of on the most reasonable terms . . .' (A. C. Prime, 'The Arts and Crafts in Philadelphia, Maryland and South Carolina', *The Walpole Society*, 1929). Married Elizabeth Edwards, 19 January 1776. Sailed from Georgetown for St. Eustatious (Dutch West Indies), July 1778, having refused as a loyalist to take the oath of allegiance to the new state. After the capture of Charlestown by the British in 1781 he returned and opened a shop in Church Street. No further record of him is found in Charlestown and he undoubtedly left the next year with the army, and was in London by 1783, when he appeared before a special committee appointed by Parliament to look into the claims of Royalists (E. Milby Burton, *South Carolina Silversmiths*). In 1785 he is found paying quarter-age to Lodge 5, Atholl Grand Lodge, meeting in the City of London. First mark entered as smallworker, 27 May 1790. Address: 207 Fleet Street. Second mark, 5 May 1810. Moved to 29 Arundell Street, Fleet Street, and third mark, 11 July 1829. Heal records him as working goldsmith and jeweller, at the first address, from 1784 (agreeing with his slightly earlier return from America) to 1796. Edward Harper, son of Thomas Harper, goldsmith, Fleet Street, was admitted to St. Paul's School, aged ten, 16 February 1788, followed by Charles, aged nine in 1799, and James, also nine, in 1801. A number of Masonic 'Jewels' bearing Harper's mark and at least one signed 'T. Harper Fleet Street Fecit' are in the Library and Museum at Freemasons' Hall, Great Queen Street. Harper played a prominent part in the union of the two Grand Lodges from 1797 and remained active till his death, 25 April 1832, at the reputed age of ninety-six (Richard J. Preece, C.B., *Notes on the Masonic Life of*

Thomas Harper, privately published from a paper read to Grand Master's Lodge, 19 March 1923). Harper's business was subsequently carried on by the firm of Acklam at 138 Strand.

HARPER, Thomas II (2792) Probably Thomas William son of John, free by patrimony 4 August 1802 as goldsmith. Mark entered as spoonmaker, 10 July 1806. Address: 11 Bell's Court, Gray's Inn Lane. Moved to 8 William Street, Gray's Inn Lane, undated.

HARRACHE, see HARACHE

HARRIS, Benjamin (931) Son of Robert Harris of Bradfordton in the County of Worcester yeoman, apprenticed to Jonathan Kirk 15 November 1689 and turned over to Nathaniel Lock. Free, 5 August 1698. Mark entered as largeworker, undated, probably April 1697 on commencement of register. Address: Without Temple Bar, where Heal records him until 1708.

HARRIS, George (820) No record of apprenticeship or freedom. Mark entered as smallworker, in partnership with Daniel May II, 30 July 1800. Address: 66 Banner Street, Bunhill Row. Heal records George Harris, silversmith, Hatton Wall, Hatton Street, 1790-3, who may be the same, and the above partnership as dissolved at the Banner Street address, 1800, which therefore appears to have been extremely ephemeral.

HARRIS, Isaac (1359, 1365) Son of Jacob Harris (below), Citizen and Goldsmith of London, apprenticed to Thomas Stackhouse 23 May 1718 on payment of £10. Free, 14 December 1725. First mark entered as smallworker, 23 September 1725. Address: Oate Lane. Second mark, 22 September 1735, same address.

HARRIS, Jacob (933) Son of Jacob Harris late Citizen and Goldsmith of London deceased, apprenticed to William Nash 27 June 1690 and re-apprenticed to Thomas Matthews 21 June 1692. Free, 6 October 1699. Mark entered as smallworker, 27 April 1705. Address: Oat Lane.

HARRIS, John I (929) Son of John Harris late of Hatton Garden cordwainer deceased, apprenticed to Thomas Holland 2 December 1708. Free, 7 March 1715. Signatory as journeyman to the petition against assaying work of foreigners not having served seven years apprenticeship, February 1716. Mark entered as largeworker, 21 March 1717. Address: Foster Lane, where Heal records him till 1734. Another John Harris, who signed the 1716 petition as liveryman, seems to have had no mark entered before this date, but he may be the John Harris, trumpet-maker, who supplied two trumpets to Bristol Corporation in 1716 and horns to the Huntsmen of the Royal Buckhounds in 1717 (M. Byrne, 'The Goldsmith-Trumpet-makers of the British Isles', *Galpin Society*, Vol. XX, 1966).

HARRIS, John II (1375) No record of apprenticeship or freedom. First mark entered as smallworker, 15 May 1761. Address: Church Yard Alley, Fetter Lane. Moved to Great New Street, 19 October (?1761). Second (incuse) mark, 2 November 1765. Moved to Gough Square, no date, where he appears as watchcasemaker in the Parl. Report list 1773. John Harris, watchcasemaker, 1812-35 (Section VI) may perhaps be a son.

HARRIS, John III (1384) Perhaps son of John Harris of Old Street St. Luke's carpenter, Citizen and Needlemaker, apprenticed to William Turner Wood Street as goldsmith 3 February 1768 and turned over to his father as carpenter 2 August 1768 and to Thomas Taylor as carpenter 13 January 1773. This turn-over, however, to apparent working carpenters makes this identification doubtful. Mark entered as plateworker, 2 March 1786. Address: 37 Monkwell Street, where Heal records him till 1793.

HARRIS, John IV (1395-8) No record of apprenticeship or freedom. First mark entered as spoonmaker, 15 January 1818. Address: 146 Aldersgate Street. Moved to 12 Well Street, Cripplegate, and second mark, 9 February 1820. Third mark, 25 January 1822. Moved to 16 Red Lion Street, Clerkenwell, 2 January 1823. Moved to 32 Charles Street, Goswell Street, 10 June 1823. Fourth mark, 12 July 1825. Moved to 27 Nelson Street, City Road, 21 January 1831.

HARRIS, John V (1399) No record of apprenticeship or freedom, but from evidence of category and third address below presumably son of the above. First mark entered as spoonmaker, 25 May 1827. Address: 43 Leather Lane. Moved to 5 West Place, John Row, City Road, no date. Second mark as smallworker, 22 November 1831. Address: 27 Nelson Street, City Road (as John Harris IV from the previous January). Third mark, 27 August 1834.

Fourth, 18 September 1839. Others 1840 and 1851. Moved to 29 Kirby Street, Hatton Garden, 23 January 1851.

HARRIS, John VI (1819) No record of apprenticeship or freedom. First mark entered as smallworker, 26 May 1818. Address: 32 St. Martin's Street, Leicester Square. Moved to 19 Queen's Street, Golden Square, and second mark, 5 May 1821. Moved to 11 Queen's Building, Knightsbridge, 27 September 1823.

*HARRIS, Simon (2537-8) No record of apprenticeship or freedom. Only mark entered as smallworker, 30 October 1795. Address: 262 Strand. Moved to 34 Great Alice Street, Goodmans Fields, 8 July 1796. Moved to 6 Clarence Place, St. George's Fields, 20 July 1807.

HARRIS, William (934) Apprenticed to Richard Lowe of the Cutlers' Company and free by service 29 November 1702. Mark entered as smallworker, 25 February 1717. Address: White Friars, near the Back Gate of the Temple. 'Free Cutler'.

HARRISON, George (815) Son of Joseph Harrison of the parish of St. Catherine in the County of Middlesex gentleman, apprenticed to John Watkins 6 December 1751 on payment of £10. 10s. Free, 7 March 1759. First mark entered as smallworker, 11 June 1760. Address: 'at Mr Jones Gunsmith in Fenchurch Street'. Second mark, 11 September 1760. Address: Fenchurch Street (Section V). Third mark (incuse), 18 December 1760. Address: Goulston Square, Whitechapel, where he appears as watchcasemaker in the Parl. Report list 1773.

HARRISON, Margaret (2031) Presumably widow of Thomas Harrison (below). Mark entered as smallworker, 21 January 1764. Address: Lamb Court, Clerkenwell Green. Second mark, 19 March 1764. Address: Shrift (?Frith) Street, Soho. The entries in a very illiterate hand. She appears without category, at her first address, in the Parl. Report list 1773.

HARRISON, Thomas (2781) No record of apprenticeship or freedom. Only mark entered as smallworker, 18 August 1758. Address: Lamb Court, Clerkenwell Green. Presumably dead by 21 January 1764, when Margaret Harrison (above) entered her mark.

HARRISON, William I (3158-9) Perhaps son of Thomas Harrison late Citizen and Haberdasher of London deceased, apprenticed to Joseph Steward 3 February 1737 on payment of £10. Freedom unrecorded. First mark entered as smallworker, 18 July 1758. Address: Monkwell Street. Second mark, 20 May 1767, same address. Heal records him as goldsmith, at this address, 1769, where he appears as bucklemaker in the Parl. Report list 1773, and entered a mark as such in 1781 (Section VIII). Perhaps the one of the same name elected to the Livery, June 1763.

HARRISON, William II (3167) No record of apprenticeship or freedom. First mark (incuse) entered as smallworker, 1 February 1804. Address: No. 1 Mitchell Street, Bunhill Row. Second mark in punch, 2 June 1810, on move to 14 North Street, City Road.

HART, Naphtali (510, 2094, 3743, 3849) Son of Jacob Hart. No record of apprenticeship or freedom. First mark entered as bucklemaker, in partnership with Duncan Urquhart, 18 October 1791. Address: Clerkenwell Green. Second mark, 20 May 1795. Third (two sizes), 19 January 1802. Fourth mark (two sizes) as plateworkers, 22 August 1805. Address: New Christopher Street, Finsbury Square. Fifth mark, alone as plateworker 10 April 1812. Address: King Street, Finsbury Square, where London directories show him alone till 1816. From 1817-27 the title is Hart and Harvey, the latter presumably Henry Harvey, his brother-in-law, goldsmith of King Street, Finsbury Square (died 1839). Hart was then joined by his son John Naphtali from 1828, the firm being styled Naphtali Hart and Son. They entered an incuse mark, in partnership as watchcasemakers, 18 January 1833 (Section V). Naphtali Hart was treasurer of Hambro Synagogue in 1807 and 1808, and later a member of Western Synagogue. He died 25 or 27 September 1834 and was buried, 28 September, Western Synagogue Cemetery, Brompton. His son entered an incuse mark as watchcasemaker, 3 January 1835 and continued in business at 5 King Street till 1848, and later at 77 Cornhill, being described as wholesale and retail watch, clock and chronometer manufacturer and silversmith. He died, 10 February 1858, at Tavistock Square (Information, R. J. D'A Hart, Esq.). Napthali Hart and Hyam Hart, jewellers, St. George's, Wapping, bankrupt September 1773 (*The Gentleman's Magazine*) may be earlier members of the family.

BIOGRAPHICAL DICTIONARY

HARTLEY, Elizabeth (595) No record of apprenticeship or freedom. A John Hartley was apprenticed to Thomas Mason in 1733, but no freedom or mark is recorded for him. It may be that Elizabeth was his widow. Mark entered as largeworker, 6 June 1748. Address: Mays Buildings. Moved to Maiden Lane, Covent Garden, 20 January 1752(?3).

HARVEY, Anne (1372) See under John Harvey II (below).

HARVEY, John I (930, 1367, 1401-4, 3644) Son of Charles Harvey, apprenticed to Mathew Judkins of the Fishmongers' Company. Free, 19 October 1737. John Harvey, goldsmith of St. Foster (Sc. St. Vedast, Foster Lane), bachelor, married to Elizabeth Haselfoot, spinster, 9 September 1737 (Fleet Register, Book 20). First mark entered as smallworker, 7 February 1738. Address: Gutter Lane. 'Fishmonger'. Second mark (New Standard), 9 January 1739. Third mark (Sterling) as largeworker, 18 June 1739. Fourth, 19 November 1745. Fifth mark, on move to Bugeons (?Prujean) Court, Old Bailey, 12 December 1746. Sixth mark, on move to Fish Street Hill, 3 October 1748. Moved to Great Kirby Street, 1 March 1750. Seventh mark, 16 August 1750. Appears as smallworker, at last address, in the Parl. Report list 1773. Heal records him as plateworker, Queen's Head, Gutter Lane, 1739-50; insolvent, Great Kirby Street, 1761; and as goldsmith, London, 1773-4, but this may refer to John Harvey II (below). The registers of St. Vedast, Foster Lane, contain baptismal entries for two daughters and three sons of John and Elizabeth Harvey between 1738 and 1745.

HARVEY, John II (1372) No record of apprenticeship or freedom, but presumably son of the above, born 24 November, baptized 4 December 1745. If however this is so, he was only fourteen when a joint mark with Anne Harvey as smallworkers, was entered, undated, between February and March 1759. This is an illiterate entry presumably in the hand of Anne who may perhaps have been a second wife of the above or, more likely, his daughter Ann, born 13 August 1739. The address for this mark is 'King Bench', which may refer to the imprisonment of John Harvey I for debt prior to his recorded insolvency in 1761. Second similar mark, for 'John Harvey Junior', 29 March 1768. Address: 'at the Crown in Bear Lane near Christchurch Surrey'. Although nearly identical to the first, this entry in a different hand. Heal records John Harvey, goldsmith, London 1773-4, without further details. He appears as smallworker, Bear Lane, Christchurch, Surrey, in the Parl. Report list 1773. There is also a John Harvey who entered an incuse mark as goldworker, 54 Snow Hill, 22 October 1773 (Section V), and who may possibly be a son.

*HARWOOD, Bartholomew (175) No record of apprenticeship or freedom. Only mark entered as smallworker, 9 July 1733. Address: 'at the Greyhound Inn in the Borough of Southwark'.

*HARWOOD, John (1368, 1411) Apprenticed to William Scarlett (q.v.) of the Broderers' Company 2 May 1722. Free, 7 May 1729, 'At Mr. Richard Scarlett's in Foster Lane Silver Smith', admitted to the freedom of the company 'On testimony of the Widow of the said William Scarlett and of the said Richard Scarlett a Member of this Company'. First mark entered as largeworker, 19 June 1739. Address: In Bunhill Row. Second mark, 29 July 1739. Address: Basing Lane, near Gerrard Hall. 'Broiderer'. John Harwood of St. Leonard, Foster Lane and Sarah Barnes of St. Michael, Crooked Lane, married 26 February 1733/4, at St. Michael, Bassishaw. Isaac, son of John and Sarah Harwood, silversmith in Basing Lane, baptised 3 May 1735, St. Mary Aldermary. In the same registers a 'List of ye Parish of St. Mary Aldermary St. Michael's Day 1734.' 'Mr. Harwood, goldsmith, family three, to church'. Heal records him as plateworker, Basing Lane, 1734; and Bunhill Row, 1739.

HASTINGS, Joseph (1383) Son of Joseph Hastings late of Fore Street Lambeth in the County of Surrey fisherman deceased, apprenticed to Benjamin Bickerton as goldsmith 7 March 1770 on payment of £10. 10s. Freedom unrecorded. Mark entered as smallworker, 11 March 1784. Address: 5 Queen Street, Borough.

HASTINGS, Rowland See below under Thomas Hastings.

HASTINGS, Thomas (2794, 2808) No record of apprenticeship or freedom, but from address probably son of Joseph Hastings (above). First mark entered as smallworker, in partnership with his presumed brother Rowland (for whom also no record of apprenticeship or freedom), 2 January 1808. Address: 53 Queen Street, Borough. Second

539

mark of Thomas alone, 30 September 1811, same address. Third mark, 16 November 1836, on moving to 36 Green Walk, Blackfriars Road.

HATFIELD, Charles (324, 335, 944) Son of John Hatfield of Tichfield in the County of Southampton, apprenticed to Joseph Barbutt 4 May 1711 on payment of £20. Turned over 11 May 1715 to David Williams (Willaume). Free, 13 April 1727. Two marks (Sterling and New Standard) entered as largeworker, 21 June 1727. Address: 'at the Golden Ball St. Martin's Lane'. Third mark, 10 August 1739. Address: St. Martin's Lane. Goldsmith. Presumably dead by 14 April 1740, on the entry of Susannah Hatfield's mark. Hatfield was one of the Subordinate Goldsmiths to the King (1723-39 (Major General H. W. D. Sitwell, 'The Jewel House and the Royal Goldsmiths', *Arch. Journ.*, CXVII, pp. 154-5). Although comparatively rare, his work is of a high standard and shows Huguenot influence, as is natural from his apprenticeship.

HATFIELD, Susannah (2541) Presumably widow of John Hatfield (above). Mark entered as largeworker, 14 April 1740. Address: St. Martin's Lane. 'Goldsmith'.

HATTERSLEY, William (2506, 3168) No record of apprenticeship or freedom. First mark as plateworker, in partnership with Samuel Dutton, 4 February 1822. Address: 7 Blewets Buildings, Fetter Lane. Partnership apparently dissolved by 8 May 1823, when Dutton entered a separate mark. Hattersley's second mark alone, 7 August 1828. Address: 7 Blewets Buildings, Holborn.

HATTON, Joseph York (1766) No record of apprenticeship or freedom. Only mark entered as smallworker, 8 June 1810. Address: Thames Street.

HATTON, Samuel (2543) No record of apprenticeship or freedom. First mark entered as smallworker, 27 September 1758. Address: Rose Street, St. Ann's, where he appears as bucklemaker in the Parl. Report list 1773, and entered two marks as such 1776-9 (Section VIII).

HATTON, Thomas (2798, 3829) No record of apprenticeship or freedom. Only mark entered as smallworker, 26 June 1762. Address: Thrif (?Frith) Street, Soho.

HAUCHAR, L. (1928) No record of apprenticeship or freedom. Only mark entered as smallworker, 16 May 1772. Address: 'Hauchar at the Comb Makers in Little Cranbourn Alley', where he appears as L. Haucher, goldworker, in the Parl. Report list 1773. Presumably concerned in mounting combs or other toilet accessories.

HAVERS, George (932) Son of John Havers, free by patrimony 20 August 1679. Mark entered as largeworker, undated, probably April 1697 on commencement of register. Address: Lillypott Lane, where Heal records him till 1705.

HAWKES, Samuel (935) Son of Thomas Hawkes of Oxted in the County of Surrey yeoman, apprenticed to John Gray 5 March 1658 for eight years 'from the XXth(?) day of February last'. There is a previous entry for him, 2 October 1657, as bound to John Brassey from 1 November following, which was presumably annulled for some unstated reason. Free, 2 March 1666. Livery, June 1682. Court, January 1694. Probably working independently by about 1670. Mark entered as largeworker, undated, presumably April 1697 on commencement of register. Address: Bishopsgate Street, where Heal records him till 1702. Warden 1704, 1710 and 1711. Died June 1711.

HAWKINS, John Lacey (1389) Son of John Lacey Hawkins of Christ's Hospital London cordwainer, apprenticed to Stephen Adams Goldsmith of St. Ann's Lane (q.v.) 5 February 1794. Free, 4 November 1801. First mark entered as spoonmaker, 2 November 1802. Address: 16 Angel Street, St. Martin's Le Grand. Second mark, 12 November 1817. Address: 17 Red Cross Square. Third mark, 18 April 1821. Fourth, 5 November 1823. Fifth, 14 April 1825. Moved to 23 Compton Street, Clerkenwell, 3 January 1826. Sixth mark, 10 October 1826. Moved to 20 Lower Northampton Street, Clerkenwell, and seventh mark, 13 September 1831. Heal records John Hawkins, jeweller, 12 Cheapside, 1795-6, but there seems no connection here.

*HAYENS, Henry (1001) No record of apprenticeship or freedom. Only mark entered as largeworker, 13 October 1749. Address: Little Windmill Street, where he still appears in the Parl. Report list 1773, as plateworker.

HAYFORD see HEYFORD

HAYNE, John (1409, 1818) No record of apprenticeship or freedom, unless to be identified with John Thomas Haines son of Joseph Haines deceased of Long's Buildings Whitecross Street undertaker, apprenticed to Thomas Johnson of Blue Anchor Alley Bunhill Row as working silversmith 6 January 1808. Freedom unrecorded. First mark entered as plateworker, 31 May 1813. Address: 23 Bowling Green Lane, Clerkenwell. Moved to 111 Goswell Street, 9 March 1814. Second mark, 21 February 1816. Third mark on move to 10 Great Sutton Place, 8 July 1817.

*HAYNE, Jonathan (1408, 2978, 3646) Son of Jonathan Hayne late of Red Lion Street Clerkenwell in the County of Middlesex surgeon deceased, apprenticed to Thomas Wallis of Red Lion Street aforesaid Goldsmith on payment of £5 of the charity of the Governors of Christ's Hospital, 1 Jan. 1796. Free, 4 June 1804. Mark entered as largeworker, 14 November 1808 (three sizes). Address: 13 Clerkenwell Close. Second mark, in partnership with Thomas Wallis II, 22 February 1810 (two sizes). Address: 16 Red Lion Street, Clerkenwell. Third mark together, 22 February 1810. Livery, 1811. Fourth mark 3 December 1817. Fifth, 17 February 1820. Sixth mark (two sizes) alone, 3 July 1821. Address: Red Lion Street, Clerkenwell. Seventh (two sizes), 19 July 1823. Eighth (two sizes), 29 October 1829. Ninth (four sizes), 12 April 1832. Tenth (five sizes), 13 May 1834. The number of marks registered and range of sizes indicates an extensive and flourishing business which is further suggested by the fact that from 1822 to 1827 Hayne took at least six apprentices. Court, 1836. Warden, 1840-42, Prime Warden, 1843. Died 19 March 1848.

HAYNE, Samuel (2546) Samuel Holditch John son of Jonathan Hayne of Red Lion Street Clerkenwell surgeon deceased and brother of Jonathan (q.v.), apprenticed to Thomas Wallis (his brother's master and partner) as goldsmith 4 January 1804 on payment of £5 of the gift of the Governors of Christ's Hospital. Freedom unrecorded. First mark as plateworker, in partnership with Dudley Cater, who had been the apprentice of Jonathan Hayne, 5 July 1836. Address: 16 Red Lion Street, Clerkenwell, when Jonathan probably retired. Second mark (two sizes), 12 April 1837. Third entry of six marks, 26 May 1842. Fourth, 1 October 1842, and later continuations.

HAYTER, George (2804) George Smith Hayter son of Thomas Hayter (below), free by patrimony 7 December 1814 as silversmith. His two names suggests that he was the godson of his father's partner George Smith. First mark, in partnership with his father Thomas (q.v.), 15 March 1816. Address: 4 Huggin Lane, Wood Street. Second mark, 7 December 1821. Livery, 1816. Court, 1846. Warden, 1851-3. Prime Warden 1854 and 1863. Died 15 September 1887.

*HAYTER, Thomas (909, 2790, 2804) Son of John Hayter of Cavendish Street Middlesex carver, apprenticed to George Smith of Huggin Lane London silversmith Citizen and Goldsmith 4 December 1782 on payment of £30. Free, 3 February 1790. Mark entered as plateworker, in partnership with George Smith II, 7 January 1792. Address: 4 Huggin Lane, Wood Street. Livery, October 1801. Second mark, alone (two sizes), 21 May 1805, same address. Third mark, in partnership with his son George Hayter (q.v.), 15 March 1816, same address. Fourth mark together, 7 December 1821. Died 2 September 1840.

HAYWARD, Joseph (1388) No record of apprenticeship or freedom. Only mark entered as smallworker, 8 October 1800. Address: York Street, St. George's Fields.

HAYWOOD, Joseph I (940) Joseph Haywood son of John of Aylesbury in the County of Buckingham maltster, apprenticed to Richard Alkyn 15 July 1670. Free, 31 August 1677. Livery, May 1694. Mark entered as smallworker, 15 February 1699. Address: 'in the Old Change'. Entry followed by 'for Buckles', suggesting an additional mark for this special purpose, although no others appear in the register under his name. He may of course have used a pre-Britannia Standard mark, not as yet recognized.

HAYWOOD, Joseph II (1364) Presumably son of Joseph Haywood Junior of Plumtree in County of Nottingham grazier, apprenticed to William Cartlitch 19 January 1725 on payment of £120 (a remarkably high premium). Free, 29 July 1736. Mark entered as smallworker, undated, but between others of November 1734. Address: Cross Street, near Golden Square, 'next dore to ye too Blew posts'.

HEAD, Thomas I (987) Son of Thomas Head late of the parish of St. Olave Southwark mariner deceased, apprenticed to Robert Bullock 13 June 1699. Free, 14 February 1708. Mark entered as smallworker, 17 January 1716. Address: Cheapside.

HEAD Thomas II (1234) No record of apprenticeship or freedom. Mark entered as spoonmaker, in partnership with John Cotton, 8 December 1809. Address: 73 Wood Street, Cheapside.

HEADLAND, Thomas Hughes (2795, 2803) No record of apprenticeship or freedom. First mark (incuse) entered as smallworker, 22 March 1834. Address: 57 Great Sutton Street, Clerkenwell. Second mark in punch, 30 May 1834. Third 7 October 1834. Moved to 13 Great Sutton Street, 2 December 1835. Fourth mark, 4 May 1837.

*HEALY, Joseph (988, 1358) Son of Joseph Healy Barber Surgeon, free by patrimony of that Company, 4 December 1724. Two marks (Sterling and New Standard) entered as largeworker, 19 August 1725. Address: 'Opposite Foster Lane Church'. 'Barber Surgeon'.

*HEARNDEN, Nicholas (3742) Son of Nicholas Hearnden late of East Mauden (?Malling) in the County of Kent gardener deceased, apprenticed to Marmaduke Daintrey 6 July 1748 and turned over to Richard Hawkins 5 July 1753. Free, 5 May 1756. No entry recorded of any mark, which probably occurred during the period of the missing register 1758-73. His name appears in the Parl. Report list 1773, as spoonmaker, Pick-Ax Street.

HEBBERD, Isaac (1394) No record of apprenticeship or freedom. First mark entered as smallworker, 14 March 1822. Address: 11 Air Street, Piccadilly. Second mark, 28 January 1825.

HEBDEN, Luke (1927) No record of apprenticeship or freedom. Only mark entered as smallworker, 17 February 1759. Address: Princess Street (Barbican), where he appears without category in the Parl. Report list 1773.

*HEBERT, Henry (999, 1000, 1008-9) No record of apprenticeship or freedom under Hebert, Herbert or Hibberd. First mark entered as largeworker, 18 January 1734. Address: At the Three Crowns, Corner of Hedge Lane, Leicester Fields. Second mark, 24 December 1735, same address. Third and fourth marks, 28 June 1739, same address. Fifth and sixth marks, 22 February 1748, on move to The Golden Hart, St. Ann's Court, Dean Street, Soho. Heal records him as Hebert or Herbert, silversmith, Three Crowns, Panton Street, Leicester Fields, 1736-40; and at Golden Hart, Dean Street,

1747. Listed by Evans as Huguenot without origin stated. Possibly from Le Mans, according to information of Sir Charles Clay. Subordinate Goldsmith to the King 1736-40 (Major General H. W. D. Sitwell, 'The Jewel House and the Royal Goldsmiths', *Arch. Journ.*, CXVII, p. 155).

HELEY, James (1357) No record of apprenticeship or freedom as Heley or Healy, but perhaps connected with John Hely following. Only mark entered as smallworker, undated, between April 1724 and June 1726. A very illiterate entry. Address: Cross Street, followed by '. . . gardn lodger shp'(?)

*HELY, John (989) Either (1) John Haley apprenticed to John Laughton of the Grocers' Company 5 July 1682, free 9 September 1689. Or (2) another of the same name apprenticed to Thomas Rogers of the same company 2 July 1685, free 1699. The first name above has a note in margin of the freedom register: 'Man: at Mr Hartwells Grocer in St. Clements Lane in Strand'. Since John Laughton is well known as a largeworker (see below) the first identity is presumably correct. Mark entered as largeworker, 11 March 1699. Address: St. Martin's Lane. 'Free Grocer'.

*HEMING, George (821-2) Son of Thomas Heming Citizen and Goldsmith of London, apprenticed to his father 2 March 1763. Freedom unrecorded. Appears as George Hemming, goldsmith, Piccadilly, in the Parl. Report list 1773, showing he had entered a mark, presumably in the missing register before that date. Mark entered as plateworker, in partnership with William Chawner, 17 November 1774. Address: Bond Street. Second mark, 15 February 1781. Address: Old Bond Street. Heal records G. Hem(m)ing, goldsmith and jeweller, Hand and Hammer opp. Black Bear Inn, Piccadilly, c. 1760-73, but from the apprenticeship above the first date is either a mistake or refers to another. Heal also finds George Heming and William Chawner, plateworkers, King's Arms, New Bond Street facing Clifford Street, 1773-81; and Heming alone, 151 New Bond Street, 1784-93, which makes it quite clear that they were successors to Thomas Heming at the same address.

*HEMING, Thomas (2796-7, 3828) Son of Richard Heming of Ludlow in the County of Salop mercer, apprenticed to Edmund Boddington 7 March 1738 on payment of

£40 and turned over the same day to Peter Archambo Butcher. Free, 7 May 1746. Mark entered as largeworker, 12 June 1745. Address: Piccadilly. Second mark unrecorded in register, presumably after 1758. Third mark, with crown above, also unrecorded, presumably not adopted until his appointment as Principal Goldsmith to the King in 1760, which appointment he held until 1782, when after a 'witch-hunt' into his charges he was supplanted by Jefferys and Jones. (Major General H. W. D. Sitwell, 'The Jewel House and the Royal Goldsmiths', *Arch. Journ.*, CXVII, p. 152.) Livery, June 1763. Appears as Thomas Hemming, goldsmith, New Bond Street, in the Parl. Report list 1773. Some of his earlier surviving pieces in the Royal collection show a French delicacy of taste and refinement of execution which is unquestionably inherited from his master Archambo. His 'masterpiece' is probably the Speaker's wine-cistern, 1770, at Belton House, Lincolnshire. Died between 1795 and 1801.

*HENNELL, David I (469, 471-2) Son of Robert Hennell of Newport Pagnell in the County of Buckingham framework knitter born 8 December 1712, apprenticed to Edward Wood 6 September 1728 on payment of £10 (another entry to the same effect, 29 November of same year). Free, 4 December 1735. Married 1 March 1736, to Hannah Broomhead 'at Wilson's' (Fleet Register of Marriages) when described as goldsmith of St. Ann, Aldersgate. First mark entered as largeworker, 23 June 1736. Address: King's Head Court, Gutter Lane, which Heal records from trade card as Flower-de Lis and Star in Gutter Lane, corner of Cary Lane, and since Edward Wood (q.v.) had moved to Cary Lane in August 1735 and incorporates a mullet or star and fleur-de-lys in his mark of that date, it seems probable that the young Hennell remained working on his recent master's premises. In April 1737 he took as apprentice his half-brother William, but the latter never entered a mark. Second mark not in register, presumably June 1739 to comply with the new Act. The Hennells had fifteen children of which only five reached maturity. John, born 1739, free of the company by patrimony but not apparently active in the trade. Robert, fifth child was apprenticed to his father, 1756 (see below). David, elected to Livery, June 1763. Third mark, in partnership with son Robert, 9 June 1763. Address: Foster Lane. Fourth mark similar, 9 July 1768. Retired from business at the request of the Company to become Deputy Warden, 1773, and gave evidence on marking procedure at the Assay Office to the Parliamentary Committee. Died 1785. This and the following entries for the family owe much to Percy Hennell ('The Hennells Identified', *The Connoisseur*, December 1955, p. 260).

HENNELL, David II (2336-7) Eldest son of Robert Hennell I, born 1767 and grandson of David I, apprenticed to his father 6 February 1782. Free, 5 August 1789. Livery 18 February 1791. First mark entered in partnership with his father, 15 July 1795. Second mark, with brother Samuel added to the partnership, 5 January 1802. Appears to have severed his connection with the business soon afterwards, since Robert and Samuel entered a new mark, October same year (but this might perhaps merely indicate David's concentration on the business rather than working side). Resigned from Livery, 4 December 1821. Date of death unknown.

HENNELL, Robert I (472, 2330-1, 2336-8) Fifth child of David Hennell I, born 1741, apprenticed to his father 5 May 1756. Free, 8 June 1763. First mark entered in partnership with his father, 9 June 1763. Livery, July 1763. Second similar mark, 9 July 1768. Third mark alone as smallworker, 30 May 1772. Appears as plateworker, Foster Lane, in the Parl. Report list 1773. Fourth mark, as 'saltmaker', 9 October 1773. Address: 16 Foster Lane. Fifth mark, in partnership with his son David II as plateworkers, 15 July 1795. Address: 11 Foster Lane. Sixth mark, with son Samuel as third partner, 5 January 1802. Seventh mark with Samuel only, 28 October 1802. Appears to have remained in business until his death in April 1811, since Samuel did not enter a mark alone till the following June. A son Robert was apprenticed to his father, Robert I, 5 April 1786, but no freedom is recorded, nor entry of a mark and he is not therefore given a separate entry here.

HENNELL, Robert II (1040, 2332) Son of John Hennell, elder brother of Robert Hennell I, who had returned to Newport Pagnell and continued his grandfather's business, described in the register as draper, Citizen and Goldsmith of London. Robert II was apprenticed to his uncle Robert

HENNELL

Hennell I 8 April 1778. Free, 1 June 1785. He was also apprenticed to John Houle (q.v.) engraver, and seems to have worked after freedom as such at Windmill Court, Smithfield, very probably executing the fine engraving typical of Robert I's pieces at the period, until first mark entered as plateworker, in partnership with Henry Nutting, 17 June 1808. Address: 38 Noble Street, Foster Lane. Second mark alone, 3 November 1809. Address: 35 Noble Street. Moved to 3 Lancaster Court, Strand, 28 June 1817. Third mark, 11 August 1820. Fourth mark, 28 January 1826. Retired 1833 when he announced in the London Gazette, 25 May, that his son Robert would take over his mark. Robert II's second mark appears on the coffin-plate of George III (illustrated, Percy Hennell., op. cit. under David I).

HENNELL, Robert III (2333) Son of Robert Hennell II (above), born 1794. Free by patrimony, 7 May 1834, as silversmith. First mark (three sizes) entered 30 June 1834. Manufactory: 14 Northumberland Street, Strand. Second mark with entry 'residence removed to Saint John's Hill, Battersea Rise', 20 May 1857. Livery, 1842. Died 1868. His son Robert Hennell IV (1826–92) was apprenticed to him and free 1849, entered marks 1869 and 1870, outside the period of this work. His younger brother James Barclay Hennell entered his mark 1877 and died 1899, when this business became extinct.

HENNELL, Samuel (2337–8, 2539, 2547) Son of Robert Hennell I, born 1778. Free by patrimony, 2 December 1800. First mark entered, as third partner to his father and brother David II, 5 January 1802. Address: 11 Foster Lane. Second mark, with Robert Hennell only, 28 October 1802. Third mark, alone, 22 June 1811. same address. Fourth mark, in partnership with John Terry (who had married one of Samuel's nieces), 6 April 1814. Apparently this partnership terminated by 27 July 1816, when a move to 8 Aldermanbury Postern is entered, again under the first entry for Samuel's separate mark. Moved again to 8 Charles Street, Goswell Street, 19 September 1816. Back to Foster Lane, 7 August 1817. To 5 Snowhill, 18 May 1818. Samuel's son Robert George, born between 1800 and 1810, began a separate business as jeweller, Southampton Street, 1835, but no mark appears to have been entered by him, although Jackson attributes one R G H, appearing on com- munion cups of 1844 at St. George's, Bloomsbury. Samuel Hennell's 1811 mark should be distinguished from those of Solomon Hougham (q.v.) working at the same time.

HENSTRIDGE, John (1362) No record of apprenticeship or freedom. Only mark entered as smallworker, 24 May 1731. Address: 'At the Crown and Pearl in Bell Alley', Lombard Street.

HENTSCH, Frederick (685) Frederick Charles son of John Frederick Hentsch of Old Street furrier, apprenticed to John Truman of City Road 7 February 1810 as plateworker and turned over 3 July 1816 to George Snook of Foundry Place, Hoxton silversmith, Citizen and Goldsmith. Free, 5 November 1817. First mark, incuse, entered as smallworker, 17 December 1818. Address: 18 Dukes Court, St. Martin's Lane. Second mark in punch, 4 November 1826. Moved to 17 Bartletts Buildings, 30 October 1827.

*HERBERT, Samuel (2542, 2545) No record of apprenticeship or freedom. First mark entered as largeworker, 9 October 1747. Address: Aldersgate Street. Second mark, with unnamed partner as Samuel Herbert and Co., 6 November 1750. Address: Foster Lane. The initials of the partner are either H.B. or possibly, but unlikely, B.H. Heal records him at both addresses, the second till 1768. Appears as plateworker, Stratford Green, in the Parl. Report list 1773. A specialist in pierced work, particularly baskets, and some epergnes.

HERIOT (alias Howard), Joseph (1370) Joseph Howard son of William Heriot late of Barnes in the County of Surrey wheelwright deceased, apprenticed to Edmund Boddington 3 September 1734 (signs with X). Free, 4 April 1750. Mark entered as largeworker, under name of Heriot but countersigned at base Joseph Howard, 30 June 1756. Address: 'Great St. Andry (Andrew's) Street, Seven Dayels', where Heal records him under Heriot from 1750 to 1778. His theatrical uncertainty of name is complicated further by the parallel existence of William Howard (q.v.), also apprenticed to Boddington, whose father also William, wheelwright of Fulham was alive in 1749. Perhaps a cousin, but the coincidence of the name and occupation adds to the mystery.

*HERNE, Lewis (1930, 3719) Son of Basil Herne of the parish of St. Gregory London gentleman, apprenticed to Richard Gurney

3 February 1748 on payment of £27. Free, 7 May 1755. Mark entered as largeworker, in partnership with Francois Butty, 13 July 1757. Address: Clerkenwell Close, whence Heal records he absconded in 1765. Livery, July 1763. *The Gentleman's Magazine* records his bankruptcy in November 1768 when he is described as goldsmith, Aldersgate Street, which would suggest that he had reappeared and set up alone. A mark which can be attributed to him at this time is that recorded by Jackson on a cup of 1766 (3719). Died between 1818 and 1822.

HERVOT, James (990, 1356) James Harvott son of James Harvott 'late of Rouen in ye Kingdome of France Dyer deced', apprenticed to Nicholas Faulcon of the Merchant Taylors' Company 1 February 1699. Free, 6 March 1706. First mark entered as smallworker, 3 October 1712. Address: Glasshouse Yard, Blackfriars. 'Free Merchant Taylor'. Second mark, 'Golde Marke', Sterling type, 20 January 1722. Address: St. Ann's, Blackfriars, over Jackson Court by Breakneck Stairs.

HEWAT, Alexander (41, 1278) No record of apprenticeship or freedom. Mark entered as largeworker, in partnership with James Ede, 6 December 1808. Address: 12 King Street, Goswell Street. Second mark alone, 3 November 1810, same address.

HEWITT, William (3169) No record of apprenticeship or freedom. First mark entered as smallworker, 24 February 1829. Address: 22 Edmunds Place, Aldersgate. Moved to 9 Great Sutton Street, Clerkenwell, and second mark, 29 January 1834. Third mark (two sizes), 28 April 1843.

HEYFORD, Daniel (467) No record of apprenticeship or freedom. Possibly the son of Humphrey Hayford, goldsmith, London, 1722 (Heal). First mark entered as smallworker, 21 February 1730. Address: Denmark Court, at Mr Pilkington's. Second mark, as Hayford, 1 May 1739. Address: Bartholomew Close, Goldsmith, where Heal records him for this year.

HICCOX, John (1361) No record of apprenticeship or freedom. Only mark entered as smallworker, 12 October 1730. Address: 'at the Dial & Crown against Hatton Garden, Holborn'. Heal records him without Christian name as goldsmith, Holborn, 1731.

HICKMAN, Edmund (1018) Son of William Hickman late Citizen and Dyer of London deceased, apprenticed to Edward Cornock 19 July 1712 on payment of £14. Free, 6 August 1719. Mark entered as largeworker, 21 August 1719 (or possibly 1720). Address: Foster Lane, where Heal records him in the same year.

HICKMAN, Henry (998) Son of Henry Hickman of London carpenter, apprenticed to Richard Wyatt of the Barber Surgeons' Company 7 December 1708. Free, 2 September 1718. Mark entered as smallworker, 8 August 1722. Address: 'at the Anchor & Crown against St. Clements Church in the Strand'. 'Free of Barber Surgeons Company'.

*HIGGINS, Francis (683-4) Son of Francis Higgins of Hosier Lane silversmith, apprenticed to George Smith of Hosier Lane aforesaid silversmith 4 December 1805 on payment of £7 14s. of the charity of the Worshipful Company of Goldsmiths Mark entered as plateworker, 31 October 1817. Address: 20 Cursitor Street, Chancery Lane. On 3 December following he is described as spoonmaker in the apprenticeship to him of Edward Kirby. Second mark, 19 January 1821. Third, 10 February 1825. Fourth, 7 August 1829. Fifth, 2 October 1829. Moved to 47 Liquerpond Street, Gray's Inn Lane, 15 November 1834. Sixth mark, 3 December 1835. Address: 40 Kerby Street, Hatton Garden. Seventh mark (two sizes), 14 June 1837. Eighth, 24 October 1843. Ninth, 14 October 1854. Tenth, 30 June 1865. Others later.

HIGGS, Edward (597) No record of apprenticeship or freedom. First mark entered as smallworker, 30 March 1763. Address: Pitfield Street, Hoxton. He appears here, as bucklemaker, in the Parl. Report list 1773 and entered three marks as such, 1782-6, and another with James Higgs, 1787, all at this address (Section VIII). Heal records Edward and James Higgs, silver button makers, 21 Peerpool Lane (Gray's Inn Lane), 1793.

HIGGS, Robert (2326) No record of apprenticeship but appears in the quarterage list of the Clockmakers' Company c. 1725 as watchcasemaker, Sweetings Alley. Only mark entered as smallworker, 25 October 1721. Address: Addell Street, Aldermanbury 'Clockmaker'.

HILL, Ann (38-9) No record of apprenticeship or freedom, although on first entry described as Free Goldsmith. First mark entered as largeworker, 15 July 1726.

Address: Great Trinity Lane. A very unusual mark in that it incorporates below the initials the year of entry as commonly in Scandinavia. Second mark, undated, between May 1734 and December 1735. Address: Albemarle Street. Presumably a widow and perhaps mother of Caleb Hill (below), since the dates of entry of her two marks span his, which would seem improbable if the latter had been her husband. Heal records her at Albemarle Street, as plateworker, till 1737.

*HILL Caleb (325) No record of apprenticeship or freedom. Presumably son of Ann Hill (above). Mark entered as largeworker, 17 September 1728. Address: Albemarle Street, Clerkenwell. Presumably dead by 1734-5, when Ann Hill's second mark was entered (see above). Heal records him at this address, 1728-35.

HILL, Charles (2634) No record of apprenticeship or freedom. Only mark entered as smallworker, in partnership with Samuel Swain, 25 July 1760. Address: New Gravel Lane, Southwark, where he appears, both alone and with the above, without category in the Parl. Report list 1773. Heal records one of the name as silversmith, London, 1781; and 3 Charing Cross, 1790-6, but connection seems unlikely with a fairly ordinary name. The Fitzwalter accounts (Essex County Archives) contain an entry under 1745: 'Char. Hill for a silver orange strainer', but this would seem too early to connect.

HILL, John (1014, 1353) Son of John Hill of Mayfold in the County of Stafford yeoman, apprenticed to Thomas Hill (his brother, q.v.) 24 May 1695. Free, 25 September 1702. Mark entered as smallworker, 27 November 1707. Address: Cannon Street. Second (Sterling) mark, undated, c. 1720. Livery, February 1726. Resigned 28 April 1743. Heal records him only as goldsmith, London, 1717.

*HILL, Robert (1011, 2335, 3775) Probably son or younger brother of Thomas Hill (below), or possibly son of Walter Hill of the parish of Ashby in the County of Worcester yeoman, apprenticed to John Austin 2 November 1689. Free, 17 July 1707. No later apprenticeship of this name before the date of first mark entered as largeworker, 13 January 1717. Address: St. Swithin's Lane. Second mark, 17 March 1740, same address, where Heal records him till 1742. The marriage entry of Robert Hill of St. Sweeting, London and Elizabeth Rood of the same parish, 4 July 1717, at St. Michael, Cornhill, would seem likely to be his. It is interesting to note that there is evidence that he received the commissions for the annual presentation dish given by the Jewish congregation of Bevis Marks to the Lord Mayor, which had earlier been made by John Ruslen (q.v.) and that the latter's address was also Swithin Lane. There seems a strong possibility therefore that Hill was Ruslen's successor (but see Thomas Hill, below). His mark is comparatively rarely found and usually on pieces of some merit. It may be that he was basically a banker-goldsmith undertaking occasional commissions such as the Jewish dishes.

HILL, Thomas (1012, 1017) Son of John Hill of Mayfield in the County of Stafford gentleman and brother to John Hill (above), apprenticed to Robert Longe 14 September 1687 and turned over to Ben. Clare. Free, 22 October 1694. First mark entered as smallworker, 27 June 1699. Address: Swithins Lane, near 'Lumbert' Street. Second mark, 9 May 1716. Address: Shadwell.

HILLAN, Christian (326, 333-4) No record of apprenticeship or freedom. From the uncertainty of spelling attached to his name he looks to have been an immigrant, perhaps Scandinavian in origin. First mark entered as largeworker, 20 April 1736. Address: Bishop's Court, Durham Yard, with later note at base 'now at the Golden Ball in Earl Street near ye 7 Dials'. The first entry appears to be in the hand of Benjamin Pyne who countersigns as Deputy or Touch warden at this period, with the name entered as Hyland, above which is a note 'ye name is Hillan'. The maker himself signs 'Hyllan' for this entry but Hillan subsequently. Second mark, 4 June 1739. Address: Great Earl Street. Third mark, undated, on move to Crown and Golden Ball, Compton Street, St. Ann's. Heal records him as Charles Hillan (the mistake in Christian name probably springing from an abbreviation), silversmith, Crown and Ball, Compton Street, Soho, 1741; and Christian Hillan, plateworker, Earl Street, 1736; and at the Compton Street address c. 1740.

HILLS, John (1378) Perhaps John Hill son of John of St. James' Clerkenwell baker deceased, apprenticed to John Brotherton 6

July 1757. Free, 5 June 1765. (But another, Thomas Hill, was apprenticed to the same master as watchcasemaker.) Only mark entered as spoonmaker, 19 November 1773. Address: 6 Paternoster Row.

HILLUM, Richard (2334) No record of apprenticeship or freedom. (Perhaps a Stationer as Richard Hillum, son of Richard, jeweller, was made free of the Goldsmiths' Company by translation from the Stationers', 1854.) First mark as plateworker, 10 September 1828. Address: 24 Myrtle Street, Hoxton. Second mark, 6 December 1831.

HILMAN, John (1363) No record of apprenticeship or freedom. Possibly free of the Cutlers' Company. Only mark entered as smallworker, annotated 'Sword Cutler', undated, between June 1731 and March 1733. Address: Russell Street, Covent Garden.

*HINDMARSH, George (807-9, 2260) No record of apprenticeship or freedom. First mark entered as largeworker, in partnership with Robert Abercromby, 11 May 1731. Address: Christopher Court, St. Martin's Le Grand. Second mark alone, 6 July 1731, same address. Third mark, undated, between 24 December 1735 and 18 March 1736. Address: Glasshouse Yard, Blackfriars. Fourth mark (two sizes), 27 June 1739, same address. Moved to Essex Street, Strand, 7 December 1748. Moved to 'ye Strand', 9 July 1753 (register entry without mark). Fifth mark, 15 September 1753. Heal records him as plateworker, St. Martin's Le Grand, 1731; Blackfriars, 1735; Glasshouse Street, 1739; and as goldsmith, Blackmoors Head, Strand, 1743; goldsmith, Tooley Street, Southwark (? another man); and jeweller and goldsmith, Crown opposite Durham Yard, Strand, and King's Arms and Birdcage, opposite Durham Yard, both *c.* 1750. Like his partner for a few months, Abercromby, Hindmarsh seems to have made practically nothing but salvers and waiters.

HINE, James (1379) No record of apprenticeship or freedom. Only mark entered as smallworker, 27 September 1774. Address: No. 14 Old Street Square.

HINTON, William (1013, 1352) Son of Henry Hinton late Citizen and Bricklayer of London deceased, apprenticed to John Cruttall 9 December 1692 and turned over to John Corey. Free, 20 September 1704. First mark entered as largeworker, 7 October 1704. Address: Red Cross Street. Second mark, undated, presumably meant for Sterling mark *c.* 1720, but since it is clearly I.H, inapplicable initials for his names, it may have been an error for H.I and not used. The occurrence is otherwise inexplicable. Heal records him as plateworker, Red Cross Street, till 1711.

HITCH, Joseph (1015) Son of William Hitch Citizen and Wax-chandler of London, apprenticed to Ralph Maunsell 7 August 1701. Free 9 December 1709. Mark entered as smallworker, 1 February 1710. Address: Gutter Lane.

HITCHCOCK, Samuel (1016, 2526-7) Son of Joseph Hitchcock late of Epsom in the County of Surrey, apprenticed to John Brace 11 August 1699. Free, 17 October 1707. Mark entered as largeworker, 24 November 1713. Address: Gutter Lane. Second (Sterling) mark, 19 October 1720. Livery, October 1721. Third mark, 5 October 1730, same address. Resigned from Livery 28 April 1743.

HITCHIN, William (3166) No record of apprenticeship or freedom. First mark entered as smallworker, 28 August 1801. Address: 4 Bridgewater Gardens. Second mark, 15 February 1825, on move to 21 Bridgewater Gardens. A William Hitchin son of John of North Street City Road jeweller was apprenticed to John Deane of Charles Street Hatton Garden as engraver and piercer 5 March 1823 and turned over to J. H. Martyn, but it is difficult to see what the connection with the above maker could be.

HOARE, Thomas (2787, 2791) No record of apprenticeship or freedom. First mark entered as smallworker, 28 April 1792. Address: 1 Bell Alley, Grub Street. Second mark, 31 March 1806. Address: 19 Grub Street.

HOBBS, James (3646) This attribution is not supported by any recorded maker's name for the period of the mark (1829) and remains doubtful.

HOBBS, Thomas (2788, 2806) No record of apprenticeship or freedom. First mark entered as smallworker, 7 May 1796. Address: 7 St. Ann's Lane. Second mark, in partnership with James Taylor as plateworkers, 27 October 1797. Address: 21 St. Ann's Lane, Aldersgate.

HOBDELL, Henry (1002) Son of Henry Hobdell of the parish of St. Andrew Holborn victualler, apprenticed to William Hunt 2 November 1732. Free, 11 January 1750. First mark entered as smallworker, 21 September 1767. Address: Silver Street. Second mark, 2 July 1770. He appears as goldworker, Silver Street, in the Parl. Report list 1773, and Heal records him as goldsmith, Aldermanbury, 1767; and Silver Street, 1773. His son Henry was apprenticed to him as goldsmith, 1767, freedom unrecorded. Richard Hobdell, goldworker (Section VII), is probably connected.

HOCKLY, Daniel (470, 473) No record of apprenticeship or freedom. First mark entered as smallworker, 16 January 1810. Address: 9 Brook Street, Holborn. Second mark, in partnership with Thomas Bosworth as smallworkers, 6 April 1815, same address. Single mark found on wine-labels.

HODGE, Thomas (2785, 2802) Son of John Hodge Citizen and Draper of London, apprenticed to Ben Newman 8 November 1737 on payment of £8. Free, 3 March 1762. First mark entered as smallworker, 10 March 1768. Address: Red Cross Street, where he appears without category in the Parl. Report list 1773. Second mark, 5 September 1785. Address: 4 Bridgwater Street, Barbican. Third mark, 30 June 1787. Moved to 6 Bear Alley, Fleet Market, 8 April 1796.

HODGES, George (806, 1055) Son of Edward Hodges of the parish of St. James' Westminster in the County of Middlesex broker apprenticed to Samuel Lea 7 November 1723 on payment of £30. Freedom unrecorded. Two Marks (Sterling and New Standard) entered as largeworker, 17 September 1728. Address: Charles Street, St. James's. Heal records Mrs Hodges, pawnbroker at the Golden Ball, Charles Street, near St. James's Square, 1704, which unless an error of date, must presumably be the mother or even grandmother of George Hodges.

HODGKINS, William I (1042) Son of Flammock Hodgkins late of Chalfont in the County of Buckingham innholder deceased, apprenticed to John Fawdery 4 March 1708. Free, 13 September 1715. Signatory as journeyman to the petition against assaying the work of foreigners not having served seven years apprenticeship, February 1716. Mark entered as largeworker, 11 September 1719 or 1720 (year omitted). Address: Dens Cort (Dean's Court), St. Martin's Le Grand. Chaffers read 'Hodgkis', and 'Dove' for Dens, followed by Jackson and Heal.

HODGKINS, William II (1541) Son of John Hodgkins late of Beambridge near Nantwich in the County Palatine of Chester maltster deceased, apprenticed to James Walters 2 December 1761 on payment of £21. Free, November 1770. Mark entered as plateworker, in partnership with James Mince, 23 November 1780. Address: 2 Bell Square, Foster Lane. Heal also records him alone as plateworker, Bell Square, 1783.

HODGKINSON, John (1386) No record of apprenticeship or freedom. Only mark entered as smallworker, 2 October 1790. Address: Fishers Street, Red Lion Square.

*HOD(G)KINSON, Thomas (2779, 3827) Thomas son of George Hodgkinson of London merchant deceased, apprenticed to Benjamin Pooll 4 November 1712. Mark entered as smallworker, 17 July 1727. Address: Goldsmiths' Court, New Street, Fetter Lane. 'Goldsmith' (whether indicating Company or working status uncertain).

HODGSON, Joseph (1400) Son of Joseph Hodgson of St. John's Court St. Martin's Le Grand peruke maker, apprenticed to James Barratt of Addle Street as silversmith 4 April 1804. Free, 1 May 1811. Mark entered as plateworker, 24 February 1827. Address: 24 Addle Street. Moved to 1 Sun Court, Cloth Fair, 24 January 1828.

HODGSON, Nicolas (2093) Probably son of William Hodgson late of Durham mercer deceased, apprenticed to Robert Mansell 31 August 1704. Freedom unrecorded. Mark entered as smallworker, 23 July 1719. Address: Little Britain. 'Gold Mark', implying he had entered another for silver, but no other entry.

HODSDON, John (767) No record of apprenticeship or freedom. Only mark entered as smallworker, in partnership with George Blackway, 14 July 1790. Address: 71 Strand.

HODSON, John (1044) Son of William Hodson of Alsford (?Alresford) in the County of Southampton tanner, apprenticed to Thomas King 14 June 1676 as from midsummer next. Free, 21 September 1683. Mark entered as largeworker, undated, probably April 1697 on commencement of register. Address: 'In Wapping', where Heal has found him recorded from 1695.

*HOGG, Andrew (40) No record of apprenticeship or freedom. Only mark entered as

BIOGRAPHICAL DICTIONARY

smallworker, 8 December 1761. Address: Northumberland Court, Strand, where the Parl. Report list records him as goldworker, 1773.

*HOLADAY, Edward (1041) Son of Edward Holaday of Malling in Kent husbandman, apprenticed to John Bache 22 December 1699. Free, 14 September 1709. Mark entered as largeworker, 1 November 1709. Address: Grafton Street. Heal records his address as Golden Cup, Grafton Street, near Newport Market, 1709-10; and Golden Cup, end of Gerrard Street near Newport Market, 1712. Signatory as 'working goldsmith' to the petition complaining of the competition of 'necessitous strangers', December 1711. Livery December 1717. Died 1719, presumably by 22 July on entry of Sarah Holaday's mark. Distinguish from Edmund Holliday (q.v.).

HOLADAY, Sarah (1052, 2529) Presumably widow of Edward Holaday (above). First mark in two sizes entered 22 July 1719, without address. Second (Sterling) mark, 15 June 1725. Address: 'Hrafton' Street (a curious aberration caused by her preoccupation with making a fine H for her own name?). Heal records her in Grafton Street until 1740. Her work while not distinguished is always of good quality.

HOLDER, Richard (2327) Son of Richard Holder of Churchstock in the County of Montgomery clerk, apprenticed to Thomas Pierce 25 September 1718 on payment of £5 and turned over 10 August 1720 to Edmund King 'in Bells Rents in ye Mint Snuffbox maker' and on 14 November 1720 to Ben. Bird in Ludgate Hill in Bell Savage Yard bucklemaker free Joyner. Free, 14 December 1725. Mark entered as smallworker, 28 January 1726. Address: Broad Street Hill. 'Free Goldsmith'. Heal records him as goldsmith, York Buildings (Strand), 1732.

HOLDUP, John (1391) No record of apprenticeship or freedom. Only mark entered as spoonmaker, 11 November 1809. Address: 24 George Street, Blackfriars Road.

HOLLAND, John I (1051, 1354) Son of Richard Holland of St. Giles without Cripplegate in the County of Middlesex victualler, apprenticed to Lawrence Coles 8 July 1703. Free, 2 August 1710. First mark entered as largeworker, 23 November 1711. Address: Foster Lane. Livery, 1717. Second (Sterling) mark, 2 July 1720. Address: Bishopsgate. Court, 1741. Heal records him as plateworker, Queen's Head, Foster Lane, 1711-12; and Bishopsgate Street, 1711-39 (but see John Holland II, below). Presumably the 'John Holland Silversmith in Bishopsgate St. London many years deputy (?Common Councillor) for Bishopsgate Ward', who died 31 August 1753 (*London Magazine* and *The Gentleman's Magazine*).

HOLLAND, John II (1405) Son of Nicholas Holland Citizen and Goldsmith of London, apprenticed to his father 4 April 1723. Freedom unrecorded. The mark entered as largeworker, 4 July 1739 (address: Bishopsgate), is apparently his, being in a different hand to that earlier of John Holland I (above). On the other hand it is in script initials conforming with the requirements of the 1738 Act, which may indicate that it is the re-entry of the former's mark. Heal records John Holland, jeweller, goldsmith and clockmaker, 5 Bishopsgate Without, from 1765-79, after the death of John I in 1753, and he appears as goldsmith, Bishopsgate Street, in the Parl. Report list 1773. The two are probably uncle and nephew. John II was elected to the Livery March 1758 and died between 1802 and 1811.

HOLLAND, Joshua (1045) Son of Thanks Holland late of St. Botolph without Aldgate London upholsterer, apprenticed to John Brace 10 May 1704. Free, 4 July 1711. Mark entered as largeworker, 22 August 1711. Address: Foster Lane, where Heal records him till 1729.

HOLLAND, Thomas I (1050) Son of John Holland of Eastbourne in the County of Sussex yeoman, apprenticed to Edward Courthope 28 November 1694. Free, 4 April 1707. Mark entered as largeworker, 23 September 1707. Address: Fleet Street, where Heal records him till 1718. Livery, October 1708. Signatory as 'working goldsmith' to the petition complaining of the competition of 'necessitous strangers', December 1711.

HOLLAND, Thomas II (2789) No record of apprenticeship or freedom. Mark entered as plateworker, 7 August 1798. Address: 21 Bell Yard, Temple Bar. Move to 47 Chancery Lane, 20 June 1809. Heal records him only at first address, the second being beyond the terminal date of his book.

HOLLIDAY, Edmund (1047) Son of Edmund Holliday of Norton Folgate in the County of Middlesex cooper, apprenticed to Benjamin

549

Nelson for nine years 'from the Feast of the Nativity of Our Saviour Christ Jesus last past' 25 February 1691. Turned over 26 October 1694 to Thomas Elton. Free, 8 July 1703. Mark entered as smallworker, 3 August 1703. Address: Horshoe Alley, Bunhill Fields. Not recorded by Heal. Distinguish from Edward Holaday (q.v.).

HOLLINSHED, Charles (331-2) Son of Thomas Hollinshed late of King Street in St. Giles in the Fields turner deceased, apprenticed to John Robins of Clerkenwell Green as goldsmith 1 March 1797. Free, 4 July 1804. First mark (two sizes) entered as plateworker, 7 February 1807. Address: 13 Clerkenwell Green. Second mark (two sizes), 23 April 1808, same address. Third mark, 16 March 1812, same address.

HOLLOWAY, John (1377, 1385) Either (1) son of William Holloway of Croydon in the County of Surrey yeoman, apprenticed to John Wirgman 4 December 1754. Free, 7 March 1770. Or possibly (2) son of Thomas Holloway of Friday Street London ticket porter, Citizen and Carpenter, apprenticed to Ralph Ayscough as goldsmith 8 August 1770. Freedom unrecorded. First mark entered as smallworker, undated, but after 30 September 1772. Address: 24 Witch Street. Second mark, 27 April 1773. Address: 24 Witch Street, Clement Danes. Third mark, 16 January 1788, same address. Heal records him as working goldsmith, 28 Wych Street, 1775-93.

HOLMAN, John (1381) No record of apprenticeship or freedom. Only mark entered as smallworker, 18 June 1778. Address: 15 Rosomons Row.

HOLMES, John (1410) No record of apprenticeship or freedom. Only mark entered as smallworker, 12 July 1733. Address: Fell Court, Fell Street, near Surgeon's Hall. Cf. Samuel Holmes, at the same address.

HOLMES, John Gwyn (1390) Son of William Holmes (below) of Clerkenwell Green silver chaser, Citizen and Lorimer, apprenticed to John Arnell as goldsmith 7 June 1780. Free, 3 October 1787. Mark entered as plateworker, 10 July 1805. Address: 12 Clerkenwell Green, probably on retirement or death of his father working at the same address.

HOLMES, Samuel (2531) No record of apprenticeship or freedom. Only mark entered as smallworker, 6 December 1734. Address: Fell Court, Fell Street, near Surgeons' Hall. See John Holmes at the same address.

*HOLMES, William (3161-2, 3176, 3526) Free of the Lorimers' Company (records destroyed 1940, but so described in later apprenticeships to him in Goldsmiths' records). Apparently working by about 1762, since pieces bearing a mark very similar to his later entered mark exist from this date till 1771. Heal records David Whyte, plateworker, Clerkenwell Green, 1766; and Whyte and Holmes, working silversmiths, Clerkenwell Green, 1770, and there can be no doubt that mark no. 3526 is theirs, found from 1764 to 1767. Heal records Holmes alone as working silversmith, 12 Clerkenwell Green, from 1768-90, and he appears as plateworker, at the same address, in the Parl. Report list 1773. His first documented mark as plateworker, in partnership with Nicholas Dumée, entered 8 September 1773. Address: 12 Clerkenwell Green. (His name is curiously missing from the Parl. Report list dated 8 March 1773, whereas David Whyte is listed at 19 Little Britain.) Second mark entered alone, 2 January 1776, same address. Third mark, 21 March 1792. Took J. S. Denwall as apprentice, 1790, and his own son John Gwyn Holmes (q.v.), 1780, who entered his mark at the same address, 10 July 1805, when presumably his father was dead or retired. 'Mrs Holmes wife of Mr Holmes silversmith Clerkenwell Green' died September 1785 (*The Gentleman's Magazine*, p. 834).

HOLYHEAD, Thomas (2780) No record of apprenticeship or freedom. Only mark entered as smallworker, 15 September 1731. Address: 'at the White Horse, Russel Street, Covent Garden'.

HOMER, William (3171) No record of apprenticeship or freedom. Only mark entered as largeworker, 8 August 1750. Address: Rose and Crown Court, Foster Lane. Heal records him as Holmer, plateworker, Foster Lane, 1750-3.

HOOD, Samuel (1043, 1046) Son of Robert Hood late of Mountsorrel in the County of Leicester gentleman deceased, apprenticed to Robert Cooper for eight years 9 December 1685. Free, 20 December 1693. Marks entered as largeworker, undated, probably April 1697 on commencement of register. Address: Maiden Lane, where Heal records him from 1694 to 1702; and at Shoreditch, 1724-7. Livery, April 1705.

BIOGRAPHICAL DICTIONARY

HOOKER, William (1053) Probably son of William Hooker free of the Dyers' Company 1688/9. Only mark entered as smallworker, 8 March 1720. Address: St. Mary Overies. 'Free Dyer'.

HOPGOOD, Metcalf (2032, 2807) No record of apprenticeship or freedom. First mark entered, in partnership with Thomas Burn Hopgood (below), 20 September 1833. Address: 202 Bishopsgate Street. Second mark alone, 14 August 1835, same address.

HOPGOOD, Thomas Burn (2705, 2807) No record of apprenticeship or freedom. First mark entered as plateworker, 23 October 1828. Address: 202 Bishopsgate. Second mark, in partnership with Metcalf Hopgood (above), 20 September 1833, same address. Partnership apparently dissolved by 14 August 1835 on entry of latter's mark alone.

HOPKINS, John (1054, 1355) Son of James Hopkins of Axbridge in the County of Somerset gentleman, apprenticed to Andrew Archer 5 June 1716. Free, 5 December 1723. Two marks (Sterling and New Standard) entered as largeworker, undated, between 1720 and 1724. Address: Rose and Crown in St. Bride's Lane, where Heal records him till 1726; also as goldsmith, Goldsmiths Arms, Bride Lane, 1730; and removed to the same sign in Fleet Street (corner of Bride Lane), 1732–6; also Golden Cup and cover, near Fleet Bridge in Fleet Street, 1736–63. Whether or no he composed himself the advertisement he inserted in the *London Evening Post*, 21 May 1736, it seems too good to ignore: 'To prevent the Decoys and Impositions the most Wary are liable to in the Goldsmiths way, from publick Sales, Auctions &c. (the Shocking Forebode of the Destruction of Trade in general) and the excessive Deceit of whited Brass, sold only by Brasiers, and by them most ridiculously call'd French Plate, John Hopkins, Goldsmith, in Fleet-Street, near Fleet-Bridge, the corner of Bride-Lane, (the other Corner a Turner's) continues making it his principal and Chief Business to deal in Second-Hand Plate, Watches, Jewels &c. and observes the Method he first began of selling at the most reasonable Prices.

'The Call he almost continually has for Quantities of various sorts of Plate Second-Hand, gives him an Opportunity of affording most Money for the same, as does the great Care he takes in employing the most experienc'd and best Workmen enable him to serve with new Plate &c. to the greatest Satisfaction, as Numbers of Quality and Gentry have sufficiently experienced.

'Note. Nothing engrav'd with Coats of Arms &c. will at any Time be exposed to Sale before the Engraving be entirely taken out, so that it shall not be known the same ever was engrav'd, which is presum'd will be most pleasing to Buyer and Seller. No Credit will be given or requir'd in either Way.'

He is possibly the —Hopkins, silversmith, died 4 August 1779 (*The Gentleman's Magazine*, p. 424), but see also William Hopkins (below).

HOPKINS, William (3155) No record of apprenticeship or freedom. First mark entered 10 October 1723. Address: Great Kerby Street, Hatton Garden. Second mark, 25 May 1739, same address, where Heal records him as plateworker the same year. See John Hopkins (above) for an obituary notice which may refer to William rather than the former.

HOPPER, W. (800) No record of apprenticeship or freedom. Only mark entered as smallworker, in partnership with George Foster, 27 August 1771. Address: White Swan, Friars Street, Blackfriars. Partnership apparently dissolved by 3 April 1772, when the latter entered a separate mark at the same address.

*HORNE, Edward I (593, 1049) Described on entry of mark as Free Clockmaker, but there is no record of him in that company's apprentice list surviving till 1700. Probably free by patrimony. First mark entered as smallworker, 25 October 1705. Address: St. Martin's Le Grand. Second (Sterling) mark, 27 July 1720. Probably a watchcasemaker.

HORNE, Edward II (598) Son of Edward Horne (above) Citizen and Clockmaker of London, apprenticed to James Mayo 7 November 1728 on payment of £30. Free, 8 November 1737. Mark entered as smallworker, 8 March 1739. Address: George Court, Benets Hall, Doctors Common. 'Goldsmith'.

HORNE, J. (1821) No record of apprenticeship or freedom. Only mark entered as smallworker, in partnership with D. S. Ash, 20 October 1800. Address: 64 St. James's Street.

HORSLEY, John (3642) No record of apprenticeship or freedom. Mark pre-

551

sumably entered in missing register c. 1760, being presumably that shown as found on candlesticks from at least 1761. His name appears only in the Parl. Report list 1773 as candlestick-maker, Haberdashers Walk, Hoxton.

HORSLEY, Matthew Coats (2034) No record of apprenticeship or freedom. Only mark entered as smallworker, in partnership with Robert Burton Cooper, 26 September 1821. Address: 461 Strand.

HORTON, William (3170) No record of apprenticeship or freedom. Only mark entered as smallworker, 29 August 1837. Address: 18 Aylesbury Street, Clerkenwell.

*HORWOOD, Nathaniel (3744) No record of apprenticeship or freedom. Mark entered in the missing register before 1773, when he appears in the Parl. Report list as plateworker, Dean Street, Soho. The mark no. 3742 might possibly be his rather than of Nicholas Hearnden (q.v.), since the latter appears as spoonmaker in the same list, and might therefore be ascribed mark no. 3744 in lieu.

*HOSIER, Elias (1048) Apprentice of Thomas Vickeridge (q.v.), 'sworne and admitted' to the freedom of the Cutlers' Company 9 April 1702. Mark entered as smallworker, 26 April 1704. Address: New Street near Shoe Lane. 'free of the Cutlers'. Not recorded by Heal. Almost certainly a haft and/or hiltmaker.

*HOUGHAM, Charles (327-9) Son of Soloman Hougham of the parish of St. John in the County of Surrey linendraper, apprenticed to Henry Corry 4 July 1764 on payment of £15. Freedom unrecorded. Mark entered as smallworker, 11 January 1769. Address: Aldersgate Street. Second mark, 11 May 1769. Appears as bucklemaker, Aldersgate Street, in the Parl. Report list 1773, and entered marks as such, 1773-9 (Section VIII). Third mark, as plateworker (two sizes), 24 January 1785. Address: 138 Aldersgate Street. Fourth entry (seven marks), 4 November 1786, same address. Heal records the above addresses and adds Charles and Solomon Hougham, goldsmiths, same address, 1790-6. Charles Hougham, goldsmith, Aldersgate Street, died 18 January 1793 (*European Magazine*, *The Gentleman's Magazine*).

*HOUGHAM, Solomon (2536, 2548) Son of Solomon Hougham, free by redemption 7 June 1786 as goldsmith. He was already an established worker, since Henry, son of Henry Hougham, was apprenticed to him in 1789. He was elected to Livery, February 1791. Partner with Charles Hougham above) from 1790, the latter dying 18 January 1793. First mark entered as plateworker 1 February 1793. Address: Aldersgate Street. Second mark (two sizes), 6 February 1793. Third mark (two sizes), 13 November 1812. Fourth mark, in partnership with Solomon Royes and John East Dix (q.v.). 13 September 1817. Address: 138 Aldersgate Street. The partnership apparently dissolved by 19 September 1818 when Royes and Dix entered a separate joint mark. Hougham died between 1818 and 1822. His marks should be distinguished from those of Samuel Hennell (q.v.).

*HOULE, John (1392) No record of apprenticeship or freedom. Mark entered as plateworker, 10 April 1811. Address: 24 Red Lion Street, Clerkenwell. Second mark, 23 February 1813. Robert Hennell II was apprenticed to him as engraver.

HOUSEHILL, Henry (1004) No record of apprenticeship or freedom. Only mark entered as smallworker, 18 May 1799. Address: Little St. Andrew's Street, Seven Dials.

HOUSTON, George (810) Described as of the Fletchers' Company on entry of mark (this company's records not extant). Mark entered as smallworker, 10 March 1737. Address: Golden Cup, Fleet Street. Heal records him as goldsmith, Golden Cup, Corner of Mitre Tavern passage, Fleet Street; or near St. Dunstan's Church, Fleet Street, 1742-73. Parl. Report list 1773 as goldsmith, Fleet Street. Bankrupt 1756 (*The Gentleman's Magazine*, p. 151).

HOW, William (3160) No record of apprenticeship or freedom. Only mark entered as smallworker, 7 August 1771. Address: 30 Quaker Buildings. Appears as bucklemaker, at this address, Parl. Report list 1773. Heal records William How and William Clerk, plateworkers, Spital Square, 1777, which may refer to the above. Less likely is William How, goldsmith and jeweller, 13 Fleet Street, 1770-4, who seems the same as William Howes or Howse, goldsmith and clockmaker, between the 2 Temple Gates, Fleet Street, 1730-74.

HOWARD, Joseph *See* HERIOT.

HOWARD, William (3174) Son of William Howard of the parish of Fulham wheelwright, apprenticed to Edmund Boddington 6 September 1749 on payment of £5 and turned over to Richard Howard Stationer 6 December 1749. Free, 6 October 1756. Mark entered as smallworker, 19 August 1760. Address: Clerkenwell Green. Moved to Wood Street, 5 May 1762. Moved to Old Bailey, 24 September 1766, this last statement signed by M. Howard (? wife). Livery, July 1763. Appears as watchcasemaker, Old Bailey, in the Parl. Report list 1773. See also Section V for one of the same name, perhaps his son. For the somewhat mysterious Joseph Howard, who seems to be related, see under Heriot (above).

HOWES, William (3173) No record of apprenticeship or freedom. Only mark entered as smallworker, 16 May 1732. Address: Lamb's Conduit Passage, Red Lyon Square. Heal records William Howes or Howse, goldsmith and clockmaker, between the two Temple Gates, Fleet Street or Temple Bar, 1730-74, but correspondence with the above seems doubtful. William Howse, goldworker, Temple Bar, appears in the Parl. Report list 1773, having entered a mark as smallworker, 7 March 1768 (Section IV).

HOWLAND, Solomon (2533-4) Son of Robert Howland of Thame in the County of Oxford carrier, apprenticed to Thomas Whipham 5 October 1752 on payment of £30 and turned over to Edward Day goldsmith 7 February 1759. Free, 9 January 1760. First mark entered as smallworker, 13 September 1760. Address: Long Lane, Smithfield. Second mark, 11 November 1760. Heal records him at this address, 1760-72.

*HUDELL, René (1074) Huguenot of undetermined origin. Mark entered as largeworker, 5 March 1718. Address: Green Street. 'Free Longbow String Maker' (this company's records not extant). Appears as witness to the marriage of Pierre Jomard and Perside Ester Hudel, daughter of Jean Hudel, 'min . et lecteur de l'eg. francoise des Grecs' in Hungerford Market Church, 9 February 1719, from which it may perhaps be assumed he was son of the same minister. Also recorded as godfather to Estienne Hanet, son of Paul Hanet, baptised 10 May 1721 at West Street Church. His work though rare is of fine quality. One suspects he may have failed to make a living on his own and later submerged his identity in a larger establishment, unless he died early.

HUDSON, Alexander (1078, 3609) Son of William Hudson of the parish of St. Michael le Querne London haberdasher, apprenticed to Andrew Raven 13 November 1697. Free, 21 November 1704. Mark entered as largeworker, 22 November 1704. Address: Bull & Mouth Street, where Heal records him from 1701 till 1705, the earlier date appearing inexplicable.

HUDSON, William (1075, 3154, 3883) Son of John Hudson of St. Giles in the Fields taylor deceased, apprenticed to Philip Rainaud 4 November 1713 on payment of £30. Free, 31 October 1722. First mark entered as smallworker, 19 November 1722. Address: St. Martin's Lane. 'Free of Goldsmiths' Company'. Second (Sterling) mark 22 April 1723, same address.

*HUGHES, Ferdinando (1083) Entry as smallworker, undated, probably April 1697 on commencement of register. The whole entry is as follows: 'Ferdinando Hughes being absent his Wife has subscribed liveing at Charing Cross free of the Lorimers the mark of Elizabeth E Hughes' (the central initial being the mark). The records of the Lorimers' Company were destroyed 1940.

HUGHES, James (1080) Probably related to Ferdinando Hughes (above), as also described on entry of mark as free Lorimer. Mark entered as smallworker, undated, probably April 1697 on commencement of register. Address: New Street, Fetter Lane.

HULL, Henry (1006) No record of apprenticeship or freedom. Only mark entered as smallworker, 3 April 1822. Address: 29 Compton Street, Clerkenwell.

HULLS, Philip (1082) No record of apprenticeship or freedom. Only mark entered as smallworker, undated, probably April 1697 on commencement of register. Address: Cock Lane, near Pye Corner.

HUMPHREY, John (1084) No record of apprenticeship or freedom unless, although so great an interval, son of John Humphrey late of Stowmarket in the county of Suffolk clothier deceased, apprenticed to William Drayton 26 July 1671, discharged 4 October 1672 and apprenticed same day to Charles Mell. Freedom unrecorded. Only mark entered as largeworker, 26 January 1711. Address: St. Martin's Le Grand. Heal records him here, 1710; and also John Humphreys, goldsmith, St. Dunstan in the West, 1717-18.

HUMPHREYS, Arthur (2888-9) Son of

James Humphreys of Addle Street founder, Citizen and Saddler, apprenticed to John Deacon of Addle Street goldsmith 5 June 1771 and turned over later to James Stamp. Freedom unrecorded. Mark entered as plateworker, in partnership with Thomas Boulton Pratt, 7 July 1780. Address: 44 Poultry.

HUMPHREYS, Samuel (2540) No record of apprenticeship or freedom. Only mark entered as plateworker, 4 March 1822. Address: 12 Green Street, Leicester Square.

HUMPHRIS, John (1412) Son of Edmund Humphris of Latin in the County of Wiltshire butcher, apprenticed to William Turner 7 October 1761. Free, 1 February 1769. Mark entered as smallworker, 10 June 1762. Address: Duke Street, York Buildings, Strand. Moved to Church Lane, Newington Butts, Surrey, 10 January 1763, where he appears as smallworker in the Parl. Report list 1773. Although there is less than a year between the date of apprenticeship and entry of a mark, it seems that the signatures to both entries, allowing for minor differences, are from the same hand. Humphris may already have been adult on apprenticeship and merely seeking freedom by routine in due course.

HUNSDON, Edward (1081) Son of Henry Hundstone of Edmonton in the County of Middlesex yeoman deceased, apprenticed to Thomas Tebb of the Joiners' Company 8 April 1673. Free, 6 February 1683. Mark entered as smallworker, undated, probably April 1697 on commencement of register. Address: Carey Lane. 'Free Joyner'. His son Edward apprenticed to Ralph Maunsell, 1705.

HUNT, Edward I (1079) Apprenticed to Thomas Williamson of the Clockmakers' Company 21 June 1677, free 30 June 1684. Mark enterd as smallworker (probably for watchcases), undated, presumably April 1697 on commencement of register. Address: Fleet Street. 'Free Clockmaker'.

HUNT, Edward II (596) Possibly son of Edward Hunt late Citizen and Barber Surgeon of London deceased, apprenticed to Alexander Johnston 1 October 1734 and turned over to Thomas Moulden 26 March 1735. Free, 16 January 1744. Mark entered as smallworker, 11 September 1762. Address: Shoe Lane, Fleet Street.

HUNT, Henry (1072) Son of Robert Hunt late Citizen and Innholder of London, apprenticed to John Hannam 27 June 1683. Free, 20 December 1695. Mark entered as smallworker, 15 October 1712. Address: Gutter Lane.

HUNT, James (1373) Son of William Hunt (below) Citizen and Goldsmith of London, apprenticed to his father 5 August 1742. Free, 7 December 1752. Livery, March 1758. Mark entered as smallworker, 30 July 1760. Address: King Street, Cheapside, where he appears as goldworker in the Parl. Report list 1773. Heal records him as at 9 King Street, 1768-77. Sworn and admitted to Freedom 'de novo', 10 April 1771, for what reason not stated. Heal also records James Hunt, goldsmith, Ironmonger Lane, deceased 1782.

HUNT, William (1077, 3886-7) Son of Edmund Hunt of Oundle in the County of Northampton gardener(?), apprenticed to John Hunt 23 December 1709. Freedom unrecorded. Mark entered as smallworker, 21 June 1725. Address: Old Change. 'Goldsmith'. Livery, 24 March 1737. His son James (above) apprenticed to him, 1742.

HUNTER, Charles (330) No record of apprenticeship or freedom. Only mark entered as smallworker, 11 October 1771. Address: Ben(jamin?) Street, Clerkenwell. Moved to Bakers Row, Whitechapel, 18 February 1772, where he appears as smallworker in the Parl. Report list 1773.

HUNTER, George I (811-4) Son of George Hunter Citizen and Barber Surgeon of London, apprenticed to John Allcock 21 May 1741 and turned over the same day to William Garrard Citizen and Carpenter in consideration of 16 guineas. Free, 8 June 1748. Mark entered as largeworker, 7 June 1748. Address: Noble Street. Moved to Silver Street, 26 September 1752. Second mark, 31 October 1755. Address: Little Britain, with note (no date): Remov'd to Cow Cross. Third mark, 21 June 1765. Address: Shoe Lane, with note (no date): 'Removed in the Old Bailey'. Fourth mark, 14 November 1767. Address: Shoe Lane. His third and fourth marks appear in the smallworkers' book but are slightly larger than the preceding ones of 1748 and 1755. Heal records him as plateworker, Shoe Lane, until 1772; and also as insolvent in 1755. He appears as smallworker, Shoe Lane, in the Parl. Report list 1773.

HUNTER, George II (817) Son of George Hunter of East Row, Hoxton silversmith, apprenticed to his brother William Hunter of Brittania (sic) Garden as silversmith 4 February 1807. Mark entered, without working category, 20 March 1817. Address: 4 East Row, City Road, with or in continuation of his father's business.

HUNTER, William I (3157, 3172, 3885) Makers of this name afford some little difficulty in differentiation (1) William son of William Hunter late of Southwark victualler, apprenticed to Thomas Chadwell 14 April 1708 and free 21 September 1715. Livery, 1746 and Court, 1752. No mark appears in the registers to match these dates (mark 3885 may relate to him, but this is doubtful). (2) William Hunter 'Jnr' son of Thomas, Citizen and Blacksmith of London, apprenticed to Samuel Wood 8 January 1746 and turned over to Thomas Hunter blacksmith (presumably his father) and then to William Hunter Goldsmith (presumably his uncle, identifiable with (1)) 4 February 1746. Free, 1 February 1753/?4. First mark entered as largeworker, 28 July 1755. Address: King Street, St Anne's. Second mark, 6 August 1756. Heal records William Hunter, plateworker at this address, 1739, but this appears to be derived from an error in Chaffers who gives correct day and month but 1739 for 1755. Heal does, however, record William Hunter (succeeded by his nephew William Hunter), goldsmith and jeweller, Anchor and Ring, (No. 51) Lombard Street, 1732; died 1762. At this address the probability of the main business being banking is of course strong, and could account for the absence of a mark. A variant of the sign as Three Golden Lions, Anchor and Ring is also noted by Heal; and William Hunter, jeweller and goldsmith, at same address, 1762-96. William Hunter, goldworker, Lombard Street, appears in the Parl. Report list 1773. Nephew followed uncle on to the Livery, 1763. Court 1787, Warden 1791-93, and Prime Warden 1794. He died between 1802 and 1811. It seems likely that the Soho address may have been purely a workshop and that although the uncle disdained a mark (probably commissioning work for his clients from others) the nephew may have started his own shop, until succeeding his uncle in Lombard Street.

HUNTER, William II (3164-5) Son of George Hunter of Hoxton in the County of Middlesex, silversmith, apprenticed to Edward Ferris of White Cross Street Citizen and Goldsmith as goldsmith 1 November 1786 on payment of £7. 14s. of the charity of the Goldsmiths' Compnay and £4 of Mr. Henry Dixon's perpetual charity of the Drapers' Company. Free, 2 April 1794. First mark entered as smallworker, 15 March 1798. Address: 3 East Row, Hoxton. Moved to 8 Britannia Gardens, Hoxton, undated. Second mark, 1 September 1824. Third mark, 25 June 1834. Address: 13 Myrtle Street, Hoxton. Fourth to eighth marks as plateworker, 1839 to 1842, same address. His brother George (q.v.) apprenticed to him 1807.

*HUNTLEY, John (1406, 3644-5) No record of apprenticeship or freedom. Only mark entered as 'smallworker in gold', 3 November 1759. Address: 'in St. Christopher's near the Bank of England, Threadneedle Street'. Heal records him as goldsmith, insolvent, near the Bank 1773, and he appears as goldworker, near the Bank, in the Parl. Report list of the same year. William Huntley (Section V) may be connected.

HUSSEY, Edward (1085, 1569) Son of Christopher Hussey Citizen and Stationer of London deceased, apprenticed to John Cooper 4 October 1716 on payment of 20 guineas. Free, 7 November 1723. Possibly the partner of Hussey and Joyce (below), 1729. Mark (New Standard) alone as smallworker entered 9 September 1753. Address: 'Fleet Street over against St. D(unstan's) C(hurch)'.

HUSSEY, Mary (2030) No record of apprenticeship or freedom. Described as widow of Edward Hussey (? an uncle perhaps of him above), on entry of her mark as smallworker, undated, between October 1723 and April 1724. 'marke entered by Eliz. Hussey free Haberdasher'. No address but another entry below without mark: 'Mary Hussey in (obliterated) in Whitecross street april ye 15 1724 ye marke of Mary Hussey X in Exechequer ally', which appears to be an amplification of the first entry.

HUSSEY, Richard (2328) Son of Seymour Hussey late Citizen and Clothworker of London deceased, apprenticed to Job Lilly 12 November 1729. Free, 31 March 1737. Mark entered as smallworker, undated in 1737. Address: Tower Street, the corner of St. Dunstan's Hill. 'Free of the Goldsmiths Company'.

HUSSEY, —— (1569) 'Hussey and Joyce', mark entered without Christian names as smallworkers, 12 May 1729. Address: Old

Boswell Court. Perhaps the Edward Hussey above, later working alone in Fleet Street.

HUTCHINSON, William I (1073) Son of Richard Hutchinson of St. Giles in the Fields taylor, apprenticed to Peter Elgar 3 March 1709. Free, 13 March 1716. Mark entered as smallworker, 23 March 1716. Address: York Street, Covent Garden. Livery, September 1746.

HUTCHINSON, William II (3156, 3884) No record of apprenticeship or freedom but the signature quite distinct from the above. Mark entered as smallworker, 18 August 1736. Address: Smart's Buildings, near the Coalyard, Holborn.

HUTSON, John (1382) Son of Henry Hutson of the Parish of St. James Clerkenwell in the County of Middlesex, hopfactor apprenticed to Richard Rugg 3 June 1761 on payment of £30. Free, 3 August 1768. Mark entered as plateworker, 2 January 1784. Address: 35 St. John's Square (Clerkenwell), where Heal records him till 1800.

HUTTON, Samuel (1076, 2528, 2544) Son of Samuel Hutton Citizen and Glover of London, apprenticed to Edward Jennings 4 April 1717 on payment of £15. Free, 7 May 1724. Mark entered as largeworker, 7 October 1724. Address: 'at the Crown, Noble Street. Goldsmith'. Second (New Standard) mark, 7 January 1725. Styled 'Spoonmaker in Noble Street' in record of the turn-over to him of Edward Bennett as apprentice, 9 April 1725. Third mark, 15 May 1734. Address: 'at the Hat and Feather, Goswell Street'. Fourth mark, 21 January 1740. Address: Goswell Street. Presumably dead by 20 June 1740, on entry of Sarah Hutton's mark.

HUTTON, Sarah (2532) Presumably widow of Samuel Hutton (above). Mark entered as largeworker, 20 June 1740. Address: Goswell Street. Goldsmith. Moved to Noble Street, 15 March 1748. Heal records her at the Hat and Feather, Goswell Street in 1740.

HYAMS, Hyam (1005) No record of apprenticeship or freedom. First mark entered as plateworker, 12 April 1821. Address: 5 Castle Street, Houndsditch. Second mark, 23 May 1821. Third mark (two sizes), 29 June 1821. Fourth and fifth marks, 5 and 6 October 1821.

HYATT, John (1369, 1690) Son of John Hyatt late of Preston in the County of Somerset clothier deceased, apprenticed to James Gould 10 May 1733, no premium stated. Free, 5 March 1741. Mark entered as largeworker, 26 January 1742. Address: Little Britain. Second mark, in partnership with Charles Semore, 24 September 1757. Address: Little Dean's Court, St. Martin's Le Grand. Moved to Noble Street, 24 October 1758. Heal records him both alone and in partnership, only in Little Britain, from 1741 to 1765. He appears without category, Little Britain, in the Parl. Report list 1773.

HYDE, Henry (1007, 2977) No record of apprenticeship or freedom. First mark entered as plateworker, in partnership with Thomas Wimbush, 27 January 1834. Address: 166 Regent Street. Second mark, alone, 23 May 1834, same address.

*HYDE, James (1380, 1407) Probably the son of Thomas Hyde, goldsmith of Gutter Lane, admitted to St. Paul's School, 24 February 1757 aged seven. No record of apprenticeship or freedom. First mark entered as smallworker, 3 November 1777. Address: 10 Gutter Lane. Second mark, 16 September 1778. Address: 38 Gutter Lane. Third and fourth marks, 10 January 1786. Heal records James and Thomas Hyde (q.v.), goldsmiths, (No. 33? or 38) Gutter Lane, 1784-96. George son of James Hyde, goldsmith of Gutter Lane, aged eight admitted to St. Paul's School, 11 July 1791.

*HYDE, Mary (2033) No record of apprenticeship or freedom. Widow of James (above) or Thomas Hyde (below). First mark entered as smallworker, in partnership with John Riley, 28 November 1799. Address: 6 Cary Lane. It appears she later married her working partner since he entered marks alone, under the spelling of Reily, from 1801 to 1826, and she as Mary Reily in partnership with Charles, presumably a son in 1826. See further under Reily.

*HYDE, Thomas (2784) Probably son of Thomas Hyde Citizen and Fishmonger, apprenticed to James Hunt 13 April 1763. Freedom unrecorded. Appears as Thomas Hyde, smallworker, Gutter Lane, as having already entered a mark, in the Parl. Report list 1773. Subsequent mark entered as smallworker, 3 February 1784. Address: 33 Gutter Lane. See his brother James Hyde and Mary Hyde (above).

BIOGRAPHICAL DICTIONARY

I

IBBOT, George (836-7, 1184) No record of apprenticeship or freedom. First mark entered as largeworker, 6 August 1753. Address: Plough Court, Fetter Lane. Second mark, 22 May 1759, same address. Third mark, 28 November 1761. Address: Portugal Street, Lincoln's Inn, where he appears without category in the Parl. Report list 1773. Heal records him only at Plough Court from first date above till 1763.

IMPEY, Dike (478-9) Son of Richard Impey late of Marston Morten in the County of Bedford gentleman deceased, apprenticed to William Lukin 9 March 1714. Free, 17 April 1727, a curiously long interval. Presumably he worked as journeyman. Described as bachelor of St. Mary le Savoy on his marriage to Mary Rawson of St. Leonard, Foster's Lane, at St. Bene't, Paul's Wharf, 2 January 1727. First mark entered as largeworker, undated, between August 1727 and March 1729. Address: Staining Lane, near Goldsmiths' Hall. 'Goldsmith'. Second mark, 6 April 1736. Address: Noble Street. Heal records him at both addresses and dates as above, and also as insolvent in Gutter Lane, 1729. The unidentified mark 3516a may possibly relate to him, although it appears very late, perhaps of a son.

INNES, Robert (2345) No record of apprenticeship or freedom. Mark entered as largeworker (two sizes), 17 January 1743. Address: Mays Buildings, St. Martin's Lane. Moved to Drury Lane, 5 April 1754. Moved to Harvie Court, Strand, (? 15 September) 1755. Heal records him only at Mays Buildings, 1742-58. From the occurrence of his mark he appears to have specialized in inkstands.

*INNOCENT, John (3647) No record of apprenticeship or freedom. His name occurs only in Parl. Report list 1773 as spoonmaker, Little Newport Street. The attributed mark must remain doubtful. See John Jackson II.

IRONSIDE, Edward (1608, 3675) Son of Edward Ironside of Bothenhampton(?) in the County of Dorset 'Esqare'(?), apprenticed to Edward Gladwin 1 August 1688 and turned over to Henry Beesley. Free, 31 March 1699. Mark entered as largeworker, 10 September 1702. Address: Lombard Street. Heal records him here from 1697 till 1736. Livery, April 1705. Court, 1726. Warden in 1731 and 1737, in which year he died in May. Heal further records Ironside and Belchier, goldsmiths, bankers and clockmakers, Black Lion, Lombard Street, 1729-44. His son Edward was apprenticed to his father in 1720, became Prime Warden of the Goldsmiths' Company 1746, and Lord Mayor in 1753, in which year he died. The firm was then Ironside, Belchier and How, as recorded by Heal till 1755.

*IRVINE, John (1425-6) No record of apprenticeship or freedom. First mark entered as smallworker, 11 August 1769. Address: Lombard Street. Second mark, 12 July 1771. Address: 127 Minories, where he appears, as spoonmaker, in the Parl. Report list 1773.

ISAACS, Michael (2040) No record of apprenticeship or freedom. First mark entered as smallworker, 15 July 1782. Address: 54 Trinity (Court), Minories. Second mark, 5 October 1784. Address: 54 Little Minories.

ISRAEL, John (1822) No record of apprenticeship or freedom. Only mark entered as smallworker, 25 April 1786. Address: 27 Berry Street, St. Mary Axe. Heal records him as goldsmith and jeweller, 110 Whitechapel, 1784; and 27 Bury Street, 1790-3.

*ISSOD, Joyce (1636) Widow of Thomas Issod (below). Mark entered as largeworker, undated, prior to 1702. Address: Fleet Street. Heal records her here in 1697 following Chaffers who regarded all the early undated entries as of April 1697.

*ISSOD, Thomas (1694) Son of John Issod of Staughton in the County of Huntinton (sic) yeoman, apprenticed to Lawrence Coles 15 July 1668. Free, 31 July 1675. Livery, June 1682. Mark entered as largeworker, undated, presumably April 1697 on commencement of register, and since Joyce Issod (above) is clearly his widow, he must have died before 1702. Address: Fleet Street. Heal records him as plateworker, White Horse, Fleet Bridge, 1690-7; and Fleet Street, 1697. In the *London Gazette*, 7 August 1690, is the following: 'Nathaniel

Whitebread, an apprentice aged 18, being a well-fed lad of a ruddy complexion, lightish brown hair, went from his master Tho. Issod, Goldsmith at the Whire (sic) Horse on Fleet Bridge the 3rd instant, with a considerable sum of money. Whoever secures and brings him to his master aforesaid shall have £5 reward and their charges.' (Quoted, F. G. Hilton Price, *Handbook of London Bankers*). From the character of Issod's recorded mark of 1697 and his freedom date, there seems little reason to ascribe to him the well-known mark of the Charles II period, T.I. between escallops, found on much important large decorative plate from the 1670s. Issod's apprenticeship to Coles (well-known as a spoonmaker from constant appearance of his mark), and the usual appearance of his mark on spoons, point to this field as his main work.

J

JACKSON, Charles (337, 339, 1095, 3611) Son of Thomas Jackson of Ashton in the County of Chester gentleman, apprenticed to John Ladyman 17 July 1700. Free, 8 February 1712. First mark entered as largeworker, 2 April 1714. Address: Cannon Street. Second (Sterling) mark, 6 July 1720. Livery, October 1721. Third mark, 18 June 1739. Address: 'at the Golden Cup in St. Swithin's Lane'. Heal records him at Cannon Street, 1714-27; Tower Street, 1734; and Golden Cup, St. Swithin's Lane, 1739.

JACKSON, Elizabeth (601) No record of apprenticeship or freedom. Possibly the widow of Charles Jackson (above). First mark entered as largeworker, 4 August 1748. Address: Paternoster Row. Subsequently remarried as Elizabeth Oldfield under which name (q.v.) she entered another mark (19 December 1750) EO, which is also struck in the book below her first entry without any explanation of the discrepancy of such initials with her previous name.

JACKSON, James (1827) Possibly son of James Jackson late of Bridgwater Gardens watchcasemaker deceased (Section VI), apprenticed to Joshua Jackson (q.v.) as goldsmith 5 March 1794 on payment of £7. 14s. of the charity of the Goldsmiths' Company. Freedom unrecorded. First mark entered as smallworker, 26 January 1805. Address: 3 Church Row, St. Luke's. Second mark, 14 February 1805. Moved to 10 Norman Street, St. Luke's, 30 April 1816. Third mark as watchcasemaker, 30 August 1832. Address: 10 'Norman Street', St. Luke's (Section VI).

JACKSON, John I (1091-2) Son of William Jackson of Bridgford in the County of Nottingham clerke, apprenticed to Richard Bransfield 10 October 1674 and turned over to John Spackman. Free, 23 December 1681. Mark entered as largeworker, undated, probably on commencement of register April 1697. Address: Fleet Street. Livery, May 1703. Heal records him at the Angel or Angel and Crown, Fleet Street, 1684-1714. F. G. Hilton Price, *Handbook of London Bankers* records that he offered a reward for the apprehension of a runaway apprentice and there described his house as being over against the Whitehorse Inn (*Post Boy*, 12 February 1713).

JACKSON, John II (3647) Son of John Jackson late Citizen and Cordwainer deceased, apprenticed to Simon Jouet 4 May 1748. Free, 5 February 1759. Appears in Parl. Report list 1773 as spoonmaker, Little Britain, and is therefore an equal candidate with John Innocent (q.v.) for the mark ascribed to him.

JACKSON, John III (1428-9, 2819) No record of apprenticeship or freedom. First mark entered as smallworker, in partnership with Thomas Jackson, probably his father (q.v.), 16 April 1790. Address: 3 Mutton Lane. Second mark alone, 31 October 1792. Address: Mutton Lane. Third mark, 5 December 1795.

JACKSON, Joshua (1427, 1436) Son of Joseph Jackson of Roachford in the County of Sussex apothecary, apprenticed to Richard Bailey 5 May 1762 and turned over same day to S. Meriton (turner). Free, 7 June 1769. First mark entered as smallworker, 6 May 1779. Address: 44 Monkwell Street. Second mark, 1 July 1784. Address: 27 New Street, Cloth Fair. Third mark, 2

October 1787. Fourth mark, 14 January 1794. Probably identifiable with the watchcasemaker of the same name 1795-8 (Section V).

*JACKSON, Orlando (1767, 2107, 2706, 3747) No record of apprenticeship or freedom. First mark entered as smallworker, undated, between August 1759 and February 1760. Address: Great Wild Street. Second mark as largeworker, in partnership with Thomas Bumfriss, 6 May 1766. Address: Little Trinity Lane, Queenhithe. Third mark as plateworker, in partnership with James Young, 17 March 1774. Address: 33 Aldersgate Street. Fourth mark, 13 May 1774. Heal records the above excepting the partnership with Bumfriss, but adding Haymarket, 1773, to the addresses, since he appears there alone as plateworker in the Parl. Report list that year.

JACKSON, Samuel (2559) Probably son of John Jackson of Potts Street Bethnal Green dyer, apprenticed to Walter Jackson of Gutter Lane as engraver 1 March 1815. Free, 6 November 1822. Mark entered as plateworker, 22 April 1822. Address: 19 Upper Street, St. Martin's Lane. Moved to 14 Newgate Street, 15 July 1823. Moved to 4 Prujean Square, Old Bailey, 3 June 1824. Further entries after 1837.

JACKSON, Thomas I (2812, 2817) Son of Joseph Jackson late of Leeds in the County of York gentleman deceased, apprenticed to William Soame of the Mercers' Company 10 October 1729 on payment of £20. Free, 1736. First mark entered as largeworker, 7 December 1736. Address: Noble Street. 'Free of Mirssers Company'. Second mark, 26 June 1739. Address: Paternoster Row. 'Mircer'. Heal records these addresses and dates and adds Mutton Lane, 1769, which however clearly belongs to Thomas Jackson II (below).

JACKSON, Thomas II (2813, 2819, 3840-1) No record of apprenticeship or freedom. First mark entered 30 September 1769 in largeworkers' book II, presumably in error for the smallworkers' book since the former had otherwise been discontinued in 1758. Address: Mutton Lane, Clerkenwell. Appears as smallworker, at this address, in the Parl. Report list 1773. Second mark, 10 May 1773. Third mark, in partnership with John Jackson III (? his son, q.v.), 16 April 1790. Address: 3 Mutton Lane. Partnership apparently dissolved by 31 October 1792 when John Jackson entered a separate mark. Heal records only Mutton Lane, 1769, as if a different address for Thomas Jackson I, for which there is no basis.

*JACOB, John (1421, 1433) No record of apprenticeship or freedom. First mark entered as largeworker, 3 May 1734. Address: Hemings Row, near St. Martin's Lane, signs 'Jean Jacob'. Second mark, 20 June 1739. Moved to Spur Street, 'lestre fil' (Leicester Fields), 7 July 1760. Still at that address, as plateworker, in Parl. Report list 1773. Heal also records him at the Acorn, Panton Street, near Leicester Fields, 1768. Married Anne, daughter of Augustine Courtauld, 1738 (J. L. Chester, *Some Earlier History of the Courtauld Family*, privately printed 1911). Listed by Evans as Huguenot (*Hug. Soc. Proc.*, 14). A good if not first rank maker whose mark is found on rococo baskets, candlesticks and hollow-ware in general.

JACOBS, Moses (2041) No record of apprenticeship or freedom. First mark, incuse as smallworker entered 22 December 1760. Address: St. James, Dukes Place, near Aldgate. Second mark in punch, 16 December 1769. Probably a watchcasemaker. Appears without category, Dukes Place, in the Parl. Report list 1773.

*JAGO, James (1824) No record of apprenticeship or freedom. Presumably son of John Jago (below). Mark entered as smallworker, 27 March 1828. Address: 6 Tabernacle Row.

*JAGO, John (1824) No record of apprenticeship or freedom. First mark entered as smallworker, 19 September 1783. Address: 16 Little Arthur Street, Goswell Street. Moved to 26 Glasshouse Yard, Aldersgate Street, 31 May 1788. Moved to 6 Tabernacle Row, City Road, 23 October 1793. Second mark, 7 December 1803. Third mark, 20 March 1804. Fourth, 21 October 1808. Fifth, 23 November 1813. Sixth, 26 August 1816. Seventh, 18 March 1818. Eighth, 3 November 1820. Ninth, 20 May 1825. Presumably succeeded by James Jago (above) in 1828.

JAGO, Mahala (2042) No record of apprenticeship or freedom. Only mark entered as smallworker, 4 September 1830. Address: 6 Tabernacle Row (as James and John Jago (above), of one of whom she was presumably widow).

JAMES, Thomas (2821) Probably son of

Thomas James of St. Martin Le Grand jeweller, Citizen and Joiner (Section VII), apprenticed to Thomas Gosling of Great Old Bailey jeweller 3 November 1779. Free, 1 April 1789. Mark entered as smallworker, 30 October 1804. Address: 98 Newgate Street. Perhaps the same as Heal's record of Thomas James, goldsmith and jeweller, 53 Tooley Street, 1790-3; and 6 St. Ann's Lane, Aldersgate Street, 1796. Thomas James, Minories, appears without category in the Parl. Report list 1773, and was possibly the father of the above.

JARMAN, Samuel *See* JERMAN.

*JARRATT, John (1423) No record of apprenticeship or freedom. Only mark entered as smallworker, 22 July 1758. Address: Hosier Lane, West Smithfield, where he appears without category in the Parl. Report list 1773.

JARVIS, John (1420) No record of apprenticeship or freedom. Only mark entered as smallworker, 30 June 1731. Address: Middlesex Court, Bartholomew Close.

JAY, Edward (602, 3545) Son of Thomas Jay late of New Sarum in the County of Wiltshire gentleman deceased, apprenticed to Gabriel Sleath 4 October 1743 on payment of £30. Free, 8 November 1751. First mark entered as largeworker, 15 April 1757. Address: Strand, near Southampton Street. Moved to Fleet Lane, 7 June 1760, the entry signed by Ann Jay, either in her husband's absence or as widow. The latter seems unlikely since Edward Jay appears in the Parl. Report list 1773 as plateworker, Salisbury Court (Fleet Street). The mark no. 3545, ascribed to him, appearing with some regularity on salvers of this period, can easily be confused with that of Elizabeth Jones, no. 600 (q.v.). There may of course have been a son of the same name working by the time of the Parl. Report.

JAY, Henry (1093) Probably son of Henry Jay of Norwich taylor, apprenticed to John Sutton 20 November 1684 for eight years. Free, 9 December 1692. Mark entered as largeworker, undated, between April 1714 and December 1719. Address: Ball Alley, Lombard Street. Heal records him here, 1716-27; also Newington, 1734, which seems unlikely to be the same man. He is presumably the 'Henry Jay Goldsmith Cheapside. Died August 1738 'Aet. 63, formerly an eminent goldsmith' (*London Magazine*, p. 412). If this identity is so, he was born in 1675 and thus apprenticed at the early age of nine, which raises doubts. On the other hand, there is no other apprenticeship record for that name within effective dates for the maker of the mark.

JEANES, Thomas (2818) Son of John Jeanes of Broughton in the County of South(ampt)on gentleman, apprenticed to Thomas Parr 6 September 1739 on payment of £84 (one of the largest sums recorded for the period). Free, 6 December 1749. Mark entered as largeworker, 14 April 1750. Address: Lombard Street, where Heal records him from this year till death in 1752.

JEFFERYS, Henry (1021) No record of apprenticeship or freedom. Only mark entered as plateworker (two sizes), 6 June 1793. Address: 91 Fleet Street. Heal records him as Henry Jefferys & Co., goldsmiths, jewellers and cutlers, 96 Fleet Street, 1790-3; at the Great Knife Case, 91 Fleet Street 1796; and 49 Salisbury Square (Heal Add.).

JEFFERYS, Samuel (1262) Son of James Jefferys of the Old Artillery Ground belonging to the Tower of London, apprenticed to William Gamble 26 October 1688. Free, 13 November 1695. Mark entered as largeworker, undated, probably April 1697 on commencement of register. Address: Near Wapping Old Stairs. Also a later undated note 'at Sunbury'. Livery, October 1720. Heal records him at Wapping Old Stairs till 1731.

JEFFERYS, Thomas (3842) No record of apprenticeship or freedom. Heal records him first as goldsmith and jeweller, Cockspur Street, 1765-77; and in partnership with William Jones at the same address, 1779-93; as Jefferys, Jones and Gilbert, 1796; and finally as Jefferys and Gilbert 1798 (Heal Add.). For the appointment of the firm as Royal Goldsmiths see William Jones II. It seems certain that they were almost entirely retailers, if not the first recorded dealers in antique plate, as exemplified by the following from the diary of Sophie v. la Roche, Friday 15 September 1786 (*Sophie in London*, 1786, translated and edited by Clare Williams, 1933): 'We visited Messrs Jeffries' silver store ... whose stock must be worth millions. It was all illuminated, and from this room, full of sparkling gold and silver moulds and vessels, with two of its walls lined with large mirrors, there is a magnificent view into two brightly lit streets, . . . I have never seen silver moulded into such noble, charming, simple forms; never in such profusion and with the added pleasure of comparing the work of previous generations with up-to-date modern creations, whereby the clients' taste and artist's workmanship at different periods may be construed and criticized. These antique, well-preserved pieces, so Mr Jeffries said, often find a purchaser more readily than the modern. This is because the English are fond of constructing and decorating whole portions of their country houses, or at least one apartment, in old Gothic style, and so are glad to purchase any accessories dating from the same or a similar period. The shelves round the window and the tables contained a number of indefinable but delicately wrought trifles, as, for instance, rings, needles, watches and bracelets, showing an inventiveness and craftsmanship almost past imagination.'

A bill dated 22 March 1786 is headed 'Bot. of Jefferys & Jones Goldsmiths & Jewellers In Cock-spur Street near Charing Cross' with the Royal arms and 'Goldsmith to His Majesty'. A cup engraved with the signature 'Jefferys & Gilbert' but bearing the mark of W. Pitts and J. Preedy, 1798, is in the Ilchester Collection. For Gilbert, see under William Jones II. The mark here attributed to Jefferys and Jones is extremely rare and does not appear in the registers. It is possible from the date of the pieces that it was cut with the intention of entering it at the Hall after Jones' appointment as Royal Goldsmith in 1783, but its use abandoned after a short time and all new plate obtained from other plateworkers.

*JELF, William (1261, 3196) Described in his entries as Free Clockmaker, but his name does not appear in the existing lists of that company (Guildhall Library). First mark (New Standard) entered, undated, between 1717 and 1720. Address: Fenchurch Street. 'Free Clockmaker'. Second (Sterling) mark, 27 July 1720. Address: Milk Street. A William Jelfe, son of Richard, deceased, was apprenticed to Henry Beesley of the Goldsmiths' Company, 1726, but the connection, if there is one, is not apparent.

JENKINS, James (1422, 1430) Son of Joseph Jenkins in the County of Surrey gentleman (town not stated), apprenticed to Samuel Hitchcock 5 July 1722 on payment of £6. 6s. Free, 4 February 1729. First mark entered as largeworker, 26 April 1731. Address: Gutter Lane. 'Free Goldsmith'. Second mark, 15 January 1739. Address: Bull Yard, Aldersgate Street. Heal records both dates and addresses and no more.

*JENKINS, Thomas (1259) Described as Free Butcher on entry of mark but no record of him in the apprentice or freedom index of that company. Mark entered as largeworker, undated, probably April 1697 on commencement of register. Address: Essex Street, without Temple Bar. 'Free Butcher'. Heal records him as goldsmith, Cornish Daw, Essex Street, 1688–1708, as does Hilton Price (*Handbook of London Bankers*). Jacob Margas was apprenticed to him 1699. Another mark very similar to that in the register but with 'E' for 'e', occurs on candlesticks of 1703 of the Fishmongers' Company.

JENNINGS, Edward (599, 1260, 1265) Son of John Jennings of the parish of St. Martin's in the Fields in the County of Middlesex gentleman, apprenticed to Charles Williams 1 May 1700. Free, 5 September 1707. First mark entered as largeworker, 26 January 1710. Address: Tower Street near the Seven Streets, 'Sehow' (Soho). Second mark, also New Standard, 30 June 1720. Third mark (Sterling) 1 July 1720. Address: Little Britain. Heal records him at both addresses, the latter till 1727. Livery, June 1725.

JENNINGS, Henry Thomas (1071) Son of Thomas Jennings of Spalding in the County of Lincoln ironmonger, apprenticed to George Smith of Huggin Lane as goldsmith 2 June 1790 on payment of £50. Free, 8 March 1798. Mark entered as plateworker, 7 May 1801. Address: 7 Crescent, Jewin Street.

JENNINGS, James (1424) Perhaps son of George Jennings of Hanslow in the County of Buckingham laceman, apprenticed to Jonah Clifton 2 December 1708. Free, 6 March 1743!) Only mark entered as smallworker 27 February 1760. Address: Bulls Head Court, Newgate Street, where he appears, without category, in the Parl. Report list 1773. It is difficult to accept the connection of this apprenticeship and mark, but there is no other available.

JENNINGS, Zachariah (2628) No record of apprenticeship or freedom. Only mark entered as smallworker, in partnership with Samuel Rudduck, 27 March 1810. Address: 35 Brunswick Street, Soho.

JERMAN

*JERMAN, Samuel (3795) Son of William Jerman late of Braintree in the County of Essex weaver, apprenticed to Edward Bennett Citizen and Goldsmith 6 October 1756 and turned over 23 February 1760 to Samuel Launder Citizen and Goldsmith. Free, 4 July 1764. Appears as Jarman, spoonmaker, Great Newport Street, in the Parl. Report list 1773.

JOHNSON, Charles (338) No record of apprenticeship or freedom. Only mark entered as largeworker, 4 August 1743. Address: Gunpowder Alley, Shoe Lane.

JOHNSON, Glover (833, 1560) Free of the Haberdashers' Company by patrimony 20 March 1695. First mark entered as largeworker, 4 August 1712. Address: Maiden Lane. 'Free Haberdasher'. Second (Sterling) mark, 29 June 1720. Address: Noble Street. Probably dead by 17 August 1727, when Mary Johnson entered her mark at the same address. Heal records him as Glover Johnson, plateworker, Maiden Lane, 1712-20, which suggests a father of the same name in the period previous to 1712, but there is no other entry as from 1697. Johnson's particular production seems from survival to have been small dredgers and trenchersalts.

JOHNSON, Henry (1022) No record of apprenticeship or freedom. Only mark entered as smallworker, 16 November 1829. Address: 4 Warwick Square, Golden Square.

JOHNSON, John I (1435, 1559) Son of Daniel Johnson Citizen and Glover of London, apprenticed to Benjamin Clare (q.v.) of the Skinners' Company 7 March 1698/9. Free, 4 November 1707. First mark entered as smallworker, 3 August 1708. Address: Gray's Inn Lane, Holborn. 'Free of the Skinners'. Second (Sterling) mark, 28 June 1720. Benjamin Clare his master, also of Gray's Inn Lane was dead when Johnson received his freedom and it seems almost certain that he carried on the business at the same address.

JOHNSON, John II (1828) Probably son of William Johnson of Martin Street City Road silversmith, apprenticed to his father as such 4 April 1827. Freedom unrecorded. Only mark entered as spoonmaker, 2 November 1835. Address: 15 Wellington Street, Kingsland Road.

JOHNSON, Lawrence (1934-5, 3722) No record of apprenticeship or freedom. First mark entered as largeworker, 3 April 1751. Address: Catherine Street. Second mark, 22 August 1752. Heal records him as working goldsmith, Katherine Street, corner of Exeter Street, near the Strand, 1751-63.

JOHNSON, Mary (2038) No record of apprenticeship or freedom. Presumably widow of Glover Johnson (q.v.). Mark entered as largeworker, 17 August 1727. Address: Noble Street, near Goldsmiths' Hall. 'Goldsmith'.

JOHNSON, Samuel (2554) Described as 'Glazier' in entry of mark. He does not appear in the only existing apprentice record of that company, the apprentice orphan list (Guildhall Library). Probably free by patrimony or redemption. Only mark entered as smallworker, undated, between 22 July and 6 October 1725 (perhaps the former date, following previous entry). Address: Wood Street, Fryingpan Alley. 'Glazier'.

JOHNSON Thomas (712, 2820) Son of Benjamin Johnson of Braintree in the County of Essex weaver, apprenticed to Robert Purton of Carey Lane as goldsmith 7 August 1782 (same day as John Gold to same master). Free, 6 February 1793. First mark entered as smallworker, in partnership with Frances Purton, 28 February 1793. Address: 2 Carey Lane. Second mark alone, 22 January 1800. Address: 26 Blue Anchor Alley, Bunhill Row.

JOHNSON, William (3204) Son of John Johnson late of Ann Street in St. George's in the East painter and glazier deceased, apprenticed to Thomas Wallis of Red Lion Street, Clerkenwell as goldsmith 2 October 1805. Free, 6 January 1813. First mark entered as spoonmaker, 9 December 1822. Address: 38 Provost Street, City Road. Moved to 1 Martin Street, City Road, 26 April 1824. Moved to 51 Ironmonger Row, 5 January 1828. Second mark, 30 May 1835.

JOHNSTON, Alexander (44-5) Son of Alexander Johnston late of St. Giles in the Fields draper deceased, apprenticed to Thomas Moulden 6 August 1724. Free, 3 September 1734. First mark entered as largeworker, 11 May 1733. Address: 'At the Crown in Foster Lane'. 'Free Goldsmith'. This entry is annotated 'dead' as so many at the period. A new entry as largeworker, 22 January 1748 (Address: 'Of Alley Villiers Street, York Buildings') seems to be in the same handwriting, but we should have expected an entry of a different mark in 1739 to comply with the Act. Moved to Panton Street, 28 July 1749. Moved to Spur Street, Leicester Fields, 9 May 1753. Moved to Old 'Jury', 10 February 1757 (both in register entry without mark). Heal records him in Panton Street, 1747; and with Charles Geddes as jewellers, Golden Ball, Panton Street, near Leicester Square, c. 1760; with another reference from the Parl. Report list 1773 as plateworker, Old Jewry. A second Alexander Johnston is recorded free by redemption, 9 February 1757, described as goldsmith. It is possible that these two entries are for entirely different persons but the position remains uncertain.

JOHNSTON, Joshua (1825-6) No record of apprenticeship or freedom. First mark entered as smallworker, 23 January 1796. Address: 8 New Castle (?Street). Second mark, 27 June 1799.

JOHNSTON, R— (2350) No record of apprenticeship or freedom. Only mark entered as smallworker, 24 March 1800. Address: 68 St. James's Street. The mark has been found by Mr. Vesey Norman of the Wallace Collection on a sword of 1809 signed 'R. Johnston 68 St. James's Str. London'. It would seem clear that he was a sword cutler, perhaps even a general outfitter.

JOLLAND, Anthony (43) Son of Anthony Jolland late of London weaver deceased, apprenticed to Humphrey Payne 21 January 1712 on payment of £20. Free, 5 February 1719. Mark entered as largeworker, 27 June 1721. Address: Staining Lane.

JONES, Dyall (3663) No record of apprenticeship or freedom. Partner as plateworker with John Moliere, 6 Clerkenwell Green, their only reference being the Parl. Report list 1773. The agreement of initials and date of the pieces on which mark no. 3663 is found appear to make its ascription to these makers certain.

JONES, Edward (1558) Son of Michael Jones Citizen and Haberdasher of London, apprenticed to Richard Palmer of the Wax Chandlers' Company 21 February 1687. The company records contain the receipt of freedom charge of £1 from Edward Jones apprentice to George Hawson (to whom perhaps he was turned over) 13 January 1697/8, but this might refer to another of the same name. Only mark entered as largeworker, undated, either April 1697 on commencement of register or shortly after receiving freedom above, since he is described as 'Free Wax Chandler'. Address: Foster Lane. (Also struck in the space allotted to him is an impression of the mark of John East, apparently in error at a later date.) Heal records Edward Jones goldsmith, London, 1676-71 and plateworker, Lombard Street, 1694 as well as Foster Lane, 1697. The earlier references must belong to another, probably the 'Edward Jones Goldsmith' whose sons and daughters appear in baptisms and burials at St. Mary Woolnoth, 1694-5.

JONES, Elizabeth (600) No record of apprenticeship or freedom. Probably widow of Robert Jones (q.v.). Mark entered as plateworker, 15 January 1783. Address: 49 Bartholomew Close. Cf. Robert Jones and John Schofield, 40 Bartholomew Close, 1776, and the apprenticeship of Robert, son of Robert Jones 'late of Bartholomew Close Goldsmith decd.' in 1787. Her mark, which is rarely found except on salvers and waiters, must be carefully distinguished from that of Edward Jay (q.v.), no. 3545, which appear too early to be hers.

JONES, George Greenhill (834-5, 1563) Son of William Jones late of Highworth in the County of Wiltshire innholder deceased, apprenticed to James Goodwyn 21 November 1711 on payment of £5 for eight years. Free, 3 December 1719. First mark entered as largeworker, 5 December 1719. Address: Foster Lane. Second (Sterling) mark, 19 February 1726, same address. (There was probably an earlier Sterling mark unentered as he is unlikely to have continued to work so long in New Standard). Third mark, 27 June 1739, same address. Heal records him here, 1724-44. Livery, July 1731. Resigned April 1748.

JONES, Isaac (1437, 1440) No record of apprenticeship or freedom. First mark entered as bucklemaker, 7 September 1780. Address: Great Wild Street, Lincoln's Inn Fields. Second and third marks, with William Jones III as such, 1787-8. Address: 26 Queen Street, Seven Dials (Section VIII). Fourth mark alone as smallworker, 3 September 1800. Address: 4 Middle Scotland Yard, Whitehall. Fifth mark, in partnership with William Jones III, 5 May 1809, same address. Moved to 3 Northumberland Court, near Northumberland House, 6 June 1812. Heal records them as J. and W. Jones, silver bucklemakers, Great St. Andrew Street, Seven Dials, 1793.

JONES, James I (1434) Presumably son of James Jones late of Fetter Lane bookbinder deceased, apprenticed to Joseph Smith 5 July 1737 on payment of £10 and turned over to Ebenezer Coker 1 October 1740. Free, 5 July 1749. Mark entered as largeworker, 27 May 1755. Address: Noble Street, near Aldersgate. Heal records him here till 1763 and he appears there without category in the Parl. Report list 1773.

JONES, James II (1693) Probably son of William Jones of St. Martin within Ludgate Citizen and Goldsmith, apprenticed to his father 3 June 1767 and turned over same day to James Jones cutler of the Mews Charing Cross in consideration of £8. 5s. of the Charity of the Goldsmiths' Company. Only mark entered as largeworker, in partnership with John Sebille (q.v.), 14 February 1798. Address: 9 Clerkenwell Close.

JONES, John I (1418-9, 1431-2, 1564, 3664) Son of Richard Jones of St. Martin's Le Grand farrier, apprenticed to James Seabrook 3 August 1715 on payment of £15 and turned over to Matthew Cooper 1 February 1719. Free, 7 February 1722. First two marks (Sterling and New Standard) entered as largeworker, 27 March 1723. Address: Maiden Lane. 'Free Goldsmith'. Third mark, 24 March 1729. Address: Salisbury Street, Rotherhithe. Fourth mark, 3 January 1733. Address: 'at the Rose and Crown St. Martin's Le Grand'. Fifth mark, 1 February 1739. Address: Cow Cross, Mr. Alcock's Rents (this last entry may possibly be for a separate maker, since the name is signed as Jon as against the previous John). Heal records all the above addresses with corresponding dates except the last but adds Foster Lane, 1719. This suggests that at or soon after the time he was turned over to Matthew Cooper he was working openly before obtaining his freedom. There seem to be other examples of this.

JONES, John II (1823) Perhaps, but unlikely, son of Henry Jones late of the parish of St. Saviour Southwark labourer deceased, apprenticed to Samuel Wood 11 January 1749 on payment of £20. Freedom unrecorded. Only mark entered as smallworker, in partnership with William Jones, 23 August 1763. Address: Middle Moorfields, where they appear without category in the Parl. Report list 1773. He is probably identifiable with the John Jones, bucklemaker, at 46 Little Minories, 1777-83 (Section VIII).

JONES, John III (1438) Perhaps, but unlikely, son of Charles Jones late of Newnham in the County of Gloucester apothecary deceased, apprenticed to Richard Sayer Arnell of Jewin Street as jeweller 4 January 1809 on payment of £20. Free, 1 May 1816. Mark entered as plateworker, 4 August 1824. Address: 1 Dean Street, Fetter Lane. Second mark, 7 February 1825. Moved to 20 Red Lion Street, Clerkenwell, 13 July 1827.

JONES, Lawrence (1557, 3665) Son of Thomas Jones of Brimhill in the County of Wiltshire yeoman, apprenticed to John King 14 June 1676 'from Midsummer next'. Free, 28 July 1686. Mark entered as largeworker, undated, presumably April 1697 on commencement of register. Address: Old Bailey. Spells his name 'Lauwrence'. Livery, 1705. Court, 1724. Warden, 1728, 1735-6. Heal records him as plateworker, Old Bailey, 1696-1720; London 1724; and Cripplegate 1734.

JONES, Robert I (2346-7, 2349) No record of apprenticeship or freedom. First mark entered as plateworker, 1 February 1774. Address: 40 Bartholomew Close. Second mark, in partnership with John Scofield, 10 February 1776, same address. Third mark alone, 14 January 1778, same address. Apparently dead by 15 January 1783, when Elizabeth Jones entered her mark at 49 Bartholomew Close, and certainly stated to be so in the apprenticeship of his son Robert (below), 1787.

JONES, Robert II (2347) Son of Robert Jones (above) late of Bartholomew Close goldsmith deceased, apprenticed to Solomon Hougham 3 October 1787 on payment of £30. Free, 5 November 1794. Mark entered as plateworker, 29 January 1796. Address: 49 Bartholomew Close, where Heal, not distinguishing between father and son, records him till 1800.

*JONES, Thomas (3840-1) Son of Thomas Jones late Citizen and Goldsmith, apprenticed to John Threadway 6 July 1748 and turned over the same day to John Wray Citizen and Tinplateworker in consideration of £18. 18s., £6. 13s. 4d. of which is paid from Christ's Hospital, £8. 5s. of the charity of the Goldsmiths' Company. Free, 3 November 1755. Appears as plateworker, Bells Buildings, Salisbury Court, in the

Parl. Report list 1773, and presumably therefore had entered a mark before that date in the missing register. Perhaps identifiable with Thomas Jones, bucklemaker at 1 Great Rider Street, St. James's, 1782-95, or Thomas Jones, bucklemaker, Buckley Court, Clerkenwell, 1792 (Section VIII).

JONES, William I (1823) Apprenticeship and freedom unestablished. Only mark entered as smallworker, in partnership with John Jones II, 23 August 1763. Address: Middle Moorfields, where they appear without category in the Parl. Report list 1773.

JONES, William II (3842) Born 1748. No record of apprenticeship or freedom. Heal records Jefferys and Jones, goldsmiths and jewellers, Cockspur Street, 1779-93; and Jefferys, Jones and Gilbert at same address, 1796. Jones succeeded as Royal Goldsmith in 1783 following the abolition of the Jewel House the previous year and after an investigation by the Lord Chamberlain into the expenses of the previous period, resulting in the dismissal of Thomas Heming. His warrant, however, was not issued until 1796 (Major General H. W. D. Sitwell, 'The Jewel House and the Royal Goldsmith's', *Arch. Journ.* CXVII, pp. 145-6). For comment on the mark attributed to Jefferys and Jones and for a description of their establishment see Thomas Jefferys. The burial of William Jones, goldsmith, Cockspur Street, forty-nine years old, appears in the register of St. Paul's Cathedral, 9 March 1797. In the same month his partner Philip Gilbert, for whom no mark is entered, was appointed Goldsmith in Ordinary to the King, and in January 1798 Jeweller in Ordinary. At the same time Rundell and Bridge were appointed as Goldsmiths and Jewellers, and royal business divided fairly equally between the two establishments until 1820 (Sitwell, *op. cit.*).

JONES, William III (1440) Perhaps son of William Jones of Tower Street Seven Dials cordwainer deceased, apprenticed to John Lambe of Fetter Lane as goldsmith 2 May 1781. Freedom unrecorded. First mark, in partnership with Isaac Jones (q.v.), as bucklemakers, 20 October 1787. Address: 26 Queen Street, Seven Dials. Second and third marks similar, 1787-8 (Section VIII). Fourth mark together as smallworkers, 5 May 1809. Address: 4 Middle Scotland Yard. Moved to 3 Northumberland Court, near Northumberland House, 6 June 1812.

JORDAN, George (839) Son of James Jordan late of Tabernacle Walk, St. Luke's Middlesex accountant deceased, apprenticed to William Turner Clark of Gee Street Goswell Street as working goldsmith 2 December 1812 on payment of £5 of the charity of the late Mr. Smith of St. Luke. Freedom unrecorded. Mark entered as smallworker, 10 March 1835. Moved to 57 Bridport Place, Hoxton, 9 February 1836.

JORDAN, Walter (3205) No record of apprenticeship or freedom. Only mark entered as plateworker, 29 March 1834. Address: 27 County Terrace, Kent Road.

JOUET, Peter (2196) No record of apprenticeship or freedom. Heal however records Pierre Jouet, goldsmith, St. Anne's, Westminster, 1699; and he appears as Peter Jouet, goldsmith, St. Giles without (Cripplegate), 1718 in the apprenticeship of his son Simon (below). Jackson also records the same name as goldsmith at Exeter, Topsham, c. 1706. Mark entered as smallworker, 23 November 1723, but so large a mark that it seems struck in the smallworkers' book in error. Address: 'Over against ye Victualing Office Little Tower Hill'. Another member of the family, although with no mark registered, was probably Samuel Juett, son of John, apprenticed to Thomas Wotton 1702.

JOUET, Simon (1561, 2553, 2556-7, 3794) Son of Peter Jouet (above) of St. Giles without Cripplegate goldsmith, apprenticed to John Orchard 3 April 1718 and turned over 20 June 1722 to Mr. Thomas Folkingham in Swithin's Lane. Free, 27 May 1725. Possibly the Simon Jovett of St. Bride's, London, bachelor, married to Sarah Browne of the same parish, 29 September 1723 at St. Bene't, Paul's Wharf. First mark (New Standard) entered as largeworker, undated, between 1724 and 1727, but presumably close to the entry of second (Sterling) mark as smallworker, 21 July 1725. Address: 'over against ye Victualing Office Little Tower Hill', as his father (above). 'Free of ye Goldsmiths Company'. Third mark, 18 June 1739. Address: White Hart, Foster Lane. Moved to Cary Lane, 9 September 1746. Fourth mark, 29 February 1748. Address: 'Now at Aldersgate April 5 1749', where Heal records him till 1752. Moved to Kingsland, 27 March 1755 (register entry without mark). Became a member of the Honourable Artillery Company, 10 January 1749.

Appears variously as Simon Jovet, Jovett or Jowett. Ensign, Yellow Trained Bands, 1749-52. Lieutenant, 1752-3. Lieutenant, White Trained Bands, 1754 (G. Goold Walker, 'Huguenots in the Trained Bands of London and the Honourable Artillery Company', *Hug. Soc. Proc.*, 15, p. 300). Listed also as Huguenot by Evans (*Hug. Soc. Proc.*, 14, p. 541).

JOYCE — (1569) Perhaps John Joyce son of Stephen Joyce of the parish of Stepney in the County of Middlesex weaver, apprenticed to Peter Platell 12 August 1708, the entry annotated with a marginal note certifying the denization of father and mother dated 20 March 1699. Freedom unrecorded. Only mark entered as smallworker, in partnership with — Hussey, 12 May 1729. Address: 'in old Boswell Court. 'Free Goldsmith'.

JOYCE, Stephen (2555) No record of apprenticeship or freedom. Only mark entered as smallworker, 4 August 1759. Address: King Street, St. Ann's. Heal records him as goldsmith, Moor Street, Soho, 1770; and King Street, Soho, 1773-8; and he appears as goldworker, at the second address, in the Parl. Report list 1773. A connection seems probable with Joseph Joyce Senior and Junior, goldsmiths, Greek Street, Soho, 1753.

JOYCE, Thomas (2816) Son of John Joyce of the City of Coventry presser deceased, apprenticed to John Bayly engraver, Citizen and Goldsmith as engraver 7 April 1773 on payment of £42. Freedom unrecorded. Mark entered as smallworker, 20 April 1791. Address: 27 Great Eastcheap. Moved to 25 John's Street, Blackfriars, 25 June 1793. Moved to 8 Russell Court, Drury Lane, 24 August 1799.

JUDKINS, Mathew (2039) Probably he of the same name apprenticed in the Fishmongers' Company 24 June 1694 and appearing as the master of an apprentice to that company in 1737. Only mark entered as smallworker, 8 May 1738. Address: Gutter Lane. 'Free Fishmonger'. St. Vedast, Foster Lane registers contain the following: 'A Female Childe of Matthew Judkins Goldsmith in Gutter Lane in this parish was Borne ye 29th day of March 1705', at which date there is no record of a mark. There may, of course, have been father and son of the same name.

*JURY, William (3201, 3203) No record of apprenticeship or freedom. First mark (two sizes) entered as smallworker, in partnership with Stephen Adams (q.v.), undated, c. 1758. Second mark, 29 October 1759. Address: Lillypot Lane. Third mark alone, 15 October 1760. Address: Long Lane, Smithfield.

JUSON, William (1728, 3690) William Jewson son of William of Shrewsbury in the County of Salop ffarier, apprenticed to William Scarlett Citizen and Broderer of London 28 August 1694. Free of the Broderers' Company, 5 March 1701. Mark entered as largeworker, 6 July 1704. Address: Foster Lane. 'Free Imbroyderer'. Heal records him here till 1714.

*JUSTIS, Thomas (2814-15, 3840-1) No record of apprenticeship or freedom. First mark entered as smallworker, 24 November 1761. Address: Well Yard, Little Britain. Second mark, 30 September 1762. Third mark, 26 September 1763. Fourth, 4 July 1764. Fifth, 20 October 1764. Sixth, 20 May 1765. Seventh, 23 November 1767. Eighth, 3 November 1768. Ninth, 8 February 1770 All the above at same address. Tenth mark, 18 October 1771. Address: as 'Thos Justis & Co', in Newgate Street. He reappears, however, as Thomas Justis, bucklemaker, Well Yard, in the Parl. Report list 1773. Heal records only Justis and Co., goldsmiths, Well Yard, St. Bartholomew's Hospital.

*JUSTIS, William (3200, 3202, 3888-9) Son of William Justis of Reading in the County of Berkshire carpenter, apprenticed to John Fawdery 17 December 1712 on payment of £4 and turned over 13 May 1718 to Richard Bayley of Foster Lane Goldsmith. Free, 5 January 1721. First mark entered as largeworker, undated, between April 1731 and January 1733. Address: Staining Lane, near Goldsmiths' Hall, Goldsmith. Second mark, 28 June 1739. Moved to Wood Street, 8 December 1750. His son William was apprenticed to him 6 May 1747, and later turned over to David Field Citizen and Turner. Mary, daughter of William and Dorothy Justis, was born 26 May 1745 (Christchurch, Newgate, incorporating St. Leonards, Foster Lane). Heal records him variously as Justis, Justise or Justus, plateworker, Golden Ball, Staining Lane near Haberdashers' Hall, 1731-55. His mark appears usually on salvers and waiters.

KANDLER, Charles I (Frederick) (341, 689, 691-2, 1540, 1862-3, 3571) No record of apprenticeship or freedom. The identity of this highly important maker remains a baffling mystery. His name is obviously German and it would seem reasonable to think, from the highly plastic quality of so much of his work, that there is some connection with the Meissen porcelain modeller of the same name. The late Norman Penzer, when working on the subject of the great wine-cooler by Kandler in the Hermitage, made considerable effort to uncover any clue to his origin but without success. His first dated marks (Sterling and New Standard) entered as largeworker, in partnership with James Murray, 29 August 1727. Address: 'in Sant Martens Lein', which appears to be in Murray's hand after his signature rather than in Kandler's. There is a third mark, New Standard, apparently entered at some time, undated, for Kandler alone, without address. In this the mitre above the initials appears, which is not in the Kandler/Murray marks, and a similar unregistered Sterling mark CK with mitre above is found on the remarkable undated kettle in the Victoria and Albert Museum. The third mark provides an important link by being restruck in the same entry as the fourth and fifth marks, 10 September 1735. These have been considered by Penzer and others to be that of a separate individual as the name is entered in Benjamin Pyne's hand (the Touch Warden of the day) as 'Charles Frederick Kandler in German Street near St. James Church', and he so signs in full, the first and last names being clearly in the same hand as those of the first two entries. This entry may have been made on Kandler's move to Jermyn Street, since it has not only the New Standard KA mark, but also the fifth mark using the initials FK for the first time. This is followed by sixth entry, 25 June 1739, in which the signature, allowing for age and the dropping of Charles, is clearly the same hand again. The last and seventh entered mark is a variant of the sixth entered below the 1739 mark and only countersigned by the Warden Joseph Howard, as usual. The discovery of a further New Standard mark in 1964 on a magnificent inkstand of 1751, in company with much other family plate bearing the earlier established marks, was an interesting addition to the documented marks. The distinction of the varying Christian names is repeated in the entries of various apprentices to Kandler in the indexes to the apprentices of Great Britain extracted from the Inland Revenue books at the Public Record Office. Charles Kandler, goldsmith of St. James's, appears as master in 1735 of Ralph Wilberforce and James Rigby. In 1743 Charles Frederick Kandler, also goldsmith, St. James's, Westminster, is listed as master of William Moody (q.v.). Again Frederick Kandler of St. James, Westminster, silversmith, appears as master of William Reynolds (q.v.) in 1748 and Peter Rooney in 1760. Frederick Kandler, plateworker, Jermyn Street, appears in the Parl. Report list 1773.

KANDLER, Charles II (342) No record of apprenticeship or freedom. Only mark entered as plateworker, 12 November 1778. Address: 100 Jermyn Street. He is clearly some relation of the above, presumably either son or grandson. Heal records him here as plateworker till 1793.

KANDLER, Frederick See **KANDLER, Charles I**.

KAY, Charles (343) No record of apprenticeship or freedom. Already working before entry of mark, as proved by the baptismal entry: 'William son of Charles and Mary Kay of Addle Street, Aldermanbury Silversmith', 18 June 1815, at St. Mary Aldermanbury. He is further described as Charles Morris Kay of 3 New Street, Blackfriars, silversmith, 3 November 1819, in the apprenticeship of another son, Charles, to Charles Reid. First mark entered as plateworker, 15 March 1822. Address: New Street, Blackfriars. Moved to 11 Addle Hill, 23 September 1823. Moved to 12 Pump Row, Old Street Road, 19 December 1825. Moved to 14 John's Row, 1827.

KEATT, Launcelot (3710) The attribution of this name to the mark in question is by Jackson, though there seems no documentary evidence from the registers and the mark fairly closely resembles that of Robert

Kempton (no. 1872), reading pellets for mullets. There is however a Lancelot Keate son of William of Mearhay County of Dorset gentleman, apprenticed to John Chadwell 18 April 1690; freedom unrecorded, which may have given rise to the ascription.

KEATT, William (1864, 1868-9) William Keate son of William of the Borough of Reading in the County of Berkshire labourer, apprenticed to John Spackman for eight years 30 November 1681. Free, 6 December 1689. Livery, April 1705. (Another of the same name, son of William of Mearhay in the County of Dorset gentleman, apprenticed to Edward Price 30 April 1693, but freedom unrecorded and seemingly not therefore entitled to work by the time of mark entry.) Three marks entered in one undated group as largeworker, the first two numbered 1 and 2, presumably April 1697 on commencement of register with 'Foster Lane' level with them; the third, presumably later, with 'now in East Smithfield'. Heal records him in Foster Lane from 1693 to 1697; Golden Cup, East Smithfield, 1697-1714; St. Martin's-in-the-Fields, 1706 till bankrupt 1710; and as London, 1724. Dead by 1735 when his son William was apprenticed to Robert Nelson.

KEBLE, Robert (1866-7, 3711) Son of Thomas Keble Citizen and Pewterer of London, apprenticed to Ralph Maunsell 11 October 1699 and turned over the same day to Thomas Brydon. Free, 11 December 1706. First mark entered as largeworker, 13 January 1707. Address: Foster Lane. Second mark, 14 July 1710. Signatory as 'working goldsmith' to the petition complaining of the competition of 'necessitous strangers', December 1711. The register of St. Vedast, Foster Lane, contains the following: 'Robert the son of Mr. Robert Keeble, a Plate worker at the signe of the City of Oxford in Gutter Lane and by Martha his wife was borne & baptized July the 11th 1709.' The register of the child's burial, 24 August 1709, follows. Arnold, a second son was born and baptized 30 July 1710, and John, born 16 December was baptized 20 December 1713.

KEDDEN, Thomas (1870) Son of Ralph Kedden of the Isle of Wight gentleman (?), apprenticed to Emanuel Russell of Bennet Hill bookbinder of the Merchant Taylors' Company 3 October 1682. Free, 1 February 1692. Mark entered as smallworker, 20 November 1700. Address: Noble Street. 'Free Merchant Taylor'. The character of his master's trade suggests a specialization in silver mounts for prayer-books etc.

KEIGWIN, John (1873) Son of John Keigwin of the parish of Paule in the County of Cornwall (?Paul Church Town, Penzance) gentleman, apprenticed to Benjamin Pyne 10 July 1703. Free, 2 August 1710. Mark entered as largeworker, 31 August 1710. Address: Snow Hill, where Heal records him, 1715-19. A John Keigwin, bachelor of the parish of St. Martin's-in-the-Fields, was married to Elizabeth Townsend of St. Clement Dane's, spinster, in St. Paul's Cathedral, 21 May 1732. This might be either the goldsmith or a putative son.

KEITH, John James (1439) No record of apprenticeship or freedom. First mark entered as plateworker, 5 May 1824. Address: 26 Union Street, Hoxton New Town. Moved to 59 Britannia Terrace, City Road, 27 November 1834. Second mark, 1 October 1839.

KELK, Charles (344) No record of apprenticeship or freedom. Small mark entered in unspecified category, 14 October 1828. Address: 10 Castle Street, Leicester Square.

KELLEY, Robert (2353) Son of Robert Kelley of Barnes in the County of Surrey gentleman, apprenticed to Stephen Adams of St. Ann's Lane as goldsmith 5 August 1789. Free, 7 June 1797. Mark entered as smallworker, 19 September 1807. Address: 15 Portugal Street, Lincoln's Inn Fields.

KELLY, Jasper (1447) No record of apprenticeship or freedom. Only mark entered as goldworker, 6 May 1779. Address: 145 Strand.

KELLY, John (1456) Perhaps (but unlikely) son of Martin Kelly of Spitalfields weaver, apprenticed to Henry Brind as working draper and taylor 3 June 1778. Freedom unrecorded. Mark entered as smallworker, in partnership with Benjamin Flight, 19 January 1791. Address: Exeter Change, Strand.

KEMBLE, John (1865) Son of Charles Kemble of St. Egidius without Cripplegate silversmith, apprenticed to John Laughton of the Grocers' Company 7 March 1699. Free, 11 June 1706 when described in the register as 'Att Mr. Bowles in Tokenhouse Yd. silversmith'. Mark entered as smallworker, 2 August 1706. Address: Red Cross Street. 'Free of the Grocers'.

BIOGRAPHICAL DICTIONARY

KEMP, John (1443) Son of John Kempe of the parish of Stepney gentleman, apprenticed to John Cooper 25 May 1715 on payment of £20. Free, 2 August 1722. Mark entered as smallworker, 4 August 1724. Address: Carey Lane, near Cheapside. Livery, March 1737. Court, 1741. Probably the 'Mr. Kemp' referred to under Francis Ruffin in Heal, the latter being described as gold chain-maker and smallworker.

KEMPTON, Robert (1872) Son of Samuel Kempton of the parish of St. Andrew's Holborn boddicemaker, apprenticed to Mathew Cooper 16 March 1703. Free, 21 April 1710. Mark entered as largeworker, 12 June 1710. Address: Foster Lane. Heal records him at this address, 1697–1718, the first date inexplicable in view of his apprenticeship date (unless derived from a mistaken ascription by Jackson).

KENDALL, Luke (182, 1904, 1936–7) Son of John Kendall late of the parish of St. Mary Whitechapel in the County of Middlesex gentleman deceased, apprenticed to Lewis Benoimont 9 November 1750. Free, 7 December 1757. First mark entered as smallworker, in partnership with Lewis Benoimont, 18 November 1761. Address: Cary Lane. (Benoimont entered a single mark, 27 August 1764.) Livery, July 1763. Second mark alone as smallworker, 18 December 1766. Address: Corner Lad Lane, Wood Street. Third mark (larger), 18 June 1772. Address: 26 Wood Street, Cheapside, where Heal records him as goldsmith and jeweller, 1768–82. He appears as goldworker here in the Parl. Report list 1773. Resigned from Livery 17 October 1810.

KENDRICK, Thomas (2822) No record of apprenticeship or freedom. Only mark entered as smallworker, 7 October 1731. Address: Water Lane, Fleet Street, over against ye Black Lion'. Heal records only —— Kendrick, jeweller, Hog Lane, St. Giles in the Fields, died 1764. This is probably William Kendrick, incuse mark entered 26 June 1760. Address: Queen Street, Seven Dials (Section V).

KENTESBER, John (1457, 3707) No record of apprenticeship or freedom. Mark entered as largeworker, in partnership with Thomas Grove, 14 June 1757. Address: Red Lion Street, St. John's, Clerkenwell, where Heal records them as plateworkers from this year till 1773, when they appear in the Parl. Report list as such. Richard, son of John Kentesber of King Street, St. Luke's, silversmith, was apprenticed to William Eley as bucklemaker, 1782, showing that the father was still then in business. There is no evidence of the spelling Kentember (as Jackson), apparently a misprint.

*KENTISH, John (3648) Son of John Kentish Citizen and Glover of London, apprenticed to James Langton Citizen and Goldsmith 2 July 1760 and turned over to his father 3 November 1763. No record of freedom unless possibly as Glover. Known only as goldworker, Cornhill, in the Parl. Report list 1773, but no mark apparently registered before or after this date.

KENTON, John (1871) Apprenticed to Henry Pointon of the Cutlers' Company. Free, 29 October 1683. Mark entered as smallworker, 8 May 1701. Address: Lombard Street. 'Free Cutler'. Presumably haft and hiltmaker, but not as yet identifiable as such.

KERSCHNER, John (1451) Son of John Kerschner of Whitechapel brushmaker, apprenticed to Richard Crossley of Giltspur Street as goldsmith 5 November 1794. Free, 2 December 1801. First mark entered as spoonmaker, 11 November 1808. Address: 4 Silver Street, Falcon Square. Second mark, 15 February 1810. Moved to 12 Clerkenwell Green, 12 March 1814. Third mark, 3 July 1814. Fourth mark (two sizes), 4 July 1814. Fifth mark, 4 September 1817. Moved to 15 Fleet Lane, Fleet Market, 9 May 1820. Moved to 15 Charterhouse Street, 29 January 1822.

KERSILL, Ann (47) No record of apprenticeship or freedom. Widow of Richard Kersill (below). Mark entered on his death as largeworker, 16 June 1747. Address: Foster Lane.

KERSILL, Richard (2352) Son of William Kersill of Highworth in the County of Wiltshire maltster, apprenticed to George Greenhill Jones 1 July 1736 on payment of £30. Free, 7 February 1744. Mark entered as largeworker, 20 April 1744. Address: Foster Lane. The registers of Christchurch, Newgate, incorporating St. Leonard, Foster Lane, record Ann daughter of Richard and Ann Kersill, born 9, baptized 24 July 1745. Richard Kersill was buried 25 May 1747 and another daughter Mary, born posthumously, 5 October 1747. Heal records Robert Kersill, goldsmith, Cheapside, bankrupt 1732, but there seems no connection; also Richard Kersill in Foster Lane till 1763, which can only be presumed as his widow carrying on the name.

KERSILL, William (3208-9) No record of apprenticeship or freedom. Perhaps a younger brother of Richard Kersill (above). First mark entered as largeworker, 21 August 1749. Address: Gutter Lane. Second mark, 2 July 1757. Prosecuted at the Old Bailey, 1768, 'for making two salt sellers worse than standard and for selling them as standard' (Parl. Report list 1773). Heal records him also as plateworker, 21 Aldersgate Street, 1772-7. He appears in the Parl. Report list 1773 as smallworker, at this address. He is perhaps the William Kersill, witness to the marriage of Thomas Kersill and Sarah Belbin 14 February 1758 (Register, St. Mary le Bowe, All Hallows, Honey Lane, and St. Pancras, Soper Lane).

KEY, Samuel (2566) Samuel Keys, son of Edward of St. Leonard's Shoreditch brickmaker, apprenticed to John Gorham 2 October 1735. Free, 1 May 1744. Mark entered, seemingly of smallworker's size, in largeworkers' book, 15 October 1745. Address: Gutter Lane. Moved to Cheapside, 26 May 1747, and to Gutter Lane, 27 April 1751 (both register entries without mark). Heal also records him in Fountain Court, 1769, as goldsmith, and he appears as smallworker, Fountain Court, Cheapside, in the Parl. Report list 1773.

KEY, Thomas (1235) No record of apprenticeship or freedom. Only mark entered as plateworker, in partnership with John Cramer(?) (q.v.), 21 September 1805. Address: 2 Pall Mall.

*KEY, William (3212) No record of apprenticeship or freedom. Mark entered as smallworker, 1 December 1783. Address: 64 Barbican, where Heal records him as goldsmith, 1790-3. His son Samuel was apprenticed to George Smith, 6 June 1787.

KIDDER, James (1450) No record of apprenticeship or freedom. Only mark entered as plateworker, 2 March 1795. Address: Hedden Street, Piccadilly. Heal however records him as goldsmith, parish of St. James', Westminster, 1765.

KIDDER, John (1448) No record of apprenticeship or freedom. Only mark entered as plateworker, 16 November 1780. Address: 14 Heydon Street, near Piccadilly, establishing his relationship, probably son, to James Kidder (above). He appears in the Parl. Report list 1773 as plateworker, Heddon Street, near Swallow Street, and Heal records him in Piccadilly, 1780-6.

KIDNEY, William (3207, 3216-7) Son of George Kidney Citizen and Merchant Taylor deceased, apprenticed to David Willaume II 22 May 1723. No premium is stated, which one might have expected from the latter. Free, 8 January 1733. First mark entered as largeworker, 7 June 1734. Address: Six Bells Court, Foster Lane. Second and third marks, 15 June 1739. Address: Foster Lane. Heal (unpublished addenda) records him as assayer and plateworker in this year. Livery, April 1740. Three sons, George, Charles and Samuel are recorded in Christchurch, Newgate (and St. Leonard, Foster Lane) registers, as born to William and Rachel Kidney, 1735-8. In view of his apprenticeship it is not surprising to find a considerable feeling for somewhat exotic rococo design in cups and sauceboats, and high technical achievement in the execution of such pieces. Cf. cup of 1740 belonging to the Goldsmiths' Company.

KILLIK, Andrew (48) Son of John Killik of Clapham in the County of Surrey carpenter, apprenticed to John Pero, 4 July 1738, on payment of £21. Free, 31 July 1745. First mark entered as largeworker, 7 September 1749. Address: Lilly Pot Lane, Noble Street. Moved to White Hart Court, Long Lane, Smithfield, 17 August 1752. Moved to Little Turnstile, Holborn, 11 May 1754. Heal records him only at first date and address.

KILMAINE, David (1876, 3517) Son of Edward Kilmaine of the parish of St. Martin in the Fields gentleman, apprenticed to George Lewis 12 April 1700. Free, 9 September 1715. Signs the apprenticeship register 'Killmain'. Mark entered as largeworker, 14 September 1715. Address: Strand. Heal however records him in this year at Snow Hill; George Horne and David Kilmaine, goldsmiths, Angel and Crown, over against New Exchange near Durham Yard, 1716 (and Hilton Price, *Handbook of London Bankers*); alone also at Angel and Crown, Strand, till death in 1728. His daughter and heiress Elizabeth married, 25 August 1741, Sir Francis Vincent, 7th Baronet, M.P. for Surrey 1761-5. She died without surviving issue, 22 November 1744 (Burke's *Peerage*). The few marks that are found of Kilmaine's were probably used on plate specially ordered by his clients.

KINCAID, John (1453) No record of apprenticeship or freedom. First mark entered as largeworker, 17 October 1743. Address: Orange Court, Leicester Fields. Second mark, 23 August 1745. A further note below reads 'Nov. 18 1748 John Kincaid at Mr. Hewit Sweep Washer in King Street'. Chaffers read the name as Kineard so followed by Heal, but there seems no doubt of the correct reading as above.

KING, Abstainando (49, 3473) No record of apprenticeship or freedom. First mark entered as snuffer maker, 8 February 1791. Address: 3 Berkly Court, St. John's Gate. Second mark, 6 July 1792. Third mark, (two sizes) 12 December 1804. Fourth mark, as smallworker, 11 April 1806. Address: 10 Berkly Street, Clerkenwell. Moved to 44 Red Lion Street, Clerkenwell, 14 March 1821.

KING, Edmund (603) Son of Charles King late Citizen and Bricklayer of London deceased, apprenticed to William Fish 3 September 1709. Free, 7 December 1716. Mark entered as smallworker, 11 January 1717. Address: Falcon Court, Lothbury. 'Free of ye Goldsmiths Company'. Described as snuffboxmaker, in Bells Rents in the Mint, 10 August 1720, on the turnover to him of Richard Holder as apprentice.

KING, George (841) Perhaps George Richard son of Richard King of Little Britain bootmaker, apprenticed to Thomas Rowe of Aldersgate Street as silverpolisher 5 October 1808. Freedom unrecorded. Mark entered as smallworker, 11 November 1819. Address: 5 Cherry Tree Court, Aldersgate Street. Moved to 9 Great Sutton Street, Goswell Street, 2 July 1823.

KING, James I (1444) No record of apprenticeship or freedom. First mark entered as smallworker, 23 February 1764. Address: Queen Street, Golden Square. Second mark on move to Kensington Gore, 1 November 1769. Appears as goldworker, Kensington Grove, in the Parl. Report list 1773, but the address in the mark entry is plainly Gore, the former clearly a compositor's guess from the original MS.

KING, James II (1458, 3648) No record of apprenticeship or freedom. Mark entered as smallworker, in partnership with William Portal, 10 November 1768. Address: Orange Street, Leicester Fields. The latter appears alone as haftmaker in Parl. Report list 1773.

*KING, Jeremiah (1441-2, 1454-5, 1875) Apprenticed to William Scarlett (q.v.) of the Broderers' Company and admitted to the freedom of that company 7 November 1722 'on Testimony of his said Master'. First and second marks, Sterling and New Standard, entered as largeworker, 11 September 1723. Address: Carey Lane. 'Imbroaderer'. Third mark, 5 June 1736. Address: Foster Lane. Fourth and fifth marks, 18 June 1739. Sixth 26 January 1743. Seventh, 14 February 1744. Heal records him as above and till 1769, but see below. Jeremiah King appears from the registers of Christchurch, Newgate, to have had a chequered and somewhat puzzling matrimonial career. He was married by licence to Sarah Scarlet, both of the parish, she presumably daughter of his master, William Scarlett, 16 April 1723. Her burial is recorded 13 October 1730, without any children of the marriage found in the register previously. The following entries then appear:

Susan, daughter of Jeremiah and Mary King, born 3, baptized 18 April 1735.

Elizabeth, daughter of Jeremiah and Elizabeth King, born 28, baptized 29 December 1738.

Sarah, daughter of Jeremiah and Sarah King, born 29 December, baptized 26 January 1740/1.

Mary and John, daughter and son of Jeremiah and Mary King, born 24 and 25 December, baptized 22 January 1741/2.

Thomas, son of Jeremiah and Mary King, born 18 March, baptized 16 April 1744.

and lastly

Jeremiah King buried 29 April 1750.

Heal's date of 1769 (above) may derive from a misascribed mark in Jackson.

KING, John (1445-6) Son of Joseph King of St. Margaret Shatton in the County of Wiltshire yeoman, apprenticed to Henry Brind 2 May 1750 on payment of £31. 10s. and turned over 2 March 1751 to William Shaw. Free, 3 August 1757. (Another of the same name, apprenticed to George King 1765, and free 1773, seems unlikely to apply.) First mark entered as plateworker, 22 April 1775. Address: 73 Little Britain. Second mark, 14 June 1775. Third, 13 June 1777. Fourth, 3 September 1779. Fifth, 11 August 1785. Address: 1 Moor Lane, Fore Street. Sixth mark, 4 September 1789. Address: Moor Lane, where Heal records him till 1800. His son Joseph was apprenticed to him 5 January 1780, when King is described as of Little Britain, plateworker, Citizen and Goldsmith.

KING, W—— (3211) Perhaps William King son of Edward King, Citizen and Barber

Surgeon of London, apprenticed to William Ewesdin 6 November 1740 on payment of £15 and turned over 16 January 1744 to Thomas Lack cordwainer. Freedom unrecorded. First mark (incuse) entered as smallworker, 21 October 1761. Second mark, 30 October 1761. Address: Cross Street, Hatton Garden. Moved to Duck Lane, Smithfield, 7 April 1762. Moved to George's Court, Clerkenwell, 13 April 1763. Moved to London House Yard, Bartholomew Close, 7 February 1764. Moved to St. John's Square, Clerkenwell, no date. Heal records him only at Cross Street, 1761-4. William King, watchcasemaker, St. John's Square, Clerkenwell, appears in the Parl. Report list 1773, presumably the same.

KING, William (3215) No record of apprenticeship or freedom. First mark entered as goldworker, 15 April 1820. Address: 39 Red Cross Street, Cripplegate (Section VII). Subsequently at 15 and 18 Bridgewater Square and 14 Red Lion Street. Second mark as plateworker, 23 November 1826. Address: 9 Great Sutton Street, Clerkenwell. Third mark as goldworker, 6 January 1829. Address: 14 Red Lion Street. Moved to 11 Tavistock Row, Covent Garden, 1834.

KINGDON, William (3213) No record of apprenticeship or freedom. Only mark entered as plateworker, 9 July 1811. Address: 8 St. John Square, Clerkenwell.

KINGSMAN, James (3648) Son of James Kingsman Citizen and Clothworker of London, apprenticed to Giles Southam Citizen and Goldsmith 10 July 1733 on payment of £31. 10s. Free, 4 December 1740. Livery, March 1758. Appears only as James Kingman, goldworker, Leadenhall Street in the Parl. Report list 1773, but no mark is registered before or after this date. Died before 1796.

KINMAN, William (3210) No record of apprenticeship or freedom. Mark entered as smallworker, 31 January 1759. Address: East Harding Street. Described as hiltmaker in Parl. Report list 1773. Another mark for him or perhaps a son of the same name entered as hiltmaker, 17 May 1782. Address: 9 New Street Square.

KIRK, William (3206) No record of apprenticeship or freedom. Only mark entered as smallworker, 26 April 1733. Address: 'at ye Green Door Turning Down by the Rissing Sun in Cloth Fair West Smithfield', a graphic picture of the out of the way corners in which some of these smallworkers must have lived and struggled to eke out an existence.

KIRKE, Jonathan (1874) Son of William Kirke of Pannal in the County of York yeoman, apprenticed to John Cruttall 14 March 1673 'from Lady day next'. Free, 30 April 1680. Mark entered as largeworker, undated, probably April 1697 on commencement of register. Address: Cannon Street. He signs as 'Jona'. Livery, May 1704. Heal records him as Jonah Kirke, goldsmith, Cannon Street, 1697 and ? 1704; also Jonathan Kirke, goldsmith, parish of St. Laurence Pountney, 1692; and Golden Cup, Lombard Street, 1703-5. It seems, since he is clearly Jonathan in the apprenticeship record, that he signed later with shortened version and that this, transcribed by Chaffers as Jonah, has been perpetuated in later lists. There was also a John Kirk elected to the Livery, October 1708, but no mark is recorded for him.

KNAGG, Thomas (1878) Apprenticed to Thomas Deane Citizen and Haberdasher of London and free of the Masons' Company 4 July 1700 'according to the late Act of Common Council'. First mark entered as smallworker, 26 October 1716. Address: Field Lane, near Holborn Bridge. 'Free of the Masons'. Second mark, incuse, 7 July 1720. Address: Lion Court, Fleet Street, perhaps as watchcasemaker (Section V).

KNIGHT, George (840) No record of apprenticeship or freedom. First mark entered as smallworker, 28 March 1818. Address: Westmorland Buildings. Second mark, 21 November 1820. Third mark (two sizes), 4 July 1821.

KNIGHT, Samuel (2565, 3218) No record of apprenticeship or freedom. First mark entered in partnership with William Knight II (q.v. ? brother) as smallworker, 24 January 1810. Address: 5 St. John's Court, St. Martin's Le Grand. Moved to 15 Bartholomew Close, 2 October 1815. Second mark alone as plateworker, 8 February 1816. Address: 7 Westmoreland Buildings, Aldersgate Street.

*KNIGHT, William I (1877) Free of the Grocers' Company by service to Hugh Humphrye 1685 (the apprentice register of this company not extant). Mark entered as hiltmaker, undated, before November 1700. Address: New Street, Shoe Lane. 'Free Grocer'.

BIOGRAPHICAL DICTIONARY

KNIGHT, William II (3214, 3218) No record of apprenticeship or freedom. First mark entered as smallworker, in partnership with Samuel Knight (? brother, above), 24 January 1810. Address: 5 St. John's Court, St. Martin's Le Grand. Moved to 15 Bartholomew Close, 20 October 1815. Second mark, alone as plateworker, 8 February 1816, same address. Moved to 7 Westmoreland Buildings (where Samuel had gone in 1816), 25 September 1827. Third mark (two sizes), 18 May 1830. Fourth mark, 20 March 1839.

KNIGHTLY, Samuel (2564) No record of apprenticeship or freedom. First mark entered as smallworker, 22 May 1761. Address: Kent Street, Southwark. Moved to the Minories, 31 May 1766. Second mark, 30 August 1769. Address: 'Alhallows Barking, Seathing Lane'. Moved to East Smithfield, 9 March 1771. Appears as bucklemaker at this last address in the Parl. Report list 1773, and entered a mark as such at this last address, 3 July 1780 (Section VIII).

*KNOPFELL, Frederick (690) No record of apprenticeship or freedom. Working as journeyman with Paul De Lamerie at the time of the latter's death in 1751 and mentioned in his will as one of the two journeymen requested to finish off the work in hand for the executors. Only mark entered 11 April 1752. Address: Little Windmill Street, St. James's, the street where Lamerie had first worked before moving to Gerrard Street, which suggests that perhaps the Windmill Street premises had been retained for some function of the business and Knopfell took them over after the estate was wound up.

KÖHLER, John I (1449) No record of apprenticeship or freedom. Only mark entered as smallworker, 1 March 1790. Address: 9 Charing Cross.

KÖHLER, John II (1452) Probably son of above, but no record of apprenticeship or freedom. Mark entered as smallworker, 3 March 1835. Address: 35 Henrietta Street, Covent Garden.

L

*LADYMAN, John (1897) Son of John Ladyman Citizen and Salter of London, apprenticed to George Watkins for nine years 2 September 1675. Free, 28 September 1687. Livery, October 1698. Only mark entered as largeworker, undated, between January and July 1699. Address: Sherborn Lane, where Heal records him, 1692-1713; and as London, 1724. The registers of St. Mary Woolnoth contain baptismal entries for four sons and two daughters of John and Sarah Ladyman, silversmith. Elizabeth, baptised 29 April 1692; John, baptised 5 November 1693, died 31 January 1694; Mary, baptised 19 November 1695; Thomas, baptised 10 June 1697; John, baptised 10 November 1697, buried next day; and John, baptised 6 January 1699.

LAIDMAN, William (1887) Free of the Merchant Taylors' Company by service to Robert Butterfield (q.v.) 12 November 1690. Mark entered as smallworker, undated, probably April 1697 on commencement of register. Address: 'in the Old Change'. 'Free Merchant Taylor'.

LAMBE, Edward (John) I (606, 612, 3546) Son of George Lambe (q.v.), late Citizen and Goldsmith of London deceased, apprenticed to his mother Jane Lambe (q.v.) widow of the said George Lambe 2 April 1731 on payment of £6. 6s. 9d. of the charity of the Worshipful Company of Goldsmiths and £3. 5s. of the charity of the Society of Working Goldsmiths London. Free by patrimony, 3 February 1742/3. Mark entered as largeworker, 31 July 1740. Address: Hunt's Court, Castle Street. Second mark, 3 September 1742. Moved to Orange Street, near Leicester Fields, 30 December 1743, and to Litchfield Street, 30 December 1745 (both register entries without mark). Dead by 5 February 1755, when his son John was apprenticed to Ebenezer Coker. Another son, George, was apprenticed to James Tookey, 4 April 1759, who may be the Edward George, father of Edward Lambe II (below), or even his grandfather.

LAMBE, Edward II (611) Edward John son of Edward George Lambe (and grandson

573

or greatgrandson of Edward Lambe I). Free by patrimony 8 December 1791, as goldsmith and jeweller. First mark entered as plateworker, 2 April 1824. Address: 8 Albemarle Street, St. John's Square. Moved to 2 Dunstan Street, Kingsland Road, 31 December 1839, and incuse mark entered. Moved to 8 Old Ivy Street, Hoxton, 30 May 1845. Moved to 1 Nursery Place, Stamford Hill, 16 August 1853.

LAMBE, George (1893) Son of William Lambe of Llanterdine (?) in the County of Hereford weaver, apprenticed to Joseph Barbutt 23 May 1706. Free, 10 June 1713. Mark entered as largeworker, 10 June 1713. Address: Heming's Row, St. Martins' Lane. Probably dead by or before July 1722, by which date his widow Jane Lambe had entered two marks. By apprenticeship George Lambe was bound to one of the principal spoonmakers of the period, and his mark is usually found on flatware, as also those of his widow and sons.

LAMBE, Jane (1463, 1895) Widow of George Lambe (above). Two marks (Sterling and New Standard) entered, undated, between January 1719 and July 1722. Address: 3 King's Court, Shandos Street. It is apparent that if both marks were entered at the same time, which seems likely, then the date is not before the return to Sterling Standard in June 1720. The Sterling mark is however entered in another line with the description 'Old Starling Marck' which may suggest it is an addition at later date, in which case the date of entry of the New Standard mark could be any time from the preceding entry of January 1719. Heal records her at Chandos Street till 1732. Her son Edward John (above) was apprenticed to her, 1731.

LAMBE, John (1472-5) Son of Edward John Lambe (q.v.), late Citizen and Goldsmith of London deceased, apprenticed to Ebenezer Coker 5 February 1755 on payment of £8. 5s. of the charity of the Goldsmiths' Company. Free, 3 November 1762. Appears as spoonmaker, Fetter Lane, in the Parl. Report List 1773, which implies a mark entered in the missing register. First recorded mark entered as spoonmaker, 8 February 1774. Address: 97 Fetter Lane. Second mark on move to 29 Fetter Lane, 25 August 1780. Third mark (two sizes), 15 February 1782. Fourth (two sizes), 9 April 1782. Fifth (two sizes), 19 September 1782. Sixth (two sizes), as plateworker, 11 February 1783. Seventh, 4 July 1785. Eighth, 21 May 1788. Ninth, 30 August 1790. Tenth, 12 February 1791. Eleventh (two sizes), 19 April 1791. Twelfth as plateworker, 17 October 1791. Heal records him as spoonmaker and watchmaker, 29 Fetter Lane, from 1783 only till 1796. His brother George, who was apprenticed to James Tookey as spoonmaker, does not appear to have entered a mark and was very probably in company with John.

*LAMBE, Jonathan (1889) Son of John Lambe of Rayne parva in the County of Essex clerk, apprenticed to Richard Conyers 26 March 1690. Free, 1 July 1697. Mark entered as largeworker, undated, between January and June 1699. Address: London Bridge, where Heal records him in 1697.

LAMBORN, Thomas (2824) No record of apprenticeship or freedom. First mark entered as smallworker, 2 September 1759. Address: Hand Court, Holborn. Second mark, 27 April 1769. Address: 2 Silver Street. Heal records the same name as goldsmith, Cold Bath Fields, no date; and Fleet Street, insolvent 1772. He appears as smallworker, at the first address above, in the Parl. Report list 1773.

LAMERIE See DE LAMERIE.

*LAMMAS, Jeremiah (1883) Either (1) Jeremy (signs Jeremiah) son of Jeremy Lammas Citizen and Stationer of London, apprenticed to Charles Round 24 May 1661. Free, 2 March 1670. Court, 1701. Warden 1713, 1719, 1720. Prime Warden, 1724. Or (2) Jeremiah son of Daniel Lammas stationer, apprenticed to Jeremiah Lammas (above) 1694. Free, 22 October 1701. Only mark entered as smallworker, 18 October 1703. Address: Whitecross Street. Heal records this name, almost certainly identifiable with the first apprentice above, as goldsmith, parish of St. Mary Staining, 1692/3-1724.

LAMPFERT, John (1489-90) No record of apprenticeship or freedom. First mark entered as largeworker, 12 November 1748. Address: Little Windmill Street. Second small mark, 24 January 1749. Moved to (?Hormelary) Street, 24 November 1749. Heal records Lampfert or Lamfert, without Christian name, plateworker, Windmill Street, 1748; and ? Windmill Street, 1769. His mark is usually found on spoons.

LANCESTER, William (3226) Son of Robert Lancester late of Wimbleton in the County of Surrey carpenter deceased, apprenticed to Alexander Johnston 4 June 1759 and turned over to John Hyatt 8 August 1761. Free, 4 February 1767. Mark entered as smallworker, 18 August 1770. Address: Noble Street, where he is so recorded in the Parl. Report list 1773. In the 1773 Register appears the entry 'William Lancester & Charles Seymour Smallworkers Noble Street. 15 July 1773. Note this is only an Extract of the Entry of their Mark in the former Mark Book', but no mark is struck in the space provided. It should be noted that Charles Seymour, mentioned above as partner to Lancester, also worked with John Hyatt to whom Lancester was turned over in 1761.

LAND, Henry (1025) No record of apprenticeship or freedom. Only mark entered as smallworker, 21 July 1767. Address: 226 Borough, Southwark. Appears without Category at this address in the Parl. Report list 1773.

LANE, Stephen (2574) Son of Thomas Lane late of Ringwood in the County of Southampton clothier deceased, apprenticed to Edward Lammas (q.v.) 14 July 1720. Free, 2 August 1727. Mark entered as smallworker, 20 April 1738. 'Goldsmith Buckel Macker in Lileypool Lane'. An illiterate entry. Lileypool is probably Lilypot Lane.

LANE, William (1888) Son of John Lane gentleman, apprenticed to James Hubbald of the Fishmongers' Company and free 14 June 1692. Mark entered as smallworker, 10 December 1697. Address: Whitechapel Bars. 'Free Fishmonger'.

LANGFORD, John I (1896) Either (1) son of Edward Langford, free by patrimony of the Merchant Taylors' Company 16 December 1686. Or (2) son of John Langford of Kingsthorpe in the County of Northampton innholder, apprenticed to Edward Taylor of Old Street carpenter June 1684. Free, 5 July 1693. Mark entered as smallworker, undated, probably April 1697 on commencement of register. Address: Whalebone Court, Lothbury. 'Free Merchant Taylor'.

*LANGFORD, John II (3656-7) No record of apprenticeship or freedom. Name found partner with John Sebille, as plateworkers, St. Martin's Le Grand, in the Parl. Report list 1773, and also as bankrupt in 1770 (*The Gentleman's Magazine*, p. 346). The mark attributed to them, recorded by Chaffers on an inkstand of 1763, seems certain from the combination of initials; it occurs principally on pierced baskets.

LANGFORD, Thomas I (1894) Son of Thomas Langford of Mansell in the County of Nottingham gentleman, apprenticed to Henry Beesley to July 1707. Free, 23 March 1715. Mark entered as largeworker, 25 March 1715. Address: Lombard Street, where Heal records him till 1720. Livery, May 1740. Edward, son of Thomas and Sarah Langford, born 21, baptised 25 December 1720, at Christchurch, Newgate, may perhaps be the goldsmith's son.

LANGFORD, Thomas II (3844) No record of apprenticeship or freedom. Name only known from Parl. Report list 1773 as plateworker, 26 Angel Street, St. Martin's Le Grand.

LANGLOIS, James Bartholomdue (sic) (1493, 3651) No record of apprenticeship or freedom. Only mark entered as largeworker, 6 April 1738. Address: St. Andrews Street, near the Seven Dials. Listed by Evans as Huguenot (*Hug. Soc. Proc.*, 14, p. 542).

*LANGTON, Dennis (480, 483, 1880, 3518) Son of Samuel Langton late of Southwark carpenter deceased, apprenticed to John Dingley of the Haberdashers' Company 2 May 1701. Free, 14 May 1708. First mark entered as smallworker, 28 March 1716. Address: Lombard Street. 'Free Haberdasher'. Second mark, 28 October 1729. Address: Twisters Alley, Bunhill Row, Bunhill Fields. Third mark, 17 March 1731. Fourth, 26 June 1732. Address: 'Ironmonger Row near ye New Church in Old Street'. Heal records him only as goldsmith, Wheatsheaf and Crown, Lombard Street, 1709-18.

LAROCHE, Louis (1941-2) No record of apprenticeship or freedom. A Lewis Roch and Mary his wife appear in the Denization List, 13 December 1664, 'born in foreign parts, with promise to pay strangers' dues and subsidy'. In their petition for denization Lewis Roach and his wife state they are French and employed as tailors to the Queen and are desirous to spend their time in England (*Hug. Soc. Pub.*, 18). They seem possibly the grandparents of the goldsmith. Louis La Roche appears as godfather to Marguerite Cuan, 16 November 1712 (Savoy register, *Hug. Soc. Pub.*, 26) and again as godfather to Jacob Louis Tabois, 19 January 1724 (Leicester Fields Church register, *Hug. Soc. Pub.*, 29). Matthew La Roche was a member of the Dublin

Goldsmiths' Company 1675-97 (Jackson, pp. 635, 656). First mark entered as largeworker, 19 November 1725. Address: 'Lumber Court, the Corner of Seven Dials neare porter Street'. Second mark, 31 July 1739, same address. Laroche was tried and convicted at the instigation of the Goldsmiths' Company for counterfeiting marks (Court Minutes, 5 August 1742). Listed by Evans as Huguenot (*Hug. Soc. Proc.*, 14, p. 542).

LAUGHTON, Ann (1890) No record of apprenticeship or freedom. Mark entered as smallworker, 'Widow' (of John Laughton q.v.), 15 December 1701. Address: Goat Alley, Whitecross Street. Heal records only Mrs. Laughton, pawnbroker, Five Bells and Candlestick (without location), 1717, which seems unlikely to correspond to the above.

LAUGHTON, Charles I (1881-2) Free by patrimony of the Grocers' Company 1685. Mark entered as smallworker, undated, probably April 1697 on commencement of register. Address: Bedfordbury, near St. Martin's Lane. 'Free Grocer'.

LAUGHTON, Charles II (355) Probably son or even grandson of Charles Laughton I and free of the Grocers' Company by patrimony, although not to be found in the company lists. First mark entered as largeworker, 15 November 1738. Address: Dawsons Alley, Bedfordbury (cf. Charles Laughton I). 'Free of Grocers Company'. Second mark, 26 August 1741, same address. Heal records him only here at the latter date.

LAUGHTON, Edward (1884) Son of John Laughton free by patrimony of the Grocers' Company 1675. Mark entered as smallworker, undated, probably April 1697 on commencement of register. Address: 'in the Old Change'. 'Free Grocer'.

LAUGHTON, Jane (1886) Possibly the widow of Charles Laughton I, although no apparent lapse of time exists between the two entries. Otherwise perhaps his sister. Described as Free Grocer but not to be found in the company index of such. Mark entered as smallworker, undated, probably April 1697 on commencement of register. Address: Bedfordbury, near St. Martin's Lane. 'Free Grocer'.

LAUGHTON, John I (1885) Son of John Laughton (also apparently goldsmith, cf. Benjamin Page's apprenticeship). Free by patrimony of the Grocers' Company, 1675. Mark entered as smallworker, undated, probably April 1697 on commencement of register. Address: Goat Alley in Whitecross Street. Dead by 15 December 1701, when Ann 'Widow' (q.v.) entered her mark at the same address.

*LAUGHTON, John II (1898-1900) Son of the preceding and brother of Edward Laughton (above). Free of the Grocers' Company. Mark entered as largeworker, undated, between January and July 1699, when he signs as 'Junior'. Address: Maiden Lane. Heal records him here (without distinction of 'Junior') from 1694-9. A number of children of John and Mary Laughton were baptised at St. John Zachary from 1693-99, and he was churchwarden at the same church, 1699 and 1700. John Laughton was buried there 17 September 1703, leaving his estate to his widow and children and 'in case my son John shall follow the same trade ... I give all my working tools ...' (Stanley Percival, 'Thomas Merry, citizen and goldsmith of London', *Connoisseur*, August 1970).

LAUGHTON, Mary (1891) No record of apprenticeship or freedom. Widow of the foregoing. Mark entered as smallworker, 31 October 1704. Address: Noble Street, where she must have moved after Thomas Merry I (q.v.) had taken over John Laughton's house.

LAUNDY, Samuel (2558, 2572-3) Son of Samuel Laundy of St. Neots in the County of Huntingdon woollendraper, apprenticed to James Goodwin 22 September 1720 on payment of 20 guineas. Free, 22 May 1728. Two marks entered as largeworker, 20 October 1727. Address: Gutter Lane. 'Moved to next door to ye Crosskeys Tavern in threedneedle Street', no date. Third mark, in partnership with Jeffery Griffith, 2 June 1731. Address: Staining Lane. The partnership apparently dissolved by 18 February 1732, when Griffith entered a separate mark. Chaffers misread or misprinted the name as Laundry, followed by others since, but the name is clear in both apprentice and mark registers. Listed by Evans as Huguenot (*Hug. Soc. Proc.*, 14, p. 542). His home town seems a little unlikely for such to have settled, but is presumably possible.

LAVER, Benjamin (188-9) Son of John Laver late of Somerton in the County of Somerset cordwainer deceased, apprenticed to Thomas Heming 4 October 1751. Free, 5 December 1764. His first mark was presumably entered in the missing largeworkers' volume of 1758-73, although there seem no surviving examples of marks at this date which might be his. His son William was apprenticed to him, 7 December 1774, when Laver is described as large plateworker of New Bond Street, and Heal records him here from 1769-79, and St. George's, Hanover Square. His second son, Thomas was apprenticed to him, 4 October 1780. What seems likely is that Laver may have been working in a similar relationship to and for Thomas Heming as the Crespells did for Parker and Wakelin (both q.v.). First (recorded) mark entered as plateworker, 20 December 1781. Address: Barlows Mews, Bruton Street, near Bond Street. Second mark, 8 September 1782. Third mark, 1 July 1789. Address: Bruton Street, Bond Street. Heal finally records him at 4 Bruton Street, Berkeley Square, 1783-1800. For his presumed elder brother see John Laver (below). What little plate has survived bearing Laver's mark shows a good standard, without any great originality of design.

LAVER, John (1468) Son of John Laver of Hanbridge in the County of Somerset gentleman (and presumably elder brother of Benjamin, above), apprenticed to James Gould 4 September 1740 on payment of £25. Freedom unrecorded. Only mark entered as largeworker, 19 May 1749. Address: Parsons Court, Bride Lane, Fleet Street. Chaffers read his name as Lavis, followed by Evans who lists him as Huguenot, presumably on evidence of this wrongly understood name (*Hug. Soc. Proc.*, 14, p. 452).

LAVER, William (3229) Either (1) son of Benjamin of New Bond Street large plateworker Citizen and Goldsmith, apprenticed to his father 7 December 1774. Or (2) son of Joseph of Great Garden Street Whitechapel dyer, apprenticed to Benjamin Laver as silversmith 18 March 1775. Free, 2 May 1787. Mark entered 7 August 1789. Address: Bridle Lane, Golden Square.

LAWLEY, Francis (699-700) No record of apprenticeship or freedom. First mark entered as smallworker, 31 December 1759. Address: Green Harbour (?Arbour) Court. Second mark, 16 May 1761. Address: Cat and Whale (?) Court, Snow Hill. He appears as hiltmaker, Green Arbor Court, in Parl. Report list 1773.

LAWLEY, Whitton (3221) No record of apprenticeship or freedom. Only mark entered as smallworker, 1 July 1729. Address: 'at ye Sugar Loaf in Long Lane, near West Smithfield'.

LAWRENCE, Thomas I (2823) From the evidence of his son's apprenticeship, free of the Dyers' Company. First mark entered as largeworker, 24 January 1743. Address: Little Arthur Street, near Golden Lane. Heal records him here, 1742 (probably not allowing for Old Style calendar). Moved to George Court, St. John's Lane, 15 March 1748. Incuse marks entered 1754, 1769 and 1770 (Section V). Moved to St. John's Square, Clerkenwell, 25 April 1755, and Francis Court, Berkley Street, 2 December 1757 (both entries without mark). Like his son (below) almost certainly a watchcasemaker.

LAWRENCE, Thomas II (2828) Son of Thomas Lawrence I (above), apprenticed to John Vowels 1756 and turned over the same day to his father a Dyer. Freedom unrecorded. Mark entered as smallworker, in partnership with James Sage, 23 March 1771. Address: Francis Court, Berkley Street, St. John's Lane, Clerkenwell (as his father from 1757), where they appear as watchcasemakers in the Parl. Report list 1773.

LAWTON, John (1485) No record of apprenticeship or freedom. First mark entered as smallworker, 30 September 1802. Address: 18 Coppice Row, Clerkenwell. Second mark, 24 October 1805. Moved to St. John Court, Cow Lane, Smithfield, 26 January 1810.

LEA, James (1830) No record of apprenticeship or freedom. Only mark entered as smallworker, 2 July 1790. Address: 19 Peppins Court, Fleet Street.

LEA, Samuel (1919, 2571) Distinguish carefully from Samuel Lee (q.v.). Son of Joseph Lea of St. Martin's in the Fields in the County of Middlesex yeoman, apprenticed to John Diggle 8 June 1698 and turned over to Philip Rollos 17 January 1700. Although the clerk enters his name as Lee he signs Lea as he does in his mark entry. First mark entered as largeworker, 13 July 1711, when he signs 'Samull' (? through nervousness). Address: Castle Street, near Hemings Row. Second (Sterling) mark, 12 December 1721. Heal records him as plateworker, Hemings Row, 1711-24.

*LEACH, John (1916) Son of John 'Leitch' of Chipping Norton in the County of Oxon. tanner, apprenticed to William Browne of the Haberdashers' Company 10 June 1675. Free, 14 July 1682. Mark entered as largeworker, undated, between January and July 1699. Address: Distaff Lane. 'Haberdasher'. Heal records him at this address, 1697; and with ?, 1698-1710.

*LEADBETTER, John Gibson (1469-70, 3653) No record of apprenticeship or freedom. First mark entered as smallworker, 28 July 1757. Address: Monkwell Street. Second mark, 18 July 1758. Third, 22 August (? 1758). Fourth, 3 February 1766. Fifth, 11 May 1767. All at same address, where he appears as bucklemaker in the Parl. Report list 1773.

LEAKE *See* LEEKE.

LEAPIDGE, Edward (609) No record of apprenticeship or freedom. Only mark entered as smallworker, 22 August 1767. Address: Purse Court, Old Change, where he appears as such in the Parl. Report list 1773.

LEASER, William (3222) No record of apprenticeship or freedom. Only mark entered as smallworker, 26 May 1738. Address: Three Kings Court, King Street, Covent Garden. Signs 'Wellyam'.

LE BAS, William (3230a) Son of David Le Bas of Long Acre in the County of Middlesex watchmaker, apprenticed to Isaac Harley 14 March 1764 and turned over same day to Samuel Meriton in consideration of £21. Free, 10 April 1771. Mark entered as saltmaker (an unusually precise description), 2 November 1773. Address: 18 Theobalds Road, Red Lyon Street, Holborn. He had previously on 30 July entered an incuse mark, B over WL (Section V), which is struck through in the register, presumably on the entry of the normal type mark. The Le Bas family have a long history in the goldsmiths' trade. The first mention of the name in the Company records is that of Guillan Le Bas, recording his production of a testimonial dated Newhaven, 4 January 1574/5, presumably as a Huguenot refugee. In 1672 Peter Le Bas, son of James Le Bas merchant of London, was apprenticed to Richard Shaw Goldsmith. David Peter, son of David Le Bas, merchant of London, was apprenticed to Stephen Goujon in 1744; his elder son George was apprenticed to John Alderhead 8 June 1757, free 4 July 1764, but no mark is entered for him. His second son is William of the present entry. William Le Bas' name appears on the payroll of the Goldsmiths' Company for some years but in what capacity remains unknown. His son James was apprenticed to his father 1 November 1786, turned over to Samuel Meriton 6 December 1786, and again to William Pitts 6 February 1793. On becoming free he moved to Dublin and commenced working at 45 Great Strand Street. His two sons, William and Robert, continued the business, the second son of William, Samuel, becoming Dublin Assaymaster 1880-90, followed by his two sons in turn from 1890 to 1941 and again by his great-grandson Captain Ronald Le Bas from 1963 till the present time, to whom these details of the family are gratefully acknowledged.

*LE CHEAUBE (CHOUABE), Pierre (323, 1906, 2145) Son of 'Thomas Cheaube of ye city of Mentz (sic) in the kingdom of France Merch(?)', apprenticed to David Williams (Willaume) 11 July 1700. A marginal note partly illegible records confirmation of the boy's being 'made a denizen of England 11 March 1700'. Free, 21 November 1707. First mark entered 21 November 1707. Address: 'in the Pelmell' (perhaps still working with Willaume). Second (Sterling) mark, 27 June 1726. Address: Glasshouse Street. 'Free of the Goldsmiths Company'. Name spelt Chouabe on this occasion. Listed by Evans as Huguenot (*Hug. Soc. Proc.*, 14, p. 542). His work is rare and it seems likely from the first address that he may have been on the Willaume payroll for most of his career.

LE CLERC, Elias (614) No record of apprenticeship or freedom. Only mark entered as goldworker, 11 January 1725. Address: Queen Street, near Seven Dials.

LEDGER, Henry (1026-7) No record of apprenticeship or freedom. First mark entered as plateworker, 26 June 1827. Address: 24 Banner Square. Second mark, 24 October 1828. William son of Henry Ledger buckram stiffener of 24 Banner Square Finsbury, apprenticed to William Chawner in 1828. What relationship there can be between the latter occupation and plateworker is obscure.

LEDIE, John (1479-80) No record of apprenticeship or freedom. First mark entered as smallworker, 30 June 1789. Address: 21 Plough Court, Fetter Lane. Second mark (three sizes), 1 April 1791. Heal records him only as jeweller, Glasshouse Yard, Water Lane, 1790-3.

LEE, Edward (605) Edward 'Lees' son of

BIOGRAPHICAL DICTIONARY

Richard of Bow in the County of Middlesex labourer, apprenticed to Nathaniel Underwood 13 January 1719. Free, 10 February 1725. Mark entered as smallworker, 13 August 1729. Address: Long Alley, near Moorfields. 'Goldsmith'. Both apprentice and mark register are signed by him with painful initials EL. Literacy was no necessary qualification for freedom of a livery company at that date or fifty years later (See e.g. Hester Bateman).

LEE, Jeremiah (1466, 1488, 3718) Son of Joseph Lee late Citizen and Shipwright of London deceased, apprenticed to Samuel Hitchcock 19 February 1717 on payment of £20. Free, 6 August 1724. First mark entered as smallworker, 6 August 1728. Address: Gutter Lane. 'Goldsmith'. Second mark, 26 June 1739. Address: Watling Street. Heal records him as plateworker only, at the latter address, 1739-42; and ? Watling Street, 1761. If the latter is related to the mark 3718, as recorded by Jackson, the identification of course remains open to others of the name. 'A List of ye Parish of St. Mary Aldermary taken on Lady Day 1733' has the following: 'Mr. Lee, Goldsmyth, to Meeting, family four' (St. Mary Aldermary register).

*LEE, John I (1465) Free Clockmaker. First mark, incuse, in partnership with Sarah Jaques, entered 21 March 1721. Address: Angel Court, Snowhill. 'free Clockmaker' (Section V). Second incuse mark alone, —1725, same address. Third mark (in punch), as smallworker with the following entry: John Lee In Angell Court On Snowhill Entered his Marke In Octo. Last. I have Altered my Marke ye Other being brock. I Promise to Abide by my New Marke November ye 12.1725.' There seems to be here a hint of some past irregularity, although the interval of time between the entry of the two marks is short and it may have perhaps been the replacement of the previous incuse mark (above) entered in 1725 without exact date.

LEE, John II (1476) Probably son of George Lee of Bishops Court Ailesbury Street Clerkenwell taylor, apprenticed to Robert Hennell of Foster Lane Goldsmith 4 May 1774. Free, 1 May 1782. Mark entered as plateworker, 2 December 1782. Address: 19 Bunhill Row. Heal records him here as goldsmith and jeweller in this year; and at 53 Rosoman Street, 1790.

LEE, John III (1477, 1832) No other suitable record of apprenticeship or freedom other than the above. There is perhaps a possibility that John Lee II is the same, but the entry signatures appear distinctive. First mark entered as goldworker, 20 March 1793. Address: 31 Noble Street, Foster Lane. Second mark, 20 July 1804, on moving to 33 Noble Street.

LEE, Richard (2356) Son of Richard Lee of Stratton in the County of Wiltshire shopkeeper, apprenticed to John King as goldsmith 5 December 1770 on payment of £10. Free, 7 January 1778. Only mark entered as plateworker, 4 May 1782. Address: 9 Lilley Pot Lane.

LEE, Samuel (1922, 2570) Distinguish carefully from Samuel Lea (q.v.). Son of George Lee late Citizen and Grocer of London, apprenticed to William Swadling 9 September 1692. Turned over to John Penford 16 June 1696 and to Francis Archbold 25 June 1697. Free, 7 August 1701. First mark entered as largeworker, 14 August 1701. Address: Newgate Street. Second (Sterling) mark, 1 July 1720. Heal records him at Newgate Street with the above dates; and as Bishopsgate without, bankrupt, 1723.

LEE *See also* LEA and LEY

*LEEKE, Ralph (1914, 3717) Ralph Leake son of Thomas of Osderston in the County of Salop yeoman, apprenticed to Thomas Littleton 15 July 1664 'from the 1st day of August next following'. Free, 20 September 1671. Heal records him as plateworker, London, 1679; Bridge Street, Covent Garden, 1686 (also Hilton Price, *Handbook of London Bankers*); Angel, Catherine Street, Strand, 1692; Covent Garden, 1697-1702. He also suggests that Ralph Leet, goldsmith, London, 1657 is identical, but the apprenticeship above seems to confute this. Mark entered as largeworker, undated, between January and July 1699. Address: Bridgett Street, Covent Garden. Court, 1703. Warden, 1714. There is a certain mystery about his work. If the mark attributed to him by Jackson before 1697 is accepted then he is shown from pieces bearing this mark to have been a fine maker whereas his 1699 mark, albeit not related to the earlier attributed mark, is rarely found.

*LEES, Edward (610) No record of apprenticeship or freedom. First mark entered as spoonmaker, 22 February 1803. Address: 14 Albemarle Street, Clerkenwell. Second

579

LEFEBURE

mark, 30 June 1806. Moved to 4 St. James' Walk, Clerkenwell, 1 March 1808. Moved to 18 Eagle Place, St. John Lane, 3 April 1810.

LEFEBURE, Daniel (1923) Son of Lewis Lefebure late of Canterbury in the County of Kent weaver deceased (and brother of John and Lewis, below), apprenticed to Peter Harrach the Younger 15 November 1701. Free, 16 November 1708. Mark entered as smallworker, 20 November 1708. Address: Dorset Street, near Whitegate Alley.

LEFEBURE, John (1459, 1921) Son of Lewis as above (and brother of Daniel), apprenticed to Peter Harach 28 May 1707 and turned over to his brother Daniel. Free, 16 June 1714. A marginal note against the apprenticeship states that the Certificate of Denization of Lewis 'La ffebure' was dated 9 April 1698. Mark entered as smallworker, 25 June 1714. Address: 'Dorcett' Street, near Spitalfields, where he presumably worked with his brother. Second mark (Sterling) entered 21 June 1720.

LEFEBURE, Lewis (1940) Also son of Lewis weaver of Canterbury (and brother of Daniel and John, above), apprenticed to his brother Daniel 9 February 1710. Free, 12 October 1721. Mark entered as smallworker, 7 October 1725. Address: King's Head Court, Petticoat Lane.

LE FRANÇOIS (FRANCIS), Abraham (56, 62) No record of apprenticeship or freedom. First mark entered as largeworker, 1 December 1742 or 1743 (the last figure blotched and read by Chaffers as 1740, but dateable from the counter-signature of Charles Alchorne as Deputy Warden to one of two years above). Address: Porter Street, St. Ann's, Soho. Second mark as Le Francis, 22 October 1746. Address: West Street, Seven Dials. Heal records him only as Le Francois at Porter Street, 1740; and West Street, 1749–50. He appears as Le Francois, without category, Porter Street, Soho, in the Parl. Report list 1773, the address presumably mistakenly taken from the first entry.

*LEGG, Henry (1024) No record of apprenticeship or freedom. Only mark entered as smallworker, 14 May 1728, with an illiterate statement following his name, apparently 'ofree Larmos Hale', which might be interpreted 'free of Lorrimers' Hall' or perhaps is the address 'opposite Lorrimers' Hall'. This company's records were destroyed in 1940.

LEY

*LE SAGE, Augustin (57, 3474) Son of John Hugh Le Sage (q.v.) and presumed younger brother of Simon. Free by patrimony as jeweller, 2 April 1782. Since he was thus free he must have been born after 25 September 1718, the date of his father's freedom. He was working however for many years before 1782. Heal records him as goldsmith and clockmaker, Corner Suffolk Street, Charing Cross, 1752–73; Cockspur Street, 1755–84; St. James', Haymarket, 1790. He appears as goldsmith, Great Suffolk Street, in the Parl. Report list 1773. His first mark must have been entered in the missing largeworkers' volume, probably soon after it was started in 1758. Its identity, since it includes the 'Golden Cup' known to have been the shop sign at Suffolk Street for father and brother, can scarcely be questioned. Listed by Evans as Huguenot (*Hug. Soc. Proc.*, 14, p. 543).

*LE SAGE, John Hugh (1646, 1680–1, 2469, 3683) Son of Hugues Le Sage late of the parish of St. Martin in the Fields gentleman deceased, apprenticed to Lewis Cuney (q.v.) 7 May 1708. Free, 25 September 1718. (The appearance of the name in the Denization List, 15 April 1693, must refer to an older man (? cousin), probably the same as the Jean le Sage whose daughter Jeanne was baptized, 17 August 1712, at Threadneedle Street Church). First mark entered as largeworker, 11 October 1718. Address: Little St. Martin's Lane, near Long Acre. Second (Sterling) mark, 26 July 1722. Address: Corner of Great Suffolk Street. 'Free Goldsmith'. Married Judith Decharmes, 'tous deux de la par. de St. Martin des Champs, Liberté de Westminster', at Hungerford Market Church, 10 April 1725. Third and fourth marks, 25 June 1739. Address: Great Suffolk Street, near ye Haymarket. Livery, April 1740. Heal records him as above till 1743, but with addition of Old Street, 1722. Listed by Evans as Huguenot (*Hug. Soc. Proc.*, 14, p. 543). Subordinate Goldsmith to the King (Major General H. W. D. Sitwell, 'The Jewel House and the Royal Goldsmiths', *Arch. Journ.*, CXVII, p. 155). The occurrence of the name as Overseer in 1718, quoted by W. H. Manchee ('Huguenot London', *Hug. Soc. Proc.*, 13, p. 70) probably refers to the Jean le Sage referred to above, married in 1712.

LE SAGE, Simon (2576–7) Son of John Hugh Le Sage (above) Citizen and Goldsmith, apprenticed to his father 6 May 1742 and turned over the same day to Peter Meure (q.v.) Citizen and Butcher in consideration of £20. Free, 5 June 1755. Two marks entered as largeworker, 5 April 1754. Address: Great Suffolk Street, Charing Cross. Heal records him as plateworker, Golden Cup, corner of Great Suffolk Street, near Haymarket, from 1739 (in which there would seem an overlap with his father) till he left off business in 1761. Subordinate Goldsmith to the King c. 1754-9 (Sitwell, *op. cit.* above). Listed by Evans as Huguenot (*op. cit.*). Among pieces made by him through the royal appointment are the imposing candelabra with royal arms at Ickworth, Suffolk.

*LESTOURGEON, Aaron (58-9, 63, 3474) No record of apprenticeship or freedom. First mark entered as smallworker, in partnership with William Lestourgeon, 17 November 1767. Address: Clements Inn Passage, near Clare Market. Second mark together, 8 December 1768. Third mark alone, 27 June 1771, same address. Appears as smallworker, at same address, in the Parl. Report list 1773. Fourth mark, 11 November 1773. Address: 49 High Holborn. Fifth mark, 4 January 1776.

*LESTOURGEON, William (63, 3227) No record of apprenticeship or freedom. First and second mark entered as smallworker, in partnership with Aaron (above). Third mark alone, 26 June 1771. Address: Mouldmaker Row, St. Martin's Le Grand.

LEVI, Jacob (2747) No record of apprenticeship or freedom. Only mark entered as smallworker, in partnership with Thomas Evans, 20 February 1784. Address: 20 Featherstone Street, near Bunhill Row. The partnership apparently dissolved by 11 September 1784 when Evans entered a further mark alone

*LEWIS, Ambrose (54-5) Only mark entered as smallworker, 12 May 1725. Address: Gutter Lane. 'Clockmaker'.

LEWIS, George (1918) Son of Philip Lewis late of Llanguner (? Llangynog) in the County of Carmarthen deceased, apprenticed to Dallington Ayers 11 March 1691. Free, 3 November 1699. Mark entered as largeworker, 22 December 1699. Address: Strand, near the New Exchange. Livery, April 1705. Heal records him as plateworker, Ange or Angel and Crown or Golden Angel and Crown, over against New Exchange, 1697-1714. Hilton Price (*Handbook of London Bankers*) quotes *London Gazette*, 1 June 1702: 'Lost a note dated May 11th 1702 given by Mr. George Lewis goldsmith against the New Exchange for £150, payable to Charles Williams Esqr or his order. All persons are desired, if offered, to stop it, Payment being already made, and whoever brings it to the said Mr. Lewis, shall have 10s. Reward'.

LEWIS, John I (1920) Probably son of Meredith Lewis late of Knighton in the County of Radnor shoemaker deceased, apprenticed to Edward Cranfield 8 July 1692 and turned over to William Westbrooke. Free, 3 March 1703. Mark entered as smallworker, 31 July 1714. Address: Giltspur Street. One of this name was elected to Livery in October 1721.

LEWIS, John II (1482) No record of apprenticeship or freedom. Mark entered as smallworker, 3 June 1794. Address: 8 Blackman Street, Southwark. Moved to 12 New White Horse Court, Borough, undated.

LEWIS, Joseph (1471, 1481, 1831) Son of Joshua Lewis of Newbury in the County of Berkshire brazier, apprenticed to John Eaton 7 February 1759. Free, 3 June 1766. First mark entered as smallworker, 30 October 1767. Address: 57 Wood Street, Cripplegate. Second mark, 4 January 1768. Address: 38 Foster Lane, where he appears as bucklemaker in the Parl. Report list 1773, and entered three marks as such, 1775-83 (Section VIII). Sixth mark as plateworker, 30 October 1792. Address: 8 Cheapside. Seventh mark, 4 April 1795. Address: 32 Norton Folgate. Moved to 20 Aldgate, 9 January 1796. Heal records him as bucklemaker and goldsmith, 38 Foster Lane, 1769-84; and at 8 Cheapside, 1790-6. His son Joseph, aged nine, was admitted to St. Paul's School, 2 April 1783.

LEWIS, William (3228) Perhaps son of William Lewis Citizen and Goldsmith, apprenticed to his father 2 May 1764. Freedom unrecorded. Only mark entered as smallworker, 18 December 1783. Address: 97 Shoe Lane. Subsequent marks as watchcasemaker, 1793-1809 (Sections V and VI). Address: 11 Bridgewater Square, 1793-1801; and 26 Red Lion Square, Clerkenwell, till 1809.

LEY, Petley (1915) Son of Timothy Ley (below) Citizen and Founder of London, apprenticed to Joseph Brandon 31 March 1704 and turned over the same day to his father. Free, 1 August 1711. Mark entered as largeworker, 30 June 1715. Address: 'within Aldgate'. Heal records him as plateworker, near the pump Aldgate, 1710; within Aldgate 1715,; and ? same address, 1721.

LEY, Timothy (1917, 3843) Timothy Leigh free of the Founders' Company 'by his fathers Coppy' (i.e. by patrimony) 2 May 1681. The Sterling mark attributed to him from its resemblance to his New Standard mark, appears before 1697. New Standard mark entered as largeworker, undated, presumably April 1697 on commencement of register. Address: Fenchurch Street. 'Free Founder'. Heal records him as Timothy Lee, goldsmith, parish of St. Gabriel, Fenchurch Street, 1692-3; and London, 1700; as Ley, plateworker, Fenchurch Street, 1697. Signatory as Timothy Lee 'working goldsmith' to the petition complaining of the competition of 'necessitous strangers', December 1711. His mark found principally on standard examples of tankards and mugs.

LHOMMEDIEU, Ozee (2108) No record of apprenticeship or freedom. Only mark entered as smallworker, undated in 1727. Address: 'St. Giles by the Seven Dials "forrenenr"'. Heal records him as Ozée L'Hommedieu, goldsmith, White Lion Street, 1715-39.

LIAS, Charles (356, 1496) No record of apprenticeship or freedom. Presumably son of John and younger brother of Henry (below). First mark entered as plateworker, as junior partner to John and Henry Lias, 7 August 1823. Address: 8 Finsbury Street. Second mark, 3 March 1828. Third mark, 24 September 1830. Fourth, 26 August 1833. Fifth mark alone, 13 May 1837. Address: 65 Crown Street, Finsbury Square. Sixth mark, 23 August 1842. Seventh, 1 March 1845. Eighth (two sizes), 26 October 1846.

LIAS, Henry John (1495-6) Son of John Lias of Finsbury Street silversmith, apprenticed to Isaac Boorman of Shaftesbury Place Aldersgate Street as silversmith 1 February 1809. Free, 1816. First mark entered as spoonmaker, in partnership with John Lias his father, 14 March 1818. Address: 8 Finsbury Street. Second mark, 2 April 1818. Third mark (two sizes), 9 October 1819. Fourth mark, in partnership with John and Charles Lias, 7 August 1823. Fifth mark, 3 March 1828. Sixth, 24 September 1830. Seventh, 26 August 1833. Eighth mark, with John Lias only, 19 May 1837. Ninth, 28 November 1839. Tenth (two sizes), 13 February 1843. Eleventh, 30 July 1845. A final note to the entry dated 8 May 1848 reads 'trading under the name of John Lias & Son'. Henry Lias elected to Livery, 1833. Court, 1851. Warden, 1858-60. Prime Warden, 1861. Died 1877.

LIAS, John (1483-4, 1495-6) No record of apprenticeship or freedom. First mark as bucklemaker, 8 November 1791. Address: 15 Great Sutton Street. Second mark as such, in partnership with Denis Charie, 29 September 1792. Address: 16 Albemarle Street, St. John's Lane. Third mark alone as such, 3 July 1794. Address: 13 Bethnal Green Road. Fourth mark as plateworker, 13 July 1799. Address: 8 Finsbury Street. Fifth mark, 15 March 1802. Sixth, 25 November 1803. Seventh, 17 August 1805. Eighth, 30 May 1810. Ninth, as spoonmaker, 31 October 1812. Tenth (two sizes), 16 June 1815. Eleventh, in partnership with his son Henry, 14 March 1818. Thence, for the partnership with Henry and Charles, see above.

LIDDIARD, Thomas (2825) No record of apprenticeship or freedom. Only mark entered as smallworker, 3 March 1770. Address: Gutter Lane. Appears as goldworker, St. Paul's Churchyard, in the Parl. Report list 1773. Heal records him as goldsmith and watchmaker, 54 St. Paul's Churchyard, 1773-95. Described as silversmith, St. Paul's Churchyard, on the admission of his sons Thomas aged thirteen, 22 May 1787, and Gilbert aged nine, 27 January 1794 to St. Paul's School. The elder son was subsequently apprenticed to Thomas Daniel, 1788.

LIGER, Isaac (1462, 1931) His name appears in the Denization List of 11 March 1700, perhaps the son of Daniel Liger, student in divinity, who appears in the Bounty List of 1687-8. A Jeanne Liger of Saumur is in the same for 1705 (Evans, *Hug. Soc. Proc.*, 14, p. 544). The freedom register of the Broderers' Company contains the following: '19 Septembris 1704. Isaac Liger in Hemming Row in the Parish of St. Martins in the ffields Goldsmith was this present day sworne and Admitted into the ffreedome of the Company of Broderers by Redemption by Order of a Court of Aldermen dated the ffourteenth day of September instant'. First mark entered 2 October 1704. Address: Hemings Row, near St. Martin's Lane. 'Free Imbroiderer'. Married, 16 October

1705, Marie Chemet at Swallow Street Church. Appears as godfather to Renée Blanchard at Hungerford Market Church, 1 November 1710. Second (Sterling) mark, 5 September 1720. Heal records him at Hemings Row till death in 1730. Liger's work appears from surviving pieces to have been of relatively small pieces of high quality with particularly outstanding engraving. Whether the latter can have been his own accomplishment is of course doubtful. His greatest client was undoubtedly the 2nd Earl of Warrington, for whom he worked from 1708 throughout his career, his work including two toilet-services of 1717 and 1728. Pieces ascribed to him in the sale catalogue of the Foley Grey Collection 1921, in which the Warrington silver was dispersed, include items dated till 1736, of which those after 1730 must almost certainly have been by his son John (following).

*LIGER, John (1467) No record of apprenticeship or freedom. Heal states he was son of Isaac Liger (above), presumably from evidence of address. Mark entered as largeworker, 9 December 1730. Address: 'at ye sign of ye Pearl in Hemings Row St. Martins Lane'. Heal records him here as plateworker till 1732, but the evidence of the Warrington silver bearing his mark (see Isaac, above) is that he worked till at least 1736. Listed by Evans as Huguenot (*Hug. Soc. Proc.*, 14, p. 544).

LILLEY, William (3224, 3231) Son of Job Lilley Citizen and Goldsmith of London (entered mark as smallworker 26 January 1727 (Section IV), recorded by Heal near Smithfield Bars 1743-55, and St. John Street 1745, elected to Livery March 1739), apprenticed to his father 3 May 1749. Free, 8 June 1757. First mark entered as smallworker, 26 July 1765. Address: Minories Second mark, 13 August 1765. Third, 30 September 1765. Appears as bucklemaker, Smithfield Bars, in the Parl. Report list 1773. Heal records him as William Lilly, goldsmith, St. John's Street, Smithfield, 1768-70; and Smithfield Bars, 1777. It would seem he took over his father's address after 1765, perhaps on the latter's death.

LINGARD, John (1460, 1932-3, 3721) Son of William Lingard of the parish of St. James Westminster chairman, apprenticed to William Fawdery 27 September 1709. Signatory as journeyman to the petition against assaying the work of foreigners not having served seven years apprenticeship, February 1716. Free, 7 November 1717. First mark entered as largeworker, 28 June 1718. Address: Fish Street. Second mark, 10 January 1719. Third mark (Sterling), 22 June 1720. Address: Maiden Lane. Heal records both dates and addresses. Listed by Evans as Huguenot (*Hug. Soc. Proc.*, 14, p. 544), but his parentage and support of the 1717 petition scarcely suggest this.

LINNEY, John (1491) No record of apprenticeship or freedom. Only mark entered as smallworker, 20 October 1769. Address: 'Hegd. Lane'. He appears misprinted as John Lilley, without category, Hedge Lane, in the Parl. Report list 1773.

LINNIT, John (1833-4) No record of apprenticeship or freedom. First mark entered as goldworker, in partnership with William Atkinson, 24 July 1809. Address: 15 Fountain Court, Strand (Section VII). Second mark as smallworker, 25 April 1815. Address: 9 Craven Buildings, Drury Lane. Third mark, 22 October 1821. Fourth mark, 31 January 1824. Moved to 10 Argyle Place, Regent Street, 25 September 1840.

LINTHWAIT, Daniel (481) No record of apprenticeship or freedom. Only mark entered as smallworker, 24 April 1761. Address: Mutton Lane, Clerkenwell, where he appears as watchcasemaker in the Parl. Report list 1773.

LISTER, Thomas, Junior (2826) No record of apprenticeship or freedom. First mark entered as smallworker, 23 November 1803. Address: 9 Great Wild Street, Lincoln's Inn Fields. Second mark (two sizes), 17 June 1828. Address: 10 Green Terrace, New River Head. Moved to 21 Charlotte Street, Fitzroy Square, 2 October 1834. In the second entry the signature appears of a different character and although there is no other evidence, it may be that this is in fact that of Thomas Wooldridge Lister, son of Thomas Lister of Green Terrace, Clerkenwell, artist; apprenticed to John Fry of Center Street, Hackney Road, silversmith, 1829.

*LITTLEBOY, George (843) Son of Richard Littleboy, admitted to the freedom of the Cutlers' Company 10 March 1731. Mark entered as smallworker, 1 December 1731. Address: Noble Street, near the coachmakers' Arms. 'Free Cutler'.

LITTLEWOOD, Samuel (2575) No record of apprenticeship or freedom. Only mark entered as smallworker, 24 January 1772. Address: 9 Lombard Street, where he appears as goldsmith in the Parl. Report list 1773.

LITZMAN, Andrew (60-1) No record of apprenticeship or freedom. First mark entered as goldworker, 3 April 1784. Address: 32 Bridges Street, Covent Garden. Second mark, 19 March 1803.

LLOYD, Griffith (1938-9) Son of Jenkin Lloyd of Llandgoidmore(?) Cardigan Doctor of Divinity, apprenticed to Isaac Smith 18 January 1671 and turned over to Walter Williams. Free, 10 September 1679. Livery, October 1698. Court, 1717. Mark entered as smallworker, undated, c. 1700. Address: Hatton Garden, where Heal records him as goldsmith, 1701.

LLOYD, Thomas (2827) Thomas Charles son of Charles Lloyd of Great Sutton Street, Clerkenwell baker, apprenticed to Thomas Paine Dexter of Goswell Place as working silversmith 6 May 1807 on payment of £25. 4s. Freedom unrecorded. Mark entered as plateworker, 27 March 1821. Address: 1 Bartholomew Place, Little Bartholomew Close.

LOCK, Joseph (1492, 1829) Son of Joseph Lock of the City of Oxford maltster, apprenticed to John Moore 6 June 1764 on payment of £20. Free, 7 August 1771. First mark entered as smallworker, 26 May 1775. Address: 7 Francis Court, Berkly Street, Clerkenwell. Second mark, 18 June 1778. Heal records him as silversmith, at this address, 1778-9.

LOCK, Nathaniel (1946-9) Son of John Lock of Warnford in the County of Hampshire yeoman, apprenticed to Roger Strickland 21 June 1680 'from the Nativity of St. John the Baptist next'. Free, 10 July 1687. Livery, April 1698. Court, 1709. First mark entered as smallworker, undated, probably April 1697 on commencement of register. Address: without Cripplegate. Signatory to the petition against the work of 'aliens and foreigners', 11 August 1697. Second, third and fourth marks in one entry as largeworker, 24 January 1699, same address. Heal records him as plateworker, Blackwell Hall Court, Cripplegate, 1692-8; and with ? for same, 1702-15. He is presumably the Nathaniel Lock buried at Christchurch, Newgate (incorporating St. Leonard, Foster Lane), 27 April 1749.

*LOCKWOOD, Richard (2357, 2359) No record of apprenticeship or freedom. First mark entered as smallworker, 20 May 1797. Address: 8 Clerkenwell Green. Second mark, 28 September 1797. Third mark, in partnership with John Douglas, 12 August 1800, same address. Fourth mark, 23 September (year omitted, presumably the same).

LOFTHOUSE, Mary (2044) No record of apprenticeship or freedom. Presumably the widow of Matthew or Seth Lofthouse (below), but of a different address to either. Mark entered as largeworker, 30 March 1731. Address: Maiden Lane, Wood Street. Signs with a badly formed cursive 'm'.

LOFTHOUSE, Matthew E. (1953, 2043, 3726) Son of Alvara Lofthouse (and younger brother of Seth below) of Manston in the County of York yeoman, apprenticed to George Hanson of the Waxchandlers' Company 20 February 1689 for eight years. Free, 29 September 1697. First mark entered as largeworker, 28 June 1705. Address: 'without Temple Bar'. 'free Waxchandler'. Second mark (Sterling), 26 June 1721. Heal records him as plateworker, Temple Bar, 1705-21; and with ? Temple Bar, 1733. His son Mathew was apprenticed to John Bodington, 16 October 1724, and turned over to his father the next day, when the latter is described as Citizen and Waxchandler of London in Maiden Lane, goldsmith. Matthew II was free 6 June 1732, but no mark appears to have been registered by him.

*LOFTHOUSE, Seth (1945) Son of Alvara Lofthouse (and elder brother of Matthew, above) of Manston 'in Comitat Ebor Agricolae' (cf. 'yeoman' in apprenticing of Matthew), apprenticed to William Wakefield of the Merchant Taylors' Company of St. Nicholas Lane goldsmith 16 February 1676. Freedom not recorded. William Bellasis was apprenticed to him in 1709 in this company. Mark entered as largeworker, undated, between January and July 1699. Address: Bishopsgate, when Lofthouse is surprisingly described as Waxchandler. How this apparent confusion with Matthew's company can have arisen is difficult to determine since the latter's first entry is later in date, but it is in another hand to Lofthouse's signature and may have been a later and mistaken addition by the clerk. Lofthouse does not appear in the Waxchandlers' freedom or apprentice list as far back as 1666. Heal records him as plateworker, Bishopsgate, 1697; White Horse, Fleet Street, near Fleet Bridge, 1712-22; and also Thomas Burgess and Seth Lofthouse, goldsmiths, White Horse, Fleet Street, 1719. He was dead by 7 February 1727 when he is so described in the record of the freedom of his former apprentice James Savage, of the Haberdashers' Company.

LOMBARD, Daniel (482) No record of apprenticeship or freedom. First mark entered as watchcasemaker, 4 March 1763. Address: Tottenham Court Road, next to the Rising Sun. Second mark, 26 November 1764. Address: 'in Prujean Court Old Bailey.' Appears however as watchcasemaker, at the first address, in the Parl. Report list 1773.

LONDON, John (1486) John Barling London son of John of St. Giles Cripplegate smith, apprenticed to Ann Trender of Princes Street, Barbican widow of Robert Trender as goldsmith 3 October 1792 and turned over 3 January 1798 to James Trender (goldsmith and cooper). Free, 1 January 1800. First mark entered as smallworker, 10 June 1808. Address: 8 Coleman Street, Bunhill Row. Second mark, undated. Address: 123 Golden Lane. Third mark (two sizes), 9 January 1818.

LONDON, William (3223, 3230) Son of John London of Coleman Street London haberdasher, apprenticed to John Goreham 6 November 1754 on payment of £15. Freedom unrecorded. First mark entered as smallworker, 4 May 1761. Address: Gutter Lane, Cheapside, 7 December 1762, where he appears without category in the Parl. Report list 1773.

LONG, Henry (1023) Son of Robert Long Citizen and Grocer of London, apprentice to Simon Bryant 25 September 1707. Free, 6 February 1716. Mark entered as smallworker, 25 August 1721. Address: Mugwell Street.

LONG, James (1478) No record of apprenticeship or freedom. Only mark entered as smallworker, 17 November 1785. Address: Royal Exchange. Incuse mark at same address as smallworker, 4 July 1797 (Section V).

LONGSTAFFE, George (845) No record of apprenticeship or freedom. First mark entered as smallworker, 5 May 1799. Address: 110 Old Street. Moved to 4 King's Head Court, St. Martin's Le Grand, 29 October 1803. Second mark, 15 April 1813. Address: 1 New Rents, St. Martin's Le Grand. Moved to 7 Fitchet Court, Noble Street, 28 January 1818.

LOOKER, William (1952, 3219, 3891) Son of Henry Looker late of the Tower of London moneyer deceased, apprenticed to Benjamin Bentley 1 May 1706. Free, 10 June 1713. First mark entered as largeworker, 12 June 1713. Address: Carey Lane. Second (Sterling) mark, 6 July 1720. Address: St. Ann's Lane. (This entry is in an unsteady hand — ?ill or drunk.) Leadenhall Street, 10 March 1724 (register entry without mark). Heal records only the first two dates and addresses.

LORD, William (3225) Son of Cornelius Lord late Citizen and Upholder of London deceased, apprenticed to William Bell Citizen and Goldsmith 5 March 1760 on payment of £5 of the charity of the Trustees of the Charity School in Bartholomew Close. Free, 5 August 1767. First mark entered as smallworker, 6 February 1770. Address: Silver Street. Second mark (incuse), 3 April 1770. Appears as watchcasemaker, at this address, in the Parl. Report list 1773.

LOVE, George (844, 1312) No record of apprenticeship or freedom. First mark entered as smallworker, 21 April 1763. Address: Grub Street. Second mark, in partnership with John Faux, 11 May 1764. Address: 'in ye Curtain Holywell Mount, Shoreditch'. Third mark, 22 December 1764. Fourth, 10 February 1767. Moved to Worship Street, near Moorfields, 14 August 1767 or later. Fifth mark, 6 February 1771. The two appear as bucklemakers, at this last address, in the Parl. Report list 1773.

LOVELL, Richard (1950, 2354) Free of the Bricklayers' Company. First mark entered as smallworker, 15 October 1701. Address: Red Lion Street. 'Free of the Bricklayers' Company'. Second (Sterling) mark, 15 August 1720. There is a confusing apprenticeship entry for Richard Lovell, son of Richard Lovell late of London cornchandler deceased, to Thomas Bushnell 17 June 1708, but it is difficult to see how this refers to the above maker.

LOVELL, Robert (1951) Son of Henry Lovell of Wooinglavon(?) in the County of Kent clerk, apprenticed to Timothy Ley of the Founders' Company 20 May 1693. Free, 3 August 1702. Mark entered as largeworker, 8 March 1703. Address: Maiden Lane. 'free of the Founders'. Signatory as 'working goldsmith' to the petition complaining of the competition of 'necessitous strangers', December 1711. Heal records him in Maiden Lane till 1708; and also 'Next the Pye tavern without Bishopsgate', 1707-15.

LOWE, Edward (607-8) No record of apprenticeship or freedom. First mark entered as smallworker, 24 September 1760. Address: St. John Street, Clerkenwell. Note at base of entry: 'Opposite Messrs Fourman's Timber Yard Old Street'. Second mark, 22 December 1769. Address: Old Street. Third mark, 26 February (?1770). Fourth, 12 September 1771. Address: Mortlake, Surrey, where he appears as smallworker in the Parl. Report list 1773. Fifth mark as plateworker, 15 August 1777.

LOWNDES, Thomas (1416) Son of Matthew Lowndes of Gravel Lane Southwark dealer in coals, apprenticed to Thomas Daniell of Carey Lane Goldsmith on payment of £31. 10s. Free, 4 July 1781. Mark entered as bucklemaker, in partnership with Edward Lycett, 1 October 1783. Address: 2 St. Ann's Lane, Aldersgate, and another with the same, 20 October 1788. Address: Noble Street (Section VIII). Third mark entered as plateworker, in partnership with Joseph Hardy, 26 May 1798. Address: 26 Clements Lane, Lombard Street. Partnership apparently dissolved by 27 April 1799 on entry of a separate mark for Hardy. Heal records him alone as silver bucklemaker and goldsmith, Round Court, 1784; St. Martins Le Grand, 1786; also with Edmund Lycett, as goldsmiths, 25 Noble Street, Foster Lane, 1789-93; and with Hardy, as plateworkers, in the year of the entry.

LUCAS, Benjamin (187) No record of apprenticeship or freedom. Only mark entered as smallworker, 24 August 1758. Address: Brabant Court, Philpot Lane, where he appears without category in the Parl. Report list 1773.

*LUCAS, Robert (2355, 2358) No record of apprenticeship or freedom. First mark entered as largeworker, 13 March 1727. Address: Three King's Court, Lombard Street. Second mark, 25 June 1739. Address: Bow Lane. Heal records him as above. He may perhaps be the Robert Lucas of St. Botolph, Aldersgate, bachelor, married to Elisabeth Linacre of St. Margaret, Westminster at St. Bene't, Paul's Wharf, 18 June 1724.

LUDLOW, John (1461, 1968, 3649) Son of Jonathan Ludlow late of the City of Cork in Ireland gentleman deceased, apprenticed to George Cox Citizen and Broderer of London 10 April 1706. Free of the Broderers' Company, 7 October 1713, being described as 'at the sign of the Spread Eagle without Aldgate Goldsmith'. First mark entered as largeworker, 15 October 1713. Address: without Aldgate. 'Free Imbroiderer'. Second (Sterling) mark, 22 June 1720. Address: Ball Alley, Lombard Street. Heal records him as for the two entries.

LUFF, John (1464, 1487, 1498, 3651) Son of John Luffe late Citizen and Butcher of London, deceased, apprenticed to William Warham 6 June 1711. Free, 3 September 1724. First and second marks entered as smallworker, 2 October 1724. Address: Gunpowder Alley, New Street, Shoe Lane. 'Free of ye Goldsmiths' Company'. Third mark, 25 June 1739. Address: Pemberton Street, Gough Square. Moved to Mrs. Bushnell's, New Street, 21 May 1750. Heal records him at Pemberton Street, 1739; and in addition Fleet Street, 1743.

*LUKIN, William I (1966, 3220) Son of Samuel Lukin of Bodicote in the County of Oxford gentleman, apprenticed to St. John Hoyte 21 June 1692 'from the 25th of this instant June' and turned over to John Shepard 1 June 1698. Free, 5 July 1699. First mark entered as largeworker, 31 July 1699. Address: Gutter Lane. Second, small mark, 12 February 1702. Third (Sterling) mark, 10 June 1725. Address: Strand. Livery, October 1708. Signed petition against assaying work of foreigners not having served seven years apprenticeship, February 1716. 'Elizabeth ye daughter of William Luken, a silversmith at ye Golden Cup in Gutter Lane in this parish and Anne his wife was borne the 27th day of November and was Baptized the 2nd day of December 1700' (Register of St. Vedast, Foster Lane). 'Robert ye son of above was buried in St. John Zachary's parish ye 8th day of June 1703' (ditto). Heal records him as silversmith, Golden Cup, Gutter Lane, 1699; Blackamoor's Head, corner of York Buildings, Strand, 1712-34; and Golden Cup, Strand, 1718; also as bankrupt, in the parish of St. George's, Hanover Square, 1751. In fact he appears as such in August 1749 (*The Gentleman's Magazine*). He resigned from the Livery 15 October 1755. Although comparatively few pieces appear to have survived bearing his mark as compared with Pyne or Nelme, for instance, it is apparent that by about 1715 Lukin was obtaining orders for expensive pieces in the Huguenot manner, and it seems probable that, as with Pyne, he was either overmarking Huguenot pieces or employing such as journeymen. His proximity in the Strand to the banking establishments of Child and Hoare may well have contributed to his clientele either directly or through orders from the banks.

*LUKIN, William II (256) No record of apprenticeship or freedom. Presumably connected with the above. Only mark (C & L.) entered as smallworker with unnamed partner, 7 November 1769. Address: 97 Royal Exchange. He appears alone as goldworker, No. 97 Cornhill, in the Parl. Report list 1773.

LUTWICH, William (1967) Son of John Luttwick of Mavorne (?Malvern) in the County of Worcester yeoman, apprenticed to Henry Ely 21 March 1683. Free, 8 May 1691. Mark entered as smallworker, undated, probably April 1697 on commencement of register. Address: Lamb Alley, Abchurch Lane.

*LUTWYCHE, William (3908) No record of apprenticeship or freedom. Possibly son of or connected with John Lutwyche son of Stocket Lutwyche late of Clyrow in the County of Radnor gentleman deceased, apprenticed to Thomas Midwinter 4 December 1733. Recorded by Heal as working goldsmith and jeweller, Anchor and Dove, 42 Lombard Street, 1766-72; Anchor and Dove, 15 Fenchurch Street, near Gracechurch Street, 1771-7; and 149 Fenchurch Street, 1777; deceased 1783. In partnership with John Henry Vere as goldsmiths, Anchor and Dove, Lombard Street, before 1766. Died 28 October 1782; described as goldsmith, Fenchurch Street (*The Gentleman's Magazine*). Lutwyche does not appear in the Parl. Report list 1773, whereas Vere is listed alone at 48 Lombard Street. The mark attributed to them, which from the unusual combination of initials will not suit any other known partnership of the time, appears mostly on pierced baskets, coasters, etc.

LYON, Henry (1969) Son of Peter Lyon of the parish of St. Giles in the Fields taylor, apprenticed to William Brand 24 March 1669. Freedom unrecorded. Mark entered as smallworker, undated, probably April 1697 on commencement of register. Address: Little Lincoln's Inn Fields. Heal records him by surname only as goldsmith, Lincoln's Inn Fields, 1701. Probably the one of the name elected to Livery, October 1708.

M

MACBRIDE, John (718, 1531) No record of apprenticeship or freedom. First mark entered as smallworker, in partnership with Francis Robine, 10 February 1810. Address: 8 New North Street, Red Lion Square. Second mark alone, 13 September 1814. Address: 33 King Street, Holborn.

*MACKDONALD, Donald (484) No record of apprenticeship or freedom. Only mark entered as smallworker, 21 July 1725. Address: 'in the little Ambrie Westminster'.

M'DUFF, Lawrence (3725) No record of apprenticeship or freedom. Appears as plateworker, Prujean Court, Old Bailey, in the Parl. Report list 1773, which implies a mark entered in the missing largeworkers' register. An undated entry in the earlier largeworkers' register reads: 'Laur^ce McDuff in Prugeon Court Vide small work Book'.

McFARLAN, Jessie (1533) No record of apprenticeship or freedom. From her address presumably widow of John Mackfarlane (below). Mark entered as largeworker, 31 October 1739. Address: New Street, Cloth Fair. Heal records her here, as plateworker, in this year only.

MACKFARLAN, John (1514, 1532) No record of apprenticeship or freedom. First mark entered as smallworker, 23 February 1734. Address: Charles Court, Strand. Second mark as largeworker, 25 June 1739, signing 'Mackfarlen'. Address: 'at the Golden Ball and Canister in New Street, Cloth Fair, West Smithfield'. Presumably dead by 31 October 1739 on the entry of Jessie McFarlan's mark in the same street. Heal records him only as plateworker, at second address and date.

McFERLAN, John (1539) No record of apprenticeship or freedom. Possibly son of above. First mark entered as smallworker, 13 March 1762. Address: 'between the two Swan Lanes Upper Thames Street', where he appears as bucklemaker in the Parl. Report list 1773, and entered three marks as such 1777 to 1784 (Section VIII). Fifth mark as plateworker, and sixth incuse, 9 May 1786. Address: 102 Thames Street.

MACKHOULE, John (1520) No record of apprenticeship or freedom. Only mark entered as smallworker, 14 January 1765. Address: 'near Porter's Block, West Smithfield.' Appears as John Mack Coull, without category, at this address, in the Parl. Report list 1773.

McINTYRE, Thomas (2842) No record of apprenticeship or freedom. Mark entered as plateworker, 7 June 1832. Address: 52 Angel Court, Skinner Street. Moved to 7 Ivy Street, Hoxton, 1 June 1837.

*MACKENZIE, Charles (360) No record of apprenticeship or freedom. Only mark entered as smallworker, 3 May 1736. Address: No. 7 Craven Buildings, near Drury Lane. Heal records him as gold snuffbox-maker, Craven Buildings, deceased 1749.

MACKENZIE, William (3240) No record of apprenticeship or freedom. Only mark entered as 'Pleatworker', 29 February 1748. Address: Windmill Street, at the corner of Angel Court. Heal records him as plateworker, Great Windmill Street, Haymarket, 1748-52.

MADDEN, Jonathan (1982, 3732) No record of apprenticeship or freedom. Presumably son or younger brother of Matthew Madden (below). Only mark entered as largeworker, 2 December 1702. Address: Ball Alley, Lombard Street (signs Jon). Heal records him there, 1702-6; and ? Lombard Street, 1723-4.

MADDEN, Matthew (1974-5) No record of apprenticeship or freedom. First mark entered as largeworker, undated, *c.* 1699 Address: Ball Alley, Lombard Street. Second mark also undated, between April and December 1700, same address. Heal records him as plateworker, parish of All Hallows, Lombard Street, 1692-3; Lombard Street 1697; and Lombard Street(?), 1695-1701. He also has Madding (or Madden)—goldsmith, Golden Bottle, upper end of Cheapside, 1716, died 1730 (also Hilton Price, *Handbook of London Bankers*).

MADDOCKS, William (3236) Possibly son of John Maddocks late of Shrewsbury in the County of Salop brewer deceased, apprenticed to Charles Jones 8 April 1730 on payment of £18. Freedom unrecorded. Incuse mark entered undated, between October 1733 and June 1735. Address: Harding Street, Fetter Lane. Second mark entered as smallworker, 16 February 1765. Address: Feild Lane, where he appears as watchcasemaker in the Parl. Report list 1773.

MAGGS, John (1504) No record of apprenticeship or freedom. Only mark entered as smallworker, 1 September 1721. Address: Foster Lane.

MAGNIAC, Francis (701) Son of Charles Magniac of the Old Change goldsmith, Citizen and Goldsmith (no mark recorded), apprenticed to his father 4 November 1767. Free, 3 December 1781. Mark entered as plateworker, 10 January 1798. Address: St. John Square, Clerkenwell. Heal records him as jeweller, St. John's Square, 1790-3; also William Magniac, same address and date, presumably a brother.

MAIDMAN, Ralph (2360) Son of Ralph Maidman of Compton in the County of Surrey, yeoman, apprenticed to Thomas Moore 6 June 1711 on payment of £4. Free, 3 March 1719. Described as bachelor of St. Mary Staining, on marriage to Sarah Lammas, widow, at St. Bene't, Paul's Wharf, 30 July 1723. Mark entered as largeworker, 31 May 1731. Address: Noble Street. Heal records him as above and insolvent, 1737. In 1728 he appears in the will of Thomas Knott, Citizen and Goldsmith, as in possession of a tenement belonging to the latter in St. Anne, Aldersgate.

MAITLAND, James (1512) Son of Richard Maitland of Richmond in the County of Surrey gentleman, apprenticed to John Pero 7 August 1718 on payment of £20. Freedom unrecorded. Mark entered as largeworker, undated, between 18 June 1728 and 24 February 1729. Address: 'at the Grasshopper the Corner of Suffolk Street'. Heal records him here, 1728-30.

MAKEMEID, Christopher (361-2) Son of William Makemeid of Hitcham in the County of Norfolk yeoman, apprenticed to John Swift 6 April 1748 on payment of £31. 10s. Free, 5 June 1755. First mark entered as smallworker, 29 November 1758. Address: Clements Inn Passage. Second mark, 11 October 1771. Address: 115 Shoe

Lane, where he appears as plateworker in the Parl. Report list 1773. Third mark, 28 June 1773. Presumably dead by 2 October 1773, when Mary Makemeid entered her mark at the same address. Heal records him as plateworker, Shoe Lane, 1773; he also informed me of Makemeid —, goldsmith, Golden Cup, Threadneedle Street, on a 'cut-out' card, c. 1760. Makemeid's son Christopher was apprenticed to William Makemeid of Mortimer Street Cavendish Square goldsmith, Citizen and Goldsmith in 1780, when his father is definitely described as dead.

MAKEMEID, Mary (2045) No record of apprenticeship or freedom. Presumably widow of Christopher Makemeid (above). Mark entered as plateworker, 2 October 1773. Address: 115 Shoe Lane.

*MAKEPEACE, Robert I (2375) Free by redemption 4 April 1759 as silversmith. Livery, 1763. Recorded by Heal as goldsmith, Serle Street, Lincoln's Inn, 1767–75, but no mark is known for this period, although possibly registered in the missing largeworkers' volume. Mark entered as plateworker, in partnership with Richard Carter, 20 January 1777. Address: Bartholomew Close. Partnership apparently dissolved by 9 December 1778, when Carter entered a new mark in partnership with Smith and Sharp. Elected to Court, 1787. Warden, 1792–4. Prime Warden, 1795. Died c. 1795–1801. Heal records Robert Makepeace and Richard Carter, goldsmiths, Serle Street, 1772–77; and also Robert Makepiece and Edward Carter, plateworkers, Bartholomew Close, 1777 (Edward probably an old directory error); next Robert Makepiece and Sons, goldsmiths, 6 Serle Street, 1784. For continuation of the firm see Robert Makepeace II (below).

MAKEPEACE, Robert II (2367, 2376) Son of Robert Makepeace of Serle Street, Lincoln's Inn Fields in the County of Middlesex goldsmith, Citizen and Goldsmith, apprenticed to his father 7 February 1776. Free, 2 April 1788. First mark entered as Robert Makepeace Junior, in partnership with his brother Thomas II (below), 8 January 1794. Address: Serle Street, Lincoln's Inn Fields. Second mark alone, 20 January 1795, same address. Livery, 18 February 1791. Court, 15 May 1801. Warden, 1812–14. Prime Warden, 1814. Died 16 December 1827. Robert II and his brother had apparently been given a share of the business by 1784 since Robert Makepeace and Sons is recorded by Heal that year.

*MAKEPEACE, Thomas I (1990, 2835) Son of Job Makepeace Citizen and Blacksmith of London, apprenticed to Nathaniel Gouldham 21 July 1709. Free, 26 July 1716. First mark entered as smallworker, 17 August 1716. Address: Ball Alley, Lombard Street. Second mark (Sterling), undated c. 1720.

MAKEPEACE, Thomas II (2376) Son of Robert Makepeace I (above) of Serle Street Lincoln's Inn Fields goldsmith, Citizen and Goldsmith, apprenticed to his father 7 October 1778. Free, 7 May 1788. Mark entered as plateworker in partnership with his brother Robert II, 8 January 1794. Address: Serle Street, Lincoln's Inn Fields. Whether Thomas died or retired soon after is not apparent, but Robert II entered a separate mark alone the next year, and whereas both his father and brother were in turn elected to Livery, Court and Prime Wardenship, there is no further sign of Thomas's participation in the affairs of his company.

MALLUSON(?), Edward (623) No record of apprenticeship or freedom. Mark entered as largeworker (although of small size), 13 June 1743. Address: 'at the Houlster in Shoe Lane'. The sign suggests a gunmount- or hiltmaker.

*MALYN, Isaac (1986) Son of Isaac Malyn late of Tilsworth in the County of Bedford gentleman deceased, apprenticed to Ralph Maunsell 17 September 1703 and turned over same day to Isaac Dighton and later to Gabriel Sleath. Free, 1 November 1710. Mark entered as largeworker, 24 November 1710. Address: Gutter Lane. Signatory as Isaac Maylin, 'working goldsmith', to the petition complaining of the competition of 'necessitous strangers', December 1711. Listed by Evans as Huguenot (*Hug. Soc. Proc.*, 14, p. 545), but neither his father's place of residence or his three masters give any real support to this suggestion, unless possibly of a family of one of the earlier Huguenot immigrations.

MANJOY, George (1978–80, 3730–1) Free by redemption as George Minjoy of the Haberdashers' Company 28 June 1685. Three marks entered as smallworker, undated, c. 1700. Address: Goodman Fields, Lombard Street. 'free Haberdasher'. Heal records George Marjoy, Margoy or Manjoy, goldsmith, Dog Row, Whitechapel, 1720, which could presumably all refer; also George Montjoy, goldsmith, Suffolk Street, 1709 which seems less likely to be connected. His mark is found on toys and it would seem possible that the GM mark found on such before 1697, formerly ascribed to George Middleton (Heal, as goldsmith and banker), is very likely his first mark.

MANLEY, George (1973) Son of Daniel Manley, apprenticed to James Hulbert of the Fishmongers' Company and free 24 October 1683. Only mark entered as smallworker, undated, probably April 1697 on commencement of the register. Address: New Street, Shoe Lane. 'Free Fishmonger'.

MANN, Thomas (1987, 2829-31, 2849) Son of James Mann Citizen and Spectaclemaker of London, apprenticed to William Juson (q.v.) of the Broderers' Company 22 October 1706. Turned over later to Henry Clark (q.v.). Free, 4 November 1713. First mark entered as largeworker, 25 November 1713. Address: Foster Lane. 'Free Imbroiderer'. Second (Sterling) mark, 1 July 1720. Third mark, 10 December 1729. Address: Haire Street, Hatton Garden. Fourth, 29 September 1736. Address: Albemarle Street, St. John's Square, Clerkenwell. Fifth, 13 July 1739, same address. Heal records him as plateworker, Foster Lane, 1713; Clerkenwell, 1736; Albemarle Street 1739; and ?Albemarle Street 1750. He also has Thomas Mann, goldsmith, Bishopsgate Street, 1743, but implies a separate identity here.

MANNERS, James (1515, 1538) No record of apprenticeship or freedom. First mark (incuse) entered 6 June 1726. Address: Great St. Andrew Street, near Seven Dials (Section V), without categorization. Second mark as largeworker, 26 April 1734. Address: 'at ye Rose in the Strand'. Third mark, 21 June 1739, same address. Moved to 'Villars' Street, York Buildings, 23 September 1745. Heal records him as silversmith, Rose, Strand, 1734-9; and James Manners Junior, plateworker, Villiers Street, Strand, 1745. The latter in fact entered an incuse mark only, 26 September 1745, at the same address as his father (Section V).

MANNING, Thomas (2844) Probably the son of Edward Manning late of St. Mary Cray in Kent gentleman deceased, apprenticed to John Swann 29 March 1716 on payment of £30. Freedom unrecorded. Mark entered as smallworker, 19 September 1738.

'Goldsmith in Holborn'. Livery, March 1740.

MANSELL, Samuel (2593) Son of Samuel Mansell late of the parish of St. Alban Wood Street turner deceased, apprenticed to Dru Drury (? Jr) 10 January 1754. Free, 11 February 1761. Mark entered as knifehaftmaker, 19 August 1773. Address: 48 Strand. Moved to Orange Court, Leicester fields, 4 June 1774. Heal records him only as silversmith, Strand, 1773.

MANSFIELD, Charles (364) No record of apprenticeship or freedom. Only mark entered as spoonmaker, 31 July 1828. Address: 16 Gough Street, Mount Pleasant. Moved to 24 Brick Lane, St. Luke's, 27 August 1828.

MANSFIELD, John (1513) Possibly son of Edward Mansfield of Clifton in the County of Bristol gentleman, apprenticed to William Warham 5 July 1704. Freedom unrecorded. Only mark entered as smallworker, 13 September 1731. Address: Rawlings Street, Hanover Square.

MARC, John Lewis (1497) No record of apprenticeship or freedom. Only mark entered as smallworker, 27 June 1726. Address: Tower Street, Soho. Heal records him as Jean Louis Marc, silversmith, Savoy, 1700-4.

*MARDER, John (1519) No record of apprenticeship or freedom. Only mark entered as smallworker, 14 October 1760. 'Entered by virtue of a Letter of Attorney by Robert Purton', no address. Possibly a provincial maker.

*MARGAS, Jacob (1510, 1983, 3733-4) Son of Samuel Margas of the parish of St. Martin's in the Fields goldsmith (who appears as 'Samuel Marga de Rouen 32 ans 20 Mars 1687' in the 'Reconnaissances' of the French Church of the Savoy (*Hug. Soc. Pub.*, 22)), apprenticed to Thomas Jenkins of the Butchers' Company 12 January 1699. Free, 7 August 1706 of that company. It is presumably his name which appears in the Denization List, 11 March 1700 (but see below for another possibility). First mark entered as largeworker, 19 August 1706. Address: St. Martin's Lane. 'free of the Butchers' Company'. Second (Sterling) mark, undated, probably 1720 but perhaps later, the next entry below being of 1728. Address: 'at ye corner of Cecil's Court St. Martin's Lane'. Heal records him as plateworker, St. Martin's Lane, 1706-20; and bankrupt, St. Martin in the Fields, 1725.

Listed by Evans as Huguenot (*Hug. Soc. Proc.*, 14, p. 545). Samuel, son of Jacob and Anne, was baptized 11 March 1719 at Leicester Fields Church, and Jacob, son of the same, was baptized 26 February 1721 at Hungerford Market Church (*Hug. Soc. Pub.*, 29 and 31). 'Old Margas' appears as one of the Subordinate Goldsmiths to the King, 1723-30 (Major General H. W. D. Sitwell, 'The Jewel House and the Royal Goldsmiths', *Arch. Journ.*, CXVII, p. 154). The disentangling of identities in the Margas family is not easy from the documentary evidence and repetition of Christian names. There is also recorded a 'Jaques Margas orfeure', married 26 December 1691 to Anne 'née Margas, presentée par Samuel son frère' at Swallow Street Church. If we assume that this Samuel is identical with the father of Jacob apprenticed in 1699 and owner of the mark entered 1706, then the Jaques of 1691 can, at nearest, be cousin to Samuel who gives away his sister Anne. It is, however, perplexing to find that Jacob's wife is also Anne, but since the birth of their son Samuel in 1719 is twenty-eight years after the marriage of Jaques and Anne, the separateness of these two namesake couples seems definite enough. Elizabeth Margas 'de Rouen' appears in the Bounty List 1706. One might have supposed her the widow of Samuel (père) but he was still obviously alive at the apprenticeship of Samuel (fils), below, in 1708. There seems in the past to have been some confusion between Margas' Britannia Standard mark and that of others of the period, and references in print are not entirely trustworthy. The ewer at Pembroke College, Cambridge, 1706 appears to be one of his earliest surviving pieces. Others are the cup and cover of 1718 (E. Alfred Jones *The Old English Plate of the Emperor of Russia*, Plate XLI) and the salver of 1725 (Farrer Collection, Ashmolean Museum). Like his brother he was chiefly occupied with domestic pieces of which his polygonal teapots are specially attractive.

MARGAS, Samuel (1988, 2588) Son of Samuel Margas of the parish of St. Martin in the Fields goldsmith, apprenticed to Jacob Margas of the Butchers' Company (his brother, above) 8 January 1708. Free of the same company 12 January 1714. Mark entered as largeworker, 14 February 1715. Address: St. Martin's Lane. 'Free Butcher'. It would seem that the two brothers worked together at least for some time. Second (Sterling) mark, 8 March 1721. Address: 'Living in King Street, Covent Garding'! The unusual 'Living in' suggests his residence rather than working address, unless the move for both was recent and he was subconsciously emphasizing independence from his brother. Heal records him as son of Jacob Margas, plateworker, St. Martin's Lane, 1714; and King Street, 1720 to 1730(?). Evans lists him as son of Jacob and Anne but this is clearly shown from apprentice and mark entries (above) to be a misinterpretation due to the duplication of names. 'Young Margas', Subordinate Goldsmith to the King, 1723-30 and 1732-3 (Major General H. W. D. Sitwell, 'The Jewel House and the Royal Goldsmiths', *Arch. Journ.*, CXVII, pp. 154-5). St. Paul's Cathedral register contains the following: 'Samuel Margas of the parish of St. Martin in ye feilds, batchelor & Judith De la Newsue* Maison of the old Artillery Ground in ye County of Middlesex, Spinster, were married with a License from Dr. Harwood in this Cathedral Church ye 3^d dat of June 1716; by me Henry Gostling Sacrist.' Samuel appears as witness (?godfather) to the baptism of Anne de la Neuve Maison, presumably a niece of Judith's, at Threadneedle Street Church, 14 August 1726, and also earlier as godfather to his nephew Samuel, son of Jacob (above), 11 May 1719 at Leicester Fields Church. The register of St. Mary Aldermanbury contains the following: 'Oct. 31. 1751. Samuel Margas of the Parish of St. Leonard Shoreditch in the County of Middlesex Widower & Sarah Pinnock of the same Parish Spinster by Mr. John Lindsay.' This might however refer to the son of Jacob and Anne. Samuel Margas' work seems rarer than that of his brother and chiefly domestic with a preponderance of candlesticks. The wine-cistern of 1714 of the Marquess of Crewe is probably his most important surviving work, with the undated ewer and dish, *c.* 1720, in the Untermyer Collection (ex Hermitage) to support it.

MARRAM, Elizabeth (1991) Presumably widow of Stephen Marram (below). Mark entered as smallworker, 6 April 1717. Address: Fenchurch Street.

---

* So the Harleian Society's printed transcript, presumably a misreading of 'Neuve', as appears in the Threadneedle Street entry.

MARRAM, Stephen (1972) Son of Stephen Marram of Luting (?Luton) in the County of Hertford gardener, apprenticed to Walter Prosser 2 October 1701. Free, 11 April 1712. Mark entered as smallworker, 21 December 1715. Address: 'Ffanchurch Street'. Presumably dead by 6 April 1717 on entry of Elizabeth Marram's mark at the same address.

MARRIOTT, Elizabeth (616) No record of apprenticeship or freedom, nor evidence of possible succession to a deceased husband. Only mark entered as smallworker, undated, between 10 and 15 May 1739. Address: 'at the Black Lion in Chancery Lane'.

MARSH, Jacob (1517, 3658) Son of George Marsh of Abbey Milton (Milton Abbas) in the County of Dorset clerk, apprenticed to William Lukin 30 September 1726 on payment of £21 and turned over to Gabriel Sleath 2 November 1731. Free, 6 November 1741. Mark entered as largeworker, 24 April 1744. Address: 'Swithings Lane, Lomber Street'. Moved to Lombard Street, 4 October 1749. Moved to Cornhill, 6 February 1761. Heal records him as plateworker, Swithin's Lane, 1744-8; and at Unicorn, 78 Lombard Street, 1753-72; also, from a trade card, 'removed from Unicorn Lombard Street to Unicorn in Cornhill circa 1760' (Heal Add). Miriam, daughter of Jacob and Elizabeth, born and baptized 17 August 1745 (presumably died at birth). A second Miriam was born to them 4 September 1746, baptized 23 September (St. Mary Woolnoth register).

*MARSH, Peter (2206) No record of apprenticeship or freedom. Only mark entered as smallworker, 26 October 1733. Address: New Street, near Shoe Lane.

MARSHALL, John (2757) No record of apprenticeship or freedom. Only mark entered as smallworker, in partnership with Thomas Freeman, 13 September 1764. Address: Princess Street, near Bridgwater Square (his partner in Little Bartholomew Close, a rare example of two addresses). Heal records them as Thomas Freeman and J. Marshall, plateworkers, Bartholomew Close, 1764. He appears without category at Westmorland Buildings, Aldersgate Street, in the Parl. Report list 1773.

MARSHALL, Samuel (2594) Son of John Marshall of Hitchin in the County of Hertford gentleman, apprenticed to George Brasier of Giltspur Street as silversmith 3 November 1784 and turned over the same day to Edward Fennell of Fetter Lane goldsmith, Citizen and Goldsmith on payment of £20, £5 whereof of the charity of Joseph Kempe of Hitchin deceased. Free, 4 January 1792. Mark entered as smallworker, 18 July 1799. Address: 23 Castle Street, Holborn. Probably identifiable with the goldworker of this name, 1821 (Section VII).

MARSON, James (1537) No record of apprenticeship or freedom. Only mark entered as smallworker, 21 March 1761. Address: Princes Street, Upper Moorfields, where he appears as watchcasemaker in the Parl. Report list 1773, and entered incuse mark at this address, 13 June 1775 (Section V). Angela Marson, presumably his widow, entered incuse mark as casemaker, 5 July 1784 at Butchers Close, Upper Moorfields (Section V).

MARSTON, Josh (1527) No record of apprenticeship or freedom. Only mark entered as smallworker, 30 January 1790. Address: 8 Steward Street, Goswell Street.

MARTIN, Charles (359, 365, 3587) Son of William Martin of Renbury in the County of Chester yeoman, apprenticed to William Darker 3 September 1719 on payment of £20 and turned over 4 October 1722 to Thomas Tearle in Foster Lane goldsmith. Free, 19 January 1726(?7). First mark entered as largeworker, undated, between 1720 and 1728. Address: Rose and Crown Brids (?Brides) Lane, Fleet Street. Second mark similar, 23 January 1730. Third mark, 20 February 1741, entered for Sarah Martin 'by power of attorney for her husband Charles Martyn (now abroad) to transact his affairs during his absence'. Heal records him as plateworker, Rose and Crown, Field Lane, 1729 (apparently following Chaffers) and London, 1740. Died 1744.

MARSHAM, Willoughby (1981) No record of apprenticeship or freedom. Only mark entered as largeworker, 24 May 1701. Address: Newgate Street, where Heal records him from 1701 to 1705.

MASON, Thomas (1971, 2832-3, 2846-8) Son of John Mason of Brockhamton in the County of Gloucester yeoman, apprenticed to Robert Timbrell 18 October 1704. Free, 4 November 1712. First mark entered as largeworker, 19 November 1716. Address: Sherborn Lane. Second (Sterling) mark, 1 July 1720. Livery, June 1725. Third mark, 28 September 1733, same address. Fourth, 6 July 1739. Address: Fish Street Hill.

Moved to Bishopsgate Street, 19 November 1740. Fifth mark, 23 September 1745. Heal records him as plateworker, at Sherborn Lane and Fish Street Hill, at dates above. He also has Thomas Mason, goldsmith, Golden Key, Lombard Street, 1706, who is clearly a separate identity.

MASSEY, Benjamin (194) No record of apprenticeship or freedom. First mark entered as plateworker, 19 August 1829. Address: 116 Leadenhall Street. Second mark, 23 September 1833. Heal (Add.) records him as goldsmith, jeweller and cutler, 116 Leadenhall Street, 1809 (? error for date above). Samuel Massey, smallworker, mark entered 12 February 1773, may perhaps be his father or other relative (Section IV).

MATHEW, John (1985) Possibly (1) John Mathews son of John of Clerkenwell in the County of Middlesex gentleman, apprenticed to John Hughes 27 September 1693. Or, more likely (2) son of William Mathew (below) Citizen and Goldsmith of London, apprenticed to his father 6 July 1704. Freedom of either unrecorded. Mark entered as largeworker, 13 September 1710. Address: Ball Alley, Lombard Street. Heal records only this address and date.

MATHEW, Mary (1984) Presumably widow of William Mathew I (below). Only mark entered as largeworker, 28 May 1707. 'Widow'. Address: George Alley, Lombard Street. Heal records her as above; and also Mary Matthew, goldsmith, London, 1700-9.

MATHEW, William I (1976-7, 3730) Son of Thomas Mathew late of Woolventon(?) in the County of Worcester, apprenticed to John Smith 28 July 1675 'from Midsummer last'. Free, 27 June 1683. First mark entered as largeworker, undated, probably April 1697 on commencement of register. Address: Foster Lane. Second mark, 20 April 1700. Address: George Alley, Lombard Street. Apparently dead by 23 May 1707 when Mary Mathew, widow (above) entered her mark at the same address. See William Mathew II (below). Heal records him as plateworker, Foster Lane, 1697; George Alley, Lombard Street, 1700; and (?) Foster Lane, 1711, but see above.

MATHEW, William II (3232-3) Son of William Mathew Citizen and Goldsmith, apprenticed to his father 4 June 1701. Freedom by patrimony, 8 February 1712. First mark entered as largeworker, 17 March 1712. Address: Minories. (An unusual New Standard mark in having the initial of Christian name over those of first two letters of surname as laid down.) Second (Sterling) mark, 20 June 1720. Heal records him as plateworker, Minories, 1711-20.

MATHEWS, Elizabeth and Robert (624) No record of apprenticeship or freedom for either. Only mark entered in partnership as plateworkers, 17 February 1825. Address: 3 Horshoe Court, Ludgate Hill. Second mark, 15 March 1825.

MATTHEWS, William (3234) Apparently distinct from William Mathew II (above), but no record of apprenticeship or freedom. Only mark entered as largeworker, undated, between 18 June 1728 and 24 February 1729. Address: Bartlets Court, Bartlet Street, Clerkenwell. Heal records him as plateworker, Clerkenwell, 1728-33.

MATTHEY, Daniel (485) No record of apprenticeship or freedom. Only mark entered as smallworker, 25 January 1737. Address: 'Living in Queen Street 7 Dyals next Door from the Green Door'.

MAY, Daniel I (367, 488, 490) No record of apprenticeship or freedom. First mark entered as smallworker, in partnership with Charles Neale, 22 March 1783. Address: 6 Air Street, Hoxton Town. Second mark together, 13 May 1783. Third mark alone, 12 January 1784, same address.

MAY, Daniel II (820) No record of apprenticeship or freedom. Presumably son of the above, the signature to this mark entry showing noticeable difference from the former. First mark entered as smallworker, in partnership with George Harris, 30 July 1800. Address: 66 Banner Street, Bunhill Row. Second mark, very small, 9 October 1800. Address: 5 Turk Street, Shoreditch.

MAY, Richard (1258, 2366, 2372) Son of Charles May of the City of Oxford grocer, apprenticed to William Dorrell 15 October 1753 on payment of £21. Free, 14 January 1761. First mark entered as smallworker, 12 May 1764. Address: Hick's Hall. Second mark also as smallworker, in partnership with Jane Dorrell (q.v.), presumably widow of William, 22 October 1766. Address: Quakers' Buildings. Third mark, 22 May 1769. Fourth mark, 3 May 1771. Address: 24 Quakers' Buildings. Fifth mark alone, 3 October 1771, same address. Sixth, 8 September 1772. Appears as smallworker, at same address, in the Parl. Report list 1773.

Seventh mark, 14 May 1778. Address: 4 St. John's Street, near Hicks Hall. Heal records him alone as goldsmith, St. John's Street, 1769; and Quakers' Buildings, which he suggests may be Quakers' Meeting House, White Hart Yard, Lombard Street, 1771-3; and in partnership with Jane Dorrell, Quakers' Buildings, 1771 and ? 1781.

MAYFIELD, Edward (621) No record of apprenticeship or freedom, but perhaps related to Thomas Mayfield. Free, 1779. Goldworker, 1790 (Section VII). Livery, 1791. Perhaps brother of Benjamin apprenticed to Thomas, 1795. Only mark entered as smallworker, 10 November 1796. Address: 3 Little Minories. Benjamin Mayfield entered two marks as goldworker at other addresses, 1824-8, and Stephen Udall Mayfield 1826-30 (Section VII).

MAYO, James (1989) Son of John Mayo late of Devizes in the County of Wiltshire goldsmith deceased, apprenticed to Philip Raynaud (Rainaud) 14 February 1708. Free, 13 April 1716. Mark entered as smallworker, 27 July 1716. Address: Little Britain.

MEACH, Richard (2363-4) No record of apprenticeship or freedom. First mark entered as smallworker, 29 March 1765. Address: Golden Cup, corner of Hatton Garden. Moved to 17 George's Court, Clerkenwell; before 1773 since he appears here as smallworker in the Parl. Report list. Second mark, 2 March 1774. Address: 17 George's Court, Clerkenwell. Moved to 156 Upper Thames Street, 14 July 1788, where Heal records him only, as working goldsmith, 1790-3.

MEALE, George (848, 2019) Son of George Males (sic) of Church Hambrough in the County of Oxford yeoman, apprenticed to Robert Turner of the Founders' Company 9 February 1708. Free, 29 October 1715. First mark (New Standard) entered as smallworker, and second, incuse (Sterling) mark, 22 June 1720. Address: Hosier Lane. 'Free Founder'. Third mark (Sterling) in punch, 15 April 1725, same address.

MEDLEY, George (849) Son of George Medley of the parish of St. Clement Danes taylor apprenticed to Samuel Edlin 12 March 1724 on payment of £10. Free, 7 February 1737. Mark entered as smallworker, 7 March 1737. Address: Plum Tree Court, Holborn. 'Goldsmith'. Livery, September 1746.

MEDLYCOTT, Edmund (617) No record of apprenticeship or freedom, but perhaps related to Edmond Medlicott (apprenticed 1685 and free 1694). Only mark entered as smallworker, 30 June 1748. Address: Foster Lane, where Heal records him at the Golden Ball as plateworker, 1748-55. Married, 27 October 1748 at St. Clement Danes, Anne Leeke of Ashbourne, County of Derby, by whom he had at least four sons. He died before 1 March 1773 when he is described as deceased, on the apprenticeship of his son John to John Hardy, clockmaker (information, Mr. M. T. Medlycott).

MEEK, John (1836) No record of apprenticeship or freedom, but possibly son of James Meek who had been apprenticed in 1788 to William Eley as bucklemaker. First mark entered as spoonmaker, 21 August 1821. Address: 43 St. John Street, Clerkenwell. Second mark, 19 March 1828.

MERCER, Thomas (2838) Son of John Mercer late of the parish of St. Andrews Holborn gentleman deceased, apprenticed to William Gardiner 8 February 1722 and turned over December 1728 to Aaron Bates Goldsmith. Free, 5 March 1728(?9). Mark entered as largeworker, 5 December 1740. Address: West Street, St. Anne's, Soho.

MERFIELD, Rebecca (2370) No record of apprenticeship or freedom, but probably widow of Samuel Flight Merefield (apprenticed to John Henderson as goldsmith 1780). Mark entered as smallworker, 27 January 1823. Address: 111 Goswell Street. Signs with +. See also James Merfield, smallworker, 28 Allen Street, Clerkenwell, 1805 (Section V).

MERITON, Samuel I (2589-90) Son of Thomas Meriton Citizen and Turner of London, apprenticed to William Wheat Citizen and Turner 10 March 1731 on payment of £12. 12s. Free, 6 September 1738. Mark entered as smallworker, 10 May 1739. Address: Cary Lane. 'Turner'. Second mark, 7 July 1746. Address: 'at the acorn in Huggin Alley Wood Street. Heal records him only at this date and address. His son Thomas (q.v.) was turned over to his father 7 February 1759, and William Le Bas (q.v.) turned over to him 14 March 1764.

MERITON, Samuel II (2591) No record of apprenticeship or freedom. Probably free of the Turners' Company by patrimony. Appears as goldworker, Foster Lane, in the Parl. Report list 1773. First mark entered as smallworker, 8 May 1775. Address: 18 Foster Lane. Second mark, 16 October 1781, same address, where Heal records him as goldsmith, 1784-96. Dead by 7 October 1800 when his son George was apprenticed to his uncle Thomas (below). For George Meriton see Sections V and VI.

MERITON, Thomas (2840) Son of Samuel Meriton I Citizen and Turner of London, apprenticed to Edward Slater 7 February 1759 and turned over the same day to his father. Free, 5 March 1766. Livery, February 1791. Mark entered as smallworker. 1 March 1791. Address: 18 Foster Lane, where Heal records him in 1800. Died 19 November 1815. There is a record of a Thomas Meriton, son of Thomas, silversmith of Wood Street, admitted aged ten to St. Paul's School, 12 July 1754, who is presumably the same, with a clerical error in his father's name.

MERRICK, Thomas (2843) No record of apprenticeship or freedom. Only mark entered as plateworker, 19 April 1834. Address: 23 Red Lion Street, Clerkenwell.

MERRY, John (1524-5) No record of apprenticeship or freedom. First mark entered as smallworker, 19 January 1782. Address: 8 King Street, Moorfields. Second mark, 24 July 1789. Address: Fore Street. Moved to 6 Addel Street, 10 July 1790. Third mark, 13 November 1799. Heal records a John Merry, jeweller, Smithfield Bars, 1747, who seems unconnected; and John Merry, silversmith, 76 Fleet Street, 1790, which seems geographically distant.

MERRY, Theophilus (2841) No record of apprenticeship or freedom. Only mark entered as smallworker 22 September 1824. Address: 9 Little Vine Street, Piccadilly.

MERRY, Thomas I (2017, 3737) Son of Thomas Merry of Collshill in the County of Berkshire cordwainer, apprenticed to Henry Grant 3 April 1693 'for 8 years from 25 March last' and turned over to John Laughton before May 1695, when he appears as 'servant' in the latter's household in tax assessment of St. Anne and St. John Zachary. Heal records him as silversmith, Maidenhead, Maiden Lane, married 1699. Free, 9 April 1701. Mark entered as smallworker, 19 June 1701. Address: Green Arbour Court, Little Old Bailey, which he shared with one Thomas Harper. He paid dues on this address only for a few months, as he is recorded as inhabitant of the parish of St. Anne and St. John Zachary for some fourteen years, having apparently taken over his late master's address by Easter 1704. Three children of Thomas and Mary Merry were baptized at the same church from 1704 to 1709. Signatory as 'working goldsmith' to the petition complaining of the competition of 'necessitous strangers', December 1711. Livery, October 1712. Churchwarden of St. John Zachary, 1714. Still voting as liveryman, 1724. His mark no. 2017 is so close in character to no. 3737 (formerly attributed to Lewis Mettayer, but which does not appear in the register and is found apparently limited to candlesticks and snuffer-stands of relevant dates) as to justify the latter's attribution to Merry. His second master Laughton was also, by the surviving evidence of his work, a candlestick maker. (See Stanley Percival, 'Thomas Merry, citizen and goldsmith of London', *Connoisseur*, August 1970.)

MERRY, Thomas II (2837) No record of apprenticeship or freedom and no address connection with the above. Mark entered as largeworker, 1 September 1731. Address: St. John's Street, by the Cross Keys. Presumably identical with T.M., plateworker, Smithfield Bars, 1727-45, as recorded by Heal; followed by St. John Street, 1731; and St. Sepulchre's, 1734.

MERRYWEATHER, Thomas (2937) Son of Roger Merryweather of St. George in the East mariner, apprenticed to Josiah Piercy of Aldersgate Street as silver polisher 4 May 1803 and turned over to Thomas Rowe 7 June 1809. Free, 5 March 1823. Mark entered as plateworker, in partnership with Timothy Smith, 10 January 1824. Address: 1 Westmorland Court, Falcon Square.

*METHAM, Robert (2368) Son of Robert Metham of Cheapside goldsmith, apprenticed to Alexander Field of Hoxton as goldsmith 5 June 1793 on payment of £20. Free, 1 July 1800. Mark entered as plateworker, 2 July 1808. Address: 57 Bartholomew Close. The father Robert appears as plateworker, 5 Butcher Hall Lane, in the Parl. Report list 1773, as having entered a mark earlier (in the missing register) but there does not appear to be any unascribed mark which might in fact be his.

METHUEN, George (852) No record of apprenticeship or freedom. First mark entered as largeworker, 3 August 1743. Address: Hemings Row, St. Martin's Lane.

Moved to Hedge Lane, Charing Cross, 28 November 1743, and back to Heming's Row, 9 June 1753 (register entry without mark). Heal records him as plateworker, Hemings Row, 1743-61. His principal output seems, from the survival of his mark, to have been salvers and dinner-plates and dishes. His work shows a high standard of design and finish. It is curious that he seems such an elusive figure.

*METTAYER, Lewis (1943, 2018, 3724) Son of Samuel Metayer, minister of La Patente Church, Crispin Street, Spitalfields, and Suzanna his wife. Appears in Denization List, 16 December 1687, with his parents, brother Samuel and sisters Mary (wife of David Willaume), Ann and Rachell. (A Francois Mettayer appears in the Bounty List in 1699 as coming from the Ile de Ré.) Louis Mettayer son of Samuel of London clerk, apprenticed to David Williams (Willaume) 29 September 1693. Free, 17 December 1700. First mark entered as largeworker, 18 December 1700. Address: 'in the Pell Mell'. Appears as godfather to Louys Car, 22 May 1701, at La Patente, Spitalfields. Married to Anne Hobbema, at Spring Garden Chapel, 16 October 1706. The interesting entry reads: 'Louis Mettayer orpheuvre, au bout de Lichefield Str, par. de Ste Anne-Anne Hobbema veuve, dem. chez Mr Harrache, orpheuvre, Suffolk Str. par. St. Martin in campis, en la Chapelle de Springarden par Mr de la Motthe, min. de la Savoye. License de L'Arch. de Canterbury. 16 Oct.' (Savoy Church register, *Hug. Soc. Pub.*, 26). Godfather to Marie Anne Bernard at La Patente, 25 December 1708. Appears in Oath Roll, Naturalization Skin for 1710. Godfather to Marie Francoise Hanet, daughter of Paul Hanet (q.v.), 22 April 1711 at West Street Church. Livery, October 1712. Godfather to Marie Madelaine Godard at Leicester Fields Church, 1 January 1720. Second mark (Sterling), 26 August 1720. Heal records him as plateworker, Acorn, Pall Mall, 1700-25; at end of Suffolk Street, 1712-16; and London, 1735. The Lichfield Street address of his marriage does not otherwise appear; it may have been only a workshop or alternately his bachelor lodgings. His son Samuel was free of the Goldsmiths by patrimony, 1741, and daughter Susanna also, 1738. He died in 1740 (Henry Wagner, *Pedigree of Willaume and Tanqueray-Williaume*. See under those two names). With a sister, the wife of David Willaume, to whom he himself was apprenticed, and a wife from the house of Pierre Harache (in whatever connection) the close ties of the Huguenot 'orfèvres' of London at that time need little further emphasizing. It must indeed have been a very 'close shop' and no doubt the English craftsmen's complaints against the foreigners may well have been stimulated as much by their clannishness as by their reputed cutting of prices. Mettayer's work, although perhaps slightly less frequently met with than that of Willaume or Harache is of equal quality and importance. His principal surviving works include two wine-cisterns of 1709 (Untermyer Collection, New York) and 1712 (The Hermitage), six candlesticks of 1711 (Earl Spencer), ewer of 1711 (Earl of Ancaster), pair of icepails 1713 (Eton College), dish with royal arms 1718 (Ex Brownlow Collection), and ewer and dish 1720 (Ex St. Martin's in the Fields).

*MEURE, Peter (2129) No record of apprenticeship or freedom. Mark entered as largeworker, in partnership with Peter Archambo II, 18 January 1750. Address: Golden Cup, Coventry Street, where Heal records them till 1755. He appears alone as Peter Muire, goldsmith, Coventry Street, in the Parl. Report list 1773, which indicates that he had entered a mark presumably between 1748 and 1773, the years covered by the missing largeworkers' register.

MEWBURN, Barak (192-3) Son of John Mewburn (below). Free by patrimony 5 Febrary 1817 as goldsmith. First mark entered as plateworker, 31 August 1826. Address: 19 Abington Row, Goswell Road. Second mark, 1 May 1830. Moved to 6 Ball Court, Giltspur Street, and third mark entered 26 January 1831.

MEWBURN, John (1528-4, 3659) Son of John Nubron of Fore Street London, mariner deceased, apprenticed as John Nubron (? through some deafness of the clerk) to John Crouch 5 February 1777. Free, 4 July 1792. First mark entered as plateworker, 2 October 1793. Address: Hare Court, Aldersgate Street. Moved to Abingdon Row, Goswell Road, undated. Livery, June 1811. Second mark, 24 March 1823. Died 27 January 1830. Heal records him as Mewburn or Newburn (cf. Nubron, above), goldsmith, Hare Court, 1793-6.

MIDDLECOTT, Edward (622, 625) No record of apprenticeship or freedom. First mark entered as plateworker, in partnership with William Esterbrooke, 29 August 1816. Address: 4 Long Acre. Second mark alone, 24 September 1817. Probably worked as spoonmakers, as Esterbrooke is so described in his separate entry of 1817.

MIDDLETON, Nicholas (2098) No record of apprenticeship or freedom. Only mark entered as smallworker, 18 May 1795. Address: 162 Strand.

MIDDLETON, William (2035) Son of Thomas Middleton of Nazing in the County of Essex husbandman, apprenticed to Mathew Mills 4 October 1661. Free, 25 November 1668. Livery, October 1698. Mark entered as largeworker, undated, between April and December 1700. Address: Leadenhall Street. Heal records him here, 1697–1705.

MIEG, Charles (363) No record of apprenticeship or freedom. Only mark entered as smallworker, 25 February 1767. Address: Porter Street, where he appears without category in the Parl. Report list 1773. Listed by Evans as Huguenot (*Hug. Soc. Proc.*, 14, p. 546).

*MILLER, Henry I (1028, 2036, 3738) Son of Henry Miller late of St. James Westminster in the County of Middlesex tanner deceased, apprenticed to Andrew Archer 18 July 1704. Free, 8 August 1711. First mark entered as largeworker, 14 July 1714. Address: Bow Lane. Second (Sterling) mark, 9 July 1720. Address: Noble Street. Heal records him also insolvent, parish of St. Sepulchre's, 1729.

MILLER, Henry II (1029) No record of apprenticeship or freedom. Only mark entered as smallworker, 8 May 1733. Address: Peter's Lane, near Hicks Hall. Heal has date under Henry Miller (above). 1739–55, but does not recognize separate identity.

MILLINGTON, John (1500, 1511, 2037) Either (1) son of Francis Millington Citizen and Goldsmith of London, apprenticed to his father 6 September 1710. Free 4 December 1718. Or, less likely (2) son of Marmaduke Millington of Wen in the County of Salop tanner, apprenticed to John Gould tanner 23 September 1698. Free 21 November 1705. First mark entered as largeworker, 22 September 1718. Address: Butchers' Hall Lane. Second (Sterling) mark, 23 June 1720. Third mark, 18 June 1728. Address: Suttons Court, Bishopsgate Street. Heal records him at both addresses and dates.

MILLS, Dorothy (489, 3519) No record of apprenticeship or freedom. Presumably widow of Hugh Mills (below). First mark identified from Heal's record of her partnership with Thomas Sarbit as goldsmith, Saffron Hill, 1746–7, and found in 1748–9. Second mark entered as largeworker, 6 April 1752. Address: Saffron Hill. Apparently married to Thomas Sarbit by 13 December 1753 when she entered another mark with that surname. Heal however records her as Dorothy Mills at Saffron Hill, 1752–4, but if this is from a directory a change of surname might well not be corrected for some time. See also under Sarbit.

MILLS, Hugh (1032–3, 3605–6) No record of apprenticeship or freedom. First mark entered as largeworker, 23 May 1739. Address: 'at the Seive on Saffron Hill'. Second mark, 14 February 1746. Address: Blue Court, Saffron Hill. Presumably dead soon after as Dorothy Mills and Thomas Sarbit are recorded by Heal at Saffron Hill, 1746 onwards. Heal however also records him till 1749, but this could be directory delay.

MILLS, Richard (2361–2, 2373, 3780, 3836) No record of apprenticeship or freedom. First mark entered as largeworker, 14 July 1755. Address: 'White Horse Alley, Cow Cross in the parish of St. "Sepulkers"'. Second mark, 11 July 1758. Third mark, 5 March 1760. Fourth, 15 December 1760. All at same address. Moved to St. Martin's Le Grand, 16 July 1763 (register entry without mark). Fifth mark, 29 June 1765. Address: Salisbury Court, Fleet Street. Sixth, 2 November 1767, same address, Heal curiously records him as plateworker, London, 1729–42, for which there is no register evidence for him or an earlier maker of the same name; also White Horse Alley, 1755, but not the later Salisbury Court. He also has Thomas Hannam (?) and Richard Mills, plateworkers, London, 1765, but this may well be taken from the ascription in Jackson (3836), which must remain open to doubt, as also definitely the present ascription of mark 3780 to Mills and David Bell.

*MINCE, James (1526, 1541, 3633) Son of James Mince of the parish of Eltham in the County of Kent gentleman, apprenticed to Jabez Daniell (q.v.) 5 July 1753. Free, 1 July 1761. Appears to have worked in partnership with Daniell from about 1766–75 from the evidence of mark no. 3633, which occurs almost entirely on castors, and Mince is described as 'castormaker' of Carey Lane in the apprenticeship to him of Thomas Tidswell, 3 February 1773. This mark would presumably have been entered in the missing register and the partnership may have been dissolved in 1773, since Jabez and Thomas Daniell appear together in the Parl. Report list of that year. Second mark entered as plateworker, in partnership with William Hodgkins II, 25 November 1780. Address: 2 Bell Square, Foster Lane. Third mark alone as smallworker, 5 February 1790, same address. Moved to 26 Phillip Lane, Aldermanbury, 28 March 1792. His son Thomas Daniell Mince was apprenticed to him 7 July 1790. The boy's second name, suggesting Jabez Daniell as godfather, supports the theory of partnership with the latter. Heal records the partnership with Hodgkins as above; and Mince alone as goldsmith, Bell Square, 1783-9.

MINCE, John (1522) No record of apprenticeship or freedom. Possibly son of Jonah Mince, watchcasemaker, mark entered 1767 (Section VI). Only mark entered as smallworker, 16 February 1773. Address: Michell Street, Old Street, where he appears as watchcasemaker in the Parl. Report list 1773. Charles, Jeremiah and Jonah Mince (Section V) are probably sons.

MITCHELL, Robert (2369) No record of apprenticeship or freedom. First mark entered as smallworker, 4 September 1821. Address: 5 Jewin Street, Aldersgate Street. Second mark, 22 May 1823.

MOLIERE, John (3663) No record of apprenticeship or freedom. Appears as plateworker in partnership with Dyall Jones, Clerkenwell Green, in the Parl. Report list 1773, this being the only record of their existence. The agreement of initials and dates of the pieces on which mark no. 3663 is found appears to make the ascription to these makers certain.

MONTAGUE See MOUNTIGUE.

MONTGOMERY, A. (64) No record of apprenticeship or freedom. Almost certainly widow of John Montgomery (below), who was dead by 21 December 1750 when his apprentice William Caldecott was turned over to Thomas Heming. Mark entered as largeworker, 27 June 1750. A very illiterate entry with the address 'Cmberedge Street' for Cambridge Street (cf. John Montgomery). Heal records A. Montgomery, plateworker, London, 1697; and Cambridge Street, 1729-50. This clearly must refer at least to one other maker and there is no evidence that ?Anne (or Alice) Montgomery was responsible for any work till the entry of her mark in 1750.

MONTGOMERY, James (1516) No record of apprenticeship or freedom. Only mark entered as smallworker, 29 September 1737. Address: 'In St. Martins Street at ye Golden Ball Leister fields'.

MONTGOMERY, John (1505-7, 1535, 2050) Either (1) son of Gilbert Montgomery of St. James's Westminster gentleman, apprenticed to John Donne 22 July 1707. Free 4 August 1714. Or (2) son of George Montgomery of St. James's Westminster goldsmith, apprenticed to Samuel Lewis 26 August 1708. Free 8 March 1716. One is tempted to see the same person in these two entries, were it not for the different freedom dates and paternal variations, which seem inexplicable, even if the second apprenticeship were in lieu of a turning over. First mark entered as smallworker, 11 March 1718. Address: Silver Street, near Golden Square, St. James's. Second (Sterling) mark, 22 November 1721, same address. Third mark as largeworker, 24 February 1729. Address: 'at the corner of Cambridge Street'. Fourth mark as smallworker, 18 October 1736. Address: 'corner of Silver Street near Golden Square'. Fifth mark as largeworker, 1 September 1742. Address: 'At the Angel the corner of Silver Street and Cambridge Street'. Heal records him only as from 1729 at the Angel, corner of Cambridge Street, Golden Square; and Angel, Silver Street, 1742-9; also London, 1750. He was dead by 21 December 1750, when William Caldecott his apprentice was turned over by the administratix (unnamed, presumably his wife A—— above) to Thomas Heming.

MOODY, George (2048) Son of Isaac Moody of Westdeane in the County of Sussex gentleman, apprenticed to Henry White Citizen and Haberdasher 29 August 1692. Free, 1 September 1699, as apprentice to Richard Allenby, presumably having been turned over at some time. Mark entered as smallworker, 17 February 1716. Address: Temple Bar. 'Free Haberdasher'.

MOODY, William (3235) Apprenticed to Charles Frederick Kandler (q.v.) goldsmith

BIOGRAPHICAL DICTIONARY

St. James 1743 on payment of £20 (Index to Apprentices from Inland Revenue books, Vol. 21, p. 4025, Public Record Office. Discovered by the late N. M. Penzer). Mark entered as largeworker, 27 August 1756. Address: 'Barwick' Street, St. James's. Moved to Taylor's Street, 25 March 1758. Heal records him at Berwick Street, 1756-60, and he still appears here, as smallworker, in the Parl. Report list 1773. William son of William Moody of Aldersgate Street silversmith was apprenticed to John Thompson as engraver 1 November 1786. The father here may be the son of the first (above), but appears to have no registered mark.

MOORE, Andrew (2047) Son of Samuel Moore Goldsmith, free by patrimony 15 July 1664. Mark entered as largeworker, undated, between April and December 1700. Address: 'in Bridewell precinct'. Heal records him as goldsmith, Bridewell, 1697, probably from Chaffers who overlooked the fact that the undated mark was not in the first group of April 1697 registrations but lay between others of 1700. He is possibly identifiable with Andrew Moore of Blackfriars, goldsmith, widower, married to Mgt. Stead of Blackfriars, spinster, 4 September 1733 (Fleet Register of Marriages), but he would have been over eighty at the time and it seems more likely that this refers to another, perhaps an otherwise unrecorded son. That Moore came of a family of goldsmiths is evident from the apprenticeship to him in 1680 of William Moore, son of Richard, late Citizen and Goldsmith of London, the former perhaps a cousin. The seventeenth century mark AM in monogram has previously been attributed to Moore through its similarity to his registered New Standard mark, but this has now been shown by Charles Oman (*Caroline Silver*, 1970) to be that of the earlier Arthur Manwaring. The most remarkable piece bearing Moore's mark is the silver table in the Royal collection presented to William III by the City of London.

MOORE, Edward (618) No record of apprenticeship or freedom. First mark entered as smallworker, 20 July 1758. Address: Ludgate Street. Second mark, 7 August 1758. Third, 14 December 1769. Address: St. Anne's Lane. Moved to Gracechurch Street, 1 July 1771, where he appears as Edward Moor, goldworker, in the Parl. Report list 1773. Heal records him only at this date and address. Presumably dead by 12 January 1774, when Esther Moor entered a mark as goldworker at 37 Gracechurch Street (Section VII).

MOORE, John (1523, 1536, 3658) Son of Francis Moore of Stamford in the County of Lincoln goldsmith, apprenticed to Fuller White 7 December 1748 on payment of £40. Free, 7 July 1756. First mark entered as largeworker, 24 January 1758. Address: Opposite St. Bride's Church, Fleet Street. Livery, July 1763. Appears as plateworker, Fleet Street, in the Parl. Report list 1773. Second mark as plateworker, 18 July 1778. Address: 17 Silver Street. His son James Henry, aged nine was admitted to St. Paul's School, 4 February 1773, when John Moore described as silversmith, Fleet Street. Heal records him as working silversmith, 118 Fleet Street, 1758-74; Silver Street, 1778; and London, 1793. He died 29 May 1807 and his mark is found until nearly this year. Heal also records John Moore, silver spurmaker at Hand and Spur, near Exeter Exchange in the Strand, c. 1750, who is apparently another, as also John Moore, smallworker, Poland Street, Soho (Parl. Report list 1773) (Section V), and John Moore, bucklemaker, 1 Great Bartholomew Close, 1787 (Section VIII).

MOORE, Thomas I (2054) Son of John Moore free of the Clothworkers' Company by patrimony 2 December 1712. Mark entered as smallworker, 27 June 1723. Address: 'in Bridewell precinct, Water Lane, Clothworker'. The entry in Heal for this name appears to refer to Thomas Moore II below). See Andrew Moore above of the same address (? uncle).

MOORE, Thomas II (2845) Son of John Moore of Ramsbury in the County of Wiltshire gentleman, apprenticed to George Greenhill Jones 7 June 1743 on payment of £30. Free, 7 September 1750. Mark entered as largeworker, 21 August 1750. Address: London Wall, Cripplegate. Second mark, 20 August 1757. Moved to Wood Street, 18 September 1758. Heal records Thomas Moore, goldsmith, Swan Alley, insolvent, 1748, who can scarcely be a boy not yet out of his indentures; also London Wall, 1750-2, which agrees with the above.

MOORE, Thomas III (1188) No record of apprenticeship or freedom. First mark entered as smallworker, in partnership with John Bourne of Abbots Bromley, Staffordshire, 26 June 1770. Address: Bartholomew

599

Close, a curious arrangement for which see John Bourne. Second mark, 12 November 1770. Third mark, as bucklemaker with Bourne, 8 February 1775, and four marks alone as such, 2 May 1776. Address: 93 Bartholomew Close, moving to 6 Butcher Hall Lane, 10 January 1783 (Section VIII). One of this name was elected to Livery, October 1801 and died November 1816.

*MOORE, William (3238) No record of apprenticeship or freedom. Only mark entered as spoonmaker 25 April 1827. Address: 33 Crispin Street, Spitalfields.

*MORDECAI, Benjamin (190, 3490) No record of apprenticeship or freedom. First mark entered as smallworker, 24 August 1770. Address: Clerkenwell Green. He appears as Mordecai, alias Mountigue, Benjamin, bucklemaker, Clerkenwell Green, in the Parl. Report list 1773, which connects him with his following entries of marks under Montigue (see below) and agrees with the entries of his buckle marks (Section VIII).

MORE, Jacob (1835) No record of apprenticeship or freedom. Only mark entered as smallworker, 16 January 1795. Address: 20 New Street, Covent Garden.

MOREL, Lewis (1944) Free by redemption 7 December 1748. Mark, however, entered as smallworker, 8 November 1737. Address: Salisbury Court, styling himself goldsmith, which must refer only at this date to trade rather than company membership.

MORISON, James (1534) A James Morrison son of Thomas late of Whitechapel shipbroker deceased was apprenticed to Charles Beard 11 January 1727 on payment of £15 and turned over to William Hinton Rogers October 1731 (neither of these appear to be working goldsmiths and the identity of the apprentice with Morison is doubtful). First mark entered as largeworker, 14 May 1740. 'Goldsmith'. Address: Bartholomew Close. Moved to Old Bailey, no date. Moved to Saffron Hill, 28 November 1744. Heal records him as Morison or Morrison, goldsmith, Bartholomew Close, 1740-52; and Giltspur Street, 1776-80. Richard Morrison, son of James of Giltspur Street Smithfield silversmith, Citizen and Goldsmith, was apprenticed to his father 6 November 1776, and a William Hollinshed to the same 3 May 1780. There seems a possibility of the intervention of another generation here.

MORISSE, Walter (3239) No record of apprenticeship or freedom. First mark entered as smallworker, 15 August 1831. Address: 52 Aldersgate Street. Moved to 5 Jewin Crescent, 24 September 1842. Second mark (two sizes), 2 May 1843. His son Walter Diederich was apprenticed to him as silversmith 6 April 1853, at the second address.

*MORISSET, James (1521) No record of apprenticeship or freedom. First recorded in partnership with his brother-in-law Louis Toussaint as supplying enamelled work to Parker and Wakelin 13 August 1767. First mark entered as smallworker, 31 August 1770. Address: Denmark Street, St. Giles, where he appears as goldworker in the Parl. Report list 1773, and where Heal records him as Morriset, goldsmith, 1773-8. Heal also records him with Gabriel Wirgman as goldsmiths, same address, partnership dissolved 1778; also R. Morriset and C. Lukin, goldsmiths and jewellers, 22 Denmark Street, 1784-96, where the firm appears correctly as Morriset, R & C. Lukin in 1780 until 1800. He entered three marks alone as goldworker, at the same address, from 1787 to 1789 (Section VII). Listed by Evans as Huguenot (*Hug. Soc. Proc.*, 14, p. 547). He was an artist of no mean achievement to judge by the gold and enamelled boxes and presentation swords of the period on which his mark is found and in which he appears to have specialized. For his work and further details see Claude Blair, '*Three Presentation Swords*', Victoria and Albert Museum. H.M.S.O. 1972.

MORLAND, George (846-7, 3588) Probably son of William Morland refiner deceased, apprenticed to William Fish 14 July 1713 on payment of £25. Free 9 September 1736. Livery, September 1746. First mark entered as 'Snuff Box Maker' in smallworkers' book, 6 September 1723. Address: Foster Lane. Second mark, 30 June 1731. Address: 'Living at Mr James Stone in Maiden Lane'.

MORLEY, Elizabeth (620) Presumably, from address, widow of Thomas Morley (below). First mark entered as smallworker, 8 August 1794. Address: 7 Westmorland Buildings. Second mark, 19 July 1796. Third, 1 October 1800. Heal records her only as E. Morley, goldsmith, London, 1799.

MORLEY, Thomas (768, 2839) No record of apprenticeship or freedom. First mark entered as plateworker, in partnership with

BIOGRAPHICAL DICTIONARY

George Baskerville, 6 May 1775. Address: 8 Albion Buildings. Second mark alone as smallworker, 20 August 1778, same address. Moved to 7 Westmorland Buildings, 15 December 1779. Third mark, 17 January 1788. Probably dead by 8 August 1794, when Elizabeth Morley's mark was entered. Heal records the partnership with Baskerville as plateworkers, Albion Buildings (Bartholomew Close), 1755-75, of which the first date seems very questionable; and Morley alone as goldsmith, Westmorland Buildings, 1790-3.

MORRIS, George (850-1) Son of Edward Morris of the parish of St. Martin in the Fields 'Colemerchant', apprenticed to Edward John Lambe 3 February 1743 and turned over 5 March 1746 to Thomas Gladwin. Free, 7 February 1750. First mark entered as largeworker, 18 May 1750. Address: Well Close Square. Moved to Foster Lane, 8 January 1751. Second mark, 12 June 1751. Heal records him as goldsmith and enameller, Well Close Square, 1750; and at the White Swan, Foster Lane, 1751-2.

MORRIS, Henry (1030-1, 1034-5, 2051, 3605-6) Son of Thomas Morris of Lutterworth in the County of Leicester baker, apprenticed to Thomas Moore 30 December 1710 on payment of £5 and turned over 30 August 1716 to William Howard in Gutter Lane and (?) John Johnson Bull and Mouth Street. Free, 4 September 1718. First mark entered as smallworker, 1 December 1718. Address: Foster Lane. Second (Sterling) mark, 24 June 1720. Address: Wood Street. Livery, July 1731. Third mark as largeworker, 3 July 1739. Address: Smithfield. 'Goldsmith'. Fourth mark on move to Fleet Street, 6 April 1744. Fifth, 5 September 1749. Heal records him as plateworker, Smithfield, 1739. His other two entries for Henry Morris, jeweller, goldsmith and toyman, Golden Key, Fleet Street, and Henry Morris & Son at the same address, appear to have no connection, nor the Henry Morris, goldsmith, Fleet Street, of the Parl. Report list 1773. Morris' mark is found almost entirely on salvers in which he seems to have specialized.

MORRISON, Richard (2365) Free by redemption as goldsmith 1 October 1760. First mark entered as smallworker, 18 October 1768. 'Goldsmith of St. Paul's Churchyard'. Second mark, 19 October 1768. Livery, December 1771. Appears as goldsmith, Cheapside, in the Parl. Report list 1773. The baptism of three daughters and son Stafford Briscoe (see below), between 1770 and 1778, is recorded at St. Vedast, Foster Lane. Heal records him as jeweller and goldsmith, St. Paul's Churchyard, 1768; and then as succeeding Stafford Briscoe at Three Kings and Golden Ball, No. 15 Cheapside, 1769-83; he previously records Briscoe and Morrison at the above address, 1763-72, and in 1781. It seems possible that the Churchyard address was a branch establishment although very close to the Cheapside shop opposite Foster Lane. Morrison died c. 1802-11. His son Stafford Briscoe (whose godfather it is not difficult to hazard) was made free by patrimony of the Goldsmiths' Company, 3 January 1798, described as gentleman. Liveryman, 1801; died 1845.

MORSE, Thomas (2053, 2834) Son of Thomas Morse late of Coxen(?) in the County of Berkshire gentleman deceased, apprenticed to Isaac Malyn 7 March 1711 on payment of £15 and turned over to Anthony Nelme 13 October 1714. Free, 17 April 1720. Mark entered as largeworker, 5 September 1718. Address: 'at the Spotted Dog', Lombard Street, where Heal records him as goldsmith, 1718-24 (also Hilton Price, *Handbook of London Bankers*). Thomas Gladwin (q.v.) was at the same address.

MORSON, James (1501, 2049) Son of James Morson of Whitechapel in the County of Middlesex cabinetmaker, apprenticed to William Keate 22 July 1708 and turned over to Joseph Smith. Free, 7 September 1715. First mark entered as largeworker, 17 October 1716. Address: Foster Lane. 'free Goldsmith'. Second (Sterling) mark, 20 June (?1720) Heal records him at Foster Lane, 1716-22.

*MORSON, Richard (2374) Son of Joseph Morson late of Westminster brewer deceased, apprenticed to Richard Gosling 16 September 1747 on payment of £84 (one of the largest premiums recorded). Free, 2 October 1754. First mark entered as smallworker, in partnership with Benjamin Stephenson, 27 October 1762. Address: Fleet Street. Second mark, 9 July 1763. Third mark 13 July (? 1763, year omitted). Moved to Ludgate Hill, 29 October 1771. Livery, December 1771. Appears with Stephenson as goldsmiths, Ludgate Hill, in the Parl. Report list 1773, there mentioned as having been prosecuted in 1770 for selling gold watchchains 'worse than standard'. He also gave evidence to the Committee of his difficulties in distinguishing between Sheffield plate and silver marks! Died between 1802 and 1811. Heal records the partnership above as goldsmiths, Golden Cup, (5) Ludgate Hill, 1760-74; also Corner of Bride Lane, 98 Fleet Street, 1760-72; and partnership dissolved 1774; after this Morson was alone, 98 Fleet Street, 1774; Ludgate Street, 1775; and 129 Ludgate Hill, 1777.

MORTIMER, H. W. (1090) No record of apprenticeship or freedom. Only mark entered as smallworker, 7 May 1798. Address: 89 Fleet Street.

MOSLEY, Richard (2371) Son of Robert Mosley of Fetter Lane jeweller (Section VII), apprenticed to David Ormond Devonshire of Old Street, St. Luke's as jeweller 1 May 1811. Free, 3 February 1819. First mark entered as goldworker, 21 February 1827. Address: 113 Fetter Lane, Holborn (his father's address) (Section VII). Second mark as smallworker, 11 February 1835. Address: 8 Hatton Garden. See also Charles and Richard Mosley, goldworkers (Section VII), who may be connected.

MOSS, Peter (2205) Son of William Moss late Citizen and Carman of London deceased, apprenticed to Hugh Spring 7 September 1721 on payment of £20 and turned over 9 January 1724 to John Mynell in the parish of St. Bride's, Salisbury Court Fleet Street watchcasemaker. Freedom unrecorded. Mark entered as smallworker, 12 August 1728. Address: Stone Cutter Street, Shoe Lane. Probably, to judge from his second master, a watchcasemaker.

MOTHERBY, John (2052) Son of William Motherby late of Wapping mariner deceased, apprenticed to Joseph Barbett (Barbut) on payment of £12. Free, 7 November 1717. Mark entered as largeworker, 22 February 1719. Address: Bull in Mouth Street, where Heal records him as plateworker, 1718.

MOTT, William (3237) No record of apprenticeship or freedom. Only mark entered as smallworker, 6 August 1802. Address: 16 York Place, Lambeth.

*MOULDON, Thomas (2836) Son of Thomas Mouldon late of Oxford farmer deceased, apprenticed to Dru Drury 6 May 1713 on payment of £5 (he signs Moulden, while the Clerk enters Moldhill) and turned over to John Taylor of Old Change watchcasemaker 4 November 1718. Free, 5 October 1721. Mark entered as smallworker, 8 February 1722. Address: Dolphin Court, Ludgate Hill. Heal records Thomas Moulden, goldsmith, Three Crowns, lower end of Cheapside 1733-9, presumably identical.

*MOULSON, William (1763, 2236) Son of Thomas Moulson of Hampton in the County of Middlesex carpenter, apprenticed to Thomas Gabriel of Banner Street Bunhill Row Citizen and Goldsmith as toolmaker 6 October 1793 on payment of £10 of the charity of the Trustees of the parish of Hampstead. Free, 4 November 1801. First mark entered as plateworker, in partnership with John Wrangham, 28 March 1822. Address: 52 Great Sutton Street, Clerkenwell. Second mark, in partnership with Paul Siddall and John Wrangham, 15 November 1823. Address: 7 White Hart Court, Castle Street, Leicester Square. Under the first entry is a note that that partnership moved to the above address, 24 January 1824.

MOULTON, Samuel (2592) Son of John Moulton of Chelsea in the County of Middlesex husbandman, apprenticed to Edward Cooke 11 January 1764 and turned over the same day to Samuel Cooke musician and on 25 February 1766 to William Harrison goldsmith. Free, 6 February 1771. First mark entered as smallworker, 30 March 1772. Address: 'at Mr Osborne 18 Little Britain', where he appears as bucklemaker in the Parl. Report list 1773. Second mark, 22 July 1774. Address: 210 Borough. Third mark, 1 June 1781. Fourth mark (incuse), 13 July 1781. Fifth mark (two sizes), 25 May 1782. Sixth, 10 December 1788. Heal records him as bucklemaker, Southwark, 1777; and 210 High Street, Borough, 1784-96, where he entered a mark as such, 28 September 1785 (Section VIII).

MOUNTFORD, John (1787) No record of apprenticeship or freedom. Only mark entered as smallworker, in partnership with John Brough, 17 October 1806. Address: 50 Aldersgate Street. The partnership apparently dissolved by 13 March 1807, when Brough entered a separate mark alone.

MOUNTFORT, Hezekiah (3739) Son of Ralph 'Monford' Citizen and Innholder of London, apprenticed to John Penkethman 20 November 1694 (when he signs 'Mumford'). Free, 16 March 1702. Livery, October 1708. His only mark in the register is an incuse one, 15 January 1712. Address: Red Lion Court, Fleet Street (Section V). The mark here attributed to him is, therefore, uncertain. He may have been a watchcasemaker.

MOUNTIGUE, Benjamin (191, 1999, 3490) No record of apprenticeship or freedom. First mark entered as smallworker, in the name of Mordecai (q.v.), 24 August 1770. Address: Clerkenwell Green. Second mark as Mountigue, 26 April 1771, same address. Third mark, 9 December 1771. Fourth, 20 June 1772, a unique example of reversed initials in a mark. Fifth, 25 July 1772. Sixth, 4 September 1772. Seventh, 26 February 1773. He appears as Mordecai, alias Mountigue, Benjamin, bucklemaker, Clerkenwell Green, in the Parl. Report list 1773, and entered seven marks as bucklemaker, from 1 October 1773 to 16 June 1784, at the same address (Section VIII). Heal records Benjamin Montague, goldsmith, 10 Clerkenwell Green, 1779-93; and Benjamin and J. J. Montague, Clerkenwell Green, 1788; as well as B.M. and Robert Pingston, at the same address, partnership dissolved 1788, but no mark is recorded for either of these combinations.

MOWDEN, David (486-7) Son of Joseph Mowden Citizen and Blacksmith of London, apprenticed to Edward Wood 13 February 1732 on payment of £15, of which £10 of the charity of Christ's Hospital London. Freedom unrecorded. First mark entered in largeworkers' book as saltmaker, 12 March 1739. Address: 'at the Crown & Seal next door to Coach makers' hall Noble street'. Second mark as smallworker, 26 October 1774. Address: 4 Addle Street. Although the lapse of thirty-five years between the two entries might normally suggest a son of the same name, the writing is similar except for a change of initial M. Heal records him as plateworker at the first address, 1738 only.

MULFORD, John (1509, 1970) No record of apprenticeship or freedom. First mark entered as smallworker, 14 November 1716. 'for Gold'. An unusual form of mark, being the initial M only crowned, perhaps regarded as a compromise for gold, being neither of the forms used for Sterling or New Standard silver. Address: Cursitors Alley, Chancery Lane. Second (Sterling) mark, 5 May 1725, same address.

MULLORD, Alexander (65) No record of apprenticeship or freedom. Only mark entered as smallworker, 6 February 1811. Address: 20 King Street, St. James's Street.

MUMFORD, Edward (615) Free of the Lorimers' Company and presumably a relative of Joseph Mumford (below). (This company's records were destroyed in 1940.) Only mark entered as smallworker, undated, between November 1721 and February 1722. Address: Leather Lane, Holborn. 'Free of Larremere'. An illiterate signature.

MUMFORD, Joseph (1502-3, 2076) Free of the Lorimers' Company (see above). Only mark entered as smallworker, 20 November 1711. Address: Field Lane. 'Free Lorrimer'. Second and third marks (Sterling), 27 July 1720, in same entry, presumably same address.

MUNDAY, John (1499, 1508, 2078-9) Son of Robert Munday, free by patrimony of the Merchant Taylors' Company 4 December 1695, described as goldsmith in Tooley Street. Mark entered as smallworker, undated, presumably April 1697 on commencement of register. Address: Whitechapel. 'Free Merchant Taylor' Second mark also undated, c. 1699. Address: 'St. folis' (St. Olave's, cf. Tooley, above) Street, Southwarke'. Apparently in Gracechurch Street 1708 (see Joseph Munday below) Third mark (Sterling), 2 August 1720. Address: 'Ould St'. Fourth mark, 27 November 1721. Address: Buckle Street, Whitechapel.

MUNDAY, Joseph (2080) 'Joseph Monday of Horsey Down Goldsmith made free by servitude to Robert Monday his Ma^r deceased on Rept. of John Monday in Gracechurch St. Goldsmith and Richard Gines in Lombard St, Silversmith', 2 June 1708 (Merchant Taylors' Company freedom list). Only mark entered as smallworker, 29 February 1716. Address: Horslydown in Southwark'. 'Free Merchant Taylor'.

MUNDAY, Robert (2077) Son of John Munday of Combe in the County of Wiltshire yeoman, apprenticed to John Crowder of Southwark of the Merchant Taylors' Company 1 January 1657. Free, 24 January 1665. Only mark entered as smallworker, undated, probably April 1697 on commencement of register. Address: 'St. Olive Street', Southwark. 'Free Merchant Taylor'. He was presumably dead by 2 June 1708, as noted in freedom entry of Joseph Munday (above).

MUNS, Elizabeth (619) No record of apprenticeship or freedom. Possibly widow of John Muns (below). Only mark entered as smallworker, 3 May 1768. Address: 3 Bull and Mouth Street, St. Martin's Le Grand.

MUNS, John (1518) Son of John Muns late of the parish of St. Ives in the County of Huntingdon butcher deceased, apprenticed to William Muns 6 March 1739. Free, 9 April 1746. First mark entered as largeworker, 27 March 1753. Address: Gold Street, Gutter Lane. Second mark, 20 August 1757. Heal records the first date and address and also London, 1776-7. He was however dead before 3 July 1776, when his son Thomas was apprenticed to Thomas Shepherd, and even possibly by 3 May 1768, if Elizabeth Muns (above) be his widow.

MURRAY, James (1540, 1863) No record of apprenticeship or freedom. Two marks entered as largeworker, in partnership with Charles Kandler I (q.v.), Sterling and New Standard, 29 August 1727. Address: St. Martin's Lane.

MYATT, John (1530) No record of apprenticeship or freedom. First mark entered as bucklemaker, 21 April 1775. Address: 10 Little Wild Street, Clare Market. Second mark as same, in partnership with John Monsell, 29 January 1780. Address: 26 Queen Street, Seven Dials. Third mark alone, at same address, 10 July 1783 (all Section VIII). Fourth mark entered as smallworker, 21 June 1799. Address: 44 Little Sutton Street, Clerkenwell.

N

NANGLE, George (858, 3244) No record of apprenticeship or freedom. First mark entered as smallworker, 30 October 1797. Address: 13 Albemarle Street, Clerkenwell. Second mark, in partnership with William and Martin Nangle as spoonmakers, 14 September 1816. Address: 32 Northampton Square. Third mark alone, 2 March 1818. Address: 25 Wilderness Row. Moved to 6 Powell Street, Goswell Street, 10 September 1819.

NANGLE, Martin (3244) No record of apprenticeship or freedom. Only mark as spoonmaker, in partnership with George and William Nangle, 14 September 1816. Address: 32 Northampton Square.

NANGLE, William (3244) No record of apprenticeship or freedom. Only mark as spoonmaker, in partnership with George and Martin Nangle (above).

NARCISSE, Desiré (491) No record of apprenticeship or freedom. First mark entered as plateworker, 9 September 1824. Address: 28 William Street, Hampstead Road; Second mark, 26 April 1825. Moved to 9 Esher Street, Westminster, 11 March 1831. Moved to 59 Regent Street, Vincent Square, 28 July 1834. Third mark (very small, ?for gold), 16 September 1842.

NASH, Bowles (195, 2083) Son of Thomas Nash late of Clint(?) in the County of Stafford gentleman deceased, apprenticed to Gabriel Sleath 25 March 1713 on payment of £30. Free, 2 March 1720. First mark entered as largeworker, 7 March 1721. Address: Round Court, St. Martin's Le Grand. Second (Sterling) mark, 7 June 1721. Heal records him as plateworker, St. Martin's Le Grand, 1720-4.

*NASH, Gawen (853-4, 859, 2084) Son of Gawen Nash late of Norwich clerk deceased, apprenticed to Thomas Merry (q.v.) 16 June 1713 on payment of £28. Free, 4 June 1724. First mark entered as smallworker, 1 July 1724. Address: Gutter Lane. 'Goldsmith'. Second mark (New Standard) as largeworker, 7 January 1726. Third mark (Sterling) 23 November 1726. Address: Wood Street. Fourth mark, 27 June 1739. Address: Carey Lane. Appears as Free 'de novo', 5 August 1742; possibly an indication that he had been expelled from the Company for some misdemeanour and later readmitted. Heal records him as plateworker, Wood Street, 1726; and Carey Lane, 1739. William-Henry, son of Gawen Nash 'from St. Martin in the Fields', was buried at St. Paul's Covent Garden, 3 March 1755, and Gawen, son of the same, was buried at the same church, 27 January 1758, presumably sons of the above. Dead by 9 December 1763 when the Court had to elect a Junior Weigher in the Assay Office in his place which he had held for several years with the following amusing comment 'it was observed that the said Gawen Nash did for sev[1] years next before his death keep a coffee house in Gutter Lane and it was alledged that it was highly inconvenient to suffer the Junior Weigher to keep a coffee house or other public house'. The Court then passed a motion forbidding any repetition of this occurrence by Nash's successors.

*NASH, Robert (2381) No record of apprenticeship or freedom. First mark entered as smallworker, 9 April 1782. Address: 2 Hanover Street, Hanover Square. Second mark, 16 November 1789. Third, 24 December 1798. Address: 3 New Street, Brompton Road. Fourth, 25 January 1799. Fifth, 5 September 1800. Moved to 1 Richmond Buildings, Soho, 27 July 1801. Heal records him as goldsmith, 20 Hanover Square, 1790-3.

*NASH, Thomas I (2852, 2860, 3846) No record of apprenticeship or freedom. First mark (incuse) entered 29 September 1759. Address: Bull and Mouth Street (Section V). Second mark as smallworker, 22 November 1759. Address: Noble Street. Moved to Fletcher's Court, Noble Street, 31 October 1761. Third mark, 14 January 1767. Address: Dalston. Fourth mark (incuse), 5 February 1767. Moved to Wood Street, 25 September 1767. Moved to Noble Street, 23 January 1768. Fifth mark, 1 March 1770. Appears as bucklemaker, Dalston, near Hackney, in the Parl. Report list 1773. Sixth and seventh marks as such, 15 October 1773. Address: 2 Water Lane, Fleet Street. Eighth mark, 3 June 1776, same address (Section VIII). Appears at this last address as bankrupt, September 1782 (*The Gentleman's Magazine*, p. 456).

NASH, Thomas II (2856) No record of apprenticeship or freedom. Perhaps identical with the preceding. Only mark entered as smallworker, 13 April 1786. Address: 6 Paul's Court, Huggin Lane. Moved to 1 Old Jury, 15 October 1789.

*NATTER, George (855-7) Son of Lawrence Natter late of Brewer Street near Golden Square in the County of Middlesex jeweller deceased, apprenticed to Charles Wright of Paternoster Row Goldsmith on payment of £40. Free, 7 April 1773, as plateworker. Three marks entered as plateworker, 23 October 1773. Address: 185 Fleet Street. His name also appears in the register in partnership with Cornelius Bland (q.v.) at the above address, 2 August 1773, but without the impression of any mark and the note against Bland's name: 'Out of Trade'. Heal records Natter as George Sigismund Natter, plateworker, Fleet Street, 1773-8, and he appears as bankrupt, 1774 (*The Gentleman's Magazine*, p. 47).

NEAL, William (3243) No record of apprenticeship or freedom. First mark entered as plateworker, 23 May 1829. Address: 43 Fetter Lane. Moved to Clerkenwell Close, 5 July 1837. Second mark, 11 September 1845. Moved to 31 Rosoman Street, Clerkenwell, 3 January 1851. Third mark, 4 June 1858. Fourth, 18 April 1860, defaced 14 March 1864, presumably on retirement.

NEALE, Charles (367, 490) Son of Ralph Neale of Hunsdown in the County of Hertford gentleman Citizen and Baker of London, apprenticed to Richard Wade of Bull and Mouth Street Citizen and Goldsmith as silver turner 2 November 1768 on payment of £15 and turned over by consent of Anne Wade widow 7 April 1773 to William Abdy. Free, 6 March 1776. First mark entered as smallworker, in partnership with Daniel May I, 22 March 1783. Address: 6 Air Street, Hoxton Town. Second mark, 13 May 1783, same address. The partnership was presumably dissolved by 12 January 1784 when May entered a separate mark. Heal records him as Charles Neale, silver turner (cf. his apprenticeship above), Wenlock Street, City Road, 1782.

*NEALE, Jacob (1546) No record of apprenticeship or freedom. First mark entered as smallworker, 25 August 1731. Address: Gun Street, Spitalfields. His writing is so illiterate that a near contemporary hand has rewritten his name and address at the base of the entry. Heal has, in unpublished addenda, Jacob Neale, senior, goldsmith, Crown and Tortoise, corner of Gun Street, Old Artillery Ground, 1723. The mark was identified on a finely chased gold snuffbox, Christie's 1967.

NEATE, John Thomas (1725) No record of apprenticeship or freedom. Only mark entered as smallworker, 21 April 1837. Address: 40 Duke Street, Manchester Square.

*NELME, Anthony (68-9, 3741) Son of John Nelme of the parish of Muchmerkle in the County of Hereford yeoman, apprenticed to Richard Rowley 1 November 1672 'from Christmas next' and later turned over to Isaac D(e)ighton. Free, 16 January 1679/

?80. His first mark, pre-1697, has long been recognized from its resemblance to the two entered undated, presumably April 1697 on commencement of register. Address: Avie Mary Lane. One of the petitioners against the work of 'aliens and foreigners', 11 August 1697. Elected Assistant to Court of the Goldsmiths 1703, and Warden 1717 and 1722. Died before 18 February 1723, the date of the granting of the administration of his goods to his widow Esther. He was married before 1683 and numerous entries for the baptism of his family at Christchurch, Newgate (incorporating St. Leonard's, Foster Lane) begin with twin sons of Anthony and Hester Nelme, Richard and John, 3 August 1683, followed by Charles 1684, Hester (entered as son, presumably in error) 1686, John 1688, Elizabeth 1690, Charles 1691 and William 1692. Heal records Nelme as goldsmith, Golden Bottle, Amen Corner, Ave Mary Lane, 1685 till death; and Foster Lane, 1691; also—Nelme, goldsmith, Golden Hart, Bishopsgate Street, 1693. There were however two other apprentices of the name to the company: (1) Charles son of John Nelme of the parish of Michaell (?Jeane, George) in the County of Gloucester shoemaker, apprenticed to Thomas Brome 6 March 1657; and (2) Jonathan son of William of Newent in the County of Gloucester, apprenticed to Anthony Nelme (senior) 7 September 1687. Nelme's surviving work shows him to have developed one of the biggest establishments by the end of the century, with considerable output of municipal pieces such as maces, as well as toilet-services and other large pieces. His work shows some effect of the Huguenot influence and it would seem probable that he had immigrant journeymen working for him, or purchased and overstruck their productions.

*NELME, Francis (67, 702) Son of Anthony Nelme (above) Citizen and Goldsmith of London, apprenticed to his father 6 March 1712. Free, 9 April 1719. Livery, October 1721. First mark entered below his father's undated large mark with the note 'Francis Nelme the same marks March 20: 1723'. Second mark, 19 June 1739. Address: Ave Mary Lane. Heal records him at the Golden Bottle, Ave Mary Lane, 1721; London, 1722-7; St. Martin's, Ludgate, 1736; and London, 1739-59. From the nature of pieces on which his mark survives, Francis Nelme does not appear to have retained the more important clients for whom his father worked, nor has his mark survived with the same frequency.

NELSON, John (1543) Possibly son of Thomas Nelson of St. Tooley (St. Olave's) Southwark gentleman, apprenticed to Benjamin Brewood 13 October 1713 on payment of £10. Free, 8 November 1726. Mark entered as smallworker, 4 January 1721. Address: 'ye Corner of Gray fryers in Newgate Street'.

*NEVILLE, John (24, 1554) No record of apprenticeship or freedom. First mark entered as largeworker, in partnership with Ann Craig (q.v.), 15 October 1740. Address: Corner of Norris Street, St. James', Haymarket. Second (small) mark, 27 May 1743. Third mark alone, 10 April 1745, presumably on Ann Craig's death or retirement. He appears as Mr. Neville, silversmith, near St. James's Markets in Norris Street, in the Fitzwalter Accounts (Essex County Archives), and Heal records him as plateworker, Hand and Ring, Norris Street, 1743-52; and as London, 1770(?). Bankrupt in January 1753 (*The Gentleman's Magazine*). When in partnership with Ann Craig, the quality of craftmanship and design in the rococo taste is of a high standard, although their mark is rare to find.

NEWBY, Thomas (2857) Son of George Newby of Foster Lane silversmith, apprenticed to Samuel Hennell of Foster Lane goldsmith 1803 and turned over to Robert Woolcomb of Pentonville silversmith, Citizen and Goldsmith 7 January 1807. Free, 7 February 1810. Mark entered as plateworker, 11 November 1816. Address: 26 New Union Street, Little Moorfields. Moved to 4 Angel Place, Grub Street, 28 March 1821.

NEWCOMB, Thomas (2851) Son of Thomas Newcomb of Newport Pagnell in the County of Buckingham shoemaker, apprenticed to David Hennell (himself also from the same place, perhaps related) 7 March 1750. Free, 7 March 1759. Mark entered as smallworker, 21 July 1760. Address: Cox's Court, Aldersgate Street: Joseph Newcomb goldworker (Section VII), may be a son, apparently succeeded by a further Joseph and William.

NEWMAN, Robert (2089, 2377) Apprenticed to Thomas Gandy of the Merchant Taylors' Company goldbeater in the Old Bailey and free of that company 1 February

1698. Mark entered as smallworker, 14 March 1720. Address: Cock Lane, near the Conduit on Snow Hill. 'Citizen and Merchant Taylor'. Second (Sterling) mark, 5 April 1721. Heal records the name as gold chainmaker, at the same address, c. 1760, which seems too late for the above but might of course be a son.

NEWTON, John (1544, 1553) Son of Peter Newton Citizen and Cordwainer of London, apprenticed to John Farnell 5 February 1719. Free, 31 March 1726. Mark entered as largeworker, 4 April 1726. Address: Staining Lane. 'Goldsmith'. Livery, March 1737. Second mark, 21 June 1739. Address: Maiden Lane, Wood Street. Heal records him as plateworker, Lombard Street, 1720 (but this is obviously a confusion with Jonathan Newton, below); also Maiden Lane, 1739-42; and goldsmith, Blackamoor's Head, within Aldgate, 1748-53, which seems probably a separate identity. Second in a line of three specialist teacaddy makers, from John Farnell his master to Samuel Taylor (q.v.), apprenticed to him in 1736.

NEWTON, Jonathan (1542, 2087-8, 3741) Son of Thomas Newton late of the City of Worcester gentleman deceased, apprenticed to William Gibson 5 October 1702. Free, 5 October 1711. First mark entered as largeworker, 17 October 1711. Address: Lad Lane, Lombard Street. Second mark, 1 May 1718. Address: Lombard Street. Third (Sterling) mark, 6 August 1720. Livery, December 1717. Heal records him as above in Lad Lane; and Anchor and Crown, Lombard Street, 1718-40; also, in partnership with Thomas Cole, at the latter address, 1744-5; and Cole and Newton, ? goldsmiths, Lombard Street, 1753-5. Hilton Price (*Handbook of London Bankers*) records the following from the *Daily Post*, 4 May 1732, under Newton's name: 'Lost 6 silver spoons. Five shillings will be paid for each spoon, if brought to his shop, provided the person who stole them is secured'.

NICHOL, Samuel (2596) Son of Thomas Nichol late of Barking in the County of Essex tanner deceased, apprenticed to Samuel Edlin 12 May 1714 on payment of £25. Free, 22 November 1722. Mark entered as smallworker, 23 March 1724. Address: 'lodging at Mr. Arnets at the blackamoors head in forster Lane'. 'Free of the Goldsmiths Company'. Livery, 1737. Court, 1741. Heal records him as Samuel Nicholl, goldsmith, within Aldgate, 1742-4; and Nicholl and Abdy, same address, 1753.

NICHOLL, Michael (2097) Son of Thomas Nicholl late of Bushey in the County of Hertford yeoman deceased, apprenticed to Benjamin Bentley 16 April 1714 on payment of £30. Free, 16 September 1723. Mark entered as largeworker, 16 November 1723. Address: Staining Lane. Heal records this address and date.

NICHOLLE, Christopher (366, 2096) Free of the Joyners' Company by an order of the Lord Mayor and Court of Alderman 11 November 1718. First mark entered as smallworker, 3 July 1719. Address: 'in Barbican'. 'free ioyner'. Second (Sterling) mark, 15 September 1720.

NICHOLLS, Robert (2380) Son of Henry Nicholls of Richmond in the County of York gentleman, apprenticed to Robert Groome silver turner of St. Martin's Le Grand Citizen and Goldsmith 14 January 1767 on payment of £30. Freedom unrecorded. Only mark entered as smallworker, 18 February 1772. Address: 'at Mr. Schuppe' (John Schuppe, q.v.), 9 New Rents, St. Martin's Le Grand. Moved to Christopher Court, St. Martin's Le Grand, 19 June 1772, where he appears as smallworker in the Parl. Report list 1773.

NICHOLLS, Thomas (2859) No record of apprenticeship or freedom. Only mark entered as plateworker, 10 August 1824. Address: 3 Fleur-de-lis Street, Norton Folgate.

NICHOLS, John (1552) No record of apprenticeship or freedom. Only mark entered as plateworker, 30 November 1825. Address: 6 Dukes Court, St. Martin's Lane. Moved to 40 Castle Street, Leicester Square, 9 June 1830.

NICHOLSON, Henry (1039) No record of apprenticeship or freedom. Only mark entered as smallworker, 29 March 1833. Address: 11 New Compton Street, Soho. Moved to 23 Chapel Place, Little Coram Street, 11 March 1835. Henry Howard Nicholson (Section VI) may be connected.

NICKLIN, John (1549) No record of apprenticeship or freedom. Only mark entered as smallworker, 25 January 1760. Address: Great Smithfield, near the Hermitage Bridge. Moved to the Curtain, near Holywell Mount, 22 July 1760, where he appears without category in the Parl. Report list 1773.

NICKOLDS, John (1551, 1556) No record of apprenticeship or freedom. First mark entered as smallworker, in partnership with (?) R. A. Roberts, 27 September 1808. Address: 3 Buckingham Place, Fitzroy Square. Second mark, in partnership with Samuel Roberts, 22 November 1813, same address. Moved to 5 Conway Street, Fitzroy Square, 16 January 1815. Third mark alone, 21 September 1818. Address: 5 Upper Conway Street. Although the name of his first partner is entered as R. A. Roberts and the entry signed thus, the mark struck against the entry is IN over SR as for the second entry. Henry Nickold, son of John, was apprenticed to George Angell as silversmith 1844.

NICKOLDS, William (3242) No record of apprenticeship or freedom. Presumably a son of John Nickolds (above). First mark entered as plateworker, 2 May 1827. Address: 5 Upper Conway Street. Moved to 3 Buckingham Place, Fitzroy Square, 27 July 1839.

NICOLSON, James (1548) No record of apprenticeship or freedom. Only mark entered as smallworker, 23 July 1735. Address: Hosier Lane, near West Smithfield, 'over against the Wheatsheaf'.

NIGHTINGALE, Richard (2095, 3745) Described in his entry as Free Founder but does not appear in the existing list of freemen of that company commencing 1681, so presumably dates from earlier. Mark entered as largeworker, undated, probably April 1697 on commencement of register. Address: Shoe Lane. 'Free Founder'. Heal records him at this address, 1697–1701.

NIXON, Michael (2046) No record of apprenticeship or freedom. First mark entered as spoonmaker, 31 March 1832. Address: 35 Broad Street, St. George's East. Second mark, 3 April 1832.

NIXON, William (3241) No record of apprenticeship or freedom. First mark entered as spoonmaker, 11 June 1817. Address: 5 Norway Street, St. Luke's. He signs with a large straggling cross. Second mark, 6 October 1817. Moved to 11 Back Church Lane, Whitechapel, 7 July 1821. Third mark, 12 October 1821.

NOAD, Stephen (2597) No record of apprenticeship or freedom. First mark entered as smallworker, 30 June 1806. Address: 5 Gunpowder Alley, Shoe Lane. Moved to 23 Charles Street, Hatton Garden, 8 October 1806. Second mark, 6 February 1835.

*NORMAN, Philip (3750) No record of apprenticeship or freedom. No entry in register. His name appears only in the Parl. Report list 1773 as plateworker, St. Martin's Lane. In the absence of any other name matching the initials of the mark attributed to him there can be little doubt as to its correctness.

NORMAN, Richard (2378–9) Son of James Norman late Citizen and Tobacconist of London deceased, apprenticed to William Dorrell 16 January 1745 on payment of £7. 10s. from Mr. Edward Deermer's Charity given by the parish of St. Gile's, Cripplegate. Free, 7 December 1757. First mark entered as smallworker, undated, after another of 21 July 1760. Address: Jerusalem Court, St. John's Square. Second mark, 31 August 1764, same address. He appears as buttonmaker here in the Parl. Report list 1773. Heal records him as silversmith, Jerusalem Court (Gracechurch Street), the latter amplification apparently in error, 1766; and Sutton Street, 1776.

NORRIS, John (1547) Two identities are possible: (1) son of Duncombe Norris late Citizen and Waxchandler of London deceased, apprenticed to Edward Blagrave 27 September 1698. Free 8 February 1712. Or (2) son of the John Norris of (1) above, apprenticed to his father 7 September 1732 on payment of £6 of the charity of Christ's Hospital. Free, 6 December 1739. The first seems more likely in view of the date of entry of the only mark as smallworker, 13 February 1735. Address: King's Head Court, Gutter Lane.

NORRIS, Thomas (2099) No record of apprenticeship or freedom. Only mark entered as smallworker, 18 June 1725. Address: Long Acre.

NORTH, Benjamin (196) No record of apprenticeship or freedom. Only mark entered as hiltmaker, 15 February 1783. Address: New Whay, St. Thomas's, Southwark. Presumably a descendant of Thomas North (below).

NORTH, Thomas (2850) Freeman of the Cutlers' Company after apprenticeship to George Wilcox (see Willcocks), 3 April 1724. Mark entered as smallworker, 4 May 1724. Address: Dean Street, Fetter Lane. 'Free Cutler'.

NORTHCOTE, Hannah (1038) Daughter of Simeon Coley (q.v.), bucklemaker, born about 1761. Married Thomas Northcote at St. Dunstan-in-the-West, 12 January 1788. First mark entered after her husband's death, 6 June 1798. Address: Barkley Street, Clerkenwell. Second mark, 3 December 1799. Moved to 9 Cross Street, Hatton Garden, 4 March 1800. Heal records her only as goldsmith, London, 1798. She died 9 September 1831 aged seventy, and was buried in Bunhill Fields, where there is a monument to her (information, Mr. Brian G. C. Brooks).

NORTHCOTE, Thomas (2853-5, 2861) Son of Richard Northcote of Well Close Square in the County of Middlesex cooper, apprenticed to Charles Hutton 23 June 1766 and turned over 'having served his indenture' to Thomas Chawner of Red Lyon Street Clerkenwell. Free, 3 July 1771. First mark entered as spoonmaker, 20 August 1776. Address: Shoemaker's Row, Blackfriars. Second mark, 29 October 1777. Third, 27 April 1779. Moved to Berkley Street, St. John's Gate, 13 January 1781. Livery, March 1781. Fourth mark, 16 May 1782. Fifth, 19 November 1784. Sixth, 27 November 1784. Seventh, 4 December 1786. Eighth, 5 March 1789. Ninth, 19 August 1789. Tenth, 10 July 1792. Eleventh, in partnership with George Bourne as plateworkers, 5 June 1794. Twelfth mark alone, 11 July 1797. 'Mr. Northcote Goldsmith Berkley St. Clerkenwell (married) to Miss Cowley of Fetter Lane 12 Jan. 1788' (*The Gentleman's Magazine*, p. 81). She was in fact Hannah Coley, daughter of Simeon Coley senior (q.v.), bucklemaker. Northcote died 22 May 1798, aged forty-nine and was buried at Bunhill Fields, his widow entering her mark in continuance of the business, 6 June following.

NORTZELL, Thomas (2858, 2862) Son of Jacob Nortzell of Mile End in County of Middlesex gentleman, apprenticed to John Berenger (q.v.) of Great New Street, Fetter Lane buttonmaker and hardwareman as metal buttonmaker 7 May 1792. Free, 7 August 1799. First mark entered as smallworker, 11 February 1817. Address: 24 Great New Street, Fetter Lane, having presumably succeeded to the business of his master Berenger. Second mark, in partnership with Henry Broughton, 29 December 1827. Address: 21 Bouverie Street, Fleet Street. His son Thomas Henry was apprenticed to him as buttonmaker and hardwareman, 1821.

*NORWOOD, Joseph (1545) Calls himself 'Stacinor' in signing his entry but untraceable in the freedom lists of the Stationer's Company. Only mark entered as smallworker, undated, between July 1728 and August 1731. Address: 'Stacinor at Green Bank Waping next doore to ye Green man'.

NUTTING, Henry (1036-7, 1040) Son of William Nutting late of Wormley in the County of Hertford maltster deceased, apprenticed to Charles Wright of Ave Maria Lane London Citizen and Goldsmith 3 July 1782 on payment of £50. Turned over to Thomas Chawner of Ave Maria Lane Goldsmith 4 February 1784. Free, 6 January 1790. First mark entered as plateworker, 9 April 1796. Address: 38 Noble Street, Foster Lane. Second mark, in partnership with Robert Hennell II (q.v.), 17 June 1808, same address. Third mark alone, 3 October 1809, same address. His son Henry was apprenticed to him 3 August 1808. The latter, rather than his father is presumably the Henry Nutting of Potters Bar Middlesex gentleman whose son John William was apprenticed, 5 October 1825, to William Simms mathematical instrument maker.

NUTTING, John George (1350, 1555) Son of Joseph Nutting (below) of King Street, Covent Garden buttonmaker apprenticed as buttonmaker to Edward Mason of Hop Gardens St. Martin's Lane buttonmaker 2 October 1793. Free, 6 January, 1801. Livery, January 1807. First mark entered as smallworker, in partnership with Joseph Nutting (below), 18 March 1803. Address: 16 King Street, Covent Garden. Second mark as plateworker, 30 March 1831. Address: Regent Street, Vincent Square. Note below: 'This mark defaced B. Preston May 24 1833', presumably on Nutting's retirement. He died April 1864.

NUTTING, Joseph (1550, 1555) No record of apprenticeship or freedom. First mark entered as smallworker, 12 February 1790. Address: 16 King Street, Covent Garden. Described as buttonmaker in apprenticeship of his son Joseph (above) October 1793. Second mark, in partnership with John George Nutting his son (above), 18 March 1803, same address.

O

OBENHAUS, Friderich (705) No record of apprenticeship or freedom. Only mark entered as smallworker, 17 July 1776. Address: Dean Court, near New Round Court, Strand.

OLDFIELD, Elizabeth (628) Apparently the widow of Charles Jackson, who entered a mark as Elizabeth Jackson (q.v.) 1748. Her mark EO entered as largeworker, 19 December 1750, below her previous entry without explanation. Address: Paternoster Row, as when Elizabeth Jackson. Second mark, 5 September 1754. Heal records her under both names as plateworker, Paternoster Row, 1748.

OLIVER, Joseph (1568) Perhaps Joseph Watkins Oliver son of Joseph of Bridgwater Gardens goldworker, apprenticed to John Barlow of Peartree Street as jeweller 1 October, 1802 and turned over to Francis Mills jeweller and weaver. Mark entered as smallworker, 23 March 1822. Address: 8 John Street, Curtain Road, Shoreditch. Moved to 53 Allerton Street, Hoxton New Town, 25 October. 1838.

OLIVEYRA See DE OLIVEYRA

ORME, John I (1565) No record of apprenticeship or freedom. Only mark entered as smallworker, 20 September. 1734. Address: Saffron Hill, near St. . .(?). Heal records John Orme, silversmith, Hand and Spur, Denmark Court, Strand, 1743; and Hand and Spur, Exeter Street, Strand, 1744.

ORME, John II (1566) No record of apprenticeship or freedom. Only mark entered as smallworker, 2 April 1796. Address: 68 Wood Street, Cheapside. Moved to 4 Coades Row, Bridge Road, Lambeth, 7 September 1798.

ORME, Thomas and William (3249) No record of apprenticeship or freedom of either. Only mark entered as smallworkers, in partnership, 21 April 1784. Address: Great Distaff Lane, Old Change. Moved to 43 Noble Street, Foster Lane, 2 March 1786.

OSBORN, John (1567) John Osborne son of John of Steyning Lane goldsmith, apprenticed to Joseph Scammell of Noble Street as goldsmith 6 January 1790 on payment of £7. 14s. and turned over to Henry Nutting 4 May 1796. Free, 3 May 1797. Mark entered as smallworker, 3 May 1797. Address: 4 Staining Lane. Moved to 16 King's Head Court, Shoe Lane, 4 January 1798 (entered as 1797, but obviously in error). Two incuse marks as watchcasemaker, 1801 and 1804. Address: 31 Primrose Street, Bishopsgate (Section V).

OSBORNE, Thomas (2109) No record of apprenticeship or freedom. Only mark entered as smallworker, 18 March 1699. Address: Tower Hill.

OTTON, Thomas Moriah (2867) Son of Thomas Otton of Park Street Islington gentleman, apprenticed to Thomas Worsley Bickerton of Jewin Street as silversmith 5 October 1808. Freedom unrecorded. Mark entered as plateworker, 4 June 1823. Address: 31 Clerkenwell Green.

*OURRY, Lewis (1954) Son of Lewis Ourry of the Isle of Jersey gentleman, apprenticed to Augustine Courtauld 5 March 1731 on payment of £15. Free, 4 September 1740. Mark entered as largeworker, 21 August 1740. Address: New Street, near Covent Garden. Heal records him as Lewis Ouvry or Ourry, plateworker, Golden Crown, New Street, Covent Garden, 1740-2. Listed by Evans as Huguenot (*Hug. Soc. Proc.*, 14, p. 54). His work is extremely rare, if indeed any has survived.

OVERING, Charles (2110) Son of Thomas Overing late of the town and County of Leicester ironmonger, apprenticed to John Crittall 13 October 1680. Free, 8 June 1692. Mark entered as largeworker, undated, probably April 1697 on commencement of register. Address: Carey Lane, where Heal records him till 1706. Thomas, son of Charles Overing and Elizabeth his wife, was born 15, baptized 25 September 1692 at St. Vedast, Foster Lane. His son John (below) was turned over to him 22 February 1717. The marriage of Mr. Charles Qvering of St. John Zachary and Mrs. Elizabeth Ludlam of St. Dunstan, Stepney, at St. Michael, Bassishaw, 4 August 1714, presumably refers to a second marriage of the same. Overing is recorded as 'Assistant in Firing' at the Assay Office in 1718, and his son Thomas as 'Drawer'.

OVERING, John (1562, 2111, 3666) Son of Charles Overing above Citizen and Goldsmith, apprenticed to John East 7 September 1715 on payment of £10 and turned over to his father 22 February 1717. Freedom unrecorded. First mark entered as largeworker, 6 January 1725. Address: Noble Street. Second (Sterling) mark, 20 February 1725. 'Free Gold smith'.

OVERTON, William (2113, 3245) Son of Henry Overton late Citizen and Stationer of London deceased, apprenticed to Richard Gines (q.v.) of the Merchant Taylors' Company 8 May 1706. Free, 7 July 1714. Mark entered as smallworker, 17 February 1716. Address: Ball Alley, in Lombard Street. 'Free Merchant Taylor'. Second (Sterling) mark, 22 June 1720.

OWEN, Mary (2055) Widow of William Owen (below). Mark entered as smallworker, 17 January 1739. Address: Cheapside. 'Widow'. Heal records her as Mrs. Mary Owen, goldsmith, Wheatsheaf, Upper end of Cheapside, 1745.

OWEN, William (2112, 3247) Son of Robert Owen of Walton-on-Thames 'armig', apprenticed to William Lane of the Fishmongers' Company 7 February 1705 and turned over to Joseph Stoakes (see Stokes). Free, 2 March 1716. Mark entered as smallworker, 12 March 1716. Address: White Hart Court, Lombard Street. 'Free of the Fishmongers'. Second (Sterling) mark, as largeworker, and the same mark in smallworkers' book, both 14 March 1724. 'free of the Fishmongers'. Address: Cheapside. Heal records him as goldsmith, Wheatsheaf, Cheapside, 1720–3; and Cheapside, 1737–40. Also listed by Hilton Price (*Handbook of London Bankers*). Dead by 17 January 1739 when his widow Mary (above) entered her mark.

OYLES, Phillip (2114) Son of George Oyles of Watford in the County of Hertford butcher, apprenticed to Samuel Hawkes 30 May 1692. Free, 6 October 1699. Mark entered as largeworker, 9 October 1699. Address: Cheapside. Philip Oyles Junr. son of Thomas Oyles of Stepney mercer, apprenticed to him 4 October 1727 was presumably a nephew. The latter does not seem to have entered a mark.

P

PACK, Nathaniel (2100) Son of Thomas Pack Citizen and Cutler of London, apprenticed to John Luffe 7 October 1724 on payment of £10 and turned over to his father 5 June 1731. Free, 5 June 1733. Mark entered as smallworker, 24 March 1732. Address: Flower de Luce Court', Fleet Street. He appears without category at Godliman Street, Doctors' Commons, in the Parl. Report list 1773. See also Isaac Pack, incuse mark PA (Section V).

PACKWOOD, John (1580) Son of George Packwood of Bromley in the County of Kent gardener, apprenticed to John Eaton 8 June 1757. Freedom unrecorded. Mark entered as smallworker, 26 October 1764. Address: Goswell Street, St. Luke's, where he appears without category in the Parl. Report list 1773.

PADMORE, George (869) No record of apprenticeship or freedom. Only mark entered as smallworker, 19 December 1764. Address: 'Thrift' Street, Soho. He appears as bucklemaker, Frith Street, Soho, in the Parl. Report list 1773, and Heal records him as goldsmith, 29 Frith Street, Soho, 1774. He was probably dead by 29 August 1774, when Eliza Padmore entered mark as bucklemaker at 19 Frith Street (Section VIII).

PAGE, Be(njamin) (2123) Free of the Grocers' Company after service to John Laughton 1660. (The apprentice lists do not survive from this period.) Mark entered as smallworker, undated, c. 1700. Address: Little Moorfields. 'Free Grocer'. Heal records him as goldsmith, Half Moon Alley, Little Moorfields, 1688–96.

PAGE, John (1593) No record of apprenticeship or freedom. Only mark entered as plateworker, 8 January 1813. Address: 4(?) Horseshoe Court, Ludgate Hill. Heal records John Page, jeweller, 8 Hind Court, Fleet Street, 1790–3, who may be connected.

PAGE, Thomas (2126, 2869) Son of John

Page of St. Andrew's Holborn barber surgeon, apprenticed to Gundry Rood 4 May 1711 on payment of £10 and turned over to John Brown in Wood Street Paul's Court 4 October 1716. Free, 8 September 1718. Mark entered as smallworker, 6 January 1719. Address: Foster Lane. Second (Sterling) mark, 12 August 1720. Address: Noble Street.

*PAGES, Francis (707, 710) Son of Solomon Pages of Farnborough(?) in the County of Somerset clerk, apprenticed to David Williams (Willaume) 6 November 1718 on payment of £30. Free, 8 January 1733. First mark entered as largeworker, 1729 (day and month missing). Address: Orange Street, Red Lion Square. Second mark, 18 June 1739. 'Gold Smith'. Same address. Livery, April 1737. Heal records him as plateworker, Golden Cup, Orange Street near Red Lion Square, 1729-39. From his surviving pieces he appears to have been a good if uninspired maker of standard forms.

PAILLET, Mark (2122) The name also spelt Pallyet or Palliett. Appears in Denization List, 25 March 1688 (*Hug. Soc. Pub.*, 18). Son of Daniel Paillet late of St. Martin's in the Fields in the County of Middlesex gentleman deceased, apprenticed to Thomas Symonds 1 August 1688. Free, 10 January 1695/?6. Mark entered as largeworker, undated, between 22 April and 21 October 1698. Address: Hemings Row, near St. Martin's Lane. Heal records him here as plateworker, 1698; and London, 1700-14. His earlier date for him as of London, 1687, in view of the apprenticeship entry, must be an error. Listed by Evans as Huguenot (*Hug. Soc. Proc.*, 14, p. 54) where it is stated that Daniel Paillet, the father was endenizened in 1687 and that a Pierre Paillet in the Bounty List for 1722-7 is said to have come from Saintonge.

PALMER, Job (1579) No record of apprenticeship or freedom. Only mark entered as smallworker, 3 August 1763. Address: 3 Coppis (Coppice) Row, Cold Bath Fields, where he appears without category in the Parl. Report list 1773. For a watchcasemaker of the same name and another, John Palmer, presumably a son, see Section VI.

*PALMER, R(?ichard) (2406) No record of apprenticeship or freedom. First mark entered incuse, as smallworker, 2 January 1759. Address: Cowcross. Second mark (cameo), 25 June 1759. Third mark, 27 May 1763. Moved to Red Lyon Street, Clerkenwell, 30 March 1764, where he appears as watchcasemaker in the Parl. Report list 1773, and entered marks as such 1769 (Section V) and 1780-95 (Section VI). Heal records Richard Palmer, watchcasemaker, 2 Red Lion Street, Clerkenwell, 1793, who may be the same or a son.

*PANTIN, Lewis I (1956, 1962) Presumably son of Simon Pantin II (q.v.). No record of apprenticeship or freedom. First mark entered as largeworker, 21 March 1734. Address: Castle Street, near Leicester Fields, where Simon Pantin II had been till 1731. Second mark, 29 June 1739. Address: 'Leicester Fields'. Heal records him as successor to Simon Pantin II, plateworker, Peacock, Castle Street, Leicester Fields, 1733-44. Listed by Evans as Huguenot (*Hug. Soc. Proc.*, 14, p. 548).

*PANTIN, Lewis II (1959) Presumably son of the above. Free by redemption, 11 March 1767. First mark entered as smallworker, 28 July 1768. Address: 45 Fleet Street, where he appears as goldworker in the Parl. Report list 1773. Second mark as goldworker, 19 October 1782. Address: 36 Southampton Street (Section VII and the following marks). Third mark, 12 April 1792. Address: 8 Sloane Square, Chelsea. Moved to 6 Crown Street, Westminster, 30 October 1795 and to 17 Alfred Place, Newington Causeway, 18 July 1800. Fourth mark, 22 June 1802. Address: 30 Marsham Street, Westminster. Moved to 5 Canterbury Place, near Manor Place, Walworth, 17 July 1805. Heal records him as goldsmith, jeweller and toyman, Crown and Sceptre, (45) Fleet Street, corner of Mitre Court, 1770-81; 36 Southampton Street, 1784; and 62 St. Martin's Le Grand, 1800, which is, however, the address of his son Lewis III (below). Lewis Pantin II was bankrupt in 1787 (*The Gentleman's Magazine*, p. 842). His three sons, Henry, George and Frederick (but not Lewis) were admitted to St. Paul's School aged eleven, nine and eight respectively in 1785, 1787 and 1788, on all which occasions Lewis Pantin is described as goldsmith, (36) Southampton Street, Strand or Covent Garden. Matthew Pantin, aged eleven, son of Lewis Pantin, goldsmith of Grafton Street, Soho, was also admitted to the same school 16 April 1795, and Charles, aged ten, son of the same (no address) 6 July 1795. These are presumably further sons of the same, although possibly of Lewis Pantin III (below), Grafton Street being perhaps a residential address.

PANTIN, Lewis III (1961) Son of Lewis Pantin II (above). Free by patrimony 3 July 1799 as goldsmith St. Martin's Le Grand. Goldworker's mark entered 22 March 1788 as Lewis Pantin Junr. Address: 36 Southampton Street, Strand. Second mark entered as smallworker, 20 December 1798. Address: 62 St. Martin's Le Grand. Signs 'Junr'. Heal records this address but as for Lewis Pantin II, 1800.

PANTIN, Mary (2056) No record of apprenticeship or freedom. From her address clearly widow of Simon Pantin II (q.v.). Mark entered as largeworker, 14 August 1733. Address: Green Street, Leicester Fields, where Heal records her till 1735. She is presumably the Marie Pantains who appears as godmother to Marie Madelaine Mallandin, 30 September 1738, at the Savoy Church. (*Hug. Soc. Pub.*, 26). Listed by Evans as Huguenot (*Hug. Soc. Proc.*, 14, p. 548).

PANTIN, Samuel. A myth for whom there is no evidence whatever. A misprint for Simon Pantin I, Jackson, page 160.

*PANTIN, Simon I (2124–5, 2606) Of a Rouen family of goldsmiths. The first of the name in England seems to be Esaie 'Pontin' who married Elizabeth Maubert 3 October 1658 at the French Church Threadneedle Street, both being described as 'natif(ve)de Rouen'. Esaie remarried in 1666 as widower, Marie Bouquet, widow of Isaac Maubert, perhaps his brother-in-law. By his first marriage Esaie had a son, also Esaie, baptized 4 March 1660, who would seem to be the Esaie Pantin, goldsmith of St. James's, Westminster, recorded by Heal, 1709, but for whom there is no entry of a mark. His daughter married Peter Courtauld in 1709 (Evans, *Hug. Soc. Proc.*, 14, p. 548). It would seem highly likely that Simon Pantin was another son of Esaie I and younger brother of Esaie II. Unfortunately the record of his apprenticeship to Peter Harrache has not survived. He was free by apprenticeship to the latter 4 June 1701. This would put his indentures at about 1694, and his likely birth about 1680. He is presumably the Simon Pantin who appears in the Denization List, 16 December 1687, and as witness to the baptism of Suzanne de Joncourt at Threadneedle Street Church, 12 December 1697. First mark entered as largeworker, 23 June 1701. Address: St. Martin's Lane. Second mark, 16 September 1717. Address: Castle Street. Third mark (Sterling), 30 June 1720, same address. Livery, October 1712. His name appears in the Naturalization Act 1709 as Simon Pantin, goldsmith, St. Martin in the Fields (*Hug. Soc. Pub.*, 18), witnesses Paul Beauvais and Henry Riboteau, and Pantin in turn as witness to four others (*Hug. Soc. Pub.*, 35). Heal records him as plateworker, Peacock Street, Martin's Lane, 1699–1701; St. Martin in the Fields, 1709–11; and as removed to Peacock, Castle Street, Leicester Fields, 1717 till death in 1728. The Peacock is included in his marks. Listed by Evans as Huguenot (*Hug. Soc. Proc.*, 14, p. 548). Although from his surviving work Pantin did not aspire to the production of the larger decorative plate of Willaume and Harrache, he obviously had a considerable clientele and output of much fine domestic plate. His masterpiece would seem to be the Bowes tea-kettle, stand and tripod table of 1719, now in the Untermyer Collection, New York. Other fine pieces include the inkstand of 1705 (Ilchester Collection), tea-kettle and stand of 1706 (ex Swaythling and Wilding Collections, British Museum), jug 1711 (Jesus College, Oxford), pair of jugs 1713 (ex Brownlow and Hearst Collections, now Untermyer Collection, New York), chamberpot 1716 (Hoare's Bank), tureen c. 1726 (The Hermitage).

PANTIN, Simon II (2607) Son of Simon Pantin (above) Citizen and Goldsmith of London, apprenticed to his father 22 May 1717. Freedom unrecorded. First mark entered 4 February 1729. Address: Castle Street, near Leicester Fields, St. Martin in ye Fields. Second mark, 23 February 1731. Address: Green Street, Leicester Fields. Heal records both addresses and dates and his death in 1733. The latter may be deduced from the entry of Mary Pantin's mark in that year (see above). Listed by Evans as Huguenot (*Hug. Soc. Proc.*, 14, p. 548).

PARADISE, William (2119, 3250) Son of William Paradise of Newbury in the County of Berkshire woollendraper, apprenticed to Joseph Ward 24 December 1708. Signatory as journeyman to the petition against assaying the work of foreigners not having served seven years apprenticeship, February 1716. Free, 5 July 1716. First mark entered as largeworker, 7 July 1718. Address: Lad Lane. Second (Sterling) mark, 24 June 1720, same address. Heal records him as above;

and London, 1724-51. Livery, October 1721.

PARFIT, Samuel (2611) No record of apprenticeship or freedom. Only mark entered as smallworker, 21 October 1734. Address: Angel Street, St. Martin's Le Grand. 'Silversmith'.

*PARGETER, Richard (2404-5, 2418) Son of Thomas Pargeter late of Clerkenwell in the County of Middlesex blacksmith deceased, apprenticed to Andrew Archer for eight years 26 March 1718 (name spelt Pargitur by Clerk, the boy signing with a cross). Turned over to James Wilkes 26 March 1724. Free, 5 August 1726. (Another of the same name (see below), apprenticed in 1724 and not free till 1734 can be disregarded on the comparison of dates.) First mark entered as largeworker, 13 October 1730. Address: East arden (?Harding) Street, near Fetter Lane. 'Free Goldsmith'. Signs with a kind of monogram 'is marke', which confirms the illiteracy of the apprenticeship entry. Second mark, 16 February 1737. Address: Frying Pan Alley, Wood Street. 'Goldsmith by Company'. Livery, March 1737. Third mark, 22 June 1739. Address: New Street, Shoe Lane. Heal records him as plateworker, Fetter Lane, 1727-30; omits Wood Street, but adds Without Aldgate, 1744. He also records Richard Pargetier, goldsmith, London, 1773. This may be connected with the other of the name, son of Richard of Tadmarton in the County of Oxford yeoman, apprenticed to John Ferris 7 May 1724 on payment of £16. Free, 1 October 1734. Livery, March 1750. John, son of Richard Pargeter, was apprenticed to his father 7 October 1761, but whether to the former or latter of the name is impossible to decide. No marks were registered for either of these. Richard Pargeter, without category, near Banbury, Oxon., appears in the Parl. Report list 1773, which suggests semi-retirement of the second Richard to his home, Tadmarton being some five miles south-west of Banbury.

*PARKER, John I (1602, 3757) Son of Thomas Parker late of Longdon in the County of Worcester gentleman deceased, apprenticed to George Wickes 5 July 1751 on payment of £50. Free, 5 May 1762. Mark entered as largeworker, in partnership with Edward Wakelin (q.v.) (successor to Wickes), some time after 1758 (the commencing year of the missing largeworker's register). Address: Panton Street, where George Wickes had moved in 1735 from Norris Street. It is interesting to note that although Wakelin had been in virtual sole charge of the business since 1747, Parker's initials on the introduction of the joint mark are placed above the latter's and it seems highly probable that Parker's entry into the firm was largely a matter of a financial injection rather than additional skill. This supposition is also supported by the high premium paid on his apprenticeship, which appears a mere formality to secure entry into the company. One of this name was called to the Livery, December 1771, but the member of the Court in 1793 and Prime Warden 1803 must surely be the following of the same name. The partnership with Wakelin presumably lasted till the entry of the mark for John Wakelin and William Taylor (q.v.) in 1776. Heal in fact records Parker and Wakelin as goldsmiths and jewellers, King's Arms, Panton Street, near St. James's, Haymarket, 1759-77, which is close confirmation of the above argued dates, and they appear together as goldsmiths, Panton Street, in the Parl. Report list 1773.

PARKER, John II (3670) Son of John Parker of St. Paul's Churchyard goldsmith and jeweller, Citizen and Carman, apprenticed to Benjamin Gurden as jeweller 2 February 1780 and turned over to his father June 1783 and by consent of his father's executor to Hannah Parker, the latter's widow, 12 November 1786. Free, 7 March 1787. Livery, February 1791. There is however no entry for him in the registers and the attribution of the above mark must remain doubtful. He died 1815-16. Heal records the father as jeweller and goldsmith, 55 St. Paul's Churchyard, 1770-81; and at 56 St. Paul's Churchyard, 1784-96, of which the last ten years must refer in fact to the widow and son. He also has John Parker silversmith and jeweller, 2 Rathbone Place, 1796, but in the case of a name of this relatively common nature this may well be another. See also John Parker 'at Phillpotts Toy Shop near the Bull and Gate High Holborn', incuse mark, 1771 (Section V).

PARKER, John III (1844) Perhaps, but probably unlikely, son of Samuel Parker of 13 Great St. Thomas Apostle tea broker, apprenticed to Frederick George Harding stationer of 24 Cornhill in 1831 on payment of £183. 15s. This figure must surely represent a future in a big concern and therefore unlikely to be the same as the owner of the mark entered as smallworker, 19 December 1836. Address: Retreat Cottage, Upper Clapton. The address indeed almost suggests the first amateur goldsmith to enter a mark.

PARKER, William (3265-6, 3270) Son of William Parker of Silver Street London gentleman, apprenticed to Thomas Phipps as goldsmith 3 December 1788 on payment of £21. Free, 3 February 1796. First mark entered as smallworker, 22 November 1798. Address: 2 Lillypot Lane. Second mark, in partnership with Benjamin Simpson (q.v.), 8 April 1799. Address: 5 Staining Lane. Partnership apparently dissolved by 4 October 1800, when Simpson entered a separate mark at another address. Third mark again alone, 25 June 1803. Moved to 5 Staining Lane, undated, below the last entry, but in fact probably referring to continuation there from the previous partnership. Moved again to 74 Little Britain, undated.

PARKES, Alexperry (76) No record of apprenticeship or freedom. Only mark entered as smallworker, 20 June 1765. Address: Old Street Square.

PARKIN, William (3269) Son of William Parkin of the Strand cutler, apprenticed to William Elliott of Compton Street Clerkenwell as silversmith 2 July 1817. Free, 5 January 1825, as cutler. (His brother James was also apprenticed to the same master in 1819, but no mark is registered for him). Mark entered as plateworker, 26 May 1824. Address, 50 Strand. From description of father and son as cutler it would see probable that their chief concern was knifehafts or other silver fittings to cutlery.

PARKYNS, William (3264) Perhaps son of William Parkyns late of Chinnor in the County of Oxford farmer deceased, apprenticed to James Baker of Northampton Court Wood Lane Clerkenwell as bucklemaker 4 February 1789. Freedom unrecorded. Mark entered as smallworker, 22 August 1792. Address: Chiswell Street. Moved to 183 High Street, Borough, 3 October 1793. Moved to 6 Wine Office Court, Fleet Street, undated.

PARR, Richard (2409) No record of apprenticeship or freedom. Only mark entered as smallworker, 22 July 1772. Address: Parsons Court, Bride Lane, Fleet Street. Signs with X. He appears as bucklemaker, at this address, in the Parl. Report list 1773, and entered two marks as such 1780 and 1786. Address: 1 Rolls Building, Fetter Lane (Section VIII).

PARR, Sarah (2610) No record of apprenticeship or freedom. Widow of Thomas Parr I (below). Mark entered below his second mark, as largeworker, 20 June 1728. Address: Cheapside. Heal records her here as plateworker, 1720-1 (which appears contradictory to the very clearly entered date of her mark); and also as London, 1732.

PARR, Thomas I (2120-1) Son of Henry Parr late of the County of Cork in the Kingdom of Ireland clerk deceased, apprenticed to Simon Noy 9 September 1687. Free, 8 August 1694. Livery, October 1712. First mark entered as largeworker, undated, probably April 1697 on commencement of register. Address: Wood Street. Second mark, 19 August 1717. Address: Cheapside. Signatory as 'working goldsmith' to the petition complaining of the competition of 'necessitous strangers', December 1711, and to that against assaying work of foreigners not having served seven years apprenticeship, February 1716. The baptisms and/or burials of eight sons and daughters of Thomas and Sarah Parr are recorded in the registers of St. Matthew, Friday Street, between 1703 and 1713 and two further sons at St. Vedast, Foster Lane, 1716 and 1718. Thomas Parr's own burial, however, appears to be unrecorded in either of these registers. He was dead by 20 June 1728, when his widow Sarah (above) entered her mark.

PARR, Thomas II (2870, 2883-4) Son of Thomas Parr I. Free by patrimony, 5 March 1733. First mark entered 9 February 1733. Address: Cheapside. 'Goldsmith'. Second and third marks, 19 June 1739, same address. Livery, January 1750. Court, February 1735. Warden, 1771-3. Recorded only by Heal as if a continuation of his father's life. He appears as Thomas Parr, goldsmith, Whetstone, in the Parl. Report list 1773, presumably on retirement.

PATTRICK, Thomas (2877) No record of apprenticeship or freedom. Only mark entered as smallworker, 2 February 1797. Address: 8 Orange Street, Leicester Square. Moved to 29 King Street, Covent Garden, 4 September 1800.

PAYNE, Ann (79) No record of apprenticeship or freedom. Presumably, from address, the widow of James Payne (q.v.). First mark entered as spoonmaker, 25 October 1834. Address: 21 Great Mitchell Street, St. Luke's. Second mark, 26 November 1834. Third mark, 5 December 1834.

PAYNE, Humphrey (1058, 1061, 2117-8) Son of Nicholas Payne of Ludlow in the County of Salop tallowchandler, apprenticed to Roger Grange 15 August 1694 and turned over to Thomas Parr. Free, 1 November 1701. First mark entered as largeworker, 3 December 1701. Address: Gutter Lane. Signatory as 'working goldsmith' to the petition complaining of the competition of 'necessitous strangers', December 1711, and to that against assaying work of foreigners not having served seven years apprenticeship, February 1716. Second and third marks (Sterling), undated, c. June 1720. Address: Cheapside. Fourth mark, 15 June 1739. Address: Cheapside. 'Silversmith'. Livery, October 1708. Court, 1734. Warden, 1747-9. Died 2 August 1751, being the same day as Paul De Lamerie. His obituary notice appeared with Lamerie's in the *London Evening Post*, Saturday 3 August-Tuesday 6 August: 'Last Friday died at Daventry in Northamptonshire Mr. Humphrey Paine, formerly an eminent Goldsmith at the Hen and Chickens in Cheapside, but having acquired a handsome Fortune, he quitted trade to his Son a few Months ago, to whom he has left the Bulk of his Estate' (P. A. S. Phillips, *Paul De Lamerie*). Heal records him as plateworker, London, 1697-9 (for which the evidence of his apprenticeship appears contradictory); Golden Cup, Gutter Lane, 1701-20; Hen and Chickens, Cheapside, 1720-40 (both these signs are incorporated in the corresponding marks); London, 1750; Humphrey and John Payne, goldsmiths and jewellers, Hen and Chickens, Cheapside, 1753-5. His work, never in any way ambitious, appears to have been limited to plain domestic pieces in the 'hollow ware' category, covered cups, tankards, mugs, tea and coffee pieces. It is doubtful whether he produced candlesticks or other castings. While thoroughly competent, his work rarely shows any individuality of design.

*PAYNE, James (1841) No record of apprenticeship or freedom. First mark entered as spoonmaker, 4 October 1824. Address: 52 Great Sutton Street, Clerkenwell. Moved to 18 Rose Street, Brick Lane, 16 August 1827. Moved to 19 Radnor Street, Ironmonger Row, St. Luke's, 26 March 1831. Moved to 21 Great Mitchell Street, St. Luke's, 30 August 1832. Second mark, 21 December 1833. Presumably dead by 25 October 1834 when Ann Payne (q.v.) entered her first mark.

PAYNE, John (1597, 3671-2) Son of Humphrey Payne (above) Citizen and Goldsmith of London, apprenticed to his father 11 January 1733. Free, 7 February 1740. Livery, April 1740. Court, February 1747. First mark entered 13 April 1751. Address: Cheapside; where he appears as goldsmith in the Parl. Report list 1773. Heal records him as goldsmith, 44 Cheapside, 1751-99. Warden, 1760-2. Prime Warden, 1765. He must be the 'Mr Payne Junior, Goldsmith. married to the only daughter of Mr Banks, Clerk to the Goldsmiths Company, £5000, 13th February 1751' (*The Gentleman's Magazine*, p. 91).

PAYNE, Richard I (2407) No record of apprenticeship or freedom. Only mark entered as smallworker, 22 October 1762. Address: Goswell Street. There is no evidence of any connection with the Cheapside family of the same name.

PAYNE, Richard II (2894) Richard Morse Payne son of John (above). Free by patrimony, 9, April 1777, as goldsmith. Mark entered as plateworker, in partnership with his brother Thomas, 30 October 1777. Address: 42 Cheapside. Heal records them here and 10 Cockspur Street, 1777-83. They appear as bankrupt, November 1780 (*The Gentleman's Magazine*, p. 544).

*PAYNE, Thomas (2894) Son of John Payne (above) of Cheapside London Goldsmith, apprenticed to his father 2 March 1768. Freedom unrecorded. Livery, November 1776. Mark entered as plateworker, in partnership with his brother Richard (q.v.). Died 25 November 1815.

PEACOCK, Edward (631, 2155, 2646) Son of Thomas Peacocke late of the Lea in the County of Wiltshire yeoman deceased, apprenticed to Dallington Ayres 30 September 1693. Free, 10 February 1700/?1. First mark entered as largeworker, in partnership with John Martin Stockar, 20 October 1705. Address: The Strand. Livery, October 1708. Second mark alone, 14 November 1710, same address. Signatory as 'working goldsmith' to the petition complaining of the competition of 'necessitous strangers', December 1711. Third mark, 5

BIOGRAPHICAL DICTIONARY

September 1724, no address. Heal records the partnership Strand, 1705-10; and Peacock as plateworker, Strand, 1710 till death in 1729; also Golden Ball, Strand, 1723 (Heal Add.).

*PEACOCK, James (1585) No record of apprenticeship or freedom. Only mark entered as smallworker, 20 December 1769. Address: 103 Minories. Appears as goldworker at this address, Parl. Report list 1773, from which presumably Heal's record comes.

PEACOCK, Thomas (2878) No record of apprenticeship or freedom. Only mark entered as smallworker, 23 October 1798. Address: 3 Amen Corner. Possibly son or relative of above.

PEAKE, Robert (2157-8) Son of Edward Peake 'late of Peekeforrest Derbyshire Myner decd.', apprenticed to John Pennock 22 April 1673 and turned over to Francis Singleton. Free, 3 November 1680. Mark entered as largeworker, undated, probably April 1697 on commencement of register. Address: Noble Street, where Heal records him from 1697 to 1704. Signatory as 'working goldsmith' to the petition complaining of the competition of 'necessitous strangers', December 1711.

*PEAKE, Vaughan (2163) No record of apprenticeship or freedom. Possibly the son of the above. Mark entered as smallworker, 27 August 1701. Address: Foster Lane, where Heal records him as insolvent, 1720.

PEARCE, Edmund (629, 2169, 3547) Son of Edmund Pearce of Tewkesbury in the County of Gloucester hatter, apprenticed to Henry Beesley 11 August 1693 'from the 24th day of June next' and turned over 10 November 1697 to Phillip Rollos. Free, 24 January 1704/?5. First mark entered as largeworker, 1 February 1705. Address: Strand, near the New Exchange. Second (Sterling) mark, 28 July 1720. Heal records him as plateworker, New Exchange, Strand, 1704-22. He also has Edward Pearce (cf. Edmund P.) goldsmith, London, 1720-1, which appears to derive from a misprint in Jackson, page 174. There seems no possible connection with Heal's Captain Pearce, goldsmith, Three Golden Cocks, upper end of Cheapside, 1700-3.

PEARCE, James (2162) Either (1) son of John Pearce, apprenticed to Richard Croome 1679. Free 11 May 1687. Or (2) son of John Pearce of Kingston-on-Thames tanner, apprenticed to Matthew Pearce 1 November 1688. Free, 26 March 1698. Mark entered as largeworker, 22 April 1698. Address: Newgate Street. Livery, October 1698. Resigned, 5 August 1736.

*PEARCE, Richard (2412, 2419) No record of apprenticeship or freedom. First mark entered as plateworker, 10 October 1812. Address: 10 Banner Street, Bunhill Row. Moved to 12 Banner Street, 24 June 1824. Second mark, in partnership with George Burrows as plateworkers, 13 November 1826. Address: 12 Banner Street, St. Luke's. Third mark (two sizes), 2 December 1835.

PEAREE (Perry?) Ann (77) No record of apprenticeship or freedom. Only mark entered as smallworker, 13 July 1765. Address: Old Street Square. A very illiterate and altered signature.

PEARSON, George (871) No record of apprenticeship or freedom. Only mark entered as smallworker, 8 May 1817. Address: 104 Dorset Court, Fleet Street.

PEARSON, William (2165-8, 3252) Son of Thomas Pearson of Spratton in the County of Northants farmer, apprenticed to Michael Bourne 11 March 1691 and turned over to Samuel Bourne. Free, 18 October 1699. First mark entered as smallworker, 22 May 1704. Address: Ball Alley, Lombard Street. Second and third marks as largeworker, 21 January 1710, same address. Fourth mark, 21 May 1717. Fifth mark (Sterling), 24 January 1721. Livery, October 1721 (as Peirson). Heal records him at this address, 1710-20.

PEASTON, Robert (3275, 3782, 3784, 3897) No record of apprenticeship or freedom. Presumably either son or younger brother of William Peaston (below). First mark entered as largeworker, in partnership with William Peaston, 12 July 1756. Address: St. Martin's Le Grand. Heal records the partnership here, 1756-63; and R. Peaston, goldsmith, St. Martin's Le Grand(?), 1762-6.

PEASTON, William (3254, 3275, 3782, 3784, 3897) No record of apprenticeship or freedom. First mark entered as largeworker, 8 January 1746. Address: New Rents, St. Martin's Le Grand. Moved to Deans Court, 8 August 1749. Second mark, in partnership with Robert Peaston (above), 12 July 1756. Address: St. Martin's Le Grand. Heal records him as working goldsmith, St. Martin's Le Grand, 1745-60; and Jewin Street, 1778; partnership with Robert,

1756-63. A William Peaston, son of George Peaston of Cranstoun Midlothian husbandman, apprenticed to Nathaniel Appleton 7 October 1761 and turned over to William Shaw and William Sheen is possibly connected with the above.

PEAVEY, William (3259) No record of apprenticeship or freedom. Only mark entered as smallworker, 13 February 1773. Address: 19 Great Russell Street, Bloomsbury, where he appears as watchcasemaker in the Parl. Report list 1773.

PEELE, Thomas (2154) Son of Thomas Peele late of Brickhill in the County of Buckingham, apprenticed to Richard Sing 9 April 1689. Free, 16 February 1705. Mark entered as largeworker, 2 March 1705. Address: Jewin Street.

PEIRCE, Thomas (2116) Son of Francis Peirce of Tunbridge Wells yeoman, apprenticed to Samuel Wallington of the Fishmongers Company June 1698 and turned over to John Trubshaw. Free, 30 May 1712. Mark entered as smallworker, 24 February 1730. Address: 'over aganst ye hors Shu ale house in West=hardin Street fetter Lane free of ye Fishmongers'. Incuse mark, at same address, 23 November 1736 (Section V).

PELL, James (745) Son of James Pell late of All Saints Huntingdon grocer deceased, apprenticed to Richard Tomkins 15 August 1717. Free, 3 September 1724. Mark entered as smallworker, in partnership with John Garbett, 30 June 1726. Address: 'at ye Half Moon and Star against ye Church in Foster Lane'. 'Free Goldsmith'. Heal records the partnership here as goldsmiths, 1726; and Garbett (q.v.) alone in Lombard Street; dead 1747.

PELTRO (?Peltreau), James (1575) No record of apprenticeship or freedom. Only mark entered as largeworker, undated, between 27 and 29 June 1739. Address: Golden Head, Heage (?Heneage) Lane. Goldsmith. Heal, probably following Chaffers, spells the name Paltro and gives only the shop sign. John and James Peltreau, sons of John, apprenticed to Joseph Lawes as engravers, 1786 and 1790, may perhaps be relations, possibly grandsons.

PENFORD, John (2156, 3674) Son of Thomas Penford of Tiltworth Hill in the County of Leicester grazier, apprenticed to Edward Hulse 14 October 1681. Free, 1 May 1689. Mark entered as largeworker, undated, probably April 1697 on commencement of register. Address: Foster Lane. Heal records him only as Penfold, here, 1696-7. The name however is quite clearly written in both apprentice and mark registers. Furthermore the following from the St. Vedast, Foster Lane register corroborates the correct version. 'A Male Child of John Penford Goldsmith a lodger in Mr Abbotts house in gutter Lane in this parish at ye signe of the Dyall was Borne the 8th day of December 1701.' Thomas, son of above, was buried 19 December 1701. Mortality was high in this family. Elizabeth 'daughter of Mr John Penford was Buried in the New Vault the 17th day of March 1696', and Carina, daughter of the same, was buried 11th May 1697 (register of St. Michael le Quern).

PENKETHMAN, John (2164) Son of Edward Penkethman Citizen and Blacksmith of London, apprenticed to William Crane 24 May 1676. Free, 15 January 1684/?5. Mark entered as smallworker, 6 May 1703. Address: Chick Lane. Livery, October 1708. Resigned, December 1740.

PENN, John (1573) No record of apprenticeship or freedom. Mark entered as largeworker, 22 April 1736. Address: 'Swan Alley over against ye man in compa(ny?)'.

PENN, Thomas (2872) Describes himself in entry as Weaver but no trace has been found in the freedom list of that Company back to 1728, nor any details of apprenticeship. Mark entered as smallworker, 3 May 1738. Address: Hide Street, Bloomsbury. 'Weaver'.

PENN, William (3267) No record of apprenticeship or freedom. Mark entered as smallworker, 5 May 1801. Address: 4 Mays Buildings, St. Martin's Lane.

PENNYFEATHER, Henry (1060) No record of apprenticeship or freedom. Incuse mark entered 22 March 1763. Address: 'Prugians' Court, Old Bailey (Section V), where he appears as watchcasemaker in the Parl. Report list 1773. Second mark entered as smallworker, 26 November 1783. Address: 13 New Rents, St. Martin's Le Grand. Heal records him here as silversmith at same address, omitting number, 1790-3.

PENSTONE, Henry (2159) Son of Francis Penstone of Maulberry (Marlborough) in the County of Wiltshire woolendraper, apprenticed to Lawrence Coles 12 January

1681. Free, 12 April 1689. Mark entered as largeworker, undated, probably April 1697 on commencement of register. Address: Gracechurch Street. Heal records him as plateworker, London, 1691-1705; and Gracechurch Street, 1697.

*PENSTONE, William I (2160) Son of Francis Penstone of Marlborough in the County of Wiltshire woolendraper (and therefore brother of Henry, above), apprenticed to William Mathew for eight years 27 May 1687. Free, 15 August 1694. Mark entered as largeworker, undated, probably April 1697 on commencement of register. Address: Foster Lane. William, son of Wm and Margaret Penston, was born 9, baptized 16 August 1696 at Christchurch, Newgate (incorporating St. Leonard, Foster Lane).

PENSTONE, William II (2161) Son of William Penstone (above). Born 9 August 1696. Free by patrimony, 3 October 1717. Signatory as journeyman to the petition against assaying the work of foreigners not having served seven years apprenticeship, Feburary 1716. Mark entered as largeworker, 4 October 1717. Address: Foster Lane. Buried at Christchurch, Newgate (incorporating St. Leonard, Foster Lane), 15 October 1741. His two sons, William and Thomas were apprenticed in 1742 and 1751 respectively. The former (for whom no mark is entered) was the father of the fourth William Penstone (below).

*PENSTONE, William III (3260) Son of William Penstone of Winchester Court near Mugwell Street Citizen and Goldsmith (who had been apprenticed to Marmaduke Daintrey in 1742, but for whom no mark is entered), apprenticed to Samuel Phipps silver turner Staining Lane 5 August 1767. Freedom unrecorded. Mark entered as spoonmaker, 17 March 1774. Address: Noble Street, where he appears as such in the Parl. Report list 1773. Heal records him as haftmaker and spoonmaker at this address, 1773, and bankrupt 1778; and also previously at Monkwell Street, which must in fact refer to his father mentioned above. There were thus four generations of William Penstones working between 1694 and 1778, of whom the third apparently has no identifiable mark.

PEPPER, Thomas I (2874) No record of apprenticeship or freedom. First mark entered as smallworker, 23 February 1767. Address: Staining Lane. Moved to Lilly Pot Lane, 27 June 1770. Second mark (incuse), 16 April 1772. Appears as watchcasemaker, Lilly Pot Lane, in the Parl. Report list 1773. Heal records Thomas Pepper, goldsmith and enameller, 5 George Street, Foster Lane, 1790-6, a date which seems to lie between this and the next of the same name, with an address different to either of them.

PEPPER, Thomas II (2881) Son of Thomas Pepper late of Wooburn in the County of Buckingham gentleman deceased, apprenticed to Alexander Field of Hoxton as goldsmith 5 October 1796 on payment of £40. Free, 3 October 1804. Mark entered as plateworker, 30 December 1809. Address: 16 Hosier Lane, Smithfield.

*PEPPIN, Robert (2413-4) No record of apprenticeship or freedom. First mark entered as spoonmaker, 15 December 1817. Address: 27 Greville Street, Hatton Garden. Second mark, 7 April 1818. Third mark, 27 January 1820. Fourth mark, 14 December 1820. Fifth, 16 May 1823. Sixth (two sizes), 21 June 1824. Moved to 15 Wilson Street, 2 December 1826. Seventh mark, 11 September 1829.

PEPPIN, Susannah (2619) Presumably widow of Sydenham William Peppin (below). Mark entered as smallworker, 9 March 1835. Address: 20 Kirby Street, Hatton Garden, as against No. 23 for Sydenham's address (below).

*PEPPIN, Sydenham William (2002, 2616) No record of apprenticeship or freedom. Probably a brother of Robert Peppin (above). First mark entered as plateworker, in partnership with Moses William Brent (q.v.), 20 December 1815. Address: 22 Greville Street (cf. 27 Greville Street, for Robert Peppin in 1817). Second mark together, 2 June 1816. Third mark alone as plateworker, 25 July 1816. Address: 22 Greville Street. Fourth mark, 3 August 1816. Moved to 23 Kirby Street, Hatton Garden, 23 October 1829. This last entry is signed by Robert Peppin.

*PERCHARD, James (1845) No record of apprenticeship or freedom. Only mark entered as smallworker, in partnership with William Brooks II (q.v.), 11 April 1808. Address: 14 Clerkenwell Green. Heal records them as goldsmiths and jewellers, 12 Charles Street, Hatton Garden, c. 1800, and at above address, 1808-17.

*PERIER, Charles (395-6, 2172) No record

of apprenticeship or freedom. The name occurs in the Naturalization Acts 6 and 7 Anne, Royal Assent 1708. Two marks (Sterling and New Standard) entered as largeworker, 6 January 1729. Address: Macclesfield Street, St. Ann's, Soho. Third mark, 21 June 1731. Address: King Street, Covent Garden. Heal, following Chaffers and Jackson, record him as plateworker, Macclesfield Street, 1727. The last figure in the mark entry appears to be a 9 altered to 8 to revert to the old calendar for the official date. It cannot in any case be taken for 7. Heal also records his bankruptcy in King Street, 1734 (*The Gentleman's Magazine*, November). Listed by Evans as Huguenot (*Hug. Soc. Proc.*, 14, p. 548). His work is very rare and his output presumably never large.

PERKINS, Jonathan I (1592, 1604, 1839) Son of Charles Perkins late of Calne in the County of Wiltshire, woolcomber deceased, apprenticed to Richard Webb 2 May 1759. Free, 7 May 1766. First mark entered as smallworker, 23 April 1772. Address: 'Goldsmith at no 5 Winchester Court Monkwell Street, Cripplegate', where he appears as bucklemaker in the Parl. Report list 1773. Second to seventh marks as bucklemaker, from 3 June 1776 to 6 November 1789. Address: 16 Hosier Lane, Smithfield (Section VIII). Eighth mark, in partnership with Jonathan Perkins Junior as plateworkers, 5 August 1795, same address. Partnership presumably ended by 29 August 1800, when J.P. senior entered ninth mark alone, at same address. Tenth mark, 19 February 1803. Died before 1811. Heal records him as working goldsmith, Mugwell (Monkwell) Street, 1772; and 16 Hosier Lane, 1781–96; also Jonathan Perkins senior and junior, plateworkers, at the same address, 1795. Charles Perkins, son of Hugh Perkins of Calne, probably a nephew, was apprenticed to him in 1783.

PERKINS, Jonathan Junior II (1604) Son of the above, apprenticed to his father 7 July 1790. Mark entered as plateworker, in partnership with his father, 5 August 1795, as above. The partnership seems to have finished by 29 August 1800, when Jonathan Perkins senior re-entered a separate mark and no further reference to the son appears.

PERKINS, Jos(eph) I (1570) Son of James Perkins late of the parish of Allhallows Barking London broker deceased, apprenticed to Richard Gines (q.v.) of the Merchant Taylors' Company 2 June 1708. Free, 2 May 1716. First mark entered as smallworker, 6 July 1720. Address: Ball Alley, Lombard Street. 'Merchant Taylor'. Second mark, 27 January 1735. Address: Great Dean Court, St. Martin's Le Grand.

PERKINS, Joseph II (1843) No record of apprenticeship or freedom. Only mark entered as smallworker, 14 March 1834. Address: 23 Crosby Row, Walworth.

PERO, Isabel (1600) No record of apprenticeship or freedom. Presumably widow of John Pero (below). Mark entered as largeworker, 1 May 1741. Address: Orange Court, near Leicester Fields. Heal records only this date and address.

*PERO, John (1571, 1599, 2171) Son of John Pero Citizen and Stationer of London, apprenticed to Thomas Farren 30 June 1709. Signatory as journeyman to the petition against assaying the work of foreigners not having served seven years apprenticeship, February 1716. Free 12 July 1717. First mark entered as largeworker, 24 August 1717. Address: Strand. Married Mary Tomkins of St. Paul at Shadwells, County of Middlesex, 14 February 1721, at Christ Church, Newgate. Second mark, 23 November 1732. Address: Corner of Suffolk Street. Married secondly Isabella Yarnton of St. Martins in the Fields, 16 December 1736, at St. Bene't, Paul's Wharf. Livery, March 1739/?40. Third mark, 22 June 1739. Address: Orange Street. Presumably dead by 1 May 1741 when his widow (above) entered her mark. Quoted as Huguenot by W. H. Manchée ('Huguenot London', *Hug. Soc. Proc.*, 13, p. 67). His work, which is rare, shows a high standard and individual character.

PERRY, James (1582, 1837–8) No record of apprenticeship or freedom. First mark entered as smallworker, 1 March 1763. Address: Shoe Lane. Moved to Holborn, and second mark, 28 June 1765. Third mark, 3 April 1767. Fourth and fifth marks, 6 June, undated, probably 1768. Sixth and seventh marks, 7 January 1773. Address: 131 Chancery Lane. He appears as hiltmaker at this address in the Parl. Report list 1773 and entered a mark as such, 18 December 1777, at 10 Crown Court, Fleet Street. His third mark has been identified on a sword hilt in the Royal Scottish Museum. Thomas Perry, Shoe Lane, 1765, incuse mark (Section V) may be connected.

PERRY, John (1577, 3668-9) Son of John Perry of the parish of Christchurch Spitalfields weaver, apprenticed to John Cafe 7 December 1750 and turned over by consent of John Winning, executor to Mr Cafe, to William Cafe 13 October 1757. Free, 1 March 1758. First mark entered as largeworker, 23 March 1757. Address: Pauls Court. Moved to Wood Street, 16 January 1759, where he appears without category in the Parl. Report list 1773. Heal records him at the first address as plateworker and as silversmith, Clerkenwell, 1772; and Holborn, 1779. Described as 'Silver candlestick maker' in apprenticeship to him of Richard Coleman 1 April 1772, and 'of Holborn silversmith' in apprenticeship of Charles Heighington 1779. Appears in the Parl. Report list 1773 as ——, Holborn.

PERTT, Robert (2416, 3785) No record of apprenticeship or freedom. Only mark entered as largeworker, 21 July 1738. Address: Newgate Street, where Heal records him, 1738-44; and also Robert Perth, goldsmith, London, 1738-55, who seems possibly the same. The signature of the entry seems definitely to be Pertt.

PETERS, John (1605) No record of apprenticeship or freedom. First mark entered as smallworker, in partnership with John Schaffer, 18 June 1810. Address: 20 Old Compton Street, Soho. Second mark (very small) alone, 10 October 1812, same address (Section IV). The John Peters, goldworker, 1822 (Section VII) would seem probably a son.

*PETERS, Richard (2402) Son of John Peters of St. Saviour's Southwark victualler, apprenticed to Jonathan Hanson of the Haberdashers' Company 11 January 1712 of St. Saviour's Southwark goldsmith. Mark entered as smallworker, 23 March 1725. Address: 'at the Gold Ring in the Borough Southwark Citizen and Haberdasher'. Heal records him as goldsmith, Gold Ring, St. Margaret's Hill, Southwark, 1724; died 1747.

PETERSON, Abraham (78, 80) No record of apprenticeship or freedom. First mark entered as plateworker, in partnership with Peter Podio (q.v.) 1 May 1783. Address: 23 Primrose Hill, Salisbury Square, Fleet Street. Second mark alone, 5 February 1790, same address. Third mark (two sizes), 6 October 1792. Moved (probably at the above date) to Fox Court, Brook Street, Holborn. Heal records him as plateworker, 23 Salisbury Court, Fleet Street, 1790-3; with Peter Podie, Salisbury Court, 1783-90; and also Podie and Peterson, 23 Salisbury Square, 1790. The inaccuracies of directories are well illustrated by these variations.

PETLEY, William (2170a, 2174, 3251) Son of James Petley of Stratford Bow in the County of Middlesex farrier, apprenticed to William Matthews 30 May 1692. Free, 5 June 1699. First mark entered as largeworker, 16 June 1699. Address: Blowbladder Street. Second mark, 22 July 1717. Third (Sterling) mark, 24 June 1720, same address. Heal records him here, 1699-1717; and London, 1717-31. 'James the son of William Petley goldsmith in horse shoe Alley in this parish and Elizabeth his wife Borne and Baptized the 2nd day of February 1699' (register of St. Michael le Quern). William, another son, was born and baptized 5 August 1702. 'Elizabeth ye wife of William Petley a Goldsmith lieving in Horse Shoue Alley in this parish was Buried in Bow by Stratford in the County of Middlsex the 28th day of June 1705' (same register). A Mary Petley was buried in the Old Vault of the same church, 13 November 1723.

PETRIJ, Jean (2170) 'Son of Bartholomy Petry by Mary his wife born at Heidelberg in the Pilatinat', so described in the Petition for Naturalization of Guy Scipio and James Peltier setting forth that the petitioners are 'Officers in Major General Levison's Regiment, where they have served above ten years; and are Refugees upon account of their religion, having no home to return to, their Commissions being all that they have to depend on'. (Royal Assent to the Bill, 4 May 1699. *Hug. Soc. Pub.*, 18.) Next appears as son of Bartholomew Petry late of Hanno in ye Empire of Germany gentleman deceased, apprenticed to David Willaume 24 November 1700. A note along side records the attesting of his naturalization under Act of Parliament. Free, 21 November 1707. Mark entered as largeworker, 21 November 1707. Address: 'in the Pelmell', where Heal records him from 1701-7. It seems probable, in view of his age when apprenticed, that he had been trained as goldsmith before entering the army and that his apprenticeship was a formality to enable him to start working immediately, either, in fact, with Willaume who was then in Pall Mall, or else nearby. A John Petry of St. Martin in the Fields married Jane Shott (or Short) of St James' at St. Lawrence, Jewry, 24 April 1687, but this seems scarcely likely to be the same man. Petrij is listed by Evans as Huguenot (*Hug. Soc. Proc.*, 14, p. 459).

PETTIT, John Cook (1232) No record of apprenticeship or freedom. First mark entered as smallworker, 30 June 1788. Address: 2 Dogwell Court, Lombard Street, Whitefriars. Second mark (incuse), 27 November 1789. Heal records him as working goldsmith, same address, 1790–3.

PETTYFOOT, Thomas (2871) No record of apprenticeship or freedom. Only mark entered as smallworker, 26 February 1733. Address: Rotten Row, Old Street, 'next to ye sign of ye bull'.

PHELPS, William (3253) Son of Thomas Phelps late of Ross in the County of Hereford joyner deceased, apprenticed to Thomas Moulden 1 July 1731 on payment of £10 of the charity of the Society of Herefordshire Gentlemen. Free, 8 November 1739. Mark entered as smallworker, 10 August 1738. Address: 'living att the three Spoons in Pater-noster-Row'. Heal records him as goldsmith, Paternoster Row, insolvent 1743.

*PHILLIPS, David (495) No record of apprenticeship or freedom. First mark entered as spoonmaker, 21 March 1834. Address: 15 Bury Street, St. Mary Axe. Second mark, 6 March 1835. Moved to 12 Wilson Street, Finsbury, 14 October 1836. Third mark, 24 May 1839.

PHILLIPS, Humphrey (1057) No record of apprenticeship or freedom. Only mark entered as smallworker, undated, between 24 February and May 1730. Address: 'in St Martins Charls Cort in the Strand'. Heal records him as working silversmith, Charles Street, Strand, 1744.

PHILLIPS, John (2115) Son of Thomas Phillips late of St Martin's Le Grand taylor deceased, apprenticed to William Lukin 27 January 1705. Free, 9 October 1712. Mark entered as largeworker, 13 February 1717. Address: Foster Lane.

*PHILLIPS, Levy (1960) No record of apprenticeship or freedom. Only mark entered as smallworker, 9 May 1770. Address: 'in St. James Sparks Court by Aldgate'. Appears as bucklemaker, Spark's Court, Duke's Place, in the Parl. Report list 1773.

*PHILLIPS, Phillip (2216) No record of apprenticeship or freedom. Only mark entered as plateworker, 28 August 1826. Address: 19 Crown Street, Finsbury. Moved to 15 Bury Street, St. Mary Axe, 27 February 1835.

PHILLIPS, William (2187) Son of Samuel Phillips Citizen and Baker of London, apprenticed to Samuel Bourne 15 September 1709. Free, 11 October 1716. Mark entered as smallworker, 11 October 1716. Address: Foster Lane. 'free of the Goldsmiths'. Livery, October 1721.

PHILLIS, Phillip (2188, 2211) Son of Phillip Phillis in the precincts of the Tower in the county of Middlesex weaver, apprenticed to Edward Vincent on payment of £15 and turned over to Francis Plymley 4 December 1716. Free, 6 August 1719. First mark entered as largeworker, 20 February 1720. Address: Cannon Street. Second (Sterling) mark, 24 June 1720, same address. Livery, October 1721. Heal records him with the alternative name Phyllis Phillip (apparently from misprint in Chaffers), plateworker, Cannon Street, 1720; Finch lane, 1727; and Friday Street, 1734. There can be no doubt of his correct name since the same occurs for father and son in the apprenticeship entry and in both mark entries of which the second appears as 'Phill. Phillis'.

PHIPPS, James I (1583, 3049) Son of William Phipps, apprenticed to William Pinnell 1741 and turned over to Robert Collier Clockmaker. Free, 1 March 1749. First mark entered as largeworker, in partnership with William Bond, 8 May 1754. Address: Foster Lane, Cheapside. Second mark as smallworker, 14 May 1767. Address: Gutter Lane. Third mark, 10 February 1772. Address: 11 Gutter Lane, where he appears as plateworker in the Parl. Report list 1773. Livery, March 1781. Died between 1795 and 1801. Heal records him as goldsmith, 40 Gutter Lane, 1769–83; also James and Thomas Phipps, goldsmiths, Gutter Lane. Partnership dissolved 1783. There is, however, no mark for this partnership. For Thomas see below.

PHIPPS, James II (2892–3) Son of Thomas Phipps (below) and grandson of James I, apprenticed to his father as goldsmith 1800. Free, 1 April 1807. First mark entered as smallworker, in partnership with his father and Edward Robinson II, the entry incomplete and undated, probably shortly after his freedom. Second mark, in partnership with Thomas Phipps, 31 January 1816.

*PHIPPS, Thomas (2891-3) Son of James Phipps I (above) of Gutter Lane London Citizen and Goldsmith, apprenticed to his father 5 April 1769. Free, 7 May 1777. Livery, February 1791. First mark entered as smallworker, in partnership with Edward Robinson II, 8 July 1783. Address: 40 Gutter Lane. Second mark (two sizes), 8 August 1789. Third mark, in partnership with the above and James Phipps II, struck in the register, but the entry unfilled except for the single signature of James Phipps and undated. Fourth mark, in partnership with James Phipps alone, 31 January 1816. Heal records him alone as goldsmith, Gutter Lane, 1788; and with Edward Robinson, 1784-96. The partnership of the three probably began after 1800. He died 31 October 1823.

PICASSE, Stephen (2615) No record of apprenticeship or freedom. Only mark entered as smallworker, 16 May 1770. Address: Denmark Street, Soho, where he appears as goldworker in the Parl. Report list 1773.

PICKERING, Charles (397) Son of Edmund Pickering Citizen and Merchant Taylor of London, apprenticed to Samuel Edlin 24 December 1729 on payment of £10 and turned over to George Baker 8 January 1736. Free, 3 March 1737. Mark entered as smallworker, undated, between May and August 1738. Address: 'at the Bunch of Grapes Foster Lane'. 'Free Goldsmith'.

PICKERING, John (1581) No record of apprenticeship or freedom. Only mark entered as smallworker, 'a chaser', 8 March 1765. Address: 'Facing the Bull and Goat Holborn', where he appears without category in the Parl. Report list 1773. Probably the only entry of a man actually described as a chaser. Perhaps identical with John Pickering, gold and metal worker, 86 Long Acre, 1790-3.

PICKERING, Matthew (2193) Son of John Pickering late of Worksworth in the County of Derby gentleman deceased, apprenticed to Nathaniel Lock 19 August 1696. Free, 8 September 1703. Mark entered as largeworker, 23 September 1703. Address: Mugwell Street. Heal records him here, Monkwell Street, as plateworker, 1703-6.

*PICKETT, William (3257) Either (1) son of William Pickett late of Stoke Newington tallowchandler deceased, apprenticed to William Hunter 5 October 1750 on payment of £50. Freedom unrecorded. Or less likely (2) son of James Pickett late of the parish of St. Andrews Holborn victualler deceased, apprenticed to the same 1755 and turned over to James Johnson (skinner) 6 August 1760. Freedom again unrecorded. Livery, 19 July 1763. Only mark entered as smallworker, 16 January 1769. Address: Ludgate Hill, where he appears as goldsmith in the Parl. Report list 1773. Heal records him, in partnership with — Thead (or Theed), as goldsmiths and jewellers, Golden Salmon, Ludgate Hill, 1758-72, which suggests Pickett's identity with the first apprentice above. According to Norman Penzer, *Paul Storr*, Pickett married into the Theed family and took Philip Rundell (q.v.) as partner in 1772. Heal records this partnership from 1777 to 1785. In 1781 Pickett had a house in Harpur Street, Holborn, where his daughter Elizabeth was burned to death while dressing for a party. He became Alderman of Cornhill Ward 1782, Sheriff 1784 and Lord Mayor 1789, having apparently retired from active business by 1785. Court of Goldsmiths' Company, May 1787. He also unsuccessfully contested Parliament for the City in 1790 and 1796, and he died 17 December in the latter year. It seems unlikely that George Pickett, goldworker, 1837 (Section VII) is connected.

PIERCE, Clifford (2191-2) Son of Henry Pierce late of Newton Coyn in the County of York clerk deceased, apprenticed to Mathew Shank 8 July 1681 (signs Piers) and re-apprenticed to Francis Cooke 13 November 1682, on this occasion his place of origin given as Newton Kyme. Free, 19 August 1690. Mark entered as smallworker, undated, probably April 1697 on commencement of register. 'Clifford Pierce being absent his wife has subscribed liveing at Smithfield barrs elisabeth peirce.' Second mark, 11 May 1705. Address: Maid Court, Moor Lane.

PIERCE, Thomas (2194) Son of Clifford Pierce (above). Free by patrimony, 21 February 1717. Mark entered as smallworker, 27 February 1717. Address: Fox and Crown, Barbican. Heal records one of the same name as goldsmith, Princes Street, Leicester Fields, 1711, but identity with the above seems doubtful since the closeness of the entry above with the grant of freedom suggests a definite decision to set up business, probably apart from his father, in 1717.

PIERCY, George (872, 1603) Son of Josiah Piercy of Aldersgate Street goldsmith, apprenticed to Thomas Wallis of Red Lion Street as goldsmith 7 November 1798. Freedom unrecorded. First mark entered as spoonmaker, in partnership with Josiah his father, 4 January 1812. Address: 17 Bartholomew Close. Second mark alone, 16 December 1819, same address. Third mark, 7 December 1820. Moved to 15 Upper Ashby Street, Goswell Road, 12 October 1826.

PIERCY, Josiah (1603, 1842) Son of Josiah Piercy of Tooley Street Southwark labourer, apprenticed to William Strowd as silver polisher 4 August 1773 on payment of £5 of the charity of the Free School of St. Olave Southwark. Free, 7 March 1781. First mark entered as spoonmaker, in partnership with his son George (above), 4 January 1812. Address: 17 Bartholomew Close. Second mark alone, 1 January 1828. Address: 15 Ashby Street, Goswell Road.

PIERCY, Robert (2410, 3783) Son of White Piercy late of Whitney in the County of Oxford blanketmaker deceased, apprenticed to Samuel Wood 7 March 1750. Free, 6 April 1757. Livery, July 1763. First mark (3783) probably entered soon after the commencement of the missing register of 1758–73, since it is found on casters and cruets and Piercy was not only apprenticed to the leading caster-maker of the previous generation, but also appears in the Wakelin ledgers as supplying casters and cruets from 1766 onwards. He appears as plateworker, Foster Lane, in the Parl. Report list 1773. Second mark (first recorded) entered as largeworker, 21 July 1775. Address: 21 Foster Lane. Moved to 57 St. Paul's Churchyard, 21 January 1780. Heal records him as plateworker, London, 1759–77; and Foster Lane, 1773–5. He died between 1795 and 1801.

PIERREPONT, George (3111) Son of George Pierrepont late Citizen and Goldsmith deceased, apprenticed to Thomas Guy 2 May 1764 and turned over the same day to John Henry Vere Poulterer on consideration of £8. 5s. of the charity of the Company. Free, 6 May 1772. Mark entered as spoonmaker, in partnership with William Eley I, 11 November 1777. Address: 46 Little Bartholomew Close. Heal records him as silversmith, Angell Street, 1786. His father of the same name, son of John Pierrepont late of the parish of St. Mary Islington gentleman, was apprenticed to William Biddle 6 May 1742, and is presumably the same as — Pierrepont, jeweller, Silver Street, Wood Street, 1753, as recorded by Heal.

PIERS, Daniel (493, 3520) No record of apprenticeship or freedom, unless he can be identified with Daniel Pearce or Peirce son of Thomas Citizen and Fishmonger, apprenticed to William Noyes 7 November 1726. Freedom unrecorded. The latter however signs 'peirce' and both the present entry and that of Mary (following) are Piers. Only mark entered as largeworker, 3 November 1746. Address: Spur Street, Leicester Fields. Presumably dead by June 1758 on the entry of Mary Piers' mark (below). Heal records him as plateworker at the above address, 1746–9; and 'Bottom of Leicester Fields', 1752–4. His work though comparatively rare shows distinction of rococo design and execution and it seems probable that he was of Huguenot extraction, as also suggested by his address.

PIERS, Mary (2057) Presumably widow of Daniel Piers (above). Only mark entered as largeworker, 2 June 1758. Address: Spur Street, Leicester Fields, where Heal records her this year, and London, 1758–62.

PIKE, William and John (3274) No record of apprenticeship or freedom of either. Mark entered as plateworkers, 10 March 1824. Address: 8 Oxford Arms Passage, Warwick Lane, Newgate Street.

PILKINGTON, Robert (2197, 2401, 2417) No record of apprenticeship or freedom. Two marks (Sterling and New Standard) entered as smallworker, undated, between June 1724 and March 1725. Address: 'at the signe of the Spectacles in Glasshouse Yard, Blackfriars'. Third mark, 20 June 1739. Address: Savoy. Heal records him, only as plateworker, at the second address and date. From the shop sign one might suppose him a silver spectacle-maker but the entry of a New Standard mark after return of Sterling and the size of the marks, although entered as smallworker, make this seem unlikely.

PILLEAU, (Alexis) Pezé (2195, 2212, 2217) Fourth son of Alexis and Madelaine Pilleau, baptized 1696. Described as son of Pezé Pilleau of Covent Garden goldsmith on his apprenticeship to John Chartier 27 April 1710. Free, 2 July 1724. Two marks (Sterling and New Standard) entered as largeworker, undated, between 30 June 1720 and September 1724, probably nearer the latter date in view of his freedom date. Address: Chandois Street. 'Free Goldsmith'. Third mark, 29 June 1739, same address. Heal records him as Pezé Pilleau Junior, goldsmith and maker of artificial teeth, Golden Cup, over against Slaughter's Coffee House, at the upper end of St. Martin's Lane, 1719; and 'removed over the way to Corner of Newport Street', St. Martin's Lane, 1719. This however must refer to the father Alexis Pilleau. Pezé Pilleau's address remained the same throughout his working career, and is given by Heal as Golden Cup, on the Paved Stones in Chandos Street, 1719–55. The fact that Pezé Pilleau did not take up his freedom till 1724, presumably indicated that he worked at first with his master Chartier or his father Alexis. He was married on Christmas Day 1724 at the Castle Street Church to Henriette Chartier, daughter of his master, by whom he had six sons and two daughters. He died 2 January 1776, but his working period seems to have ended about 1755. His work, though comparatively rare, is characterized by fine proportion and finish; he seems to have specialized in an unusual design of jug with facetted body, to which there are German parallels. The Pilleau family have been the subject of two studies by Sir Charles Clay, F.S.A.: 1. 'Notes on the Ancestors and Descendants of Pezé Pilleau, the London Goldsmith' (*Hug. Soc. Proc.*, 16, p. 338 et seq.), and 2. 'The Register of the Reformed Church at Le Mans' (with appendix by the present author on Pezé Pilleau) (*Hug. Soc. Pub.*, 47, 1961). The earliest recorded member of the family is Alexis Pilleau, goldsmith, who executed a reliquary for the cathedral of Le Mans in 1612. He was the great-grandfather of Alexis Pilleau, merchant goldsmith of Le Mans, born 1658, who married Madelaine Pézé in 1683 and arrived in England by 1688 when he joined the Threadneedle Street Church as Alexis Pilleau of Le Mans. Although recorded as goldsmith and artificial teeth maker from 1703 to 1719 there is no entry of any mark for him, but if his principal work was the teeth-making it was presumably considered exempt from marking.

Pezé Pilleau and Henriette Chartier had six sons and two daughters, all recorded in the Castle Street register, of whom apparently all but Isaac and Susan were already dead, as well as their mother, by the time Pezé made his will in 1762. In this his son Isaac is described as 'A clerk in the Bank of England'. Susan and Francis Perigal, watchmaker at the Royal Exchange, are named as executors, the latter presumably the son of Henriette Pilleau's sister Susanne who had married Francois Perigal of the Dieppe watch-making Huguenot family. In his will Pilleau left to his daughter an estate at Wigborough, Essex, formerly left to him by Isaac Houssaye of Colchester, whose mother, Marie Blondeau, was related to Pezé's grandmother. Suzanne Pilleau founded the Lying-In Charity at Colchester in 1796 and died 1814. Isaac, born 1734, is said to have had a reputation as an art connoisseur and to have assisted Lord Liverpool in the formation of his collection of pictures and engravings. He married Jane Crispin or Crespin, probably a member of the goldsmith Paul Crespin's family, and died in 1812. Isaac's son Henry, civil servant, had four sons and five daughters from whom descended a number of distinguished military and medical personalities of the nineteenth century.

PINARD, Paul (2214) No record of apprenticeship or freedom. Only mark entered as largeworker, 12 October 1751. Address: Hog Lane. Heal records him as goldsmith and laceman, at this address; and also Crown, (No. 27) New Street, Covent Garden, c. 1760–84. Listed by Evans as Huguenot (*Hug. Soc. Proc.*, 14, p. 549).

*PINCKNEY, Israel (2190) Son of John Pinckney of Longstock in the County of Southampton clerk, apprenticed to John King 24 June 1673. Free, 1 July 1680, when he signs 'Pynckney'. He appears as Pinckney in the apprenticeship to him of George Titterton in 1687. Mark entered as largeworker, undated, probably April 1697 on commencement of register. Address: St. James's Street. Heal records him as Pincking following a misreading of the entry signature by Chaffers, where it is spelt Pinckny, the latter two letters in somewhat cramped formation. There were also, as recorded by Heal, three other goldsmiths of the name of Pinckney in Fleet Street in the seventeenth century, to whom Israel may well have been related.

PINDER, William (3258) No record of apprenticeship or freedom. First mark entered as smallworker, 3 February 1770. Address: 'near Featherstone Street, Bunhill Row'. Second mark, 30 May 1771. He appears as bucklemaker, at the same address, in the Parl. Report list 1773, and entered a mark as such, 5 September 1775. Address: 57 Bunhill Row (Section VIII). Heal omits the above dates and address but records him as goldsmith, 67 Aldersgate Street, 1779; and Noble Street, Foster Lane, 1784.

PINNELL, George Frederick (799) Son of John Pinnell of Islington gentleman, apprenticed to William Barrett of Deans Court, St. Martin's Le Grand as silversmith 4 October 1815. Free, 5 October 1831. First mark entered as smallworker, 27 September 1830. Address: 21 Hill Street, Jewin Street. Second mark, on move to 18 Red Cross Square, 10 November 1840. Third mark, 10 February 1841. Fourth, 23 November 1841. Fifth, 4 July 1842. Dead and mark defaced, 7 February 1852.

PITCHES, George (573, 630) Son of Anthony Pitches of Hastead (sic) in Suffolk clerk, apprenticed to Thomas Folkingham 20 December 1706. Free, 13 July 1715. Two marks (Sterling and New Standard) entered as largeworker, in partnership with John Edwards II, 6 December 1723. Address: St. Swithin's Lane, near Lombard Street. The partnership apparently dissolved by 27 April 1724, when Edwards entered two further marks alone.

PITTS, John (1598) No record of apprenticeship or freedom. Only mark entered 26 October 1730. Address: 'Brick Lane in ye Rope walk near Old Street'.

*PITTS, Thomas I (2875) Son of Thomas Pitts of the parish of St. Mary Whitechapel, apprenticed to Charles Hatfield 6 December 1737 and turned over to David Willaume (II) February 1742. Free, 16 January 1744. The mark now attributed here to him must have been entered not long after the start of the missing register of 1758-73, and he appears as plateworker, Air Street, St. James's, in the Parl. Report list 1773. Heal records him as working silversmith and chaser, Golden Cup, 20 Air Street, Piccadilly, 1767-93. The 'Workmens' Ledgers' of Parker and Wakelin (Garrard MSS., Victoria and Albert Museum) contain many pages of accounts from Pitts for epergnes from 1766, from which the identification of the mark, formerly attributed to Thomas Powell in the absence of any other evidence, was natural enough. His three sons Thomas, William and Joseph were all apprenticed to him in Air Street, 1767, 1769 and 1772. It is interesting to note that Joseph was apprenticed to his father and turned over the same day to Philip Day plate casemaker and leatherseller and described as plate casemaker on attaining his freedom in 1781. The continuous need for cases for the output of epergnes and centrepieces must have led to a close connection with Day and probably a desire to have a member of the family sharing in the business arising.

PITTS, Thomas II (2876) Perhaps son of Thomas Pitts I (above), apprenticed to his father of Hare (!) Street in the parish of St. James' Westminster Citizen and Goldsmith 4 February 1767. Free, 11 January 1775. Mark entered as plateworker, 5 April 1804. Address: London Field, Hackney. This identification, however, appears rather unlikely in view of the lapse of nearly thirty years between freedom and mark entry, and the fact that William Pitts (q.v.) was still working in continuation of the family business.

PITTS, William (3263, 3272) Son of Thomas Pitts I (above), apprenticed to his father of Air Street Piccadilly goldsmith, Citizen and Goldsmith 1 March 1769. Free, 3 November 1784. First mark entered as plateworker, 18 December 1781. Address: 17 St. Martin's Street, Leicester Fields. Second mark, 4 May 1786. Address: 26 Litchfield Street, Soho. Third mark, in partnership with Joseph Preedy, 11 January 1791, same address. Moved to 8 Newport Street, St. Ann's, 3 August 1795. Fourth mark alone, 21 December 1799. Address: 15 Little Wild Street, Lincoln's Inn Fields. Fifth mark, 5 March 1806. Address: 14 James Street, Lambeth Marsh. His son, William was apprenticed to his father 5 February 1806; the latter was then already at James Street, where he or William II still was in 1818 on the apprenticeship to him of John Childers, when Pitts was described as silversmith and chaser. Heal records all the above addresses and dates up to 1800. In his production of epergnes and dessert-baskets and stands, both alone and with Preedy, William Pitts shows himself specializing in exactly the same work as his father. In the Regency period he turned to the production of ornate cast candelabra in the neo-rococo style.

PIX, John (2199) Son of Charles Pix of Hawcus (?Hawkhurst) in Kent gentleman, apprenticed to Jeremy Lammas Jr. 27 February 1710 on payment of £12. Free, 12

June 1718. Mark entered as smallworker, with year 1725 only. Address: Swan Court, Grub Street.

PIZEY, George (873, 2670) No record of apprenticeship or freedom. First mark entered as plateworker, in partnership with Samuel Whitford, 27 August 1810. Address: 15 Denmark Court. There is an additional signature of Whitford below, against a change of address to 25 Grafton Street, but no date. Second mark alone, 23 December 1828. Address: 8 Acton Street, Gray's Inn Lane.

*PLANK, Lewis (1955) No record of apprenticeship or freedom. Only mark entered as jeweller, 26 August 1730. Address: Little Love Lane, Wood Street. Probably connected with Anthony Planck recorded by Heal as jeweller in Foster Lane and Bread Street from 1699 to 1727; and a second of the name, 1749-77. Peter Planck was apprenticed 1727, free 1744, and appears in Heal as refiner, Long Acre, to whom two sons William and Peter were apprenticed in 1768 and 1769.

*PLATEL, Philip (2213) No record of apprenticeship or freedom and relationship, if any, to Pierre (below) undetermined. Only mark entered as largeworker, 25 November 1737. Address: 'at ye Blackmores Head ye Corner of York Buildings in the Strand'. Heal records no more. Listed by Evans as Huguenot (*Hug. Soc. Proc.*, 14, p. 549).

PLATEL, Pierre (2200) Youngest son of Jean Batiste Bertrand Platel du Plateau of Lille, born c. 1664. The family are traced back at Lille to Jean Platel du Plateau whose son Luc was 'very old' in 1550. Jean Batiste fled as refugee to Flanders in 1685 and Pierre and his brother Claude arrived in England in 1688 in the train of William III (*Domestic State Papers*). Appears as Petro Platel in the Denization List, 8 May 1697, with his brother Claudius, and the names of Lewis Cuny and John Chartier adjacent. Free by redemption by order of the Court of Aldermen 14 June 1699. Mark entered as largeworker, 28 June 1699. Address: Pall Mall. Heal records him as plateworker, 'over against the Duke of Schomberg's in Pall Mall', 1699-1707; and 'The Lower end of Pall Mall at the Iron Rails', 1716. That these are separate addresses is confirmed by the St. James's rate books in which Platel appears from 1699 till 1704 in Pall Mall North (South in 1702, presumably in error), and from 1716-18 in Pall Mall South (the books are missing in the intervening years). Married Elizabeth Peterson, aged sixteen (?), 16 April 1700 at St. James', Piccadilly, he described as 'above 32 years', silversmith of St. James's'. Their son Peter was born 6 and baptized 19 September 1701 at St. James', and daughter Martha was born 4 and baptized 8 February 1703 at the same. Livery, 26 October 1708. He died and was buried at St. James's Piccadilly, 21 May 1719, leaving no will, but administration of his estate was entered in the Principal Probate Registry, 2 June 1719. His son Peter (Queen's College, Cambridge, B.A. 1726, M.A. 1730) became vicar of Yeldham Magna, Essex in 1732, curate, Chipping Barnet 1745-7, vicar of Ashburton, Devon 1749, and of Newport, Essex 1769, where he died. He appears as himself in Hogarth's engraving of 'The Sheriff's Banquet' (plate 8 of *The Idle and Industrious Apprentices*). His great-great-great-grandson Francis Vittery Platel was born 1908 (Major, George Medal) and died in 1944 leaving one son John Chamberlain Platel born 1937 (B.A., Trinity College, Oxford). (The author is indebted to Mrs F. V. Platel for much of the above family history supplementing and in parts correcting the chapter on Pierre Platel in P. A. S. Phillips, *Paul de Lamerie*, 1935.) It is significant that some of Platel's most important pieces including the rare and jewel-like gold ewer and dish of 1701 belong either to the Bentinck or Cavendish families, so closely associated with William III. The items at Welbeck are the toilet-service of 1701 (some pieces later by Clausen and Pyne) and a set of casters of 1709. Those at Chatsworth are the gold ewer and dish and cup and cover of 1717. A chocolate-pot of 1702 and cup and cover of 1705 are in the Farrer Collection, Ashmolean Museum.

PLATT, Robert (2408) No record of apprenticeship or freedom. First mark entered as smallworker, 21 September 1764. Address: Long Lane, Smithfield. Second mark, 8 June 1768. Address: New Turnstile, Holborn, where he appears as smallworker in the Parl. Report list 1773.

PLAYER, Gabriel (2201) Son of Isaac (Izack) Player late of Owldford(?) in the County of Middlesex yeoman, apprenticed to John Hudson for eight years 'from the 24th June last' 6 July 1687. Free, 24 June 1696. Livery, October 1708. Mark entered as largeworker, 3 August 1700. Address: 'at Ratcliff'. Heal records him as plateworker, Ratcliff, 1700–4; near Wapping Dock, 1710; and Malling Kent, 1727.

PLAYFAIR, William (3276) No record of apprenticeship or freedom. Only mark entered as spoonmaker, in partnership with William Wilson, 16 May 1782. Address: 2 Portland Road, Great Portland Street, Marybone. Heal records no more.

PLIMMER, John (1586) No record of apprenticeship or freedom. Only mark entered as smallworker, 18 December 1771. Address: 'the corner of the Great old bailey at No. 5 near Newgate', where he appears as smallworker in the Parl. Report list 1773.

PLIMPTON, Charles (400) Son of Thomas Plimpton of Gravel Lane Southwark dealer, apprenticed to William Frisbee of Snow Hill as goldsmith 1 March 1797 on payment of £20. Free, 2 January 1805. Mark entered as plateworker, 27 May 1805. Address: 10 Robert Street, Blackfriars Road. Moved to 26 Great Surrey Street, Blackfriars Road, no date.

PLUMLEY, Charles and John (403) No record of apprenticeship or freedom of either. Only mark entered as plateworkers, 24 April 1822. Address: 43 Ludgate Hill. Charles alone entered incuse mark as plateworker, 27 October 1830. Address: 231 Strand (Section V).

PLUMMER, Michael (2058) Son of William Plummer (below). Free of the Clothworkers' Company by patrimony, 1 July 1795 as silversmith 35 Noble Street. Mark entered as plateworker, 5 October 1791. Address: 47 Gutter Lane. Moved to 35 Noble Street, no date. Heal records him at Gutter Lane, 1791–5.

*PLUMMER, William (3255) Apprenticed to Edward Aldridge (q.v.) Clothworker 4 February 1746 (?7) Free, 5 February 1755. First mark entered as largeworker, 8 April 1755. Address: Foster Lane. Moved to Gutter Lane, 11 September 1757, where he appears as plateworker in the Parl. Report list 1773. Second mark, 17 March 1774. Address: 47 Gutter Lane. Third mark, 7 May 1789, same address. Heal records him at Foster Lane, 1755–63; Gutter Lane, 1773–89 (in 1784, No. 47); and 40 (or 43) Gutter Lane, 1790–3. His son William was apprenticed to Thomas Whipham as goldsmith in 1777, when William I is described as Citizen and Clothworker. William II appears as son of Wm. and Esther Plummer, born 11 May, baptized 18 May 1763, in St. Vedast, Foster Lane register. A daughter Eliz^a. is also recorded, born 1765. 'William Plummer buried in the Church Vault Novr 27th 1791. Aged 52 years', would almost certainly seem to refer to the same (compare the date of the entry of Michael Plummer's mark above), but his age given would make him only sixteen at the entry of his first mark in 1755. His work is almost entirely confined to pierced saw-cut pieces as cake-baskets, sugar and cream-baskets and strainers. He must have had a reasonably sized establishment since piercing is of necessity a slow process and from their survival rate his output of such pieces was high.

*PLUMPTON, Henry (1059) No record of apprenticeship or freedom. Only mark entered as smallworker, 14 November 1761. Address: Maiden Lane. He appears as smallworker, near Wapping Old Stairs, in the Parl. Report list 1773.

PLUMPTON, James (1584) No record of apprenticeship or freedom. Only mark entered as smallworker, 5 June 1767. Address: 13 Hosier Lane, where he appears as watchcasemaker in the Parl. Report list 1773.

PLYMLEY, Francis (2202) Son of John Plymley of Wolverhampton in the County of Stafford clerk, apprenticed to Samuel Wastell 26 January 1706. Free, 7 September 1715. Mark entered as largeworker, 12 October 1715. Address: Nicholas Lane. Heal records him as goldsmith here, at this date; and at Finch Lane, insolvent, 1723.

*POCOCK, Edward (81, 632, 993) No record of apprenticeship or freedom. A Henry Pocock, son of Edward was free in 1679, perhaps his father. First mark entered as largeworker, in partnership with Hugh Arnett, 15 February 1720. Second (Sterling) mark, 22 June 1720. Address: Foster Lane. Third mark alone, 11 December 1728, same address. Heal records him in partnership, London, 1719–24; and, in unpublished addenda, Blackmoors Head, Foster Lane, 1723; also alone, Foster Lane, 1728–34.

PODIE, See PODIO.

PODIO, Joseph Felix (2198) No record of apprenticeship or freedom. Possibly son of Peter Podio (below). Only mark entered as plateworker, 2 August 1806. Address: 6 Back Hill, Hatton Garden. Moved to 12

Croford Buildings, Clerkenwell, 13 October 1807.

PODIO, Peter (80, 2215) No record of apprenticeship or freedom. First mark entered as plateworker, in partnership with Abraham Peterson (q.v.), 1 May 1783. Address: 23 Primrose Hill, Salisbury Square, Fleet Street. In this entry the clerk wrote Podie but the signature and second entry are clearly Podio. Second mark alone, 12 February 1790. Address: King Edward Street, Bridewell Precinct. Heal records him in partnership as Podie, but not his working alone.

POLLOCK, John (1572, 1596) No record of apprenticeship or freedom. First mark entered as largeworker, 16 October 1734. Address: 'in Lon Acre over against the bird & hand'. Second mark 26 June 1739, same address. Moved to Belton Street, Long Acre, 26 January 1744. Heal records him Long Acre, 1734-9; Old Belton Street, Long Acre, 1748; and London, 1752-3.

PONT, John (1574, 1578) Son of Thomas Pont late of Huntingdon draper deceased, apprenticed to Dru Drury 23 June 1713 on payment of £20. Free, 5 October 1732. Mark entered as largeworker, 19 March 1739. Address: Staining Lane. Second mark as smallworker, 5 February 1762. Address: Maiden Lane. Appears as haft or hiltmaker at this address Parl. Report list 1773. Since from his apprenticeship date he must have been born c. 1700, the latter address and date may refer to a son of the same name. Heal records the two addresses and dates of the marks.

*PONTIFEX, Daniel (494, 3128) No record of apprenticeship or freedom. First mark entered as plateworker, in partnership with William Fountain (q.v.), 29 July 1791. Address: 13 Hosier Lane, West Smithfield. Partnership apparently dissolved by 1 September 1794, when Fountain entered a separate mark. Second mark alone, 10 September 1794, same address. Moved to 8 St. John's Square, Clerkenwell, 1 April 1811. Heal records the partnership as above and Pontifex alone, both same dates; and then Pontifex and Fountain, silversmiths, same address, 1796. His work, particularly fine silver-gilt dessert-dishes and baskets shows a high standard of execution and delicacy of design.

POOLE, Benjamin (2210) Son of John Poole late of Bubbingworth in the County of Essex gentleman deceased, apprenticed to Simon Knight 23 February 1699. Free, 27 February 1709. Livery, October 1708. Mark entered as smallworker, 31 May 1717. Address: Foster Lane.

POPE, Abraham (72, 2208) Son of William Pope late of the City of Westminster marriner deceased, apprenticed to Alexander Bower of the Leathersellers' Company 16 March 1691. Free, 20 July 1703 Mark entered as smallworker, 30 August 1703. Address: Holborn. 'Free of the Leathersellers'. Second (Sterling) mark, 30 July 1720. Heal records him as goldsmith, Ball Court in Salisbury Court, Fleet Street, 1716.

PORT, Thomas (2209) Son of Nicholas Port of Kingston on Thames in the County of Surrey tanner, apprenticed to Richard Sing 8 November 1699. Free, 17 October 1707. Mark entered as largeworker, 3 June 1713. Address: Queen Street. Livery, October 1721. Heal records him as above and 'Prince of Wale's Head over against the Bank in the Poultry', 1717-30. He died 10 February 1733 (*London Magazine*, p. 98, *The Gentleman's Magazine*, p. 101), then described as an eminent goldsmith in the Poultry, Common Councilman for Cheap Ward.

*PORTAL, Abraham (73) Member of a Huguenot family originating in Bagnols-sur Ceze, Languedoc. Guillaume Portal, born 1639, was 'of the Great Wardrobe' of William III and Anne. His brother Jean Francois also fled to England, father of three sons and seven daughters. The second son Pierre Guillaume became rector of Clowne, County Derby, c. 1724 and of South Fambridge, County of Essex in 1734. His first son Andrew took orders and was vicar of St. Helen's, Abingdon. Abraham, his second son, described as son of William Portal of Prittlewell in the County of Essex clerk, was apprenticed to Paul De Lamerie 3 July 1740 on payment of £35. Free, 7 March 1749. Mark entered as largeworker, 26 October 1749. Address: Rose Street, Soho. Moved into the precinct of the Savoy, 29 September 1750. Moved to the Strand, 1 June 1753. Livery, June 1763. Heal records him as goldsmith, jeweller and dramatist, Rose Street, Soho, 1749; Salmon and Pearl, 34 Ludgate Hill, 1763-78; and Castle Street, Holborn, 1795; died 1809; also in partnership with Harry Gearing as goldsmiths, jewellers and toymen, at the Ludgate Hill address, 1774; bankrupt 1778. He appears as goldsmith, Ludgate Hill, in the Parl. Report list 1773. His brother William (q.v.) was apprenticed to him, 1750. Abraham married firstly Elizabeth Nethersole, who died without issue 1758, and secondly in that year Elizabeth Bedwell of Abingdon (where his brother was vicar), who bore him two sons and four daughters, one of whom, Anne, married Moreton Walhouse and became mother of Edward, 1st Lord Hatherton.

Portal is one of the very few goldsmiths to appear in the *Dictionary of National Biography*, on account of his literary activities. He first appears in *Biographica Dramatica* (1812): 'Failing in this (i.e. as a goldsmith) he commenced bookselling in the Strand (cf. the move of 1753, above) in which he was more successful. He finished his career as box-keeper at Drury Lane Theatre but we cannot learn the time of his death'. His first play was *Olindo and Sophronia*, a tragedy, 1758. 'This play is a very indifferent one and was never brought on the stage. The story of it is taken from Tasso's *Gieruselemme Liberata*. The author tells us that this was his virgin tragedy, the effort of almost unassisted nature, the solace and amusement of the leisure hours of one who has hitherto passed his time not in the learned and peaceful retreats of the Muses, but in the rude and noisy shop of Vulcan'. Portal's further plays published were *The Indiscreet Lover*, comedy 1768; *The Cady of Bagdad*, opera 1778, performed for one night at Drury Lane (the songs only printed); and *Vortimer or The True Patriot* 1796. In 1781 he produced a volume of *Poems* with dedicatory lines to Richard Brinsley Sheridan, with whom he claimed friendship, and containing a Sonnet to Sheridan's wife, the beautiful Elizabeth Linley and a Monody on the death of her brother Thomas. Portal's second son was christened Richard Brinsley, whose godfather seems little in doubt.

Portal's work, as may be expected from his flirting with the literary muse, is fairly rare, but shows on occasions a reasonable accomplishment, perhaps the work of his journeymen. His evidence to the Parl. Report Committee in 1773, of the difficulty he found in distinguishing the marks on Sheffield plate from those on silver, leaves doubts as to whether bad eye-sight, ineptitude or business spite was the reason. He died in Castle Street, Holborn, January 1809 and was buried at St. Andrew's, leaving less than £1000. (For some of the above details cf. Sir William Portal, Bart., *Abraham Portal and his descendants*, 1925.)

PORTAL, Louis (1957) No record of apprenticeship or freedom. Only mark entered as smallworker, 10 August 1758. Address: St. Martin's Le Grand. Possibly connected with the Hector Portal apprenticed in 1698.

*PORTAL, William (1458, 3256) Son of William Portal of South Hambridge in the County of Essex clerk, apprenticed to his brother Abraham Portal (q.v.) 1750 on payment of £20. Free, 11 February 1761. Mark entered as smallworker, 11 August 1760. Address: Orange Street near Leicester Square. Second mark, 7 September, presumably 1760. Third, 21 April 1764. Fourth, 20 March 1767. Fifth mark, in partnership with James King II, 10 November 1768. Livery, December 1771. Appears as haftmaker, Orange Street, Parl. Report list 1773. Heal records him only as haftmaker, 1768–73. Died September 1815. Did he, one wonders, supply the swords for his brother's one night opera, *The Cady of Bagdad* in 1778 ?

PORTER, John (2207, 3751–2) Son of Francis Porter late of Danberry in the County of Essex yeoman deceased, apprenticed to John Sutton 3 July 1684. Free, 22 April 1692. Mark entered as largeworker, 21 October 1698. Address: Strand. Heal also records him at Clare Court, Drury Lane, 1705; and London, 1712.

POTTER, William (3261) No record of apprenticeship or freedom. Only mark entered as spoonmaker, 26 February 1777. Address: Little Wild Street, Lincoln's Inn Fields. Heal records him here as plateworker, 1777–8.

POTTICARY, Christopher (399) Son of Christopher Potticary of St. Mary Whitechapel gentleman, apprenticed to William Burton 1 October 1751 on payment of £15. Free, 5 May 1758. Mark entered as smallworker, 7 January 1767. Address: Silver Street, Bridgewater Square. Described as watchcasemaker in apprenticeship to him of his son Nathaniel in 1768, and also as such in the Parl. Report list 1773. Nathaniel entered an incuse mark, 1 November 1783 at 1 Bridgewater Square (Section V). Samuel Potticary, goldworker (Section VII), may be connected.

POULDEN, Richard (2415) No record of apprenticeship or freedom. First mark entered as smallworker, 13 November 1818. Address: 46 St. John Street, Clerkenwell. Second mark, 13 October 1822. Moved to 13 Manchester Street, Bethnal Green, 15 August 1827. Moved to 15 Little Nelson Street, City Road, 21 February 1828.

POWELL, Francis (709, 711) No record of apprenticeship or freedom. First mark entered as smallworker, in partnership with Robert Coates, 6 January 1818. Address: 4 Fann Street. Second mark alone, 7 May 1818, same address. Moved to 13 College Street, Tooley Street, 13 May 1826; to Christopher Court, St. Martin's Le Grand, 27 March 1834; to 10 Green Lane, Stoke Newington, 16 September 1835; to 14 Pauls Alley, Red Cross Street, Cripplegate, 6 June 1839; to 4 Fann Street, Aldersgate Street, 5 July 1850.

POWELL, George (870) No record of apprenticeship or freedom. Only mark entered as smallworker, 9 August 1771. Address: 9 Habedsher (Haberdasher) Walk, Hoxton, where he appears without category in the Parl. Report list 1773.

POWELL, Thomas (2885) No record of apprenticeship or freedom. First mark entered as largeworker, 5 May 1756. Address: Mouldmakers Row, St. Martin's Le Grand. Moved to New Court, New Street, Fetter Lane, 16 July 1757. Second mark, on move to Bolt Court, Fleet Street, 10 February 1758. Heal records him as plateworker, St. Martin's Le Grand, 1756; Bolt Court, 1758; and Craig's Court, Charing Cross, 1773-89. He appears as plateworker, near Craig's Court, in the Parl. Report list 1773, but the later date in Heal may perhaps be derived from the attribution by Jackson to him of Thomas Pitts' mark (q.v.). Thomas Powell, goldsmith, St. Martin in the Fields, appears as bankrupt in *The Gentleman's Magazine*, June 1777. Heal also has Thomas Powell, jeweller Peacock, Gutter Lane, Cheapside, c. 1760, who would appear from address and date to be another. The name also occurs without category, Noble Street, St. Luke's in the Parl. Report list 1773, immediately above the Craig's Court entry, clearly indicating a separate identity.

POWELL, William (1804) Three apprenticeships of this name and relative date appear in the records but no identification is possible. Only mark entered as largeworker, in partnership with James Davis, 2 October 1826. Address: 7 Queen Square, Aldersgate Street.

POYNTON, Thomas (2873) No record of apprenticeship or freedom. Only mark entered as smallworker, 22 August 1758. Address: Old Street Square. Elizabeth Poynton, bucklemaker, appears at this address in the Parl. Report list 1773, presumably his widow.

PRATT, James (1594) Either (1) son of Thomas Boulton Pratt (q.v.) of Gutter Lane Goldsmith, apprenticed to his father as goldsmith 3 February 1796. Freedom unrecorded. Or (2) son of Richard Pratt of Greenhill Rents Smithfield Row cabinetmaker, apprenticed to Charles Clopton Price of City Road Goldsmith as working goldsmith 4 July 1804 on payment of £20. Freedom unrecorded. Mark entered as plateworker, 11 August 1818. Address: 47 Rowston Street, Clerkenwell.

PRATT, Richard (2403) No record of apprenticeship or freedom, unless, but unlikely, Richard Pratt son of John, apprenticed to John Watts 1735. Mark entered as smallworker, 4 May 1730. Address: Of Alley, York Buildings, Strand.

PRATT, Thomas Boulton (2888-9) Son of Charles Pratt of Greenwich in the County of Kent gardener, apprenticed to John Payne 11 January 1753 on payment of £50. Free, 6 February 1760. Livery, July 1763. Mark entered as plateworker, in partnership with Arthur Humphreys, 7 July 1780. Address: 44 Poultry. His son Thomas was apprenticed to him 6 April 1785, when the father's address is recorded as Gutter Lane. Heal records him here as goldsmith, 1774-90; also with Arthur Humphreys, 44 Poultry, 1780 (probably Gutter Lane his workshop and the Poultry address a retail establishment); also with William Edward Smith and Joseph Hardy as goldsmiths and jewellers, 82 Cheapside, 1790, partnership dissolved 1796. Two further sons were apprenticed to him: John, 5 May 1790 and James, 3 February 1796. He died 2 December 1796 (*The Gentleman's Magazine*).

*PREEDY, Joseph (1587-8, 3272) Son of the Rev. Benjamin Preedy of St. Albans in the County of Hertford clerk, apprenticed to Thomas Whipham 2 October 1765 and turned over 9 June 1766 to William Plummer of Gutter Lane goldsmith, Citizen and Clothworker on consideration of £21. Free, 4 August 1773 as plateworker. First mark

PREIST (or PRIEST)

entered as plateworker, 3 February 1777. Address: Westmoreland Buildings, Aldersgate Street. Second mark, in partnership with William Pitts, 11 January 1791. Address: Litchfield Street, St. Ann's. Moved to 8 Newport Street, St. Ann's, 3 August 1795. The partnership was apparently dissolved by 21 December 1799 when Pitts entered a single mark. Third mark alone, 20 January 1800. Address: 8 Great Newport Street. Heal records all the above addresses and dates, and also Preedy alone in Litchfield Street in 1791, the year of the commencement of the partnership with Pitts.

PREIST (or PRIEST), James (3271) Son of William Preist deceased, apprenticed to William Preist (presumably his brother) 1750. Free, 4 July 1764. Mark presumably entered, in partnership with his brother William, shortly after this date in the missing register of largeworkers. Recorded by Heal together as goldsmiths, 30 Whitecross Street, from 1764 to 1773, and they appear in the Parl. Report list of this latter date. His son, James Hammond Preist was apprenticed to him 1 January 1783, when James Preist is described as goldsmith of Watling Street, Citizen and Goldsmith. Heal also records this address and date.

PREIST (or PRIEST), John (1576, 3668) Son of John Priest Citizen and Barber Surgeon of London, apprenticed to William Gould 6 February 1739 on payment of £18. Free, 7 June 1749. Mark entered as largeworker, 24 June 1748. Address: Salisbury Court, Fleet Street. Moved to Prugions (sic) Court, Old Bailey, 29 February 1760. Heal records him as plateworker, Salisbury Court, 1748-51, but not the latter address. His connection with James and William Preist (above and below) is not apparent. Like his master William Gould he was a specialist candlestick maker and it is doubtful if his mark will be found on any other category of plate.

*PREIST, William (3271, 3335) Son of William Preist Citizen and Armourer and Brazier of London, apprenticed to Richard Gurney 30 July 1740 on payment of £27. 6s. Free, 6 September 1749. First mark entered as largeworker, in partnership with William Shaw, 12 October 1749. Address: Maiden Lane. Moved to Wood Street, 2 January 1751. Livery, March 1758. Second mark together, 27 June 1759. Recorded by Heal on his own as goldsmith, corner of Lad Lane, Wood Street, 1763. Third mark, with James Preist, presumably his brother (q.v.), presumably entered shortly after the latter's freedom, July 1764. Heal then records them together at 30 Whitecross Street till 1773 when he appears, with James as plateworkers, in the Parl. Report list of that year. He died between 1802 and 1811. Heal records also William Preist, goldsmith, Hackney, 1782, whose identity with the above remains open to question.

*PRESTON, Benjamin (206) Son of Benjamin Preston of the Assay Office Goldsmiths' Hall London, apprenticed to Edward Barnard of Paternoster Row as silversmith 7 November 1810 on payment of £20. Free, 3 December 1817. Mark entered as plateworker, 16 September 1825. Address: 41 Coppice Row, Clerkenwell. Livery, April 1835. Died September 1887.

PRETTY, Catherine (398) No record of apprenticeship or freedom. Only mark entered as smallworker, 13 March 1759. Address: Gorgs (?George's) Court, St. John's Lane, Clerkenwell. Moved to Duck Lane, Smithfield, 21 March 1761.

PREW, Thomas (2222, 2868) Son of William Prew of Charlcott in Warwick yeoman, apprenticed to Thomas Ripsheire of the Grocers' Company in Gutter Lane silversmith for seven years 20 July 1708. Free, 9 July 1718, when noted 'Man & Ma^r. both in Gutter Lane silversmiths'. First mark entered as smallworker, 16 July 1718. Address: Gutter Lane. 'Free Grocer.' Second (Sterling) mark, 4 July 1720, same address.

PRICE, Andrew (74-5) No record of apprenticeship or freedom. First mark entered as smallworker, 4 May 1763. Address: Noble Street, St. Luke's. Second mark, 12 September 1766, same address.

PRICE, Charles (401-2) Probably Charles Clapton Price son of John Price of St. Luke Street sawyer, apprenticed to Carnelius Bland of Aldersgate Street as goldsmith 2 December 1789. Free, 1 February 1797. First mark entered as plateworker, 11 February 1812. Address: 1 Cross Street, Sutton Street (Hatton Garden). Moved to 25 St. John Street, Clerkenwell, 11 October 1819. Second mark, 27 November 1823. Third mark, 20 November 1826.

PRICE, Harvey (1056) Son of Charles Price of Prestaign in the County of Radnorshire mercer, apprenticed to George Lambe 7 December 1715 on payment of £20. Turned over 3 September 1718 to George Lamb in Little Newport Street. This one would suppose a mistake for the name of his new master, but on the other hand he was turned over to Jane Lambe (widow of George) in 'Shandos' Street 31 May 1722. Free, 8 April 1725. Mark entered as largeworker, 10 February 1727. Address: Wine Street, near Round Court in the Strand. 'Free of Gouldsmith'. Later undated address: 'in flowr de luce Court in fleet street'. Heal records him as in Wine Street (?Court), before 1726, but the mark entry is clearly dated 10 February 1726/7. He also gives Flower de Luce Court as 1726, but this address follows the other in the entry and is clearly subsequent to it.

PRICE, Joseph (1840, 3273) Son of William Price of Love Grove Fleet Market poulterer, apprenticed to Mary Crosswell of Monkwell Street (widow of Henry) as silversmith 6 January 1808 and turned over to Edward Rigby and again to Mary Crosswell on payment of £3 charity money by the treasurer of the parish of St. Sepulchre. Free, 6 December 1815. First mark as smallworker, in partnership with his brother William (q.v.), 28 January 1820. Address: 5 Silver Street, Wood Street. Second mark alone, 10 August 1821, same address. Moved to 49 Red Lion Street, Clerkenwell, 18 June 1825.

PRICE, Sarey (2614, 2620) No record of apprenticeship or freedom. First mark entered as smallworker, 27 June 1761. Address: Blue Anchor Alley, Bunhill Row. Signs with X. Second mark, 14 June 1763.

PRICE, Thomas (2879) No record of apprenticeship or freedom. Only mark entered as smallworker, 6 August 1802. Address: 13 Weston Street, Pentonville.

PRICE, William (3268, 3273) Son of William Price of St. Bride's Fleet Street poulterer, apprenticed to Richard Crosswell of Monkwell Street, as goldsmith 11 August 1802 and turned over to Henry Crosswell 2 May 1804. Free, 6 June 1810. First mark entered as smallworker, 17 March 1812. Address: 15 Shoe Lane. Moved to 5 Silver Street, Wood Street, 23 December 1814. Second mark, in partnership with his brother Joseph (q.v.), 28 January 1820, same address. Partnership probably dissolved by 10 August 1821, when Joseph entered a separate mark. William alone moved to 72 Wood Street, 22 June 1825. Presumably the William Archer Price elected to Livery, 23 January 1822. Died 1859-62.

PRICHARD, Thomas (2219-20) 'Thomas Thomas als Prichard' son of Richard Thomas 'de Grithland(?)' in the County of Flint yeoman, apprenticed to Charles Laughton of the Grocers' Company silversmith Bedfordbury Covent Garden 3 October 1687. Free, 1 July 1695. First mark entered as smallworker, undated, probably April 1697 on commencement of register. Address: New Round Court, Strand. 'Free Grocer'. Second mark, 30 November 1709. Address: Drury Lane. Heal records him as Thomas Prichard or Pritchard, plateworker, against the Red Bull in Drury Lane, 1709-11. He was master of John Edwards II (q.v.).

PRIEST *See* PREIST

PRIEST, Samuel (2613) No record of apprenticeship or freedom. Only mark entered as smallworker, 24 March 1760. Address: Old Street, near Goswell Street. Samuel Priest and John Rawley appear as partners without category at Crown Court, Charterhouse Lane, in the Parl. Report list 1773, having entered an incuse mark, 28 March 1761, at the same address (Section V).

PRIESTMAN, John (1589) No record of apprenticeship or freedom. Only mark entered as spoonmaker, 23 February 1786. Address: 18 Bartholomew Close. Moved to 11 Great Sutton Street, Clerkenwell, no date.

PRITCHARD, John (1591) No record of apprenticeship or freedom. First mark entered as bucklemaker, 19 October 1778. Address: 13 Sutton Street, Goswell Street (Section VIII). Second mark entered as smallworker, 2 April 1799. Address: Rawstone Street, St. John Street Road.

PRITCHARD, Joseph (1595) No record of apprenticeship or freedom. Only mark entered as plateworker, 10 February 1825. Address: 4 Swinton Place, Bagnage Road. Moved to 28 Steward Street, 13 August (year omitted). Probably dead by 19 February 1831, when Sarah Pritchard (below) entered her mark at the same address. Probably a specialist knifehaftmaker as Sarah Pritchard (below).

PRITCHARD, Sarah (2618) No record of apprenticeship or freedom. Presumably widow of Joseph Pritchard (above). Mark entered as knifehaft-maker, 19 February 1831. Address: 28 Seward (sic) Street, Goswell Street. Signs with X.

PROC(K)TER, Edmund (2218) Son of John Procter late Citizen and Salter of London deceased, apprenticed to Robert Timbrell 12 July 1692 (Signs register Procter). Free, 6 October 1699. Mark entered as largeworker, 8 October 1700. Address: St. Ann's Lane. Heal records nothing further.

PROSSER, John (1590) No record of apprenticeship or freedom. Only mark entered as smallworker, 4 April 1796. Address: 9 Charing Cross. A well-known swordmaker, whose signature is found on fine presentation swords of the early nineteenth century.

PROSSER, Walter (2221) Either (1) Son of Walter Prosser late of Llantission(?) in the County of Monmouth clerk deceased, apprenticed to Katherine Stevens widow of Roger 13 October 1676. Free, 21 November 1684. Or, possibly (2) son of the above. Mark entered as smallworker, 23 March 1708. Address: London Wall, near Moorgate.

PROTHERO, Thomas P. (2880) No record of apprenticeship or freedom. Only mark entered as smallworker, 29 October 1802. Address: 36 Brownlow Street, Drury Lane.

*PRYOR, William (496) No record of apprenticeship or freedom. Only mark entered as largeworker, in partnership with Edward Dobson and James Williams (qq.v.), 10 February 1755. Address: Paternoster Row. Partnership dissolved 26 July 1755. Heal also records William Pryor, silversmith, 82 Minories, 1784-93; and Savory and Pryor, cutlers and silversmiths, 10 Poultry, 1793-6, who may well relate to the above.

PURRIER, William (3262) No record of apprenticeship or freedom. Only mark entered as smallworker, 27 October 1778. Address: 53 Long Lane, Smithfield.

PURSE, William (3895) No record of apprenticeship or freedom. The name is only found as an attribution by Jackson to the mark in question appearing on a beaker of 1804. I can find no authority behind the attribution.

PURTON, Frances (708, 712) Widow of Robert Purton (below). First mark entered as smallworker, 4 March 1783. Address: 2 Cary Lane. Second mark, 16 June 1787. Third mark, in partnership with Thomas Johnson, 28 February 1793, same address. Fourth mark alone, 28 January 1795. Heal records her as Francis at this address, 1788-93. Her identity is established by the apprenticeship to her in 1790 of Joseph Thredder.

PURTON, Robert (2411) Son of Michael Purton Citizen and Fishmonger of London, apprenticed to David Hennell 6 January 1765. Free, 11 March 1772 as goldsmith, Mortlake, Surrey. First mark entered as smallworker, 23 January 1779. Address: 3 Ball Court, Bunhill Row. Second mark, 13 April 1779. Third mark, 23 February 1780. Address: 2 Cary Lane, Foster Lane. Probably dead by 4 March 1783, when his widow Frances entered her first mark (above).

PURVER, Sarah (2617) No record of apprenticeship or freedom. Presumably widow of Thomas Purver (below). Only mark entered as spoonmaker, 23 September 1817. Address: 2 Clerkenwell Close.

PURVER, Thomas (2882, 2890) Son of John Purver of Chedingford in the County of Surrey labourer, apprenticed to William Sumner as goldsmith 6 August 1783. Free, 6 July 1791. First mark entered as spoonmaker, 6 October 1814. Address: 2 Clerkenwell Close. Second mark, in partnership with Edward Furnice, 17 April 1815, same address. Presumably dead by 23 September 1817 when Sarah Purver (above) entered her mark at the same address.

PYE, Thomas (2886-7) Son of Thomas Pye Citizen and Ironmonger of London, apprenticed to William Petley 25 June 1706. Free, 1 June 1715. Signatory as journeyman to the petition against assaying the work of foreigners not having served seven years apprenticeship, February 1716. First mark entered as largeworker, 17 July 1738. Address: Carey Lane. Second mark, 14 June 1739, same address. Heal records him here for 1738-9.

PYKE, William (2246) Son of Richard Pike of Cambridge gentleman, apprenticed to John Cooke 26 April 1683 for eight years. Free, 10 July 1691. Mark entered as smallworker, undated, probably April 1697 on commencement of register. Address: Petty France, near Bishopsgate.

*PYNE, Benjamin (2244-5, 3748) Son of Humfry Pyne late of St. Mary Ottery in the County of Devon gentleman deceased, apprenticed to George Bowers 23 October 1667 for eight years. Free, 1 September 1676. The unusual mark of a single letter P crowned, which is found from shortly after 1680, appears on the 1697 copperplate at Goldsmiths' Hall, and reappears after 1720, again unentered, can safely be attributed to him. His only authenticated marks are the two entered as largeworker, undated, probably April 1697 on commencement of register. Address: St. Martin's Le Grand. Heal records him as goldsmith, George Street 1693-6; St. Martin's Le Grand, 1697; and London, 1700-27. He can almost certainly be identified with the Benjamin Pine of St. Leonard, Foster Lane, married to Susanna Salisbury of St. Bridget, London at St. Lawrence Jewry, 25 December 1682. The register of Christchurch, Newgate, contains baptismal entries for six sons and two daughters of Benjamin and Susanna Pine between 1683 and 1699, of whom all but one son and one daughter were buried in near infancy. In 1685 Pyne was working for Sir Richard Hoare, as his account for 14 September that year includes 'A chocolate dish of Esqr Peypes' (Hilton Price, *Handbook of London Bankers*) whose private account was kept at Hoare's from 1680 till 1701 (Heal). He signed the petition against the work of 'aliens or foreigners', 11 August 1697, and in 1699 he was elected Renter Warden but paid £30 fine to be excused office. Court, May 1703. Warden, 1715, 1720 and 1721 and Prime Warden, 1725. He held the position of Subordinate Goldsmith to the King for the coronation of George I only (Major General H. W. D. Sitwell, 'The Jewel House and the Royal Goldsmiths', *Arch. Journ.*, CXVII, p. 154). His son Benjamin was apprenticed to him 21 October 1708, free 8 May 1716, and was elected Assistant Assayer in 1720. This Benjamin II is not apparently identifiable in the register of Christchurch, Newgate, referred to above. The first entry is tantalisingly for Benjamin dau. (sic) of Benjamin and Susanna Pine, baptized 1683 and buried 1688. The next use of the name is for a son born January 1692/3 and buried 1 August 1694, and there is no further record of another of the same name. It was of course quite usual to re-use names of dead children on another occasion and presumably Benjamin II was baptized elsewhere. By the end of the seventeenth century Pyne was obviously, from his surviving work, in the front rank of London goldsmiths and with Anthony Nelme shared the main responsibility of upholding native standards against Huguenot competition, although like Nelme it is more than probable that he employed (or bought up and remarked the work of) the latter to some extent. His connection with Hoare's bank may well have continued for a considerable time and perhaps be responsible for the number of orders for municipal maces and regalia and church plate he received. However the end of his life was sad. On 17 January 1727, when he must have been nearly seventy-five he resigned from the Livery and petitioned with others for the place of Beadle to the Company, vacant by the death of John Bodington (q.v.), and was elected the same day to the post. He was buried at Christchurch, Newgate, 9 April 1732 and on 23 June 1732 the Court of Assistants received a petition from 'Mary and Ann Pyne, Dau^{rs} of the late beadle Benj^a. Pyne deceased, in effect setting forth that their father had faithfully served all offices in the Comp^a. and after many years trade was reduced so that he dyed in Debt tho he had been Beadle some time. That the pet^{rs}. were educated and maintained with hope of a decent provision and not bro^t. up to any business & are now destitute of any support & uncapable of getting their bread & therefore pray for such annuall pencons or other Relief as the Court shall think fitt'. They were accordingly awarded a payment of £5 each immediately and their case referred to the next Court for further relief under the Middleton Charity. They received annual payments of £5 until 1734, after which names are omitted in the Court minutes. The two daughters were however made free by patrimony, 7 February 1737/8, after the death of their brother Benjamin II (buried at Christchurch, 20 September 1737), who in February 1736 had also presented a petition to the Company, when he was described as Common Assayers Assistant, that 'he has served 16 years in a place of great trust which is very laborious and requires a constant attendance and is very prejudicial to his eyesight and health; that he has been appointed to retry the plate in doubt which tho' a favour is adding much more to the Pet^{rs}. care and charge and he hopes he may ask leave to have his salary augmented, which is so small that in case of sickness he should find it hard to support himself and that as he has never given the Court any trouble for so many years he hopes they will take it into consideration and raise his salary to £70 a year or what the Court shall think proper'. As a result his salary was raised to the sum asked, which was a considerable concession since after his death the new Assistant was appointed at only £45. Both Benjamin Pyne Senior and Junior appear jointly as lessees of a property in Yapton, Sussex from one Lawrence Eliot of Yapton Place, 5 November 1718 (West Sussex Records Office, Add. MSS. 129 167).

PYNETON, Ellize (1958) No record of apprenticeship or freedom. Only mark entered as smallworker, 9 September 1760. Address: Old Street Square. It is curious that although the Christian name is clearly written Ellize, the first initial of the mark is L., as if the order to the mark cutter had been given verbally and misunderstood and the error allowed to remain.

Q

QUANTOCK, John (1606-7) Son of Thomas Quantock of the parish of Kingsbury in the County of Somerset yeoman, apprenticed to James Gould 14 January 1726 on payment of £20. Free, 9 January 1738/?9. First mark entered as largeworker, undated, after 3 July 1739. Address: 'Facing Hugging Alley in Wood Street'. Second mark, 30 May 1754. Heal records him here from 1734-54 and from the Parl. Report list still there 1773, although this is later than his mark seems to be found. Like his master James Gould, Quantock was a specialist candlestick maker and it is extremely doubtful if his mark will be found on any other category of plate.

R

RADBURN, John (1617) No record of apprenticeship or freedom. First mark entered as smallworker, 13 February 1762. Address: New Street, Fetter Lane. Second mark, 18 April 1769. Heal records John Raeburn, haftmaker and goldsmith, at the same address, 1773, apparently a misprint for the same. He appears as hiltmaker, at this address, in the Parl. Report list 1773.

RADCLIFFE, Thomas (2910) Possibly (if apprenticed while already working to obtain freedom of the company) son of Edward Radcliffe of Union Street Southwark founder, apprenticed to John Peter Elvin engraver of Monmouth Court Whitcomb Street 7 December 1803. Free, 6 November 1811. First mark entered as smallworker, 6 November 1802. Address: 29 Great Sutton Street, Clerkenwell. Moved to 2 Elbow Place, City Road, 14 September 1814; to 47 St. John Street, Smithfield, 3 January 1821; to 48 Wellington Street, Goswell Street, 19 February 1822; to 13 Long Lane, Smithfield, 25 October 1823. Second mark as snuffermaker, 28 November 1826. Address: 136 Goswell Street. Third mark as smallworker, 18 March 1828. Address: 36 King Street, Clerkenwell. Moved to 15 Adam Street, New Kent Road, 10 January 1831; to 63 St. John Street, West Smithfield, 26 April 1836.

RAINAUD, Philip (2225, 2251) Appears as Philip Reynaud in the Denization List 11 March 1699/1700 and in an unpassed Naturalization Bill of 1702/3 as Philip Rainaud son of James and Ann Rainaud, born at Rochovar, Poictou (*Hug. Soc. Pub.*, 18 and 27). Apprenticed, as son of James Rainaud late in Poictou in the kingdom of France gentleman deceased, to Peter Platel 29 May 1700. A note alongside the entry, signed by Thomas Lawrence, Notary Public, attests his denization. Free, 13 February 1707/8. First mark entered as largeworker, 14 February 1708. Address: Corner of Suffolk Street. Second (Sterling) mark, 26 October 1720. Livery, October 1721. Heal records him as plateworker, Suffolk Street, 1707 till bankruptcy in 1728. Listed by Evans as Huguenot (*Hug. Soc. Proc.*, 14, p. 550). His work is rare and on a modest scale of domestic pieces.

RAINBOW, Stephen (2623) Son of Stephen Rainbow of St. Ann's Westminster in the County of Middlesex joyner, apprenticed to Peter Harach Junior 24 February 1708/9. Free, 5 October 1721. The apprenticeship entry bears a note, 'A certificate from J. Sperling curate that the Appr. was born in St. Anne's pish'. Mark entered as smallworker, undated, c. 1721. Address: Newport Court, in the parish of St. Anne, in the liberties of Westminster. 'Free Goldsmith'.

RAINE, Richard (2252) Son of Ambrose Raine of Coneysthorpe in the County Palatine of Durham yeoman, apprenticed to William Gibson 3 November 1699. Free, 8 February 1711/12. (The place name spelt 'Conneysthpe' presumably Coneysthorpe now Yorkshire.) Mark entered as largeworker, 21 June 1712. Address: 'in fleet street' and below 'out of England'. Heal adds nothing further.

RALPH, William (3281) No record of apprenticeship or freedom. Only mark entered as smallworker, 26 August 1772. Address: Saffron Hill, where he appears as bucklemaker in the Parl. Report list 1773.

RAMSAY, James (1615) No record of apprenticeship or freedom. Only mark entered as smallworker, 18 February 1725. Address: 'At the Green and white door within three doors of the reid Lyon Tavern Clerinwell Green' (unquestionably the most charmingly precise address in the registers).

RAND, John (2247) Free of the Merchant Taylors' Company by service to Thomas Batsford of Lombard Street goldsmith, 2 October 1695. Livery of the same company, 22 September 1710. Mark entered as largeworker, 13 January 1704. Address: Lombard Street. 'Free Merchant Taylor.' Signatory as 'working goldsmith' to the petition complaining of the competition of 'necessitous strangers', December 1711. Thomas Gladwin (q.v.) was apprenticed to him 1712. Heal records him as plateworker, Black Dog, Lombard Street, 1703-13.

RAVEN, Andrew (2248-9, 3475) Free by redemption on the order of the Court of Aldermen 11 August 1697. Mark entered as largeworker, undated, probably April 1697 on commencement of register. Address: Round Court, St. Martin's Le Grand, where Heal records him this year, and as London, 1706-28. Livery, October 1698.

RAVEN[S], Edward (633, 2250) Son of Thomas Raven of Islington tallow chandler, apprenticed to William Knight of the Grocers' Company in New Street Shoe Lane silversmith 2 April 1688. Free, 3 February 1695/6, through service to William Knight, both in New Street, silversmith. First mark entered as smallworker, undated, probably April 1697 on commencement of register. Address: New Street, Fetter Lane. 'free Grocer'. Second mark (Sterling), 4 July 1720. Both signatures as 'Ravens'.

*RAWLE, W(illiam) (3279) No record of apprenticeship or freedom. Only mark entered as smallworker, 11 May 1769. Address: 'Corner Castle Court Strand'. He appears in the Parl. Report list 1773 as hiltmaker, Corner of Castle Street, Strand, and is so listed by Heal.

RAWLINGS, Charles (409-10, 414) Son of William Rawlings deceased late of York Place Westminster capilliare (? wig) maker, apprenticed to Edward Coleman of Henry Place Westminster as watch finisher 7 February 1810. Freedom unrecorded. First mark entered as plateworker, 3 July 1817. Address: 12 Well Street. Second mark, 28 October 1819, 9 Brook Street, Holborn. Third mark, 13 June 1822. Fourth, 12 October 1826. Fifth, 24 October 1826. Sixth mark, in partnership with William Summers, 6 April 1829. Address: Brook Street, Holborn. Moved to 10 Great Marlborough Street, Regent Street, 9 January 1839. Six new marks, 2 December 1840. The partnership produced excellent snuffboxes well into the Victorian period.

RAY, Clifford (408) No record of apprenticeship or freedom. Only mark entered as smallworker, 6 June 1737. Address: 'at Mrs Male in Cow Lane Smithfield'. 'No Free Man'. The latter note is probably unique in the registers.

RAY, Thomas (2902) Son of William Ray Citizen and Cooper of London, apprenticed to William Richards 7 November 1738 on payment of £30. Free, 13 January 1747/?8. Mark entered as smallworker, 12 April 1759. Address: Bridewell Precinct, where he appears as watchcasemaker in the Parl.

Report list 1773, and entered marks as such, 14 June 1777 (Sections V and VI). Heal records the name as watchcasemaker, Water Street, 1768, who is perhaps the same.

RAYMOND, John (1618, 1633) Son of Rowland Raymond Citizen and Joyner of London deceased, apprenticed to Thomas Manning 6 November 1735 on payment of £28. 7s. Free, 8 November 1743. First mark entered as smallworker, 19 August 1762. Address: 'Near the Star & Garter Islington'. Second mark, 26 September 1768. Address: 'in Islington', where he appears as bucklemaker in the Parl. Report list 1773. He may be identifiable with Heal's John Raymond, goldsmith, Boy and Coral, Gutter Lane, c. 1755.

RAYNES, John (2247a, 2259) Son of John Raynes of St. Olave's Southwark grocer, apprenticed to Samuel Bourne 12 December 1717 on payment of £5. Freedom unrecorded. Two marks (New Standard and a rare full surname Sterling mark) entered as smallworker, 28 September 1736. Address: 'at the sign of Pallas Foster Lane', 'Free of Goldsmiths Company'. Heal records him as goldsmith, Gutter Lane, married in 1725; and as at the sign of Pallas, insolvent in 1743.

READ, Edward (636-7) No record of apprenticeship or freedom. First mark entered as smallworker, 3 March 1768. Address: 2 Oat Lane. Second mark, 16 March 1768. He appears as such, at the same address, in the Parl. Report list 1773.

READ, John (2302, 2442) Either (1) son of Mathew Read of Preston in the County of Lancashire farrier, apprenticed to Richard Barnet 28 September 1677 'From Christmas next'. Free, 15 September 1693. Or (2) John Reade son of John of Litchfield in the County of Stafford, apprenticed to John Archbold 13 October 1686 'from the 5th of November next' and turned over to Robert Timbrell. Free, 9 May 1694. Livery, October 1708. First mark entered as largeworker, in partnership with Daniel Sleamaker (q.v.), 17 October 1701. Address: Lawrence Pountney Lane. Second mark alone, 22 July 1704, same address. Heal records him as above; and London, 1705-12. Signatory as 'working goldsmith' to the petition complaining of the 'competition of necessitous strangers', December 1711.

READ, Josepheus (sic) (1846) 'Joseph' son of Robert Read of Hosier Lane, Smithfield Clothworker, apprenticed to Henry Hardy as card maker (?) 2 December 1800 and turned over to his father 4 November 1804. Free, 4 January 1809, as Clothworker (whereas, normally, freedom is of the company to which the boy was first apprenticed, despite turnover to another). Mark entered as plateworker, 10 August 1816. Address: 6 Baron Buildings, Great Surrey Street. Moved to 6 Island Yard, St. Andrew's Hill, no date. Moved to 12 Water Lane, Blackfriars, 4 February 1824.

READ, Thomas (2903, 2919) No record of apprenticeship or freedom. First mark entered as smallworker, in partnership with Thomas Smith, 14 March 1771. Address: 17 Bartholomew Close. Second mark alone, 1 April 1772, same address. They appear together however, as bucklemakers, at this address, in the Parl. Report list 1773. Third mark alone as bucklemaker, 11 June 1776. Address: Caley Court, Holborn. Fourth and fifth marks, 1789, same address (Section VIII).

READSHAW, Joshua (2303) Son of John Readshaw late of Hartlepool in the County of York merchant deceased, apprenticed to George Garthorne 22 June 1687. Free, 22 June 1694. Livery, April 1705. Mark entered as largeworker, undated, probably April 1697 on commencement of register. Address: 'At the Golden ball in St. Anne's Lane'. Heal records him here and as bankrupt, Wood Street, 1728.

REASEY, James (1621) No record of apprenticeship or freedom. Only mark entered as smallworker, 23 October 1769. Address: Little Compton Street, Soho. Presumably dead by 2 March 1773 when Mary Reasey's mark is entered.

REASEY, Mary (2063) No record of apprenticeship or freedom. Presumably widow of James Reasey (above). Mark entered as smallworker, 2 March 1773. Address: Compton Street, Soho, where she appears as watchcasemaker in the Parl. Report list of the same year.

*REASON, John (2305) Free of the Cutlers' Company by service to John Witton 4 April 1698. Mark entered as smallworker, 23 June 1698. Address: Heart Street in Covent Garden. 'Free Cutler'.

REASON, Joseph (1611, 2304) Free of the Cutlers' Company by service to Daniell Wilson 13 April 1697. Probably, from closeness of date, a brother of John Reason (above). First mark entered as smallworker, undated, probably April 1697 on commencement of register. Address: Bourley (Burleigh) Street, Strand. 'free Cutler'. Second (Sterling) mark, 17 June 1720.

REDHEAD, Thomas (2306, 2897) Son of John Redhead of St. Stephen Coleman blacksmith, apprenticed to Thomas Steed of the Merchant Taylors' Company 5 July 1710. Free, 12 November 1718. First mark entered as smallworker, 4 May 1719. Address: Tokenhouse Yard, Lothbury. 'free Merchant Taylor'. Second mark (Sterling), 29 June 1720.

*REDRICK, Richard (2423) No record of apprenticeship or freedom. First mark entered as smallworker, 7 April 1762. Address: 'at Mr Beucer in St. John Street'. Second mark, 30 May 1763. Third mark, 4 March 1768. Address: Aldermanbury, where he appears as watchcasemaker in the Parl. Report list 1773. Charles Redrick entered as the same in 1796, 37 Aldermanbury (Section VI), is presumably his son.

REEVE, William (3277) Either (1) son of William Reeve late Citizen and Dyer of London deceased, apprenticed to William Fawdery 26 October 1715 on payment of £20. Free, 4 July 1723. Or (2) son of Henry Reeve Citizen and Goldsmith of London deceased, apprenticed to John Holland 4 September 1718 on payment of £25. Free 31 March 1726. Mark entered as largeworker, 14 May 1731. Address: 'At the Blackmoors Head in the Minories', where Heal records him at this date, and also London, 1735–53. He was bankrupt June 1735 (*The Gentleman's Magazine*, p. 333) as goldsmith, Lombard Street.

REID, George (886) No record of apprenticeship or freedom. First mark entered as smallworker, 6 March 1811. Address: 32 Rose Lane, Spitalfields. Moved to 22 Dean Street, Fetter Lane, 3 September 1812. Second mark, 23 June 1817. Third, 20 February 1824. Fourth, 25 February 1824. Fifth (two sizes), 26 June 1824. Sixth, 13 August 1825. Seventh (two sizes), 13 March 1828. Eighth mark, as plateworker, 27 July 1829. Address: 18 Cross Street, Hatton Garden. Ninth mark, as smallworker, 11 March 1830, same address.

REID, William Ker (1236, 3217a, 3286) Son of Christian Ker Reid (of Newcastle, q.v., Section II) free by redemption 2 November 1814. First mark entered as plateworker, in partnership with Joseph Cradock (q.v.), 8 June 1812. Address: 67 Leather Lane. Moved, before 19 August 1819, to 3 Carey Street, Lincoln's Inn Fields. Second mark (two sizes), 19 August 1819. Third mark, 24 September 1824. Fourth mark alone as plateworker, 8 November 1825. Address: 5 Bream's Buildings, Chancery Lane. Fifth mark, 21 February 1826. Sixth (three sizes), 3 May 1828. Elected Livery, April 1818. His son William Ker Jr. was apprenticed to him 1846, and another Edward, free by patrimony 1844. William senior died 1 February 1868.

REILLY, Joseph Charles (1795) No record of apprenticeship or freedom. Only mark entered as plateworker, 19 July 1819. Address: 12 Middle Row, Holborn.

*REILY, Charles (413, 2066) Son of John Reily (below). No record of apprenticeship or freedom. First mark entered as smallworker, in partnership with his mother Mary Reily (below), 31 May 1826. Address: 6 Carey Lane. Second mark as plateworker, in partnership with George Storer, 1 January 1829, same address. Moved to 3 Lovel's Court, Paternoster Row, 26 June 1835, and back to 6 Carey Lane, 16 February 1836. Third mark (two sizes), 18 June 1840. Their later marks are found principally on fine quality snuff-boxes and other small pieces.

REILY, John (1627-8, 2033) No record of apprenticeship or freedom. First mark as Riley, in partnership with Mary Hyde (q.v.) as smallworkers, 28 November 1799. Address: 6 Carey Lane. Apparently soon after this he married the latter and his second mark as smallworker appears alone, 20 February 1801, same address. Third mark, 24 September 1802. Fourth mark (two sizes), 15 February 1805. Fifth mark, 9 April 1823. Buried 15 May 1826. His widow's and son's joint mark entered 31 May following.

REILY, Mary (2066) Originally Mary Hyde (q.v.). Apparently married to John Reily above (previously Riley) between 28 November 1799, when she appears as Mary Hyde on entry of their joint mark, and 20 February 1801, when he entered a mark alone. Her second mark entered as smallworker, in partnership with Charles Reily, presumably son, 31 May 1826. Address: 6 Carey Lane. She presumably retired or may have died by 1 January 1829 when the latter entered another mark with George Storer.

REMMETT, Thomas (789, 2907) No record of apprenticeship or freedom. First mark entered as smallworker, in partnership with George Dixon, 6 February 1797. Address: Heming's Row, St. Martin's Lane. Second mark alone, 17 October 1798, same address. Third mark, 15 January 1799. Fourth, 26 January 1804.

RENAUD, Henry (1063) No record of apprenticeship or freedom. Only mark entered as smallworker, 27 March 1727. Address: St. Andrew Street, near the Seven Dials.

RENOU, Timothy (2904-6) No record of apprenticeship or freedom. First mark entered as plateworker, 11 February 1792. Address: 45 St. John's Street, West Smithfield. Second mark, 2 August 1800. Third, 8 August 1800. Heal records him as Thomas (clearly a directory misprint), plateworker, St. John Street, 1792; and as Timothy, goldsmith, London, 1800-4. Although the company records show no signs of his connections it seems likely that Renou came from a considerable family of goldsmiths. Philippe Renou, probably a refugee of c. 1685, appears as 'orfebure' in the register of Le Carré Church 1692, Abraham as 'orfèvre dem(eurant) en Newport Market' 'married to Susanne Godefroy, 27 June 1704 (also at Le Carré), and Jacques 'orphèvre' married to Marie Renou both of the parish of St. Ann's, Westminster, at Swallow Street Church, 11 August 1709. James Renou entered incuse marks c. 1725 and 1735, and E. Renou an incuse mark, 19 May 1735. Address: 'Lumber Street in ye mint Southwark'. Timothy Renou (? a grandfather of the subject of this entry) entered an incuse mark 4 December 1737 'at Linnin Draper (?Hall) Freeman of the Farer (sic) Company'. (For all these see Section V.) After these references, however, there is a gap until the entry of 1792, above. A Timothy Renou, perhaps son of the goldsmith, served as a midshipman in H.M.S. *Colossus* at Trafalgar. He was born at Berwick in 1789, which seems, however, to make the connection unlikely (*The Nelson Collection at Lloyds*, 1932, p. 10, footnote 25). Renou's mark is usually found on dinner plate, dishes and to a limited extent salvers, all of good quality and refinement of design.

REW, Robert (2422) No record of apprenticeship or freedom. Only mark entered as largeworker, 10 August 1754. Address: Greenhill Rents, where he appears without category in the Parl. Report list 1773. The old confusion between the mark of this maker and that of Richard Rugg (q.v.) can be removed by a comparison of the relative size of their two marks.

*REYNOLDS, John (1620) No record of apprenticeship or freedom. First mark entered as smallworker, 10 October 1768. Address: New Street, Fetter Lane. He appears as hiltmaker, 25 New Street, in the Parl. Report list 1773. Second mark as hiltmaker, 7 September 1775. Address: 36 Little Old Bailey.

*REYNOLDS(ON), William (3278, 3899) A William Reynolds was apprenticed to Frederick Kandler (q.v.) of St. James' Westminster in 1748 (Index to Apprentices in Inland Revenue Books, Public Record Office, Vol. 25, p. 4887); and William son of James Reynolds of the parish of St. James Clerkenwell butcher, to Peter Archambo 19 April 1751 on payment of £40. Free, 4 April 1759. Having regard to the status of Kandler and Archambo this may well indicate a turn-over of the apprentice to a member of the Goldsmiths' Company for his freedom, since the former was apparently not free of the company. The entry of the mark as largeworker, 12 October 1757 (Address: South side of St. James' Market) provides further doubts. Firstly it is eighteen months earlier than the freedom of William Reynolds, although if he was the same as the apprentice of Kandler in 1748, he had already had nine years at the craft and was obviously competent to work. But there is another problem. The name can be read, as Chaffers did, as 'Reynoldson' or, as seems more possible, 'Reynolds on / South side of St. James Market'. The latter seems supported by the fact that the Parl. Report list 1773 has only William Reynolds, plateworker, Swallow Street, St. James's. Since Archambo and Kandler worked respectively in Coventry Street, and Jermyn Street the likelihood of a pupil remaining in the same general area seems strong and suggests identity between him of St. James' Market in 1757 and Swallow Street in 1773.

RIBOULEAU, Isaac (1610, 2342) Son of Stephen Ribouleau of Hammersmith distiller, apprenticed to Augustine Courtauld 5 July 1716 on payment of £10. Free, 2 July

1724. The father's name has previously been read as Hopkin but although badly written it is definitely Stephen. One of this name appears in the Denization List of 1687, and is clearly the father of Isaac. Two marks (New Standard and Sterling) entered as largeworker, 16 July 1724. Address: St. Martin's Lane. 'Free Goldsmith'. Through nervousness, apparently, the goldsmith wrote the date as 1714, and this has given rise to confusion and the invention of two Isaacs, senior and junior. The position of the entry in the register clearly indicates the correct version of the year, lying as it does between John Robinson of November 1723 and Thomas Rush of November 1724, which agrees with the freedom date and also accounts for the entry of marks for both standards, the Sterling mark not being required in 1714. Heal and Evans both attempt to distinguish between Isaac Ribouleau senior and junior, the former with mark entered 1714 (now shown to be an error for 1724) and the latter as apprenticed above. Heal also records him as Lombard Street, insolvent, 1729. His work is rare but when found of high quality.

RIBOULEAU, Jason (1963) No record of apprenticeship or freedom. Possibly a grandson or other descendant of Isaac Ribouleau (above). Only mark entered as smallworker, 6 May 1761. Address: Little St. Andrews Street, Seven Dials. Moved to Hozier Lane, Smithfield, no date. He appears here as watchcasemaker in the Parl. Report list 1773.

RICCARD, William (3282) No record of apprenticeship or freedom. First mark entered as smallworker, 18 November 1775. Address: Castle Street, Leicester Fields. Second mark, 8 March 1781. Heal records him as Riccard, William, goldsmith and jewller, at the same address, 1774-93.

RICH, Charles Hastings (336, 411) No record of apprenticeship or freedom. First mark entered as plateworker, 25 July 1817. Address: 17 Finsbury Street, Finsbury Square. Second mark, in partnership with Elizabeth Adams, 13 June 1823. Address: St. Ann's Lane.

RICH, John (1635) No record of apprenticeship or freedom. Only mark entered as smallworker, 13 June 1765. Address: 'at the Back of Tottenham Court Road Near Withfield (sic for Whitfield's) Chappel Jno. Row'. He appears as bucklemaker, Tottenham Court Road, in the Parl. Report list 1773, and entered two marks as such 15 August 1780. Address: 14 Tottenham Court Road (Section VIII).

RICHARDS, George (887) Possibly George John son of William, free by patrimony 6 February 1839 as silversmith. Livery, 1864, and died 1876. First mark entered as plateworker, 30 July 1830. Address: 24 Bartlett Buildings, Holborn. Others 1844-5.

RICHARDS, Thomas (2911) Son of Thomas, free by patrimony 2 October 1811 as silversmith. Mark entered as plateworker, 23 May 1812. Address: 10 Bridgwater Square.

RICHARDS, William (2343) Son of Leonard Richards Citizen and Clockmaker of London, apprenticed to Henry Duck 15 June 1712 on payment of £12. Free, 4 September 1719. Mark entered as smallworker, 2 November 1719. Address: Half Moon Court, Ludgate Hill. He also entered an incuse mark WR, presumably for gold. Heal records only William Richards, goldsmith, London, 1730.

RICHARDSON, George (884) No record of apprenticeship or freedom. Only mark entered as smallworker, 12 July 1760. Address: St. John's Square, nigh Clerkenwell. Presumably dead by 9 June 1763, when Mary Richardson entered her mark at the same address.

RICHARDSON, John I (1612, 2344, 3778) Son of George Richardson of Foremark in the County of Derby yeoman, apprenticed to Richard Watts 27 September 1715 on payment of £25. Free, 4 July 1723. Two marks (New Standard and Sterling) entered as largeworker, 8 July 1723. Address: Gutter Lane. 'Goldsmith'. Below this at a later date and in another rather erratic hand is written: 'a Trooper for K. Gorg', which implies that Richardson did not remain long at the bench. Heal records him as above and continues with addresses and dates belonging to John Richardson II (below).

RICHARDSON, John II (1632) Son of James Richardson of Tilson in the County of Chester clerk, apprenticed to Henry Morris 8 November 1739 on payment of £42 (a high premium). Freedom unrecorded. Mark entered as largeworker, 13 August 1752. Address: Greenhill Rents, Smithfield, where he appears without category in the Parl. Report list 1773. Heal records him, as if identical with John Richardson I (above), as plateworker, Smithfield, 1752; and London, 1768. He specialized like his master Henry Morris in salvers and waiters.

RICHARDSON, Mary (2061) No record of apprenticeship or freedom. Presumably the widow of George Richardson (above). First mark entered as smallworker, 9 June 1763. Address: St. John's Square, Clerkenwell. Second mark, 7 October 1763. Third, 12 July 1765. She appears as bucklemaker, at this address, in the Parl. Report list 1773.

RIDLEY, Joseph (1609) Son of Robert Ridley of Peterborough in the County of Northampton apothecary, apprenticed to John Penkethman 19 September 1688. Free, 13 November 1696. Mark entered as smallworker, 30 August 1710. Address: Bell Alley in Coleman Street.

*RIDOUT, George (883) No record of apprenticeship or freedom. Only mark entered as largeworker, 17 October 1743. Address: Lombard Street, preceded by 'Goldsmith', which in this position more probably indicates occupation than freedom of the company. Heal records only this date and address.

RILEY, Christopher (2339) Son of Richard Ryley of Wellborne in the County of Lincoln esquire, apprenticed to John Sutton 25 February 1681 'from fifth and twentieth day of March next'. Free, 30 March 1688. Livery, October 1708. Mark entered as largeworker, undated, probably April 1697 on commencement of register. Address: Strand. Heal records him here, same date; and London, 1686(?)–1709.

RILEY, John (2033) No record of apprenticeship or freedom. First mark entered as smallworker, in partnership with Mary Hyde (q.v.), 28 November 1799. Address: 6 Cary Lane. See under Reily for continuation of his career.

RIPSHEAR, Martha (2059) No record of apprenticeship or freedom. Presumably widow of Thomas Ripshear (below). Mark entered as smallworker, 1 December 1720. Address: Gutter Lane. She signs only her surname as above in childish and bungled hand and the clerk enters 'Marthea Ripshaw' below.

RIPSHEAR, Thomas (2340-1) Son of John Ripsheire labourer, apprenticed to John Laughton of the Grocers' Company 6 August 1688 for eight years and free of that company 17 September 1696. Mark entered as smallworker, undated, probably April 1697 on commencement of register. Address: Fore Street. 'Free Grocer'. Presumably dead by 1 December 1720 when Martha Ripshear (above) entered her mark at the same address. The register of St. Vedast, Foster Lane, contains the entry of birth and death of 'a Male Childe of Thomas Rypsheir a silversmith in Dove Courte in gutter lane', 14 May and 17 June 1702, and a daughter Margaret, born or baptized 20 September 1703 and buried 4 July 1708. There is also an entry: John Ripshire 'Father of Thomas Ripshire was buried at Old Bethlem May 9th 1710'.

*RIPSHER, William (3288) No record of apprenticeship or freedom. First mark entered as smallworker, 27 August 1834. Address: 19 Ratcliffe Row, St. Lukes. Moved to 7 Garden Walk, Willow Walk, Shoreditch, 25 March 1844. Second mark, 27 April 1849.

ROBERT, Abraham (86, 3475) No record of apprenticeship or freedom. Only mark entered as smallworker, 14 April 1727. Address: Garrard (?Gerard) Street, St. Ann, Old Soho.

*ROBERT, John (1625) No record of apprenticeship or freedom. Only mark entered as smallworker, 14 October 1795. Address: 98 Bishopsgate Street.

ROBERTS, Hugh (2382) Hugh Roberts (alias Humphreys) son (?stepson) of Robert Humphreys of the parish of Eggishway(?) in the County of Derby yeoman, apprenticed to Augustine Dudley 31 January 1672. Free, 14 February 1679. Court, 1704. Mark entered as largeworker, undated, probably April 1697 on commencement of register. Address: Newgate Street. Heal records him here and London, 1697–1714.

*ROBERTS, John (2385) Described on entry of mark as Free Cutler but there is no trace of apprenticeship or freedom in that company's records. Mark entered as smallworker, 16 April 1716. Address: Threadneedle Street. 'Free Cutler'.

ROBERTS, R. A. (1556) Possibly father or brother of Samuel Roberts (below), since he signs entry for mark of latter with John Nickolds, 27 September 1808.

ROBERTS, Samuel (1556, 2625) No record of apprenticeship or freedom. First mark entered as smallworker, in partnership with John Nickolds, 27 September 1808. Address: 3 Buckingham Place, Fitzroy Square, although the entry signed 'R. A. Roberts'.

BIOGRAPHICAL DICTIONARY

Second mark as plateworker with the same, 22 November 1813. Moved to 5 Conway Street, Fitzroy Square, 16 January 1815. Third mark entered alone as plateworker, 22 July 1818. Address: 251 High Holborn. Moved to 8 Arlington Street, Camden Town, 15 May 1820. Moved to Founders Court, Lothbury, 9 March 1825. Moved to 6 Bridgwater Square, 30 November 1825.

ROBERTS, Thomas (2391, 2898) As John Roberts (above) described on entry of mark as Free Cutler, but there is no trace of apprenticeship or freedom in that company's records. First mark entered as smallworker, 20 November 1703. Address: Bread Street. 'Free Cutler'. Second (Sterling) mark, 6 July 1720. Address: Newgate Street.

ROBERTS, W. (3287) No record of apprenticeship or freedom. Only mark entered as smallworker, 20 March 1830. Address: 9 Exmouth Street.

ROBERTSON, James Jordan (1847) No record of apprenticeship or freedom. Only mark entered as smallworker, 15 July 1826. Address: 2 Cobourg Street, Clerkenwell.

ROBERTSON, John (1629) No record of apprenticeship or freedom. First mark entered as smallworker, 14 September 1802. Address: 2 Hen and Chicken Court, Fleet Street. Second mark, 8 October 1802. Third mark (very small), 28 June 1805, same address (Section IV). Cf. also the same name 1822 (Section V) at 26 Villiers Street, and 1826 at Clarendon Street (Section VII).

ROBERTSON, William (3289-90) No record of apprenticeship or freedom. First mark entered as largeworker, 3 October 1753. Address: Porter Street. Second mark, 23 September 1755. Moved to Newport Street, 10 January 1756, where he appears as plateworker in the Parl. Report list 1773.

ROBINE, Francis (718) No record of apprenticeship or freedom. Only mark entered as smallworker, in partnership with John Macbride, 10 February 1810. Address: 8 New North Street, Red Lion Square.

*ROBINS, John (1623, 3678) Son of John Robins of Brewton (Bruton) in the County of Somerset mason, apprenticed to Richard Wade 3 October 1764 on payment of £20 and turned over 27 January 1766 to David Whyte Citizen and Goldsmith consideration being paid over to him. Free, 6 November 1771. First mark entered as plateworker, 20 October 1774. Address: 5 St. John Street. Moved to 67 Aldersgate Street, 18 July 1781. Livery, March 1781. Second mark (two sizes), 7 August 1787. Moved to 13 Clerkenwell Green, 5 February 1794. Heal records him as if two separate identities, one as plateworker, St. John's Street, 1774-1800, and Clerkenwell Green, 1795; the other as goldsmith, Aldersgate Street. Died 2 September 1831.

ROBINS, Thomas (2915) Son of Thomas Robins of Bruton Somersetshire mason (presumably a brother of the mason John, above), apprenticed to John Robins of Aldersgate Street London goldsmith (presumably cousin) 6 December 1786. Free, 6 August 1794. Mark (two sizes) entered as plateworker, 10 January 1801. Address: 35 St. John Square. Livery, June 1811. Died 22 August 1859. Heal records only Thomas Robins, goldsmith, Stationers' Hall Court, Ludgate Hill, 1800, which seems to indicate a separate identity. His mark is found on dinner plate of good quality, chiefly entrée dishes.

ROBINSON, Edward I (2390) Apprenticeship and parentage untraced but free of the Vintners' Company 7 March 1670. Mark entered as smallworker, 10 December 1702. Address: Warwick Lane. 'Vintner'. Heal records him as goldsmith, Warwick Lane near Newgate, 1716.

*ROBINSON, Edward II (2891-2) Son of Edward Robinson of the Little Minories London taylor apprenticed to James Phipps of Gutter Lane 7 October 1772 on payment of £10. Free, 2 February 1780. First mark entered as smallworker, in partnership with Thomas Phipps II, 8 July 1783. Address: 40 Gutter Lane. Second mark (two sizes), 8 August 1789. Third mark, in partnership with Thomas and James Phipps II, struck in register but entry never completed and date a blank. Livery, February 1791. Died 10 January 1816. Heal records him alone as goldsmith, Gutter Lane, 1783, and with Thomas Phipps, 1784-96.

ROBINSON, John I (1613, 2400) Son of Henry Robinson late of the Island of Garne Key (? sic) 'in the coast of France' (deleted) (presumably Guernsey), apprenticed to David Williams (Willaume) 6 April 1710. Free, 2 May 1717. Two marks (New Standard and Sterling) entered as largeworker, 4 November 1723. Address: 'at the Golden Crown in Orange Street by Leicester Fields'. Heal records him as Jonathan Robinson, plateworker, at this address and date. The

643

mark entry is signed Joⁿ which was mis-misprinted by Chaffers as 'Jonhn', causing this error to creep in.

ROBINSON, John II (1614, 1630, 3676) Described as Cordwainer on entry of mark and possibly therefore son of William Robinson late of Leeds in the County of York vintner, apprenticed to Thomas Bayley Citizen and Cordwainer 25 August 1727 on payment of £2. There are, however, others of the name about this time in the same company's apprentice register and identification is not certain. First mark entered as largeworker, 9 February 1738. Address: Porter Street, St. Ann's Soho. 'Cordwainer'. Second mark, 3 July 1739. Address: Long's Court, Leicester Fields. Moved to New Bond Street by Hanover Square, 8 September 1742. Heal records him as plateworker, Porter Street, 1738; Leicester Fields, 1739-42; and goldsmith, Star and Ring, New Bond Street, St. George Hanover Square, 1759-69; as well as plateworker, New Bond Street, 1773. The Parl. Report list 1773 describes him here as goldsmith.

ROBINSON, Philip (2226, 2397) Son of James Robinson late of Wormingford in the County of Essex clerk deceased, apprenticed to Thomas Sadler 2 September 1702. Free, 19 February 1714. First mark entered as largeworker, 10 March 1714. Address: Fleet Street. Second (Sterling) mark, 29 April 1723, same address. Livery, October 1721. Elected to Court, 1732 but did not serve. Heal records him as goldsmith, Golden Parrot, Cheapside, 1714-15, which appears to contradict the address of the mark entry; Golden Ball, corner of Salisbury Court, Fleet Street, 1713-28; and Fleet Street, 1734, till decease in 1744.

ROBINSON, Thomas I (2908-9) Son of William Robinson of Goswell Street victualler, apprenticed to John Robins of Aldersgate Street as goldsmith 4 January 1792. Free, 1 January 1800. First mark entered as plateworker, 5 March 1802. Address: 24 Red Lion Street, Clerkenwell. Moved to 13 St. John Square, 25 October 1810. Second mark, 2 December 1813. Address: 25 Fleet Lane, Old Bailey.

ROBINSON, Thomas II (2918) No record of apprenticeship or freedom. Only mark entered as smallworker, in partnership with S. Harding, 31 March 1810. Address: 4 Dean's Court, St. Martin's Le Grand.

ROBSON, William (3285) No record of apprenticeship or freedom. First mark entered as smallworker, 23 July 1819. Address: 1 St. Dunstan's Hill, Tower Street. Second mark, 17 June 1822.

*ROBY, Samuel (2624) No record of apprenticeship or freedom. Only mark entered as largeworker, 18 February 1740. Address: Bell Court, Foster Lane. Moved to Monkwell Street, 31 May 1743. Heal records him only at the first address and date.

RODENBOSTEL, George (885) No record of apprenticeship or freedom. Only mark entered as plateworker, 5 December 1778. Address: Piccadilly. He married, 8 October 1776 at St. George's, Hanover Square, Katherina Dorothy, daughter of John Christopher Hoffmaster, trumpetmaker, whose business he had taken over on the latter's death in 1763. He voted in the Westminster election of 1780 giving his trade as French horn maker. He died before 1790, when his widow is recorded at 70 Piccadilly (M. Byrne, 'The Goldsmith Trumpet-makers of the British Isles', Galpin Society, Vol. XIX, 1966). Heal records only his address and date of mark entry.

ROE, Ebenezer (2393) Parentage and apprenticeship untraced but free of the Vintners' Company 3 October 1699. Mark entered as largeworker, 20 May 1709. Address: Maiden Lane. 'Free Vintner'.

ROE, Nathaniel (2396) Son of Mathew Roe late of the City of Norwich cutler deceased, apprenticed to William Scarlett Citizen and Broderer of London 16 December 1702. Free of the Broderers' Company, 12 December 1710. Mark entered as largeworker, undated, between October 1710 and June 1712, probably December 1710. Address: Foster Lane. 'Free Imbroiderer'. His son John was born 14, baptized 26 March and buried 30 March 1717 at Christchurch, Newgate. Roe's entry is annotated at the bottom: 'Gon to live at Norwich', where he was by 1734 when he was ordered to melt down plate for the Corporation weighing 273 oz. 15d. In March 1735 he supplied new plate of which the surviving pieces, sauce-boats and salt-cellars were made by Joseph Sanders and James Smith of London (C. C. Oman, The Connoisseur, Vol. CLVI, pp. 6-14, 1964). Heal records him as a sheriff of Norwich, 1737.

ROE, Nicholas (2389) Son of Nicholas Roe free by patrimony of the Clothworkers'

Company 4 May 1687. Mark entered as smallworker, undated, probably April 1697 on commencement of register. Address: Smithfield. 'Free Clothworker'.

ROGERS, William (1622) No record of apprenticeship or freedom. Only mark entered as smallworker, 11 April 1770. Address: Ludgate Hill, where he appears without category in the Parl. Report list 1773.

ROKER, Elizabeth (639) No record of apprenticeship or freedom. Presumably widow of Philip Roker III (below). Mark entered as plateworker, 11 October 1776. Address: Bishopsgate without.

*ROKER, John (1631) Son (probably the eldest) of Philip Roker II Citizen and Goldsmith of London, apprenticed to his father 25 May 1737 on payment of £8. 5s. the gift of the Company. Freedom unnoted. Mark entered as largeworker, 13 September 1743. 'Goldsmith'. Address: in Bishopsgate Street, where Heal records him as working goldsmith, Golden Cup, without Bishopsgate, 1740-5. He was dead by 3 August 1759 when his son Thomas was apprenticed to Beauchamp Warwick.

ROKER, Mathew (2065) Son (probably the third) of Philip Roker II, free by patrimony 12 June 1754. Mark entered as largeworker, 29 April 1755. Address: at 'Greenwich Kent', where Heal records him from this date till 1773 when he appears as spoonmaker, Greenwich, in the Parl. Report list 1773. His father had moved to Greenwich at an unspecified date and it seems probable that Mathew took over as from the date of the entry of his mark.

ROKER, Philip I (2384, 3781) Philip Ludford son of Thomas Roker late of the parish of St. Saviours in Southwark bricklayer deceased, apprenticed to Edward Gladwyn 26 April 1676 'from the Feast of Philip & Jacob next' (1 May). Freedom unrecorded. Married by about mid 1683. A son Thomas, of Phillip and Ellenor Rooker, silversmith, was baptized 2 March 1684 at St. Mary Woolnoth, followed by three more sons and five daughters till 1701. Mark entered as largeworker, undated, probably April 1697 on commencement of register. Address: Sherborne Lane. Heal records him as silversmith, parish of St. Mary Woolnoth, 1683-1701 (from the register quoted above); plateworker, Sherborne Lane, 1697; and Long Acre and King Street, 1720 and 1739, but these two last refer to his son Philip II (below).

ROKER, Philip II (2223, 2229, 2398, 3753-5) Son of Philip I (above) baptized 7 May 1693 at St. Mary Woolnoth. Apprenticed to Joseph Barbutt (specialist spoonmaker, q.v.) 1 November 1707. Free, 7 April 1720. First mark entered as largeworker, 7 April 1720. Address: Long Acre. Second (Sterling) mark, 17 August 1720. Third mark, 20 June 1739. Address: King Street, Westminster. Later moved to Greenwich, date unspecified. His eldest son John was apprenticed to him in 1737, the next, Philip III, to his brother John in 1743; the third, Mathew, was free by patrimony 1754; and the fourth, William, was apprenticed to Henry Bickerton 6 April 1757, when his father is described as dead. This may have been about the time of Mathew's entry of mark, 1755, to carry on the business.

*ROKER, Philip III (2227) Son (probably the second) of Philip II Citizen and Goldsmith of London, apprenticed to his brother John 10 January 1743. Freedom unrecorded. Mark entered as spoonmaker, 28 June 1776. Address: 96 Bishopsgate Street without, where John had worked from 1743 till his death before 1759. Heal records Philip at Bishopsgate Street from 1768, but this still leaves a hiatus between the latest date of John's death and the latter's recorded mark. It seems probable that as long as John was alive Philip III did not enter a mark and that, after the former's death, he first did so in the missing register c. 1758, and in consequence appears as spoonmaker in the Parl. Report list 1773.

ROLLOS, Philip I (2383) Appears in the Denization List of 5 March 1690/1 as Phillips Rollos without any indication of place of origin. Free by redemption, 11 August 1697. Livery, October 1698. Mark entered in two sizes as largeworker, undated, probably April 1697 on commencement of register. Address: 'over against Bull Inn Court, Strand'. His name and that of Philip II were misread or misprinted as Rolles by Chaffers, followed by Jackson and partly by Heal, who records the name as plateworker, London, as early as 1675, and it may be that the mark PR in plain oblong punch with slightly pointed base, occurring at about 1680 onwards particularly on candlesticks and footed salvers of Huguenot style, is his. Rollos held the post of Subordinate Goldsmith to William III and Anne, to be followed by his son (Major General H. W. D. Sitwell, 'The Jewel House and the Royal Goldsmiths', *Arch. Journ.*, CXVII, p. 154). As well as Philip II, another son, Jacob was apprenticed to him in 1703, but no mark is entered to him. Rollos' major surviving works are the cisterns of 1699 in the Hermitage, Leningrad; that of 1701 in the Marlborough ambassadorial plate at Althorp; another of the same date from the Foley Grey Collection; and another, undated, at Burghley. Undated sconces of about 1697 are in the Ilchester Collection, another set of 1700 were formerly in the Sneyd Heirlooms, and firedogs of 1704 are at Welbeck Abbey. In general it may be not unfairly said that his work lacks the refinement of detail shown by the Haraches and Willaume, while at the same time possessing a breadth of design and sense of scale which make his larger pieces always imposing.

ROLLOS, Philip II (2224, 2392) Son of Philip Rollos (above) of St. Martin's in the Fields in the County of Middlesex goldsmith, apprenticed to Dallington Ayres 2 December 1692 and turned over to his father. Free, 26 July 1705. First mark entered as largeworker, 20 August 1705. Address: Heath Cock Court, Strand. Livery, October 1712. Second (Sterling) mark, 28 September 1720, same address. The first entry is signed 'Philip Rollos Jnr'. Like his father, a Subordinate Goldsmith to the Crown. Among unusual pieces bearing his mark are the covered bowl, with arms of Queen Anne, 1710, from the Brownlow Collection; the chocolate-pot of the same year at Knole; a wine-cistern of 1712 from the Earl of Home's collection (now Wilding Collection, British Museum); and the pair of highly decorated cups of 1714 from the Methuen and Sassoon Collections. These pieces in general all show more refinement of detail and richness of effect than his father's work.

ROMAN, Ann (2386-7) No record of apprenticeship or freedom. Only mark entered as largeworker, undated, probably April 1697 on commencement of register. Address: Water Lane, Fleet Street.

ROMER, Emick (638) Emmich Römer, son of Michel Michelsen Römer, goldsmith of Oslo (1682–1739) born 2 August 1724. Lived in Bragernaes and apprenticed in 1749. Recorded in 1751 as living in Strömso. After this, Norwegian records show a gap till 5 May 1795 when he was settled in Halden, Southern Norway. The mark attributed to him, which must have been entered in the missing register after 1758, is based on the appearance of his name in the Parl. Report list 1773 as plateworker, 123 High Holborn, and there is no other possible candidate for these initials in the list. Identification is confirmed by the fact that Romer appears as supplying sugar and cream-baskets to Parker and Wakelin, 1770–1 (Garrard MSS, Victoria and Albert Museum Library). His mark appears on a number of pierced epergnes of about 1765–75. (Norwegian history information of Jorunn Fossberg per Judith Banister.)

*ROMER, John (3677) No record of apprenticeship or freedom and connection, if any, with Emick Romer (above) not apparent. The mark attributed to him is based on his appearance in the Parl. Report list 1773 as plateworker, Compton Street, Soho. It seems quite reasonable to believe him, as well as Stephen Romer, goldsmith and jeweller, Covent Garden (Heal), to be sons of Emick.

RONGENT, Etienne (634) No record of apprenticeship or freedom. Only mark as largeworker entered undated, c. 1731. Address: 'at ye Golden Cup, Church Street, St. Ann's Soho'. Heal records this, and London, 1755; also Rongent, jeweller, Hemings Row, St. Martin's Lane, 1748, who may perhaps be the same. Listed by Evans as Huguenot (*Hug. Soc. Proc.*, 14, p. 551).

ROOD See ROODE.

ROODE, Alexander (2388) Son of Thomas Roode of Glastonbury in the County of Somerset innholder, apprenticed to John Ruslen 31 March 1669. Free, 14 December 1676. Livery, November 1687. Court, 1704. Mark entered as largeworker, undated, probably April 1697 on commencement of register. Address: Cannon Street. Signatory to the petitition against the work of 'aliens or foreigners', 11 August 1697. Heal records him as plateworker, parish of St. Martin Ongar, 1692; and Ship, Cannon Street, 1694–1706.

ROODE, Elizabeth (635) No record of apprenticeship or freedom. Presumably widow of Gundry Roode (below). Only mark entered as smallworker, 24 October 1738. Address: Golden Lane.

ROODE, Gundry (880-1, 2394, 3592) Either (1) Son of Thomas Roode late of Glaston in the County of Somerset yeoman deceased, apprenticed to Alexander Roode (above), his brother 30 June 1682. Or (2) son of Gundry Roode late of Glassingbury in the County of Somerset grocer deceased, apprenticed to Alexander Roode 18 December 1696 (presumably his cousin). The freedom of neither Gundry recorded. First mark entered as largeworker, 1 March 1710. Address: Staining Lane. Second (Sterling) mark, 21 May 1721. Address: Queen Street in ye Mint. Third mark, 9 September 1737. Address: 'over against ye Kings Road in golden lane'. The registers of St. Michael le Quern contain entries for Elizabeth, daughter of Mr Gundry Rude by Elizabeth his wife, born 27 October, baptized 24 November 1713: Oliver and Jane, twins, born 6 November 1714, Jane buried five days later and Oliver three weeks after birth; lastly Gundry, born 6 January 1715 and buried 3 March following.

ROOD(E), James (2395) Son of James Roode late of Bridgwater in the County of Somerset soapboiler, apprenticed to Alexander Roode 11 July 1700. Free, 5 October 1710. Mark entered as largeworker, 27 October 1710. Address: Bow Lane, Signatory as 'working goldsmith' to the petition complaining of the competition of 'necessitous strangers', December 1711. Heal records him as above, and Angel Precinct, 1718.

ROOD(E), Mary (2060, 2399) No record of apprenticeship or freedom. Perhaps widow of James (above). Two marks (Sterling and New Standard) entered as largeworker, 2 December 1721. Address: Maiden Lane. Heal records her here, 1720-1.

ROOKE, Michael (2064) No record of apprenticeship or freedom. Only mark entered as smallworker, 4 April 1796. Address: 15 Little New Street, Shoe Lane.

ROPER, William (3280) No record of apprenticeship or freedom. Only mark entered as smallworker, 13 October 1770. Address: St. Martin's Lane. Appears in Parl. Report list 1773, without category, at this address. Heal records him here till 1777, and 2 Great Queen Street, Lincoln's Inn Fields, 1779.

ROSS, Bartholomew (224) Son of Bartholomew Ross late of Crown Court Covent Garden taylor deceased, apprenticed to Thomas Ross (his brother, below) as silver polisher 1 August 1804. Freedom unrecorded. Mark entered as smallworker, 15 July 1822. Address: 13 Church Court, Strand.

ROSS, Robert (2428) No record of apprenticeship or freedom. First mark entered as spoonmaker, 13 October 1774. Address: 10 Bells Building, Salisbury Court, where he so appears in the Parl. Report list 1773. Moved to New Street, Covent Garden, 2 February 1776. Moved to '2 Conquest Buildings, Blackfryars New Road Surrye Side', 18 February 1778. Heal records him only at New Street, 1774-6.

ROSS, Thomas (2912, 2916-7) Son of Bartholomew Ross of Wardour Street Soho taylor, apprenticed to Thomas Rowe of Gutter Lane as silver polisher 6 August 1794. Free, 7 July 1802. His brother Bartholomew (above) was apprenticed to him 1804, when Thomas was of Hooper Street, Clerkenwell. First mark entered as plateworker, 10 November 1819. Address: 19 Green Street, Leicester Square. Second mark, 14 February 1821. Third mark, 11 November 1825. Moved to 39 Princes Street, Leicester Square, 16 November 1837.

ROTTON, John (1626) No record of apprenticeship or freedom. Only mark entered as smallworker 16 March 1797. Address: 3 Burleigh Street, Strand.

ROUS, George (888, 3593) No record of apprenticeship or freedom. Only mark entered as smallworker, 17 January 1765. Address: Rose and Crown Court, Foster Lane.

ROWE, John (1616) Son of John Rowe late of Lynn Regis in the County of Norfolk musician deceased, apprenticed to Richard Bailey 3 December 1741. Free, 1 February 1749. Mark entered as largeworker, 3 June 1749. Address: Gutter Lane. Heal records him as plateworker, London, 1724 (apparently for another otherwise unrecorded); Gutter Lane, 1749-73 (as in the Parl. Report list for the latter years); and Monkwell Street, 1778.

ROWE, Thomas (2901) No record of apprenticeship. Probably the Thomas Rowe free by redemption as goldsmith 10 January 1754. Mark entered as largeworker, 29 December 1753. Address: Cannon Street. Second mark, 23 February 1760. Address: St. Dunstan's, Tower Street where he appears without category in the Parl. Report list 1773.

ROWNEY, Richard (2424) No record of apprenticeship or freedom. First mark entered as smallworker, 1 April 1785. Address: 95 Holborn Hill. Second mark, 30 August 1785. Address: 'The corner of King Street, St. Giles'.

ROYES, Solomon (2548, 2626-7) Son of John Royes late of Canterbury weaver deceased, apprenticed to Solomon Hougham of Aldersgate Street as goldsmith 5 August 1789. Free, 6 December 1797. First mark entered as plateworker, in partnership with Solomon Hougham and John East Dix, 13 September 1817. Address: 138 Aldersgate Street. Second mark with Dix only, 19 September 1818, same address. Third mark alone, 22 February 1820, same address. Fourth mark, 26 November 1822. He seems to have been adept in getting rid of his partners in quick succession while retaining his hold on the premises.

RUDDUCK, Samuel (2628) No record of apprenticeship or freedom. Only mark entered as smallworker, in partnership with Zachariah Jennings, 27 March 1810. Address: 35 Brunswick Street, Soho. Samuel Ruddock, goldworker, 1831 (Section VII) seems probably a son.

RUDKINS, Appolone (87) No record of apprenticeship or freedom. Only mark entered as smallworker, 6 December 1766. Address: Great Earl Street, Seven Dials.

RUDKINS, James (1619) No record of apprenticeship or freedom. Only mark entered as smallworker, 26 July 1763. Address: Little Winchester Street, near Little Moorgate.

RUDKINS, William (3283-4) No record of apprenticeship or freedom. First mark entered as smallworker, 12 March 1789. Address: 22 Torrington Street, Cold Bath Fields. Second mark, 16 January 1796. Address: 57 Gee Street, Goswell Street. Third mark, under address of first entry, 31 March 1797.

RUELL, James (1624) No record of apprenticeship or freedom. Mark entered as smallworker, 28 April 1795. Address: 1 Goldsmith Street, Gough Square. Moved to 13 Little Wild Street, 16 June 1801.

RUGG, Richard (2420-1) Son of Richard Rugg late of Limington in the County of Somerset husbandman deceased, apprenticed to James Gould 10 January 1738 on payment of £25. Free, 3 September 1746. First mark entered as largeworker, 30 May 1754. Address: Caroline Court, Saffron Hill. Moved to Clerkenwell Green, 15 July 1754. Appears as plateworker, St. John's Square, Clerkenwell, in the Parl. Report list 1773. Second mark as plateworker, 18 March 1775. Address: St. John Square. Heal records the Saffron Hill address and date, and St. John's Square, 1766-75. His son Richard was apprenticed to his father 2 November 1763, free 7 November 1770. Livery, December 1771, and died between 1795 and 1801. It has in the past been considered impossible to distinguish between the marks of Rugg and Robert Rew (q.v.). The size of the only similar mark which each entered is, however, so widely different from the other that there need be no doubt in the matter.

*RUNDELL, Philip (2228, 3764) Son of Thomas Rundell doctor of Widcombe Bath, born 1743. Apprenticed 1760 to William Rogers jeweller of Bath on payment of £20. Arrived in London, 1767 or 1769, as shopman to Theed and Pickett (q.v.), Ludgate Hill, at a salary of £20 p.a. Made partner with Pickett 1772 and acquired sole ownership of the business in 1785-6. Took John Bridge (q.v.) into partnership 1788, and his nephew Edmund Walter Rundell by 1803, the firm being styled Rundell, Bridge and Rundell from 1805. Appointed Goldsmith and Jeweller to the King in 1797, due it is said, to George III's acquaintanceship with John Bridge's relative, a farmer near Weymouth. Took Paul Storr (q.v.) into working partnership in 1807, an arrangement which lasted till 1819, when the latter regained independence. Only then was Rundell's first mark entered as plateworker, 4 March 1819 (two sizes). Address: 76 Dean Street, Soho (the workshop). Second mark (two sizes), 25 May 1819. Third mark (two sizes), 31 October 1822. The following year John Bridge entered his first mark and it seems probable therefore that it was about this time that Rundell retired. He did not die however till 1827, leaving his fortune of £1¼ million to his nephew Joseph Nield. For Rundell's eccentric and unpleasant character see the manuscript of George Fox Junior (Harvard University Library) quoted by N. M. Penzer (*Paul Storr*, pp. 67 et seq.) from whom much of the above is acknowledged. Two marble portrait busts, identified as Rundell, by E. H. Bailey, who designed for the firm, were in the Grittleton Marbles of the Nield family dispersed in 1966. Joseph Nield was of course the millionaire who left his fortune to Queen Victoria. Burke's *Peerage* contains the statement (Goldney, Baronets) that 'Eleonora, daughter of Richard Rundell of Philips Norton, Wilts and Sister of the millionaire Philip Rundell of Ludgate Hill, goldsmith', married Samuel Goldney of Bath and died in 1816. It seems more probable that she was in fact sister of Edmund Rundell, Philip's nephew.

RUSH, Thomas (2899-2900, 2913-4) Son of Samuel Rush Citizen and Haberdasher of London, apprenticed to Joseph Clare 30 March 1715 on payment of £20. Free, 24 May 1722. First mark entered as largeworker, 25 November 1724. 'Goldsmith living at the Acorne in Foster Lane'. Second mark, 1 November 1731. Address: 'at the Acorne in St. Ann's Lane'. Third mark, 18 June 1739. Address: 'of the parish of Ann's Aldersgate removed to Aldersgate Street'. Heal records him as plateworker, Acorn or Acron, Fetter Lane, 1724, following Chaffers who misread Fetter for Foster in the first entry; London, 1734-44; and Acorn, Aldersgate Street, 1739-73. There is, however, no mention of him in the Parl. Report list for 1773 and it is unlikely, though of course possible, that he was still working at the age of seventy-two or more.

*RUSLEN, John (2450) Son of Thomas Ruslen Citizen and Clothworker of London, apprenticed to Thomas George 14 November 1656 'from the Feast of the Birth of our Lord God next coming'. Free, 8 January 1664. Livery, June 1682. Court, 1693. Warden, 1702, 1707-8. Prime Warden, 1712. His first mark, pre-Britannia period, is recognisable from its resemblance to his only recorded mark as largeworker, undated, probably April 1697 on commencement of the register. Address: 'at the Golden Cup St. Swithin's Lane'. Heal records him here as goldsmith, 1690-1715 (also Hilton-Price, *Handbook of London Bankers*). John, son of John and Sarah 'Ruston', Goldsmith, baptized 5 October 1693 at St. Mary Woolnoth, is probably a son. Ruslen signed the Committee report on the present state of the Company, 29 April 1708, as John Rusten, but appears as Mr Warden Ruslen in 1712. Ruslen's marks both before and after 1697 appear on a number of good quality pieces although there is no suggestion of serious rivalry with the Huguenots. He was apparently for some length of time patronised by the Jewish congregation of Bevis Marks for the making of their annual presentation dish to the Lord Mayor, of which several have survived.

RUSSEL, John (1280, 1634) No record of apprenticeship or freedom. First mark entered as smallworker, in partnership with James Evans, 31 August 1761. Address: Golden Head, Greek Street, Soho. Second mark alone as smallworker, 25 August 1764. Address: 'at Mr Edwards Engraver opposite the Savoy Gate Strand'. Third mark, 6 March 1767. Address: Northumberland Street, Strand. Fourth mark, 6 November 1769. He appears here as goldworker in the Parl. Report list 1773, where he is mentioned as having been prosecuted in 1770 for making gold watch-chains 'worse than standard'. Another John Russell, of no category, St. John's Street, Clerkenwell, in the same list appears a separate person.

RUSSELL, Abraham (2452, 3787) Son of John Russell Citizen and Fishmonger of London, apprenticed to Jonathan Kirk 20 March 1695. Free, 17 July 1702. Mark entered as largeworker, 24 July 1702. Address: St. Ann's Lane. Heal records him here, 1702-3; and London, 1710-11. Listed by Evans as Huguenot (*Hug. Soc. Proc.*, 14, p. 552).

*RUSSELL, Elias (3553-4) No record of apprenticeship or freedom, nor entry of mark. Heal records him as goldsmith, Suffolk Street, 1755-73, and he appears as goldworker in the Parl. Report list for the latter year. His mark is identifiable from his appearance in the Wakelin Ledgers as goldworker from 1767-73, and from the discovery of mark 3553 on a fine gold snuffbox of 1761, in a strong French taste, also engraved with the signature of Parker and Wakelin (Loan, British Museum). It is clear from the one or two examples so far recognized that he was a box maker of the highest standards and perhaps French or French trained. He is possibly related to Peter Russell (or Roussel), toyman at Chevenix's Toy Shop, facing Suffolk Street, Charing Cross, 1759 (Heal).

*RUTLAND, Robert (2425-7). No record of apprenticeship or freedom. First mark entered as spoonmaker, 21 August 1807. Address: 13 Lisle Street, Leicester Square. Second mark, 31 May 1808. Third, 4 July

649

1811. Address: 15 Lisle Street. Fourth mark, 24 April 1812. Address: 13 Lisle Street. Fifth, 30 May 1815. Sixth, 21 August 1819. Seventh, 29 November 1821. Eighth, 9 October 1822. Ninth, 18 August 1824. Tenth, 10 June 1826.

RYDER, Mary (2062) No record of apprenticeship or freedom. Only mark entered as smallworker, 4 July 1769. Address: Wich Street. She so appears in the Parl. Report list 1773.

RYVES, Keirk (1879) No record of apprenticeship or freedom. Only mark entered as smallworker, 20 January 1729. Address: Cloth Fair, Smithfield. The actual entry. runs: 'Jenever the 20 1728/9. Liueth in clauth in fauer Smith feld', a charming piece of illiteracy.

S

SADLER, John (1665) No record of apprenticeship or freedom. Only mark entered as smallworker, 15 April 1772. Address: Drury Lane, opposite Brownlow Street, where he appears without category in the Parl. Report list 1773.

SADLER, Thomas (2466, 2921) Son of Thomas Sadler late of Much horsley (?Great Horkesley) in the County of Essex yeoman deceased, apprenticed to Lawrence Cole 10 March 1692. Free, 16 January 1700. Two marks entered as largeworker, 25 August 1701. Address: Foster Lane. Livery, April 1705. Third (Sterling) mark, undated c. 1720. Probably the Thomas Sadler of (St.) 'Vedast Fostèr' (Lane) married to Frances Roberts of Christchurch, Newgate, at the latter church, 20 April 1704. Heal records him as plateworker, Foster Lane, 1701-20.

SAGE, James (2828) No record of apprenticeship or freedom. Only mark as smallworker, in partnership with Thomas Lawrence Junior, entered 23 March 1771. Address: Francis Court, Berkley Street, St. John's Square, Clerkenwell, where they appear as watchcasemakers in the Parl. Report list 1773. James Sage, watchcasemaker, 1779 (Section VI) may be connected.

SALLAM, Robert (2433) Son of Robert Sallam late of the parish of St. Mary Whitechapel watchmaker deceased, apprenticed to Richard Gurney 1 July 1736. Free, 6 September 1749. Mark entered as smallworker, 6 November 1765. Address: Watling Street, where he appears as plateworker in the Parl. Report list 1773, so quoted by Heal. He is distinct from Robert Salmon in the same list, spoonmaker, St. Martin's Churchyard, to whom the mark of Robert Sharp (q.v.) has been long attributed, but for whom no mark appears in the surviving registers but was presumably entered between 1758 and 1773.

SAMBROOK, James (1851) No record of apprenticeship or freedom. Mark entered as smallworker, 28 August 1819. Address: 38 Baltic Street, St. Luke's. Moved to 24 Wynyatt Street, Clerkenwell, 19 January 1835.

SAMPEL, William (769, 3305) No record of apprenticeship or freedom. First mark entered as largeworker, in partnership with George Baskerville, 27 January 1755. Address: New Inn Passage, Clare Court. Second mark alone, 29 August 1755. Address: 1 Baldwin's Gardens. Recorded by Heal as 'Sempel', in partnership with Baskerville; and as 'Sampel' alone, as above; and London, 1763.

SAMWAYS, Joseph (1852) No record of apprenticeship or freedom. Only mark entered as plateworker, 26 June 1832. Address: Near Falcon Place, Falcon Square.

SANDEN, William (3304) No record of apprenticeship or freedom. Only mark entered as largeworker, 30 June 1755. Address: St. Martin's 'La' Grand. Heal records this, and London, 1785. The only signature has been so read by Chaffers, followed by Jackson and Heal, but it seems highly probable that it is in fact Sanders and is presumably identical with William Sanders, smallworker, Old Bailey, in the Parl. Report list 1773.

SANDERS, Benjamin (225, 235, 3494) Son of William Sanders of Wickham in the County of Buckingham yeoman, apprenticed to John Sanders 4 April 1721. Free, 5 February 1733/?4. First mark entered as largeworker, 1 April 1737. Address: Staining Lane. 'Goldsmith'. Second mark, 28 June 1739, the very feeble writing suggestive of illness or drunkenness (?). Heal records him in Staining Lane, 1737-44.

SANDERS, John I (1638, 2467) Son of William Sanders of Mill End in the County of Bucks yeoman, apprenticed to William Gamble 25 September 1706. Free, 3 August 1715. Signatory as journeyman to the petition against assaying the work of foreigners not having served seven years apprenticeship, February 1716. First mark entered as largeworker, 5 July 1717. Address: Oving (? Oring) Street, Red Lion Square. Second (Sterling) mark, 27 June 1720, no address. Heal records him as plateworker, Oring (sic) Street, 1717; and London, 1720-48.

SA(U)NDERS, John II (1668, 3687) Son of Archibald Sanders of Rotherhithe in the County of Surrey yeoman, apprenticed to John Westray 2 July 1760. Free, 5 July 1769. Mark entered as smallworker, 8 March 1775. (Clerk enters Saunders, but maker signs Sanders.) Address: 4 Fans Alley, Aldersgate Street. Heal records only John Sanders, silversmith, White Horse Court, 1782, who may be the same.

SANDERS, Joseph (1655, 1679) Son of William Sanders of High Wickham in the County of Buckingham yeoman (and probably therefore younger brother of John Sanders I (q.v.), apprenticed to Thomas Ewesdin 1 September 1714 on payment of £12. Turned over 4 September 1719 to Joseph Belcher in Maiden Lane London. Free, 11 January 1721/?2. Livery, March 1727/8. First mark entered as largeworker, 7 December 1730. Address: Carey Lane. 'Free Goldsmith'. Second mark, 22 June 1739. Address: Maiden Lane. Heal records him as plateworker, Carey Lane, 1730; and London, 1732-42. Resigned from Livery 18 May 1748.

SANDERS, William *See* SANDEN.

SARBITT, Dorothy (501) Formerly Dorothy Mills (q.v.). Having been in partnership with Thomas Sarbitt (below), she must have been married to him by 13 December 1753, when her first mark alone as Sarbitt was entered. Address: Saffron Hill, as with the former marks, perhaps on widowhood.

SARBITT, Thomas (3519) No record of apprenticeship or freedom. Mark, in partnership with Dorothy Mills, identified from the record by Heal of the partnership and found on pieces of 1748-9. Apparently married to Dorothy Mills (q.v.) before December 1753. Heal records John Sarbitt (possibly their son), goldsmith, Martin's Court, Leicester Square, 1790-6.

SARDET, Henry (1068) No record of apprenticeship or freedom. Only mark entered as smallworker, 17 April 1765. Address: High Holborn near the Coal Yard. Heal records him as plateworker, at this address, 1773-7, whereas he appears as goldworker, High Holborn, in the Parl. Report list 1773.

SARSON, Thomas (2935) Son of Thomas Sarson of Hoxton in the County of Middlesex mariner, apprenticed to Basill Denn 22 December 1729 on payment of £15 and turned over 5 January 1734/5 to Edward Burcomb (Leather Seller). Freedom unrecorded. Mark entered as smallworker, 6 May 1737. Address: Wood Street, Cheapside. 'Goldsmith'. Heal records him as goldsmith, at this address, 1745, fugitive for debt.

SAUNDERS, Alexander (92, 94) Son of Benjamin Saunders late of the parish of St. Giles without Cripplegate brassfounder deceased, apprenticed to Walter Brind 1 February 1748/9. Free, 5 August 1756. First mark entered as largeworker, 3 September 1757. Address: Foster Lane, Noble Street. Second mark as smallworker, 17 July 1778. Address: No. 3 Hare Court, Aldersgate Street. He also appears in Parl. Report list 1773 as plateworker, St. Martin's Churchyard. Heal records him Noble Street 1757; Foster Lane, 1766; and St. Martin's Churchyard but not Hare court.

SAUNDERS, Hugh (2468) Son of William Saunders of London gentleman, apprenticed to Thomas Nicholls of the Haberdashers' Company 9 February 1705. Freedom not traced. Mark entered as largeworker, 23 June 1718. Address: St. Bride's Lane. 'Haberdasher'. Heal records him at this address till 1726.

SAVAGE, James (1650) Apprenticed about 1720 to Seth Lofthouse of the Merchant Taylors' Company and free 7 February 1727 as 'James Savage Work[g] Goldsmith in East Hardin St by Shoe Lane to Seth Lofthouse decd. made free on rept. of Rich[d] Cox Citizen and Carpenter and Joshua ffrensham Citizen and Goldsmith'. Only mark entered as largeworker, 23 May 1728. Address: East Harding Street, near Fetter Lane. 'ye Merchant Taylor Company'. Heal records him at this address till 1733.

SAVORY, Adey Bellamy (15-7, 96) Son of Joseph Savory (below). Free by patrimony 8 October 1802 as coal merchant (!). First mark entered as plateworker, 14 February 1826. Address: 54 Cornhill. Second mark, 13 October 1826. Third mark (six sizes), 11 November 1826. Fourth mark, 11 November 1829. Fifth, 3 April 1830. Sixth, 26 January 1832. Seventh mark, in partnership with Joseph and Albert Savory, 7 September 1833. Address: 14 Cornhill; Manufactories: 15 George Street, Goswell Street, 5 Finsbury South. Eighth mark (two sizes), in partnership, 5 July 1834. For Heal's records of this firm before 1800 see Joseph Savory (below).

SAVORY, Albert (96, 1853) Son of Adey Savory (above). Free by patrimony, 4 December 1833, as silversmith. First mark entered as plateworker, in partnership with his father and brother Joseph II, 7 September 1833. Address: 14 Cornhill etc. Second mark (two sizes), 5 July 1834. Third mark, in partnership with Joseph only, 2 January 1835, trading as A. B. Savory and Sons, same address. Fourth mark, 14 November 1835.

SAVORY, Joseph I (1664) Son of Moses Savory of Wandsworth in the County of Surrey fisherman, apprenticed to James Hunt 2 July 1760. Free, 3 February 1768. First mark entered as smallworker, 31 January 1772. Address: Old Fish Street, where he appears without category in the Parl. Report list 1773. Second mark as goldworker, 22 January 1782. Address: 48 Cheapside (Section VII). Heal records him as goldsmith, cutler and jeweller, Strand, 1777; and Golden Fleece, No. 48 near Bow Church, Cheapside, 1782-8; also Thomas Barnard and Joseph Savory, goldsmiths, Adam Street, Adelphi, 1779-81 (the partnership dissolved 1781, Barnard continuing the business); Savory, Farrand and Co., goldsmiths and jewellers, 48 Strand, 1790-6; Savory, Farrand and Sheldrake, same address, 1793-1809; Savory and Pryor, cutlers and silversmiths, 10 Poultry. There are no recorded marks for any of the above partnerships, which were presumably retailing businesses only. William Savory, goldworker, 2 Lillypot Lane, 1805 (Section VII) may possibly be connected.

SAVORY, Joseph II (96, 1853) Son of Adey Bellamy Savory (above). Free by patrimony, 4 December 1833, as silversmith. First mark, in partnership with his father Joseph and brother Albert, 7 September 1833. Address: 14 Cornhill etc. (See also under Adey and Albert Savory, above.)

SAVORY, Thomas Cox (2724) Son of Adey Bellamy Savory (above). Free by patrimony 2 December 1829 as silversmith. First mark entered as plateworker, 13 September 1827. Address: 54 Cornhill (with his father). Second mark, 2 November 1827. Third mark (two sizes), 27 January 1832.

SCAMMELL, Joseph (1688) Son of John Scammell of Tetbury in the County of Gloucester weaver, apprenticed to William Abdy as goldsmith 2 December 1767. Free, 7 December 1774. Mark entered as plateworker, 11 August 1788. Address: 7 Staining Lane. Heal records him as silversmith, 38 Noble Street, 1788-93. He was dead by 1800 when his son Joseph was apprenticed to William Pitts.

SCARLETT, Richard (2429-30, 2487) Son of William Scarlett (below) of the Broderers' Company, apprenticed to his father 12 December 1710. Free, 5 February 1718, of that company. First mark entered as largeworker, 24 September 1719. Address: Foster Lane. 'Free Imbroder'. Second (Sterling) mark, 24 June 1720. Third mark, 11 September 1723. Address: Foster Lane. 'Imbroder', Junior. This would at first sight suggest a second of the name but from the known facts this seems impossible and is presumably a sudden recollection that William is still alive. Richard Scarlett of St. Leonard, Foster Lane and Dorothy Arnold of the same were married 28 March 1719, at Christchurch, Newgate. They cannot therefore have had a son of the same name old enough to enter a mark in 1723. Dorothy Scarlett was buried at Christchurch, Newgate, 3 December 1736. Heal records Scarlett as plateworker, Foster Lane, 1719-30.

SCARLETT, William (2484, 3292-3) William son of Thomas Scarlett late of Dereham in the County of Norfolk cooper deceased, apprenticed to Simon Scott 27 April 1687 may or may not be the same person. It is not possible to settle this, as, although Scarlett is described as 'Free Imbroyder' in his mark entries, the freedom books of that company now commence only in 1694 and it is obvious from Heal that he was at work before this. First mark as largeworker entered, undated, probably April 1697 on commencement of register. Address: Foster

Lane. 'Free Imbroyder'. Second mark (Sterling), 29 June 1720. Third mark, 25 September 1722. Fourth, 18 October 1725. Heal records him as William Scarlet, goldsmith, Cradle Court, Cripplegate Ward, 1692-3; and plateworker, Foster Lane, 1697-1725. He was Master of the Broderers' Company in 1726 and was dead by 7 May 1729 (see John Harwood). He is presumably the William Scarlett of St. Leonard's, Foster Lane, married to Mary Flaskett widow, by licence, at St. Mary Woolnoth, 29 May 1701. He must presumably also have been a widower, and Richard (above) born of a previous marriage which has not come to light.

SCHAFFER, John (1605) No record of apprenticeship or freedom. Only mark entered as smallworker, in partnership with John Peters, 18 June 1810. Address: 20 Old Compton Street, Soho.

SCHOFIELD See SCOFIELD.

SCHOFIELD, Robert (3779) Attributed with John Sc(h)ofield to the mark in question by Jackson. There seems, however, to be no other evidence for this name and it must be remembered that the mark of Robert Jones and John Scofield, entered in 1776, is found before that date and had probably been entered in the missing register of 1758-73. It seems likely that the mark above was an alternative of the recorded one, in which the 'I' of Jones was not apparent for reproduction.

SCHOFIELD, William (3326) Perhaps son of William Scholefield of Crown Court Fleet Street mathematical instrument maker, apprenticed to George Grace of St. John's Lane Clerkenwell as mathematical instrument maker 3 May 1786. Free, 7 April 1802. First mark entered as spoonmaker, 10 November 1820. Address: 2 Clerkenwell Close. Second mark, 17 May 1833. Address: 10 Sarah Place, Old Street Road.

SCHUPPE, John (1686) No record of apprenticeship or freedom. Believed from his name and work to be an immigrant Dutchman. Mark entered as largeworker, 28 June 1753. Address: Little Deans Court, St. Martin's Le Grand. Moved to 6 New Rents, 17 July 1755. Heal records him as plateworker, Deans Court, 1753-73, but he appears as plateworker, at the second address above, in the Parl. Report list 1773. His mark appears almost entirely on creamjugs modelled in the Dutch taste as cows, but is occasionally met with on other small fancies such as figure tapersticks.

*SCHURMAN, Albertus (91, 3478) No record of apprenticeship or freedom. Only mark entered as largeworker, 4 March 1756. Address: 'at Mr Ashley Peruke maker opposite bull and gate Holborn'. Moved to Bedford Court, Red Lyon Street, 9 April 1757, where Heal records him (without the first address) as plateworker, 1756-62.

*SCOFIELD, John (1670, 2349, 3709, 3779) Although widely known as Schofield, both the clerk's entry and signature of this maker are as above. No record of apprenticeship or freedom, which for a maker who occupied such a prominent position in the plateworking of the late part of the century is tantalizing. First mark entered as plateworker, in partnership with Robert Jones, 10 February 1776. Address: 40 Bartholomew Close. Second mark alone, 13 January 1778. Address: 29 Bell Yard, Temple Bar. Third mark, 1 October 1787. Heal records him always as Schofield, with all the above addresses and dates, and with 1796 as later date for Bell Yard. He also records Robert and John Schofield, 1772-6, for which see under Schofield (above).

In his candlesticks and candelabra Scofield displays a high degree of elegant design executed with impeccable craftsmanship, which rivals at best the contemporary French goldsmith Henri Auguste. It was perhaps the restrained taste of the period that prevented Scofield from displaying a virtuosity which might well have given him a reputation equal with Lamerie or Storr. No one could mount glass better, as is shown by his cruet in the Rotch Collection (Victoria and Albert Museum). It seems likely that he worked for Jefferys, Jones and Gilbert, the then Royal goldsmiths, and that he may have had considerable commissions for Carlton House

SCOTT, Digby (504-5, 3522) No record of apprenticeship or freedom. Very probably acquainted or working with Benjamin Smith II (q.v.) in Birmingham in association with Matthew Boulton, although no mention of him appears in the Boulton papers (Birmingham Assay Office). On the other hand it should be noted that Benjamin Smith's third son, born 1797, was christened Digby before the father had left Birmingham for Greenwich, which seems a significant pointer to Scott's presence in Birmingham at that date. First mark entered as plateworker, in partnership with Benjamin Smith II, 4 October 1802. Address: Limekiln Lane, Greenwich. Second mark, 21 March 1803. The partnership apparently dissolved by 11 May 1807, when Smith entered a separate mark. There would seem to be a return to a triple partnership with the addition of James Smith in 1811, if the existence of mark no. 3522 is to be relied upon, but it seems otherwise unknown than as represented by Jackson and may stem from some error of reproduction (cf. Benjamin and James Smith).

SCRIVENER, Dor (? Dorah or Dorothy) (2486) 'Widow'. Only mark entered as smallworker, undated, probably April 1697 on commencement of register. Address: White Alley, Chancery Lane. 'Free Cutler'. The only one of this name in the Cutlers' Company records appears to be George Scrivener (below), whose apprentice John Wilkins was made free in 1689, and who may therefore have been related to the above.

SCRIVENER, George (2485) No record of apprenticeship or freedom. Only mark entered as smallworker, undated, probably April 1697 on commencement of register. Address: Fetter Lane. He is perhaps the George Scrivener, Free Cutler, referred to in the previous entry, but can scarcely be the husband of the above since both entries are apparently almost simultaneous at the start of the new register.

SEABROOK, James (1642, 2507) Son of Robert Seabrook late Citizen and Lorimer of London deceased, apprenticed to Thomas Merry 1 April 1706. Free, 6 October 1714. Mark entered as largeworker, 11 October 1714. Address: Wood Street. Second (Sterling) mark, 22 July 1720. Address: St. Ann's Lane. Seabrook seems to have had a chequered matrimonial and professional career. He is probably the James Seabrook of St. John Zachary, bachelor, married to Elizabeth Gamble of St. Leonard, Foster Lane, spinster, at St. Bene't, Paul's Wharf, 23 April 1716. A daughter Elizabeth died 1 July 1718 and was buried at St. John Zachary. Heal records him of the parish of St. John Zachary in 1723. James Seabrook, goldsmith of Cripplegate, widower, married Jane Dawson of the same, widow, 17 September 1740 (Fleet register of marriages). James Seabrook of St. Luke's, Goldsmith, bachelor, was married to Eliz. Livings of the same parish, widow, 22 January 1745/6 (Fleet register), and James Seabrook, goldsmith of St. John Zachary, widower, was married to Eliz. Clegg, widow, 7 October 1749 (Fleet register). Heal records him as insolvent, of the parish of St. Giles, Cripplegate, and it appears he was in and out of the Fleet Prison at frequent intervals acquiring a new wife from time to time. He appears in the Minutes of the Company, 5 August 1742, 'one of the 10 new almesmen of the Company' as having petitioned against the Company's displeasure after absconding from subpoena as a witness against Richard Gosling (whom he had served near ten years) for counterfeiting marks (of which Gosling was convicted). Seabrook was discharged from his pension and rendered incapable of partaking of any alms or charity of the Company for the future. A sad story, reminiscent of Hogarth's Idle Apprentice.

SEAMAN, William (3322) Son of John Seaman late of St. Andrew Holborn cabinetmaker deceased, apprenticed to Thomas Streetin of Great Sutton Street Clerkenwell as goldsmith 6 April 1796 on payment of £20. Free, 7 December 1803. First mark entered as spoonmaker, 29 February 1804. Address: 6 Coopers Court, Seward Street, Goswell Street. Second mark, on move to 9 Great Sutton Street, 15 October 1810. Third mark (three sizes), 18 October 1810. Fourth mark, 16 October 1818. Fifth, 3 January 1820. Sixth, 4 September 1822. Moved to 1 New Gloucester Place, Hoxton, 9 June 1823.

SEBILLE, John (1693, 3656-7) No record of apprenticeship or freedom. Appears with his partner John Langford (q.v.) as bankrupt in 1770 (*The Gentleman's Magazine*, p. 346), and in the Parl. Report list as plateworkers, St. Martin's Le Grand, 1773. The mark attributed to them with virtual certainty from Chaffers onwards must have been entered in the missing register between 1758 and 1763 when it is recorded by Chaffers. Second mark as plateworker, in partnership with James Jones II, 14 February 1798. Address: 9 Clerkenwell Close. This might possibly be a son of the same name. Listed by Evans as Huguenot, quoting one of the same name, 'A French Refugee' who was admitted Freeman of the Cork Goldsmiths' Company in 1685 (*Journal of the Royal Society of Antiquities of Ireland*, XXV, p. 218).

SELLERS, George (901) No record of apprenticeship or freedom. Only mark entered as smallworker, 25 May 1802. Address: 12 Cross Street, Hatton Garden. Moved to 70 Bunhill Row, 1 November 1820

SEMORE, Charles (1690) No record of apprenticeship or freedom. Mark entered as largeworker, in partnership with John Hyatt, 24 September 1757. Address: Little Dean's Court, St. Martin's Le Grand. Moved to Noble Street, 24 October 1758. Heal records them as goldsmiths, Little Britain, 1750-65. Semore (or as then spelt, Seymour) was also in partnership in 1773 with William Lancester (q.v.) as smallworkers in Noble Street, according to an entry of the names, without any mark struck, in the 1773 register.

*SHALLIS, James (1850) Son of John Shallis of the Vineyard Gardens, Clerkenwell chip hat bleacher, apprenticed to Joseph Beckwith of Clerkenwell Green as bright engraver 3 August 1803. Free, 7 November 1810. Mark entered as plateworker, 8 May 1811. Address: 8 Wineyard Gardens, Clerkenwell. (The entry unsigned by the maker.) Livery, December 1839. Died 8 May 1859.

SHARP, John (1678) No record of apprenticeship or freedom. Only mark entered as plateworker, 19 September 1821. Address: 30 Fish Street Hill.

SHARP, Robert (506-8, 2293, 2436, 3523) Son of Robert Sharp of Newcastle on Tyne yeoman, apprenticed to Gawen Nash 4 February 1747 and turned over the same day to Thomas Gladwin (q.v.) Citizen and Merchant Taylor. Free, 4 May 1757. First mark in partnership with Daniel Smith (q.v.) apparently entered by 1763 (3523) in the missing register. The firm appears as supplying plate to Parker and Wakelin in the latters' ledger for 1766 (Garrard MSS, Victoria and Albert Museum). Address by 1770: Aldermanbury, when a second Robert Sharp (presumably a nephew), son of John Sharp late of Newcastle upon Tyne brewer deceased, was apprenticed to his uncle (he plays no further part however in the firm). Livery, December 1771. Appears with Daniel Smith as plateworkers, Aldermanbury, in the Parl. Report list 1773. Second mark as plateworker, in partnership with Richard Carter (q.v.) and Daniel Smith, 9 December 1778. Address: 14 Westmoreland Buildings, Aldersgate Street. Third, fourth and fifth marks, in partnership with Smith only again, 7 February 1780, same address. Sixth mark alone, 7 January 1788, same address. This last mark has been ascribed previously to Robert Salmon, spoonmaker (Parl. Report list 1773), for whom there is no recorded mark in the existing registers. A curious characteristic of the marks of Smith and Sharp after the Carter partnership was over, and of Sharp alone in 1788, is that each shows at the top edge of the punch traces of the bottom of the initials of the former partner (above), apparently intentionally. It can scarcely be likely with all the work of the firm that the old punch was good enough cut down, and it seems a whim to suggest the change of the firm's make-up. Robert Sharp died in 1803. Heal records him alone as goldsmith, Aldermanbury, 1770; and Westmoreland Buildings, 1789; with Daniel Smith as plateworkers, London, 1763-89; at 50 Aldermanbury, 1763-77; Westmoreland Buildings, 1780; and 14 Bartolomew Close, 1779-96; also Carter, Smith and Sharp, Westmoreland Buildings, 1778. The firm were the principal exponents of the magnificent racecups, particularly for Doncaster, in the Adam taste, and in at least one case, that of one won by the Marquess of Zetland, designed by Adam himself (Robert Rowe, *Adam Silver*). Candelabra of French classical flavour were another important production, and much dinner plate. The firm almost certainly must have supplied both Parker and Wakelin (as mentioned above) and Wakelin and Taylor later, and also Jefferys, Jones and Gilbert after the latters' appointment as Royal Goldsmiths in 1784. One imagines, as with Scofield above, that the plate at Carlton House may largely have come from their hands.

SHARP, William (3325) William Henry son of John Sharp of Fish Street Hill, Colchester clockmaker, apprenticed to Samuel Wheatley of Old Street St. Luke's as silversmith 7 March 1810 on payment of £36. 15s. Free, 2 July 1817. First mark entered as plateworker, 31 March 1817. Address: 3 Old Street, St. Luke's. Moved to 16 Red Cross Square, 23 January 1818. Second mark, 16 September 1824.

*SHARRATT, Thomas (2929) Apprenticed to John Haygarth of the Founders' Company and turned over to John Jarratt of the same.

Free of the Founders' Company, 28 December 1752. First mark (incuse), 8 December 1768. Address: 'Ozier' Lane, West Smithfield (Section V). Second mark as smallworker, 23 April 1772, same address, with addition of 'Founder'. Appears as smallworker, at this address, in the Parl. Report list 1773. Third mark, 22 February 1776. Address: 17 Hosiers Lane, Smithfield.

SHAW, Daniel (500) No record of apprenticeship or freedom. Only mark entered as largeworker, 7 December 1748. Address: Great Arthur Street, Goswell Street.

*SHAW, George (891) Apprenticed to George Shaw (presumably his father) and free of the Cutlers' Company 15 June 1717. Mark entered as swordcutler, 28 June 1720. Address: 'at ye flaming Sword in fullwoods Rents, Holbourn in St. Andrews parrish'.

SHAW, Philip (2231-2) Described as Free Butcher in his entry, but no trace of his name appears in the index to apprentices or freemen of that company. First mark entered as smallworker, 17 September 1730. Address: 'Living at Mr Alcocoks Goldsmith at ye Cup & Ring at Cripplegate' (see John Alcock). 'Free Butcher'. Second mark, 18 October 1733. Address: Peartree Street, Brisk Lane, Old Street. Heal records him only as silversmith, late of Bishopsgate, in prison for debt, 1720.

SHAW, Thomas (2934) No record of apprenticeship or freedom. Only mark entered as smallworker, 22 June 1785. Address: 6 Gloucester Row, Curtain Road, Shoreditch.

SHAW, William I (2530, 3299-300, 3329) Son of Thomas Shaw late of Atherstone in the County of Warwick clerk deceased, apprenticed to Edward Holliday 9 March 1715 on payment of £20. Free, 12 November 1724. First and second marks (Sterling and New Standard) entered as largeworker, 16 January 1729. Address: Gerrard Street, Soho. 'of Goldsmiths Company'. Third mark, 24 June 1739, same address. Fourth mark, 24 April 1745. Heal records him as goldsmith, Corner of Maxfield's Street (?Macclesfield), facing Gerrard Street, 1725; Gerrard Street, Soho, 1727; and Golden Ball, Gerrard Street, 1743-5. He appears as William Shaw, goldsmith, St. Anne, Westminster, bankrupt, July 1745 (*The Gentleman's Magazine*, p. 389).

SHAW, William II (3301, 3335) Son of Thomas Shaw of the parish of All Hallows the Less London dry cooper, apprenticed to John Swift 11 November 1736 (the premium erased). Free, 6 April 1748. Livery, April 1751. First mark entered as largeworker, 3 January 1749. Address: Maiden Lane. Second mark, in partnership with William Priest (q.v.), 12 October 1749, same address. Moved to Wood Street, 2 January 1751. Third mark with Priest, 27 June 1759. Heal records him as plateworker, Maiden Lane, 1749; goldsmith, 22 Wood Street, Cheapside, 1763-72; and plateworker, Bishopsgate Street, 1769-73 (where he appears in the Parl. Report List 1773); with William Priest, as working goldsmiths, Unicorn, Wood Street, near Maiden Lane, 1749-58. Either alone or with Priest his mark occurs on good, if not inspired, hollow-ware, coffee-pots, tankards and some waiters.

SHEA, John (1849, 2448) No record of apprenticeship or freedom. First mark entered as spoonmaker, 6 November 1807. Address: 17 Duke Street, Westminster Road. Second mark, in partnership with Richard Turner as spoonmakers, 23 April 1808. Address: 31 St. John's Square, Clerkenwell.

SHEEN *See* SKEEN.

SHEENE, Alice (2522) No record of apprenticeship or freedom. Presumably widow of Joseph Sheene (below). Mark entered as largeworker, 29 April 1700. Address: Ball Alley, Lombard Street. Heal records her here till 1715.

SHEENE, Joseph (2521) Son of Joseph Sheene of Tewkesbury in the County of Gloucester mercer, apprenticed to Benjamin Bradford 4 April 1677. Freedom unrecorded. James Chadwick apprenticed to him, 22 September 1686. Mark entered as largeworker, undated, probably April 1697 on commencement of register. Address: Ball Alley, Lombard Street. Livery, October 1698. Presumably dead by 29 April 1700, on entry of Alice Sheene's mark at the same address. Heal records him as plateworker, parish of All Hallows, Lombard Street, 1692-3; London, 1697-1710; and Lombard Street, 1710. The last dates seem open to doubt.

SHEKLETON, John (1674, 1677) No record of apprenticeship or freedom. First mark entered as smallworker, 15 April 1799. Address: 13 Old Street. Moved to 4 Prugan (?) Square, Old Bailey, 6 October 1802. Second mark, 9 March 1809. Third mark, 8

March 1821. Address: 1 Pontipool Place, Blackfriars Road.

SHEKLETON, Thomas (2932) No record of apprenticeship or freedom. Presumably son or younger brother of John Shekleton (above). Mark entered as smallworker, 10 February 1810. Address: 4 Prugun Square, Old Bailey.

SHELLEY, Samuel I (2629) No record of apprenticeship or freedom. Only mark entered as smallworker, 24 October 1728. Address: Bell Alley, Goswell Street.

SHELLEY, Samuel II (2632, 3799) No record of apprenticeship or freedom. First mark entered as smallworker, 6 December 1758. Address: Exeter Court, Barthow (Bartholomew) Close. Second mark, 3 July 1772. Blue Court, Saffron Hill. He appears as goldworker, Christopher's Court, Bartholomew Close, in the Parl. Report list 1773. His second mark which appears nearly identical with the first, is, however, signed Shilley and he so appears as a separate entity in the Parl. Report list. Heal records him as goldsmith, Bartholomew Close, 1773; 149 Strand, 1784–93; also Shelley and Co., 61 St. Paul's Churchyard, 1774–7; Shelley and King, jewellers, Strand, 1770–2; 146 Strand, 1772; and 110 Oxford Street, 1779–81. *The Gentleman's Magazine*, 28 February 1781: 'At this Sessions (of the Old Bailey) among many other felons was Samuel Shelley, for purchasing plate knowing the same to be stolen. He was, before this, accounted a very reputable silversmith in the Strand. He was sentenced to one's years labour on the Thames.' (i.e. the 'hulks', cf. *Great Expectations*).

SHELMERDINE, Daniel (499, 2523–4) Apprenticed to Francis Williams of the Cutlers' Company and free of that company 29 October 1681. First mark entered as smallworker, undated, probably April 1697 on commencement of register. Address: Exchange Alley, Cornhill. 'Cutler'. Second mark, 17 May 1717, no address. Third mark, 22 June 1720 as 'sword cutler'. Address: 'at the Golden Dagger in New Street by Shoe Lane, St. Brides Parish'. Heal records him only as silversmith, Noble Street, by Foster Lane, insolvent, 1729.

SHEPHERD, John (2520) Probably John Sheppard son of John of Home Lacey in the County of Hereford yeoman, apprenticed to Sir Thomas Vyner Knight and Baronet 'for 8 years from Lady Day last past' 17 June 1664. Freedom unrecorded. Mark entered as largeworker, undated, probably April 1697. Address: Gutter Lane. The mark was entered twice with no discernible difference in two separate entries. Heal records him as plateworker, Gutter Lane, 1685(?)–97.

SHEPHERD, Thomas (2926–8) Son of Thomas Shepherd late of Auborn in the County of Wiltshire baker deceased, apprenticed to John Munns 6 October 1762 and turned over to Robert Salmon 3 November 1768. Free, 1 November 1769. First mark entered as smallworker, 18 December 1769. Address: Bull and Mouth Street, where he so appears in the Parl. Report list 1773. Second mark, 27 April 1773. Third, 6 November 1782. Address: 11 Glasshouse Yard, Aldersgate Street. Fourth, 20 October 1785. Fifth, 5 April 1786. Moved to Seven Bridges, Reading, Berkshire, 17 May 1792. Heal records him as working silversmith, Bull and Mouth Street, 1771; and Glasshouse Yard, Aldersgate Street, 1785–9.

SHERMER, Thomas (2525) Son of William Shermer of Highworth in the County of Wiltshire Mercer apprenticed to Richard Bailey 3 August 1708. Signatory as journeyman to the petition against assaying the work of foreigners not having served seven years apprenticeship, February 1716. Free, 8 March 1716. Mark entered as largeworker, 12 September 1717. Address: Foster Lane. The entry contains no less than eleven attempts at a good impression of his mark! Heal records him at the same address, 1717–20.

SHINTON, Humphrey (1065) No record of apprenticeship or freedom. Only mark entered as smallworker, 21 January 1730. Address: Chick Lane. Below the entry 'silver mark', suggesting he was more accustomed to working in some other material. Perhaps a purveyor of one or other of the many silver-mounted accessories or cases of the time.

SHIPWAY, Charles (417) No record of apprenticeship or freedom. First mark entered as spoonmaker, 25 January 1826. Address: 28 Rahere Street, Goswell Street. Second mark, 8 May 1829. Moved to 82 Nicholas Street, New North Road, 20 March 1832. Third mark, 17 June 1836. Moved to 13 Shaftesbury Street, New North Road, 17 April 1844. Moved to 162 Goswell Street, St. Luke's, 25 March 1847.

*SHRUDER, James (1653, 1682–3) No

record of apprenticeship or freedom. First mark entered as largeworker, 1 August 1737. Address: Wardour Street, St. Ann's, Westminster. Second and third marks, 25 June 1739. Address: Greek Street, Soho. Below this an undated note, 'James Shruder at the Golden Ewer in Spur Street, Leicester Square'. Bankrupt, June 1749 as Goldsmith, St. Martin's in the Fields (*The Gentleman's Magazine*, p. 285). Heal records him as above, with the addition of the sign of the Golden Ewer in Greek Street; as well as Corner of Hedge Lane, Leicester Square, from 1744. The character of his work, at its best some of the finest rococo plate of the day, suggests a German origin and training to match his name. His power as a designer is exemplified by his highly original tradecard (Heal, plate LXV) signed 'J. Shruder Inv.' and engraved by J. Warburton.

SIBLEY, Mary (2067) No record of apprenticeship or freedom. Presumably widow of Richard Sibley I (below). Mark entered as plateworker, in partnership with Richard Sibley II, 23 February 1836. Address: 30 Red Lion Street, Clerkenwell.

SIBLEY, Richard I (2438, 2440, 2748, 3050) Son of John Sibley of Bath in the County of Somerset goldsmith deceased, apprenticed to Fendall Rushworth of Carey Lane London 2 November 1785 and turned over the same day to Daniel Smith of Bartholomew Close Citizen and Merchant Taylor and again 2 March 1791 to Robert Sharp Citizen and Goldsmith. Free, 2 October 1793. Livery, June 1811. First mark entered as plateworker, in partnership with Thomas Ellerton, 14 November 1803. Address: 14 Bartholomew Close. Second mark alone, 11 March 1805, same address. Third mark, in partnership with William Burwash, 7 October 1805, same address. Fourth mark alone again, 13 July 1812. Address: 30 Red Lion Street, Clerkenwell. His various apprentices included the son of William Burwash in 1806, and his own son in 1821. He died 1836. His work whether alone or in partnership is of a high standard of design and execution in a restrained key of Regency taste.

SIBLEY, Richard II (2067, 2440) Son of Richard Sibley I (above), apprenticed to his father as silversmith 7 February 1821. Free, 4 February 1829. First mark as plateworker, in partnership with Mary Sibley his mother, 23 February 1836. Address: 30 Red Lion Street, Clerkenwell. Second mark alone as spoonmaker, 15 March 1837, same address. Third mark, 21 June 1839, on move to 10 Dufours Place, Broad Street, Golden Square. Moved to 30 Poland Street, Oxford Street, 6 September 1853. Moved to 18 Poland Street, 30 July 1858. Moved to 13 Oxford Market, Oxford Street, 2 July 1862.

SIDAWAY, John (1669) No record of apprenticeship or freedom. Only mark entered as smallworker, 23 April 1777. Address: 10 Little Britain, where Heal records him as silversmith, 1790-3.

SIDDALL, Paul (2236) No record of apprenticeship or freedom. Only mark entered as plateworker, in partnership with John Wrangham and William Moulson, 15 November 1823. Address: 7 White Hart Court, Castle Street, Leicester Square.

SIEBER, Ernest (640) No record of apprenticeship or freedom. Only mark entered as largeworker, 2 June 1746. Address: 'in Walkers Court near Crown Court old Soho St James'. Heal records him as plateworker, Crown Street, 1746. His work is very rare and seems almost confined to candlesticks, with an emphasis on examples with cast figure stems. His name suggests a German origin, but, if so, he was of an itinerant nature, since by 1752 he was in The Hague, where he produced a pair of figure candlesticks to match a previous pair bearing his mark made in London in 1748 (Christie's, 17 May 1967). A mark very close to his London mark was used and is recorded by Voet (*Haagsche Meesterteekens*, no. 176) on pieces dating about 1780. It is possible of course that this might be for a son of the same name.

SIERVENT, Samuel (2631) No record of apprenticeship or freedom. Mark entered as largeworker, 20 June 1755. Address: St. Martin's Lane. Moved to Foster Buildings, White Cross Street, 1 October 1756. Heal records only the former address. His mark is very rarely found. Listed by Evans as Huguenot (*Hug. Soc. Proc.*, 14, p. 552).

SILK, Charles (416) No record of apprenticeship or freedom. Only mark entered as smallworker, 26 August 1817. Address: 4 Green Street, Leicester Square.

SIMCOE, Joseph (1639, 2551) Son of William Simcoe of Chick Lane taylor, apprenticed to Benjamin Thompson 25 November 1707. Free, 27 November 1716. First mark entered as smallworker, 1

December 1716. Address: Foster Lane. Second (Sterling) mark, 29 June 1720, same address. Presumably dead by 20 February 1724 on entry of Rachel Simcoe's mark.

SIMCOE, Rachel (2431) No record of apprenticeship or freedom. Presumably widow of Joseph Simcoe (above). Mark entered as smallworker, 20 February 1724. Address: Maiden Lane.

SIMKISS, Richard (2435) No record of apprenticeship or freedom. Only mark entered as smallworker, 5 March 1770. Address: Noble Street. Appears as goldworker, Maiden Lane, Wood Street, in the Parl. Report list 1773, where he is mentioned as having been prosecuted in 1770 for making gold watchchains 'worse than standard'.

SIMON, Peter (2230, 2552) No record of apprenticeship or freedom. New Standard and Sterling marks entered as largeworker, 14 May 1725. Address: Earl Street, near Seven Dials. Probably a Huguenot although omitted by Evans (*Hug. Soc. Proc.*, 14). Pierre Simon, eighteen years old, with his parents Jean and Anne from Rouen, appears in the Reconnaissances of the French Church of the Savoy, 18 September 1687 (*Hug. Soc. Pub.*, 22), and Peter Simon in the Denization List, 31 January 1689/90 (*Hug. Soc. Pub.*, 18). Peter Simon (perhaps the son of the above) appears in the Oath Roll Naturalization of 1710 (*Hug. Soc. Pub.*, 27), and Pierre Simond, 'marchand par. St. Nicollas Acons dans la cite de Londres' married Susanne Grostete de la Buffière at the Spring Garden Chapel, 11 January 1725/?6. Another Pierre Simon, son of Louis and Marie (née Bellier), was baptized at the Church of the Artillery, Spitalfields, 28 February 1697/?8.

SIMONS, Barnett (226) No record of apprenticeship or freedom. Two marks, one incuse, entered as smallworker, 9 February 1767. Address: Duke Lane, Smithfield. Third mark, 11 June 1767. Address: Mould Makers Row, St. Martin's Le Grand, where he appears as smallworker in the Parl. Report list 1773. Perhaps a watchcasemaker. The name suggests a Jewish origin.

SIMONS, William (3314) Son of George Simons of the parish of Dinton near Ailesbury in the County of Buckingham victualler, apprenticed to Richard Hawkins 2 November 1757 and turned over (having served out his indenture) to Robert Salmon (spoonmaker). Free, 8 August 1770. First mark entered as plateworker, 18 January 1776. Address: Lambeth Walk. Second mark, 13 February 1776. Heal records him as spoonmaker, 6 Barbican, 1771-3, as he appears in the Parl. Report list for the latter year, and he may well have entered an earlier mark in the missing register prior to 1773. He is described as spoonmaker of the parish of St. Mary, Lambeth, in the apprenticeship to him of George Whittington in 1776.

SIMPSON, Benjamin (228, 3270) No record of apprenticeship or freedom. First mark entered as smallworker, in partnership with William Parker (q.v.), 8 April 1799. Address: 5 Staining Lane. Second mark alone, 4 October 1800. Address: 15 Fountain Court, Strand.

SIMPSON, Lancelot (1964) No record of apprenticeship or freedom. Only mark entered as smallworker, 7 November 1769. Address: Great Turnstile, Holborn, where he appears without category in the Parl. Report list 1773. Heal records only Launcelot Simpson, goldsmith, Moorfields, 1780.

SIMPSON, Richard (2434) No record of apprenticeship or freedom. Only mark entered as smallworker, 31 July 1767. Address: Albion Buildings, near Aldersgate Street, where he appears as watchcasemaker in the Parl. Report list 1773, and entered three marks as such, 1776-1800 (Section VI).

SIMSON, Joseph (2549) Son of Joseph Simpson late of the parish of St. Giles Cripplegate vintner deceased, apprenticed to Matthew Cuthbert 29 September 1696. Free, 20 October 1703. Mark entered as smallworker, 25 October 1703. Address: Aldersgate Street. Heal records only Simson, goldsmith, Golden Lion, over against Short's gardens in Drury Lane, 1710. There is perhaps a possibility that we have here an entry for Joseph Sympson (so signs) Senior, the engraver.

SING See SYNG.

SINGLETON, Francis (2550) Francis 'Shingleton' son of Joseph of Wickham in the County of Buckingham yeoman, apprenticed to Robert Stephens 6 May 1659. Free, 15 April 1668. Livery, 1687. His son Joseph was apprenticed to him 18 December 1690. Mark entered as largeworker, undated, probably April 1697 on commencement of register. Address: Foster Lane. Heal records him as plateworker, London, 1677–1702; and Foster Lane, 1697.

SKEEN, William (3306–7) Free by redemption as goldsmith 4 March 1761, but first mark entered as largeworker, 4 December 1755. Address: Old Bolton Street, Long Acre. Moved to St. Ann's Lane near Aldersgate, 11 February 1761, where he appears as plateworker in the Parl. Report list 1773. Second mark as plateworker, 26 June 1775. Address: No. 37 Green Hill (sic) Rents, Cow Cross. Third mark, 5 May 1783. Address: 16 Well Street, Faulkner Square. Heal records him as William Sheen, plateworker, for the first three addresses, and under Skeen, as goldsmith, St. Ann's Lane, 1767–8; Greenhill's Rents, 1775; and Well Street, Falcon Street, 1783.

SKIDMAN, Henry (1067) No record of apprenticeship or freedom. First mark entered as silverworker, 1 May 1821. Address: 6 Suffolk Street, St. Pancras. Second mark, 3 April 1822. Moved to 3 Coldbath Square, Clerkenwell, 11 May 1822.

SKINNER, Abel (2563) Son of Matthew Skinner late of Bampton of the Bush in the County of Oxford butcher deceased, apprenticed to Thomas Woodward of the Joiners' Company 11 January 1676. Free of that company, 6 February 1683. Mark entered as smallworker, 19 April 1715. Address: Cheapside. 'Free Joyner'.

SKINNER, Daniel (503, 2562) Son of Corbett Skinner of Great Torrington in the County of Devon gentleman, apprenticed to Maurice Boheme 11 May 1703. Free, 6 June 1710. First mark entered as smallworker, 3 July 1710. Address: Silver Street. Second mark, 13 Feburary 1716. Third mark (Sterling), 20 June 1720.

SKUPHOLME, George (2560) Son of George Skupholme late Citizen and Haberdasher of London deceased, apprenticed to William Crane 25 September 1667. Free, 9 or 19 January 1675/?8. Livery, November 1687. Mark entered as smallworker, undated, probably April 1697 on commencement of register. Address: Maiden Lane. Perhaps dead or retired by 25 April 1705, the date of the entry of his son John's mark (see below).

SKUPHOLME, John (2561) Son of George Skupholme (above), apprenticed to his father 9 March 1694. Free, 15 February 1703/?4. Mark entered as smallworker, 25 April 1705. Address: Maiden Lane.

SLATER, James (1647) Son of James Slater of St. Ann's Aldersgate shoemaker, apprenticed to John fford of the Merchant Taylors' Company 2 July 1718 on payment of £15. Described as goldsmith journeyman with Wm(?) Hill Trinity Lane turned over to Thomas Kidder and from him to John Allbright (q.v.). Free of the same company, 7 July 1725. First mark entered as largeworker, undated, between October 1725 and January 1728, probably earlier than later. Address: Garland Court, Great Trinity Lane. 'Merchant Taylors Company'. Heal records him as plateworker, Great Trinity Lane, 1732.

SLEAMAKER, Daniel (2442, 2567) Son of Thomas Sleamaker late of Brinley in the County of Warwick husbandman deceased, apprenticed to Robert Timberley 14 January 1691. Free, 29 July 1698. Livery, April 1705. First mark entered as largeworker, in partnership with John Read (q.v.), 17 October 1701. Address: Laurence Pountney Lane. Read entered a separate mark on 22 July 1704, and Sleamaker his second mark alone, 15 October 1704. Address: Swithins Lane. Heal records him as plateworker, with these addresses and dates; and also London, 1707–32.

SLEATH, Gabriel (890, 904, 907, 2568–9) Born 11 January 1674 in the parish of Friern Barnet. Son of Gabriel Sleath Citizen and Tallow Chandler of London, apprenticed to Thomas Cooper 27 November 1691. Free, 22 October 1701. Married before 1704 and before entering a mark, apparently working for Isaac Dighton (q.v.), since the register of St. Vedast, Foster Lane, has the following entry. 'Thomas the son of Gabriell Sleath a Goldsmith Lieuing in Captain Isaac Dightons house in gutter Lane in this parish and Anne his wife was Borne and Baptized the 27th day of July 1704 in Edward Hathaway House in gutter Lane'. The child was buried on 18 August 1704. Sleath entered his first mark as largeworker, 14 March 1707. Address: Gutter Lane. Livery, October 1712. Signatory as 'working goldsmith' to the petition complaining of the competition of 'necessitous strangers', December 1711, and to that against assaying work of foreigners not having served seven years apprenticeship, February 1716. Second (Sterling) mark, 17 June 1720. Third mark, 18 June 1739. Address: Gutter Lane. Fourth mark, in partnership with Francis Crump (who had been apprenticed to him), 22 November 1753, same address. By 1729 Sleath had acquired property at or was living at Friern Barnet, as Anne Sleath was buried there, 14 April 1729. Sleath was next married to Jane Crane, both of St. Vedast, at St. Helen's Bishopsgate, 17 August 1729. He was buried at Friern Barnet, 21 March 1756. His will, dated 9 March preceding, names his wife Joan and directs the sale of 'all my Stock in Trade and also the Lease of my House in Gutter Lane'. He leaves £5 to his sister Sarah Wood, otherwise everything to his wife. Witnesses to the will include Francis Crump. A son Gabriel born 1707 may perhaps be identified with one of the name buried at St Saviour's, Southwark 1739 as butcher. Heal records Sleath as plateworker, Gutter Lane, 1669(?) and 1704; also the partnership with Crump, 1753-5; he also has Heath (due presumably to misprints in original sources, Sl cursive being read as H.), Gutter Lane, 1706-39; and Heath and Crumpe, 1753. From the evidence of his surviving pieces Sleath appears to have had an extensive business in the production of standard types of hollow-ware, coffee-pots, tankards, cups and covers. His major works are the wine-cisterns in the Hermitage and that of the Grocers' Company. (I am indebted to Miss Grimshaw for much of the above information.)

SMALLWOOD, John (1648) Son of John Smallwood pencil-maker of St. Clement Danes, apprenticed to John Seagood 13 October 1713 on payment of £25 and turned over to James Catliffe. Freedom unrecorded. Mark entered as smallworker, undated, between November 1725 and July 1726. Address: Drury Lane, near Long Acre.

SMART, Francis (2583) Son of Francis Smart Citizen and Armourer of London, apprenticed to Edward Blagrave 11 August 1693. Free, 7 December 1702. Mark entered as smallworker, 22 January 1703. Address: Maiden Lane.

SMITH, Alexander (93) No record of apprenticeship or freedom. First mark entered as smallworker, 8 March 1819. Address: 3 Bedfordbury, Covent Garden. Second (incuse) mark, on move to 6 Rose Street, 7 May 1827.

SMITH, Ann (2582) Free of the Coopers' Company, probably by patrimony. Only mark as smallworker, undated, probably April 1697 on commencement of register. 'Widdow at Cripple gate free Cooper'. Heal records her as Mrs Smith, goldsmith, Cock Alley, without Cripplegate, 1692-8.

SMITH, Anne (97) No record of apprenticeship or freedom. Only mark as smallworker, in partnership with Nathaniel Appleton, 26 July 1771. Address: Aldersgate Street. They appear as smallworkers, Cox's Court, Aldersgate Street, in the Parl. Report list 1773. The mark is frequently met with on small cream-jugs and salt-cellars of a somewhat pedestrian quality.

*SMITH, Benjamin I (2584) Freeman of the Cordwainers' Company. Only mark entered as smallworker, 26 July 1706. Address: near Cripplegate. 'Free Cordwainer'. From the address it seems possible that he was the son of Ann Smith (above), although not free of the same company.

*SMITH, Benjamin II (229-30, 237-8, 504-5, 3522) Son of Ralph Smith of Birmingham, born 15 December 1764. Married firstly, 8 October 1788, Mary Adams at Edgbaston parish church. Apparently to be identified with 'Mr Smith' introduced through James Alston, on the recommendation of 'Mr Nevill', to Matthew Boulton at Birmingham (letter dated 18 May 1790. Birmingham Assay Office), then described as 'an Ingenious Chaser'. By September 1792 the firm of Boulton and Smith, latchet manufacturers was in existence, from the evidence of a specification endorsed 'Smith Buckle Invention' signed James Smith, from which it is clear that both Benjamin and James were with Boulton. In March 1794 they were joined by John Lander, jeweller, who had invented an 'Elastic Shoe Latchet', when Benjamin and James are described as button makers. Disagreement developed in 1801 when Benjamin threatened to withdraw and go to London and a new partnership was drawn up between Boulton and James in 1802. On 1 February 1802, Benjamin married secondly Mary Shiers at Greenwich Church, by which time he was presumably setting up the workshop there. First mark, in partnership with Digby Scott, 4 October 1802. Address: Limekiln Lane, Greenwich. Second mark together, 21 March 1803. The partnership apparently dissolved by 11 May 1807, when Smith entered a third separate mark. Fourth mark, 25 June 1807. Fifth, in partnership with his brother James, 23 February 1809. Sixth separate mark, 14 October 1812.

Seventh mark, 15 January 1814. Eighth mark, in partnership with his son Benjamin, 5 July 1816. Address: Camberwell. Ninth mark alone again, 25 June 1818. By his first marriage Smith had four sons, of whom Benjamin was the eldest, and three daughters, and by Mary Shiers a fourth daughter in 1803 at Greenwich. His third son Digby, born 2 June 1797, may be assumed to be the godson of Digby Scott. There seems little doubt from the accounts preserved in the Boulton papers at Birmingham that Smith was of a difficult and probably irascible nature and this is borne out by the variations in his entry of marks with and without partners. His firm was of course, together with Storr, manufacturing almost entirely for Rundell and Bridge, and it seems possible that the latter may have supported Smith's move to London. The firm's most important production is probably the Jamaica service of 1803 in the Royal Collection. The silver-gilt trays, baskets and wine-coasters with openwork vine borders are among their most distinctive and accomplished achievements. The designs, so closely related to those of Storr, must almost certainly have stemmed from central control by Rundell and Bridge. (Family and Birmingham information by kindness of Mrs Shirley Bury, from Mrs Jane Vickers and Mr Hamil Westwood).

SMITH, Benjamin III (231, 236-7) Eldest son of Benjamin Smith II, born 6 October 1793 at 12 Hockley Row near Birmingham, apprenticed to his father as silversmith 6 July 1808. Free, 3 January 1821. First mark, (two sizes) in partnership with his father, entered 5 July 1816. Address: Camberwell. Second mark alone, 15 July 1818. Moved to 12 Duke Street, Lincoln's Inn Fields, and third mark, 24 July 1822 (two sizes). Fourth mark (two sizes), 1 December 1837. Livery, April 1842(?). Died 1850.

SMITH, Daniel (506-8, 2293, 3521, 3523) Son of William Smith late of Hawick in Cumberland gentleman deceased, apprenticed to Thomas Gladwin (q.v.) of the Merchant Taylors' Company 6 November 1740. Free, 7 February 1753 (4?). Livery, 25 November 1765. First mark possibly as early as 1759 (352). Second mark, in partnership with Robert Sharp, found as early as 1765 (353). Both these would of course have appeared in the missing register, since they appear together as plateworkers, Aldermanbury, in the Parl. Report list 1773. Third mark, in partnership with Richard Carter and Robert Sharp, 9 December 1778. Address: 14 Westmoreland Buildings. Fourth mark, in partnership with Robert Sharp only, 7 February 1780, same address. This partnership was apparently dissolved, possibly by Smith's retirement, 7 January 1788, when Sharp entered a separate mark. Heal records Smith and Sharp, plateworkers, London, 1763-89; 50 Aldermanbury, 1763-77; Westmoreland Building, 1780; and 14 Bartholomew Close, 1779-96. Smith and Sharp appear in the 'Workmens Ledger' of Parker and Wakelin as supplying plate in 1766. For remarks on their productions see Robert Sharp.

SMITH, George I (895, 905, 908) Possibly son of George Smith of St. Martin's in the Fields, victualler, apprenticed to Edmund Pearce 3 March 1705 and turned over to John Smith. Free, 23 May 1718. A second possibility is son of George Smith Citizen and Goldsmith (presumably the above), apprenticed to Gabriel Sleath 31 November 1728. Free, 7 December 1750. First mark entered as largeworker, 28 February 1732. Address: Gutter Lane. 'Free Goldsmith'. Second mark, 4 September 1739, same address. Third mark, in partnership with Samuel Smith III, 13 December 1750. Address: Foster Lane. The partnership presumably dissolved by 1754, when Samuel Smith entered a separate mark. Heal records him as plateworker, Gutter Lane, 1732-9; and London, 1742; and G. & S. Smith, plateworkers, Foster Lane, 1751.

*SMITH, George II (896-8, 909) Son of John Smith of the parish of St. George Middlesex waterman, apprenticed to William Aldridge 2 May 1750 on payment of £10. Free, 3 May 1758. First mark entered as smallworker, undated, before 7 August 1758. Address: Red Cross Street. Second mark as smallworker, 21 November 1767. Address: Huggins Alley, Wood Street. Third mark, 9 August 1771, added to the above entry. Livery, December 1771. Nine marks as bucklemaker, all at 4 Huggin Lane, from 1775 to 1789 (Section VIII). He appears as bucklemaker, Hogan Lane, in the Parl. Report list 1773. Thirteenth mark, in partnership with Thomas Hayter as plateworkers, 7 January 1792, same address. There is a confusion by Heal between this worker and George Smith III, who is clearly distinguishable by mark and signature as well as his specialization as spoonmaker. Heal's only certain references to George Smith II is as goldsmith and bucklemaker, 4 Huggin Lane, Wood Street; and with Thomas Hayter as goldsmiths, Huggin Lane, 1792-6. Probably died between 1802 and 1811.

*SMITH, George III (906, 910) Son of Thomas Smith of Wolverhampton in the County of Stafford butcher, apprenticed to Thomas Chawner of Paternoster Row London spoonmaker, Citizen and Goldsmith 'to learn the art of a Spoonmaker' 4 December 1765 and turned over to Pierce Tempest. Freedom unrecorded. First mark as spoonmaker, 1 February 1774. Address: 110 Wood Street. Second mark, 12 August 1775. Third, 23 July 1776. Fourth, 22 October 1776. Fifth, 20 October 1778. Address: 60 Paternoster Row. Sixth, 17 July 1780 (two sizes). Seventh, 10 August 1782 (five punches). Eighth, in partnership with William Fearn, 3 November 1786, same address. Moved to 1 Lovell's Court, Paternoster Row, 29 June 1790. Heal appears to overlap him with George Smith II as buckle and haftmaker, 110 Wood Street, 1765-82. He also records George Smith, plateworker, Bartholomew Close, 1774; Wood Street, 1782; spoonmaker, 60 Paternoster Row, 1783-4; with William Fearn as goldsmiths, Lovell Court, Paternoster Row, 1786-9. A very high percentage of the surviving flat-ware of the years 1775-90 bears the mark of this maker or of him and his partner Fearn. For a continuation of the firm see William Eley, Fearn (above) and William Chawner.

*SMITH, George IV (899-900, 2294) Presumably son of the above. No record of apprenticeship or freedom. Described as 'Junior' on entry of first mark as spoonmaker, 20 June 1799. Address: 1 Lovell Court, Paternoster Row. Second mark, 8 November 1803. Address: 31 St. John's Square, Clerkenwell. Moved to 16 Hosier Lane, Smithfield, 16 February 180(?6). Third mark, in partnership with Richard Crossley, 9 April 1807. Address: Giltspur Street. Fourth mark alone again, 20 January 1812. Address: 16 Hosier Lane (as previously, probably having continued at this address during the above partnership).

SMITH, George V (903) Apparently no connection with the above. The former always signs 'Geo' against the present 'George' and the writing differs considerably. No record of apprenticeship or freedom. Only mark entered as plateworker, 5 January 1828. Address: 19 Cross Street, Leonard Street.

SMITH, James I (1643, 2586) There are three possible apprenticeship entries, of which the most likely appears to be that for the son of Thomas Smith of Hampstead (?Hemsted) in the County of Hereford yeoman, apprenticed to Peter White 20 March 1710. Signatory as journeyman to the petition against assaying the work of foreigners not having served seven years apprenticeship, February 1716. Free, 3 April 1718. First mark entered as largeworker, 22 April 1718. Address: Foster Lane. Second (Sterling) mark, 25 August 1720. Heal and Hilton Price record James Smith, goldsmith, Lombard Street, 1710; and London, bankrupt, 1713, which can scarcely be the same; also plateworker, Foster Lane, 1718-34; goldsmith, London, 1720-8; and goldsmith, 'Hen And Chickens', Tooley Street, 1731, who may correspond with the one of this name elected to the Livery, May 1731. One of this name was prosecuted by the Company for counterfeiting marks (Minutes, 5 August 1742).

SMITH, James II (1658, 1685) Possibly (1) son of Nehemiah Smith late of the parish of St. Botolph without Aldersgate wheelwright deceased, apprenticed to John Gammon 6 May 1735 on payment of £9. Freedom unrecorded. Or (2) son of James Smith late Citizen and Tinplate worker of London deceased, apprenticed to John Ferris 4 September 1735 on payment of £21. and turned over 5 December 1738 to John Montgomery in consideration of £21. Free, 5 July 1743. First mark entered as largeworker, 14 September 1744. Address: Winchester Court, Monkwell Street. Second mark, 25 September 1746. Address: Old Bailey. Heal records the above two addresses and also silversmith, Angel, Fleet Street, 1750-1; Corner of Raquet Court, Fleet Street, 1751-62; 115 Fleet Street (as identical with above), 1760-80; also working goldsmith, Angel, Great Old Bailey, near Newgate, c. 1760; and goldsmith, parish of St. John Zachary, died 1771. Appears as goldsmith, Fleet Street, in the Parl. Report list 1773. William Boyce Smith, son of James Smith, goldsmith of Fleet Street, was admitted to St. Paul's School, 29 April 1763 (Admission Registers, St. Paul's School).

SMITH, James III (238, 3522) Son of Ralph Smith of Birmingham and brother of Benjamin Smith II (above). For his early career with Matthew Boulton see the entry for his brother. James appears to have remained with Boulton, after Benjamin's move to London, until his mark was entered as plateworker, in partnership with Benjamin Smith II, 23 February 1809. Address: Lime Kiln Lane, Greenwich. The partnership apparently dissolved by 14 October 1812, when Benjamin entered a separate mark. The mark with Digby Scott and Benjamin Smith in a triple partnership, recorded in 1811 (3522), does not appear in the register and appears of doubtful origin (see Digby Scott, above).

SMITH, John I (2579-80) Perhaps (1) son of Thomas Smith of Betchton in the County of Chester gentleman, apprenticed to Thomas Marmion 7 October 1681. Free 14 January 1690. Or (2) son of Richard Smith of the parish of St. Bride's London brasier, apprenticed to William Buckler 12 August 1685 and turned over to Osmond Strickland. Free, 26 August 1692. Mark entered as largeworker, undated, probably April 1697 on commencement of register. Address: Holborn. Heal records John Smith, goldsmith, White's Alley, Holborn, 1692; and John or Jonathan Smith, goldsmith, Holborn, 1697. Will dated 1703-10.

SMITH, John II (1663, 1672) No record of apprenticeship or freedom. First mark entered as smallworker, 19 February 1769. Address: Blue Anchor Alley, Bunhill Row, where he appears without category in the Parl. Report list 1773. A Benjamin Smith is also listed separately at the same address. Second mark, 28 February 1782. Address: 4 Bull Head Court, Jewin Street.

SMITH, Joseph I (1640-1, 2585) Probably son of William Smith of Wolton(?) in the County of Northampton, apprenticed to Richard Overing 12 August 1696. Turned over 29 May 1700 to Benjamin Watts. Free, 27 March 1707. (Another was son of Edward Smith of London engraver, apprenticed to Richard Gutter 17 May 1699. Free 8 October 1707.) First mark entered as largeworker, 11 April 1707. Address: Foster Lane. Second (Sterling) mark, 6 July 1720. Address: Well Yard, Little Britain. Third mark, 30 September 1723, same address. Fourth mark, 3 May 1728. Address: Clerkenwell Close. 'ye Goldsmiths Company'.

Another entry without mark, 26 June 1739. Address: Clerkenwell Close. His 1723 mark, presumably by mere accident, appears identical with that of James Seabrook's of 1720 (no. 1642). Heal records him as plateworker, Foster Lane, 1707; and Clerkenwell, 1728-33. He seems to have been the earliest maker to establish himself in Clerkenwell.

SMITH, Joseph II (1676) No record of apprenticeship or freedom. Only mark entered as smallworker, 18 August 1808. Address: 2 Little Bartholomew Close.

SMITH, Samuel I (2578) Probably son of Samuel Smith of Edgware in the County of Middlesex clerk, apprenticed to John Jackson 5 April 1692. Free, 20 September 1700. Mark entered as largeworker, 27 September 1700. Address: Sweethings (St. Swithin's) Lane, where Heal records him as plateworker, 1700-4. Livery, January 1714/15. Court, May 1716. Warden, 1730-1. Prime Warden, 1734.

SMITH, Samuel II (2587) Either (1) son of Thomas Smith late of the town and County of Nottingham mercer deceased, apprenticed to John Eggleton 11 July 1700. Free, 28 April 1708. Or (2) son of Edward Smith Citizen and Joiner of London, apprenticed to William Twell 25 May 1710. Free, 18 July 1717. Mark entered as largeworker, 26 September 1719. Address: Gutter Lane. The signature in the entry is clearly different from that of Samuel Smith I. Heal records only the above date and address.

SMITH, Samuel III (908, 2630) Either (1) son of Samuel Smith (I or II above) late Citizen and Goldsmith of London deceased apprenticed to Samuel Wood 6 December 1743 on payment of £5 of the charity of the Governors of Christ's Hospital. Free, 11 January 1750/?1. Or (2) son of Samuel, free by patrimony 1 March 1748/?9. First mark entered as largeworker, in partnership with George Smith I, 13 December 1750. Address: Foster Lane. Livery, March 1751/2. Court, February 1752/3. Second mark alone, 14 February 1754, same address. Warden, 1769-72. Prime Warden, 1776. Samuel Smith 'Junior' elected to Livery 1776, and Court 1777, is presumably his son. Heal records Samuel Smith, plateworker, Foster Lane, 1754; also Samuel Smith, goldsmith and banker, 12 Aldermanbury, 1773-1800, whose identity with

Samuel Smith III appears doubtful, but may refer to the son.

SMITH, Thomas I (2923) The number of apprentice entries of this name makes identification virtually impossible, and there is no freedom date close enough to the mark entry to suggest the most likely. Mark entered as largeworker, 16 October 1750. Address: Wood Street, near Cripplegate, 'Removed to the above place', implying a previous entry and address for which there is no evidence. Heal records the above date and address; also Thomas Smith, goldsmith, Hare, Lombard Street, 1755; and London, 1774. Thomas Smith, smallworker, Wood Street, in the Parl. Report list 1773 presumably refers to the above.

SMITH, Thomas II (2919) No apprenticeship or freedom identifiable. First mark entered as smallworker, in partnership with Thomas Read, 14 March 1771. Address: 17 Bartholomew Close. Second mark alone, 1 April 1772, same address. They appear together as bucklemakers at this address in the Parl. Report list 1773.

SMITH, Timothy (2933, 2937) Perhaps Timothy Green Smith son of Charles, free by patrimony as silversmith 4 June 1817. First mark entered as plateworker, in partnership with Thomas Merryweather, 10 January 1824. Address: 1 Westmorland Court, Falcon Square. Second mark alone, 21 July 1825, same address.

SMITH, William I (3308-9) Son of Samuel Smith Citizen and Goldsmith, apprenticed to his father 4 February 1742. Free, 6 March 1749. Livery, March 1751/2. First mark entered as smallworker, 28 October 1758. Address: Cheapside. Second mark, 12 June 1762. Court, February 1763. Third mark 30 October 1764. Fourth, 25 September 1769. Appears as goldsmith, Cheapside, in the Parl. Report list 1773, and gave evidence to the committee of the purchase of sub-standard punch-ladles from Sheffield manufacturers. Fifth mark, 13 July 1774. Address: 32 Cheapside. Probably dead by 16 March 1781, when Wildman Smith (below) entered a mark at the same address. Heal records William Smith, jeweller and working goldsmith, Blackmoor's Head, opp. Gutter Lane (No. 32), Cheapside, 1760-79; also 30 Milk Street, 1769-79.

SMITH, William II (3315) A number of nearly contemporary apprentice records of this name make identification impossible. Only mark entered as smallworker, 10 June 1777. Address: 12 Bentinck Street, Cavendish Square.

SMITH, Wildman (3316) No record of apprenticeship or freedom. Probably son of William Smith I (above). Mark entered as haftmaker 16 March 1781. Address: 32 Cheapside.

SMITHSEND, John (2581) Free of the Haberdashers' Company by service to Isaac Dighton 20 December 1692. (The entry of his apprenticeship not traced.) Mark entered as largeworker, undated, probably April 1697 on commencement of register. Address: Minories. 'Free Haberdasher'.

SNATT, Josiah (1848) No record of apprenticeship or freedom. Only mark entered as smallworker, 10 January 1798. Address: 4 Fan Street, Aldersgate. Probably dead by 10 September 1817, on entry of Sarah Snatt's mark at same address.

SNATT, Sarah (2633) No record of apprenticeship or freedom. Presumably widow of the above. Only mark entered as smallworker, 10 September 1817. Address: 4 Fan Street, Aldersgate Street.

SNELLING, John (2595) Son of William Snelling of Pickwick in the parish of Corsham Wiltshire yeoman, apprenticed to Arthur Mannering 20 February 1674 and turned over to William Hall. Free 14 October 1681. Mark entered as largeworker, undated, probably April 1697 on commencement of register. Address: Holborn. Heal records him here as plateworker, 1697-1704; and Mrs Snelling, goldsmith, Lock and Key, Holborn, over against Hatton Garden, 1716 (presumably his widow).

*SOAME, William (2599, 3295-7, 3328) Son of Stephen Soame Citizen and Mercer, apprenticed to Samuel Hitchcock 4 February 1713 on payment of £20. Free by patrimony of the Mercers' Company, 1720. First two marks (Sterling and New Standard) entered as largeworker, 19 January 1723. Address: Friday Street. 'free of ye Mercers Company'. Third mark, 23 August 1732. Address: Cheapside. Fourth mark, 11 February 1739. Fifth, 20 June 1739. Heal records him at both addresses and dates to 1739 and that he died 1772, 'having retired many years'.

SOLOMON, David (502) No record of apprenticeship or freedom. First, incuse, mark entered as smallworker, 29 May 1813.

Address: 72 Long Acre. Moved to 2 Surrey foot, Westminster, 9 September 1817. Second mark, 19 September 1817.

SOLOMON, William (3302-3) No record of apprenticeship or freedom. First two marks entered as largeworker, 19 October 1747. Address: Church Street, St. Ann's, Soho. Third mark, 12 September(?)·1751. Heal records only the first date and address.

SOLORO, Gorspor (?Jasper) (893) No record of apprenticeship or freedom. Only mark entered as smallworker, 1 May 1724. Address: Great St. Andrew's Street, Seven Dials. He made two attempts at his signature, the first reading apparently 'garpa soloro' and the second as used above. One is left uncertain of his identity or origin.

SOMERSALL, William Nathaniel (2261) No record of apprenticeship or freedom. First mark entered as plateworker, in partnership with R. W. Atkins, 26 July 1824. Address: 11 Bridgwater Square. Second mark, 31 March 1825. Third mark, 6 February 1830.

SOUTH, William (2598) Son of Edward South Citizen and Goldsmith of London, apprenticed to James Harrison 8 February 1661 and turned over to his father. Apparently re-apprenticed to Henry Whittingham, 18 December 1663. Free, 1 March 1670. Mark entered as smallworker, undated, probably April 1697 on commencement of register. Address: Foster Lane.

SOUTHAM, Giles (894) Son of Giles Southam of Banbury in the County of Oxford gentleman, apprenticed to Edward Chowne 14 December 1721 on payment of £20. Free, 4 June 1729. Livery, April 1737. Mark entered as smallworker, 10 October 1734. Address: 'near Smithfield bars'. 'Goldsmith'. Heal records him as goldsmith and jeweller, Little Britain, 1745, died 1747, when he was apparently succeeded by Thomas Caldecott whom Heal records 'removed to the late Mr Southam's opposite Bartholomew Close in Little Britain' (no date).

*SOUTHEY, William James (3323-4) William Smalt(?) son of John Southey of Aldersgate Buildings carpenter, apprenticed to William Chawner of Aldersgate Street as spoonmaker 3 July 1793 and turned over to John Blake of Leicester Square spoonmaker 5 February 1794. Free, 2 May 1810 as silversmith. First mark entered as spoonmaker, 3 February 1810. Address: 1 Bowling Green Lane, Clerkenwell. Moved to 10 Church Row, St. Luke's, 5 April 1821. Second mark, 2 January 1822. Third as plateworker, 9 December 1825. Address: 34 Radnor Street, St. Luke's.

SOUX, John (1652) No record of apprenticeship or freedom. Perhaps son or nephew of Daniel Soux (recorded by Heal as goldsmith, Goulston Square, near Whitechapel Bars, 1701;' and as—Suks, George Yard, Holborn, 1712). Only mark entered as smallworker, undated, between May and October 1728. Address: Eagle Street, near Red Lion Square.

SPACKMAN, John I (2604) Two of this name appear in the apprentice records of the time. (1) Son of Thomas Spackman of Marlborough in the County of Wiltshire, apprenticed to Roger Stephens 15 April 1668. Free, 1 September 1676. Livery, November 1687. (2) Son of Joseph Spackman (presumably the brother of Thomas, above) of Marlborough taylor, apprenticed to the earlier John Spackman (his cousin?) 7 April 1693. Freedom unrecorded. Mark entered as largeworker, undated, probably April 1697 on commencement of register. Address: Charing Cross. Heal records him as plateworker, Spreadeagle, Strand, 1694; and Charing Cross, 1697; also London, 1724. John, son of John and Elizabeth 'Spakeman', baptized 2 September 1684 at Christchurch, Newgate, was presumably a son. Elizabeth, daughter of John and Honor Spakeman, born 8 December, baptized 10 January 1714 at the same church, was presumably the latter's child. The relationship of the following members of the family is complicated. It appears that the Thomas mentioned above had also a son Thomas, as also did Joseph (above), so that there were two John and two Thomas Spackmans as well as William, the youngest son of Joseph, all members of the Company at the same period. John (Junior) was elected to Livery, August 1720.

SPACKMAN, John II (1656-7) Son of Thomas Spackman (q.v.) late Citizen and Goldsmith of London deceased, apprenticed to Elizabeth Goodwin widow of James Goodwin deceased 21 October 1730 on payment of £8 of the Charity of Christ's Hospital. Turned over 29 November 1734 to William Justus. Free, 6 December 1737. Mark entered as largeworker, 11 September 1741. Address: Foster Lane. 'Goldsmith'.

Moved to Gutter Lane, 24 November 1742, and second mark entered: 'The above mark being lost the other was Entred at ye time of Removal'. Heal records him only at Foster Lane.

*SPACKMAN, Thomas (2600-1) Either (1) son of Thomas Spackman of Marlborough in the County of Wiltshire grocer, apprenticed to William Swadling 19 November 1690 and turned over 16 June 1696 to John Spackman, his brother. Free 17 May 1700. Livery October 1708. Or (2) son of Joseph Spackman late of Marlborough in the County of Wiltshire chapman, apprenticed to John Spackman 5 November 1701. Freedom unrecorded. The probability seems in favour of the earlier of the two cousins, as the owner of the two marks entered as largeworker, 25 May 1700. Address: Foster Lane. Third mark, 15 January 1707. Signatory as 'working goldsmith' to the petition complaining of the competition of 'necessitous strangers', December 1711. He appears to have been a spoonmaker. Heal records him as plateworker, Foster Lane, 1700 to bankruptcy in 1719. It is possible that he renounced London and return to his native town, since Thomas Spackman of Marlborough entered his mark as smallworker, 1 November 1725 (see Provincial Section), but the record of marriage of one of this name at Marlborough in 1714 suggests another identity for the latter.

SPACKMAN, William (2609, 3294) (Third) son of Joseph Spackman late of Marlborough in ye County of Wiltshire chapman, apprenticed to William Andrews 27 July 1703 for eight years and turned over 30 April 1706 to Nathaniel Lock. Free, 4 November 1712. First mark entered as largeworker, 1 November 1714. Address: Lillypot Lane. Second (Sterling) mark, 14 July 1720, same address. Third and fourth marks (New Standard and Sterling) entered, undated, between September 1723 and May 1725. Heal records him at Lillypot Lane, 1714-26.

SPENCER, John (1654) Free by patrimony of the Haberdashers' Company 9 February 1739 'of Little Morefields'. Only mark entered as smallworker, 8 March 1739. Address: Ropemaker Alley, Little Moorfields. 'Free haberdasher'.

*SPILSBURY, Francis I (719-20, 2621) Son of Edward Spilsbury late Citizen and Cook of London, apprenticed to Richard Green 2 November 1708 for eight years. Signatory as journeyman to the petition against assaying the work of foreigners not having served seven years apprenticeship. February 1716. Free, 12 July 1717. First mark entered as largeworker, 24 July 1729. Address: Foster Lane. 'Free Goldsmith'. Livery, March 1737. Second mark, 15 June 1739, same address. Third mark, 12 December 1739. Heal records him as plateworker, Spread Eagle, Foster Lane, 1729-39.

*SPILSBURY, Francis II (721) Son of the above, born 1733. Free by patrimony, 2 November 1757. Livery, July 1763. Mark entered as smallworker, 24 November 1767. Address: 24 Gutter Lane. Heal records him here as plateworker, 1767-73, and he so appears at the same address in the Parl. Report list 1773, when he gave evidence to the committee of the leakage of new designs for plate at the Assay Office and of corruption in the staff. He found 'giving liquor at the Hall' prevented trouble with the assay. He also informed the committee that 'he sells his manufactures viz. Cruet Frames, Bottle Stands, Pails, Mustard Pots and Salts in general to shopkeepers in London and receives old silver for the weight of the Plate and Money for the fashion'. He knew of examples of the cutting out of marks but had avoided trouble by not reporting them. He died, 6 August 1793, 'At Hampstead aged 60, Mr Spilsbury of Soho Sq. proprietor of the anti-scorbutic drops. He was a silversmith in Noble St. Cheapside & turned quack about 25 years ago when he first kept a shop in Mount Row Lambeth. By his 2nd wife who survives him he has left a numerous young family.' (*The Gentleman's Magazine*, p. 773). Robert Spilsbury goldworker (Section VII) may perhaps be connected.

SPO[O]NER, John (2612) No record of apprenticeship or freedom. Only mark entered as smallworker, 25 January 1736. Address: Wood Street.

SPRAGE, Charles (415) Son of Wadham Sprage of the parish of Bayford in the County of Hertford gentleman, apprenticed to John White 4 May 1724 on payment of £21. Freedom unrecorded. Mark entered as largeworker, 4 February 1734. Address: 'corner of Chapel Court near Oxford Chapel'. Heal records only this date and address.

SPREE, Henry (1066) No record of apprenticeship or freedom. Only mark entered as smallworker, 1 May 1738. Address: 'in hockle hole' (Hockley in the Hole).

SPRENKELSEN, Niccolas (2101) No record of apprenticeship or freedom. Only mark entered as smallworker, 8 July 1766. Address: Little St. Andrew Street, Seven Dials.

*SPRIMONT, Nicholas (2102) Son of Peter Sprimont and Getrude Goffin, born at Liège, 23 January 1716. Apprenticed as silversmith to his uncle and godfather Nicholas Joseph Sprimont at Rue du Pont 16. Arrived in England probably early in 1742 as he married, 13 November that year, at Knightsbridge Chapel, Ann Protin of Kensington, spinster. Only mark entered as largeworker, 25 January 1743. Address: Compton Street, St. Ann's, Soho. The rate books show him as tenant of a house on the north side of Compton Street and two years later with an additional back-shop. He remained in occupation here till 1748. He also appears from 1747 in the Chelsea rate book as occupying half of Monmouth House in Lawrence Street, and from then onwards it seems clear that the new venture of porcelain manufacture was to absorb his full interest and time (F. Severne Mackenna, *Chelsea Porcelain*, 1948, based on the researches of Major W. H. Tapp). After the sale of the Chelsea business to Duesbury of Derby, James Christie sold the remaining Chelsea productions which Sprimont appears to have retained as his own property. He remained living in Chelsea and Richmond till his death later that year at the early age of fifty-four, since Christie's catalogue of his picture collection, sold 26–27 March 1771, describes them as brought from his houses in these two places. The pictures of the Italian, French, Flemish and Dutch schools in 173 lots realized the high total for the time of £1,239. Sprimont is buried in Petersham Church below Richmond Hill. His surviving marked pieces of silver are excessively rare and all lie between 1742 and 1747. The best known are the two pairs of marine salts of 1742, the dishes of 1743 and sauce-boats of 1743–4, all in the Royal Collection. His largest pieces known are a jardinière of 1745 (Christie's, 15 February 1905 and Rovensky Collection, Parke-Bernet, 19 January 1957) and the Ashburnham centrepiece or covered basket of 1747 (Christie's, 24 March 1914, now Victoria and Albert Museum). Another important item is the tea-kettle of 1745 in the Russian Royal Collection (E. A. Jones, *The Old English Plate of the Emperor of Russia*, Plate XLIX). For a discussion of the possible relationship in the work of Sprimont and Paul Crespin see A. G. Grimwade, 'Crespin or Sprimont?', *Apollo*, August 1969.

SPRING, Hugh (1064, 2608) Son of Hugh Spring Citizen and Joyner of London, apprenticed to Joseph Ward for eight years 3 November 1699 'from St. Thomas Day next'. Free, 5 October 1710. Signatory as journeyman to the petition against assaying the work of foreigners not having served seven years apprenticeship, February 1716. First mark (New Standard) entered 22 December 1721. Address: Foster Lane. Second (Sterling) mark, 27 October 1722, same address. Heal records him as plateworker, Foster Lane, 1721; insolvent 1729. Hugh Spring of St. Martin, Ludgate, bachelor, was married to Mary Pulford of St. Brides, spinster, 26 December 1709 at St. Bene't, Paul's Wharf (Joseph Ward worked in Fleet Street at this time which makes the identification reasonably likely). 'Hugh Spring of ye parish of St. Andrews Holbourn and Anne Tooly of ye same parish were lawfully married with Licence in ye parish of St. Vedast al's Fosters, London Novemb[r] the 29th 1716 by Mr Pattison' (Register, St. Vedast). Two sons and daughters of Hugh Spring and Ann his wife were buried at St. Michael le Quern between 1719 and 1722, and there is also an entry: 'Hugh Spring was Buried in ye New Vault March ye 27th 1725'. This last entry conflicts with Heal's record of insolvency in 1729.

SPRING, William (2602–3) Son of William Spring Citizen and Goldsmith of London, apprenticed to John Hoyte 13 June 1693 and turned over to Samuel Hood. Free, 23 August 1700. Mark entered as largeworker, 30 August 1701. Address: Strand near Charing Cross. Heal records him as plateworker, Golden Cup, near Hungerford Market, Strand, 1701–27; and Strand, 1734. Livery, October 1712.

SPRINGGALL, Francis (2605) Son of Henry Springall late of Newington Butts in the County of Surrey gardiner, apprenticed to William Chebsey of the Leathersellers' Company 13 August 1686. Free, 18 January 1693. Mark entered as smallworker, 15 December 1698. Address: New Street. 'Free Leatherseller and Hilt Maker'.

SQUIRE, George (892, 2622) Son of William Squire vintner of the Inner Temple, apprenticed to Richard Green 23 June 1713 on payment of £30. Free, 7 July 1720. First mark (New Standard) entered 15 September 1720. Address: 'at the Golden Angel Fleet Street'. Second (Sterling) mark, 25 November 1720. Heal records him, mysteriously, as plateworker, London, 1697-9; and as above and London, 1723-9.

STACKHOUSE, Thomas (2639, 2920) Son of Christopher Stackhouse Citizen and Merchant Taylor of London, apprenticed to Philip Rollos Junior 19 November 1706. Free, 18 November 1715. First mark entered as smallworker, 30 December 1715. Address: Clerkenwell. Second (Sterling) mark, 21 June 1720. Address: Gutter Lane. Third mark, 6 May 1728, same address. 'Free Goldsmith'. Fourth mark, 9 August 1738. Address: Fleet Lane. 'Free Blacksmith' (the latter apparently an aberration of the Clerk's, since the signature is undoubtedly of the same). Fifth mark, 16 January 1739, same address. Heal records him as silversmith, Candlestick and Snuffers, Gutter Lane, 1724; and Blue Ball Court, Salisbury Court, Fleet Street, no date.

STAMMERS, Edward (641) No record of apprenticeship or freedom. First mark entered as smallworker, 31 May 1816. Address: 99 Strand. Second mark (two sizes) as plateworker, 10 July 1828, same address.

STAMP, Frances (722-3) No record of apprenticeship or freedom. Presumably widow of James Stamp (below). Mark entered as plateworker, 12 May 1780. Address: 86 Cheapside.

STAMP, James (1666-7, 1691) Free by redemption as goldsmith 2 May 1764. First mark entered as smallworker, in partnership with John Baker I, 18 April 1764. Address: Cow Cross. Moved to Ludgate Street, apparently 18 February 1765, when second mark entered. Third mark in partnership, 29 April 1768. Livery, December 1771. Fourth mark alone as plateworker, 6 July 1774. Address: 86 Cheapside, where he had already appeared as such in the Parl. Report list 1773. Fifth mark, 8 May 1776. Sixth mark (two sizes), 12 March 1777. Seventh (two sizes), 14 October 1777. Eighth, 7 January 1779. Ninth, 22 July 1779. The rapid succession of new punches indicates a quickly expanding business, brought to an unexpected stop by Stamp's death, 11 April 1780 (*The Gentleman's Magazine*, p. 203), although his widow Frances appears to have carried on probably only for winding up or selling the business, which was subsequently succeeded at the same address by Sutton and Bult and after by Godbehere, Wigan and Bult (q.v.). Heal records Stamp as working goldsmith and jeweller, Ludgate Street, 1766; with John Barker as the same and at same address, 1768, partnership dissolved 1770; Stamp alone, 86 Cheapside, 1772-9; and James and Francis (sic) Stamp (succeeded by James Sutton), 1780.

STAMPER, John (528) Son of George Stamper of the City of Chichester gentleman, apprenticed to William Darker 15 December 1731 on payment of £63 (an extremely high premium) and turned over to John Hopkins 10 July 1735. Free, 7 February 1739/?40. Mark entered as largeworker, in partnership with Edward Aldridge, 20 July 1753, no address. Livery, June 1763. Dead before 1796. Heal records him as goldsmith and jeweller, London, 1743; Star, corner of Hind Court opposite Water Lane in Fleet Street, 1762-6; and 148 Fleet Street, 1772; with Edward Aldridge as plateworkers, London, 1753-7.

STAPLER, John (1675) No record of apprenticeship or freedom. Only mark entered as smallworker, 9 February 1807. Address: 106 York Street, Commercial Road.

STARKEY, Michael (2069) No record of apprenticeship or freedom. First mark entered as plateworker, 19 January 1809. Address: 28 North Street, City Road. Second mark, 24 September 1822. Third, 4 July 1834. Address: 28 Cowper Street, City Road. Edward Starkey, partner with David Simpson, as also Samuel Starkey, both entered as goldworkers (Section VII), may be connected.

STEED, Thomas (2641, 2922) Free of the Merchant Taylors' Company by service to James Walker in Old Bailey gilder 1 February 1687. Livery, 1 June 1708. Court, 24 February 1725. First mark entered as smallworker, undated, probably April 1697 on commencement of register. Address: Whalebone Court, Lothbury. Second (Sterling) mark, 24 January 1723, same address.

*STEPHENS, Benoni (232-4) No record of apprenticeship or freedom. First mark entered as spoonmaker, 14 August 1834. Address: 19 Myrtle Street, Hoxton. Second mark, 9 October 1834. Address: 76 Houndsditch. Third mark, 1 May 1835. Address: 9 Camomile Street. Fourth, 18 June 1835. Fifth, 24 August 1836.

STEPHENS, Daniel (2644) Son of Benjamin Stephens Citizen and Mercer of London, apprenticed to Benjamin Pooll of the Mercers' Company 15 April 1713 on payment of £25. Free by patrimony of that company, 1719. Mark entered as smallworker, 3 October 1720. Address: Crown Court, Cheapside. 'Mercer'. Since Cheapside was in any case a considerable centre for the mercers' trade (witness the site of their Hall) one wonders whether Stephens' mark was intended for silver accessories—buttons or buckles—for his main business.

*STEPHENSON, Benjamin (227, 2374) Free by redemption as goldsmith 4 February 1756. First mark entered as smallworker, in partnership with Richard Morson, 27 October 1762. Address: Fleet Street. Second mark, 9 July 1763. Third, 13 July, year omitted (?1763). Moved to Ludgate Hill, 1771, where the two appear, as goldsmiths, in the Parl. Report list 1773, there mentioned as having been prosecuted in 1770 for selling gold watch chains 'worse than standard'. Fourth mark (two sizes) alone, 26 January 1775. Address: 5 Ludgate Hill. Heal records Morson and Stephenson as goldsmiths, Golden Cup, (No. 5) Ludgate Hill, 1760-74; and Corner of Bride Lane, 98 Fleet Street, 1760-72; partnership dissolved, Stephenson alone as plateworker, 5 Ludgate Hill, 1774-9.

STEPHENSON, William (3312-3) Free of the Girdlers' Company by Redemption 22 July 1774. First mark entered as smallworker, 1 December 1775. Address: 9 Pelican Court, Old Bailey. Moved to 16 Gutter Lane, 25 July 1776. Second mark, 5 April 1780. Moved to 35 Lombard Street, 27 November 1781. Third mark as plateworker, 17 June 1786. Fourth (two sizes) as smallworker, 23 June 1787. Moved to 27 Lombard Street, 8 January 1790. Fifth mark (two sizes), same date. Sixth (two sizes), 7 December 1792. Described as Citizen and Girdler in the turning over to him of John Moore, 1789. Heal records him as silversmith, 27 Lombard Street, 1786-96.

STEVENSON, Ambrose (89, 2638) Ambrose Stephens (sic) son of Thomas of Giles Cripplegate Citizen and Haberdasher, apprenticed to his father September 1692. Free of the Haberdashers' Company, 1701. First mark entered as largeworker, 1 February 1707. Address: Barbican. 'Free Haberdasher'. Signatory as 'working goldsmith' to the petition complaining of the competition of 'necessitous strangers', December 1711. Second (Sterling) mark, 22 June 1720. Address: Round Court in St. Martin's (sc. Le Grand). Heal records him only at the first address, 1706-20.

STEVENSON, Robert (2437) No record of apprenticeship or freedom. Only mark entered as smallworker, 5 August 1802. Address: 51 Fetter Lane.

STEWARD, John (1673, 1687) Son of Joseph Steward II (below) of Wood Steet Citizen and Goldsmith, apprenticed to his father as goldsmith 2 May 1770. Free, 1 October 1777. First mark entered as smallworker, 26 June 1784. Address: 98 Wood Street. Second mark, 22 July 1784. Third, 25 November 1785. Fourth, 19 May 1786. Fifth, 1 September 1790. Sixth, 27 July 1791. Seventh, 4 March 1796. Address: 116 Bunhill Row. Eighth, 20 August 1800. Moved to 73 Lower East Smithfield, 24 May 1810. Livery, February 1791. Died between 1818 and 1822. Heal records him as goldsmith, 99 Wood Street, Cheapside, 1789-96; and Bunhill Row, 1789-96. Heal's entry of John Steward, Grub Street, 1755, is clearly an error, either his or his source, for Joseph Steward II (below).

STEWARD, Joseph I (1644, 1684, 2643) Son of Joseph Steward of Hornchurch in the County of Essex blacksmith, apprenticed to Peter White 22 October 1709. Signatory as journeyman to the petition against assaying the work of foreigners not having served seven years apprenticeship, February 1716. Free, 13 May 1718. First mark entered as largeworker, 18 November 1719. Address: 'Maden Lane'. Second (Sterling) mark, 7 September 1720. Third mark, 28 June 1739. Address: Maiden Lane 'Goldsmith'. For his son Joseph II see below. Heal records him as plateworker, Maiden Lane, 1719-39. His two other entries for the same name belong to Joseph II.

STEWARD, Joseph II (1659-62, 3681) Son of the above, apprenticed to Richard Pargeter 5 March 1745/?6 and turned over to Richard Bailey 4 October 1751. Freedom unrecorded. First mark entered as largeworker, 29 January 1755. Address: Haberdasher Square, Grub Street. Second mark (two sizes), 8 April 1755. Third mark as smallworker, 9 September 1762. Address: Foster Lane. Fourth mark as the same, 14 March 1768. Address: Gutter Lane. Fifth mark as the same, 7 March 1770. Address: Wood Street. Livery, December 1771. Sixth mark, 3 June 1773. Seventh, 18 June 1773. Eighth, 4 April 1780. Address: 98 Wood Street. Ninth, 23 May 1783. His son John (above) was apprenticed to him in 1770. Heal records him without differentiation from his father as smallworker, Gutter Lane, 1765-6; and 89 or 98 (?) Wood Street, 1770-93. He appears as smallworker, Wood Street, in the Parl. Report list 1773, and entered an incuse mark as such, 8 July 1775 (Section V).

STEWART, Charles (418, 2647) Son of Cuthbert Stewart late of Bloomsbury in the County of Middlesex bricklayer deceased, apprenticed to Joshua Readshaw 26 August 1698 and turned over to Michael Denny. Free, 3 October 1707. Two marks (Sterling and New Standard) as largeworker, in partnership with an unnamed worker whose initials in the mark are W. Ho., 4 July 1722. Address: Newport Street, Lower end of Long Acre. Heal has no obvious candidate for the initials W.Ho., but see possibly William Hodgkin or William Hopkins (above).

STEWART, John (1314) No record of apprenticeship or freedom. Only mark entered as plateworker, in partnership with John Foskett, 20 February 1810. Address: 27 St. John's Square.

STILWELL, Thomas (2936) Free of the Joiners' Company. Only mark entered as smallworker, in partnership with Thomas Burbidge, 9 August 1763. Address: White Friars Gateway, Fleet Street. They subsequently entered an incuse mark TSB (Section V), signed only by Stilwell, at the same address, 14 December 1763. Third mark (incuse) alone without category, 13 September 1764. Address: Noble Street (Section V), then described as Free Joyner. Appears as watchcasemaker, Bride Lane, in the Parl. Report list 1773.

*STOCKAR, John Martin (2635-6, 2646) Son of John Stockar of Canterbury in the County of Kent clerk, apprenticed to Michael Fenton 27 January 1688. Free, 20 February 1695. First mark entered as largeworker undated, probably April 1697 on commencement of register. Address: Strand. Second mark in partnership with Edward Peacock, 20 October 1705, same address. Third mark alone, 1 July 1710, same address. Signatory as 'working goldsmith' to the petition complaining of the competition of 'necessitous strangers' December 1711. Heal records him as Stocker (or -ar) plateworker, Mitre, near York Buildings, Strand, 1705-12; and with Peacock as goldsmiths, Strand, 1705-10. A curious entry in the register of St. Michael le Quern must from its mention of Canterbury be surely connected with the goldsmith: 'Mr John Bix, a Lodger at Mr Stockars (a Stranger) was Carried to Canterbury to be buried August ye 3rd 1708.' Does 'Stranger' refer to Bix or Stockar and as a non-parishioner or foreigner to England? Both names have a Germanic sound, as does the combination of Stockar's Christian names.

STOCKING, William (3330) No record of apprenticeship or freedom. Only mark entered as smallworker, 21 February 1725. Address: 'at the Crown and Gold Chains in Horseshoe Passage, St. Martins le Grand'.

STOKES, Joseph (2640) Son of Thomas Stokes of St. Olave's Southwark Baker, apprenticed to Samuel Hawkes 3 August 1687. Free, 8 August 1694. Livery, October 1698. Only mark entered as largeworker, undated, probably April 1697 on commencement of register. Address: St. Olave's, Southwark.

STONE, James (1649) Son of Henry Stone of Haversham in the County of Westmorland yeoman, apprenticed to James Roode 11 August 1715. Free, 6 September 1722. Mark entered as smallworker, 14 April 1726. Address: 'at Mr Stewards in Maiden Lane near Goldsmiths Hall, Free Goldsmith'. (See Joseph Steward I, above.)

STONHOUSE, George (902) No record of apprenticeship or freedom. First mark entered as plateworker, 9 August 1824. Address: 2 Elm Street, Gray's Inn Lane. Second mark on move to 42 Gun Street, Blackfriars Road, 19 November 1825. Third mark (two sizes), 14 December 1837. Moved to 19 Eltham Street, Blandon Street, New Kent Road, no date.

*STORER, George (413) Son of James Storer of Clerkenwell watchmaker, apprenticed to Richard Hislop of Clerkenwell as watchmaker, 5 March 1800 on payment of £21.

Freedom unrecorded. First mark entered as plateworker, in partnership with Charles Reily, 1 January 1829. Address: 6 Carey Lane. Moved to 3 Lovel's Court, Paternoster Row, 26 June 1835. Moved back to 6 Carey Lane, 16 February 1836. Second mark (two sizes), 18 June 1840.

*STORR, Paul (2233-5, 3133) Son of Thomas Storr of Westminster, first silver-chaser, later innkeeper, born 1771. Apprenticed c. 1785 to Andrew Fogelberg of Church Street, Soho, at which address Storr's first separate mark is also entered. First mark entered as plateworker, in partnership with William Frisbee (q.v.), 2 May 1792. Address: 5 Cock Lane, Snow Hill. Second mark alone, 12 January 1793. Address: 30 Church Street, Soho. Third mark, 27 April 1793. Fourth 8 August 1794. Moved to 20 Air Street, 8 October 1796 (at which address Thomas Pitts had worked till at least 1793). Fifth mark, 29 November 1799. Sixth, 21 August 1807. Address: 53 Dean Street, Soho. Seventh, 10 February 1808. Eighth, 15 December 1808. Ninth (three sizes), 21 October 1813. Tenth (three sizes), 12 September 1817. Moved to Harrison Street, Gray's Inn Road, 4 March 1819, after severing his connection with Rundell, Bridge and Rundell. Eleventh mark (two sizes), 2 September 1833. Address: 17 Harrison Street. Twelfth and last mark, 17 December 1834. Heal records him both in partnership with Frisbee and alone at Cock Lane in 1792, and at the other addresses and dates above, except Harrison Street. Storr married in 1801, Elizabeth Susanna Beyer of the Saxon family of piano and organ builders of Compton Street, by whom he had ten children. He retired in 1838 to live at Hill House, Tooting. He died 18 March 1844 and is buried in Tooting Churchyard. His will, proved 3 April 1844, shows an estate of £3,000. A memorial to him in Otley Church, Suffolk was put up by his son Francis the then incumbent of the parish. See N. M. Penzer, *Paul Storr*, 1954, from which the above brief personal details and apprenticeship are taken and where much interesting and colourful detail of Storr's family and relationships with Rundell, Bridge and Rundell are fully related. Storr's reputation rests on his mastery of the grandiose neo-Classical style developed in the Regency period. His early pieces up to about 1800 show restrained taste and average execution, although by 1797 he had produced the remarkable gold font for the Duke of Portland. Here, however, the modelling of the classical figures must presumably have been the work of a professional sculptor, as yet unidentified, and many of the pieces produced by him for Rundell and Bridge in the Royal Collection must have sprung from designs commissioned by that firm rather than from his own invention. On the other hand there still existed in his Harrison Street workshop, until destroyed in World War II (then belonging to Messrs J. W. Benson, the commercial descendants of Hunt and Roskell), a group of Piranesi engravings of classical vases and monuments bearing his signature, presumably used as source material for designs. The massiveness of the best of his compositions is well shown by the fine urns of 1800 at Woburn Abbey, but the purity of the Theocritus Cup in the Royal Collection must be essentially ascribed to the restraint of its designer John Flaxman, while not denying to Storr its superb execution. Lord Spencer's vine-pattern ice-pails of 1817 show similar quality. Not all Storr's best work, however, was classical in inspiration. The candelabra of 1807 at Woburn derive from candlesticks by Paul Crespin of the George II period, formerly part of the Bedford Collection, and he attempted essays in floral rococo creations from time to time, which it must be admitted, however, tend to over-floridity. On occasions the excellence of his technical qualities was marred by a lack of good proportions, as in the chalices of the church plate of St. Pancras, 1821. In spite of small lapses, however, there is no doubt that Storr rose to the demands made upon him as the author of more fine display plate than any other English goldsmith, including Lamerie, was ever called upon to produce.

STORY, Joseph William (1761-2) No record of apprenticeship or freedom. First mark entered as smallworker, 7 July 1803. Address: 4 Charterhouse Lane. Second mark as plateworker, in partnership with William Elliott, 6 October 1809. Address: 25 Compton Street, Clerkenwell. The partnership was apparently dissolved by 7 September 1813, when Elliott entered a separate mark. No further mark for Story, however, appears.

STRACHAN, Alexander James (46) Free by redemption as goldsmith 4 June 1817. First

BIOGRAPHICAL DICTIONARY

mark entered as smallworker, 21 September 1799. Address: 30 Long Acre. Moved to 7 Mercer Street, Long Acre, 18 July 1803. Second mark, 6 August 1823. Moved to 125 Long Acre, 6 November 1828. His sons John, Alexander James and Edward were apprenticed to him in 1817, 1818 and 1823 respectively. Livery, January 1822. Died between 1842 and 1850. The 'Paul Storr' of gold boxes, doubly so from the accomplishment of his technique and also that he was clearly the principal supplier of gold boxes to Rundell, Bridge and Rundell for Royal presentation purposes and official occasions. Some of his finest recognized pieces are in the Wellington Collection, Apsley House.

*STRANGE, William (3298) Free by service to John Carman of the Cutlers' Company 13 October 1724. Only mark entered as smallworker, 9 June 1725. Address: New Street Square. 'Cutler'. Heal records him as silversmith, New Street, St. Bride's, insolvent, 1743.

STREET, William (2642, 3291) Son of William Street of Harrow on the Hill yeoman, apprenticed to Andrew Archer 3 December 1706. Free, 27 May 1715. First mark entered as largeworker, 25 February 1717. Address: Staining Lane. Second (Sterling) mark, 23 June 1720. Heal records only the above.

STREETIN, Thomas (2930-1) Son of Richard Streetin of Plough Court Fetter Lane watchmaker, Citizen and Clockmaker, apprenticed to John Lambe of Fetter Lane silver spoonmaker 5 November 1783 on payment of £10 of the charity of the trustees of the late Doctor Bromfield deceased. Free, 1 December 1790, as silversmith. First mark entered as plateworker, 15 August 1794. Address: 18 Plough Court, Fetter Lane (his home address). Moved to 1 Great Sutton Street, Goswell Street, 28 March 1794. (?) Second mark, on move to 17 Clerkenwell Green, 10 August 1798. Third mark as spoonmaker, 25 October 1799. Fourth mark, 20 September 1802. Moved to 34 Great Sutton Street, 18 April 1806. Fifth mark, 27 June 1806. Sixth mark (two sizes) and seventh, 16 July 1810. Eighth, 13 April 1820. Heal records him as plateworker, 1 Plough Court, 1791-2; Great Sutton Street, 1796; and Clerkenwell Green, 1799. His son Henry was apprenticed to him 6 March 1816.

STROUD, William (3321, 3332) Son of John Stroud of Burleigh Street Strand polisher, Citizen and Blacksmith, apprenticed to John Wirgman of Princes Street Leicester Fields as goldsmith 4 October 1769 on payment of £10 and turned over to Benjamin Laver of New Bond Street 4 December 1771. Free, 6 November 1776. First mark entered as plateworker, 7 July 1788. Address: 4 Burleigh Street Strand. Second mark, 9 March 1821. Moved to 2 Red Lion Court, Fleet Street, 27 August 1823. Heal records William Stroud, goldsmith, Maiden Lane, Wood Street, 1761, who must be an earlier separate individual for whom there is no entry of a mark; also William Strowd, goldsmith, Burleigh Street, Strand, 1792-1804. Thomas Stroud, goldworker, 1829 (Section VII) may be connected.

*STUART, Isaa(c) (1645) Free of the Cutlers' Company by service to Thomas Bass 27 April 1721. Only mark entered as smallworker, 27 October 1721. Address: New Street, Shoe Lane, 'Cutler'.

STURT, Thomas (2637) Son of Thomas Sturt Citizen and Merchant Taylor of London, apprenticed to Ralph Crowther 2 December 1664 and turned over to Robert Munday. Free, 6 December 1671. Livery, November 1687. Court, 1704. Only mark entered as smallworker, undated, probably April 1697 on commencement of register. Address: Holborn. Heal records him as goldsmith and pawnbroker, Castle Yard, near Holborn Bars, 1701-7, and quotes the following from the *London Gazette*, 3 April 1701: 'All persons that have any jewels Plate or other goods Pawned to Mr Thos Sturt, goldsmith in Castle Yard Holborn are desired to redeem them by 24 June next or they'll be dispos'd of—he having left off taking in Pawns'.

SUDELL, William (3310-1) Son of John Sudell Citizen and Wax Chandler of London, apprenticed to Richard Wade 1 March 1758 and turned over to William Yearley (Fishmonger) the same day. Free, 5 February 1766. First mark entered as smallworker, 16 February 1767. Address: Butlers Alley, Grub Street. Moved to Silver Street, no date. Second mark, 19 April 1774. Address: 3 Monkwell Street. Moved to 5 Pillikin (sic, for Pelican) Court, Little Britain, 4 May 1775. Third mark (two sizes), 16 November 1779. Fourth mark (two sizes), 16 June 1788, same address. Heal records him as goldsmith, Butlers

673

Alley, 1770; and Pelican Court, 1776-85. He appears as smallworker, Monkwell Street, in the Parl. Report list 1773, before the entry of his second mark at that address.

SULLIVAN, Richard (2439) No record of apprenticeship or freedom. Only mark entered as smallworker, 11 July 1826. Address: 11 Blackheath Hill, Greenwich.

SUMMERS, William (414) Distinguish from William Sumner I and II (below). Son of Thomas Summers, free by patrimony 1 March 1826 as goldsmith and jeweller. First mark entered as goldworker, 16 March 1826. Address: 19 Little Britain (Section VII). Second mark as smallworker, in partnership with Charles Rawlings, 6 April 1829. Address: Brook Street, Holborn. Moved to 10 Great Marlborough Street, Regent Street, 9 January 1839. Six new marks, 2 December 1840. Marks defaced (see Book no. 6, page 127). Livery, February 1850. Makers of good quality snuffboxes, wine-labels and other small items. Died 15 January 1890. His four sons William, Edward, James Lea and Henry were all free by patrimony between 1858 and 1866.

SUMNER, Eliza (2070) No record of apprenticeship or freedom. Presumably daughter of Mary and William Sumner (q.v.). First mark entered as spoonmaker, in partnership with Mary Sumner, 31 August 1809. Address: 1 Clerkenwell Close. Second mark, 21 August 1810.

SUMNER, Mary (2068, 2070) No record of apprenticeship or freedom. Presumably widow of William Sumner I (below). First mark entered as spoonmaker, 18 March 1807. Address: 1 Clerkenwell Close. Second mark, in partnership with Eliza (above), 31 August 1809, same address. Third mark with the same, 21 August 1810.

SUMNER, William (3318-9, 3331, 3334) Son of Gilbert Sumner late of Hadley in the County of Essex farmer deceased, apprenticed to Thomas Chawner 5 October 1763 on payment of £25. Free, 7 November 1770. First mark entered as plateworker, in partnership with Richard Crossley (q.v.), 1 May 1775. Address: 1 Clerkenwell Close. Second mark (two sizes), 27 January 1776. Described as spoonmaker of Clerkenwell Close, in the apprenticeship to him of Thomas Wheeler 6 March 1776. Third mark, 10 May 1777. Fourth, 27 January 1780. Fifth mark alone as plateworker, 6 April 1782, same address. Sixth mark, 14 December 1784. Seventh (two sizes), 9 May 1787. Eighth as spoonmaker, 7 June 1788, same address. Ninth and tenth marks undated. Livery, February 1791. Eleventh mark, 15 October 1802. Twelfth (two sizes), 31 March 1803. Probably dead before 18 March 1807, when Mary Sumner entered her first mark. Heal records him as goldsmith, 1 Clerkenwell Close, 1773-96; and with Richard Crossley as plateworkers, Clerkenwell, 1775-80. His other entry for the name refers to William Sumner II (below).

SUMNER, William II (3320) Although no record of apprenticeship or freedom, he appears to be quite distinct from the above, his signature being quite irreconcilable with the former's in the same year. Only mark entered as smallworker, 12 May 1787. Address: 9 Albion Buildings, Bartholomew Close. This address does not appear at all for William Sumner I.

SUTTON, James (1671, 1692, 3625) Free by redemption as goldsmith 18 August 1780. Presumably brother of William Sutton (q.v.). First mark entered as plateworker, 7 July 1780. Address: 86 Cheapside, next door to Mercers' Chapel. Second mark, in partnership with James Bult, 4 October 1782. Address: 86 Cheapside. Heal records him as working goldsmith and jeweller (successor to James and Francis Stamp) at the above address, 1780-2; and with Bult as plateworkers, 1782-93. Since William Sutton and Co are also described by Heal as successors to the Stamps, but at 85 Cheapside, it would seem that the establishment was to all intents one, even if the brothers tried to maintain some semblance of independence from each other. Sutton and Bult are listed as bankrupt, July 1784 in *The Gentleman's Magazine*, page 559.

*SUTTON, John (2649) Son of Thomas Sutton of Brignelt(?) in the County of York gentleman, apprenticed to John Winterton 8 February 1661. Free, 19 February 1668. Livery, September 1674. Warden 1696, 1701, 1703. Prime Warden, 1707. His mark is the first entered in the largeworkers' book started April 1697, and is awarded the distinction of a large ornamental script as 'present Touchwarden', 15 April 1697. Address: Lombard Street. Heal records him as plateworker, parish of St. Mary Woolnoth, 1674-1707. The register of that church contain entries for the burial of Ann, daughter of John Sutton, goldsmith, 25 January 1680, and the baptisms of two sons, John and Thomas and three daughters Sarah and two further Anns, from 1683 to 1693. Sutton was signatory of the Committee Report on the present state of the Goldsmiths' Company, 29 April 1708, towards the end of his year as Prime Warden, when he was about sixty.

SUTTON, Thomas (2648, 3800) Either (1) son of Charles Sutton Citizen and Butcher of London, apprenticed to John Ladyman 14 July 1702 'from 29th of September next'. Free, 5 December 1711. Or (2) son of John Sutton (above) Citizen and Goldsmith of London, apprenticed to his father 1 December 1699. Freedom unrecorded. Only mark entered as largeworker, 7 January 1712. Address: Mugwell (? Monkwell) Street. Heal records only this address and date.

SUTTON, William (3317) No record of apprenticeship or freedom. Presumably brother of James Sutton (above). First mark entered as smallworker, 26 August 1784. Address: 85 Cheapside. Second mark, 27 October 1784, same address. Heal records William Sutton and Co., successors to James Stamp, goldsmiths, 85 Cheapside, 1782–93; and William Sutton and Isaac Cooper, goldsmiths, Cheapside, 1786. See James Sutton for the adjacent address, suggesting a kind of double establishment.

SWAIN, Samuel (2634) No record of apprenticeship or freedom. Only mark entered as smallworker, in partnership with Charles Hill, 25 July 1760. Address: New Gravel Lane, Southwark, where they appear without category in the Parl. Report list 1773.

SWANN, John (1637, 2651) Son of John Swann late of Lewes in the County of Sussex yeoman deceased, apprenticed to Henry Leyon 31 July 1695. Free, 17 June 1709, and again 26 March 1712 (? a mysterious duplication). First mark entered as smallworker, 18 June 1714, although in New Standard period, using initials IS, presumably for gold only, unless a mistake corrected by the second mark, 19 December 1715, SW.

SWANSON, Robert (2432, 2441) No record of apprenticeship or freedom. First mark entered as smallworker, 18 March, year omitted, probably 1730. Address: 'at the Crown in Foster Lane'. Second mark, 18 October 1743. Address: Haulse Court, Blackman Street, Southwark. Heal records only the second address and date.

SWIFT, John (1651, 1689, 3686, 3708) Son of Anthony Swift late of St. Olave's Southwark in the County of Surrey merchant taylor deceased, apprenticed to Thomas Langford 6 March 1718 on payment of £20. Turned over 6 April 1719 to William Paradise and again 9 May 1723 to Thomas Serle in Gutter Lane. Free, 10 June 1725. Married Margaret Gray of St. Olave, Silver Street, 14 November 1725 at St. Ben't, Paul's Wharf, when Swift 'of St. Vedast als. Foster Bachelor'. First mark entered as smallworker, undated, between May and October 1728. Address: Staining Lane. 'Goldsmith'. Second mark as largeworker, 29 June 1739. Address: Noble Street. Third mark (small size), 18 July 1757. Fourth, 22 August 1757. Livery, March 1758. Heal records him as plateworker, Noble Street, near Goldsmiths' Hall, 1728–73, but the latter date presumably refers to his son John who was apprenticed to him 15 June 1750 and who died before 1796. The entry John Swift, plateworker, Noble Street, in the Parl. Report list 1773 does not clarify the problem as to when the son succeeded his father nor is there the entry of any mark for the son. Swift's work appears mostly to have been hollow-ware, tankards, coffee-pots and teapots with an attractive repertoire of rococo and Chinoiserie motifs.

SWIFT, Thomas (2924–5) Son of John Swift of Bletchingham in the County of Oxford yeoman, apprenticed to Thomas Moulden 1 October 1729 on payment of £40. Free, 16 January 1744/?5. First mark entered as largeworker, 7 August 1758. Address: Bell Court, Foster Lane. Moved to Old Bailey, 18 June 1762. Second mark, 10 July 1762. Heal records him as haftmaker, 1773–7, as he appears in the Parl. Report list for the former year.

SWIFT, William (3327) No record of apprenticeship or freedom. Only mark entered as smallworker, 21 April 1726. Address: 'at Mr Harris's in Forrington (?Faringdon) Street near the Cold Bath'.

SYNG, Richard (2673) Son of George Sing of London gentleman, apprenticed to Abraham Hinde 2 April 1679 'for 8 years from Christmas last'. Free, 23 November 1687. Livery, April 1705. Mark entered as largeworker, undated, probably April 1697 on commencement of register. Address: 'in Carey Lane', misread by Chaffers who attached the 'in' to Syng, to be followed by Jackson and Heal. There is however a clear colon between name and 'in', and of course the apprenticeship and other records to corroborate. 'Joseph son of Mr Richard Synge and Rebecca his wife was Borne and Bapt. the 24th day of February 1691' (Register of St. Vedast, Foster Lane). This son was apprenticed to his father 19 September 1711, but does not seem to have entered a mark. Syng was signatory to the petition against foreign workmen, 1 October 1703. He was churchwarden of St. John Zachary in 1706 and 1707.

T

TABART, Pet(t)er (2237-8, 2677) Probably related to 'Jacobus' Tabart denizened 29 September 1698 (*Hug. Soc. Pub.*, 18), and Claude Tabart 'F. du S*r* Pierre et de Magdeleine' baptized 'dans la rue de Grafton vis à vis l'enseigne du grand seigneur' 10 December 1706 (West Street Church Register, *Hug. Soc. Pub.*, 32). First mark entered as largeworker, 7 July 1725. Silversmite in emensirau (?)'. This very illiterately written word was read by Chaffers as 'Wendisau' for Windsor, but careful examination disproves this, since there is a clearly recognizable first letter 'e' matching the same letter in Petter. The word is probably an attempt at Heming's Row, where other Huguenot smiths were situated. Second (Sterling) mark added below the first, perhaps, though not necessarily, at a later date. 'Peter Tabart of St. Giles in the Fields co. Midd. & Anne Jonquerie of Christchurch Spitalfields in the same co. (married) by Mr Bethune; by lic(ence)', 18 May 1731 (Register of St. Michael, Cornhill). Peter Tabart appears as godfather to Pierre Combettes, 14 November 1731 (Savoy Church Register), and to Daniel Tabart son of Daniel and Marianne, 12 February 1735, at the same church. Listed by Evans as Huguenot working at Windsor (following Chaffers) (*Hug. Soc. Proc.*, 14, p. 552).

TACONET, Joseph (1714) No record of apprenticeship or freedom. Only mark entered as smallworker, 20 February 1799. Address: 7 Phoenix Street, Soho.

TANNER, William (3345) No record of apprenticeship or freedom. First mark entered as goldworker, 10 October 1803. Address: 8 Georges Row, City Road (Section VII). Second mark entered as smallworker, 26 September 1811. Address: 4 Badger Yard, Clerkenwell.

TANQUERAY, Anne (100, 2676) Elder daughter and first child of David Willaume I (q.v.), baptized in 'Sohaut' 14 July 1691. Married David Tanqueray (q.v.), 1717. On her husband's death she entered two marks (Sterling and New Standard) which were struck alongside his own in the original entry for him of 1713; his name was struck through and hers written above. This is the only occurrence of this alteration to an entry that appears to have happened, the usual practice being for a widow to be given a fresh entry in the correct chronological position in the register. The date of David's death is not yet known, but Anne's second son Thomas was not born till September 1724, which gives January of that year as a *terminus a quo*. Chaffers, misled by the unusual entry, gives the date of Anne's mark as 1720, but this is obviously too early. Heal, also misled, records her as plateworker, Pall Mall, 1713-31. She died and was buried at Tingrith, Bedfordshire (for which see Willuame), 25 July 1733; her will was proved 21 November 1733 (Wagner, quoted under David Tanqueray, below). The work bearing her mark is clearly that of the journeymen employed by the establishment, and there is no reason to think she herself was a qualified goldsmith. The quality of her sauce-boats and inkstands is particularly outstanding.

TANQUERAY, David (509, 2675) Son of David Tanqueray late of St. Lô in the province of Normandy in the Kingdom of France, apprenticed to David Williams (Willaume) 16 September 1708. David Tanqueray of St. Lô, weaver, appears in the Bounty List for 1710 (Evans, *Hug. Soc.*

Proc., 15, p. 553). A note alongside the apprenticeship entry reads: 'Ao.60 Anne Rne no 42 Naturalized by Act of Parliament as appeared by a copy signed by Matt. Johnson . . .'. In the Act his mother's name appears as Sarah. He was not made free till 4 October 1722, but he entered his first mark as largeworker, 23 December 1713. Address: Green Street, 'near Leister fields'. Second (Sterling) mark, 12 August 1720. Address: Pall Mall. Heal records the first address and date, and Pall Mall, 1720-5. Tanqueray married his master's elder and only surviving daughter, Anne (see above) in 1717, by whom he had two sons (1) David, born 1721, matriculated Christ Church, Oxford 1741. Rector of Cranley 1751-60, and Bow Brickhill, Bucks 1760-82; and (2) Thomas, born September 1724, matriculated Christ Church, Oxford 1743. Rector of Tingrith 1751, till death in 1783 (for Tingrith, Bedfordshire see David Willaume I). His son succeeded to the living for fifty-nine years and the latter's son for fifty-one, totalling 150 years between them. Tanqueray is recorded as Subordinate Goldsmith to the King in 1729 and 1732 (Major General H. W. D. Sitwell, 'The Jewel House and the Royal Goldsmiths', *Arch. Journ.*, CXVII, pp. 164-5), but it seems likely that by this time he was dead and that Anne was in charge of the business, no doubt with her brother David Willaume II to keep a friendly eye on affairs for her. In fact one wonders whether the Tanqueray workshop may not have been, all the time, an ancillary to the Willaume establishment. (Henry Wagner, 'Pedigree of the Huguenot Refugee Families of Willaume and Tanqueray-Willaume', *Miscellanea Genealogica et Heraldica*, 4th Series, Vol. III, p. 92 et. seq.) Tanqueray's surviving work is relatively rare but contains one remarkable piece, the gilt wine-cistern of 1718 at Chatsworth which demonstrates the widest mastery of Huguenot technique. Otherwise his known work seems of more standard type as strapwork cups, salvers and salt-cellars.

TANT, William (3904-5) Son of William Tant of the parish of St. Giles without Cripplegate buckle-carver, apprenticed to Thomas Swift 3 May 1758 and turned over to Benjamin Cartwright Citizen and Blacksmith 24 May 1758. Free, 5 February 1766. Mark presumably entered in the missing register soon after freedom. He appears as William Tant, Junior, spoonmaker in the Parl. Report list 1773. Address: Haberdasher's Square, Grub Street.

TAPLEY, John (1720-1) No record of apprenticeship or freedom. First mark entered as silverworker, 7 December 1833. 'Manufactory': 24 Lower Edmond Street, King's Cross. Second mark (two sizes), 21 February 1834. Moved to 23 Winchester Street, Pentonville, 24 June 1834. Moved to 4 Horse Shoe Court, Ludgate Hill, 10 September 1835. Third mark (two sizes), 8 July 1836. Fourth mark, 20 October 1840. Moved to 40 Russell Street, Cornwall Road, Waterloo Road, 30 September 1844.

*TATUM, John Senior and John Junior (1727) Although there is a John Tatum apprenticed in 1734, it seems impossible that he could have been still working at the date of this mark. John Tatum Senior is therefore probably son of William, Citizen and Cooper of London, apprenticed to Dru Drury Junior 6 May 1761. Free, 6 July 1768. John Junior is probably his son, for whom there is, in this event, no apprenticeship record. John I entered first mark (very small) as smallworker, before 1790, and second mark, 22 October 1790. Address: 4 Poppins Court, Fleet Street (Section IV). Third mark, in partnership with John Junior as smallworkers, 21 July 1794. Address: Poppins Court Fleet Street. Fourth mark together, 28 February 1798. John Junior entered final mark alone, 28 March 1799, same address (Section IV).

TAYLER, John (1696-7) Son of Thomas Tayler of Highclear in the County of Southampton yeoman, apprenticed to Henry Green 5 October 1714 on payment of £20. Free, 15 February 1722. First mark entered as largeworker, 6 June 1728. Address: Gutter Lane. 'free Goldsmith' Second mark, 14 January 1734. Heal records him as plateworker, Gutter Lane, 1728-34; also John Taylor, goldsmith, Golden Cup, against Southampton Street, Strand, 1728-34; and Peter and John Taylor, goldsmiths, same address, 1740.(See Peter Taylor, below.)

TAYLER, Thomas (2945) Son of William Tayler of Highwood hill in the parish of Hendon Middlesex gardener, apprenticed to William Turton of Gutter Lane Cheapside as goldsmith 2 February 1774. Freedom unrecorded. Mark entered as smallworker, 21 May 1791. Address: 2 Bear Alley, Fleet Market.

TAYLER, William (1764) Son of William

Tayler Citizen and Leatherseller of London, apprenticed to John Eaton 6 February 1765 and turned over the same day to his father. Free, 1 April 1772. First mark entered as plateworker, in partnership with John Wakelin, 25 September 1776. Address: Panton Street. Second mark, 9 May 1777. Heal records them as John Wakelin and William Taylor (successors to Parker and Wakelin), goldsmiths, Panton Street, 1776-96. The latter spelling of the surname is normally now used but both the clerk's entry and signature are spelt Tayler. This partnership constituted the fourth link in the connection between George Wickes and Robert Garrard. Taylor died 29 July 1792: 'At Stockwell Surrey after a lingering illness Mr Wm. Taylor goldsmith of Panton Street' (*The Gentleman's Magazine*, p. 575 and *European Magazine*, p. 480).

TAYLEUR, John (1707) Possibly (1) son of Thomas Taylor late of Pembridge in the County of Hereford husbandman deceased, apprenticed to Thomas Heming 1 April 1761. Free 2 July 1794 as 'Gentleman' (an odd note). Or (2) son of Henry Tayleur late of Hammersmith victualler deceased, apprenticed to Isaac River as goldsmith 11 January 1769. Free, 7 February 1776. First mark entered as plateworker, 15 April 1775. Address: 18 Newgate (appears as if Mewgat in entry) Street. Second mark, 4 December 1776. Moved to 14 Red Lyon Street, 18 September 1780. Heal records him as plateworker, Newgate Street, 1775-84.

TAYLOR, Abraham (101) No record of apprenticeship or freedom. First mark entered as smallworker, 6 February 1795. Address: 1 Wenlock Street, St. Luke's. Second mark, 26 January 1796. Third mark, (two sizes), 2 November 1798. Fourth (two sizes), 2 August 1803. Moved to 8 Church Street, Spitalfields, no date.

TAYLOR, Elizabeth (645) No record of apprenticeship or freedom. Presumably widow of William Taylor (below). First mark entered as smallworker, 26 February 1767. Address: Hugin Alley. Second mark, 26 February 1771. Appears as bucklemaker, Hogan Alley, in the Parl. Report list 1773. But see also William Taylor, bucklemaker, 1774 (Section VIII).

TAYLOR, George (912) George Augustus son of William Taylor late of Foster Lane ironmonger deceased, apprenticed to William Sumner of Clerkenwell as spoonmaker 4 April 1792 on payment of £21. Free, 12 June 1799 as silversmith. First mark entered as smallworker, 26 March 1802. Address: 10 Fell Street, Wood Street. Moved to 10 Queen Anne Street, Whitechapel Road, 6 March 1808.

TAYLOR, Ja(mes) (2806) Son of John Taylor of Water Lane Blackfriars wire drawer, apprenticed to James Kirk of St. Paul's Churchyard as jeweller and toyman 7 May 1787. Free, 2 May 1798. Mark entered as plateworker, in partnership with Thomas Hobbs, 27 October 1797. Address: 12 St. Ann's Lane, Aldersgate. Heal records only James Taylor, cutler and silversmith, 121 Cheapside, 1796, who is presumably a different individual.

TAYLOR, Peter (2239) No record of apprenticeship or freedom. Only mark entered as largeworker, 11 November 1740. Address: Golden Cup, Strand. Heal records him as plateworker, Golden Cup, against Southampton Street or corner of Cecil Street, Strand, 1740-53; and Peter and John Taylor, goldsmiths, at the same address, 1740. Peter Taylor, goldsmith, Strand, appears in the Parl. Report list 1773, rather surprisingly, as there seems no other supporting evidence for his working so long and certainly no record of any mark at this date. Although rare, his work when found shows a high standard of craftsmanship coupled with a nice use of rococo ornament.

TAYLOR, Samuel (2645) Son of Thomas Taylor Citizen and Weaver of London, apprenticed to John Newton 3 March 1737 on payment of £18.18s. Free, 3 April 1744. Livery, May 1751. First mark entered as largeworker, 3 May 1744. Address: Maiden Lane, Wood Street. Second mark, 27 January 1757. He appears as plateworker, at the same address, in the Parl. Report list 1773. Heal records the name as jeweller, corner of Lad Lane, Wood Street, 1744-57; jeweller, Bartholomew Close, 1762 (perhaps another); jeweller and clockmaker, Maiden Lane, Wood Street, 1773; and 10 Ball Alley, Lombard Street, 1807-10 (the latter undoubtedly another). Like his master, whose business he probably succeeded to, since Newton was finally in Maiden Lane, Taylor was a specialist in tea-caddies and sugar-bowls, and his mark is rarely, if ever, found on pieces outside this category. His work is competent, if somewhat monotonous in its constant use of floral chasing.

BIOGRAPHICAL DICTIONARY

TAYLOR, Thomas I (2943) No record of apprenticeship or freedom. First mark entered as smallworker, 16 February 1767. Address: Little Minories. Moved to Paternoster Row, Spitalfields, no date. Second mark, 5 July 1771. Address: White Cross Street. Third mark, 6 June 1772. Address: Chequer Alley, Bunhill Row, where he appears as bucklemaker in the Parl. Report list 1773, and also separately without category at White Cross Street. Fourth mark as bucklemaker, 3 May 1774, and another, 11 August 1775. Address for both: White Cross Street (Section VIII).

TAYLOR, Thomas II (2946) No record of apprenticeship or freedom. Only mark entered as smallworker, 19 October 1793. Address: 1 Back Hill, Hatton Garden.

*TAYLOR, Trevillion (2948) No record of apprenticeship or freedom. Only mark entered as smallworker, 10 February 1760. Address: 'next to the Black Bull, Rotten Row, Old Street', where he appears as bucklemaker in the Parl. Report list 1773.

TAYLOR, William (3340) No record of apprenticeship or freedom. First mark entered as smallworker, 2 October 1764. Address: Huggin Alley, Gutter Lane, where Heal records him as silver bucklemaker, c. 1780. This may be an error or the name of a son, since it would seem probable that he was dead by 26 February 1767, when Elizabeth Taylor (above) entered her first mark. On the other hand the signature of William Taylor entered as bucklemaker, 10 June 1774, at 9 Huggin Lane, appears identical (Section VIII).

TEARE, John (1855) No record of apprenticeship or freedom. First mark entered as smallworker, 17 March 1828. Address: 23 Charles Street, City Road. Moved to 11 Henry Street, Waterloo Road, 5 July 1828. Moved to 7 York Terrace, York Road, Lambeth, and second mark, 18 September 1833. 'And at 86 Crown Court Temple', 10 May 1838. Third mark, 27 February 1840. Fourth 22 February 1842.

TEARLE, Thomas (2740, 2938, 2947) Son of Thomas Tearle of Stanbridge in the County of Bedford yeoman, apprenticed to Gabriel Sleath 23 September 1707. Free, 7 September 1715. Signatory as journeyman to the petition against assaying the work of foreigners not having served seven years apprenticeship, February 1716. First mark entered as largeworker, 9 February 1719. Address: Foster Lane. Second (Sterling) mark, 30 June 1720. Third mark, 22 June 1739. Address: Russell Street, Covent Garden. Moved to Shurbin (?Sherborne) Lane, 6 May 1740. Heal records him as plateworker, Foster Lane, 1719-25; and Russell Street, 1739-42, the second with a variant spelling Turle. The registers of St. Vedast, Foster Lane, contain the following: 'Elizabeth the daughter of Tho. Tiarle and Ann his wife Born ye 5 of April 1726 and Baptised ye 24 of ye same month'. Rebecca, daughter of Tho. Tearle, was born 5 May, baptized 11 May 1727, and John, son of the same, was born 11 March, baptized 12 March 1729-30. As one would expect from his apprenticeship Tearle is an excellent general maker of cups, tankards and salvers, without ever aspiring to important pieces, or displaying great originality.

TEMPEST, Benjamin Charles (239-40) Son of Richard Tempest late of Goswell Street warehouseman deceased, apprenticed to William Seaman of Great Sutton Street Clerkenwell as silversmith 4 November 1812. Free, 4 October 1820. First mark entered as spoonmaker, 14 April 1826. Address: 53 Great Sutton Street, Clerkenwell (presumably with or succeeding to his master). Second mark, 2 May 1826. Third mark, and moved to 29 Great Sutton Street, no date.

TERREY, John Edward (1281, 2547) No record of apprenticeship. Free of the Vintners' Company by patrimony, 3 June 1812. Address: City of London Tavern, presumably that of his father, an innkeeper. That this freedom refers to this maker is proved by his appearing as silversmith of Hatton Garden, Citizen and Vintner, in the turn-over to him of William Morris, 7 March 1821. First mark entered as plateworker, in partnership with Samuel Hennell (q.v.), 6 April 1814. Address: Foster Lane. Second mark alone as plateworker, 26 January 1816. Address: Foster Lane. Moved to 31 Hatton Garden, 9 May 1819. Third mark (two sizes), 3 October 1828. Fourth mark, 18 February 1835. Against the last mark is the following note: 'This mark was withdrawn and defaced 9 Oct. 1848 Josiah Stamp'. This date presumably agrees with Terrey's retirement or death.

TERRY, John (1719) No record of apprenticeship or freedom. Only mark entered as smallworker, 5 May 1818. Address: 3 Cross Street, Hatton Garden.

TEULINGS, Constantine (419) No record of apprenticeship or freedom. Only mark entered as largeworker, 16 June 1755. 'Silversmith'. Address: Dean Street, St. Ann's, Soho. Heal records him here as plateworker, at this date; and also Duke's Court, St. Martin's Lane, 1762-73 (as he appears in the Parl. Report list 1773); and 15 Charing Cross, 1762-93. In spite of his long working career his work seems scarce, if indeed it has ever been identified, and it seems probable that he was mainly a retailer, or as a maker in a very small way of business.

TEY, William (3337) Son of Richard Tey late of the parish of St. Giles Cripplegate blacksmith deceased, apprenticed to William Fish 25 May 1715 for eight years. Free, 25 July 1723. Mark entered as smallworker, 15 November 1725. Address: New Street, Blackfriars. 'Goldsmith'.

THEOBALDS, William (3350-1, 3354) Son of William Theobalds of Charles Street Christchurch Surrey silversmith, apprenticed to John Kerschner of Clerkenwell Green as silver spoonmaker 6 November 1815 and turned over to Charles Eley 5 April 1820. Free, 3 December 1823 as silversmith. First mark entered as plateworker, 14 January 1829. Address: 3 Lovel(ls) Court, Paternoster Row (the address of Eley, Fearn and Chawner at this date). Moved to 7 Salisbury Court, Fleet Street, 20 November 1829. Second mark (six punches), 23 January 1834. Third mark (three punches), 15 July 1834. Fourth mark (seven punches), 12 February 1835. Addresses: Salisbury Court and Lovels Court. Fifth mark, as plate and spoonmaker, in partnership with Lockington Bunn (q.v.), 30 June 1835. Address: 7 Salisbury Court, Fleet Street. Sixth mark (five punches) alone, 27 February 1836.

THEREMIN, Frances (725) No record of apprenticeship or freedom. Only mark entered as smallworker, 24 April 1772. Address: Spur Street, Leicester Fields, where she so appears in the Parl. Report list 1773.

THOMAS, Evan (643) No record of apprenticeship or freedom. Only mark entered as smallworker, 25 April 1735. Address: Bishop Court, Clerkenwell. Heal records the name as goldsmith, London, 1774, who may perhaps be the same.

THOMAS, James (1854) James Edward, son of Edward Thomas of Vineyard Gardens, Clerkenwell pocket-book maker, apprenticed to William Seaman of Great Sutton Street Clerkenwell as silversmith 7 August 1816. Free, 5 August 1824. Mark entered as spoonmaker, 10 August 1824. Address: 29 Great Sutton Street, Clerkenwell. Moved to 20 Vineyard Gardens, Clerkenwell (? his father's address), 9 March 1825.

THOMAS, Richard (2445) No record of apprenticeship or freedom. Only mark entered as largeworker, 20 March 1755. Address: Kings Arms Passage, Ludgate Hill. Heal records him as plateworker, King's Arms Yard, 1755-64.

THOMASSON, James (2800) Son of Robert Thomason of Linley in the County of Lancaster yeoman, apprenticed to Ralph Gerrard Citizen and Waxchandler 13 October 1694. Free, 2 February 1705. Mark entered as smallworker, 17 March 1717. Address: Lombard Street. 'free of the Wax Chandlers'. Heal records him as goldsmith, parish of St. Mary Woolnoth, 1706-23; and Golden Key, Lombard Street, 1725-45 (Heal Add.); and as goldsmith and jeweller, near Cullum Street, in Fenchurch Street, 1745-55, who may perhaps be a son; also Thomas Thomason, goldsmith, London, 1706; and the same name, Fenchurch Street, bankrupt 1744.

*THOMEGAY, Mark (2075) No record of apprenticeship or freedom. First mark entered as smallworker, 10 September 1763. Address: Middle Moorfields. Second (incuse) mark, 3 March 1770. Appears as goldworker, Middle Moorfields, in the Parl. Report list 1773, where Mark Thomegay and Son are mentioned as having been prosecuted in 1770 for making gold watchchains 'worse than standard'. Heal records him as gold and silver manufacturer, 12 Middle Moorfields, 1760-93. His son Richard was apprenticed to Nicholas Biggs as goldsmith, 1776.

THOMPSON, Edward I (642) Son of Edward Thompson late Citizen and Joyner of London, free by patrimony of the Joyners' Company 3 December 1706. Mark entered as smallworker, undated, between 1717 and 1720. Address: Staining Lane. 'Free Joyner'. Apparently dead by 2 April 1728, when his son Edward (below) was made free of the same company as his father. Heal records Edward Thompson, goldsmith, parish of St. Mary Staining, bankrupt 1729, but this could perhaps be his son (below).

THOMPSON, Edward II (646) Son of Edward Thompson (above) late Citizen and Joyner of London, free of the Joyners' Company 2 April 1728. Only mark entered as smallworker, 19 March 1728/?9. 'Edward Thompson Junr'. Address: Staining Lane. 'Free Joyner'. See above for Heal's record of bankruptcy.

THOMPSON, Francis (2776) Son of John Thompson Citizen and Draper of London, free by patrimony of his father's company 4 October 1699. Only mark entered as smallworker, 21 October 1699. Address: Abchurch Lane 'Free Draper'. One of the same name (possibly a son), appears in the Drapers' Company records as paying quarterage as silver hilt-maker in 1725.

THOMPSON, Henry (1069) Possibly another son of Edward Thompson I (above). Described on entry of his mark as Free Joyner, but does not appear in the index to that Company's register, nor in the individual entries back to 1725. Mark entered as smallworker, 1 September 1730. Address: Silver Street. 'Free Joyner'.

THOMPSON, John I (1695, 2801) Son of Jonas Thompson of the parish of Clayton in the County of York yeoman, apprenticed to Christopher Allison of the Skinners' Company 2 November 1698. Free, 2 April 1706, having been turned over to William Gardiner, Citizen and Goldsmith. First mark entered as smallworker, 9 April 1711. Address: St. John Street. 'Free Skinner'. Second (Sterling) mark, 15 August 1720. Address: Wood Street.

THOMPSON, John II (2778) Clearly distinct from above in his hand. No record of apprenticeship or freedom. Mark entered 10 May 1717, with the unusual accompaniment 'maketh all sorts of knifes & forks in Carey Lane'.

THOMPSON, William I (2777) Free of the Blacksmiths' Company, but not traceable in the existing records. Mark entered as smallworker, 26 September 1701. Address: Snow Hill. 'Free Blacksmith'.

THOMPSON, William II (3344, 3355) The entry of several apprentices at suitable dates makes identification with the above uncertain. First mark entered as smallworker, 19 October 1802. Address: 29 Grafton Street, Soho. Second mark, 24 April 1804. Moved to 35 Piccadilly, no date, and to 54 Jermyn Street, St. James', and 11 Air Street, Piccadilly, all without date. Second mark as plateworker, in partnership with William Frost, 16 June 1818. Address: 11 Air Street.

THOMPSON, William III (3344) Apparently distinct by signature and address from the above, although mark almost identical and represented by the same entry no. 3344. Only mark entered as smallworker, 4 November 1807. Address: 15 Mitchell Street, Brick Lane. Moved to 10 St. John's Row, Brick Lane, St. Luke's, 6 April 1812.

THOMSON, Benjamin (2773) Probably son of Thomas Thomson Citizen and Cordwainer of London, apprenticed to Walter Prosser 2 July 1700 and turned over to Edward Horne. Free, 3 October 1707. Mark entered as smallworker, 6 January 1716. Address: Dean's Court, St. Martin's Lane.

THORNBURGH, Nicholas (2103) No record of apprenticeship or freedom. Only mark entered as smallworker, 15 March 1738. Address: 'within three Doors of the fountain Tavern in ye Strand'.

THORNE, Samuel (2774) Son of John Thorne of Remingham(?) in the County of Berkshire yeoman, apprenticed to Benjamin Trehearn 27 August 1683. Free, 27 April 1694. Mark entered as largeworker, undated, probably April 1697 on commencement of register. Address: Cannon Street. His mark has the unusual feature of a punning device in the crown of thorns encircling the initials. Heal records him as plateworker, Cannon Street, 1697-1700.

THORNE, Thomas (2939) Possibly son of Thomas Thorne of Reading in the County of Berkshire tanner, apprenticed to Robert White 8 May 1707. Free, 29 June 1715. Mark entered as smallworker, 14 May 1736. Address: Wood Street. 'Goldsmith'. His son Thomas was apprenticed to him in 1738 and recorded by Heal as goldsmith, 23 Wood Street, Cheapside, 1760-72; he appears as smallworker in the Parl. Report list 1773, having been elected to the Livery 1751, Court 1763, Warden 1776-8 and Prime Warden 1780. He died 2 May 1785 (*The Gentleman's Magazine*, p. 403). In spite of this prominence in the Company, no mark can be traced for him.

THREDDER, Joseph (1715) Son of Henry 'Threader' of Barking in Essex fisherman, apprenticed to Frances Purton widow of

Robert as goldsmith 5 April 1790 on payment of £21. Free, 7 June 1797. Mark entered as plateworker, 19 August 1802. Address: 2 Priest Court, Foster Lane.

THRISCROSS, Simon (2775) Son of Simon Thriscross late citizen and Draper of London deceased a tallow chandler in Trinity Lane, apprenticed to Thomas Mann of the Drapers' Company 23 March 1676. Free, 15 September 1686. In 1695 he appears in the same company's books as paying quarterage (fine) as 'working goldsmith', Ludgate Hill. Mark entered as largeworker, undated, probably April 1697 on commencement of register. Address: Smithfield Bars. 'Free Draper'. Heal records him in surname only at this date and address.

*THURKLE, Abraham (102) No record of apprenticeship or freedom. Probably son of George Thurkle (below). Only mark entered as smallworker, 9 February 1827. Address: 5 New Street Square.

*THURKLE, George (911) No record of apprenticeship or freedom. Probably son of Francis Thurkle, hiltmaker (Section IX), 15 New Street Square, who entered his first mark in 1783. First mark entered as smallworker, 19 March 1800. Address: 15 New Street Square. Second mark, 10 August 1821. Address: 5 New Street Square. See Abraham Thurkle (above), presumably his son and successor.

TIFFIN, John (2811) Son of John Tiffin of Souldroff in the County of Bedford clerk, apprenticed to Samuel Hood 1 March 1694. Free, 9 April 1701. Mark entered as largeworker, 12 May 1701. Address: Watling Street.

*TIMBERLAKE, James (1701-2) No record of apprenticeship or freedom. The name James, perfectly written in the mark entry, was abbreviated in error by Chaffers as Jos. and read by Jackson and Heal as Joseph in consequence. First mark entered as largeworker, 19 April 1743. Address: Castle Street, near Seven Dials. Second mark, 5 April 1755. Heal records only the first date (with the error of Christian name mentioned above).

TIMBRELL, Robert (2707, 2810) Son of Thomas Timbrell of Brouckington(?) in the County of Gloucester yeoman, apprenticed to Augustine Dudley 9 November 1678. Free, 3 February 1685/?6. Court, August 1705. First mark entered as largeworker, undated, probably April 1697 on commencement of register. Address: Sherborne Lane. Second mark below also undated, presumably after October 1707, in partnership with Joseph Bell I, whose name alone is written alongside. Chaffers, although reproducing the mark, overlooked the signature of Bell, and omitted any identification of him as partner, resulting in an ascription by Jackson of the mark to Timbrell and Benjamin Bentley, who had been working alone at another address from 1698. Heal records Robert Timbrell, goldsmith, Sherborne Lane, 1690-1715 (also Hilton-Price *Handbook of London Bankers*); and following Jackson's error, with Benjamin Bentley, goldsmiths, London, 1714-15. That Timbrell was acting as banker as early as 1693 is proved by two entries in the day book of C. Peers, London Merchant 1689-95 (kindly communicated to me by the late Wilfred Samuel F.S.A.): 'Dec. 5 1693. Charles Jones Jr. Richard Crossley's bill dated Bristol 2nd inst. at 10 days sight in favour of Jones on Robert Timbrell of London. Endorsed remitted £200 to C. Peers', and, under 26 July 1694, another bill on Timbrell in favour of the same Jones for £125. He was one of the petitioners against the work of 'aliens or foreigners', 11 August 1697.

TIPPEN, Henry (1070) No record of apprenticeship or freedom. First mark entered as smallworker, 29 January 1805. Address: Ratcliff Row, City Road. Second mark, 6 June 1805. Third, 20 March 1808. Fourth, 13 October 1809. Moved to Richmond Building, Soho, no date. Presumably dead by 10 October 1821, on entry of Maria Tippen's mark (below).

TIPPEN, Maria (2074) Presumably widow of Henry Tippen (above). No record of apprenticeship or freedom. Mark entered as smallworker, 10 October 1821. Address: 1 Richmond Buildings, Soho.

TITTERTON, George (2809) Son of George Titterton late of Leek in the County of Stafford yeoman, apprenticed to Israel Pickney 27 July 1687. Free, 4 June 1695. Mark entered as largeworker, undated, probably April 1697 on commencement of register. Address: Shipp Yard, without Temple Bar. Heal records this address and date; and London, 1708-9.

*TOKETT, Marmaduke (2071) No record of apprenticeship or freedom. Only mark entered as smallworker, 24 July 1762. Address: 'next door to the Golden Lion,

Wardour Street, Soho'. Appears as gold-worker, Wardour Street, in the Parl-Report list 1773, and so Heal.

TOMBS, John (1699) No record of apprenticeship or freedom. Only mark entered as smallworker, 3 January 1738. Address: 'at the 2 Brewers and Horns, Old Street'.

TOMBS, Thomas (2940) No record of apprenticeship or freedom. Only mark entered as smallworker, 14 June 1738. Address: Dean's Court, St. Martin's Le Grand.

TOMKINS, Richard (2866) Son of Richard Tomkins late Citizen and Clothworker of London deceased, apprenticed to Samuel Day 20 February 1701. Free, 19 April 1709. Mark entered as smallworker, 4 May 1709. Address: Gutter Lane. Incuse (Sterling) mark entered later, undated *c.* 1730. Address: 'in Joneses lane ouver against the Spread ghalesq (?eagle) (Section V).

*TOOKEY, Elizabeth (3558-9) No record of apprenticeship or freedom. Presumably the widow of James Tookey and mother of Thomas (below) since she appears in the Parl. Report list 1773 as spoonmaker, Silver Street and must have entered a mark in the missing register. The marks attributed to her, found on spoons, seem therefore to be acceptable.

*TOOKEY, James (1703-4) Son of Charles Tookey late of the parish of St. Giles without Cripplegate baker deceased, apprenticed to Henry Green 5 April 1733. Free, 2 July 1741. Mark entered as largeworker, 11 May 1750. Address: Noble Street, Foster Lane. Moved to Silver Street, 26 September 1752. Livery, March 1758. Second mark as smallworker, 25 January 1762. Address: Silver Street. Called spoonmaker in the apprenticeship to him of his son Thomas (below) 1766. Heal records him only as plateworker, Noble Street, 1750. He was presumably dead by early 1773, since Elizabeth Tookey appears alone in the Parl. Report list dated 29 April of that year.

*TOOKEY, Thomas (2944, 2949) Son of Thomas (a clerical error obviously for James, above) Tookey of Silver Street London spoonmaker, Citizen and Goldsmith, apprenticed to his father 'to learn his art of a spoonmaker' 9 April 1766. Free, 5 May 1773. First mark entered as spoonmaker, 30 October 1773. Address: 12 Silver Street. Second mark, 2 November 1775. Third, 24 March 1779. Moved to 35 Monkwell Street, and fourth mark, 5 December 1780. Heal records him as plateworker, Silver Street, 1773; and Monkwell Street, 1779.

TOONE, William (2863, 3336) Son of William Toone of St. Giles without Cripplegate threadthroster, apprenticed to Joseph Smith 23 May 1718 on payment of £12 and turned over to Charles Jackson in Cannon Street 9 May 1723. Free, 10 June 1725. Two marks (Sterling and New Standard) entered as largeworker, 3 November 1725. Address: More Lane, near Cripplegate. 'Freeman of the Goldsmiths Company'. Heal records him as plateworker, Cripplegate, 1725.

TOULIET, John (1710) No record of apprenticeship or freedom. First mark entered as smallworker, 26 April 1784. Address: Whitcombe Street, Leicester Fields. Second mark, 9 February 1792.

TOWNRAW, Thomas (2941-2) Son of Rothwell Townraw of the City of Lincoln gentleman, apprenticed to John Luff 1 July 1731 on payment of £31.10s. Free, 4 July 1738. First mark entered as smallworker, 21 September 1738. Address: St. Martin's Lane. 'Free Goldsmith'. Second mark, 13 November 1753. Address: Dolphin Court, Noble Street. Third mark, 29 October 1754. Chaffers misread the name as Towman from the 1753 entry (not concerning himself with the first mark as smallworker) followed by Heal. Townraw does not appear in the Parl. Report list 1773 so was presumably dead or retired before then. His son Richard was apprenticed to Richard Pargeter in 1754.

TOWNSEND, Edmund (2864) Son of Edmund Townsend in the Town and County of Leicester pewterer(?), apprenticed to Samuel Hawkes 19 May 1680 'from Midsummer next'. Freedom unrecorded. Mark entered as largeworker, undated, probably April 1697 on commencement of register. Address: Without Cripplegate.

TOWNSEND, George (2865) Son of Edward Townsend late of Stonfold(?) in the County of Gloucester glazier deceased, apprenticed to George Greenhill 12 September 1677. Free, 28 September 1687. Mark entered as smallworker, 10 March 1701. Address: Eagle and Child Alley, Shoe Lane. Livery, October 1712.

TRAHERNE, Benjamin (2895) Son of Thomas Traherne of Lugwardine in the County of Hereford yeoman, apprenticed at Goldsmiths' Hall to Philip Traherne 'a goldsmith free of the Grocers' 15 September 1699. Free, 22 September 1676. Mark entered as largeworker, undated, probably April 1697 on commencement of register. Address: St. Martin Le Grand. Heal records him as plateworker, St. Martin's Lane, following a misreading of Chaffers, 1697–1700.

*TRAIES, William (3347–9) No record of apprenticeship or freedom. First mark entered as spoonmaker, 4 June 1822. Address: 2 Cherry Tree Court, Aldersgate Street. Second mark, 13 October 1823. Move to 6 Powell Street, Goswell Street, 1 April 1824. Third mark, 8 November 1824. Fourth (two sizes), 25 August 1825.

TREEN, William (3352) No record of apprenticeship or freedom. Only mark entered as spoonmaker, 11 January 1833. Address: 3 Essex Street, Battle Bridge.

TRENDER, Ann (1726) No record of apprenticeship or freedom. Possibly the widow of Robert Trender apprenticed in 1776 to William Sudell and turned over to William Turton. Free, 1783. Heal records him as goldsmith, Aldersgate Street, 1790. Her mark entered as smallworker, in partnership with James Trender, 29 November 1792. Address: 10 Princes Street, Barbican. Partnership apparently dissolved on entry of separate mark of James Trender, 1806 (below). Heal records her as goldsmith, Barbican, 1795.

*TRENDER, James (1717, 1726) No record of apprenticeship or freedom. Probably son of Robert and Ann (see above). First mark entered as smallworker, in partnership with Ann Trender, 29 November 1792. Address: 10 Princes Street, Barbican. Second mark alone as bucklemaker, 19 April 1793, same address. Third mark as such, 9 August 1797. Address: 7 Long Lane, West Smithfield. Moved later (no date) to Dove Court, 4 Leather Lane. (Section VIII). Fourth mark as smallworker, 27 August 1806. Address: 43 Baldwins Gardens, Leather Lane. Heal records him as goldsmith, Barbican, 1795.

TRENHOLME, Jonathan (1698) Son of William Trenholme late of Harlsen in the County of York gentleman deceased, apprenticed to Dru Drury 10 June 1719 on payment of £35. Free, 5 October 1732. Only mark entered as smallworker, 14 June 1734. Address: Wood Street. Heal records him as haftmaker and smallworker, Case of Knives and Forks and Goldsmiths' Arms, Wood Street; c. 1760. It is clear from this sign and his apprenticeship to Drury (q.v.) that he was a specialist knife, and perhaps sword-hilt, maker.

TRENHOLME, William (3338) Appears in the Quarterage list of the Clockmakers' Company, c. 1730 as casemaker 'with Mr Bayly'. Only mark entered as smallworker, 23 October, undated between 1730 and 1733. Address: Maiden Lane, near Goldsmiths' Hall. 'Clockmaker'.

TRINGHAM, John (1708) Son of William Tringham Citizen and Goldsmith of London, apprenticed to William Hunt 5 June 1740 on payment of £16.15s., £8.5s. of the charity of the Goldsmiths' Company and £8.10s. by the treasurer of the Working Goldsmith's feast. Free, 7 December 1752, as gold chainmaker. Free 'de novo', 10 April 1771. Mark entered as goldworker, 9 March 1779. Address: 3 Queenshead Passage, Newgate Street. Also incuse mark entered at same date. Heal records him as goldsmith, Newgate Street, 1780. Alice Tringham, presumably his widow, entered an incuse mark as goldworker, at 3 Queens head Passage, 30 May 1789 (Section V). James Tringham also as goldworker (Section VII), at 22 Noble Street, 1791. Also John, Thomas and Ann Tringham, goldworkers, 7 Preist Court, Foster Lane, 1803.

TRIPLAND, John (1718) No record of apprenticeship or freedom. Only mark entered as smallworker, 8 April 1812. Address: 12 Evangelist Court, Blackfriars.

*TRIPP, Job (1705, 1723) Son of Job Trip late of the parish of St. Martin in the Fields broker deceased, apprenticed to William Williams 12 June 1745 on payment of £50 and turned over April 1748 to William Cripps. Free, 2 July 1752. First mark entered as largeworker, 31 December 1754. Address: St. Martin's Lane. Second mark, 27 July 1757. Moved to Leadenhall Street, no date. Livery, July 1763. Appears as bucklemaker, King Street, Westminster in the Parl. Report list 1773. Died before 1796. Heal records him as plateworker, Golden Ball, St. Martin's Lane, facing May's buildings, 1754; and Bridge Street, Westminster, 1769–78.

TROBY, John (1711–2) No record of apprenticeship or freedom. First mark entered as smallworker, 29 March 1787.

Address: Ship Court, Old Bailey. Second mark, 14 May 1791. Third, 19 December 1791. Fourth, 6 June 1800. Fifth entry as plateworker, 20 April 1803, same address. Presumably dead by 17 December 1804, on entry of Mary Troby's mark (below). William Bamforth Troby son of John Troby deceased was apprenticed to John Fosket 1809.

TROBY, Mary (2073) Presumably widow of John Troby (above). Mark entered as smallworker, 17 December 1804. Address: 2 Ship Court, Old Bailey.

TROBY, William (3346) William Bamforth Troby son of John Troby late of Ship Court Old Bailey silversmith deceased, apprenticed to John Fosket of St. John's Square as silversmith 7 June 1809. Freedom unrecorded. First mark entered as largeworker ('Large Plate'), 3 March 1812. Address: 3 Prujeans Square, Old Bailey. Second mark (two sizes), as plateworker, 18 July 1821, same address.

TRUEMAN, Isaac (1713) No record of apprenticeship or freedom. First mark entered as smallworker, 28 October 1788. Address: 64 Queen Street, Cheapside. Second mark, 26 November 1789.

TRUSS, William (2896, 3454, 3468) Son of Charles Truss of Reading in the County of Berkshire bargeman, apprenticed to John ffodrey (?Fawdery) 27 July 1703. Free, 19 August 1713. Mark entered as largeworker, undated, before December 1713, probably shortly after freedom. Address: Foster Lane, with 'at Reding berkesheare' added in another hand, probably at the time of his return to his native town, which from the other two entries for him was before 22 September 1721. In this respect it is interesting to find that Heal records him at Foster Lane, 1710-21. From the evidence of surviving examples of his mark, he appears to have been a knife-haft maker. (See further under Reading in Provincial Section, following.)

TUCKWELL, Joseph (1724, 2954) Son of Francis Tuckwell Citizen and Hatbandmaker of London, apprenticed to Thomas Steed of the Merchant Taylors' Company 5 April 1704. Free, 1 October 1712. First mark entered as smallworker, 15 April 1713. Address: Castle Alley in Burchin lalee (?Alley, but if so, why when the previous spelling is correct). 'Free Merchant Taylor'. Second mark (Sterling), 22 July 1720.

Livery of the Merchant Taylors, 29 November 1726.

TUITE, Elizabeth (644, 3557) No record of apprenticeship or freedom. Presumably widow of John Tuite (below), on the evidence of the ewer incorporated in both marks. Mark entered as largeworker, 7 January 1741. Address: George Street, York Buildings. Heal records her as plateworker, York Buildings (Strand), 1741 and (?) 1769.

TUITE, John (1700, 1722) According to Jackson, son of James Tuite of Drogheda merchant, apprenticed to John Matthews of Dublin goldsmith in 1703, and working in Dublin from 1710 to 1720, using the same, or a similar mark to that entered later in London to which he moved in 1723 and where Jackson says he died in 1740. First mark entered as largeworker, undated, between September 1721 and July 1725. Address: Ireland's Yard, Blackfriars. Moved to Litchfield Street, near Newport Market, also undated. Second mark, 27 June 1739. Address: Litchfield Street, St. Ann's, Westminster. Heal records him as goldsmith, Irelands Yard, 1721; Green Door, Litchfield Street, near Newport Street, 1721-39; and George Street, York Buildings, Strand, 1745. This last address may perhaps have been in fact that of Elizabeth his widow (see above). Heal also has John Tuite, goldsmith, London, 1763, but this appears probably based on a mis-attributed mark of another maker, or misprint for William (following). In spite of the elegant ewer incorporated in both his marks Tuite appears to have specialized in the making of salvers.

TUITE, William (3339, 3900-3) No record of apprenticeship or freedom, and no known connection with the foregoing. Mark entered as largeworker, undated, between December 1755 and March 1758. Address: King Street, Golden Square. Heal records him here as goldsmith, 1756; and 41 Great Queen Street, Lincoln's Inn Fields, 1761-75, where he appears as plateworker in the Parl. Report list 1773. William Tuite of the parish of St. Giles in the Fields, bachelor, and Catherine Reddan of St. Paul's, Covent Garden, spinster married at the latter church by licence, 24 March 1761. Tuite was bankrupt February 1770 (*The Gentleman's Magazine*, p. 96). At 41 Great Queen Street in 1774, Heal also records

William Tuffley, previously at Cannon Street from 1742 to bankruptcy in 1756. He was apprenticed in 1726 and elected to Livery in 1750, but no mark is recorded. Whether he succeeded Tuite is not established.

TURBITT, William (2952) Son of William Turbitt late of Kingston on Thames in the County of Surrey waterman deceased, apprenticed to Thomas Spackman 5 August 1701. Free, 5 July 1710. Mark entered as largeworker, 7 July 1710. Address: Bell Court, Foster Lane. The entry is annotated 'dead at virginneay'. Heal records him as goldsmith, Foster Lane, 1711-13.

TURNER, Francis (724, 2950-1, 3576) Son of John Turner in Crake County of York clerk, apprenticed to Thomas Prichard of the Grocers' Company 8 October 1700. Free, 13 November 1707, 'in bull & mouth str near Moorgate silversmith'. Mark entered as largeworker, 5 April 1709. Address: St. Ann's Lane. 'Free Grocer'. Signatory as 'working goldsmith' to the petition complaining of the competition of 'necessitous strangers', December 1711. Second (Sterling) mark, 5 August 1720. Third (New Standard) mark, 25 February 1721. Address: St. Ann's Lane. His mark seems to occur principally on candlesticks.

*TURNER, George (913-4) No record of apprenticeship or freedom. First mark entered as spoonmaker, in partnership with W. Biddell, 29 March 1820. Address: 55 Drury Lane. Second mark alone, 22 November 1823, same address. Moved to 28 Devonshire Street, Queen Square, 27 February 1824.

TURNER, James (307, 1716) No record of apprenticeship or freedom. First mark entered as plateworker, in partnership with Charles Fox, 20 October 1801. Address: 3 Old Street, Goswell Street. The partnership dissolved by 5 September 1804, when Fox entered a separate mark. Turner's second mark alone, 17 September 1804, same address.

TURNER, John (1706) No record of apprenticeship or freedom. First mark entered as smallworker, 26 February 1759, with accompanying incuse mark. Address: Deean (sic) Rents, Cow Cross. Appears as watchcasemaker, Quaker's Buildings, Cow Cross, in the Parl. Report list 1773, and entered three marks as such 1777-93 (Section V).

One of the same name, probably a son, entered an incuse mark as watchcasemaker, 1804, at Greenhills Rents, Cow Cross (Section VI).

*TURNER, Richard (2447-8) No record of apprenticeship or freedom. Perhaps son of Richard Turner, bucklemaker, 15 St. John Square, 1789 (Section VIII). First mark entered as smallworker, 28 October 1801. Address: 3 Amen Corner. Moved to 31 St. John's Square, 10 May 1802. Second mark as spoonmaker, in partnership with John Shea, 23 April 1808, same address. Third mark alone, 16 November 1809. Moved to 4 Islington Road, 3 February 1813.

TURNER, Robert (2443, 2953) Free of the Founders' Company by service to his brother 5 August 1695. First mark entered as smallworker, 29 June 1703. Address: Shoe Lane. 'Free of the Founders'. Second (Sterling) mark, 17 March 1726.

TURNER, William (2674, 3353, 3906) Either (1) son of Richard Turner of the parish of St. Mary le Bone blacksmith, apprenticed to James Wilks 5 March 1741. Free 5 April 1749. Livery, 8 March 1758. Or, less likely (2) son of William Turner late Citizen and Turner of London deceased, apprenticed to Charles Davis 4 October 1739. Freedom unrecorded. First mark entered as largeworker, in partnership with James Williams, 9 August 1753. Address: Staining Lane. Moved to Addle Street, 20 September 1753. Second mark alone, 21 June 1754. Address: Addle Street. Moved to Wood Street, 3 May 1758. Livery March 1758. Court, May 1758. Heal records him as plateworker, Addle Street, 1754-6; and spoonmaker, Wood Street, 1767-8. He died 1772.

TURRILL, John (1856) No record of apprenticeship or freedom. Only mark entered as smallworker, 14 May 1836. Address: 250 Regent Street.

TURTON, Mehatabell (2072) No record of apprenticeship or freedom. Probably widow of William Turton (below). Only mark entered as smallworker, 10 October 1798. Address: 31 Monkwell Street. Signs 'Mehatell' in somewhat laboured hand.

TURTON, William (3341-2, 3356) Son of Thomas Turton late of Horsleydown in the parish of St. John Southwark shovelmaker deceased, apprenticed to William Dorell 5 October 1757 on payment of £18.18s. Free,

5 December 1764. Appears as smallworker, Parish Street, Horsleydown, Southwark, in the Parl. Report list 1773, so must have already entered a mark before that date in the missing register. First mark as smallworker entered 4 October 1773. Address: 10 Gutter Lane. Moved to Charterhouse Lane, 22 February 1776. Moved to 18 Little Britain, and second mark, 22 May 1780. Third mark, 6 May 1782. Fourth, 24 October 1783. Fifth, in partnership with William Walbancke, 8 April 1784. Sixth mark, also in partnership, 26 June 1788, on move to 8 Fore Street. Seventh mark alone, 6 March 1791. Address: 43 Grub Street. Moved to 78 Chiswell Street, 9 October 1795. His son William was apprenticed to him 1779 and free 1787. Heal records him as smallworker in silver, Little Britain, 1777–9; and 43 Grub Street, Cripplegate, 1792; also Turton and Walbancke, jewellers, 8 Fore Street, Cripplegate, 1790–3.

TWEEDIE, John (1709) No record of apprenticeship or freedom. Presumably son or younger brother of Walter Tweedie (below). Only mark entered as plateworker, 1 December 1783. Address: 7 Holiwell, St. Clements. Heal records him here as plateworker, 1783.

TWEEDIE, Walter (3343, 3353a) No record of apprenticeship or freedom. First mark entered as spoonmaker, 7 December 1775. Address: Holywell Street, Strand, but he appears as spoonmaker, at the same address, in the Parl. Report list 1773, so was already established with an earlier mark in the missing register by then. Second mark as plateworker (two sizes), 25 September 1779. Third mark (two sizes), 29 October 1781. Heal records him as plateworker, Holywell Street, 1775–86.

TWELL, William (2956) Son of William Twell of the parish of St. James' Clerkenwell in the County of Middlesex labourer, apprenticed to Thomas Gardiner 27 April 1699 for eight years and turned over next day to Joseph Bird. Free, 3 March 1707. Mark entered as largeworker, 28 March 1709. Address: Gutter Lane. Signatory as 'working goldsmith' to the petition complaining of the competition of 'necessitous strangers', December 1711. Heal records him as plateworker, Gutter Lane (married) 1702–11.

TWYFORD, Robert (2446) No record of apprenticeship or freedom. Only mark entered as smallworker, 23 June 1784. Address: 40 Strand.

TYRILL, Robert (135, 2444, 2449) Son of Thomas Tyrrill of the parish of Leatherhead in the County of Surrey, apprenticed to John White 1 September 1720 on payment of £8.8s. Freedom unrecorded. First mark entered as largeworker, in partnership with Bennett Bradshaw, 21 March 1737. Address: at the Golden Ball, Oxford Chapel, Cavendish Square. 'Free Goldsmiths'. Second mark together, 2 July 1739. Address: Oxford Chapel. Third mark alone, 10 May 1742. Address: Angel Court, Strand. Moved to Wytch Street, 11 October 1752. Heal records the partnership as silversmiths, Golden Ball, Oxford Chapel (Chapel Court, Henrietta Street, Marylebone), 1737–9; and Tyrril alone as goldsmith, Angel Court, Strand, 1742–57. Oxford Chapel is now St. Peter's, Vere Street, originally a proprietary chapel of the Earl of Oxford and Mortimer.

U

UNDERWOOD, A. (3479) There is no evidence for the existence of this maker other than the attribution attached to the mark in question by Jackson. John Underwood, goldworker, Noble Street, appears in the Parl. Report list 1773, and was elected to the livery, January 1751. The probability would appear to be that of a mis-read mark of some other maker.

UNDERWOOD, Nathaniel (2104, 2981) Son of John Underwood late Citizen and Silk Stocking Framework Knitter of London deceased, apprenticed to Thomas Adams 21 November 1679. Free, 1 March 1688. First mark entered as smallworker, 12 January 1701. Address: Shadwell. Second (Sterling) mark, 19 December 1722. Address: Horshell (?Horseshoe) Alley, Moorfields. Livery, October 1721, and resigned May 1740. Heal records only ——Underwood, goldsmith, Three Flower-de-Luces, Holborn, 1701-2, who might possibly be identical; and ——Underwood, jeweller, facing the terrace in St. James's Street, 1750, who is probably the John Underwood mentioned above.

URQUHART, Duncan (510, 3849) No record of apprenticeship or freedom. First mark entered as bucklemaker, in partnership with Napthali Hart (q.v.), 18 October 1791. Address: Clerkenwell Green. Second mark, 20 May 1795. Third mark (two sizes), 19 January 1802. Fourth mark as plateworkers (two sizes), 22 August 1805. Address: New Christopher Street, Finsbury Square. Heal records the firm as goldsmiths, London, 1791-1805. Apart from buckles their principal output seems to have been tea-services of standard design.

URQUHART, Robert (2451) No record of apprenticeship or freedom. Only mark entered as smallworker, 10 February 1801. Address: Little Britain. Moved to 179 Strand, 10 August 1805.

V

VAEN, John (627, 3850-1) John Vain (signs thus) son of Charles late of Tredennock in the County of Monmouth yeoman deceased, apprenticed to Benjamin Watts 27 July 1706 and turned over to Timothy Ley. Free, 7 July 1714. Mark entered as largeworker, in partnership with William England, 22 July 1714. Address: Bow Lane. Heal records this date and address. Although it is tempting to ascribe the otherwise unattributed marks nos. 3850-1 to Vaen, it seems impossible to do so unless the apprenticeship was a mere late formality to obtain freedom. Otherwise these interesting marks remain without any putative owner.

VALE, James (1857) No record of apprenticeship or freedom. Only mark entered as gold and silverworker, 30 January 1836. Address: 7 Bennett Street, Charlotte Street, Fitzroy Square.

VARDON, Samuel (2650) No record of apprenticeship or freedom. Only mark entered as smallworker, in partnership with Thomas Vardon, 13 December 1775. Address: 39 Frith Street, Soho. Moved to 23 Soho Square, 21 February 1789. Heal records them as goldsmiths, 29 Frith Street, Soho, 1779-93; and in unpublished addenda, 144 Tottenham Court Road, 1798.

VARDON, Thomas (2650) See above.

VENN, Thomas (2955) No record of apprenticeship or freedom. Only mark entered as smallworker, 26 March 1764. Address: Lepherds Court, Baldwin Garden, Leather Lane. Appears as watchcasemaker, Leopard's Court, Baldwin's Gardens, in the Parl. Report list 1773, and entered an incuse mark as such, 26 October 1774, at this latter address (Section V), and moved to 18 Clerkenwell Green, 10 February 1778.

VERDIER, Francis (729) No record of apprenticeship or freedom. Only mark entered as smallworker, 6 December 1730. Address: Long Court, Leicester Fields.

*VERE, John Henry (1417, 3562, 3908) John Vere son of Samuel late of the City of Coventry silkman deceased, apprenticed to James Watkins 3 January 1745 on payment of £80. Free, 7 February 1753. Livery, July 1763. Court, 1777. Apparently in partnership with Edward Aldridge Junior, 1763-5, the mark so attributed presumably entered in the missing register. Heal records John Henry Vere and William Lutwyche, goldsmiths, Anchor and Dove, Lombard Street, before 1766, and there can be no doubt that the mark 3908 must be ascribed to this partnership, although it seems to overlap the other with Aldridge. Vere's only documented mark is as smallworker, 31 October 1769. Address: 48 Lombard Street. He appears here as goldworker in the Parl. Report list 1773, John Henry Vere of Allhallows, Lombard Street, bachelor, married Mary Andrews of St. Clement, Eastcheap, widow, 3 July 1766 at St. Clement, Eastcheap, when one of the witnesses signed Eliezer Eldridge which suggests a connection with Edward Aldridge. He is curiously styled 'Poulterer' in the apprenticeship to him of George Pierrepont (q.v.) 1764 and was presumably for some reason also free of that Company.

VERLANDER, John (1730, 1732) Son of

Simon Verlander of Colchester in the County of Essex, apprenticed to John Gammond 13 August 1727 on payment of £10. Free, 4 March 1735. First mark entered as largeworker, 9 August 1739. Address: 'Harty Chock' (?Artichoke) Court, White Cross Street. 'Free Goldsmith'. Second mark, on move to Brick Lane, Old Street, 15 April 1747. Heal records him as silversmith, Artichoke Court, Whitecross Street, 1739; insolvent 1743. He appears however as plateworker, Brick Lane, in the Parl. Report list 1773, so presumably recovered from his embarrassments.

VERNON, George (917) Free of the Joyners' Company, apparently before 1725 and not traceable. Only mark entered as smallworker, 19 July 1728. Address: Hemings Row. 'Free Joyners Company'.

VICARIDGE, Thomas (2982) Free of the Cutlers' Company by apprenticeship to Joseph Jones 2 April 1682. Mark entered as smallworker, undated, probably April 1697 on commencement of register and at latest before 1700. Address: New Street. 'Free Cutler and hiltmaker'. John Carman (q.v.) was apprenticed to him in the Cutlers' Company, 19 April 1716. His mark has been identified on a fine swordhilt of the Queen Anne period.

VICKERMAN, John (1731) Son of John Vickerman of Maiden Lane Wood Street carpenter, Citizen and Carpenter, apprenticed to Nathaniel Appleton Goldsmith 6 August 1777. Free, 6 October 1784. One of the same name entered a mark as smallworker, 20 May 1768. Address: Bridgewater Gardens, where he appears without category in the Parl. Report list 1773. Whether there is any connection or identity here it seems impossible to say.

VIDEAU, Aymé (106-7) The name first appears in the Denization List of 1681 for one Peter Videau and reappears for the same in 1687. Ayme Vedeau son of John Vedeau of the parish of St. Martin's in the Fields gentleman, apprenticed to David Willaume 3 May 1723 on payment of £20. Free, 8 January 1733/?4, and 'de novo', 5 August 1742. Livery, September 1746. The entry for his first mark as largeworker is missing, as are others of initial 'V', but it was entered presumably about the time of his freedom. The entry in Jackson for 1726 may possibly be explained by a not uncommon accident of reading the date-letter 'T' upside down as 'L', if poorly struck on the piece from which the impression was taken. Second mark, 18 June 1739. Address: Green Street, Leicester Fields, where Heal records him as plateworker, 1739-73. He appears misspelt as Ayrne Vedeau, plateworker, Green Street, in the Parl. Report list 1773, but his mark never seems to be found at this late date and he may perhaps have become retailer only or partly retired with others taking charge. Listed as Huguenot by Evans who records that he made the baptismal bowl of the Hamburg Lutheran Church, Dalston (*Hug. Soc. Proc.*, 14, p. 553). He appears as godfather to Aume Foquelin at Hungerford Market Church, 18 October 1730. The majority of his output seems to have been hollow-ware, coffee-pots, tea-caddies etc., of high quality and, from the mid-thirties, with particularly graceful flat chasing.

*VINCENT, Edmund (3561) Son of Arthur Vincent of the parish of St. Brides baker, apprenticed to Edward Feline 6 July 1750 on payment of £20. Free, 2 November 1763. The mark attributed to him here must have been entered in the missing register of 1758-73, since it has been found on pieces from 1765-70. He appears in the Parl. Report list 1773 as plateworker, King's Arms Court, Ludgate Hill. Heal also records him as plateworker, St. Ann's, Soho, 1768. There is no other recorded name at this date which matches these initials.

*VINCENT, Edward (648-9, 2983, 3560, 3852) The name occurs three times in the apprenticeship register at dates which might apply to the maker of this name who is only identifiable by the entry of a mark in 1739, since there is no page for the letter V in the first largeworkers' register. The most likely apprentice, to judge from a comparison of signature, the status of his master and the subsequent quality of his work, is Edward son of William Vincent of Hendon parish in the County of Middlesex yeoman, apprenticed to Robert Cooper 20 December 1699. Free, 23 July 1712. The first two marks now attributed to him, first Britannia Standard mark, and second Sterling mark, c. 1720, are not to be found in the first largeworkers' register (the page for V presumably having fallen out in the past). Third mark entered as largeworker, 25 June 1739. Address: Dean Street, Fetter Lane. Heal records him as goldsmith, London,

VINCENT

1713; and Strand, 1716; bankrupt 1722; also Dean Street, 1739, as above; bankrupt again 1743. Owing to the existence of two other apprentices of the same name and period, however, some of these entries may refer to another. Edward Vincent signs the 1716 petition against foreign workmen as journeyman in a hand quite different from that of the 1739 mark entry, which appears to match that of an apprentice entered in 1711 and not free till 1719. The maker of the recorded marks is of considerable rank producing high quality hollow-ware, coffee-pots, cups and salvers. His masterpiece is with little doubt the superb oblong salver of 1729 of the Middle Temple of which Lamerie would not have been ashamed.

VINCENT, Henry (1086) No record of apprenticeship or freedom. Only mark entered as smallworker, 22 August 1783. Address: 117 Swallow Street, St. James'.

VINCENT, John (1729) Free of the Clockmakers' Company (?). Only mark entered as smallworker, undated, c. 1730. Address: Angle Court on Snowhill. 'Free Clockmaker'. 'Knife handle maker'. One wonders if in fact 'Free Clockmaker' is an aberration by the clerk for 'Free Cutler' in view of his specialization and the location on Snowhill where so many of the cutlers were situated.

VINCENT, Philip (2240) Son of Clement Vincent of Lambeth in the County of Surrey gentleman, apprenticed to Philip Roker 23 October 1723 on payment of £15. Freedom unrecorded. Mark entered as largeworker, 29 November 1757. Address: Little Earl Street, Seven Dials, where Heal records him from this date till 1764. He appears here also in the Parl. Report list 1773, without category.

*VINCENT, William (3357) There are three possible apprentice candidates for identification with this maker: (1) Son of William Vincent of Aylesworth (?Halesworth) in the County of Suffolk glazier, apprenticed to Isaac Duke 10 January 1750 on payment of £30. Free 6 July 1757. (2) Son of William Vincent of Whitechapel buttonmaker, apprenticed to Peter Culver 2 October 1754 on payment of £20. Free 5 May 1762. (3) William Warren Vincent son of William late of Chatham in the County of Kent gentleman deceased, apprenticed to Spencer Burgis Citizen and Goldsmith 2 May 1764 on payment of £30. Freedom unrecorded. Of these possible candidates (1) seems the most likely. The mark of this maker is missing from the registers, presumably entered in the missing one after 1758, but it is frequently met with on teapots and caddies of good quality in the decades of the '70s and '80s. He appears as plateworker, St. Ann's Lane, in the Parl. Report list 1773, and Heal records him as plateworker, 8 St. Ann's Lane, Wood Street, 1766–93.

*VONHAM, Frederick (730, 3578) No record of apprenticeship or freedom. Mark entered as largeworker, 22 December 1752. Address: George Street, York Buildings. The second mark attributed to him can scarcely belong to any other. Heal records him as silversmith, Eagle Street, Strand, 1751; George Street, 1752; and York Buildings, Strand, 1773. He appears as plateworker, George Street, York Buildings, in the Parl. Report list 1773.

W

WADE, Frederick (735) No record of apprenticeship or freedom. Only mark entered as smallworker, 12 July 1820. Address: 77 Great Guilford Street, Southwark. Moved to 48 John Street, Blackfriars Road, 5 March 1821. Moved to 7 John Street, 4 April 1823. Moved to 10 John Street, 1 August 1827.

WADE, Thomas (2970) No record of apprenticeship or freedom. First mark entered as smallworker, 21 May 1808. Address: Brunswick Row, Queen Square. Moved to Hemings Row, St. Martin's Lane, 20 July 1810. Second mark, 15 March 1814. Third mark, 8 December 1821.

WAKEFIELD, John (1749) Son of James Wakefield late of Goswell Street broker deceased, apprenticed to Thomas Brough of Aldersgate Street as goldsmith 1 August 1798 on payment of £30. Free, 1 October 1806. First mark entered as smallworker, 12 February 1806. Address: 45 Goswell Street.

Second mark, 22 August 1806. Moved to 2 King Street, Goswell Street, and third mark, 21 March 1818. Fourth mark, 15 May 1818.

*WAKELIN, Edward (656, 1602, 3757) Son of Edward Wakelin late of Uttoxeter in the County of Stafford baker deceased, apprenticed to John Le Sage 3 June 1730 on payment of £21. Free, 7 September 1748. By 2 November 1747 he had joined George Wickes (q.v.) at Panton Street, since the latter's ledger (Garrard MSS, Victoria and Albert Museum Library) under that date shows the transfer of 'a Moiety of the Stock in Trade' of Wickes to Wakelin. First mark (modelled on that of Wickes and differing only in the initial letter of the Christian name, and that in 'black letter' capital nearly indistinguishable) entered as largeworker, 17 November 1747 (two sizes). Address: 'Panton Street near ye Haymarket'. It is doubtful if, after this date, any plate is found with Wickes' mark and it is obvious that Wakelin took virtual charge, at least of the silversmith's side of the business, from then. The ledgers from 1747 to 1760 contain stock-taking balances each year of the partnership showing first Wickes', and then from 1750 Wickes' and Netherton's (for whom see Wickes) indebtedness in stock to the partnership and, to their credit, their outgoings. The lease of the house was assigned, presumably to Wakelin (but this is not actually stated), on 2 April 1748 for £400, and the annual rent was £40.0s.10d. No jewellery appears in the annual valuation of stock and it seems that this was no concern of Wakelin's, presumably being in the hands of Netherton. Second mark, in partnership with John Parker I (q.v.), sometime after 1758 and therefore in the missing register. Parker's initials placed above Wakelin's suggest that he became senior partner, and since he had been apprenticed to Wickes rather than Wakelin, this may be so. At any rate, by 14 December 1761 the firm is self-styled Parker and Wakelin in a reference in the ledger of the time to their own day-book. The partnership appears to have lasted till 1777, when the next one of John Wakelin, Edward's son, and William Taylor begins (q.v.). Heal records Wakelin alone as goldsmith, Panton Street, 1747-66; and Parker and Wakelin (successors to Wickes and Netherton), (King's Arms), Panton Street, near St. James', Haymarket, 1759-77. His obituary notice read: 'At Mitcham Surrey Mr Edw. Wakelin formerly a goldsmith in Panton Street. Died, 7 Feb. 1784' (*The Gentleman's Magazine*, page 152). The following September Samuel Netherton, presumably as Wakelin's executor, is recorded as paying a legacy of £20 to J. Wakelin. How practical a craftsman Wakelin was is somewhat difficult to assess. That he had drive and business building qualities is apparent by the growth and continuity of this famous establishment. The setting up of the Crespel business must have been his idea, and he it is who must have taken the orders of half the nobility of England to enlarge their plate-closets on marriage to an heiress or elevation to higher rank. There would seem little doubt that once Lamerie was dead in 1751, the centre of production for fine work was divided between Panton Street and Thomas Heming's establishment. The best productions of Parker and Wakelin of the '60s and '70s show considerable awareness of French taste and technique and it would be extremely interesting to know the personnel, other than the Crespels (q.v.), in the workshops behind the façade of the 'King's Arms' during that time.

WAKELIN, John (1760, 1764) Son of Edward Wakelin (above) of Panton Street in the County of Middlesex goldsmith, apprenticed to his father 5 March 1766. Free, 6 January 1779. First mark entered as plateworker, in partnership with William Taylor (q.v.), 25 September 1776. Address: Panton Street. Second mark with the same, 9 May 1777. Third mark, in partnership with Robert Garrard I (q.v.), 20 October 1792. Heal records the first partnership as successors to Parker and Wakelin, goldsmiths, Panton Street, 1776-96; and Wakelin and Garrard as the same, 1792-1805. John Wakelin appears in the Jewel Office accounts in 1797 as Goldsmith and Jeweller to the King for a few items only (Major General H. W. D. Sitwell, 'The Jewel Office and the Royal Goldsmiths', *Arch. Journ.*, CXVII, page 153). It is interesting to see that whereas Edward Wakelin's position in the previous partnership with Parker seems second, his son, from the leading position of his initials in the mark, and the styling of the firm, returned to the senior position of the partnership. It seems probable that at this time the competition of Jeffreys, Jones and Gilbert (q.v.) must have been considerable, but as virtually no plate bears their mark, and must have been supplied by others such as Smith and Sharp and Scofield, it is difficult to judge where the commissions largely went.

WALBANCKE, William (3356) No record of apprenticeship or freedom. First mark entered as smallworker in partnership with William Turton, 8 April 1784. Address: 18 Little Britain. Second mark with the same, 26 June 1788, on move to 8 Fore Street. The partnership apparently dissolved by 6 March 1791, when Turton entered a further mark alone. Three sons of Walbancke were apprenticed to members of the Goldsmiths' Company between 1795 and 1823.

WALDGRAVE, Charles (425) No record of apprenticeship or freedom. Only mark entered as bucklemaker, 21 January 1736. Address: Four Dove Court, St. Martin's Le Grand.

*WALKER, Bowyer (253) No record of apprenticeship or freedom. Only mark entered as largeworker, 10 April 1735. Address: 'near the two pumps in St. Thomas's Southwark'. Heal records this date and address only, as plateworker.

WALKER, Robert (2457) No record of apprenticeship or freedom. Only mark entered as smallworker, 9 September 1731. Address: 'at the Crown and Two Watchchains in Hoxton Market Place'.

*WALKER, Thomas (2968) No record of apprenticeship or freedom. First mark (incuse), in partnership with James Styring, 30 July 1800. Address: 15 Dorrington Street, Cold Bath Fields (Section V). Second mark (incuse) alone, 1 September 1800. Third mark as smallworker, 20 October 1800. Address: 10 Rolles Buildings, Fetter Lane. Fourth mark (incuse), 17 October 1810. Address: 6 Lamb Passage, Chiswell Street.

WALL, John (1745, 2737) Son of Charles Wall Citizen and Haberdasher of London, apprenticed to John Stamper 1 October 1760. Free, 5 July 1769. First mark entered as plateworker, in partnership with Thomas Daniel, 13 June 1781. Address: Foster Lane. The partnership apparently dissolved by 8 October 1782, when Daniel entered a separate mark. Wall's second mark as plateworker, 7 January 1783. Address: 24 Wood Street, Cheapside. (His name is mispelt by the clerk 'Whall' but signed by Wall normally.) Heal records the partnership for its brief spell, and Wall alone as silversmith, 24 Wood Street, 1783–93. Mary Wall, who entered an incuse mark as bucklemaker, 1792 (Section V), may perhaps be connected.

WALL, Thomas (2995) Son of Joseph Wall of Wilton in the County of Wiltshire clerk apprenticed to William Gamble 10 September 1700. Free, 28 April 1708. Mark entered as largeworker, 25 September 1708. Address: Ball Alley, Lombard Street. Heal records him as plateworker, Lombard Street, 1708; and London, 1739. The latter date seems open to some doubt.

WALLIS, Robert (2462) No record of apprenticeship or freedom. First mark entered as spoonmaker, 28 November 1836. Address: 11 Queen Street, Pitfield Street, Hoxton Market. Second mark, 19 December 1836. Moved to 6 President Street, East King Square, 16 November 1841. Third mark, 15 March 1843. Fourth, 22 October 1845. Fifth, 6 October 1849.

*WALLIS, Thomas I (2962) Son of John Wallis of the City of Coventry butcher, apprenticed to William Jones 7 June 1749 on payment of £26.5s. Free, 1 December 1756. First mark (two sizes) entered as largeworker, 8 March 1758. Address: Little Britain. Second mark (two sizes), 22 January 1763, same address. Moved to Aldersgate Street, 13 September 1764, where Heal records him in 1765. Livery, December 1771. By October 1771, when Thomas Wallis II (below) was apprenticed to him, he was in Monkwell Street, where he appears as plateworker in the Parl. Report list 1773. He died about 1818–22.

*WALLIS, Thomas II (2963, 2975, 2978) Son of Billers Wallis late of Shadwell in the County of Middlesex victualler deceased, apprenticed to Thomas Wallis of Monkwell Street goldsmith (above) 2 October 1771. Free, 3 February 1779. First mark entered as plateworker, 7 November 1778. Address: Monkwell Street. Four marks as bucklemaker, 6 January 1780 to 26 June 1789. Address: 54 Red Lion Street, Clerkenwell (Section VIII). Livery, April 1791. Sixth mark as plateworker (two sizes), 15 September 1792, same address. Seventh mark (six punches), 16 August 1796. Eighth mark (six punches), 14 September 1801. Ninth mark (two sizes), in partnership with Jonathan Hayne as plateworkers, 22 February 1810. Address: 16 Red Lion Street. Tenth mark (three sizes), 3 December 1817. Eleventh mark, 17 February 1820. Partnership dissolved by 3 July 1821, when Hayne entered a separate mark. Francis Mayor, apprenticed to Wallis in 1816, was turned over to Hayne 3 October 1821, which also suggests the retirement of Wallis. He died 10 June 1836.

WALPOLE, Henry (1088) No record of apprenticeship or freedom. Only mark entered as smallworker, 26 February 1765. Address: near the Kings Road, Gray's Inn Lane. Appears in the Parl. Report list as watchcasemaker, at this address, 1773. Heal records him as goldsmith, London, 1773.

WALSH, White (2985) Son of Thomas Walsh of Oakford Fitzpain in the County of Dorset gentleman, apprenticed to Richard Sing 19 June 1691. Free, 11 November 1698. Mark entered as largeworker, 25 November 1698, no address. Heal records him as Walter Walsh, goldsmith, London, 1698–1702. His Christian name, however is clearly White in both apprenticeship and mark registers.

WALTERS, William (2996) Son of Thomas Walters of Putnam in the County of Buckingham taylor, apprenticed to Edward Hitchcock of the Merchant Taylors' Company 8 January 1697 and free of that company by service to Mary widow of Edward Hitchcock 6 November 1717. Only mark entered as smallworker, 5 March 1716. Address: Market Lane, near St. James' Market. 'Free Merchant Taylor'. The name is spelt Waters in the first apprenticeship entry, Walters in the freedom entry and might be Watters in the mark entry. In none of these forms is he identifiable in Heal.

WALTHER, Herman James (1020) No record of apprenticeship or freedom. The name suggests a German origin. Only mark entered as smallworker, 2 April 1770. Address: 8 Spawfields(?), Clerkenwell, where he appears as goldworker in the Parl. Report list 1773.

WARD, Joseph (2989, 3856) Son of Aron Ward late of Eckenton(?) in the County of Worcester shoemaker deceased, apprenticed to Joseph Slicer 4 October 1672. Free, 4 January 1689. First mark entered as largeworker, undated, probably April 1697 on commencement of register. Signatory to the petition against the work of 'aliens or forreigners', 11 August 1697, again to the petition of 1 October 1703 against marking foreigners' work and extending the freedom 'to certain Frenchmen', and as 'working goldsmith' to that complaining of the competition of 'necessitous strangers', 1 December 1711. Livery, April 1705. Court, October 1714. Second mark, 19 September 1717. Address: St. Paul's Churchyard. In 1716 Ward was appointed Assistant Assayer at Goldsmiths' Hall, in spite of which the fine tea-kettle by him belonging to the service of 1719 in the Company's collection is a 'duty-dodger'! Heal records him as plateworker, Water Lane, 1697; Rose and Crown, Cornhill, 1706–8; St. Paul's Churchyard, 1717; Foster Lane (bankrupt), 1723; and Goldsmiths' Hall, 1727–34. He was obviously a colourful character, since in 1722 the Court of the Company passed an order that he was not to be admitted to any further meetings (later rescinded) and there are references to his having made public apologies for having used 'unbecoming langugage'. He resigned from the Court January 1726.

WARD, Michael (2081) No record of apprenticeship or freedom. Only mark entered as largeworker, undated between July 1750 and February 1752. Address: Middle Street, Cloth Fair. Heal records him as plateworker, London, 1720 (curiously early compared with the entry); and Cloth Fair, 1750.

*WARHAM, William I (2993, 3859) Son of Anthony Warham of Windborne (?Wimborne) in the County of Dorset yeoman, apprenticed to Charles Eyston 1 August 1677. Free, 3 November 1703 (a very odd delay). Mark entered as largeworker, 12 November 1703. Address: Shear Lane. Livery, October 1708. Heal records him as plateworker, Golden Cup, Shire Lane, 1698– bankrupt 1722 (also Hilton Price, *Handbook of London Bankers*).

*WARHAM, William II (2994, 3858) Son of Anthony Warham of Lyd in the County of Dorset (? a cousin of William Warham I), apprenticed to John Cuthbert 11 September 1695. Free, 5 July 1704. Mark entered as William Warham Junior, as largeworker, 7 April 1705. Address: Chancery Lane. Heal records him as plateworker, Chancery Lane, 1705–27; Star over against the Black Spread Eagle in Chancery Lane, 1708–12; near King's Head Tavern, Chancery Lane, 1711; and By the pump Chancery Lane, 1715. (The vagaries of eighteenth century addresses are thus clearly illustrated.) Hilton Price (*Handbook of London Bankers*) records Warham, advertising for a lost lottery order, as in Chancery Lane, 1721.

WARNER, John George (1351) No record of apprenticeship or freedom. First mark entered as smallworker, 3 June 1819. Address: 152 Drury Lane. Second mark as goldworker, in partnership with Robert Latham, 23 March 1830. Address: 17 Denmark Street (Section VII, RL & IW).

WARREN, John (1747) No record of apprenticeship or freedom. Only mark entered as smallworker, 19 December 1788. Address: 20 Strand.

WARTER, Richard (2988) Son of John Warter late Citizen and Goldsmith of London deceased, apprenticed to Benjamin Braford 30 March 1686. Free, 1 May 1696. Mark entered as smallworker, undated, probably April 1697 on commencement of register. Address: Barbican. Livery, October 1708. Court, 1732. Warden, 1745, 1747. Died November 1747 (*London Magazine*, p. 532). Heal records him as silversmith, Golden Lion, Holborn Bridge, 1708; died in 1747. Alxo Hilton Price, *Handbook of London Bankers*.

*WASTELL, Samuel (2990-1, 3801) Son of Henry Wastell of (?) in the County of Norfolk clerk, apprenticed to Benjamin Braford 8 August 1694 and turned over to John Fawdery 11 December 1699. Free, 10 October 1701. Mark entered as largeworker, 20 October 1701. Address: Finch Lane. Heal records him here as plateworker, same date; and Mitre, Leadenhall Street, 1705-8.

WATERHOUSE, Thomas (2992) Son of Mathew Waterhouse of Neatherstreetelington (sic) in the County of York yeoman, apprenticed to Henry Lee 21 December 1680. Free, 29 June 1688. Mark entered as largeworker, 22 July 1702. Address: Silver Street. Heal records him as goldsmith, at this address and date.

WATERS, James (1743-4) Presumably son of Charles Waters late of the parish of St. Clement Danes yeoman deceased, apprenticed to James Stone 7 January 1730. Free, 24 March 1737. Livery, March 1758. First mark entered as smallworker, 24 May 1769. Address: Foster Lane. Moved to Ludgate Street, 4 July 1772. Second mark, 11 July 1775. Address: 4 Cornhill. Heal records him only as goldsmith, Foster Lane, 1770-3, but the Parl. Report list 1773 confirms the mark register by showing him as smallworker, Ludgate Street. Died before 1796.

WATERS, Robert (2460) No record of apprenticeship or freedom. Only mark entered as smallworker, 29 July 1800. Address: 4 Bishops Court, Clerkenwell Green.

WATERS, William *See* WALTERS.

WATKINS, William (518, 2739, 3374, 3857, 3910) Son of John Watkins of Warbleton in the County of Sussex farmer, apprenticed to Ebenezer Coker 14 April 1747. Free, 12 June 1754. First mark entered as largeworker, 9 February 1756. Address: Paternoster Row. In the same entry, and presumably the same date, second mark, in partnership with Thomas Devonshire. Third mark together, 10 March 1756. Fourth, 24 June 1766. Heal records him alone as plateworker, Paternoster Row, 1756-73(?); and with Devonshire, at same address, 1756. Watkins does not appear in the Parl. Report list 1773. He had been elected to the Livery June 1763, but resigned 11 July 1765, presumably through ill health or poverty.

WATSON, Thomas (2967) Certain identification in apprenticeship register difficult due to several possible entries, but perhaps son of Thomas Watson late Citizen and Innholder deceased, apprenticed to Simon Gordon 4 October 1758 on payment of £80. Free, 3 December 1766. Only mark entered as plateworker, 1 January 1784. Address: 23 Aldersgate Street. Heal records William Cox and Thomas Watson as goldsmiths and jewellers, 23 Aldersgate Street, 1777; partnership dissolved 1784; and Watson alone at the same address, 1784-96. It is clear therefore that he did not enter a mark until running the business on his own. One of this name elected to Livery, November 1776, and Court, February 1787.

*WATTS, Benjamin (251, 2984) Son of Benjamin Watts of Barnshall in the County of York gentleman, apprenticed to Walter Bradley 3 August 1691. Free, 11 November 1698. First mark entered as largeworker, 21 November 1698. Address: Carey Lane. Livery, April 1705. Signatory as 'working goldsmith' to the petition complaining of the competition of 'necessitous strangers', December 1711. Second mark (Sterling), 7 September 1720. Address: 'at the Golden snale in Fleet Street'. Heal records him as plateworker, Carey Lane, 1698; Golden

Snail, Fleet Street, 1720-1; and Fleet Street, 1724-7. From the survival of his marks he seems to have been principally a spoonmaker.

WATTS, Charles (429) No record of apprenticeship or freedom. First mark, incuse entered as smallworker, 20 September 1783. Address: 16 Wheeler Street, Spitalfields (Section V). Second mark entered as smallworker, 5 January 1788, same address. Third mark, 28 November 1799. Fourth mark, 3 August 1808. Fifth 31 December 1813, same address.

WATTS, Richard (2453-4, 2986-7, 3788) Son of William Watts Citizen and Lorimer of London, apprenticed to Christopher Canner 8 December 1698. Free, 17 March 1707/?8. First mark entered as largeworker, 10 February 1710. Address: Maiden Lane. Second (Sterling) mark, 24 June 1720. Address: Gutter Lane. Heal records both addresses and dates, the latter till 1723.

WAYSMITH, Francis (734) No record of apprenticeship or freedom. Only mark entered as smallworker, 20 August 1757. Address: King's Arms Court, Ludgate Hill. He appears without category at the same address in the Parl. Report list 1773.

WEAVER, Henry (3091) Son of Henry Weaver of Crew in the County of Cheshire yeoman, apprenticed to John Wright 8 July 1692 and turned over to Samuel Hood. Free, 10 March 1700/?1. Mark entered as smallworker, 10 April 1701. Address: 'at the Golden Acorn in Church Lane over ag^t York house in ye Strand'. In the apprenticeship register the name is spelt 'Weaver', in mark register he signs 'Weever'.

WEAVER, Richard (2458) Son of William Weaver of Nuneaton in the County of Warwick yeoman, apprenticed to James Gatcliffe 1 May 1718 on payment of £25. Free, 13 September 1727. Mark entered as smallworker, 4 May 1738. 'Snuffbox maker'. Address: Addle Hill, near Doctors Commons. 'Free Goldsmith'.

WEBB, George (3597) The name to which Jackson ascribed the mark in question. There appears however to be no record of the entry of the mark either before or after 1837 (its date) to such a maker, nor any record of apprenticeship or freedom of the name.

WEBSTER, Henry (1089) No record of apprenticeship or freedom. Only mark entered as smallworker, 29 December 1837. Address: 21 Bedford Street, Strand.

WEBSTER, Samuel I (2671) Son of William Webster of Portpool Lane in the County of Middlesex porter, apprenticed to John Tatum of Dorset Street Salisbury Square as goldsmith 2 March 1796. Freedom unrecorded. Mark entered as smallworker, in partnership with John Bunn, 7 January 1806. Address: 23 Charles Street, Hatton Garden. The partnership apparently over by 10 May 1806, when Bunn entered a single mark.

WEBSTER, Samuel II (2665) No record of apprenticeship or freedom and no apparent connection with the previous name. Only mark entered as spoonmaker, 28 June 1826. Address: 33 Aylesbury Street, Clerkenwell.

WEIR, George (920, 3098) No record of apprenticeship or freedom. Two marks (Sterling and New Standard) entered as largeworker, 27 July 1727. Address: Hemings Row, St. Martin's Lane. Heal records only this address and date.

WEISS, Frederick Foveaux (681) No record of apprenticeship or freedom. Only mark entered as smallworker, 30 June 1836. Address: 62 Strand.

WELDER, Samuel (2654-5, 3092-3, 3802-3, 3870) Son of Samuel Welder Citizen and Draper of London, apprenticed to Robert Keble 10 July 1707. Free, 4 August 1714. First mark entered as largeworker, 11 August 1714. Address: Gutter Lane. Second mark, 30 September 1717, same address. Third (Sterling) mark, 28 July 1720. Address: 'at ye Oxford City in Gutter Lane Cheapside'. Fourth mark, 1 October 1729. Address: Foster Lane. 'Goldsmith'. Heal records him as plateworker, Oxford City, Gutter Lane, 1714-20; and Foster Lane, 1729-33. The registers of St. Vedast, Foster Lane, record the birth of two sons: 'Samuell ye son of Sam^{ll} Welder by Elizabeth his wife' 26 March 1716, and Thomas 23 September 1717, followed by four daughters from 1719 to 1728 and another at Christchurch, Newgate (incorporating St. Leonard's, Foster Lane), 1732. Welder's chief productions appear to have been casters. His mark no. 2655 is inconviently close in appearance to that of Samuel Wood, also caster-maker, no. 2657.

WELDRING, John (3696-9) No record of apprenticeship or freedom. Appears as plateworker, opposite St. Clement's Church, Strand, in the Parl. Report list 1773, as having entered a mark before that date. Process of elimination leaves him or James Wiburd as candidates for the attribution of these closely similar marks. Heal records him as above; and London, 1790.

WELLES, Samuel Wight (2667) Son of Dabee (sic) Welles Citizen and Leatherseller of London, apprenticed to John Swift 28 September 1730 on payment of £30. Free, 5 July 1739. Mark entered as largeworker, 2 March 1741. Address: Staining Lane. 'removed into Maiden Lane', 7 November 1744. Moved to St. Ann's Lane, 7 April 1755. Heal records him only as plateworker, Staining Lane, 1740; and London, 1750.

WELLS, Daniel (513) No record of apprenticeship or freedom. Only mark entered as smallworker, 23 September 1723. Address: Salisbury Court, Fleet Street. Heal records Daniel and Jane Wells, silversmiths, next door to Rose and Crown, Salisbury Court, Fleet Street, 1725.

WELLS, Francis (3095) Son of Ralph Wells of Watterton (?) in the County of Oxford clerk, apprenticed to Ralph Leventhorp 30 June 1671. Free, 3 July 1678. Only mark entered as smallworker, 19 August 1702. Address: Angel Street. His son Francis was apprenticed to his father, 22 June 1709, and turned over to Thomas Lumpkin, Clockmaker. Free, 6 March 1717.

WELLS, John (3097) Son of Francis Wells (above). Free by patrimony 19 June 1718. Mark entered as smallworker, 29 November 1718. Address: Friday Street. Heal records him as goldsmith, West Smithfield, insolvent, 1730.

WELLS, Thomas (2969) No record of apprenticeship or freedom. Only mark entered as smallworker, 29 August 1806. Address: 22 Well Street, Cripplegate.

WERRITZER, Peter (2242, 3756) No record of apprenticeship or freedom. Only mark entered as largeworker, 23 July 1750. Address: Salisbury Court, Strand. Moved to Denmark Court, Strand, 16 June 175(?4), the last figure blotched. Heal records him as plateworker, London, 1739 (seemingly of doubtful authenticity); and Salisbury Street, 1750-2.

WEST, Benjamin (254-5) Son of William West of Chesham in the County of Buckingham gentleman, apprenticed to James Smith as plateworker 6 September 1725 on payment of £20. Free, 10 May 1733. First mark entered as largeworker, 14 January 1738. Address: Carey Lane. 'Free of Goldsmiths Company'. Second mark, 8 June 1739. Address: Foster Lane. Heal records him as plateworker, Carey Lane, 1737; and Foster Lane, 1739-46. Benjamin, son of Benjamin and Margaret West, was born and baptized 28 December 1738 and buried 11 January 1739 (Register, Christchurch, Newgate, incorporating St. Leonard, Foster Lane). Benjamin, son of above, was born 25 November, baptized 3 December 1739, and Sarah, daughter of same, was born 27 November baptized 9 December 1741.

WEST, James (1742) Son of James West of the City of Chichester glover, apprenticed to Richard Gosling 1 July 1731 on payment of £50. Free, 5 September 1738. Mark entered as largeworker, 29 June 1739. Address: 'at the Blackmoor's Head, Foster Lane'. 'Goldsmith'. Heal records him here as plateworker, 1734-9, the former date somewhat doubtful in view of his apprenticeship dates.

WEST, Mathew (3094) Son of William West late of Cossum (?Corsham) in the County of Wiltshire cooper deceased, apprenticed to John Spackman 26 October 1682. Free, 6 December 1689. Only mark entered as largeworker, undated, probably April 1697 on commencement of register. Address: Foster Lane. Livery, April 1705. Heal records him as plateworker, London, 1673 (presumably an earlier goldsmith of the same name); Foster Lane, 1697-1707; goldsmith, Seven Stars, Clare Street, Clare Market, 1697-1731; and Seven Stars, over against Sun tavern, Old Bailey, 1731-5. There seems a possibility of a separate identity for the last two addresses. F. G. Hilton Price (*Handbook of London Bankers*) records West as having advertised in the *Flying Post* of 1713 that he had purchased a number of lottery tickets which he wished to dispose of. Another notice in the *London Journal*, 19 May 1722 runs: 'MATTHEW WEST, Goldsmith at the Seven Stars in Clare street, Clare Market, gives Notice that he is impowered by the Director of the Lottery set forth by the States of Groningen in Holland, to dispose of 10000 Tickets, viz. from No. 16001 to 26000 inclusive, it being the most advantagious that hath been set on Foot, consisting of 25000 Tickets being Prizes, and 7000 Premiums which are given in gratis. This Lottery is divided into 10 Classes, the Subscribers only paying 5s. in the 1st Class, 10s. for the 2d., 15s. for the 3d, £1 for the 4th, and £1.5s. for the 5th Class. Credit is given by the States for the other 5 Classes; and may gain by one Ticket from £1000 to £9000 upwards, as may be seen by the Scheme at large, given Gratis at my house aforesaid or at my Office's at North's Coffee house in Exchange Alley; likewise at Mr Isaac Barbutt's Merchant, at the Blue Ball in Great St. Hellen, Bishopsgate street, who is impowered by the Director to dispose of the like Number, viz. from 38001 to 48000 inclusive.' West's scheme was apparently an attempt to get round the law suppressing lotteries which had been passed in 1689, and his ingenuity 'sparked off' a new crop of complicated lottery schemes run by City sharks. In consequence the fine for defying the law was raised to £600. It was not till 1736 that an Act was passed legalizing draws to raise funds for Westminster Bridge' (Alan Hess, *Illustrated London News*. 6 April 1968).

WEST, William (3372, 3909) Son of Richard West of the parish of Ware in the County of Somerset Doctor of Laws deceased, apprenticed to William Wildboar 4 March 1725 on payment of £42. Freedom unrecorded. Mark entered as largeworker, 8 August 1738. Address: Longs Court, near Leicester fields. 'Goldsmith'. Heal records only this date and address.

WESTON, Charles (430) Son of William Weston of Islington silversmith (who appears as spoonmaker, Silver Street, Wood Street, in the Parl. Report list 1773, but for whom no mark is recorded or can be conjectured), apprenticed to George Day of Vinegar Yard St. John's Lane Clerkenwell as silver spoonmaker 6 April 1814 on payment of £10 by the Worshipful Company of Goldsmiths of the gifts of John Smith and Francis Ash deceased. Freedom unrecorded. Mark entered as spoonmaker, 13 October 1821. Address: 30 King Street, Islington, where William Weston (below), presumably his brother, had been working from 1810.

WESTON, William (3368-9) Free by patrimony as Goldsmith 7 October 1794, presumably son of William Weston as Charles (above). First mark entered as plateworker, 18 September 1810. Address: 30 King Street, Islington. Second mark as spoonmaker, 5 September 1822, same address.

WETHERED, James (3096) Son of William Wethered of Enfield in the County of Middlesex scrivener, apprenticed to Matthew West 14 August 1701. Free, 14 September 1709, and 'de novo', 18 May 1739. Only mark entered as largeworker, 24 September 1709. Address: 'in Catherin Street in St. Catherin'. Heal records him only at this date, Catherine Street.

WETHERELL, John (3695) Son of John Wetherell of Croft in the County of York yeoman, apprenticed to John Foster 7 February 1754. Freedom unrecorded. His mark, if entered, would presumably have occurred in the period of the missing register, 1758-73. There must, however, be some mistake in Jackson's attribution to him of the above mark in 1751, before his apprenticeship began, and the mystery is increased by Heal's entry of John Wetherell, goldsmith, London, 1739-52.

WHEAT, Samuel (2659, 2668, 3807) Son of William Wheat late Citizen and Turner of London deceased, apprenticed to Henry Bickerton 3 September 1746. Free, 7 April 1756. First mark entered as largeworker, 11 May 1756. Address: Maiden Lane, Wood Street. Second mark, 20 April 1757. Appears as goldworker, Maiden Lane, in the Parl. Report list 1773, and Heal records him as goldsmith, 1756-73. He is presumably the Samuel Wheat, bachelor, married to Ann Chittle of St. Ann, Westminster at St. Lawrence Jewry, 24 October 1756, Wheat being 'of this parish' (i.e. St. Lawrence Jewry).

WHEATCROFT, William (3371) No record of apprenticeship or freedom. Only mark entered as smallworker, 9 February 1831. Address: 18 Berkeley Street, Clerkenwell.

WHEATLEY, Samuel (2664, 2672) Son of James Wheatley of Lombard Street Whitefriars Gold and Silver Wire Drawer and Citizen, apprenticed to Ann Chesterman widow of Fleet Market silversmith 5 February 1777 and turned over 5 April 1780 by Sarah Chesterman executrix of Ann Chesterman to Charles Chesterman of Fleet Market goldsmith, Citizen and Goldsmith. Free, 5 May 1784. First mark entered as plateworker, in partnership with John Evans I, 27 April 1810. Address: 3 Old Street, Goswell Street. Second mark alone as plateworker, 23 August 1811, same address. The interval between the dates of freedom and entry of mark is such that we are possibly dealing with a son of the apprentice although there is no evidence of this from the registers.

WHEELER, Thomas (2960) Son of Thomas Wheeler late of St. Giles in the Fields carpenter, apprenticed to John Wade of the Founders' Company, 4 December 1704. Free, 4 February 1712. Only mark entered as smallworker, 10 January 1723. Address: Lily Pot Lane. 'Free Founder'.

*WHIPHAM, Thomas (2961, 2974, 2976, 2979, 3510, 3847) Son of William Whipham of Layton in the County of Bedford innkeeper, apprenticed to Thomas Farren 3 July 1728 on payment of £25. Free, 7 June 1737. First mark entered as largeworker, 20 June 1737. Address: Foster Lane. 'Goldsmith'. Second mark, 18 June 1739. Third mark, in partnership with William Wiliams I (also apprenticed to Farren in 1731, q.v.), 1 May 1740, same address. 'Goldsmiths'. Livery, September 1746. Court, 1752. Moved to Ave Mary Lane, 23 July 1753. Fourth mark, in partnership with Charles Wright, 24 October 1757, same address. Warden 1765–7, and Prime Warden 1771. Appears alone as goldsmith, Fleet Street, in the Parl. Report list 1773, and was apparently still in business in 1780 when he purchased the church plate of Stoke Bruern, Northants, for £50.12s.8d., the new set having been made by his partner Wright in 1776. Heal records him as working silversmith, Foster Lane, 1737–9; Ave Mary Lane, 1751–6; and Grasshopper, (No. 61) Fleet Street, 1760–84; with William Williams as plateworkers, (Spread eagle), Foster Lane, 1740–6; with Charles Wright as plateworkers, 9 Ave Mary Lane, 1757–75; and Whipham and Williams, goldsmiths, Angel and Crown, in Foster Lane, c. 1760 (unpublished addenda). In 1743 Whipham entered the widow Ann Farren's mark on the death of Thomas Farren (see above) by power of attorney, and it seems probable that he was acting as Farren's executor. Whether he succeeded to the business is not apparent, but at least he did not move to Farren's address. It seems possible that his wife was a Farren, but his marriage has not been traced. Frances, daughter of Thomas and Frances Whipham, born 4, baptized 23 July 1741 at Christchurch, Newgate (incorporating St. Leonard, Foster Lane) is followed by Anne, daughter of the same, born 7, baptized 17 August 1742 at St. Michael le Quern (possibly named after her maternal grandmother, if the latter was indeed Ann Farren), Mary, another daughter 1744, and Thomas 1747 at the same church. Frances Whipham, buried at St. Michael le Quern 19 August 1745, was presumably the eldest daughter. Whipham's obituary appeared in *The Gentleman's Magazine*: 'Mr Whipham senior formerly a silversmith Fleet Street at St. Albans Died 27 Aug. 1785' (page 748). His son Thomas appears to have been his successor, as Heal records Whipham and North, goldsmiths and jewellers, 61 Fleet Street, 1790–1802, but there is no evidence of his entering a separate mark. Thomas junior was free by patrimony, 7 December 1768, Livery 1769, Court 1777, and Prime Warden 1790. He died 1815. Through the nineteenth century and into this one, several generations of the family were freemen of the company.

WHITE, Fuller (731–3, 1316, 3579) Son of Fuller White late of Great Hallenbury(?) in the County of Essex deceased, apprenticed to Edward Feline 8 January 1734 on payment of £30. Free, 5 December 1744. First mark entered as largeworker, 31 December 1744. Address: Golden Ball and Pearl in Noble Street. Second mark in partnership with John Fray, 4 March 1745, same address. The partnership apparently dissolved by 4 January 1748, when Fray entered a separate mark at Foster Lane. White's third mark alone, 9 January 1750/?1. Fourth mark, 5 July 1758. Livery, March 1750. Died 2 July 1775. Heal records him as plateworker, Golden Ball and Pearl, Noble Street, 1742–73; and with John Fray at same address, 1750. He appears alone as plateworker, Noble Street, in the Parl. Report list 1773. His work, mostly hollowware, tankards and coffee-pots, is good but rarely inspired.

*WHITE, John (1735, 1751, 3153, 3882) Son of Christopher White of Wareham in the County of Dorset apothecary, apprenticed to Robert Cooper 8 September 1711 on payment of £32.5s. Free, 3 December 1719. First mark entered as largeworker, 10 December 1719. Address: Corner of Arundel Street, Strand. Second (Sterling) mark, 4 January 1725. Third mark, 26 June 1739. Address: Corner of Green Street, near Leicester Fields. Heal records him as plateworker, Golden Cup, Arundel Street, Strand, 1719–24; goldsmith, London, 1720–33; and plateworker, Green Street, 1739. He also has John White, goldsmith, London,

1772, who may be the same, although nothing with his mark is found as late as this. However one of the name was elected to the Livery March 1758, and Court February 1763. Warden 1778-80, and Prime Warden 1782, dying 9 May 1789. If the latter is identical with the goldsmith above, he must have been about ninety at death. White is a mysterious figure, as his work, somewhat rare, is of high quality and Huguenot character, without there being any apparent connection in his training or parentage with the immigré school. He either was, or employed, a particularly fine engraver who made considerable use of a grinning mask of Hogarthian type in the cartouches enclosing coats-of-arms and in strapwork borders.

*WHITE, Robert (2455) Apprenticed to John Laughton of the Grocers' Company 6 May 1683. Free 1 March 1692, 'Att his M$_a^r$ (master's) in Maiden Lane Wood Street'. Only mark entered as smallworker, 27 May 1723. Address: Bedfordbury Green, against the Black Lion. 'Grocer'. Heal records Robert White, goldsmith, King's Head Court (?), Fetter Lane, 1705 (Fetter apparently a misprint for Gutter, since this name and address appears in the St. Vedast, Foster Lane registers). There does not seem, however, any obvious identity with the above, although there is a long gap between freedom and entry of the only recorded mark.

WHITE, Samuel (3804, 3807-8) Son of James White late of the parish of Nalmanton in the County of York husbandman deceased, apprenticed to John Swift 8 November 1758 on payment of £31.10s. Free, 5 February 1766. Livery, November 1766. Appears as plateworker, Oat Lane, in the Parl. Report list 1773 as having entered a mark prior to that date. Heal records him as such 1773-6. The attribution of any mark to him is unfortunately uncertain owing to the contemporary existence of Samuel Wheat and Samuel Whitford (q.v.), but the latter, described as smallworker or bucklemaker, may perhaps be rejected for the larger pieces on which mark no. 3804 occurs. Samuel White died November 1815.

WHITEHEAD, Thomas (2972) No record of apprenticeship or freedom. Only mark entered as smallworker, 2 January 1822. Address: 115 Dorset Square, Salisbury Square, Fleet Street.

WHITEHOUSE, David (516) No record of apprenticeship or freedom. First mark entered as smallworker, 25 November 1790. Address: Holywell Mount. Second (incuse) mark as smallworker, 11 December 1799. Address: 4 St. John's Street, Clerkenwell, and moved to 2 Sandyard, Turnmill Street, 28 June 1810 (Section V). See also Nathaniel Whitehouse, 1810-25 (Section IV).

WHITFORD, George (2519) No record of apprenticeship or freedom. Only mark entered as plateworker in partnership with Samuel Whitford II (q.v.), 23 July 1802. Address: 15 Denmark Court, Strand. The partnership apparently dissolved by 5 October 1807 on re-entry of Samuel's single mark.

WHITFORD, Samuel I (2661, 3804) No record of apprenticeship or freedom. Only mark entered as smallworker, 27 March 1764. Address: St. Martin's Le Grand. Appears as bucklemaker, at the same address, in the Parl. Report list 1773. Heal records him as goldsmith, London, 1773-90. Thomas Whitford, smallworker, 6 King's Head Court, St. Martin's Le Grand, who entered an incuse mark 1774 (Section V), would seem connected, as also Mary Whitford, as such at the same address, 1778-9, as bucklemaker (Section VIII).

WHITFORD, Samuel II (2519, 2663, 2669-70) No record of apprenticeship or freedom. First mark entered as plateworker, 10 June 1800. Address: 1 Smithfield Bars. Second mark, in partnership with George Whitford (q.v.), 23 July 1802. Address: 15 Denmark Court, Strand. Third mark (two sizes) alone, 5 October 1807, same address. Fourth mark, in partnership with George Pizey, 27 August 1810, same address. Fifth mark alone again (two sizes), 4 May 1812. Address: 25 Grafton Street, Soho. Sixth mark, 17 March 1817. Address: 4 Porter street, Newport Market. Seventh, 7 October 1817. The base of the last entry is minuted 'Died prior to Sept. 1856'.

*WHITING, John James (1757) No record of apprenticeship or freedom. First mark entered as spoonmaker, 7 October 1833. Address: 19 Myrtle Street, Hoxton. Second mark, 30 October 1833. Third, 18 September 1834. Fourth, 10 March 1835. Fifth, 11 May 1840. Sixth, 24 August 1842. Moved to 107 Bunhill Row, 5 July 1845. Seventh mark, 8 May 1846. Eighth, 22 December 1847 (two punches).

*WHITTINGHAM, John (1746) No record

of apprenticeship or freedom. First mark entered as smallworker, 1 February 1788. Address: 13 Staining Lane. Second mark, 13 August 1788.

*WHYTE, David (3525-6) Free by redemption as plateworker 2 October 1765. The mark which can reasonably be attributed to him is found from 1762 and would therefore have been entered in the missing register. He appears in the Parl. Report list 1773 as plateworker, 19 Little Britain. Heal records him as plateworker, Clerkenwell, 1766; and 19 Little Britain, 1766-74; also Whyte and Holmes, working silversmiths, No. 12 Clerkenwell Green, 1770. The mark 3526, which is obviously theirs, is found however on pieces as early as 1763-7. (See also William Holmes.)

WIBURD, James (3696-9) Son of James Wyburd (sic) of the parish of St. Mary Overs in the County of Surrey gentleman, apprenticed to Charles Woodward 10 September 1741 on payment of £26.5s. Appears as plateworker, Tooley Street, in the Parl. Report list 1773 as having entered a mark before that date. Process of elimination leaves him or John Weldring for these closely similar marks. Heal records him as plateworker, at this address, 1766-73.

WICHEHALLIS, John (1737) Free of the Scriveners' Company but no records are available of this company to expand this. Only mark entered as largeworker, undated, between April 1728 and April 1729. Address: 'at Detfort (?Deptford) Bridge Freemon of Scribner Compney'. Heal records him as John Wichhaller or Wichehaller, goldsmith, Deptford, 1728, based presumably on Chaffers' reading of the entry, but I am satisfied that the last two letters of the signature are 'is' or possibly 'es'.

*WICKES, George (918, 921, 927, 3197) Son of James Wickes late of St. Edmondsbury in the County of Suffolk upholsterer deceased, apprenticed to Samuel Wastell 2 December 1712 on payment of £30 (he signs Wicks). Free, 16 June 1720. Two marks (Sterling and New Standard) entered as largeworker, 3 February 1722. Address: Threadneedle Street. Third mark, 30 June 1735. Address: Panton Street, Haymarket. Livery, March 1739/40. Fourth mark, 6 July 1739. Address: 'at the King Arms, Panton Street near the Haymarket'. More, however, is known of his working life than revealed in his mark entries. Heal records him as plateworker, Leadenhall Street, before 1721, when he was presumably still working with Wastell, who was there at least 1705-8 (Heal). By c. 1730 he was in partnership with John Craig (see Ann Craig) at the Corner of Norris Street, Haymarket, almost opposite his final situation. There is no recorded mark for this partnership, but a supporting fact to its existence is the apprenticeship to Wickes in 1731 of David Craig. Heal records the death of John Craig in 1735 or 1736, the former year that in which Wickes entered his Panton Street marks and it is clear from the surviving ledger (Messrs Garrard's) that this is when Wickes began a really independent existence. The Panton Street mark was entered on 30 June and the ledger's first entry is dated the 23rd of the same month. One folio (31) of the ledger is headed 'My House' and under 24 June appears the entry 'To the King's Arms and feathers £14.3.6', providing a *terminus a quo* for Wickes' appointment to Frederick, Prince of Wales, who was later to cause him considerable trouble. Heal records him as King's Arms, Panton Street, two doors from Haymarket, 1735-61; and in partnership with Samuel Netherton as goldsmiths and jewellers, at the same address, 1751, left off business 1759. There is no mark for this partnership and, as will be seen below, it would seem as if Wickes renounced the silversmith's side of the business to Edward Wakelin (q.v.) in 1747 and remained a sleeping partner with Netherton attending to the jewellery side. With the growth of the business by this time, as witnessed by the list of distinguished clients in the ledgers, there must have been of necessity a division of responsibility. The first ledger which runs from 1735 to 1741 contains, among others, accounts for the Dukes of Devonshire and Chandos, Dowager Duchess of Norfolk, Marquess of Caernarvon, Earl Inchiquin and many 'Lords'. In the next volume he added the Dukes of Kingston, Roxburgh, Montrose and Bridgwater, the Earls of Scarborough, Kildare and others, Admiral Vernon and Arthur Onslow, the Speaker. Bishops appear from time to time to add dignity to the list.

The account of Frederick, Prince of Wales commences on 24 March 1735/6 with a tactful gesture, 'To a Black Eboney Handle for a tea kettle and a Button fo a teapot 0s.0d.' The next entries set a more realistic standard: 'May 1. To a fine cup & cover 124oz.17d. £80. To a fine Bread Baskett 87oz.9d. £50'. There are several entries for the hire of plate for parties in November, December, January and August, the last 'To the use of Plate for ye Oxford & Cambridge Entertainment £6.6.0'. Frederick had been living at an extravagant rate and in September 1737 he was banished by George II to cool his heels at Kew and made attempts to retrench. 'The Prince reduced the number of his inferior servants which made many enemies among the lower sort of people and did not save him money. He put off all his horses too that were not absolutely necessary and farmed all his tables, even that of the Princess and himself' (i.e. contracted his catering) (Hervey's *Memoirs*). The blow fell, too, on Wickes who entered in his ledger: 'September 20 To the Damadge and Loss to me in a Large Parcell of Plate Bespoke and ordered by the Prince which was in such forwardedness when countermand(ed) as amounts to more than £500'. Later Wickes allows in credit 'Sold Six Dozen of Plates and twelve Dishes at 6d per oz 2000 oz. £50', obviously the charge for the plate tax, which he seems already to have charged his royal client. Then he cooled off and added 'The Damadge on the other side (i.e. debit account) being Reduced by executing part of the work intended and I have now taken of token of the whole Damadge altho' I have not Recd it any other wise than by the profitt of the work made ... £450', thus writing off the matter. However, by February 1738 he had a new order from the Prince for '18 chased Sconces weighing 426 oz. at 5/11 per oz. £126.1.6 plus £5.5. for making each', and from here the royal account returned to a satisfactory conduct. The most important piece recognizable in the account is the silver-gilt epergne designed by William Kent and still, though added to by Rundell and Bridge, in the Royal Collection: 'Nov. 11.1745 To a silver gilt Epergne, a Table, 4 Saucers, 4 Casters, 8 Branch Lights and Pegs 845 oz.9d. at 15/8 per oz £662.5.4. To Graving the Table 4 Saucers and Casters £23.16.0. To 6 Glass Saucers £3.3.0. To 2 Wainscot Cases £6.10.0.' After the Prince's death Wickes continued to work for his widow and in 1759 a modest account starts for 'Their Royal Highnesses Prince William and Henry', the third and fourth sons of Frederick, then only sixteen and fourteen years old.

The largest of Wickes' productions for one client to have survived intact would seem to be the service of 1745-7 made for James Fitzgerald, Viscount Leinster, subsequently Duke of Leinster, on his marriage to Emilia, daughter of the 2nd Duke of Richmond. This numbers some one hundred and seventy pieces, including an arbor epergne (Collection Walter Chrysler Jr., Parke-Bernet, New York, 1960).

Other outstanding pieces are the ewer and dish of 1735 formerly in the Wertheimer collection (Jackson, *History of English Plate*), a group of gilt dishes made for Frederick, Prince of Wales, 1739 now dispersed (Sterling Clark Institute, Williamstown, Mass., the late Sir Philip Sassoon and others), and a pair of candelabra with nymph and faun figures of 1744 made for the Earl of Kildare (Christie's, 1926).

There is little doubt that from 1735 onwards Wickes' clientele was as large and important as (if not possibly more so than) Lamerie's and the quality of his productions, whoever the executants, in no way inferior to the latter's.

WIDDOWSON, Joseph (1861) Free by redemption as Goldsmith, 7 May 1828. Mark entered as plateworker, 2 January 1829. Address: 100 Fleet Street.

WIGAN, Edward (2516-7) Son of Thomas Wigan of the City of Bristol goldsmith, apprenticed to James Stamp of Cheapside goldsmith 2 December 1772 on payment of £20. Free, 1 March 1786. First mark entered as plateworker, in partnership with Samuel Godbehere (q.v.), 13 September 1786. Address: 86 Cheapside. Second mark (three sizes) with the same, 14 August 1789. Third (three sizes) with the same, 26 July 1792. Fourth mark, in partnership with Godbehere and James Bult (q.v.) as S. Goodbehere and Co., 15 March 1800. He disappears from the partnership by 16 September 1818, when Godbehere and Bult re-entered a new mark without his initials. His son Edward was apprenticed to him 2 December 1800. It should be noted that Bult had also been apprenticed to James Stamp in 1774 so the two partners had been together long before the entry of their joint mark.

WILCOCKE, Henry (1087) Son of Joseph Wilcocks Citizen and Goldsmith of London (below), apprenticed to Maurice Boheme 6 December 1707. Signatory as journeyman to the petition against assaying the work of foreigners not having served seven years apprenticeship, February 1716. Free, 8 March 1715/?16. Only mark entered as smallworker, 5 June 1721. Address: Wood Street. 'Goldsmith'.

WILCOCKE, Joseph (3185) Son of Henry Wilcocks of Kingston in the County of Surrey gentleman, apprenticed to William Wynn 12 December 1679. Free, 5 January 1686. Only mark entered as smallworker, 20 June 1701. Address: Bishopsgate Street.

*WILDBIRD, John (3190) No record of apprenticeship or freedom. Only mark entered as smallworker, 14 September 1715. Address: Little Britain. 'Diamond Cutter' (in another hand at base of entry).

WILDMAN, Thomas (2957) Free of the Blacksmiths' Company. Only mark entered as smallworker, 17 August 1720. Address: 'Parish of St. Pulcher (St. Sepulchre) Snow Hill'. 'of ye Blacksmit Compie'. Heal records him as goldsmith, Black-a-Moor's Head, Cheapside, 1742–62 (unless a son).

WILDMAN, William (3178) Probably father or brother of the above. Free of the Blacksmiths' Company. Signatory as 'working goldsmith' to the petition complaining of the competition of 'necessitous strangers', December 1711. First mark entered as smallworker, 15 April 1712. Address: Sherborne Lane. 'Free Blacksmith'. Second (Sterling) mark, 22 July 1720.

WILFORD, Starling (2652–3, 3191, 3802–3) Son of Starling Wilford of Edmonton in the County of Middlesex victualler, apprenticed to Thomas Allen 28 June 1709. Free, 26 July 1716. First mark entered as largeworker, 17 January 1718. Address: Gutter Lane. Second (Sterling) mark, 30 June 1720. Third mark, 22 April 1729. Address: 'Leven In Sene Pulkes (St. Sepulchre's) parshe ner the old bale' (Bailey). Orthography was not Wilford's strong point! Livery, May 1737. Heal records him as plateworker, Gutter Lane, 1717–29; and as the above illiterate entry for 1729; and London, 1730–7. He appears to have been still active in 1751, when on 8 March of that year Edward Aldridge, son of Charles Aldridge of Cambridge staymaker, was apprenticed to him but turned over the same day to the other Edward Aldridge Citizen and Clothworker.

His mark should be distinguished from the contemporary mark of Samuel Welder.

WILKES See WILKS.

*WILKINS, John (3181) Free of the Cutlers' Company by service to George Scrivener (q.v.) 27 March 1689 (?, the entry torn). Only mark entered as smallworker, undated, c. 1699. Address: Exchange Alley. 'Free Cutler'.

WILKINS, Micah (2082, 3186) Free of the Bakers' Company. First mark entered as smallworker, 16 March 1702. Address: Lothbury. 'Free Baker'. Second (Sterling) mark, 11 June 1720. Address: Foster Lane.

WILKINSON, Thomas (2966) Son of John Wilkinson late Citizen and Mercer of London deceased, apprenticed to John Andrews 6 November 1754. Free, 14 July 1762. First mark entered as smallworker, 7 November 1763. Address: Brick Lane, Old Street. Second mark, 6 June 1767. Address: Pear Tree Street, near Old Street, where he appears as bucklemaker in the Parl. Report list 1773.

WILKS, Denis (515, 519, 521) No record of apprenticeship or freedom. First mark entered as largeworker, 29 September 1737. Address: Henry Street, Old Street. Second mark, 2 July 1739, same address. Moved to Golden Ball, Fore Street, 27 November 1740. Third mark, 30 November 1747, on move to New Street, Old Street. Fourth mark, in partnership with John Fray (q.v.), 19 July 1753. Address: Fore Street. The partnership apparently dissolved by 28 August 1756, when Fray entered a separate mark at another address. Heal records Wilks as plateworker, London, 1728–36; and Old Street, 1737–9; and with John Fray as plateworkers, Fore Street, 1753.

WILKS, James (1734, 1753, 1758, 3198) Either (1) son of Thomas Wilkes of Charterhouse Lane in the County of Middlesex shoemaker, apprenticed to Andrew Archer for eight years 10 October 1711. Free 4 July 1720. Livery March 1736/7. Or (2) son of John Wilkes in the parish of St. Andrew's Holborn gentleman, apprenticed to Thomas Colvill 15 August 1715 on payment of £22. Free, 6 September 1722. There seems no way of establishing which of these clearly differentiated apprentices is to be identified with the above. Two marks (Sterling and New Standard) entered, 31 December 1722. Address: Golden Lane. 'Free Goldsmith'. Second small mark (Sterling), undated, between April 1728 and April 1729. Address: St. Mary Axe. 'Free Goldsmith'. Third mark, 20 June 1739. Address: Fell Court, Fell Street, Wood Street. Fourth mark, 16 July 1742. Moved to Wood Street, 2 October 1747. Heal records him as Wilkes or Wilks, plateworker, at Golden Lane 1722; St. Mary Axe 1728; and Fell Street (Wood Street), 1739. Also James Wilks, goldsmith, Golden Ball, Wood Street, near Cripplegate 1735. There is perhaps a possibility of the entries for 1722 and 1728-9 being in different hands, and in the latter the names is spelt Wilkes as against Wilks in 1722 and 1739. There are, however, common features in all signatures as well as variations, and the point remains obscure.

WILLATS, Thomas (2971) No record of apprenticeship or freedom. Only mark entered as smallworker, 15 July 1809. Address: 8 Fore Street. For Moses Willats, perhaps connected, 1762, see Section IV.

WILLAUME, David I (512, 3192-4, 3859) Son of Adam Willaume goldsmith of Metz on the Pont des Morts and Anne Philippe his wife, born 7 June 1658. He presumably learnt his trade from his father or another Metz goldsmith. His denization appears in State Papers, Car. II, Entry Book 67, under date 16 December 1687, where the name is spelt Williamme (or Villiamme). Heal's reference to him, therefore, as being in London in 1674 is manifestly an error, perhaps deriving from a misattribution of a mark. He does, however, record Willaume at the Windsor Castle, Charing Cross from 1686, by which time he may well have reached London, denization following later. The identity of his pre-1697 mark or marks remains doubtful. He married at the French Chapel of La Patente, Spitalfields 19 October 1690, Marie, daughter of Samuel Mettayer, Minister of that church and sister of Lewis Mettayer (q.v.). Free by order of the Court of Aldermen as David Williams 27 January 1693/?4. Livery, October 1698. Court, February 1724/5. First mark as largeworker, undated, probably April 1697 on commencement of register. Address: 'in the pell-mell'. Second and third marks added to the first entry, 29 January 1719. Address: St. James's Street. Fourth (Sterling) mark, 27 July 1720, same address. Heal records him as David Willaume senior, goldsmith and banker, London, 1674-1712, of which (as shown above) the first date is erroneous; and Windsor Castle, Charing Cross, 1686-90; and Golden Ball, Pall Mall, 1697-1712. Heal gives the St. James Street address only to David Willaume II (q.v.), but it is clear that the father was in St. James' Street by January 1719 where Chaffers states he is recorded as keeping 'running cashes' (i.e. banking); the 1720 entry appears to be in his son's hand, although he was not free till 1723, presumably acting for his father. He is also recorded by Hilton Price (*Handbook of London Bankers*). The children of his marriage were Anne, born 1691, wife of David Tanqueray (both q.v.), David, born 1693 (see below) and Adam and Suzanne born 1694 and 1696, both dead in infancy. Willaume makes frequent appearances in the Huguenot church registers of London as witness or godfather, and it is clear that he was an outstanding member of the community. He first appears as godfather to David Surel at Hungerford Market Church, 5 August 1688, and 'assisted' (? gave away) at the marriage of his sister-in-law Marie Mettayer (bearing curiously the same name as his wife) to Simon Gribelin, the engraver, 1 January 1691 at La Patente, Spitalfields, which (as mentioned above) was the church of which Samuel Mettayer was minister. The entry of his own marriage runs: 'David Willaume marchand orfebure en cette ville, f.d' Adam Willaume, marchand dem^t à Metz et d'Anne Philippe-et Marie Mettyaer ff.de Maître Samuel Mettayer, l'un des ministres de cette eglise et de Susanne Fremin. Led. epoux assisté du Sr Philippe Ostome et du Sr Willaume Crommelin, marchand, dem^{ts} en cette ville; et lad. epose assistée de Samuel Mettayer son père, et Samuel Mettayer, son frère, dem^{ts} aussi en cette ville. Samuel Mettayer, min.' Willaume appears to have retired about 1728 (when David II entered a mark of distinctly different type to that of his father), and purchased the Manor of Tingrith, Bedfordshire in 1730, from which time the family became seated there, intermarrying with the Tanquerays and later being styled Tanqueray-Willaume. (See Wagner, 'Pedigree of the Huguenot Refugee Families of Willaume and Tanqueray-Willaume', *Miscellanea Genealogia et Heraldica*, 4th Series, Vol. III, from which the main genealogical details above are derived.) He died before 22 January 1741 (E. A. Jones, note in MS Catalogue, Chatsworth).

There can be no doubt, on the evidence of his surviving work, that Willaume enjoyed the patronage of the wealthiest clients in England from the latter part of the reign of William III to the end of George I's reign. Among so many outstanding pieces it is difficult to select any pre-eminent masterpiece, when all display the highest qualities of rich design and impeccable execution. The following is a short list of important works:

1698 Pair of wine-coolers. Duke of Devonshire
1699 Ewer and dish. Queen's College, Cambridge
1699 Pair of sconces. Lord Brownlow
1700 Ewer and dish. Duke of Portland
1701 Ewer and dish. Duke of Abercorn
1701 Wine fountain. Duke of Buccleuch
1704 etc. Toilet service. Luton Hoo Collection
1706 Ewer and dish. Fishmongers' Company
1708 Wine-cistern and fountain. Duke of Brunswick
1711 Pair of mounted ivory vases. Wilding Collection, British Museum
1713 Punch-bowl and cover. Trinity Hall, Cambridge
1718 Ewer and dish. Ex Hearst Collection 1938
1725 Toilet service. Ex collection of Viscountess Cowdray
1726 Ewer and dish. Earl Fitzwilliam

WILLAUME, David II (514, 517, 3195) Son of David Willaume I, Citizen and Goldsmith of London, born 5 March 1693 and apprenticed to his father 6 March 1707. While still in his apprenticeship he was sent by his father in 1716 to Metz to claim his inheritance. Free, 2 May 1723 and also recorded as free by patrimony the same date, making his apprenticeship a mere formality. Livery, March 1727/6. Married firstly, 17 April 1721, Marianne, daughter of Samuel Le Fébure (le Fèvre) at the church of Le Carré, then described as 'orfévre, par(oisse) de St. Martin des Champs'. Subsequently married Elizabeth, daughter of Charles Dymoke of Ampthill, Bedfordshire. Settlement dated 23 November 1733. First and second marks (New and Sterling Standards) entered as largeworker, 2 April 1728, on or about the date of his father's retirement. Address: 'in St James Street of St. George Hanover Square'. Third (Sterling) mark, 19 June 1739, entered by Edward Jordens 'by Verteu of a Letter of Eturney'. The phrase 'of St. George Hanover Square' is presumably to indicate his private address. Heal records him from the date of his apprenticeship in 1706 to 1746, of which he gives his address as the Golden Ball, on the terrace in St. James's Street, 1716-20, but this, as has been shown above, must apply to David I, and in any case the son was not free till 1723, though no doubt he may well have been playing an active part in the business by then, since it is clearly his signature in the entry of his father's Sterling mark in 1720. Heal also records him as in St. Martin's in the Fields, 1721, based on the register of his first marriage, which then presumably referred to his residence. He is presumably the —Williams, Subordinate Goldsmith to the King, 1744 and 1746 (Major General H. W. D. Sitwell, 'The Jewel House and the Royal Goldsmiths', *Arch. Journ.*, CXVIII, p. 155). He became High Sheriff of Bedfordshire in 1737. His wife Elizabeth died and was buried at Tingrith, 20 June 1746, and Willaume died 26 January 1761. By his second marriage there were four sons and two daughters. The eldest child Mary married her cousin Rev. Thomas Tanqueray, rector of Tingrith (cf. David Willaume I). The eldest son, Edward, became in due course holder of his brother-in-law's benefice. The Willaumes' belief in family solidarity is clearly apparent. The quality of work bearing David II's mark is not so strongly marked in character as that of his father, and it would seem fairly evident that the business had grown to the extent that he had little to do with the plate bearing his mark, which scarcely shows Huguenot influence, probably being largely executed by native English journeymen. Presumably the banking side of the business continued to flourish and indeed there is little doubt that it was this and not plateworking which formed the foundation of the family fortunes (Wagner, *op. cit.* under David Willaume I, above).

WILLCOCKS, George (919, 3189) Free of the Cutlers' Company. Record of his apprenticeship and freedom not traceable, but he appears as Wilcox as master to Thomas North (q.v.), 1725. First mark entered as smallworker, 2 May 1715. Address: Wine Office Court, Fleet Street. 'Free Cutler'. Second mark (Sterling), 22 June 1720.

WILLIAMS, Charles (3182-4) Son of Charles Williams Citizen and Painter Stainer of London, apprenticed to Edward Hulse 1 March 1689 and turned over to John Ladyman. Free, 12 March 1697. Three marks entered as largeworker, undated, probably April 1697 on commencement of register. Address: Lamb Alley, Sherborne Lane, where Heal records him from 1697-1704.

WILLIAMS, David *See* WILLAUME.

*WILLIAMS, James (496, 1755, 2674) Son of James Williams of the Little Minnories in the County of Middlesex yeoman, apprenticed to John Gorham 3 July 1745. Free, 5 July 1753. First mark entered as largeworker, in partnership with William Turner, 9 August 1753. Address: Staining Lane. Moved to Addle Street, 20 September 1753. The partnership presumably dissolved by 21 June 1754, when Turner entered a separate mark. Second mark, in partnership with Edward Dobson and William Pryor, 10 February 1755. Address: Paternoster Row. Third mark alone, 30 July 1755, same address. Heal records him only as plateworker, Paternoster Row, 1755-6.

WILLIAMS, John (3377) Three of this name appear as apprentices and free from 1758, but there is no evidence to establish identity with the above. First mark entered as smallworker, in partnership with William Williams II (q.v.), 14 April 1780. Address: 45 and 103 St. Martin's Lane. Second mark alone as bucklemaker, 13 November 1790. Address: 45 St. Martin's Lane (Section VIII). Heal records John Williams, goldsmith and watchmaker, Union Court, 1770; and the same or another as jeweller and goldsmith, Bartholomew Close, 1773-93, but there is no apparent relationship with the entry above.

WILLIAMS, Richard (3188) Son of Francis Williams of the parish of Hanford(?) in the County of Salop yeoman, apprenticed to Edward Ironside 6 August 1703. Free, 1 August 1711. Mark entered as largeworker, 11 April 1712. Address: Gutter Lane. Signatory as journeyman to the petition against assaying the work of foreigners not having served seven years apprenticeship, February 1716.

WILLIAMS, Robert (2456, 3199) Son of Tobias Williams late of the Town and County of Brecknock clerk deceased, apprenticed to William Lukin 30 June 1709. Free, 3 November 1726. Two marks (Sterling and New Standard) entered as largeworker, 2 October 1726. Address: Golden Unicorn in King Street, Westminster. 'free of Goldsmith Company'. Heal records the above date and address, and also 'Buried 1762'.

*WILLIAMS, Walter I (3376) No record of apprenticeship or freedom. Only mark entered as smallworker, 7 October 1775. Address: Earls Court, Cranbourne Alley, Leicester Fields.

WILLIAMS, Walter II (3370) No record of apprenticeship or freedom and no apparent connection, except closeness of address, with the above. Only mark entered as plateworker, 31 October 1815. Address: 103 St. Martin's Lane, Charing Cross.

WILLIAMS, William I (2979, 3362-3) Son of William Williams of Hitchin in the County of Hertford shopkeeper, apprenticed to Thomas Farren 1 September 1731 on payment of £21. Free, 5 December 1738. (His partner Whipham (q.v.) was also apprenticed to Farren.) Two marks entered as largeworker, one in partnership with Thomas Whipham, the other a single WW, 1 May 1740. Address: Foster Lane. 'Goldsmith'. Third mark alone, 10 September 1742. Address: Spread Eagle, Foster Lane. Livery, September 1746. Heal records him in partnership with Whipham, 1740-6; and alone as working goldsmith, Spread Eagle, Foster Lane, 1742-8, i.e. overlapping by four years the period of the partnership. Other examples of this kind of arrangement seem to have occurred and it is not clear what the business arrangements may have been. His separate mark is rarely met with, and may perhaps have been entered for a special occasion or commission.

WILLIAMS, William II (3367, 3377) No record of apprenticeship or freedom. First mark entered as smallworker, in partnership with John Williams (q.v.), 14 April 1780. Address: 45 and 103 St. Martin's Lane. Second mark alone, 8 February 1797. Address: 103 St. Martin's Lane. Third mark, 16 July 1800.

WILLIS, James (1739) No record of apprenticeship or freedom. Only mark entered as smallworker, undated between June 1732 and July 1735. Address: 'Cross Street, Golden Square at Mr Eavens'(?). An illiterate entry with two attempts at the address.

WILLIS, John (1748) Son of John Willis of

Farnborough in the County of Kent yeoman, apprenticed to Thomas Harding as goldsmith 6 February 1782. Free, 7 October 1789. First mark entered as smallworker, 20 March 1789. Address: Mile's Court, Chiswell Street. Moved to 70 Old Street, 21 April 1790. Moved to 28 Blue Anchor Alley, 6 July 1791. Moved to 81 Bishopsgate Without, 29 July 1794. Second mark, 31 March 1796. Address: 28 Blue Anchor Alley, Bishopsgate Without. Heal records John Willis, goldsmith, New Bond Street, 1784; and St. John's Lane, 1786, but there seems no connection between these addresses, either with each other or the entry above.

WILLMORE, Joseph (1859) No record of apprenticeship or freedom. It seems very probable that this is, in fact, an entry by the well-known Birmingham maker, to enable him to set up a London workshop. First mark (two sizes) as smallworker entered 21 February 1805. Address: 14 Bouverie Street, Fleet Street. Moved to 11 Thavies Inn, Holborn, 6 March 1823. Second mark (two sizes), 14 March 1840.

WILLMOT, James (1752) No record of apprenticeship or freedom. Only mark entered as largeworker, 3 August 1741. Address: 'at the Flying Horse near the Fountaine Tavern Strand'. His trade card, illustrated by Heal, styles him as goldsmith and jeweller, Flying Horse, between the Savoy and the Fountain Tavern, Strand. His mark is rarely found.

WILLSON, William (3359) Son of Richard Wilson late of London cartman deceased, apprenticed to George Wilcox (see Willcocks above) of the Cutlers' Company 23 March 1719 and later turned over to Thomas North. Free, 21 April 1726. Only mark entered as smallworker, 9 May 1726. Address: New Street. 'Free of Cutlers Company'.

WILSON, Thomas (2965) No record of apprenticeship or freedom. First mark entered as smallworker, 2 April 1761. Address: 'of Deptford in ye County of Kent'. Second mark, 25 August 1770. Third, 3 November 1770. Incuse mark as bucklemaker, 26 June 1775 (Section V), and two others, cameo, 24 April 1776. Address: 'Near the Lower Water Gate, Deptford' (Section VIII). A clearer indication of his speciality of mariners' shoebuckles it would be harder to find.

WILSON, William (3276) Perhaps son of John Wilson of the parish of St. George in the County of Middlesex yeoman, apprenticed to James Coby 1 April 1761 on payment of £10. Free, 1 March 1769. Mark entered as spoonmaker, in partnership with William Playfair, 16 May 1782. Address: 2 Portland Road, Great Portland Street, St. Marybone. Heal records them at this address and date, as plateworkers; and as Playfair Wilson and Co., working silversmiths, near Rathbone Place, 1784. He seems distinct from the William Wilson, bucklemaker, 1785 (Section VIII).

WIMANS, Edward (3179-80) No record of apprenticeship or freedom. Mark entered as largeworker, undated, probably April 1697 on commencement of register. Address: Foster Lane. Immediately below the first mark is struck a second in lozenge-shaped punch, against which is written the word 'Widdow', without her name and also undated. For some reason Chaffers omitted to print the Christian name of this maker although clearly written in the entry and this lacuna is perpetuated in Jackson and Heal.

WIMBUSH, Thomas (2973, 2977) No record of apprenticeship or freedom. First mark entered as plateworker, 27 November 1828. Address: 21 Red Lion Street. Moved to 166 Regent Street, 17 August 1833. Second mark, in partnership with Henry Hyde, 27 January 1834. The partnership dissolved, 20 May 1834, 'by mutual consent' (*London Gazette*), and on 17 June 1834 Wimbush made indenture of assignment of all his effects to Thomas Smith of Ramsbury Manor, Wiltshire, and George Osborne of Brentford, in trust for his creditors. The Post Office directory of 1834 records him as Manufacturing Gold and Silversmith to the King, 166 Regent Street, and a coffeepot of Gothic style, bearing his mark, 1829, is engraved with the cypher of George IV. He later married Sarah Hanley Broughton at St. Mary, Newington, Surrey, 21 May 1840, and entered new marks, 13 October 1840 at 33 Newington Crescent, and 3 July 1845 at 1 Penton Place, Clerkenwell. My thanks are due to an anonymous informant for much of the above.

WINDSOR, David (3524) No record of apprenticeship or freedom and nothing appears recorded of this maker, except the attribution of the particular mark to him by Jackson.

WINGLER, John (1741) No record of

apprenticeship or freedom. Only mark entered as snuffbox maker, 6 April 1738. Address: Cockpit Court, Jewin Street.

WINKINGS, Nicelas (sic) (2105) No record of apprenticeship or freedom. Only mark entered as largeworker, 21 September 1751. Address: Red Lion Street, Holborn, where Heal records him (as Nicholas) at the same date. He is however identifiable as one of the leading trumpet-makers of the time. In 1763 he is described as 'Horn Maker to the Royal Hunt' in Mortimer's *Directory*. Granted letters of denization, 13 March 1767, then described as ironmonger and brazier. Probate of his will granted, 2 May 1782, to his wife Abigail and Thomas Willet of Moulsey, Surrey. To his son John he left the lease of his house and to another son, Samuel, £100 or vice versa if John did not want the house. Samuel took the house and retained it for two years, and it was later taken in 1784 by William Shaw, also trumpet maker (M. Byrne, 'The Goldsmith Trumpet-makers of the British Isles', *Galpin Society*, Vol. XIX, 1966).

WINNE, Grace (3177) No record of apprenticeship or freedom. Only mark entered as smallworker, 13 February 1702. Address: Wood Street.

WINNE, William (3358) Son of John Winne of the City of Coventry taylor, apprenticed to Mary Fenton widow of Michael 2 July 1701. Free, 21 April 1710. Mark entered as smallworker, 26 October 1720. Address: Minories. 'Goldsmith'. Heal records William Winn, goldsmith, near Hermitage Stairs, Wapping, 1712, who could, from the date of his above freedom, be the same; followed by Minories, 1724-34; and in unpublished addenda Gold Ring, Minories, 1726. He also records William Winn, goldsmith, near Aldgate, 1744, who might be a son. The William Wynn, watchcasemaker, incuse mark, 1732 (Section V), appears to have different signature and address, but may be the same.

WINTER, William (3375) No record of apprenticeship or freedom. Only mark entered as smallworker, 25 January 1769. Address: 21 Bunhill Row, St. Luke's, Old Street, where he appears, as goldworker, in the Parl. Report list 1773. Heal records him at this address as goldsmith, 1772-9.

WINTLE, Eden (654) No record of apprenticeship or freedom. Only mark entered as spoonmaker, 8 May 1828. Address: 34 Commercial Road, Lambeth. From name and occupation he is presumably connected with James Wintle (below), possibly a brother.

*WINTLE, George (923-6) No record of apprenticeship or freedom. First mark entered as plateworker, 2 January 1787. Address: 2 'Angle' Street, St. Martin's Le Grand. Second mark, 25 June 1789. Address: 147 Aldersgate Street. Third mark (incuse) as plateworker, 7 October 1790 (Section V). Fourth, 28 February 1791. Moved to 14 Glasshouse Yard, Aldersgate Street, 3 May 1792. Fifth mark, 6 December 1794. Moved to 19 Long Lane, Southwark, 29 April 1797. Sixth mark as spoonmaker, 4 May 1801. Address: 9 Twisters Alley, Bunhill Row. Seventh mark, 14 December 1804. Moved to 3 Bell Savage Yard, 14 October 1812. Eighth mark, 15 May 1813. Moved to 3 Union Street, St. George's Fields, 8 August 1814; to 11 Joiners Street, Westminster Road, 22 October 1814. Ninth mark, 10 March 1818. Tenth, 23 February 1820. Moved to 34 Commercial Road, Lambeth, 17 August 1820. Eleventh mark, 22 July 1823. Heal records him as silver spoonmaker, Angel Street, 1787; and 147 Aldersgate Street, 1790-3.

*WINTLE, James (1750, 1860) Probably son of the above from the coincidence of the second address, but there is no record of apprenticeship or freedom. First mark entered as spoonmaker, 19 October 1812. Address: 3 Borough Road, St. George's Fields. Moved to 3 Bell Savage Yard, Ludgate Hill, 6 November 1812. Back to 3 Borough Road, 5 June 1813. Moved to 30 North Street, City Road, 14 January 1815. Second mark, 3 February 1818. Third mark, 25 August 1820. Fourth mark, 10 November 1820. Fifth mark, 19 January 1821. Sixth mark, 15 February 1821. Seventh mark, 14 September 1826. Moved to 4 John Street, Waterloo Road, 8 May 1827. Eighth mark, 21 August 1829. Ninth mark, 31 December 1833. Moved to 11 Rupel Street, Blackfriars Road, 16 January 1834. Tenth mark, 25 September 1838. Eleventh mark, 6 October 1838.

*WINTLE, Samuel (2662) No record of apprenticeship or freedom. First mark entered as bucklemaker, in partnership with Thomas Wintle, 1 October 1778. Address: 2 Blue Coat Building, Butcher Hall Lane. Moved to 118 Fleet Street, 16 July 1779.

Second mark alone as same, 31 July 1779. Address: 'facing the Coach & Horses, Long Lane Southwark' (Section VIII). Third mark as smallworker, 27 May 1783. Address: Long Lane, Southwark 'near the Coach and Horses'. Moved to Surrey Square, Kent Road, no date. Fourth mark, 2 August 1792. Address: 35 Seward Street. Heal records him only as goldsmith, London, 1783.

WIRGMAN, Gabriel (922) No record of apprenticeship or freedom. Presumably son of John Wirgman (below) and grandson of Peter I (q.v.). First mark entered as smallworker, 22 June 1772. Address: 14 Red Lion Street, Clerkenwell, where he appears as goldworker in the Parl. Report list 1773, but had in fact been working as early as 1767 (Bill, Heal Addenda). In partnership with James Morisset, 11 Denmark Street from 1776-8, after which he appears also at same address as jeweller, goldsmith and enameller. Second mark as goldworker (Section VII), 3 November 1785, at 11 Denmark Street, where Heal records him 1778-83. His will, proved 23 September 1791, bears a codicil dated 9 August 1791, 'in my way home in Devizes in the County of Wilts'. His name was confused with that of his apparently better known brother Peter Wirgman II, which resulted in the obituary in *The Gentleman's Magazine*, 12 September 1791: 'At Devizes, Wilts, Mr Peter Wirgman working jeweller and goldsmith of Denmark St. Soho, one of the most eminent artists in his line, having distinguished himself in the finishing of a box in which the freedom of the City of London was presented to Lord Keppel, and in many other public exhibitions of skill. Mr Wirgman left a numerous family'. In fact Peter Wirgman II, who has no recorded mark, is recorded by Heal as toyman, jeweller and enameller, 69 St. James's Street, 1784-96; and also 11 Denmark Street, Soho (as above for Gabriel). The firm also appears as Wirgman, Son and Colibert at 11 Denmark Street, 1796. They were already in St. James's Street by 1778 when Dr. Johnson bought his shoe-buckles there (Boswell's *Life*, 28 April 1778; 'Wirgman's the well known toy-shop in St. James's Street at the corner of St. James's Place'). Peter Wirgman appears in directories till 1798; his will was proved 20 April 1801, in which his cousin Thomas is mentioned, whose name appears in St. James's Street in directories 1805-11. (Information, Mr Claude Blair.)

WIRGMAN, John (1754) Son of Peter Wirgman (below) of the parish of St. Mary le Strand in the County of Middlesex goldsmith, apprenticed to Edward Feline 5 June 1733 on payment of £20. Free, 3 July 1740. Mark entered as largeworker, 13 May 1751 (twenty-three days after his father's death). Address: Windsor Court, Strand (his father's address). Moved to Castle Court, Strand, 12 November 1751. Moved to opposite Durham Yard, Strand, 27 May 1761. Heal records him as plateworker, Strand, 1745; and Princes Street, 1766-72. In view of his apprenticeship it is not surprising to find him the only Wirgman concerned with plateworking rather than gold and enamel work.

*WIRGMAN, Peter I (2241) No record of apprenticeship or freedom. Probably related to Petter Wirgman, born 1707, son of Abraham Wirgman, working in Gothenberg, Sweden, as goldsmith 1733-7 (Gustaf Upmark, *Guld och Silversmeden i Sverige 1520-1850*, 1943). Mark entered as smallworker, 17 May 1738. Address: 'Winsor' Court near the New Church in the Strand. Foriner'. He was however previously described as goldsmith of the parish of St. Mary le Strand, in 1733, when his son John (q.v.) was apprenticed. He died Saturday 20 April 1751 (*London General Evening Post*). For the further history of his firm see under Gabriel Wirgman (above).

WIRGMAN, Peter II *See* under WIRGMAN, Gabriel.

WISDOME, John (1733, 3187) Son of Phillip Wisdom of Chipping Norton in the County of Oxford upholsterer, apprenticed to John Leach Citizen and Haberdasher of London 14 July 1694. Free of the Haberdashers, 13 December 1700. First mark entered as largeworker, 17 June 1704. Address: Watling Street. 'Free Haberdasher'. Second mark, 7 August 1717, same address. Third (Sterling) mark, 26 August 1720. Fourth, 14 October 1723. Heal records him as plateworker, Watling Street, 1704 till death in 1731.

WISE, Thomas (1788) No record of apprenticeship or freedom. Only mark entered as smallworker, in partnership with Joshua Butler II, 30 May 1835. Address: 30 Coppice Row, Clerkenwell. For other smaller marks, 1837-8, Section IV.

*WITHAM, Edward (653) Son of Edward, free by patrimony as silversmith 7 October

1807. First mark entered as smallworker, 16 July 1813. Address: 19 Silver Street. Second mark, 17 February 1814. The father Edward (also son of Edward) Witham of Long Lane near West Smithfield taylor, Citizen and Merchant Taylor, was apprenticed to Harman Smith of Noble Street as silversmith 2 December 1767, free 1776, Livery October 1806 and died 1818-22. It is therefore just possible that this mark although so much nearer in date to the son's freedom of 1807, might have been entered by the father, although then about sixty.

WITHERS, William (3365) No record of apprenticeship or freedom. Only mark entered as smallworker, 17 August 1762. Address: Turks Head Court, Golden Lane, Old Street.

WOOD, Benjamin (252) Perhaps son of Thomas Wood of Cheadle in the County of Stafford gentleman, apprenticed to Francis Smart 11 September 1705. Freedom unrecorded. Only mark entered as smallworker, 28 August 1729. Address: 'at ye Golden Legg in turne-stile alley'.

WOOD, Edward (651-2, 655, 3246) Son of John Wood Citizen and Turner of London, apprenticed to James Roode 6 July 1715 on payment of £20. Free, 2 August 1722. Two marks (Sterling and New Standard) entered as largeworker, 18 August 1722. Address: 'on Puddle-dock hill ye end of Great Carter Lane'. Third mark, 26 August 1735. Address: Carey Lane. Fourth, 30 September 1740, same address. Livery, March 1737. Heal records him as plateworker, Puddle Dock (Upper Thames Street), 1722; and Carey Lane, 1735 till death in 1752. He is probably the Edward Wood of St. Michael, Queenhithe, bachelor, married to Ann Booth of St. Gabriel, Fenchurch, spinster at St. Bene't, Paul's Wharf, 11 September 1723. It is interesting to find Wood in the line of specialist salt-cellar makers, since his master Roode appears to have produced little else and Wood in his turn appears equally limited in his output and became in 1728 the master of the young David Hennell, than whom, probably, no-one in London in the mid eighteenth century made more salt-cellars.

WOOD, Samuel (2656-8, 2666, 3808) Born c. 1704. Son of George Wood late of Carswell in the County of Stafford gentleman deceased, apprenticed to Thomas Bamford 7 June 1721 on payment of £15. Free, 5 March 1730/?1. First mark entered as largeworker, 3 July 1733. Address: Gutter Lane by Cheapside. Livery, April 1737. Second mark undated, between September 1737 and August 1738, same address. Third mark, 15 June 1739. Court, May 1745. Moved to Foster Lane, and fourth mark entered, 15 July 1754. Fifth mark, 2 October 1756. Warden 1758-60, and Prime Warden 1763. Appears as plateworker, Southgate, in the Parl. Report list 1773. Heal records him as plateworker, Gutter Lane, 1733-40; and Southgate (?St. Paul's Churchyard), 1773. That Southgate was, however, the northern suburb is clear from his obituary (below). Elizabeth, daughter of Samuel and Elizabeth Wood, baptized 30 May 1738 at St. Vedast, Foster Lane, is presumably his child. No others appear recorded. Wood's obituary notice in *The Gentleman's Magazine*, 6 October 1794, paints the picture of a stalwart character: 'at Southgate aged 90 of a second paralytic stroke, Mr Wood, goldsmith of London. His daughter married Mr Howitt, mercer of London whose only daughter is married to Mr James Moore of Cheapside. For the last two years of his life he used to ride to town every week, to transact business at Goldsmiths Hall, being the father and oldest member of that company'. Through his apprenticeship to Thomas Bamford, who himself had been bound to Charles Adam, Wood came of a continuous line of specialist caster-makers, and in turn trained both Jabez Daniell and Robert Piercey (q.v.), both clearly established also in the same line of production. Wood's cruets and individual casters, to judge from the very large number surviving, must have been produced on a wholesale manufacturing basis, but are, no less for that, of a uniformly high standard and one of the most attractively designed smaller items of plate, without which no reasonably equipped table of the eighteenth century appears to have been complete.

WOODCOCK, William (3361) No record of apprenticeship or freedom. Only mark entered as smallworker, 7 January (?) 1736. Address: Sword and Buckler Court, Ludgate Hill.

WOODHOUSE, Richard (3248) Son of James Woodhouse late Citizen and Haberdasher of London deceased, apprenticed to Abell Skinner Junior Citizen and Joiner 25 March 1718. Free, 4 May 1725. New Standard mark entered as smallworker, 15

October 1725. Address: 'Broad Street behind the Change, free of Joyners Company'. He does not appear to have entered a Sterling mark, which is somewhat curious by 1725.

WOODHOUSE, Thomas (2964) No record of apprenticeship or freedom. Only mark entered as smallworker, 4 October 1758. Address: 'at the Hermitage, St. John's Wapping'. Signs with X. Appears without category in the Parl. Report list of 1773, address Hermitage.

*WOODS, Christopher (427) No record of apprenticeship or freedom. Only mark entered as plateworker, 12 June 1775. Address: King Street, St. Ann's, Soho. He may be identical with Christopher Fly Wood, recorded with Thomas Filkin as spoonmakers, Battersea, in the Parl. Report list 1773.

WOODWARD, Charles (426) Son of Robert Woodward of the parish of St. Olave's Southwark butcher, apprenticed to George Wickes 13 September 1727 on payment of £20. Free, 4 September 1740. Only mark entered as largeworker, 10 April 1741 when he signs 'Woodard'. Address: Tooley Street, Southwark. The mark entry is signed Woodard but this is presumably due to nervousness at the occasion. The apprenticeship entry is clearly Woodward.

*WOODWARD, John (1738) Perhaps son of James Woodward of Clapham in the County of Surrey ironmonger, apprenticed to Richard Gutter 7 July 1709. Freedom unrecorded. Only mark entered as smallworker, 24 November 1730. Address: Round Court, St. Martin's Le Grand.

WOODWARD, William (3360, 3373) Son of Henry Woodard (sic) late of St. Olave's Southwark in the County of Surrey butcher deceased, apprenticed to William Pearson 17 February 1719 on payment of £26.5s. and turned over 8 October 1722 to George Wickes in Threadneedle Street. Free, 16 June 1726. (Cf. Charles Woodward above, apparently a cousin and apprenticed also to Wickes.) First mark entered as largeworker, 20 August 1731. Address: Fenchurch Street. 'Goldsmith'. Second mark, 19 October 1743, same address. Heal records the same address and two dates; also London, 1752.

WOOLCOMB, Robert (2461) Robert Woolcomb late of the Foundling Hospital, apprenticed to Charles Chesterman of Fleet Market as silversmith 1 June 1791 on payment of £20 of the charity of Francis Newham. Free, 1 May 1799. Only mark entered as plateworker, 12 November 1818. Address: 8 Collier Street, Pentonville.

WOOLLER, William (3364) No record of apprenticeship or freedom. Only mark entered as largeworker, 14 May 1750. Address: New Street, Cloth Fair. Heal records this address and date; and London, 1767.

*WORBOYS, Arthur (108) Free by redemption as jeweller 6 October 1762. Mark, however, as smallworker entered 23 September 1758. Address: Vinson (?Vincent) Court, Silver Street. Heal records him as jeweller, 4 Wine Office Court, Fleet Street, 1767-79; and 94 Fleet Street, near Bride Lane, 1774-87. He appears in the Parl. Report list 1773 as Arthur Worboyes, goldworker, Wine Office Court. Livery, December 1771. His three sons John, Thomas and Arthur were apprenticed to him 1771, 1776 and 1780. He met a tragic end, as his obituary in *The Gentleman's Magazine* records, 21 July 1787: 'Burnt in a dreadful fire which consumed his house in Fleet Street Mr Arthur Worboys, silversmith, of whom next month'. There is however nothing further following. Thomas Worboys (Section V) entered as goldworker, 9 Bell's Buildings, Salisbury Square, 7 November 1787, is presumably son and successor.

WORTHINGTON, William (3366) Free by redemption as gilder, 6 May 1767. First mark entered as smallworker, 14 May 1771. Address: 158 Fleet Street. Second mark, 12 February 1772. Heal records him as goldsmith and gilder, 158 Fleet Street, 1767-73. Appears as goldworker, at the same address, in the Parl. Report list 1773, and entered mark as such, 13 March 1776, at same address (Section VII).

WOTTON, Richard Lewis (2459) No record of apprenticeship or freedom. Only mark entered as smallworker, 30 July 1760. Address: Hoxton Market. Appears in the Parl. Report list 1773, at the same address, as smallworker.

*WRANGHAM, John (1763, 2236) No record of apprenticeship or freedom. First mark entered as plateworker, in partnership with William Moulson (q.v.), 28 March 1822. Address: 52 Great Sutton Street, Clerkenwell. Second mark, in partnership with Paul Siddall (q.v.) and William Moulson, 15

November 1823. Address: 7 White Hart Court, Castle Street, Leicester Square.

WREN, John II (1756) Son of William Wren Citizen and Haberdasher of London, apprenticed to William Abdy 2 August 1759. Free, 4 February 1767. Mark entered as spoonmaker, 27 February 1777. Address: 95 Bishopsgate Street without. Heal records him as plateworker, Worship Street, 1776; 95 Bishopsgate without, 1777-85; and London, 1795.

WRENN, John I (1736) Son of John Wren late of the parish of St. Olave's Southwark in the County of Surrey lighterman deceased, apprenticed to William Howard 21 October 1721 on payment of £10 and turned over 12 June 1723 to John Mapp in Noble Street. Free, 5 March 1728/?9. Although the Clerk spells the name Wren in the apprentice register, the boy signs Wrenn both there and later on entering mark as smallworker, 14 November 1728. Address: Six Bell Court, Foster Lane. 'Free Goldsmith'.

*WRIGHT, Charles (428, 2976, 3510-1) Son of Thomas Wright of Sheffield in the County of York carrier, apprenticed to Thomas Whipham 3 June 1747 on payment of £40. Free, 3 July 1754. First mark entered as largeworker, in partnership with Thomas Whipham, 24 October 1757. Address: Ave Mary Lane, where he appears alone as plateworker in the Parl. Report list 1773. He gave evidence to the Committee of the Report on frauds by the sale of mixed silver and plated wares at the same rate per ounce. Second mark alone, 22 July 1775. Address: 9 Ave Maria Lane. Third mark (two sizes), 3 February 1780. Fourth, 25 August 1780. Heal records him as goldsmith, 9 Ave Mary Lane, married 1764, there till 1780; 76 Strand, 1784-8; and 94 Watling Street, 1790. He was elected to Livery, 1758. Court 1777 and Warden, 1783-5. Resigned 1790, when he probably also retired from business, and died 1815. The Ave Mary Lane address was occupied from 1783 by Thomas Chawner (q.v.).

WRIGHT, James (1740) Probably son of Robert Wright of Witney in the County of Oxford blacksmith, apprenticed to Joseph Sanders 14 January 1725 on payment of £5. Freedom unrecorded. Mark entered as smallworker, 24 July 1735. Address: Cary Lane over against ye Wheatsheaf.

WRIGHT, Paul (2243) Son of the Rev. Paul Wright of Oakley Essex clerk, apprenticed to Edward Smith 13 January 1762 on payment of £20 by the charity of the Stewards of the Feast of the Sons of the Clergy. Free, 4 October 1769 as jeweller. First mark entered as smallworker, 3 January 1771. Address: 12 Foster Lane. Second mark (very small, presumably for gold), 15 May 1771. Heal records him as goldsmith, successor to Edward Smith at the Parrot and Pearl, 12 Foster Lane, 1771-3. He appears as goldworker, 12 Foster Lane, in the Parl. Report list 1773, and entered a mark as such, 23 March 1782. Address: 10 George Yard, Aldersgate Street (Section VII).

WRIGHT, Sacheverel (2660) No record of apprenticeship or freedom. Only mark entered as smallworker, 23 August 1758. Address: The Star and George, Noble Street, St. Luke's. He appears without category, at Noble Street, in the Parl. Report list 1773. Heal records him as goldsmith, London, 1771-3.

WRIGHT, Thomas (2958-9, 3847) Probably son of Thomas Wright late Citizen and Cooper of London, apprenticed to Joseph Heywood 30 March 1688 for eight years. Free, 15 January 1705. (A previous entry in register for similar names 1686.) First mark entered as largeworker, 6 September 1721. Address: Maiden Lane. Second mark as smallworker, 9 November 1722, same address, with the note 'Small old Sta(ndard) marke wittniss my hand Tho Wright free Goldsmith'. Heal records him as goldsmith, late of Shoe Lane, 1720; and Maiden Lane, 1721. The mark no. 3847, formerly attributed to him, seems more probably that of Thomas Whipham.

WYATT, Joseph (1858) Son of William Wyatt of Rotherhithe Wall in the County of Surrey miller, apprenticed to William Suddell of Pelican Court Little Britain as silversmith 8 April 1778. Free, 4 May 1785. Mark entered as smallworker, 1 October 1789. Address: 12 Angel Street, St. Martin's Le Grand. Heal records him as goldsmith, Angel Street, 1790.

Y

*YERBURY, Daniel (3380) Free of the Haberdashers' Company by redemption 11 November 1715. Mark entered as largeworker, 29 February 1716. Address: Bread Street. 'Free Haberdasher'. Heal records him at this address, 1715 (not allowing for old calendar). He was, however, already in the neighbourhood since the register of All Hallows, Bread Street contains entries for the baptism of six children of Daniel and Susannah Yerbury from 10 December 1714 to 30 April 1727. His identity therein is proved by one entry '3 July 1718 John son of Daniel & Susannah Yerbery, silversmith by trade'.

YORKE, Edward (657, 3381) Son of John Yorke late of the parish of Eddington in the County of Wiltshire yeoman deceased, apprenticed to John Bayly 28 March 1693 and turned over to William Fawdery 30 November 1697. Free, 9 April 1701. First mark entered as largeworker, 3 July 1705. Address: Holborn. Second (Sterling) mark, 26 November 1730. Address: King Street, Westminster. Signs the second entry York. Heal records Edward York or Yorke, plateworker, parish of St. Mary Staining, 1692–3, but from the evidence of apprenticeship this must refer to an earlier maker of the same name, for whom there seems no other evidence. Subsequently, under the same heading, London, 1699–1705; Holborn, 1705; and King Street, Westminster, 1717–32.

YORKE, Thomas (2980) Son of Thomas Yorke Citizen and Framework-knitter, apprenticed to Edward York (see above, ? uncle or cousin) 18 October 1711. Free, 4 May 1721. Mark entered as smallworker, 9 August 1721. Address: 'Bayleys Place near ye Wittelling Office' (presumably an anticipatory Wellerian version of Victualling). Thomas York, incuse mark, 1722 (Section V), has a different signature and address and appears a separate maker.

*YOUNG, George (928) Free of the Cutlers' Company. First mark (incuse) entered, 18 May 1723, as smallworker. Address: Glasshouse Yard, Blackfriars. 'free Cutler' (Section V). Second mark as largeworker, 17 June 1746. Address: Shoe Alley, Moorfields. Third mark (incuse), 15 October 1746. Heal records him as goldsmith, Glasshouse Street, 1722; Broken Wharf (Upper Thames Street), 1723; and plateworker, Moorfields, 1746–9.

YOUNG, James (1765, 1767) Presumably son of Richard Young Citizen and Carter of London, apprenticed to John Muns (q.v.) 4 October 1749 on payment of £5 of the charity of Christ's Hospital. Freedom unrecorded. First mark entered as smallworker, 21 July 1760. Address: Basinghall Street. Moved to Clerkenwell, 22 January 1766. Second mark, in partnership with Orlando Jackson (q.v.), 17 March 1774. Address: 33 Aldersgate Street, where he already appears alone as plateworker in the Parl. Report list 1773. Third mark with the same, 13 May 1774. Fourth mark alone as plateworker, 15 April 1775. Address: 5 Aldersgate Street. Fifth mark, 28 April 1781. Moved to 70 Little Britain, 13 November 1788. His son James was apprenticed to William Peaston 5 August 1778 and turned over to his father 3 February 1779. In this entry James Senior is described as Citizen and Carman, presumably free by patrimony of the Carters' Company in accordance with his father's description in 1749. Heal records him as plateworker, 32 Aldersgate Street, 1773–90; James Young and Son, 70 Little Britain, 1790–3; and with Orlando Jackson, Aldersgate, 1774. His work alone or jointly is of elegant neo-Classical design and fine finish, particularly his epergnes.

*YOUNG, Nat(hanie)l (2106) No record of apprenticeship or freedom. Only mark entered as smallworker, undated, between 1723 and 1736. Address: 'New Street, Fetter Lane near ye Three Tuns, London'.

*YOUNG, William (3378–9) No record of apprenticeship or freedom. First mark entered as largeworker, 31 March 1735. Address: St. Andrew's Street, Seven Dials, St. Giles. Second mark, 29 June 1739. Heal records him as plateworker, St. Andrew's Street, 1735–9; High Holborn, 1744–7; and Golden Cup, Holborn Bridge, 1752; died 1755. He also has William Young, jeweller, Christopher's Court, 1767, but this seems unlikely to be the same.

BIOGRAPHICAL DICTIONARY

Z

ZOUCH, Richard (2464-5) Son of Edward Zouch of the parish of St. James Westminster gentleman, apprenticed to Francis Plymley 13 December 1720 and turned over to William Darker in the Strand plateworker 25 September 1725. Free, 8 November 1737. First mark entered as largeworker, 31 March 1735. Address: Chequer Court, Charing Cross. Second mark, 27 June 1739, same address.

Notices of Provincial Makers whose Marks Appear in the London Registers

ANDOVER

MENEFY, Richard (3435) Only mark entered as spoonmaker, 28 November 1793. Address: Andover, Hampshire. His name cannot be found in any document or records of Andover. There is however one occurrence of the surname in 1851 for a bank clerk.

AYLESBURY

CAMPBELL, Neil. Only mark a very small NC in script entered as smallworker, 3 April 1776. Address: Aylesbury (Section IV). He appears as bucklemaker, Aylesbury, Buckinghamshire, in the Parl. Report list 1773. There is no record of this maker as such in Aylesbury records. The name however occurs in the Buckinghamshire Quarter Sessions in 1723-4, and in land tax records as owner of house and land in 1780, presumably for father and son or grandfather and grandson. The mark NC in roman capitals accompanied by lion passant, on a pair of buckles in a facetted 'cut-steel' design in the Maufe Collection, is probably also his.

STONE, John. Bucklemaker, 1776 (Section VIII).

BANBURY

BAXTER, John (3619) Mark attributed to him by Jackson on strength of his entry in the Parl. Report list 1773 as goldsmith, Banbury, Oxfordshire. Mark presumably entered in the missing register between 1758 and 1773.

BATH

*BASNETT, William (3462-3) Two marks entered as plateworker, 3 September 1784. Address: Bath. The name, also spelt Bassnett, occurs in Bath directories from 1784-1846. First address: 1 Bond Street. 1812: moved to 28 Milsom Street. 1833: at 32 Rivers Street. 1837: 15 Ruby Place.

BOTTLE, James (3419) Mark entered as plateworker, 16 January 1819. Address: Bridge Street, Bath. John Bottle, working silversmith, appears in Bath directory, 2 Garrard Street, 1800.

BOTTLE, William (3464-5) First mark entered as plateworker, in partnership with Jeremiah Willsher (below). Address: Bath. Second mark alone as plateworker, 6 March 1800. Entered by power of attorney and signed by Samuel Goodbehere, Alderman. The Bath directories record William Bottle at 41 Walcot Street, 1805-46; also at 43 Walcot Street, in 1819; and 3 St. James Parade, 1833. He appears as Overseer of the poor of St. Michael's parish, 1826.

BRETTON, Lionel (3427) Mark entered as plateworker, 18 November 1784. Address: Bath. The name occurs in directories from 1784-1812, at 46 Milsom Street, variously as Messrs Bretton and Bretton and Son. The Christian name used is John, presumably that of the son.

BURDEN, James (3449) Mark entered as plateworker, in partnership with Thomas Mitchell and Thomas Merrifield, 21 February 1831. Address: Bath. The mark entered by power of attorney, signed by George Fred. Bult 'Attorney to the said firm'. It is interesting to note that William Bottle's power of attorney was given to Samuel Goodbehere and it seems likely that the G. F. Bult above may have been a member of the family of James Bult, partner in the firm of Goodbehere, Wigan and Bult of Cheapside, who would thus appear to have had business relationships with both Bottle and Burden. James Burden 'of Mitchell & Co' appears in directories 1837-41 at 6 Paradise Street, Wells Road. In 1841 Stephen Burden appears as a member of the firm.

FORD, John (3407) First mark entered as smallworker, in partnership with John Williams, 10 March 1767. Address: Bath. Second mark, 6 May 1782. Address: Bath. The second entry signed 'Joseph Walley by Power of Attorney'. No references in Bath directories have been found to these makers. They appear as bucklemakers, Bath, in the Parl. Report list 1773.

*GRAHAM, Thomas (3444-5) Mark entered as plateworker in partnership with Jacob Willis, 29 June 1789. Address: Walcot

BATH

BATH—contd.
Street, Bath. Signed by power of attorney by Fendall Rushforth. Second mark alone, 14 May 1792. Address: No ( ) Walcot Street (Willis (q.v.) having moved to Frome). There is no directory entry for these makers.

HARRIS, Thomas. Mark entered as watch-casemaker, 1805. Address: Horse Street. (Section VI.)

*HOWELL, Thomas (3446-7) Appears as plateworker, Bath, with a mark entered at London in the Parl. Report list 1773. First recorded mark entered as plateworker, 27 May 1784. Address: Burton Street. Second mark (two sizes), 11 June 1791. Entered by power of attorney, signed by Fendall Rushforth. Same address. Third mark (two sizes), 26 July 1792. His son Thomas was apprenticed to Benjamin Laver (q.v.) of Bruton Street, Berkeley Square 3 December 1783, when the father is described as Goldsmith of the City of Bath. Thomas Howell Senior was apparently dead by 1800, in which year the only directory reference to the firm appears as Ann Howell and Son, Burton Street.

*MERRETT, Peter (3429) Mark entered as smallworker, 28 January 1793. Address: Bath. He appears in directories from 1812-19 as working jeweller, 13 Beaufort Square (in the last year the number is given as 14).

MERRIFIELD, Thomas (3449) Mark entered as plateworker, in partnership with James Burden and Thomas Mitchell (q.v.), 21 February 1831. Address: Bath. Mark entered by power of attorney, signed by George Frederick Bult 'Attorney to the said firm'. Merrifield appears in directories at 10 King Street, between 1826 and 1846, and in 1833 at 23 Kingsmead Terrace.

MITCHELL, Thomas (3449) Mark entered, in partnership with James Burden and Thomas Merrifield (above), 21 February 1831. His name appears in directories from 1837-46 at 23 Kingsmead Terrace. In 1848 the firm appears as Mitchell and Merrifield silversmiths and water gilders.

TOWNSEND, John (3416) Mark (two sizes) entered as plateworker, 10 September 1783. Address: Walcot Street. No references found in directories. Presumably son or brother of the following.

*TOWNSEND, William (3469) Mark entered as plateworker, 7 September 1774. Address: Walcot Street, Bath. The entry not signed by him, only by the Warden. He had, however, appeared as plateworker, Bath, in the Parl. Report list of 1773 and must therefore have entered an earlier mark in the missing register before that year. He appears in the directory for 1791 as working silversmith, 27 Walcot Street, and as freeman (? of the City of Bath). He does not appear in the freeman's register at Goldsmiths' Hall. There is also a Thomas Townsend, High Street, 1784, who may be connected.

WELSHMAN, James (3418) First mark entered as plateworker, 22 July 1813. Address: 43 Walcot Street, Bath. Second mark (two sizes), 3 September 1819. Third mark (two sizes), 13 August 1822. Fourth (two sizes), 13 August 1823. He appears in directories at the above address, 1819-29, and in 1826 also at 23 Kingsmead Terrace, the address of Merrifield and Mitchell (above), but whether connected with them or possibly temporarily sheltered by them does not appear.

WILLIAMS, John (3407) First mark entered as smallworker, in partnership with John Ford, 10 March 1767. Address: Bath. Appears as bucklemaker, Bath, in the Parl. Report list 1773. Second mark, 6 May 1782, entered by power of attorney signed Joseph Walley. No reference to either in directories.

WILLIS, Jacob (3445) Mark entered as plateworker, in partnership with Thomas Graham (above), 29 June 1789. Address: Walcot Street, Bath. By power of attorney signed by Fendall Rushforth. See also under Frome.

*WILLSHER, Jeremiah (3465) Mark entered as plateworker, in partnership with William Bottle (above), 27 October 1796. Address: Bath. By power of attorney signed by Fendall Rushforth.

WYNNE, Thomas (3457) Mark entered as largeworker, 18 October 1754. Address: Bath. His is the earliest mark of a Bath maker appearing in the register, and his name appears without category in the Parl. Report list 1773.

BIRMINGHAM

BALDWIN, John. Mark entered as goldworker, 1817. Address: Whitale Street. (Section VII).

BICKLEY, William. Mark entered, in partnership with Samson Tomlinson, as goldworkers, 1793. Address: Moor Street. (Section VII).

BIRMINGHAM—contd.

CARTWRIGHT, William. Mark entered, in partnership with Samuel Horton, as goldworkers, 1804 (Section VII).

CATER, Thomas (3439-40) Mark entered as smallworker, 13 June 1764. Address: Edmond Street, Birmingham. Second mark, 2 November 1765. Appears both as Thomas Carter and Cater, without category, Edmond Street, Birmingham, in the Parl. Report list 1773.

CLARK, Francis (673) Two marks entered as plateworker, 26 December 1826. Address: 52 Lionel Street. Birmingham. (Included in error in Section I).

COOKE, Elizabeth. Mark entered as goldworker, 1792. No address except town. (Section VII).

COOPER, Benjamin. Incuse mark entered without category, 1749. No address except 'Buringham'. (Section V).

EVANS, Richard (3430) Mark entered as smallworker, 1 June 1787. No address except town. See under Shrewsbury for further details.

GREEN, Thomas (3443) Mark entered as smallworker, 17 March 1766. Address: Birmingham. Appears as bucklemaker, Birmingham, in the Parl. Report list 1773.

HANCOCK, Charles. Mark entered as goldworker, 1799-1814. Address: New Street. (Section VII).

HORTON, George. Mark entered as goldworker, 1824. Address: 66 New Town Row. (Section VII).

HORTON, Samuel. Mark entered, in partnership with William Cartwright, as goldworkers. No address except town. (Section VII).

*JACKSON, James. Mark entered as smallworker, 27 March 1773, by power of attorney. Address: Birmingham (Section IV). Second mark as ringmaker, 28 October 1779 (Secion VII). Appears without category in the Parl. Report list 1773.

MITCHELL, Robert (3453) Mark entered as smallworker, in partnership with Thomas Pemberton, 21 July 1813, by power of attorney signed by Pemberton for both. Address: Snow Hill, Birmingham.

MOORE, John. Mark entered as goldworker, 1811. Address: Caroline Street. (Section VII).

PARKES, Thomas. Mark entered as goldworker, 1826. Address: Town only. (Section VII).

PARSONS, Thomas. Mark entered as goldworker, 1793. Address: Town only. (Section VII).

PEMBERTON, Samuel. Mark entered as goldworker, 1778. Address: Town only. (Section VII).

PEMBERTON, Thomas (3453) See Robert Mitchell (above). Also entered marks alone as goldworker, 1807 and 1826. Address: Snow Hill. (Section VII).

SMITH, John (3423) Mark entered as smallworker, 25 February 1762, by letter of attorney. 'James S. Smith'. Address: Town only. Appears without category in the Parl. Report list 1773.

TOMLINSON, Samuel. Mark entered, in partnership with William Bickley as goldworkers, 1793. Address: Moor Street. (Section VII).

TONGUE, William. Mark entered as goldworker, 1810. Address: 22 High Street. (Section VII).

WALKER, Joseph (3426) Mark entered as plateworker, 27 June 1823. Address: Birmingham. Second mark, 24 December 1823.

WILLMORE, Thomas (3458) Mark entered as plateworker, 23 March 1790. Address: Birmingham.

WOODHILL, James. Mark entered as goldworker, 1823. (Section VII).

WOOLLEY, William. Mark entered as pendant maker (watches), 1813. No address except town. (Section VI).

BRADFORD, WILTSHIRE

*SPENDER. George (3393) Mark entered as smallworker, 6 June 1763, by letter of attorney. Address: Bradford, Wiltshire. The entry is headed 'Spender tone Mark' which seems inexplicable. He is probably the George Spender, son of Thomas Spender victualler, and Sarah, mentioned in the will of the former, 1765, and again in that of Sarah Spender of Newtown, Bradford, 1774. He appears without category in the Parl. Report list 1773.

BRISTOL

BRIMBLECOME, William (3461) Mark entered as smallworker, 11 June 1762. Address: Bristol. Son of Richard Brimblecome porter deceased, apprenticed to

BRISTOL   COLCHESTER

BRISTOL—contd.

Thomas Wigan (of Bristol, q.v.) silversmith and Sarah his wife 23 December 1755. Burgess, 16 February 1763. Appears as bucklemaker, Bristol, in the Parl. Report list 1773.

CHANDLER, Walter. Mark entered as bucklemaker, 1785. No address except town. (Section VII).

COVE, John (3386) Mark entered as large-worker, 4 January 1697–8. 'Free Currier', 'of Bristoll'. 'Entered by Mr Timothy Griffith'. Cove is recorded as having voted in the 1722 election as 'Goldsmith St. Michael's Parish'.

DANIEL, Phineas (3428) Mark entered as smallworker, 6 June 1790. Address: Bristol. By letter of attorney signed Joseph Griffin.

DELANY, Samuel (2505) Mark entered as smallworker, 5 January 1796, in partnership with John Lee. Address: Adam and Eve Lane, Bristol. (Included by error in Section I).

FARR, John (3406) Son of John Farr of Henbury yeoman, apprenticed to William Sladen (or Sloden, q.v.) Goldsmith and Rachel his wife 11 December 1771 on payment of £10 the gift of the Gloucester Society in Bristol. Burgess, 5 September 1780. First mark entered as smallworker, 3 January 1784. Address: Merryport Street, Bristol. Second mark, 21 May 1791.

FRENCH, Joshua (3422, 3635) Mark entered as smallworker, 8 June 1763. Address: Horsefair, Bristol. Appears in partnership with George Spenderlon as bucklemakers, Bristol, in the Parl. Report list 1773.

HOSKINS, Richard (3434) Mark entered as smallworker, 6 May 1791. Address: John's Street, Bristol.

JONES, Frederick. Mark entered as goldworker, 1833. Address: Adam and Eve Passage. (Section VIII).

LEE, John (2505) Mark entered as smallworker, in partnership with Samuel Delany (above). Address: Adam and Eve Lane, Bristol. (Included by error in Section I).

MILLER, Ann (3382) Mark entered as smallworker, 16 January 1764, by letter of attorney signed by James Tooker. Address: Bristol. She was probably the widow of one 'Miller, Jeweller, Broad Street died Saturday last' (Felix Farley's *Journal*, 18 December 1762). Appears as bucklemaker, Bristol, in the Parl. Report list 1773.

MORGAN, Charles (3385) Mark entered as smallworker, 9 February 1807. Address: Nicholas Street, Bristol. A Charles Morgan, jeweller, appears as Burgess, 27 July 1830, son of Joseph Morgan, pewterer, deceased, of Maryport Churchyard and is further mentioned in 1836 and 1865, but this must be too late for identification with the entry above and may perhaps be a relation.

MORGAN, John. Mark entered, in partnership with Samuel Sowerby as goldworkers, 1800. Address: Wine Street. Alone, 1806, no address. (Section VII).

PALMER, Thomas. Mark entered as goldworker, 1791. Address: 13 St. John Street. (Section VIII).

PEIRCE, Thomas (3452) First mark entered as smallworker, 8 November 1763, by power of attorney by Mr Stamp. Address: Bristol. Second mark larger, 21 August 1765. The name appears as Thomas Pierce, watchmaker, moved from Wine Street to Corn Street, 1746. Died 1771, in spite of which he (or perhaps a son) appears without category in the Parl. Report list 1773.

POWELL, John (3412–13) Son of John Powell of Henbury gardener, apprenticed to John Farr (q.v.) 18 December 1793. First mark entered as smallworker, in partnership with Thomas Williamson (below), 8 October 1802. Address: St. Nichols Street, Bristol. Second mark alone, 12 November 1806. Address: 'at Mrs Phillips's', 36 Nicholas Street, Bristol. Described as Goldsmith on becoming Burgess, 16 June 1818.

SEEDE, John. Name entered without mark as plateworker, 25 June 1773. Address: Barton Alley, near St. James's Church Yard, Bristol. Below appears 'Note this is only an Extract of the Entry of his Mark in the former Mark Book' (referring to the missing register of 1758–73).

SLODEN, William (3467) Mark entered as smallworker, 6 October 1764, by letter of attorney signed Walter Hattam (?Hallam). Address: Bristol. He is described as William Sladen Goldsmith in the apprenticeship to him of John Farr (above) 1771, and appears without category, Bristol, in the Parl. Report list 1773.

SOWERBY, Samuel. Mark entered, in partnership with John Morgan as goldworkers, 1800. Address: Wine Street. Alone, 1806. Address: High Street. (Section VII).

TANNER, John. Mark entered as gold-

NOTICES OF PROVINCIAL MAKERS

BRISTOL—contd.
worker, 1788. Address: St. Mary Port Street; St. Augustine's Back, 1795. (Section VII).

TAYLOR, Charles (3388) Son of William Taylor of Clearwell Gloucestershire yeoman, apprenticed to John Tanner jeweller and Mary his wife 10 March 1796 on payment of 70 guineas. Burgess, 28 August 1812, as jeweller. Mark entered as plateworker, in partnership with Thomas Terrett Taylor, 11 January 1837, by power of attorney signed by the latter. Address: High Street, Bristol. City Councillor, 1846-59(?). Died 17 November 1861, aged eighty.

TAYLOR, Thomas Terrett (3388) Presumably son of the above. Probably born 1814. Mark entered, in partnership with Charles Taylor, 1837. Member of City Council, 1859-80. Died 27 June 1880, aged sixty-six.

WIGAN, Thomas (3459) Mark entered as smallworker, 11 July 1763. Address: Bristol. Appears as bucklemaker, Bristol, in the Parl. Report list 1773. Thomas Wigan, son of Thomas Wigan, silversmith (presumably the above), was described as Goldsmith on becoming Burgess, 22 June 1778. He apparently started a banking business with Messrs Jane and Heaven, which failed 1793 (Cave, *History of Banking in Bristol*).

WILLIAMSON, Thomas (3413) Mark entered as smallworker, in partnership with John Powell (above), 8 October 1802. Address: St. Nichols Street, Bristol. The partnership presumably ended by 12 November 1806, when Powell entered a separate mark.

CAMBRIDGE

COULDEN, John. Mark entered as goldworker, 1831. Address: 15 Rose Crescent. (Section VII).

URLING, Samuel (3460) Two marks entered as largeworker, 30 September 1701. Address: Cambridge. 'Entered by Me Jnº Parke'

CHATHAM

BAKER, Samuel (2477) Mark entered as smallworker, 20 December 1731. Address: 'In Chatham free Goldsmith'. His name appears in the Poor Law rate books for the West Borough of Chatham from 1729 to 1754. He was buried at Chatham Parish Church, 29 September 1757. (Included by error in Section I).

CHELMSFORD

CARTER, William. Mark entered as goldworker, 1821. Address: Mousham. (Section VII).

HUNSDON, Thomas Hinde, Mark entered as bucklemaker, 1775. Address: Town only. (Section VIII).

CHESTER

LOWE, George (3392) Two marks entered as smallworker, 21 January 1791. Address: Town only.

CHICHESTER

CHALDECOTT, John (3403) Three marks, one very small, entered as jeweller, 7 June 1769. Address: 'in the City of Chichester in the County of Sussex'. Appears as goldworker in the Parl. Report list 1773.

CHALDECOT(T), Thomas. Presumably a son of the above. Mark entered as smallworker, 12 August 1792. Address: East Street, Chichester, Sussex, by letter of attorney signed Fendall Rushforth. (Section IV).

CIRENCESTER

PADBURY, John. Mark entered as goldworker, 1802. Address: Town only. (Section VII).

COLCHESTER

HUTCHINSON, Richard I (3397) Born 1676, son of Richard Hutchinson (who died 1680) late of Colchester in the County of Essex. Goldsmith, apprenticed to John Sutton (of London, q.v.) 17 December 1690 for eight years. Freedom unrecorded. Admitted Free Burgess of Colchester, 1700. Mark entered as largeworker, 13 December 1699. Address: 'in Colchester'. He died 1701-2. The mark however is found on church plate up till at least 1714 and the business may therefore have been carried on by his widow, or son Richard (below), using his father's mark (*Essex Review*, Vol. LX, No. 239, July 1951, pp. 162-3).

HUTCHINSON, Richard II (3433) Son of the above. Mark entered as largeworker, 28 June 1727. Address: 'at Colchester'; 'entered by Tho. Thorne over against Maiden lane in Wood Street'. The business was carried on in the parishes of St. Nicholas and St. Runwald. 'Mr. Hutchinson' is rated at £17 in the latter parish, 1755. One of the same name moved to Norwich in 1764, but this may have been another Richard of the next generation. The name however

COLCHESTER—contd.

appears as voting in the Colchester parliamentary elections of 1768 to 1790. His mark appears on a number of pieces of church plate in Essex. There is presumably a connection between the Thomas Thorne who entered Hutchinson's mark for him and the following maker.

THORN, James (3415) Mark (two sizes) entered as smallworker, 20 September 1758, by power of attorney. Address: 'of Colchester'. He was described as clockmaker on his marriage to Hester, daughter of Isaac Green of Lexden, Colchester, gentleman, and died in 1762 (will proved 18 May). His son James Thorn, silversmith, died in 1799. (L. C. Sier, 'Colchester Clock Makers', *Essex Review*, Vol. XLIX.) The entry James Thorn, without category, appears in the Parl. Report list 1773, presumably for the son in continuation of the business.

COVENTRY

BROWN, William. Mark entered as watchcasemaker, 1822. Address: Well Street. (Section VI).

DERBY

BROCKES, Edward (3383) Mark entered as largeworker, undated, probably April 1697 on commencement of register. Address: 'in Darby', followed by the signature of Francis Garthorne, presumably acting on his behalf.

DEVIZES

BURROUGH, Thomas (3438) First mark entered as smallworker, 26 May 1759. Address: Devizes, Wiltshire. Second mark as silversmith, 11 October 1769, by letter of attorney signed Sam. Meriton (q.v.). Third mark similar, 18 October 1769. Fourth (TB Roman capitals), 8 November 1769. Fifth mark smaller, 23 February 1778. Burrough was first recorded as jeweller of Devizes on the apprenticeship to him of Isaac Tricker, 24 May 1751; as bookseller and goldsmith (Waylen's *History of Devizes*) 1756, when he was collecting money for a new road. He published a map of Devizes in 1759 and other books up to 1776. He appears as bucklemaker, Devizes, Wiltshire, in the Parl. Report list 1773. Died 17 February 1781. His will, proved 2 April, mentions five daughters, of whom Frances was wife of Bennett Swaine (sic, for Benjamin Swayne below)

SWAYNE, Benjamin (3384) Mark entered as smallworker, 14 May 1781. Address: Devizes. The date strongly suggests that he had succeeded with his wife Frances to the business of his father-in-law, Thomas Burrough (above). He was probably dead by 9 April 1783, when Frances entered two marks as bucklemaker (Section VIII).

*EXETER

*ADAMS, John (3399) Mark entered as smallworker, 17 April 1787. Address: Exeter, Devonshire. He was entered as a member of the Exeter Goldsmiths' Company, 7 August 1780. Warden 1781-3, 1788-9 and 1793-5. Accountant to the Company 1785, 1789 and 1797 till his death in March 1806.

*EUSTACE, Thomas (3442) Mark entered as plateworker, 20 April 1779. Address: Exeter, Devonshire. He was entered as a member of the Exeter Goldsmiths' Company, 7 August 1774. Warden, 1777-9. Bankrupt and discharged from the Company, 1789.

FARNHAM, SURREY

NEWLAND, Ridg(ewa)y William (2463) Mark entered as smallworker, 15 March 1800. Address: Farnham, Surrey. Referred to as clockmaker by Nigel Temple, *Farnham Buildings and People*, 1963. (Included by error in Section I).

FROME

WILLIS, Jacob (3425) Mark entered as smallworker, 7 April 1792. Address: Frome, Somerset. He had previously worked at Bath, under which see also.

GAINSBOROUGH, LINCOLNSHIRE

DICKINSON, Joseph (3405) Mark entered as smallworker, 21 April 1780. Address: Gainsborough, County of Lincoln, by letter of attorney signed Daniel Wall, Joseph Dickinson, described as Goldsmith, jeweller, bachelor, married Ann Bate, 3 November 1754, both of Gainsborough. He is described as silversmith on the burial of his son, 1755, and subsequently so till 1762. Died November 1782; described in his will as jeweller and silversmith, the business to be carried on in the joint names of his widow and son Joseph (born 1756). The mark entered may therefore be of either father or son. The name disappears from the rate book in 1797.

GLOUCESTER

*WASHBOURN, George (3394) Mark entered as smallworker, 7 April 1773. Address: Gloucester. His name is entered again, without mark, as ringmaker with the same date, Gloucester, signed by Thos Wallis, Attorney, with the statement 'Note this is only an Extract of the Entry of his Mark in the former Mark Book'.

HASTINGS

WILLIAMS, Henry. Mark entered as goldworker, 1834. Address: 52 High Street. (Section VII).

HITCHIN

FIELD, Daniel. Mark entered as goldworker, 1780. Address: Town only. Earlier at Luton. (Section VII).

HUNGERFORD

BANCE, Matthew. Mark entered as goldworker, 1780. Address: Town only. (Section VII).

IPSWICH

DALLINGER, Joseph (3421) First mark entered as plateworker, 15 May 1824. Address: Church Lane, St. Matthew's, Ipswich. Second mark, 2 May 1828. Address: 21 Davey Place, Norwich. Dallinger does not appear in Ipswich directories, burgess rolls or poll books. William Henry Dallinger, presumably a son, appears as copper-plate printer and stationer from 1846 to 1866. See further under Norwich.

LEICESTER

ANDREWS, George (3391) Mark entered as smallworker, 24 November 1737, by letter of attorney signed Clifford Ray. No trace of this maker can be found in local records.

LITTLE RISENDON, GLOUCESTER

*HOYTE, Frances (3396) Mark entered as largeworker, undated, probably April 1697 on commencement of register. Described as 'Widd', presumably still responsible in retirement, of a London establishment. It is however curious that there appears to be no record of any male goldsmith of this name working earlier in London.

LIVERPOOL

COAKLEY, John (3420) Mark entered as plateworker, 3 September 1832. Address: 18 Arley Street, Vauxhall Road, Liverpool, by power of attorney, by Benjamin Ward, Attorney to the said John Coakley. This maker appears as silversmith, 18 Arley Street, in the Liverpool directory for 1829.

JONES, Robert. Mark entered as goldworker, 1790. Address: 1 Water Street. (Section VII).

SAMUEL, Lewis (1965) First mark entered as spoonmaker, 3 September 1830. Address: 4 Lord Street, Liverpool. Second mark, 11 June 1835. Lewis Samuel, born 11 March 1783. Married Catherine Yates, 1804. Died 1854. Appears in the Liverpool directories as silversmith, goldsmith, watch manufacturer and jeweller, 1805-53. Address: Pool Lane until 1813, then various addresses in Lord Street till 1848, when retirement presumed. Thereafter at 16 Percy Street. (*History and Genealogy of the Jewish families of Yates and Samuel of Liverpool*; ed. L. Wolf, 1958.) (Included by error in Section I.)

LUTON

FIELD, Daniel. Mark entered as goldworker, 1780. Later at Hitchin. (Section VII).

MANCHESTER

OLLIVANT, Thomas (3450-1) First mark entered as plateworker, 12 May 1789. Address: Manchester. Second mark, 3 November 1830. Address: 16 Exchange Street, Manchester. The directories from 1794 onwards show various entries for the firm: Ollivant, Sons and Nephew, silversmiths, 18 Exchange Street; Mr Ollivant, silversmith; house Hulme and 4 Marsden -c(?). Ollivant died in 1868. In about 1855 he was joined by J. W. Botsford, and as Ollivant and Botsford the firm still remains in existence.

ORME, Joseph Boardman (3402) Mark entered as plateworker, 14 February 1793. Address: Manchester. He appears as jeweller, hardware and toy merchant, 102 Market Street Lane, in the Manchester directory for 1794.

PIPE, J. Wil^{on}. Mark entered as goldworker, 1825. Address: Market Street. (Section VII).

MARLBOROUGH

SPACKMAN, Thomas (3455) Mark entered as smallworker, 1 November 1725. Address: Marlborough. A Thomas Spackman of Hankerton married Elizabeth King at St.

721

MARLBOROUGH

MARLBOROUGH—contd.
Mary's, Marlborough, 6 September 1714. The relationship of this maker to the London goldsmiths of the same name (q.v.) remains obscure.

NEWBURY

*GRANTHAM, John (3408) Mark entered as smallworker, 17 April 1771. Address: 'Newbury Barckshire'. Appears as goldworker, Newbury, Berkshire, in the Parl. Report list 1773.

LOVIDGE, Thomas (3448) Mark entered as goldworker, 12 March 1778. Address: 'Newbury Bercks'. He appears as goldsmith, Newbury, Berkshire, in the Parl. Report list 1773 as already having entered a mark. Second mark as goldworker, 23 October 1793 (Section VII).

NEWCASTLE

COHEN, David. Mark entered as smallworker, 17 June 1830. Address: 5 Collingwood Street, Newcastle. Below this is pencilled 'qu; 79 Grey Street Newcastle' presumably a later address of the same. (Section IV).

LANGLANDS, John (3411) Mark entered as plateworker, in partnership with John Robertson, 3 March 1780. Address: Newcastle upon Tyne, by letter of attorney signed Charles Storey. It is difficult to think why such a well-established firm as this in a town with a properly conducted assay office thought it necessary to enter a mark for London use. Was it perhaps to avoid some kind of leakage of trade secrets in their own town?

REID, Christian Ker and David (3387) First mark entered as plateworkers, 10 October 1815, by power of attorney signed by William Ker Reid, Attorney to Christian Ker Reid. Address: Dean Street, Newcastle. Second mark small, for Christian Reid only, 30 July 1817. Second mark of the partnership (three sizes), 16 May 1828.

ROBERTSON, John (3411) See under Langlands (above).

'NORFOK'

BRINDS, Jon (3400) Mark entered as smallworker, undated, c. November–December 1721. The entry is in a peculiar form 'Hereunder is the Certificat of Jon Brinds being the Owner of this Mark Norfok'.

SHEFFIELD

NORTHAMPTON

SHARP, James (3424) Mark entered as plateworker, 3 December 1817, by power of attorney signed Jas. M. Jeyes (?). Address: Northampton. He first appears in the Northampton Pollbook as watchmaker, Mercers Row, 1818; as silversmith, 1820 and 1824; watchmaker, 1826–35, in the latter year at The Drapery. He advertised in *Northampton Mercury*, 8 April 1837, that he had sold his business of clock and watchmaker, silversmith and jeweller to William Kirk.

NORWICH

BIDWELL, Joseph (1786) Mark entered as smallworker, 16 January 1830. Address: Red Lyon Street, Norwich. He is recorded here as engraver and copperplate printer from 1830–54. (Included by error in Section I).

DALLINGER, Joseph (3421) First mark entered at Ipswich (see above). Second mark, 21 Davey Place, Norwich, 2 May 1828, where he is recorded as engraver, lithographer and copperplate printer.

FOLGATE, W. (3466) Mark entered as plateworker, in partnership with William Osborne, 18 November 1825, by power of attorney signed by Wm. Osborne. Address: Norwich. He is recorded as working jeweller till 1830 at 20 The Gentlemen's Walk.

HERBERT, John (1820) First mark entered as smallworker, 22 April 1828. Address: 9 Rampant Horse Street, Norwich. Second mark (two sizes) 23 July 1836, on move to 31 Pottergate Street, Norwich. He is noted as heraldic chaser and hairworker until 1836. (Included by error in Section I).

LEVI, Myer. Mark entered as goldworker, 1823. Address: 10 Rampant Horse Street. (Section VII)

OSBORNE, William (3466) Mark entered as plateworker, in partnership with W. Folgate (above), 18 November 1825.

SULLIVAN, Charles. Mark entered as goldworker, 1828. Address: 20 Goat Street; St. Andrew's Street, 1831. (Section VII).

WOODS, Robert (3436) Mark entered as smallworker, 14 March 1822. Address: Old King's Head Yard, St. Stephen's Street, Norwich. Also noted as working jeweller in Red Lion Street till 1842.

NOTICES OF PROVINCIAL MAKERS

Nottingham

GREEN, John. Mark entered as goldworker, 1776. Address: Town only. (Section VII).

GREEN, Thomas. Mark entered as goldworker, 1783. Address: Town only. (Section VII).

Oxford

GOLDWIRE, Richard (3431-2, 3770) First mark entered as smallworker, 28 March 1753. Address: Oxford. Second mark, 15 September 1763. Address: 'of the Parish of St. Clement near the City of Oxford in the County Thereoff'. He is recorded in the Survey of Oxford, 1772, as owner or occupier of a house in St. Clement's parish (H. E. Salter, *Surveys and Tokens*, Oxford Historical Society, 1923). There seems a strong possibility that earlier than his first Oxford mark he had been working in Salisbury. See no. 3770 for a mark (RG) noted on a snuffbox of 1744 which itself was engraved 'Richard Goldwyer Sarum'. Appears as Richard Gladwire, plateworker, Oxford, in the Parl. Report list 1773.

LOCK, Edward (3389) Mark entered as smallworker, 30 July 1762. Address: Oxford. Frequently recorded in the City's archives as silversmith or goldsmith. Freeman, 1759. Appears without category in the Parl. Report list 1773. Mayor, 1776 and 1791. Also held offices as Key Keeper, Chamberlain and Senior Bailiff. No address is recorded however. (M. G. Hobson, *Oxford Council Acts 1752-1801*, Oxford Historical Society, 1957, and H. E. Salter, *Oxford City Properties*, Oxford Historical Society, 1926.)

Plymouth

BROWN, Jnº (3401) Mark entered as smallworker, 23 July 1771, by letter of attorney signed by Robt. A. Cox (presumably the London worker of that name, q.v.). 'Goldsmith'. Address: Plymouth. John Brown of Plymouth appears in the assay books of the Exeter Goldsmiths' Company from 1765 to 1783. His entire output consisted of buckles and chapes for naval shoes and swords. He appears as goldsmith, Plymouth, in the Parl. Report list 1773, and entered second mark as bucklemaker, 1778 (Section VIII).

NATHAN, Jacob. Mark entered as goldworker, 1813. Address: Stonehouse. (Section VII).

Portsmouth

The four following makers all entered their marks in April 1759, which clearly suggests a visitation by the Goldsmiths' Company.

*BOURN, Loader. Mark entered as smallworker, 20 April 1759. Address: Portsmouth (Section IV). Appears without category, at Portsmouth, in the Parl. Report list 1773.

HARDING, John (3409) Mark entered as smallworker, 5 April 1759. Address: Portsmouth. The Portsmouth rate books show John Harden, High Street, 1759; and John Harding, 1 Broad Street, and 78 High Street, 1781. He appears without category in the Parl. Report list 1773.

PICOTT, Thomas. Mark entered as smallworker, 5 April 1759. Address: Portsmouth. The mark entered by 'Sam: Eaton of London'. (Section IV.) He appears without category, Portsmouth, in the Parl. Report list 1773.

SAMUEL, Merducea. Mark entered as smallworker, 2 April 1759. Address: 'of Portsmouth Comon' (Section IV). Appears as Mordecai Samuel, without category, Portsmouth Common, in the Parl. Report list 1773. Perhaps the Samuel Mordecai in Colledge Street, 1780-6. The name suggests a Jewish 'slop-seller' to the Navy, the mark probably for shoebuckles.

Reading

TRUSS, William (2896, 3454, 3468) See under London for his apprenticeship and entry of first mark c. 1713. According to Heal he is recorded in London till 1721. He then entered two marks as largeworker (Sterling and New Standard), 22 September 1721. Address: 'att Reading', where he presumably had returned and continued to work. There are, however, no traces of him in Reading records. William Truss, plumber, is recorded 1754-82, perhaps a son.

Salisbury

JEBOULT, Hugh (3395) Mark entered as smallworker, 25 May 1787. Address: Salisbury. Signs as Hugh Jeboult Jr. There is no trace of him in Salisbury records.

Sheffield

HARWOOD, Samuel (3437) Mark entered as spoonmaker, 25 April 1836. Address: Union Street, Sheffield. He had previously entered a mark at the Sheffield Assay

SHEFFIELD

SHEFFIELD—contd.

Office, 1835, and appears in the Sheffield trade directory, 1833 as Samuel Harwood and Co. merchants and manufacturers of table-knives and silver and plated dessert and fruit-knives etc., 99 Norfolk Street and 12 Norfolk Lane, Sheffield. They do not appear in the next directory of 1849.

HIRST, John (3410) First mark entered as smallworker, 25 February 1765. Address: Farfield, near Sheff^d, Yorkshire. Second mark, 26 February 1770. He is first mentioned as Cutler of Sheffield, 1753; and as John Hirst and Co., bucklemakers of Far Field, 1760. He appears in the Parl. Report list 1773 as haftmaker. Died 1774.

NOWILL, Thomas. Mark entered as goldworker, 1779. Address: High Street. (Section VII).

RO(W)BOT(H)AM, John (3414) Mark entered as smallworker, 14 December 1768. Address: Sheffield, Yorkshire, by letter of attorney signed Wm. Rogers. He appears without category in the Parl. Report list 1773. Son of John Rowbotham carpenter, apprenticed at Sheffield as cutler 1729. Free of the Cutlers' Company (of Sheffield), 1751. One of the original thirty Guardians of the Standard of Wrought Plate appointed for life on the establishment of the Sheffield Assay Office in 1773. He entered a mark with William Hancock at Sheffield in 1773, and others in 1774 and 1776. Address: Norfolk Street. Appears in the Sheffield trade directory, 1774 as John Rowbotham and Co., silversmiths and platers, Norfolk Street. Died 1781.

TYAS, Thomas, Junior (3456) Mark entered as smallworker, 18 May 1769. Address: Sheffield, Yorkshire, by power of attorney signed by Daniel Cookson. Son of Thomas Tyas, cutler, free of the Cutlers' Company (of Sheffield), 1767. Appears without category in the Parl. Report list 1773, and in the Sheffield trade directory, 1774, as table-knife cutler, Lambert Knole, Sheffield. Not in the second directory of 1787.

VAVASOUR, Walter. Mark entered as goldworker, 1774. (Section VII).

SHREWSBURY

EVANS, Richard (3430) Mark entered as smallworker, 3 May 1779. Address: Shrewsbury. He was probably son of James Evans of Shrewsbury, watchmaker, and grandson of Jenkin Evans of Oswestry, clerk, baptized 17 March 1754. Admitted to the Company of Mercers, Goldsmiths etc. of Shrewsbury, 1780, and Burgess of the town the same year. An elder brother, Pryce James Evans was a watchmaker in Cornmarket, Shrewsbury for many years. Richard Evans subsequently entered a second mark at Goldsmiths' Hall as of Birmingham, 1787 (see above).

SUNDERLAND

THOMPSON, John (3417) Mark entered as plateworker, 12 May 1785. Address: Sunderland. Son of George and Isabel Thompson, born 5 September 1746 in Sunderland. Described as goldsmith on signing marriage bond for William Barnes of Sunderland in 1787. Mentioned in a list of 'goldsmiths trading in places where there was no assay in the habit of bringing their plate to Newcastle to be touched', as having died 30 May 1801, aged fifty-four (*Archeologia Aeliana*, 3rd Series, XI.116).

THAME, OXFORD

STONE, Edward (3390) Mark entered as smallworker, 1 July 1761. Address: Thame in Oxfordshire. He appears as bucklemaker in the Parl. Report list 1773.

THURSLEY, SURREY

LOWE, Caleb. Mark entered as smallworker, 20 September 1790. Address: 'Thursbye near Godalman Surrey' (Section IV). This is presumably the village of Thursley, just off the Portsmouth road before reaching the Devil's Punchbowl at Hindhead. One does not imagine a very brisk trade for Mr Lowe in this rural retreat, but perhaps he pursued the craft as a hobby in retirement.

WALSALL

ADAMS, Joseph (3398) Mark entered as smallworker, 25 September 1772. Address: Walsall, Staffordshire. Joseph and Chape Adams, bucklemakers, Adams Row, appear in Sketchley and Adams, *Directory of Walsall*, 1767; Joseph Adams, bucklemaker, same address 1771, and again 1790. Mark entered as bucklemaker, 1783 (Section VIII).

WIGAN

DONCASTER, Thomas (3441) Mark entered as smallworker, 5 September 1758, by letter of attorney signed F. Pages. Address: Wigan, in Lankashire. Doncaster

WIGAN—contd.
petitioned vainly for freedom as watchmaker and silversmith, 1755. He married Hannah Rizley, 2 January 1756. Further petition for freedom, October 1756, rejected through opposition of tinsmiths who claimed Doncaster's intention to practice as a tinman. Freedom was finally granted as watchmaker, silversmith and tinsmith, 31 December 1763. Appears without category, 'Wiggan Lancashire', in the Parl. Report list 1773. Burgess, 1788. Bailiff, 1789. Married secondly, Ann Scott, 1792. Alderman and Mayor, 1795 and 1798. Described as banker, 1800. Died after 1802. (Arthur J. Hawkes, *Clockmakers and Watchmakers of Wigan*.)

WOLVERHAMPTON

CROWLEY, John Junior (3404) Mark entered as smallworker, 24 August 1803. Address: Wolverhampton. He appears as 'Optician', 6 Court, 3 Lichfield Street, Wolverhampton, in the rate books from about 1802 to 1811. The mark was therefore presumably for spectacle frames.

Addenda to Notices of Provincial Makers

BATH

BASNETT, William (page 715) Described as jeweller on the apprenticeship to him of George Brown, 1 May 1778. (I.R., R.B.)

GRAHAM, Thomas (page 715) Apprenticed to William Townshend (sic) of Bath (q.v.), silversmith, 10 September 1768 for seven years on payment of £42. (I.R. 1/25 f.193, R.B.)

HOWELL, Thomas (page 716) Described as working jeweller on apprenticeship of Peter Merrett to him 1775, as working goldsmith on taking Jeremiah Willsher apprentice 1788 and as goldsmith for apprenticeship of Daniel P. Bishop, 16 January 1797. (I.R., R.B.)

MERRETT, Peter (page 716) Apprenticed to Thomas Howell of the City of Bath, working jeweller, 2 January 1775 for seven years on payment of £20. (I.R. 1/28 f.114, R.B.)

TOWNSEND, William (page 716) Son of Henry Townsend, apprenticed to Nathaniell Nangle of the City of Bristol, jeweller (possibly related to George Nangle of London, q.v.), 12 April 1743 for seven years on payment of 5 shillings. He was described as silversmith on taking Thomas Graham and Richard Berryman Symons apprentices in 1768 and 1775 respectively. (I.R. 1/16 f.228 et al., R.B.)

WILLSHER, Jeremiah (page 716) Apprenticed to Thomas Howell of Bath, Somerset, working goldsmith, 2 August 1788 for seven years on payment of £42. (I.R. 1/34 f.8, R.B.)

BIRMINGHAM

JACKSON, James (page 717) He was first Assaymaster of the Birmingham Assay Office on its foundation 1773. (Information Mr Hamil Westwood.)

BRADFORD, WILTSHIRE

SPENDER, George (page 717) His parentage is now confirmed as son of Thomas Spender of Bradford, Wilts., victualler, apprenticed to John Forster, Citizen and Goldsmith of London, 2 June 1756 for seven years on payment of £12. 12s. and turned over 5 September 1760 to William Shaw II (q.v.). Spender did not, however, take up the freedom of the Goldsmiths' Company. (R.B.)

EXETER

ADAMS, John (page 720) Apprenticed to James & Foy of Taunton, goldsmiths, 10 October 1772 for seven years on payment of £90. (I.R. 1/58 f.164, R.B.)

EUSTACE, Thomas (page 720) Apprenticed to Richard Jenkins of the City of Exon, 'jeweller &ca', 1 May 1766 for seven years on payment of £36. 15s. (I.R. 1/24 f.211, R.B.)

MARDER, John See Biographical Addendum, page 758.

GLOUCESTER

WASHBOURN, George (page 721) Well known in Gloucester as a watch- and clockmaker, a member of a family of clockmakers (G. Dowler, *Gloucester Clock and Watchmakers*). He appears to have undertaken some silversmithing as the Cathedral Treasury Accounts for 1797 contain an

GLOUCESTER

GLOUCESTER—*contd.*
entry 'To George Wasbourne for gilding and repairing the candlesticks at the communion table 11–00–00'. (Information Mr A. J. H. Sale.)

LITTLE RISENDON, GLOUCESTER

HOYTE, Frances (page 721) She was the widow of St. John Hoyte, 'Citizen and Goldsmith of London of St. John Zachary, London', appointed executrix in his will, proved in 1693. (Information Mr A. J. H. Sale.)

PORTSMOUTH

NEWBURY

GRANTHAM, John (page 722) Possibly identifiable with John Grantham, apprenticed to Jo: Francis Bomreliet(?) of St. Clement's, jeweller, 7 September 1762 for seven years on payment of £31. 10s. (I.R. 1/23 f.113, R.B.)

PORTSMOUTH

BOURN, Loader (page 723) Presumably to be identified with Loader, son of James Bourn of Sheerness, apprenticed to Michael Lade of the City of Canterbury, goldsmith, 22 April 1730 for seven years on payment of £100. (I.R. 1/49 f.187, R.B.)

III
Notes to Makers listed in Part One, Sections IV, V, VI and VII

BOURNE, Aaron (pages 281, 355) He appears as goldsmith, Maiden Lane, Covent Garden, Baldwin's *New Complete Guide*, 1770 and 1777. (R.B.)

COOPER, Benjamin (page 289) He is probably the one of that name who appears in Parker and Wakelin's Workmen's Ledger No. 2 as supplying chain, hussar, swan neck and plain spurs from December 1770.

DROZ, Frederick (page 360) Probably of Swiss origin. Jean Fredrich Humbert Droz, journeyman watchmaker from Le Locle, was executed for murder in Amsterdam, 1766. Charles Humbert Droz, goldsmith from Neuchâtel, acquired Amsterdam citizenship in 1804. (Information Mr K. Citroen.)

FLOWER, Edward (page 359) Edward Flower, jeweller and toyman, Rolls Building, Fetter Lane, presumably father of the above, appears in Baldwin's *New Complete Guide*, 1770, and at Chichester Rents, Chancery Lane in 1777. (R.B.)

GIBBS, Solomon (page 318) The year of mark entry should read 1718.

GURDEN, Benjamin (pages 281, 356) Benjamin Gurden and Son appear as jeweller (sic), 114 Wood Street, in the *New Complete Guide*, 1777. (R.B.)

HANET, George (page 336) John and George Hanet, probably his sons, appear as goldworkers, Porter Street near Leicester Fields in the *London Directory*, 1768 and Baldwin's *New Complete Guide*, 1770. (R.B.)

REDRICK, Charles (page 335) Should read Christopher Richard Redrick who was son of Richard Redrick, watchcase-maker, Aldermanbury, of the Drapers' Company, apprenticed to his father 26 November 1782 for seven years and free 4 May 1790. (Drapers' Company records, S.T.)

WORSDELL, William (page 386) Born at Devizes, Wiltshire. Emigrated to Holland 1775 and became free of the Haarlem Corporation as able to employ six journeymen. In 1776 asked permission to change his mark WW to that of 'a lion passant', first granted by the Corporation, but then cancelled by the Masters of the Mint foreseeing difficulties because of his intention to export his work, mainly buttons, to England. (Information Mr K. Citroen.)

Appendix

Index of Goldsmiths recorded in the Biographical Dictionary and Addenda who were Freemen of Livery Companies other than the Goldsmiths

APOTHECARIES
Sydenham William Peppin

BAKERS
Micah Wilkins

BARBER SURGEONS
William Cartlidge
Joseph Healy
Henry Hickman

BLACKSMITHS
William Thompson
Thomas Wildman
William Wildman

BOWYERS
Edmund Cooper

BREWERS
Joseph Bird

BRICKLAYERS
Richard Lovell

BRODERERS
John Beauchamp
Robert Burton
Henry Clarke I
George Cox
Andrew Dalton
Edward Dymond
John Harwood
Caleb Hill
William Juson
Jeremiah King
Isaac Liger
John Liger
John Ludlow
Wiliam Lutwyche
Thomas Mann
Nathaniel Roe
Richard Scarlett
William Scarlett
Bowyer Walker

BUTCHERS
Peter Archambo I
Thomas Jenkins
Jacob Margas
Samuel Margas
Peter Meure
Philip Shaw

CARPENTERS
William Burkitt
John Edwards III

CARTERS
James Young

CLOCKMAKERS
Edward Bayley
John Berry
William Bertram
Christopher Cutting
James Delander
Anne Fletcher
Edward Fletcher
Robert Higgs
Edward Horne I and II
Edward Hunt I
William Jelf
Ambrose Lewis
Philip Phillips
William Trenholme
John Vincent(?)

CLOTHWORKERS
Charles Aldridge
Edward Aldridge I
Richard Atkins
Henry Bailey
Thomas Burwash
William Burwash
Robert Cates
Burrage Davenport
Daniel Denney
Charles Fox I and II
Philip Freeman
Henry Green
Samuel Herbert
John Langford II
Thomas Moore I
Richard Pearce
William Plummer
Joseph Read
Nicholas Roe

COOPERS
Henry Avery
John Cann (?)
Ann Smith

CORDWAINERS
John Robinson II
Benjamin Smith I

CUTLERS
Thomas Bass
John Bennett II
Hugh Brawne
Henry Bruin
Thomas Bulley
John Carman I and II
Richard Chapman
Benjamin Corbett
Thomas Dealtry
William Deards
William Harris
Elias Hosier
John Kenton
George Littleboy
Peter Marsh
Thomas North
John Reason
Joseph Reason
John Roberts
Thomas Roberts
George Shaw
Daniel Shelmerdine
William Strange
Isaac Stuart
Abraham Thurkle
Francis Thurkle
George Francis Thurkle
Thomas Vicaridge
John Wilkins
George Willcocks
William Willson
George Young
Nathaniel Young

DRAPERS
James Beattie
Richard Botfield
Charles Bull
Richard Calvert
Daniel Cole
Thomas Cole
John Eckford I
Andrew Hogg
John Jarratt
Richard Lockwood
Richard Palmer
Christopher Richard Redrick
Richard Redrick
William Ripsher

APPENDIX

Drapers—*contd.*
Philip Rundell
Simon Thriscross
Thomas Walker

Dyers
William Hooker
Thomas Lawrence I and II

Farriers
Peter Cramillion

Fishmongers
John Harvey I
Mathew Judkins
William Lane
George Manley
William Owen
Thomas Peirce

Fletchers
George Houston

Founders
John Allen II
Michael Barnett
Robert Bodley
Timothy Ley
Robert Lovell
George Meale
Richard Nightingale
Thomas Sharratt
Robert Turner
Thomas Wheeler

Girdlers
Charles Aldridge
Adrian Eastwick
Francis Garthorne
Henry Green
William Stephenson

Glaziers
Samuel Johnson

Glovers
John Allen I
William Allen I
Joseph Ash I
Roger Biggs
Henry Dell
Frederick De Veer
George Evans
Richard Glanville
William Key
William Lukin II

Grocers
Abel Brokesby
John Edwards II
Robert Garrard I and II

John Hely
John Kemble
William Knight I
Charles Laughton I and II
Edward Laughton
Jane Laughton
John Laughton I and II
Benjamin Page
Thomas Prew
Thomas Prichard
Edward Raven
John Reynolds
George Ridout
Thomas Ripshear
Taylor Trevillion
Francis Turner
Robert White

Haberdashers
John Alderhead
John Brockus
William Bull
Nicholas Clausen
Benjamin Cooper I
Isaac Dighton
James Englie
Thomas Fawler
Jacob Foster
Richard Gardiner
Edward Gibson
George Giles
Bartholomew Harwood
Dennis Langton
John Leach
Robert Lucas
George Manjoy
George Moody
Vaughan Peake
Charles Perier
Richard Peters
Lewis Plank
Edward Pocock
Hugh Saunders
John Smithsend
Ambrose Stevenson
John Wisdome
Daniel Yerbury

Innholders
Richard Turner

Joiners
James Barker
Benjamin Bird
Benjamin Blakely
John Cooke II
Robert Dennison
Edward Hunsdon

Christopher Nicholle
Abel Skinner
Edward Thompson I and II
Henry Thompson
George Vernon
Richard Woodhouse

Leathersellers
Richard Burcombe
John Burgh
John Carter I
George Chebsey
William Chebsey
William Coles
Robert Collier
Samuel Eaton
Robert Elliot
Richard Fuller
Abraham Pope
Francis Springgall

Longbowstringmakers
Paul Callard
Paul Crespin
John Goode
Paul Hanet
Rene Hudell
John Innocent
William Pryor
Christopher Woods
William Young

Loriners
Stephen Adams I
William Bedford
John Betts
John Hague I
William Holmes
Ferdinando Hughes
James Hughes
William Jury
Edward Mumford
Joseph Mumford

Mercers
Christopher Barker
Thomas W. Barker
James Britton
Thomas Jackson I
Samuel Roby
Daniel Stephens

Merchant Taylors
William Atkinson
Charles Bagshaw
William Bellassyse
John Blunt
Thomas Brydon
Robert Butterfield

730

APPENDIX

MERCHANT TAYLORS—contd.
Daniel Chapman
Thomas Corbet
Walter Crisp
Epaphroditus Fowler
John Furnivall
George Gines
Richard Gines
Thomas Gladwin
Samuel Green
James Hervot
James Jago
John Jago
Thomas Justis
Thomas Kedden
William Laidman
John Langford I
John Gibson Leadbetter
Seth Lofthouse
John Munday
Joseph Munday
Robert Munday
Jacob Neale
Robert Newman
William Overton
Joseph Perkins I
Henry Plumpton
John Rand
Thomas Redhead
James Savage
James Slater
Daniel Smith
Thomas Steed
Joseph Tuckwell
William Walters
 (? Watters)

MUSICIANS
George Hindmarsh
James Peacock

NEEDLEMAKERS
William Chandless
William Eaton
Samuel Godbehere
Mark Thomegay

PEWTERERS
John Blake
John William Blake
William Chawner I
Clement Cheese
Robert Rutland
George Smith III

PLAISTERERS
John James Whiting

POULTERERS
John Gray

SADDLERS
John Everit

SCRIVENERS
John Wichehallis

SKINNERS
Charles Archer
George Beale
Abraham Buteux
Benjamin Clare
Benjamin Davis
Anthony Francia
John Johnson I
John Thompson I

SPECTACLEMAKERS
Thomas Bumfriss
Thomas Cutmore
Orlando Jackson
Arthur Worboys

STATIONERS
Thomas Bowen I
Richard Hillum (?)
Joseph Norwood (?)

TURNERS
Samuel Meriton I and II (?)

VINTNERS
Joseph Bell III
William Broadbent
John Durandeau
John Hague II
John Houle
Edward Lees
Edward Robinson I
Ebenezer Roe
Paul Storr
John Edward Terrey
George Wintle
James Wintle
Thomas Wintle

WAXCHANDLERS
George Brome
George Ellis
William Fordham
Edward Jones
Matthew E. Lofthouse
Seth Lofthouse
James Thomasson

WEAVERS
Thomas Penn (?)

The following goldsmiths appear as Liverymen of the Companies listed below in Supplement to the *British Directory for 1792* by P. Barfoot and J. Wilkes, in addition to those in Appendix above. (R.B.)

CURRIERS
Charles Hougham
John Cook Pettit

FARRIERS
William Pryor

FISHMONGERS
William J. Edwards
James Hyde
Thomas Hyde

GIRDLERS
John Lambe

GLOVERS
George Evans

PEWTERERS
George Smith III

TURNERS
David Field
Thomas Harper

WEAVERS
Edward Darvill

Addenda to Biographical Dictionary

Much of the new parental and apprenticeship information now added below derives from the Inland Revenue Record of Taxes paid on Apprentice Indentures in the Public Record Office, referred to as I.R., with volume and folio number. New freedom details are from individual Companies and also from the City Freedom Records in the Guildhall Library, referred to as C.F.1. The contributions of Robert Barker and Sarah Tanner from these sources are indicated by their initials. Bankruptcy details derive from the Public Record Office Docket Books B3 and 4 by courtesy of John Culme, and certain information from Parker and Wakelin's Workmen's Ledger No. 2 (*Garrard MSS*, National Art Library) from Helen Clifford. Further information has come from the extracts from the Sun Insurance records supplied to Goldsmiths' Hall Library by Mr S. B. Turner and his associates.

It should be noted that whereas in previous editions it was stated that the records of both the Loriners' and Longbowstringmakers' Companies had been destroyed in 1940, this has been found to be erroneous and they have provided information on a number of makers now incorporated below. Note further that in the original Biographical Dictionary the name of the Loriners' Company was spelt Lorimers, as invariably in the original mark entries in question. The correct modern usage is as above.

Addenda to Biographical Dictionary
including those of the Second Edition

ABDY, William I (page 419) Recorded as son of Mathew Abdy of Sheffield, Yorkshire. (C.F.1, R.B.)

ABERCROMBY, Robert (page 419) The lack of apprenticeship or freedom record is due to the fact that he began his career in Newcastle where he is recorded as journeyman to John Carnaby, goldsmith of that town, 3 May 1720. He presumably moved to London, probably in company with George Hindmarsh (q.v. below), shortly before they entered their joint mark in May 1731. (Information Mrs G. E. P. How.)

ADAM, Charles (page 419) He was born 1667. His tombstone at Thornhill, Yorkshire, describes him as 'Charles Adam late of London Citizen and Goldsmith', 23 August 1738 in his seventy-first year. (Information Mr C. Blair.)

ADAMS, Stephen I (page 419) Son of Stephen Adams. Free by patrimony of the Loriners' Company, 1 August 1759. No apprenticeship recorded in Inland Revenue lists. Elected to the Livery of the Loriners 1773 and Master in 1789. (S.T.)

ALDERHEAD, John (page 420) Son of Joseph Alderhead of Mortlake, Surrey, butcher, apprenticed to Robert Lucas (q.v.) of the Haberdashers' Company, silversmith of Bow Lane, 8 November 1734 for seven years on payment of £20. (C.F.1, R.B.) As previously recorded he was, however, free of the Goldsmiths by redemption.

ALDRIDGE, Edward I (page 421) Son of William Aldridge of the Clothworkers' Company, deceased, apprenticed to George Beckler (alias Berklear) of St. Martin's-le-Grand, silversmith, 29 March 1715 for seven years on payment of £10. Free of the Clothworkers by patrimony 4 February 1724, one day before the entry of his mark. Between 1736 and 1758 he took five apprentices, all of whom were to specialize in basket-making and be closely connected: Samuel Herbert, Henry Bailey, William Plummer, Edward Aldridge II, and Charles Aldridge (all q.v.). (Information Mr D. E. Wickham, Archivist, Clothworkers' Company, R.B. and S.T.)

ALDRIDGE, Edward II (page 421) The attribution of mark no. 3562 to him is no longer tenable. See John Arnell and Edmund Vincent below.

ALLEINE, Jonathan (page 422) The attribution of mark no. 1109 to this name is now to be considered almost certainly that of John Arnell (q.v. below). Since Jackson's attribution of mark no. 3703 to him is very questionable as suggested (page 263) it remains doubtful if he was more than a retailer.

ALLEN, John I (page 422) Son of James Allen of St. Leonard, Shoreditch, Middlesex, apprenticed to William Allen of the Glovers' Company, 10 August 1724, for seven years. Free of the City March 1735 by service of the Glovers (the company records for the date not extant). The reverse of the original indenture (City Records office) bears notes of orders placed by clients for stock and shoe buckles and stay hooks, a clear indication of Allen's specialization. (C.F.1, R.B. and S.T.)

ALLEN, John III (page 422) He may perhaps be the same as John Allen, jeweller and goldsmith, 42 Poultry in the *New Complete Guide*, 1777. (R.B.)

ALLEN, Thomas (page 422) His pre-1687 mark TA, three pellets above, cinquefoil below, is recognized as that of a spoonmaker. (T. A. Kent, *London Silver Spoonmakers*, 1981.)

ALLEN, William I (page 423) Son of James Allen of St. Leonard, Shoreditch, Middlesex (elder brother of John I above), apprenticed to Thomas Jefferies of the Glovers' Company, 7 January 1710. Free of the City February 1720 by service of the Glovers (the company records for the date not extant).

ANDREWS, Richard (page 423) Son of Henry Andrews of Little Britain, apprenticed to Thomas Green of Christ Church, London, jeweller, 24 August 1732 for seven years on payment of £26. 5s. (P.R.O., I.R. 1/13 f.76, R.B.) Since his only recorded mark was not entered until 1773, it is possible that an earlier one was entered in the missing smallworkers' volume. Otherwise there is an alternative that the 1773 mark is that of a son of the same name.

ANGEL(L), John and Joseph (page 424) The confusing nomenclature of this family resulted in an erroneous claim that it was John Charles who entered the partnership mark of 1831 with his uncle, whereas it was in fact Joseph's brother John, who as stated under the former's entry was apprenticed to William Elliott in 1799 as son of Joseph Angel of Battle Bridge, weaver, and was free 1 January 1807. John Charles was in fact apprenticed to his own father, and was free by service in 1832. Joseph's eldest son Charles was apprenticed to his father but does not appear to have taken up his freedom and perhaps did not remain with the firm. The brothers' partnership appears to have come to an end by mid-1840, since John (Charles) and George, sons of John, entered a separate mark at 51 Compton Street, 19 June 1840, and another in July 1844, whereas Joseph Snr and Jnr continued at 55 Compton Street entering their mark 6 July 1840. Another son of each brother was free by patrimony, but pursued other occupations, Walter, third son of John, described as silver-plate engraver when made free in 1850, and Thomas, third son of Joseph, as solicitor, free in 1841. (Information Mr David Beasley, Goldsmiths' Hall.)

ANNESLEY, Arthur (page 424) A list of members of the Rotterdam silversmiths' guild, recently discovered, includes that of this maker recording his mark there as 'A.A with a star'. Several pieces with this mark and the Rotterdam date-letters for 1767–78 have been identified showing English characteristics. Annesley presumably moved to Holland shortly after his bankruptcy in 1762 in order to have worked there long enough to have qualified as a full member of the guild by 1768, since the regulations involved a two-year apprenticeship and then appointment as 'Poorter' or 'Burger' before acceptance as a guild member. (Information Miss S. Hare.) He may also possibly be identified with one of the same name made free of the Dublin Goldsmiths' Company in 1752 who died in 1795. (D. Bennett, *Irish Georgian Silver*, London, 1972.)

ARNELL, John (not previously included) It now seems certain that mark no. 1109 is his rather than Jonathan Alleine's as previously suggested. Arnell appears in the Parker and Wakelin Workmen's Ledger No. 2 as a supplier of candlesticks; his account, brought forward from the missing ledger begun in 1760, runs from March 1767. (H.C.) Son of John Arnell of Paddington, Middlesex, weaver, he was apprenticed to John Quantock (q.v.), a specialist candlestickmaker, 5 October 1752 for seven years. Free 2 November 1763, the same day as Edmund Vincent (q.v.) in partnership with whom mark no. 3562 can now be definitely ascribed, in view of its observed occurrence on candlesticks only; the partnership apparently dissolved by 1767.

ASH, Joseph I (page 426) Son of Samuel Ash of the parish of St. John Horleydown, victualler, apprenticed to Roger Biggs (q.v.) of the Glovers' Company, 7 May 1793 for seven years on payment of £10. Free of that company 15 September 1801, one day after entering his first mark. Two apprentices of his former master were turned over to him the following month. (Glovers' Company records, S.T.)

ATKINS, Richard William (page 426) Son of Michael Thomas Atkins of the Clothworkers' Company, watchmaker. Free by patrimony of that company 7 May 1823 as silversmith, Red Lion Street, Clerkenwell. Described as silver chaser in an apprenticeship to him 1830, then at Bridgwater Square. Livery of the Clothworkers 1831. Master 1867. Died 3 January 1874. (Information Mr D. E. Wickham, Archivist, Clothworkers' Company, and S.T.)

AVERY, Henry (page 427) Son of William Avery of Henley-on-Thames, Oxfordshire, gentleman, apprenticed to Ann Smith of the Coopers' Company (q.v.), 2 July 1700 for eight years and subsequently turned over to Maurice Boheme (q.v.). Free of the Coopers 1 August 1710. (Coopers' Company records, S.T. and R.B.)

BAILEY, Henry (page 428) Son of Henry Bailey of Ringwood, County of Southton (Southampton), apprenticed to Edward Aldridge (I) of the Clothworkers' Company, goldsmith, of Lillipot Lane, for seven years on payment of £15. 15s. Free 8 October 1746 as goldsmith, journeyman to Edward Aldridge. Although he entered his only mark in June 1750, there seems a strong possibility that he was in fact the unnamed partner of Samuel Herbert in the double mark SH.HB, entered in November following. (R.B.) In the same month he took Francis Spilsbury II as apprentice.

BAKER

(Information Mr D. E. Wickham, Archivist, Clothworkers' Company, and S.T.)

BAKER, John I and II (page 429) Renewed examination of the available evidence suggests that these two are indeed one man for whom the first identity as son of Benjamin Baker apprenticed in 1740 is correct. The first mark listed under Baker II is therefore his first mark alone after severing partnership with James Stamp. Certainly the latter (q.v.) was listed alone in the Parl. Report list 1773. The two entries on page 429 should therefore be read as a continuous whole, ignoring the previous suggestion made of identity with the John Baker free in 1765. John Baker, Livery 1771, must also be the same.

BARBE, John (page 429) He is possibly related to the two silversmiths of this name at The Hague, Holland: Jacob Barbe, 1735-73, and Jacob Abraham Barbe, 1765-92. (Information Mr K. Citroen.)

BARBOT, John (page 430) Son of James Barbot of Maryland in Virginia, merchant, deceased, apprenticed to Pierre La Brosse of St. Ann's, Westminster, silversmith, 26 April 1717 for seven years on payment of £16 (I.R. 1/5 f.117, R.B.). He appears as supplier of gold rings, toothpick cases, cane heads and smelling bottles in Parker and Wakelin's Workmen's Ledger No. 2 from December 1767. (H.C.)

BARKER, Christopher (page 430) Son of Thomas Barker of Tadcaster, Yorkshire, skinner, apprenticed to John Jackson of the Mercers' Company, goldsmith, Little Britain, 13 October 1765 and turned over 29 June 1770 to George Smith, citizen and pewterer. Free of the Mercers' Company 18 December 1772. He first appears at 60 Paternoster Row, 1784-5. (S.T.)

BARKER, James (page 430) Son of Thomas Barker of the Joyners' Company, apprenticed to Thomas Gilpin of St. Clement Danes, Middlesex, goldsmith, 17 June 1735 for seven years on payment of £52. 10s. Since Gilpin was never free of the Goldsmiths' Company, Barker also could not acquire that status. (R.B.)

BARKER, Thomas Wilkes (page 430) Free of the Mercers' Company by patrimony as son of Christopher Barker above. (S.T.) Presumably this freedom was the reason why he did not take that of the Goldsmiths, even though apprenticed to William Fearn.

BARNARD, Edward I (page 430) He married in 1791 Mary Boosey of the music publishing family. One daughter, Sarah, married Michael Faraday the scientist. Others, Mary and Elizabeth, were the wives respectively of William Ker Reid 1812 (q.v., page 639) and his brother David 1815 of the Newcastle firm of silversmiths with whom the Barnard establishment had close business connections. The Barnard firm, the longest surviving extant London business, derives its continuous history from the purchase by Thomas Whipham of Francis Nelme's business in 1739, thence to Charles Wright 1756, Thomas Chawner 1783, Henry Chawner 1786, his partner John Emes and the latter's widow Rebeccah's partnership with Edward Barnard 1808. (John Culme, *Nineteenth Century Silver*, 1977.) For a full discussion of the varied extra-London trade connections of the firm and business details see Judith Banister, 'The Barnard Ledgers', *Society of Silver Collectors Proceedings*, Vol. II, p. 165.

BLAKE

BARNETT, Michael (page 431) He appears as brass and silver caster, 36 Cock Lane, and liveryman of the Founders' Company in Barfoot and Wilkes, *List of the Livery*, 1792, his description and company reflecting the nature of cast sword hilts, pommels and guards of the day.

BASS, Thomas (page 433) Son of Thomas Bass of St. Andrew's, Holborn, cabinetmaker, apprenticed as previously stated 22 January 1701. (Cutlers' Company records and C.F.1, S.T.)

BATEMAN, Hester (page 433) For interesting factual detail on the premises, equipment and general business activities of the Bateman family concern see John Culme, *Nineteenth Century Silver*, 1977.

BATEMAN, Jonathan (page 433) It is interesting to note that he was made free by redemption of the Goldsmith's Company on 7 April 1784, presumably for the main purpose of apprenticing his son to himself. The son, also Jonathan, was free by servitude 5 October 1791, the date previously given in error for the father's supposed election to the Livery, when he was in fact already dead. Since there is no mark for the son individually, or in partnership with his mother, uncle or brother, it seems he either remained outside the partnership or pursued another career.

BATEMAN, Peter (page 433) The date of his apprenticeship to Richard Clarke was 15 September 1755.

BEALE, George (page 435) Described as

736

BIOGRAPHICAL DICTIONARY: ADDENDA

'Being about to leave off his Trade', 11 November 1715 when he remitted the remainder of his apprentice Daniel Yerbury's term. (C.F.1, R.B.)

BEATTIE, James (page 435) Son of William Beattie late of Fettresso in North Britain, farmer, deceased, apprenticed to Andrew Hogg (q.v.) of the Drapers' Company, 22 December 1756 for seven years. Free of that company 21 November 1764 as smallworker in gold, Red Lyon Court, Fleet Street. Livery 1787 to 1801. Described in 1787 as smallworker in gold, pocketbook-maker. Address from 1797 to 1801 York Street, Covent Garden. His wife Ann appears as pensioner 1807-29. (Drapers' Company records and C.F.1, S.T.)

BEATTY, James (page 435) He can probably be identified as James, son of Adam Beatty of Shipwash, Devon, mercer, apprenticed to John Elston of Exeter, goldsmith, and Mary his wife 27 May 1721 for seven years on payment of £40. (I.R. 1/47, f.71, R.B.)

BEAUCHAMP, John (page 435) Son of Edward Beauchamp of St. Andrew's, Holborn, silversmith of the Broderers' Company (who was free by redemption 1777 as pawnbroker at the Golden Ball, Holborn), apprenticed to his father 25 May 1795. Free of the Broderers 2 June 1802, as 'lives with his father No. 14 Holborn, a silversmith and pawnbroker'. Apparently Master of that company 1812, 1828 and 1829. (Broderers' Company records, S.T.)

BEDFORD, William (page 436) Son of William Bedford of St. James's, Clerkenwell, gentleman, apprenticed to James Hughes (q.v.) of the Loriners' Company, 13 March 1695 for seven years. Free of the City June 1702 after becoming free of the Loriners. (Records not surviving for that year. C.F.1, S.T.)

BELL, Joseph III (page 437) Son of George Bell of Salisbury Court, London, soap-maker, apprenticed to George Wintle (q.v.) of the Vintners' Company, silversmith, Bunhill Row, 3 February 1808 on payment of £19. 19s. Free of that company 5 June 1816. Address 10 Mint, Borough. (Vintners' Company records, S.T.)

BENNETT, John II (page 438) The previous suggestion of parentage and apprenticeship now disproved. Son of Peter Bennett of Hammersmith in the parish of Fulham, Middlesex, labourer, apprenticed to John Carman I (q.v.) of the Cutlers' Company, 11 April 1723 for seven years. Free 12 October 1731. Livery 1772 as Threadneedle Street sword cutler. (Cutlers' Company records, S.T.)

BENOIMENT, Louis (page 438) He appears as Lovic Victor Benoiment, son of Louis Victor Benoiment, schoolmaster, of St. Ann's, Soho, 'a native of France of the Reformed Religion', apprenticed to Samuel Phillipon of St. Martin-in-the-Fields, jeweller, 17 June 1736 for seven years on payment of £30. Free of the Goldsmiths' Company 6 September 1749 by redemption as a jeweller. (I.R.1/14 f.167, and C.F.1, R.B.)

BIGGS, Roger (page 440) Son of Thomas Biggs of Leather Lane, St. Andrew's, Holborn, apprenticed to William Key (q.v.) of the Glovers' Company, 12 March 1784 for seven years on payment of £10. 10s. Free of that company 15 March 1791 as goldsmith, 12 Laystall Street, Cold Bath Fields.

BINGER, Christopher (page 441) He appears as smallworker in gold of St. Pancras, Middlesex in the apprenticeship to him of Philip Cornman (q.v.) 22 March 1768, three years before the entry of his only mark. (I.R. 1/25 f.164, R.B.) He was a minor supplier to Wakelin and Garrard from 1793 to 1803 of chased and dengrave gold- or silver-mounted bottles, silver-gilt snuff boxes, etc. (H.C.)

BINLEY, Margaret (page 441) She appears in Parker and Wakelin's Workmen's Ledger No. 2 as supplying buttons, buckles and bottle tickets from November 1767. (H.C.)

BIRD, Benjamin (page 441) He was probably dead before 7 November 1721 when Rebekah Bird, now established as his widow (q.v.), entered her mark.

BIRD, Joseph (page 441) The suggested probability that he was master of David Green (q.v.), as stated in his entry (page 528), was in fact so. The latter was turned over to Bird after initial apprenticeship to Thomas Gardner.

BIRD, Rebekah (page 442) Described as widow of Benjamin Bird, late citizen and joiner of London, deceased 8 December 1724 on taking Robert Dennison (q.v.) apprentice. (Joyners' Company registers, R.B.)

BLAKE, John (page 442) Son of John Blake, late of Harwich, butcher, deceased, apprenticed to George Smith (III q.v.), silversmith of the Pewterers' Company, 24 June

737

1779. Free of that company 22 August 1786. Livery 1793. Warden 1804–6. Described as refiner in company records 1806. (Pewterers' Company records, S.T.)

BLAKE, John William (page 442) Son of the above, apprenticed to his father 5 August 1802. Free of the Pewterers' Company.

BLAND, Cornelius (page 443) He was already in Aldersgate Street by September 1771, when his Sun Insurance policy describes him as silver chaser, which as previously stated he was termed in 1779. (Information Mr S. B. Turner, R.B.)

BLAND, James (page 443) He was made free by patrimony 7 October 1794, when his second name appears as Hewitt rather than the misreading of Huell from his apprenticeship entry.

BLUNT, John I (page 443) Son of William Blunt of St. Leonard's, Shoreditch, Middlesex, baker, deceased, apprenticed to William Overton (q.v.) of the Merchant Taylors' Company, 3 March 1725 for seven years on payment of £15 and later turned over to William Allen (q.v.), Citizen and Glover. Free of the Merchant Taylors 4 October 1732 as silversmith of Brick Lane, Old Street. (Merchant Taylors' records, R.B. and S.T.)

BODINGTON, John (page 444) His date of death was correctly 1728.

BORCHERS, Albrecht (page 445) He was almost certainly a German immigrant. The name occurs frequently in Hamburg and neighbourhood. (Information Mr K. Citroen.)

BOTFIELD, Richard (page 445) Son of Richard Botfield of the Coopers' Company apprenticed to Thomas Cole (q.v.) of the Drapers' Company, 12 March 1718 for seven years on payment of £13. Free of the Drapers 24 March 1725 as chainmaker, Saffron Hill. Cf. Daniel Cole below. (R.B.)

BRASSEY, John (page 447) In 1716 the South Sea Company purchased a cup and salver from a William Brassey for whom no mark is recorded. It is suggested that he may have been related to and working in the firm of John and Nathaniel Brassey, a possibility made reasonable in view of the Brasseys' banking activities from 1730–40. (Rosemary Weinstein, *Antique Collector*, October 1983.)

BRAWNE, Hugh (page 447) Son of Hugh Brawne of St. Martin-in-the-Fields, taylor, apprenticed to Henry Panton of the Cutlers' Company, 14 April 1696 for seven years. Free of that company 16 November 1703, the same day as the entry of his mark. (Cutlers' Company records and C.F.1, S.T.)

BRIDGE, John (page 448) He was free by redemption in April 1788. His nephew John Gawler Bridge became the dominant partner from about 1825. That year he laid the foundation of the new premises on Ludgate Hill designed by his brother-in-law, the architect J. C. Mead. John Bridge Snr died at his house at Hammersmith in 1834. In that year the senior partners were Bigge and Edward Rundell, who soon withdrew, while Bigge as head lost interest, and John Gawler Bridge was eventually left to wind up the business for the other partners. (John Culme, *Nineteenth Century Silver*, 1977 and Sotheby's *Catalogue*, 6 February 1986.)

BRIND, Walter (page 449) He appears as supplier of panakins, papboats, children's mugs and cream-boats in Parker and Wakelin's Workmen's Ledger No. 2, November 1768, his account brought forward from the earlier missing ledger begun in 1760. Mark no. 3865 can therefore reasonably be attributed to him in addition to no. 3864. (H.C.) The previous suggestion that his third son Thomas was the Prime Warden of that name is incorrect. The latter was son of Thomas Brind, silver turner, possibly a brother of Walter and Henry.

BRITTON, James (page 449) Son of Mary Britton, Clerkenwell, widow, apprenticed to Thomas Wilkes Barker, of the Mercers' Company, silversmith, Cross Street, Hatton Garden for seven years gratis. Free of the Mercers' Company January 1810. He appears in the Mercers' freedom list for 1814 at Mr Barker's, 6 Kirby Street, Hatton Garden and still there as a liveryman 1820. Still listed with Barker 1833–4, but alone 1840. (S.T.)

BROADHURST, Ed. (page 450) Perhaps identical with one of the same name recorded in the Exeter Assay Book as working in Plymouth Dock from 1757. (Information Mr T. Kent.)

BROCKUS, John (page 450) Son of Charles Brochus (sic) of the Haberdashers' Company, apprenticed to Robert Pilkington, silversmith ye Savoy (q.v.), 21 July 1741 for seven years on payment of £10. 10s. (I.R. 1/16 f.80, R.B.) Free of the Haberdashers by patrimony 7 March 1748, then

BIOGRAPHICAL DICTIONARY: ADDENDA

described as silversmith, Stanhope Street, Clare Market, when he may have entered a mark in the missing Smallworkers' Book.

BROCKWELL, Henry (page 450) Son of Henry Brockwell of Brooks Row, St. Pancras, silversmith, apprenticed to William Fearn (q.v.), spoonmaker, Lovell's Court, Paternoster Row, 5 December 1804. Free of the Goldsmiths 1 April 1802. (S.T.)

BULL, Charles (page 453) Son of William Bull, late of St. Bennet's Hill, Doctors Common, glazier, deceased, apprenticed to Thomas Walker (q.v.) of the Drapers' Company, goldsmith, Moles Buildings, Fetter Lane, 2 August 1803 for seven years on payment of £8. Free of that company 20 December 1811 as pawnbroker, 25 Castle Street, Holborn. In 1828 described as goldsmith, 10 New Court, Fleet Street, as on the entry of his mark four years later. (Drapers' Company records, S.T.)

BULL, William (page 453) Son of John Bull, Vintners' Company, apprenticed to John Glover of the Haberdashers' Company, 29 April 1681 for eight years. Free 18 March 1692 (correct year). (C.F.1 and Haberdashers' Company records, R.B. and S.T.)

BUMFRISS, Thomas (page 453) Son of Joseph Bumfriss of St. Giles-in-the-Fields, brewer, deceased. Free by redemption of the Spectacle-makers' Company as chaser 23 April 1766. Address Old Bailey, Gran Arborn(?) Court (Break Neck Stairs). (C.F.1 and Spectacle-makers' Register, R.B.) Orlando Jackson, his partner from 1776–73 (not 1783 as previously stated), also became free of the same company on the same date, obviously chosen for low cost. Since Bumfriss is recorded as chaser in the apprenticeship of his son in 1760 it is clear he was of ripe years by then.

BURDETT, Henry (page 454) Son of Theophilus Burdett, late of Hallerton, Leics., clerk, deceased. (C.F.1, R.B.)

BURROWS, John (page 455) Son of Richard Burrows, apprenticed to Abraham Cooke of St. Clement Deans (sic), Snuffboxmaker, 24 August 1751 on payment of £5. (I.R. 1/19 f.37, R.B.)

BURTON, Robert (page 455) Son of Robert Burton of St. Giles, Cripplegate, London, shoemaker, deceased, apprenticed to Jeremiah King of the Broderers' Company, goldsmith (q.v.), 2 April 1746 for seven years on payment of £7. 10s. by charity. Turned over by King's widow and executrix to James Tookey (q.v.) 20 June 1750. Free of the Broderers 6 June 1753 as silversmith at Mr Tookey in Silver Street, where he presumably continued to work as journeyman until entering his mark in 1758. (S.T.)

BURTT, Joseph Josiah (page 455) Son of Thomas Burtt of Northampton Street, Clerkenwell, silversmith apprenticed to John William Blake (q.v.) of the Pewterers' Company, silversmith, Long Acre, 12 December 1822 on payment of £30. Not made free of the Pewterers. (S.T.)

BURTT, Thomas (page 455) From the above record the previous suggestion that he was presumably son or brother of the above, although arguable, may still be valid as a younger brother of their father's name.

BURWASH, Thomas (page 455) Son of William Burwash (as previously surmised) of the Clothworkers' Company, silversmith, 14 Bartholomew Close, apprenticed to his father 2 March 1808. Free of the Clothworkers 1 November 1815 as watchmaker, probably working with his uncle Thomas, also Clothworker, free 1791 as watchpendant-maker of 69 St. John Street, where he entered a mark in 1813 (page 319). (Information Mr D. E. Wickham, Archivist, Clothworkers' Company, and S.T.)

BURWASH, William (page 455) Son of Thomas Burwash of Mortimer Street, Cavendish Square, bricklayer, apprenticed to John Rogers of the Clothworkers' Company, packer, of Old Broad Street, 1 April 1772. Free of the Clothworkers as packer of 79 Broad Street. He had, however, changed his occupation when his brother Thomas was apprenticed to him as watchpendant-maker of 5 Red Lion Street, Clerkenwell where William entered a mark as casemaker 1802 (page 326) and only in the apprenticeship to him of his son Thomas (above) is he described as silversmith of 14 Bartholomew Close. It is now clear that he is in fact identical with the husband of Elizabeth Salt, married in 1781. The year of the entry of his first mark should of course read 1805. (Acknowledgements as above.)

BUTEUX, Abraham (page 455) His insurance policy of 16 September 1721 gives his address as 'at the Golden Ewer in Green Street in Leicester Fields' and covers only household goods and stock. It seems probable that there is a working connection with the Pantin family, as previously suggested, since Lewis Pantin I (q.v. below) was at the

Golden Ewer, Castle Street in 1735. (Sun Insurance policy information Mr S. B. Turner, and R.B.)

BUTTY, Francis (page 456) Butty and Co. appear as minor suppliers of salts, coffee-pots, tureens and dishes in Parker and Wakelin's Workmen's Ledger No. 2 from February 1771. (H.C.)

CAFE, John (page 456), and CAFE, William (page 457) For a full discussion of these candlestickmakers see J. P. Fallon, 'The Goulds and Cafes, Candlestick makers', *Society of Silver Collectors Proceedings*, Vol. II, p. 146. He reads their father's name as Giles, and states that John was free in 1741, correcting for a presumed Old Style calendar entry, but dates appear to be sometimes in New Style by this time and the correct year here remains doubtful, lacking evidence from surrounding entries. John Cafe died before 27 August 1757, when probate of his will was proved (Fallon). He left the lease of his house in Gutter Lane to his brother William and £7500 cash, from which his executors, Marmaduke Daintrey (q.v.) and John Winning, were to permit his brother the use of £500 to carry on his business for seven years. His Somerset properties passed to his wife and their five children. His brother William died early in 1802, his will being proved in that March, in which he left all to his second wife, Jane (Fallon, op. cit.).

CALLARD, Isaac (page 457) The possibility that he had a son of the same name is perhaps implied by its appearance as supplier of forks, spoons and strainers in Parker and Wakelin's Workmen's Ledger No. 2 from March 1766, the account brought forward from the earlier missing ledger. (H.C.)

CALLARD, Paul (page 457) Apprenticed to Paul Hanet (his godfather) of the Longbowstringmakers, 7 October 1737. Free of that company 6 April 1748. As Warden of that company he signed the freedom papers of John Innocent (q.v.) 1763. (S.T.)

CALVERT, Richard (page 457) Son of Peter Calvert of Blackfriars, London, apprenticed to Daniel Cole of the Drapers' Company, 23 October 1751 for seven years on payment of £20. Free of that company 15 November 1758 as watchcasemaker, Blackfriars, and shortly after, as their joint mark shows, joined his master in partnership. (Drapers' Company records, S.T.)

CARMAN, John I (page 458) Son of Richard Carman, deceased, of the parish of St. Margaret's, Westminster, apprenticed 1 July 1708 to Thomas Vicaridge of the Cutlers' Company (q.v.). Freedom as previously stated of that company. (S.T.)

CARTER, John II (page 459) Hammond and Carter, goldsmiths, 45 St. Martin's-le-Grand, appear in the *London Directory*, 1768 and at Westmoreland Buildings in Baldwin's *New Complete Guide*, 1770. The fluctuating partnerships of Carter, Crouch, Makepeace and Hannam remain difficult to disentangle. Hammond and Company appear in Parker and Wakelin's ledger from April 1766, the account brought forward from the missing previous ledger, and from 1767 the account is under Carter's name alone. (R.B. and H.C.)

CARTER, Richard (page 459) For the descent of Carter and Makepeace from the Langleys through Thomas Gilpin to the present-day firm of A. Woodhouse and Son, see John Culme, *Directory of Gold and Silversmiths*, pp. 179-80.

CARTIER, David (page 460) Probably identical with one of the same name recorded in Amsterdam in 1740 as a silverworker from Neuchâtel. (Information Mr K. Citroen.) Was he perhaps a watchcasemaker?

CARTLIDGE, William (page 460) Son of William Cartlidge of Pell Street, Wood Street, labourer, apprenticed to John Parker of the Barber Surgeons' Company, pawnbroker, London Wall, 3 May 1796 on payment of £25 and later turned over to Henry Colcott, Citizen and Glover, carpenter, Little Bell Alley, Coleman Street. Free of the Barber Surgeons 1 January 1811 as silversmith, King Street, Middlesex. Livery 1827. (Barber Surgeons' records, S.T.)

CHANDLESS, William (page 461) Son of Thomas Chandless of 13 White Hart Row, Kennington, Middlesex, gentleman, apprenticed to William Eaton (q.v.) of the Needlemakers' Company, 31 July 1822 on payment of £5 of Christ's Hospital Charity. Free of that company 13 November 1832 as silversmith, 1 Crown Court, Aldersgate Street. (Needlemakers' Company records, S.T.)

CHARTIER, John (page 462) The previous suggestion that mark no. 1194 is his rather than his son's is supported by the fact that the latter was apprenticed to Henry Bodker of St. Giles's, chaser, 15 January 1718 for seven years. (I.R. 1/6 f.21, R.B.)

BIOGRAPHICAL DICTIONARY: ADDENDA

CHAWNER, Henry (page 463) For the statement that he took over the business of Charles Wright (q.v.) in 1786 and the descent to Edward Barnard, see John Culme, *Directory of Gold and Silversmiths*, under the latter name, quoting an anonymous article in the *Watchmaker, Jeweller and Silversmith*, 1899, including a description of Chawner's art collection at his Hampshire home.

CHAWNER, William I (page 463) Son of John Chawner of Muce(?) Lane, Derbyshire, yeoman (and therefore brother of Thomas Chawner (q.v.), as previously suggested), apprenticed to Francis Piggott of the Pewterers' Company, 8 June 1750 on payment of £35. Free of that company 20 October 1757. Livery 1761. (Pewterers' Company records, S.T.)

CHEBSEY, George (page 464) Now confirmed as the son of William Chebsey, apprenticed to his father of the Leathersellers' Company, 25 March 1681 and free by service 26 April 1692. (S.T.)

CHEESE, Clement (page 464) Son of John Cheese of Aylesbury, Bucks., sack manufacturer, apprenticed to John William Blake (q.v.), the Pewterers' Company, 24 August 1815 on payment of £50. Free 12 June 1828 as silversmith of 14 Vineyard Walk, Clerkenwell, although he had entered his first mark five years earlier, a year after his presumed term of service had ended. (S.T.)

CLARK, Thomas (page 465) Heal's second entry for this name must be the man declared bankrupt 12 July 1736 at St. Clements Dane, toyman, the petitioning creditor being Thomas Timbrell, Lombard Street, goldsmith. (B 4/8, 244, J.C.)

CLARKE, John II (page 466) No date is recorded for his move to Broad Street. That of 18 March 1819 is for the move to Charterhouse Street.

CLAUSEN, Nicholas (page 466) According to his insurance policy originally issued 18 July 1712 at the Golden Head in Orange Street (Sun Office no. 2216), he 'removd into St Martins Street July 18th 1718'. Another policy of 27 April 1724 covers both his Orange Street address and 'House being the next house to the sign of the Black Crow in Lissen Green (Lissom Grove) near Paddington in Mdx'. (Information Mr S. B. Turner.) He was dead by December 1732 when his apprentice Charles Perier (q.v.) took up his freedom of the Haberdashers' Company. (Haberdashers' Company register, S.T.)

CLAYTON, David (page 466) Declared bankrupt 13 September 1711 on the petition of Thomas (Genoese?) London, merchant. (B 4/1, 83, J.C.)

COLE, Daniel (page 468) Son of James Cole of Barkley (sic), Glos., apprenticed to Thomas Cole (q.v.) of the Drapers' Company, 6 May 1730. Free of that company 20 June 1739 as watch-chainmaker, Cow Cross, Smithfield. (Drapers' Company records, S.T.)

COLE, Thomas (page 468) Free of the Drapers' Company by redemption 31 July 1717 as watch-chainmaker, Cow Cross.

COOK, Abraham (page 470) In 1751 he took as apprentice John Burrows (see above), some seven and a half years before the date of his first registered mark. It seems probable that he had entered an earlier mark in the missing Smallworkers' register. (R.B.)

COOPER, Edmund (page 471) Son of John Cooper of the Bowyers' Company, free by patrimony 20 April 1699. He took at least five apprentices up to 1727. (Bowyers' Company records, C.F.1, S.T.)

CORBETT, Benjamin (page 472) Son of Benjamin Corbit (sic) of East Smithfield, glass grinder, apprenticed 20 June 1717 to Charles Jackson as previously stated. (S.T.)

CORNMAN, Philip (page 473) Apprenticed to Christopher Binger I (q.v.) of St. Pancras, Middlesex, smallworker in gold, 22 March 1768 for seven years on payment of £2. (I.R. 1/25 f.164, R.B.) He was presumably turned over later to Herman Jacobi (*vice* James) Walther (q.v.) who is named as his master from whom he 'departed without consent' 29 April 1772 (*The Public Advertiser*, 1 May 1772). It seems likely that he was of Teutonic extraction, as equally, from their names, his two masters. He next appears as sculptor, 5 Great Newport Street, exhibiting models and portraits in wax at the Royal Academy 1788-92, the address being that entered with his mark as smallworker, 1793. This was significantly close to that of William Pitts and Joseph Preedy from 1795. The royal communion service of Quebec Cathedral of 1802 and 1803 bears a large unregistered mark PC, which can only be that of Cornman working to designs of J. B. Boileau, and in this service the alms dish is by Joseph Preedy. (A. G. Grimwade, 'New Light on Canadian Treasure', *Country Life*, 31 January 1985.) By 1807 his son

Henry (q.v.) had joined his father and they appear as Cornman & Son, gold and silver workers, at Newport Street in the London Postal Directory until 1820, after that as Cornman Son & Bridges, 22 Newman Street until 1826. Henry also exhibited models and portraits in wax. Philip Cornman died in 1822, will proved 14 October, leaving 'all my Working Tools Stock in Trade and Implements of my Trade' to his son. Henry retired from business in 1825/6 and died 10 November 1830, leaving an unwitnessed will, the signature of which was attested by two jewellers, Noah Goetze and Thomas Dee, suggesting continued trade in jewellery and plate. (John Culme, Sotheby's *Catalogue*, 24 October 1985.) He appears to have had a number of activities. His insurance policy of 10 December 1781 describes him as engraver of 7 Little St. Martin's Lane. Another policy of 23 March 1786 again as engraver at 5 Newport Street, and a third of 4 November 1791 as engraver and printseller, both before the entry of his first mark. (Sun Insurance policies, information Mr S. Allaway and Mr S. B. Turner, and R.B.)

COURTAULD, Samuel I (page 475) He appears in 1762 as Samuel Courtwould in a notice of silver stolen from a Peter Laprimaudaye, to be referred to if any items were 'offered for sale, pawned or valued', and gave evidence at the trial of the thief, a German surgeon Autenreith, that a saltcellar recovered by the owner in the thief's house had been made by him. (*The Public Advertiser*, 30 October 1762, and London Sessions Papers. Quoted by John Culme, 'Periodical Reflections', *The Antique Collector*, February 1987.)

COWLES, George (page 475) His partnership with Louisa Courtauld was announced by Cowles in the *Gloucester Journal*, 29 September 1777 as 'this day dissolved' with his move to the Lombard Street address of his second mark entry. In the same paper, 19 January 1778, he announced his move to Cornhill 'where he proposes carrying on the Manufacturing Business'. His advertisements in Gloucester suggest he had maintained business contacts in that city of his birth. (Information Mr A. J. H. Sale through R.B.) On 2 November 1787 he petitioned the Goldsmiths' Company for the office of Beadle, a fact suggesting he had by then given up business and needed assistance.

COX, George (page 476) Son of Andrew Cox, deceased, of the Leathersellers' Company, apprenticed to William Scarlett (q.v.) of the Broderers' Company, 31 January 1690 for eight years. (C.F.1, R.B.)

COX, Robert Albin (page 476) The village of origin of this maker, as his brother William (below), is correctly Brewham. He of the same name, to whom reference was previously made as presumably a son, was in fact son of William Cox III (below), presumably with his uncle as godfather. Robert Albin Cox appears as supplier of unwrought silver to specialist manufacturers and suppliers in Parker and Wakelin's Workmen's Ledger No. 2 from March 1769. In spite of entering three marks as large-worker up to 1759 it seems probable that he had changed his business to bullion merchant sometime after. (H.C.)

COX, William III (page 477) The previous statement that there is no record of apprenticeship or freedom is incorrect. He was the son of Edward Cox, late of Brewham in the County of Somerset gentleman deceased, apprenticed to his brother Robert Albin Cox (above) 11 January 1753. Free, 6 February 1760. His son Robert Albin Cox II was free by patrimony 5 April 1786 and eventually Prime Warden 1818 as stated under his uncle's entry (page 476). He founded the most important London refinery of the time, which became Cox & Merle in 1781, then Merle & Co. in 1817. The firm appears as Merle Son & Co., bankers and gold refiners of 2 Cox's Court, Little Britain (the address of Robert Albin Cox I from 1769), from 1818 to 1821 (F. G. Hilton Price, *A Handbook of London Bankers*, 1890). Robert II was the plaintiff in the *cause célèbre* in 1825 against the actor Edmund Kean for criminal conversation with Cox's second wife Charlotte, for which damages of £800 were awarded him (*Dict. Nat. Biog.*, 'Edmund Kean' and other biographies of the same). He was Sheriff 1801–1802, Alderman for Aldersgate Ward 1813–1826, dying that year 19 June.

CRESPEL, Sebastian I (page 477) Son of Honor Crespell, apprenticed to George Methuen of St. Martin Fields, Middlesex, goldsmith (q.v.) for seven years from 13 November 1745 on payment of £14. 14s. (I.R. 1/17 f.174, R.B.)

CRESPIN, Paul (page 479) The portrait previously referred to was acquired by the Victoria and Albert Museum (Sotheby's

Catalogue, November 1985). When exhibited at 'The Quiet Conquest', London Museum, 1985 it was tentatively attributed to Pierre Soubeyras working in Toulouse, Paris and Rome, but there is as yet no evidence of Crespin's going abroad (Tessa Murdoch, Sotheby's *News Letter*, January 1986). His freedom of the Longbowstringmakers, already recorded, was obtained by redemption 25 April 1721, which suggests that the entry of his first mark was about this date. A curious discrepancy has been found in the City Freedom paper for him, where he is described as son of Abram of ye Isle of Guernsie (S.T.). In view of his cleric son's ultimate appointment as Dean of that island, there is obviously some connection. Paul's father Daniel, so definitely given as such in his apprenticeship, may have had two names and by 1721 retired to Guernsey.

CRIPPS, William (page 479) He appears in the Rate Book for the area as a tenant at the Crown and Golden Ball, Compton Street for the Michaelmas quarter of 1742 in succession to Christian Hillan (q.v.) and next door to Nicholas Sprimont (q.v.). From 1746, when he moved to St. James's Street, he may probably have become a retail trader as well as manufacturer. His death was announced in *The Public Advertiser*, 2 January 1766: 'Yesterday Evening died at his House in St. James's-Street of a Fit of Apoplexy, Mr Crips a Gold and Silver-Smith of great Business. He was suddenly seized after Supper on Tuesday Night, and continued in great Agonies till he expired.' A second notice two days later stated: 'On Thursday last the Surgeons opened the Head of the late Mr. Cripps, Goldsmith and Jeweller of St. James's-Street, who died on Wednesday Evening; and we hear his sudden death was occasioned by the bursting of a Vein in his Head.' His will proved 6 January 1766 mentions neither wife nor children, but a half, quarter and eighth of his effects to his three brothers and the remaining eighth to Joseph Partridge, apothecary. The premises were taken over by George Coyte & Co as retail silversmiths, to be succeeded by Mark Cripps, apparently of the same generation as William, perhaps a cousin and not, as previously suggested, his son. In his will proved in 1776 Mark Cripps describes himself as of Newport Pagnell and mentions beneficiaries of William. (John Culme, Sotheby's *Catalogue*, 24 October 1985.)

CRUICKSHANK, Robert (page 481) He appears as goldsmith and jeweller in Baldwin's *New Complete Guide*, 1770. (R.B.) He may just possibly be identical with the silversmith of the same name working in Montreal, Canada by or before 1774 until 1809, whose mark RC in script, pellet between in double-lobed punch is somewhat similar to mark no. 3769, previously tentatively ascribed to Robert Cox. In Montreal Cruickshank was a prominent citizen with a hardware business as well as a silver workshop, and was also closely connected with the fur trade. His silver teapots show close affinities with English models. It should be noted, however, that the Montreal Cruickshank has been said to have been born in Aberdeen in 1748, whereas the London goldsmith from Aberbrothock was apprenticed in 1759, implying the age of only eleven in the latter year if the identity is accepted. But the earlier date is apparently unsubstantiated. (Information Mr Ross, A. C. Fox, *Quebec and Related Silver* at The Detroit Institute of Arts, 1978; Ramsay Traquair, *The Old Silver of Quebec*, 1940.)

CRUMP, Francis (page 481) His fourth son Sleath could not have had Crump's former master and partner as godfather, as previously suggested, since the latter had died in 1756 and the child must have been named in memory of him.

CUNST, Jasper (page 482) He was perhaps related to Willem Kunst, silversmith, free of the Amsterdam corporation in 1740. (Information Mr K. Citroen.) He was declared bankrupt 24 July 1741, with address St. Bride's, London (adjoining Salisbury Court), goldsmith and snuffboxmaker, on the petition of William Jackson, goldsmith, of Old Street Square, St. Luke's, Middlesex. (B 4/10, 94, J.C.)

CUTMORE, Thomas (page 482) Son of John Cutmore of Blackfriars Road, gentleman, free by redemption of the Spectaclemakers' Company, 13 March 1829 as silver spoon manufacturer. John Cutmore, presumably his brother, was for five years 'superintendant' to William Eley (q.v.) and after for fourteen years the same for Bateman and Ball, Bunhill Row, the subsequent style of the Bateman family business (John Culme, *Nineteenth Century Silver*). An apprentice of William Eley of 1826 was turned over to Thomas Cutmore in 1829 and then elsewhere in 1830 as Cutmore had 'changed his trade', these facts and the address confirming the previous suggestion that the Cutmores and Eley were closely connected. (Spectacle-makers' Company records, S.T.)

DANIELL, Jabez (page 483) He died 4 September 1777. His tombstone, St. Anne and St. Agnes, Gresham Street (now Lutheran Church), records him as 'late a Goldsmith of the Parish of St. John Zachary but had retired from business'. His will signed 1 March 1776 contained the clause 'James Mince my late Servant owes me a considerable sum of money which I am persuaded he is not able to pay. I do therefore hereby acquit release and discharge the same and every part thereof.' He also left Mince 'ten pounds for Mourning'. For the probable godpaternal relationship of Daniell to Mince's son, see page 598. (John Culme, 'Periodical Reflections', *The Antique Collector*, February 1987.)

DANIELL, Thomas (page 484) *The London Chronicle*, reporting the celebrations of George III's recovery, 13 March 1789, records: 'Among the illuminations on Tuesday evening, few exceeded in brilliancy that of the London Silver Plate Manufactory in Foster Lane, the large premises of which were lighted up with solid silver three-light branches of candlesticks.' In the same year a handbill of Daniell's claimed 'Twenty Thousand Ounces of every species of Silver Goods ... finished in the highest elegance of patterns, and peculiarly excellent workmanship and embellishments from the best and latest designs always on hand' (John Culme, 'Periodical Reflections', *The Antique Collector*, February 1987). It is clear that Thomas Daniell was a believer in publicity.

DARVILL, Edward (page 484) He is presumably to be identified with Edward Darvis, supplier of tea chests and canisters in Parker and Wakelin's Workmen's Ledger No. 2, August 1773. (H.C.)

DAVENPORT, Burrage (page 484) Son of William Davenport, late of St. Luke's, Middlesex, carrier, deceased, apprenticed to Samuel Herbert (q.v.), silversmith of Foster Lane, Clothworker 13 April 1763. Free of the Clothworkers by service 3 October 1770 as goldsmith of Foster Lane. He appears to have lived until a great age, since he witnessed the freedom of an apprentice to him in 1843, when he must have been about ninety-four, the apprenticeship being probably only a formality for admittance to the company, his address in 1792 being given as Newington, Surrey. (Information Mr D. E. Wickham, Archivist, Clothworkers' Company, through R.B.)

DAVIS, Benjamin (page 485) Son of Joseph Davis of St. John Street, Middlesex, hatter, of the Skinners' Company, apprenticed to his father 2 June 1802 on payment of £5 from Christ's Hospital Charity (perhaps surprising but probably a regular occurrence of that charitable education). Free of the Skinners 5 September 1809 as at Messrs Turner & Co., working silversmiths, St. John's Square, Clerkenwell. Described on an apprenticeship to him 1826 as spoonmaker. He may have ceased working in 1833 as two apprentices were turned over elsewhere that year. (Skinners' Company records, S.T.)

DAY, Charles (page 486) Born 1797 and apprenticed as previously stated, he did not take the freedom of the Goldsmiths until 1863, in order to qualify as a pensioner of the company. The Male Petitioners' Book of the company contains a pathetic story. Formerly employed with Lias and Sons (q.v.) he left and became a greengrocer, losing his savings of £300, and was left with £16, a sick wife, and unable to work, depending on their son. He was duly elected a pensioner. (S.T.)

DEARDS, William (page 487) His daughter (?Mary) married Paul Daniel Chevenix and with him traded as 'Toymen' 'at the sign of the Golden Door over against Suffolk Street'. She sold her lease of the original Strawberry Hill cottage to Horace Walpole in 1747. 'It is a little plaything that I got out of Mrs Chevenix shop ...'. The Deard(s) family also had a toyshop in the Strand at the western end of Craven Street and evidently used the second half of the Chevenix shop as a branch under the Deard name for they issued a trade-card bearing this address. Deard also had a branch in Bath. (Hugh Phillips, *Mid-Georgian London*, 1964.)

DE LAMERIE, Paul (page 488) It has recently been established by careful investigation and inspection of a number of pieces of the New Sterling Standard by this maker that he used two varying unregistered versions of his first mark. The first, in use from 1716 until about 1720, has a pear-shaped outline to the punch around the fleur-de-lys below and fan-shaped outline around the coronet and mullet above. The second, in use from about 1720 until the registration of his sterling mark in 1732, shows a fleur-de-lys of considerably larger proportion than that of the earlier marks and a rounded outline to the punch around the coronet, which is of crown nature with arches (Goldsmiths' Company *Review*, 1984-5, p. 9).

A hitherto unknown relationship between Lamerie and the engraver Ellis Gamble, master of William Hogarth and, on the evidence of his trade card (Heal, *London Goldsmiths*), a retail goldsmith, is established by the discovery of an insurance policy in the joint names of Gamble and Lamerie, giving the former's address at the Golden Angel in Cranbourn Street 'for their Goods and Merchandize in their now Dwelling house only situate as aforesaid' in the sum of £1000, 11 October 1723 (Sun Insurance policy no. 30100). In 1726 Lamerie took out a separate policy for £500 at his Great Windmill address for household goods and stock-in-trade and in October 1728 both he and Gamble took separate policies at their individual addresses covering 'Household Goods and Utensils in Trade' for £200 and £100 respectively, 'Stock in Trade consisting of Wrought Plate only', both at £800 and 'Wearing Apparel' at £100. It seems probable that the first policy of 1723 was intended to cover Lamerie's work while in Gamble's hands for engraving or perhaps sale, and that the relationship may have been terminated at the time of the separate policies of 1728. (Sun Insurance policies, information Mr S. B. Turner.) Gamble was made bankrupt January 1733 with Lamerie as creditor. (B 4/7, 210, R.B.)

DELISLE, Louis (page 488) He is probably identical with Louis Rousseaux de L'Isle recorded as silverworker from Auxarne, Burgundy, in Amsterdam 1781. (Information Mr K. Citroen.)

DELMESTRE, John (page 489) Son of Daniel Delmester of St. Paul, Shadwell, surgeon apprenticed to Charles Legg of St. Martin-in-the-Fields, silversmith, 15 August 1717 for seven years on payment of £10. (I.R. 1/5 f.175, R.B.) The interval from his presumed freedom in 1724 to the only entry of a mark in his name appears unusually long, though always possible, and may perhaps be that of a son of the same name.

DENNEY, Daniel (page 489) Son of William Denney, blacksmith, deceased, of Lothbury, London, apprenticed to Henry Green (q.v.) of the Clothworkers' Company, silversmith, of Aldersgate Street, 6 May 1778 for seven years on payment of £25. Free 1 June 1785. (Information Mr D. E. Wickham, Archivist, Clothworkers' Company, and S.T.)

DENNISON, Robert (page 489) Son of Robert Dennison, late of Mortlake, Surrey, victualler, deceased, apprenticed to John Boyce of the Joyners' Company, 8 December 1724 for seven years on payment of £5 and turned over the same day to Rebekah Bird, widow of Benjamin Bird (both q.v.) 'to learn the trade of a Joyner'. Free 3 July 1733. (Joyners' Company registers, R.B.) Despite the standard phrase of the apprenticeship it is clear that Bird and Dennison were working bucklemakers.

DENNY, William (page 490) His place of birth is probably correctly read as 'Tuexbury', i.e. Tewkesbury. His first address should read 'Dove Court'. The date of entry of his mark alone may perhaps be on or about 1 November 1700, the date of John Bache's second mark on parting company. 'Swaything' Lane is of course St. Swithin's Lane.

DE OLIVEYRA, Abraham Lopez (page 490) His insurance policy of 15 June 1723 gives his address as 'next to the pump at Mrs Morais's in Little St. Helens in Bishopsgate Street' and another of 1733 as 'next door to the Ben Johnson's Head in Houndsditch'. (Sun Insurance policy, information Mr S. B. Turner, and R.B.) He is named eight times as supplying the Lord Mayor's salvers to Bevis Marks, first in 1724 and lastly in 1738. (Information Dr R. Barnett.)

DESREUMAUX, James (page 490) Samuel des Rumeaux, diamond worker in Amsterdam 1767, is probably related. (Information Mr K. Citroen.)

DE VEER, Frederick (page 491) Son of Frederick De Veer of Hamborough (? Hamburg), silversmith, deceased. Free of the Glovers' Company by redemption 14 March 1732. He appears as jeweller at his Angel Court address in the Glovers list of 1779. (S.T.) A large gold snuffbox signed 'Deveer, London' bearing the Amsterdam hallmarks for 1756, presumably on importation by one of his relatives, Abraham de Veer (1703-95) or Justus de Veer (1696-1762), is in the Rijksmuseum. (Information Mr K. Citroen.)

DICKER, William (page 492) The correct date of his bankruptcy was 7 June 1727 on the petition of Thomas Dicker, Salhurst, Sussex, yeoman, presumably a member of his family, possibly an older brother (B 4/5, 311, J.C.)

DODDS, Joseph (page 493) He is perhaps identifiable with 'Jos: Dodds', apprenticed to Matthew Derbyshire of Kingston-upon-Hull, jeweller and goldsmith, 17 July 1773 for seven years on payment of £42. (I.R. 1/58 f.209, R.B.)

DOVEY, Richard (page 494) His trade-card, in the possession of the Hon. C. Lennox-Boyd, describes him as 'at the Boot and Crown opposite Exeter Exchange in the Strand Small Worker in Gold, Silver, Amber and Tortoiseshell; Tipps China & Glass &c'. This address may postdate that of Pimlico in 1777.

DOXSEY, Thomas (page 494) The ascription of mark no. 3818 to him should be deleted, since there is no evidence that he was other than goldworker. The mark may be that of Thomas Devonshire (q.v.) although the latter appears to have remained in partnership with William Watkins (q.v.) until 1766. (Information Mr P. Dane.)

DRINKWATER, Sandylands (page 494) He does not appear to have been turned over to Robert White's widow Elizabeth as previously stated. Her name appears in his freedom grant in testimony of his service, implying the recent death of her husband. His will dated 14 June 1776 at St. Albans was proved 23 October that year. In it he left to his nephew of the same name (not his son as previously suggested) his freehold, etc. at St. Albans. To his wife Katherine an annuity of £20 p.a. and all his household goods, furniture, linen, plate, jewels and wearing apparel and fifty volumes at choice from his library. To Thomas Whipham (q.v.) of St. Albans, gentleman, and Charles Wright (q.v.) of Amen Corner, London, Goldsmith, his executors, £6700 in three per cent consolidated annuities in trust for his wife for £200 p.a. To his nephew Sandylands the remainder of his books and two bookcases on payment to his wife at fair appraisal. His executors to have £50 each and his nephew to be sole remaining beneficiary. (Information Mr T. Ingalls.)

DRURY, Dru II (page 495) A drawing dated 1834, perhaps by G. Scharf, shows the shop-window of 'Drury, silversmith and jeweller' at the corner of Villiers Street with the Strand (Hugh Phillips, *Mid-Georgian London*, 1964, Fig. 148A). The creditors listed in Drury's bankruptcy records reveal the extent of his involvement with the active members of the trade of the day. His debts were proved in seven entries from 18 December 1777 up to 7 November 1782. The list includes twenty-five working gold- or silversmiths, all recorded in the main Biographical Dictionary, preceding, as follows: William Abdy, Margaret Binley, Walter Brind, George Burrows, Robert Albin Cox, Thomas Daniel, Burrage Davenport, Richard Dovey, Philip Freeman, Peter Gillois, Thomas Hallows, John Holloway, William Holmes, James Hunt, John Kidder, Samuel Meriton, James Morisset, Richard Morrison, John Myatt, Elias Russell, John Scofield, Mark Thomegay, Walter Tweedie, Gabriel Wirgman and Charles Wright. Another was Aaron Barling, goldworker (Section VII, page 355, wrongly listed as Banting). (B 3/1257, J.C.)

DUCOMMIEU, Louis (page 497) He is described in his insurance policy of 14 May 1777 surprisingly as silversmith and cook at the corner of Greese Street in Stephen Street in Rathbone Place. (Sun Insurance policy information Mr S. B. Turner, and R.B.)

DUPONT, Louis (page 497) His wife Rachel Marie was the daughter of the Amsterdam goldworker Olivier Migault, whose mother Elisabeth Fourestier was a distant relative of Lewis Mettayer (q.v.). Dupont was probably related to the Amsterdam silversmith Jean Maximien du Pont. (Information Mr K. Citroen.)

DURANDEAU, John Edward (page 498) Son of Philip Durandeau of Clerkenwell, Middlesex, watchmaker, apprenticed to James Wintle (q.v.) of the Vintners' Company, 7 May 1817 on payment of £20. Free of that company 9 February 1853, then in Liverpool.

DUTTON, John (page 498) An alternative identity for this maker may well be son of John Dutton of St. Thomas the Apostle, Southwark, of the Dyers' Company, apprenticed to John Arnell, silversmith, Little Britain (q.v. above), 6 August 1766 on payment of £12. 12s., £10 being of the charity of the Society of St. Thomas aforesaid. Free 11 August 1791 as vintner, Walworth. Described thus on taking up his freedom so long after apprenticeship may imply change of business, possibly from the address carrying on his father's occupation. (R.B.)

BIOGRAPHICAL DICTIONARY: ADDENDA

DYMOND, Edward (page 498) Son of Robert Dymond of the Leathersellers' Company, apprenticed to George Cox of the Broderers' Company (q.v.), 7 May 1712 for seven years on payment of £30 and afterwards turned over to Richard Gines Merchant Taylor (q.v.). Free of the Broderers 1 March 1721 as goldsmith, Lombard Street, presumably still working for Gines. (P.R.O. I.R. 1/1 f.104 and Broderers' registers, R.B. and S.T.)

EAST, John (page 498) The Prime Warden mentioned under this heading is probably 'John East a goldsmith' buried at St. Clement Danes, 14 March 1707.

EATON, William (page 499) Born 1788. Son of William Eaton of the Needlemakers' Company, free by redemption 1784, the bucklemaker (pp. 404–5), apprenticed to his father 6 January 1802 and turned over to Alexander Field (q.v.). Free of the Needlemakers' Company by patrimony 9 January 1810 as silversmith, 30 Addle Street. Livery 1812. He was dead by August 1856 when his son John was made free of the Needlemakers as silversmith, 16 Jewin Street.

EDWARDS, James I (page 501) Probably son of James Edwards of the Strand, London, apprenticed to William Daniell of St. Bartholomew the Great, jeweller, 25 May 1725 for five years on payment of £10. 10s. (I.R. 1/10 f.194, R.B.)

EDWARDS, John II (page 501) He appears in the Fitzwalter Accounts '11 May 1738. Paid Edwards, silversmith in Lombard Street for 14 tickets, silver, for wine bottles at 5s 6d each £3 17 0' (Essex County Records).

ELEY, William I (page 502) The insurance policy of the partnership with Fearn, 1 March 1802, gives the address as 1 and 2 Lovell's Court 'On their house being two laid into one with new workshop and offices' covered for £2000 and 'utensils and stock therein' for £900. (Sun Insurance policy information Mr S. B. Turner and R.B.)

ELEY, William II (page 502) He was connected with J. L. Barritt, book-cover maker and binder (probably as supplying silver clasps and mounts) and was an active partner in Eley Brothers Patent Cartridge. His death was in fact due to an explosion caused by his own careless stirring of a mixture of fulminate of mercury in an experiment (*The Times*, 28 June 1841).

EMES, John (page 504) For the statement that Emes, following his apprenticeship, worked as an engraver and brought further capital into the expanding business of Henry Chawner (q.v.), see John Culme, *Directory of Gold and Silversmiths*, under Edward Barnard, quoting an anonymous article in *Watchmaker, Jeweller and Silversmith*, 1899.

EMES, Rebecca (page 504) She retired in 1829, when Edward Barnard succeeded to the business (op.cit. above).

ESTERBROOK, William (page 504) He is possibly identifiable with one of the same name shown in the Exeter Freeman records as made free 18 October 1806, then apprentice of Richard Jenkins, a prolific maker of spoons. (S.T.)

EVANS, George (page 504) Parentage unestablished. Apprenticed to John Allen I (q.v.) of the Glovers' Company, 12 July 1749. Free 26 May 1763. In Glovers' Company list 1779 as silversmith, Fore Street. (Glovers' Company records, S.T.)

EVANS, James (page 504) He appears as James Morley Evans, supplier of gold buckles, buttons and chains in Parker and Wakelin's Workmen's Ledger No. 2 from August 1766, his account brought forward from the earlier missing ledger. (H.C.)

EVERIT, John (page 505) Son of Abraham Everett (sic) of the Saddlers' Company. Free of the City October 1701, having become free of the Saddlers by patrimony. (C.F.1, S.T.)

FARRELL, Edward (page 506) He was born about 1780 and working at King's Head Court from 1801. The previous suggestion that he was maker for Thomas Hamlet is now disproved by the evidence of his work for Kensington Lewis, the St. James's Street retailer and entrepreneur for the Duke of York and others from about 1816–34. (John Culme, *Nineteenth Century Silver*, 1977.)

FARREN, Thomas (page 506) For his master 'John' Denny, read William Denny. Farren served St. Mary Woolnoth as sidesman and collector of the poor in 1716 and was nominated churchwarden in 1728 but exempted. He was one of four members of the Court of the Goldsmiths' Company entrusted with making of new plate in 1740, his contribution being the four rococo cups and covers and pair of finely engraved salvers forming part of the principal buffet display. He was buried at St. Mary Woolnoth, 14 October 1743. (Rosemary Weinstein, 'The South Sea Company Plate', *The Antique Collector*, October 1983.) His will proved 21 October 1743: 'unto my dear and loving wife Ann Farren all my ready monies, stock in trade, plate, goods, Chattells... and all other personal estate whatsoever', she as sole executrix. (Information Mr T. Kent.)

FIELD, Daniel (not previously included) The mark no. 3514 (page 250) may now be justifiably attributed to this maker. He appears as silversmith prosecuting his journeyman Christian Robinson at the Old Bailey, March 1762 on a charge of stealing fifteen silver boxes formed as barrels, eggs or vases valued at a few shillings apiece. Robinson had worked for Field 'near 35 years', implying the latter must have been in business since about 1727, covering the dates of the pieces recorded under mark no. 3514. Field died in September 1770 leaving an unsigned will which was attested by William Justis the younger who had been his apprentice and Samuel Meriton (q.v.). (London Session Papers quoted by John Culme, 'Periodical Reflections', *The Antique Collector*, February 1987.)

FISH, William (page 509) Correctly free by redemption 7 May 1706.

FITCH, Daniel (page 509) He is presumably the Daniel Fitch apprenticed to Peter Paupard of Old Artillery Ground, jeweller, 24 November 1762 for seven years on payment of £10. (I.R. 1/23 f.131, R.B.)

FOGELBERG, Andrew (page 511) His arrival in London can now be predated by the existence of a Sun Insurance policy of 16 February 1767, in the name of Andrew Fogelberg of St. Ann's Court, Dean Street, Soho, silversmith (policy no. 242671). Another dated 22 February 1782, while giving his Church Street address, appears only to cover household goods in a dwelling house at Pond Street, Hampstead (Sun Insurance policy information Ann Paton). He died before 3 February 1815, the date of proving his will. In this he remembered his sister Christina Bergstrom and her son Bengt, also a silversmith, of Laholm, Sweden, clearly establishing his origin. His widow Susanna sold the Hampstead property to Paul Storr, evidence of the latter's continuing friendship. (John Culme, *Nineteenth Century Silver*, 1977.)

FOX, Charles I (page 513) Son of Thomas Fox, gentleman, of St. Andrew's, Holborn, Middlesex, apprenticed to Henry Green (q.v.), goldsmith, Aldersgate, of the Clothworkers' Company, 1 August 1792 for seven years and turned over 2 May 1799 to Thomas Fray Citizen and Goldsmith. Free of the Clothworkers 2 April 1800 as silversmith, 92 Fetter Lane, probably his master's address. (Information Mr D. E. Wickham, Archivist, Clothworkers' Company, and S.T.)

FOX, Charles II (page 513) Now confirmed as son of above. Born 1801. Free of the Clothworkers' Company by patrimony 7 March 1827 as working silversmith, 139 Old Street, where he had entered his mark five years earlier. (Information as above.)

FRENCH, John (page 515) He came from Newcastle where he was apprentice and journeyman to Jonathan French and admitted to the guild 2 September 1727. He voted in elections there in 1734 and 1741 and 'from London' 1780. He presumably came south shortly before being made free in London. (Information Mrs G. E. P. How.) Described as goldsmith by trade, son of Joshua French of Lemington in the County of Northumberland, gentleman. (C.F.1, R.B.)

FULLER, Crispin (page 516) Born 5 December 1755. Unrecorded as already stated for apprenticeship at Goldsmiths' Hall, he was however apprenticed to Hester Bateman (herself never free of the Company) as silversmith 5 October 1769. He married the latter's granddaughter, Sarah, daughter of Letitia (Hester's daughter) and Richard Clark 6 October 1781. His son Jeremiah was first apprenticed to his father as a working silversmith 18 September 1812 before subsequent apprenticeship to James Shallis as previously recorded, the latter in fact his brother-in-law married to Esther Fuller. Jeremiah later became assayer at Goldsmiths' Hall, living over the premises, and retired in 1864. (Information Mr Jasper Fuller, grandson of Jeremiah, born 1904, his own father, Jeremiah's son, having been born at Goldsmiths' Hall in 1840.)

GALLANT, Jane (page 517) Probably the widow of William Gallant of St. Giles, Middlesex, watchcase-maker, to whom his son John was apprenticed 1 January 1753 for seven years on payment of 5s. (I.R. 1/19 f.79, R.B.)

GARDEN, Phil(l)ip(s) (page 518) The mark entry dates should read 'Third and

BIOGRAPHICAL DICTIONARY: ADDENDA

fourth marks 12 March 1744. St. Paul's Churchyard. Fifth mark 29 October 1748. Sixth 18 April 1751. Seventh 28 April 1756'. The date of his bankruptcy was 26 June 1762 when the petitioning creditors were Lewis Herne and Francis Butty, St. James's, Clerkenwell, silversmiths and partners (q.v.). (B 4/16, 221, J.C.)

GARDNER, Richard (page 519) The attribution of marks nos. 3771-2 to him is strengthened by the fact that he appears as supplier of saucepans, coffee-pots, sauceboats and chocolate-pots in Parker and Wakelin's Workmen's Ledger No. 2 from July 1770. (H.C.)

GARFIELD, Jeremiah (page 519) Tried and convicted in 1822 'for selling twelve silver teaspoons with a counterfeit duty mark on them' and sentenced to seven years' transportation. Sailed aboard the *Eliza* to New South Wales. Petitioned the Governor in 1823, naming his crime, and was assigned to a silversmith/retailer Jacob Josephson, but appears never to have practised his trade. In the 1828 census lists he appears, aged forty-eight, as a constable in Bathurst, N.S.W. (Information Mr J. Warwick-James.)

GARRARD, Robert II (page 519) Apprenticed to his father Robert Garrard I of the Grocers' Company, 1 June 1809 for seven years and free by service rather than patrimony as previously stated. (Grocers' Company records, S.T.)

GARTHORNE, George (page 520) His death occurred in October 1730.

GIGNAC, Benjamin (page 522) The previous suggestion of Flemish or German origin is clarified by the fact that he was born in Amsterdam 1713, apprenticed there in 1724 and moved to London 1735. (Information Mr K. Citroen.)

GILES, George (page 522) Son of John Giles, late of St. Mary Aldermanbury, founder, deceased, apprenticed to Thomas Leach of the Haberdashers' Company, goldsmith, Lombard Street, 18 July 1754 for seven years on payment of £60 (a large sum for the period). Free 2 December 1761 as goldsmith near Cripplegate, London Wall. (Haberdashers' Company registers, R.B.) For another possibly related to Giles's master see John Leach (page 577).

GILPIN, Thomas (page 523) An account of the coronation of George III describes the ancient custom that the new sovereign should dine on the first Lord Mayor's day after his coronation with the Chief Magistrate and Corporation and quotes from 'a long descriptive letter published at the time' as follows: 'I must not forget to tell you that the grand service of plate at the King's table was entirely new and made by Mr Gilpin. The City exchanged with him the old plate for his new to do honour to this grand occasion ... on the table between each service (i.e. course) was placed near 100 cold ornamentals (sic) and a grand silver epergne filled with various kinds of shellfish of different colours' (*A Faithful Account of the Coronations of the Kings and Queens of England exemplified in that of King George III and Queen Caroline*, ed. Richard Thomson, 1820). For.the succession from Haldanby Langley to Gilpin and onwards through Makepeace and Carter to the present firm of A. Woodhouse and Son, see John Culme, *Directory of Gold and Silversmiths*, pp. 179-80. Gilbert Langley, a self-confessed rogue and wastrel, was fellow apprentice of Gilpin about 1726 and began to pilfer silver in the shop, unsuspected by his father or Gilpin. (*Life and Adventures of Gilbert Langley*, written by himself, London, 1740, J.C.)

GLADMAN, Samuel (not previously included) Partner with Samuel Bellingham (q.v.) on entry of their mark as goldworkers, 12 October 1793. His will, proved 1804, describes him as a gold chainmaker. (MS note Goldsmiths' Hall copy of *London Goldsmiths*.)

GLANVILLE, Richard (page 523) Son of Samuel Glanville, late of the parish of St. Bartholomew behind the Exchange, cutler, deceased, apprenticed to Frederick De Veer (q.v. above) of the Grocers' Company, 27 September 1743 for seven years on payment of one penny (!) Free of that company 10 July 1752. Appears in the Glovers' List 1779 as Strand, jeweller. (Glovers' Company Freedom register, S.T.)

GODBEHERE, Samuel (page 524) Son of Edmund Godbehere of Workworth, Derbyshire, grocer. Free of the Needlemakers' Company by redemption, 10 September 1784 as silversmith. Livery 1787. Master 1804. Died between December 1818 and January 1819. (S.T.)

GODFREY, Benjamin (page 524) Son of William Godfrey of Surrey, gentleman, apprenticed to John Craig of St. James's, Middlesex, jeweller, 17 April 1716 for seven years from 25 December 1715 on payment of £20. (I.R. 1/4 f.156, R.B.) Considering his father's description and the relatively high premium for the period it seems likely that the Norris Street business was principally a retail one, a supposition strengthened by his widow's trade card as appointed to the Duke of Cumberland.

GODFREY, Elizabeth (page 524) She appears in the Fitzwalter Accounts '4 May 1745. Paid Mrs Godfrey silversmith for a large silver milk jug £2 0 0' (Essex County Records).

GOODE, John (page 525) Son of John Goode of St. Martin-in-the-Fields, sword cutler apprenticed to Robert Loader of the Longbowstringmakers' Company, 9 November 1692 for seven years. Free of that company 18 July 1701. Indenture signed Gaude (C.F.1, R.B.) Is this corroboration of the previous suggestion of Huguenot origin?

GOULD, James (page 526), Mary and William (page 527) For a full discussion of these candlestickmakers, see J. P. Fallon, 'The Goulds and Cafes, Candlestick makers', *Society of Silver Collectors Proceedings*, Vol. II, p. 146. The correct date for the move by James Gould from Gutter Lane is 1741. He died in 1750 described in his will as gentleman of Islington, London, stipulating burial in his vault in Kingsbury Churchyard, Somersetshire, leaving all his properties in Somerset to his widowed sister, Hannah Baker, for her lifetime and then to his nephew James, son of William Gould (q.v.). This nephew must have been the James Gould, candlestickmaker, of the Parl. Report list, since Fallon states that James's own son of the same name had died during apprenticeship before 1750. In the light of her husband's death, established as 1750, the mark signed by her must have been entered by her in her husband's sickness or absence and should therefore be regarded as his still in business. In discussing William Gould's history after the affair of the Fishmongers' chandelier, Fallon records three further apprentices taken by him in 1753, including his son James and others in 1755 and 1761, while also recording Richard Webb goldsmith as occupying Gould's premises in Foster Lane in 1756. Any working activity by Gould at this period remains in doubt.

GOULD, William (page 527) Declared bankrupt 8 July 1762 as silversmith, Foster Lane, on the petition of James Gould, South Petherton, Somerset, gentleman, no doubt a senior family member. (B 4/16, 225 J.C.)

GREEN, Henry (page 528) Son of Henry Green, late of Hendon, Middlesex, farmer, deceased, apprenticed to Edward Aldridge I (q.v.) of the Clothworkers' Company, goldsmith, Foster Lane, 8 October 1746 for seven years on payment of £20. Free 5 February 1755 as journeyman to his master. The Clothworkers' Company has a bill for silver dated 28 August 1794 headed Henry Green and Charles Aldridge with the latter's name deleted, evidence of the termination of the partnership before that date. Green was dead by 2 May 1799 when his apprentice Charles Fox I (q.v.) was turned over to Thomas Fray. (Information Mr D. E. Wickham, Archivist, Clothworkers' Company, and S.T.) The fact that both Henry Green and Charles Aldridge also took the freedom of the Girdlers' Company may have been for social reasons, rather than as previously suggested to qualify for business.

GREEN, Samuel (page 528) He was also again declared bankrupt 7 November 1729 as goldsmith and silversmith, Lombard Street, on the petition of Samuel Wise, St. Saviour's, Southwark, gentleman. (B. 4/5, 196, J.C.)

HAGUE, John I (page 531) Son of John Hague of St. Andrew's, Holborn, gentleman, apprenticed to Joseph Mumford (q.v.) of the Loriners' Company, 20 September 1718 for seven years on payment of £20. Free 25 February 1731, described as 'Lives in Grey Fryers; works at Mr Morris's a Silver Plate Worker near Pye Corner, Smithfield' (cf. Henry Morris, page 601). After freedom Hague agreed to serve four years as an indentured servant in the West Indies, which he seems to have done, since his first mark was not entered until December 1735. (I.R. 1/6 f.125, Loriners' Company records and C.F.1, R.B. and S.T.)

HAGUE, John II (page 531) Son of Joseph Hague of Bethnal Street, Middlesex, weaver (and therefore seemingly unlikely to have been grandson of John Hague I as previously suggested), apprenticed to Edward Lees (q.v.) of the Vintners' Company, Albemarle Street, Clerkenwell, 5 December 1804 on payment of £2 paid by Langbourn Ward Charity School. Subsequently turned over to George Burrows II (q.v.). Free of the Vintners 3 March 1813, then of Fork Buildings, Pentonville. (S.T.)

BIOGRAPHICAL DICTIONARY: ADDENDA

HALL, Daniel (page 531) Son of Daniel Hall of the Hatbandmakers' Company, apprenticed to John Hall of the Drapers' Company, recorded in 1732 as silversmith, Abchurch Lane, Blackfriars, 8 July 1725 for seven years and turned over 8 March 1728 to John Wynel, Citizen and Broderer. Free of the Drapers 27 July 1732 as watchcasemaker, Fleet Street. Livery 1765 to 1775 (presumed date of death). Described as pawnbroker in an apprenticeship to him, 1771. Following his death, his widow Elizabeth took further apprentices in 1779 and 1784. (Drapers' Company records, S.T.)

HAMON, Louis (page 532) Appears as Lewis Hamand of St. James's, Westminster, apprenticed to John Lesage of St. Martin-in-the-Fields, goldsmith, 10 November 1725 for seven years on payment of £15. This is an unusual instance of a master, free of the Goldsmiths' Company, omitting to record the boy's apprenticeship in the company's register, perhaps because Lesage was working out of the City jurisdiction. (I.R. 1/11 f.46, R.B.)

HANET, Paul (page 532) His freedom by redemption is recorded on 7 March 1716, the same day as entry of his first mark when he was described as 'of great St. Andrews street in the parish of St. Giles-in-the-Fields in the County of Middx Goldsmith'. (Longbowstringmakers' Company Freedom register, S.T.)

HARACHE, Francis (page 533) He appears as Francis Harrach of St. Giles-in-the-Fields, apprenticed to Isaac Cabane of St. Martin's Westr, silversmith, 31 May 1725 for seven years on payment of £10. 10s. (I.R. 1/10 f.184, R.B.) In 1732 Harache is described as snuffbox-maker in the apprenticeship to him of Thomas Harache. The latter, for whom no mark is recorded, is described as silversmith in the apprenticeship to him of John Jacob, 1743, and as snuffbox-maker in the apprenticeship of Thomas Danser in 1744. (R.B.)

HARACHE, Jean (page 533) His working life can now be predated to 1710 by a Sun Insurance policy of 20 December that year for 'John Harache of Little Newport Street in the Parish of St. Ann's Westr. Com Middx Goldsmith for his Goods'. (Information Mr S. B. Turner.)

HARACHE, Peter I (page 533) It is now established that he came from a long line of Rouen goldsmiths, the earliest of whom, Jehan and Pierre, were masters in 1570 (C. G. Cassan, *Les Orfèvres de Normandie*, p. 217, where he is listed as Harach Pierre (VI) but without indication of his relationship to other members of the family).

HARACHE, Peter II (page 534) Son of Pierre Harache of Rouen and Isabeau Guerain, the former dead in 1679 so not identifiable with Peter I above. He married Jeanne Lemaignen (alias le Magnon or Mannaye) 21 July 1681 and is recorded as renouncing the Huguenot faith 2 November 1685 when working as a journeyman. In view of his denization date in England of 1698 it would appear probable that he arrived about then to join his namesake, of whatever relationship to the latter, the former suggestion that he was his son remaining undetermined (Cassan, op.cit. above). Harache's wife was probably related to Jean Magnan, recorded as a goldsmith's apprentice in Amsterdam, 1686. (Information Mr K. Citroen.)

HARRIS, Simon (page 538) After 1811 he appears in the records of the Exeter Assay Office as 'of Plymouth Dock', presumably principally supplying naval shoe-buckles, etc. (Information Mr T. Kent.)

HARWOOD, Bartholomew (page 539) Son of Bartholomew Harwood of St. Saviour's, Southwark, soap factor, deceased, apprenticed to Richard Peters (q.v.) of the Haberdashers' Company of St. Saviour's, Southwark, goldsmith, 4 June 1725 for seven years on payment of £20. Appears not to have taken the freedom of the Haberdashers, but since working in Southwark had no need to. (I.R. 1/10 f.194 and Haberdashers' Company records, R.B.)

HARWOOD, John (page 539) Son of Kommit Harwood, late of London, cabinet-maker, deceased. Apprenticed and free as previously stated. (Broderers' Company records, S.T.)

HATTON, Margaret (not previously included. See page 148n) Presumably the widow of Thomas Hatton (q.v.). Only mark entered as smallworker, 19 March 1764. Address Shrift (Frith) Street, Soho, as for the latter.

HAYENS, Henry (page 540) He appears as supplier and mender of filigree work in Parker and Wakelin's Workmen's Ledger No. 2, August 1770, brought forward from the earlier missing ledger. (H.C.)

HAYNE, Jonathan (page 541) For date of freedom read 4 January 1804.

HAYTER, Thomas (page 541) He married Martha, eldest daughter of his master and subsequent partner, George Smith II. She died aged sixty-six in 1834 (memorial plaque St. Michael, Wood Street).

HEALY, Joseph (page 542) He was actually apprenticed to David Green of the Goldsmiths' Company, 5 September 1717 for seven years on payment of the sum of £20, but as previously mentioned took up the freedom of the Barber Surgeons by patrimony. (Goldsmiths' Apprentice Book 5, f.82, R.B.)

HEARNDEN, Nicholas (page 542) The mark no. 3742 is now recognized as that of Naphthali Hart (q.v.), the date-letter of the teapot from which the mark was taken by Jackson being almost certainly a misreading for that of 1818 (both lower case 'e'). Hearnden's description of spoonmaker and that of his first master Daintry in 1773 supports the attribution of no. 3744 to him rather than Nathaniel Horwood as previously suggested. (Information Mr Ian Pickford.)

HEBERT, Henry (page 542) He appears twice in the Fitzwalter Accounts. '6 October 1739. Paid Hebert silversmith for two silver ladles for the tureens, &ca and in full £9. 19s. 6d.' and '11 December 1739 . . . for a silver standish weight about 50 ounces at 2s. 6d. per ounce fashion of which allowed at the Jewel Office 32 ounces and for what is over and above I now pay said Hebert £8 8s. . . .' (Essex County Records). The reference to the Jewel Office indicates that the piece in question was official or 'indenture plate', the allowance for which had been exceeded by the recipient. This transaction agrees with Hebert's position as a royal goldsmith. Apart from the suggestion of a Le Mans origin for the name of Hebert, it also occurs for many goldsmiths in Amsterdam and The Hague. (Information Mr K. Citroen.)

HELY, John (page 542) Now to be identified as son of John Healey of Nash, Bucks., labourer, apprenticed and free as previously stated as alternative (1) for this maker. (S.T.)

HEMING, George (page 542) It is now established that he was not the son of Thomas Heming as previously stated, but in fact his brother. He appears as son of Richard Heming, late of Ludlow, Salop, mercer, deceased (as did Thomas in his father's lifetime), apprenticed to Richard Lewis of the Musicians' Company, 7 May 1746 for seven years on payment of £31. 10s. Free of the Musicians 8 August 1754 as druggist, Lad Lane, but later described as 'now of Piccadilly, goldsmith'. This being so, he may well have been in Piccadilly from c. 1760 as Heal suggests and appears to have had a separate business, certainly when in partnership with William Chawner (q.v.), from that of his brother Thomas. Whether George, son of Thomas, ever joined his father remains unknown. (Musicians' Company registers, R.B.)

HEMING, Thomas (page 542) His birth was in 1722–3, his death at the age of seventy-eight being 9 April 1801 on his memorial in Hillingdon Church, Middlesex. He appears as holding silver for Lady Mary Coke at the time of a burglary she suffered in 1774. Her journal for 10 June that year records: 'In looking among some papers yesterday . . . I found a paper of a very alarming nature for my plate which is now at Mr Hemming's: 'tis a note of eight of the silver dishes being in pawn; there is however a line drawn across the writing, which gives me some hopes that he had redeemed them . . .' (*The Letters and Journals of Lady Mary Coke*, Vol. IV). The German sage Gottfried Lichterberg wrote in his commonplace book, probably in 1775: 'A silver service worth 30,000 pounds has been ordered from the famous silversmith in Bond Street Mr Hemmins some days ago. It will go abroad and even he does not know the recipient. He makes it on the order of two City merchants. Hemmins has a fine country seat near Uxbridge: I passed it on 6th April; what a difference between him and Kramer (a Gottingen silversmith).' (Information Mr K. Citroen.) It seems very probable that this service can be equated with that ordered for the Governors of Tula, Russia, which included 38 candlesticks, 31 meat-dishes and 9 salvers by Heming, 1776 and 1777, and some by G. Heming and W. Chawner (E. Alfred Jones, *The Old English Plate of the Emperor of Russia*, p. 92, Pl. XLVI). Some of this service was disposed of by the Soviets and appeared on the London market in 1934 (Christie's *Catalogues*, 11 and 18 July 1934, and Crichton Bros.' advertisement in *Connoisseur*, February 1936). Heming was the first President of The Guardians, otherwise known as the Society for the Protection of Trade against Swindlers and Sharpers, founded March 1776. A silver-mounted

BIOGRAPHICAL DICTIONARY: ADDENDA

ebony gavel survives with his name as President (Sotheby's *Catalogue*, 22 November 1984, where a full account of the society by John Culme is given). Other goldsmiths serving on the committee were Richard Morson as Vice-President, Treasurer and Secretary, Thomas Jefferys, Augustus Le Sage, Thomas Payne, Thomas Whipham and Charles Wright (all q.v.). Others were general members.

HENNELL, David I (page 543) David Hennell and Son appear as regular suppliers of salts and their glasses in Parker and Wakelin's Workmen's Ledger No. 2, October 1766, brought forward from earlier missing ledger. From August 1769 the firm appears as David and Robert Hennell. (H.C.)

HERBERT, Samuel (page 544) Son of Thomas Herbert, late of Ilford, Essex, gentleman, deceased, apprenticed to Edward Aldridge I, of the Clothworkers' Company, goldsmith of Gutter Lane, 6 April 1736 for seven years on payment of £10 10s. Free of the Clothworkers as goldsmith, New Court, Bunhill Fields, 4 September 1744. For the identity of his unnamed partner in his mark entry see Henry Bailey above. In 1763 he took Burrage Davenport as apprentice, establishing a nexus of makers of pierced baskets springing from Aldridge and all free of the Clothworkers. (Information Mr D. E. Wickham, Archivist, Clothworkers' Company, through R.B.)

HERNE, Lewis (page 544) Mark no. 3719 can now be confidently regarded as his, since he appears as supplier of a range of items including plates, sauce-boats, tureens and tea vases in Parker and Wakelin's Workmen's Ledger No. 2 in 1767, the account brought forward from the earlier missing ledger, supporting the previous suggestion that he had set up alone after 1765. (H.C.)

HIGGINS, Francis (page 545) Free by patrimony 5 January 1814 as silversmith, Hosier Lane. Correct date of third mark 18 February 1825.

HILL, Caleb (page 546) Kaleb, son of Allen Hill of Chippenham, Wilts., parchment maker, apprenticed to Thomas Mann (q.v.) of the Broderers' Company, 4 January 1721 for seven years on payment of £20. (I.R. 1/8 f.88, R.B.)

HILL, Robert (page 546) His name appears in the Bevis Marks records in 1720 and 1721. (Information Dr R. Barnett.)

HINDMARSH, George (page 547) His identity is now clearly established as the George Hymers, son of George Hymers of Newcastle, skinner, apprenticed to Jonathon French 30 August 1721 for seven years on payment of £25. Subsequently as son of George Hindmarsh late of New Castle-upon-Tine, skinner, deceased, he was made free of the Musicians' Company by redemption 4 May 1736, probably because with Robert Abercromby they had moved into the City by the time of their third mark before 18 March 1736. The Musicians' Company, from other evidence, appears to have offered freedom at a cheap rate. (Musicians' Company records, R.B.) Hindmarsh was declared bankrupt 8 February 1746, described as jeweller and goldsmith, Strand, St. Martin-in-the-Fields, on the petition of Robert Macmorran, London, merchant. (B 4/11, 136, J.C.)

HOD(G)KINSON, Thomas (page 548) Later recorded as gold and silver worker in Amsterdam 1737. (Information Mr K. Citroen.)

HOGG, Andrew (page 548) Son of Alexander Hogg of Aberdeen in North Britain, yeoman, apprenticed to Joseph Barker of the Drapers' Company, silversmith, Bread Street Hill, 15 September 1742 for seven years on payment of £4, being Mr Dixon's gift paid by the company. Free of that company 20 September 1749 as jeweller and goldsmith, Great Russell Street. Livery 1759. Court 1779. Master 1793. Subsequent addresses: 1776, Castle Street, Leicester Square; 1784, Chapel Row, Little Chelsea; 1791, Queen Street, Brompton; 1794-9, Upper Belgrave Place, Chelsea. (Drapers' Company records, S.T.)

HOLADAY, Edward (page 549) His last home, still standing, was Swanton Street Farm, Bredgar, near Sittingbourne, Kent. (Information present owner from title deeds through Revd P. Hawker.)

HOLMES, William (page 550) Son of John Holmes of the Loriners' Company, apprenticed to Erasmus Christian Hoffman, 'Chasser' of St. Martin-in-the-Fields, 4 April 1747 for seven years on payment of £6. (I.R. 1/18 f.143 R.B.) Free by patrimony of the Loriners 7 August 1765 (Loriners' Company register). On taking an apprentice in September 1765 he is described as a chaser of Clerkenwell Green. Master of the Loriners 1781 and resigned from the company 1804. (S.T.)

HORNE, Edward I (page 551) Son of Charles Horne of Burntwood (Brentwood), Essex, innholder, apprenticed to Thomas Elton of the Clockmakers' Company, 15 March 1697 for seven years. Free of that company 4 December 1704 by service and not as previously suggested by patrimony. (Clockmakers' Company records and C.F.1, S.T.)

HORWOOD, Nathaniel (page 552) Son of Nathaniel Horwood, apprenticed to Frederick Venham (? Vonham, q.v.), chaser, of St. Luke's, Middlesex, 19 October 1744 for seven years on payment of £6. (I.R. 1/17 f.101, R.B.) The previous attribution of mark no. 3744 to him should now be disregarded. See Nicholas Hearnden above.

HOSIER, Elias (page 552) Son of Elias (Ellis) Hosier of Hooton (? Wooton) under Hedge, cutler, apprenticed 17 March 1694 to Thomas Vicaridge as previously stated. (S.T.)

HOUGHAM, Charles (page 552) Born 1749. Died aged forty-four 18 January 1793. (Source as below.)

HOUGHAM, Solomon (page 552) Born c. 1746. Died 17 August 1818, aged seventy-two. (Monument St. Botolph's without Aldersgate.)

HOULE, John (page 552) Son of John Houle of New Street Square, London, chaser, apprenticed to Paul Storr of the Vintners' Company, 7 November 1798. Free 4 February 1807. Address Garden Court, St. Giles. Livery of the Vintners 14 April 1818 as silversmith, Red Lion Street. Took seven apprentices, two of them his sons, the last in 1826. (S.T.) He had been working as a chaser from at least 1795, when his insurance policy describes him as such at 17 New Street Square near Shoe Lane, and another of 1 April 1802 again as chaser at Garden Court, Great Turnstile, Lincoln's Inn Fields, when his books were covered for the surprisingly high figure for the time of £470.

HUDELL, René (page 553) He was made free of the Longbowstringmakers by redemption 3 March 1717/18, two days before the entry of his only mark, an obvious arrangement to enable him to work as goldsmith. (S.T.)

HUGHES, Ferdinando (page 553) Son of James Hughes of Bromham, Wilts., gentleman, apprenticed to Edward Pilsworth of the Loriners' Company, 28 April 1662. Free 17 December 1690. (S.T.)

HUNTLEY, John (page 555) Son of Stephen Huntly, apprenticed to Peter Tabois of St. Giles, London, snuffbox-maker, 3 July 1752 for seven years on payment of £21. Freedom not found. (I.R. 1/19 f.50, R.B.)

HYDE, James (page 556) Born 29 January 1748, son of Thomas and Anna Maria Hyde (register, St. Vedast, Foster Lane); his age in the St. Paul's School register apparently in error. Dead by 28 November 1799 when his widow Mary (below) entered her mark with John Riley.

HYDE, Mary (page 556) Definitely established as the wife of James (above). A number of children born to them are recorded in the St. Vedast, Foster Lane registers between 1782 and 1799, including George as previously recorded as James's son on entering St. Paul's School, who was born 1782.

HYDE, Thomas (page 556) The elder brother of James above, born 23 December 1746 and apparently to be identified with 'John Hyde', son of Thomas H. goldsmith of Gutter Lane, admitted to St. Paul's School 1756. The difference in name may be the result of a clerical error or perhaps a second name was added after baptism to distinguish him from his father. (Information on Hyde family Miss M. Grimshaw.)

INNOCENT, John (page 557) Son of John Innocent of St. Ann's, Soho, silversmith, apprenticed to Paul Callard of the Longbowstringmakers, 20 December 1754 and free of that company 5 January 1763. (S.T.) His insurance policy of 10 January 1794 describes him as silversmith, Newport Street. (Sun Insurance policy information Mr S. B. Turner, R.B.)

IRVINE, John (page 557) Apprenticed to James Hill, goldsmith, in Edinburgh, 18 May 1753 for seven years on payment of £35, a high figure for the time. (I.R. 1/51 f.261, R.B.) He is probably the one of the same name made free of the Scriveners' Company by redemption as goldsmith 25 April 1769 (Scriveners' Company records and C.F.1, S.T.)

ISSOD, Joyce (page 557) Her mark has been noted on a piece with hallmark for 1698, antedating her husband's death to approximately this year. (Information Mrs G. E. P. How.)

ISSOD, Thomas (page 557) The previously expressed supposition that the mark T.I.

between escallops is not his is now confirmed by the identification of Thomas Jenkins (q.v. below) with that mark.

JACKSON, Orlando (page 559) Son of Thomas Jackson of Heddington (near Edinburgh), apprenticed to John Welch, goldsmith, in Edinburgh, 21 November 1750 on payment of £10. (I.R. 1/52 f.50.) He must have arrived in London soon after obtaining his freedom in Edinburgh, since his first mark was entered before February 1760. He was subsequently made free of the Spectaclemakers' Company by redemption 23 April 1766, described as chaser, on the same day as Thomas Bumfriss, with whom he was to enter a mark 6 May following in order to work within the City at Queenhithe. The Spectacle-makers appear to have provided a cheap entry to freedom. (C.F.1 and Spectacle-makers' register, R.B.)

JACOB, John (page 559) Delete 'No record of apprenticeship or freedom'. He was apprenticed to Thomas Harache, silversmith (for whom no mark is recorded) in 1743.

JAGO, James (page 559) Son of John Jago (q.v.) of the Merchant Taylors' Company, silversmith, St. Luke's, Old Street, apprenticed to his father 5 September 1798. Free of that company 2 March 1825. (Merchant Taylors' Company records, S.T.)

JAGO, John (page 559) Son of Thomas Jago of St. Luke's, Old Street, sawyer, apprenticed to William Carter of the Merchant Taylors' Company, silversmith, Newgate Street, 7 December 1774. Free of that company 5 July 1786, three years after the entry of his first mark.

JARRATT, John (page 560) Son of William Jarratt of St. Sepulchre, London, watchgilder, apprenticed to James Knight of the Drapers' Company, 4 August 1741 for seven years. Free 14 August 1756 as gilder and chaser, Mile End. (S.T.)

JELF, William (page 561) Son of William Jelfe of Southwold, Essex (? in error for Suffolk), carpenter, apprenticed to Edward Horne I (q.v.) of the Clockmakers' Company. Free 3 June 1717. (S.T.)

JENKINS, Thomas (page 561) Appears as Thomas Jenken, son of Thomas Jenken of Madren in co. Cornwall, yeoman, apprenticed to John Seale, Citizen and Butcher, of London, 8 May 1661 for seven years. Free 15 July 1668. (C.F.1, R.B.) Master of Butchers' Company 1699. He is now established as the maker of many important pieces of the Restoration period, using the mark T.I. between escallops, similar in form and escallops to his 1697 mark no. 1259. (A. Grimwade and J. Banister, 'Thomas Jenkins Unveiled', *Connoisseur*, July 1977.)

JERMAN, Samuel (page 562) A mark S J in rectangle with indented upper edge and sides which would appear to be attributable to this maker found on a marrowspoon of 1766. (Information Mr M. G. Barnett.)

JONES, Thomas (page 564) The attribution of marks nos. 3840-1 is confirmed by his appearance as supplier of coffee-pots, tea vases, chafing dishes, salts, saucepans and sauce-boats, address Rupert Street, in Parker and Wakelin's Workmen's Ledger No. 2, August 1767. (H.C.)

JURY, William (page 566) Son of Thomas Jury, late Citizen and Haberdasher of London, deceased, apprenticed to John Hague (q.v.) of the Loriners' Company, 22 April 1752 on payment of £5. Free 15 December 1759 as silversmith of Lillipot Lane, near Noble Street. (S.T.)

JUSTIS, Thomas (page 566) Son of William Justis, deceased, of the Carpenters' Company, and therefore probably a younger brother of William Justis (q.v.), apprenticed to William Overton (q.v.) of the Merchant Taylors' Company, 2 December 1730 for seven years on payment of £10 and later turned over to John Edwards, citizen and grocer. Free of the Merchant Taylors 7 September 1748 as working silversmith, Bartholomew Close. He was dead by 1 March 1790 when his apprentice John Lemay was made free. (Merchant Taylors' records, R.B. and S.T.)

JUSTIS, William (page 566) Justis and Company goldsmiths, Well Yard, Bartholomew's Hospital in the *London Directory*, 1768 and Baldwin's *New Complete Guide*, 1770 may perhaps be a later address for his son. (R.B.)

KENTISH, John (page 569) The attribution of mark no. 3648 to this name is now to be disregarded. There were father and son of the same name. The former, son of John Kentish of Hitchin, Herts., linen draper, was apprenticed to Frederick De Veer (q.v.) of the Glovers' Company, 20 August 1736. Free 15 December 1747. On the Court 1776 and 1778 as jeweller, Cornhill, where he was already recorded in 1768 in the *London Directory* and as Kentish and Turner in the

New Complete Guide, 1777. The possibility that the son joined his father in business seems likely but unestablished. Since all references are as a jeweller it suggests that Jackson's first attribution of the mark in question is most unlikely. (Glovers' Company records and C.F.1, S.T. and R.B.)

KEY, William (page 570) Son of James Key of St. Martin-in-the-Fields, taylor, apprenticed to John Mitchell of the Glovers' Company, 4 September 1760 for seven years. Free of the City May 1769 by service but no entry in Glovers' Freedom Book. (Glovers' Company records and C.F.1, S.T.)

KING, Jeremiah (page 571) Son of Thomas King of Langley, Herts., yeoman, apprenticed as previously stated to William Scarlett 1 June 1715 for seven years on payment of £20. His second marriage appears in the register of St. Clement, Eastcheap, 21 February 1733(?4) 'Jeremiah King widower of St. Leonard, Foster Lane and Mary Bayley of Christchurch'. (Broderers' Company records, S.T.)

KNIGHT, William I (page 572) A mark W K conjoined found on the Lichfield 'Bearing Sword' of 1685 may be the pre-1697 mark of this goldsmith. A plug bayonet in the National Museum of Wales has the same mark (see Jackson, page 143, possibly from the same piece). (Information Mr A. Vesey Norman.)

KNOPFELL, Frederick (page 573) He is almost certainly to be identified with Frederick Klupfel(l) jeweller of the parish of St. Martin's-le-Grand (Heal) who was related to Sigismund Godhelp Dinglinger, recorded by Heal as jeweller at the Diamond Cross, St. Martin's-le-Grand 1749, a member of the famous family of Dresden royal goldsmiths. (Information Mr K. Citroen.)

LADYMAN, John (page 573) The entry date of his mark is more probably April 1697 together with the other first entries, all undated, under John Sutton's initial entry of 15 April that year.

LAMBE, Jonathan (page 574) His undated mark was probably entered on or soon after obtaining his freedom July 1697.

LAMMAS, Jeremiah (page 574) The suggested identity (1) in this maker's entry should be disregarded. (Note: This addendum appeared in the 2nd Edition with name misprinted as 'Kammas'.)

LANGFORD, John II (page 575) Son of Nicholas Langford of the Merchant Taylors' Company, apprenticed to Henry Bailey of the Clothworkers' Company, goldsmith, Foster Lane, 20 September 1752 for seven years on payment of £25. Free 6 February 1760 as journeyman to his master. (Information Mr D. E. Wickham, Archivist, Clothworkers' Company, and S.T.) Langford and Sebille appear as suppliers of a wide range of pierced work including bottle stands, salts, bread baskets and cream pails in Parker and Wakelin's Workmen's Ledger No. 2 from November 1766, the account brought forward from the earlier missing ledger. (H.C.)

LANGTON, Dennis (page 575) He is almost certainly the one of the same name, whose executrix Mary Mordaunt petitioned for the bankruptcy of Thomas Mouldon 11 July 1739. (B 4/9 217, J.C.)

LAUGHTON, John II (page 576) The entry date of his mark is more probably April 1697 together with the other first entries, all undated. (See John Ladyman above.)

LAWFORD, John (not previously included) Son of James Lawford of Dartford, Kent, carpenter, apprenticed to Isaac Duke (q.v.) 6 September 1751. Free 8 November 1758. Hitherto unidentified as a plateworker, he appears as partner to William Vincent (q.v. page 690 and below), also apprenticed to Duke, in Parker and Wakelin's Workmen's Ledger No. 2 as Messrs Vincent and Lawford, suppliers of bread baskets, cream pails, sugar baskets, etc. between September 1767 and September 1768. The partners then appear to have parted, supplying similar pieces separately, Lawford continuing until at least December 1770. He does not appear in the Parliamentary Report of 1773. These facts suggest that mark no. 3653 may perhaps be ascribed to him when working alone. (H.C. and R.B.)

LEACH, John (page 577) The entry date of his mark is more probably April 1697 together with the other first entries, all undated. He was dead by 19 May 1713 when his apprentice Daniel Yerbury (q.v.) was turned over to George Beale.

LEADBETTER, John Gibson (page 578) Son of John Leadbetter, deceased, of the Barber Surgeons' Company, apprenticed to Thomas Justis (q.v.) of the Merchant Taylors' Company, 5 October 1748 for seven years on payment of £5. Free 3 December 1755 as working goldsmith, journeyman with Thomas Justis. (Merchant Taylors' records, S.T.)

BIOGRAPHICAL DICTIONARY: ADDENDA

LE CHEAUBE, Pierre (page 578) Mark no. 1906 is not his. See page 140n.

LEE, John I (page 579) He is recorded as a goldworker in Amsterdam in 1731 and admitted to the guild there the following year. (Information Mr K. Citroen.)

LEEKE, Ralph (page 579) His mark may have been entered as early as July 1697 or until July 1699 as previously stated.

LEES, Edward (page 579) Son of John Lees of Christ Church, Surrey soap boiler, apprenticed to Thomas Wintle (Samuel Wintle, q.v.) of the Vintners' Company, silversmith, Queen's Row, Walworth, 6 December 1786 and turned over to George Wintle (q.v.) 1 December 1790. Free of the Vintners 17 October 1795, then at 5 Shorts Buildings, Clerkenwell. Described as spoonmaker in apprenticeship to him of James Payne, 1808.

LEGG, Henry (page 580) Son of John Legg of the Merchant Taylors' Company, apprenticed to Joseph Mumford (q.v.) of the Loriners' Company, 1 June 1720 for seven years on payment of £10. Free of that company, as previously suggested, 7 June 1727 as 'at ye Sign of ye Helmet in Holborn near Bernards Inn in Butler (? illegible)' (Loriners' Company records, R.B.) His insurance policy of 9 October 1729 gives the address as 'at the Crown in Brook Street in Holborn', elucidating the above. (Sun Insurance policy information Mr S. B. Turner, R.B.)

LE SAGE, Augustin (page 580) Apprenticed as Augustus Le Sage to Sampson Bishop, Suffolk Street, Middlesex, jeweller, 19 June 1749 for seven years on payment of £35. (I.R. 1/18 f.195, R.B.) Since, as previously recorded, he appears as goldsmith and clockmaker in Suffolk Street as early as 1752, it would seem his apprenticeship was a very nominal status, although, curiously, he did not take his freedom of the Goldsmiths by patrimony until 1782.

LE SAGE, John Hugh (page 580) For his first Sterling mark, omitted by some mischance from the register, see note on page 261 describing added mark no. 3678A. He appears in the Fitzwalter Accounts: '20 June 1747. Paid Mr John Le Sage for a silver standish for my lady Fitzwalter £5 12s. 6d.' (Essex County Records).

LESTOURGEON, Aaron (page 581) His insurance policy of 14 February 1777 gives his address as 'at Mr Douxsaints (toyseller) 49 High Holborn' and his trade as silversmith. (Sun Insurance policy information Ann Paton, R.B.) 'Douxsaints' is obviously in error for Toussaint, partner of James Moriset (q.v. below).

LESTOURGEON, William (page 581) He and Aaron, his son, appear as suppliers of 'tea tubs', cork stoppers, mustard pots, ladles, funnels and nutmeg graters in Parker and Wakelin's Workmen's Ledger No. 2 on 20 March 1766, the account brought forward from the missing ledger begun in 1760. From May 1769 the account is titled William Lestourgeon & Son or Messrs Lestourgeon and from 1771 as Aaron Lestourgeon alone. On this evidence and the inclusion of the fish above, the initials mark no. 3893 can reasonably be attributed to William. (H.C.)

LEWIS, Ambrose (page 581) Son of Ambrose Lewis of Kingswood, Wilts., maltster, apprenticed to William Jelfe (q.v.) of the Clockmakers' Company, 23 September 1717 for seven years on payment of £12. Free 5 April 1725. (I.R. 1/5 f.189 and C.F.1, R.B. and S.T.)

LIGER, John (page 583) Son of Isaac Liger, deceased, goldsmith, of the Broderers' Company. Free of the Broderers by patrimony 2 July 1735 as goldsmith of Green Street, Leicester Fields. (S.T.) This suggests that he had moved from Heming's Row sometime after 1732 without re-entering his mark or at least noting the change of address in the register.

LITTLEBOY, George (page 583) His father Richard was deceased when the son was apprenticed to Thomas Cooke of the Goldsmiths' Company, 4 November 1712 for seven years on payment of £15 and then turned over 26 November 1718 to Thomas Redhead of the Merchant Taylors' Company (Goldsmiths' Apprentice Book 5 f.38, R.B.). In spite of this he was, as previously noted, later made free of the Cutlers, his father's company, presumably to allow him to work in the city.

LOCKWOOD, Richard (page 584) Son of Thomas Lockwood of Cow Cross, deceased, apprenticed to James Beattie (q.v.) of the Drapers' Company, goldworker, Saffron Hill, St. Andrew's, Holborn, 13 April 1775 for seven years. Free of that company 15 April 1783 as silversmith, Cow Cross (probably his father's house). (Drapers' Company records, S.T.)

LOFTHOUSE, Seth (page 584) The entry date of his mark is more probably April

757

1697 together with the other first entries, all undated.

LUCAS, Robert (page 586) Son of John Lucas of Guilsborough, Northamptonshire, gentleman, apprenticed to John Wisdome (q.v.), silversmith, Watling Street, of the Haberdashers' Company, 2 December 1715 for seven years on payment of £26. Free 24 March 1727 (eleven days after entering his first mark). (Haberdashers' registers and C.F.1, R.B. and S.T.)

LUKIN, William I (page 586) A Sun Insurance policy of 3 February 1716 gives his address as 'at the golden Cup in the Strand in the parish of St. Mary Le Savoy Goldsmith' and an endorsement of 14 April 1721 'Remov'd to Buckingham Street end in the Strand in the parish of St Martin in the ffield'. (Information Mr S. B. Turner.)

LUKIN, William II (page 587) Son of William Lukin of Brocksted, Essex, farmer, apprenticed to John Kentish (q.v.) of the Glovers' Company, 4 September 1755 on payment of 1 penny. Free of that company 15 February 1769. The Glovers' Livery List, 1779 shows him at 9 Cornhill (gone away). (Glovers' Company records, S.T.)

LUTWYCHE, William (page 587) The previous suggestion of his possible parentage is now corrected by the entry of his freedom by patrimony of the Broderers' Company as son of John Lutwych, late Citizen and Broderer of London, deceased, on 4 April 1764, when described as 'a Goldsmith in Lombard Street'. (Broderers' registers, R.B.) The mark no. 3908, previously attributed to him in partnership with John Henry Vere, must now almost certainly be considered that of William Vincent and John Lawford (q.v. above and below). It seems very probable that Lutwyche and Vere were retailers, as their addresses suggest. (H.C.)

MACKDONALD, Donald (page 587) Son of John McDonald of Balcony, deceased, apprenticed to Colin McKenzie, Goldsmith and Burgess of Edinburgh, 27 March 1717 for seven years on payment of 700 Merks or £38.17.9½. (I.R. 1/45 f.32, R.B.)

MACKENZIE, Charles (page 588) Son of Collin McKenzie of Rosend, apprenticed to James Mitchelson, Goldsmith and Burgess of Edinburgh, 20 November 1717 for seven years on payment of 600 Merks or £33.6.8. (I.R. 1/45 f.69, R.B.) His arrival in London can be predated to 13 November 1730 by a Sun Insurance policy: 'Charles Mackenzie in Tower Street near Seven Dials Snuff Box maker on his Household Goods and Stock in Trade including his Manufactured and Wrought Plate ... not exceeding £400'. (Information Mr S. B. Turner.)

MAKEPEACE, Robert I (page 589) He was admitted to the Newcastle Guild of Goldsmiths 1 July 1755 and is recorded as having 'voted from London' in 1774 and 1777. He presumably reached London shortly before obtaining his freedom at Goldsmiths' Hall. (Information Mrs G. E. P. How.) A Sun Insurance policy of 27 August 1761 names him as Robert Makepeace in Maiden Lane, Wood Street, goldsmith, an earlier different address than previously recorded. (Information Mr S. B. Turner.) For the descent of Makepeace and Carter from the Langleys through Thomas Gilpin to the present-day firm of A. Woodhouse and Son, see John Culme, *Directory of Gold and Silversmiths*, pp. 179–80.

MAKEPEACE, Thomas I (page 589) He may possibly be identified with one of the same name entered in the Newcastle Guild 3 May 1745 as 'London Goldsmith', in which case perhaps the father of Robert above. (Information as above.)

MALYN, Isaac (page 589) A Sun Insurance policy of 7 October 1717 shows him to have moved across the Thames. 'Isaac Malyn near the Queens head in the Park in the Parish of St. Saviour's, Southwark, goldsmith'. (Information Mr S. B. Turner.)

MARDER, John (page 590) The Exeter Assay Book records the name of one Marder (without Christian name) as submitting two dozen spoons for assay 29 April 1758. Since his London mark was entered by power of attorney there seems some likelihood that he was from Exeter. (Information Mr T. Kent.)

MARGAS, Jacob (page 590) The publication of *Les Orfèvres de Normandie* by C. G. Cassan 1980 has established further facts about this family of goldsmiths. The founder of the line, Samuel, born about 1627, married Martha Harache and died in 1683 aged fifty-six. His son Samuel, born about 1656, married Madeleine Pantin in Rouen in 1681 and Jacob was born 19 March 1684 and a daughter Anne in 1685. By March 1688 the family had reached London, Samuel being then thirty-two and apparently using his original Rouen maker's mark very similar to that of his father (see addendum to mark

3796, page 269). It seems probable that the second son Samuel (page 591) was born in London about 1690. The 'Jaques Margas orfeure' who married Anne Margas in 1691 is clearly not of this line and must at nearest have been a younger brother of the second Samuel as previously suggested.

MARSH, Peter (page 592) Son of Timothy Marsh of London, mariner, apprenticed to John Carman I (q.v.) of the Cutlers' Company, 7 January 1724 for seven years on payment of £10. 10s. Free 7 October 1731. (Cutlers' Company registers and I.R. 1/9 f.198, R.B. and S.T.)

METHAM, Robert (page 595) Robert Snr was son of Robert Metham of St. Mary the Virgin, Aldermanbury, publican, apprenticed to William Plummer of the Clothworkers' Company, goldsmith, Gutter Lane, 5 October 1757 on payment of £21. Free 6 December 1766 as silversmith, Butcher Hall Lane, Newgate Street, confirming the presumption that he had entered a mark in the missing register. (Information Mr D. E. Wickham, Archivist, Clothworkers' Company and S.T.) He appears as an occasional supplier of bread baskets, soy and cruet frames in Parker and Wakelin's Workmen's Ledger No. 2 from December 1769. (H.C.)

METTAYER, Lewis (page 596) His brother-in-law Estienne Hobbema was married to Anne Harache, sister of Peter Harache II (q.v.). As previously stated, when widowed she married Mettayer. In 1708 he stood as godfather to Marie Anne Bernard. In Amsterdam the goldsmith Antoine Bernard was brother-in-law of his colleague Philippe Mettayer. Although not yet definitely established, the family connections between the Mettayers of London and Amsterdam seem very probable. (Information Mr K. Citroen.)

MEURE, Peter (page 596) Son of Antony Meare (sic), of St. Mary Savoy, bookseller, deceased, apprenticed to Peter Archambo I of the Butchers' Company (his uncle), 4 January 1722. Free 5 July 1739. (Butchers' Company records, R.B.)

MILLER, Henry (page 597) Henry Miller 'of the Parish of St. Bride's Goldsmith', whose wife eloped July 1712 (*London Gazette*, No. 5026) would appear to be another person.

MINCE, James (page 598) The working relationship between Mince and Hodgkins from 1780–90 and Thomas Daniell (q.v.) is emphasized by a pair of tea-caddies of 1788 with the formers' joint mark overstruck by that of Daniell in his main capacity at the time of retailer. See also under Jabez Daniell in Addenda above. (John Culme, 'Periodical Reflections', *The Antique Collector*, February 1987.)

MOORE, William (page 600) Son of Isaac Moore of Crispin Street, Spitalfields, carpenter, deceased, apprenticed to Robert Turner (q.v.) of the Innholders' Company, silversmith, 6 October 1817. He does not appear to have taken up freedom of his master's company. His mark entry address suggests he worked in his late father's residence. (Innholders' Company records, S.T.)

MORDECAI, Benjamin (page 600) Described as Benj. Mordecai of Clerkenwell, silversmith, etc., when he took Levy Phillips (q.v.) apprentice 14 August 1767, strengthening the attribution of mark no. 3490 to him. (I.R. 1/26 f.139, R.B.)

MORISSET, James (page 600) Toussaint and Morisset appear as suppliers of enamelled buttons, watchcases, chains and jewellery in Parker and Wakelin's Workmen's Ledger No. 2 from August 1767. (H.C.)

MORSON, Richard (page 601) In spite of his former prosecution for selling below-standard gold watchchains (perhaps a case of the captain of the ship being held responsible for his subordinate's misdemeanours), Morson is recorded as Vice-President, Treasurer and Secretary of The Guardians or Society for the Protection of Trade against Swindlers and Sharpers, founded in 1776 (see also Thomas Heming in Addendum above). (John Culme, 'Periodical Reflections', *The Antique Collector*, February 1987.)

MOULDON, Thomas (page 602) He is also presumably identifiable with Thomas Moulden, late of Cheapside, goldsmith, declared bankrupt 26 March 1734 on the petition of John Harkness, London merchant, and again on 11 July 1739 as of Fleet Street, goldsmith, on the petition of Mary Mordaunt, Fleet Street, widow, executrix of Dennis Langton, deceased (q.v.). (B 4/8, 36 and B 4/7, 217, J.C.)

MOULSON, William (page 602) He was assistant, and his partner Wrangham foreman, to Francis Lambert and William Rawlings, retailers of Coventry Street, who acquired the business of Thomas Hamlet (Chaffers, *Gilda Aurifabrorum*).

MUMFORD, Edward (page 603) Son of John Mumford of Walsall, Staffs., carpenter, apprenticed to his elder brother Joseph (q.v. below) of the Loriners' Company, 23 March 1714 for seven years. Free by September 1721 when he took up freedom of the City of London. (A gap in Loriners' records at this date, S.T.) The variation of both father's trade in his apprenticeship entry and that of his brother below as well as the alias of Mountford in the latter shows a carefree attitude characteristic of such records.

MUMFORD, Joseph (page 603) An alias for Mountford. Son of John Mountford of Walsall, Staffs., hardwareman, apprenticed to John Walsh of Newcastle-upon-Tyne, Citizen and Loriner of London, 1 February 1699 for seven years. Free about July 1711, when he took up freedom of the City of London. (A gap in Loriners' records at this date, S.T.)

NASH, Gawen (page 604) Declared bankrupt 8 March 1740 as silversmith, St. John Zachary, on the petition of John Clarkson, Citizen and Ironmonger of London, and Jane Haynes of St. John Zachary, widow, the executors of Robert Haynes, late Citizen and Haberdasher, deceased. (B 4/9, 280, J.C.)

NASH, Robert (page 605) Son of William Nash of Swindon, Wilts., butcher, apprenticed to Andrew Hunter, silversmith, of the Drapers' Company, 21 November 1760 for seven years on payment of £20 and turned over 1 July 1765 to George Nash, Citizen and Haberdasher, Andrew Hunter being dead. He did not, however, take up freedom of either company. (Drapers' Company records, S.T.)

NASH, Thomas I (page 605) He appears as supplier of cruet frames, pierced bottle stands, salts and 'salt trowels' in Parker and Wakelin's Workmen's Ledger No. 2, October 1768. (H.C.)

NATTER, George (page 605) His apprenticeship date was 5 March 1766. (R.B.)

NEALE, Jacob (605) Son of Jacob Neale of Stepney, Middlesex, silversmith, apprenticed to Nathaniel Firmin of the Merchant Taylors' Company, 3 October 1716 for seven years. Free of that company 2 December 1724. (Merchant Taylors' records and C.F.1, R.B.)

NELME, Anthony (page 605) His actual date of death was 23 January 1723 at Goldsmiths' Hall. The parish of Charles Nelme, apprenticed in 1657, has now been identified as Mitcheldeane. The previous suggestion that he may have employed immigrant journeymen, in spite of having supported the petition of 1697 against aliens and foreigners, is confirmed by an entry in the Court of Aldermen Papers, September 1706 (City Records Office) that Nelme 'lately in extraordinary hast to work up divers parcells of Silver Plate and being at a Loss for a Journeyman in one particular part of yor Peticoners said Trade Did for that purpose entertaine one John Christian Volage a Germane'. The latter (? a chaser), apparently not free of the City, was in consequence discharged from Nelme's service. (R.B.)

NELME, Francis (page 606) For the statement that Thomas Whipham (q.v.) took over his business in 1739 see John Culme, *Directory of Gold and Silversmiths*, quoting an anonymous article in the *Watchmaker, Jeweller and Silversmith*, 1899. He was, however, declared bankrupt 6 January 1741 as silversmith of Amen Corner on the petition of William Hart, goldsmith, Fleet Street. (B 4/10, 38, J.C.) It is possible that debts responsible for the petition were outstanding from his active business period.

NEVILLE, John (page 606) His mention in the Fitzwalter Accounts is dated 30 January 1738, suggesting that he was working alone before partnership with Ann Craig. As well as his bankruptcy, previously recorded, he was also made bankrupt 10 June 1746 as jeweller and goldsmith, Haymarket, on the petition of David Armorer, wine cooper. (B 4/11, 156, J.C.) His creditors then included a long list of the leading goldsmiths of the time, among them Abercromby, Cripps, Drinkwater, Heming, Jacob, Methuen, Wood, etc. He must have been buying large amounts of plate for retailing and failing to settle. This would account for the rarity of pieces bearing his mark. In 1753 George Methuen was the petitioning creditor. (B 1/22.52, 1/23.262 and 4/12.302, R.B. and J.C.)

NORMAN, Philip (page 608) He appears as supplier of stewing dishes, dish rings, sauce-boats, spoons, tureens, cream pails, gravy pots and cheese plates in Parker and Wakelin's Workmen's Ledger No. 2 from December 1768. In view of this range of production it is surprising that his mark is not met with more frequently in surviving pieces. (H.C.)

BIOGRAPHICAL DICTIONARY: ADDENDA

NORWOOD, Joseph (page 609) Son of William Norwood of the Stationers' Company, apprenticed to Thomas Ripsheire (or Ripshear, q.v.) of the Grocers' Company, 9 July 1718 for seven years on payment of £10. (I.R. 1/6 f.105, R.B.) Since he describes himself as 'Stacinor' in his mark entry, he may have been free of that company by patrimony.

OURRY, Lewis (page 610) The doubts of survival of his work previously expressed are removed by the discovery of a dessert spoon of 1740 bearing his clearly identifiable mark. (Information Mr A. E. Gover.) Nevertheless, his work is extremely rare.

PAGES, Francis (page 612) His birthplace was correctly Farmborough, eight miles from Bath. The church contains memorial tablets to his father, the Revd Solomon Pages, Rector, died 1725, and his mother Lucy, died 1745, as also of his brother Alexander who succeeded his father as Rector and died 1785. (Information Mr Timothy Kent.)

PALMER, Richard (page 612) Son of Richard Palmer of St. Faith's, London, cornfactor, apprenticed to Daniel Cole (q.v.) of the Drapers' Company, 12 June 1746 for seven years on payment of £20. Free 19 February 1755 as watchcase-maker, Georges Court, near Red Lion Street, Clerkenwell. Livery of Drapers' Company 1771, Court 1790, Master 1803. His son Richard was apprenticed to him in 1764. (Drapers' Company records, S.T.)

PANTIN, Lewis I (page 612) His insurance policy of 5 July 1735 gives his address as 'at the Golden Ewer in Castle St near Leicester Fields', a specific mention of a different sign to that given for the family from 1699. Is there some indication here of a connection with James Shruder (q.v.) whose sign was the golden ewer at various addresses? (Sun Insurance policy information Mr S. B. Turner, R.B.) See also Abraham Buteux above whose address in 1721 was the Golden Ewer, Green Street, Leicester Fields and who was son-in-law of Simon Pantin I.

PANTIN, Lewis II (page 612) Apprenticed to John Passavant of St. Clement's, smallworker in gold, etc., 25 October 1753 for seven years on payment of £25. (I.R. 1/19 f.155, R.B.) A Philip Passavant, probably the son of the above master, entered a mark as goldworker 1785 (page 375), but the former has no mark entry. In addition to his bankruptcy of 1787 previously stated, Pantin had been in trouble in 1781, when an insurance policy of 30 November was effected by Benjamin Garden, Richard Andrews and Edward Holmes in trust for the creditors of Lewis Pantin on the latter's utensils and stock in 45 Fleet Street. Almost immediately he seems to have moved, as another policy of 1 January 1782 is for 36 Southampton Street. (Sun Insurance policies information Mr S. B. Turner, R.B.) Pantin's end was a sad one. Elected Beadle of the Goldsmiths' Company 2 November 1787, presumably following his bankruptcy of that year, with salary and 'the Beadle's usual dwelling and Perquisites', he was dismissed from this office 4 December 1789 'heavily in debt' and then given £60 per annum (Goldsmiths' Company Minutes). His son Lewis III seems to have been unsupportive.

PANTIN, Simon I (page 613) His parentage has now been established by the discovery of an original indenture of apprenticeship for him in the City Freedom records, where he is described as 'Simon Pontaine, the sonne of Simon Pontaine of the pish of St. Giles in the ffields in the County of middx Goldsmith apprenticed to Peter Arrach of the pish of St. Martin in the ffields Goldsmith' 30 September 1686 for seven years, one witness being James Guerrier, probably a relative of John Peter Guerrier (q.v.), later also apprenticed to Harache. Free as previously stated 4 June 1701. It is now clear that he was born earlier than before suggested, probably about 1672, and also that Simon Pantin of the Denization List 1687 may in fact be his father. (R.B.) 'Simon Pantin North side St. Martin's Court' appears in the St. Martin's Poor Rate Book for 1698, rated at 16s. 8d. He was perhaps already working in his own shop as journeyman to Pierre Harache. His move to Castle Street can be predated to 3 May 1710, the date of a Sun Insurance policy, 'Mr Simon Panting at the Golden Ball in Castle Street ... Silversmith'. Another of October 1725 repeats this address, again like Lewis Pantin above, a specific difference from the well-authenticated Peacock sign. An explanation seems difficult to determine. (Information Mr S. B. Turner.)

PARGETER, Richard (page 614) It has recently been suggested that mark no. 3897 (there attributed to W. and R. Peaston) is in fact, from its form and device similar to that of W. and J. Preist (no. 3271), more probably the mark of William Preist and Richard Pargeter describing themselves as goldsmiths of Wood Street in a charge against Abraham Bassett for stealing silver and wire cuttings, September 1763. This is confirmed by the Rate Books for Wood Street where Preist and Pargeter are entered as sharing two houses there in 1762–4. (John Culme, 'Periodical Reflections', *The Antique Collector*, February 1987.) Preist had been in Wood Street from 1751 and did not enter his combined mark with his brother James until 1764. In support of this theory it should be observed that the mark registered by William and Robert Peaston in 1756 (no. 3275) is in a quatrefoil punch and the only one entered in their joint names.

PARKER, John (page 614) His partnership with Edward Wakelin existed from October 1760 until June 1776. There is no evidence to suggest that the firm had any manufacturing or repair facilities. It subcontracted all commissions to outworkers or suppliers who also supplied items for stock. The firm's mark has been found on articles made by John Ansill and Stephen Gilbert (the latter q.v.) who were both apprentices of Wakelin and on work supplied by Sebastian and James Crespell (q.v.). (H.C.) For a full account of the interesting family connections between Wickes, Wakelin and Parker see Elaine Barr, *George Wickes, Royal Goldsmith*, 1980.

PAYNE, James (page 616) Son of Holman Payne of Golden Lane, brewer's servant, apprenticed to Edward Lees (q.v.) of the Vintners' Company, spoonmaker, St. James's Walk, Clerkenwell, 3 February 1808. He does not appear to have taken up freedom of his master's company. (Vintners' Company records.)

PAYNE, Thomas (page 616) Delete freedom unrecorded. He was free by patrimony 2 February 1774 as goldsmith in Cheapside.

PEACOCK, James (page 617) Free of the Musicians' Company 6 February 1770 as 'goldsmith in the Minories', without mention of parentage. Since he had entered his mark the previous December this was presumably by redemption, taking advantage of the low cost of freedom in this company. (R.B.)

PEAKE, Vaughan (page 617) Not as previously suggested the son of Robert Peake but of William Peake of the Haberdashers' Company, free by patrimony 23 February 1700. Described as a silversmith on taking William Halsey as apprentice in 1709. (Haberdashers' Company records and C.F.1, R.B.)

PEARCE, Richard (617) Son of John Pearce late of St. Mary, Bermondsey, Surrey, wool stapler, deceased, apprenticed to Charles Fox I (q.v.) of the Clothworkers' Company, 1 May 1805 for seven years. Free of that company 6 May 1812 as silversmith, No. 3 Bermondsey Street. (Information Mr D. F. Wickham, Archivist, Clothworkers' Company, and S.T.)

PENSTONE, William I (page 619) Listed as spoonmaker by T. A. Kent, *London Silver Spoonmakers*. He appears as 'Mr Penniston, a Freeman in the Old Bailey' in a case brought against one Nicholas Davois, a French refugee silversmith, for working in the city, not being free who had several times brought silver to him 'to be wrought into Spoons'. In 1703 Davois took him seven ounces of silver to be made into two dozen spoons (apparently teaspoons) in two days, and when these were unfinished in the time Penstone suggested Davois should help him finish them and while so doing 'in comes the officer and Arrests him upon this' (City Records Office, R.B.)

PENSTONE, William III (page 619) He appears to have been working by 1772. See footnote to his mark no. 3260, page 231.

PEPPIN, Robert (page 619) Son of Samuel Bishop Peppin of the Society of Apothecaries. Free by patrimony of that society 2 February 1818, probably to enable him to take an apprentice, which he did the following May. (R.B.)

PEPPIN, Sydenham William (page 619) Now confirmed as brother of Robert Peppin above. Free of the Society of Apothecaries by patrimony 4 February 1817. (R.B.)

PERCHARD, James (page 619) He was perhaps related to Peter and Peter Perchard, goldsmiths, 15 Abchurch Lane, Lombard Street, in the *London Directory*, 1768 and *New Complete Guide*, 1772. (R.B.)

PERIER, Charles (page 619) Son of John Perrier of St. Ann's (? Soho), distiller, apprenticed to Nicholas Clausen (q.v.) of the Haberdashers' Company, silversmith, St. Martin-in-the-Fields, 5 September 1712 for seven years on payment of £30. He did not bother to take up his freedom of that

BIOGRAPHICAL DICTIONARY: ADDENDA

company until 1 December 1732 as goldsmith, King's Street, Common (sic) Garden, his former master being then deceased. (I.R. 1/1 f.161 and Haberdashers' register, R.B. and S.T.)

PERO, John (page 620) He was probably related to the Amsterdam goldsmith Daniel Perault *c.* 1710 and Guillaume Pereau, goldsmith and citizen of the same city, 1722. (Information Mr K. Citroen.) His insurance policy of 9 February 1722 gives his address as 'New Round Court in the Strand'. (Sun Insurance policy information Mr S. B. Turner, R.B.)

PETERS, Richard (page 621) His apprenticeship premium to Jonathan Hanson was £20. He was free of the Haberdashers' Company 15 May 1719. (Haberdashers' register, R.B. and S.T.)

PHILLIPS, David (page 622) Son of Phillip Phillips (q.v.) of 15 Bury Street, St. Mary, Axe, watchmaker of the Clockmaker's Company, apprenticed to his father 2 July 1832, but does not appear to have taken his freedom of that company, in spite of the fact that he entered his first mark in 1834. (S.T.)

PHILLIPS, Levy (page 622) Apprenticed to Benjamin Mordecai (q.v.) of Clerkenwell in Middlesex, silversmith, etc., 14 August 1767 for seven years on payment of £50. (I.R. 1/26 f.139, R.B.)

PHILLIPS, Phillip (page 622) Son of Joseph Phillips, 'a native of Germany', born in England. Free of the Clockmakers' Company by redemption 15 February 1832, although he had entered his mark as plateworker 1826. His son Joel was apprenticed to him on the same date as his son David (above), 2 July 1832, when the indenture already gives the father's address as Bury Street, watchmaker. Joel's son, Solomon Joel, founded the well-known firm of S. J. Phillips of Bond Street. The latter's only son Edmund dying without issue in 1934, the firm descended to his nephews Richard and Martin Norton, sons of his sister. (Information Mr R. M. Norton.)

PHIPPS, Thomas (page 623) His third mark with Robinson and James Phipps, although undated, can be fixed as about 1811 from its place in the register.

PICKETT, William (page 623) It is now established that he was the previously first-mentioned apprentice of William Hunter, made free by redemption 6 April 1757 after applying to the Corporation for remission of his last seven months of service, 'an opportunity offering to his advantage', and to be admitted to the freedom of the City by redemption in the Goldsmiths' Company. The second William Pickett apprenticed to Hunter may perhaps have been a cousin. For a full discussion of Pickett's career see John Culme, *Nineteenth Century Silver*, 1977. Pickett appears alone as goldsmith and toyman, 32 Ludgate Street, in Baldwin's *New Guide*, 1770 and *New Complete Guide*, 1777 but also as Thead and Pickett with same description and address, *London Directory*, 1768 and Baldwin, 1770, an example of the casualness of these references. (R.B.)

PINCKNEY, Israel (page 625) The Poor Rate Book of St. James's Piccadilly shows him already in St. James's Street in 1695.

PITTS, Thomas I (page 626) He is described as silversmith, jeweller and cutler in his insurance policy of 14 November 1777 with address 'near Half Moon Street in Piccadilly', a somewhat vague location in view of the fact that 'household goods in dwelling house' are covered as well as 'Plate in trade, paste and garnet work' with jewels excepted for £500. Air Street, his trade address, scarcely seems 'near Half Moon Street', the latter presumably being the private address. (Sun Insurance policy information Mr I. M. Garner, R.B.)

PLANK, Lewis (page 627) Son of Isaac Planck of St. Martin-in-the-Fields, gentleman, apprenticed to George Allmand, jeweller, 'fflettditch' of the Haberdashers' Company, 1 December for seven years on payment of £5. Freedom unrecorded. (Haberdashers' register.) The second Anthony Planck, previously noted, also appears as jeweller, Sergeant's Inn, Fleet Street in the *London Directory*, 1763, Baldwin's *New Complete Guide*, 1770 and at 63 Great Queen Street, Lincoln's Inn Fields, in the *New Complete Guide*, 1777. (R.B.)

PLATEL, Philip (page 627) Son of Peter Platell (q.v.), Citizen and Goldsmith, deceased, apprenticed to Nicholas Clausen of the Haberdashers' Company, 6 November 1719 for seven years on payment of £30. Freedom unrecorded. (I.R. 1/7 f.57 and Haberdashers' register, R.B.)

PLUMMER, William (page 628) Son of George Plummer of Evington, Leics., grazier, apprenticed as previously stated to Edward Aldridge, goldsmith, Foster Lane, of the Clothworkers' Company, 4 February 1746/7 for seven years on payment of £21 and when made free on date given was described as goldsmith in Green Street, Leicester Fields, which points to a quick move to Foster Lane where his mark was entered on 8 April following. Was Green Street another workshop of Aldridge's? (Information Mr D. E. Wickham, Archivist, Clothworkers' Company, through R.B.)

PLUMPTON, Henry (page 628) Son of John Plumpton, late of St. John's, Wapping, Middlesex, mariner, deceased, apprenticed to John Blunt I (q.v. above) of the Merchant Taylors' Company, 4 April 1733 for seven years on payment of £20. Free of that company 2 April 1740 as journeyman goldsmith with John Blunt. It is interesting to see, as previously stated, that by 1773 he had returned to his father's place of Wapping. (Merchant Taylors' Company records, R.B.)

POCOCK, Edward (page 628) The previous suggestion of his parentage is to be ignored. He was son of Edward Pocock of Ore, Berks., gentleman, apprenticed to John Wisdome (q.v.), goldsmith, Watling Street, of the Haberdashers' Company, 6 October 1710 for seven years on payment of £20. Free 5 February 1720 as silversmith, Watling Street, presumably then still with his master. He was dead by 6 July 1750 when his former apprentice John Weston was made free. (Haberdashers' Company registers, R.B.)

PONTIFEX, Daniel (page 629) He was second son of William Pontifex of Iver, Bucks., baptized at Beaconsfield 23 March 1767. Apprenticed to Robert Jones, Coppersmith (probably Robert Jones I (q.v.)) and applied for freedom of the Armourers' and Brasiers' Company 20 November 1792, but refused as not having served his time with the master to whom he was bound. He appears from the records of the above company to have emigrated to America before 1815, when Henry Daniel son of Daniel Pontifex of New York silversmith was apprenticed to John Pontifex of the same company, to be followed by Charles son of Daniel Pontifex of Boston, U.S.A. in 1824 and Robert son of Daniel Pontifex again of New York 1825. His descendant Mr Claude Pontifex, however, states that Daniel never went to America but moved to Trelleck, Monmouth in 1815, adopting at the same time the name of Price. This apparent contradiction coupled with the earlier dispute over his freedom suggests that the silversmith was given to light-hearted disregard for establishment procedures, to say the least. (Information Mr Claude Pontifex through Mr C. Blair.)

PORTAL, Abraham (page 629) The date of his freedom should read 7 March 1750. His partnership with Harry Gearing began earlier than previously indicated. Together they signed as retailers 'Portal and Gearing Fecit Ludgate Hill' on the cup made by John Romer in 1772 for presentation by the City to the former Lord Mayor, Brass Crosby. (Judith Banister, 'In the Cause of Liberty', *Country Life*, 12 November 1981.)

PORTAL, William (page 630) He appears as supplier of knife handles, silver blades and forks in Parker and Wakelin's Workmen's Ledger No. 2, October 1766, the account brought forward from the earlier missing ledger. (H.C.)

PREEDY, Joseph (page 631) His insurance policy of 28 February 1805 shows him still at 8 Great Newport Street with utensils and stock including patterns covered for £500 and the same in workshop for £300. His business was still obviously considerable. (Sun Insurance policy information Mr S. B. Turner, R.B.)

PREIST, William (page 632) For new attribution of mark no. 3897 see Richard Pargeter above.

PRESTON, Benjamin (page 632) Like Edward Farrell (q.v. above) he worked to the order of Kensington Lewis, retailer of St. James's Street from 1834 to 1836. (John Culme, *Nineteenth Century Silver*, 1977.)

PRYOR, William (page 634) As William Pryer, son of William Pryer of St. Bartholomew the Great, barber, apprenticed to William Young (q.v.) of the Longbowstringmakers' Company, 3 November 1743 for seven years on payment of one penny (!) Free of that company 8 November 1750. (S.T.)

PYNE, Benjamin (page 635) The year of his election to Beadle was 1728.

RAWLE, William (page 637) Although no example of his mark has yet been recorded on silver-hilted swords, his name has been found on a few pistols, probably as retailer, of which one example has silvermounts with the maker's mark T I, probably that of Thomas Jackson II (q.v.). Rawle's obituary (*Gentleman's Magazine*, November 1789) describes him as 'accoutrement maker in the Strand well known to the gentlemen of the army for his improvements in that branch and equally well known to the lovers of virtu for his valuable collection of medals, bronzes, arms and other curiosities'. His collections were dispersed in a series of auction sales by Mr Hutchins, King Street, Covent Garden. These included two days of prints, drawings and books; two of antiquities and curiosities; three of coins and medals; and another of pictures, miniatures, etc. Rawle was also a medallist, although only one example attributed to him of Thomas Snelling in the British Museum is known. (Howard L. Blackmore, 'William Rawle', *Apollo*, February 1988.)

REASON, John (page 638) Son of John Reason, late of Challden, Dorset, tallowchandler, deceased, apprenticed to John Whitton of the Cutlers' Company, 19 November 1678 for seven years. Free 4 April 1698, thirteen years later than the expiry of his apprenticeship, previous to entering his only mark. Presumably working as journeyman until then. (S.T.)

REDRICK, Richard (page 639) Son of Thomas Redrick of Arcall, Salop, farmer, apprenticed to Richard Palmer (q.v.) of the Drapers' Company, 19 February 1755 for seven years on payment of £15. Free of the Drapers 20 October 1762 as watchcasemaker, St. John Street, Clerkenwell. (Drapers' Company records, S.T.)

REILY, Charles (page 639) He was born 6 July 1803.

REYNOLDS, John (page 640) Son of Edward Reynolds of St. Mary Magdalen, Bermondsey, Surrey, gentleman, apprenticed to Richard Glanville (q.v.) of the Grocers' Company, 21 September 1753 for seven years on payment of £10. Free 12 July 1763. (S.T.)

REYNOLDS(ON), William (page 640) Mark no. 3278 must be that of the firstmentioned William Reynolds, son of George Reynolds, apprenticed to Frederick Kandler 25 March 1749 (corrected year) for seven years on payment of £30. (I.R. 1/18 f.173, R.B.) He would therefore have been free early in 1756 before the entry of his mark in 1757. Mark no. 3899, unregistered but found on pieces of 1759, could then well be that of the second of the name free, as previously stated in that year.

RIDOUT, George (page 642) Son of Isaac Ridout of St. Martin-in-the-Fields, mariner, apprenticed to John Edwards II (q.v.) of the Grocers' Company, goldsmith, Swithens Lane, 7 May 1736 for seven years on payment of £20. Free 2 June 1743. (Grocers' Company records, S.T. and R.B.)

RIPSHER, William Gladwin (page 642) Son of William Ripsher of Silver Street, Stepney, labourer, apprenticed to Robert Scantlebury of the Drapers' Company, silversmith, Chapel Row, Spa Fields, on payment of £4, 26 April 1816. Free of that company 6 August 1833 as silversmith, 5 Broughton Place, Hackney Road. Died 1856. (Drapers' Company records, S.T.)

ROBERT, John (page 642) His apprenticeship and freedom are in fact recorded. Son of Isaiah Robert, late of Long Alley, Moorfields, Middlesex, engraver, deceased, apprenticed to John Whittingham (q.v.) of Staining Lane, engraver, Citizen and Goldsmith of London, to learn the art of engraver, on payment of £5 of the charity of Christ's Hospital, London. Free 4 March 1789 as engraver, a rare example of a mention of the craft in the Company's records.

ROBERTS, John (page 642) Son of Edward Roberts of Broqbourne (Broxbourne) in Herts., apprenticed to Thomas Roberts (q.v.), perhaps an elder brother, of the Cutlers' Company, 19 June 1706 for seven years. Free 29 October 1714. (S.T.)

ROBINS, John (page 643) His daughter Frances Anne, who lived with her father at Norwood Green, Heston, near Hounslow, married Colonel John Utterton (1778–1843) and succeeded to her father's house and furniture after his death. Their son John Sutton Utterton, born 1814, married Eleanor fifth daughter of Paul Storr in 1839 and became Bishop of Guildford in 1874, dying in 1879. His sister Susan married Paul Storr's eldest son Paul in 1836. (N. M. Penzer, *Paul Storr*.)

ROBINSON, Edward II (page 643) His third mark in partnership with Thomas and James Phipps can be dated from about 1811 from its place in the register.

ROBY, Samuel (page 644) Son of William Roby of St. Ebbs in the City of Oxford, gentleman, apprenticed to William Soame (q.v.) of the Mercers' Company, 26 January 1733 for seven years on payment of £47. 5*s*. Free of the Mercers 28 March 1740. (Mercers' Company records, R.B. and S.T.)

ROKER, John (page 645) His freedom is recorded as by patrimony 19 December 1743.

ROKER, Philip III (page 645) His freedom

is recorded as by patrimony 1 December 1756.

ROMER, John (page 646) His full name was John Christopher and he signs thus in the ledgers of Parker and Wakelin, his first account being prior to May 1752. He appears to have acted in a managerial position to that firm from 1760, since the lease of 'the house' (presumably workshop) was transferred to him that October. (Elaine Barr, *George Wickes, Royal Goldsmith*, 1980.) He was born about 1715, and may therefore have been perhaps a rather older brother of Emick Romer, or a cousin. He was married as bachelor aged twenty-nine at St. James's, Piccadilly, 2 February 1744 to Millecent Bennett of Clifton, Gloucestershire. In 1757 he took as apprentices Edward Norton Storr and Thomas Storr, the latter the father of Paul. (Judith Banister, 'In the Cause of Liberty', *Country Life*, 12 November 1981.)

RUNDELL, Philip (page 648) His identity as son of Thomas Rundell as conjectured by Penzer (op.cit.) is now refuted. His father's name is omitted from the record of his apprenticeship as 'Rundall' to William Rogers, 24 May 1760 on payment of £20. The latter was also master of John Bridge (q.v.). Rundell was made free of the Drapers' Company 29 October 1771 on a 'fine' of £2. 6s. 8d., then described as son of Francis (Rundell) of Rolvenden in Kent, Officer of Excise, jeweller of Ludgate Hill. (Presumably the parent had moved from Bath after Rundell's apprenticeship began.) Livery of the Drapers 1772. Assistant 1792 but later fined for non-service as Junior Warden and Master. His Bath family origins are confirmed by the apprenticeship to him of his nephew Samuel Goldney, son of the same name of the City of Bath in 1784, free in 1791 as jeweller, Ludgate Hill, and later member of the Stock Exchange and Master of his company 1841. (Drapers' Company records, S.T.) Joseph Neeld (*vice* Nield) who was left only part of Rundell's fortune was in fact his great-nephew, being grandson of the latter's favourite sister Elizabeth. He had, it seems, quitted his profession and devoted himself to Rundell's care for thirteen years. (The *Annual Biography* for the year 1828 quoted by John Culme, Sotheby's *Catalogue*, 24 October 1985.) The previous suggestion that he was identical with Queen Victoria's benefactor is erroneous. The latter was John Camden Neild, son of James Neild, jeweller of St. James's Street and philanthropist.

RUSLEN, John (page 649) His name first occurs in the Bevis Marks records in 1688 and lastly in 1716. (Information Dr R. Barnett.)

RUSSELL, Elias (page 649) He may perhaps have been the son or a relation of Isaac Roussell described in a Sun Insurance policy of 5 December 1716 'at Mr Remys against Shandois Street ... Goldsmith'. The earliest reference to Russell as yet recorded is as a creditor of John Neville (q.v.), bankrupt 10 June 1746, and in a Sun Insurance policy of 1 July following as 'next door to Mr Nash's in Orange Street in the Parish of St. Martin in the Fields Goldsmith'. Another policy of 18 January 1786 gives the address as 18 Duke's Court, St. Martin's Lane, silversmith. (Information Mr S. B. Turner.) The gold snuffbox of 1761 previously recorded is now in the collection of the Goldsmiths' Company.

RUTLAND, Robert (page 649) Son of Jonathan Rutland of Oxford Street, Middlesex, goldsmith, apprenticed to John Blake (q.v.) of the Pewterers' Company, 29 August 1799 on payment of £31. 10s. Free of that company 18 December 1806. Dead by 4 March 1828 when 'the widow of Robert Rutland, a maker of silver spoons in Lisle Street, Leicester Square received a visit from burglars who stole about sixty pounds of lead mouldings' (*Police Gazette*, p. 59C). (Pewterers' Company records, S.T.)

SCHURMAN, Albertus (page 653) Probably an immigrant worker. The name is found for silversmiths in Elberfeld, Germany. (Information Mr K. Citroen.)

SCOFIELD, John (page 653) The origins of this important maker remain regrettably undetermined. He appears in the Wakelin and Garrard ledgers as supplying items up to 15 June 1799 with a final payment to 'Mr. Cook for the Executors' 25 July of that year. He was buried in St. Dunstan's-in-the-West 27 May 1799, will proved 8 July following, in which he left substantial monetary legacies to his widow, a second wife and two daughters, one of each marriage. (P.R.O. PROB 11/1327 p. 391, R.B.)

SHALLIS, James (page 655) He married Esther, daughter of Crispin Fuller (q.v.), and was master of his brother-in-law Jeremiah Fuller, on whose apprenticeship

BIOGRAPHICAL DICTIONARY: ADDENDA

he was curiously described as 'oil and colourman'. (Information Mr Jasper Fuller.)

SHARRATT, Thomas (page 655) Son of Adam Sharratt, his apprenticeship to John Haygarth is dated 2 September 1745 for seven years on payment of £15. (P.R.O. I.R. 1/17 f.166, R.B.)

SHAW, George (page 656) His apprenticeship to his father George is dated 1 July 1708 for seven years. Rather naturally no premium was paid. (S.T.)

SHRUDER, James (page 657) He appears as 'Chasser &c' of St. Ann's, Westminster, in the apprenticeship to him of Julian Crispin (perhaps an otherwise unrecorded son of Paul Crespin, q.v.) for seven years from 11 May 1733 on payment of £32. (I.R. 1/13 f.181 R.B.) Since his first mark was not entered until 1737 it is now clear that he was practising as a chaser from the earlier date, probably at the same address. He is further described in Mortimer's *Universal Director*, 1763 as 'Shrouder, James Modeller and Papier Mache Manufacturer. Great Marlborough-street, Carnaby Market'. Since he appears to have had links with the Crespin family and was also one of the witnesses to Paul De Lamerie's will dated 24 May 1751, it is tempting to consider that he may be the actual modeller of much of the important rococo work of these makers and possibly of George Wickes also. (R.B.) The petitioning creditor for his previously mentioned bankruptcy 1749 was George Hindmarsh (q.v.). (J.C.)

SMITH, Benjamin I (page 661) Described as son of Ralph Smith of Wolverhampton, Staffs., coal miner, in the granting of his freedom. (C.F.1, R.B.)

SMITH, Benjamin II (page 661) He became free of the Goldsmiths' Company by redemption 2 December 1807. Why he waited five years after entering his first mark at the Hall is unexplained. He died 28 August 1823.

SMITH, George II (page 662) He died 1 May 1805 aged sixty-six. His eldest daughter Martha married his partner Thomas Hayter and died at Pentonville 10 April 1834 aged sixty-six (memorial plaque formerly in St. Michael, Wood Street).

SMITH, George III (page 663) Probably the George son of Thomas Smith baptized at Wolverhampton 19 May 1746. Before his apprenticeship to Thomas Chawner, previously stated, he had under the same statement of parentage been apprenticed to William Chawner I of the Pewterers' Company, 16 October 1760, and was made free of that company 17 March 1768. Livery 1772. Master 1795. That he was also apprenticed to William's brother Thomas Chawner, as previously stated, may have resulted from some personal reason on either side, but the previous statement that he was turned over to Pierce Tempest is in error for another goldsmith's apprentice. Through the Pewterers' Company he had three apprentices bound to him and three turned over, when he is twice described as silver spoonmaker.

SMITH, George IV (page 663) Apprenticed to William Fearn (q.v.) of Paternoster Row, 5 August 1789. Free by service 5 October 1796.

SOAME, William (page 665) He turned over an apprentice, John Weston, to his own former apprentice Samuel Roby (q.v.) 11 February 1743, which may possibly have been on retirement. The Mercers' Company Livery List, August 1752 describes him as 'Now of Little Thurlow, Suffolk, formerly a silversmith in Cheapside'. (Mercers' Company records, S.T.)

SOUTHEY, William (page 666) The previous entry under this name is now separated for two makers, confusingly only recognizable by their second names. 1. William Smalt Southey, son of John Southey of Aldersgate Buildings, carpenter, apprenticed to William Champion (q.v., not Chawner as previously), spoonmaker, Aldersgate Street, 3 July 1793, turned over to John Blake as stated 1794. Free 2 May 1810. 2. William James Southey, son of William Southey of Broad Street, Old Gravel Lane, Middlesex, spoonmaker, apprenticed to Joseph Angel (q.v.) 4 November 1818 on payment of £10 of the charity of the Goldsmiths' Company. Free 7 December 1825 as silversmith, Radnor Street, St. Luke's. His only mark (as opposed to the earlier marks of William Smalt Southey) WS without pellet, entered 9 December 1825. (S.T.)

SPACKMAN, Thomas (page 667) Bankrupt 2 October 1717 as goldsmith of London on the petition of William Swadlin, London, goldsmith (P.R.O. B 4/2, 182, J.C.)

SPILSBURY, Francis I (page 667) Described as deceased on the apprenticeship of his son Francis (below) 12 September 1750.

SPILSBURY, Francis II (page 667) Son of the above, deceased, apprenticed to Henry

Bailey (q.v.) of the Clothworkers' Company, goldsmith, Foster Lane, 12 September 1750 for seven years on payment of £20. Free of the Goldsmiths as previously stated. (Mr D. E. Wickham, Archivist, Clothworkers' Company, and S.T.)

SPRIMONT, Nicholas (page 668) He was clearly established at his address by the end of 1742 since he took an apprentice James Lamistre on 12 December that year. (I.R. 1/16 f.206, R.B.)

STEPHENS, Benoni (page 669) Born 1795. Son of William Stephens of Bridport, Dorset, gentleman, made free of the Goldsmiths' Company by redemption 10 January 1837, then described as 'of the age of 42 years occupying premises at No. 9 Camomile Street ... carrying on the business of a manufacturing Silversmith'. (C.F.1, S.T.)

STEPHENSON, Benjamin (page 670) The son of Jon Stephenson of Raby in the County of Durham, Taylor, goldsmith by trade. (C.F.1, R.B.)

STOCKAR, John Martin (page 671) He appears to have been closing down business towards the end of 1716 since, as already stated, his apprentice Thomas England (q.v.) was turned over to Samuel Margas that October and another, James Cranwell, to Edward Vincent (q.v.) 12 February 1717. Stockar died in the West Indies in that year. (R.B.)

STORER, George (page 671) The previous statement of his parentage and apprenticeship is erroneous. There is no such record for him.

STORR, Paul (page 672) The previous statement that he was apprenticed to Andrew Fogelberg, as originally claimed by N. M. Penzer, *Paul Storr*, 1954 is now disproved. Storr was in fact apprenticed as the son of Thomas Storr of Union Street, New Palace Yard, Westminster, victualler, to William Rock of the Vintners' Company of Parliament Street, 7 July 1784 for seven years, and was made free of the Vintners' Company and City of London 5 October 1791, then of Tothill Fields, Westminster. Livery 1804 as silversmith, Gray's Inn Lane. Court 1837. Between 1794 and 1831 no fewer than twenty-six apprentices were bound to him. (S.T.) One apprentice, Peter Bogerts, bound 6 December 1809, appears to be identical with Peter Bogaerts named jointly with Storr in Sun Insurance policy of 18 October 1809 as Carvers and Gilders, covering models in shop behind 22 Air Street. Other policies give addresses 20 and 23 Air Street. In 1807 a similar policy names Storr with Philip and Edmund Waller Rundell, John Bridge and William Theed (the sculptor) covering 'dwelling house, casting room under the yard behind the workshops all communicating in the said yard' in the sum of £3000. (Sun Insurance policies information Mr S. B. Turner and associates.)

STRANGE, William (page 673) Son of William Strange, shoemaker, of St. Bride's, London, apprenticed to John Carman 7 September 1716 and free of the Cutlers' Company as previously noted. (S.T.)

STUART, Isaac (page 673) Son of Andrew Stewart of St. Andrew's, Holborn, joiner, apprenticed to Thomas Bass 28 August 1712 for seven years on payment of £10 and free of the Cutlers' Company as already stated. (I.R. 1/2 f.29, R.B.)

SUTTON, John (674) For his birthplace 'Brignelt(?)' read Brignell. After his apprenticeship to Winterton he was at an unrecorded date turned over to Arthur Manwaring.

TATUM, John (page 677) John Tatum, son of John Tatum, was free by patrimony 5 June 1793, confirming his parentage as previously surmised.

TAYLOR, Trevillion (page 679) Son of Marmaduke Taylor, late of Derby, apothecary, deceased, apprenticed to John Allen, silversmith, of the Glovers' Company (perhaps John Allen I (q.v.)), 4 October 1736 on payment of £21. A memorandum of 20 February 1741 states that Allen 'hath left of Trade' and that Taylor was to be turned over to 'some other Freeman using the trade of a Silver Smith'. The following 4 April Taylor was turned over to John Wiberd, 'Goldsmith of the same trade', with whom he then migrated to the West Indies, where Wiberd died in January 1743, Taylor becoming sole executor of his estate and remaining in the West Indies working as a journeyman in early 1746. He returned to London by 13 February 1754 when he took up his freedom of the Grocers' Company, although he appears not to have completed his full term of apprenticeship. (Original apprentice indenture. Glovers' Company freedom register, S.T. Notes on West Indian goldsmiths, R.B.)

THOMEGAY, Mark (page 680) Apprenticed to Richard Clark, Citizen and Needlemaker

BIOGRAPHICAL DICTIONARY: ADDENDA

of London, for seven years from 23 January 1760 on payment of £30. (I.R. 1/22 f.82, R.B.) Since his first mark was entered in 1763, this apprenticeship was probably a formality for entrance to the Needlemakers.

THURKLE, Abraham (page 682) Son of George Moses Thurkle (q.v.) of the Cutlers' Company, apprenticed to his father, sword cutler of New Street Square, 20 October 1818. Free 20 May 1826 by patrimony as sword cutler, New Street Square. (S.T.)

THURKLE, George Moses (page 682) Son of Francis Thurkle, sword cutler of the Cutlers' Company, apprenticed to Francis Thurkle Jnr, chaser of the same company, 8 August 1782. Free 9 November 1789 as sword cutler, 15 New Street Square. There were therefore four members of the family working at this address until at least 1827. (S.T.)

TIMBERLAKE, James (page 682) Son of James Timberlake of St. Martin-in-the-Fields, apprenticed to Melchshere Rogers of St. Martin-in-the-Fields, 'chacer', 9 September 1714 for seven years on payment of £7. (I.R. 1/8 f.26, R.B.) Assuming he was free in 1721, but did not enter a mark until 1743, he must have worked as a journeyman for over twenty years, unless the mark is that of a son of the same name.

TOKETT, Marmaduke (page 682) Apprenticed to Joseph Joyce of St. Ann's, Westminster, goldsmith, 24 June 1743 for seven years on payment of £10. 10s. (I.R. 1/17 f.22, R.B.) Heal records Joseph Joyce in Greek Street, Soho, 1753, but no mark appears to be recorded for him. Stephen Joyce (q.v.) seems related. Tokett does not appear to have freedom of a company.

TOOKEY, Elizabeth (page 683) Definitely established as the widow of James and mother of Thomas Tookey (below) on the evidence of the latter's freedom entry. Mark no. 3559 has been found on a pair of marrowscoops of 1767, suggesting that her husband was dead by early 1768 at latest. (Information Lt. Col. P. G. Collyer.)

TOOKEY, James (page 683) As argued above he was apparently dead by the early part of 1768, i.e. before the end of the dateletter year of 1767-8 in May. He appears as supplier of tea and salt spoons in Parker and Wakelin's Workmen's Ledger No. 2 from March 1766, the account brought forward from the missing ledger begun in 1760. (H.C.)

TOOKEY, Thomas (page 683) In his freedom entry he is described as son of James Tookey deceased ... made free with consent of Elizabeth his mother and executrix. He is probably the one of the name buried 11 September 1791 aged forty, at Bunhill Fields Cemetery.

TRAIES, William (page 684) Son of James Traies of Crediton, jeweller and engraver, made free of the city of Exeter 'by succession' (? patrimony) 8 February 1817, then described as of Dartmouth, watchmaker. He can be identified with the entry of the mark of 1822. Henry Ellis of Exeter mentions in his diary that Traies moved to London to become a flatware maker, with whom Ellis subsequently opened an account for the supply of spoons and forks. (Information Mr T. A. Kent through S.T.)

TRENDER, James (page 684) He can be identified with James Trinder, son of Robert Trinder, Citizen and Cooper of London, born 1767, made free of the Coopers' Company by patrimony 7 August 1792, and with him of the same name of Leather Lane in the apprenticeship to him of John Anderson, to be taught the trade of a goldsmith, 1799, and of Baldwins Gardens in the apprenticeship of Alexander Foster, 1807. (Coopers' Company records and C.F.1, R.B.)

TRIPP, Job (page 684) He also appears as jeweller and watchmaker, Bridge Street, Westminster, in the *London Directory*, 1768. (R.B.)

TURNER, George (page 686) Son of Richard Turner of 31 St. John's Square, silversmith (q.v.) of the Innholders' Company, apprenticed to his father 21 September 1808. He does not appear to have taken freedom of that company. (Innholders' Company records, S.T.)

TURNER, Richard (page 686) Son of Robert Turner of Wolverhampton, bucklemaker, free by redemption of the Innholders' Company, 7 October 1793. Took eight apprentices, including his two sons, from 1798 to 1817.

VERE, John Henry (page 688) The mark no. 3908 previously attributed to him in partnership with William Lutwyche must now almost certainly be attributed to William Vincent and John Lawford (q.v. above and below). It seems very probable that Lutwyche and Vere were retailers, as their addresses suggest. (H.C.)

VINCENT, Edmund (page 689) Appears in partnership with John Arnell (q.v. above) as suppliers of candlesticks in Parker and Wakelin's Workmen's Ledger No. 2 up to 1767, agreeing with dates of candlesticks on which mark no. 3562 has been found. The partners were fittingly enough both made free on the same day, 2 November 1763, although with different masters. The records of the Sun Insurance Company show Vincent in West Street, Seven Dials from mid-1765 and still there 1767, by which time Arnell had moved to Little Britain. (Information Mr S. B. Turner, R.B.)

VINCENT, Edward (page 689) He was also bankrupt earlier than previously stated, 12 September 1720, as late of London, goldsmith, on the petition of James Ravener, Westminster, butcher. (B 4/3, 138, J.C.) It is however possible that this record might refer to another of the three entries in the apprenticeship registers previously noted.

VINCENT, William (page 690) It is now clear that the first option of identification of apprenticeship previously suggested is correct. Vincent was to form partnership with his co-apprentice John Lawford (q.v. above), made free the following year. Messrs Vincent and Lawford appear as suppliers of chased bread baskets, pierced cream pails and ladles in Parker and Wakelin's Workmen's Ledger No. 2, November 1767, the account brought forward from the earlier missing ledger. After October 1768 the account continues in the name of Lawford alone. It is now clear that mark no. 3908, from the more normal arrangement of the initials read vertically and horizontally rather than diagonally, is more likely to be theirs than the previous attribution to John Vere and William Lutwyche. (H.C.)

VONHAM, Frederick (page 690) He may possibly be identified with Frederick Venham, chaser, St. Luke's, Middlesex, to whom Nathaniel Horwood (q.v.) was apprenticed in 1744. (I.R. 1/17 f.101, R.B.)

WAKELIN, Edward (page 691) For a full account of the interesting family connections between Wickes, Parker and Wakelin, see Elaine Barr, *George Wickes, Royal Goldsmith*, 1980.

WALKER, Bowyer (page 692) Son of William Walker of Dizworth, Leics., gentleman, apprenticed to Henry Clarke I (q.v.) of the Broderers' Company, 1 September 1725 for seven years on payment of £10. (I.R. 1/11 f.15, R.B.) Turned over 12 June 1729 to John Gorham (q.v.), Citizen and Goldsmith. Free 7 March 1733 of the Broderers' Company. (Broderers' Company records, S.T.)

WALKER, Thomas (page 692) Son of William Walker of Jewin Street, perukemaker, apprenticed to James Beattie (q.v. above) of the Drapers' Company, 18 April 1783. Free of that company 26 June 1792 as goldsmith, 393 Strand. Livery 1802. Court 1832–50, when he died. Master 1844. The company records give further addresses to those for his mark entries, as follows: 1793, Ray Street, Clerkenwell; 1796, Pemberton Row, Gough Square, Fleet Street; 1805–30, Tabernacle Walk; 1831, Wanstead; 1832, Hampstead; 1833–7, Wanstead; 1838–46, Holloway Place; 1847–50, Peckham Rye. (Drapers' Company records, S.T.)

WALLIS, Thomas I (page 692) He also appears as silversmith, 37 Monkwell Street, in Baldwin's *New Complete Guide*, 1770 and the *New Complete Guide*, 1777. Mark no. 2963 is also his. See page 211n. (R.B.)

WALLIS, Thomas II (page 692) Delete mark no. 2693 from this entry. The suggestion that Billers Wallis was brother to Thomas Wallis I is refuted by Mrs A. Taylor (née Wallis, descendant of the latter) who states that the brothers of Thomas Wallis I were John and Clement.

WARHAM, William I (page 693) Heal's notice of him as the bankrupt of 1722 is an error for William Warham II below.

WARHAM, William II (page 693) Declared bankrupt 18 December 1722 as goldsmith, Chancery Lane, on the petition of Evan Davies of Chancery Lane, cyder merchant (B 4/3, 310, J.C.) and again 12 May 1727 on the petition of William Shemell, West Horndon, Essex, gentleman. (B 4/5, 294.)

WASTELL, Samuel (page 694) The badly written town name in the apprenticeship entry appears to read 'Lin', i.e. King's Lynn, from where an apprentice to him, Thomas Sharp, is also recorded.

WATTS, Benjamin (page 694) Declared bankrupt 14 June 1720 as goldsmith, London, on the petition of Edward Cornock, goldsmith, London (q.v.). (B 4/3, 125, J.C.)

WHIPHAM, Thomas (page 698) He is stated to have acquired the business of Francis Nelme (q.v.) in 1739 (John Culme, *Nineteenth Century Silver*, 1977). For the descent of the business to Messrs Barnard, see Edward Barnard above. It is now established that he died in 1756, to be succeeded by his

BIOGRAPHICAL DICTIONARY: ADDENDA

son Thomas Whipham II, to whom the mark no. 2976 in partnership with Charles Wright must be correctly ascribed. Thomas Whipham II retired in 1775 and entered the retail trade at 61 Fleet Street as recorded by Heal. (John Culme, *Directory of Gold and Silversmiths*, under Edward Barnard and Sons, quoting an anonymous article in *Watchmaker, Jeweller and Silversmith*, 1899.)

WHITE, John (page 698) He appears with a curious qualification in the Fitzwalter Accounts '25 March 1729. To Mr White silversmith and excise officer, a bill for plate £14 14s on my brother Fitzwalter's account £17 8s 0d' (Essex County Records). He was declared bankrupt 24 April 1740 as silversmith, St. Martin-in-the-Fields, on the petition of John Lee, Norfolk Street, Strand, gentleman. (B 4/9, 293, J.C.)

WHITE, Robert (page 699) Dead before 22 December 1726 when his widow Elizabeth testified to the service of Sandylands Drinkwater as apprentice to White for the grant of his freedom.

WHITING, John James (page 699) Son of John Whiting, late of Montague Street, Whitechapel, millwright, deceased, apprenticed to Thomas Willats (q.v.) of the Plaisterers' Company, 1 June 1810 and turned over to William Eaton (q.v.) 6 December 1811. Free of the Plaisterers 12 January 1819. Livery 1843. His son of same name, apprenticed to him 1840, entered his mark as spoonmaker at his father's address 1857. (Plaisterers' Company records, S.T.)

WHITTINGHAM, John (page 699) He appears as engraver in the apprenticeship to him of John Robert (q.v. in Addenda above).

WHYTE, David (page 700) He appears as supplier of cups and covers in Parker and Wakelin's Workmen's Ledger No. 2 from October 1770. (H.C.)

WICKES, George (page 700) The definitive work on this important goldsmith is by Elaine Barr, *George Wickes, Royal Goldsmith*, 1980, containing much information on his family connections and clients as well as his relationships with Edward Wakelin and John Parker (q.v.).

WILDBIRD, John (page 702) This name should read Wildbore. John son of Joseph Wildbore citizen and mercer apprenticed to William Pearson (q.v.) 18 September 1705. Free 23 September 1712. His brother William apprenticed to him June 1713, two years before the entry of John's mark as previously recorded above.

WILKINS, Micah (page 702) Son of Micah Wilkins, deceased, of Marlborough, Wilts., turner, apprenticed to James Dancer of the Bakers' Company, 4 June 1694 for seven years. Free of that company *c.* January 1702. (C.F.1, Bakers' Company records, not precise, S.T.)

WILLIAMS, James (page 705) Declared bankrupt as late of Paternoster Row, London, silversmith, on the petition of William Oldfield, goldsmith, of Paternoster Row, perhaps the son of Elizabeth Oldfield (q.v.). (B 4/13, 263, J.C.)

WILLIAMS, Walter I (page 705) He can probably be identified with the apprentice of that name bound to Christian Felpur(?) of St. Martin-in-the-Fields, buttonmaker, 27 October 1768 for the usual term of seven and a half years on payment of £10. (I.R. 1/25 f.199, R.B.)

WINTLE, George (page 707) Son of James Wintle of St. Mary Magdalen, Bermondsey, Officer of Excise, apprenticed to Thomas Wintle (his brother) of the Vintners' Company, of Gwyn's Buildings, Islington, 5 November 1777. Free of that company 6 October 1790. He took in all thirteen apprentices from 1790 to 1822, when described as working silversmith or silversmith. In 1812 he was prosecuted at the Old Bailey for producing flatware with forged hall and duty marks, but found not guilty. (Vintners' Company records, S.T.)

WINTLE, James (page 707) Son of George Wintle of the Vintners' Company, of Christian Alley, Bunhill Row, working silversmith, apprenticed to his father 6 July 1803. Free of that company 2 April 1817 at 13 North Street, City Road. (Vintners' Company records, S.T.)

WINTLE, Thomas (page 707 under Samuel Wintle) Son of James Wintle of the Vintners' Company, free of that company by patrimony 1 October 1777. Address Gwyn's Buildings, Islington. His brother George apprenticed to him 5 November 1777. He was ordered to be prosecuted by the Goldsmiths' Company 13 April 1778 for selling a gold stock buckle worse than standard and fined £10 February 1779 (Minute Book). Described as engraver in an apprenticeship to him 1786, as also silversmith the same year, then in Walworth and Battersea 1790. (Vintners' Company records, S.T.)

WIRGMAN, Peter (page 708) His address

in Windsor Court in the Strand can now be pre-dated to 15 July 1723 when he took out a Sun Insurance policy there for 'his Goods and Merchandize in his said dwelling house' at £500. (Information Mr S. B. Turner.)

WITHAM, Edward (page 708) Son of Edward Witham of St. Ann's, Blackfriars, gentleman, of the Goldsmiths' Company, apprenticed to Roger Biggs (q.v.) of the Glovers' Company 12 July 1800 for seven years on payment of £21. Turned over to Thomas Ash (q.v.) 15 October 1801. Free of the Goldsmiths' Company as previously stated. The previous suggestion that the mark entered in 1813 might be that of his father should be ignored. (Glovers' Company records, S.T.)

WOODS, Christopher (page 710) As Christopher Fly Woods, son of John Woods of Hayes, Middlesex, yeoman, apprenticed to Paul Callard (q.v.) of the Longbowstringmakers' Company, 13 January 1762. Free of that company 7 July 1773. It should be noted that his address on entering his mark 1775 is the same street as Callard's. (Longbowstringmakers' Company records, S.T.)

WOODWARD, John (page 710) A more likely identity for this maker than that previously suggested is son of Samuel Woodward of St. Andrew's, Holborn, gentleman, apprenticed to George Berkler (alias Berklear) of St. Martin's-le-Grand, silversmith, 11 November 1723 for seven years on payment of £15. (I.R. 1/9 f.149, R.B.) The entry of the mark is a mere thirteen days after the presumed termination of service and the address the same as Berkler's.

WORBOYS, Arthur (page 710) As Arthur Warboyes made free of the Spectaclemakers' Company by redemption 14 September 1762, then described as jeweller, Wine Office Court. He thus appears to have been made free of the former company before becoming free of the Goldsmiths three weeks later. Was he under threat to become free without delay, having entered his mark as recorded in 1758? (Spectaclemakers' registers, R.B.)

WRANGHAM, John (page 710) He was foreman and his partner Moulson assistant to Francis Lambert and William Rawlings, retailers of Coventry Street, who acquired the business of Thomas Hamlet (Chaffers, *Gilda Aurifabrorum*).

WRIGHT, Charles (page 711) For the statement that his business at 9 Ave Maria Lane was amalgamated with that of Henry Chawner in 1786 and the descent to Edward Barnard, see John Culme, *Directory of Gold and Silversmiths*, under the latter name, quoting an anonymous article in the *Watchmaker, Jeweller and Silversmith*, 1899. On 18 May 1787 Wright wrote to the Goldsmiths' Company desiring to be excused the office of Prime Warden as he was then resident in Wales.

YERBURY, Daniel (page 712) Son of Daniel Yerbury of the City of Salisbury, gentleman, apprenticed to John Leach (q.v.) of the Haberdashers' Company, goldsmith, Distaff Lane, 21 April 1710 for seven years and turned over 19 May 1713 to George Beale (q.v.), Citizen and Skinner of London, following Leach's death. Free of the Haberdashers 11 November 1715 as silversmith, Bread Street, by redemption, since his full term had not expired as Beale was 'about to leave off his Trade and willing to remit to the Petitioner (Yerbury) the Remainder of his Apprenticeship'. (Haberdashers' Company register and C.F.1, R.B.)

YOUNG, George (page 712) Son of Thomas Young of Riply, Surrey, yeoman, apprenticed to John Hughes of the Cutlers' Company, 19 October 1711 for seven years on payment of £10. Free of that company 15 January 1719. (Cutlers' Company records, R.B.)

YOUNG, Nathaniel (page 712) Son of Isaac Young of Watchfield, Berks., maltster, apprenticed to Joseph Hobbs of the Cutlers' Company 3 March 1713 and turned over the same day to Edward Bacon, Citizen and Cutler of the same art. Free of that company 22 June 1720. (Cutlers' Company records, R.B.)

YOUNG, William (page 712) Almost certainly identical with the son of George Young of St. Saviour's, Southwark, hair seller, apprenticed to Paul Hanet (q.v.) of the Longbowstringmakers' Company 5 February 1724 for seven years. Free of that company 30 August 1739. Both master and apprentice have the same address on entering marks and it seems possible that Young succeeded to Hanet's establishment. (Longbowstringmakers' Company records, R.B.)

Further information on a number of the names in the Biographical Dictionary, chiefly concerning the descent of their firms after 1837, is to be found in John Culme, *The Directory of Gold and Silversmiths 1838–1914*. These names are listed below. When not under the original name in Culme, reference is made to that under which they appear. Information from the same work of pre-1837 date has been included in the Addenda to the Biographical Dictionary.

Aldridge, James
Angell, Joseph
Barnard, Edward
Barton, Edward
Bateman, William
Boyton, Charles
Brent, Moses William
 (under Cook, Thurston)
Brown, William
Brunt, John Eldershaw
Bunn, Lockington
 (under Theobalds, William)
Butler, Joshua
Carsberg, George
Cater, Dudley
 (under Hayne and Cater)
Cowie, George
Crespel, Sebastian II
Death, Robert
Dexter, Thomas Paine
Diller, Thomas
 (under Harris and Brownett)
Douglas, Archibald
Eaton, William
Edington, James
Edington, John
Edwards, Thomas
Elliott, William
Emanuel, Michael
 (under Emanuel, Harry)
Evans, John II
Figg, John
Fox, Charles I and II
Garrard, Robert I
Harris, John IV and V
 (under C. S. Harris and Sons)
Hayne, Jonathan
Hennell, Robert II
Higgins, Francis
Hitchin, William
Houle, John
Hunter, William II
Jackson, James
Jackson, Samuel
Jago, John
Keith, John James
Kohler, John II
Lias, Henry John
Linnit, John

Morisse, Walter
Neal, William
Nicholls, Thomas
Nutting, Joseph
 (under Sherlock and Co.)
Pearce, Richard
Peppin, Sydenham William
 (under Cook, Thurston)
Phillips, Phillip
 (under Phillips, S. J.)
Piercey, Josiah
Pike, William and John
 (under Pike, Ann)
Pinnell, George Frederick
 (under Pinnell, Jane)
Rawlings, Charles
Reid, George
Reid, William Ker
Rudduck, Samuel
 (under Ruddock, Samuel)
Rundell, Philip
Savory, Joseph
Scott, Digby
 (under Smith, Nicholson & Co)
Sibley, Richard II
Smith, Benjamin II and III
 (under Smith, Nicholson & Co)
Smith, James III
 (as above)
Tapley, John
Teare, John
Theobalds, William
Thurkle, George
 (under Thurkle, Benjamin)
Wallis, Robert
 (under Wallis, Charles)
Wallis, Thomas I and II
 (under Hayne and Cater)
Whitford, George
Whitford, Samuel II
Whiting, John James
Wimbush, Thomas
Wintle, James
 (under Wintle, Jacob)
Wise, Thomas
Wrangham, John

Paul Storr	Plate Worker	No. 30 Church Street Soho
		New Mark
		New Mark
		Removed to No. 20 Air St. James
Mary Jackson	Case Maker	No. 2 Bridgewater Gardens

Paul Storr	Plateworker	No. 53 Dean St. Soho New Mark
		New Mark
		New Marks
		New Marks
		Removed to Harrison Street Grays Inn Road

Paul Storr	Plate Worker	No. 17 Harrison Street Grays Inn Road
		2 New Marks